THE CIA WORLD FACTBOOK
FULL-SIZE 2020 EDITION

VOLUME 2:
The Gambia ~ Poland

CENTRAL INTELLIGENCE AGENCY
UNITED STATES OF AMERICA

The CIA World Factbook Volume 2 — Full-Size 2020 Edition

Giant Format, 600+ Pages: The #1 Global Reference, Complete & Unabridged — Vol. 2 of 3, The Gambia ~ Poland

Central Intelligence Agency

This edition first published 2020 by Carlile Intelligence Library. "Carlile Intelligence Library" and its associated logos and devices are trademarks. Carlile Intelligence Library is an imprint of Carlile Media (a division of Creadyne Developments LLC). The appearance of U.S. Government visual information does not imply or constitute U.S. Government endorsement. This book is published for information purposes only.

New material copyright © 2020 Carlile Media. **All rights reserved.**

Published in the United States of America.

ISBN-13: 978-1-949117-14-1
ISBN-10: 1949117146

WWW.CARLILE.MEDIA

2020 CIA WORLD FACTBOOK VOLUME ISBNS

Use these International Standard Book Numbers to obtain the other volumes of this year's Factbook from your book vendor.

VOLUME 1: ISBN-13: 978-1-949117-13-4
ISBN-10: 1949117138

VOLUME 2: ISBN-13: 978-1-949117-14-1
ISBN-10: 1949117146

VOLUME 3: ISBN-13: 978-1-949117-15-8
ISBN-10: 1949117154

Note: ISBN-10s are provided (without hyphens) for online retailers.

TABLE OF CONTENTS

GAMBIA, THE :: 1

GAZA STRIP :: 8

GEORGIA :: 13

GERMANY :: 21

GHANA :: 29

GIBRALTAR :: 37

GREECE :: 42

GREENLAND :: 50

GRENADA :: 56

GUAM :: 62

GUATEMALA :: 67

GUERNSEY :: 75

GUINEA :: 79

GUINEA-BISSAU :: 87

GUYANA :: 94

HAITI :: 102

HEARD ISLAND AND MCDONALD ISLAND :: 110

HOLY SEE (VATICAN CITY) :: 112

HONDURAS :: 116

HONG KONG :: 123

HUNGARY :: 130

ICELAND :: 138

INDIA :: 145

INDIAN OCEAN :: 154

INDONESIA :: 156

IRAN :: 164

IRAQ :: 173

IRELAND :: 182

ISLE OF MAN :: 190

ISRAEL :: 194

ITALY :: 202

JAMAICA :: 210

JAN MAYEN :: 217

JAPAN :: 219

JERSEY :: 227

JORDAN :: 231

KAZAKHSTAN :: 239

KENYA :: 247

KIRIBATI :: 256

KOREA, NORTH :: 262

KOREA, SOUTH :: 269

KOSOVO :: 277

KUWAIT :: 284

KYRGYZSTAN :: 291

LAOS :: 298

LATVIA :: 305

LEBANON :: 312

LESOTHO :: 320

LIBERIA :: 327

LIBYA :: 335

LIECHTENSTEIN :: 343

LITHUANIA :: 348

LUXEMBOURG :: 355

MACAU :: 362

MADAGASCAR :: 368

MALAWI :: 376

MALAYSIA :: 383

MALDIVES :: 392

MALI :: 399

MALTA :: 407

MARSHALL ISLANDS :: 414

MAURITANIA :: 420

MAURITIUS :: 428

MEXICO :: 436

MICRONESIA :: 445

MOLDOVA :: 451

MONACO :: 459

MONGOLIA :: 464

MONTENEGRO :: 471

MONTSERRAT :: 478

MOROCCO :: 483

MOZAMBIQUE :: 491

NAMIBIA :: 499

NAURU :: 507

NAVASSA ISLAND :: 512

NEPAL :: 514

NETHERLANDS :: 522

NEW CALEDONIA :: 530

NEW ZEALAND :: 536

NICARAGUA :: 543

NIGER :: 550

NIGERIA :: 558

NIUE :: 566

NORFOLK ISLAND :: 570

NORTH MACEDONIA :: 573

NORTHERN MARIANA ISLANDS :: 580

NORWAY :: 585

OMAN :: 593

PACIFIC OCEAN :: 600

PAKISTAN :: 602

PALAU :: 611

PANAMA :: 616

PAPUA NEW GUINEA :: 623

PARACEL ISLANDS :: 631

PARAGUAY :: 633

PERU :: 641

PHILIPPINES :: 650

PITCAIRN ISLANDS :: 659

POLAND :: 662

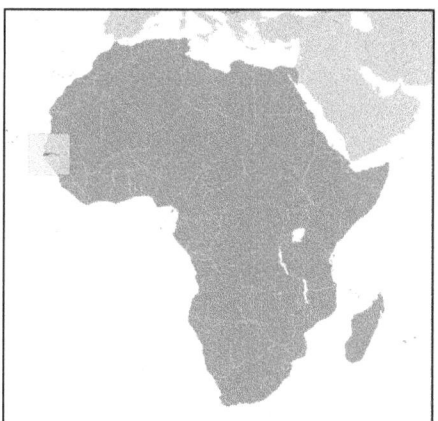

AFRICA :: GAMBIA, THE

INTRODUCTION :: GAMBIA, THE

BACKGROUND:
The Gambia gained its independence from the UK in 1965. Geographically surrounded by Senegal, it formed a short-lived Confederation of Senegambia between 1982 and 1989. In 1991, the two nations signed a friendship and cooperation treaty, although tensions flared up intermittently during the regime of Yahya JAMMEH. JAMMEH led a military coup in 1994 that overthrew the president and banned political activity. A new constitution and presidential election in 1996, followed by parliamentary balloting in 1997, completed a nominal return to civilian rule. JAMMEH was elected president in all subsequent elections including most recently in late 2011. After 22 years of increasingly authoritarian rule, President JAMMEH was defeated in free and fair elections in December 2016. Due to The Gambia's poor human rights record under JAMMEH, international development partners had distanced themselves, and substantially reduced aid to the country. These channels have now reopened under the administration of President Adama BARROW, who took office in January 2017. The US and The Gambia currently enjoy improved relations. US assistance to the country has supported military education and training programs, as well as various capacity building and democracy strengthening activities.

GEOGRAPHY :: GAMBIA, THE

LOCATION:
Western Africa, bordering the North Atlantic Ocean and Senegal

GEOGRAPHIC COORDINATES:
13 28 N, 16 34 W

MAP REFERENCES:
Africa

AREA:
total: 11,300 sq km
land: 10,120 sq km
water: 1,180 sq km
country comparison to the world: 166

AREA - COMPARATIVE:
slightly less than twice the size of Delaware

LAND BOUNDARIES:
total: 749 km
border countries (1): Senegal 749 km

COASTLINE:
80 km

MARITIME CLAIMS:
territorial sea: 12 nm
contiguous zone: 18 nm
continental shelf: extent not specified
exclusive fishing zone: 200 nm

CLIMATE:
tropical; hot, rainy season (June to November); cooler, dry season (November to May)

TERRAIN:
flood plain of the Gambia River flanked by some low hills

ELEVATION:
mean elevation: 34 m
lowest point: Atlantic Ocean 0 m
highest point: unnamed elevation 53 m

NATURAL RESOURCES:
fish, clay, silica sand, titanium (rutile and ilmenite), tin, zircon

LAND USE:
agricultural land: 56.1% (2011 est.)
arable land: 41% (2011 est.) / permanent crops: 0.5% (2011 est.) / permanent pasture: 14.6% (2011 est.)
forest: 43.9% (2011 est.)
other: 0% (2011 est.)

IRRIGATED LAND:
50 sq km (2012)

POPULATION DISTRIBUTION:
settlements are found scattered along the Gambia River; the largest communities, including the capital of Banjul, and the country's largest city, Serekunda, are found at the mouth of the Gambia River along the Atlantic coast

NATURAL HAZARDS:
droughts

ENVIRONMENT - CURRENT ISSUES:
deforestation due to slash-and-burn agriculture; desertification; water pollution; water-borne diseases

ENVIRONMENT - INTERNATIONAL AGREEMENTS:
party to: Biodiversity, Climate Change, Climate Change-Kyoto Protocol, Desertification, Endangered Species, Hazardous Wastes, Law of the Sea, Ozone Layer Protection, Ship Pollution, Wetlands, Whaling
signed, but not ratified: none of the selected agreements

GEOGRAPHY - NOTE:
almost an enclave of Senegal; smallest country on the African mainland

PEOPLE AND SOCIETY :: GAMBIA, THE

POPULATION:
2,092,731 (July 2018 est.)

country comparison to the world: 148

NATIONALITY:

noun: Gambian(s)

adjective: Gambian

ETHNIC GROUPS:

Mandinka/Jahanka 34%, Fulani/Tukulur/Lorobo 22.4%, Wolof 12.6%, Jola/Karoninka 10.7%, Serahuleh 6.6%, Serer 3.2%, Manjago 2.1%, Bambara 1%, Creole/Aku Marabout 0.7%, other 0.9%, non-Gambian 5.2%, no answer 0.6% (2013 est.)

LANGUAGES:

English (official), Mandinka, Wolof, Fula, other indigenous vernaculars

RELIGIONS:

Muslim 95.7%, Christian 4.2%, none 0.1%, no response 0.1% (2013 est.)

DEMOGRAPHIC PROFILE:

The Gambia's youthful age structure – almost 60% of the population is under the age of 25 – is likely to persist because the country's total fertility rate remains strong at nearly 4 children per woman. The overall literacy rate is around 55%, and is significantly lower for women than for men. At least 70% of the populace are farmers who are reliant on rain-fed agriculture and cannot afford improved seeds and fertilizers. Crop failures caused by droughts between 2011 and 2013 have increased poverty, food shortages, and malnutrition.

The Gambia is a source country for migrants and a transit and destination country for migrants and refugees. Since the 1980s, economic deterioration, drought, and high unemployment, especially among youths, have driven both domestic migration (largely urban) and migration abroad (legal and illegal). Emigrants are largely skilled workers, including doctors and nurses, and provide a significant amount of remittances. The top receiving countries for Gambian emigrants are Spain, the US, Nigeria, Senegal, and the UK. While the Gambia and Spain do not share historic, cultural, or trade ties, rural Gambians have migrated to Spain in large numbers because of its proximity and the availability of jobs in its underground economy (this flow slowed following the onset of Spain's late 2007 economic crisis).

The Gambia's role as a host country to refugees is a result of wars in several of its neighboring West African countries. Since 2006, refugees from the Casamance conflict in Senegal have replaced their pattern of flight and return with permanent settlement in The Gambia, often moving in with relatives along the Senegal-Gambia border. The strain of providing for about 7,400 Casamance refugees has increased poverty among Gambian villagers.

AGE STRUCTURE:

0-14 years: 36.97% (male 388,615/female 385,172)

15-24 years: 20.31% (male 210,217/female 214,807)

25-54 years: 34.9% (male 357,934/female 372,428)

55-64 years: 4.26% (male 42,655/female 46,591)

65 years and over: 3.55% (male 34,328/female 39,984) (2018 est.)

DEPENDENCY RATIOS:

total dependency ratio: 92.3 (2015 est.)

youth dependency ratio: 87.8 (2015 est.)

elderly dependency ratio: 4.5 (2015 est.)

potential support ratio: 22.3 (2015 est.)

MEDIAN AGE:

total: 21.3 years (2018 est.)

male: 20.9 years

female: 21.6 years

country comparison to the world: 184

POPULATION GROWTH RATE:

1.99% (2018 est.)

country comparison to the world: 48

BIRTH RATE:

28.6 births/1,000 population (2018 est.)

country comparison to the world: 43

DEATH RATE:

6.9 deaths/1,000 population (2018 est.)

country comparison to the world: 132

NET MIGRATION RATE:

-1.8 migrant(s)/1,000 population (2018 est.)

country comparison to the world: 157

POPULATION DISTRIBUTION:

settlements are found scattered along the Gambia River; the largest communities, including the capital of Banjul, and the country's largest city, Serekunda, are found at the mouth of the Gambia River along the Atlantic coast

URBANIZATION:

urban population: 61.9% of total population (2019)

rate of urbanization: 4.07% annual rate of change (2015-20 est.)

MAJOR URBAN AREAS - POPULATION:

443,000 BANJUL (capital) (2019)

note: includes the local government areas of Banjul and Kanifing

SEX RATIO:

at birth: 1.03 male(s)/female

0-14 years: 1.01 male(s)/female

15-24 years: 0.98 male(s)/female

25-54 years: 0.96 male(s)/female

55-64 years: 0.92 male(s)/female

65 years and over: 0.86 male(s)/female

total population: 0.98 male(s)/female (2018 est.)

MOTHER'S MEAN AGE AT FIRST BIRTH:

20.9 years (2013 est.)

note: median age at first birth among women 25-29

MATERNAL MORTALITY RATE:

597 deaths/100,000 live births (2017 est.)

country comparison to the world: 13

INFANT MORTALITY RATE:

total: 58.4 deaths/1,000 live births (2018 est.)

male: 63.7 deaths/1,000 live births

female: 52.9 deaths/1,000 live births

country comparison to the world: 16

LIFE EXPECTANCY AT BIRTH:

total population: 65.4 years (2018 est.)

male: 63 years

female: 67.8 years

country comparison to the world: 181

TOTAL FERTILITY RATE:

3.42 children born/woman (2018 est.)

country comparison to the world: 44

CONTRACEPTIVE PREVALENCE RATE:

9% (2013)

DRINKING WATER SOURCE:

improved:

urban: 94.2% of population

rural: 84.4% of population

total: 90.2% of population

unimproved:

urban: 5.8% of population

rural: 15.6% of population

total: 9.8% of population (2015 est.)

CURRENT HEALTH EXPENDITURE:

4.4% (2016)

PHYSICIANS DENSITY:

0.11 physicians/1,000 population (2015)

HOSPITAL BED DENSITY:

1.1 beds/1,000 population (2011)

SANITATION FACILITY ACCESS:

improved:

urban: 61.5% of population (2015 est.)

rural: 55% of population (2015 est.)

total: 58.9% of population (2015 est.)

unimproved:

urban: 38.5% of population (2015 est.)

rural: 45% of population (2015 est.)

total: 41.1% of population (2015 est.)

HIV/AIDS - ADULT PREVALENCE RATE:

1.9% (2018 est.)

country comparison to the world: 26

HIV/AIDS - PEOPLE LIVING WITH HIV/AIDS:

26,000 (2018 est.)

country comparison to the world: 76

HIV/AIDS - DEATHS:

<1000 (2018 est.)

MAJOR INFECTIOUS DISEASES:

degree of risk: very high (2016)

food or waterborne diseases: bacterial and protozoal diarrhea, hepatitis A, and typhoid fever (2016)

vectorborne diseases: malaria and dengue fever (2016)

water contact diseases: schistosomiasis (2016)

animal contact diseases: rabies (2016)

respiratory diseases: meningococcal meningitis (2016)

OBESITY - ADULT PREVALENCE RATE:

10.3% (2016)

country comparison to the world: 139

CHILDREN UNDER THE AGE OF 5 YEARS UNDERWEIGHT:

16.5% (2013)

country comparison to the world: 37

EDUCATION EXPENDITURES:

3.1% of GDP (2016)

country comparison to the world: 136

LITERACY:

definition: age 15 and over can read and write

total population: 55.5%

male: 63.9%

female: 47.6% (2015 est.)

SCHOOL LIFE EXPECTANCY (PRIMARY TO TERTIARY EDUCATION):

total: 9 years

male: 9 years

female: 9 years (2010)

UNEMPLOYMENT, YOUTH AGES 15-24:

total: 13.1%

male: 9.1%

female: 17.2% (2012 est.)

country comparison to the world: 107

GOVERNMENT :: GAMBIA, THE

COUNTRY NAME:

conventional long form: Republic of The Gambia

conventional short form: The Gambia

etymology: named for the Gambia River that flows through the heart of the country

GOVERNMENT TYPE:

presidential republic

CAPITAL:

name: Banjul

geographic coordinates: 13 27 N, 16 34 W

time difference: UTC 0 (5 hours ahead of Washington, DC, during Standard Time)

etymology: Banjul is located on Saint Mary's Island at the mouth of the Gambia River; the Mandinka used to gather fibrous plants on the island for the manufacture of ropes; "bang julo" is Mandinka for "rope fiber"; mispronunciation over time caused the term became the word Banjul

ADMINISTRATIVE DIVISIONS:

5 regions, 1 city*, and 1 municipality**; Banjul*, Central River, Kanifing**, Lower River, North Bank, Upper River, West Coast

INDEPENDENCE:

18 February 1965 (from the UK)

NATIONAL HOLIDAY:

Independence Day, 18 February (1965)

CONSTITUTION:

history: previous 1965 (Independence Act), 1970; latest adopted 8 April 1996, approved by referendum 8 August 1996, effective 16 January 1997; note - referendum on new constitution planned over the next 2 years

amendments: proposed by the National Assembly; passage requires at least three-fourths majority vote by the Assembly membership in each of several readings and approval by the president of the republic; a referendum is required for amendments affecting national sovereignty, fundamental rights and freedoms, government structures and authorities, taxation, and public funding; passage by referendum requires participation of at least 50% of eligible voters and approval by at least 75% of votes cast; amended 2001, 2004, 2010 (2017)

LEGAL SYSTEM:

mixed legal system of English common law, Islamic law, and customary law

INTERNATIONAL LAW ORGANIZATION PARTICIPATION:

accepts compulsory ICJ jurisdiction with reservations; accepts ICCt jurisdiction

CITIZENSHIP:

citizenship by birth: yes

citizenship by descent only: yes

dual citizenship recognized: no

residency requirement for naturalization: 5 years

SUFFRAGE:

18 years of age; universal

EXECUTIVE BRANCH:

chief of state: President Adama BARROW (since 19 January 2017); Vice President Isatou TOURAY (since 15 March 2019); note - the president is both chief of state and head of government

head of government: President Adama BARROW (since 19 January 2017); Vice President Isatou TOURAY (since 15 March 2019)

cabinet: Cabinet appointed by the president

elections/appointments: president directly elected by simple majority popular vote for a 5-year term (no term limits); election last held on 1 December 2016 (next to be held in 2021); vice president appointed by the president

election results: Adama BARROW elected president; percent of vote - Adama BARROW (Coalition 2016) 43.3%, Yahya JAMMEH (APRC) 39.6%, Mamma KANDEH (GDC) 17.1%

LEGISLATIVE BRANCH:

description: unicameral National Assembly (58 seats; 53 members directly elected in single-seat constituencies by simple majority vote and 5 appointed by the president; members serve 5-year terms)

elections: last held on 6 April 2017 (next to be held in 2022)

election results: percent of vote by party - UDP 37.5%, GDC 17.4%, APRC 16%, PDOIS 9%, NRP 6.3%, PPP 2.5%, other 1.7%, independent 9.6%; seats by party - UDP 31, APRC 5, GDC 5, NRP 5, PDOIS 4, PPP 2, independent 1; composition - men 52, women 6, percent of women 10.3%

JUDICIAL BRANCH:

highest courts: Supreme Court of The Gambia (consists of the chief justice and 6 justices; court sessions held with 5 justices)

judge selection and term of office: justices appointed by the president after consultation with the Judicial Service Commission, a 6-member independent body of high-level judicial officials, a presidential appointee, and a National Assembly appointee; justices appointed for life or until mandatory retirement at age 75

subordinate courts: Court of Appeal; High Court; Special Criminal Court; Khadis or Muslim courts; district tribunals; magistrates courts; cadi courts

POLITICAL PARTIES AND LEADERS:

Alliance for Patriotic Reorientation and Construction or APRC [Fabakary JATTA]
Coalition 2016 [collective leadership] (electoral coalition includes UDP, PDOIS, NRP, GMC, GDC, PPP, and GPDP)
Gambia Democratic Congress or GDC [Mama KANDEH]
Gambia Moral Congress or GMC [Mai FATTY]
Gambia Party for Democracy and Progress or GPDP [Sarja JARJOU]
National Convention Party or NCP [Yaya SANYANG and Majanko SAMUSA (both claiming leadership)]
National Democratic Action Movement or NDAM [Lamin Yaa JUARA]
National Reconciliation Party or NRP [Hamat BAH]
People's Democratic Organization for Independence and Socialism or PDOIS [Sidia JATTA]
People's Progressive Party or PPP [Yaya CEESAY]
United Democratic Party or UDP [Ousainou DARBOE]

INTERNATIONAL ORGANIZATION PARTICIPATION:

ACP, AfDB, AU, ECOWAS, FAO, G-77, IBRD, ICAO, ICCt, ICRM, IDA, IDB, IFAD, IFC, IFRCS, ILO, IMF, IMO, Interpol, IOC, IOM, IPU, ISO (correspondent), ITSO, ITU, ITUC (NGOs), MIGA, MINUSMA, NAM, OIC, OPCW, UN, UNAMID, UNCTAD, UNESCO, UNIDO, UNMIL, UNOCI, UNWTO, UPU, WCO, WFTU (NGOs), WHO, WIPO, WMO, WTO

DIPLOMATIC REPRESENTATION IN THE US:

Ambassador Dawda D. FADERA (since 24 January 2018)

chancery: 5630 16th Street NW, Washington, DC 20011

telephone: [1] (202) 785-1399

FAX: [1] (202) 342-0240

DIPLOMATIC REPRESENTATION FROM THE US:

chief of mission: Ambassador Richard "Carl" PASCHALL (since 9 April 2019)

telephone: [220] 439-2856

embassy: Kairaba Avenue, Fajara, P.M.B.19, Banjul

mailing address: P.M.B. 19, Banjul

FAX: [220] 439-2475

FLAG DESCRIPTION:

three equal horizontal bands of red (top), blue with white edges, and green; red stands for the sun and the savannah, blue represents the Gambia River, and green symbolizes forests and agriculture; the white stripes denote unity and peace

NATIONAL SYMBOL(S):

lion; national colors: red, blue, green, white

NATIONAL ANTHEM:

name: For The Gambia, Our Homeland

lyrics/music: Virginia Julie HOWE/adapted by Jeremy Frederick HOWE

note: adopted 1965; the music is an adaptation of the traditional Mandinka song "Foday Kaba Dumbuya"

ECONOMY :: GAMBIA, THE

ECONOMY - OVERVIEW:

The government has invested in the agriculture sector because three-quarters of the population depends on the sector for its livelihood and agriculture provides for about one-third of GDP, making The Gambia largely reliant on sufficient rainfall. The agricultural sector has untapped potential - less than half of arable land is cultivated and agricultural productivity is low. Small-scale manufacturing activity features the processing of cashews, groundnuts, fish, and hides. The Gambia's reexport trade accounts for almost 80% of goods exports and China has been its largest trade partner for both exports and imports for several years.

The Gambia has sparse natural resource deposits. It relies heavily on remittances from workers overseas and tourist receipts. Remittance inflows to The Gambia amount to about one-fifth of the country's GDP. The Gambia's location on the ocean and proximity to Europe has made it one of the most frequented tourist destinations in West Africa, boosted by private sector investments in eco-tourism and facilities. Tourism normally brings in about 20% of GDP, but it suffered in 2014 from tourists' fears of Ebola virus in neighboring West African countries. Unemployment and underemployment remain high.

Economic progress depends on sustained bilateral and multilateral aid, on responsible government economic management, and on continued technical assistance from multilateral and bilateral donors. International donors and lenders were concerned about the quality of fiscal management under the administration of former President Yahya JAMMEH, who reportedly stole hundreds of millions of dollars of the country's funds during his 22 years in power, but anticipate significant improvements under the new administration of President Adama BARROW, who assumed power in early 2017. As of April 2017, the IMF, the World Bank, the European Union, and the African Development Bank were all negotiating with the new government of The Gambia to provide financial support in the coming months to ease the country's financial crisis.

The country faces a limited availability of foreign exchange, weak agricultural output, a border closure with Senegal, a slowdown in tourism, high inflation, a large fiscal deficit, and a high domestic debt burden that has crowded out private sector investment and driven interest rates to new highs. The government has committed to taking steps to reduce the deficit, including through expenditure caps, debt consolidation, and reform of state-owned enterprises.

GDP (PURCHASING POWER PARITY):

$5.556 billion (2017 est.)

$5.314 billion (2016 est.)

$5.292 billion (2015 est.)

note: data are in 2017 dollars

country comparison to the world: 176

GDP (OFFICIAL EXCHANGE RATE):

$1.482 billion (2017 est.)

GDP - REAL GROWTH RATE:

4.6% (2017 est.)

0.4% (2016 est.)

5.9% (2015 est.)

country comparison to the world: 62

GDP - PER CAPITA (PPP):

$2,600 (2017 est.)

$2,600 (2016 est.)

$2,700 (2015 est.)

note: data are in 2017 dollars

country comparison to the world: 197

GROSS NATIONAL SAVING:

6.8% of GDP (2017 est.)

7.1% of GDP (2016 est.)

3.7% of GDP (2015 est.)

country comparison to the world: 172

GDP - COMPOSITION, BY END USE:

household consumption: 90.7% (2017 est.)

government consumption: 12% (2017 est.)

investment in fixed capital: 19.2% (2017 est.)

investment in inventories: -2.7% (2017 est.)

exports of goods and services: 20.8% (2017 est.)

imports of goods and services: -40% (2017 est.)

GDP - COMPOSITION, BY SECTOR OF ORIGIN:

agriculture: 20.4% (2017 est.)

industry: 14.2% (2017 est.)

services: 65.4% (2017 est.)

AGRICULTURE - PRODUCTS:

rice, millet, sorghum, peanuts, corn, sesame, cassava (manioc, tapioca), palm kernels; cattle, sheep, goats

INDUSTRIES:

peanuts, fish, hides, tourism, beverages, agricultural machinery assembly, woodworking, metalworking, clothing

INDUSTRIAL PRODUCTION GROWTH RATE:

-0.8% (2017 est.)

country comparison to the world: 175

LABOR FORCE:

777,100 (2007 est.)

country comparison to the world: 150

LABOR FORCE - BY OCCUPATION:

agriculture: 75%

industry: 19%

services: 6% (1996 est.)

UNEMPLOYMENT RATE:

NA

POPULATION BELOW POVERTY LINE:

48.4% (2010 est.)

HOUSEHOLD INCOME OR CONSUMPTION BY PERCENTAGE SHARE:

lowest 10%: 2%

highest 10%: 36.9% (2003)

DISTRIBUTION OF FAMILY INCOME - GINI INDEX:

50.2 (1998)

country comparison to the world: 18

BUDGET:

revenues: 300.4 million (2017 est.)

expenditures: 339 million (2017 est.)

TAXES AND OTHER REVENUES:

20.3% (of GDP) (2017 est.)

country comparison to the world: 148

BUDGET SURPLUS (+) OR DEFICIT (-):

-2.6% (of GDP) (2017 est.)

country comparison to the world: 117

PUBLIC DEBT:

88% of GDP (2017 est.)

82.3% of GDP (2016 est.)

country comparison to the world: 28

FISCAL YEAR:

calendar year

INFLATION RATE (CONSUMER PRICES):

8% (2017 est.)

7.2% (2016 est.)

country comparison to the world: 196

CENTRAL BANK DISCOUNT RATE:

9% (31 December 2009)

11% (31 December 2008)

country comparison to the world: 31

COMMERCIAL BANK PRIME LENDING RATE:

29% (31 December 2017 est.)

30.4% (31 December 2016 est.)

country comparison to the world: 7

STOCK OF NARROW MONEY:

$297.2 million (31 December 2017 est.)

$279.5 million (31 December 2016 est.)

country comparison to the world: 181

STOCK OF BROAD MONEY:

$297.2 million (31 December 2017 est.)

$279.5 million (31 December 2016 est.)

country comparison to the world: 184

STOCK OF DOMESTIC CREDIT:

$552.5 million (31 December 2017 est.)

$499 million (31 December 2016 est.)

country comparison to the world: 175

MARKET VALUE OF PUBLICLY TRADED SHARES:

NA

CURRENT ACCOUNT BALANCE:

-$194 million (2017 est.)

-$85 million (2016 est.)

country comparison to the world: 97

EXPORTS:

$72.9 million (2017 est.)

$106.6 million (2016 est.)

country comparison to the world: 201

EXPORTS - PARTNERS:

Guinea-Bissau 51.9%, Vietnam 14.6%, Senegal 8.8%, Mali 7.2% (2017)

EXPORTS - COMMODITIES:

peanut products, fish, cotton lint, palm kernels

IMPORTS:

$376.9 million (2017 est.)

$310.5 million (2016 est.)

country comparison to the world: 201

IMPORTS - COMMODITIES:

foodstuffs, manufactures, fuel, machinery and transport equipment

IMPORTS - PARTNERS:

Cote dIvoire 11.5%, Brazil 10.6%, Spain 10.2%, China 7.8%, Russia 6.4%, Netherlands 5.3%, India 5% (2017)

RESERVES OF FOREIGN EXCHANGE AND GOLD:

$170 million (31 December 2017 est.)

$87.64 million (31 December 2016 est.)

country comparison to the world: 179

DEBT - EXTERNAL:

$586.8 million (31 December 2017 est.)

$571.2 million (31 December 2016 est.)

country comparison to the world: 175

EXCHANGE RATES:

dalasis (GMD) per US dollar -

49.74 (2017 est.)

43.8846 (2016 est.)

43.8846 (2015 est.)

41.89 (2014 est.)

41.733 (2013 est.)

ENERGY :: GAMBIA, THE

ELECTRICITY ACCESS:

population without electricity: 1 million (2017)

electrification - total population: 47.8% (2016)

electrification - urban areas: 69% (2016)

electrification - rural areas: 15.5% (2016)

ELECTRICITY - PRODUCTION:

304.1 million kWh (2016 est.)

country comparison to the world: 182

ELECTRICITY - CONSUMPTION:

282.8 million kWh (2016 est.)

country comparison to the world: 186

ELECTRICITY - EXPORTS:

0 kWh (2016 est.)

country comparison to the world: 138

ELECTRICITY - IMPORTS:

0 kWh (2016 est.)

country comparison to the world: 151

ELECTRICITY - INSTALLED GENERATING CAPACITY:

117,000 kW (2016 est.)

country comparison to the world: 178

ELECTRICITY - FROM FOSSIL FUELS:

97% of total installed capacity (2016 est.)

country comparison to the world: 34

ELECTRICITY - FROM NUCLEAR FUELS:

0% of total installed capacity (2017 est.)

country comparison to the world: 94

ELECTRICITY - FROM HYDROELECTRIC PLANTS:

0% of total installed capacity (2017 est.)

country comparison to the world: 172

ELECTRICITY - FROM OTHER RENEWABLE SOURCES:

3% of total installed capacity (2017 est.)

country comparison to the world: 125

CRUDE OIL - PRODUCTION:

0 bbl/day (2018 est.)

country comparison to the world: 140

CRUDE OIL - EXPORTS:

0 bbl/day (2015 est.)

country comparison to the world: 128

CRUDE OIL - IMPORTS:

0 bbl/day (2015 est.)

country comparison to the world: 131

CRUDE OIL - PROVED RESERVES:

0 bbl (1 January 2018 est.)

country comparison to the world: 135

REFINED PETROLEUM PRODUCTS - PRODUCTION:

0 bbl/day (2017 est.)

country comparison to the world: 148

REFINED PETROLEUM PRODUCTS - CONSUMPTION:

3,800 bbl/day (2016 est.)

country comparison to the world: 185

REFINED PETROLEUM PRODUCTS - EXPORTS:

42 bbl/day (2015 est.)

country comparison to the world: 122

REFINED PETROLEUM PRODUCTS - IMPORTS:

3,738 bbl/day (2015 est.)

country comparison to the world: 181

NATURAL GAS - PRODUCTION:

0 cu m (2017 est.)

country comparison to the world: 136

NATURAL GAS - CONSUMPTION:

0 cu m (2017 est.)

country comparison to the world: 149

NATURAL GAS - EXPORTS:

0 cu m (2017 est.)

country comparison to the world: 108

NATURAL GAS - IMPORTS:

0 cu m (2017 est.)

country comparison to the world: 129

NATURAL GAS - PROVED RESERVES:

0 cu m (1 January 2014 est.)

country comparison to the world: 138

CARBON DIOXIDE EMISSIONS FROM CONSUMPTION OF ENERGY:

607,300 Mt (2017 est.)

country comparison to the world: 180

COMMUNICATIONS :: GAMBIA, THE

TELEPHONES - FIXED LINES:

total subscriptions: 37,969

subscriptions per 100 inhabitants: 2 (July 2016 est.)

country comparison to the world: 162

TELEPHONES - MOBILE CELLULAR:

total subscriptions: 2,838,127

subscriptions per 100 inhabitants: 138 (July 2016 est.)

country comparison to the world: 141

TELEPHONE SYSTEM:

general assessment: adequate microwave radio relay and open-wire network; state-owned Gambia

Telecommunications partially privatized but still retaining a monopoly; multiple mobile networks offering effective competition; three licensed ISPs which serve local area without much competion (2018)

domestic: fixed-line stands at 2 per 100 subscriptions with one dominant company and mobile-cellular teledensity, aided by multiple mobile-cellular providers, is over 138 per 100 persons (2018)

international: country code - 220; landing points for the ACE submarine cable to West Africa and Europe; microwave radio relay links to Senegal and Guinea-Bissau; satellite earth station - 1 Intelsat (Atlantic Ocean) (2019)

BROADCAST MEDIA:

1 state-run TV-channel; one privately-owned TV-station; 1 Online TV-station; three state-owned radio station and 31 privately owned radio stations; eight community radio stations; transmissions of multiple international broadcasters are available, some via shortwave radio; cable and satellite TV subscription services are obtainable in some parts of the country

(2019)

INTERNET COUNTRY CODE:

.gm

INTERNET USERS:

total: 371,785

percent of population: 18.5% (July 2016 est.)

country comparison to the world: 153

BROADBAND - FIXED SUBSCRIPTIONS:

total: 3,750

subscriptions per 100 inhabitants: less than 1 (2017 est.)

country comparison to the world: 180

MILITARY AND SECURITY :: GAMBIA, THE

MILITARY EXPENDITURES:

3% of GDP (2018)
1.48% of GDP (2015)
1.72% of GDP (2014)
1.15% of GDP (2013)
1.22% of GDP (2012)

country comparison to the world: 23

MILITARY AND SECURITY FORCES:

Office of the Chief of Defense Staff: Gambian National Army (GNA), Gambian Navy (GN), Republican National Guard (RNG) (2018)

MILITARY SERVICE AGE AND OBLIGATION:

18 years of age for male and female voluntary military service; no conscription; service obligation 6 months (2012)

TRANSPORTATION :: GAMBIA, THE

CIVIL AIRCRAFT REGISTRATION COUNTRY CODE PREFIX:

C5 (2016)

AIRPORTS:

1 (2013)

country comparison to the world: 221

AIRPORTS - WITH PAVED RUNWAYS:

total: 1 (2019)

over 3,047 m: 1

ROADWAYS:

total: 2,977 km (2011)

paved: 518 km (2011)

unpaved: 2,459 km (2011)

country comparison to the world: 157

WATERWAYS:

390 km (on River Gambia; small oceangoing vessels can reach 190 km) (2010)

country comparison to the world: 88

MERCHANT MARINE:

total: 9

by type: other 9 (2018)

country comparison to the world: 154

PORTS AND TERMINALS:

major seaport(s): Banjul

TRANSNATIONAL ISSUES :: GAMBIA, THE

DISPUTES - INTERNATIONAL:

attempts to stem refugees, cross-border raids, arms smuggling, and other illegal activities by separatists from southern Senegal's Casamance region, as well as from conflicts in other west African states

TRAFFICKING IN PERSONS:

current situation: The Gambia is a source and destination country for women and children subjected to forced labor and sex trafficking; Gambian women, girls, and, to a lesser extent, boys are exploited for prostitution and domestic servitude; women, girls, and boys from West African countries are trafficked to The Gambia for commercial sexual exploitation, particularly by European sex tourists; boys in some Koranic schools are forced into street vending or begging; some Gambian children have been identified as victims of forced labor in neighboring West African countries

tier rating: Tier 3 – The Gambia does not fully comply with the minimum standards for the elimination of trafficking and is not making significant efforts to do so; the government demonstrated minimal anti-trafficking law enforcement efforts, investigating one trafficking case but not prosecuting or convicting any offenders in 2014; authorities did not investigate, prosecute, or convict any government employees complicit in trafficking, although corruption was a serious problem; the government identified and repatriated 19 Gambian girls subjected to domestic servitude in Lebanon but did not identify or provide protective services to any trafficking victims in The Gambia; a government program continued to provide resources and financial support to 12 Koranic schools on the condition that their students were not forced to beg (2015)

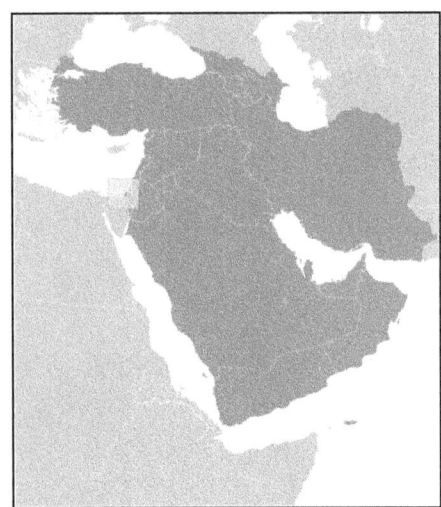

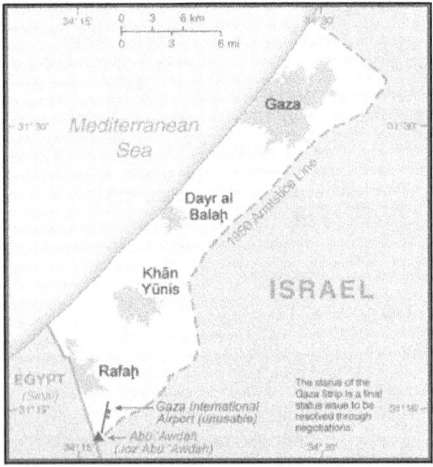

MIDDLE EAST :: GAZA STRIP

INTRODUCTION :: GAZA STRIP

BACKGROUND:

Inhabited since at least the 15th century B.C., Gaza has been dominated by many different peoples and empires throughout its history; it was incorporated into the Ottoman Empire in the early 16th century. Gaza fell to British forces during World War I, becoming a part of the British Mandate of Palestine. Following the 1948 Arab-Israeli War, Egypt administered the newly formed Gaza Strip; it was captured by Israel in the Six-Day War in 1967. Under a series of agreements known as the Oslo accords signed between 1994 and 1999, Israel transferred to the newly-created Palestinian Authority (PA) security and civilian responsibility for many Palestinian-populated areas of the Gaza Strip as well as the West Bank. Negotiations to determine the permanent status of the West Bank and Gaza Strip stalled in 2001, after which the area witnessed a violent intifada or uprising.

Israel by late 2005 unilaterally withdrew all of its settlers and soldiers and dismantled its military facilities in the Gaza Strip, but it continues to control the Gaza Strip's land and maritime borders and airspace. In early 2006, the Islamic Resistance Movement (HAMAS) won a majority in the Palestinian Legislative Council election. Attempts to form a unity government between Fatah and HAMAS failed and violent clashes between their respective supporters ensued, culminating in HAMAS's violent seizure of all military and governmental institutions in the Gaza Strip in June 2007. Since HAMAS's takeover, Israel and Egypt have enforced tight restrictions on movement and access of goods and individuals into and out of the territory. Fatah and HAMAS have since reached a series of agreements aimed at restoring political unity between the Gaza Strip and the West Bank but have struggled to effect them; a reconciliation agreement signed in October 2017 remains unimplemented.

In July 2014, HAMAS and other Gaza-based militant groups engaged in a 51-day conflict with Israel culminating in late August with an open-ended truce that was punctured with periodic rocket attacks and air strikes in 2018 and 2019. Since March 2018, Hamas has coordinated demonstrations along the Gaza security fence, many of which turned violent and resulted in one Israeli soldier death and several Israeli soldier injuries as well as more than 200 Palestinian deaths and thousands of live fire injuries. In 2018 and 2019, Palestinian militants launched thousands of rockets and mortar toward Israeli communities, and the IDF launched air strikes in return, resulting in multiple deaths on both sides. Egypt and the UN Special Coordinator for the Middle East Peace Process have negotiated multiple ceasefires to avert a broader conflict.

The UN in 2015 published a study assessing that the Gaza Strip could become uninhabitable by 2020 unless steps are taken to address Gaza's economic and humanitarian situation. In September 2018, the UN reported that conditions were worse than when its experts made that prediction.

GEOGRAPHY :: GAZA STRIP

LOCATION:

Middle East, bordering the Mediterranean Sea, between Egypt and Israel

GEOGRAPHIC COORDINATES:

31 25 N, 34 20 E

MAP REFERENCES:

Middle East

AREA:

total: 360 sq km

land: 360 sq km

water: 0 sq km

country comparison to the world: 207

AREA - COMPARATIVE:

slightly more than twice the size of Washington, DC

LAND BOUNDARIES:

total: 72 km

border countries (2): Egypt 13 km, Israel 59 km

COASTLINE:

40 km

MARITIME CLAIMS:

see entry for Israel
note: effective 3 January 2009, the Gaza maritime area is closed to all maritime traffic and is under blockade imposed by Israeli Navy until further notice

CLIMATE:

temperate, mild winters, dry and warm to hot summers

TERRAIN:

flat to rolling, sand- and dune-covered coastal plain

ELEVATION:

lowest point: Mediterranean Sea 0 m

highest point: Abu 'Awdah (Joz Abu 'Awdah) 105 m

NATURAL RESOURCES:

arable land, natural gas

IRRIGATED LAND:

240 sq km; note - includes the West Bank (2012)

POPULATION DISTRIBUTION:

population concentrated in major cities, particularly Gaza City in the north

NATURAL HAZARDS:

droughts

ENVIRONMENT - CURRENT ISSUES:

soil degradation; desertification; water pollution from chemicals and pesticides; salination of fresh water; improper sewage treatment; water-borne disease; depletion and contamination of underground water resources

GEOGRAPHY - NOTE:

strategic strip of land along Mideast-North African trade routes has experienced an incredibly turbulent history; the town of Gaza itself has been besieged countless times in its history; there are no Israeli settlements in the Gaza Strip; the Gaza Strip settlements were evacuated in 2005

PEOPLE AND SOCIETY :: GAZA STRIP

POPULATION:

1,836,713 (July 2018 est.)

country comparison to the world: 152

NATIONALITY:

noun: NA

adjective: NA

ETHNIC GROUPS:

Palestinian Arab

LANGUAGES:

Arabic, Hebrew (spoken by many Palestinians), English (widely understood)

RELIGIONS:

Muslim 98.0 - 99.0% (predominantly Sunni), Christian <1.0%, other, unaffiliated, unspecified <1.0% (2012 est.)

note: dismantlement of Israeli settlements was completed in September 2005; Gaza has had no Jewish population since then

AGE STRUCTURE:

0-14 years: 44.1% (male 415,746 /female 394,195)

15-24 years: 21.34% (male 197,797 /female 194,112)

25-54 years: 28.5% (male 256,103 /female 267,285)

55-64 years: 3.48% (male 33,413 /female 30,592)

65 years and over: 2.58% (male 24,863 /female 22,607) (2018 est.)

DEPENDENCY RATIOS:

total dependency ratio: 75.8 (2015 est.)

youth dependency ratio: 70.5 (2015 est.)

elderly dependency ratio: 5.2 (2015 est.)

potential support ratio: 19.1 (2015 est.)

note: data represent Gaza Strip and the West Bank

MEDIAN AGE:

total: 17.4 years (2018 est.)

male: 17.1 years

female: 17.8 years

country comparison to the world: 219

POPULATION GROWTH RATE:

2.25% (2018 est.)

country comparison to the world: 35

BIRTH RATE:

30.5 births/1,000 population (2018 est.)

country comparison to the world: 34

DEATH RATE:

3 deaths/1,000 population (2018 est.)

country comparison to the world: 222

NET MIGRATION RATE:

-5 migrant(s)/1,000 population (2018 est.)

country comparison to the world: 194

POPULATION DISTRIBUTION:

population concentrated in major cities, particularly Gaza City in the north

URBANIZATION:

urban population: 76.4% of total population (2019)

rate of urbanization: 3% annual rate of change (2015-20 est.)

note: data represent Gaza Strip and the West Bank

SEX RATIO:

at birth: 1.06 male(s)/female

0-14 years: 1.05 male(s)/female

15-24 years: 1.02 male(s)/female

25-54 years: 0.96 male(s)/female

55-64 years: 1.09 male(s)/female

65 years and over: 1.1 male(s)/female

total population: 1.02 male(s)/female (2018 est.)

MATERNAL MORTALITY RATE:

27 deaths/100,000 live births (2017 est.)

note: data represent Gaza Strip and the West Bank

country comparison to the world: 117

INFANT MORTALITY RATE:

total: 16 deaths/1,000 live births (2018 est.)

male: 17.1 deaths/1,000 live births

female: 14.9 deaths/1,000 live births

country comparison to the world: 96

LIFE EXPECTANCY AT BIRTH:

total population: 74.4 years (2018 est.)

male: 72.7 years

female: 76.2 years

country comparison to the world: 124

TOTAL FERTILITY RATE:

3.97 children born/woman (2018 est.)

country comparison to the world: 32

CONTRACEPTIVE PREVALENCE RATE:

57.2% (2014)

note: includes Gaza Strip and West Bank

DRINKING WATER SOURCE:

improved:

urban: 50.7% of population

rural: 81.5% of population

total: 58.4% of population

unimproved:

urban: 49.3% of population

rural: 18.5% of population

total: 41.6% of population (2015 est.)

note: includes Gaza Strip and the West Bank

PHYSICIANS DENSITY:

2.2 physicians/1,000 population (2014)

HOSPITAL BED DENSITY:

1.3 beds/1,000 population (2017)

SANITATION FACILITY ACCESS:

improved:

urban: 93% of population (2015 est.)

rural: 90.2% of population (2015 est.)

total: 92.3% of population (2015 est.)

unimproved:

urban: 7% of population (2015 est.)

rural: 9.8% of population (2015 est.)

total: 7.7% of population (2015 est.)

note: note includes Gaza Strip and the West Bank

HIV/AIDS - ADULT PREVALENCE RATE:
NA

HIV/AIDS - PEOPLE LIVING WITH HIV/AIDS:
NA

HIV/AIDS - DEATHS:
NA

CHILDREN UNDER THE AGE OF 5 YEARS UNDERWEIGHT:
1.4% (2014)

note: estimate is for Gaza Strip and the West Bank

country comparison to the world: 117

EDUCATION EXPENDITURES:
5.3% of GDP (2017)

note: includes Gaza Strip and the West Bank

country comparison to the world: 49

LITERACY:
definition: age 15 and over can read and write

total population: 96.9%

male: 98.6%

female: 95.2% (2016 est.)

note: estimates are for Gaza and the West Bank

SCHOOL LIFE EXPECTANCY (PRIMARY TO TERTIARY EDUCATION):
total: 13 years

male: 12 years

female: 14 years (2017)

note: data represent Gaza Strip and the West Bank

UNEMPLOYMENT, YOUTH AGES 15-24:
total: 46.9%

male: 40.5%

female: 75.3% (2018 est.)

note: includes the West Bank

country comparison to the world: 6

GOVERNMENT :: GAZA STRIP

COUNTRY NAME:
conventional long form: none

conventional short form: Gaza Strip

local long form: none

local short form: Qita' Ghazzah

etymology: named for the largest city in the region, Gaza, whose settlement can be traced back to at least the 15th century B.C. (as "Ghazzat")

ECONOMY :: GAZA STRIP

ECONOMY - OVERVIEW:
Movement and access restrictions, violent attacks, and the slow pace of post-conflict reconstruction continue to degrade economic conditions in the Gaza Strip, the smaller of the two areas comprising the Palestinian territories. Israeli controls became more restrictive after HAMAS seized control of the territory in June 2007. Under Hamas control, Gaza has suffered from rising unemployment, elevated poverty rates, and a sharp contraction of the private sector, which had relied primarily on export markets.

Since April 2017, the Palestinian Authority has reduced payments for electricity supplied to Gaza and cut salaries for its employees there, exacerbating poor economic conditions. Since 2014, Egypt's crackdown on the Gaza Strip's extensive tunnel-based smuggling network has exacerbated fuel, construction material, and consumer goods shortages in the territory. Donor support for reconstruction following the 51-day conflict in 2014 between Israel and HAMAS and other Gaza-based militant groups has fallen short of post-conflict needs.

GDP (PURCHASING POWER PARITY):
see entry for the West Bank

GDP (OFFICIAL EXCHANGE RATE):
$2.938 billion (2014 est.) (2014 est.)

note: excludes the West Bank

GDP - REAL GROWTH RATE:
-15.2% (2014 est.)

5.6% (2013 est.)

7% (2012 est.)

note: excludes the West Bank

country comparison to the world: 223

GDP - PER CAPITA (PPP):
see entry for the the West Bank

GDP - COMPOSITION, BY END USE:
household consumption: 88.6% (2017 est.)

government consumption: 26.3% (2017 est.)

investment in fixed capital: 22.4% (2017 est.)

investment in inventories: 0% (2017 est.)

exports of goods and services: 18.6% (2017 est.)

imports of goods and services: -55.6% (2017 est.)

note: data exclude the West Bank

GDP - COMPOSITION, BY SECTOR OF ORIGIN:
agriculture: 3% (2017 est.)

industry: 21.1% (2017 est.)

services: 75% (2017 est.)

note: data exclude the West Bank

AGRICULTURE - PRODUCTS:
olives, fruit, vegetables, flowers; beef, dairy products

INDUSTRIES:
textiles, food processing, furniture

INDUSTRIAL PRODUCTION GROWTH RATE:
2.2% (2017 est.)

note: see entry for the West Bank

country comparison to the world: 125

LABOR FORCE:
1.24 million (2017 est.)

note: excludes the West Bank

country comparison to the world: 138

LABOR FORCE - BY OCCUPATION:
agriculture: 5.2%

industry: 10%

services: 84.8% (2015 est.)

note: data exclude the West Bank

UNEMPLOYMENT RATE:
27.9% (2017 est.)

27% (2016 est.)

note: data exclude the West Bank

country comparison to the world: 201

POPULATION BELOW POVERTY LINE:

30% (2011 est.)

note: data exclude the West Bank

BUDGET:

see entry for the West Bank

FISCAL YEAR:

calendar year

INFLATION RATE (CONSUMER PRICES):

0.2% (2017 est.)

-0.2% (2016 est.)

note: excludes the West Bank

country comparison to the world: 16

COMMERCIAL BANK PRIME LENDING RATE:

see entry for the West Bank

STOCK OF NARROW MONEY:

see entry for the West Bank

STOCK OF BROAD MONEY:

$2.901 billion (31 December 2017 est.)

$2.538 billion (31 December 2016 est.)

country comparison to the world: 129

STOCK OF DOMESTIC CREDIT:

$2.041 billion (31 December 2017 est.)

$1.712 billion (31 December 2016 est.)

country comparison to the world: 149

CURRENT ACCOUNT BALANCE:

-$1.444 billion (2017 est.)

-$1.348 billion (2016 est.)

note: excludes the West Bank

country comparison to the world: 152

EXPORTS:

$1.955 billion (2017 est.)

$1.827 billion (2016 est.)

country comparison to the world: 142

EXPORTS - COMMODITIES:

strawberries, carnations, vegetables, fish (small and irregular shipments, as permitted to transit the Israeli-controlled Kerem Shalom crossing)

IMPORTS:

$8.59 billion (2018 est.)

$7.852 billion (2017 est.)

see entry for the West Bank

country comparison to the world: 109

IMPORTS - COMMODITIES:

food, consumer goods, fuel

RESERVES OF FOREIGN EXCHANGE AND GOLD:

$446.3 million (31 December 2017 est.)

$583 million (31 December 2015 est.)

country comparison to the world: 156

DEBT - EXTERNAL:

see entry for the West Bank

EXCHANGE RATES:

see entry for the West Bank

ENERGY :: GAZA STRIP

ELECTRICITY ACCESS:

population without electricity: 80,930 (2012)

electrification - total population: 98% (2012)

electrification - urban areas: 99% (2012)

electrification - rural areas: 93% (2012)

note: data for Gaza Strip and West Bank combined

ELECTRICITY - PRODUCTION:

51,000 kWh (2011 est.)

country comparison to the world: 218

ELECTRICITY - CONSUMPTION:

202,000 kWh (2009 est.)

country comparison to the world: 216

ELECTRICITY - EXPORTS:

0 kWh (2011 est.)

country comparison to the world: 139

ELECTRICITY - IMPORTS:

193,000 kWh (2011 est.)

country comparison to the world: 117

CRUDE OIL - PROVED RESERVES:

0 bbl (1 January 2010 est.)

country comparison to the world: 136

COMMUNICATIONS :: GAZA STRIP

TELEPHONES - FIXED LINES:

total subscriptions: 432,000 (includes the West Bank); (July 2016 est.)

subscriptions per 100 inhabitants: 9 (includes the West Bank); (July 2016 est.) (July 2016 est.)

country comparison to the world: 101

TELEPHONES - MOBILE CELLULAR:

total subscriptions: 3,531,000 (includes the West Bank)

subscriptions per 100 inhabitants: 76 (includes the West Bank) (July 2016 est.)

TELEPHONE SYSTEM:

general assessment: Israel has final say in allocating frequencies in the Gaza Strip and does not permit anything beyond a 2G network (2018)

domestic: Israeli company BEZEK and the Palestinian company PALTEL are responsible for fixed-line services; the Palestinian JAWWAL company provides cellular services; a slow 2G network allows calls and limited data transmission (2018)

international: country code - 970 (2018)

BROADCAST MEDIA:

1 TV station and about 10 radio stations; satellite TV accessible

INTERNET COUNTRY CODE:

.ps note - same as the West Bank

INTERNET USERS:

total: 2.673 million (includes the West Bank)

percent of population: 57.4% (July 2016 est.)

country comparison to the world: 100

BROADBAND - FIXED SUBSCRIPTIONS:

total: 320,500

subscriptions per 100 inhabitants: 14 (2016 est.)

note: includes West Bank

country comparison to the world: 93

MILITARY AND SECURITY :: GAZA STRIP

MILITARY AND SECURITY FORCES:

HAMAS does not have a conventional military in the Gaza Strip but maintains security forces in addition to its military wing, the 'Izz al-Din al-Qassam Brigades; the military wing reports to the Hamas Political Bureau leadership; there are several other militant groups operating in Gaza, most notably the al-Quds Brigades of Palestinian Islamic Jihad, that are usually but not always beholden to Hamas' authority (2019)

TRANSPORTATION :: GAZA STRIP

AIRPORTS:

1 (2013)

country comparison to the world: 222

AIRPORTS - WITH PAVED RUNWAYS:

total: 1 (2019)
under 914 m: 1
note - non-operational

HELIPORTS:
1 (2013)

ROADWAYS:
note: see entry for the West Bank

PORTS AND TERMINALS:
major seaport(s): Gaza

TERRORISM :: GAZA STRIP

TERRORIST GROUPS - HOME BASED:

Army of Islam (AOI): aim(s): stage attacks against Israel and Egypt from the Gaza Strip and, ultimately, establish an Islamic emirate in the region
area(s) of operation: headquartered in Gaza; heaviest presence and operational activity is in the Gaza Strip
note: operatives have a history of launching low-impact rockets into Israeli and Egyptian territory; the Army of Islam (Jaish al-Islam, JAI) in Syria is unrelated to AOI (2018)

HAMAS: aim(s): maintain control of the Gaza Strip to facilitate Palestinian nationalist aims
area(s) of operation: headquartered in Gaza (2018)

Mujahidin Shura Council in the Environs of Jerusalem (MSC): aim(s): bolster its staging capabilities in the Gaza Strip against Israel and, ultimately, destroy the state of Israel
area(s) of operation: headquartered in Gaza, although present in Egypt, Libya, Syria, and Israel (2018)

Palestine Islamic Jihad (PIJ): aim(s): enhance its staging capabilities in the Gaza Strip to launch attacks against Israel
area(s) of operation: stages rocket attacks against civilians and military personnel primarily in southern Israel (2018)

Palestine Liberation Front (PLF):
aim(s): bolster its staging capabilities in the Gaza Strip against Israel and, ultimately, destroy the state of Israel in order to establish a secular, Marxist Palestinian state with Jerusalem as its capital
area(s) of operation: based in Gaza; maintains a recruitment and paramilitary training presence in most of the refugee camps across the Gaza Strip (2018)

PFLP-General Command (PFLP-GC):
aim(s): bolster its staging capabilities to prepare fighters for deployment to Syria and to launch occasional attacks inside Israel; ultimately, seeks to establish a Palestinian state
area(s) of operation: headquartered in Gaza; as a longtime supporter of the Syrian Government, the group trains and deploys fighters to Syria to fight on behalf of President Bashar al-ASAD; stages occasional small-scale attacks inside Israel (2018)

Popular Front for the Liberation of Palestine (PFLP): aim(s): destroy the state of Israel and, ultimately, establish a secular, Marxist Palestinian state
area(s) of operation: headquartered in Gaza, recruiting and training fighters; stages limited attacks against Israel (2018)

TERRORIST GROUPS - FOREIGN BASED:

Abdallah Azzam Brigades (AAB):
aim(s): bolster its staging capabilities in the Gaza Strip against Israel to continue its attempts to disrupt Israel's economy and its efforts to establish security
area(s) of operation: launches homemade rockets from the Gaza Strip into populated Israeli territory, primarily the cities of Nahariya and Ashkelon (2018)

al-Aqsa Martyrs Brigade (AAMB):
aim(s): bolster its staging capabilities in the Gaza Strip against Israel and, ultimately, establish a Palestinian state comprising the West Bank, Gaza Strip, and Jerusalem

area(s) of operation: stages attacks from the Gaza Strip against Israeli soldiers and civilians inside Israel, including launching rockets and missiles (2018)

Islamic Revolutionary Guard Corps -- Qods Force (IRGC-QF):
aim(s): supports the destruction of Israel through funding, training, and weapons
area(s) of operation: Gaza Strip

(2019)

Islamic State of Iraq and ash-Sham (ISIS)-Sinai:
aim(s): bolster its staging capabilities in the Gaza Strip against Israel and, ultimately, establish a regional Islamic caliphate
area(s) of operation: stages attacks against Egyptian forces along the Gaza Strip-Egypt border and launches rockets into southern Israel from the border closest to Israel
note: formerly known as Ansar Bayt al-Maqdis (2018)

TRANSNATIONAL ISSUES :: GAZA STRIP

DISPUTES - INTERNATIONAL:
the status of the Gaza Strip is a final status issue to be resolved through negotiations; Israel removed settlers and military personnel from Gaza Strip in September 2005

REFUGEES AND INTERNALLY DISPLACED PERSONS:
refugees (country of origin): 1,421,282 (Palestinian refugees) (2019)

IDPs: 238,000 (includes persons displaced within the Gaza Strip due to the intensification of the Israeli-Palestinian conflict since June 2014 and other Palestinian IDPs in the Gaza Strip and West Bank who fled as long ago as 1967, although confirmed cumulative data do not go back beyond 2006) (2018)

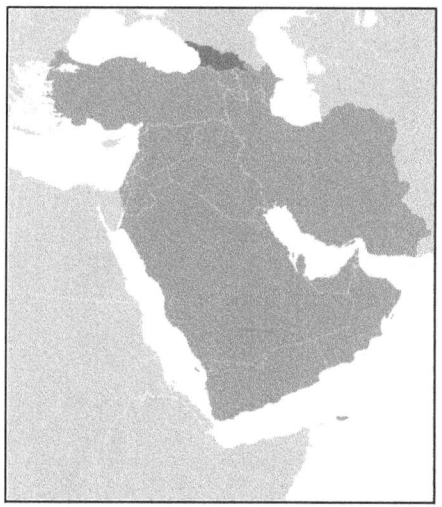

MIDDLE EAST :: GEORGIA

INTRODUCTION :: GEORGIA

BACKGROUND:

The region of present day Georgia contained the ancient kingdoms of Colchis and Kartli-Iberia. The area came under Roman influence in the first centuries A.D., and Christianity became the state religion in the 330s. Domination by Persians, Arabs, and Turks was followed by a Georgian golden age (11th-13th centuries) that was cut short by the Mongol invasion of 1236. Subsequently, the Ottoman and Persian empires competed for influence in the region. Georgia was absorbed into the Russian Empire in the 19th century. Independent for three years (1918-1921) following the Russian revolution, it was forcibly incorporated into the USSR in 1921 and regained its independence when the Soviet Union dissolved in 1991.

Mounting public discontent over rampant corruption and ineffective government services, followed by an attempt by the incumbent Georgian Government to manipulate parliamentary elections in November 2003, touched off widespread protests that led to the resignation of Eduard SHEVARDNADZE, president since 1995. In the aftermath of that popular movement, which became known as the "Rose Revolution," new elections in early 2004 swept Mikheil SAAKASHVILI into power along with his United National Movement (UNM) party. Progress on market reforms and democratization has been made in the years since independence, but this progress has been complicated by Russian assistance and support to the separatist regions of Abkhazia and South Ossetia. Periodic flare-ups in tension and violence culminated in a five-day conflict in August 2008 between Russia and Georgia, including the invasion of large portions of undisputed Georgian territory. Russian troops pledged to pull back from most occupied Georgian territory, but in late August 2008 Russia unilaterally recognized the independence of Abkhazia and South Ossetia, and Russian military forces remain in those regions.

Billionaire Bidzina IVANISHVILI's unexpected entry into politics in October 2011 brought the divided opposition together under his Georgian Dream coalition, which won a majority of seats in the October 2012 parliamentary elections and removed UNM from power. Conceding defeat, SAAKASHVILI named IVANISHVILI as prime minister and allowed Georgian Dream to create a new government. Giorgi MARGVELASHVILI was inaugurated as president on 17 November 2013, ending a tense year of power-sharing between SAAKASHVILI and IVANISHVILI. At the time, these changes in leadership represented unique examples of a former Soviet state that emerged to conduct democratic and peaceful government transitions of power. IVANISHVILI voluntarily resigned from office after the presidential succession, and Georgia's legislature on 20 November 2013 confirmed Irakli GARIBASHVILI as his replacement. GARIBASHVILI was replaced by Giorgi KVIRIKASHVILI in December 2015. KVIRIKASHVILI remained Prime Minister following Georgian Dream's success in the October 2016 parliamentary elections, where the party won a constitutional majority. IVANISHVILI reemerged as Georgian Dream party chairman in April 2018. KVIRIKASHVILI resigned in June 2018 and was replaced by Mamuka BAKHTADZE. Popular and government support for integration with the West is high in Georgia. Joining the EU and NATO are among the country's top foreign policy goals.

GEOGRAPHY :: GEORGIA

LOCATION:

Southwestern Asia, bordering the Black Sea, between Turkey and Russia, with a sliver of land north of the Caucasus extending into Europe; note - Georgia views itself as part of Europe; geopolitically, it can be classified as falling within Europe, the Middle East, or both

GEOGRAPHIC COORDINATES:

42 00 N, 43 30 E

MAP REFERENCES:

Asia

AREA:

total: 69,700 sq km

land: 69,700 sq km

water: 0 sq km

note: approximately 12,560 sq km, or about 18% of Georgia's area, is Russian occupied; the seized area includes all of Abkhazia and the breakaway region of South Ossetia, which consists of the northern part of Shida Kartli, eastern slivers of the Imereti region and Racha-Lechkhumi and Kvemo Svaneti, and part of western Mtskheta-Mtianeti

country comparison to the world: 122

AREA - COMPARATIVE:

slightly smaller than South Carolina; slightly larger than West Virginia

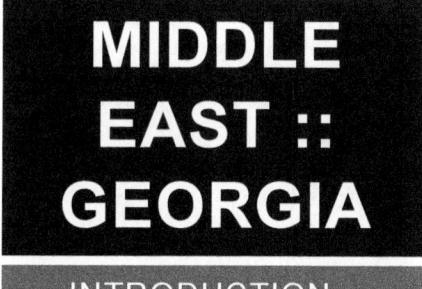

LAND BOUNDARIES:

total: 1,814 km

border countries (4): Armenia 219 km, Azerbaijan 428 km, Russia 894 km, Turkey 273 km

COASTLINE:

310 km

MARITIME CLAIMS:

territorial sea: 12 nm

exclusive economic zone: 200 nm

CLIMATE:

warm and pleasant; Mediterranean-like on Black Sea coast

TERRAIN:

largely mountainous with Great Caucasus Mountains in the north and Lesser Caucasus Mountains in the south; Kolkhet'is Dablobi (Kolkhida Lowland) opens to the Black Sea in the west; Mtkvari River Basin in the east; fertile soils in river valley flood plains and foothills of Kolkhida Lowland

ELEVATION:

mean elevation: 1,432 m

lowest point: Black Sea 0 m

highest point: Mt'a Shkhara 5,193 m

NATURAL RESOURCES:

timber, hydropower, manganese deposits, iron ore, copper, minor coal and oil deposits; coastal climate and soils allow for important tea and citrus growth

LAND USE:

agricultural land: 35.5% (2011 est.)

arable land: 5.8% (2011 est.) / permanent crops: 1.8% (2011 est.) / permanent pasture: 27.9% (2011 est.)

forest: 39.4% (2011 est.)

other: 25.1% (2011 est.)

IRRIGATED LAND:

4,330 sq km (2012)

POPULATION DISTRIBUTION:

settlement concentrated in the central valley, particularly in the capital city of Tbilisi in the east; smaller urban agglomerations dot the Black Sea coast, with Bat'umi being the largest

NATURAL HAZARDS:

earthquakes

ENVIRONMENT - CURRENT ISSUES:

air pollution, particularly in Rust'avi; heavy water pollution of Mtkvari River and the Black Sea; inadequate supplies of potable water; soil pollution from toxic chemicals; land and forest degradation; biodiversity loss; waste management

ENVIRONMENT - INTERNATIONAL AGREEMENTS:

party to: Air Pollution, Biodiversity, Climate Change, Climate Change-Kyoto Protocol, Desertification, Endangered Species, Hazardous Wastes, Law of the Sea, Ozone Layer Protection, Ship Pollution, Wetlands

signed, but not ratified: none of the selected agreements

GEOGRAPHY - NOTE:

note 1: strategically located east of the Black Sea; Georgia controls much of the Caucasus Mountains and the routes through them

note 2: the world's four deepest caves are all in Georgia, including two that are the only known caves on earth deeper than 2,000 m: Krubera Cave at -2,197 m (-7,208 ft; reached in 2012) and Veryovkina Cave at -2,212 (-7,257 ft; reached in 2018)

PEOPLE AND SOCIETY :: GEORGIA

POPULATION:

4.003 million (July 2018 est.)

country comparison to the world: 128

NATIONALITY:

noun: Georgian(s)

adjective: Georgian

ETHNIC GROUPS:

Georgian 86.8%, Azeri 6.3%, Armenian 4.5%, other 2.3% (includes Russian, Ossetian, Yazidi, Ukrainian, Kist, Greek) (2014 est.)

LANGUAGES:

Georgian (official) 87.6%, Azeri 6.2%, Armenian 3.9%, Russian 1.2%, other 1% (2014 est.)

note: Abkhaz is the official language in Abkhazia

RELIGIONS:

Orthodox (official) 83.4%, Muslim 10.7%, Armenian Apostolic 2.9%, other 1.2% (includes Catholic, Jehovah's Witness, Yazidi, Protestant, Jewish), none 0.5%, unspecified/no answer 1.2% (2014 est.)

AGE STRUCTURE:

0-14 years: 18.23% (male 469,163 /female 428,734)

15-24 years: 11.45% (male 299,362 /female 264,456)

25-54 years: 40.89% (male 984,275 /female 1,029,902)

55-64 years: 13.17% (male 289,337 /female 359,444)

65 years and over: 16.27% (male 314,467 /female 486,947) (2018 est.)

DEPENDENCY RATIOS:

total dependency ratio: 50 (2015 est.)

youth dependency ratio: 28.1 (2015 est.)

elderly dependency ratio: 21.9 (2015 est.)

potential support ratio: 4.6 (2015 est.)

MEDIAN AGE:

total: 38.3 years (2018 est.)

male: 35.5 years

female: 41.1 years

country comparison to the world: 59

POPULATION GROWTH RATE:

0.01% (2018 est.)

country comparison to the world: 190

BIRTH RATE:

12.1 births/1,000 population (2018 est.)

country comparison to the world: 163

DEATH RATE:

10.9 deaths/1,000 population (2018 est.)

country comparison to the world: 23

NET MIGRATION RATE:

-1.1 migrant(s)/1,000 population (2018 est.)

country comparison to the world: 141

POPULATION DISTRIBUTION:

settlement concentrated in the central valley, particularly in the capital city of Tbilisi in the east; smaller urban agglomerations dot the Black Sea coast, with Bat'umi being the largest

URBANIZATION:

urban population: 59% of total population (2019)

rate of urbanization: 0.42% annual rate of change (2015-20 est.)

note: data include Abkhazia and South Ossetia

MAJOR URBAN AREAS - POPULATION:

1.077 million TBILISI (capital) (2019)

SEX RATIO:

at birth: 1.06 male(s)/female

0-14 years: 1.09 male(s)/female

15-24 years: 1.13 male(s)/female

25-54 years: 0.96 male(s)/female

55-64 years: 0.8 male(s)/female

65 years and over: 0.65 male(s)/female

total population: 0.92 male(s)/female (2018 est.)

MOTHER'S MEAN AGE AT FIRST BIRTH:

24.5 years (2014 est.)

note: data do not cover Abkhazia and South Ossetia

MATERNAL MORTALITY RATE:

25 deaths/100,000 live births (2017 est.)

country comparison to the world: 121

INFANT MORTALITY RATE:

total: 14.7 deaths/1,000 live births (2018 est.)

male: 16.8 deaths/1,000 live births

female: 12.5 deaths/1,000 live births

country comparison to the world: 99

LIFE EXPECTANCY AT BIRTH:

total population: 76.6 years (2018 est.)

male: 72.5 years

female: 80.9 years

country comparison to the world: 84

TOTAL FERTILITY RATE:

1.76 children born/woman (2018 est.)

country comparison to the world: 158

CONTRACEPTIVE PREVALENCE RATE:

53.4% (2010)

note: percent of women aged 15-44

DRINKING WATER SOURCE:

improved:

urban: 100% of population

rural: 100% of population

total: 100% of population

unimproved:

urban: 0% of population

rural: 0% of population

total: 0% of population (2015 est.)

CURRENT HEALTH EXPENDITURE:

8.4% (2016)

PHYSICIANS DENSITY:

5.1 physicians/1,000 population (2015)

HOSPITAL BED DENSITY:

2.6 beds/1,000 population (2013)

SANITATION FACILITY ACCESS:

improved:

urban: 95.2% of population (2015 est.)

rural: 75.9% of population (2015 est.)

total: 86.3% of population (2015 est.)

unimproved:

urban: 4.8% of population (2015 est.)

rural: 24.1% of population (2015 est.)

total: 13.7% of population (2015 est.)

HIV/AIDS - ADULT PREVALENCE RATE:

0.4% (2018 est.)

country comparison to the world: 79

HIV/AIDS - PEOPLE LIVING WITH HIV/AIDS:

9,400 (2018 est.)

country comparison to the world: 101

HIV/AIDS - DEATHS:

<500 (2018 est.)

OBESITY - ADULT PREVALENCE RATE:

21.7% (2016)

country comparison to the world: 86

CHILDREN UNDER THE AGE OF 5 YEARS UNDERWEIGHT:

1.1% (2009)

country comparison to the world: 121

EDUCATION EXPENDITURES:

3.8% of GDP (2017)

country comparison to the world: 117

LITERACY:

definition: age 15 and over can read and write

total population: 99.8%

male: 99.8%

female: 99.7% (2015 est.)

SCHOOL LIFE EXPECTANCY (PRIMARY TO TERTIARY EDUCATION):

total: 15 years

male: 15 years

female: 16 years (2017)

UNEMPLOYMENT, YOUTH AGES 15-24:

total: 30.5%

male: 26.3%

female: 32.7% (2017 est.)

country comparison to the world: 29

GOVERNMENT :: GEORGIA

COUNTRY NAME:

conventional long form: none

conventional short form: Georgia

local long form: none

local short form: Sak'art'velo

former: Georgian Soviet Socialist Republic

etymology: the Western name may derive from the Persian designation "gurgan" meaning "Land of the Wolves"; the native name "Sak'art'velo" means "Land of the Kartvelians" and refers to the core central Georgian region of Kartli

GOVERNMENT TYPE:

semi-presidential republic

CAPITAL:

name: Tbilisi

geographic coordinates: 41 41 N, 44 50 E

time difference: UTC+4 (9 hours ahead of Washington, DC, during Standard Time)

etymology: the name in Georgian means "warm place," referring to the numerous sulfuric hot springs in the area

ADMINISTRATIVE DIVISIONS:

9 regions (mkharebi, singular - mkhare), 1 city (kalaki), and 2 autonomous republics (avtomnoy respubliki, singular - avtom respublika)

regions: Guria, Imereti, Kakheti, Kvemo Kartli, Mtskheta Mtianeti, Racha-Lechkhumi and Kvemo Svaneti, Samegrelo and Zemo Svaneti, Samtskhe-Javakheti, Shida Kartli; note - the breakaway region of South Ossetia consists of the northern part of Shida Kartli, eastern slivers of the Imereti region and Racha-Lechkhumi and Kvemo Svaneti, and part of western Mtskheta-Mtianeti;

city: Tbilisi;

autonomous republics: Abkhazia or Ap'khazet'is Avtonomiuri Respublika (Sokhumi), Ajaria or Acharis Avtonomiuri Respublika (Bat'umi)

note: the administrative centers of the two autonomous republics are shown in parentheses

note: the United States recognizes the breakaway regions of Abkhazia and South Ossetia to be part of Georgia

INDEPENDENCE:
9 April 1991 (from the Soviet Union); notable earlier date: A.D. 1008 (Georgia unified under King BAGRAT III)

NATIONAL HOLIDAY:
Independence Day, 26 May (1918); note - 26 May 1918 was the date of independence from Soviet Russia, 9 April 1991 was the date of independence from the Soviet Union

CONSTITUTION:
history: previous 1921, 1978 (based on 1977 Soviet Union constitution); latest approved 24 August 1995, effective 17 October 1995

amendments: proposed as a draft law supported by more than one half of the Parliament membership or by petition of at least 200,000 voters; passage requires support by at least three fourths of the Parliament membership in two successive sessions three months apart and the signature and promulgation by the president of Georgia; amended several times, last in 2018 (2019)

LEGAL SYSTEM:
civil law system

INTERNATIONAL LAW ORGANIZATION PARTICIPATION:
accepts compulsory ICJ jurisdiction; accepts ICCt jurisdiction

CITIZENSHIP:
citizenship by birth: no

citizenship by descent only: at least one parent must be a citizen of Georgia

dual citizenship recognized: no

residency requirement for naturalization: 10 years

SUFFRAGE:
18 years of age; universal

EXECUTIVE BRANCH:
chief of state: President Salome ZOURABICHVILI (since 16 December 2018)

head of government: Prime Minister Giorgi GAKHARIA (since 8 September 2019)

cabinet: Cabinet of Ministers

elections/appointments: president directly elected by absolute majority popular vote in 2 rounds if needed for a 5-year term (eligible for a second term); election last held on 28 November 2018 (next to be held in 2024); prime minister nominated by Parliament, appointed by the president

note - 2017 constitutional amendments made the 2018 election the last where the president was directly elected; future presidents will be elected by a 300-member College of Electors; in light of these changes, ZOURABICHVILI was allowed a six-year term

election results: Salome ZOURABICHVILI elected president in runoff; percent of vote - Salome ZOURABICHVILI (independent, backed by Georgian Dream) 59.5%, Grigol VASHADZE (UNM) 40.5%; Giorgi GAKHARIA approved as prime minister by Parliamentary vote 98-0

LEGISLATIVE BRANCH:
description: unicameral Parliament or Sakartvelos Parlamenti (150 seats; 77 members directly elected in a single nationwide constituency by closed, party-list proportional representation vote and 73 directly elected in single-seat constituencies by simple majority vote; members serve 4-year terms)

elections: last held on 8 October and 30 October 2016 (next to be held in 2020)

election results: percent of vote by party - Georgian Dream 48.7%, UNM 27.1%, Alliance of Patriots 5%, other 19.2%; seats by party - Georgian Dream 115, UNM 27, Alliance of Patriots 6, IWSG 1, independent 1; composition - men 126, women 24, percent of women 16%; note - European Georgia split from UNM in January 2017 taking 20 of 27 parliamentary seats; composition as of 1 July 2019: Georgian Dream 106, European Georgia 20, UNM 7, Alliance of Patriots 7, independent 10

JUDICIAL BRANCH:
highest courts: Supreme Court (consists of 28 judges organized into several specialized judicial chambers; number of judges determined by the president of Georgia); Constitutional Court (consists of 9 judges); note - the Abkhazian and Ajarian Autonomous republics each have a supreme court and a hierarchy of lower courts

judge selection and term of office: Supreme Court judges nominated by the High Council of Justice (a 14-member body consisting of the Supreme Court chairperson, common court judges, and appointees of the president of Georgia) and appointed by Parliament; judges appointed for life; Constitutional Court judges appointed 3 each by the president, by Parliament, and by the Supreme Court judges; judges appointed for 10-year terms

subordinate courts: Courts of Appeal; regional (town) and district courts

POLITICAL PARTIES AND LEADERS:
Alliance of Patriots [Irma INASHVILI]
Democratic Movement-United Georgia [Nino BURJANADZE]
Development Movement [Davit USPASHVILI]
European Georgia [Davit BAKRADZE] (split from UNM)
For Justice Party [Eka BESELIA]
Free Democrats or FD [Shalva SHAVGULIDZE]
Georgian Dream-Democratic Georgia [Bidzina IVANISHVILI]
Girchi (Pinecone) [Zurab JAPARIDZE]
Industry Will Save Georgia (Industrialists) or IWSG [Giorgi TOPADZE]
Labor Party [Shalva NATELASHVILI]
New Georgia [Giorgi VASHADZE]
Republican Party [Khatuna SAMNIDZE]
United National Movement or UNM [Grigol VASHADZE]

INTERNATIONAL ORGANIZATION PARTICIPATION:
ADB, BSEC, CD, CE, CPLP (associate), EAPC, EBRD, FAO, G-11, GCTU, GUAM, IAEA, IBRD, ICAO, ICC (national committees), ICCt, ICRM, IDA, IFAD, IFC, IFRCS, ILO, IMF, IMO, Interpol, IOC, IOM, IPU, ISO (correspondent), ITSO, ITU, ITUC (NGOs), MIGA, OAS (observer), OIF (observer), OPCW, OSCE, PFP, SELEC (observer), UN, UNCTAD, UNESCO, UNIDO, UNWTO, UPU, WCO, WHO, WIPO, WMO, WTO

DIPLOMATIC REPRESENTATION IN THE US:
Ambassador David BAKRADZE (since 18 January 2017)

chancery: 1824 R Street NW, Washington, DC 20009

telephone: [1] (202) 387-2390

FAX: [1] (202) 387-0864

consulate(s) general: New York

DIPLOMATIC REPRESENTATION FROM THE US:

chief of mission: Ambassador (vacant); Charge d'Affaires Elizabeth ROOD (since 13 May 2019)

telephone: [995] (32) 227-70-00

embassy: 29 Georgian-American Friendship Avenue, Didi Dighomi, Tbilisi 0131

mailing address: 7060 T'bilisi Place, Washington, DC 20521-7060

FAX: [995] (32) 253-23-10

FLAG DESCRIPTION:

white rectangle with a central red cross extending to all four sides of the flag; each of the four quadrants displays a small red bolnur-katskhuri cross; sometimes referred to as the Five-Cross Flag; although adopted as the official Georgian flag in 2004, the five-cross design appears to date back to the 14th century

NATIONAL SYMBOL(S):

Saint George, lion; national colors: red, white

NATIONAL ANTHEM:

name: "Tavisupleba" (Liberty)

lyrics/music: Davit MAGRADSE/Zakaria PALIASHVILI (adapted by Joseb KETSCHAKMADSE)

note: adopted 2004; after the Rose Revolution, a new anthem with music based on the operas "Abesalom da Eteri" and "Daisi" was adopted

ECONOMY :: GEORGIA

ECONOMY - OVERVIEW:

Georgia's main economic activities include cultivation of agricultural products such as grapes, citrus fruits, and hazelnuts; mining of manganese, copper, and gold; and producing alcoholic and nonalcoholic beverages, metals, machinery, and chemicals in small-scale industries. The country imports nearly all of its needed supplies of natural gas and oil products. It has sizeable hydropower capacity that now provides most of its electricity needs.

Georgia has overcome the chronic energy shortages and gas supply interruptions of the past by renovating hydropower plants and by increasingly relying on natural gas imports from Azerbaijan instead of from Russia. Construction of the Baku-Tbilisi-Ceyhan oil pipeline, the South Caucasus gas pipeline, and the Baku-Tbilisi-Kars railroad are part of a strategy to capitalize on Georgia's strategic location between Europe and Asia and develop its role as a transit hub for gas, oil, and other goods.

Georgia's economy sustained GDP growth of more than 10% in 2006-07, based on strong inflows of foreign investment, remittances, and robust government spending. However, GDP growth slowed following the August 2008 conflict with Russia, and sank to negative 4% in 2009 as foreign direct investment and workers' remittances declined in the wake of the global financial crisis. The economy rebounded in the period 2010-17, but FDI inflows, the engine of Georgian economic growth prior to the 2008 conflict, have not recovered fully. Unemployment remains persistently high.

The country is pinning its hopes for faster growth on a continued effort to build up infrastructure, enhance support for entrepreneurship, simplify regulations, and improve professional education, in order to attract foreign investment and boost employment, with a focus on transportation projects, tourism, hydropower, and agriculture. Georgia had historically suffered from a chronic failure to collect tax revenues; however, since 2004 the government has simplified the tax code, increased tax enforcement, and cracked down on petty corruption, leading to higher revenues. The government has received high marks from the World Bank for improvements in business transparency. Since 2012, the Georgian Dream-led government has continued the previous administration's low-regulation, low-tax, free market policies, while modestly increasing social spending and amending the labor code to comply with International Labor Standards. In mid-2014, Georgia concluded an association agreement with the EU, paving the way to free trade and visa-free travel. In 2017, Georgia signed Free Trade Agreement (FTA) with China as part of Tbilisi's efforts to diversify its economic ties. Georgia is seeking to develop its Black Sea ports to further facilitate East-West trade.

GDP (PURCHASING POWER PARITY):

$39.85 billion (2017 est.)

$37.96 billion (2016 est.)

$36.91 billion (2015 est.)

note: data are in 2017 dollars

country comparison to the world: 118

GDP (OFFICIAL EXCHANGE RATE):

$15.16 billion (2017 est.)

GDP - REAL GROWTH RATE:

5% (2017 est.)

2.8% (2016 est.)

2.9% (2015 est.)

country comparison to the world: 50

GDP - PER CAPITA (PPP):

$10,700 (2017 est.)

$10,300 (2016 est.)

$9,900 (2015 est.)

note: data are in 2017 dollars

country comparison to the world: 138

GROSS NATIONAL SAVING:

23% of GDP (2017 est.)

19.9% of GDP (2016 est.)

19.5% of GDP (2015 est.)

country comparison to the world: 75

GDP - COMPOSITION, BY END USE:

household consumption: 62.8% (2017 est.)

government consumption: 17.1% (2017 est.)

investment in fixed capital: 29.5% (2017 est.)

investment in inventories: 2.4% (2017 est.)

exports of goods and services: 50.4% (2017 est.)

imports of goods and services: -62.2% (2017 est.)

GDP - COMPOSITION, BY SECTOR OF ORIGIN:

agriculture: 8.2% (2017 est.)

industry: 23.7% (2017 est.)

services: 67.9% (2017 est.)

AGRICULTURE - PRODUCTS:

citrus, grapes, tea, hazelnuts, vegetables; livestock

INDUSTRIES:

steel, machine tools, electrical appliances, mining (manganese, copper, gold), chemicals, wood products, wine

INDUSTRIAL PRODUCTION GROWTH RATE:

6.7% (2017 est.)

country comparison to the world: 34

LABOR FORCE:

1.998 million (2016 est.)

country comparison to the world: 125

LABOR FORCE - BY OCCUPATION:

agriculture: 55.6%

industry: 8.9%

services: 35.5% (2006 est.)

UNEMPLOYMENT RATE:

NA% (2017 est.)

11.8% (2016 est.)

country comparison to the world: 156

POPULATION BELOW POVERTY LINE:

9.2% (2010 est.)

HOUSEHOLD INCOME OR CONSUMPTION BY PERCENTAGE SHARE:

lowest 10%: 2%

highest 10%: 31.3% (2008)

DISTRIBUTION OF FAMILY INCOME - GINI INDEX:

40.1 (2014)

46 (2011)

country comparison to the world: 66

BUDGET:

revenues: 4.352 billion (2017 est.)

expenditures: 4.925 billion (2017 est.)

TAXES AND OTHER REVENUES:

28.7% (of GDP) (2017 est.)

country comparison to the world: 91

BUDGET SURPLUS (+) OR DEFICIT (-):

-3.8% (of GDP) (2017 est.)

country comparison to the world: 153

PUBLIC DEBT:

44.9% of GDP (2017 est.)

44.4% of GDP (2016 est.)

note: data cover general government debt and include debt instruments issued (or owned) by government entities other than the treasury; the data include treasury debt held by foreign entities; the data include debt issued by subnational entities; Georgia does not maintain intragovernmental debt or social funds

country comparison to the world: 116

FISCAL YEAR:

calendar year

INFLATION RATE (CONSUMER PRICES):

6% (2017 est.)

2.1% (2016 est.)

country comparison to the world: 185

CENTRAL BANK DISCOUNT RATE:

7% (23 September 2015)

6.5% (7)

note: this is the Refinancing Rate, the key monetary policy rate of the National Bank of Georgia

country comparison to the world: 49

COMMERCIAL BANK PRIME LENDING RATE:

11.49% (31 December 2017 est.)

12.62% (31 December 2016 est.)

country comparison to the world: 70

STOCK OF NARROW MONEY:

$2.301 billion (31 December 2017 est.)

$1.933 billion (31 December 2016 est.)

country comparison to the world: 131

STOCK OF BROAD MONEY:

$2.301 billion (31 December 2017 est.)

$1.933 billion (31 December 2016 est.)

country comparison to the world: 139

STOCK OF DOMESTIC CREDIT:

$8.961 billion (31 December 2017 est.)

$7.753 billion (31 December 2016 est.)

country comparison to the world: 111

MARKET VALUE OF PUBLICLY TRADED SHARES:

$1.155 billion (31 December 2015 est.)

$943.4 million (31 December 2012 est.)

$795.7 million (31 December 2011 est.)

country comparison to the world: 104

CURRENT ACCOUNT BALANCE:

-$1.348 billion (2017 est.)

-$1.84 billion (2016 est.)

country comparison to the world: 151

EXPORTS:

$3.566 billion (2017 est.)

$2.831 billion (2016 est.)

country comparison to the world: 122

EXPORTS - PARTNERS:

Russia 14.5%, Azerbaijan 10%, Turkey 7.9%, Armenia 7.7%, China 7.6%, Bulgaria 6.6%, Ukraine 4.6%, US 4.5% (2017)

EXPORTS - COMMODITIES:

vehicles, ferro-alloys, fertilizers, nuts, scrap metal, gold, copper ores

IMPORTS:

$7.415 billion (2017 est.)

$6.747 billion (2016 est.)

country comparison to the world: 115

IMPORTS - COMMODITIES:

fuels, vehicles, machinery and parts, grain and other foods, pharmaceuticals

IMPORTS - PARTNERS:

Turkey 17.2%, Russia 9.9%, China 9.2%, Azerbaijan 7.6%, Ukraine 5.6%, Germany 5.4% (2017)

RESERVES OF FOREIGN EXCHANGE AND GOLD:

$3.039 billion (31 December 2017 est.)

$2.756 billion (31 December 2016 est.)

country comparison to the world: 108

DEBT - EXTERNAL:

$16.99 billion (31 December 2017 est.)

$14.08 billion (31 December 2016 est.)

country comparison to the world: 100

STOCK OF DIRECT FOREIGN INVESTMENT - AT HOME:

$17.47 billion (31 December 2017 est.)

$14.66 billion (31 December 2016 est.)

country comparison to the world: 84

STOCK OF DIRECT FOREIGN INVESTMENT - ABROAD:

$2.477 billion (31 December 2017 est.)

$2.185 billion (31 December 2016 est.)

country comparison to the world: 81

EXCHANGE RATES:

laris (GEL) per US dollar -

2.535 (2017 est.)

2.3668 (2016 est.)

2.3668 (2015 est.)

2.2694 (2014 est.)

1.7657 (2013 est.)

ENERGY :: GEORGIA

ELECTRICITY ACCESS:

electrification - total population: 100% (2016)

ELECTRICITY - PRODUCTION:

13.24 billion kWh (2016 est.)

country comparison to the world: 91

ELECTRICITY - CONSUMPTION:

12.37 billion kWh (2016 est.)

country comparison to the world: 87

ELECTRICITY - EXPORTS:

560 million kWh (2016 est.)

country comparison to the world: 66

ELECTRICITY - IMPORTS:

1.329 billion kWh (2016 est.)

country comparison to the world: 63

ELECTRICITY - INSTALLED GENERATING CAPACITY:

4.641 million kW (2016 est.)

country comparison to the world: 84

ELECTRICITY - FROM FOSSIL FUELS:

35% of total installed capacity (2016 est.)

country comparison to the world: 179

ELECTRICITY - FROM NUCLEAR FUELS:

0% of total installed capacity (2017 est.)

country comparison to the world: 95

ELECTRICITY - FROM HYDROELECTRIC PLANTS:

65% of total installed capacity (2017 est.)

country comparison to the world: 22

ELECTRICITY - FROM OTHER RENEWABLE SOURCES:

0% of total installed capacity (2017 est.)

country comparison to the world: 187

CRUDE OIL - PRODUCTION:

400 bbl/day (2018 est.)

country comparison to the world: 93

CRUDE OIL - EXPORTS:

3,006 bbl/day (2017 est.)

country comparison to the world: 68

CRUDE OIL - IMPORTS:

2,660 bbl/day (2015 est.)

country comparison to the world: 78

CRUDE OIL - PROVED RESERVES:

35 million bbl (1 January 2018 est.)

country comparison to the world: 80

REFINED PETROLEUM PRODUCTS - PRODUCTION:

247 bbl/day (2017 est.)

country comparison to the world: 106

REFINED PETROLEUM PRODUCTS - CONSUMPTION:

27,000 bbl/day (2016 est.)

country comparison to the world: 122

REFINED PETROLEUM PRODUCTS - EXPORTS:

2,052 bbl/day (2015 est.)

country comparison to the world: 104

REFINED PETROLEUM PRODUCTS - IMPORTS:

28,490 bbl/day (2015 est.)

country comparison to the world: 101

NATURAL GAS - PRODUCTION:

7.363 million cu m (2017 est.)

country comparison to the world: 95

NATURAL GAS - CONSUMPTION:

2.294 billion cu m (2017 est.)

country comparison to the world: 83

NATURAL GAS - EXPORTS:

0 cu m (2017 est.)

country comparison to the world: 109

NATURAL GAS - IMPORTS:

2.294 billion cu m (2017 est.)

country comparison to the world: 50

NATURAL GAS - PROVED RESERVES:

8.495 billion cu m (1 January 2018 est.)

country comparison to the world: 80

CARBON DIOXIDE EMISSIONS FROM CONSUMPTION OF ENERGY:

9.912 million Mt (2017 est.)

country comparison to the world: 109

COMMUNICATIONS :: GEORGIA

TELEPHONES - FIXED LINES:

total subscriptions: 713,826

subscriptions per 100 inhabitants: 14 (2017 est.)

country comparison to the world: 86

TELEPHONES - MOBILE CELLULAR:

total subscriptions: 5,730,625

subscriptions per 100 inhabitants: 116 (2017 est.)

country comparison to the world: 116

TELEPHONE SYSTEM:

general assessment: fixed-line telecommunications network has limited coverage outside Tbilisi; multiple mobile-cellular providers provide services to an increasing subscribership throughout the country; broadband subscribers steadily increasing; with the recent investment in infrastructure customers are moving from copper to fiber networks (2018)

domestic: fixed-line 14 per 100, cellular telephone networks cover the entire country; mobile-cellular teledensity roughly 116 per 100 persons; intercity facilities include a fiber-optic line between T'bilisi and K'ut'aisi (2018)

international: country code - 995; landing points for the Georgia-Russia, Diamond Link Global, and Caucasus Cable System fiber-optic submarine cable provides connectivity to Russia, Romania and Bulgaria; international service is available by microwave, landline, and satellite through the Moscow switch; international electronic mail and telex service are available (2019)

BROADCAST MEDIA:

The Tbilisi-based Georgian Public Broadcaster (GPB) includes Channel 1, Channel 2 as well as the Batumi-based Adjara TV, and the State Budget funds all three; there are also a number of independent commercial television broadcasters, such as Imedi, Rustavi 2, Pirveli TV, Maestro, Kavkasia, Georgian Dream Studios (GDS), Obiektivi, and a small Russian language operator TOK TV; Tabula and Post TV are web-based television outlets; all of these broadcasters and web-based television outlets, except GDS, carry the news; the Georgian Orthodox Church also operates a satellite-based television station called Unanimity; there are 26 regional television broadcasters across Georgia that are members of the Georgian Association of Regional Broadcasters and/or the Alliance of Georgian Broadcasters; the broadcaster organizations seek to strengthen the regional media's capacities and distribution of regional products: a nationwide digital switchover occurred in 2015; there are several dozen private radio stations; GPB operates 2 radio stations

(2019)

INTERNET COUNTRY CODE:

.ge

INTERNET USERS:

total: 2,464,107

percent of population: 50% (July 2016 est.)

country comparison to the world: 105

BROADBAND - FIXED SUBSCRIPTIONS:

total: 770,113

subscriptions per 100 inhabitants: 16 (2017 est.)

country comparison to the world: 73

MILITARY AND SECURITY :: GEORGIA

MILITARY EXPENDITURES:

2.1% of GDP (2018)

2% of GDP (2017)

2.23% of GDP (2016)

2.34% of GDP (2015)

2.26% of GDP (2014)

country comparison to the world: 45

MILITARY AND SECURITY FORCES:

Georgian Defense Forces: Land Forces (include Air and Air Defense Forces); separatist Abkhazia Armed Forces: Ground Forces, Air Forces; separatist South Ossetia Armed Forces (2019)

note: Georgian naval forces have been incorporated into the Coast Guard, which is part of the Ministry of Internal Affairs rather than the Ministry of Defense

MILITARY SERVICE AGE AND OBLIGATION:

18 to 27 years of age for compulsory and voluntary active duty military service; conscript service obligation is 12 months (2017)

MILITARY - NOTE:

Georgia does not have any military stationed in the separatist territories of Abkhazia and South Ossetia, but large numbers of Russian servicemen have been stationed in these regions since the 2008 Russia-Georgia War (2019)

TRANSPORTATION :: GEORGIA

NATIONAL AIR TRANSPORT SYSTEM:

number of registered air carriers: 5 (2015)

inventory of registered aircraft operated by air carriers: 13 (2015)

annual passenger traffic on registered air carriers: 232,263 (2015)

annual freight traffic on registered air carriers: 185,040 mt-km (2015)

CIVIL AIRCRAFT REGISTRATION COUNTRY CODE PREFIX:

4L (2016)

AIRPORTS:

22 (2013)

country comparison to the world: 135

AIRPORTS - WITH PAVED RUNWAYS:

total: 18 (2017)

over 3,047 m: 1 (2017)

2,438 to 3,047 m: 7 (2017)

1,524 to 2,437 m: 3 (2017)

914 to 1,523 m: 5 (2017)

under 914 m: 2 (2017)

AIRPORTS - WITH UNPAVED RUNWAYS:

total: 4 (2013)

1,524 to 2,437 m: 1 (2013)

914 to 1,523 m: 2 (2013)

under 914 m: 1 (2013)

HELIPORTS:

2 (2013)

PIPELINES:

1596 km gas, 1175 km oil (2013)

RAILWAYS:

total: 1,363 km (2014)

narrow gauge: 37 km 0.912-m gauge (37 km electrified) (2014)

broad gauge: 1,326 km 1.520-m gauge (1,251 km electrified) (2014)

country comparison to the world: 84

ROADWAYS:

total: 20,295 km (2018)

country comparison to the world: 111

MERCHANT MARINE:

total: 82

by type: bulk carrier 1, general cargo 24, oil tanker 2, other 55 (2018)

country comparison to the world: 96

PORTS AND TERMINALS:

major seaport(s): Black Sea - Bat'umi, P'ot'i

TRANSNATIONAL ISSUES :: GEORGIA

DISPUTES - INTERNATIONAL:

Russia's military support and subsequent recognition of Abkhazia and South Ossetia independence in 2008 continue to sour relations with Georgia

REFUGEES AND INTERNALLY DISPLACED PERSONS:

IDPs: 293,000 (displaced in the 1990s as a result of armed conflict in the breakaway republics of Abkhazia and South Ossetia; displaced in 2008 by fighting between Georgia and Russia over South Ossetia) (2018)

stateless persons: 566 (2018)

ILLICIT DRUGS:

limited cultivation of cannabis and opium poppy, mostly for domestic consumption; used as transshipment point for opiates via Central Asia to Western Europe and Russia

EUROPE :: GERMANY

INTRODUCTION :: GERMANY

BACKGROUND:

As Europe's largest economy and second most populous nation (after Russia), Germany is a key member of the continent's economic, political, and defense organizations. European power struggles immersed Germany in two devastating world wars in the first half of the 20th century and left the country occupied by the victorious Allied powers of the US, UK, France, and the Soviet Union in 1945. With the advent of the Cold War, two German states were formed in 1949: the western Federal Republic of Germany (FRG) and the eastern German Democratic Republic (GDR). The democratic FRG embedded itself in key western economic and security organizations, the EC (now the EU) and NATO, while the communist GDR was on the front line of the Soviet-led Warsaw Pact. The decline of the USSR and the end of the Cold War allowed for German reunification in 1990. Since then, Germany has expended considerable funds to bring eastern productivity and wages up to western standards. In January 1999, Germany and 10 other EU countries introduced a common European exchange currency, the euro.

GEOGRAPHY :: GERMANY

LOCATION:

Central Europe, bordering the Baltic Sea and the North Sea, between the Netherlands and Poland, south of Denmark

GEOGRAPHIC COORDINATES:

51 00 N, 9 00 E

MAP REFERENCES:

Europe

AREA:

total: 357,022 sq km

land: 348,672 sq km

water: 8,350 sq km

country comparison to the world: 64

AREA - COMPARATIVE:

three times the size of Pennsylvania; slightly smaller than Montana

LAND BOUNDARIES:

total: 3,714 km

border countries (9): Austria 801 km, Belgium 133 km, Czech Republic 704 km, Denmark 140 km, France 418 km, Luxembourg 128 km, Netherlands 575 km, Poland 467 km, Switzerland 348 km

COASTLINE:

2,389 km

MARITIME CLAIMS:

territorial sea: 12 nm

exclusive economic zone: 200 nm

continental shelf: 200-m depth or to the depth of exploitation

CLIMATE:

temperate and marine; cool, cloudy, wet winters and summers; occasional warm mountain (foehn) wind

TERRAIN:

lowlands in north, uplands in center, Bavarian Alps in south

ELEVATION:

mean elevation: 263 m

lowest point: Neuendorf bei Wilster -3.5 m

highest point: Zugspitze 2,963 m

NATURAL RESOURCES:

coal, lignite, natural gas, iron ore, copper, nickel, uranium, potash, salt, construction materials, timber, arable land

LAND USE:

agricultural land: 48% (2011 est.)

arable land: 34.1% (2011 est.) / permanent crops: 0.6% (2011 est.) / permanent pasture: 13.3% (2011 est.)

forest: 31.8% (2011 est.)

other: 20.2% (2011 est.)

IRRIGATED LAND:

6,500 sq km (2012)

POPULATION DISTRIBUTION:

most populous country in Europe; a fairly even distribution throughout most of the country, with urban areas attracting larger and denser populations, particularly in the far western part of the industrial state of North Rhine-Westphalia

NATURAL HAZARDS:

flooding

ENVIRONMENT - CURRENT ISSUES:

emissions from coal-burning utilities and industries contribute to air pollution; acid rain, resulting from sulfur dioxide emissions, is damaging forests; pollution in the Baltic Sea from raw sewage and industrial effluents from rivers in eastern Germany; hazardous waste disposal; government established a mechanism for ending the use of nuclear power by 2022; government working to meet EU commitment to identify nature preservation areas in line with the

EU's Flora, Fauna, and Habitat directive

ENVIRONMENT - INTERNATIONAL AGREEMENTS:

party to: Air Pollution, Air Pollution-Nitrogen Oxides, Air Pollution-Persistent Organic Pollutants, Air Pollution-Sulfur 85, Air Pollution-Sulfur 94, Air Pollution-Volatile Organic Compounds, Antarctic-Environmental Protocol, Antarctic-Marine Living Resources, Antarctic Seals, Antarctic Treaty, Biodiversity, Climate Change, Climate Change-Kyoto Protocol, Desertification, Endangered Species, Environmental Modification, Hazardous Wastes, Law of the Sea, Marine Dumping, Ozone Layer Protection, Ship Pollution, Tropical Timber 83, Tropical Timber 94, Wetlands, Whaling

signed, but not ratified: none of the selected agreements

GEOGRAPHY - NOTE:

strategic location on North European Plain and along the entrance to the Baltic Sea; most major rivers in Germany - the Rhine, Weser, Oder, Elbe - flow northward; the Danube, which originates in the Black Forest, flows eastward

PEOPLE AND SOCIETY :: GERMANY

POPULATION:

80,457,737 (July 2018 est.)

country comparison to the world: 19

NATIONALITY:

noun: German(s)

adjective: German

ETHNIC GROUPS:

German 87.2%, Turkish 1.8%, Polish 1%, Syrian 1%, other 9% (2017 est.)

note: data represent population by nationality

LANGUAGES:

German (official)

note: Danish, Frisian, Sorbian, and Romani are official minority languages; Low German, Danish, North Frisian, Sater Frisian, Lower Sorbian, Upper Sorbian, and Romani are recognized as regional languages under the European Charter for Regional or Minority Languages

RELIGIONS:

Roman Catholic 28.2%, Protestant 26%, Muslim 5%, Orthodox 1.9%, other Christian 1.1%, other .9%, none 37% (2017 est.)

AGE STRUCTURE:

0-14 years: 12.83% (male 5,299,798 /female 5,024,184)

15-24 years: 9.98% (male 4,092,901 /female 3,933,997)

25-54 years: 39.87% (male 16,181,931 /female 15,896,528)

55-64 years: 14.96% (male 5,989,111 /female 6,047,449)

65 years and over: 22.36% (male 7,930,590 /female 10,061,248) (2018 est.)

DEPENDENCY RATIOS:

total dependency ratio: 52.1 (2015 est.)

youth dependency ratio: 19.9 (2015 est.)

elderly dependency ratio: 32.1 (2015 est.)

potential support ratio: 3.1 (2015 est.)

MEDIAN AGE:

total: 47.4 years (2018 est.)

male: 46.2 years

female: 48.5 years

country comparison to the world: 3

POPULATION GROWTH RATE:

-0.17% (2018 est.)

country comparison to the world: 208

BIRTH RATE:

8.6 births/1,000 population (2018 est.)

country comparison to the world: 213

DEATH RATE:

11.8 deaths/1,000 population (2018 est.)

country comparison to the world: 19

NET MIGRATION RATE:

1.5 migrant(s)/1,000 population (2018 est.)

country comparison to the world: 56

POPULATION DISTRIBUTION:

most populous country in Europe; a fairly even distribution throughout most of the country, with urban areas attracting larger and denser populations, particularly in the far western part of the industrial state of North Rhine-Westphalia

URBANIZATION:

urban population: 77.4% of total population (2019)

rate of urbanization: 0.27% annual rate of change (2015-20 est.)

MAJOR URBAN AREAS - POPULATION:

3.557 million BERLIN (capital), 1.791 million Hamburg, 1.521 million Munich, 1.108 million Cologne (2019)

SEX RATIO:

at birth: 1.05 male(s)/female

0-14 years: 1.05 male(s)/female

15-24 years: 1.04 male(s)/female

25-54 years: 1.02 male(s)/female

55-64 years: 0.99 male(s)/female

65 years and over: 0.79 male(s)/female

total population: 0.96 male(s)/female (2018 est.)

MOTHER'S MEAN AGE AT FIRST BIRTH:

29.4 years (2015 est.)

MATERNAL MORTALITY RATE:

7 deaths/100,000 live births (2017 est.)

country comparison to the world: 154

INFANT MORTALITY RATE:

total: 3.4 deaths/1,000 live births (2018 est.)

male: 3.7 deaths/1,000 live births

female: 3.1 deaths/1,000 live births

country comparison to the world: 202

LIFE EXPECTANCY AT BIRTH:

total population: 80.9 years (2018 est.)

male: 78.6 years

female: 83.4 years

country comparison to the world: 37

TOTAL FERTILITY RATE:

1.46 children born/woman (2018 est.)

country comparison to the world: 204

CONTRACEPTIVE PREVALENCE RATE:

80.3% (2011)

note: percent of women aged 18-49

DRINKING WATER SOURCE:

improved:

urban: 100% of population

rural: 100% of population

total: 100% of population

unimproved:

urban: 0% of population

rural: 0% of population

total: 0% of population (2015 est.)

CURRENT HEALTH EXPENDITURE:

11.1% (2016)

PHYSICIANS DENSITY:

4.21 physicians/1,000 population (2016)

HOSPITAL BED DENSITY:

8.3 beds/1,000 population (2013)

SANITATION FACILITY ACCESS:

improved:

urban: 99.3% of population (2015 est.)

rural: 99% of population (2015 est.)

total: 99.2% of population (2015 est.)

unimproved:

urban: 0.7% of population (2015 est.)

rural: 1% of population (2015 est.)

total: 0.8% of population (2015 est.)

HIV/AIDS - ADULT PREVALENCE RATE:

0.1% (2018 est.)

country comparison to the world: 123

HIV/AIDS - PEOPLE LIVING WITH HIV/AIDS:

87,000 (2018 est.)

country comparison to the world: 46

HIV/AIDS - DEATHS:

<500 (2018 est.)

OBESITY - ADULT PREVALENCE RATE:

22.3% (2016)

country comparison to the world: 79

EDUCATION EXPENDITURES:

4.8% of GDP (2015)

country comparison to the world: 75

SCHOOL LIFE EXPECTANCY (PRIMARY TO TERTIARY EDUCATION):

total: 17 years

male: 17 years

female: 17 years (2016)

UNEMPLOYMENT, YOUTH AGES 15-24:

total: 6.8%

male: 7.6%

female: 5.8% (2017 est.)

country comparison to the world: 158

GOVERNMENT :: GERMANY

COUNTRY NAME:

conventional long form: Federal Republic of Germany

conventional short form: Germany

local long form: Bundesrepublik Deutschland

local short form: Deutschland

former: German Reich

etymology: the Gauls (Celts) of Western Europe may have referred to the newly arriving Germanic tribes who settled in neighboring areas east of the Rhine during the first centuries B.C. as "Germani," a term the Romans adopted as "Germania"; the native designation "Deutsch" comes from the Old High German "diutisc" meaning "of the people"

GOVERNMENT TYPE:

federal parliamentary republic

CAPITAL:

name: Berlin

geographic coordinates: 52 31 N, 13 24 E

time difference: UTC+1 (6 hours ahead of Washington, DC, during Standard Time)

daylight saving time: +1hr, begins last Sunday in March; ends last Sunday in October

etymology: the origin of the name is unclear but may be related to the old West Slavic (Polabian) word "berl" or "birl," meaning "swamp"

ADMINISTRATIVE DIVISIONS:

16 states (Laender, singular - Land); Baden-Wuerttemberg, Bayern (Bavaria), Berlin, Brandenburg, Bremen, Hamburg, Hessen (Hesse), Mecklenburg-Vorpommern (Mecklenburg-Western Pomerania), Niedersachsen (Lower Saxony), Nordrhein-Westfalen (North Rhine-Westphalia), Rheinland-Pfalz (Rhineland-Palatinate), Saarland, Sachsen (Saxony), Sachsen-Anhalt (Saxony-Anhalt), Schleswig-Holstein, Thueringen (Thuringia); note - Bayern, Sachsen, and Thueringen refer to themselves as free states (Freistaaten, singular - Freistaat), while Bremen calls itself a Free Hanseatic City (Freie Hansestadt) and Hamburg considers itself a Free and Hanseatic City (Freie und Hansestadt)

INDEPENDENCE:

18 January 1871 (establishment of the German Empire); divided into four zones of occupation (UK, US, USSR, and France) in 1945 following World War II; Federal Republic of Germany (FRG or West Germany) proclaimed on 23 May 1949 and included the former UK, US, and French zones; German Democratic Republic (GDR or East Germany) proclaimed on 7 October 1949 and included the former USSR zone; West Germany and East Germany unified on 3 October 1990; all four powers formally relinquished rights on 15 March 1991; notable earlier dates: 10 August 843 (Eastern Francia established from the division of the Carolingian Empire); 2 February 962 (crowning of OTTO I, recognized as the first Holy Roman Emperor)

NATIONAL HOLIDAY:

German Unity Day, 3 October (1990)

CONSTITUTION:

history: previous 1919 (Weimar Constitution); latest drafted 10-23 August 1948, approved 12 May 1949, promulgated 23 May 1949, entered into force 24 May 1949

amendments: proposed by Parliament; passage and enactment into law require two-thirds majority vote by both the Bundesrat (upper house) and the Bundestag (lower house) of Parliament; articles including those on basic human rights and freedoms cannot be amended; amended many times, last in 2017 (2018)

LEGAL SYSTEM:

civil law system

INTERNATIONAL LAW ORGANIZATION PARTICIPATION:

accepts compulsory ICJ jurisdiction with reservations; accepts ICCt jurisdiction

CITIZENSHIP:

citizenship by birth: no

citizenship by descent only: at least one parent must be a German citizen or a resident alien who has lived in Germany at least 8 years

dual citizenship recognized: yes, but requires prior permission from government

residency requirement for naturalization: 8 years

SUFFRAGE:

18 years of age; universal; age 16 for some state and municipal elections

EXECUTIVE BRANCH:

chief of state: President Frank-Walter STEINMEIER (since 19 March 2017)

head of government: Chancellor Angela MERKEL (since 22 November 2005)

cabinet: Cabinet or Bundesminister (Federal Ministers) recommended by the chancellor, appointed by the president

elections/appointments: president indirectly elected by a Federal Convention consisting of all members of the Federal Parliament (Bundestag) and an equivalent number of delegates indirectly elected by the state parliaments; president serves a 5-year term (eligible for a second term); election last held on 12 February 2017 (next to be held in February 2022); following the most recent Federal Parliament election, the party or coalition with the most representatives usually elects the chancellor (Angela Merkel since 2005) and appointed by the president to serve a renewable 4-year term; Federal Parliament vote for chancellor last held on 14 March 2018 (next to be held after the Bundestag elections in 2021)

election results: Frank-Walter STEINMEIER elected president; Federal Convention vote count - Frank-Walter STEINMEIER (SPD) 931, Christopher BUTTERWEGGE (The Left) 128, Albrecht GLASER (Alternative for Germany AfD) 42, Alexander HOLD (BVB/FW) 25, Engelbert SONNEBORN (Pirates) 10; Angela MERKEL (CDU) reelected chancellor; Federal Parliament vote - 364 to 315

LEGISLATIVE BRANCH:

description: bicameral Parliament or Parlament consists of: Federal Council or Bundesrat (69 seats; members appointed by each of the 16 state governments) Federal Diet or Bundestag (709 seats - total seats can vary each electoral term; approximately one-half of members directly elected in multi-seat constituencies by proportional representation vote and approximately one-half directly elected in single-seat constituencies by simple majority vote; members serve 4-year terms)

elections: Bundesrat - none; composition is determined by the composition of the state-level governments; the composition of the Bundesrat has the potential to change any time one of the 16 states holds an election Bundestag - last held on 24 September 2017 (next to be held in 2021); most postwar German governments have been coalitions

election results: Bundesrat - composition - men 50, women 19, percent of women 27.5% Bundestag - percent of vote by party - CDU/CSU 33%, SPD 20.5%, AfD 12.6%, FDP 10.7%, The Left 9.2%, Alliance '90/Greens 8.9%, other 5%; seats by party - CDU/CSU 246, SPD 152, AfD 91, FDP 80, The Left 69, Alliance '90/Greens 67; composition - men 490, women 219, percent of women 30.5%; note - total Parliament percent of women 30.5%

JUDICIAL BRANCH:

highest courts: Federal Court of Justice (court consists of 127 judges, including the court president, vice presidents, presiding judges, other judges and organized into 25 Senates subdivided into 12 civil panels, 5 criminal panels, and 8 special panels); Federal Constitutional Court or Bundesverfassungsgericht (consists of 2 Senates each subdivided into 3 chambers, each with a chairman and 8 members)

judge selection and term of office: Federal Court of Justice judges selected by the Judges Election Committee, which consists of the Secretaries of Justice from each of the 16 federated states and 16 members appointed by the Federal Parliament; judges appointed by the president; judges serve until mandatory retirement at age 65; Federal Constitutional Court judges - one-half elected by the House of Representatives and one-half by the Senate; judges appointed for 12-year terms with mandatory retirement at age 68

subordinate courts: Federal Administrative Court; Federal Finance Court; Federal Labor Court; Federal Social Court; each of the 16 federated states or Land has its own constitutional court and a hierarchy of ordinary (civil, criminal, family) and specialized (administrative, finance, labor, social) courts

POLITICAL PARTIES AND LEADERS:

Alliance '90/Greens [Annalena BAERBOCK and Robert HABECK]
Alternative for Germany or AfD [Alexander GAULAND and Joerg MEUTHEN]
Christian Democratic Union or CDU [Annegret KRAMP-KARRENBAUER]
Christian Social Union or CSU [Markus SOEDER]
Free Democratic Party or FDP [Christian LINDNER]
The Left or Die Linke [Katja KIPPING and Bernd RIEXINGER]
Social Democratic Party or SPD [Andrea NAHLES]

INTERNATIONAL ORGANIZATION PARTICIPATION:

ADB (nonregional member), AfDB (nonregional member), Arctic Council (observer), Australia Group, BIS, BSEC (observer), CBSS, CD, CDB, CE, CERN, EAPC, EBRD, ECB, EIB, EITI (implementing country), EMU, ESA, EU, FAO, FATF, G-5, G-7, G-8, G-10, G-20, IADB, IAEA, IBRD, ICAO, ICC (national committees), ICCt, ICRM, IDA, IEA, IFAD, IFC, IFRCS, IGAD (partners), IHO, ILO, IMF, IMO, IMSO, Interpol, IOC, IOM, IPU, ISO, ITSO, ITU, ITUC (NGOs), MIGA, MINURSO, MINUSMA, NATO, NEA, NSG, OAS (observer), OECD, OPCW, OSCE, Pacific Alliance (observer), Paris Club, PCA, Schengen Convention, SELEC (observer), SICA (observer), UN, UNAMID, UNCTAD, UNESCO, UNHCR, UNIDO, UNIFIL, UNMISS, UNRWA, UNWTO, UPU, WCO, WHO, WIPO, WMO, WTO, ZC

DIPLOMATIC REPRESENTATION IN THE US:

Ambassador Emily Margarethe HABER (since 22 June 2018)

chancery: 4645 Reservoir Road NW, Washington, DC 20007

telephone: [1] (202) 298-4000

FAX: [1] (202) 298-4249

consulate(s) general: Atlanta, Boston, Chicago, Houston, Los Angeles, Miami, New York, San Francisco

DIPLOMATIC REPRESENTATION FROM THE US:

chief of mission: Ambassador Richard GRENELL (since 8 May 2018)

telephone: [49] (30) 8305-0

embassy: Clayallee 170, 14191 Berlin

mailing address: Clayallee 170, 14191 Berlin

FAX: [49] (30) 8305-1215

consulate(s) general: Dusseldorf, Frankfurt am Main, Hamburg, Leipzig, Munich

FLAG DESCRIPTION:

three equal horizontal bands of black (top), red, and gold; these colors have played an important role in German history and can be traced back to the medieval banner of the Holy Roman Emperor - a black eagle with red claws and beak on a gold field

NATIONAL SYMBOL(S):

eagle; national colors: black, red, yellow

NATIONAL ANTHEM:

name: "Das Lied der Deutschen" (Song of the Germans)

lyrics/music: August Heinrich HOFFMANN VON FALLERSLEBEN/Franz Joseph HAYDN

note: adopted 1922; the anthem, also known as "Deutschlandlied" (Song of Germany), was originally adopted for its connection to the March 1848 liberal revolution; following appropriation by the Nazis of the first verse, specifically the phrase, "Deutschland, Deutschland ueber alles" (Germany, Germany above all) to promote nationalism, it was banned after 1945; in 1952, its third verse was adopted by West Germany as its national anthem; in 1990, it became the national anthem for the reunited Germany

ECONOMY :: GERMANY

ECONOMY - OVERVIEW:

The German economy - the fifth largest economy in the world in PPP terms and Europe's largest - is a leading exporter of machinery, vehicles, chemicals, and household equipment. Germany benefits from a highly skilled labor force, but, like its Western European neighbors, faces significant demographic challenges to sustained long-term growth. Low fertility rates and a large increase in net immigration are increasing pressure on the country's social welfare system and necessitate structural reforms.

Reforms launched by the government of Chancellor Gerhard SCHROEDER (1998-2005), deemed necessary to address chronically high unemployment and low average growth, contributed to strong economic growth and falling unemployment. These advances, as well as a government subsidized, reduced working hour scheme, help explain the relatively modest increase in unemployment during the 2008-09 recession - the deepest since World War II. The German Government introduced a minimum wage in 2015 that increased to $9.79 (8.84 euros) in January 2017.

Stimulus and stabilization efforts initiated in 2008 and 2009 and tax cuts introduced in Chancellor Angela MERKEL's second term increased Germany's total budget deficit - including federal, state, and municipal - to 4.1% in 2010, but slower spending and higher tax revenues reduced the deficit to 0.8% in 2011 and in 2017 Germany reached a budget surplus of 0.7%. A constitutional amendment approved in 2009 limits the federal government to structural deficits of no more than 0.35% of GDP per annum as of 2016, though the target was already reached in 2012.

Following the March 2011 Fukushima nuclear disaster, Chancellor Angela MERKEL announced in May 2011 that eight of the country's 17 nuclear reactors would be shut down immediately and the remaining plants would close by 2022. Germany plans to replace nuclear power largely with renewable energy, which accounted for 29.5% of gross electricity consumption in 2016, up from 9% in 2000. Before the shutdown of the eight reactors, Germany relied on nuclear power for 23% of its electricity generating capacity and 46% of its base-load electricity production.

The German economy suffers from low levels of investment, and a government plan to invest 15 billion euros during 2016-18, largely in infrastructure, is intended to spur needed private investment. Domestic consumption, investment, and exports are likely to drive German GDP growth in 2018, and the country's budget and trade surpluses are likely to remain high.

GDP (PURCHASING POWER PARITY):

$4.199 trillion (2017 est.)

$4.099 trillion (2016 est.)

$4.012 trillion (2015 est.)

note: data are in 2017 dollars

country comparison to the world: 5

GDP (OFFICIAL EXCHANGE RATE):

$3.701 trillion (2017 est.)

GDP - REAL GROWTH RATE:

2.5% (2017 est.)

2.2% (2016 est.)

1.5% (2015 est.)

country comparison to the world: 128

GDP - PER CAPITA (PPP):

$50,800 (2017 est.)

$49,800 (2016 est.)

$49,100 (2015 est.)

note: data are in 2017 dollars

country comparison to the world: 27

GROSS NATIONAL SAVING:

28% of GDP (2017 est.)

28.2% of GDP (2016 est.)

28.1% of GDP (2015 est.)

country comparison to the world: 40

GDP - COMPOSITION, BY END USE:

household consumption: 53.1% (2017 est.)

government consumption: 19.5% (2017 est.)

investment in fixed capital: 20.4% (2017 est.)

investment in inventories: -0.5% (2017 est.)

exports of goods and services: 47.3% (2017 est.)

imports of goods and services: -39.7% (2017 est.)

GDP - COMPOSITION, BY SECTOR OF ORIGIN:

agriculture: 0.7% (2017 est.)

industry: 30.7% (2017 est.)

services: 68.6% (2017 est.)

AGRICULTURE - PRODUCTS:

potatoes, wheat, barley, sugar beets, fruit, cabbages; milk products; cattle, pigs, poultry

INDUSTRIES:

among the world's largest and most technologically advanced producers of iron, steel, coal, cement, chemicals, machinery, vehicles, machine tools, electronics, automobiles, food and beverages, shipbuilding, textiles

INDUSTRIAL PRODUCTION GROWTH RATE:

3.3% (2017 est.)

country comparison to the world: 95

LABOR FORCE:

45.9 million (2017 est.)

country comparison to the world: 14

LABOR FORCE - BY OCCUPATION:

agriculture: 1.4%

industry: 24.2%

services: 74.3% (2016)

UNEMPLOYMENT RATE:

3.8% (2017 est.)

4.2% (2016 est.)

country comparison to the world: 46
POPULATION BELOW POVERTY LINE:
16.7% (2015 est.)

HOUSEHOLD INCOME OR CONSUMPTION BY PERCENTAGE SHARE:

lowest 10%: 3.6%

highest 10%: 24% (2000)

DISTRIBUTION OF FAMILY INCOME - GINI INDEX:
27 (2006)
30 (1994)

country comparison to the world: 145
BUDGET:
revenues: 1.665 trillion (2017 est.)
expenditures: 1.619 trillion (2017 est.)

TAXES AND OTHER REVENUES:
45% (of GDP) (2017 est.)

country comparison to the world: 22
BUDGET SURPLUS (+) OR DEFICIT (-):
1.3% (of GDP) (2017 est.)

country comparison to the world: 25
PUBLIC DEBT:
63.9% of GDP (2017 est.)
67.9% of GDP (2016 est.)

note: general government gross debt is defined in the Maastricht Treaty as consolidated general government gross debt at nominal value, outstanding at the end of the year in the following categories of government liabilities (as defined in ESA95): currency and deposits (AF.2), securities other than shares excluding financial derivatives (AF.3, excluding AF.34), and loans (AF.4); the general government sector comprises the sub-sectors of central government, state government, local government and social security funds; the series are presented as a percentage of GDP and in millions of euros; GDP used as a denominator is the gross domestic product at current market prices; data expressed in national currency are converted into euro using end-of-year exchange rates provided by the European Central Bank

country comparison to the world: 61
FISCAL YEAR:
calendar year

INFLATION RATE (CONSUMER PRICES):
1.7% (2017 est.)
0.4% (2016 est.)

country comparison to the world: 92
CENTRAL BANK DISCOUNT RATE:
0% (31 December 2017)
0% (31 December 2010)

note: this is the European Central Bank's rate on the marginal lending facility, which offers overnight credit to banks in the euro area

country comparison to the world: 154
COMMERCIAL BANK PRIME LENDING RATE:
1.67% (31 December 2017 est.)
1.78% (31 December 2016 est.)

country comparison to the world: 187
STOCK OF NARROW MONEY:
$2.453 trillion (31 December 2017 est.)
$2.016 trillion (31 December 2016 est.)

note: see entry for the European Union for money supply for the entire euro area; the European Central Bank (ECB) controls monetary policy for the 18 members of the Economic and Monetary Union (EMU); individual members of the EMU do not control the quantity of money circulating within their own borders

country comparison to the world: 4
STOCK OF BROAD MONEY:
$2.453 trillion (31 December 2017 est.)
$2.016 trillion (31 December 2016 est.)

country comparison to the world: 4
STOCK OF DOMESTIC CREDIT:
$5.033 trillion (31 December 2017 est.)
$4.433 trillion (31 December 2016 est.)

country comparison to the world: 4
MARKET VALUE OF PUBLICLY TRADED SHARES:
$1.716 trillion (31 December 2015 est.)
$1.739 trillion (31 December 2014 est.)
$1.936 trillion (31 December 2013 est.)

country comparison to the world: 6
CURRENT ACCOUNT BALANCE:
$291 billion (2017 est.)
$297.5 billion (2016 est.)

country comparison to the world: 1
EXPORTS:
$1.434 trillion (2017 est.)
$1.322 trillion (2016 est.)

country comparison to the world: 3
EXPORTS - PARTNERS:
US 8.8%, France 8.2%, China 6.8%, Netherlands 6.7%, UK 6.6%, Italy 5.1%, Austria 4.9%, Poland 4.7%, Switzerland 4.2% (2017)

EXPORTS - COMMODITIES:
motor vehicles, machinery, chemicals, computer and electronic products, electrical equipment, pharmaceuticals, metals, transport equipment, foodstuffs, textiles, rubber and plastic products

IMPORTS:
$1.135 trillion (2017 est.)
$1.022 trillion (2016 est.)

country comparison to the world: 3
IMPORTS - COMMODITIES:
machinery, data processing equipment, vehicles, chemicals, oil and gas, metals, electric equipment, pharmaceuticals, foodstuffs, agricultural products

IMPORTS - PARTNERS:
Netherlands 13.8%, China 7%, France 6.6%, Belgium 5.9%, Italy 5.4%, Poland 5.4%, Czechia 4.8%, US 4.5%, Austria 4.3%, Switzerland 4.2% (2017)

RESERVES OF FOREIGN EXCHANGE AND GOLD:
$200.1 billion (31 December 2017 est.)
$173.7 billion (31 December 2015 est.)

country comparison to the world: 13
DEBT - EXTERNAL:
$5.326 trillion (31 March 2016 est.)
$5.21 trillion (31 March 2015 est.)

country comparison to the world: 4
STOCK OF DIRECT FOREIGN INVESTMENT - AT HOME:
$1.653 trillion (31 December 2017 est.)
$1.391 trillion (31 December 2016 est.)

country comparison to the world: 5
STOCK OF DIRECT FOREIGN INVESTMENT - ABROAD:
$2.298 trillion (31 December 2017 est.)
$1.981 trillion (31 December 2016 est.)

country comparison to the world: 3
EXCHANGE RATES:
euros (EUR) per US dollar -
0.885 (2017 est.)
0.903 (2016 est.)

0.9214 (2015 est.)
0.885 (2014 est.)
0.7634 (2013 est.)

ENERGY :: GERMANY

ELECTRICITY ACCESS:

electrification - total population: 100% (2016)

ELECTRICITY - PRODUCTION:

612.8 billion kWh (2016 est.)

country comparison to the world: 7

ELECTRICITY - CONSUMPTION:

536.5 billion kWh (2016 est.)

country comparison to the world: 6

ELECTRICITY - EXPORTS:

78.86 billion kWh (2016 est.)

country comparison to the world: 1

ELECTRICITY - IMPORTS:

28.34 billion kWh (2016 est.)

country comparison to the world: 5

ELECTRICITY - INSTALLED GENERATING CAPACITY:

208.5 million kW (2016 est.)

country comparison to the world: 6

ELECTRICITY - FROM FOSSIL FUELS:

41% of total installed capacity (2016 est.)

country comparison to the world: 166

ELECTRICITY - FROM NUCLEAR FUELS:

5% of total installed capacity (2017 est.)

country comparison to the world: 21

ELECTRICITY - FROM HYDROELECTRIC PLANTS:

2% of total installed capacity (2017 est.)

country comparison to the world: 137

ELECTRICITY - FROM OTHER RENEWABLE SOURCES:

52% of total installed capacity (2017 est.)

country comparison to the world: 4

CRUDE OIL - PRODUCTION:

41,000 bbl/day (2018 est.)

country comparison to the world: 56

CRUDE OIL - EXPORTS:

6,569 bbl/day (2017 est.)

country comparison to the world: 63

CRUDE OIL - IMPORTS:

1.836 million bbl/day (2017 est.)

country comparison to the world: 6

CRUDE OIL - PROVED RESERVES:

129.6 million bbl (1 January 2018 est.)

country comparison to the world: 65

REFINED PETROLEUM PRODUCTS - PRODUCTION:

2.158 million bbl/day (2017 est.)

country comparison to the world: 9

REFINED PETROLEUM PRODUCTS - CONSUMPTION:

2.46 million bbl/day (2017 est.)

country comparison to the world: 9

REFINED PETROLEUM PRODUCTS - EXPORTS:

494,000 bbl/day (2017 est.)

country comparison to the world: 17

REFINED PETROLEUM PRODUCTS - IMPORTS:

883,800 bbl/day (2017 est.)

country comparison to the world: 9

NATURAL GAS - PRODUCTION:

7.9 billion cu m (2017 est.)

country comparison to the world: 45

NATURAL GAS - CONSUMPTION:

93.36 billion cu m (2017 est.)

country comparison to the world: 8

NATURAL GAS - EXPORTS:

34.61 billion cu m (2017 est.)

country comparison to the world: 11

NATURAL GAS - IMPORTS:

119.5 billion cu m (2017 est.)

country comparison to the world: 1

NATURAL GAS - PROVED RESERVES:

39.5 billion cu m (1 January 2018 est.)

country comparison to the world: 64

CARBON DIOXIDE EMISSIONS FROM CONSUMPTION OF ENERGY:

847.6 million Mt (2017 est.)

country comparison to the world: 6

COMMUNICATIONS :: GERMANY

TELEPHONES - FIXED LINES:

total subscriptions: 44.4 million

subscriptions per 100 inhabitants: 55 (2017 est.)

country comparison to the world: 4

TELEPHONES - MOBILE CELLULAR:

total subscriptions: 106 million

subscriptions per 100 inhabitants: 132 (2017 est.)

country comparison to the world: 15

TELEPHONE SYSTEM:

general assessment: one of the world's most technologically advanced telecommunications systems; as a result of intensive capital expenditures since reunification, the formerly backward system of the eastern part of the country, dating back to World War II, has been modernized and integrated with that of the western part; universal 3G available infrastructure and LTE networks; penetration in broadband and mobile sectors average for region (2018)

domestic: extensive system of automatic telephone exchanges connected by modern networks of fiber-optic cable, coaxial cable, microwave radio relay, and a domestic satellite system; cellular telephone service is widely available, expanding rapidly, and includes roaming service to many foreign countries; 55 per 100 for fixed-line and 132 per 100 for mobile-cellular (2018)

international: country code - 49; landing points for SeaMeWe-3, TAT-14, AC-1, CONTACT-3, Fehmarn Balt, C-Lion1, GC1, GlobalConnect-KPN, and Germany-Denmark 2 & 3 submarine cables to Europe, Africa, the Middle East, Asia, Southeast Asia and Australia; as well as earth stations in the Inmarsat, Intelsat, Eutelsat, and Intersputnik satellite systems (2019)

BROADCAST MEDIA:

a mixture of publicly operated and privately owned TV and radio stations; 70 national and regional public broadcasters compete with nearly 400 privately owned national and regional TV stations; more than 90% of households have cable or satellite TV; hundreds of radio stations including multiple national radio networks, regional radio networks, and a large number of local radio stations

INTERNET COUNTRY CODE:

.de

INTERNET USERS:

total: 72,365,643

percent of population: 89.6% (July 2016 est.)

country comparison to the world: 8

BROADBAND - FIXED SUBSCRIPTIONS:

total: 33.217 million

subscriptions per 100 inhabitants: 41 (2017 est.)

country comparison to the world: 4

MILITARY AND SECURITY :: GERMANY

MILITARY EXPENDITURES:
1.24% of GDP (2018)
1.24% of GDP (2017)
1.2% of GDP (2016)
1.18% of GDP (2015)
1.18% of GDP (2014)

country comparison to the world: 101

MILITARY AND SECURITY FORCES:
Federal Armed Forces (Bundeswehr): Army (Heer), Navy (Deutsche Marine, includes naval air arm), Air Force (Luftwaffe), includes air defense), Joint Support Service (Streitkraeftebasis, SKB), Central Medical Service (Zentraler Sanitaetsdienst, ZSanDstBw), Cyber and Information Space Command (Kommando Cyber- und Informationsraum, Kdo CIR) (2019)

MILITARY SERVICE AGE AND OBLIGATION:
17-23 years of age for male and female voluntary military service; conscription ended 1 July 2011; service obligation 8-23 months or 12 years; women have been eligible for voluntary service in all military branches and positions since 2001 (2013)

TRANSPORTATION :: GERMANY

NATIONAL AIR TRANSPORT SYSTEM:
number of registered air carriers: 20 (2015)

inventory of registered aircraft operated by air carriers: 1,113 (2015)

annual passenger traffic on registered air carriers: 115,540,886 (2015)

annual freight traffic on registered air carriers: 6,985,007,915 mt-km (2015)

CIVIL AIRCRAFT REGISTRATION COUNTRY CODE PREFIX:
D (2016)

AIRPORTS:
539 (2013)

country comparison to the world: 13

AIRPORTS - WITH PAVED RUNWAYS:
total: 318 (2017)
over 3,047 m: 14 (2017)
2,438 to 3,047 m: 49 (2017)
1,524 to 2,437 m: 60 (2017)
914 to 1,523 m: 70 (2017)
under 914 m: 125 (2017)

AIRPORTS - WITH UNPAVED RUNWAYS:
total: 221 (2013)
1,524 to 2,437 m: 1 (2013)
914 to 1,523 m: 35 (2013)
under 914 m: 185 (2013)

HELIPORTS:
23 (2013)

PIPELINES:
37 km condensate, 26985 km gas, 2400 km oil, 4479 km refined products, 8 km water (2013)

RAILWAYS:
total: 33,590 km (2017)
standard gauge: 33,331 km 1.435-m gauge (19,973 km electrified) (2015)
narrow gauge: 220 km 1.000-m gauge (79 km electrified)
15 km 0.900-m gauge, 24 km 0.750-m gauge (2015)

country comparison to the world: 7

ROADWAYS:
total: 625,000 km (2017)
paved: 625,000 km (includes 12,996 km of expressways) (2017)
note: includes local roads

country comparison to the world: 12

WATERWAYS:
7,467 km (Rhine River carries most goods; Main-Danube Canal links North Sea and Black Sea) (2012)

country comparison to the world: 18

MERCHANT MARINE:
total: 629
by type: bulk carrier 1, container ship 107, general cargo 92, oil tanker 36, other 393 (2018)

country comparison to the world: 33

PORTS AND TERMINALS:
major seaport(s): Baltic Sea - Rostock

oil terminal(s): Brunsbuttel Canal terminals

container port(s) (TEUs): Bremen/Bremerhaven (5,510,000), Hamburg (8,860,000) (2017)

LNG terminal(s) (import): Hamburg

river port(s): Bremen (Weser)

North Sea - Wilhelmshaven Bremerhaven (Geeste) Duisburg, Karlsruhe, Neuss-Dusseldorf (Rhine) Brunsbuttel, Hamburg (Elbe) Lubeck (Wakenitz)

TRANSNATIONAL ISSUES :: GERMANY

DISPUTES - INTERNATIONAL:
none

REFUGEES AND INTERNALLY DISPLACED PERSONS:
refugees (country of origin): 532,065 (Syria), 136,463 (Iraq), 126,018 (Afghanistan), 55,334 (Eritrea), 41,150 (Iran), 24,036 (Turkey), 23,581 (Somalia), 9,155 (Serbia and Kosovo), 8,119 (Russia), 7,454 (Pakistan), 6,453 (Nigeria) (2018)

stateless persons: 14,779 (2018)

ILLICIT DRUGS:
source of precursor chemicals for South American cocaine processors; transshipment point for and consumer of Southwest Asian heroin, Latin American cocaine, and European-produced synthetic drugs; major financial center

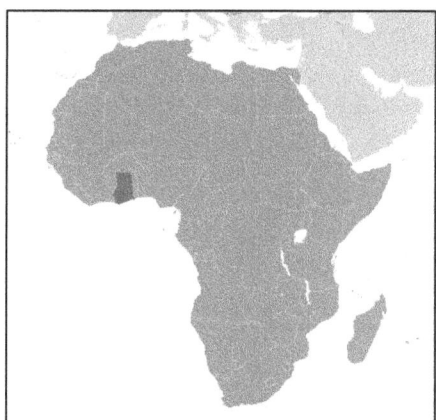

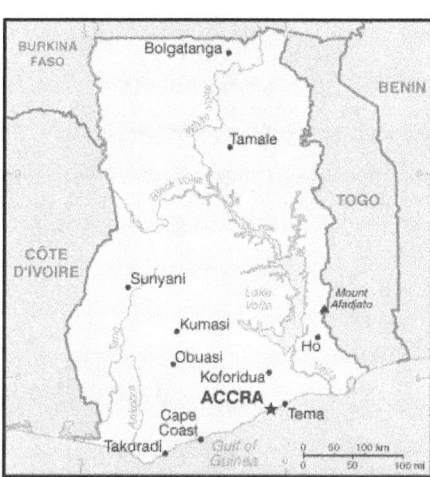

AFRICA :: GHANA

INTRODUCTION :: GHANA

BACKGROUND:

Formed from the merger of the British colony of the Gold Coast and the Togoland trust territory, Ghana in 1957 became the first sub-Saharan country in colonial Africa to gain its independence. Ghana endured a series of coups before Lt. Jerry RAWLINGS took power in 1981 and banned political parties. After approving a new constitution and restoring multiparty politics in 1992, RAWLINGS won presidential elections in 1992 and 1996 but was constitutionally prevented from running for a third term in 2000. John KUFUOR of the opposition New Patriotic Party (NPP) succeeded him and was reelected in 2004. John Atta MILLS of the National Democratic Congress won the 2008 presidential election and took over as head of state, but he died in July 2012 and was constitutionally succeeded by his vice president, John Dramani MAHAMA, who subsequently won the December 2012 presidential election. In 2016, however, Nana Addo Dankwa AKUFO-ADDO of the NPP defeated MAHAMA, marking the third time that the Ghana's presidency has changed parties since the return to democracy.

GEOGRAPHY :: GHANA

LOCATION:
Western Africa, bordering the Gulf of Guinea, between Cote d'Ivoire and Togo

GEOGRAPHIC COORDINATES:
8 00 N, 2 00 W

MAP REFERENCES:
Africa

AREA:
total: 238,533 sq km

land: 227,533 sq km

water: 11,000 sq km

country comparison to the world: 83

AREA - COMPARATIVE:
slightly smaller than Oregon

LAND BOUNDARIES:
total: 2,420 km

border countries (3): Burkina Faso 602 km, Cote d'Ivoire 720 km, Togo 1098 km

COASTLINE:
539 km

MARITIME CLAIMS:
territorial sea: 12 nm

exclusive economic zone: 200 nm

contiguous zone: 24 nm

continental shelf: 200 nm

CLIMATE:
tropical; warm and comparatively dry along southeast coast; hot and humid in southwest; hot and dry in north

TERRAIN:
mostly low plains with dissected plateau in south-central area

ELEVATION:
mean elevation: 190 m

lowest point: Atlantic Ocean 0 m

highest point: Mount Afadjato 885 m

NATURAL RESOURCES:
gold, timber, industrial diamonds, bauxite, manganese, fish, rubber, hydropower, petroleum, silver, salt, limestone

LAND USE:
agricultural land: 69.1% (2011 est.)

arable land: 20.7% (2011 est.) / permanent crops: 11.9% (2011 est.) / permanent pasture: 36.5% (2011 est.)

forest: 21.2% (2011 est.)

other: 9.7% (2011 est.)

IRRIGATED LAND:
340 sq km (2012)

POPULATION DISTRIBUTION:
population is concentrated in the southern half of the country, with the highest concentrations being on or near the Atlantic coast

NATURAL HAZARDS:
dry, dusty, northeastern harmattan winds from January to March; droughts

ENVIRONMENT - CURRENT ISSUES:
recurrent drought in north severely affects agricultural activities; deforestation; overgrazing; soil erosion; poaching and habitat destruction threaten wildlife populations; water pollution; inadequate supplies of potable water

ENVIRONMENT - INTERNATIONAL AGREEMENTS:
party to: Biodiversity, Climate Change, Climate Change-Kyoto Protocol, Desertification, Endangered Species, Environmental Modification, Hazardous Wastes, Law of the Sea, Ozone Layer Protection, Ship Pollution, Tropical Timber 83, Tropical Timber 94, Wetlands

signed, but not ratified: Marine Life Conservation

GEOGRAPHY - NOTE:

Lake Volta is the world's largest artificial lake (manmade reservoir) by surface area (8,482 sq km; 3,275 sq mi); the lake was created following the completion of the Akosombo Dam in 1965, which holds back the White Volta and Black Volta Rivers

PEOPLE AND SOCIETY :: GHANA

POPULATION:

28,102,471 (July 2018 est.)

note: estimates for this country explicitly take into account the effects of excess mortality due to AIDS; this can result in lower life expectancy, higher infant mortality, higher death rates, lower population growth rates, and changes in the distribution of population by age and sex than would otherwise be expected

country comparison to the world: 49

NATIONALITY:

noun: Ghanaian(s)

adjective: Ghanaian

ETHNIC GROUPS:

Akan 47.5%, Mole-Dagbon 16.6%, Ewe 13.9%, Ga-Dangme 7.4%, Gurma 5.7%, Guan 3.7%, Grusi 2.5%, Mande 1.1%, other 1.4% (2010 est.)

LANGUAGES:

Asante 16%, Ewe 14%, Fante 11.6%, Boron (Brong) 4.9%, Dagomba 4.4%, Dangme 4.2%, Dagarte (Dagaba) 3.9%, Kokomba 3.5%, Akyem 3.2%, Ga 3.1%, other 31.2% (2010 est.)

note: English is the official language

RELIGIONS:

Christian 71.2% (Pentecostal/Charismatic 28.3%, Protestant 18.4%, Catholic 13.1%, other 11.4%), Muslim 17.6%, traditional 5.2%, other 0.8%, none 5.2% (2010 est.)

DEMOGRAPHIC PROFILE:

Ghana has a young age structure, with approximately 57% of the population under the age of 25. Its total fertility rate fell significantly during the 1980s and 1990s but has stalled at around four children per woman for the last few years. Fertility remains higher in the northern region than the Greater Accra region. On average, desired fertility has remained stable for several years; urban dwellers want fewer children than rural residents. Increased life expectancy, due to better health care, nutrition, and hygiene, and reduced fertility have increased Ghana's share of elderly persons; Ghana's proportion of persons aged 60+ is among the highest in sub-Saharan Africa. Poverty has declined in Ghana, but it remains pervasive in the northern region, which is susceptible to droughts and floods and has less access to transportation infrastructure, markets, fertile farming land, and industrial centers. The northern region also has lower school enrollment, higher illiteracy, and fewer opportunities for women.

Ghana was a country of immigration in the early years after its 1957 independence, attracting labor migrants largely from Nigeria and other neighboring countries to mine minerals and harvest cocoa – immigrants composed about 12% of Ghana's population in 1960. In the late 1960s, worsening economic and social conditions discouraged immigration, and hundreds of thousands of immigrants, mostly Nigerians, were expelled.

During the 1970s, severe drought and an economic downturn transformed Ghana into a country of emigration; neighboring Cote d'Ivoire was the initial destination. Later, hundreds of thousands of Ghanaians migrated to Nigeria to work in its booming oil industry, but most were deported in 1983 and 1985 as oil prices plummeted. Many Ghanaians then turned to more distant destinations, including other parts of Africa, Europe, and North America, but the majority continued to migrate within West Africa. Since the 1990s, increased emigration of skilled Ghanaians, especially to the US and the UK, drained the country of its health care and education professionals. Internally, poverty and other developmental disparities continue to drive Ghanaians from the north to the south, particularly to its urban centers.

AGE STRUCTURE:

0-14 years: 37.83% (male 5,344,146 /female 5,286,383)

15-24 years: 18.61% (male 2,600,390 /female 2,629,660)

25-54 years: 34.21% (male 4,663,234 /female 4,950,888)

55-64 years: 5.05% (male 690,327 /female 727,957)

65 years and over: 4.3% (male 557,155 /female 652,331) (2018 est.)

DEPENDENCY RATIOS:

total dependency ratio: 73 (2015 est.)

youth dependency ratio: 67.1 (2015 est.)

elderly dependency ratio: 5.9 (2015 est.)

potential support ratio: 17.1 (2015 est.)

MEDIAN AGE:

total: 21.2 years (2018 est.)

male: 20.7 years

female: 21.7 years

country comparison to the world: 185

POPULATION GROWTH RATE:

2.16% (2018 est.)

country comparison to the world: 40

BIRTH RATE:

30.2 births/1,000 population (2018 est.)

country comparison to the world: 35

DEATH RATE:

6.8 deaths/1,000 population (2018 est.)

country comparison to the world: 134

NET MIGRATION RATE:

-1.7 migrant(s)/1,000 population (2018 est.)

country comparison to the world: 155

POPULATION DISTRIBUTION:

population is concentrated in the southern half of the country, with the highest concentrations being on or near the Atlantic coast

URBANIZATION:

urban population: 56.7% of total population (2019)

rate of urbanization: 3.34% annual rate of change (2015-20 est.)

MAJOR URBAN AREAS - POPULATION:

3.206 million Kumasi, 2.475 million ACCRA (capital), 900,000 Sekondi Takoradi (2019)

SEX RATIO:

at birth: 1.03 male(s)/female

0-14 years: 1.01 male(s)/female

15-24 years: 0.99 male(s)/female

25-54 years: 0.94 male(s)/female

55-64 years: 0.95 male(s)/female

65 years and over: 0.85 male(s)/female

total population: 0.97 male(s)/female (2018 est.)

MOTHER'S MEAN AGE AT FIRST BIRTH:

22.3 years (2017 est.)

note: median age at first birth among women 25-29

MATERNAL MORTALITY RATE:

308 deaths/100,000 live births (2017 est.)

country comparison to the world: 36

INFANT MORTALITY RATE:

total: 34.1 deaths/1,000 live births (2018 est.)

male: 38 deaths/1,000 live births

female: 30.1 deaths/1,000 live births

country comparison to the world: 52

LIFE EXPECTANCY AT BIRTH:

total population: 67.4 years (2018 est.)

male: 64.9 years

female: 70 years

country comparison to the world: 172

TOTAL FERTILITY RATE:

3.96 children born/woman (2018 est.)

country comparison to the world: 34

CONTRACEPTIVE PREVALENCE RATE:

30.8% (2017)

DRINKING WATER SOURCE:

improved:

urban: 92.6% of population

rural: 84% of population

total: 88.7% of population

unimproved:

urban: 7.4% of population

rural: 16% of population

total: 11.3% of population (2015 est.)

CURRENT HEALTH EXPENDITURE:

4.4% (2016)

PHYSICIANS DENSITY:

0.18 physicians/1,000 population (2017)

HOSPITAL BED DENSITY:

0.9 beds/1,000 population (2011)

SANITATION FACILITY ACCESS:

improved:

urban: 20.2% of population (2015 est.)

rural: 8.6% of population (2015 est.)

total: 14.9% of population (2015 est.)

unimproved:

urban: 79.8% of population (2015 est.)

rural: 91.4% of population (2015 est.)

total: 85.1% of population (2015 est.)

HIV/AIDS - ADULT PREVALENCE RATE:

1.7% (2018 est.)

country comparison to the world: 29

HIV/AIDS - PEOPLE LIVING WITH HIV/AIDS:

330,000 (2018 est.)

country comparison to the world: 22

HIV/AIDS - DEATHS:

14,000 (2018 est.)

country comparison to the world: 16

MAJOR INFECTIOUS DISEASES:

degree of risk: very high (2016)

food or waterborne diseases: bacterial and protozoal diarrhea, hepatitis A, and typhoid fever (2016)

vectorborne diseases: malaria, dengue fever, and yellow fever (2016)

water contact diseases: schistosomiasis (2016)

animal contact diseases: rabies (2016)

respiratory diseases: meningococcal meningitis (2016)

OBESITY - ADULT PREVALENCE RATE:

10.9% (2016)

country comparison to the world: 136

CHILDREN UNDER THE AGE OF 5 YEARS UNDERWEIGHT:

11.2% (2014)

country comparison to the world: 57

EDUCATION EXPENDITURES:

4.5% of GDP (2017)

country comparison to the world: 88

LITERACY:

definition: age 15 and over can read and write

total population: 76.6%

male: 82%

female: 71.4% (2015 est.)

SCHOOL LIFE EXPECTANCY (PRIMARY TO TERTIARY EDUCATION):

total: 12 years

male: 12 years

female: 11 years (2017)

UNEMPLOYMENT, YOUTH AGES 15-24:

total: 15.2%

male: 15.8%

female: 14.6% (2015 est.)

country comparison to the world: 91

GOVERNMENT :: GHANA

COUNTRY NAME:

conventional long form: Republic of Ghana

conventional short form: Ghana

former: Gold Coast

etymology: named for the medieval West African kingdom of the same name but whose location was actually further north than the modern country

GOVERNMENT TYPE:

presidential republic

CAPITAL:

name: Accra

geographic coordinates: 5 33 N, 0 13 W

time difference: UTC 0 (5 hours ahead of Washington, DC, during Standard Time)

etymology: the name derives from the Akan word "nkran" meaning "ants," and refers to the numerous anthills in the area around the capital

ADMINISTRATIVE DIVISIONS:

16 regions; Ahafo, Ashanti, Bono, Bono East, Central, Eastern, Greater Accra, North East, Northern, Oti, Savannah, Upper East, Upper West, Volta, Western, Western North

INDEPENDENCE:

6 March 1957 (from the UK)

NATIONAL HOLIDAY:

Independence Day, 6 March (1957)

CONSTITUTION:

history: several previous; latest drafted 31 March 1992, approved and promulgated 28 April 1992, entered into force 7 January 1993

amendments: proposed by Parliament; consideration requires prior referral to the Council of State, a body of prominent citizens who advise the president of the republic; passage of amendments to "entrenched" constitutional articles (including those on national sovereignty, fundamental rights and freedoms, the structure and authorities of the branches of government, and amendment procedures) requires approval in a referendum by at least 40%

participation of eligible voters and at least 75% of votes cast, followed by at least two-thirds majority vote in Parliament, and assent of the president; amendments to non-entrenched articles do not require referenda; amended 1996 (2017)

LEGAL SYSTEM:
mixed system of English common law and customary law

INTERNATIONAL LAW ORGANIZATION PARTICIPATION:
has not submitted an ICJ jurisdiction declaration; accepts ICCt jurisdiction

CITIZENSHIP:
citizenship by birth: no

citizenship by descent only: at least one parent or grandparent must be a citizen of Ghana

dual citizenship recognized: yes

residency requirement for naturalization: 5 years

SUFFRAGE:
18 years of age; universal

EXECUTIVE BRANCH:
chief of state: President Nana Addo Dankwa AKUFO-ADDO (since 7 January 2017); Vice President Mahamudu BAWUMIA (since 7 January 2017); the president is both chief of state and head of government

head of government: President Nana Addo Dankwa AKUFO-ADDO (since 7 January 2017); Vice President Mahamudu BAWUMIA (since 7 January 2017)

cabinet: Council of Ministers; nominated by the president, approved by Parliament

elections/appointments: president and vice president directly elected on the same ballot by absolute majority popular vote in 2 rounds if needed for a 4-year term (eligible for a second term); election last held on 7 December 2016 (next to be held in December 2020)

election results: Nana Addo Dankwa AKUFO-ADDO elected president in the first round; percent of vote - Nana Addo Dankwa AKUFO-ADDO (NPP) 53.7%, John Dramani MAHAMA (NDC) 44.5%, other 1.8%

LEGISLATIVE BRANCH:
description: unicameral Parliament (275 seats; members directly elected in single-seat constituencies by simple majority vote to serve 4-year terms)

elections: last held on 7 December 2016 (next to be held in December 2020)

election results: percent of vote by party - NPP 54%, NDC 44%, other 2%; seats by party - NPP 171, NDC 104; composition - men 240, women 35, percent of women 12.7%

JUDICIAL BRANCH:
highest courts: Supreme Court (consists of the chief justice and 12 justices)

judge selection and term of office: chief justice appointed by the president in consultation with the Council of State (a small advisory body of prominent citizens) and with the approval of Parliament; other justices appointed by the president upon the advice of the Judicial Council (an 18-member independent body of judicial, military and police officials, and presidential nominees) and on the advice of the Council of State; justices can retire at age 60, with compulsory retirement at age 70

subordinate courts: Court of Appeal; High Court; Circuit Court; District Court; regional tribunals

POLITICAL PARTIES AND LEADERS:
note: Ghana has more than 20 registered parties; included are 5 of the more popular parties as of May 2017

INTERNATIONAL ORGANIZATION PARTICIPATION:
ACP, AfDB, AU, C, ECOWAS, EITI (compliant country), FAO, G-24, G-77, IAEA, IBRD, ICAO, ICC (national committees), ICCt, ICRM, IDA, IFAD, IFC, IFRCS, ILO, IMF, IMO, IMSO, Interpol, IOC, IOM, IPU, ISO, ITSO, ITU, ITUC (NGOs), MIGA, MINURSO, MINUSMA, MONUSCO, NAM, OAS (observer), OIF, OPCW, UN, UNAMID, UNCTAD, UNESCO, UNHCR, UNIDO, UNIFIL, UNISFA, UNMIL, UNMISS, UNOCI, UNWTO, UPU, WCO, WFTU (NGOs), WHO, WIPO, WMO, WTO

DIPLOMATIC REPRESENTATION IN THE US:
Ambassador Barfour ADJEI-BARWUAH (since 21 July 2017)

chancery: 3512 International Drive NW, Washington, DC 20008

telephone: [1] (202) 686-4520

FAX: [1] (202) 686-4527

consulate(s) general: New York

DIPLOMATIC REPRESENTATION FROM THE US:
chief of mission: Ambassador Stephanie S. SULLIVAN (since 30 November 2018)

telephone: [233] 030-274-1000

embassy: 24 Fourth Circular Rd., Cantonments, Accra
P.O. Box GP2288, Accra

mailing address: P.O. Box 194, Accra

FAX: [233] 030-274-1389

FLAG DESCRIPTION:
three equal horizontal bands of red (top), yellow, and green, with a large black five-pointed star centered in the yellow band; red symbolizes the blood shed for independence, yellow represents the country's mineral wealth, while green stands for its forests and natural wealth; the black star is said to be the lodestar of African freedom

note: uses the popular Pan-African colors of Ethiopia; similar to the flag of Bolivia, which has a coat of arms centered in the yellow band

NATIONAL SYMBOL(S):
black star, golden eagle; national colors: red, yellow, green, black

NATIONAL ANTHEM:
name: God Bless Our Homeland Ghana

lyrics/music: unknown/Philip GBEHO

note: music adopted 1957, lyrics adopted 1966; the lyrics were changed twice, in 1960 when a republic was declared and after a 1966 coup

ECONOMY :: GHANA

ECONOMY - OVERVIEW:
Ghana has a market-based economy with relatively few policy barriers to trade and investment in comparison with other countries in the region, and Ghana is endowed with natural resources. Ghana's economy was strengthened by a quarter century of relatively sound management, a competitive business environment, and sustained reductions in poverty levels, but in recent years has suffered the consequences of loose fiscal policy, high budget and current account deficits, and a depreciating currency.

Agriculture accounts for about 20% of GDP and employs more than half of the workforce, mainly small landholders. Gold, oil, and cocoa exports, and individual remittances, are major sources of foreign exchange. Expansion of Ghana's nascent oil industry has boosted economic growth, but the fall in oil prices since 2015 reduced by half Ghana's oil revenue. Production at Jubilee, Ghana's first commercial offshore oilfield, began in mid-December 2010. Production from two more fields, TEN and Sankofa, started in 2016 and 2017 respectively. The country's first gas processing plant at Atuabo is also producing natural gas from the Jubilee field, providing power to several of Ghana's thermal power plants.

As of 2018, key economic concerns facing the government include the lack of affordable electricity, lack of a solid domestic revenue base, and the high debt burden. The AKUFO-ADDO administration has made some progress by committing to fiscal consolidation, but much work is still to be done. Ghana signed a $920 million extended credit facility with the IMF in April 2015 to help it address its growing economic crisis. The IMF fiscal targets require Ghana to reduce the deficit by cutting subsidies, decreasing the bloated public sector wage bill, strengthening revenue administration, boosting tax revenues, and improving the health of Ghana's banking sector. Priorities for the new administration include rescheduling some of Ghana's $31 billion debt, stimulating economic growth, reducing inflation, and stabilizing the currency. Prospects for new oil and gas production and follow through on tighter fiscal management are likely to help Ghana's economy in 2018.

GDP (PURCHASING POWER PARITY):

$134 billion (2017 est.)

$123.6 billion (2016 est.)

$119.2 billion (2015 est.)

note: data are in 2017 dollars

country comparison to the world: 80

GDP (OFFICIAL EXCHANGE RATE):

$47.02 billion (2017 est.)

GDP - REAL GROWTH RATE:

8.4% (2017 est.)

3.7% (2016 est.)

3.8% (2015 est.)

country comparison to the world: 7

GDP - PER CAPITA (PPP):

$4,700 (2017 est.)

$4,500 (2016 est.)

$4,400 (2015 est.)

note: data are in 2017 dollars

country comparison to the world: 172

GROSS NATIONAL SAVING:

9% of GDP (2017 est.)

7.8% of GDP (2016 est.)

9% of GDP (2015 est.)

country comparison to the world: 167

GDP - COMPOSITION, BY END USE:

household consumption: 80.1% (2017 est.)

government consumption: 8.6% (2017 est.)

investment in fixed capital: 13.7% (2017 est.)

investment in inventories: 1.1% (2017 est.)

exports of goods and services: 43% (2017 est.)

imports of goods and services: -46.5% (2017 est.)

GDP - COMPOSITION, BY SECTOR OF ORIGIN:

agriculture: 18.3% (2017 est.)

industry: 24.5% (2017 est.)

services: 57.2% (2017 est.)

AGRICULTURE - PRODUCTS:

cocoa, rice, cassava (manioc, tapioca), peanuts, corn, shea nuts, bananas; timber

INDUSTRIES:

mining, lumbering, light manufacturing, aluminum smelting, food processing, cement, small commercial ship building, petroleum

INDUSTRIAL PRODUCTION GROWTH RATE:

16.7% (2017 est.)

country comparison to the world: 2

LABOR FORCE:

12.49 million (2017 est.)

country comparison to the world: 47

LABOR FORCE - BY OCCUPATION:

agriculture: 44.7%

industry: 14.4%

services: 40.9% (2013 est.)

UNEMPLOYMENT RATE:

11.9% (2015 est.)

5.2% (2013 est.)

country comparison to the world: 158

POPULATION BELOW POVERTY LINE:

24.2% (2013 est.)

HOUSEHOLD INCOME OR CONSUMPTION BY PERCENTAGE SHARE:

lowest 10%: 2%

highest 10%: 32.8% (2006)

DISTRIBUTION OF FAMILY INCOME - GINI INDEX:

42.3 (2012-13)
41.9 (2005-06)

BUDGET:

revenues: 9.544 billion (2017 est.)

expenditures: 12.36 billion (2017 est.)

TAXES AND OTHER REVENUES:

20.3% (of GDP) (2017 est.)

country comparison to the world: 149

BUDGET SURPLUS (+) OR DEFICIT (-):

-6% (of GDP) (2017 est.)

country comparison to the world: 183

PUBLIC DEBT:

71.8% of GDP (2017 est.)

73.4% of GDP (2016 est.)

country comparison to the world: 46

FISCAL YEAR:

calendar year

INFLATION RATE (CONSUMER PRICES):

12.4% (2017 est.)

17.5% (2016 est.)

country comparison to the world: 206

CENTRAL BANK DISCOUNT RATE:

20% (31 December 2017)

25.5% (31 December 2016)

country comparison to the world: 5

COMMERCIAL BANK PRIME LENDING RATE:

30.35% (31 December 2017 est.)

31.26% (31 December 2016 est.)

country comparison to the world: 4

STOCK OF NARROW MONEY:

$7.018 billion (31 December 2017 est.)

$6.472 billion (31 December 2016 est.)

country comparison to the world: 91

STOCK OF BROAD MONEY:

$7.018 billion (31 December 2017 est.)

$6.472 billion (31 December 2016 est.)

country comparison to the world: 93

STOCK OF DOMESTIC CREDIT:

$14.25 billion (31 December 2017 est.)

$13.67 billion (31 December 2016 est.)

country comparison to the world: 99
MARKET VALUE OF PUBLICLY TRADED SHARES:
$13.41 billion (31 December 2017 est.)
$13.48 billion (31 December 2016 est.)
$15.11 billion (31 December 2015 est.)
country comparison to the world: 69
CURRENT ACCOUNT BALANCE:
-$2.131 billion (2017 est.)
-$2.86 billion (2016 est.)
country comparison to the world: 168
EXPORTS:
$13.84 billion (2017 est.)
$11.14 billion (2016 est.)
country comparison to the world: 78
EXPORTS - PARTNERS:
India 23.8%, UAE 13.4%, China 10.8%, Switzerland 10.1%, Vietnam 5.2%, Burkina Faso 4% (2017)
EXPORTS - COMMODITIES:
oil, gold, cocoa, timber, tuna, bauxite, aluminum, manganese ore, diamonds, horticultural products
IMPORTS:
$12.65 billion (2017 est.)
$12.91 billion (2016 est.)
country comparison to the world: 93
IMPORTS - COMMODITIES:
capital equipment, refined petroleum, foodstuffs
IMPORTS - PARTNERS:
China 16.8%, US 8%, UK 6.2%, Belgium 5.9%, India 4.1% (2017)
RESERVES OF FOREIGN EXCHANGE AND GOLD:
$7.555 billion (31 December 2017 est.)
$6.162 billion (31 December 2016 est.)
country comparison to the world: 81
DEBT - EXTERNAL:
$22.14 billion (31 December 2017 est.)
$16.5 billion (31 December 2016 est.)
country comparison to the world: 90
STOCK OF DIRECT FOREIGN INVESTMENT - AT HOME:
$19.85 billion (31 December 2013 est.)
$118 million (31 December 2012 est.)
country comparison to the world: 79
STOCK OF DIRECT FOREIGN INVESTMENT - ABROAD:
$16.62 billion (31 December 2013 est.)
$109 million (31 December 2012 est.)
country comparison to the world: 59
EXCHANGE RATES:
cedis (GHC) per US dollar -
4.385 (2017 est.)
3.909 (2016 est.)
3.909 (2015 est.)
3.712 (2014 est.)
2.895 (2013 est.)

ENERGY :: GHANA

ELECTRICITY ACCESS:
population without electricity: 5 million (2017)
electrification - total population: 79.3% (2016)
electrification - urban areas: 89.8% (2016)
electrification - rural areas: 66.6% (2016)
ELECTRICITY - PRODUCTION:
12.52 billion kWh (2016 est.)
country comparison to the world: 94
ELECTRICITY - CONSUMPTION:
9.363 billion kWh (2016 est.)
country comparison to the world: 99
ELECTRICITY - EXPORTS:
187 million kWh (2016 est.)
country comparison to the world: 76
ELECTRICITY - IMPORTS:
511 million kWh (2016 est.)
country comparison to the world: 79
ELECTRICITY - INSTALLED GENERATING CAPACITY:
3.801 million kW (2016 est.)
country comparison to the world: 92
ELECTRICITY - FROM FOSSIL FUELS:
58% of total installed capacity (2016 est.)
country comparison to the world: 135
ELECTRICITY - FROM NUCLEAR FUELS:
0% of total installed capacity (2017 est.)
country comparison to the world: 96
ELECTRICITY - FROM HYDROELECTRIC PLANTS:
42% of total installed capacity (2017 est.)
country comparison to the world: 48
ELECTRICITY - FROM OTHER RENEWABLE SOURCES:
1% of total installed capacity (2017 est.)
country comparison to the world: 153

CRUDE OIL - PRODUCTION:
173,000 bbl/day (2018 est.)
country comparison to the world: 37
CRUDE OIL - EXPORTS:
104,000 bbl/day (2017 est.)
country comparison to the world: 34
CRUDE OIL - IMPORTS:
6,220 bbl/day (2015 est.)
country comparison to the world: 74
CRUDE OIL - PROVED RESERVES:
660 million bbl (1 January 2018 est.)
country comparison to the world: 41
REFINED PETROLEUM PRODUCTS - PRODUCTION:
2,073 bbl/day (2015 est.)
country comparison to the world: 104
REFINED PETROLEUM PRODUCTS - CONSUMPTION:
90,000 bbl/day (2016 est.)
country comparison to the world: 83
REFINED PETROLEUM PRODUCTS - EXPORTS:
2,654 bbl/day (2015 est.)
country comparison to the world: 100
REFINED PETROLEUM PRODUCTS - IMPORTS:
85,110 bbl/day (2015 est.)
country comparison to the world: 59
NATURAL GAS - PRODUCTION:
914.4 million cu m (2017 est.)
country comparison to the world: 68
NATURAL GAS - CONSUMPTION:
1.232 billion cu m (2017 est.)
country comparison to the world: 87
NATURAL GAS - EXPORTS:
0 cu m (2017 est.)
country comparison to the world: 110
NATURAL GAS - IMPORTS:
317.4 million cu m (2017 est.)
country comparison to the world: 68
NATURAL GAS - PROVED RESERVES:
22.65 billion cu m (1 January 2018 est.)
country comparison to the world: 73
CARBON DIOXIDE EMISSIONS FROM CONSUMPTION OF ENERGY:
13.67 million Mt (2017 est.)
country comparison to the world: 96

COMMUNICATIONS :: GHANA

TELEPHONES - FIXED LINES:

total subscriptions: 301,551

subscriptions per 100 inhabitants: 1 (2017 est.)

country comparison to the world: 112

TELEPHONES - MOBILE CELLULAR:

total subscriptions: 36,751,761

subscriptions per 100 inhabitants: 134 (2017 est.)

country comparison to the world: 38

TELEPHONE SYSTEM:

general assessment: primarily microwave radio relay; wireless local loop has been installed; 2019 to bring universal access licenses; government invested in fiber infrastructure; one of the most active mobile markets in Africa (2018)

domestic: fixed-line 1 per 100 subscriptions; competition among multiple mobile-cellular providers has spurred growth with a subscribership of more than 140 per 100 persons and rising (2018)

international: country code - 233; landing point for the SAT-3/WASC, MainOne, ACE, WACS and GLO-1 fiber-optic submarine cables that provide connectivity to South and West Africa, and Europe; satellite earth stations - 4 Intelsat (Atlantic Ocean); microwave radio relay link to Panaftel system connects Ghana to its neighbors (2019)

BROADCAST MEDIA:

state-owned TV station, 2 state-owned radio networks; several privately owned TV stations and a large number of privately owned radio stations; transmissions of multiple international broadcasters are accessible; several cable and satellite TV subscription services are obtainable

INTERNET COUNTRY CODE:

.gh

INTERNET USERS:

total: 9,328,018

percent of population: 34.7% (July 2016 est.)

country comparison to the world: 49

BROADBAND - FIXED SUBSCRIPTIONS:

total: 56,810

subscriptions per 100 inhabitants: less than 1 (2017 est.)

country comparison to the world: 128

MILITARY AND SECURITY :: GHANA

MILITARY EXPENDITURES:

0.41% of GDP (2018)

0.4% of GDP (2017)

0.38% of GDP (2016)

0.52% of GDP (2015)

0.68% of GDP (2014)

country comparison to the world: 150

MILITARY AND SECURITY FORCES:

Ghana Armed Forces: Army, Navy, Air Force (2019)

MILITARY SERVICE AGE AND OBLIGATION:

18-26 years of age for voluntary military service, with basic education certificate; no conscription; must be HIV/AIDS negative (2012)

MARITIME THREATS:

West African piracy more than doubled in 2018 to become the most dangerous area in the World; the waters off of Ghana saw a dramatic increase with 10 attacks reported in 2018 compared with only one in 2017; eight ships were boarded, one hijacked, and 47 crew taken hostage or kidnapped

TRANSPORTATION :: GHANA

NATIONAL AIR TRANSPORT SYSTEM:

number of registered air carriers: 4 (2015)

inventory of registered aircraft operated by air carriers: 8 (2015)

annual passenger traffic on registered air carriers: 390,457 (2015)

annual freight traffic on registered air carriers: 844,630 mt-km (2015)

CIVIL AIRCRAFT REGISTRATION COUNTRY CODE PREFIX:

9G (2016)

AIRPORTS:

10 (2013)

country comparison to the world: 155

AIRPORTS - WITH PAVED RUNWAYS:

total: 7 (2017)

over 3,047 m: 1 (2017)

2,438 to 3,047 m: 1 (2017)

1,524 to 2,437 m: 3 (2017)

914 to 1,523 m: 2 (2017)

AIRPORTS - WITH UNPAVED RUNWAYS:

total: 3 (2013)

914 to 1,523 m: 3 (2013)

PIPELINES:

394 km gas, 20 km oil, 361 km refined products (2013)

RAILWAYS:

total: 947 km (2014)

narrow gauge: 947 km 1.067-m gauge (2014)

country comparison to the world: 92

ROADWAYS:

total: 109,515 km (2009)

paved: 13,787 km (2009)

unpaved: 95,728 km (2009)

country comparison to the world: 45

WATERWAYS:

1,293 km (168 km for launches and lighters on Volta, Ankobra, and Tano Rivers; 1,125 km of arterial and feeder waterways on Lake Volta) (2011)

country comparison to the world: 56

MERCHANT MARINE:

total: 44

by type: general cargo 6, oil tanker 2, other 36 (2018)

country comparison to the world: 116

PORTS AND TERMINALS:

major seaport(s): Takoradi, Tema

TRANSNATIONAL ISSUES :: GHANA

DISPUTES - INTERNATIONAL:

disputed maritime border between Ghana and Cote d'Ivoire

REFUGEES AND INTERNALLY DISPLACED PERSONS:

refugees (country of origin): 6,517 (Cote d'Ivoire) (flight from 2010 post-election fighting) (2019)

IDPs: 5,000 (land disputes between ethnic communities in the north in 2018) (2018)

TRAFFICKING IN PERSONS:

current situation: Ghana is a source, transit, and destination country for men, women, and children subjected to forced labor and sex trafficking; the trafficking of Ghanaians, particularly children, internally is more common than the trafficking of foreign nationals; Ghanian children are subjected to forced labor in fishing, domestic service, street hawking, begging, portering, mining, quarrying, herding, and agriculture, with girls, and to a lesser extent boys, forced into prostitution; Ghanian women, sometimes lured with legitimate job offers, and girls are sex trafficked in West Africa, the Middle East, and Europe; Ghanian men fraudulently recruited for work in the Middle East are subjected to forced labor or prostitution, and a few Ghanian adults have been identified as victims of false labor in the US; women and girls from Vietnam, China, and neighboring West African countries are sex trafficked in Ghana; the country is also a transit point for sex trafficking from West Africa to Europe

tier rating: Tier 2 Watch List - Ghana does not fully comply with the minimum standards for the elimination of trafficking; however, it is making significant efforts to do so; Ghana continued to investigate and prosecute trafficking offenses but was unable to ramp up its anti-trafficking efforts in 2014 because the government failed to provide law enforcement or protection agencies with operating budgets; victim protection efforts decreased in 2014, with significantly fewer victims identified; most child victims were referred to NGO-run facilities, but care for adults was lacking because the government did not provide any support to the country's Human Trafficking Fund for victim services or its two shelters; anti-trafficking prevention measures increased modestly, including reconvening of the Human Trafficking Management Board, public awareness campaigns on child labor and trafficking, and anti-trafficking TV and radio programs (2015)

ILLICIT DRUGS:

illicit producer of cannabis for the international drug trade; major transit hub for Southwest and Southeast Asian heroin and, to a lesser extent, South American cocaine destined for Europe and the US; widespread crime and money-laundering problem, but the lack of a well-developed financial infrastructure limits the country's utility as a money-laundering center; significant domestic cocaine and cannabis use

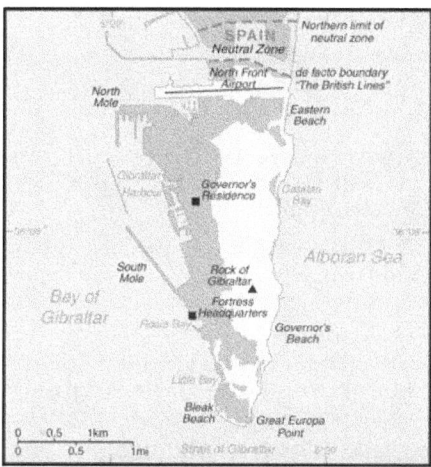

EUROPE :: GIBRALTAR

INTRODUCTION :: GIBRALTAR

BACKGROUND:

Strategically important, Gibraltar was reluctantly ceded to Great Britain by Spain in the 1713 Treaty of Utrecht; the British garrison was formally declared a colony in 1830. In a referendum held in 1967, Gibraltarians voted overwhelmingly to remain a British dependency. The subsequent granting of autonomy in 1969 by the UK led Spain to close the border and sever all communication links. Between 1997 and 2002, the UK and Spain held a series of talks on establishing temporary joint sovereignty over Gibraltar. In response to these talks, the Gibraltar Government called a referendum in late 2002 in which the majority of citizens voted overwhelmingly against any sharing of sovereignty with Spain. Since late 2004, Spain, the UK, and Gibraltar have held tripartite talks with the aim of cooperatively resolving problems that affect the local population, and work continues on cooperation agreements in areas such as taxation and financial services; communications and maritime security; policy, legal and customs services; environmental protection; and education and visa services. A new noncolonial constitution came into force in 2007, and the European Court of First Instance recognized Gibraltar's right to regulate its own tax regime in December 2008. The UK retains responsibility for defense, foreign relations, internal security, and financial stability.

Spain and the UK continue to spar over the territory. Throughout 2009, a dispute over Gibraltar's claim to territorial waters extending out three miles gave rise to periodic non-violent maritime confrontations between Spanish and UK naval patrols and in 2013, the British reported a record number of entries by Spanish vessels into waters claimed by Gibraltar following a dispute over Gibraltar's creation of an artificial reef in those waters. Spain renewed its demands for an eventual return of Gibraltar to Spanish control after the UK's June 2016 vote to leave the EU, but London has dismissed any connection between the vote and its continued sovereignty over Gibraltar. The EU has said that Gibraltar will be ouside the territorial scope of any future UK-EU trade deal and that separate agreements between the EU and UK regarding Gibraltar would require Spain's prior approval.

GEOGRAPHY :: GIBRALTAR

LOCATION:

Southwestern Europe, bordering the Strait of Gibraltar, which links the Mediterranean Sea and the North Atlantic Ocean, on the southern coast of Spain

GEOGRAPHIC COORDINATES:

36 08 N, 5 21 W

MAP REFERENCES:

Europe

AREA:

total: 6.5 sq km

land: 6.5 sq km

water: 0 sq km

country comparison to the world: 245

AREA - COMPARATIVE:

more than 10 times the size of The National Mall in Washington, D.C.

LAND BOUNDARIES:

total: 1.2 km

border countries (1): Spain 1.2 km

COASTLINE:

12 km

MARITIME CLAIMS:

territorial sea: 3 nm

CLIMATE:

Mediterranean with mild winters and warm summers

TERRAIN:

a narrow coastal lowland borders the Rock of Gibraltar

ELEVATION:

lowest point: Mediterranean Sea 0 m

highest point: Rock of Gibraltar 426 m

NATURAL RESOURCES:

none

LAND USE:

agricultural land: 0% (2011 est.)

arable land: 0% (2011 est.) / permanent crops: 0% (2011 est.) / permanent pasture: 0% (2011 est.)

forest: 0% (2011 est.)

other: 100% (2011 est.)

IRRIGATED LAND:

NA

NATURAL HAZARDS:

occasional droughts; no streams or large bodies of water on the peninsula (all potable water comes from desalination)

ENVIRONMENT - CURRENT ISSUES:

limited natural freshwater resources: more than 90% of drinking water supplied by desalination, the remainder from stored rainwater; a separate supply of saltwater used for sanitary services

GEOGRAPHY - NOTE:

note 1: strategic location on Strait of Gibraltar that links the North Atlantic Ocean and Mediterranean Sea

note 2: one of only two British territories where traffic drives on the right, the other being the island of Diego Garcia in the British Indian Ocean Territory

PEOPLE AND SOCIETY :: GIBRALTAR

POPULATION:

29,461 (July 2018 est.)

country comparison to the world: 218

NATIONALITY:

noun: Gibraltarian(s)

adjective: Gibraltar

ETHNIC GROUPS:

Gibraltarian 79%, other British 13.2%, Spanish 2.1%, Moroccan 1.6%, other EU 2.4%, other 1.6% (2012 est.)

note: data represent population by nationality

LANGUAGES:

English (used in schools and for official purposes), Spanish, Italian, Portuguese

RELIGIONS:

Roman Catholic 72.1%, Church of England 7.7%, other Christian 3.8%, Muslim 3.6%, Jewish 2.4%, Hindu 2%, other 1.1%, none 7.1%, unspecified 0.1% (2012 est.)

AGE STRUCTURE:

0-14 years: 20.29% (male 3,064 /female 2,915)

15-24 years: 13.76% (male 2,110 /female 1,944)

25-54 years: 40.35% (male 6,094 /female 5,794)

55-64 years: 9.31% (male 1,183 /female 1,560)

65 years and over: 16.28% (male 2,336 /female 2,461) (2018 est.)

MEDIAN AGE:

total: 35 years (2018 est.)

male: 34.1 years

female: 36 years

country comparison to the world: 83

POPULATION GROWTH RATE:

0.21% (2018 est.)

country comparison to the world: 180

BIRTH RATE:

13.9 births/1,000 population (2018 est.)

country comparison to the world: 136

DEATH RATE:

8.5 deaths/1,000 population (2018 est.)

country comparison to the world: 78

NET MIGRATION RATE:

-3.3 migrant(s)/1,000 population (2018 est.)

country comparison to the world: 182

URBANIZATION:

urban population: 100% of total population (2019)

rate of urbanization: 0.45% annual rate of change (2015-20 est.)

MAJOR URBAN AREAS - POPULATION:

35,000 GIBRALTAR (capital) (2018)

SEX RATIO:

at birth: 1.07 male(s)/female

0-14 years: 1.05 male(s)/female

15-24 years: 1.09 male(s)/female

25-54 years: 1.05 male(s)/female

55-64 years: 0.76 male(s)/female

65 years and over: 0.95 male(s)/female

total population: 1.01 male(s)/female (2018 est.)

INFANT MORTALITY RATE:

total: 5.8 deaths/1,000 live births (2018 est.)

male: 6.5 deaths/1,000 live births

female: 5.1 deaths/1,000 live births

country comparison to the world: 167

LIFE EXPECTANCY AT BIRTH:

total population: 79.7 years (2018 est.)

male: 76.8 years

female: 82.8 years

country comparison to the world: 48

TOTAL FERTILITY RATE:

1.9 children born/woman (2018 est.)

country comparison to the world: 131

HIV/AIDS - ADULT PREVALENCE RATE:

NA

HIV/AIDS - PEOPLE LIVING WITH HIV/AIDS:

NA

HIV/AIDS - DEATHS:

NA

EDUCATION EXPENDITURES:

NA

GOVERNMENT :: GIBRALTAR

COUNTRY NAME:

conventional long form: none

conventional short form: Gibraltar

etymology: from the Spanish derivation of the Arabic "Jabal Tariq," which means "Mountain of Tariq" and which refers to the Rock of Gibraltar

DEPENDENCY STATUS:

overseas territory of the UK

GOVERNMENT TYPE:

parliamentary democracy (Parliament); self-governing overseas territory of the UK

CAPITAL:

name: Gibraltar

geographic coordinates: 36 08 N, 5 21 W

time difference: UTC+1 (6 hours ahead of Washington, DC, during Standard Time)

daylight saving time: +1hr, begins last Sunday in March; ends last Sunday in October

etymology: from the Spanish derivation of the Arabic "Jabal Tariq," which means "Mountain of Tariq" and which refers to the Rock of Gibraltar

ADMINISTRATIVE DIVISIONS:

none (overseas territory of the UK)

INDEPENDENCE:

none (overseas territory of the UK)

NATIONAL HOLIDAY:

National Day, 10 September (1967); note - day of the national referendum to decide whether to remain with the UK or join Spain

CONSTITUTION:

history: previous 1969; latest passed by referendum 30 November 2006, entered into effect 14 December 2006, entered into force 2 January 2007

amendments: proposed by Parliament and require prior consent of the British monarch (through the

Secretary of State); passage requires at least three-fourths majority vote in Parliament followed by simple majority vote in a referendum; note – only sections 1 through 15 in Chapter 1 (Protection of Fundamental Rights and Freedoms) can be amended by Parliament (2016)

LEGAL SYSTEM:
the laws of the UK, where applicable, apply

CITIZENSHIP:
see United Kingdom

SUFFRAGE:
18 years of age; universal; and British citizens with six months residence or more

EXECUTIVE BRANCH:
chief of state: Queen ELIZABETH II (since 6 February 1952); represented by Governor Lt. Gen. Edward DAVIS (since 19 January 2016)

head of government: Chief Minister Fabian PICARDO (since 9 December 2011)

cabinet: Council of Ministers appointed from among the 17 elected members of Parliament by the governor in consultation with the chief minister

elections/appointments: the monarchy is hereditary; governor appointed by the monarch; following legislative elections, the leader of the majority party or majority coalition usually appointed chief minister by the governor

LEGISLATIVE BRANCH:
description: unicameral Parliament (18 seats; 17 members directly elected in a single nationwide constituency by majority vote and 1 appointed by Parliament as speaker; members serve 4-year terms) (e.g. 2019)

elections: last held on 17 October 2019 (next to be held in 2023) (e.g. 2019)

election results: percent of vote by party - GSLP-Liberal Alliance 52.5% (GSLP 37.0%, LPG 15.5%), GSD 25.6%; seats by party - GSLP-Liberal Alliance 10 (GSLP 7, LPG 3), GSD 6; composition of elected members - men 15, women 2, percent of women 11.8% (e.g. 2019)

JUDICIAL BRANCH:
highest courts: Court of Appeal (consists of at least 3 judges, including the court president); Supreme Court of Gibraltar (consists of the chief justice and 3 judges); note - appeals beyond the Court of Appeal are heard by the Judicial Committee of the Privy Council (in London)

judge selection and term of office: Court of Appeal and Supreme Court judges appointed by the governor upon the advice of the Judicial Service Commission, a 7-member body of judges and appointees of the governor; tenure of the Court of Appeal president based on terms of appointment; Supreme Court chief justice and judges normally appointed until retirement at age 67 but tenure can be extended 3 years

subordinate courts: Court of First Instance; Magistrates' Court; specialized tribunals for issues relating to social security, taxes, and employment

POLITICAL PARTIES AND LEADERS:
Gibraltar Liberal Party or Liberal Party of Gibraltar or LPG [Joseph GARCIA]
Gibraltar Social Democrats or GSD [Keith AZOPARDI]
Gibraltar Socialist Labor Party or GSLP [Fabian PICARDO]
GSLP-Liberal Alliance (includes GSLP and LPG)
Together Gibraltar or TG [Marlene HASSAN-NAHON]

INTERNATIONAL ORGANIZATION PARTICIPATION:
ICC (NGOs), Interpol (subbureau), UPU

DIPLOMATIC REPRESENTATION IN THE US:
none (overseas territory of the UK)

DIPLOMATIC REPRESENTATION FROM THE US:
none (overseas territory of the UK)

FLAG DESCRIPTION:
two horizontal bands of white (top, double width) and red with a three-towered red castle in the center of the white band; hanging from the castle gate is a gold key centered in the red band; the design is that of Gibraltar's coat of arms granted on 10 July 1502 by King Ferdinand and Queen Isabella of Spain; the castle symbolizes Gibraltar as a fortress, while the key represents Gibraltar's strategic importance - the key to the Mediterranean

NATIONAL SYMBOL(S):
Barbary macaque; national colors: red, white, yellow

NATIONAL ANTHEM:
name: Gibraltar Anthem

lyrics/music: Peter EMBERLEY

note: adopted 1994; serves as a local anthem; as a territory of the United Kingdom, "God Save the Queen" is official (see United Kingdom)

ECONOMY :: GIBRALTAR

ECONOMY - OVERVIEW:
Self-sufficient Gibraltar benefits from an extensive shipping trade, offshore banking, and its position as an international conference center. Tax rates are low to attract foreign investment. The British military presence has been sharply reduced and now contributes about 7% to the local economy, compared with 60% in 1984. In recent years, Gibraltar has seen major structural change from a public to a private sector economy, but changes in government spending still have a major impact on the level of employment.

The financial sector, tourism (over 11 million visitors in 2012), gaming revenues, shipping services fees, and duties on consumer goods also generate revenue. The financial sector, tourism, and the shipping sector contribute 30%, 30%, and 25%, respectively, of GDP. Telecommunications, e-commerce, and e-gaming account for the remaining 15%.

GDP (PURCHASING POWER PARITY):
$2.044 billion (2014 est.)

$1.85 billion (2013 est.)

$2 billion (2012 est.)

note: data are in 2014 dollars

country comparison to the world: 196

GDP (OFFICIAL EXCHANGE RATE):
$2.044 billion (2014 est.) (2014 est.)

GDP - PER CAPITA (PPP):
$61,700 (2014 est.)

$43,000 (2008 est.)

$41,200 (2007 est.)

country comparison to the world: 17

GDP - COMPOSITION, BY SECTOR OF ORIGIN:
agriculture: 0% (2016 est.)

industry: 0% (2008 est.)

services: 100% (2016 est.)

AGRICULTURE - PRODUCTS:

none

INDUSTRIES:
tourism, banking and finance, ship repairing, tobacco

INDUSTRIAL PRODUCTION GROWTH RATE:
NA

LABOR FORCE:
24,420 (2014 est.)

country comparison to the world: 209

LABOR FORCE - BY OCCUPATION:
agriculture: NEGL
industry: 1.8%
services: 98.2% (2014 est.)

UNEMPLOYMENT RATE:
1% (2016 est.)

country comparison to the world: 9

POPULATION BELOW POVERTY LINE:
NA

HOUSEHOLD INCOME OR CONSUMPTION BY PERCENTAGE SHARE:
lowest 10%: NA
highest 10%: NA

BUDGET:
revenues: 475.8 million (2008 est.)
expenditures: 452.3 million (2008 est.)

TAXES AND OTHER REVENUES:
23.3% (of GDP) (2008 est.)

country comparison to the world: 127

BUDGET SURPLUS (+) OR DEFICIT (-):
1.1% (of GDP) (2008 est.)

country comparison to the world: 31

PUBLIC DEBT:
7.5% of GDP (2008 est.)
8.4% of GDP (2006 est.)

country comparison to the world: 200

FISCAL YEAR:
1 July - 30 June

INFLATION RATE (CONSUMER PRICES):
2.5% (2013 est.)
2.2% (2012 est.)

country comparison to the world: 123

EXPORTS:
$202.3 million (2014 est.)
$271 million (2004 est.)

country comparison to the world: 189

EXPORTS - PARTNERS:
Spain 27.1%, Germany 20.4%, Netherlands 10.8%, Poland 8.6%, France 6.6%, Italy 5.7%, Cote dIvoire 4.5% (2017)

EXPORTS - COMMODITIES:
(principally reexports) petroleum 51%, manufactured goods (2010 est.)

IMPORTS:
$2.967 billion (2004 est.)

country comparison to the world: 149

IMPORTS - COMMODITIES:
fuels, manufactured goods, foodstuffs

IMPORTS - PARTNERS:
Spain 15.6%, Italy 13.4%, US 13.3%, Netherlands 10.9%, Greece 8.5%, Russia 6.6%, UK 5.8%, Belgium 4.4% (2017)

DEBT - EXTERNAL:
NA

EXCHANGE RATES:
Gibraltar pounds (GIP) per US dollar -
0.885 (2017 est.)
0.903 (2016 est.)
0.9214 (2015 est.)
0.885 (2014 est.)
0.7634 (2013 est.)

ENERGY :: GIBRALTAR

ELECTRICITY - PRODUCTION:
238.8 million kWh (2016 est.)

country comparison to the world: 187

ELECTRICITY - CONSUMPTION:
230.8 million kWh (2016 est.)

country comparison to the world: 189

ELECTRICITY - EXPORTS:
0 kWh (2016 est.)

country comparison to the world: 140

ELECTRICITY - IMPORTS:
0 kWh (2016 est.)

country comparison to the world: 152

ELECTRICITY - INSTALLED GENERATING CAPACITY:
43,000 kW (2016 est.)

country comparison to the world: 196

ELECTRICITY - FROM FOSSIL FUELS:
100% of total installed capacity (2016 est.)

country comparison to the world: 8

ELECTRICITY - FROM NUCLEAR FUELS:
0% of total installed capacity (2017 est.)

country comparison to the world: 97

ELECTRICITY - FROM HYDROELECTRIC PLANTS:
0% of total installed capacity (2017 est.)

country comparison to the world: 173

ELECTRICITY - FROM OTHER RENEWABLE SOURCES:
0% of total installed capacity (2017 est.)

country comparison to the world: 188

CRUDE OIL - PRODUCTION:
0 bbl/day (2018 est.)

country comparison to the world: 141

CRUDE OIL - EXPORTS:
0 bbl/day (2015 est.)

country comparison to the world: 129

CRUDE OIL - IMPORTS:
0 bbl/day (2015 est.)

country comparison to the world: 132

CRUDE OIL - PROVED RESERVES:
0 bbl (1 January 2018 est.)

country comparison to the world: 137

REFINED PETROLEUM PRODUCTS - PRODUCTION:
0 bbl/day (2017 est.)

country comparison to the world: 149

REFINED PETROLEUM PRODUCTS - CONSUMPTION:
78,000 bbl/day (2016 est.)

country comparison to the world: 88

REFINED PETROLEUM PRODUCTS - EXPORTS:
0 bbl/day (2015 est.)

country comparison to the world: 158

REFINED PETROLEUM PRODUCTS - IMPORTS:
74,200 bbl/day (2015 est.)

country comparison to the world: 66

NATURAL GAS - PRODUCTION:
0 cu m (2017 est.)

country comparison to the world: 137

NATURAL GAS - CONSUMPTION:
0 cu m (2017 est.)

country comparison to the world: 150

NATURAL GAS - EXPORTS:
0 cu m (2017 est.)

country comparison to the world: 111

NATURAL GAS - IMPORTS:
0 cu m (2017 est.)

country comparison to the world: 130

NATURAL GAS - PROVED RESERVES:

0 cu m (1 January 2014 est.)

country comparison to the world: 139

CARBON DIOXIDE EMISSIONS FROM CONSUMPTION OF ENERGY:

13.34 million Mt (2017 est.)

country comparison to the world: 98

COMMUNICATIONS :: GIBRALTAR

TELEPHONES - FIXED LINES:

total subscriptions: 19,753

subscriptions per 100 inhabitants: 67 (2017 est.)

country comparison to the world: 179

TELEPHONES - MOBILE CELLULAR:

total subscriptions: 41,035

subscriptions per 100 inhabitants: 140 (2017 est.)

country comparison to the world: 204

TELEPHONE SYSTEM:

general assessment: adequate, automatic domestic system and adequate international facilities (2018)

domestic: automatic exchange facilities; 67 per 100 fixed-line and 140 per 100 mobile-cellular (2018)

international: country code - 350; landing point for the EIG to Europe, Asia, Africa and the Middle East via submarine cables; radiotelephone; microwave radio relay; satellite earth station - 1 Intelsat (Atlantic Ocean) (2019)

BROADCAST MEDIA:

Gibraltar Broadcasting Corporation (GBC) provides TV and radio broadcasting services via 1 TV station and 4 radio stations; British Forces Broadcasting Service (BFBS) operates 1 radio station; broadcasts from Spanish radio and TV stations are accessible

INTERNET COUNTRY CODE:

.gi

INTERNET USERS:

total: 27,699

percent of population: 94.4% (July 2016 est.)

country comparison to the world: 203

BROADBAND - FIXED SUBSCRIPTIONS:

total: 17,373

subscriptions per 100 inhabitants: 59 (2017 est.)

country comparison to the world: 154

MILITARY AND SECURITY :: GIBRALTAR

MILITARY AND SECURITY FORCES:

Royal Gibraltar Regiment (2019)

MILITARY - NOTE:

defense is the responsibility of the UK; the Royal Gibraltar Regiment replaced the last British regular infantry forces in 1991 (2019)

TRANSPORTATION :: GIBRALTAR

CIVIL AIRCRAFT REGISTRATION COUNTRY CODE PREFIX:

VP-G (2016)

AIRPORTS:

1 (2013)

country comparison to the world: 223

AIRPORTS - WITH PAVED RUNWAYS:

total: 1 (2017)

1,524 to 2,437 m: 1 (2017)

ROADWAYS:

total: 29 km (2007)

paved: 29 km (2007)

country comparison to the world: 212

MERCHANT MARINE:

total: 250

by type: bulk carrier 11, container ship 26, general cargo 81, oil tanker 27, other 105 (2018)

country comparison to the world: 59

PORTS AND TERMINALS:

major seaport(s): Gibraltar

TRANSNATIONAL ISSUES :: GIBRALTAR

DISPUTES - INTERNATIONAL:

in 2002, Gibraltar residents voted overwhelmingly by referendum to reject any "shared sovereignty" arrangement; the Government of Gibraltar insists on equal participation in talks between the UK and Spain; Spain disapproves of UK plans to grant Gibraltar even greater autonomy

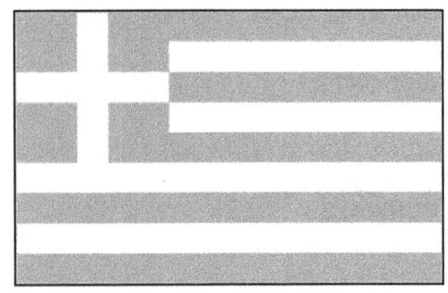

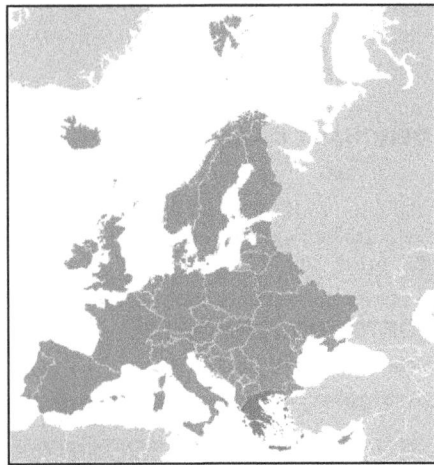

EUROPE :: GREECE

INTRODUCTION :: GREECE

BACKGROUND:

Greece achieved independence from the Ottoman Empire in 1830. During the second half of the 19th century and the first half of the 20th century, it gradually added neighboring islands and territories, most with Greek-speaking populations. In World War II, Greece was first invaded by Italy (1940) and subsequently occupied by Germany (1941-44); fighting endured in a protracted civil war between supporters of the king and other anti-communist and communist rebels. Following the latter's defeat in 1949, Greece joined NATO in 1952. In 1967, a group of military officers seized power, establishing a military dictatorship that suspended many political liberties and forced the king to flee the country. In 1974 following the collapse of the dictatorship, democratic elections and a referendum created a parliamentary republic and abolished the monarchy. In 1981, Greece joined the EC (now the EU); it became the 12th member of the European Economic and Monetary Union (EMU) in 2001. Greece has suffered a severe economic crisis since late 2009, due to nearly a decade of chronic overspending and structural rigidities. Beginning in 2010, Greece entered three bailout agreements - with the European Commission, the European Central Bank (ECB), the IMF, and the third in 2015 with the European Stability Mechanism (ESM) - worth in total about $300 billion. The Greek Government formally exited the third bailout in August 2018.

GEOGRAPHY :: GREECE

LOCATION:
Southern Europe, bordering the Aegean Sea, Ionian Sea, and the Mediterranean Sea, between Albania and Turkey

GEOGRAPHIC COORDINATES:
39 00 N, 22 00 E

MAP REFERENCES:
Europe

AREA:
total: 131,957 sq km

land: 130,647 sq km

water: 1,310 sq km

country comparison to the world: 98

AREA - COMPARATIVE:
slightly smaller than Alabama

LAND BOUNDARIES:
total: 1,110 km

border countries (4): Albania 212 km, Bulgaria 472 km, Macedonia 234 km, Turkey 192 km

COASTLINE:
13,676 km

MARITIME CLAIMS:
territorial sea: 12 nm

continental shelf: 200-m depth or to the depth of exploitation

CLIMATE:
temperate; mild, wet winters; hot, dry summers

TERRAIN:
mountainous with ranges extending into the sea as peninsulas or chains of islands

ELEVATION:
mean elevation: 498 m

lowest point: Mediterranean Sea 0 m

highest point: Mount Olympus 2,917

note: Mount Olympus actually has 52 peaks but its highest point, Mytikas (meaning "nose"), rises to 2,917 meters; in Greek mythology, Olympus' Mytikas peak was the home of the Greek gods

NATURAL RESOURCES:
lignite, petroleum, iron ore, bauxite, lead, zinc, nickel, magnesite, marble, salt, hydropower potential

LAND USE:
agricultural land: 63.4% (2011 est.)

arable land: 19.7% (2011 est.) / permanent crops: 8.9% (2011 est.) / permanent pasture: 34.8% (2011 est.)

forest: 30.5% (2011 est.)

other: 6.1% (2011 est.)

IRRIGATED LAND:
15,550 sq km (2012)

POPULATION DISTRIBUTION:
one-third of the population lives in and around metropolitan Athens; the remainder of the country has moderate population density mixed with sizeable urban clusters

NATURAL HAZARDS:
severe earthquakes

volcanism: Santorini (367 m) has been deemed a Decade Volcano by the International Association of Volcanology and Chemistry of the Earth's Interior, worthy of study due to its explosive history and close proximity to human populations;

although there have been very few eruptions in recent centuries, Methana and Nisyros in the Aegean are classified as historically active

ENVIRONMENT - CURRENT ISSUES:

air pollution; air emissions from transport and electricity power stations; water pollution; degradation of coastal zones; loss of biodiversity in terrestrial and marine ecosystems; increasing municipal and industrial waste

ENVIRONMENT - INTERNATIONAL AGREEMENTS:

party to: Air Pollution, Air Pollution-Nitrogen Oxides, Air Pollution-Sulfur 94, Antarctic-Environmental Protocol, Antarctic-Marine Living Resources, Antarctic Treaty, Biodiversity, Climate Change, Climate Change-Kyoto Protocol, Desertification, Endangered Species, Environmental Modification, Hazardous Wastes, Law of the Sea, Marine Dumping, Ozone Layer Protection, Ship Pollution, Tropical Timber 83, Tropical Timber 94, Wetlands

signed, but not ratified: Air Pollution-Persistent Organic Pollutants, Air Pollution-Volatile Organic Compounds

GEOGRAPHY - NOTE:

strategic location dominating the Aegean Sea and southern approach to Turkish Straits; a peninsular country, possessing an archipelago of about 2,000 islands

PEOPLE AND SOCIETY :: GREECE

POPULATION:

10,761,523 (July 2018 est.)

country comparison to the world: 84

NATIONALITY:

noun: Greek(s)

adjective: Greek

ETHNIC GROUPS:

Greek 91.6%, Albanian 4.4%, other 4% (2011)

note: data represent citizenship; Greece does not collect data on ethnicity

LANGUAGES:

Greek (official) 99%, other (includes English and French) 1%

RELIGIONS:

Greek Orthodox (official) 81-90%, Muslim 2%, other 3%, none 4-15%, unspecified 1% (2015 est.)

AGE STRUCTURE:

0-14 years: 13.72% (male 760,615 /female 716,054)

15-24 years: 9.68% (male 531,957 /female 509,671)

25-54 years: 42.18% (male 2,259,672 /female 2,279,464)

55-64 years: 13.28% (male 699,205 /female 729,655)

65 years and over: 21.14% (male 997,359 /female 1,277,871) (2018 est.)

DEPENDENCY RATIOS:

total dependency ratio: 52.7 (2015 est.)

youth dependency ratio: 22.2 (2015 est.)

elderly dependency ratio: 30.5 (2015 est.)

potential support ratio: 3.3 (2015 est.)

MEDIAN AGE:

total: 44.9 years (2018 est.)

male: 43.8 years

female: 45.9 years

country comparison to the world: 7

POPULATION GROWTH RATE:

-0.07% (2018 est.)

country comparison to the world: 203

BIRTH RATE:

8.3 births/1,000 population (2018 est.)

country comparison to the world: 218

DEATH RATE:

11.4 deaths/1,000 population (2018 est.)

country comparison to the world: 21

NET MIGRATION RATE:

2.3 migrant(s)/1,000 population (2018 est.)

country comparison to the world: 46

POPULATION DISTRIBUTION:

one-third of the population lives in and around metropolitan Athens; the remainder of the country has moderate population density mixed with sizeable urban clusters

URBANIZATION:

urban population: 79.4% of total population (2019)

rate of urbanization: 0.22% annual rate of change (2015-20 est.)

MAJOR URBAN AREAS - POPULATION:

3.154 million ATHENS (capital), 811,000 Thessaloniki (2019)

SEX RATIO:

at birth: 1.06 male(s)/female

0-14 years: 1.06 male(s)/female

15-24 years: 1.04 male(s)/female

25-54 years: 0.99 male(s)/female

55-64 years: 0.96 male(s)/female

65 years and over: 0.78 male(s)/female

total population: 0.95 male(s)/female (2018 est.)

MOTHER'S MEAN AGE AT FIRST BIRTH:

29.8 years (2014 est.)

MATERNAL MORTALITY RATE:

3 deaths/100,000 live births (2017 est.)

country comparison to the world: 178

INFANT MORTALITY RATE:

total: 4.5 deaths/1,000 live births (2018 est.)

male: 5 deaths/1,000 live births

female: 4.1 deaths/1,000 live births

country comparison to the world: 181

LIFE EXPECTANCY AT BIRTH:

total population: 80.8 years (2018 est.)

male: 78.2 years

female: 83.6 years

country comparison to the world: 40

TOTAL FERTILITY RATE:

1.44 children born/woman (2018 est.)

country comparison to the world: 207

DRINKING WATER SOURCE:

improved:

urban: 100% of population

rural: 100% of population

total: 100% of population

unimproved:

urban: 0% of population

rural: 0% of population

total: 0% of population (2015 est.)

CURRENT HEALTH EXPENDITURE:

8.5% (2016)

PHYSICIANS DENSITY:

4.59 physicians/1,000 population (2016)

HOSPITAL BED DENSITY:

4.3 beds/1,000 population (2015)

SANITATION FACILITY ACCESS:

improved:

urban: 99.2% of population (2015 est.)

rural: 98.1% of population (2015 est.)

total: 99% of population (2015 est.)

unimproved:

urban: 0.8% of population (2015 est.)

rural: 1.9% of population (2015 est.)

total: 1% of population (2015 est.)

HIV/AIDS - ADULT PREVALENCE RATE:

0.2% (2017 est.)

country comparison to the world: 98

HIV/AIDS - PEOPLE LIVING WITH HIV/AIDS:

14,000 (2017 est.)

country comparison to the world: 92

HIV/AIDS - DEATHS:

<100 (2017 est.)

OBESITY - ADULT PREVALENCE RATE:

24.9% (2016)

country comparison to the world: 54

EDUCATION EXPENDITURES:

NA

LITERACY:

definition: age 15 and over can read and write

total population: 97.7%

male: 98.5%

female: 96.9% (2015 est.)

SCHOOL LIFE EXPECTANCY (PRIMARY TO TERTIARY EDUCATION):

total: 18 years

male: 18 years

female: 18 years (2016)

UNEMPLOYMENT, YOUTH AGES 15-24:

total: 43.6%

male: 39.3%

female: 48.2% (2017 est.)

country comparison to the world: 12

GOVERNMENT :: GREECE

COUNTRY NAME:

conventional long form: Hellenic Republic

conventional short form: Greece

local long form: Elliniki Dimokratia

local short form: Ellas or Ellada

former: Hellenic State, Kingdom of Greece

etymology: the English name derives from the Roman (Latin) designation "Graecia," meaning "Land of the Greeks"; the Greeks call their country "Hellas" or "Ellada"

GOVERNMENT TYPE:

parliamentary republic

CAPITAL:

name: Athens

geographic coordinates: 37 59 N, 23 44 E

time difference: UTC+2 (7 hours ahead of Washington, DC, during Standard Time)

daylight saving time: +1hr, begins last Sunday in March; ends last Sunday in October

etymology: according to tradition, the city is named after Athena, the Greek goddess of wisdom; in actuality, the appellation probably derives from a lost name in a pre-Hellenic language

ADMINISTRATIVE DIVISIONS:

13 regions (perifereies, singular - perifereia) and 1 autonomous monastic state* (aftonomi monastiki politeia); Agion Oros* (Mount Athos), Anatoliki Makedonia kai Thraki (East Macedonia and Thrace), Attiki (Attica), Dytiki Ellada (West Greece), Dytiki Makedonia (West Macedonia), Ionia Nisia (Ionian Islands), Ipeiros (Epirus), Kentriki Makedonia (Central Macedonia), Kriti (Crete), Notio Aigaio (South Aegean), Peloponnisos (Peloponnese), Sterea Ellada (Central Greece), Thessalia (Thessaly), Voreio Aigaio (North Aegean)

INDEPENDENCE:

3 February 1830 (from the Ottoman Empire); note - 25 March 1821, outbreak of the national revolt against the Ottomans; 3 February 1830, signing of the London Protocol recognizing Greek independence by Great Britain, France, and Russia

NATIONAL HOLIDAY:

Independence Day, 25 March (1821)

CONSTITUTION:

history: many previous; latest entered into force 11 June 1975

amendments: proposed by at least 50 members of Parliament and agreed by three-fifths majority vote in two separate ballots at least 30 days apart; passage requires absolute majority vote by the next elected Parliament; entry into force finalized through a "special parliamentary resolution"; articles on human rights and freedoms and the form of government cannot be amended; amended 1986, 2001, 2008 (2016)

LEGAL SYSTEM:

civil legal system based on Roman law

INTERNATIONAL LAW ORGANIZATION PARTICIPATION:

accepts compulsory ICJ jurisdiction with reservations; accepts ICCt jurisdiction

CITIZENSHIP:

citizenship by birth: no

citizenship by descent only: at least one parent must be a citizen of Greece

dual citizenship recognized: yes

residency requirement for naturalization: 10 years

SUFFRAGE:

17 years of age; universal and compulsory

EXECUTIVE BRANCH:

chief of state: President Prokopios (Prokopis) PAVLOPOULOS (since 13 March 2015)

head of government: Prime Minister Kyriakos MITSOTAKIS (since 8 July 2019)

cabinet: Cabinet appointed by the president on the recommendation of the prime minister

elections/appointments: president elected by Hellenic Parliament for a 5-year term (eligible for a second term); election last held on 18 February 2015 (next to be held by February 2020); president appoints as prime minister the leader of the majority party or coalition in the Hellenic Parliament

election results: Prokopios PAVLOPOULOS (ND) elected president by Parliament - 233 of 300 votes

LEGISLATIVE BRANCH:

description: unicameral Hellenic Parliament or Vouli ton Ellinon (300 seats; 280 members in multi-seat constituencies and 12 members in a single nationwide constituency directly elected by open party-list proportional representation vote; 8

members in single-seat constituencies elected by simple majority vote; members serve up to 4 years); note - only parties surpassing a 3% threshold are entitled to parliamentary seats; parties need 10 seats to become formal parliamentary groups but can retain that status if the party participated in the last election and received the minimum 3% threshold

elections: last held on 7 July 2019 (next to be held by July 2023)

election results: percent of vote by party - ND 39.9%, SYRIZA 31.5%, KINAL 8.1%, KKE 5.3%, Greek Solution 3.7%, MeRA25 3.4%, other 8.1%; seats by party - ND 158, SYRIZA 86, KINAL 22, KKE 15, Greek Solution 10, MeRA25 9; composition - men 244, women 56, percent of women 18.7%

JUDICIAL BRANCH:

highest courts: Supreme Civil and Criminal Court or Areios Pagos (consists of 56 judges, including the court presidents); Council of State (supreme administrative court) (consists of the president, 7 vice presidents, 42 privy councilors, 48 associate councilors and 50 reporting judges, organized into six 5- and 7-member chambers; Court of Audit (government audit and enforcement) consists of the president, 5 vice presidents, 20 councilors, and 90 associate and reporting judges

judge selection and term of office: Supreme Court judges appointed by presidential decree on the advice of the Supreme Judicial Council (SJC), which includes the president of the Supreme Court, other judges, and the prosecutor of the Supreme Court; judges appointed for life following a 2-year probationary period; Council of State president appointed by the Greek Cabinet to serve a 4-year term; other judge appointments and tenure NA; Court of Audit president appointed by decree of the president of the republic on the advice of the SJC; court president serves a 4-year term or until age 67; tenure of vice presidents, councilors, and judges NA

subordinate courts: Courts of Appeal and Courts of First Instance (district courts)

POLITICAL PARTIES AND LEADERS:

Anticapitalist Left Cooperation for the Overthrow or ANTARSYA [collective leadership]
Coalition of the Radical Left or SYRIZA [Alexios (Alexis) TSIPRAS]
Communist Party of Greece or KKE [Dimitrios KOUTSOUMBAS]
Democratic Left or DIMAR [Athanasios (Thanasis) THEOCHAROPOULOS]
European Realistic Disobedience Front or MeRA25 [Yanis VAROUFAKIS]
Greek Solution [Kyriakos VELOPOULOS]
Independent Greeks or ANEL [Panagiotis (Panos) KAMMENOS]
Movement for Change or KINAL [Foteini (Fofi) GENIMMATA]
New Democracy or ND [Kyriakos MITSOTAKIS]
People's Association-Golden Dawn [Nikolaos MICHALOLIAKOS]
Popular Unity or LAE [Panagiotis LAFAZANIS]
The River (To Potami) [Stavros THEODORAKIS]
Union of Centrists or EK [Vasileios (Vasilis) LEVENTIS]

INTERNATIONAL ORGANIZATION PARTICIPATION:

Australia Group, BIS, BSEC, CD, CE, CERN, EAPC, EBRD, ECB, EIB, EMU, ESA, EU, FAO, FATF, IAEA, IBRD, ICAO, ICC (national committees), ICCt, ICRM, IDA, IEA, IFAD, IFC, IFRCS, IGAD (partners), IHO, ILO, IMF, IMO, IMSO, Interpol, IOC, IOM, IPU, ISO, ITSO, ITU, ITUC (NGOs), MIGA, NATO, NEA, NSG, OAS (observer), OECD, OIF, OPCW, OSCE, PCA, Schengen Convention, SELEC, UN, UNCTAD, UNESCO, UNHCR, UNIDO, UNIFIL, UNWTO, UPU, WCO, WFTU (NGOs), WHO, WIPO, WMO, WTO, ZC

DIPLOMATIC REPRESENTATION IN THE US:

Ambassador Theocharis LALAKOS (since 27 June 2016)

chancery: 2217 Massachusetts Avenue NW, Washington, DC 20008

telephone: [1] (202) 939-1300

FAX: [1] (202) 939-1324

consulate(s) general: Boston, Chicago, Los Angeles, New York, Tampa (FL), San Francisco

consulate(s): Atlanta, Houston

DIPLOMATIC REPRESENTATION FROM THE US:

chief of mission: Ambassador Geoffrey R. PYATT (since 24 October 2016)

telephone: [30] (210) 721-2951

embassy: 91 Vasillisis Sophias Avenue, 10160 Athens

mailing address: PSC 108, APO AE 09842-0108

FAX: [30] (210) 645-6282

consulate(s) general: Thessaloniki

FLAG DESCRIPTION:

nine equal horizontal stripes of blue alternating with white; a blue square bearing a white cross appears in the upper hoist-side corner; the cross symbolizes Greek Orthodoxy, the established religion of the country; there is no agreed upon meaning for the nine stripes or for the colors

note: Greek legislation states that the flag colors are cyan and white, but cyan can mean "blue" in Greek, so the exact shade of blue has never been set and has varied from a light to a dark blue over time; in general, the hue of blue normally encountered is a form of azure

NATIONAL SYMBOL(S):

Greek cross (white cross on blue field, arms equal length); national colors: blue, white

NATIONAL ANTHEM:

name: "Ymnos eis tin Eleftherian" (Hymn to Liberty)

lyrics/music: Dionysios SOLOMOS/Nikolaos MANTZAROS

note: adopted 1864; the anthem is based on a 158-stanza poem by the same name, which was inspired by the Greek Revolution of 1821 against the Ottomans (only the first two stanzas are used); Cyprus also uses "Hymn to Liberty" as its anthem

ECONOMY :: GREECE

ECONOMY - OVERVIEW:

Greece has a capitalist economy with a public sector accounting for about 40% of GDP and with per capita GDP about two-thirds that of the leading euro-zone economies. Tourism provides 18% of GDP. Immigrants make up nearly one-fifth of the work force, mainly in agricultural and unskilled jobs. Greece is a major beneficiary of EU aid, equal to about 3.3% of annual GDP.

The Greek economy averaged growth of about 4% per year between 2003 and 2007, but the economy went into recession in 2009 as a result of the world financial crisis, tightening credit conditions, and Athens' failure to address a growing budget deficit. By 2013, the economy had contracted 26%, compared with the pre-crisis level of 2007. Greece met the EU's Growth and Stability Pact budget deficit criterion of no more than 3% of GDP in 2007-08, but violated it in 2009, when the deficit reached 15% of GDP. Deteriorating public finances, inaccurate and misreported statistics, and consistent underperformance on reforms prompted major credit rating agencies to downgrade Greece's international debt rating in late 2009 and led the country into a financial crisis. Under intense pressure from the EU and international market participants, the government accepted a bailout program that called on Athens to cut government spending, decrease tax evasion, overhaul the civil-service, health-care, and pension systems, and reform the labor and product markets. Austerity measures reduced the deficit to 1.3% in 2017. Successive Greek governments, however, failed to push through many of the most unpopular reforms in the face of widespread political opposition, including from the country's powerful labor unions and the general public.

In April 2010, a leading credit agency assigned Greek debt its lowest possible credit rating, and in May 2010, the IMF and euro-zone governments provided Greece emergency short- and medium-term loans worth $147 billion so that the country could make debt repayments to creditors. Greece, however, struggled to meet the targets set by the EU and the IMF, especially after Eurostat - the EU's statistical office - revised upward Greece's deficit and debt numbers for 2009 and 2010. European leaders and the IMF agreed in October 2011 to provide Athens a second bailout package of $169 billion. The second deal called for holders of Greek government bonds to write down a significant portion of their holdings to try to alleviate Greece's government debt burden. However, Greek banks, saddled with a significant portion of sovereign debt, were adversely affected by the write down and $60 billion of the second bailout package was set aside to ensure the banking system was adequately capitalized.

In 2014, the Greek economy began to turn the corner on the recession. Greece achieved three significant milestones: balancing the budget - not including debt repayments; issuing government debt in financial markets for the first time since 2010; and generating 0.7% GDP growth — the first economic expansion since 2007.

Despite the nascent recovery, widespread discontent with austerity measures helped propel the far-left Coalition of the Radical Left (SYRIZA) party into government in national legislative elections in January 2015. Between January and July 2015, frustrations grew between the SYRIZA-led government and Greece's EU and IMF creditors over the implementation of bailout measures and disbursement of funds. The Greek government began running up significant arrears to suppliers, while Greek banks relied on emergency lending, and Greece's future in the euro zone was called into question. To stave off a collapse of the banking system, Greece imposed capital controls in June 2015, then became the first developed nation to miss a loan payment to the IMF, rattling international financial markets. Unable to reach an agreement with creditors, Prime Minister Alexios TSIPRAS held a nationwide referendum on 5 July on whether to accept the terms of Greece's bailout, campaigning for the ultimately successful "no" vote. The TSIPRAS government subsequently agreed, however, to a new $96 billion bailout in order to avert Greece's exit from the monetary bloc. On 20 August 2015, Greece signed its third bailout, allowing it to cover significant debt payments to its EU and IMF creditors and to ensure the banking sector retained access to emergency liquidity. The TSIPRAS government — which retook office on 20 September 2015 after calling new elections in late August — successfully secured disbursal of two delayed tranches of bailout funds. Despite the economic turmoil, Greek GDP did not contract as sharply as feared, boosted in part by a strong tourist season.

In 2017, Greece saw improvements in GDP and unemployment. Unfinished economic reforms, a massive non-performing loan problem, and ongoing uncertainty regarding the political direction of the country hold the economy back. Some estimates put Greece's black market at 20- to 25% of GDP, as more people have stopped reporting their income to avoid paying taxes that, in some cases, have risen to 70% of an individual's gross income.

GDP (PURCHASING POWER PARITY):

$299.3 billion (2017 est.)

$295.3 billion (2016 est.)

$296 billion (2015 est.)

note: data are in 2017 dollars

country comparison to the world: 56

GDP (OFFICIAL EXCHANGE RATE):

$200.7 billion (2017 est.)

GDP - REAL GROWTH RATE:

1.4% (2017 est.)

-0.2% (2016 est.)

-0.3% (2015 est.)

country comparison to the world: 176

GDP - PER CAPITA (PPP):

$27,800 (2017 est.)

$27,400 (2016 est.)

$27,300 (2015 est.)

note: data are in 2017 dollars

country comparison to the world: 75

GROSS NATIONAL SAVING:

10.9% of GDP (2017 est.)

9.5% of GDP (2016 est.)

9.6% of GDP (2015 est.)

country comparison to the world: 159

GDP - COMPOSITION, BY END USE:

household consumption: 69.6% (2017 est.)

government consumption: 20.1% (2017 est.)

investment in fixed capital: 12.5% (2017 est.)

investment in inventories: -1% (2017 est.)

exports of goods and services: 33.4% (2017 est.)

imports of goods and services: -34.7% (2017 est.)

GDP - COMPOSITION, BY SECTOR OF ORIGIN:

agriculture: 4.1% (2017 est.)

industry: 16.9% (2017 est.)

services: 79.1% (2017 est.)

AGRICULTURE - PRODUCTS:

wheat, corn, barley, sugar beets, olives, tomatoes, wine, tobacco, potatoes; beef, dairy products

INDUSTRIES:

tourism, food and tobacco processing, textiles, chemicals, metal products; mining, petroleum

INDUSTRIAL PRODUCTION GROWTH RATE:

3.5% (2017 est.)

country comparison to the world: 85

LABOR FORCE:

4.769 million (2017 est.)

country comparison to the world: 84

LABOR FORCE - BY OCCUPATION:

agriculture: 12.6%

industry: 15%

services: 72.4% (30 October 2015 est.)

UNEMPLOYMENT RATE:

21.5% (2017 est.)

23.6% (2016 est.)

country comparison to the world: 189

POPULATION BELOW POVERTY LINE:

36% (2014 est.)

HOUSEHOLD INCOME OR CONSUMPTION BY PERCENTAGE SHARE:

lowest 10%: 1.7%

highest 10%: 26.7% (2015 est.)

DISTRIBUTION OF FAMILY INCOME - GINI INDEX:

36.7 (2012 est.)

35.7 (2011)

country comparison to the world: 86

BUDGET:

revenues: 97.99 billion (2017 est.)

expenditures: 96.35 billion (2017 est.)

TAXES AND OTHER REVENUES:

48.8% (of GDP) (2017 est.)

country comparison to the world: 17

BUDGET SURPLUS (+) OR DEFICIT (-):

0.8% (of GDP) (2017 est.)

country comparison to the world: 36

PUBLIC DEBT:

181.8% of GDP (2017 est.)

183.5% of GDP (2016 est.)

country comparison to the world: 2

FISCAL YEAR:

calendar year

INFLATION RATE (CONSUMER PRICES):

1.1% (2017 est.)

0% (2016 est.)

country comparison to the world: 59

CENTRAL BANK DISCOUNT RATE:

0.05% (31 March 2016)

0.15% (11 June 2014)

note: this is the European Central Bank's rate on the marginal lending facility, which offers overnight credit to banks in the euro area

country comparison to the world: 144

COMMERCIAL BANK PRIME LENDING RATE:

5.25% (31 December 2017 est.)

5.62% (31 December 2016 est.)

country comparison to the world: 144

STOCK OF NARROW MONEY:

$106.6 billion (31 December 2017 est.)

$86.53 billion (31 December 2016 est.)

note: see entry for the European Union for money supply for the entire euro area; the European Central Bank (ECB) controls monetary policy for the 18 members of the Economic and Monetary Union (EMU); individual members of the EMU do not control the quantity of money circulating within their own borders

country comparison to the world: 39

STOCK OF BROAD MONEY:

$106.6 billion (31 December 2017 est.)

$86.53 billion (31 December 2016 est.)

country comparison to the world: 39

STOCK OF DOMESTIC CREDIT:

$248.7 billion (31 December 2017 est.)

$231.4 billion (31 December 2016 est.)

country comparison to the world: 41

MARKET VALUE OF PUBLICLY TRADED SHARES:

$42.08 billion (31 December 2015 est.)

$55.15 billion (31 December 2014 est.)

$82.59 billion (31 December 2013 est.)

country comparison to the world: 56

CURRENT ACCOUNT BALANCE:

-$1.596 billion (2017 est.)

-$2.072 billion (2016 est.)

country comparison to the world: 158

EXPORTS:

$31.54 billion (2017 est.)

$27.1 billion (2016 est.)

country comparison to the world: 64

EXPORTS - PARTNERS:

Italy 10.6%, Germany 7.1%, Turkey 6.8%, Cyprus 6.5%, Bulgaria 4.9%, Lebanon 4.3% (2017)

EXPORTS - COMMODITIES:

food and beverages, manufactured goods, petroleum products, chemicals, textiles

IMPORTS:

$52.27 billion (2017 est.)

$45.45 billion (2016 est.)

country comparison to the world: 52

IMPORTS - COMMODITIES:

machinery, transport equipment, fuels, chemicals

IMPORTS - PARTNERS:

Germany 10.4%, Italy 8.2%, Russia 6.8%, Iraq 6.3%, South Korea 6.1%, China 5.4%, Netherlands 5.3%, France 4.3% (2017)

RESERVES OF FOREIGN EXCHANGE AND GOLD:

$7.807 billion (31 December 2017 est.)

$6.026 billion (31 December 2015 est.)

country comparison to the world: 80

DEBT - EXTERNAL:

$506.6 billion (31 March 2016 est.)

$468.2 billion (31 March 2015 est.)

country comparison to the world: 23

STOCK OF DIRECT FOREIGN INVESTMENT - AT HOME:

$35.48 billion (31 December 2017 est.)

$30.8 billion (31 December 2016 est.)

country comparison to the world: 67

STOCK OF DIRECT FOREIGN INVESTMENT - ABROAD:

$29.64 billion (31 December 2017 est.)

$32.91 billion (31 December 2016 est.)

country comparison to the world: 49

EXCHANGE RATES:

euros (EUR) per US dollar -

0.885 (2017 est.)

0.903 (2016 est.)

0.9214 (2015 est.)

0.885 (2014 est.)

0.7634 (2013 est.)

ENERGY :: GREECE

ELECTRICITY ACCESS:

electrification - total population: 100% (2016)

ELECTRICITY - PRODUCTION:

52.05 billion kWh (2016 est.)

country comparison to the world: 53

ELECTRICITY - CONSUMPTION:

56.89 billion kWh (2016 est.)

country comparison to the world: 45

ELECTRICITY - EXPORTS:

1.037 billion kWh (2016 est.)

country comparison to the world: 58
ELECTRICITY - IMPORTS:
9.833 billion kWh (2016 est.)

country comparison to the world: 27
ELECTRICITY - INSTALLED GENERATING CAPACITY:
19.17 million kW (2016 est.)

country comparison to the world: 46
ELECTRICITY - FROM FOSSIL FUELS:
57% of total installed capacity (2016 est.)

country comparison to the world: 137
ELECTRICITY - FROM NUCLEAR FUELS:
0% of total installed capacity (2017 est.)

country comparison to the world: 98
ELECTRICITY - FROM HYDROELECTRIC PLANTS:
14% of total installed capacity (2017 est.)

country comparison to the world: 105
ELECTRICITY - FROM OTHER RENEWABLE SOURCES:
29% of total installed capacity (2017 est.)

country comparison to the world: 19
CRUDE OIL - PRODUCTION:
4,100 bbl/day (2018 est.)

country comparison to the world: 80
CRUDE OIL - EXPORTS:
3,229 bbl/day (2017 est.)

country comparison to the world: 67
CRUDE OIL - IMPORTS:
484,300 bbl/day (2017 est.)

country comparison to the world: 20
CRUDE OIL - PROVED RESERVES:
10 million bbl (1 January 2018 est.)

country comparison to the world: 90
REFINED PETROLEUM PRODUCTS - PRODUCTION:
655,400 bbl/day (2017 est.)

country comparison to the world: 28
REFINED PETROLEUM PRODUCTS - CONSUMPTION:
304,100 bbl/day (2017 est.)

country comparison to the world: 43
REFINED PETROLEUM PRODUCTS - EXPORTS:
371,900 bbl/day (2017 est.)

country comparison to the world: 22
REFINED PETROLEUM PRODUCTS - IMPORTS:
192,200 bbl/day (2017 est.)

country comparison to the world: 35
NATURAL GAS - PRODUCTION:
8 million cu m (2017 est.)

country comparison to the world: 93
NATURAL GAS - CONSUMPTION:
4.927 billion cu m (2017 est.)

country comparison to the world: 61
NATURAL GAS - EXPORTS:
0 cu m (2017 est.)

country comparison to the world: 112
NATURAL GAS - IMPORTS:
4.984 billion cu m (2017 est.)

country comparison to the world: 36
NATURAL GAS - PROVED RESERVES:
991.1 million cu m (1 January 2018 est.)

country comparison to the world: 100
CARBON DIOXIDE EMISSIONS FROM CONSUMPTION OF ENERGY:
69.37 million Mt (2017 est.)

country comparison to the world: 51

COMMUNICATIONS :: GREECE

TELEPHONES - FIXED LINES:
total subscriptions: 5,176,475

subscriptions per 100 inhabitants: 48 (2017 est.)

country comparison to the world: 28
TELEPHONES - MOBILE CELLULAR:
total subscriptions: 12,937,106

subscriptions per 100 inhabitants: 120 (2017 est.)

country comparison to the world: 72
TELEPHONE SYSTEM:

general assessment: adequate, modern networks reach all areas; good mobile telephone and international service; 3 mobile network operators; 2019 5G trials and LTE use; despite rough economic conditions broadband penetration developing (2018)

domestic: microwave radio relay trunk system; extensive open-wire connections; submarine cable to offshore islands; 48 per 100 for fixed-line and 120 per 100 for mobile-cellular (2018)

international: country code - 30; landing points for the SEA-ME-WE-3, Adria-1, Italy-Greece 1, OTEGLOBE, MedNautilus Submarine System, Aphrodite 2, AAE-1 and Silphium optical telecommunications submarine cable that provides links to Europe, the Middle East, Africa, Southeast Asia, Asia and Australia; tropospheric scatter; satellite earth stations - 4 (2 Intelsat - 1 Atlantic Ocean and 1 Indian Ocean, 1 Eutelsat, and 1 Inmarsat - Indian Ocean region) (2019)

BROADCAST MEDIA:
broadcast media dominated by the private sector; roughly 150 private TV channels, about 10 of which broadcast nationwide; 1 government-owned terrestrial TV channel with national coverage; 3 privately owned satellite channels; multi-channel satellite and cable TV services available; upwards of 1,500 radio stations, all of them privately owned; government-owned broadcaster has 2 national radio stations

INTERNET COUNTRY CODE:
.gr

INTERNET USERS:
total: 7,443,016

percent of population: 69.1% (July 2016 est.)

country comparison to the world: 57
BROADBAND - FIXED SUBSCRIPTIONS:
total: 3,778,263

subscriptions per 100 inhabitants: 35 (2017 est.)

country comparison to the world: 32

MILITARY AND SECURITY :: GREECE

MILITARY EXPENDITURES:
2.39% of GDP (2018)

2.52% of GDP (2017)

2.56% of GDP (2016)

2.54% of GDP (2015)

2.34% of GDP (2014)

country comparison to the world: 36
MILITARY AND SECURITY FORCES:
Hellenic Armed Forces: Hellenic Army (Ellinikos Stratos, ES; includes National Guard reserves), Hellenic Navy (Elliniko Polemiko Navtiko, EPN), Hellenic Air Force (Elliniki Polemiki Aeroporia, EPA; includes air defense). (2019)

MILITARY SERVICE AGE AND OBLIGATION:
19-45 years of age for compulsory military service; during wartime the law allows for recruitment beginning

January of the year of inductee's 18th birthday, thus including 17 year olds; 18 years of age for volunteers; conscript service obligation is 1 year for the Army and 9 months for the Air Force and Navy; women are eligible for voluntary military service (2014)

TRANSPORTATION :: GREECE

NATIONAL AIR TRANSPORT SYSTEM:

number of registered air carriers: 9 (2015)

inventory of registered aircraft operated by air carriers: 93 (2015)

annual passenger traffic on registered air carriers: 12,583,541 (2015)

annual freight traffic on registered air carriers: 27,452,961 mt-km (2015)

CIVIL AIRCRAFT REGISTRATION COUNTRY CODE PREFIX:

SX (2016)

AIRPORTS:

77 (2013)

country comparison to the world: 69

AIRPORTS - WITH PAVED RUNWAYS:

total: 68 (2017)

over 3,047 m: 6 (2017)

2,438 to 3,047 m: 15 (2017)

1,524 to 2,437 m: 19 (2017)

914 to 1,523 m: 18 (2017)

under 914 m: 10 (2017)

AIRPORTS - WITH UNPAVED RUNWAYS:

total: 9 (2013)

914 to 1,523 m: 2 (2013)

under 914 m: 7 (2013)

HELIPORTS:

9 (2013)

PIPELINES:

1329 km gas, 94 km oil (2013)

RAILWAYS:

total: 2,548 km (2014)

standard gauge: 1,565 km 1.435-m gauge (764 km electrified) (2014)

narrow gauge: 961 km 1.000-m gauge (2014)

22 0.750-m gauge

country comparison to the world: 67

ROADWAYS:

total: 117,000 km (2018)

country comparison to the world: 42

WATERWAYS:

6 km (the 6-km-long Corinth Canal crosses the Isthmus of Corinth; it shortens a sea voyage by 325 km) (2012)

country comparison to the world: 106

MERCHANT MARINE:

total: 1,343

by type: bulk carrier 191, container ship 6, general cargo 136, oil tanker 405, other 605 (2018)

country comparison to the world: 21

PORTS AND TERMINALS:

major seaport(s): Aspropyrgos, Pachi, Piraeus, Thessaloniki

oil terminal(s): Agioi Theodoroi

container port(s) (TEUs): Piraeus (4,145,079) (2017)

LNG terminal(s) (import): Revithoussa

TERRORISM :: GREECE

TERRORIST GROUPS - HOME BASED:

Revolutionary Struggle (RS): aim(s): disrupt the influence of globalization and international capitalism on Greek society and, ultimately, overthrow the Greek Government

area(s) of operation: operates exclusively inside Greece, primarily in Athens

note: largely inactive in recent years, with the exception of shootouts with police officers trying to arrest members (2018)

TRANSNATIONAL ISSUES :: GREECE

DISPUTES - INTERNATIONAL:

Greece and Turkey continue discussions to resolve their complex maritime, air, territorial, and boundary disputes in the Aegean Sea; the mass migration of unemployed Albanians still remains a problem for developed countries, chiefly Greece and Italy

REFUGEES AND INTERNALLY DISPLACED PERSONS:

refugees (country of origin): 23,931 (Syria), 9,291 (Afghanistan) (2018)

stateless persons: 198 (2018)

note: 1,183,767 estimated refugee and migrant arrivals (January 2015-December 2019); as of the end of February 2019, an estimated 80,600 migrants and refugees are stranded in Greece since 2015-16; 50,215 migrant arrivals in 2018

ILLICIT DRUGS:

a gateway to Europe for traffickers smuggling cannabis and heroin from the Middle East and Southwest Asia to the West and precursor chemicals to the East; some South American cocaine transits or is consumed in Greece; money laundering related to drug trafficking and organized crime

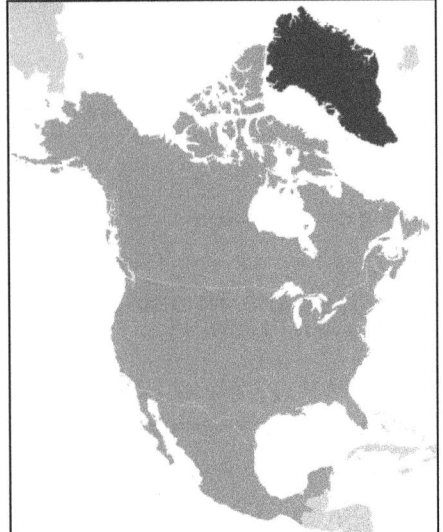

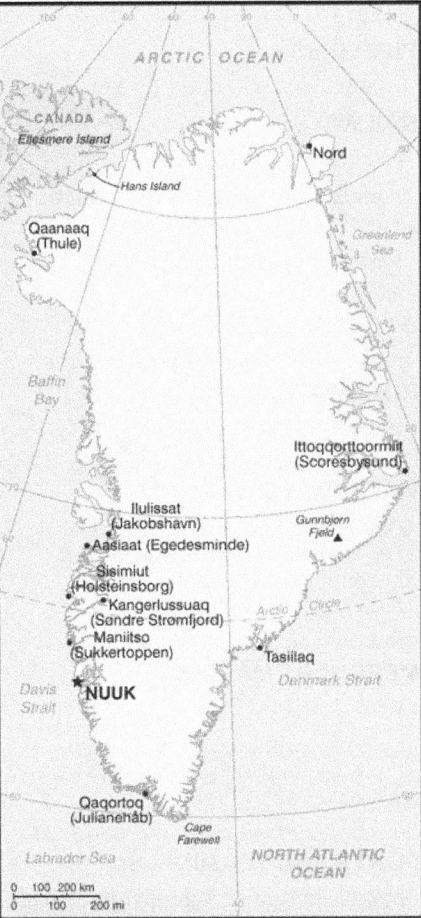

NORTH AMERICA :: GREENLAND

INTRODUCTION :: GREENLAND

BACKGROUND:

Greenland, the world's largest island, is about 80% ice-capped. Vikings reached the island in the 10th century from Iceland; Danish colonization began in the 18th century, and Greenland became an integral part of the Danish Realm in 1953. It joined the European Community (now the EU) with Denmark in 1973 but withdrew in 1985 over a dispute centered on stringent fishing quotas. Greenland remains a member of the Overseas Countries and Territories Association of the EU. Greenland was granted self-government in 1979 by the Danish parliament; the law went into effect the following year. Greenland voted in favor of increased self-rule in November 2008 and acquired greater responsibility for internal affairs when the Act on Greenland Self-Government was signed into law in June 2009. Denmark, however, continues to exercise control over several policy areas on behalf of Greenland, including foreign affairs, security, and financial policy in consultation with Greenland's Self-Rule Government.

GEOGRAPHY :: GREENLAND

LOCATION:
Northern North America, island between the Arctic Ocean and the North Atlantic Ocean, northeast of Canada

GEOGRAPHIC COORDINATES:
72 00 N, 40 00 W

MAP REFERENCES:
Arctic Region

AREA:
total: 2,166,086 sq km

land: 2,166,086 sq km (approximately 1,710,000 sq km ice-covered)

country comparison to the world: 13

AREA - COMPARATIVE:
slightly more than three times the size of Texas

LAND BOUNDARIES:
0 km

COASTLINE:
44,087 km

MARITIME CLAIMS:
territorial sea: 3 nm

continental shelf: 200 nm or agreed boundaries or median line

exclusive fishing zone: 200 nm or agreed boundaries or median line

CLIMATE:
arctic to subarctic; cool summers, cold winters

TERRAIN:
flat to gradually sloping icecap covers all but a narrow, mountainous, barren, rocky coast

ELEVATION:

mean elevation: 1,792 m

lowest point: Atlantic Ocean 0 m

highest point: Gunnbjorn Fjeld 3,694 m

NATURAL RESOURCES:

coal, iron ore, lead, zinc, molybdenum, diamonds, gold, platinum, niobium, tantalite, uranium, fish, seals, whales, hydropower, possible oil and gas

LAND USE:

agricultural land: 0.6% (2011 est.)

arable land: 0% (2011 est.) / permanent crops: 0% (2011 est.) / permanent pasture: 0.6% (2011 est.)

forest: 0% (2011 est.)

other: 99.4% (2011 est.)

IRRIGATED LAND:

NA

POPULATION DISTRIBUTION:

settlement concentrated on the southwest shoreline, with limited settlements scattered along the remaining coast; interior is uninhabited

NATURAL HAZARDS:

continuous permafrost over northern two-thirds of the island

ENVIRONMENT - CURRENT ISSUES:

especially vulnerable to climate change and disruption of the Arctic environment; preservation of the Inuit traditional way of life, including whaling and seal hunting

GEOGRAPHY - NOTE:

dominates North Atlantic Ocean between North America and Europe; sparse population confined to small settlements along coast; close to one-quarter of the population lives in the capital, Nuuk; world's second largest ice sheet after that of Antarctica covering an area of 1.71 million sq km (660,000 sq mi) or about 79% of the island, and containing 2.85 million cu km (684 thousand cu mi) of ice (this is almost 7% of all of the world's fresh water); if all this ice were converted to liquid water, one estimate is that it would be sufficient to raise the height of the world's oceans by 7.2 m (24 ft)

PEOPLE AND SOCIETY :: GREENLAND

POPULATION:

57,691 (July 2018 est.)

country comparison to the world: 206

NATIONALITY:

noun: Greenlander(s)

adjective: Greenlandic

ETHNIC GROUPS:

Greenlandic 89.7%, Danish 7.8%, other Nordic 1.1%, and other 1.4% (2018 est.)

note: data represent population by country of birth

LANGUAGES:

Greenlandic (West Greenlandic or Kalaallisut is the official language), Danish, English

RELIGIONS:

Evangelical Lutheran, traditional Inuit spiritual beliefs

AGE STRUCTURE:

0-14 years: 21% (male 6,151 /female 5,962)

15-24 years: 15.1% (male 4,388 /female 4,321)

25-54 years: 40.83% (male 12,349 /female 11,209)

55-64 years: 13.5% (male 4,259 /female 3,529)

65 years and over: 9.57% (male 2,944 /female 2,579) (2018 est.)

MEDIAN AGE:

total: 34 years (2018 est.)

male: 35 years

female: 32.9 years

country comparison to the world: 89

POPULATION GROWTH RATE:

-0.04% (2018 est.)

country comparison to the world: 200

BIRTH RATE:

14.3 births/1,000 population (2018 est.)

country comparison to the world: 133

DEATH RATE:

8.8 deaths/1,000 population (2018 est.)

country comparison to the world: 69

NET MIGRATION RATE:

-6 migrant(s)/1,000 population (2018 est.)

country comparison to the world: 201

POPULATION DISTRIBUTION:

settlement concentrated on the southwest shoreline, with limited settlements scattered along the remaining coast; interior is uninhabited

URBANIZATION:

urban population: 87.1% of total population (2019)

rate of urbanization: 0.42% annual rate of change (2015-20 est.)

MAJOR URBAN AREAS - POPULATION:

18,000 NUUK (capital) (2018)

SEX RATIO:

at birth: 1.05 male(s)/female

0-14 years: 1.03 male(s)/female

15-24 years: 1.02 male(s)/female

25-54 years: 1.1 male(s)/female

55-64 years: 1.21 male(s)/female

65 years and over: 1.14 male(s)/female

total population: 1.09 male(s)/female (2018 est.)

INFANT MORTALITY RATE:

total: 8.7 deaths/1,000 live births (2018 est.)

male: 9.9 deaths/1,000 live births

female: 7.4 deaths/1,000 live births

country comparison to the world: 147

LIFE EXPECTANCY AT BIRTH:

total population: 72.9 years (2018 est.)

male: 70.2 years

female: 75.8 years

country comparison to the world: 145

TOTAL FERTILITY RATE:

1.97 children born/woman (2018 est.)

country comparison to the world: 122

DRINKING WATER SOURCE:

improved:

urban: 100% of population

rural: 100% of population

total: 100% of population

unimproved:

urban: 0% of population

rural: 0% of population

total: 0% of population (2015 est.)

PHYSICIANS DENSITY:

1.87 physicians/1,000 population (2016)

HOSPITAL BED DENSITY:

8.2 beds/1,000 population (2015)

SANITATION FACILITY ACCESS:

improved:

urban: 100% of population (2015 est.)

rural: 100% of population (2015 est.)

total: 100% of population (2015 est.)

unimproved:

urban: 0% of population (2015 est.)

rural: 0% of population (2015 est.)

total: 0% of population (2015 est.)

HIV/AIDS - ADULT PREVALENCE RATE:
NA

HIV/AIDS - PEOPLE LIVING WITH HIV/AIDS:
NA

HIV/AIDS - DEATHS:
NA

EDUCATION EXPENDITURES:
NA

LITERACY:

definition: age 15 and over can read and write

total population: 100%

male: 100%

female: 100% (2015 est.)

GOVERNMENT :: GREENLAND

COUNTRY NAME:

conventional long form: none

conventional short form: Greenland

local long form: none

local short form: Kalaallit Nunaat

note: named by Norwegian adventurer Erik THORVALDSSON (Erik the Red) in A.D. 985 in order to entice settlers to the island

DEPENDENCY STATUS:

part of the Kingdom of Denmark; self-governing overseas administrative division of Denmark since 1979

GOVERNMENT TYPE:

parliamentary democracy (Parliament of Greenland or Inatsisartut)

CAPITAL:

name: Nuuk (Godthaab)

geographic coordinates: 64 11 N, 51 45 W

time difference: UTC-3 (2 hours ahead of Washington, DC, during Standard Time)

daylight saving time: +1hr, begins last Sunday in March; ends last Sunday in October

note: Greenland has four time zones

etymology: "nuuk" is the Inuit word for "cape" and refers to the city's position at the end of the Nuup Kangerlua fjord

ADMINISTRATIVE DIVISIONS:

5 municipalities (kommuner, singular kommune); Avannaata, Kujalleq, Qeqertalik, Qeqqata, Sermersooq

note: Northeast Greenland National Park (Kalaallit Nunaanni Nuna Eqqissisimatitaq) and the Thule Air Base in Pituffik (in northwest Greenland) are two unincorporated areas; the national park's 972,000 sq km - about 46% of the island - makes it the largest national park in the world and also the most northerly

INDEPENDENCE:

none (extensive self-rule as part of the Kingdom of Denmark; foreign affairs is the responsibility of Denmark, but Greenland actively participates in international agreements relating to Greenland)

NATIONAL HOLIDAY:

National Day, June 21; note - marks the summer solstice and the longest day of the year in the Northern Hemisphere

CONSTITUTION:

history: previous 1953 (Greenland established as a constituency in the Danish constitution), 1979 (Greenland Home Rule Act); latest 21 June 2009 (Greenland Self-Government Act)

LEGAL SYSTEM:

the laws of Denmark apply where applicable and Greenlandic law applies to other areas

CITIZENSHIP:

see Denmark

SUFFRAGE:

18 years of age; universal

EXECUTIVE BRANCH:

chief of state: Queen MARGRETHE II of Denmark (since 14 January 1972), represented by High Commissioner Mikaela ENGELL (since April 2011)

head of government: Premier Kim KIELSEN (since 30 September 2014)

cabinet: Self-rule Government (Naalakkersuisut) elected by the Parliament (Inatsisartut) on the basis of the strength of parties

elections/appointments: the monarchy is hereditary; high commissioner appointed by the monarch; premier indirectly elected by Parliament for a 4-year term

election results: Kim KIELSEN elected premier; Parliament vote - Kim KIELSEN (S) 27.2%, Sara OLSVIG (IA) 25.5%, Randi Vestergaard EVALDSEN (D) 19.5%, other 27.8%

LEGISLATIVE BRANCH:

description: unicameral Parliament or Inatsisartut (31 seats; members directly elected in multi-seat constituencies by proportional representation vote to serve 4-year terms)

Greenland elects 2 members to the Danish Parliament to serve 4-year terms

elections: Greenland Parliament - last held on 24 April 2018 (next to be held by 2022)

Greenland members to Danish Parliament - last held on 18 June 2015 (next to be held by June 2019)

election results: Greenland Parliament percent of vote by party - S 27.2%, IA 25.5%, D 19.5%, PN 13.4%, A 5.9%, SA 4.1%, NQ 3.4% other 1%; seats by party - S 9, IA 8, D 6, PN 4, A 2, SA 1, NQ 1; composition - men 19, women 12, percent of women 38.7%

Greenland members in Danish Parliament - percent of vote by party - NA; seats by party - IA 1, S 1; composition - 2 women

JUDICIAL BRANCH:

highest courts: High Court of Greenland (consists of the presiding professional judge and 2 lay assessors); note - appeals beyond the High Court of Greenland can be heard by the Supreme Court (in Copenhagen)

judge selection and term of office: judges appointed by the monarch upon the recommendation of the Judicial Appointments Council, a 6-member independent body of judges and lawyers; judges appointed for life with retirement at age 70

subordinate courts: Court of Greenland; 18 district or magistrates' courts

POLITICAL PARTIES AND LEADERS:

Cooperation Party (Suleqatigiissitsisut or Samarbejdspartiet) or SA [Michael ROSING]

Democrats Party (Demokraatit) or D [Niels THOMSEN]

Forward Party (Siumut) or S [Kim KIELSEN]

Inuit Community (Inuit Ataqatigiit)

or IA [Sara OLSVIG]
Our Country's Future (Nunatta Qitornai) or NQ [Vittus QUJAUKITSOQ]
Signpost Party (Partii Naleraq) or PN [Hans ENOKSEN]
Fellowship Party (Atassut) or A [Siverth Karl HEILMANN]

INTERNATIONAL ORGANIZATION PARTICIPATION:

Arctic Council, ICC, NC, NIB, UPU

DIPLOMATIC REPRESENTATION IN THE US:

none (self-governing overseas administrative division of Denmark); note - Greenland has an office in the Danish Embassy in the US; it also has offices in the Danish consulates in Chicago and New York

DIPLOMATIC REPRESENTATION FROM THE US:

none (self-governing overseas administrative division of Denmark)

FLAG DESCRIPTION:

two equal horizontal bands of white (top) and red with a large disk slightly to the hoist side of center - the top half of the disk is red, the bottom half is white; the design represents the sun reflecting off a field of ice; the colors are the same as those of the Danish flag and symbolize Greenland's links to the Kingdom of Denmark

NATIONAL SYMBOL(S):

polar bear; national colors: red, white

NATIONAL ANTHEM:

name: "Nunarput utoqqarsuanngoravit" ("Our Country, Who's Become So Old" also translated as "You Our Ancient Land")

lyrics/music: Henrik LUND/Jonathan PETERSEN

note: adopted 1916; the government also recognizes "Nuna asiilasooq" as a secondary anthem

ECONOMY :: GREENLAND

ECONOMY - OVERVIEW:

Greenland's economy depends on exports of shrimp and fish, and on a substantial subsidy from the Danish Government. Fish account for over 90% of its exports, subjecting the economy to price fluctuations. The subsidy from the Danish Government is budgeted to be about $535 million in 2017, more than 50% of government revenues, and 25% of GDP.

The economy is expanding after a period of decline. The economy contracted between 2012 and 2014, grew by 1.7% in 2015 and by 7.7% in 2016. The expansion has been driven by larger quotas for shrimp, the predominant Greenlandic export, and also by increased activity in the construction sector, especially in Nuuk, the capital. Private consumption and tourism also are contributing to GDP growth more than in previous years. Tourism in Greenland grew annually around 20% in 2015 and 2016, largely a result of increasing numbers of cruise lines now operating in Greenland's western and southern waters during the peak summer tourism season.

The public sector, including publicly owned enterprises and the municipalities, plays a dominant role in Greenland's economy. During the last decade the Greenland Self Rule Government pursued conservative fiscal and monetary policies, but public pressure has increased for better schools, health care, and retirement systems. The budget was in deficit in 2014 and 2016, but public debt remains low at about 5% of GDP. The government plans a balanced budget for the 2017–20 period.

Significant challenges face the island, including low levels of qualified labor, geographic dispersion, lack of industry diversification, the long-term sustainability of the public budget, and a declining population due to emigration. Hydrocarbon exploration has ceased with declining oil prices. The island has potential for natural resource exploitation with rare-earth, uranium, and iron ore mineral projects proposed, but a lack of infrastructure hinders development.

GDP (PURCHASING POWER PARITY):

$2.413 billion (2015 est.)

$2.24 billion (2014 est.)

$2.203 billion (2013 est.)

note: data are in 2015 US dollars

country comparison to the world: 193

GDP (OFFICIAL EXCHANGE RATE):

$2.221 billion (2015 est.) (2015 est.)

GDP - REAL GROWTH RATE:

7.7% (2016 est.)

1.7% (2015 est.)

-0.8% (2014 est.)

country comparison to the world: 11

GDP - PER CAPITA (PPP):

$41,800 (2015 est.)

$38,800 (2014 est.)

$38,500 (2013 est.)

country comparison to the world: 44

GDP - COMPOSITION, BY END USE:

household consumption: 68.1% (2015 est.)

government consumption: 28% (2015 est.)

investment in fixed capital: 14.3% (2015 est.)

investment in inventories: -13.9% (2015 est.)

exports of goods and services: 18.2% (2015 est.)

imports of goods and services: -28.6% (2015 est.)

GDP - COMPOSITION, BY SECTOR OF ORIGIN:

agriculture: 15.9% (2015 est.)

industry: 10.1% (2015 est.)

services: 73.9% (2015)

AGRICULTURE - PRODUCTS:

sheep, cow, reindeer, fish, shellfish

INDUSTRIES:

fish processing (mainly shrimp and Greenland halibut); anorthosite and ruby mining; handicrafts, hides and skins, small shipyards

INDUSTRIAL PRODUCTION GROWTH RATE:

NA

LABOR FORCE:

26,840 (2015 est.)

country comparison to the world: 207

LABOR FORCE - BY OCCUPATION:

agriculture: 15.9%

industry: 10.1%

services: 73.9% (2015 est.)

UNEMPLOYMENT RATE:

9.1% (2015 est.)

10.3% (2014 est.)

country comparison to the world: 132

POPULATION BELOW POVERTY LINE:

16.2% (2015 est.)

HOUSEHOLD INCOME OR CONSUMPTION BY PERCENTAGE SHARE:

lowest 10%: NA

highest 10%: NA

DISTRIBUTION OF FAMILY INCOME - GINI INDEX:

33.9 (2015 est.)

34.3 (2014 est.)

country comparison to the world: 107

BUDGET:

revenues: 1.719 billion (2016 est.)

expenditures: 1.594 billion (2016 est.)

TAXES AND OTHER REVENUES:

77.4% (of GDP) (2016 est.)

country comparison to the world: 3

BUDGET SURPLUS (+) OR DEFICIT (-):

5.6% (of GDP) (2016 est.)

country comparison to the world: 5

PUBLIC DEBT:

13% of GDP (2015 est.)

country comparison to the world: 196

FISCAL YEAR:

calendar year

INFLATION RATE (CONSUMER PRICES):

0.3% (January 2017 est.)

1.2% (January 2016 est.)

country comparison to the world: 19

CENTRAL BANK DISCOUNT RATE:

NA

EXPORTS:

$407.1 million (2015 est.)

$599.7 million (2014 est.)

country comparison to the world: 183

EXPORTS - PARTNERS:

Denmark 82.5%, Iceland 4.4% (2017)

EXPORTS - COMMODITIES:

fish and fish products 91% (2015 est.)

IMPORTS:

$783.5 million (2015 est.)

$866.1 million (2014 est.)

country comparison to the world: 191

IMPORTS - COMMODITIES:

machinery and transport equipment, manufactured goods, food, petroleum products

IMPORTS - PARTNERS:

Denmark 69.7%, Sweden 10.6% (2017)

DEBT - EXTERNAL:

$36.4 million (2010)

$58 million (2009)

country comparison to the world: 197

EXCHANGE RATES:

Danish kroner (DKK) per US dollar -

6.586 (2017 est.)

6.7309 (2016 est.)

6.7309 (2015 est.)

6.7326 (2014 est.)

5.6125 (2013 est.)

ENERGY :: GREENLAND

ELECTRICITY ACCESS:

electrification - total population: 100% (2016)

ELECTRICITY - PRODUCTION:

538 million kWh (2016 est.)

country comparison to the world: 163

ELECTRICITY - CONSUMPTION:

468 million kWh (2016 est.)

country comparison to the world: 170

ELECTRICITY - EXPORTS:

0 kWh (2016 est.)

country comparison to the world: 141

ELECTRICITY - IMPORTS:

0 kWh (2016 est.)

country comparison to the world: 153

ELECTRICITY - INSTALLED GENERATING CAPACITY:

187,000 kW (2016 est.)

country comparison to the world: 167

ELECTRICITY - FROM FOSSIL FUELS:

51% of total installed capacity (2016 est.)

country comparison to the world: 149

ELECTRICITY - FROM NUCLEAR FUELS:

0% of total installed capacity (2017 est.)

country comparison to the world: 99

ELECTRICITY - FROM HYDROELECTRIC PLANTS:

49% of total installed capacity (2017 est.)

country comparison to the world: 42

ELECTRICITY - FROM OTHER RENEWABLE SOURCES:

0% of total installed capacity (2017 est.)

country comparison to the world: 189

CRUDE OIL - PRODUCTION:

0 bbl/day (2018 est.)

country comparison to the world: 142

CRUDE OIL - EXPORTS:

0 bbl/day (2015 est.)

country comparison to the world: 130

CRUDE OIL - IMPORTS:

0 bbl/day (2015 est.)

country comparison to the world: 133

CRUDE OIL - PROVED RESERVES:

0 bbl (1 January 2018 est.)

country comparison to the world: 138

REFINED PETROLEUM PRODUCTS - PRODUCTION:

0 bbl/day (2015 est.)

country comparison to the world: 150

REFINED PETROLEUM PRODUCTS - CONSUMPTION:

4,000 bbl/day (2016 est.)

country comparison to the world: 184

REFINED PETROLEUM PRODUCTS - EXPORTS:

0 bbl/day (2015 est.)

country comparison to the world: 159

REFINED PETROLEUM PRODUCTS - IMPORTS:

3,973 bbl/day (2015 est.)

country comparison to the world: 177

NATURAL GAS - PRODUCTION:

0 cu m (2017 est.)

country comparison to the world: 138

NATURAL GAS - CONSUMPTION:

0 cu m (2017 est.)

country comparison to the world: 151

NATURAL GAS - EXPORTS:

0 cu m (2017 est.)

country comparison to the world: 113

NATURAL GAS - IMPORTS:

0 cu m (2017 est.)

country comparison to the world: 131

NATURAL GAS - PROVED RESERVES:

0 cu m (1 January 2014 est.)

country comparison to the world: 140

CARBON DIOXIDE EMISSIONS FROM CONSUMPTION OF ENERGY:

613,800 Mt (2017 est.)

country comparison to the world: 179

COMMUNICATIONS :: GREENLAND

TELEPHONES - FIXED LINES:

total subscriptions: 16,000

subscriptions per 100 inhabitants: 28 (July 2016 est.)

country comparison to the world: 186

TELEPHONES - MOBILE CELLULAR:

total subscriptions: 61,000

subscriptions per 100 inhabitants: 106 (July 2016 est.)

country comparison to the world: 199

TELEPHONE SYSTEM:

general assessment: adequate domestic and international service provided by satellite, cables, and microwave radio relay; the fundamental telecommunications infrastructure consists of a digital radio link from Nanortalik in south Greenland to Uummannaq in north Greenland; satellites cover north and east Greenland for domestic and foreign telecommunications; a marine cable connects south and west Greenland to the rest of the world, extending from Nuuk and Qaqortoq to Canada and Iceland (2018)

domestic: 14 per 100 for fixed-line subscriptions and 111 per 100 for mobile-cellular (2018)

international: country code - 299; landing points for Greenland Connect, Greenland Connect North, Nunavut Undersea Fiber System submarine cables to Greenland, Iceland, and Canada; satellite earth stations - 15 (12 Intelsat, 1 Eutelsat, 2 Americom GE-2 (all Atlantic Ocean)) (2019)

BROADCAST MEDIA:

the Greenland Broadcasting Company provides public radio and TV services throughout the island with a broadcast station and a series of repeaters; a few private local TV and radio stations; Danish public radio rebroadcasts are available (2019)

INTERNET COUNTRY CODE:

.gl

INTERNET USERS:

total: 39,544

percent of population: 68.5% (July 2016 est.)

country comparison to the world: 198

MILITARY AND SECURITY :: GREENLAND

MILITARY AND SECURITY FORCES:

no regular military forces or conscription. (2019)

MILITARY - NOTE:

The Danish military's Joint Arctic Command in Nuuk is responsible for territorial defense of Greenland (2019)

TRANSPORTATION :: GREENLAND

NATIONAL AIR TRANSPORT SYSTEM:

number of registered air carriers: 1 (registered in Denmark) (2015)

inventory of registered aircraft operated by air carriers: 8 (registered in Denmark) (2015)

CIVIL AIRCRAFT REGISTRATION COUNTRY CODE PREFIX:

OY-H (2016)

AIRPORTS:

15 (2013)

country comparison to the world: 146

AIRPORTS - WITH PAVED RUNWAYS:

total: 10 (2019)

2,438 to 3,047 m: 2

1,524 to 2,437 m: 1

914 to 1,523 m: 1

under 914 m: 6

AIRPORTS - WITH UNPAVED RUNWAYS:

total: 5 (2013)

1,524 to 2,437 m: 1 (2013)

914 to 1,523 m: 2 (2013)

under 914 m: 2 (2013)

ROADWAYS:

note: although there are short roads in towns, there are no roads between towns; inter-urban transport is either by sea or by air

MERCHANT MARINE:

total: 8

by type: general cargo 1, other 7 (2018)

country comparison to the world: 157

PORTS AND TERMINALS:

major seaport(s): Sisimiut

TRANSNATIONAL ISSUES :: GREENLAND

DISPUTES - INTERNATIONAL:

managed dispute between Canada and Denmark over Hans Island in the Kennedy Channel between Canada's Ellesmere Island and Greenland; Denmark (Greenland) and Norway have made submissions to the Commission on the Limits of the Continental Shelf (CLCS) and Russia is collecting additional data to augment its 2001 CLCS submission

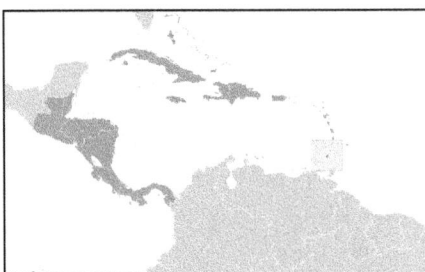

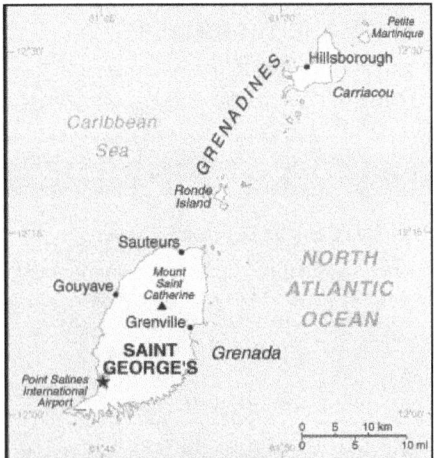

CENTRAL AMERICA :: GRENADA

INTRODUCTION :: GRENADA

BACKGROUND:

Carib Indians inhabited Grenada when Christopher COLUMBUS discovered the island in 1498, but it remained uncolonized for more than a century. The French settled Grenada in the 17th century, established sugar estates, and imported large numbers of African slaves. Britain took the island in 1762 and vigorously expanded sugar production. In the 19th century, cacao eventually surpassed sugar as the main export crop; in the 20th century, nutmeg became the leading export. In 1967, Britain gave Grenada autonomy over its internal affairs. Full independence was attained in 1974 making Grenada one of the smallest independent countries in the Western Hemisphere. In 1979, a leftist New Jewel Movement seized power under Maurice BISHOP ushering in the Grenada Revolution. On 19 October 1983, factions within the revolutionary government overthrew and killed BISHOP and members of his party. Six days later the island was invaded by US forces and those of six other Caribbean nations, which quickly captured the ringleaders and their hundreds of Cuban advisers. The rule of law was restored and democratic elections were reinstituted the following year and have continued since then.

GEOGRAPHY :: GRENADA

LOCATION:
Caribbean, island between the Caribbean Sea and Atlantic Ocean, north of Trinidad and Tobago

GEOGRAPHIC COORDINATES:
12 07 N, 61 40 W

MAP REFERENCES:
Central America and the Caribbean

AREA:
total: 344 sq km

land: 344 sq km

water: 0 sq km

country comparison to the world: 208

AREA - COMPARATIVE:
twice the size of Washington, DC

LAND BOUNDARIES:
0 km

COASTLINE:
121 km

MARITIME CLAIMS:
territorial sea: 12 nm

exclusive economic zone: 200 nm

CLIMATE:
tropical; tempered by northeast trade winds

TERRAIN:
volcanic in origin with central mountains

ELEVATION:
lowest point: Caribbean Sea 0 m

highest point: Mount Saint Catherine 840 m

NATURAL RESOURCES:
timber, tropical fruit

LAND USE:
agricultural land: 32.3% (2011 est.)

arable land: 8.8% (2011 est.) / permanent crops: 20.6% (2011 est.) / permanent pasture: 2.9% (2011 est.)

forest: 50% (2011 est.)

other: 17.7% (2011 est.)

IRRIGATED LAND:
20 sq km (2012)

POPULATION DISTRIBUTION:
approximately one-third of the population is found in the capital of St. George's; the island's population is concentrated along the coast

NATURAL HAZARDS:
lies on edge of hurricane belt; hurricane season lasts from June to November

volcanism: Mount Saint Catherine (840 m) lies on the island of Grenada; Kick 'em Jenny, an active submarine volcano (seamount) on the Caribbean Sea floor, lies about 8 km north of the island of Grenada; these two volcanoes are at the southern end of the volcanic island arc of the Lesser Antilles that extends up to the Netherlands dependency of Saba in the north

ENVIRONMENT - CURRENT ISSUES:
deforestation causing habitat destruction and species loss; coastal erosion and contamination; pollution and sedimentation; inadequate solid waste management

ENVIRONMENT - INTERNATIONAL AGREEMENTS:
party to: Biodiversity, Climate Change, Climate Change-Kyoto Protocol, Desertification, Endangered Species, Law of the Sea, Ozone Layer Protection, Whaling

signed, but not ratified: none of the selected agreements

GEOGRAPHY - NOTE:
the administration of the islands of the Grenadines group is divided between Saint Vincent and the Grenadines and Grenada

PEOPLE AND SOCIETY :: GRENADA

POPULATION:
112,207 (July 2018 est.)

country comparison to the world: 190

NATIONALITY:
noun: Grenadian(s)

adjective: Grenadian

ETHNIC GROUPS:
African descent 82.4%, mixed 13.3%, East Indian 2.2%, other 1.3%, unspecified 0.9% (2011 est.)

LANGUAGES:
English (official), French patois

RELIGIONS:
Protestant 49.2% (includes Pentecostal 17.2%, Seventh Day Adventist 13.2%, Anglican 8.5%, Baptist 3.2%, Church of God 2.4%, Evangelical 1.9%, Methodist 1.6%, other 1.2%), Roman Catholic 36%, Jehovah's Witness 1.2%, Rastafarian 1.2%, other 5.5%, none 5.7%, unspecified 1.3% (2011 est.)

AGE STRUCTURE:
0-14 years: 23.84% (male 13,901/female 12,851)

15-24 years: 14.61% (male 8,196/female 8,201)

25-54 years: 40.27% (male 23,121/female 22,067)

55-64 years: 10.97% (male 6,284/female 6,023)

65 years and over: 10.31% (male 5,377/female 6,186) (2018 est.)

DEPENDENCY RATIOS:
total dependency ratio: 50.7 (2015 est.)

youth dependency ratio: 39.9 (2015 est.)

elderly dependency ratio: 10.8 (2015 est.)

potential support ratio: 9.3 (2015 est.)

MEDIAN AGE:
total: 32.1 years (2018 est.)

male: 32 years

female: 32.2 years

country comparison to the world: 105

POPULATION GROWTH RATE:
0.42% (2018 est.)

country comparison to the world: 161

BIRTH RATE:
15.2 births/1,000 population (2018 est.)

country comparison to the world: 122

DEATH RATE:
8.2 deaths/1,000 population (2018 est.)

country comparison to the world: 83

NET MIGRATION RATE:
-2.8 migrant(s)/1,000 population (2018 est.)

country comparison to the world: 174

POPULATION DISTRIBUTION:
approximately one-third of the population is found in the capital of St. George's; the island's population is concentrated along the coast

URBANIZATION:
urban population: 36.4% of total population (2019)

rate of urbanization: 0.76% annual rate of change (2015-20 est.)

MAJOR URBAN AREAS - POPULATION:
39,000 SAINT GEORGE'S (capital) (2018)

SEX RATIO:
at birth: 1.1 male(s)/female

0-14 years: 1.08 male(s)/female

15-24 years: 1 male(s)/female

25-54 years: 1.05 male(s)/female

55-64 years: 1.04 male(s)/female

65 years and over: 0.87 male(s)/female

total population: 1.03 male(s)/female (2018 est.)

MATERNAL MORTALITY RATE:
25 deaths/100,000 live births (2017 est.)

country comparison to the world: 122

INFANT MORTALITY RATE:
total: 9.4 deaths/1,000 live births (2018 est.)

male: 9 deaths/1,000 live births

female: 9.9 deaths/1,000 live births

country comparison to the world: 140

LIFE EXPECTANCY AT BIRTH:
total population: 74.8 years (2018 est.)

male: 72.1 years

female: 77.6 years

country comparison to the world: 120

TOTAL FERTILITY RATE:
2 children born/woman (2018 est.)

country comparison to the world: 117

DRINKING WATER SOURCE:
improved:

urban: 99% of population

rural: 95.3% of population

total: 96.6% of population

unimproved:

urban: 1% of population

rural: 4.7% of population

total: 3.4% of population (2015 est.)

CURRENT HEALTH EXPENDITURE:
5.2% (2016)

PHYSICIANS DENSITY:
1.45 physicians/1,000 population (2017)

HOSPITAL BED DENSITY:
3.7 beds/1,000 population (2014)

SANITATION FACILITY ACCESS:
improved:

urban: 97.5% of population (2015 est.)

rural: 98.3% of population (2015 est.)

total: 98% of population (2015 est.)

unimproved:

urban: 2.5% of population (2015 est.)

rural: 1.7% of population (2015 est.)

total: 2% of population (2015 est.)

HIV/AIDS - ADULT PREVALENCE RATE:
0.5% (2018)

country comparison to the world: 70

HIV/AIDS - PEOPLE LIVING WITH HIV/AIDS:
<500 (2018)

HIV/AIDS - DEATHS:
<100 (2018)

MAJOR INFECTIOUS DISEASES:
note: active local transmission of Zika virus by Aedes species mosquitoes has been identified in this country (as of August 2016); it poses an important risk (a large number of cases possible) among US citizens if bitten by an infective mosquito; other less common ways to get Zika are through sex, via blood transfusion, or during pregnancy, in which the pregnant woman passes Zika virus to her fetus

OBESITY - ADULT PREVALENCE RATE:
21.3% (2016)

country comparison to the world: 90

EDUCATION EXPENDITURES:

10.3% of GDP (2016)

country comparison to the world: 3

LITERACY:

definition: age 15 and over can read and write

total population: 98.6%

male: 98.6%

female: 98.6% (2014 est.)

SCHOOL LIFE EXPECTANCY (PRIMARY TO TERTIARY EDUCATION):

total: 17 years

male: 16 years

female: 17 years (2017)

GOVERNMENT :: GRENADA

COUNTRY NAME:

conventional long form: none

conventional short form: Grenada

etymology: derivation of the name remains obscure; some sources attribute the designation to Spanish influence (most likely named for the Spanish city of Granada), with subsequent French and English interpretations resulting in the present-day Grenada; in Spanish "granada" means "pomegranate"

GOVERNMENT TYPE:

parliamentary democracy under a constitutional monarchy; a Commonwealth realm

CAPITAL:

name: Saint George's

geographic coordinates: 12 03 N, 61 45 W

time difference: UTC-4 (1 hour ahead of Washington, DC, during Standard Time)

etymology: the 1763 Treaty of Paris transferred possession of Grenada from France to Great Britain; the new administration renamed Ville de Fort Royal (Fort Royal Town) to Saint George's Town, after the patron saint of England; eventually the name became simply Saint George's

ADMINISTRATIVE DIVISIONS:

6 parishes and 1 dependency*; Carriacou and Petite Martinique*, Saint Andrew, Saint David, Saint George, Saint John, Saint Mark, Saint Patrick

INDEPENDENCE:

7 February 1974 (from the UK)

NATIONAL HOLIDAY:

Independence Day, 7 February (1974)

CONSTITUTION:

history: previous 1967; latest presented 19 December 1973, effective 7 February 1974, suspended 1979 following a revolution but restored in 1983

amendments: proposed by either house of Parliament; passage requires two-thirds majority vote by the membership in both houses and assent of the governor general; passage of amendments to constitutional sections, such as personal rights and freedoms, the structure, authorities, and procedures of the branches of government, the delimitation of electoral constituencies, or the procedure for amending the constitution, also requires two-thirds majority approval in a referendum; amended 1991, 1992 (2018)

LEGAL SYSTEM:

common law based on English model

INTERNATIONAL LAW ORGANIZATION PARTICIPATION:

has not submitted an ICJ jurisdiction declaration; accepts ICCt jurisdiction

CITIZENSHIP:

citizenship by birth: yes

citizenship by descent only: yes

dual citizenship recognized: yes

residency requirement for naturalization: 7 years for persons from a non-Caribbean state and 4 years for a person from a Caribbean state

SUFFRAGE:

18 years of age; universal

EXECUTIVE BRANCH:

chief of state: Queen ELIZABETH II (since 6 February 1952); represented by Governor General Cecile LA GRENADE (since 7 May 2013)

head of government: Prime Minister Keith MITCHELL (since 20 February 2013)

cabinet: Cabinet appointed by the governor general on the advice of the prime minister

elections/appointments: the monarchy is hereditary; governor general appointed by the monarch; following legislative elections, the leader of the majority party or majority coalition usually appointed prime minister by the governor general

LEGISLATIVE BRANCH:

description: bicameral Parliament consists of:
Senate (13 seats; members appointed by the governor general - 10 on the advice of the prime minister and 3 on the advice of the leader of the opposition party; members serve 5-year terms)
House of Representatives (15 seats; members directly elected in single-seat constituencies by simple majority vote to serve 5-year terms)

elections: Senate - last appointments on 27 April 2018 (next no later than 2023)
House of Representatives - last held on 13 March 2018 (next no later than 2023)

election results: Senate - percent by party - NA; seats by party - NA; composition - men 11, women 2 percent of women 15.4%
House of Representatives - percent of vote by party - NNP 58.9%, NDC 40.5%; other 0.6% seats by party - NNP 15; composition - men 8, women 7, percent of women 46.7%; note - total Parliament percent of women 32.1%

JUDICIAL BRANCH:

highest courts: regionally, the Eastern Caribbean Supreme Court (ECSC) is the superior court of the Organization of Eastern Caribbean States; the ECSC - headquartered on St. Lucia - consists of the Court of Appeal - headed by the chief justice and 4 judges - and the High Court with 18 judges; the Court of Appeal is itinerant, traveling to member states on a schedule to hear appeals from the High Court and subordinate courts; High Court judges reside in the member states, with 2 in Grenada; appeals beyond the ECSC in civil and criminal matters are heard by the Judicial Committee of the Privy Council (in London)

judge selection and term of office: chief justice of Eastern Caribbean Supreme Court appointed by Her Majesty, Queen ELIZABETH II; other justices and judges appointed by the Judicial and Legal Services Commission, and independent body of judicial officials; Court of Appeal justices appointed for life with mandatory retirement at age 65; High Court judges appointed for life with mandatory retirement at age 62

subordinate courts: magistrates' courts; Court of Magisterial Appeals

POLITICAL PARTIES AND LEADERS:

National Democratic Congress or NDC [Nazim BURKE]
New National Party or NNP [Keith MITCHELL]

INTERNATIONAL ORGANIZATION PARTICIPATION:

ACP, AOSIS, C, Caricom, CDB, CELAC, FAO, G-77, IBRD, ICAO, ICCt (signatory), ICRM, IDA, IFAD, IFC, IFRCS, ILO, IMF, IMO, Interpol, IOC, ITU, ITUC, LAES, MIGA, NAM, OAS, OECS, OPANAL, OPCW, Petrocaribe, UN, UNCTAD, UNESCO, UNIDO, UPU, WHO, WIPO, WTO

DIPLOMATIC REPRESENTATION IN THE US:

Ambassador Ethelstan Angus FRIDAY (since 3 September 2013)

chancery: 1701 New Hampshire Avenue NW, Washington, DC 20009

telephone: [1] (202) 265-2561

FAX: [1] (202) 265-2468

consulate(s) general: Miami

DIPLOMATIC REPRESENTATION FROM THE US:

chief of mission: the US does not have an official embassy in Grenada; the US Ambassador to Barbados is accredited to Grenada

telephone: [1] (473) 444-1173 through 1176

embassy: Lance-aux-Epines Stretch, Saint George's, Grenada

mailing address: P. O. Box 54, Saint George's

FAX: [1] (473) 444-4820

FLAG DESCRIPTION:

a rectangle divided diagonally into yellow triangles (top and bottom) and green triangles (hoist side and outer side), with a red border around the flag; there are seven yellow, five-pointed stars with three centered in the top red border, three centered in the bottom red border, and one on a red disk superimposed at the center of the flag; there is also a symbolic nutmeg pod on the hoist-side triangle (Grenada is a leading nutmeg producer); the seven stars stand for the seven administrative divisions, with the central star denoting the capital, St. George; yellow represents the sun and the warmth of the people, green stands for vegetation and agriculture, and red symbolizes harmony, unity, and courage

NATIONAL SYMBOL(S):

Grenada dove, bougainvillea flower; national colors: red, yellow, green

NATIONAL ANTHEM:

name: Hail Grenada

lyrics/music: Irva Merle BAPTISTE/Louis Arnold MASANTO

note: adopted 1974

ECONOMY :: GRENADA

ECONOMY - OVERVIEW:

Grenada relies on tourism and revenue generated by St. George's University - a private university offering degrees in medicine, veterinary medicine, public health, the health sciences, nursing, arts and sciences, and business - as its main source of foreign exchange. In the past two years the country expanded its sources of revenue, including from selling passports under its citizenship by investment program. These projects produced a resurgence in the construction and manufacturing sectors of the economy.

In 2017, Grenada experienced its fifth consecutive year of growth and the government successfully marked the completion of its five-year structural adjustment program that included among other things austerity measures, increased tax revenue and debt restructuring. Public debt-to-GDP was reduced from 100% of GDP in 2013 to 71.8% in 2017.

GDP (PURCHASING POWER PARITY):

$1.634 billion (2017 est.)

$1.555 billion (2016 est.)

$1.5 billion (2015 est.)

note: data are in 2017 dollars

country comparison to the world: 198

GDP (OFFICIAL EXCHANGE RATE):

$1.119 billion (2017 est.)

GDP - REAL GROWTH RATE:

5.1% (2017 est.)

3.7% (2016 est.)

6.4% (2015 est.)

country comparison to the world: 46

GDP - PER CAPITA (PPP):

$15,100 (2017 est.)

$14,500 (2016 est.)

$14,000 (2015 est.)

note: data are in 2017 dollars

country comparison to the world: 110

GROSS NATIONAL SAVING:

11.7% of GDP (2017 est.)

17% of GDP (2016 est.)

13.9% of GDP (2015 est.)

country comparison to the world: 153

GDP - COMPOSITION, BY END USE:

household consumption: 63% (2017 est.)

government consumption: 12% (2017 est.)

investment in fixed capital: 20% (2017 est.)

investment in inventories: -0.1% (2017 est.)

exports of goods and services: 60% (2017 est.)

imports of goods and services: -55% (2017 est.)

GDP - COMPOSITION, BY SECTOR OF ORIGIN:

agriculture: 6.8% (2017 est.)

industry: 15.5% (2017 est.)

services: 77.7% (2017 est.)

AGRICULTURE - PRODUCTS:

bananas, cocoa, nutmeg, mace, soursop, citrus, avocados, root crops, corn, vegetables, fish

INDUSTRIES:

food and beverages, textiles, light assembly operations, tourism, construction, education, call-center operations

INDUSTRIAL PRODUCTION GROWTH RATE:

10% (2017 est.)

country comparison to the world: 16

LABOR FORCE:

55,270 (2017 est.)

country comparison to the world: 189

LABOR FORCE - BY OCCUPATION:

agriculture: 11%

industry: 20%

services: 69% (2008 est.)

UNEMPLOYMENT RATE:

24% (2017 est.)

28.2% (2016 est.)

country comparison to the world: 195

POPULATION BELOW POVERTY LINE:

38% (2008 est.)

HOUSEHOLD INCOME OR CONSUMPTION BY PERCENTAGE SHARE:

lowest 10%: NA

highest 10%: NA

BUDGET:

revenues: 288.4 million (2017 est.)

expenditures: 252.3 million (2017 est.)

TAXES AND OTHER REVENUES:

25.8% (of GDP) (2017 est.)

country comparison to the world: 116

BUDGET SURPLUS (+) OR DEFICIT (-):

3.2% (of GDP) (2017 est.)

country comparison to the world: 12

PUBLIC DEBT:

70.4% of GDP (2017 est.)

82% of GDP (2016 est.)

country comparison to the world: 50

FISCAL YEAR:

calendar year

INFLATION RATE (CONSUMER PRICES):

0.9% (2017 est.)

1.7% (2016 est.)

country comparison to the world: 45

CENTRAL BANK DISCOUNT RATE:

6.5% (31 December 2009)

6.5% (31 December 2008)

country comparison to the world: 59

COMMERCIAL BANK PRIME LENDING RATE:

8.31% (31 December 2017 est.)

8.64% (31 December 2016 est.)

country comparison to the world: 101

STOCK OF NARROW MONEY:

$223.3 million (31 December 2017 est.)

$214 million (31 December 2016 est.)

country comparison to the world: 182

STOCK OF BROAD MONEY:

$223.3 million (31 December 2017 est.)

$214 million (31 December 2016 est.)

country comparison to the world: 185

STOCK OF DOMESTIC CREDIT:

$550 million (31 December 2017 est.)

$566.3 million (31 December 2016 est.)

country comparison to the world: 176

MARKET VALUE OF PUBLICLY TRADED SHARES:

NA

CURRENT ACCOUNT BALANCE:

-$77 million (2017 est.)

-$34 million (2016 est.)

country comparison to the world: 83

EXPORTS:

$39.9 million (2017 est.)

$44.2 million (2016 est.)

country comparison to the world: 205

EXPORTS - PARTNERS:

US 25.3%, Japan 10.1%, Guyana 8.7%, Dominica 6.6%, St. Lucia 6.4%, Netherlands 4.7%, Barbados 4.1%, St. Kitts and Nevis 4% (2017)

EXPORTS - COMMODITIES:

nutmeg, bananas, cocoa, fruit and vegetables, clothing, mace, chocolate, fish

IMPORTS:

$316 million (2017 est.)

$314.7 million (2016 est.)

country comparison to the world: 203

IMPORTS - COMMODITIES:

food, manufactured goods, machinery, chemicals, fuel

IMPORTS - PARTNERS:

US 31.7%, Trinidad and Tobago 24.9%, China 6.7% (2017)

RESERVES OF FOREIGN EXCHANGE AND GOLD:

$199.1 million (31 December 2017 est.)

$198 million (31 December 2015 est.)

country comparison to the world: 175

DEBT - EXTERNAL:

$793.5 million (2017 est.)

$682.3 million (2016 est.)

country comparison to the world: 169

EXCHANGE RATES:

East Caribbean dollars (XCD) per US dollar -

2.7 (2017 est.)

2.7 (2016 est.)

2.7 (2015 est.)

2.7 (2014 est.)

2.7 (2013 est.)

ENERGY :: GRENADA

ELECTRICITY ACCESS:

electrification - total population: 92.3% (2016)

electrification - urban areas: 92.3% (2016)

electrification - rural areas: 92.3% (2016)

ELECTRICITY - PRODUCTION:

202.1 million kWh (2016 est.)

country comparison to the world: 192

ELECTRICITY - CONSUMPTION:

185.1 million kWh (2016 est.)

country comparison to the world: 194

ELECTRICITY - EXPORTS:

0 kWh (2016 est.)

country comparison to the world: 142

ELECTRICITY - IMPORTS:

0 kWh (2016 est.)

country comparison to the world: 154

ELECTRICITY - INSTALLED GENERATING CAPACITY:

51,100 kW (2016 est.)

country comparison to the world: 191

ELECTRICITY - FROM FOSSIL FUELS:

96% of total installed capacity (2016 est.)

country comparison to the world: 39

ELECTRICITY - FROM NUCLEAR FUELS:

0% of total installed capacity (2017 est.)

country comparison to the world: 100

ELECTRICITY - FROM HYDROELECTRIC PLANTS:

0% of total installed capacity (2017 est.)

country comparison to the world: 174

ELECTRICITY - FROM OTHER RENEWABLE SOURCES:

4% of total installed capacity (2017 est.)

country comparison to the world: 112

CRUDE OIL - PRODUCTION:

0 bbl/day (2018 est.)

country comparison to the world: 143

CRUDE OIL - EXPORTS:

0 bbl/day (2015 est.)

country comparison to the world: 131

CRUDE OIL - IMPORTS:

0 bbl/day (2015 est.)

country comparison to the world: 134

CRUDE OIL - PROVED RESERVES:

0 bbl (1 January 2018 est.)

country comparison to the world: 139

REFINED PETROLEUM PRODUCTS - PRODUCTION:

0 bbl/day (2015 est.)

country comparison to the world: 151

REFINED PETROLEUM PRODUCTS - CONSUMPTION:

2,000 bbl/day (2016 est.)

country comparison to the world: 194
REFINED PETROLEUM PRODUCTS - EXPORTS:
0 bbl/day (2015 est.)

country comparison to the world: 160
REFINED PETROLEUM PRODUCTS - IMPORTS:
1,886 bbl/day (2015 est.)

country comparison to the world: 191
NATURAL GAS - PRODUCTION:
0 cu m (2017 est.)

country comparison to the world: 139
NATURAL GAS - CONSUMPTION:
0 cu m (2017 est.)

country comparison to the world: 152
NATURAL GAS - EXPORTS:
0 cu m (2017 est.)

country comparison to the world: 114
NATURAL GAS - IMPORTS:
0 cu m (2017 est.)

country comparison to the world: 132
NATURAL GAS - PROVED RESERVES:
0 cu m (1 January 2014 est.)

country comparison to the world: 141
CARBON DIOXIDE EMISSIONS FROM CONSUMPTION OF ENERGY:
283,600 Mt (2017 est.)

country comparison to the world: 193

COMMUNICATIONS :: GRENADA

TELEPHONES - FIXED LINES:
total subscriptions: 32,491
subscriptions per 100 inhabitants: 29 (2017 est.)
country comparison to the world: 169

TELEPHONES - MOBILE CELLULAR:
total subscriptions: 113,177
subscriptions per 100 inhabitants: 101 (2017 est.)
country comparison to the world: 191

TELEPHONE SYSTEM:
general assessment: adequate, automatic, island-wide telephone system; lack of local competition but telecoms are a high contributor to overall GDP (2018)
domestic: interisland VHF and UHF radiotelephone links; 29 per 100 for fixed-line and 101 per 100 for mobile-cellular (2018)
international: country code - 1-473; landing points for the ECFS, Southern Caribbean Fiber and CARCIP submarine cables with links to 13 Caribbean islands extending from the British Virgin Islands to Trinidad & Tobago including Puerto Rico and Barbados; SHF radiotelephone links to Trinidad and Tobago and Saint Vincent; VHF and UHF radio links to Trinidad (2019)

BROADCAST MEDIA:
multiple publicly and privately owned television and radio stations; Grenada Information Service (GIS) is government-owned and provides television and radio services; the Grenada Broadcasting Network, jointly owned by the government and the Caribbean Communications Network of Trinidad and Tobago, operates a TV station and 2 radio stations; Meaningful Television (MTV) broadcasts island-wide and is part of a locally-owned media house, Moving Target Company, that also includes an FM radio station and a weekly newspaper; multi-channel cable TV subscription service is provided by Columbus Communications Grenada (FLOW GRENADA) and is available island wide; approximately 25 private radio stations also broadcast throughout the country (2019)

INTERNET COUNTRY CODE:
.gd

INTERNET USERS:
total: 62,123
percent of population: 55.9% (July 2016 est.)
country comparison to the world: 185

BROADBAND - FIXED SUBSCRIPTIONS:
total: 22,235
subscriptions per 100 inhabitants: 20 (2017 est.)
country comparison to the world: 148

MILITARY AND SECURITY :: GRENADA

MILITARY AND SECURITY FORCES:
no regular military forces; Royal Grenada Police Force (includes Coast Guard) (2019)

TRANSPORTATION :: GRENADA

NATIONAL AIR TRANSPORT SYSTEM:
number of registered air carriers: 0 (2015)
inventory of registered aircraft operated by air carriers: 0 (2015)
annual passenger traffic on registered air carriers: 0 (2015)
annual freight traffic on registered air carriers: 0 mt-km (2015)

CIVIL AIRCRAFT REGISTRATION COUNTRY CODE PREFIX:
J3 (2016)

AIRPORTS:
3 (2013)
country comparison to the world: 195

AIRPORTS - WITH PAVED RUNWAYS:
total: 3 (2017)
2,438 to 3,047 m: 1 (2017)
1,524 to 2,437 m: 1 (2017)
under 914 m: 1 (2017)

ROADWAYS:
total: 1,127 km (2017)
paved: 902 km (2017)
unpaved: 225 km (2017)
country comparison to the world: 176

MERCHANT MARINE:
total: 6
by type: general cargo 3, other 3 (2018)
country comparison to the world: 161

PORTS AND TERMINALS:
major seaport(s): Saint George's

TRANSNATIONAL ISSUES :: GRENADA

DISPUTES - INTERNATIONAL:
none

ILLICIT DRUGS:
small-scale cannabis cultivation; lesser transshipment point for marijuana and cocaine to US

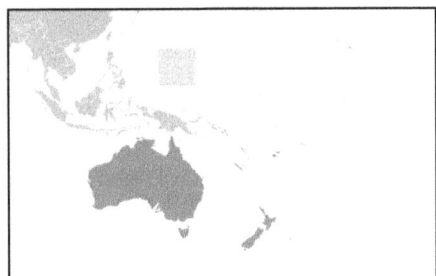

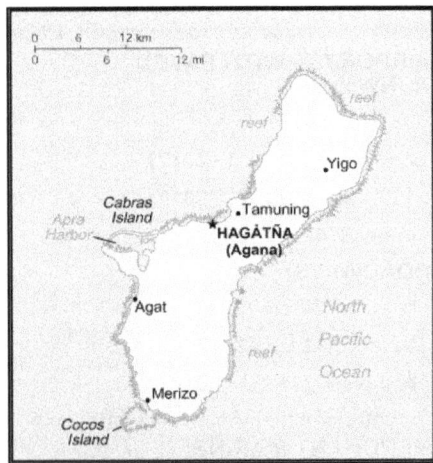

AUSTRALIA - OCEANIA :: GUAM

INTRODUCTION :: GUAM

BACKGROUND:
Spain ceded Guam to the US in 1898. Captured by the Japanese in 1941, it was retaken by the US three years later. The military installations on the island are some of the most strategically important US bases in the Pacific; they also constitute the island's most important source of income and economic stability.

GEOGRAPHY :: GUAM

LOCATION:
Oceania, island in the North Pacific Ocean, about three-quarters of the way from Hawaii to the Philippines

GEOGRAPHIC COORDINATES:
13 28 N, 144 47 E

MAP REFERENCES:
Oceania

AREA:
total: 544 sq km
land: 544 sq km
water: 0 sq km
country comparison to the world: 195

AREA - COMPARATIVE:
three times the size of Washington, DC

LAND BOUNDARIES:
0 km

COASTLINE:
125.5 km

MARITIME CLAIMS:
territorial sea: 12 nm
exclusive economic zone: 200 nm

CLIMATE:
tropical marine; generally warm and humid, moderated by northeast trade winds; dry season (January to June), rainy season (July to December); little seasonal temperature variation

TERRAIN:
volcanic origin, surrounded by coral reefs; relatively flat coralline limestone plateau (source of most fresh water), with steep coastal cliffs and narrow coastal plains in north, low hills in center, mountains in south

ELEVATION:
lowest point: Pacific Ocean 0 m
highest point: Mount Lamlam 406 m

NATURAL RESOURCES:
aquatic wildlife (supporting tourism), fishing (largely undeveloped)

LAND USE:
agricultural land: 33.4% (2011 est.)
arable land: 1.9% (2011 est.) / permanent crops: 16.7% (2011 est.) / permanent pasture: 14.8% (2011 est.)
forest: 47.9% (2011 est.)
other: 18.7% (2011 est.)

IRRIGATED LAND:
2 sq km (2012)

POPULATION DISTRIBUTION:
no large cities exist on the island, though large villages (municipalities) attract much of the population; the largest of these is Dededo

NATURAL HAZARDS:
frequent squalls during rainy season; relatively rare but potentially destructive typhoons (June to December)

ENVIRONMENT - CURRENT ISSUES:
fresh water scarcity; reef damage; inadequate sewage treatment; extermination of native bird populations by the rapid proliferation of the brown tree snake, an exotic, invasive species

GEOGRAPHY - NOTE:
largest and southernmost island in the Mariana Islands archipelago and the largest island in Micronesia; strategic location in western North Pacific Ocean

PEOPLE AND SOCIETY :: GUAM

POPULATION:
167,772 (July 2018 est.)
country comparison to the world: 186

NATIONALITY:
noun: Guamanian(s) (US citizens)
adjective: Guamanian

ETHNIC GROUPS:
Chamorro 37.3%, Filipino 26.3%, white 7.1%, Chuukese 7%, Korean 2.2%, other Pacific Islander 2%, other Asian 2%, Chinese 1.6%, Palauan 1.6%, Japanese 1.5%, Pohnpeian 1.4%, mixed 9.4%, other 0.6% (2010 est.)

LANGUAGES:
English 43.6%, Filipino 21.2%, Chamorro 17.8%, other Pacific island languages 10%, Asian languages 6.3%, other 1.1% (2010 est.)

RELIGIONS:
Roman Catholic 85%, other 15% (1999 est.)

AGE STRUCTURE:
0-14 years: 27.48% (male 23,893 /female 22,207)
15-24 years: 16.4% (male 14,692 /female 12,816)

25-54 years: 37.18% (male 32,170 /female 30,207)

55-64 years: 10.05% (male 8,627 /female 8,236)

65 years and over: 8.9% (male 6,947 /female 7,977) (2018 est.)

DEPENDENCY RATIOS:

total dependency ratio: 52.3 (2015 est.)

youth dependency ratio: 38.8 (2015 est.)

elderly dependency ratio: 13.6 (2015 est.)

potential support ratio: 7.4 (2015 est.)

MEDIAN AGE:

total: 29.1 years (2018 est.)

male: 28.4 years

female: 29.9 years

country comparison to the world: 127

POPULATION GROWTH RATE:

0.23% (2018 est.)

country comparison to the world: 179

BIRTH RATE:

19.4 births/1,000 population (2018 est.)

country comparison to the world: 81

DEATH RATE:

6 deaths/1,000 population (2018 est.)

country comparison to the world: 164

NET MIGRATION RATE:

-11 migrant(s)/1,000 population (2018 est.)

country comparison to the world: 217

POPULATION DISTRIBUTION:

no large cities exist on the island, though large villages (municipalities) attract much of the population; the largest of these is Dededo

URBANIZATION:

urban population: 94.9% of total population (2019)

rate of urbanization: 0.92% annual rate of change (2015-20 est.)

MAJOR URBAN AREAS - POPULATION:

147,000 HAGATNA (capital) (2018)

SEX RATIO:

at birth: 1.07 male(s)/female

0-14 years: 1.08 male(s)/female

15-24 years: 1.15 male(s)/female

25-54 years: 1.06 male(s)/female

55-64 years: 1.05 male(s)/female

65 years and over: 0.87 male(s)/female

total population: 1.06 male(s)/female (2018 est.)

INFANT MORTALITY RATE:

total: 11.9 deaths/1,000 live births (2018 est.)

male: 11.8 deaths/1,000 live births

female: 12.1 deaths/1,000 live births

country comparison to the world: 115

LIFE EXPECTANCY AT BIRTH:

total population: 76.4 years (2018 est.)

male: 73.9 years

female: 78.9 years

country comparison to the world: 86

TOTAL FERTILITY RATE:

2.92 children born/woman (2018 est.)

country comparison to the world: 57

DRINKING WATER SOURCE:

improved:

urban: 99.5% of population

rural: 99.5% of population

total: 99.5% of population

unimproved:

urban: 0.5% of population

rural: 0.5% of population

total: 0.5% of population (2015 est.)

SANITATION FACILITY ACCESS:

improved:

urban: 89.8% of population (2015 est.)

rural: 89.8% of population (2015 est.)

total: 89.8% of population (2015 est.)

unimproved:

urban: 10.2% of population (2015 est.)

rural: 10.2% of population (2015 est.)

total: 10.2% of population (2015 est.)

HIV/AIDS - ADULT PREVALENCE RATE:

NA

HIV/AIDS - PEOPLE LIVING WITH HIV/AIDS:

NA

HIV/AIDS - DEATHS:

NA

EDUCATION EXPENDITURES:

NA

UNEMPLOYMENT, YOUTH AGES 15-24:

total: 29.4%

male: 29.7%

female: 28.9% (2011 est.)

country comparison to the world: 34

GOVERNMENT :: GUAM

COUNTRY NAME:

conventional long form: none

conventional short form: Guam

local long form: none

local short form: Guahan

abbreviation: GU

etymology: the native Chamorro name for the island "Guahan" (meaning "we have" or "ours") was changed to Guam in the 1898 Treaty of Paris, whereby Spain relinquished Guam, Cuba, Puerto Rico, and the Philippines to the US

DEPENDENCY STATUS:

unincorporated organized territory of the US with policy relations between Guam and the federal government under the jurisdiction of the Office of Insular Affairs, US Department of the Interior

GOVERNMENT TYPE:

republican form of government with separate executive, legislative, and judicial branches; unincorporated organized territory of the US with local self-government

CAPITAL:

name: Hagatna (Agana)

geographic coordinates: 13 28 N, 144 44 E

time difference: UTC+10 (15 hours ahead of Washington, DC, during Standard Time)

etymology: the name is derived from the Chamoru word "haga," meaning "blood", and may refer to the bloodlines of the various families that established the original settlement

ADMINISTRATIVE DIVISIONS:

none (territory of the US)

INDEPENDENCE:

none (territory of the US)

NATIONAL HOLIDAY:

Discovery Day (or Magellan Day), first Monday in March (1521)

CONSTITUTION:

history: effective 1 July 1950 (Guam Act of 1950 serves as a constitution)

amendments: amended many times, last in 2015 (2017)

LEGAL SYSTEM:

common law modeled on US system; US federal laws apply

CITIZENSHIP:

see United States

SUFFRAGE:

18 years of age; universal; note - Guamanians are US citizens but do not vote in US presidential elections

EXECUTIVE BRANCH:

chief of state: President Donald J. TRUMP (since 20 January 2017); Vice President Michael R. PENCE (since 20 January 2017)

head of government: Governor Lourdes LEON GUERRERO (since 7 January 2019); Lieutenant Governor Josh TENORIO (since 7 January 2019)

cabinet: Cabinet appointed by the governor with the consent of the Legislature

elections/appointments: president and vice president indirectly elected on the same ballot by an Electoral College of 'electors' chosen from each state to serve a 4-year term (eligible for a second term); under the US Constitution, residents of unincorporated territories, such as Guam, do not vote in elections for US president and vice president; however, they may vote in Democratic and Republican presidential primary elections; governor and lieutenant governor elected on the same ballot by absolute majority vote in 2 rounds if needed for a 4-year term (eligible for 2 consecutive terms); election last held on 6 November 2018 (next to be held in November 2022)

election results: Lourdes LEON GUERRERO elected governor; percent of vote - Lourdes LEON GUERRERO (Democratic Party) 50.7%, Ray TENORIO (Republican Party) 26.4%; Josh TENORIO (Democratic Party) elected lieutenant governor

LEGISLATIVE BRANCH:

description: unicameral Legislature of Guam or Liheslaturan Guahan (15 seats; members elected in a single countrywide constituency by simple majority vote to serve 2-year terms)

elections: last held on 6 November 2018 (next to be held in November 2020)

election results: percent of vote by party - NA; seats by party - Democratic Party 10, Republican Party 5; composition - men 5, women 10, percent of women 66.7%

note: Guam directly elects 1 member by simple majority vote to serve a 2-year term as a delegate to the US House of Representatives; the delegate can vote when serving on a committee and when the House meets as the Committee of the Whole House, but not when legislation is submitted for a "full floor" House vote; election of delegate last held on 6 November 2018 (next to be held in November 2020); election results - seat by party - Democratic Party 1; composition 1 man

JUDICIAL BRANCH:

highest courts: Supreme Court of Guam (consists of 3 justices); note - appeals beyond the Supreme Court of Guam are referred to the US Supreme Court

judge selection and term of office: justices appointed by the governor and confirmed by the Guam legislature; justices appointed for life subject to retention election every 10 years

subordinate courts: Superior Court of Guam - includes several divisions; US Federal District Court for the District of Guam (a US territorial court; appeals beyond this court are heard before the US Court of Appeals for the Ninth Circuit)

POLITICAL PARTIES AND LEADERS:

Democratic Party [Joaquin "Kin" PEREZ]
Republican Party [Jerry CRISOSTOMO]

INTERNATIONAL ORGANIZATION PARTICIPATION:

AOSIS (observer), IOC, PIF (observer), SPC, UPU

DIPLOMATIC REPRESENTATION IN THE US:

none (territory of the US)

DIPLOMATIC REPRESENTATION FROM THE US:

none (territory of the US)

FLAG DESCRIPTION:

territorial flag is dark blue with a narrow red border on all four sides; centered is a red-bordered, pointed, vertical ellipse containing a beach scene, a proa or outrigger canoe with sail, and a palm tree with the word GUAM superimposed in bold red letters; the proa is sailing in Agana Bay with the promontory of Punta Dos Amantes, near the capital, in the background; the shape of the central emblem is that of a Chamorro sling stone, used as a weapon for defense or hunting; blue represents the sea and red the blood shed in the struggle against oppression

note: the US flag is the national flag

NATIONAL SYMBOL(S):

coconut tree; national colors: deep blue, red

NATIONAL ANTHEM:

name: "Fanohge Chamoru" (Stand Ye Guamanians)

lyrics/music: Ramon Manalisay SABLAN [English], Lagrimas UNTALAN [Chamoru]/Ramon Manalisay SABLAN

note: adopted 1919; the local anthem is also known as "Guam Hymn"; as a territory of the United States, "The Star-Spangled Banner," which generally follows the playing of "Stand Ye Guamanians," is official (see United States)

ECONOMY :: GUAM

ECONOMY - OVERVIEW:

US national defense spending is the main driver of Guam's economy, followed closely by tourism and other services. Guam serves as a forward US base for the Western Pacific and is home to thousands of American military personnel. Total federal spending (defense and non-defense) amounted to $1.988 billion in 2016, or 34.2 of Guam's GDP. Of that total, federal grants and cover-over payments amounted to $3444.1 million in 2016, or 35.8% of Guam's total revenues for the fiscal year. In 2016, Guam's economy grew 0.3%. Despite slow growth, Guam's economy has been stable over the last decade. National defense spending cushions the island's economy against fluctuations in tourism. Service exports, mainly spending by foreign tourists in Guam, amounted to over $1 billion for the first time in 2016, or 17.8% of GDP.

GDP (PURCHASING POWER PARITY):

$5.793 billion (2016 est.)

$5.697 billion (2015 est.)

$5.531 billion (2014 est.)

country comparison to the world: 174

GDP (OFFICIAL EXCHANGE RATE):

$5.793 billion (2016 est.) (2016 est.)

GDP - REAL GROWTH RATE:

0.4% (2016 est.)

0.5% (2015 est.)

1.6% (2014 est.)

country comparison to the world: 192

GDP - PER CAPITA (PPP):

$35,600 (2016 est.)

$35,200 (2015 est.)

$34,400 (2014 est.)

country comparison to the world: 56

GDP - COMPOSITION, BY END USE:

household consumption: 56.2% (2016 est.)

government consumption: 55% (2016 est.)

investment in fixed capital: 20.6% (2016 est.)

investment in inventories: NA (2016 est.)

exports of goods and services: 19.4% (2016 est.)

imports of goods and services: -51.2% (2016 est.)

GDP - COMPOSITION, BY SECTOR OF ORIGIN:

agriculture: NA

industry: NA

services: 58.4% NA (2015 est.)

AGRICULTURE - PRODUCTS:

fruits, copra, vegetables; eggs, pork, poultry, beef

INDUSTRIES:

national defense, tourism, construction, transshipment services, concrete products, printing and publishing, food processing, textiles

INDUSTRIAL PRODUCTION GROWTH RATE:

NA

LABOR FORCE:

73,210 (2016 est.)

note: includes only the civilian labor force

country comparison to the world: 184

LABOR FORCE - BY OCCUPATION:

agriculture: 0.3%

industry: 21.6%

services: 78.1% (2013 est.)

UNEMPLOYMENT RATE:

4.5% (2017 est.)

3.9% (2016 est.)

country comparison to the world: 64

POPULATION BELOW POVERTY LINE:

23% (2001 est.)

HOUSEHOLD INCOME OR CONSUMPTION BY PERCENTAGE SHARE:

lowest 10%: NA

highest 10%: NA

BUDGET:

revenues: 1.24 billion (2016 est.)

expenditures: 1.299 billion (2016 est.)

TAXES AND OTHER REVENUES:

21.4% (of GDP) (2016 est.)

country comparison to the world: 139

BUDGET SURPLUS (+) OR DEFICIT (-):

-1% (of GDP) (2016 est.)

country comparison to the world: 78

PUBLIC DEBT:

22.1% of GDP (2016 est.)

32.1% of GDP (2013)

country comparison to the world: 184

FISCAL YEAR:

1 October - 30 September

INFLATION RATE (CONSUMER PRICES):

1% (2017 est.)

0% (2016 est.)

country comparison to the world: 52

EXPORTS:

$1.124 billion (2016 est.)

$1.046 billion (2015 est.)

country comparison to the world: 157

EXPORTS - PARTNERS:

Palau 13.6% (2017)

EXPORTS - COMMODITIES:

transshipments of refined petroleum products, construction materials, fish, foodstuffs and beverages

IMPORTS:

$2.964 billion (2016 est.)

$3.054 billion (2015 est.)

country comparison to the world: 150

IMPORTS - COMMODITIES:

petroleum and petroleum products, food, manufactured goods

IMPORTS - PARTNERS:

Singapore 41.7%, Japan 30.6%, Hong Kong 10.6% (2017)

DEBT - EXTERNAL:

NA

STOCK OF DIRECT FOREIGN INVESTMENT - AT HOME:

(31 December 2009 est.)

EXCHANGE RATES:

the US dollar is used

ENERGY :: GUAM

ELECTRICITY ACCESS:

electrification - total population: 100% (2016)

ELECTRICITY - PRODUCTION:

1.722 billion kWh (2016 est.)

country comparison to the world: 141

ELECTRICITY - CONSUMPTION:

1.601 billion kWh (2016 est.)

country comparison to the world: 146

ELECTRICITY - EXPORTS:

0 kWh (2016 est.)

country comparison to the world: 143

ELECTRICITY - IMPORTS:

0 kWh (2016 est.)

country comparison to the world: 155

ELECTRICITY - INSTALLED GENERATING CAPACITY:

560,000 kW (2016 est.)

country comparison to the world: 143

ELECTRICITY - FROM FOSSIL FUELS:

94% of total installed capacity (2016 est.)

country comparison to the world: 46

ELECTRICITY - FROM NUCLEAR FUELS:

0% of total installed capacity (2017 est.)

country comparison to the world: 101

ELECTRICITY - FROM HYDROELECTRIC PLANTS:

0% of total installed capacity (2017 est.)

country comparison to the world: 175

ELECTRICITY - FROM OTHER RENEWABLE SOURCES:

6% of total installed capacity (2017 est.)

country comparison to the world: 98

CRUDE OIL - PRODUCTION:

0 bbl/day (2018 est.)

country comparison to the world: 144

CRUDE OIL - EXPORTS:

0 bbl/day (2015 est.)

country comparison to the world: 132

CRUDE OIL - IMPORTS:

0 bbl/day (2015 est.)

country comparison to the world: 135

CRUDE OIL - PROVED RESERVES:

0 bbl (1 January 2018 est.)

country comparison to the world: 140

REFINED PETROLEUM PRODUCTS - PRODUCTION:

0 bbl/day (2015 est.)

country comparison to the world: 152

REFINED PETROLEUM PRODUCTS - CONSUMPTION:

14,000 bbl/day (2016 est.)

country comparison to the world: 153

REFINED PETROLEUM PRODUCTS - EXPORTS:

0 bbl/day (2015 est.)

country comparison to the world: 161

REFINED PETROLEUM PRODUCTS - IMPORTS:

13,500 bbl/day (2015 est.)

country comparison to the world: 141

NATURAL GAS - PRODUCTION:

0 cu m (2017 est.)

country comparison to the world: 140

NATURAL GAS - CONSUMPTION:

0 cu m (2017 est.)

country comparison to the world: 153

NATURAL GAS - EXPORTS:

0 cu m (2017 est.)

country comparison to the world: 115

NATURAL GAS - IMPORTS:

0 cu m (2017 est.)

country comparison to the world: 133

NATURAL GAS - PROVED RESERVES:

0 cu m (1 January 2014 est.)

country comparison to the world: 142

CARBON DIOXIDE EMISSIONS FROM CONSUMPTION OF ENERGY:

2.214 million Mt (2017 est.)

country comparison to the world: 157

COMMUNICATIONS :: GUAM

TELEPHONES - FIXED LINES:

total subscriptions: 68,000

subscriptions per 100 inhabitants: 42 (July 2016 est.)

country comparison to the world: 151

TELEPHONES - MOBILE CELLULAR:

total subscriptions: 181,000

subscriptions per 100 inhabitants: 113 (July 2016 est.)

country comparison to the world: 182

TELEPHONE SYSTEM:

general assessment: modern system, integrated with US facilities for direct dialing, including free use of 800 numbers (2018)

domestic: three major companies provide both fixed-line and mobile services, as well as access to the Internet; fixed-line 42 per 100 and 113 per 100 for mobile-cellular (2018)

international: country code - 1-671; major landing points for Atisa, HANTRU1, HK-G, JGA-N, JGA-S, PIPE-1, SEA-US, SxS, Tata TGN-Pacific, AJC, GOKI, AAG, AJC and Mariana-Guam Cable submarine cables between Asia, Australia, and the US (Guam is a transpacific communications hub for major carriers linking the US and Asia); satellite earth stations - 2 Intelsat (Pacific Ocean) (2019)

BROADCAST MEDIA:

about a dozen TV channels, including digital channels; multi-channel cable TV services are available; roughly 20 radio stations

INTERNET COUNTRY CODE:

.gu

INTERNET USERS:

total: 125,328

percent of population: 77% (July 2016 est.)

country comparison to the world: 174

MILITARY AND SECURITY :: GUAM

MILITARY - NOTE:

defense is the responsibility of the US

TRANSPORTATION :: GUAM

AIRPORTS:

5 (2013)

country comparison to the world: 179

AIRPORTS - WITH PAVED RUNWAYS:

total: 4 (2017)

over 3,047 m: 2 (2017)

2,438 to 3,047 m: 1 (2017)

914 to 1,523 m: 1 (2017)

AIRPORTS - WITH UNPAVED RUNWAYS:

total: 1 (2013)

under 914 m: 1 (2013)

ROADWAYS:

total: 1,045 km (2008)

country comparison to the world: 178

MERCHANT MARINE:

total: 3

by type: other 3 (2018)

country comparison to the world: 168

PORTS AND TERMINALS:

major seaport(s): Apra Harbor

TRANSNATIONAL ISSUES :: GUAM

DISPUTES - INTERNATIONAL:

none

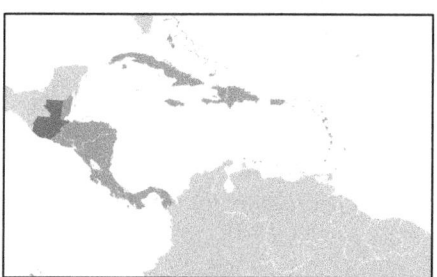

CENTRAL AMERICA :: GUATEMALA

INTRODUCTION :: GUATEMALA

BACKGROUND:
The Maya civilization flourished in Guatemala and surrounding regions during the first millennium A.D. After almost three centuries as a Spanish colony, Guatemala won its independence in 1821. During the second half of the 20th century, it experienced a variety of military and civilian governments, as well as a 36-year guerrilla war. In 1996, the government signed a peace agreement formally ending the internal conflict.

GEOGRAPHY :: GUATEMALA

LOCATION:
Central America, bordering the North Pacific Ocean, between El Salvador and Mexico, and bordering the Gulf of Honduras (Caribbean Sea) between Honduras and Belize

GEOGRAPHIC COORDINATES:
15 30 N, 90 15 W

MAP REFERENCES:
Central America and the Caribbean

AREA:
total: 108,889 sq km
land: 107,159 sq km
water: 1,730 sq km
country comparison to the world: 108

AREA - COMPARATIVE:
slightly smaller than Pennsylvania

LAND BOUNDARIES:
total: 1,667 km
border countries (4): Belize 266 km, El Salvador 199 km, Honduras 244 km, Mexico 958 km

COASTLINE:
400 km

MARITIME CLAIMS:
territorial sea: 12 nm
exclusive economic zone: 200 nm
continental shelf: 200-m depth or to the depth of exploitation

CLIMATE:
tropical; hot, humid in lowlands; cooler in highlands

TERRAIN:
two east-west trending mountain chains divide the country into three regions: the mountainous highlands, the Pacific coast south of mountains, and the vast northern Peten lowlands

ELEVATION:
mean elevation: 759 m
lowest point: Pacific Ocean 0 m
highest point: Volcan Tajumulco (highest point in Central America) 4,220 m

NATURAL RESOURCES:
petroleum, nickel, rare woods, fish, chicle, hydropower

LAND USE:
agricultural land: 41.2% (2011 est.)
arable land: 14.2% (2011 est.) / permanent crops: 8.8% (2011 est.) / permanent pasture: 18.2% (2011 est.)
forest: 33.6% (2011 est.)
other: 25.2% (2011 est.)

IRRIGATED LAND:
3,375 sq km (2012)

POPULATION DISTRIBUTION:
the vast majority of the populace resides in the southern half of the country, particularly in the mountainous regions; more than half of the population lives in rural areas

NATURAL HAZARDS:
numerous volcanoes in mountains, with occasional violent earthquakes; Caribbean coast extremely susceptible to hurricanes and other tropical storms

volcanism: significant volcanic activity in the Sierra Madre range; Santa Maria (3,772 m) has been deemed a Decade Volcano by the International Association of Volcanology and Chemistry of the Earth's Interior, worthy of study due to its explosive history and close proximity to human populations; Pacaya (2,552 m), which erupted in May 2010 causing an ashfall on Guatemala City and prompting evacuations, is one of the country's most active volcanoes with frequent eruptions since 1965; other historically active volcanoes include Acatenango, Almolonga, Atitlan, Fuego, and Tacana; see note 2 under "Geography - note"

ENVIRONMENT - CURRENT ISSUES:
deforestation in the Peten rainforest; soil erosion; water pollution

ENVIRONMENT - INTERNATIONAL AGREEMENTS:
party to: Antarctic Treaty, Biodiversity, Climate Change, Climate Change-Kyoto Protocol, Desertification, Endangered Species, Environmental Modification, Hazardous Wastes, Law of the Sea, Marine Dumping, Ozone Layer Protection, Ship Pollution, Wetlands, Whaling

signed, but not ratified: none of the selected agreements

GEOGRAPHY - NOTE:

note 1: despite having both eastern and western coastlines (Caribbean Sea and Pacific Ocean respectively), there are no natural harbors on the west coast

note 2: Guatemala is one of the countries along the Ring of Fire, a belt of active volcanoes and earthquake epicenters bordering the Pacific Ocean; up to 90% of the world's earthquakes and some 75% of the world's volcanoes occur within the Ring of Fire

PEOPLE AND SOCIETY :: GUATEMALA

POPULATION:
16,581,273 (July 2018 est.)

country comparison to the world: 67

NATIONALITY:
noun: Guatemalan(s)

adjective: Guatemalan

ETHNIC GROUPS:
mestizo (mixed Amerindian-Spanish - in local Spanish called Ladino) 56%, Maya 41.7%, Xinca (indigenous, non-Maya) 1.8%, African descent .2%, Garifuna (mixed West and Central African, Island Carib, and Arawak) .1%, foreign .2% (2018 est.)

LANGUAGES:
Spanish (official) 69.9%, Maya languages 29.7% (Q'eqchi' 8.3%, K'iche 7.8%, Mam 4.4%, Kaqchikel 3%, Q'anjob'al 1.2%, Poqomchi' 1%, other 4%), other 0.4% (includes Xinca and Garifuna) (2018 est.)

note: the 2003 Law of National Languages officially recognized 23 indigenous languages, including 21 Maya languages, Xinca, and Garifuna

RELIGIONS:
Roman Catholic, Protestant, indigenous Maya

DEMOGRAPHIC PROFILE:
Guatemala is a predominantly poor country that struggles in several areas of health and development, including infant, child, and maternal mortality, malnutrition, literacy, and contraceptive awareness and use. The country's large indigenous population is disproportionately affected. Guatemala is the most populous country in Central America and has the highest fertility rate in Latin America. It also has the highest population growth rate in Latin America, which is likely to continue because of its large reproductive-age population and high birth rate. Almost half of Guatemala's population is under age 19, making it the youngest population in Latin America. Guatemala's total fertility rate has slowly declined during the last few decades due in part to limited government-funded health programs. However, the birth rate is still more close to three children per woman and is markedly higher among its rural and indigenous populations.

Guatemalans have a history of emigrating legally and illegally to Mexico, the United States, and Canada because of a lack of economic opportunity, political instability, and natural disasters. Emigration, primarily to the United States, escalated during the 1960 to 1996 civil war and accelerated after a peace agreement was signed. Thousands of Guatemalans who fled to Mexico returned after the war, but labor migration to southern Mexico continues.

AGE STRUCTURE:
0-14 years: 34.55% (male 2,919,281 /female 2,810,329)

15-24 years: 20.23% (male 1,688,900 /female 1,665,631)

25-54 years: 35.47% (male 2,878,075 /female 3,002,920)

55-64 years: 5.28% (male 407,592 /female 468,335)

65 years and over: 4.46% (male 336,377 /female 403,833) (2018 est.)

DEPENDENCY RATIOS:
total dependency ratio: 68.7 (2015 est.)

youth dependency ratio: 61.1 (2015 est.)

elderly dependency ratio: 7.6 (2015 est.)

potential support ratio: 13.1 (2015 est.)

MEDIAN AGE:
total: 22.5 years (2018 est.)

male: 22 years

female: 23.1 years

country comparison to the world: 179

POPULATION GROWTH RATE:
1.72% (2018 est.)

country comparison to the world: 59

BIRTH RATE:
24.6 births/1,000 population (2018 est.)

country comparison to the world: 50

DEATH RATE:
5 deaths/1,000 population (2018 est.)

country comparison to the world: 194

NET MIGRATION RATE:
-2.4 migrant(s)/1,000 population (2018 est.)

country comparison to the world: 168

POPULATION DISTRIBUTION:
the vast majority of the populace resides in the southern half of the country, particularly in the mountainous regions; more than half of the population lives in rural areas

URBANIZATION:
urban population: 51.4% of total population (2019)

rate of urbanization: 2.68% annual rate of change (2015-20 est.)

MAJOR URBAN AREAS - POPULATION:
2.891 million GUATEMALA CITY (capital) (2019)

SEX RATIO:
at birth: 1.05 male(s)/female

0-14 years: 1.04 male(s)/female

15-24 years: 1.01 male(s)/female

25-54 years: 0.96 male(s)/female

55-64 years: 0.87 male(s)/female

65 years and over: 0.83 male(s)/female

total population: 0.99 male(s)/female (2018 est.)

MOTHER'S MEAN AGE AT FIRST BIRTH:
21.2 years (2014/15 est.)

note: median age at first birth among women 25-29

MATERNAL MORTALITY RATE:
95 deaths/100,000 live births (2017 est.)

country comparison to the world: 72

INFANT MORTALITY RATE:
total: 23.3 deaths/1,000 live births (2018 est.)

male: 25.6 deaths/1,000 live births

female: 20.9 deaths/1,000 live births

country comparison to the world: 70

LIFE EXPECTANCY AT BIRTH:
total population: 71.8 years (2018 est.)

male: 69.8 years

female: 73.9 years

country comparison to the world: 149

TOTAL FERTILITY RATE:

2.87 children born/woman (2018 est.)

country comparison to the world: 58

CONTRACEPTIVE PREVALENCE RATE:

60.6% (2014/15)

DRINKING WATER SOURCE:

improved:

urban: 98.4% of population

rural: 86.8% of population

total: 92.8% of population

unimproved:

urban: 1.6% of population

rural: 13.2% of population

total: 7.2% of population (2015 est.)

CURRENT HEALTH EXPENDITURE:

5.8% (2016)

PHYSICIANS DENSITY:

0.36 physicians/1,000 population (2018)

HOSPITAL BED DENSITY:

0.6 beds/1,000 population (2014)

SANITATION FACILITY ACCESS:

improved:

urban: 77.5% of population (2015 est.)

rural: 49.3% of population (2015 est.)

total: 63.9% of population (2015 est.)

unimproved:

urban: 22.5% of population (2015 est.)

rural: 50.7% of population (2015 est.)

total: 36.1% of population (2015 est.)

HIV/AIDS - ADULT PREVALENCE RATE:

0.4% (2018 est.)

country comparison to the world: 80

HIV/AIDS - PEOPLE LIVING WITH HIV/AIDS:

47,000 (2018 est.)

country comparison to the world: 61

HIV/AIDS - DEATHS:

2,200 (2018 est.)

country comparison to the world: 44

MAJOR INFECTIOUS DISEASES:

degree of risk: high (2016)

food or waterborne diseases: bacterial diarrhea, hepatitis A, and typhoid fever (2016)

vectorborne diseases: dengue fever and malaria (2016)

note: active local transmission of Zika virus by Aedes species mosquitoes has been identified in this country (as of August 2016); it poses an important risk (a large number of cases possible) among US citizens if bitten by an infective mosquito; other less common ways to get Zika are through sex, via blood transfusion, or during pregnancy, in which the pregnant woman passes Zika virus to her fetus

OBESITY - ADULT PREVALENCE RATE:

21.2% (2016)

country comparison to the world: 93

CHILDREN UNDER THE AGE OF 5 YEARS UNDERWEIGHT:

12.4% (2015)

country comparison to the world: 53

EDUCATION EXPENDITURES:

2.8% of GDP (2017)

country comparison to the world: 149

LITERACY:

definition: age 15 and over can read and write

total population: 81.5%

male: 87.4%

female: 76.3% (2015 est.)

SCHOOL LIFE EXPECTANCY (PRIMARY TO TERTIARY EDUCATION):

total: 11 years

male: 11 years

female: 11 years (2014)

UNEMPLOYMENT, YOUTH AGES 15-24:

total: 5%

male: 3.7%

female: 8% (2017 est.)

country comparison to the world: 164

GOVERNMENT :: GUATEMALA

COUNTRY NAME:

conventional long form: Republic of Guatemala

conventional short form: Guatemala

local long form: Republica de Guatemala

local short form: Guatemala

etymology: the Spanish conquistadors used many native Americans as allies in their conquest of Guatemala; the site of their first capital (established in 1524), a former Maya settlement, was called "Quauhtemallan" by their Nahuatl-speaking Mexican allies, a name that means "land of trees" or "forested land", but which the Spanish pronounced "Guatemala"; the Spanish applied that name to a re founded capital city three years later and eventually it became the name of the country

GOVERNMENT TYPE:

presidential republic

CAPITAL:

name: Guatemala City

geographic coordinates: 14 37 N, 90 31 W

time difference: UTC-6 (1 hour behind Washington, DC, during Standard Time)

etymology: the Spanish conquistadors used many native Americans as allies in their conquest of Guatemala; the site of their first capital (established in 1524), a former Maya settlement, was called "Quauhtemallan" by their Nahuatl-speaking Mexican allies, a name that means "land of trees" or "forested land", but which the Spanish pronounced "Guatemala"; the Spanish applied that name to a re founded capital city three years later and eventually it became the name of the country

ADMINISTRATIVE DIVISIONS:

22 departments (departamentos, singular - departamento); Alta Verapaz, Baja Verapaz, Chimaltenango, Chiquimula, El Progreso, Escuintla, Guatemala, Huehuetenango, Izabal, Jalapa, Jutiapa, Peten, Quetzaltenango, Quiche, Retalhuleu, Sacatepequez, San Marcos, Santa Rosa, Solola, Suchitepequez, Totonicapan, Zacapa

INDEPENDENCE:

15 September 1821 (from Spain)

NATIONAL HOLIDAY:

Independence Day, 15 September (1821)

CONSTITUTION:

history: several previous; latest adopted 31 May 1985, effective 14 January 1986; suspended and reinstated in 1994

amendments: proposed by the president of the republic, by agreement of 10 or more deputies of

Congress, by the Constitutional Court, or by public petition of at least 5,000 citizens; passage requires at least two-thirds majority vote by the Congress membership and approval by public referendum, referred to as "popular consultation"; constitutional articles such as national sovereignty, the republican form of government, limitations on those seeking the presidency, or presidential tenure cannot be amended; amended 1994 (2018)

LEGAL SYSTEM:

civil law system; judicial review of legislative acts

INTERNATIONAL LAW ORGANIZATION PARTICIPATION:

has not submitted an ICJ jurisdiction declaration; accepts ICCt jurisdiction

CITIZENSHIP:

citizenship by birth: yes

citizenship by descent only: yes

dual citizenship recognized: yes

residency requirement for naturalization: 5 years with no absences of six consecutive months or longer or absences totaling more than a year

SUFFRAGE:

18 years of age; universal; note - active duty members of the armed forces and police by law cannot vote and are restricted to their barracks on election day

EXECUTIVE BRANCH:

chief of state: President Jimmy Ernesto MORALES Cabrera (since 14 January 2016); Vice President Jafeth CABRERA Franco (since 14 January 2016); note - the president is both chief of state and head of government

head of government: President Jimmy Ernesto MORALES Cabrera (since 14 January 2016); Vice President Jafeth CABRERA Franco (since 14 January 2016)

cabinet: Council of Ministers appointed by the president

elections/appointments: president and vice president directly elected on the same ballot by absolute majority popular vote in 2 rounds if needed for a 4-year term (not eligible for consecutive terms); election last held on 16 June 2019 with a runoff on 11 August 2019 (next to be held in June 2023)

election results: Alejandro GIAMMATTEI elected president; percent of vote in first round - Sandra TORRES (UNE) 25.54%, Alejandro GIAMMATTEI (VAMOS) 13.95%, Edmond MULET (PHG) 11.21%, Thelma CABRERA (MLP) 10.37%, Roberto ARZU (PAN-PODEMOS) 6.08%; percent of vote in second round - Alejandro GIAMMATTEI (VAMOS) 58%, Sandra TORRES (UNE) 42%; note - the new president will be inaugurated on 14 January 2020

LEGISLATIVE BRANCH:

description: unicameral Congress of the Republic or Congreso de la Republica (158 seats; 127 members directly elected in multi-seat constituencies in the country's 22 departments by simple majority vote and 31 directly elected in a single nationwide constituency by closed-list, proportional representation vote; members serve 4-year terms); note - two additional seats will be added to the new congress when it is seated in January 2020

elections: last held on 16 June 2019 (next to be held on June 2023)

election results: percent of vote by party - NA; seats by party - UNE 53, VAMOS 16, UCN 12, VALOR 9, BIEN 8, FCN-NACION 8, SEMILLA 7, TODOS 7, VIVA 7, CREO 6, PHG 6, VICTORIA 4, Winaq 4, PC 3, PU 3, URNG 3, PAN 2, MLP 1, PODEMOS 1

note: current seats by party as of 1 June 2019 - FCN 37, UNE 32, MR 20, TODOS 17, AC 12, EG 7, UCN 6, CREO 5, LIDER 5, VIVA 4, Convergence 3, PAN 3, PP 2, FUERZA 1, PU 1, URNG 1, Winaq 1, independent 1; composition - men 136, women 22, percent of women 13.9%

JUDICIAL BRANCH:

highest courts: Supreme Court of Justice or Corte Suprema de Justicia (consists of 13 magistrates, including the court president and organized into 3 chambers); note - the court president also supervises trial judges countrywide; Constitutional Court or Corte de Constitucionalidad (consists of 5 titular magistrates and 5 substitute magistrates)

judge selection and term of office: Supreme Court magistrates elected by the Congress of the Republic from candidates proposed by the Postulation Committee, an independent body of deans of the country's university law schools, representatives of the country's law associations, and representatives of the Courts of Appeal; magistrates elected for concurrent, renewable 5-year terms; Constitutional Court judges - 1 elected by the Congress of the Republic, 1 by the Supreme Court, 1 by the president of the republic, 1 by the (public) University of San Carlos, and 1 by the Assembly of the College of Attorneys and Notaries; judges elected for renewable, consecutive 5-year terms; the presidency of the court rotates among the magistrates for a single 1-year term

subordinate courts: numerous first instance and appellate courts

POLITICAL PARTIES AND LEADERS:

Bienestar Nacional or BIEN [Alfonso PORTILLO and Evelyn MORATAYA]
Citizen Alliance or AC
Citizen Prosperity or PC [Dami Anita Elizabeth KRISTENSON Sales]
Commitment, Renewal, and Order or CREO [Roberto GONZALEZ Diaz-Duran]
Convergence [Sandra MORAN]
Encounter for Guatemala or EG [Nineth MONTENEGRO Cottom]
Everyone Together for Guatemala or TODOS [Felipe ALEJOS]
Force or FUERZA [Mauricio RADFORD]
Guatemalan National Revolutionary Unity or URNG-MAIZ or URNG [Gregorio CHAY Laynez]
Humanist Party of Guatemala or PHG [Edmond MULET]
Movement for the Liberation of Peoples or MLP [Thelma CABRERA]
Movimiento Semilla or SEMILLA [Thelma ALDANA]
National Advancement Party or PAN [Harald JOHANNESSEN]
National Convergence Front or FCN-NACION or FCN [Jimmy MORALES]
National Unity for Hope or UNE [Sandra TORRES]
Nationalist Change Union or UCN [Mario ESTRADA]
Patriotic Party or PP
PODEMOS [Jose Raul VIRGIL Arias]
Political Movement Winaq or Winaq [Sonia GUTIERREZ Raguay]
Reform Movement or MR
Renewed Democratic Liberty or LIDER (dissolved mid-February 2016)
TODOS [Felipe ALEJOS]
Unionista Party or PU [Alvaro ARZU Escobar]
Value or VALOR [Zury RIOS]
Vamos por una Guatemala Diferente or VAMOS [Alejandro GIAMMATTEI]
Victory or VICTORIA [Amilcar RIVERA]

Vision with Values or VIVA [Armando Damian CASTILLO Alvarado]

note: parties represented in the last election, but have since dissolved - FCN (2017), LIDER (2016), and PP (2017)

INTERNATIONAL ORGANIZATION PARTICIPATION:

BCIE, CACM, CD, CELAC, EITI (compliant country), FAO, G-24, G-77, IADB, IAEA, IBRD, ICAO, ICC (national committees), ICCt (signatory), ICRM, IDA, IFAD, IFC, IFRCS, IHO, ILO, IMF, IMO, Interpol, IOC, IOM, IPU, ISO (correspondent), ITSO, ITU, ITUC (NGOs), LAES, LAIA (observer), MIGA, MINUSTAH, MONUSCO, NAM, OAS, OPANAL, OPCW, Pacific Alliance (observer), PCA, Petrocaribe, SICA, UN, UNCTAD, UNESCO, UNIDO, UNIFIL, Union Latina, UNISFA, UNITAR, UNMISS, UNOCI, UNWTO, UPU, WCO, WFTU (NGOs), WHO, WIPO, WMO, WTO

DIPLOMATIC REPRESENTATION IN THE US:

Ambassador Manuel Alfredo ESPINA Pinto (since 8 September 2017)

chancery: 2220 R Street NW, Washington, DC 20008

telephone: [1] (202) 745-4952

FAX: [1] (202) 745-1908

consulate(s) general: Atlanta, Chicago, Del Rio (TX), Denver, Houston, Los Angeles, McAllen (TX), Miami, New York, Oklahoma City, Philadelphia, Phoenix, Providence (RI), Raleigh (NC), San Bernardino (CA), San Francisco, Seattle

consulate(s): Lake Worth (FL), Tucson (AZ)

DIPLOMATIC REPRESENTATION FROM THE US:

chief of mission: Ambassador Luis E. ARREAGA (since 4 October 2017)

telephone: [502] 2326-4000

embassy: 7-01 Avenida Reforma, Zone 10, Guatemala City

mailing address: DPO AA 34024

FAX: [502] 2326-4654

FLAG DESCRIPTION:

three equal vertical bands of light blue (hoist side), white, and light blue, with the coat of arms centered in the white band; the coat of arms includes a green and red quetzal (the national bird) representing liberty and a scroll bearing the inscription LIBERTAD 15 DE SEPTIEMBRE DE 1821 (the original date of independence from Spain) all superimposed on a pair of crossed rifles signifying Guatemala's willingness to defend itself and a pair of crossed swords representing honor and framed by a laurel wreath symbolizing victory; the blue bands represent the Pacific Ocean and Caribbean Sea; the white band denotes peace and purity

note: one of only two national flags featuring a firearm, the other is Mozambique

NATIONAL SYMBOL(S):

quetzal (bird); national colors: blue, white

NATIONAL ANTHEM:

name: "Himno Nacional de Guatemala" (National Anthem of Guatemala)

lyrics/music: Jose Joaquin PALMA/Rafael Alvarez OVALLE

note: adopted 1897, modified lyrics adopted 1934; Cuban poet Jose Joaquin PALMA anonymously submitted lyrics to a public contest calling for a national anthem; his authorship was not discovered until 1911

ECONOMY :: GUATEMALA

ECONOMY - OVERVIEW:

Guatemala is the most populous country in Central America with a GDP per capita roughly half the average for Latin America and the Caribbean. The agricultural sector accounts for 13.5% of GDP and 31% of the labor force; key agricultural exports include sugar, coffee, bananas, and vegetables. Guatemala is the top remittance recipient in Central America as a result of Guatemala's large expatriate community in the US. These inflows are a primary source of foreign income, equivalent to two-thirds of the country's exports and about a tenth of its GDP.

The 1996 peace accords, which ended 36 years of civil war, removed a major obstacle to foreign investment, and Guatemala has since pursued important reforms and macroeconomic stabilization. The Dominican Republic-Central America Free Trade Agreement (CAFTA-DR) entered into force in July 2006, spurring increased investment and diversification of exports, with the largest increases in ethanol and non-traditional agricultural exports. While CAFTA-DR has helped improve the investment climate, concerns over security, the lack of skilled workers, and poor infrastructure continue to hamper foreign direct investment.

The distribution of income remains highly unequal with the richest 20% of the population accounting for more than 51% of Guatemala's overall consumption. More than half of the population is below the national poverty line, and 23% of the population lives in extreme poverty. Poverty among indigenous groups, which make up more than 40% of the population, averages 79%, with 40% of the indigenous population living in extreme poverty. Nearly one-half of Guatemala's children under age five are chronically malnourished, one of the highest malnutrition rates in the world.

GDP (PURCHASING POWER PARITY):

$138.1 billion (2017 est.)

$134.4 billion (2016 est.)

$130.4 billion (2015 est.)

note: data are in 2017 dollars

country comparison to the world: 77

GDP (OFFICIAL EXCHANGE RATE):

$75.62 billion (2017 est.)

GDP - REAL GROWTH RATE:

2.8% (2017 est.)

3.1% (2016 est.)

4.1% (2015 est.)

country comparison to the world: 123

GDP - PER CAPITA (PPP):

$8,200 (2017 est.)

$8,100 (2016 est.)

$8,000 (2015 est.)

note: data are in 2017 dollars

country comparison to the world: 150

GROSS NATIONAL SAVING:

13.6% of GDP (2017 est.)

14.4% of GDP (2016 est.)

13.5% of GDP (2015 est.)

country comparison to the world: 141

GDP - COMPOSITION, BY END USE:

household consumption: 86.3% (2017 est.)

government consumption: 9.7% (2017 est.)

investment in fixed capital: 12.3% (2017 est.)

investment in inventories: -0.2% (2017 est.)

exports of goods and services: 18.8% (2017 est.)

imports of goods and services: -26.9% (2017 est.)

GDP - COMPOSITION, BY SECTOR OF ORIGIN:

agriculture: 13.3% (2017 est.)

industry: 23.4% (2017 est.)

services: 63.2% (2017 est.)

AGRICULTURE - PRODUCTS:

sugarcane, corn, bananas, coffee, beans, cardamom; cattle, sheep, pigs, chickens

INDUSTRIES:

sugar, textiles and clothing, furniture, chemicals, petroleum, metals, rubber, tourism

INDUSTRIAL PRODUCTION GROWTH RATE:

1.8% (2017 est.)

country comparison to the world: 136

LABOR FORCE:

6.664 million (2017 est.)

country comparison to the world: 69

LABOR FORCE - BY OCCUPATION:

agriculture: 31.4%

industry: 12.8%

services: 55.8% (2017 est.)

UNEMPLOYMENT RATE:

2.3% (2017 est.)

2.4% (2016 est.)

country comparison to the world: 23

POPULATION BELOW POVERTY LINE:

59.3% (2014 est.)

HOUSEHOLD INCOME OR CONSUMPTION BY PERCENTAGE SHARE:

lowest 10%: 1.6%

highest 10%: 38.4% (2014)

DISTRIBUTION OF FAMILY INCOME - GINI INDEX:

53 (2014 est.)

56 (2011)

country comparison to the world: 10

BUDGET:

revenues: 8.164 billion (2017 est.)

expenditures: 9.156 billion (2017 est.)

TAXES AND OTHER REVENUES:

10.8% (of GDP) (2017 est.)

country comparison to the world: 212

BUDGET SURPLUS (+) OR DEFICIT (-):

-1.3% (of GDP) (2017 est.)

country comparison to the world: 85

PUBLIC DEBT:

24.7% of GDP (2017 est.)

24.5% of GDP (2016 est.)

country comparison to the world: 175

FISCAL YEAR:

calendar year

INFLATION RATE (CONSUMER PRICES):

4.4% (2017 est.)

4.4% (2016 est.)

country comparison to the world: 165

CENTRAL BANK DISCOUNT RATE:

7.53% (31 December 2015 est.)

6.5% (31 December 2010)

country comparison to the world: 41

COMMERCIAL BANK PRIME LENDING RATE:

13.05% (31 December 2017 est.)

13.1% (31 December 2016 est.)

country comparison to the world: 59

STOCK OF NARROW MONEY:

$12.23 billion (31 December 2017 est.)

$10.81 billion (31 December 2016 est.)

country comparison to the world: 80

STOCK OF BROAD MONEY:

$12.23 billion (31 December 2017 est.)

$10.81 billion (31 December 2016 est.)

country comparison to the world: 81

STOCK OF DOMESTIC CREDIT:

$32.31 billion (31 December 2017 est.)

$30.44 billion (31 December 2016 est.)

country comparison to the world: 78

MARKET VALUE OF PUBLICLY TRADED SHARES:

NA

CURRENT ACCOUNT BALANCE:

$1.134 billion (2017 est.)

$1.023 billion (2016 est.)

country comparison to the world: 47

EXPORTS:

$11.12 billion (2017 est.)

$10.58 billion (2016 est.)

country comparison to the world: 89

EXPORTS - PARTNERS:

US 33.8%, El Salvador 11.1%, Honduras 8.8%, Nicaragua 5.1%, Mexico 4.7% (2017)

EXPORTS - COMMODITIES:

sugar, coffee, petroleum, apparel, bananas, fruits and vegetables, cardamom, manufacturing products, precious stones and metals, electricity

IMPORTS:

$17.11 billion (2017 est.)

$15.77 billion (2016 est.)

country comparison to the world: 84

IMPORTS - COMMODITIES:

fuels, machinery and transport equipment, construction materials, grain, fertilizers, electricity, mineral products, chemical products, plastic materials and products

IMPORTS - PARTNERS:

US 39.8%, China 10.7%, Mexico 10.7%, El Salvador 5.3% (2017)

RESERVES OF FOREIGN EXCHANGE AND GOLD:

$11.77 billion (31 December 2017 est.)

$9.156 billion (31 December 2016 est.)

country comparison to the world: 71

DEBT - EXTERNAL:

$22.92 billion (31 December 2017 est.)

$21.45 billion (31 December 2016 est.)

country comparison to the world: 89

STOCK OF DIRECT FOREIGN INVESTMENT - AT HOME:

$16.2 billion (2017 est.)

$14.6 billion (2016 est.)

country comparison to the world: 88

EXCHANGE RATES:

quetzales (GTQ) per US dollar -

7.323 (2017 est.)

7.5999 (2016 est.)

7.5999 (2015 est.)

7.6548 (2014 est.)

7.7322 (2013 est.)

ENERGY :: GUATEMALA

ELECTRICITY ACCESS:

population without electricity: 1 million (2017)

electrification - total population: 91.8% (2016)

electrification - urban areas: 96.8% (2016)

electrification - rural areas: 86.4% (2016)

ELECTRICITY - PRODUCTION:

12.12 billion kWh (2016 est.)

country comparison to the world: 96

ELECTRICITY - CONSUMPTION:

10.1 billion kWh (2016 est.)

country comparison to the world: 96

ELECTRICITY - EXPORTS:

1.858 billion kWh (2017 est.)

country comparison to the world: 47

ELECTRICITY - IMPORTS:

747 million kWh (2016 est.)

country comparison to the world: 75

ELECTRICITY - INSTALLED GENERATING CAPACITY:

4.605 million kW (2016 est.)

country comparison to the world: 85

ELECTRICITY - FROM FOSSIL FUELS:

41% of total installed capacity (2016 est.)

country comparison to the world: 167

ELECTRICITY - FROM NUCLEAR FUELS:

0% of total installed capacity (2017 est.)

country comparison to the world: 102

ELECTRICITY - FROM HYDROELECTRIC PLANTS:

31% of total installed capacity (2017 est.)

country comparison to the world: 67

ELECTRICITY - FROM OTHER RENEWABLE SOURCES:

28% of total installed capacity (2017 est.)

country comparison to the world: 23

CRUDE OIL - PRODUCTION:

9,600 bbl/day (2018 est.)

country comparison to the world: 78

CRUDE OIL - EXPORTS:

9,383 bbl/day (2017 est.)

country comparison to the world: 59

CRUDE OIL - IMPORTS:

0 bbl/day (2015 est.)

country comparison to the world: 136

CRUDE OIL - PROVED RESERVES:

83.07 million bbl (1 January 2018 est.)

country comparison to the world: 71

REFINED PETROLEUM PRODUCTS - PRODUCTION:

1,162 bbl/day (2015 est.)

country comparison to the world: 105

REFINED PETROLEUM PRODUCTS - CONSUMPTION:

89,000 bbl/day (2016 est.)

country comparison to the world: 84

REFINED PETROLEUM PRODUCTS - EXPORTS:

10,810 bbl/day (2015 est.)

country comparison to the world: 80

REFINED PETROLEUM PRODUCTS - IMPORTS:

97,900 bbl/day (2015 est.)

country comparison to the world: 55

NATURAL GAS - PRODUCTION:

0 cu m (2017 est.)

country comparison to the world: 141

NATURAL GAS - CONSUMPTION:

0 cu m (2017 est.)

country comparison to the world: 154

NATURAL GAS - EXPORTS:

0 cu m (2017 est.)

country comparison to the world: 116

NATURAL GAS - IMPORTS:

0 cu m (2017 est.)

country comparison to the world: 134

NATURAL GAS - PROVED RESERVES:

2.96 billion cu m (1 January 2006 est.)

country comparison to the world: 94

CARBON DIOXIDE EMISSIONS FROM CONSUMPTION OF ENERGY:

17.15 million Mt (2017 est.)

country comparison to the world: 91

COMMUNICATIONS :: GUATEMALA

TELEPHONES - FIXED LINES:

total subscriptions: 2,461,109

subscriptions per 100 inhabitants: 16 (2017 est.)

country comparison to the world: 54

TELEPHONES - MOBILE CELLULAR:

total subscriptions: 19,986,482

subscriptions per 100 inhabitants: 129 (2017 est.)

country comparison to the world: 57

TELEPHONE SYSTEM:

general assessment: fairly modern network centered in the city of Guatemala; one of the lowest teledensities in the region especially in the country; state-owned telecommunications company privatized in the late 1990s opened the way for competition; steady improvement of fixed-line which has also spurred growth in mobile-cellular and broadband; open regulatory framework coupled with competion and greater disposable household revenue spurs growth (2018)

domestic: fixed-line teledensity roughly 15 per 100 persons; fixed-line investments are being concentrated on improving rural connectivity; mobile-cellular teledensity about 129 per 100 persons (2018)

international: country code - 502; landing points for the ARCOS, AMX-1, American Movil-Texius West Coast Cable and the SAm-1 fiber-optic submarine cable system that, together, provide connectivity to South and Central America, parts of the Caribbean, and the US; connected to Central American Microwave System; satellite earth station - 1 Intelsat (Atlantic Ocean) (2019)

BROADCAST MEDIA:

4 privately owned national terrestrial TV channels dominate TV broadcasting; multi-channel satellite and cable services are available; 1 government-owned radio station and hundreds of privately owned radio stations (2019)

INTERNET COUNTRY CODE:

.gt

INTERNET USERS:

total: 5,241,952

percent of population: 34.5% (July 2016 est.)

country comparison to the world: 74

BROADBAND - FIXED SUBSCRIPTIONS:

total: 506,000

subscriptions per 100 inhabitants: 3 (2017 est.)

country comparison to the world: 81

MILITARY AND SECURITY :: GUATEMALA

MILITARY EXPENDITURES:

0.35% of GDP (2018)

0.36% of GDP (2017)

0.39% of GDP (2016)

0.43% of GDP (2015)

0.45% of GDP (2014)

country comparison to the world: 151

MILITARY AND SECURITY FORCES:

Army of Guatamala (Ejercito de Guatamala): Land Forces (Fuerzas de Tierra), Naval Forces (Fuerza de Mar), and Air Force (Fuerza de Aire). (2019)

MILITARY SERVICE AGE AND OBLIGATION:
all male citizens between the ages of 18 and 50 are eligible for military service; in practice, most of the force is volunteer, however, a selective draft system is employed, resulting in a small portion of 17-21 year-olds conscripted; conscript service obligation varies from 1 to 2 years; women can serve as officers (2013)

TRANSPORTATION :: GUATEMALA

NATIONAL AIR TRANSPORT SYSTEM:
number of registered air carriers: 3 (2015)

inventory of registered aircraft operated by air carriers: 8 (2015)

annual passenger traffic on registered air carriers: 93,129 (2015)

annual freight traffic on registered air carriers: 455,520 mt-km (2015)

CIVIL AIRCRAFT REGISTRATION COUNTRY CODE PREFIX:
TG (2016)

AIRPORTS:
291 (2013)

country comparison to the world: 23

AIRPORTS - WITH PAVED RUNWAYS:
total: 16 (2017)

2,438 to 3,047 m: 2 (2017)

1,524 to 2,437 m: 4 (2017)

914 to 1,523 m: 6 (2017)

under 914 m: 4 (2017)

AIRPORTS - WITH UNPAVED RUNWAYS:
total: 275 (2013)

2,438 to 3,047 m: 1 (2013)

1,524 to 2,437 m: 2 (2013)

914 to 1,523 m: 77 (2013)

under 914 m: 195 (2013)

HELIPORTS:
1 (2013)

PIPELINES:
480 km oil (2013)

RAILWAYS:
total: 800 km (2018)

narrow gauge: 800 km 0.914-m gauge (2018)

note: despite the existence of a railway network, all rail service was suspended in 2007 and no passenger or freight train currently runs in the country (2018)

country comparison to the world: 97

ROADWAYS:
total: 17,621 km (2016)

paved: 7,489 km (2016)

unpaved: 10,132 km (includes 4,960 km of rural roads) (2016)

country comparison to the world: 117

WATERWAYS:
990 km (260 km navigable year round; additional 730 km navigable during high-water season) (2012)

country comparison to the world: 65

MERCHANT MARINE:
total: 9

by type: oil tanker 1, other 8 (2018)

country comparison to the world: 155

PORTS AND TERMINALS:
major seaport(s): Puerto Quetzal, Santo Tomas de Castilla

TRANSNATIONAL ISSUES :: GUATEMALA

DISPUTES - INTERNATIONAL:
annual ministerial meetings under the Organization of American States-initiated Agreement on the Framework for Negotiations and Confidence Building Measures continue to address Guatemalan land and maritime claims in Belize and the Caribbean Sea; Guatemala persists in its territorial claim to half of Belize, but agrees to Line of Adjacency to keep Guatemalan squatters out of Belize's forested interior; both countries agreed in April 2012 to hold simultaneous referenda, scheduled for 6 October 2013, to decide whether to refer the dispute to the ICJ for binding resolution, but this vote was suspended indefinitely; Mexico must deal with thousands of impoverished Guatemalans and other Central Americans who cross the porous border looking for work in Mexico and the US

REFUGEES AND INTERNALLY DISPLACED PERSONS:
IDPs: 242,000 (more than three decades of internal conflict that ended in 1996 displaced mainly the indigenous Maya population and rural peasants; ongoing drug cartel and gang violence) (2018)

ILLICIT DRUGS:
major transit country for cocaine and heroin; it is estimated that 1,000 mt of cocaine are smuggled through the country each year, primarily destined for the US market; in 2016, the Guatamalan government estimated that an average of 4,500 hectares of opium poppy were being cultivated; marijuana cultivation for mostly domestic consumption; proximity to Mexico makes Guatemala a major staging area for drugs (particularly for cocaine); money laundering is a serious problem; corruption is a major problem

EUROPE :: GUERNSEY

INTRODUCTION :: GUERNSEY

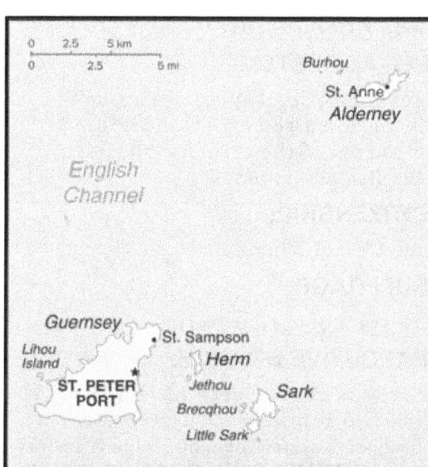

BACKGROUND:
Guernsey and the other Channel Islands represent the last remnants of the medieval Duchy of Normandy, which held sway in both France and England. The islands were the only British soil occupied by German troops in World War II. The Bailiwick of Guernsey is a self-governing British crown dependency that is not part of the United Kingdom. However, the UK Government is constitutionally responsible for its defense and international representation. The Bailiwick of Guernsey consists of the main island of Guernsey and a number of smaller islands including Alderney, Sark, Herm, Jethou, Brecqhou, and Lihou.

GEOGRAPHY :: GUERNSEY

LOCATION:
Western Europe, islands in the English Channel, northwest of France

GEOGRAPHIC COORDINATES:
49 28 N, 2 35 W

MAP REFERENCES:
Europe

AREA:
total: 78 sq km

land: 78 sq km

water: 0 sq km

note: includes Alderney, Guernsey, Herm, Sark, and some other smaller islands

country comparison to the world: 228

AREA - COMPARATIVE:
about one-half the size of Washington, DC

LAND BOUNDARIES:
0 km

COASTLINE:
50 km

MARITIME CLAIMS:
territorial sea: 3 nm

exclusive fishing zone: 12 nm

CLIMATE:
temperate with mild winters and cool summers; about 50% of days are overcast

TERRAIN:
mostly flat with low hills in southwest

ELEVATION:
lowest point: English Channel 0 m

highest point: Le Moulin on Sark 114 m

NATURAL RESOURCES:
cropland

IRRIGATED LAND:
NA

NATURAL HAZARDS:
very large tidal variation and fast currents can make local waters dangerous

ENVIRONMENT - CURRENT ISSUES:
coastal erosion, coastal flooding; declining biodiversity due to land abandonment and succession to scrub or woodland

GEOGRAPHY - NOTE:
large, deepwater harbor at Saint Peter Port

PEOPLE AND SOCIETY :: GUERNSEY

POPULATION:
66,697 (July 2018 est.)

country comparison to the world: 204

NATIONALITY:
noun: Channel Islander(s)

adjective: Channel Islander

ETHNIC GROUPS:
Guernsey 52%, UK and Ireland 23.7%, Portugal 2.1%, Latvia 1.5%, other 6.7%, unspecified 14.1%

note: data represent population by country of birth; the native population is of British and Norman-French descent

LANGUAGES:
English, French, Norman-French dialect spoken in country districts

RELIGIONS:
Protestant (Anglican, Presbyterian, Baptist, Congregational, Methodist), Roman Catholic

AGE STRUCTURE:
0-14 years: 14.51% (male 4,994 /female 4,686)

15-24 years: 10.89% (male 3,711 /female 3,553)

25-54 years: 41.41% (male 13,958 /female 13,658)

55-64 years: 13.38% (male 4,425 /female 4,496)

65 years and over: 19.81% (male 6,038 /female 7,178) (2018 est.)

DEPENDENCY RATIOS:

total dependency ratio: 47.1 (2015 est.)

youth dependency ratio: 21.6 (2015 est.)

elderly dependency ratio: 25.4 (2015 est.)

potential support ratio: 3.9 (2015 est.)

note: data represent the Guernsey and Jersey

MEDIAN AGE:

total: 44 years (2018 est.)

male: 42.7 years

female: 45.3 years

country comparison to the world: 14

POPULATION GROWTH RATE:

0.28% (2018 est.)

country comparison to the world: 174

BIRTH RATE:

9.8 births/1,000 population (2018 est.)

country comparison to the world: 194

DEATH RATE:

9 deaths/1,000 population (2018 est.)

country comparison to the world: 61

NET MIGRATION RATE:

2.1 migrant(s)/1,000 population (2018 est.)

country comparison to the world: 49

URBANIZATION:

urban population: 30.9% of total population (2019)

rate of urbanization: 0.46% annual rate of change (2015-20 est.)

note: data represent Guernsey and Jersey

MAJOR URBAN AREAS - POPULATION:

16,000 SAINT PETER PORT (capital) (2018)

SEX RATIO:

at birth: 1.05 male(s)/female

0-14 years: 1.07 male(s)/female

15-24 years: 1.04 male(s)/female

25-54 years: 1.02 male(s)/female

55-64 years: 0.98 male(s)/female

65 years and over: 0.84 male(s)/female

total population: 0.99 male(s)/female (2018 est.)

INFANT MORTALITY RATE:

total: 3.4 deaths/1,000 live births (2018 est.)

male: 3.7 deaths/1,000 live births

female: 3.1 deaths/1,000 live births

country comparison to the world: 203

LIFE EXPECTANCY AT BIRTH:

total population: 82.7 years (2018 est.)

male: 80 years

female: 85.5 years

country comparison to the world: 9

TOTAL FERTILITY RATE:

1.57 children born/woman (2018 est.)

country comparison to the world: 186

CURRENT HEALTH EXPENDITURE:

HIV/AIDS - ADULT PREVALENCE RATE:

NA

HIV/AIDS - PEOPLE LIVING WITH HIV/AIDS:

NA

HIV/AIDS - DEATHS:

NA

EDUCATION EXPENDITURES:

NA

GOVERNMENT :: GUERNSEY

COUNTRY NAME:

conventional long form: Bailiwick of Guernsey

conventional short form: Guernsey

former: Norman Isles

etymology: the name is of Old Norse origin, but the meaning of the root "Guern(s)" is uncertain; the "-ey" ending means "island"

DEPENDENCY STATUS:

British crown dependency

GOVERNMENT TYPE:

parliamentary democracy (States of Deliberation)

CAPITAL:

name: Saint Peter Port

geographic coordinates: 49 27 N, 2 32 W

time difference: UTC 0 (5 hours ahead of Washington, DC, during Standard Time)

daylight saving time: +1hr, begins last Sunday in March; ends last Sunday in October

etymology: Saint Peter Port is the name of the town and its surrounding parish; the "port" distinguishes this parish from that of Saint Peter on the other side of the island

ADMINISTRATIVE DIVISIONS:

none (British crown dependency); there are no first-order administrative divisions as defined by the US Government, but there are 10 parishes: Castel, Forest, Saint Andrew, Saint Martin, Saint Peter Port, Saint Pierre du Bois, Saint Sampson, Saint Saviour, Torteval, Vale

note: two additional parishes for Guernsey are sometimes listed - the parish of Saint Anne on the island of Alderney and the parish of Saint Peter on the island of Sark - but they are generally not included in the enumeration of parishes

INDEPENDENCE:

none (British crown dependency)

NATIONAL HOLIDAY:

Liberation Day, 9 May (1945)

CONSTITUTION:

history: unwritten; includes royal charters, statutes, and common law and practice

amendments: new laws or changes to existing laws are initiated by the States of Deliberation; passage requires majority vote (2018)

LEGAL SYSTEM:

customary legal system based on Norman customary law; includes elements of the French civil code and English common law

CITIZENSHIP:

see United Kingdom

SUFFRAGE:

16 years of age; universal

EXECUTIVE BRANCH:

chief of state: Queen ELIZABETH II (since 6 February 1952); represented by Lieutenant-Governor Vice Admiral Ian CORDER (since 14 March 2016)

head of government: Chief Minister Gavin ST PIER (since 6 May 2016); Bailiff Sir Richard COLLAS (since 23 March 2012); note - the chief minister is the president of the Policy and Resources Committee and is the de facto head of government; the Policy and Resources Committee, elected by the States of Deliberation, functions as the executive; the 5 members all have equal voting rights

cabinet: none

elections/appointments: the monarchy is hereditary; lieutenant governor and bailiff appointed by the monarch;

chief minister, who is the president of the Policy and Resources Committee indirectly elected by the States of Deliberation for a 4-year term; last held on 6 May 2016 (next to be held in 2020)

election results: Gavin ST PIER (independent) elected president of the Policy and Resources Committee and chief minister

LEGISLATIVE BRANCH:

description: unicameral States of Deliberation (40 seats; 38 People's Deputies and 2 representatives of the States of Alderney; members directly elected by majority vote to serve 4-year terms); note - non-voting members include the bailiff (presiding officer), attorney-general, and solicitor-general

elections: last held on 27 April 2016 (next to be held in 2020)

election results: percent of vote - NA; seats - independent 38; composition - men 27, women 13, percent of women 32.5%

JUDICIAL BRANCH:

highest courts: Guernsey Court of Appeal (consists of the Bailiff of Guernsey, who is the ex-officio president of the Guernsey Court of Appeal, and at least 12 judges); Royal Court (organized into 3 divisions - Full Court sits with 1 judge and 7 to 12 jurats acting as judges of fact, Ordinary Court sits with 1 judge and normally 3 jurats, and Matrimonial Causes Division sits with 1 judge and 4 jurats); note - appeals beyond Guernsey courts are heard by the Judicial Committee of the Privy Council (in London)

judge selection and term of office: Royal Court Bailiff, Deputy Bailiff, and Court of Appeal justices appointed by the British Crown and hold office at Her Majesty's pleasure; jurats elected by the States of Election, a body chaired by the Bailiff and a number of jurats

subordinate courts: Court of Alderney; Court of the Seneschal of Sark; Magistrates' Court (includes Juvenile Court); Contracts Court; Ecclesiastical Court; Court of Chief Pleas

POLITICAL PARTIES AND LEADERS:

none; all independents

INTERNATIONAL ORGANIZATION PARTICIPATION:

UPU

DIPLOMATIC REPRESENTATION IN THE US:

none (British crown dependency)

DIPLOMATIC REPRESENTATION FROM THE US:

none (British crown dependency)

FLAG DESCRIPTION:

white with the red cross of Saint George (patron saint of England) extending to the edges of the flag and a yellow equal-armed cross of William the Conqueror superimposed on the Saint George cross; the red cross represents the old ties with England and the fact that Guernsey is a British Crown dependency; the gold cross is a replica of the one used by Duke William of Normandy at the Battle of Hastings in 1066

NATIONAL SYMBOL(S):

Guernsey cow, donkey; national colors: red, white, yellow

NATIONAL ANTHEM:

name: "Sarnia Cherie" (Guernsey Dear)

lyrics/music: George DEIGHTON/Domencio SANTANGELO

note: adopted 1911; serves as a local anthem; as a British crown dependency, "God Save the Queen" is official (see United Kingdom)

ECONOMY :: GUERNSEY

ECONOMY - OVERVIEW:

Financial services accounted for about 21% of employment and about 32% of total income in 2016 in this tiny, prosperous Channel Island economy. Construction, manufacturing, and horticulture, mainly tomatoes and cut flowers, have been declining. Financial services, professional services, tourism, retail, and the public sector have been growing. Light tax and death duties make Guernsey a popular offshore financial center.

GDP (PURCHASING POWER PARITY):

$3.465 billion (2015 est.)

$3.451 billion (2014 est.)

$3.42 billion (2013 est.)

note: data are in 2015 dollars

country comparison to the world: 184

GDP (OFFICIAL EXCHANGE RATE):

$2.742 billion (2005 est.) (2005 est.)

GDP - REAL GROWTH RATE:

0.4% (2015 est.)

1.2% (2014 est.)

4.2% (2012 est.)

country comparison to the world: 193

GDP - PER CAPITA (PPP):

$52,500 (2014 est.)

country comparison to the world: 24

GDP - COMPOSITION, BY SECTOR OF ORIGIN:

agriculture: 3% (2000)

industry: 10% (2000)

services: 87% (2000)

AGRICULTURE - PRODUCTS:

tomatoes, greenhouse flowers, sweet peppers, eggplant, fruit; Guernsey cattle

INDUSTRIES:

tourism, banking

INDUSTRIAL PRODUCTION GROWTH RATE:

NA

LABOR FORCE:

31,470 (March 2006)

country comparison to the world: 203

UNEMPLOYMENT RATE:

1.2% (2016 est.)

country comparison to the world: 13

POPULATION BELOW POVERTY LINE:

NA

HOUSEHOLD INCOME OR CONSUMPTION BY PERCENTAGE SHARE:

lowest 10%: NA

highest 10%: NA

BUDGET:

revenues: 563.6 million (2005)

expenditures: 530.9 million (2005 est.)

TAXES AND OTHER REVENUES:

20.6% (of GDP) (2005)

country comparison to the world: 146

BUDGET SURPLUS (+) OR DEFICIT (-):

1.2% (of GDP) (2005)

country comparison to the world: 29

FISCAL YEAR:

calendar year

INFLATION RATE (CONSUMER PRICES):

3.4% (June 2006 est.)

country comparison to the world: 141

EXPORTS:

NA

EXPORTS - COMMODITIES:

tomatoes, flowers and ferns, sweet peppers, eggplant, other vegetables

IMPORTS:

NA

IMPORTS - COMMODITIES:

coal, gasoline, oil, machinery, and equipment

DEBT - EXTERNAL:

NA

EXCHANGE RATES:

Guernsey pound per US dollar

0.7836 (2017 est.)

0.738 (2016 est.)

0.738 (2015)

0.6542 (2014)

0.607 (2013)

ENERGY :: GUERNSEY

ELECTRICITY ACCESS:

electrification - total population: 100% (2016)

COMMUNICATIONS :: GUERNSEY

TELEPHONES - FIXED LINES:

total subscriptions: 36,547

subscriptions per 100 inhabitants: 60 (July 2016 est.)

country comparison to the world: 164

TELEPHONES - MOBILE CELLULAR:

total subscriptions: 71,249

subscriptions per 100 inhabitants: 113 (July 2016 est.)

country comparison to the world: 197

TELEPHONE SYSTEM:

general assessment: high performance global connections with quality service; connections to major cities around the world to rival and attract future investment and future needs of islanders and businesses (2018)

domestic: fixed-line 60 per 100 and mobile-cellular 113 per 100 persons (2018)

international: country code - 44; landing points for Guernsey-Jersey, HUGO, INGRID, Channel Islands -9 Liberty and UK-Channel Islands-7 submarine cable to UK and France (2019)

BROADCAST MEDIA:

multiple UK terrestrial TV broadcasts are received via a transmitter in Jersey with relays in Jersey, Guernsey, and Alderney; satellite packages are available; BBC Radio Guernsey and 1 other radio station operating

INTERNET COUNTRY CODE:

.gg

INTERNET USERS:

total: 55,050

percent of population: 83.3% (July 2016 est.)

country comparison to the world: 190

MILITARY AND SECURITY :: GUERNSEY

MILITARY - NOTE:

defense is the responsibility of the UK

TRANSPORTATION :: GUERNSEY

NATIONAL AIR TRANSPORT SYSTEM:

number of registered air carriers: 2 (registered in UK) (2015)

inventory of registered aircraft operated by air carriers: 11 (registered in UK) (2015)

AIRPORTS:

2 (2013)

country comparison to the world: 200

AIRPORTS - WITH PAVED RUNWAYS:

total: 2 (2019)

1,524 to 2,437 m: 1

under 914 m: 1

ROADWAYS:

total: 260 km (2017)

country comparison to the world: 198

PORTS AND TERMINALS:

major seaport(s): Braye Bay, Saint Peter Port

TRANSNATIONAL ISSUES :: GUERNSEY

DISPUTES - INTERNATIONAL:

none

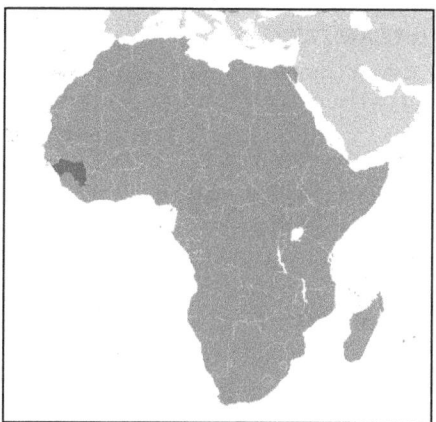

AFRICA :: GUINEA

INTRODUCTION :: GUINEA

BACKGROUND:

Guinea is at a turning point after decades of authoritarian rule since gaining its independence from France in 1958. Sekou TOURE ruled the country as president from independence to his death in 1984. Lansana CONTE came to power in 1984 when the military seized the government after TOURE's death. Gen. CONTE organized and won presidential elections in 1993, 1998, and 2003, though results were questionable due to a lack in transparency and neutrality in the electoral process. Upon CONTE's death in December 2008, Capt. Moussa Dadis CAMARA led a military coup, seizing power and suspending the constitution. His unwillingness to yield to domestic and international pressure to step down led to heightened political tensions that peaked in September 2009 when presidential guards opened fire on an opposition rally killing more than 150 people. In early December 2009, CAMARA was wounded in an assassination attempt and exiled to Burkina Faso. A transitional government led by Gen. Sekouba KONATE paved the way for Guinea's transition to a fledgling democracy. The country held its first free and competitive democratic presidential and legislative elections in 2010 and 2013 respectively, and in October 2015 held a second consecutive presidential election. Alpha CONDE was reelected to a second five-year term as president in 2015, and the National Assembly was seated in January 2014. CONDE's first cabinet is the first all-civilian government in Guinea. The country held a successful political dialogue in August and September 2016 that brought together the government and opposition to address long-standing tensions. Local elections were held in February 2018, and disputed results in some of the races resulted in ongoing protests against CONDE's government.

GEOGRAPHY :: GUINEA

LOCATION:
Western Africa, bordering the North Atlantic Ocean, between Guinea-Bissau and Sierra Leone

GEOGRAPHIC COORDINATES:
11 00 N, 10 00 W

MAP REFERENCES:
Africa

AREA:
total: 245,857 sq km

land: 245,717 sq km

water: 140 sq km

country comparison to the world: 80

AREA - COMPARATIVE:
slightly smaller than Oregon; slightly larger than twice the size of Pennsylvania

LAND BOUNDARIES:
total: 4,046 km

border countries (6): Cote d'Ivoire 816 km, Guinea-Bissau 421 km, Liberia 590 km, Mali 1062 km, Senegal 363 km, Sierra Leone 794 km

COASTLINE:
320 km

MARITIME CLAIMS:
territorial sea: 12 nm

exclusive economic zone: 200 nm

CLIMATE:
generally hot and humid; monsoonal-type rainy season (June to November) with southwesterly winds; dry season (December to May) with northeasterly harmattan winds

TERRAIN:
generally flat coastal plain, hilly to mountainous interior

ELEVATION:
mean elevation: 472 m

lowest point: Atlantic Ocean 0 m

highest point: Mont Nimba 1,752 m

NATURAL RESOURCES:
bauxite, iron ore, diamonds, gold, uranium, hydropower, fish, salt

LAND USE:
agricultural land: 58.1% (2011 est.)

arable land: 11.8% (2011 est.) / permanent crops: 2.8% (2011 est.) / permanent pasture: 43.5% (2011 est.)

forest: 26.5% (2011 est.)

other: 15.4% (2011 est.)

IRRIGATED LAND:
950 sq km (2012)

POPULATION DISTRIBUTION:
areas of highest density are in the west and south; interior is sparsely populated

NATURAL HAZARDS:
hot, dry, dusty harmattan haze may reduce visibility during dry season

ENVIRONMENT - CURRENT ISSUES:
deforestation; inadequate potable water; desertification; soil contamination and erosion;

overfishing, overpopulation in forest region; poor mining practices lead to environmental damage; water pollution; improper waste disposal

ENVIRONMENT - INTERNATIONAL AGREEMENTS:

party to: Biodiversity, Climate Change, Climate Change-Kyoto Protocol, Desertification, Endangered Species, Hazardous Wastes, Law of the Sea, Ozone Layer Protection, Ship Pollution, Wetlands, Whaling

signed, but not ratified: none of the selected agreements

GEOGRAPHY - NOTE:

the Niger and its important tributary the Milo River have their sources in the Guinean highlands

PEOPLE AND SOCIETY :: GUINEA

POPULATION:

11,855,411 (July 2018 est.)

country comparison to the world: 75

NATIONALITY:

noun: Guinean(s)

adjective: Guinean

ETHNIC GROUPS:

Fulani (Peuhl) 33.4%, Malinke 29.4%, Susu 21.2%, Guerze 7.8%, Kissi 6.2%, Toma 1.6%, other/foreign .4% (2018 est.)

LANGUAGES:

French (official), Pular, Maninka, Susu, other native languages

note: about 40 languages are spoken; each ethnic group has its own language

RELIGIONS:

Muslim 89.1%, Christian 6.8%, animist 1.6%, other .1%, none 2.4% (2014 est.)

DEMOGRAPHIC PROFILE:

Guinea's strong population growth is a result of declining mortality rates and sustained elevated fertility. The population growth rate was somewhat tempered in the 2000s because of a period of net outmigration. Although life expectancy and mortality rates have improved over the last two decades, the nearly universal practice of female genital cutting continues to contribute to high infant and maternal mortality rates. Guinea's total fertility remains high at about 5 children per woman because of the ongoing preference for larger families, low contraceptive usage and availability, a lack of educational attainment and empowerment among women, and poverty. A lack of literacy and vocational training programs limit job prospects for youths, but even those with university degrees often have no option but to work in the informal sector. About 60% of the country's large youth population is unemployed.

Tensions and refugees have spilled over Guinea's borders with Sierra Leone, Liberia, and Cote d'Ivoire. During the 1990s Guinea harbored as many as half a million refugees from Sierra Leone and Liberia, more refugees than any other African country for much of that decade. About half sought refuge in the volatile "Parrot's Beak" region of southwest Guinea, a wedge of land jutting into Sierra Leone near the Liberian border. Many were relocated within Guinea in the early 2000s because the area suffered repeated cross-border attacks from various government and rebel forces, as well as anti-refugee violence.

AGE STRUCTURE:

0-14 years: 41.4% (male 2,473,486 /female 2,435,139)

15-24 years: 19.23% (male 1,145,488 /female 1,134,103)

25-54 years: 30.8% (male 1,827,246 /female 1,824,162)

55-64 years: 4.72% (male 269,995 /female 289,164)

65 years and over: 3.85% (male 203,754 /female 252,874) (2018 est.)

DEPENDENCY RATIOS:

total dependency ratio: 84.2 (2015 est.)

youth dependency ratio: 78.6 (2015 est.)

elderly dependency ratio: 5.6 (2015 est.)

potential support ratio: 17.8 (2015 est.)

MEDIAN AGE:

total: 19 years (2018 est.)

male: 18.8 years

female: 19.3 years

country comparison to the world: 204

POPULATION GROWTH RATE:

2.75% (2018 est.)

country comparison to the world: 13

BIRTH RATE:

36.4 births/1,000 population (2018 est.)

country comparison to the world: 16

DEATH RATE:

8.9 deaths/1,000 population (2018 est.)

country comparison to the world: 64

NET MIGRATION RATE:

0 migrant(s)/1,000 population (2018 est.)

country comparison to the world: 85

POPULATION DISTRIBUTION:

areas of highest density are in the west and south; interior is sparsely populated

URBANIZATION:

urban population: 36.5% of total population (2019)

rate of urbanization: 3.54% annual rate of change (2015-20 est.)

MAJOR URBAN AREAS - POPULATION:

1.889 million CONAKRY (capital) (2019)

SEX RATIO:

at birth: 1.03 male(s)/female

0-14 years: 1.02 male(s)/female

15-24 years: 1.01 male(s)/female

25-54 years: 1 male(s)/female

55-64 years: 0.93 male(s)/female

65 years and over: 0.81 male(s)/female

total population: 1 male(s)/female (2018 est.)

MOTHER'S MEAN AGE AT FIRST BIRTH:

19.5 years (2018 est.)

note: median age at first birth among women 25-29

MATERNAL MORTALITY RATE:

576 deaths/100,000 live births (2017 est.)

country comparison to the world: 14

INFANT MORTALITY RATE:

total: 55.3 deaths/1,000 live births (2018 est.)

male: 60.4 deaths/1,000 live births

female: 50.1 deaths/1,000 live births

country comparison to the world: 19

LIFE EXPECTANCY AT BIRTH:

total population: 62.1 years (2018 est.)

male: 60.4 years

female: 64 years

country comparison to the world: 201

TOTAL FERTILITY RATE:

4.98 children born/woman (2018 est.)

country comparison to the world: 14

CONTRACEPTIVE PREVALENCE RATE:

8.7% (2016)

DRINKING WATER SOURCE:

improved:

urban: 92.7% of population

rural: 67.4% of population

total: 76.8% of population

unimproved:

urban: 7.3% of population

rural: 32.6% of population

total: 23.2% of population (2015 est.)

CURRENT HEALTH EXPENDITURE:

5.5% (2016)

PHYSICIANS DENSITY:

0.08 physicians/1,000 population (2016)

HOSPITAL BED DENSITY:

0.3 beds/1,000 population (2011)

SANITATION FACILITY ACCESS:

improved:

urban: 34.1% of population (2015 est.)

rural: 11.8% of population (2015 est.)

total: 20.1% of population (2015 est.)

unimproved:

urban: 65.9% of population (2015 est.)

rural: 88.2% of population (2015 est.)

total: 79.9% of population (2015 est.)

HIV/AIDS - ADULT PREVALENCE RATE:

1.4% (2018 est.)

country comparison to the world: 34

HIV/AIDS - PEOPLE LIVING WITH HIV/AIDS:

120,000 (2018 est.)

country comparison to the world: 40

HIV/AIDS - DEATHS:

4,300 (2018 est.)

country comparison to the world: 30

MAJOR INFECTIOUS DISEASES:

degree of risk: very high (2016)

food or waterborne diseases: bacterial and protozoal diarrhea, hepatitis A, and typhoid fever (2016)

vectorborne diseases: malaria, dengue fever, and yellow fever (2016)

water contact diseases: schistosomiasis (2016)

animal contact diseases: rabies (2016)

aerosolized dust or soil contact diseases: Lassa fever (2016)

OBESITY - ADULT PREVALENCE RATE:

7.7% (2016)

country comparison to the world: 158

CHILDREN UNDER THE AGE OF 5 YEARS UNDERWEIGHT:

18.3% (2016)

country comparison to the world: 31

EDUCATION EXPENDITURES:

2.2% of GDP (2017)

country comparison to the world: 165

LITERACY:

definition: age 15 and over can read and write

total population: 30.4%

male: 38.1%

female: 22.8% (2015 est.)

SCHOOL LIFE EXPECTANCY (PRIMARY TO TERTIARY EDUCATION):

total: 9 years

male: 10 years

female: 8 years (2014)

UNEMPLOYMENT, YOUTH AGES 15-24:

total: 1%

male: 1.5%

female: 0.6% (2012 est.)

country comparison to the world: 178

GOVERNMENT :: GUINEA

COUNTRY NAME:

conventional long form: Republic of Guinea

conventional short form: Guinea

local long form: Republique de Guinee

local short form: Guinee

former: French Guinea

etymology: the country is named after the Guinea region of West Africa that lies along the Gulf of Guinea and stretches north to the Sahel

GOVERNMENT TYPE:

presidential republic

CAPITAL:

name: Conakry

geographic coordinates: 9 30 N, 13 42 W

time difference: UTC 0 (5 hours ahead of Washington, DC, during Standard Time)

ADMINISTRATIVE DIVISIONS:

7 regions administrative and 1 gouvenorat*; Boke, Conakry*, Faranah, Kankan, Kindia, Labe, Mamou, N'Zerekore

INDEPENDENCE:

2 October 1958 (from France)

NATIONAL HOLIDAY:

Independence Day, 2 October (1958)

CONSTITUTION:

history: previous 1958, 1990; latest promulgated 19 April 2010, approved 7 May 2010

amendments: proposed by the National Assembly or by the president of the republic; consideration of proposals requires approval by simple majority vote by the Assembly; passage requires approval in referendum; the president can opt to submit amendments directly to the Assembly, in which case approval requires at least two-thirds majority vote (2017)

LEGAL SYSTEM:

civil law system based on the French model

INTERNATIONAL LAW ORGANIZATION PARTICIPATION:

accepts compulsory ICJ jurisdiction with reservations; accepts ICCt jurisdiction

CITIZENSHIP:

citizenship by birth: no

citizenship by descent only: at least one parent must be a citizen of Guinea

dual citizenship recognized: no

residency requirement for naturalization: na

SUFFRAGE:

18 years of age; universal

EXECUTIVE BRANCH:

chief of state: President Alpha CONDE (since 21 December 2010)

head of government: Prime Minister Ibrahima FOFANA (since 22 May 2018)

cabinet: Council of Ministers appointed by the president

elections/appointments: president directly elected by absolute majority popular vote in 2 rounds if needed for a 5-year term (eligible for a second term); election last held on 11 October 2015 (next to be held in 2020); prime minister appointed by the president

election results: Alpha CONDE reelected president in the first round; percent of vote - Alpha CONDE (RPG) 57.8%, Cellou Dalein DIALLO (UFDG) 31.4%, other 10.8%

LEGISLATIVE BRANCH:

description: unicameral People's National Assembly or Assemblee Nationale Populaire (114 seats; 76 members directly elected in a single nationwide constituency by proportional representation vote and 38 directly elected in single-seat constituencies by simple majority vote; members serve 5-year terms)

elections: last held on 28 September 2013 (next was schelduled for January 2019, but postponed indefinitely)

election results: percent of vote by party - NA; seats by party - RPG 53, UFDG 37, UFR 10, PEDN 2, UPG 2, other 10; composition - men 89, women 25, percent of women 21.9%

JUDICIAL BRANCH:

highest courts: Supreme Court or Cour Supreme (organized into Administrative Chamber and Civil, Penal, and Social Chamber; court consists of the first president, 2 chamber presidents, 10 councilors, the solicitor general, and NA deputies); Constitutional Court (consists of 9 members)

judge selection and term of office: Supreme Court first president appointed by the national president after consultation with the National Assembly; other members appointed by presidential decree; members serve until age 65; Constitutional Court member appointments - 2 by the National Assembly and the president of the republic, 3 experienced judges designated by their peers, 1 experienced lawyer, 1 university professor with expertise in public law designated by peers, and 2 experienced representatives of the Independent National Institution of Human Rights; members serve single 9-year terms

subordinate courts: Court of Appeal or Cour d'Appel; High Court of Justice or Cour d'Assises; Court of Account (Court of Auditors); Courts of First Instance (Tribunal de Premiere Instance); labor court; military tribunal; justices of the peace; specialized courts

POLITICAL PARTIES AND LEADERS:

Bloc Liberal or BL [Faya MILLIMONO]
National Party for Hope and Development or PEDN [Lansana KOUYATE]
Rally for the Guinean People or RPG [Alpha CONDE]
Union for the Progress of Guinea or UPG
Union of Democratic Forces of Guinea or UFDG [Cellou Dalein DIALLO]
Union of Republican Forces or UFR [Sidya TOURE]

INTERNATIONAL ORGANIZATION PARTICIPATION:

ACP, AfDB, AU, ECOWAS, EITI (compliant country), FAO, G-77, IBRD, ICAO, ICCt, ICRM, IDA, IDB, IFAD, IFC, IFRCS, ILO, IMF, IMO, Interpol, IOC, IOM, IPU, ISO (correspondent), ITSO, ITU, ITUC (NGOs), MIGA, MINURSO, MINUSMA, MONUSCO, NAM, OIC, OIF, OPCW, UN, UNCTAD, UNESCO, UNHCR, UNIDO, UNISFA, UNMISS, UNOCI, UNWTO, UPU, WCO, WFTU (NGOs), WHO, WIPO, WMO, WTO

DIPLOMATIC REPRESENTATION IN THE US:

Ambassador Kerfalla YANSANE (since 24 January 2018)

chancery: 2112 Leroy Place NW, Washington, DC 20008

telephone: [1] (202) 986-4300

FAX: [1] (202) 986-3800

DIPLOMATIC REPRESENTATION FROM THE US:

chief of mission: Ambassador Simon HENSHAW (since 4 March 2019)

telephone: [224] 655-10-40-00

embassy: Transversale #2, Center Administratif de Koloma, Commune de Ratoma, Conakry

mailing address: P.O. Box 603, Transversale No. 2, Centre Administratif de Koloma, Commune de Ratoma, Conakry

FAX: [224] 655-10-42-97

FLAG DESCRIPTION:

three equal vertical bands of red (hoist side), yellow, and green; red represents the people's sacrifice for liberation and work; yellow stands for the sun, for the riches of the earth, and for justice; green symbolizes the country's vegetation and unity

note: uses the popular Pan-African colors of Ethiopia; the colors from left to right are the reverse of those on the flags of neighboring Mali and Senegal

NATIONAL SYMBOL(S):

elephant; national colors: red, yellow, green

NATIONAL ANTHEM:

name: "Liberte" (Liberty)

lyrics/music: unknown/Fodeba KEITA

note: adopted 1958

ECONOMY :: GUINEA

ECONOMY - OVERVIEW:

Guinea is a poor country of approximately 12.9 million people in 2016 that possesses the world's largest reserves of bauxite and largest untapped high-grade iron ore reserves, as well as gold and diamonds. In addition, Guinea has fertile soil, ample rainfall, and is the source of several West African rivers, including the Senegal, Niger, and Gambia. Guinea's hydro potential is enormous and the country could be a major exporter of electricity. The country also has tremendous agriculture potential. Gold, bauxite, and diamonds are Guinea's main exports. International investors have shown interest in Guinea's unexplored mineral reserves, which have the potential to propel Guinea's future growth.

Following the death of long-term President Lansana CONTE in 2008 and the coup that followed, international donors, including the G-8, the IMF, and the World Bank, significantly curtailed their development programs in Guinea. However, the IMF approved a 3-year Extended Credit Facility arrangement in 2012, following the December 2010 presidential elections. In September 2012, Guinea achieved Heavily Indebted Poor Countries completion point status. Future access to international assistance and investment will depend on the government's ability to be transparent, combat corruption, reform its banking system, improve its business environment, and build infrastructure. In April 2013, the government amended its mining code to reduce taxes and royalties. In 2014, Guinea complied with requirements of the

Extractive Industries Transparency Initiative by publishing its mining contracts. Guinea completed its program with the IMF in October 2016 even though some targeted reforms have been delayed. Currently Guinea is negotiating a new IMF program which will be based on Guinea's new five-year economic plan, focusing on the development of higher value-added products, including from the agro-business sector and development of the rural economy.

Political instability, a reintroduction of the Ebola virus epidemic, low international commodity prices, and an enduring legacy of corruption, inefficiency, and lack of government transparency are factors that could impact Guinea's future growth. Economic recovery will be a long process while the government adjusts to lower inflows of international donor aid following the surge of Ebola-related emergency support. Ebola stalled promising economic growth in the 2014-15 period and impeded several projects, such as offshore oil exploration and the Simandou iron ore project. The economy, however, grew by 6.6% in 2016 and 6.7% in 2017, mainly due to growth from bauxite mining and thermal energy generation as well as the resiliency of the agricultural sector. The 240-megawatt Kaleta Dam, inaugurated in September 2015, has expanded access to electricity for residents of Conakry. An combined with fears of Ebola virus, continue to undermine Guinea's economic viability.

Guinea's iron ore industry took a hit in 2016 when investors in the Simandou iron ore project announced plans to divest from the project. In 2017, agriculture output and public investment boosted economic growth, while the mining sector continued to play a prominent role in economic performance.

Successive governments have failed to address the country's crumbling infrastructure. Guinea suffers from chronic electricity shortages; poor roads, rail lines and bridges; and a lack of access to clean water - all of which continue to plague economic development. The present government, led by President Alpha CONDE, is working to create an environment to attract foreign investment and hopes to have greater participation from western countries and firms in Guinea's economic development.

GDP (PURCHASING POWER PARITY):
$27.97 billion (2017 est.)

$25.84 billion (2016 est.)

$23.39 billion (2015 est.)

   note: data are in 2017 dollars

   country comparison to the world: 138

GDP (OFFICIAL EXCHANGE RATE):
$10.25 billion (2017 est.)

GDP - REAL GROWTH RATE:
8.2% (2017 est.)

10.5% (2016 est.)

3.8% (2015 est.)

   country comparison to the world: 8

GDP - PER CAPITA (PPP):
$2,200 (2017 est.)

$2,000 (2016 est.)

$1,900 (2015 est.)

   note: data are in 2017 dollars

   country comparison to the world: 205

GROSS NATIONAL SAVING:
5.1% of GDP (2017 est.)

-6.3% of GDP (2016 est.)

-5.3% of GDP (2015 est.)

   country comparison to the world: 176

GDP - COMPOSITION, BY END USE:
   household consumption: 80.8% (2017 est.)

   government consumption: 6.6% (2017 est.)

   investment in fixed capital: 9.1% (2017 est.)

   investment in inventories: 18.5% (2017 est.)

   exports of goods and services: 21.9% (2017 est.)

   imports of goods and services: -36.9% (2017 est.)

GDP - COMPOSITION, BY SECTOR OF ORIGIN:
   agriculture: 19.8% (2017 est.)

   industry: 32.1% (2017 est.)

   services: 48.1% (2017 est.)

AGRICULTURE - PRODUCTS:
rice, coffee, pineapples, mangoes, palm kernels, cocoa, cassava (manioc, tapioca), bananas, potatoes, sweet potatoes; cattle, sheep, goats; timber

INDUSTRIES:
bauxite, gold, diamonds, iron ore; light manufacturing, agricultural processing

INDUSTRIAL PRODUCTION GROWTH RATE:
11% (2017 est.)

   country comparison to the world: 9

LABOR FORCE:
5.558 million (2017 est.)

   country comparison to the world: 75

LABOR FORCE - BY OCCUPATION:
   agriculture: 76%

   industry: 24% (2006 est.)

UNEMPLOYMENT RATE:
2.7% (2017 est.)

2.8% (2016 est.)

   country comparison to the world: 28

POPULATION BELOW POVERTY LINE:
47% (2006 est.)

HOUSEHOLD INCOME OR CONSUMPTION BY PERCENTAGE SHARE:
   lowest 10%: 2.7%

   highest 10%: 30.3% (2007)

DISTRIBUTION OF FAMILY INCOME - GINI INDEX:
39.4 (2007)

40.3 (1994)

   country comparison to the world: 72

BUDGET:
   revenues: 1.7 billion (2017 est.)

   expenditures: 1.748 billion (2017 est.)

TAXES AND OTHER REVENUES:
16.6% (of GDP) (2017 est.)

   country comparison to the world: 178

BUDGET SURPLUS (+) OR DEFICIT (-):
-0.5% (of GDP) (2017 est.)

   country comparison to the world: 61

PUBLIC DEBT:
37.9% of GDP (2017 est.)

41.8% of GDP (2016 est.)

   country comparison to the world: 137

FISCAL YEAR:
calendar year

INFLATION RATE (CONSUMER PRICES):
8.9% (2017 est.)

8.2% (2016 est.)

   country comparison to the world: 200

CENTRAL BANK DISCOUNT RATE:

22.25% (31 December 2005)

country comparison to the world: 2

COMMERCIAL BANK PRIME LENDING RATE:

22.2% (31 December 2017 est.)

22.2% (31 December 2016 est.)

country comparison to the world: 10

STOCK OF NARROW MONEY:

$1.84 billion (31 December 2017 est.)

$1.61 billion (31 December 2016 est.)

country comparison to the world: 135

STOCK OF BROAD MONEY:

$1.84 billion (31 December 2017 est.)

$1.61 billion (31 December 2016 est.)

country comparison to the world: 144

STOCK OF DOMESTIC CREDIT:

$1.762 billion (31 December 2017 est.)

$1.931 billion (31 December 2016 est.)

country comparison to the world: 157

MARKET VALUE OF PUBLICLY TRADED SHARES:

NA

CURRENT ACCOUNT BALANCE:

-$705 million (2017 est.)

-$2.705 billion (2016 est.)

country comparison to the world: 128

EXPORTS:

$3.514 billion (2017 est.)

$1.954 billion (2016 est.)

country comparison to the world: 124

EXPORTS - PARTNERS:

China 35.8%, Ghana 20.1%, UAE 11.6%, India 4.3% (2017)

EXPORTS - COMMODITIES:

bauxite, gold, diamonds, coffee, fish, agricultural products

IMPORTS:

$4.799 billion (2017 est.)

$4.43 billion (2016 est.)

country comparison to the world: 133

IMPORTS - COMMODITIES:

petroleum products, metals, machinery, transport equipment, textiles, grain and other foodstuffs

IMPORTS - PARTNERS:

Netherlands 17.2%, China 13.2%, India 11.8%, Belgium 10%, France 6.9%, UAE 4.5% (2017)

RESERVES OF FOREIGN EXCHANGE AND GOLD:

$331.8 million (31 December 2017 est.)

$383.4 million (31 December 2016 est.)

country comparison to the world: 165

DEBT - EXTERNAL:

$1.458 billion (31 December 2017 est.)

$1.462 billion (31 December 2016 est.)

country comparison to the world: 160

STOCK OF DIRECT FOREIGN INVESTMENT - AT HOME:

$3.174 billion (31 December 2017 est.)

$2.391 billion (31 December 2016 est.)

country comparison to the world: 114

STOCK OF DIRECT FOREIGN INVESTMENT - ABROAD:

$1.8 million (31 December 2017 est.)

$69.19 million (31 December 2016 est.)

country comparison to the world: 118

EXCHANGE RATES:

Guinean francs (GNF) per US dollar -

9,230 (2017 est.)

9,085 (2016 est.)

9,085 (2015 est.)

7,485.5 (2014 est.)

7,014.1 (2013 est.)

ENERGY :: GUINEA

ELECTRICITY ACCESS:

population without electricity: 11 million (2017)

electrification - total population: 33.5% (2016)

electrification - urban areas: 82.2% (2016)

electrification - rural areas: 6.9% (2016)

ELECTRICITY - PRODUCTION:

598 million kWh (2016 est.)

country comparison to the world: 162

ELECTRICITY - CONSUMPTION:

556.1 million kWh (2016 est.)

country comparison to the world: 168

ELECTRICITY - EXPORTS:

0 kWh (2016 est.)

country comparison to the world: 144

ELECTRICITY - IMPORTS:

0 kWh (2016 est.)

country comparison to the world: 156

ELECTRICITY - INSTALLED GENERATING CAPACITY:

550,000 kW (2016 est.)

country comparison to the world: 145

ELECTRICITY - FROM FOSSIL FUELS:

33% of total installed capacity (2016 est.)

country comparison to the world: 182

ELECTRICITY - FROM NUCLEAR FUELS:

0% of total installed capacity (2017 est.)

country comparison to the world: 103

ELECTRICITY - FROM HYDROELECTRIC PLANTS:

67% of total installed capacity (2017 est.)

country comparison to the world: 20

ELECTRICITY - FROM OTHER RENEWABLE SOURCES:

0% of total installed capacity (2017 est.)

country comparison to the world: 190

CRUDE OIL - PRODUCTION:

0 bbl/day (2018 est.)

country comparison to the world: 145

CRUDE OIL - EXPORTS:

0 bbl/day (2015 est.)

country comparison to the world: 133

CRUDE OIL - IMPORTS:

0 bbl/day (2015 est.)

country comparison to the world: 137

CRUDE OIL - PROVED RESERVES:

0 bbl (1 January 2018 est.)

country comparison to the world: 141

REFINED PETROLEUM PRODUCTS - PRODUCTION:

0 bbl/day (2017 est.)

country comparison to the world: 153

REFINED PETROLEUM PRODUCTS - CONSUMPTION:

19,000 bbl/day (2016 est.)

country comparison to the world: 143

REFINED PETROLEUM PRODUCTS - EXPORTS:

0 bbl/day (2015 est.)

country comparison to the world: 162

REFINED PETROLEUM PRODUCTS - IMPORTS:

18,460 bbl/day (2015 est.)

country comparison to the world: 128

NATURAL GAS - PRODUCTION:

0 cu m (2017 est.)

country comparison to the world: 142

NATURAL GAS - CONSUMPTION:

0 cu m (2017 est.)

country comparison to the world: 155

NATURAL GAS - EXPORTS:

0 cu m (2017 est.)

country comparison to the world: 117

NATURAL GAS - IMPORTS:
0 cu m (2017 est.)

country comparison to the world: 135

NATURAL GAS - PROVED RESERVES:
0 cu m (1 January 2014 est.)

country comparison to the world: 143

CARBON DIOXIDE EMISSIONS FROM CONSUMPTION OF ENERGY:
2.794 million Mt (2017 est.)

country comparison to the world: 149

COMMUNICATIONS :: GUINEA

TELEPHONES - FIXED LINES:
total subscriptions: 0

subscriptions per 100 inhabitants: less than 1 (2017 est.)

country comparison to the world: 219

TELEPHONES - MOBILE CELLULAR:
total subscriptions: 10.8 million

subscriptions per 100 inhabitants: 87 (July 2016 est.)

country comparison to the world: 81

TELEPHONE SYSTEM:
general assessment: huge improvement over the last ten years; in May 2019, 4G wifi was launched in the capital; the capital and the regional administrative centers have 3G access; in 2018 the set up of an IXP (Internet Exchange Point) will reduce cost of Internet bandwidth and improve infrastructure (2018)

domestic: there is national coverage and Conakry is reasonably well-served; coverage elsewhere remains inadequate but is improving; fixed-line teledensity less than 1 per 100 persons; mobile-cellular subscribership is expanding rapidly and now approaches 90 per 100 persons (2018)

international: country code - 224; ACE submarine cable connecting Guinea with 20 landing points in Western and South Africa and Europe; satellite earth station - 1 Intelsat (Atlantic Ocean (2019)

BROADCAST MEDIA:
government maintains marginal control over broadcast media; single state-run TV station; state-run radio broadcast station also operates several stations in rural areas; a dozen private television stations; a steadily increasing number of privately owned radio stations, nearly all in Conakry, and about a dozen community radio stations; foreign TV programming available via satellite and cable subscription services

(2019)

INTERNET COUNTRY CODE:
.gn

INTERNET USERS:
total: 1,185,148

percent of population: 9.8% (July 2016 est.)

country comparison to the world: 129

BROADBAND - FIXED SUBSCRIPTIONS:
total: 1,100

subscriptions per 100 inhabitants: less than 1 (2017 est.)

country comparison to the world: 190

MILITARY AND SECURITY :: GUINEA

MILITARY EXPENDITURES:
2.47% of GDP (2018)

2.71% of GDP (2017)

2.49% of GDP (2016)

3.31% of GDP (2015)

2.97% of GDP (2014)

country comparison to the world: 33

MILITARY AND SECURITY FORCES:
National Armed Forces: Army, Guinean Navy (Armee de Mer or Marine Guineenne, includes Marines), Guinean Air Force (Force Aerienne de Guinee), Republican Guard, Gendarmerie, People's Militia (Reserves) (2019)

MILITARY SERVICE AGE AND OBLIGATION:
no compulsory military service (2017)

TRANSPORTATION :: GUINEA

CIVIL AIRCRAFT REGISTRATION COUNTRY CODE PREFIX:
3X (2016)

AIRPORTS:
16 (2013)

country comparison to the world: 143

AIRPORTS - WITH PAVED RUNWAYS:
total: 4 (2017)

over 3,047 m: 1 (2017)

1,524 to 2,437 m: 3 (2017)

AIRPORTS - WITH UNPAVED RUNWAYS:
total: 12 (2013)

1,524 to 2,437 m: 7 (2013)

914 to 1,523 m: 3 (2013)

under 914 m: 2 (2013)

RAILWAYS:
total: 1,086 km (2017)

standard gauge: 279 km 1.435-m gauge (2017)

narrow gauge: 807 km 1.000-m gauge (2017)

country comparison to the world: 88

ROADWAYS:
total: 44,301 km (2018)

paved: 3,346 km (2018)

unpaved: 40,955 km (2018)

country comparison to the world: 84

WATERWAYS:
1,300 km (navigable by shallow-draft native craft in the northern part of the Niger River system) (2011)

country comparison to the world: 54

MERCHANT MARINE:
total: 1

by type: other 1 (2018)

country comparison to the world: 171

PORTS AND TERMINALS:
major seaport(s): Conakry, Kamsar

TRANSNATIONAL ISSUES :: GUINEA

DISPUTES - INTERNATIONAL:
Sierra Leone considers Guinea's definition of the flood plain limits to define the left bank boundary of the Makona and Moa Rivers excessive and protests Guinea's continued occupation of these lands, including the hamlet of Yenga, occupied since 1998

TRAFFICKING IN PERSONS:
current situation: Guinea is a source, transit, and, to a lesser extent, a destination country for men, women, and children subjected to forced labor and sex trafficking; the majority of trafficking victims are Guinean children, and trafficking is more prevalent among Guineans than foreign national migrants; Guinean

girls are subjected to domestic servitude and commercial sexual exploitation, while boys are forced to beg or to work as street vendors, shoe shiners, or miners; Guinea is a source country and transit point for West African children forced to work as miners in the region; Guinean women and girls are subjected to domestic servitude and sex trafficking in West Africa, the Middle East, the US, and increasingly Europe, while Thai, Chinese, and Vietnamese women are forced into prostitution and some West Africans are forced into domestic servitude in Guinea

tier rating: Tier 2 Watch List – Guinea does not fully comply with the minimum standards for the elimination of trafficking; however, it is making significant efforts to do so; in 2014, Guinea was granted a waiver from an otherwise required downgrade to Tier 3 because its government has a written plan that, if implemented would constitute making significant efforts to bring itself into compliance with the minimum standards for the elimination of trafficking; no new investigations were conducted in 2014, and the one ongoing case led to the prosecution of four offenders for forced child labor, three of whom were convicted but given inadequate sentences for the crime; the government did not identify or provide protective services to victims and did not support NGOs that assisted victims but continued to refer child victims to NGOs on an ad hoc basis; Guinean law does not prohibit all forms of trafficking, excluding, for example, debt bondage; the 2014 Ebolavirus outbreak negatively affected Guinea's ability to address human trafficking (2015)

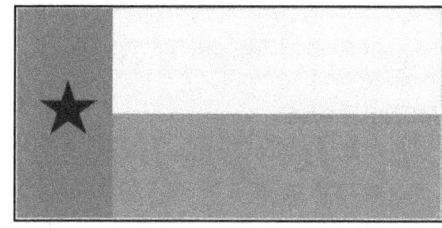

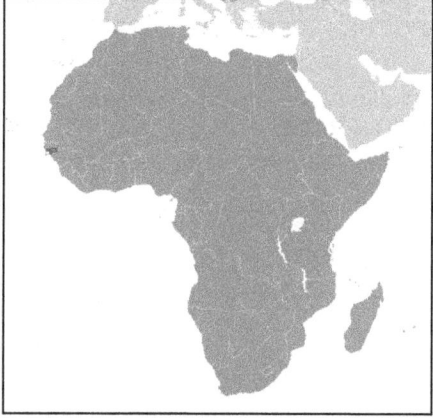

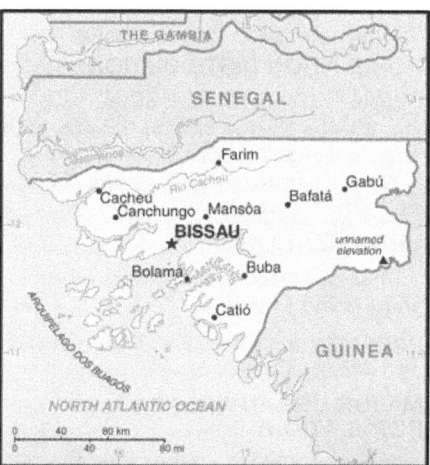

AFRICA :: GUINEA-BISSAU

INTRODUCTION :: GUINEA-BISSAU

BACKGROUND:

Since independence from Portugal in 1974, Guinea-Bissau has experienced considerable political and military upheaval. In 1980, a military coup established authoritarian General Joao Bernardo 'Nino' VIEIRA as president. Despite eventually setting a path to a market economy and multiparty system, VIEIRA's regime was characterized by the suppression of political opposition and the purging of political rivals. Several coup attempts through the 1980s and early 1990s failed to unseat him. In 1994 VIEIRA was elected president in the country's first free, multiparty election. A military mutiny and resulting civil war in 1998 eventually led to VIEIRA's ouster in May 1999. In February 2000, a transitional government turned over power to opposition leader Kumba YALA after he was elected president in transparent polling. In September 2003, after only three years in office, YALA was overthrown in a bloodless military coup, and businessman Henrique ROSA was sworn in as interim president. In 2005, former President VIEIRA was reelected, pledging to pursue economic development and national reconciliation; he was assassinated in March 2009. Malam Bacai SANHA was elected in an emergency election held in June 2009, but he passed away in January 2012 from a long-term illness. A military coup in April 2012 prevented Guinea-Bissau's second-round presidential election - to determine SANHA's successor - from taking place. Following mediation by the Economic Community of Western African States, a civilian transitional government assumed power in 2012 and remained until Jose Mario VAZ won a free and fair election in 2014. Beginning in 2015, a political dispute between factions in the ruling PAIGC party brought government gridlock. It was not until April 2018 that a consensus prime minister could be appointed, the national legislature reopened (having been closed for two years), and a new government formed under Prime Minister Aristides GOMES. In March 2019, the government held legislative elections, voting in the PAIGC as the ruling party; however, President VAZ continues to perpetuate a political stalemate by refusing to name PAICG President Domingos SIMOES PEREIRA Prime Minister.

GEOGRAPHY :: GUINEA-BISSAU

LOCATION:

Western Africa, bordering the North Atlantic Ocean, between Guinea and Senegal

GEOGRAPHIC COORDINATES:

12 00 N, 15 00 W

MAP REFERENCES:

Africa

AREA:

total: 36,125 sq km

land: 28,120 sq km

water: 8,005 sq km

country comparison to the world: 138

AREA - COMPARATIVE:

slightly less than three times the size of Connecticut

LAND BOUNDARIES:

total: 762 km

border countries (2): Guinea 421 km, Senegal 341 km

COASTLINE:

350 km

MARITIME CLAIMS:

territorial sea: 12 nm

exclusive economic zone: 200 nm

CLIMATE:

tropical; generally hot and humid; monsoonal-type rainy season (June to November) with southwesterly winds; dry season (December to May) with northeasterly harmattan winds

TERRAIN:

mostly low-lying coastal plain with a deeply indented estuarine coastline rising to savanna in east; numerous off-shore islands including the Arquipelago Dos Bijagos consisting of 18 main islands and many small islets

ELEVATION:

mean elevation: 70 m

lowest point: Atlantic Ocean 0 m

highest point: unnamed elevation in the eastern part of the country 300 m

NATURAL RESOURCES:

fish, timber, phosphates, bauxite, clay, granite, limestone, unexploited deposits of petroleum

LAND USE:

agricultural land: 44.8% (2011 est.)

arable land: 8.2% (2011 est.) / permanent crops: 6.9% (2011 est.) / permanent pasture: 29.7% (2011 est.)

forest: 55.2% (2011 est.)

other: 0% (2011 est.)

IRRIGATED LAND:

250 sq km (2012)

POPULATION DISTRIBUTION:

approximately one-fifth of the population lives in the capital city of Bissau along the Atlantic coast; the remainder is distributed among the eight other, mainly rural, regions

NATURAL HAZARDS:

hot, dry, dusty harmattan haze may reduce visibility during dry season; brush fires

ENVIRONMENT - CURRENT ISSUES:

deforestation (rampant felling of trees for timber and agricultural purposes); soil erosion; overgrazing; overfishing

ENVIRONMENT - INTERNATIONAL AGREEMENTS:

party to: Biodiversity, Climate Change, Climate Change-Kyoto Protocol, Desertification, Endangered Species, Hazardous Wastes, Law of the Sea, Ozone Layer Protection, Wetlands

signed, but not ratified: none of the selected agreements

GEOGRAPHY - NOTE:

this small country is swampy along its western coast and low-lying inland

PEOPLE AND SOCIETY :: GUINEA-BISSAU

POPULATION:

1,833,247 (July 2018 est.)

country comparison to the world: 153

NATIONALITY:

noun: Bissau-Guinean(s)

adjective: Bissau-Guinean

ETHNIC GROUPS:

Fulani 28.5%, Balanta 22.5%, Mandinga 14.7%, Papel 9.1%, Manjaco 8.3%, Beafada 3.5%, Mancanha 3.1%, Bijago 2.1%, Felupe 1.7%, Mansoanca 1.4%, Balanta Mane 1%, other 1.8%, none 2.2% (2008 est.)

LANGUAGES:

Crioulo (lingua franca), Portuguese (official; largely used as a second or third language), Pular (a Fula language), Mandingo

RELIGIONS:

Muslim 45.1%, Christian 22.1%, animist 14.9%, none 2%, unspecified 15.9% (2008 est.)

DEMOGRAPHIC PROFILE:

Guinea-Bissau's young and growing population is sustained by high fertility; approximately 60% of the population is under the age of 25. Its large reproductive-age population and total fertility rate of more than 4 children per woman offsets the country's high infant and maternal mortality rates. The latter is among the world's highest because of the prevalence of early childbearing, a lack of birth spacing, the high percentage of births outside of health care facilities, and a shortage of medicines and supplies.

Guinea-Bissau's history of political instability, a civil war, and several coups (the latest in 2012) have resulted in a fragile state with a weak economy, high unemployment, rampant corruption, widespread poverty, and thriving drug and child trafficking. With the country lacking educational infrastructure, school funding and materials, and qualified teachers, and with the cultural emphasis placed on religious education, parents frequently send boys to study in residential Koranic schools (daaras) in Senegal and The Gambia. They often are extremely deprived and are forced into street begging or agricultural work by marabouts (Muslim religious teachers), who enrich themselves at the expense of the children. Boys who leave their marabouts often end up on the streets of Dakar or other large Senegalese towns and are vulnerable to even worse abuse.

Some young men lacking in education and job prospects become involved in the flourishing international drug trade. Local drug use and associated violent crime are growing.

AGE STRUCTURE:

0-14 years: 43.55% (male 400,666/female 397,704)

15-24 years: 20.23% (male 181,286/female 189,515)

25-54 years: 29.9% (male 259,762/female 288,300)

55-64 years: 3.29% (male 27,621/female 32,611)

65 years and over: 3.04% (male 24,331/female 31,451) (2018 est.)

DEPENDENCY RATIOS:

total dependency ratio: 80.4 (2015 est.)

youth dependency ratio: 75.2 (2015 est.)

elderly dependency ratio: 5.2 (2015 est.)

potential support ratio: 19.3 (2015 est.)

MEDIAN AGE:

total: 17.8 years (2018 est.)

male: 17.2 years

female: 18.5 years

country comparison to the world: 216

POPULATION GROWTH RATE:

2.48% (2018 est.)

country comparison to the world: 23

BIRTH RATE:

37.3 births/1,000 population (2018 est.)

country comparison to the world: 13

DEATH RATE:

8.5 deaths/1,000 population (2018 est.)

country comparison to the world: 79

NET MIGRATION RATE:

-4 migrant(s)/1,000 population (2018 est.)

country comparison to the world: 185

POPULATION DISTRIBUTION:

approximately one-fifth of the population lives in the capital city of Bissau along the Atlantic coast; the remainder is distributed among the eight other, mainly rural, regions

URBANIZATION:

urban population: 43.8% of total population (2019)

rate of urbanization: 3.41% annual rate of change (2015-20 est.)

MAJOR URBAN AREAS - POPULATION:

579,000 BISSAU (capital) (2019)

SEX RATIO:

at birth: 1.03 male(s)/female

0-14 years: 1.01 male(s)/female

15-24 years: 0.96 male(s)/female

25-54 years: 0.9 male(s)/female

55-64 years: 0.85 male(s)/female

65 years and over: 0.77 male(s)/female

total population: 0.95 male(s)/female (2018 est.)

MATERNAL MORTALITY RATE:

667 deaths/100,000 live births (2017 est.)

country comparison to the world: 8

INFANT MORTALITY RATE:

total: 54.8 deaths/1,000 live births (2018 est.)

male: 61 deaths/1,000 live births

female: 48.4 deaths/1,000 live births

country comparison to the world: 20

LIFE EXPECTANCY AT BIRTH:

total population: 61.4 years (2018 est.)

male: 59.2 years

female: 63.6 years

country comparison to the world: 204

TOTAL FERTILITY RATE:

4.81 children born/woman (2018 est.)

country comparison to the world: 18

CONTRACEPTIVE PREVALENCE RATE:

16% (2014)

DRINKING WATER SOURCE:

improved:

urban: 98.8% of population

rural: 60.3% of population

total: 79.3% of population

unimproved:

urban: 1.2% of population

rural: 39.7% of population

total: 20.7% of population (2015 est.)

CURRENT HEALTH EXPENDITURE:

6.1% (2016)

PHYSICIANS DENSITY:

0.2 physicians/1,000 population (2015)

HOSPITAL BED DENSITY:

1 beds/1,000 population (2009)

SANITATION FACILITY ACCESS:

improved:

urban: 33.5% of population (2015 est.)

rural: 8.5% of population (2015 est.)

total: 20.8% of population (2015 est.)

unimproved:

urban: 66.5% of population (2015 est.)

rural: 91.5% of population (2015 est.)

total: 79.2% of population (2015 est.)

HIV/AIDS - ADULT PREVALENCE RATE:

3.5% (2018 est.)

country comparison to the world: 17

HIV/AIDS - PEOPLE LIVING WITH HIV/AIDS:

44,000 (2018 est.)

country comparison to the world: 64

HIV/AIDS - DEATHS:

1,800 (2018 est.)

country comparison to the world: 48

MAJOR INFECTIOUS DISEASES:

degree of risk: very high (2016)

food or waterborne diseases: bacterial and protozoal diarrhea, hepatitis A, and typhoid fever (2016)

vectorborne diseases: malaria, dengue fever, and yellow fever (2016)

water contact diseases: schistosomiasis (2016)

animal contact diseases: rabies (2016)

OBESITY - ADULT PREVALENCE RATE:

9.5% (2016)

country comparison to the world: 144

CHILDREN UNDER THE AGE OF 5 YEARS UNDERWEIGHT:

17% (2014)

country comparison to the world: 34

EDUCATION EXPENDITURES:

2.1% of GDP (2013)

country comparison to the world: 167

LITERACY:

definition: age 15 and over can read and write

total population: 59.9%

male: 71.8%

female: 48.3% (2015 est.)

GOVERNMENT :: GUINEA-BISSAU

COUNTRY NAME:

conventional long form: Republic of Guinea-Bissau

conventional short form: Guinea-Bissau

local long form: Republica da Guine-Bissau

local short form: Guine-Bissau

former: Portuguese Guinea

etymology: the country is named after the Guinea region of West Africa that lies along the Gulf of Guinea and stretches north to the Sahel; "Bissau," the name of the capital city, distinguishes the country from neighboring Guinea

GOVERNMENT TYPE:

semi-presidential republic

CAPITAL:

name: Bissau

geographic coordinates: 11 51 N, 15 35 W

time difference: UTC 0 (5 hours ahead of Washington, DC, during Standard Time)

ADMINISTRATIVE DIVISIONS:

9 regions (regioes, singular - regiao); Bafata, Biombo, Bissau, Bolama/Bijagos, Cacheu, Gabu, Oio, Quinara, Tombali

INDEPENDENCE:

24 September 1973 (declared); 10 September 1974 (from Portugal)

NATIONAL HOLIDAY:

Independence Day, 24 September (1973)

CONSTITUTION:

history: promulgated 16 May 1984; note - constitution suspended following military coup in April 2012 and restored in 2014

amendments: proposed by the National People's Assembly if supported by at least one third of its members, by the Council of State (a presidential consultant body), or by the government; passage requires approval by at least two-thirds majority vote of the Assembly; constitutional articles on the republican and secular form of government and national sovereignty cannot be amended; amended 1991, 1993, 1996 (2017)

LEGAL SYSTEM:

mixed legal system of civil law, which incorporated Portuguese law at independence and influenced by Economic Community of West African States (ECOWAS), West African Economic and Monetary Union (UEMOA), African Francophone Public Law, and customary law

INTERNATIONAL LAW ORGANIZATION PARTICIPATION:

accepts compulsory ICJ jurisdiction; non-party state to the ICCt

CITIZENSHIP:

citizenship by birth: yes

citizenship by descent only: yes

dual citizenship recognized: no

residency requirement for naturalization: 5 years

SUFFRAGE:

18 years of age; universal

EXECUTIVE BRANCH:

chief of state: President Jose Mario VAZ (since 17 June 2014)

head of government: (vacant)

cabinet: Cabinet nominated by the prime minister, appointed by the president

elections/appointments: president directly elected by absolute majority popular vote in 2 rounds if needed for a 5-year term; election last held on 13 April 2014 with a runoff on 18 May 2014 (next to be held on 24 November 2019); prime minister appointed by the president after consultation with party leaders in the National People's Assembly; note - the president cannot apply for a third consecutive term, nor during the 5 years following the end of the second term

election results: Jose Mario VAZ elected president in second round; percent of vote in first round - Jose Mario VAZ (PAIGC) 41%, Nuno Gomez NABIAM (independent) 25.1%, other 33.9%; percent of vote in second round - Jose Mario VAZ 61.9%, Nuno Gomez NABIAM 38.1%

LEGISLATIVE BRANCH:

description: unicameral National People's Assembly or Assembleia Nacional Popular (102 seats; 100 members directly elected in 27 multi-seat constituencies by closed party-list proportional representation vote and 2 elected in single-seat constituencies for citizens living abroad (1 for Africa, 1 for Europe); all members serve 4-year terms)

elections: last held on 10 March 2019 (next to be held in March 2023)

election results: percent of vote by party - PAIGC 35.2%, Madem G-15 21.1%, PRS 21.1%, other 22.6%; seats by party - PAIGC 47, Madem G-15 27, PRS 21, other 7; composition - men 88, women 14, percent of women 13.7%

JUDICIAL BRANCH:

highest courts: Supreme Court or Supremo Tribunal de Justica (consists of 9 judges and organized into Civil, Criminal, and Social and Administrative Disputes Chambers); note - the Supreme Court has both appellate and constitutional jurisdiction

judge selection and term of office: judges nominated by the Higher Council of the Magistrate, a major government organ responsible for judge appointments, dismissals, and judiciary discipline; judges appointed by the president for life

subordinate courts: Appeals Court; regional (first instance) courts; military court

POLITICAL PARTIES AND LEADERS:

African Party for the Independence of Guinea-Bissau and Cabo Verde or PAIGC [Domingos SIMOES PEREIRA]
Democratic Convergence Party or PCD [Vicente FERNANDES]
Movement for Democratic Alternation Group of 15 or MADEM-G15 [Braima CAMARA]
National People's Assembly – Democratic Party of Guinea Bissau or APU-PDGB [Nuno Gomes NABIAM]
New Democracy Party or PND [Mamadu Iaia DJALO]
Party for Social Renewal or PRS [Alberto NAMBEIA]
Republican Party for Independence and Development or PRID [Aristides GOMES]
Union for Change or UM [Agnelo REGALA]

INTERNATIONAL ORGANIZATION PARTICIPATION:

ACP, AfDB, AOSIS, AU, CPLP, ECOWAS, FAO, FZ, G-77, IBRD, ICAO, ICRM, IDA, IDB, IFAD, IFC, IFRCS, ILO, IMF, IMO, Interpol, IOC, IOM, IPU, ITSO, ITU, ITUC (NGOs), MIGA, MINUSMA, NAM, OIC, OIF, OPCW, UN, UNCTAD, UNESCO, UNIDO, UNWTO, UPU, WADB (regional), WAEMU, WCO, WFTU (NGOs), WHO, WIPO, WMO, WTO

DIPLOMATIC REPRESENTATION IN THE US:

none; note - Guinea-Bissau does not have official representation in Washington, DC

DIPLOMATIC REPRESENTATION FROM THE US:

the US Embassy suspended operations on 14 June 1998; the US Ambassador to Senegal is accredited to Guinea-Bissau

FLAG DESCRIPTION:

two equal horizontal bands of yellow (top) and green with a vertical red band on the hoist side; there is a black five-pointed star centered in the red band; yellow symbolizes the sun; green denotes hope; red represents blood shed during the struggle for independence; the black star stands for African unity

note: uses the popular Pan-African colors of Ethiopia; the flag design was heavily influenced by the Ghanaian flag

NATIONAL SYMBOL(S):

black star; national colors: red, yellow, green, black

NATIONAL ANTHEM:

name: "Esta e a Nossa Patria Bem Amada" (This Is Our Beloved Country)

lyrics/music: Amilcar Lopes CABRAL/XIAO He

note: adopted 1974; a delegation from then Portuguese Guinea visited China in 1963 and heard music by XIAO He; Amilcar Lopes CABRAL, the leader of Guinea-Bissau's independence movement, asked the composer to create a piece that would inspire his people to struggle for independence

ECONOMY :: GUINEA-BISSAU

ECONOMY - OVERVIEW:

Guinea-Bissau is highly dependent on subsistence agriculture, cashew nut exports, and foreign assistance. Two out of three Bissau-Guineans remain below the absolute poverty line. The legal economy is based on cashews and fishing. Illegal logging and trafficking in narcotics also play significant roles. The combination of limited economic prospects, weak institutions, and favorable geography have made this West African country a way station for drugs bound for Europe.

Guinea-Bissau has substantial potential for development of mineral resources, including phosphates, bauxite, and mineral sands. Offshore oil and gas exploration has begun. The country's climate and soil make it feasible to grow a wide range of cash crops, fruit, vegetables, and tubers; however, cashews generate more than 80% of export receipts and are the main source of income for many rural communities.

The government was deposed in August 2015, and since then, a political stalemate has resulted in weak governance and reduced donor support.

The country is participating in a three-year, IMF extended credit facility program that was suspended because of a planned bank bailout. The program was renewed in 2017, but the major donors of direct budget support (the EU, World Bank, and African Development Bank) have halted their programs indefinitely. Diversification of the economy remains a key policy goal, but Guinea-Bissau's poor infrastructure and business climate will constrain this effort.

GDP (PURCHASING POWER PARITY):

$3.171 billion (2017 est.)

$2.994 billion (2016 est.)

$2.817 billion (2015 est.)

note: data are in 2017 dollars

country comparison to the world: 188

GDP (OFFICIAL EXCHANGE RATE):

$1.35 billion (2017 est.)

GDP - REAL GROWTH RATE:

5.9% (2017 est.)

6.3% (2016 est.)

6.1% (2015 est.)

country comparison to the world: 36

GDP - PER CAPITA (PPP):

$1,900 (2017 est.)

$1,800 (2016 est.)

$1,700 (2015 est.)

note: data are in 2017 dollars

country comparison to the world: 212

GROSS NATIONAL SAVING:

8.6% of GDP (2017 est.)

10.1% of GDP (2016 est.)

10.5% of GDP (2015 est.)

country comparison to the world: 168

GDP - COMPOSITION, BY END USE:

household consumption: 83.9% (2017 est.)

government consumption: 12% (2017 est.)

investment in fixed capital: 4.1% (2017 est.)

investment in inventories: 0.2% (2017 est.)

exports of goods and services: 26.4% (2017 est.)

imports of goods and services: -26.5% (2017 est.)

GDP - COMPOSITION, BY SECTOR OF ORIGIN:

agriculture: 50% (2017 est.)

industry: 13.1% (2017 est.)

services: 36.9% (2017 est.)

AGRICULTURE - PRODUCTS:

rice, corn, beans, cassava (manioc, tapioca), cashew nuts, peanuts, palm kernels, cotton; timber; fish

INDUSTRIES:

agricultural products processing, beer, soft drinks

INDUSTRIAL PRODUCTION GROWTH RATE:

2.5% (2017 est.)

country comparison to the world: 117

LABOR FORCE:

731,300 (2013 est.)

country comparison to the world: 151

LABOR FORCE - BY OCCUPATION:

agriculture: 82%

industry and services: 18% (2000 est.)

UNEMPLOYMENT RATE:

NA

POPULATION BELOW POVERTY LINE:

67% (2015 est.)

HOUSEHOLD INCOME OR CONSUMPTION BY PERCENTAGE SHARE:

lowest 10%: 2.9%

highest 10%: 28% (2002)

BUDGET:

revenues: 246.2 million (2017 est.)

expenditures: 263.5 million (2017 est.)

TAXES AND OTHER REVENUES:

18.2% (of GDP) (2017 est.)

country comparison to the world: 162

BUDGET SURPLUS (+) OR DEFICIT (-):

-1.3% (of GDP) (2017 est.)

country comparison to the world: 86

PUBLIC DEBT:

53.9% of GDP (2017 est.)

57.9% of GDP (2016 est.)

country comparison to the world: 87

FISCAL YEAR:

calendar year

INFLATION RATE (CONSUMER PRICES):

1.1% (2017 est.)

1.5% (2016 est.)

country comparison to the world: 60

CENTRAL BANK DISCOUNT RATE:

4.25% (31 December 2009)

4.75% (31 December 2008)

country comparison to the world: 94

COMMERCIAL BANK PRIME LENDING RATE:

5.5% (31 December 2017 est.)

5.3% (31 December 2016 est.)

country comparison to the world: 134

STOCK OF NARROW MONEY:

$583.6 million (31 December 2017 est.)

$489.2 million (31 December 2016 est.)

country comparison to the world: 166

STOCK OF BROAD MONEY:

$583.6 million (31 December 2017 est.)

$489.2 million (31 December 2016 est.)

country comparison to the world: 170

STOCK OF DOMESTIC CREDIT:

$250.3 million (31 December 2017 est.)

$232.4 million (31 December 2016 est.)

country comparison to the world: 182

MARKET VALUE OF PUBLICLY TRADED SHARES:

NA

CURRENT ACCOUNT BALANCE:

-$27 million (2017 est.)

$16 million (2016 est.)

country comparison to the world: 75

EXPORTS:

$328.1 million (2017 est.)

$278.6 million (2016 est.)

country comparison to the world: 185

EXPORTS - PARTNERS:

India 67.1%, Vietnam 21.1% (2017)

EXPORTS - COMMODITIES:

fish, shrimp; cashews, peanuts, palm kernels, raw and sawn lumber

IMPORTS:

$283.5 million (2017 est.)

$136.5 million (2016 est.)

country comparison to the world: 206

IMPORTS - COMMODITIES:

foodstuffs, machinery and transport equipment, petroleum products

IMPORTS - PARTNERS:

Portugal 47.8%, Senegal 12.1%, China 10.4%, Netherlands 8.1%, Pakistan 5.4% (2017)

RESERVES OF FOREIGN EXCHANGE AND GOLD:

$356.4 million (31 December 2017 est.)

$349.4 million (31 December 2016 est.)

country comparison to the world: 163

DEBT - EXTERNAL:

$1.095 billion (31 December 2010 est.)

$941.5 million (31 December 2000 est.)

country comparison to the world: 164

EXCHANGE RATES:

Communaute Financiere Africaine francs (XOF) per US dollar -

605.3 (2017 est.)

593.01 (2016 est.)

593.01 (2015 est.)

591.45 (2014 est.)

494.42 (2013 est.)

ENERGY :: GUINEA-BISSAU

ELECTRICITY ACCESS:

population without electricity: 2 million (2017)

electrification - total population: 14.7% (2016)

electrification - urban areas: 29.8% (2016)

electrification - rural areas: 4% (2016)

ELECTRICITY - PRODUCTION:

39 million kWh (2016 est.)

country comparison to the world: 208

ELECTRICITY - CONSUMPTION:

36.27 million kWh (2016 est.)

country comparison to the world: 208

ELECTRICITY - EXPORTS:

0 kWh (2016 est.)

country comparison to the world: 145

ELECTRICITY - IMPORTS:

0 kWh (2016 est.)

country comparison to the world: 157

ELECTRICITY - INSTALLED GENERATING CAPACITY:

28,300 kW (2016 est.)

country comparison to the world: 200

ELECTRICITY - FROM FOSSIL FUELS:

99% of total installed capacity (2016 est.)

country comparison to the world: 24

ELECTRICITY - FROM NUCLEAR FUELS:

0% of total installed capacity (2017 est.)

country comparison to the world: 104

ELECTRICITY - FROM HYDROELECTRIC PLANTS:

0% of total installed capacity (2017 est.)

country comparison to the world: 176

ELECTRICITY - FROM OTHER RENEWABLE SOURCES:

1% of total installed capacity (2017 est.)

country comparison to the world: 154

CRUDE OIL - PRODUCTION:

0 bbl/day (2018 est.)

country comparison to the world: 146

CRUDE OIL - EXPORTS:

0 bbl/day (2015 est.)

country comparison to the world: 134

CRUDE OIL - IMPORTS:

0 bbl/day (2015 est.)

country comparison to the world: 138

CRUDE OIL - PROVED RESERVES:

0 bbl (1 January 2018 est.)

country comparison to the world: 142

REFINED PETROLEUM PRODUCTS - PRODUCTION:

0 bbl/day (2015 est.)

country comparison to the world: 154

REFINED PETROLEUM PRODUCTS - CONSUMPTION:

2,700 bbl/day (2016 est.)

country comparison to the world: 190

REFINED PETROLEUM PRODUCTS - EXPORTS:

0 bbl/day (2015 est.)

country comparison to the world: 163

REFINED PETROLEUM PRODUCTS - IMPORTS:

2,625 bbl/day (2015 est.)

country comparison to the world: 186

NATURAL GAS - PRODUCTION:

0 cu m (2017 est.)

country comparison to the world: 143

NATURAL GAS - CONSUMPTION:

0 cu m (2017 est.)

country comparison to the world: 156

NATURAL GAS - EXPORTS:

0 cu m (2017 est.)

country comparison to the world: 118

NATURAL GAS - IMPORTS:

0 cu m (2017 est.)

country comparison to the world: 136

NATURAL GAS - PROVED RESERVES:

0 cu m (1 January 2014 est.)

country comparison to the world: 144

CARBON DIOXIDE EMISSIONS FROM CONSUMPTION OF ENERGY:

397,900 Mt (2017 est.)

country comparison to the world: 188

COMMUNICATIONS :: GUINEA-BISSAU

TELEPHONES - FIXED LINES:

0

country comparison to the world: 220

TELEPHONES - MOBILE CELLULAR:

total subscriptions: 1,434,822

subscriptions per 100 inhabitants: 80 (2017 est.)

country comparison to the world: 155

TELEPHONE SYSTEM:

general assessment: small system including a combination of microwave radio relay, open-wire lines, radiotelephone, and mobile cellular communications; 2 mobile network operators (MTN and Orange) (2018)

domestic: fixed-line teledensity less than 1 per 100 persons; mobile cellular teledensity is roughly 70 per 100 persons (2018)

international: country code - 245; ACE submarine cable connecting Guinea-Bissau with 20 landing points in Western and South Africa and Europe (2019)

BROADCAST MEDIA:

1 state-owned TV station, Televisao da Guine-Bissau (TGB) and a second station, Radio e Televisao de Portugal (RTP) Africa, is operated by Portuguese public broadcaster (RTP); 1 state-owned radio station, several private radio stations, and some community radio stations; multiple international broadcasters are available (2019)

INTERNET COUNTRY CODE:

.gw

INTERNET USERS:

total: 66,169

percent of population: 3.8% (July 2016 est.)

country comparison to the world: 183

BROADBAND - FIXED SUBSCRIPTIONS:

total: 629

subscriptions per 100 inhabitants: less than 1 (2017 est.)

MILITARY AND SECURITY :: GUINEA-BISSAU

MILITARY EXPENDITURES:
1.64% of GDP (2015)
2.04% of GDP (2014)
2.08% of GDP (2013)
1.46% of GDP (2012)
1.6% of GDP (2011)

country comparison to the world: 70

MILITARY AND SECURITY FORCES:
People's Revolutionary Armed Force (FARP): Army, Navy, National Air Force (Forca Aerea Nacional); Guard Nacional (2019)

MILITARY SERVICE AGE AND OBLIGATION:
18-25 years of age for selective compulsory military service (Air Force service is voluntary); 16 years of age or younger, with parental consent, for voluntary service (2013)

TRANSPORTATION :: GUINEA-BISSAU

CIVIL AIRCRAFT REGISTRATION COUNTRY CODE PREFIX:
J5 (2016)

AIRPORTS:
8 (2013)

country comparison to the world: 160

AIRPORTS - WITH PAVED RUNWAYS:
total: 2 (2017)
over 3,047 m: 1 (2017)
1,524 to 2,437 m: 1 (2017)

AIRPORTS - WITH UNPAVED RUNWAYS:
total: 6 (2013)
1,524 to 2,437 m: 1 (2013)
914 to 1,523 m: 2 (2013)
under 914 m: 3 (2013)

ROADWAYS:
total: 4,400 km (2018)
paved: 453 km (2018)
unpaved: 3,947 km (2018)

country comparison to the world: 146

WATERWAYS:
(rivers are partially navigable; many inlets and creeks provide shallow-water access to much of interior) (2012)

MERCHANT MARINE:
total: 9
by type: general cargo 5, other 4 (2018)

country comparison to the world: 156

PORTS AND TERMINALS:
major seaport(s): Bissau, Buba, Cacheu, Farim

TRANSNATIONAL ISSUES :: GUINEA-BISSAU

DISPUTES - INTERNATIONAL:
a longstanding low-grade conflict continues in parts of Casamance, in Senegal across the border; some rebels use Guinea-Bissau as a safe haven

REFUGEES AND INTERNALLY DISPLACED PERSONS:
refugees (country of origin): 10,000 (Senegal) (2018)

TRAFFICKING IN PERSONS:
current situation: Guinea-Bissau is a source country for children subjected to forced labor and sex trafficking; the extent to which adults are trafficked for forced labor or forced prostitution is unclear; boys are forced into street vending in Guinea-Bissau and manual labor, agriculture, and mining in Senegal, while girls may be forced into street vending, domestic service, and, to a lesser extent, prostitution in Guinea and Senegal; some Bissau-Guinean boys at Koranic schools are forced into begging by religious teachers

tier rating: Tier 3 - Guinea-Bissau does not fully comply with the minimum standards for the elimination of trafficking and is not making significant efforts to do so; despite enacting an anti-trafficking law and adopting a national action plan in 2011, the country failed to demonstrate any notable anti-trafficking efforts for the third consecutive year; existing laws prohibiting all forms of trafficking were not used to prosecute any trafficking offenders in 2014, and only one case of potential child labor trafficking was under investigation; authorities continued to rely entirely on NGOs and international organizations to provide victims with protective services; no trafficking prevention activities were conducted (2015)

ILLICIT DRUGS:
increasingly important transit country for South American cocaine en route to Europe; enabling environment for trafficker operations due to pervasive corruption; archipelago-like geography near the capital facilitates drug smuggling

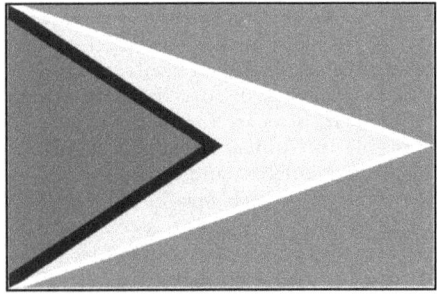

INTRODUCTION :: GUYANA

BACKGROUND:

Originally a Dutch colony in the 17th century, by 1815 Guyana had become a British possession. The abolition of slavery led to settlement of urban areas by former slaves and the importation of indentured servants from India to work the sugar plantations. The resulting ethnocultural divide has persisted and has led to turbulent politics. Guyana achieved independence from the UK in 1966, and since then it has been ruled mostly by socialist-oriented governments. In 1992, Cheddi JAGAN was elected president in what is considered the country's first free and fair election since independence. After his death five years later, his wife, Janet JAGAN, became president but resigned in 1999 due to poor health. Her successor, Bharrat JAGDEO, was elected in 2001 and again in 2006. Early elections held in May 2015 resulted in the first change in governing party and the replacement of President Donald RAMOTAR by current President David GRANGER. After a December 2018 no-confidence vote against the GRANGER government, national elections will be held before the scheduled spring 2020 date.

GEOGRAPHY :: GUYANA

LOCATION:
Northern South America, bordering the North Atlantic Ocean, between Suriname and Venezuela

GEOGRAPHIC COORDINATES:
5 00 N, 59 00 W

MAP REFERENCES:
South America

AREA:
total: 214,969 sq km

land: 196,849 sq km

water: 18,120 sq km

country comparison to the world: 86

AREA - COMPARATIVE:
slightly smaller than Idaho; almost twice the size of Tennessee

LAND BOUNDARIES:
total: 2,933 km

border countries (3): Brazil 1308 km, Suriname 836 km, Venezuela 789 km

COASTLINE:
459 km

MARITIME CLAIMS:
territorial sea: 12 nm

exclusive economic zone: 200 nm

continental shelf: 200 nm or to the outer edge of the continental margin

CLIMATE:
tropical; hot, humid, moderated by northeast trade winds; two rainy seasons (May to August, November to January)

TERRAIN:
mostly rolling highlands; low coastal plain; savanna in south

ELEVATION:
mean elevation: 207 m

lowest point: Atlantic Ocean 0 m

highest point: Laberintos del Norte on Mount Roraima 2,775 m

NATURAL RESOURCES:
bauxite, gold, diamonds, hardwood timber, shrimp, fish

LAND USE:
agricultural land: 8.4% (2011 est.)

arable land: 2.1% (2011 est.) / permanent crops: 0.1% (2011 est.) / permanent pasture: 6.2% (2011 est.)

forest: 77.4% (2011 est.)

other: 14.2% (2011 est.)

IRRIGATED LAND:
1,430 sq km (2012)

POPULATION DISTRIBUTION:
population is heavily concentrated in the northeast in and around Georgetown, with noteable concentrations along the Berbice River to the east; the remainder of the country is sparsely populated

NATURAL HAZARDS:
flash flood threat during rainy seasons

ENVIRONMENT - CURRENT ISSUES:
water pollution from sewage and agricultural and industrial chemicals; deforestation

ENVIRONMENT - INTERNATIONAL AGREEMENTS:
party to: Biodiversity, Climate Change, Climate Change-Kyoto Protocol, Desertification, Endangered Species, Hazardous Wastes, Law of the Sea, Ozone Layer Protection, Ship

Pollution, Tropical Timber 83, Tropical Timber 94

signed, but not ratified: none of the selected agreements

GEOGRAPHY - NOTE:

the third-smallest country in South America after Suriname and Uruguay; substantial portions of its western and eastern territories are claimed by Venezuela and Suriname respectively; contains some of the largest unspoiled rainforests on the continent

PEOPLE AND SOCIETY :: GUYANA

POPULATION:

740,685 (July 2018 est.)

note: estimates for this country explicitly take into account the effects of excess mortality due to AIDS; this can result in lower life expectancy, higher infant mortality, higher death rates, lower population growth rates, and changes in the distribution of population by age and sex than would otherwise be expected

country comparison to the world: 166

NATIONALITY:

noun: Guyanese (singular and plural)

adjective: Guyanese

ETHNIC GROUPS:

East Indian 39.8%, African descent 29.3%, mixed 19.9%, Amerindian 10.5%, other 0.5% (includes Portuguese, Chinese, white) (2012 est.)

LANGUAGES:

English (official), Guyanese Creole, Amerindian languages (including Caribbean and Arawak languages), Indian languages (including Caribbean Hindustani, a dialect of Hindi), Chinese (2014 est.)

RELIGIONS:

Protestant 34.8% (Pentecostal 22.8%, Seventh Day Adventist 5.4%, Anglican 5.2%, Methodist 1.4%), Hindu 24.8%, Roman Catholic 7.1%, Muslim 6.8%, Jehovah's Witness 1.3%, Rastafarian 0.5%, other Christian 20.8%, other 0.9%, none 3.1% (2012 est.)

DEMOGRAPHIC PROFILE:

Guyana is the only English-speaking country in South America and shares cultural and historical bonds with the Anglophone Caribbean. Guyana's two largest ethnic groups are the Afro-Guyanese (descendants of African slaves) and the Indo-Guyanese (descendants of Indian indentured laborers), which together comprise about three quarters of Guyana's population. Tensions periodically have boiled over between the two groups, which back ethnically based political parties and vote along ethnic lines. Poverty reduction has stagnated since the late 1990s. About one-third of the Guyanese population lives below the poverty line; indigenous people are disproportionately affected. Although Guyana's literacy rate is reported to be among the highest in the Western Hemisphere, the level of functional literacy is considerably lower, which has been attributed to poor education quality, teacher training, and infrastructure.

Guyana's emigration rate is among the highest in the world - more than 55% of its citizens reside abroad - and it is one of the largest recipients of remittances relative to GDP among Latin American and Caribbean counties. Although remittances are a vital source of income for most citizens, the pervasive emigration of skilled workers deprives Guyana of professionals in healthcare and other key sectors. More than 80% of Guyanese nationals with tertiary level educations have emigrated. Brain drain and the concentration of limited medical resources in Georgetown hamper Guyana's ability to meet the health needs of its predominantly rural population. Guyana has one of the highest HIV prevalence rates in the region and continues to rely on international support for its HIV treatment and prevention programs.

AGE STRUCTURE:

0-14 years: 25.38% (male 95,740/female 92,282)

15-24 years: 21.55% (male 81,676/female 77,942)

25-54 years: 38.52% (male 149,199/female 136,129)

55-64 years: 8.15% (male 27,684/female 32,678)

65 years and over: 6.39% (male 19,336/female 28,019) (2018 est.)

DEPENDENCY RATIOS:

total dependency ratio: 53.5 (2015 est.)

youth dependency ratio: 45.8 (2015 est.)

elderly dependency ratio: 7.7 (2015 est.)

potential support ratio: 13.3 (2015 est.)

MEDIAN AGE:

total: 26.7 years (2018 est.)

male: 26.3 years

female: 27 years

country comparison to the world: 148

POPULATION GROWTH RATE:

0.48% (2018 est.)

country comparison to the world: 156

BIRTH RATE:

15.4 births/1,000 population (2018 est.)

country comparison to the world: 118

DEATH RATE:

7.4 deaths/1,000 population (2018 est.)

country comparison to the world: 115

NET MIGRATION RATE:

-3.2 migrant(s)/1,000 population (2018 est.)

country comparison to the world: 180

POPULATION DISTRIBUTION:

population is heavily concentrated in the northeast in and around Georgetown, with noteable concentrations along the Berbice River to the east; the remainder of the country is sparsely populated

URBANIZATION:

urban population: 26.7% of total population (2019)

rate of urbanization: 0.83% annual rate of change (2015-20 est.)

MAJOR URBAN AREAS - POPULATION:

110,000 GEORGETOWN (capital) (2018)

SEX RATIO:

at birth: 1.05 male(s)/female

0-14 years: 1.04 male(s)/female

15-24 years: 1.05 male(s)/female

25-54 years: 1.1 male(s)/female

55-64 years: 0.85 male(s)/female

65 years and over: 0.69 male(s)/female

total population: 1.02 male(s)/female (2018 est.)

MOTHER'S MEAN AGE AT FIRST BIRTH:

20.8 years (2009 est.)

note: median age at first birth among women 25-29

MATERNAL MORTALITY RATE:

667 deaths/100,000 live births (2017 est.)

country comparison to the world: 9

INFANT MORTALITY RATE:

total: 29.5 deaths/1,000 live births (2018 est.)

male: 33.2 deaths/1,000 live births

female: 25.5 deaths/1,000 live births

country comparison to the world: 63

LIFE EXPECTANCY AT BIRTH:

total population: 68.9 years (2018 est.)

male: 65.9 years

female: 72.1 years

country comparison to the world: 164

TOTAL FERTILITY RATE:

1.97 children born/woman (2018 est.)

country comparison to the world: 123

CONTRACEPTIVE PREVALENCE RATE:

33.9% (2014)

DRINKING WATER SOURCE:

improved:

urban: 98.2% of population

rural: 98.3% of population

total: 98.3% of population

unimproved:

urban: 1.8% of population

rural: 1.7% of population

total: 1.7% of population (2015 est.)

CURRENT HEALTH EXPENDITURE:

4.2% (2016)

PHYSICIANS DENSITY:

0.8 physicians/1,000 population (2018)

HOSPITAL BED DENSITY:

1.6 beds/1,000 population (2014)

SANITATION FACILITY ACCESS:

improved:

urban: 87.9% of population (2015 est.)

rural: 82% of population (2015 est.)

total: 83.7% of population (2015 est.)

unimproved:

urban: 12.1% of population (2015 est.)

rural: 18% of population (2015 est.)

total: 16.3% of population (2015 est.)

HIV/AIDS - ADULT PREVALENCE RATE:

1.4% (2018 est.)

country comparison to the world: 35

HIV/AIDS - PEOPLE LIVING WITH HIV/AIDS:

8,200 (2018 est.)

country comparison to the world: 107

HIV/AIDS - DEATHS:

<200 (2018 est.)

MAJOR INFECTIOUS DISEASES:

degree of risk: very high (2016)

food or waterborne diseases: bacterial and protozoal diarrhea, hepatitis A, and typhoid fever (2016)

vectorborne diseases: dengue fever and malaria (2016)

note: active local transmission of Zika virus by Aedes species mosquitoes has been identified in this country (as of August 2016); it poses an important risk (a large number of cases possible) among US citizens if bitten by an infective mosquito; other less common ways to get Zika are through sex, via blood transfusion, or during pregnancy, in which the pregnant woman passes Zika virus to her fetus

OBESITY - ADULT PREVALENCE RATE:

20.2% (2016)

country comparison to the world: 103

CHILDREN UNDER THE AGE OF 5 YEARS UNDERWEIGHT:

8.2% (2014)

country comparison to the world: 70

EDUCATION EXPENDITURES:

6.3% of GDP (2017)

country comparison to the world: 28

LITERACY:

definition: age 15 and over has ever attended school

total population: 88.5%

male: 87.2%

female: 89.8% (2015 est.)

SCHOOL LIFE EXPECTANCY (PRIMARY TO TERTIARY EDUCATION):

total: 11 years

male: 11 years

female: 12 years (2012)

UNEMPLOYMENT, YOUTH AGES 15-24:

total: 21.6%

male: 17.3%

female: 28% (2017 est.)

country comparison to the world: 62

GOVERNMENT :: GUYANA

COUNTRY NAME:

conventional long form: Cooperative Republic of Guyana

conventional short form: Guyana

former: British Guiana

etymology: the name is derived from Guiana, the original name for the region that included British Guiana, Dutch Guiana, and French Guiana; ultimately the word is derived from an indigenous Amerindian language and means "Land of Many Waters" (referring to the area's multitude of rivers and streams)

GOVERNMENT TYPE:

parliamentary republic

CAPITAL:

name: Georgetown

geographic coordinates: 6 48 N, 58 09 W

time difference: UTC-4 (1 hour ahead of Washington, DC, during Standard Time)

etymology: when the British took possession of the town from the Dutch in 1812, they renamed it Georgetown in honor of King George III

ADMINISTRATIVE DIVISIONS:

10 regions; Barima-Waini, Cuyuni-Mazaruni, Demerara-Mahaica, East Berbice-Corentyne, Essequibo Islands-West Demerara, Mahaica-Berbice, Pomeroon-Supenaam, Potaro-Siparuni, Upper Demerara-Berbice, Upper Takutu-Upper Essequibo

INDEPENDENCE:

26 May 1966 (from the UK)

NATIONAL HOLIDAY:

Republic Day, 23 February (1970)

CONSTITUTION:

history: several previous; latest promulgated 6 October 1980

amendments: proposed by the National Assembly; passage of amendments affecting constitutional articles, such as national sovereignty, government structure and powers, and constitutional amendment procedures, requires approval by the Assembly membership, approval in a referendum, and assent of the president; other amendments only require Assembly approval; amended many times, last in 2016 (2018)

LEGAL SYSTEM:

common law system, based on the English model, with some Roman-Dutch civil law influence

INTERNATIONAL LAW ORGANIZATION PARTICIPATION:

has not submitted an ICJ jurisdiction declaration; accepts ICCt jurisdiction

CITIZENSHIP:

citizenship by birth: yes

citizenship by descent only: yes

dual citizenship recognized: no

residency requirement for naturalization: na

SUFFRAGE:

18 years of age; universal

EXECUTIVE BRANCH:

chief of state: President David GRANGER (since 16 May 2015); Vice Presidents Sydney ALLICOCK, Carl Barrington GREENIDGE, Moses Veerasammy NAGAMOOTOO, and Hemraj RAMJATTAN (since 20 May 2015); Prime Minister Moses Veerasammy NAGAMOOTOO (since 20 May 2015); note - the president is both chief of state and head of government

head of government: President David GRANGER (since 16 May 2015); Vice Presidents Sydney ALLICOCK, Carl Barrington GREENIDGE, Moses Veerasammy NAGAMOOTOO, and Hemraj RAMJATTAN (since 20 May 2015); Prime Minister Moses Veerasammy NAGAMOOTOO (since 20 May 2015)

cabinet: Cabinet of Ministers appointed by the president, responsible to the National Assembly

elections/appointments: the predesignated candidate of the winning party in the last National Assembly election becomes president for a 5-year term (no term limits); election last held on 11 May 2015 (next to be held no later than 2020); prime minister appointed by the president

election results: David GRANGER (APNU-AFC) designated president by the majority party in the National Assembly

LEGISLATIVE BRANCH:

description: unicameral National Assembly (65 seats; 40 members directly elected in a single nationwide constituency and 25 directly elected in multi-seat constituencies - all by closed list proportional representation vote; members serve 5-year terms)

elections: last held on 11 May 2015 (next to be held on 2 March 2020)

election results: percent of vote by party - APNU-AFC 50.3%, PPP/C 49.2%, other 0.5%; seats by party - APNU-AFC 33, PPP/C 32; composition - men 44, women 21, percent of women 32.3%

JUDICIAL BRANCH:

highest courts: Supreme Court of Judicature (consists of the Court of Appeal with a chief justice and 3 justices, and the High Court with a chief justice and 10 justices organized into 3- or 5-judge panels); note - in 2009, Guyana acceded to the Caribbean Court of Justice as the final court of appeal in civil and criminal cases, replacing that of the Judicial Committee of the Privy Council (in London)

judge selection and term of office: Court of Appeal and High Court chief justices appointed by the president; other judges of both courts appointed by the Judicial Service Commission, a body appointed by the president; judges appointed for life with retirement at age 65

subordinate courts: Land Court; magistrates' courts

POLITICAL PARTIES AND LEADERS:

A Partnership for National Unity or APNU [David A. GRANGER]
Alliance for Change or AFC [Raphael TROTMAN]
Justice for All Party [C.N. SHARMA]
National Independent Party or NIP [Saphier Husain SUBEDAR]
People's Progressive Party/Civic or PPP/C [Donald RAMOTAR]
The United Force or TUF [Manzoor NADIR]
United Republican Party or URP [Vishnu BANDHU]

INTERNATIONAL ORGANIZATION PARTICIPATION:

ACP, AOSIS, C, Caricom, CD, CDB, CELAC, FAO, G-77, IADB, IBRD, ICAO, ICCt, ICRM, IDA, IFAD, IFC, IFRCS, ILO, IMF, IMO, Interpol, IOC, IOM, ISO (correspondent), ITU, LAES, MIGA, NAM, OAS, OIC, OPANAL, OPCW, PCA, Petrocaribe, UN, UNASUR, UNCTAD, UNESCO, UNIDO, UPU, WCO, WFTU (NGOs), WHO, WIPO, WMO, WTO

DIPLOMATIC REPRESENTATION IN THE US:

Ambassador Riyad David INSANALLY (since 16 Sept 2016)

chancery: 2490 Tracy Place NW, Washington, DC 20008

telephone: [1] (202) 265-6900

FAX: [1] (202) 232-1297

consulate(s) general: New York

DIPLOMATIC REPRESENTATION FROM THE US:

chief of mission: Ambassador Sarah-Ann LYNCH (since 13 March 2019)

telephone: [592] 225-4900 through 4909

embassy: US Embassy, 100 Young and Duke Streets, Kingston, Georgetown

mailing address: P. O. Box 10507, Georgetown; US Embassy, 3170 Georgetown Place, Washington DC 20521-3170

FAX: [592] 225-8497

FLAG DESCRIPTION:

green with a red isosceles triangle (based on the hoist side) superimposed on a long, yellow arrowhead; there is a narrow, black border between the red and yellow, and a narrow, white border between the yellow and the green; green represents forest and foliage; yellow stands for mineral resources and a bright future; white symbolizes Guyana's rivers; red signifies zeal and the sacrifice of the people; black indicates perseverance

NATIONAL SYMBOL(S):

Canje pheasant (hoatzin), jaguar, Victoria Regia water lily; national colors: red, yellow, green, black, white

NATIONAL ANTHEM:

name: Dear Land of Guyana, of Rivers and Plains

lyrics/music: Archibald Leonard LUKERL/Robert Cyril Gladstone POTTER

note: adopted 1966

ECONOMY :: GUYANA

ECONOMY - OVERVIEW:

The Guyanese economy exhibited moderate economic growth in recent years and is based largely on agriculture and extractive industries. The economy is heavily dependent upon the export of six commodities - sugar, gold, bauxite, shrimp, timber, and rice - which represent nearly 60% of the country's GDP and are highly susceptible to adverse weather conditions and fluctuations in commodity prices. Guyana closed or consolidated several sugar estates in 2017, reducing production of sugar to a forecasted 147,000 tons in 2018, less than half of 2017 production. Much of Guyana's growth in recent years has come from a surge in gold production. With a record-breaking 700,000 ounces of gold produced in 2016, Gold production in Guyana has offset the economic effects of declining sugar production. In January 2018, estimated 3.2 billion barrels of oil were found offshore and Guyana is scheduled to become a petroleum producer by March 2020.

Guyana's entrance into the Caricom Single Market and Economy in January 2006 broadened the country's export market, primarily in the raw materials sector. Guyana has experienced positive growth almost every year over the past decade. Inflation has been kept under control. Recent years have seen the government's stock of debt reduced significantly - with external debt now less than half of what it was in the early 1990s. Despite these improvements, the government is still juggling a sizable external debt against the urgent need for expanded public investment. In March 2007, the Inter-American Development Bank, Guyana's principal donor, canceled Guyana's nearly $470 million debt, equivalent to 21% of GDP, which along with other Highly Indebted Poor Country debt forgiveness, brought the debt-to-GDP ratio down from 183% in 2006 to 52% in 2017. Guyana had become heavily indebted as a result of the inward-looking, state-led development model pursued in the 1970s and 1980s. Chronic problems include a shortage of skilled labor and a deficient infrastructure.

GDP (PURCHASING POWER PARITY):

$6.301 billion (2017 est.)

$6.169 billion (2016 est.)

$5.969 billion (2015 est.)

note: data are in 2017 dollars

country comparison to the world: 171

GDP (OFFICIAL EXCHANGE RATE):

$3.561 billion (2017 est.)

GDP - REAL GROWTH RATE:

2.1% (2017 est.)

3.4% (2016 est.)

3.1% (2015 est.)

country comparison to the world: 146

GDP - PER CAPITA (PPP):

$8,100 (2017 est.)

$8,000 (2016 est.)

$7,800 (2015 est.)

note: data are in 2017 dollars

country comparison to the world: 151

GROSS NATIONAL SAVING:

10.5% of GDP (2017 est.)

15% of GDP (2016 est.)

8.8% of GDP (2015 est.)

country comparison to the world: 161

GDP - COMPOSITION, BY END USE:

household consumption: 71.1% (2017 est.)

government consumption: 18.2% (2017 est.)

investment in fixed capital: 25.4% (2017 est.)

investment in inventories: 0% (2017 est.)

exports of goods and services: 47.8% (2017 est.)

imports of goods and services: -63% (2017 est.)

GDP - COMPOSITION, BY SECTOR OF ORIGIN:

agriculture: 15.4% (2017 est.)

industry: 15.3% (2017 est.)

services: 69.3% (2017 est.)

AGRICULTURE - PRODUCTS:

sugarcane, rice, edible oils; beef, pork, poultry; shrimp, fish

INDUSTRIES:

bauxite, sugar, rice milling, timber, textiles, gold mining

INDUSTRIAL PRODUCTION GROWTH RATE:

-5% (2017 est.)

country comparison to the world: 196

LABOR FORCE:

313,800 (2013 est.)

country comparison to the world: 162

LABOR FORCE - BY OCCUPATION:

agriculture: NA

industry: NA

services: NA

UNEMPLOYMENT RATE:

11.1% (2013)

11.3% (2012)

country comparison to the world: 151

POPULATION BELOW POVERTY LINE:

35% (2006 est.)

HOUSEHOLD INCOME OR CONSUMPTION BY PERCENTAGE SHARE:

lowest 10%: 1.3%

highest 10%: 33.8% (1999)

DISTRIBUTION OF FAMILY INCOME - GINI INDEX:

44.6 (2007)

43.2 (1999)

country comparison to the world: 42

BUDGET:

revenues: 1.002 billion (2017 est.)

expenditures: 1.164 billion (2017 est.)

TAXES AND OTHER REVENUES:

28.1% (of GDP) (2017 est.)

country comparison to the world: 96

BUDGET SURPLUS (+) OR DEFICIT (-):

-4.5% (of GDP) (2017 est.)

country comparison to the world: 165

PUBLIC DEBT:

52.2% of GDP (2017 est.)

50.7% of GDP (2016 est.)

country comparison to the world: 95

FISCAL YEAR:

calendar year

INFLATION RATE (CONSUMER PRICES):

2% (2017 est.)

0.8% (2016 est.)

country comparison to the world: 105

CENTRAL BANK DISCOUNT RATE:

5.5% (31 December 2011)

4.25% (31 December 2010)

country comparison to the world: 75

COMMERCIAL BANK PRIME LENDING RATE:

13% (31 December 2017 est.)

13% (31 December 2016 est.)

country comparison to the world: 62

STOCK OF NARROW MONEY:

$758.4 million (31 December 2017 est.)

$701.4 million (31 December 2016 est.)

country comparison to the world: 163

STOCK OF BROAD MONEY:

$758.4 million (31 December 2017 est.)

$701.4 million (31 December 2016 est.)

country comparison to the world: 167
STOCK OF DOMESTIC CREDIT:
$1.903 billion (31 December 2017 est.)
$1.875 billion (31 December 2016 est.)
country comparison to the world: 153
MARKET VALUE OF PUBLICLY TRADED SHARES:
$610.9 million (31 December 2012 est.)
$440.4 million (31 December 2011 est.)
$339.8 million (31 December 2010 est.)
country comparison to the world: 110
CURRENT ACCOUNT BALANCE:
-$237 million (2017 est.)
$13 million (2016 est.)
country comparison to the world: 100
EXPORTS:
$1.439 billion (2017 est.)
$1.38 billion (2016 est.)
country comparison to the world: 150
EXPORTS - PARTNERS:
Canada 24.9%, US 16.5%, Panama 9.6%, UK 7.7%, Jamaica 5.1%, Trinidad and Tobago 5% (2017)
EXPORTS - COMMODITIES:
sugar, gold, bauxite, alumina, rice, shrimp, molasses, rum, timber
IMPORTS:
$1.626 billion (2017 est.)
$1.341 billion (2016 est.)
country comparison to the world: 173
IMPORTS - COMMODITIES:
manufactures, machinery, petroleum, food
IMPORTS - PARTNERS:
Trinidad and Tobago 27.5%, US 26.5%, China 8.9%, Suriname 6.1% (2017)
RESERVES OF FOREIGN EXCHANGE AND GOLD:
$565.4 million (31 December 2017 est.)
$581 million (31 December 2016 est.)
country comparison to the world: 146
DEBT - EXTERNAL:
$1.69 billion (31 December 2017 est.)
$1.542 billion (31 December 2016 est.)
country comparison to the world: 157
EXCHANGE RATES:
Guyanese dollars (GYD) per US dollar -
207 (2017 est.)
206.5 (2016 est.)
206.5 (2015 est.)
206.5 (2014 est.)
206.45 (2013 est.)

ENERGY :: GUYANA

ELECTRICITY ACCESS:
electrification - total population: 84.2% (2016)
electrification - urban areas: 90.2% (2016)
electrification - rural areas: 81.9% (2016)
ELECTRICITY - PRODUCTION:
1.01 billion kWh (2016 est.)
country comparison to the world: 151
ELECTRICITY - CONSUMPTION:
790.1 million kWh (2016 est.)
country comparison to the world: 161
ELECTRICITY - EXPORTS:
0 kWh (2016 est.)
country comparison to the world: 146
ELECTRICITY - IMPORTS:
0 kWh (2016 est.)
country comparison to the world: 158
ELECTRICITY - INSTALLED GENERATING CAPACITY:
428,000 kW (2016 est.)
country comparison to the world: 151
ELECTRICITY - FROM FOSSIL FUELS:
89% of total installed capacity (2016 est.)
country comparison to the world: 57
ELECTRICITY - FROM NUCLEAR FUELS:
0% of total installed capacity (2017 est.)
country comparison to the world: 105
ELECTRICITY - FROM HYDROELECTRIC PLANTS:
0% of total installed capacity (2017 est.)
country comparison to the world: 177
ELECTRICITY - FROM OTHER RENEWABLE SOURCES:
11% of total installed capacity (2017 est.)
country comparison to the world: 78
CRUDE OIL - PRODUCTION:
0 bbl/day (2018 est.)
country comparison to the world: 147
CRUDE OIL - EXPORTS:
0 bbl/day (2015 est.)
country comparison to the world: 135
CRUDE OIL - IMPORTS:
0 bbl/day (2015 est.)
country comparison to the world: 139
CRUDE OIL - PROVED RESERVES:
0 bbl (1 January 2018 est.)
country comparison to the world: 143
REFINED PETROLEUM PRODUCTS - PRODUCTION:
0 bbl/day (2015 est.)
country comparison to the world: 155
REFINED PETROLEUM PRODUCTS - CONSUMPTION:
14,000 bbl/day (2016 est.)
country comparison to the world: 154
REFINED PETROLEUM PRODUCTS - EXPORTS:
0 bbl/day (2015 est.)
country comparison to the world: 164
REFINED PETROLEUM PRODUCTS - IMPORTS:
13,720 bbl/day (2015 est.)
country comparison to the world: 140
NATURAL GAS - PRODUCTION:
0 cu m (2017 est.)
country comparison to the world: 144
NATURAL GAS - CONSUMPTION:
0 cu m (2017 est.)
country comparison to the world: 157
NATURAL GAS - EXPORTS:
0 cu m (2017 est.)
country comparison to the world: 119
NATURAL GAS - IMPORTS:
0 cu m (2017 est.)
country comparison to the world: 137
NATURAL GAS - PROVED RESERVES:
0 cu m (1 January 2014 est.)
country comparison to the world: 145
CARBON DIOXIDE EMISSIONS FROM CONSUMPTION OF ENERGY:
2.131 million Mt (2017 est.)
country comparison to the world: 158

COMMUNICATIONS :: GUYANA

TELEPHONES - FIXED LINES:
total subscriptions: 135,795
subscriptions per 100 inhabitants: 18 (2017 est.)
country comparison to the world: 135

TELEPHONES - MOBILE CELLULAR:

total subscriptions: 643,210

subscriptions per 100 inhabitants: 87 (2017 est.)

country comparison to the world: 165

TELEPHONE SYSTEM:

general assessment: reliable international long distance service; 100% digital network; national transmission supported by fiber optic cable and rural network by microwaves; more than 150,000 lines; many areas still lack fixed-line telephone services; 2019 budget allocates funds for ICT (Information and Communications Technology) development (2018)

domestic: fixed-line teledensity is about 20 per 100 persons; mobile-cellular teledensity about 87 per 100 persons (2018)

international: country code - 592; landing point for the SG-SCS submarine cable to Suriname, and the Caribbean; satellite earth station - 1 Intelsat (Atlantic Ocean) (2019)

BROADCAST MEDIA:

government-dominated broadcast media; the National Communications Network (NCN) TV is state-owned; a few private TV stations relay satellite services; the state owns and operates 2 radio stations broadcasting on multiple frequencies capable of reaching the entire country; government limits on licensing of new private radio stations has constrained competition in broadcast media

INTERNET COUNTRY CODE:

.gy

INTERNET USERS:

total: 262,425

percent of population: 35.7% (July 2016 est.)

country comparison to the world: 163

BROADBAND - FIXED SUBSCRIPTIONS:

total: 64,889

subscriptions per 100 inhabitants: 9 (2017 est.)

country comparison to the world: 126

MILITARY AND SECURITY :: GUYANA

MILITARY EXPENDITURES:

1.69% of GDP (2018)

1.68% of GDP (2017)

1.51% of GDP (2016)

1.46% of GDP (2015)

1.28% of GDP (2014)

country comparison to the world: 68

MILITARY AND SECURITY FORCES:

Guyana Defense Force: Army, Air Corps, Coast Guard (2019)

MILITARY SERVICE AGE AND OBLIGATION:

18 years of age or older for voluntary military service; no conscription (2014)

TRANSPORTATION :: GUYANA

NATIONAL AIR TRANSPORT SYSTEM:

number of registered air carriers: 2 (2015)

inventory of registered aircraft operated by air carriers: 12 (2015)

annual passenger traffic on registered air carriers: 43,835 (2015)

annual freight traffic on registered air carriers: 0 mt-km (2015)

CIVIL AIRCRAFT REGISTRATION COUNTRY CODE PREFIX:

8R (2016)

AIRPORTS:

117 (2013)

country comparison to the world: 49

AIRPORTS - WITH PAVED RUNWAYS:

total: 11 (2017)

1,524 to 2,437 m: 2 (2017)

914 to 1,523 m: 1 (2017)

under 914 m: 8 (2017)

AIRPORTS - WITH UNPAVED RUNWAYS:

total: 106 (2013)

1,524 to 2,437 m: 1 (2013)

914 to 1,523 m: 16 (2013)

under 914 m: 89 (2013)

ROADWAYS:

total: 3,995 km (2019)

paved: 799 km (2019)

unpaved: 3,196 km (2019)

country comparison to the world: 151

WATERWAYS:

330 km (the Berbice, Demerara, and Essequibo Rivers are navigable by oceangoing vessels for 150 km, 100 km, and 80 km respectively) (2012)

country comparison to the world: 91

MERCHANT MARINE:

total: 55

by type: general cargo 26, oil tanker 7, other 22 (2018)

country comparison to the world: 111

PORTS AND TERMINALS:

major seaport(s): Georgetown

TRANSNATIONAL ISSUES :: GUYANA

DISPUTES - INTERNATIONAL:

all of the area west of the Essequibo River is claimed by Venezuela preventing any discussion of a maritime boundary; Guyana has expressed its intention to join Barbados in asserting claims before UN Convention on the Law of the Sea (UNCLOS) that Trinidad and Tobago's maritime boundary with Venezuela extends into their waters; Suriname claims a triangle of land between the New and Kutari/Koetari Rivers in a historic dispute over the headwaters of the Courantyne

TRAFFICKING IN PERSONS:

current situation: Guyana is a source and destination country for men, women, and children subjected to sex trafficking and forced labor – children are particularly vulnerable; women and girls from Guyana, Venezuela, Suriname, Brazil, and the Dominican Republic are forced into prostitution in Guyana's interior mining communities and urban areas; forced labor is reported in mining, agriculture, forestry, domestic service, and shops; Guyanese nationals are also trafficked to Suriname, Jamaica, and other Caribbean countries for sexual exploitation and forced labor

tier rating: Tier 2 Watch List – Guyana does not fully comply with the minimum standards for the elimination of trafficking; however, it is making significant efforts to do so; in 2014, Guyana was granted a waiver from an otherwise required downgrade to Tier 3 because its government has a written plan that, if implemented would constitute making significant efforts to bring itself into compliance with the minimum standards for the elimination of trafficking; the government released its anti-trafficking action plan in June 2014 but made uneven efforts to implement it; law enforcement was weak, investigating seven trafficking cases, prosecuting four alleged traffickers, and convicting one trafficker – a police officer – who was released on bail pending appeal; in 2014, as in previous years, Guyanese courts dismissed the majority of ongoing trafficking prosecutions; the government referred some victims to care services, which were provided by NGOs with little or no government support (2015)

ILLICIT DRUGS:

transshipment point for narcotics from South America - primarily Venezuela - to Europe and the US; producer of cannabis; rising money laundering related to drug trafficking and human smuggling

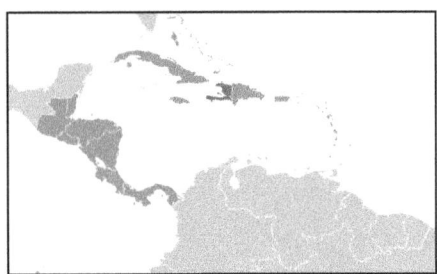

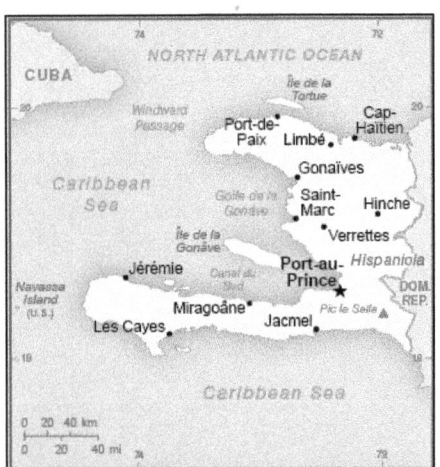

CENTRAL AMERICA :: HAITI

INTRODUCTION :: HAITI

BACKGROUND:

The native Taino - who inhabited the island of Hispaniola when Christopher COLUMBUS first landed on it in 1492 - were virtually wiped out by Spanish settlers within 25 years. In the early 17th century, the French established a presence on Hispaniola. In 1697, Spain ceded to the French the western third of the island, which later became Haiti. The French colony, based on forestry and sugar-related industries, became one of the wealthiest in the Caribbean but relied heavily on the forced labor of enslaved Africans and environmentally degrading practices. In the late 18th century, Toussaint L'OUVERTURE led a revolution of Haiti's nearly half a million slaves that ended France's rule on the island. After a prolonged struggle, and under the leadership of Jean-Jacques DESSALINES, Haiti became the first country in the world led by former slaves after declaring its independence in 1804, but it was forced to pay an indemnity to France for more than a century and was shunned by other countries for nearly 40 years. After the US occupied Haiti from 1915-1934, Francois "Papa Doc" DUVALIER and then his son Jean-Claude "Baby Doc" DUVALIER led repressive and corrupt regimes that ruled Haiti from 1957-1971 and 1971-1986, respectively. A massive magnitude 7.0 earthquake struck Haiti in January 2010 with an epicenter about 25 km (15 mi) west of the capital, Port-au-Prince. Estimates are that over 300,000 people were killed and some 1.5 million left homeless. The earthquake was assessed as the worst in this region over the last 200 years. On 4 October 2016, Hurricane Matthew made landfall in Haiti, resulting in over 500 deaths and causing extensive damage to crops, houses, livestock, and infrastructure. Currently the poorest country in the Western Hemisphere, Haiti continues to experience bouts of political instability.

GEOGRAPHY :: HAITI

LOCATION:
Caribbean, western one-third of the island of Hispaniola, between the Caribbean Sea and the North Atlantic Ocean, west of the Dominican Republic

GEOGRAPHIC COORDINATES:
19 00 N, 72 25 W

MAP REFERENCES:
Central America and the Caribbean

AREA:
total: 27,750 sq km

land: 27,560 sq km

water: 190 sq km

country comparison to the world: 148

AREA - COMPARATIVE:
slightly smaller than Maryland

LAND BOUNDARIES:
total: 376 km

border countries (1): Dominican Republic 376 km

COASTLINE:
1,771 km

MARITIME CLAIMS:
territorial sea: 12 nm

exclusive economic zone: 200 nm

contiguous zone: 24 nm

continental shelf: to depth of exploitation

CLIMATE:
tropical; semiarid where mountains in east cut off trade winds

TERRAIN:
mostly rough and mountainous

ELEVATION:
mean elevation: 470 m

lowest point: Caribbean Sea 0 m

highest point: Chaine de la Selle 2,680 m

NATURAL RESOURCES:
bauxite, copper, calcium carbonate, gold, marble, hydropower, arable land

LAND USE:
agricultural land: 66.4% (2011 est.)

arable land: 38.5% (2011 est.) / permanent crops: 10.2% (2011 est.) / permanent pasture: 17.7% (2011 est.)

forest: 3.6% (2011 est.)

other: 30% (2011 est.)

IRRIGATED LAND:
970 sq km (2012)

POPULATION DISTRIBUTION:
fairly even distribution; largest concentrations located near coastal areas

NATURAL HAZARDS:
lies in the middle of the hurricane belt and subject to severe storms from June to October; occasional flooding and earthquakes; periodic droughts

ENVIRONMENT - CURRENT ISSUES:
extensive deforestation (much of the remaining forested land is being cleared for agriculture and used as fuel); soil erosion; overpopulation leads to inadequate supplies of potable water and and a lack of sanitation; natural disasters

ENVIRONMENT - INTERNATIONAL AGREEMENTS:

party to: Biodiversity, Climate Change, Climate Change-Kyoto Protocol, Desertification, Law of the Sea, Marine Dumping, Marine Life Conservation, Ozone Layer Protection

signed, but not ratified: Hazardous Wastes

GEOGRAPHY - NOTE:

shares island of Hispaniola with Dominican Republic (western one-third is Haiti, eastern two-thirds is the Dominican Republic); it is the most mountainous nation in the Caribbean

PEOPLE AND SOCIETY :: HAITI

POPULATION:

10,788,440 (July 2018 est.)

note: estimates for this country explicitly take into account the effects of excess mortality due to AIDS; this can result in lower life expectancy, higher infant mortality, higher death rates, lower population growth rates, and changes in the distribution of population by age and sex than would otherwise be expected

country comparison to the world: 83

NATIONALITY:

noun: Haitian(s)

adjective: Haitian

ETHNIC GROUPS:

black 95%, mixed and white 5%

LANGUAGES:

French (official), Creole (official)

RELIGIONS:

Roman Catholic 54.7%, Protestant 28.5% (Baptist 15.4%, Pentecostal 7.9%, Adventist 3%, Methodist 1.5%, other 0.7%), Vodou 2.1%, other 4.6%, none 10.2% (2003 est.)

note: many Haitians practice elements of Vodou in addition to another religion, most often Roman Catholicism; Vodou was recognized as an official religion in 2003

AGE STRUCTURE:

0-14 years: 32.27% (male 1,733,920 /female 1,747,387)

15-24 years: 21.11% (male 1,139,188 /female 1,137,754)

25-54 years: 37.32% (male 1,997,816 /female 2,028,495)

55-64 years: 5.1% (male 262,494 /female 287,515)

65 years and over: 4.21% (male 199,617 /female 254,254) (2018 est.)

DEPENDENCY RATIOS:

total dependency ratio: 62.3 (2015 est.)

youth dependency ratio: 54.8 (2015 est.)

elderly dependency ratio: 7.5 (2015 est.)

potential support ratio: 13.3 (2015 est.)

MEDIAN AGE:

total: 23.3 years (2018 est.)

male: 23.1 years

female: 23.6 years

country comparison to the world: 172

POPULATION GROWTH RATE:

1.31% (2018 est.)

country comparison to the world: 84

BIRTH RATE:

22.6 births/1,000 population (2018 est.)

country comparison to the world: 65

DEATH RATE:

7.5 deaths/1,000 population (2018 est.)

country comparison to the world: 111

NET MIGRATION RATE:

-2 migrant(s)/1,000 population (2018 est.)

country comparison to the world: 163

POPULATION DISTRIBUTION:

fairly even distribution; largest concentrations located near coastal areas

URBANIZATION:

urban population: 56.2% of total population (2019)

rate of urbanization: 2.9% annual rate of change (2015-20 est.)

MAJOR URBAN AREAS - POPULATION:

2.704 million PORT-AU-PRINCE (capital) (2019)

SEX RATIO:

at birth: 1.01 male(s)/female

0-14 years: 0.99 male(s)/female

15-24 years: 1 male(s)/female

25-54 years: 0.98 male(s)/female

55-64 years: 0.91 male(s)/female

65 years and over: 0.79 male(s)/female

total population: 0.98 male(s)/female (2018 est.)

MOTHER'S MEAN AGE AT FIRST BIRTH:

22.8 years (2016/7 est.)

note: median age at first birth among women 25-29

MATERNAL MORTALITY RATE:

480 deaths/100,000 live births (2017 est.)

country comparison to the world: 22

INFANT MORTALITY RATE:

total: 45.4 deaths/1,000 live births (2018 est.)

male: 51.5 deaths/1,000 live births

female: 39.2 deaths/1,000 live births

country comparison to the world: 35

LIFE EXPECTANCY AT BIRTH:

total population: 64.6 years (2018 est.)

male: 61.9 years

female: 67.2 years

country comparison to the world: 186

TOTAL FERTILITY RATE:

2.66 children born/woman (2018 est.)

country comparison to the world: 65

CONTRACEPTIVE PREVALENCE RATE:

34.3% (2016/17)

DRINKING WATER SOURCE:

improved:

urban: 64.9% of population

rural: 47.6% of population

total: 57.7% of population

unimproved:

urban: 35.1% of population

rural: 52.4% of population

total: 42.3% of population (2015 est.)

CURRENT HEALTH EXPENDITURE:

5.4% (2016)

PHYSICIANS DENSITY:

0.23 physicians/1,000 population (2018)

HOSPITAL BED DENSITY:

0.7 beds/1,000 population (2013)

SANITATION FACILITY ACCESS:

improved:

urban: 33.6% of population (2015 est.)

rural: 19.2% of population (2015 est.)

total: 27.6% of population (2015 est.)

unimproved:

urban: 66.4% of population (2015 est.)

rural: 80.8% of population (2015 est.)

total: 72.4% of population (2015 est.)

HIV/AIDS - ADULT PREVALENCE RATE:

2% (2018 est.)

country comparison to the world: 24

HIV/AIDS - PEOPLE LIVING WITH HIV/AIDS:

160,000 (2018 est.)

country comparison to the world: 33

HIV/AIDS - DEATHS:

2,700 (2018 est.)

country comparison to the world: 38

MAJOR INFECTIOUS DISEASES:

degree of risk: very high (2016)

food or waterborne diseases: bacterial and protozoal diarrhea, hepatitis A and E, and typhoid fever (2016)

vectorborne diseases: dengue fever and malaria (2016)

note: active local transmission of Zika virus by Aedes species mosquitoes has been identified in this country (as of August 2016); it poses an important risk (a large number of cases possible) among US citizens if bitten by an infective mosquito; other less common ways to get Zika are through sex, via blood transfusion, or during pregnancy, in which the pregnant woman passes Zika virus to her fetus

OBESITY - ADULT PREVALENCE RATE:

22.7% (2016)

country comparison to the world: 72

CHILDREN UNDER THE AGE OF 5 YEARS UNDERWEIGHT:

9.5% (2017)

country comparison to the world: 66

EDUCATION EXPENDITURES:

2.4% of GDP (2016)

country comparison to the world: 162

LITERACY:

definition: age 15 and over can read and write

total population: 60.7%

male: 64.3%

female: 57.3% (2015 est.)

GOVERNMENT :: HAITI

COUNTRY NAME:

conventional long form: Republic of Haiti

conventional short form: Haiti

local long form: Republique d'Haiti/Repiblik d Ayiti

local short form: Haiti/Ayiti

etymology: the native Taino name means "Land of High Mountains" and was originally applied to the entire island of Hispaniola

GOVERNMENT TYPE:

semi-presidential republic

CAPITAL:

name: Port-au-Prince

geographic coordinates: 18 32 N, 72 20 W

time difference: UTC-5 (same time as Washington, DC, during Standard Time)

daylight saving time: +1hr, begins second Sunday in March; ends first Sunday in November

etymology: according to tradition, in 1706, a Captain de Saint-Andre named the bay and its surrounding area after his ship Le Prince; the name of the town that grew there means, "the Port of The Prince"

ADMINISTRATIVE DIVISIONS:

10 departments (departements, singular - departement); Artibonite, Centre, Grand'Anse, Nippes, Nord, Nord-Est, Nord-Ouest, Ouest, Sud, Sud-Est

INDEPENDENCE:

1 January 1804 (from France)

NATIONAL HOLIDAY:

Independence Day, 1 January (1804)

CONSTITUTION:

history: many previous; latest adopted 10 March 1987

amendments: proposed by the executive branch or by either the Senate or the Chamber of Deputies; consideration of proposed amendments requires support by at least two-thirds majority of both houses; passage requires at least two-thirds majority of the membership present and at least two-thirds majority of the votes cast; approved amendments enter into force after installation of the next president of the republic; constitutional articles on the democratic and republican form of government cannot be amended; amended 2011, 2012 (2018)

LEGAL SYSTEM:

civil law system strongly influenced by Napoleonic Code

INTERNATIONAL LAW ORGANIZATION PARTICIPATION:

accepts compulsory ICJ jurisdiction; non-party state to the ICCt

CITIZENSHIP:

citizenship by birth: no

citizenship by descent only: at least one parent must be a native-born citizen of Haiti

dual citizenship recognized: no

residency requirement for naturalization: 5 years

SUFFRAGE:

18 years of age; universal

EXECUTIVE BRANCH:

chief of state: President Jovenel MOISE (since 7 February 2017)

head of government: Prime Minister Fritz William MICHEL (since 22 July 2019); note - Prime Minister Jean Michel LAPIN resigned on 22 July 2019

cabinet: Cabinet chosen by the prime minister in consultation with the president; parliament must ratify the Cabinet and Prime Minister's governing policy

elections/appointments: president directly elected by absolute majority popular vote in 2 rounds if needed for a 5-year term (eligible for a single non-consecutive term); last election originally scheduled for 9 October 2016 but postponed until 20 November 2016 due to Hurricane Matthew

election results: Jovenel MOISE elected president in first round; percent of vote - Jovenel MOISE (PHTK) 55.6%, Jude CELESTIN (LAPEH) 19.6%, Jean-Charles MOISE (PPD) 11%, Maryse NARCISSE (FL) 9%; other 4.8%

LEGISLATIVE BRANCH:

description: bicameral legislature or le Corps l'egislatif ou le Parlement consists of:
le S'enat or Senate (30 seats, 29 filled as of June 2019; members directly elected in multi-seat constituencies by absolute majority vote in 2 rounds if needed; members serve 6-year terms

with one-third of the membership renewed every 2 years)
la Chambre de deput'es or Chamber of Deputies (119 seats; 116 filled as of June 2019; members directly elected in single-seat constituencies by absolute majority vote in 2 rounds if needed; members serve 4-year terms); note - when the 2 chambers meet collectively it is known as L'Assembl'ee nationale or the National Assembly and is convened for specific purposes spelled out in the constitution

elections:
Senate - last held on 20 November 2016 with runoff on 29 January 2017 (next scheduled for 27 October 2019)
Chamber of Deputies - last held on 9 August 2015 with runoff on 25 October 2015 and 20 November 2016 (next scheduled for 27 October 2019)

election results:
Senate - percent of vote by party - NA; seats by party - NA; composition - men 27, women 1, percent of women 3.6%
Chamber of Deputies - percent of vote by party - NA; seats by party - NA; composition - men 115, women 3, percent of women 2.5%; note - total legislature percent of women 2.7%

JUDICIAL BRANCH:

highest courts: Supreme Court or Cour de cassation (consists of a chief judge and other judges); note - Haiti is a member of the Caribbean Court of Justice

judge selection and term of office: judges appointed by the president from candidate lists submitted by the Senate of the National Assembly; note - Article 174 of Haiti's constitution states that judges of the Supreme Court are appointed for 10 years, whereas Article 177 states that judges of the Supreme Court are appointed for life

subordinate courts: Courts of Appeal; Courts of First Instance; magistrate's courts; land, labor, and children's courts

note: the Superior Council of the Judiciary or Conseil Superieur du Pouvoir Judiciaire is a 9-member body charged with the administration and oversight of the judicial branch of government

POLITICAL PARTIES AND LEADERS:

Alternative League for Haitian Progress and Empowerment or LAPEH [Jude CELESTIN]
Christian Movement for a New Haiti or MCNH [Luc MESADIEU]
Christian National Movement for the Reconstruction of Haiti or UNCRH [Chavannes JEUNE]
Convention for Democratic Unity or KID [Evans PAUL]
Cooperative Action to Rebuild Haiti or KONBA [Jean William JEANTY]
December 16 Platform or Platfom 16 Desanm [Dr. Gerard BLOT]
Democratic Alliance Party or ALYANS [Evans PAUL] (coalition includes KID and PPRH)
Democratic Centers' National Council or CONACED [Osner FEVRY]
Dessalinian Patriotic and Popular Movement or MOPOD [Jean Andre VICTOR]
Effort and Solidarity to Create an Alternative for the People or ESKAMP [Joseph JASME]
Fanmi Lavalas or FL [Jean-Bertrand ARISTIDE]
For Us All or PONT [Jean-Marie CHERESTAL]
Fusion of Haitian Social Democrats or FHSD [Edmonde Supplice BEAUZILE]
Grouping of Citizens for Hope or RESPE [Charles-Henri BAKER]
Haitians for Haiti [Yvon NEPTUNE]
Haitian Tet Kale Party or PHTK [Ann Valerie Timothee MILFORT]
Haiti in Action or AAA [Youri LATORTUE]
Independent Movement for National Reconstruction or MIRN [Luc FLEURINORD]
Konbit Pou refe Ayiti or KONBIT
Lavni Organization or LAVNI [Yves CRISTALIN]
Liberal Party of Haiti or PLH [Jean Andre VICTOR]
Love Haiti or Renmen Ayiti [Jean-Henry CEANT, Camille LEBLANC]
Mobilization for National Development or MDN [Hubert de RONCERAY]
New Christian Movement for a New Haiti or MOCHRENA [Luc MESADIEU]
Organization for the Advancement of Haiti and Haitians or OLAHH
Party for the Integral Advancement of the Haitian People or PAIPH
Patriotic Unity or IP [Marie Denise CLAUDE]
Peasant's Response or Repons Peyizan [Michel MARTELLY]
Platform Alternative for Progress and Democracy or ALTENATIV [Victor BENOIT and Evans PAUL]
Platform of Haitian Patriots or PLAPH [Dejean BELISAIRE, Himmler REBU]
Platform Pitit Desaline or PPD [Jean-Charles MOISE]
Pont
Popular Party for the Renewal of Haiti or PPRH [Claude ROMAIN]
PPG18
Rally of Progressive National Democrats or RDNP [Mirlande MANIGAT]
Renmen Ayiti or RA [Jean-Henry CEANT]
Reseau National Bouclier or Bouclier
Respect or RESPE
Strength in Unity or Ansanm Nou Fo [Leslie VOLTAIRE]
Struggling People's Organization or OPL [Jacques-Edouard ALEXIS]
Truth (Verite)
Union [Chavannes JEUNE]
Unity or Inite [Levaillant LOUIS-JEUNE]
Vigilance or Veye Yo [Lavarice GAUDIN]

INTERNATIONAL ORGANIZATION PARTICIPATION:

ACP, AOSIS, Caricom, CD, CDB, CELAC, FAO, G-77, IADB, IAEA, IBRD, ICAO, ICC (NGOs), ICRM, IDA, IFAD, IFC, IFRCS, ILO, IMF, IMO, Interpol, IOC, IOM, IPU, ITSO, ITU, ITUC (NGOs), LAES, MIGA, NAM, OAS, OIF, OPANAL, OPCW, PCA, Petrocaribe, UN, UNCTAD, UNESCO, UNIDO, Union Latina, UNWTO, UPU, WCO, WFTU (NGOs), WHO, WIPO, WMO, WTO

DIPLOMATIC REPRESENTATION IN THE US:

Ambassador Paul Getty ALTIDOR (since 2 May 2012)

chancery: 2311 Massachusetts Avenue NW, Washington, DC 20008

telephone: [1] (202) 332-4090

FAX: [1] (202) 745-7215

consulate(s) general: Atlanta, Boston, Chicago, Miami, Orlando (FL), New York, San Juan (Puerto Rico)

DIPLOMATIC REPRESENTATION FROM THE US:

chief of mission: Ambassador Michele SISON (since 21 February 2018)

telephone: [509] 229-8000

embassy: Tabarre 41, Route de Tabarre, Port-au-Prince

mailing address: (in Haiti) P.O. Box 1634, Port-au-Prince, Haiti; (from abroad) 3400 Port-au-Prince, State Department, Washington, DC 20521-3400

FAX: [509] 229-8028

FLAG DESCRIPTION:

two equal horizontal bands of blue (top) and red with a centered white rectangle bearing the coat of arms, which contains a palm tree flanked by flags and two cannons above a scroll bearing the motto L'UNION FAIT LA FORCE (Union Makes Strength); the colors are taken from the French Tricolor and represent the union of blacks and mulattoes

NATIONAL SYMBOL(S):

Hispaniolan trogon (bird), hibiscus flower; national colors: blue, red

NATIONAL ANTHEM:

name: "La Dessalinienne" (The Dessalines Song)

lyrics/music: Justin LHERISSON/Nicolas GEFFRARD

note: adopted 1904; named for Jean-Jacques DESSALINES, a leader in the Haitian Revolution and first ruler of an independent Haiti

ECONOMY :: HAITI

ECONOMY - OVERVIEW:

Haiti is a free market economy with low labor costs and tariff-free access to the US for many of its exports. Two-fifths of all Haitians depend on the agricultural sector, mainly small-scale subsistence farming, which remains vulnerable to damage from frequent natural disasters. Poverty, corruption, vulnerability to natural disasters, and low levels of education for much of the population represent some of the most serious impediments to Haiti's economic growth. Remittances are the primary source of foreign exchange, equivalent to more than a quarter of GDP, and nearly double the combined value of Haitian exports and foreign direct investment.

Currently the poorest country in the Western Hemisphere, with close to 60% of the population living under the national poverty line, Haiti's GDP growth rose to 5.5% in 2011 as the Haitian economy began recovering from the devastating January 2010 earthquake that destroyed much of its capital city, Port-au-Prince, and neighboring areas. However, growth slowed to below 2% in 2015 and 2016 as political uncertainty, drought conditions, decreasing foreign aid, and the depreciation of the national currency took a toll on investment and economic growth. Hurricane Matthew, the fiercest Caribbean storm in nearly a decade, made landfall in Haiti on 4 October 2016, with 140 mile-per-hour winds, creating a new humanitarian emergency. An estimated 2.1 million people were affected by the category 4 storm, which caused extensive damage to crops, houses, livestock, and infrastructure across Haiti's southern peninsula.

US economic engagement under the Caribbean Basin Trade Partnership Act (CBTPA) and the 2008 Haitian Hemispheric Opportunity through Partnership Encouragement Act (HOPE II) have contributed to an increase in apparel exports and investment by providing duty-free access to the US. The Haiti Economic Lift Program (HELP) Act of 2010 extended the CBTPA and HOPE II until 2020, while the Trade Preferences Extension Act of 2015 extended trade benefits provided to Haiti in the HOPE and HELP Acts through September 2025. Apparel sector exports in 2016 reached approximately $850 million and account for over 90% of Haitian exports and more than 10% of the GDP.

Investment in Haiti is hampered by the difficulty of doing business and weak infrastructure, including access to electricity. Haiti's outstanding external debt was cancelled by donor countries following the 2010 earthquake, but has since risen to $2.6 billion as of December 2017, the majority of which is owed to Venezuela under the PetroCaribe program. Although the government has increased its revenue collection, it continues to rely on formal international economic assistance for fiscal sustainability, with over 20% of its annual budget coming from foreign aid or direct budget support.

GDP (PURCHASING POWER PARITY):

$19.97 billion (2017 est.)

$19.74 billion (2016 est.)

$19.46 billion (2015 est.)

note: data are in 2017 dollars

country comparison to the world: 150

GDP (OFFICIAL EXCHANGE RATE):

$8.608 billion (2017 est.)

GDP - REAL GROWTH RATE:

1.2% (2017 est.)

1.5% (2016 est.)

1.2% (2015 est.)

country comparison to the world: 181

GDP - PER CAPITA (PPP):

$1,800 (2017 est.)

$1,800 (2016 est.)

$1,800 (2015 est.)

note: data are in 2017 dollars

country comparison to the world: 213

GROSS NATIONAL SAVING:

24.9% of GDP (2017 est.)

29.5% of GDP (2016 est.)

29.3% of GDP (2015 est.)

country comparison to the world: 61

GDP - COMPOSITION, BY END USE:

household consumption: 99.1% (2017 est.)

government consumption: 10% (2016 est.)

investment in fixed capital: 32.6% (2016 est.)

investment in inventories: -1.4% (2017 est.)

exports of goods and services: 20% (2017 est.)

imports of goods and services: -60.3% (2017 est.)

note: figure for household consumption also includes government consumption

GDP - COMPOSITION, BY SECTOR OF ORIGIN:

agriculture: 22.1% (2017 est.)

industry: 20.3% (2017 est.)

services: 57.6% (2017 est.)

AGRICULTURE - PRODUCTS:

coffee, mangoes, cocoa, sugarcane, rice, corn, sorghum; wood, vetiver

INDUSTRIES:

textiles, sugar refining, flour milling, cement, light assembly using imported parts

INDUSTRIAL PRODUCTION GROWTH RATE:

0.9% (2017 est.)

country comparison to the world: 161

LABOR FORCE:

4.594 million (2014 est.)

note: shortage of skilled labor; unskilled labor abundant

country comparison to the world: 88

LABOR FORCE - BY OCCUPATION:

agriculture: 38.1%

industry: 11.5%

services: 50.4% (2010)

UNEMPLOYMENT RATE:

40.6% (2010 est.)

note: widespread unemployment and underemployment; more than two-thirds of the labor force do not have formal jobs

country comparison to the world: 215

POPULATION BELOW POVERTY LINE:

58.5% (2012 est.)

HOUSEHOLD INCOME OR CONSUMPTION BY PERCENTAGE SHARE:

lowest 10%: 0.7%

highest 10%: 47.7% (2001)

DISTRIBUTION OF FAMILY INCOME - GINI INDEX:

60.8 (2012)

59.2 (2001)

country comparison to the world: 4

BUDGET:

revenues: 1.567 billion (2017 est.)

expenditures: 1.65 billion (2017 est.)

TAXES AND OTHER REVENUES:

18.2% (of GDP) (2017 est.)

country comparison to the world: 163

BUDGET SURPLUS (+) OR DEFICIT (-):

-1% (of GDP) (2017 est.)

country comparison to the world: 79

PUBLIC DEBT:

31.1% of GDP (2017 est.)

33.9% of GDP (2016 est.)

country comparison to the world: 164

FISCAL YEAR:

1 October - 30 September

INFLATION RATE (CONSUMER PRICES):

14.7% (2017 est.)

13.4% (2016 est.)

country comparison to the world: 211

COMMERCIAL BANK PRIME LENDING RATE:

13.1% (31 December 2017 est.)

13.23% (31 December 2016 est.)

country comparison to the world: 58

STOCK OF NARROW MONEY:

$1.273 billion (31 December 2017 est.)

$1.049 billion (31 December 2016 est.)

country comparison to the world: 151

STOCK OF BROAD MONEY:

$1.273 billion (31 December 2017 est.)

$1.049 billion (31 December 2016 est.)

country comparison to the world: 156

STOCK OF DOMESTIC CREDIT:

$3.112 billion (31 December 2017 est.)

$2.253 billion (31 December 2016 est.)

country comparison to the world: 138

MARKET VALUE OF PUBLICLY TRADED SHARES:

NA

CURRENT ACCOUNT BALANCE:

-$348 million (2017 est.)

-$83 million (2016 est.)

country comparison to the world: 108

EXPORTS:

$980.2 million (2017 est.)

$995 million (2016 est.)

country comparison to the world: 161

EXPORTS - PARTNERS:

US 80.6%, Dominican Republic 4.9% (2017)

EXPORTS - COMMODITIES:

apparel, manufactures, oils, cocoa, mangoes, coffee

IMPORTS:

$3.618 billion (2017 est.)

$3.183 billion (2016 est.)

country comparison to the world: 144

IMPORTS - COMMODITIES:

food, manufactured goods, machinery and transport equipment, fuels, raw materials

IMPORTS - PARTNERS:

US 20.7%, China 18.8%, Netherlands Antilles 15.7%, Indonesia 8.5% (2017)

RESERVES OF FOREIGN EXCHANGE AND GOLD:

$2.361 billion (31 December 2017 est.)

$2.11 billion (31 December 2016 est.)

country comparison to the world: 117

DEBT - EXTERNAL:

$2.762 billion (31 December 2017 est.)

$2.17 billion (31 December 2016 est.)

country comparison to the world: 146

STOCK OF DIRECT FOREIGN INVESTMENT - AT HOME:

$1.46 billion (31 December 2017 est.)

$1.37 billion (31 December 2016 est.)

country comparison to the world: 122

EXCHANGE RATES:

gourdes (HTG) per US dollar -

65.21 (2017 est.)

63.34 (2016 est.)

63.34 (2015 est.)

50.71 (2014 est.)

45.22 (2013 est.)

ENERGY :: HAITI

ELECTRICITY ACCESS:

population without electricity: 8 million (2017)

electrification - total population: 38.7% (2016)

electrification - urban areas: 65.4% (2016)

electrification - rural areas: 0.5% (2016)

ELECTRICITY - PRODUCTION:

1.023 billion kWh (2016 est.)

country comparison to the world: 149

ELECTRICITY - CONSUMPTION:

406.2 million kWh (2016 est.)

country comparison to the world: 173

ELECTRICITY - EXPORTS:

0 kWh (2016 est.)

country comparison to the world: 147

ELECTRICITY - IMPORTS:

0 kWh (2016 est.)

country comparison to the world: 159

ELECTRICITY - INSTALLED GENERATING CAPACITY:

332,000 kW (2016 est.)

country comparison to the world: 155

ELECTRICITY - FROM FOSSIL FUELS:

82% of total installed capacity (2016 est.)

country comparison to the world: 78

ELECTRICITY - FROM NUCLEAR FUELS:

0% of total installed capacity (2017 est.)

country comparison to the world: 106

ELECTRICITY - FROM HYDROELECTRIC PLANTS:

18% of total installed capacity (2017 est.)

country comparison to the world: 94

ELECTRICITY - FROM OTHER RENEWABLE SOURCES:

0% of total installed capacity (2017 est.)

country comparison to the world: 191

CRUDE OIL - PRODUCTION:

0 bbl/day (2018 est.)

country comparison to the world: 148

CRUDE OIL - EXPORTS:

0 bbl/day (2015 est.)

country comparison to the world: 136

CRUDE OIL - IMPORTS:

0 bbl/day (2015 est.)

country comparison to the world: 140

CRUDE OIL - PROVED RESERVES:

0 bbl (1 January 2018 est.)

country comparison to the world: 144

REFINED PETROLEUM PRODUCTS - PRODUCTION:

0 bbl/day (2015 est.)

country comparison to the world: 156

REFINED PETROLEUM PRODUCTS - CONSUMPTION:

21,000 bbl/day (2016 est.)

country comparison to the world: 137

REFINED PETROLEUM PRODUCTS - EXPORTS:

0 bbl/day (2015 est.)

country comparison to the world: 165

REFINED PETROLEUM PRODUCTS - IMPORTS:

20,030 bbl/day (2015 est.)

country comparison to the world: 122

NATURAL GAS - PRODUCTION:

0 cu m (2017 est.)

country comparison to the world: 145

NATURAL GAS - CONSUMPTION:

0 cu m (2017 est.)

country comparison to the world: 158

NATURAL GAS - EXPORTS:

0 cu m (2017 est.)

country comparison to the world: 120

NATURAL GAS - IMPORTS:

0 cu m (2017 est.)

country comparison to the world: 138

NATURAL GAS - PROVED RESERVES:

0 cu m (1 January 2014 est.)

country comparison to the world: 146

CARBON DIOXIDE EMISSIONS FROM CONSUMPTION OF ENERGY:

3.595 million Mt (2017 est.)

country comparison to the world: 141

COMMUNICATIONS :: HAITI

TELEPHONES - FIXED LINES:

total subscriptions: 5,703

subscriptions per 100 inhabitants: less than 1 (2017 est.)

country comparison to the world: 204

TELEPHONES - MOBILE CELLULAR:

total subscriptions: 6,486,549

subscriptions per 100 inhabitants: 61 (2017 est.)

country comparison to the world: 109

TELEPHONE SYSTEM:

general assessment: telecommunications infrastructure is among the least-developed in Latin America and the Caribbean; domestic cell service is functional (2018)

domestic: fixed-line is less than 1 per 100; mobile-cellular telephone services have expanded greatly in the last decade due to low-cost GSM (Global Systems for Mobile) phones and pay-as-you-go plans; mobile-cellular teledensity is 61 per 100 persons (2018)

international: country code - 509; landing points for the BDSNi and Fibralink submarine cables to 14 points in the Bahamas and Dominican Republic; satellite earth station - 1 Intelsat (Atlantic Ocean) (2019)

BROADCAST MEDIA:

98 television stations throughout the country, including 1 government-owned; cable TV subscription service available; 850 radio stations (of them, only 346 are licensed), including 1 government-owned; more than 100 community radio stations; over 64 FM stations in Port-au-Prince alone; VOA Creole Service broadcasts daily on 30 affiliate stations

(2016)

INTERNET COUNTRY CODE:

.ht

INTERNET USERS:

total: 1,282,686

percent of population: 12.2% (July 2016 est.)

country comparison to the world: 127

BROADBAND - FIXED SUBSCRIPTIONS:

total: 29,900

subscriptions per 100 inhabitants: less than 1 (2017 est.)

country comparison to the world: 141

MILITARY AND SECURITY :: HAITI

MILITARY AND SECURITY FORCES:

the Haitian Armed Forces (FAdH), disbanded in 1995, began to be reconstituted in 2017 to assist with natural disaster relief, border security, and combating transnational crime; the small Coast Guard is not part of the military, but rather the Haitian National Police. (2019)

TRANSPORTATION :: HAITI

NATIONAL AIR TRANSPORT SYSTEM:

number of registered air carriers: 1 (2015)

inventory of registered aircraft operated by air carriers: 1 (2015)

CIVIL AIRCRAFT REGISTRATION COUNTRY CODE PREFIX:

HH (2016)

AIRPORTS:

14 (2013)

country comparison to the world: 149

AIRPORTS - WITH PAVED RUNWAYS:

total: 4 (2017)

2,438 to 3,047 m: 2 (2017)

914 to 1,523 m: 2 (2017)

AIRPORTS - WITH UNPAVED RUNWAYS:

total: 10 (2013)

914 to 1,523 m: 2 (2013)

under 914 m: 8 (2013)

ROADWAYS:

total: 4,266 km (2009)

paved: 768 km (2009)

unpaved: 3,498 km (2009)

country comparison to the world: 148

MERCHANT MARINE:

total: 4

by type: general cargo 3, other 1 (2018)

country comparison to the world: 165

PORTS AND TERMINALS:

major seaport(s): Cap-Haitien, Gonaives, Jacmel, Port-au-Prince

TRANSNATIONAL ISSUES :: HAITI

DISPUTES - INTERNATIONAL:

since 2004, peacekeepers from the UN Stabilization Mission in Haiti have assisted in maintaining civil order in Haiti; the mission currently includes 6,685 military, 2,607 police, and 443 civilian personnel; despite efforts to control illegal migration, Haitians cross into the Dominican Republic and sail to neighboring countries; Haiti claims US-administered Navassa Island

REFUGEES AND INTERNALLY DISPLACED PERSONS:

IDPs: 34,508 (includes only IDPs from the 2010 earthquake living in camps or camp-like situations; information is lacking about IDPs living outside of camps or who have left camps) (2019)

stateless persons: 2,992 (2018); note - individuals without a nationality who were born in the Dominican Republic prior to January 2010

TRAFFICKING IN PERSONS:

current situation: Haiti is a source, transit, and destination country for men, women, and children subjected to forced labor and sex trafficking; most of Haiti's trafficking cases involve children in domestic servitude vulnerable to physical and sexual abuse; dismissed and runaway child domestic servants often end up in prostitution, begging, or street crime; other exploited populations included low-income Haitians, child laborers, and women and children living in IDP camps dating to the 2010 earthquake; Haitian adults are vulnerable to fraudulent labor recruitment abroad and, along with children, may be subjected to forced labor in the Dominican Republic, elsewhere in the Caribbean, South America, and the US; Dominicans are exploited in sex trafficking and forced labor in Haiti

tier rating: Tier 2 Watch List – Haiti does not fully comply with the minimum standards for the elimination of trafficking; however, it is making significant efforts to do so; in 2014, Haiti was granted a waiver from an otherwise required downgrade to Tier 3 because its government has a written plan that, if implemented would constitute making significant efforts to bring itself into compliance with the minimum standards for the elimination of trafficking; in 2014, Haiti developed a national anti-trafficking action plan and enacted a law prohibiting all forms of human trafficking, although judicial corruption hampered its implementation; progress was made in investigating and prosecuting suspected traffickers, but no convictions were made; the government sustained limited efforts to identify and refer victims to protective services, which were provided mostly by NGOs without government support; campaigns to raise awareness about child labor and child trafficking continued (2015)

ILLICIT DRUGS:

Caribbean transshipment point for cocaine en route to the US and Europe; substantial bulk cash smuggling activity; Colombian narcotics traffickers favor Haiti for illicit financial transactions; pervasive corruption; significant consumer of cannabis

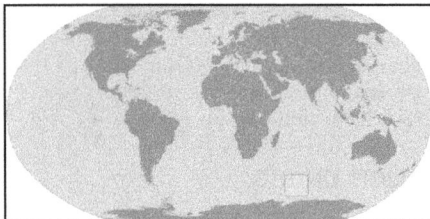
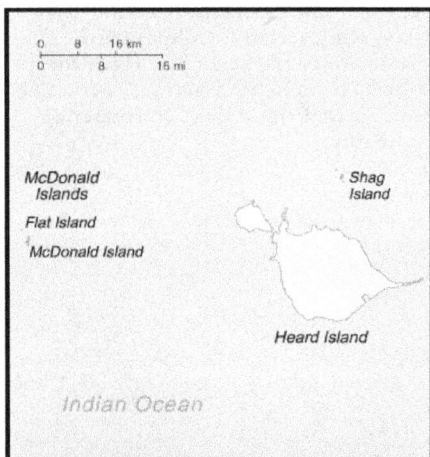

ANTARCTICA :: HEARD ISLAND AND MCDONALD ISLANDS

INTRODUCTION :: HEARD ISLAND AND MCDONALD ISLANDS

BACKGROUND:
The UK transferred these uninhabited, barren, sub-Antarctic islands to Australia in 1947. Populated by large numbers of seal and bird species, the islands have been designated a nature preserve.

GEOGRAPHY :: HEARD ISLAND AND MCDONALD ISLANDS

LOCATION:
islands in the Indian Ocean, about two-thirds of the way from Madagascar to Antarctica

GEOGRAPHIC COORDINATES:
53 06 S, 72 31 E

MAP REFERENCES:
Antarctic Region

AREA:
total: 412 sq km

land: 412 sq km

water: 0 sq km

country comparison to the world: 203

AREA - COMPARATIVE:
slightly more than two times the size of Washington, DC

LAND BOUNDARIES:
0 km

COASTLINE:
101.9 km

MARITIME CLAIMS:
territorial sea: 12 nm

exclusive fishing zone: 200 nm

CLIMATE:
antarctic

TERRAIN:
Heard Island - 80% ice-covered, bleak and mountainous, dominated by a large massif (Big Ben) and an active volcano (Mawson Peak); McDonald Islands - small and rocky

ELEVATION:
lowest point: Indian Ocean 0 m

highest point: Mawson Peak on Big Ben volcano 2,745 m

NATURAL RESOURCES:
fish

LAND USE:
agricultural land: 0% (2011 est.)

arable land: 0% (2011 est.) / permanent crops: 0% (2011 est.) / permanent pasture: 0% (2011 est.)

forest: 0% (2011 est.)

other: 100% (2011 est.)

NATURAL HAZARDS:
Mawson Peak, an active volcano, is on Heard Island

ENVIRONMENT - CURRENT ISSUES:
none; uninhabited and mostly ice covered

GEOGRAPHY - NOTE:
Mawson Peak on Heard Island is the highest Australian mountain (at 2,745 meters, it is taller than Mt. Kosciuszko in Australia proper), and one of only two active volcanoes located in Australian territory, the other being McDonald Island; in 1992, McDonald Island broke its dormancy and began erupting; it has erupted several times since, most recently in 2005

PEOPLE AND SOCIETY :: HEARD ISLAND AND MCDONALD ISLANDS

POPULATION:
uninhabited

GOVERNMENT :: HEARD ISLAND AND MCDONALD ISLANDS

COUNTRY NAME:
conventional long form: Territory of Heard Island and McDonald Islands

conventional short form: Heard Island and McDonald Islands

abbreviation: HIMI

etymology: named after American Captain John HEARD, who sighted the island on 25 November 1853, and American Captain William McDONALD, who discovered the islands on 4 January 1854

DEPENDENCY STATUS:
territory of Australia; administered from Canberra by the Department of Sustainability, Environment, Water, Population and Communities (Australian Antarctic Division)

LEGAL SYSTEM:
the laws of Australia apply where applicable

DIPLOMATIC REPRESENTATION IN THE US:
none (territory of Australia)

DIPLOMATIC REPRESENTATION FROM THE US:
none (territory of Australia)

FLAG DESCRIPTION:
the flag of Australia is used

ECONOMY :: HEARD ISLAND AND MCDONALD ISLANDS

ECONOMY - OVERVIEW:
The islands have no indigenous economic activity, but the Australian Government allows limited fishing in the surrounding waters. Visits to Heard Island typically focus on terrestrial and marine research and infrequent private expeditions.

COMMUNICATIONS :: HEARD ISLAND AND MCDONALD ISLANDS

INTERNET COUNTRY CODE:
.hm

MILITARY AND SECURITY :: HEARD ISLAND AND MCDONALD ISLANDS

MILITARY - NOTE:
defense is the responsibility of Australia; Australia conducts fisheries patrols

TRANSPORTATION :: HEARD ISLAND AND MCDONALD ISLANDS

RAILWAYS:
ROADWAYS:
PORTS AND TERMINALS:
none; offshore anchorage only

TRANSNATIONAL ISSUES :: HEARD ISLAND AND MCDONALD ISLANDS

DISPUTES - INTERNATIONAL:
none

EUROPE :: HOLY SEE (VATICAN CITY)

INTRODUCTION :: HOLY SEE (VATICAN CITY)

BACKGROUND:
Popes in their secular role ruled portions of the Italian peninsula for more than a thousand years until the mid-19th century, when many of the Papal States were seized by the newly united Kingdom of Italy. In 1870, the pope's holdings were further circumscribed when Rome itself was annexed. Disputes between a series of "prisoner" popes and Italy were resolved in 1929 by three Lateran Treaties, which established the independent state of Vatican City and granted Roman Catholicism special status in Italy. In 1984, a concordat between the Holy See and Italy modified certain of the earlier treaty provisions, including the primacy of Roman Catholicism as the Italian state religion. Present concerns of the Holy See include religious freedom, threats against minority Christian communities in Africa and the Middle East, the plight of refugees and migrants, sexual misconduct by clergy, international development, interreligious dialogue and reconciliation, and the application of church doctrine in an era of rapid change and globalization. About 1.3 billion people worldwide profess Catholicism - the world's largest Christian faith.

GEOGRAPHY :: HOLY SEE (VATICAN CITY)

LOCATION:
Southern Europe, an enclave of Rome (Italy)

GEOGRAPHIC COORDINATES:
41 54 N, 12 27 E

MAP REFERENCES:
Europe

AREA:
total: 0.44 sq km
land: 0.44 sq km
water: 0 sq km
country comparison to the world: 258

AREA - COMPARATIVE:
about 0.7 times the size of the National Mall in Washington, DC

LAND BOUNDARIES:
total: 3.4 km
border countries (1): Italy 3.4 km

COASTLINE:
0 km (landlocked)

MARITIME CLAIMS:
none (landlocked)

CLIMATE:
temperate; mild, rainy winters (September to May) with hot, dry summers (May to September)

TERRAIN:
urban; low hill

ELEVATION:
lowest point: Saint Peter's Square 19 m
highest point: Vatican Gardens (Vatican Hill) 78 m

NATURAL RESOURCES:
none

LAND USE:
agricultural land: 0% (2011 est.)
arable land: 0% (2011 est.) / permanent crops: 0% (2011 est.) / permanent pasture: 0% (2011 est.)
forest: 0% (2011 est.)
other: 100% (2011 est.)

NATURAL HAZARDS:
occasional earthquakes

ENVIRONMENT - CURRENT ISSUES:
some air pollution from the surrounding city of Rome

ENVIRONMENT - INTERNATIONAL AGREEMENTS:
party to: Ozone Layer Protection
signed, but not ratified: Air Pollution, Environmental Modification

GEOGRAPHY - NOTE:
landlocked; an enclave in Rome, Italy; world's smallest state; beyond the territorial boundary of Vatican City, the Lateran Treaty of 1929 grants the Holy See extraterritorial authority over 23 sites in Rome and five outside

of Rome, including the Pontifical Palace at Castel Gandolfo (the Pope's summer residence)

PEOPLE AND SOCIETY :: HOLY SEE (VATICAN CITY)

POPULATION:
1,000 (2017 est.)

country comparison to the world: 236

NATIONALITY:

noun: none

adjective: none

ETHNIC GROUPS:
Italian, Swiss, Argentinian, and other nationalities from around the world (2017)

LANGUAGES:
Italian, Latin, French, various other languages

RELIGIONS:
Roman Catholic

POPULATION GROWTH RATE:
0% (2014 est.)

country comparison to the world: 192

URBANIZATION:

urban population: 100% of total population (2019)

rate of urbanization: -0.05% annual rate of change (2015-20 est.)

MAJOR URBAN AREAS - POPULATION:
1,000 VATICAN CITY (capital) (2018)

HIV/AIDS - ADULT PREVALENCE RATE:
NA

HIV/AIDS - PEOPLE LIVING WITH HIV/AIDS:
NA

HIV/AIDS - DEATHS:
NA

EDUCATION EXPENDITURES:
NA

GOVERNMENT :: HOLY SEE (VATICAN CITY)

COUNTRY NAME:

conventional long form: The Holy See (Vatican City State)

conventional short form: Holy See (Vatican City)

local long form: La Santa Sede (Stato della Citta del Vaticano)

local short form: Santa Sede (Citta del Vaticano)

etymology: "holy" comes from the Greek word "hera" meaning "sacred"; "see" comes from the Latin word "sedes" meaning "seat," and refers to the episcopal chair; the term "Vatican" derives from the hill Mons Vaticanus on which the Vatican is located and which comes from the Latin "vaticinari" (to prophesy), referring to the fortune tellers and soothsayers who frequented the area in Roman times

GOVERNMENT TYPE:
ecclesiastical elective monarchy; self-described as an "absolute monarchy"

CAPITAL:

name: Vatican City

geographic coordinates: 41 54 N, 12 27 E

time difference: UTC+1 (6 hours ahead of Washington, DC, during Standard Time)

daylight saving time: +1hr, begins last Sunday in March; ends last Sunday in October

ADMINISTRATIVE DIVISIONS:
none

INDEPENDENCE:
11 February 1929; note - the three treaties signed with Italy on 11 February 1929 acknowledged, among other things, the full sovereignty of the Holy See and established its territorial extent; however, the origin of the Papal States, which over centuries varied considerably in extent, may be traced back to A.D. 754

NATIONAL HOLIDAY:
Election Day of Pope FRANCIS, 13 March (2013)

CONSTITUTION:

history: previous 1929, 1963; latest adopted 26 November 2000, effective 22 February 2001 (Fundamental Law of Vatican City State); note - in October 2013, Pope Francis instituted a 9-member Council of Cardinal Advisors to reform the administrative apparatus of the Holy See (Roman Curia) to include writing a new constitution

amendments: note - although the Fundamental Law of Vatican City State makes no mention of amendments, Article Four (drafting laws), states that this legislative responsibility resides with the Pontifical Commission for Vatican City State; draft legislation is submitted through the Secretariat of State and considered by the pope (2016)

LEGAL SYSTEM:
religious legal system based on canon (religious) law

INTERNATIONAL LAW ORGANIZATION PARTICIPATION:
has not submitted an ICJ jurisdiction declaration; non-party state to the ICCt

CITIZENSHIP:

citizenship by birth: no

citizenship by descent only: no

dual citizenship recognized: no

residency requirement for naturalization: not applicable

note: in the Holy See, citizenship is acquired by law, ex iure, or by adminstrative decision; in the first instance, citizenship is a function of holding office within the Holy See as in the case of cardinals resident in Vatican City or diplomats of the Holy See; in the second instance, citizenship may be requested in a limited set of circumstances for those who reside within Vatican City under papal authorization, as a function of their office or service, or as the spouses and children of current citizens; citizenship is lost once an individual no longer permanently resides in Vatican City, normally reverting to the citizenship previously held

SUFFRAGE:
election of the pope is limited to cardinals less than 80 years old

EXECUTIVE BRANCH:

chief of state: Pope FRANCIS (since 13 March 2013)

head of government: Secretary of State Cardinal Pietro PAROLIN (since 15 October 2013); note - Head of Government of Vatican City is President Cardinal Giuseppe BERTELLO (since 1 October 2011)

cabinet: Pontifical Commission for the State of Vatican City appointed by the pope

elections/appointments: pope elected by the College of Cardinals, usually for life or until voluntary resignation; election last held on 13 March 2013 (next to be held after the death or resignation of the current pope); Secretary of State appointed by the pope

election results: Jorge Mario BERGOGLIO, former Archbishop of Buenos Aires, elected Pope FRANCIS

LEGISLATIVE BRANCH:

description: unicameral Pontifical Commission for Vatican City State or Pontificia Commissione per lo Stato della Citta del Vaticano (7 seats; members appointed by the pope to serve 5-year terms)

elections: last held on 11 July 2018

election results: composition - men 7, women 0

JUDICIAL BRANCH:

highest courts: Supreme Court or Supreme Tribunal of the Apostolic Signatura (consists of the cardinal prefect, who serves as ex-officio president of the court, and 2 other cardinals of the Prefect Signatura); note - judicial duties were established by the Motu Proprio, papal directive, of Pope PIUS XII on 1 May 1946; most Vatican City criminal matters are handled by the Republic of Italy courts

judge selection and term of office: cardinal prefect appointed by the pope; the other 2 cardinals of the court appointed by the cardinal prefect on a yearly basis

subordinate courts: Appellate Court of Vatican City; Tribunal of Vatican City

POLITICAL PARTIES AND LEADERS:

none

INTERNATIONAL ORGANIZATION PARTICIPATION:

CE (observer), IAEA, Interpol, IOM, ITSO, ITU, ITUC (NGOs), OAS (observer), OPCW, OSCE, Schengen Convention (de facto member), SICA (observer), UN (observer), UNCTAD, UNHCR, Union Latina (observer), UNWTO (observer), UPU, WIPO, WTO (observer)

DIPLOMATIC REPRESENTATION IN THE US:

Apostolic Nuncio Archbishop Christophe PIERRE (since 27 June 2016)

chancery: 3339 Massachusetts Avenue NW, Washington, DC 20008

telephone: [1] (202) 333-7121

FAX: [1] (202) 337-4036

DIPLOMATIC REPRESENTATION FROM THE US:

chief of mission: Ambassador Callista GINGRICH (since 22 December 2017)

telephone: [39] (06) 4674-1

embassy: American Embassy to the Holy See, Via Sallustiana, 49, 00187 Rome, Italy

mailing address: Unit 5660, Box 66, DPO AE 09624-0066

FAX: [39] (06) 4674-3412

FLAG DESCRIPTION:

two vertical bands of yellow (hoist side) and white with the arms of the Holy See, consisting of the crossed keys of Saint Peter surmounted by the three-tiered papal tiara, centered in the white band; the yellow color represents the pope's spiritual power, the white his worldly power

NATIONAL SYMBOL(S):

crossed keys beneath a papal tiara; national colors: yellow, white

NATIONAL ANTHEM:

name: "Inno e Marcia Pontificale" (Hymn and Pontifical March); often called The Pontifical Hymn

lyrics/music: Raffaello LAVAGNA/Charles-Francois GOUNOD

note: adopted 1950

ECONOMY :: HOLY SEE (VATICAN CITY)

ECONOMY - OVERVIEW:

The Holy See is supported financially by a variety of sources, including investments, real estate income, and donations from Catholic individuals, dioceses, and institutions; these help fund the Roman Curia (Vatican bureaucracy), diplomatic missions, and media outlets. Moreover, an annual collection taken up in dioceses and from direct donations go to a non-budgetary fund, known as Peter's Pence, which is used directly by the pope for charity, disaster relief, and aid to churches in developing nations.

The separate Vatican City State budget includes the Vatican museums and post office and is supported financially by the sale of stamps, coins, medals, and tourist mementos as well as fees for admission to museums and publication sales. Revenues increased between 2010 and 2011 because of expanded operating hours and a growing number of visitors. However, the Holy See did not escape the financial difficulties experienced by other European countries; in 2012, it started a spending review to determine where to cut costs to reverse its 2011 budget deficit of $20 million. The Holy See generated a modest surplus in 2012 before recording a $32 million deficit in 2013, driven primarily by the decreasing value of gold. The incomes and living standards of lay workers are comparable to those of counterparts who work in the city of Rome so most public expenditures go to wages and other personnel costs;. In February 2014, Pope FRANCIS created the Secretariat of the Economy to oversee financial and administrative operations of the Holy See, part of a broader campaign to reform the Holy See's finances.

GDP (PURCHASING POWER PARITY):

NA

INDUSTRIES:

printing; production of coins, medals, postage stamps; mosaics, staff uniforms; worldwide banking and financial activities

LABOR FORCE:

4,822 (2016)

country comparison to the world: 221

LABOR FORCE - BY OCCUPATION:

note: essentially services with a small amount of industry; nearly all dignitaries, priests, nuns, guards, and the approximately 3,000 lay workers live outside the Vatican

POPULATION BELOW POVERTY LINE:

NA

BUDGET:

revenues: 315 million (2013)

expenditures: 348 million (2013)

TAXES AND OTHER REVENUES:

NA

BUDGET SURPLUS (+) OR DEFICIT (-):

NA

FISCAL YEAR:

calendar year

EXCHANGE RATES:

euros (EUR) per US dollar -

0.885 (2017 est.)

0.903 (2016 est.)

0.9214 (2015 est.)

0.885 (2014 est.)

0.7634 (2013 est.)

COMMUNICATIONS :: HOLY SEE (VATICAN CITY)

TELEPHONE SYSTEM:

general assessment: automatic digital exchange (2018)

domestic: connected via fiber-optic cable to Telecom Italia network (2018)

international: country code - 39; uses Italian system

BROADCAST MEDIA:

the Vatican Television Center (CTV) transmits live broadcasts of the Pope's Sunday and Wednesday audiences, as well as the Pope's public celebrations; CTV also produces documentaries; Vatican Radio is the Holy See's official broadcasting service broadcasting via shortwave, AM and FM frequencies, and via satellite and Internet connections

INTERNET COUNTRY CODE:

.va

COMMUNICATIONS - NOTE:

the Vatican Apostolic Library is one of the world's oldest libraries, formally established in 1475, but actually much older; it holds a significant collection of historic texts including 1.1 million printed books and 75,000 codices (manuscript books with handwritten contents); it serves as a research library for history, law, philosophy, science, and theology; the library's collections have been described as "the world's greatest treasure house of the writings at the core of Western tradition"

MILITARY AND SECURITY :: HOLY SEE (VATICAN CITY)

MILITARY AND SECURITY FORCES:

Pontifical Swiss Guard Corps (Corpo della Guardia Svizzera Pontificia); The Gendarmerie Corps of Vatican City is a police force that helps augment the Pontifical Swiss Guard during the Pope's appearances, as well as providing general security, traffic direction, and investigative duties for the Vatican City State (2019)

MILITARY SERVICE AGE AND OBLIGATION:

Pontifical Swiss Guard Corps (Corpo della Guardia Svizzera Pontificia): 19-30 years of age for voluntary military service; no conscription; must be Roman Catholic, a single male, and a Swiss citizen, with a secondary education (2019)

MILITARY - NOTE:

defense is the responsibility of Italy

TRANSPORTATION :: HOLY SEE (VATICAN CITY)

RAILWAYS:

TRANSNATIONAL ISSUES :: HOLY SEE (VATICAN CITY)

DISPUTES - INTERNATIONAL:

none

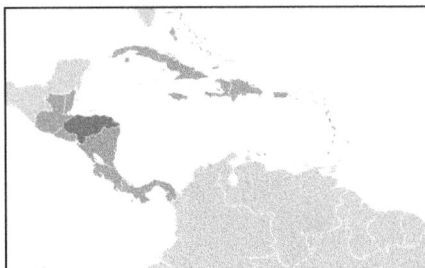

CENTRAL AMERICA :: HONDURAS

INTRODUCTION :: HONDURAS

BACKGROUND:

Once part of Spain's vast empire in the New World, Honduras became an independent nation in 1821. After two and a half decades of mostly military rule, a freely elected civilian government came to power in 1982. During the 1980s, Honduras proved a haven for anti-Sandinista contras fighting the Marxist Nicaraguan Government and an ally to Salvadoran Government forces fighting leftist guerrillas. The country was devastated by Hurricane Mitch in 1998, which killed about 5,600 people and caused approximately $2 billion in damage. Since then, the economy has slowly rebounded.

GEOGRAPHY :: HONDURAS

LOCATION:
Central America, bordering the Caribbean Sea, between Guatemala and Nicaragua and bordering the Gulf of Fonseca (North Pacific Ocean), between El Salvador and Nicaragua

GEOGRAPHIC COORDINATES:
15 00 N, 86 30 W

MAP REFERENCES:
Central America and the Caribbean

AREA:
total: 112,090 sq km

land: 111,890 sq km

water: 200 sq km

country comparison to the world: 104

AREA - COMPARATIVE:
slightly larger than Tennessee

LAND BOUNDARIES:
total: 1,575 km

border countries (3): Guatemala 244 km, El Salvador 391 km, Nicaragua 940 km

COASTLINE:
823 km (Caribbean Sea 669 km, Gulf of Fonseca 163 km)

MARITIME CLAIMS:
territorial sea: 12 nm

exclusive economic zone: 200 nm

contiguous zone: 24 nm

continental shelf: natural extension of territory or to 200 nm

CLIMATE:
subtropical in lowlands, temperate in mountains

TERRAIN:
mostly mountains in interior, narrow coastal plains

ELEVATION:
mean elevation: 684 m

lowest point: Caribbean Sea 0 m

highest point: Cerro Las Minas 2,870 m

NATURAL RESOURCES:
timber, gold, silver, copper, lead, zinc, iron ore, antimony, coal, fish, hydropower

LAND USE:
agricultural land: 28.8% (2011 est.)

arable land: 9.1% (2011 est.) / permanent crops: 4% (2011 est.) / permanent pasture: 15.7% (2011 est.)

forest: 45.3% (2011 est.)

other: 25.9% (2011 est.)

IRRIGATED LAND:
900 sq km (2012)

POPULATION DISTRIBUTION:
most residents live in the mountainous western half of the country; unlike other Central American nations, Honduras is the only one with an urban population that is distributed between two large centers - the capital of Tegucigalpa and the city of San Pedro Sula; the Rio Ulua valley in the north is the only densely populated lowland area

NATURAL HAZARDS:
frequent, but generally mild, earthquakes; extremely susceptible to damaging hurricanes and floods along the Caribbean coast

ENVIRONMENT - CURRENT ISSUES:
urban population expanding; deforestation results from logging and the clearing of land for agricultural purposes; further land degradation and soil erosion hastened by uncontrolled development and improper land use practices such as farming of marginal lands; mining activities polluting Lago de Yojoa (the country's largest source of fresh water), as well as several rivers and streams, with heavy metals

ENVIRONMENT - INTERNATIONAL AGREEMENTS:
party to: Biodiversity, Climate Change, Climate Change-Kyoto Protocol, Desertification, Endangered Species, Hazardous Wastes, Law of the Sea, Marine Dumping, Ozone Layer Protection, Ship Pollution, Tropical Timber 83, Tropical Timber 94, Wetlands

signed, but not ratified: none of the selected agreements

GEOGRAPHY - NOTE:

has only a short Pacific coast but a long Caribbean shoreline, including the virtually uninhabited eastern Mosquito Coast

PEOPLE AND SOCIETY :: HONDURAS

POPULATION:
9,182,766 (July 2018 est.)

note: estimates for this country explicitly take into account the effects of excess mortality due to AIDS; this can result in lower life expectancy, higher infant mortality, higher death rates, lower population growth rates, and changes in the distribution of population by age and sex than would otherwise be expected

country comparison to the world: 95

NATIONALITY:
noun: Honduran(s)

adjective: Honduran

ETHNIC GROUPS:
mestizo (mixed Amerindian and European) 90%, Amerindian 7%, black 2%, white 1%

LANGUAGES:
Spanish (official), Amerindian dialects

RELIGIONS:
Roman Catholic 46%, Protestant 41%, atheist 1%, other 2%, none 9% (2014 est.)

DEMOGRAPHIC PROFILE:
Honduras is one of the poorest countries in Latin America and has one of the world's highest murder rates. More than half of the population lives in poverty and per capita income is one of the lowest in the region. Poverty rates are higher among rural and indigenous people and in the south, west, and along the eastern border than in the north and central areas where most of Honduras' industries and infrastructure are concentrated. The increased productivity needed to break Honduras' persistent high poverty rate depends, in part, on further improvements in educational attainment. Although primary-school enrollment is near 100%, educational quality is poor, the drop-out rate and grade repetition remain high, and teacher and school accountability is low.

Honduras' population growth rate has slowed since the 1990s, but it remains high at nearly 2% annually because the birth rate averages approximately three children per woman and more among rural, indigenous, and poor women. Consequently, Honduras' young adult population - ages 15 to 29 - is projected to continue growing rapidly for the next three decades and then stabilize or slowly shrink. Population growth and limited job prospects outside of agriculture will continue to drive emigration. Remittances represent about a fifth of GDP.

AGE STRUCTURE:
0-14 years: 32.37% (male 1,518,526 /female 1,453,891)

15-24 years: 20.88% (male 977,899 /female 939,490)

25-54 years: 37.07% (male 1,724,257 /female 1,679,694)

55-64 years: 5.27% (male 229,066 /female 255,169)

65 years and over: 4.41% (male 174,771 /female 230,003) (2018 est.)

DEPENDENCY RATIOS:
total dependency ratio: 59.8 (2015 est.)

youth dependency ratio: 52.7 (2015 est.)

elderly dependency ratio: 7.1 (2015 est.)

potential support ratio: 14.2 (2015 est.)

MEDIAN AGE:
total: 23.3 years (2018 est.)

male: 23 years

female: 23.7 years

country comparison to the world: 173

POPULATION GROWTH RATE:
1.56% (2018 est.)

country comparison to the world: 68

BIRTH RATE:
22 births/1,000 population (2018 est.)

country comparison to the world: 68

DEATH RATE:
5.3 deaths/1,000 population (2018 est.)

country comparison to the world: 185

NET MIGRATION RATE:
-1.1 migrant(s)/1,000 population (2018 est.)

country comparison to the world: 142

POPULATION DISTRIBUTION:
most residents live in the mountainous western half of the country; unlike other Central American nations, Honduras is the only one with an urban population that is distributed between two large centers - the capital of Tegucigalpa and the city of San Pedro Sula; the Rio Ulua valley in the north is the only densely populated lowland area

URBANIZATION:
urban population: 57.7% of total population (2019)

rate of urbanization: 2.75% annual rate of change (2015-20 est.)

MAJOR URBAN AREAS - POPULATION:
1.403 million TEGUCIGALPA (capital), 876,000 San Pedro Sula (2019)

SEX RATIO:
at birth: 1.05 male(s)/female

0-14 years: 1.04 male(s)/female

15-24 years: 1.04 male(s)/female

25-54 years: 1.03 male(s)/female

55-64 years: 0.9 male(s)/female

65 years and over: 0.76 male(s)/female

total population: 1.01 male(s)/female (2018 est.)

MOTHER'S MEAN AGE AT FIRST BIRTH:
20.4 years (2011/12 est.)

note: median age a first birth among women 25-29

MATERNAL MORTALITY RATE:
65 deaths/100,000 live births (2017 est.)

country comparison to the world: 86

INFANT MORTALITY RATE:
total: 16.7 deaths/1,000 live births (2018 est.)

male: 18.9 deaths/1,000 live births

female: 14.4 deaths/1,000 live births

country comparison to the world: 93

LIFE EXPECTANCY AT BIRTH:
total population: 71.3 years (2018 est.)

male: 69.6 years

female: 73 years

country comparison to the world: 152

TOTAL FERTILITY RATE:
2.61 children born/woman (2018 est.)

country comparison to the world: 70

CONTRACEPTIVE PREVALENCE RATE:
73.2% (2011/12)

DRINKING WATER SOURCE:

improved:

urban: 97.4% of population

rural: 83.8% of population

total: 91.2% of population

unimproved:

urban: 2.6% of population

rural: 16.2% of population

total: 8.8% of population (2015 est.)

CURRENT HEALTH EXPENDITURE:

8.4% (2016)

PHYSICIANS DENSITY:

0.31 physicians/1,000 population (2017)

HOSPITAL BED DENSITY:

0.7 beds/1,000 population (2014)

SANITATION FACILITY ACCESS:

improved:

urban: 86.7% of population (2015 est.)

rural: 77.7% of population (2015 est.)

total: 82.6% of population (2015 est.)

unimproved:

urban: 13.3% of population (2015 est.)

rural: 22.3% of population (2015 est.)

total: 17.4% of population (2015 est.)

HIV/AIDS - ADULT PREVALENCE RATE:

0.3% (2018 est.)

country comparison to the world: 88

HIV/AIDS - PEOPLE LIVING WITH HIV/AIDS:

23,000 (2018 est.)

country comparison to the world: 80

HIV/AIDS - DEATHS:

<1000 (2018 est.)

MAJOR INFECTIOUS DISEASES:

degree of risk: high (2016)

food or waterborne diseases: bacterial diarrhea, hepatitis A, and typhoid fever (2016)

vectorborne diseases: dengue fever and malaria (2016)

note: active local transmission of Zika virus by Aedes species mosquitoes has been identified in this country (as of August 2016); it poses an important risk (a large number of cases possible) among US citizens if bitten by an infective mosquito; other less common ways to get Zika are through sex, via blood transfusion, or during pregnancy, in which the pregnant woman passes Zika virus to her fetus

OBESITY - ADULT PREVALENCE RATE:

21.4% (2016)

country comparison to the world: 89

CHILDREN UNDER THE AGE OF 5 YEARS UNDERWEIGHT:

7.1% (2012)

country comparison to the world: 73

EDUCATION EXPENDITURES:

6% of GDP (2017)

country comparison to the world: 35

LITERACY:

definition: age 15 and over can read and write

total population: 89%

male: 89%

female: 88.9% (2016 est.)

SCHOOL LIFE EXPECTANCY (PRIMARY TO TERTIARY EDUCATION):

total: 10 years

male: 10 years

female: 11 years (2014)

UNEMPLOYMENT, YOUTH AGES 15-24:

total: 7.9%

male: 5.6%

female: 12.1% (2017 est.)

country comparison to the world: 146

GOVERNMENT :: HONDURAS

COUNTRY NAME:

conventional long form: Republic of Honduras

conventional short form: Honduras

local long form: Republica de Honduras

local short form: Honduras

etymology: the name means "depths" in Spanish and refers to the deep anchorage in the northern Bay of Trujillo

GOVERNMENT TYPE:

presidential republic

CAPITAL:

name: Tegucigalpa; note - article eight of the Honduran constitution states that the twin cities of Tegucigalpa and Comayaguela, jointly, constitute the capital of the Republic of Honduras; however, virtually all governmental institutions are on the Tegucigalpa side, which in practical terms makes Tegucigalpa the capital

geographic coordinates: 14 06 N, 87 13 W

time difference: UTC-6 (1 hour behind Washington, DC during Standard Time)

ADMINISTRATIVE DIVISIONS:

18 departments (departamentos, singular - departamento); Atlantida, Choluteca, Colon, Comayagua, Copan, Cortes, El Paraiso, Francisco Morazan, Gracias a Dios, Intibuca, Islas de la Bahia, La Paz, Lempira, Ocotepeque, Olancho, Santa Barbara, Valle, Yoro

INDEPENDENCE:

15 September 1821 (from Spain)

NATIONAL HOLIDAY:

Independence Day, 15 September (1821)

CONSTITUTION:

history: several previous; latest approved 11 January 1982, effective 20 January 1982

amendments: proposed by the National Congress with at least two-thirds majority vote of the membership; passage requires at least two-thirds majority vote of Congress in its next annual session; constitutional articles, such as the form of government, national sovereignty, the presidential term, and the procedure for amending the constitution, cannot be amended; amended many times, last in 2015; note - the 2015 amendment struck down several constitutional articles on presidential term limits (2018)

LEGAL SYSTEM:

civil law system

INTERNATIONAL LAW ORGANIZATION PARTICIPATION:

accepts compulsory ICJ jurisdiction with reservations; accepts ICCt jurisdiction

CITIZENSHIP:

citizenship by birth: yes

citizenship by descent only: yes

dual citizenship recognized: yes

residency requirement for naturalization: 1 to 3 years

SUFFRAGE:

18 years of age; universal and compulsory

EXECUTIVE BRANCH:

chief of state: President Juan Orlando HERNANDEZ Alvarado (since 27 January 2014); Vice Presidents Ricardo ALVAREZ, Maria RIVERA, and Olga ALVARADO (since 26 January 2018); note - the president is both chief of state and head of government

head of government: President Juan Orlando HERNANDEZ Alvarado (since 27 January 2014); Vice Presidents Ricardo ALVAREZ, Maria RIVERA, and Olga ALVARADO (since 26 January 2018)

cabinet: Cabinet appointed by president

elections/appointments: president directly elected by simple majority popular vote for a 4-year term; election last held on 26 November 2017 (next to be held in November 2021); note - in 2015, the Constitutional Chamber of the Honduran Supreme Court struck down the constitutional provisions on presidential term limits

election results: Juan Orlando HERNANDEZ Alvarado reelected president; percent of vote Juan Orlando HERNANDEZ Alvarado (PNH) 43%, Salvador NASRALLA (Alianza de Oposicion conta la Dictadura) 41.4%, Luis Orlando ZELAYA Medrano (PL) 14.7%, other .9%

LEGISLATIVE BRANCH:

description: unicameral National Congress or Congreso Nacional (128 seats; members directly elected in multi-seat constituencies by closed, party-list proportional representation vote; members serve 4-year terms)

elections: last held on 27 November 2017 (next to be held on 28 November 2021)

election results: percent of vote by party - PNH 47.7%, LIBRE 23.4%, PL 20.3%, AP 3.1%, PINU 3.1%, DC 0.8%, PAC 0.8%, UD 0.8%; seats by party - PNH 61, LIBRE 30, PL 26, AP 4, PINU 4, DC 1, PAC 1, UD 1; composition - men 101, women 27, percent of women 21.1%

JUDICIAL BRANCH:

highest courts: Supreme Court of Justice or Corte Suprema de Justicia (15 principal judges, including the court president, and 7 alternates; court organized into civil, criminal, constitutional, and labor chambers); note - the court has both judicial and constitutional jurisdiction

judge selection and term of office: court president elected by his peers; judges elected by the National Congress from candidates proposed by the Nominating Board, a diverse 7-member group of judicial officials and other government and non-government officials nominated by each of their organizations; judges elected by Congress for renewable, 7-year terms

subordinate courts: courts of appeal; courts of first instance; justices of the peace

POLITICAL PARTIES AND LEADERS:

Alliance against the Dictatorship or Alianza de Oposicion conta la Dictadura [Salvador NASRALLA] (electoral coalition)
Anti-Corruption Party or PAC [Marlene ALVARENGA]
Christian Democratic Party or DC [Lucas AGUILERA]
Democratic Unification Party or UD [Alfonso DIAZ]
Freedom and Refoundation Party or LIBRE [Jose Manuel ZELAYA Rosales]
Honduran Patriotic Alliance or AP [Romeo VASQUEZ Velasquez]
Liberal Party or PL [Luis Orlando ZELAYA Medrano]
National Party of Honduras or PNH [Reinaldo SANCHEZ Rivera]
Innovation and Unity Party or PINU [Guillermo VALLE]

INTERNATIONAL ORGANIZATION PARTICIPATION:

BCIE, CACM, CD, CELAC, EITI (candidate country), FAO, G-11, G-77, IADB, IAEA, IBRD, ICAO, ICCt, ICRM, IDA, IFAD, IFC, IFRCS, ILO, IMF, IMO, Interpol, IOC (suspended), IOM, IPU, ISO (subscriber), ITSO, ITU, ITUC (NGOs), LAES, LAIA (observer), MIGA, MINURSO, MINUSTAH, NAM, OAS, OPANAL, OPCW, Pacific Alliance (observer), PCA, Petrocaribe, SICA, UN, UNCTAD, UNESCO, UNIDO, Union Latina, UNWTO, UPU, WCO (suspended), WFTU (NGOs), WHO, WIPO, WMO, WTO

DIPLOMATIC REPRESENTATION IN THE US:

Ambassador Marlon Ramsses TABORA Munoz (since 24 April 2017)

chancery: Suite 700, 1250 Connecticut Avenue NW, Washington, DC 20036

telephone: [1] (202) 966-7702

FAX: [1] (202) 966-9751

consulate(s) general: Atlanta, Chicago, Houston, Los Angeles, Miami, New Orleans, New York, San Francisco

consulate(s): Dallas, McAllen (TX)

DIPLOMATIC REPRESENTATION FROM THE US:

chief of mission: Ambassador (vacant); Charge d'Affaires Colleen A. HOEY (since August 2019)

telephone: [504] 2236-9320, 2238-5114

embassy: Avenida La Paz, Tegucigalpa M.D.C.

mailing address: American Embassy, APO AA 34022, Tegucigalpa

FAX: [504] 2236-9037

FLAG DESCRIPTION:

three equal horizontal bands of cerulean blue (top), white, and cerulean blue, with five cerulean, five-pointed stars arranged in an X pattern centered in the white band; the stars represent the members of the former Federal Republic of Central America: Costa Rica, El Salvador, Guatemala, Honduras, and Nicaragua; the blue bands symbolize the Pacific Ocean and the Caribbean Sea; the white band represents the land between the two bodies of water and the peace and prosperity of its people

note: similar to the flag of El Salvador, which features a round emblem encircled by the words REPUBLICA DE EL SALVADOR EN LA AMERICA CENTRAL centered in the white band; also similar to the flag of Nicaragua, which features a triangle encircled by the words REPUBLICA DE NICARAGUA on top and AMERICA CENTRAL on the bottom, centered in the white band

NATIONAL SYMBOL(S):

scarlet macaw, white-tailed deer; national colors: blue, white

NATIONAL ANTHEM:

name: "Himno Nacional de Honduras" (National Anthem of Honduras)

lyrics/music: Augusto Constancio COELLO/Carlos HARTLING

note: adopted 1915; the anthem's seven verses chronicle Honduran history; on official occasions, only the chorus and last verse are sung

ECONOMY :: HONDURAS

ECONOMY - OVERVIEW:

Honduras, the second poorest country in Central America, suffers from extraordinarily unequal distribution of income, as well as high underemployment. While historically dependent on the export of bananas and coffee, Honduras has diversified its export base to include apparel and automobile wire harnessing.

Honduras's economy depends heavily on US trade and remittances. The US-Central America-Dominican Republic Free Trade Agreement came into force in 2006 and has helped foster foreign direct investment, but physical and political insecurity, as well as crime and perceptions of corruption, may deter potential investors; about 15% of foreign direct investment is from US firms.

The economy registered modest economic growth of 3.1%-4.0% from 2010 to 2017, insufficient to improve living standards for the nearly 65% of the population in poverty. In 2017, Honduras faced rising public debt, but its economy has performed better than expected due to low oil prices and improved investor confidence. Honduras signed a three-year standby arrangement with the IMF in December 2014, aimed at easing Honduras's poor fiscal position.

GDP (PURCHASING POWER PARITY):

$46.3 billion (2017 est.)

$44.18 billion (2016 est.)

$42.58 billion (2015 est.)

note: data are in 2017 dollars

country comparison to the world: 112

GDP (OFFICIAL EXCHANGE RATE):

$22.98 billion (2017 est.)

GDP - REAL GROWTH RATE:

4.8% (2017 est.)

3.8% (2016 est.)

3.8% (2015 est.)

country comparison to the world: 56

GDP - PER CAPITA (PPP):

$5,600 (2017 est.)

$5,400 (2016 est.)

$5,300 (2015 est.)

note: data are in 2017 dollars

country comparison to the world: 170

GROSS NATIONAL SAVING:

22.1% of GDP (2017 est.)

20.6% of GDP (2016 est.)

20.5% of GDP (2015 est.)

country comparison to the world: 83

GDP - COMPOSITION, BY END USE:

household consumption: 77.7% (2017 est.)

government consumption: 13.8% (2017 est.)

investment in fixed capital: 23.1% (2017 est.)

investment in inventories: 0.7% (2017 est.)

exports of goods and services: 43.6% (2017 est.)

imports of goods and services: -58.9% (2017 est.)

GDP - COMPOSITION, BY SECTOR OF ORIGIN:

agriculture: 14.2% (2017 est.)

industry: 28.8% (2017 est.)

services: 57% (2017 est.)

AGRICULTURE - PRODUCTS:

bananas, coffee, citrus, corn, African palm; beef; timber; shrimp, tilapia, lobster, sugar, oriental vegetables

INDUSTRIES:

sugar processing, coffee, woven and knit apparel, wood products, cigars

INDUSTRIAL PRODUCTION GROWTH RATE:

4.5% (2017 est.)

country comparison to the world: 65

LABOR FORCE:

3.735 million (2017 est.)

country comparison to the world: 96

LABOR FORCE - BY OCCUPATION:

agriculture: 39.2%

industry: 20.9%

services: 39.8% (2005 est.)

UNEMPLOYMENT RATE:

5.6% (2017 est.)

6.3% (2016 est.)

note: about one-third of the people are underemployed

country comparison to the world: 82

POPULATION BELOW POVERTY LINE:

29.6% (2014)

HOUSEHOLD INCOME OR CONSUMPTION BY PERCENTAGE SHARE:

lowest 10%: 1.2%

highest 10%: 38.4% (2014)

DISTRIBUTION OF FAMILY INCOME - GINI INDEX:

47.1 (2014)

45.7 (2009)

country comparison to the world: 26

BUDGET:

revenues: 4.658 billion (2017 est.)

expenditures: 5.283 billion (2017 est.)

TAXES AND OTHER REVENUES:

20.3% (of GDP) (2017 est.)

country comparison to the world: 150

BUDGET SURPLUS (+) OR DEFICIT (-):

-2.7% (of GDP) (2017 est.)

country comparison to the world: 120

PUBLIC DEBT:

39.5% of GDP (2017 est.)

38.5% of GDP (2016 est.)

country comparison to the world: 131

FISCAL YEAR:

calendar year

INFLATION RATE (CONSUMER PRICES):

3.9% (2017 est.)

2.7% (2016 est.)

country comparison to the world: 152

CENTRAL BANK DISCOUNT RATE:

6.25% (31 December 2010)

country comparison to the world: 66

COMMERCIAL BANK PRIME LENDING RATE:

19.26% (31 December 2017 est.)

19.33% (31 December 2016 est.)

country comparison to the world: 16

STOCK OF NARROW MONEY:

$2.827 billion (31 December 2017 est.)

$2.455 billion (31 December 2016 est.)

country comparison to the world: 123

STOCK OF BROAD MONEY:

$2.827 billion (31 December 2017 est.)

$2.455 billion (31 December 2016 est.)

country comparison to the world: 130

STOCK OF DOMESTIC CREDIT:

$13.3 billion (31 December 2017 est.)

$12.67 billion (31 December 2016 est.)

country comparison to the world: 103

MARKET VALUE OF PUBLICLY TRADED SHARES:

NA

CURRENT ACCOUNT BALANCE:

-$380 million (2017 est.)

-$587 million (2016 est.)

country comparison to the world: 110

EXPORTS:

$8.675 billion (2017 est.)

$7.841 billion (2016 est.)

country comparison to the world: 95

EXPORTS - PARTNERS:

US 34.5%, Germany 8.9%, Belgium 7.7%, El Salvador 7.3%, Netherlands 7.2%, Guatemala 5.2%, Nicaragua 4.8% (2017)

EXPORTS - COMMODITIES:

coffee, apparel, coffee, shrimp, automobile wire harnesses, cigars, bananas, gold, palm oil, fruit, lobster, lumber

IMPORTS:

$11.32 billion (2017 est.)

$10.56 billion (2016 est.)

country comparison to the world: 97

IMPORTS - COMMODITIES:

communications equipment, machinery and transport, industrial raw materials, chemical products, fuels, foodstuffs

IMPORTS - PARTNERS:

US 40.3%, Guatemala 10.5%, China 8.5%, Mexico 6.2%, El Salvador 5.7%, Panama 4.4%, Costa Rica 4.2% (2017)

RESERVES OF FOREIGN EXCHANGE AND GOLD:

$4.708 billion (31 December 2017 est.)

$3.814 billion (31 December 2016 est.)

country comparison to the world: 96

DEBT - EXTERNAL:

$8.625 billion (31 December 2017 est.)

$7.852 billion (31 December 2016 est.)

country comparison to the world: 118

EXCHANGE RATES:

lempiras (HNL) per US dollar -

23.74 (2017 est.)

22.995 (2016 est.)

22.995 (2015 est.)

22.098 (2014 est.)

21.137 (2013 est.)

ENERGY :: HONDURAS

ELECTRICITY ACCESS:

population without electricity: 2 million (2017)

electrification - total population: 87.6% (2016)

electrification - urban areas: 100% (2016)

electrification - rural areas: 72.2% (2016)

ELECTRICITY - PRODUCTION:

8.501 billion kWh (2016 est.)

country comparison to the world: 108

ELECTRICITY - CONSUMPTION:

7.22 billion kWh (2016 est.)

country comparison to the world: 107

ELECTRICITY - EXPORTS:

536 million kWh (2015 est.)

country comparison to the world: 67

ELECTRICITY - IMPORTS:

195 million kWh (2016 est.)

country comparison to the world: 94

ELECTRICITY - INSTALLED GENERATING CAPACITY:

2.546 million kW (2016 est.)

country comparison to the world: 108

ELECTRICITY - FROM FOSSIL FUELS:

40% of total installed capacity (2016 est.)

country comparison to the world: 169

ELECTRICITY - FROM NUCLEAR FUELS:

0% of total installed capacity (2017 est.)

country comparison to the world: 107

ELECTRICITY - FROM HYDROELECTRIC PLANTS:

25% of total installed capacity (2017 est.)

country comparison to the world: 77

ELECTRICITY - FROM OTHER RENEWABLE SOURCES:

34% of total installed capacity (2017 est.)

country comparison to the world: 11

CRUDE OIL - PRODUCTION:

0 bbl/day (2018 est.)

country comparison to the world: 149

CRUDE OIL - EXPORTS:

0 bbl/day (2015 est.)

country comparison to the world: 137

CRUDE OIL - IMPORTS:

0 bbl/day (2015 est.)

country comparison to the world: 141

CRUDE OIL - PROVED RESERVES:

0 bbl (1 January 2018 est.)

country comparison to the world: 145

REFINED PETROLEUM PRODUCTS - PRODUCTION:

0 bbl/day (2017 est.)

country comparison to the world: 157

REFINED PETROLEUM PRODUCTS - CONSUMPTION:

59,000 bbl/day (2016 est.)

country comparison to the world: 97

REFINED PETROLEUM PRODUCTS - EXPORTS:

12,870 bbl/day (2015 est.)

country comparison to the world: 77

REFINED PETROLEUM PRODUCTS - IMPORTS:

56,120 bbl/day (2015 est.)

country comparison to the world: 75

NATURAL GAS - PRODUCTION:

0 cu m (2017 est.)

country comparison to the world: 146

NATURAL GAS - CONSUMPTION:

0 cu m (2017 est.)

country comparison to the world: 159

NATURAL GAS - EXPORTS:

0 cu m (2017 est.)

country comparison to the world: 121

NATURAL GAS - IMPORTS:

0 cu m (2017 est.)

country comparison to the world: 139

NATURAL GAS - PROVED RESERVES:

0 cu m (1 January 2014 est.)

country comparison to the world: 147

CARBON DIOXIDE EMISSIONS FROM CONSUMPTION OF ENERGY:

9.436 million Mt (2017 est.)

country comparison to the world: 110

COMMUNICATIONS :: HONDURAS

TELEPHONES - FIXED LINES:

total subscriptions: 491,107

subscriptions per 100 inhabitants: 5 (2017 est.)

country comparison to the world: 96

TELEPHONES - MOBILE CELLULAR:

total subscriptions: 8,233,499

subscriptions per 100 inhabitants: 91 (2017 est.)

country comparison to the world: 98

TELEPHONE SYSTEM:

general assessment: fixed-line connections are increasing but still limited; competition among multiple providers of mobile-cellular services is contributing to a sharp increase in subscribership; demand for broadband increasing and some investment needed in network upgrades; mobile penetration below regional average (2018)

domestic: private sub-operators allowed to provide fixed lines in order to expand telephone coverage contributing to a small increase in fixed-line teledensity 5 per 100; mobile-cellular subscribership is roughly 91 per 100 persons (2018)

international: country code - 504; landing points for both the ARCOS and the MAYA-1 fiber-optic submarine cable systems that together provide connectivity to South and Central America, parts of the Caribbean, and the US; satellite earth stations - 2 Intelsat (Atlantic Ocean); connected to Central American Microwave System (2019)

BROADCAST MEDIA:
multiple privately owned terrestrial TV networks, supplemented by multiple cable TV networks; Radio Honduras is the lone government-owned radio network; roughly 300 privately owned radio stations

INTERNET COUNTRY CODE:
.hn

INTERNET USERS:
total: 2,667,978

percent of population: 30% (July 2016 est.)

country comparison to the world: 102

BROADBAND - FIXED SUBSCRIPTIONS:
total: 232,990

subscriptions per 100 inhabitants: 3 (2017 est.)

country comparison to the world: 104

MILITARY AND SECURITY :: HONDURAS

MILITARY EXPENDITURES:
1.71% of GDP (2018)

1.74% of GDP (2017)

1.68% of GDP (2016)

1.68% of GDP (2015)

4.62% of GDP (2014)

country comparison to the world: 66

MILITARY AND SECURITY FORCES:
Honduran Armed Forces (Fuerzas Armadas de Honduras, FFAA): Army, Honduran Naval Force (FNH; includes marines), Honduran Air Force (Fuerza Aerea Hondurena, FAH), Honduran Public Order Military Police (PMOP) (2019)

MILITARY SERVICE AGE AND OBLIGATION:
18 years of age for voluntary 2- to 3-year military service; no conscription (2018)

TRANSPORTATION :: HONDURAS

NATIONAL AIR TRANSPORT SYSTEM:
number of registered air carriers: 5 (2015)

inventory of registered aircraft operated by air carriers: 10 (2015)

annual passenger traffic on registered air carriers: 251,149 (2015)

annual freight traffic on registered air carriers: 502,372 mt-km (2015)

CIVIL AIRCRAFT REGISTRATION COUNTRY CODE PREFIX:
HR (2016)

AIRPORTS:
103 (2013)

country comparison to the world: 54

AIRPORTS - WITH PAVED RUNWAYS:
total: 13 (2017)

2,438 to 3,047 m: 3 (2017)

1,524 to 2,437 m: 3 (2017)

914 to 1,523 m: 4 (2017)

under 914 m: 3 (2017)

AIRPORTS - WITH UNPAVED RUNWAYS:
total: 90 (2013)

1,524 to 2,437 m: 1 (2013)

914 to 1,523 m: 16 (2013)

under 914 m: 73 (2013)

RAILWAYS:
total: 699 km (2014)

narrow gauge: 164 km 1.067-m gauge (2014)

115 km 1.057-m gauge
420 km 0.914-m gauge

country comparison to the world: 101

ROADWAYS:
total: 14,742 km (2012)

paved: 3,367 km (2012)

unpaved: 11,375 km (1,543 km summer only) (2012)

note: an additional 8,951 km of non-official roads used by the coffee industry

country comparison to the world: 123

WATERWAYS:
465 km (most navigable only by small craft) (2012)

country comparison to the world: 84

MERCHANT MARINE:
total: 550

by type: container ship 1, general cargo 249, oil tanker 89, other 211 (2018)

country comparison to the world: 40

PORTS AND TERMINALS:
major seaport(s): La Ceiba, Puerto Cortes, San Lorenzo, Tela

TRANSNATIONAL ISSUES :: HONDURAS

DISPUTES - INTERNATIONAL:
International Court of Justice (ICJ) ruled on the delimitation of "bolsones" (disputed areas) along the El Salvador-Honduras border in 1992 with final settlement by the parties in 2006 after an Organization of American States survey and a further ICJ ruling in 2003; the 1992 ICJ ruling advised a tripartite resolution to a maritime boundary in the Gulf of Fonseca with consideration of Honduran access to the Pacific; El Salvador continues to claim tiny Conejo Island, not mentioned in the ICJ ruling, off Honduras in the Gulf of Fonseca; Honduras claims the Belizean-administered Sapodilla Cays off the coast of Belize in its constitution, but agreed to a joint ecological park around the cays should Guatemala consent to a maritime corridor in the Caribbean under the OAS-sponsored 2002 Belize-Guatemala Differendum

REFUGEES AND INTERNALLY DISPLACED PERSONS:
IDPs: 190,000 (violence, extortion, threats, forced recruitment by urban gangs) (2016)

ILLICIT DRUGS:
transshipment point for drugs and narcotics; illicit producer of cannabis, cultivated on small plots and used principally for local consumption; corruption is a major problem; some money-laundering activity

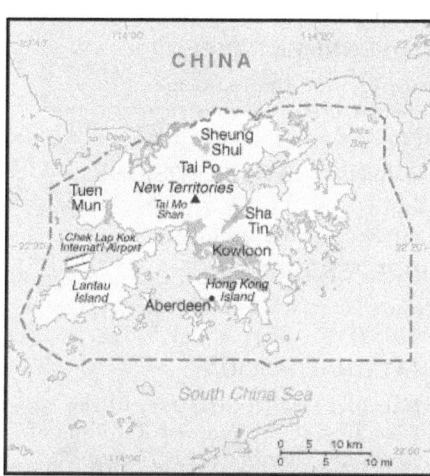

EAST ASIA / SOUTHEAST ASIA :: HONG KONG

INTRODUCTION :: HONG KONG

BACKGROUND:

Occupied by the UK in 1841, Hong Kong was formally ceded by China the following year; various adjacent lands were added later in the 19th century. Pursuant to an agreement signed by China and the UK on 19 December 1984, Hong Kong became the Hong Kong Special Administrative Region of the People's Republic of China on 1 July 1997. In this agreement, China promised that, under its "one country, two systems" formula, China's socialist economic system would not be imposed on Hong Kong and that Hong Kong would enjoy a "high degree of autonomy" in all matters except foreign and defense affairs for the subsequent 50 years.

GEOGRAPHY :: HONG KONG

LOCATION:
Eastern Asia, bordering the South China Sea and China

GEOGRAPHIC COORDINATES:
22 15 N, 114 10 E

MAP REFERENCES:
Southeast Asia

AREA:
total: 1,108 sq km
land: 1,073 sq km
water: 35 sq km
country comparison to the world: 184

AREA - COMPARATIVE:
six times the size of Washington, DC

LAND BOUNDARIES:
total: 33 km
regional borders (1): China 33 km

COASTLINE:
733 km

MARITIME CLAIMS:
territorial sea: 12 nm

CLIMATE:
subtropical monsoon; cool and humid in winter, hot and rainy from spring through summer, warm and sunny in fall

TERRAIN:
hilly to mountainous with steep slopes; lowlands in north

ELEVATION:
lowest point: South China Sea 0 m
highest point: Tai Mo Shan 958 m

NATURAL RESOURCES:
outstanding deepwater harbor, feldspar

LAND USE:
agricultural land: 5% (2011 est.)
arable land: 3.2% (2011 est.) / permanent crops: 0.9% (2011 est.) / permanent pasture: 0.9% (2011 est.)
forest: 0% (2011 est.)
other: 95% (2011 est.)

IRRIGATED LAND:
10 sq km (2012)

POPULATION DISTRIBUTION:
population fairly evenly distributed

NATURAL HAZARDS:
occasional typhoons

ENVIRONMENT - CURRENT ISSUES:
air and water pollution from rapid urbanization; urban waste pollution; industrial pollution

ENVIRONMENT - INTERNATIONAL AGREEMENTS:
party to: Marine Dumping (associate member), Ship Pollution (associate member)

GEOGRAPHY - NOTE:
consists of a mainland area (the New Territories) and more than 200 islands

PEOPLE AND SOCIETY :: HONG KONG

POPULATION:
7,213,338 (July 2018 est.)
country comparison to the world: 102

NATIONALITY:
noun: Chinese/Hong Konger
adjective: Chinese/Hong Kong

ETHNIC GROUPS:
Chinese 92%, Filipino 2.5%, Indonesian 2.1%, other 3.4% (2016 est.)

LANGUAGES:
Cantonese (official) 88.9%, English (official) 4.3%, Mandarin (official) 1.9%, other Chinese dialects 3.1%, other 1.9% (2016 est.)

RELIGIONS:
Buddhist or Taoist 27.9%, Protestant 6.7%, Roman Catholic 5.3%, Muslim 4.2%, Hindu 1.4%, Sikh 0.2%, other or none 54.3% (2016 est.)

note: many people practice Confucianism, regardless of their religion or not having a religious affiliation

AGE STRUCTURE:
0-14 years: 12.38% (male 471,983 /female 420,977)

15-24 years: 9.89% (male 372,991 /female 340,221)

25-54 years: 43.96% (male 1,354,676 /female 1,816,303)

55-64 years: 16.64% (male 571,329 /female 628,774)

65 years and over: 17.14% (male 580,248 /female 655,836) (2018 est.)

DEPENDENCY RATIOS:
total dependency ratio: 35.9 (2015 est.)

youth dependency ratio: 15.2 (2015 est.)

elderly dependency ratio: 20.7 (2015 est.)

potential support ratio: 4.8 (2015 est.)

MEDIAN AGE:
total: 44.8 years (2018 est.)

male: 43.7 years

female: 45.5 years

country comparison to the world: 8

POPULATION GROWTH RATE:
0.29% (2018 est.)

country comparison to the world: 172

BIRTH RATE:
8.8 births/1,000 population (2018 est.)

country comparison to the world: 209

DEATH RATE:
7.6 deaths/1,000 population (2018 est.)

country comparison to the world: 103

NET MIGRATION RATE:
1.7 migrant(s)/1,000 population (2018 est.)

country comparison to the world: 54

POPULATION DISTRIBUTION:
population fairly evenly distributed

URBANIZATION:
urban population: 100% of total population (2019)

rate of urbanization: 0.82% annual rate of change (2015-20 est.)

MAJOR URBAN AREAS - POPULATION:
7.491 million Hong Kong (2019)

SEX RATIO:
at birth: 1.08 male(s)/female

0-14 years: 1.12 male(s)/female

15-24 years: 1.1 male(s)/female

25-54 years: 0.75 male(s)/female

55-64 years: 0.91 male(s)/female

65 years and over: 0.88 male(s)/female

total population: 0.87 male(s)/female (2018 est.)

MOTHER'S MEAN AGE AT FIRST BIRTH:
29.8 years (2008 est.)

INFANT MORTALITY RATE:
total: 2.7 deaths/1,000 live births (2018 est.)

male: 2.9 deaths/1,000 live births

female: 2.5 deaths/1,000 live births

country comparison to the world: 213

LIFE EXPECTANCY AT BIRTH:
total population: 83.1 years (2018 est.)

male: 80.4 years

female: 86 years

country comparison to the world: 6

TOTAL FERTILITY RATE:
1.2 children born/woman (2018 est.)

country comparison to the world: 221

CONTRACEPTIVE PREVALENCE RATE:
74.8% (2012)

PHYSICIANS DENSITY:
1.96 physicians/1,000 population (2018)

HOSPITAL BED DENSITY:
5.4 beds/1,000 population (2018)

HIV/AIDS - ADULT PREVALENCE RATE:
NA

HIV/AIDS - PEOPLE LIVING WITH HIV/AIDS:
NA

HIV/AIDS - DEATHS:
NA

EDUCATION EXPENDITURES:
3.3% of GDP (2017)

country comparison to the world: 130

SCHOOL LIFE EXPECTANCY (PRIMARY TO TERTIARY EDUCATION):
total: 16 years

male: 16 years

female: 16 years (2014)

UNEMPLOYMENT, YOUTH AGES 15-24:
total: 8.7%

male: 9.3%

female: 8.2% (2017 est.)

country comparison to the world: 138

GOVERNMENT :: HONG KONG

COUNTRY NAME:
conventional long form: Hong Kong Special Administrative Region

conventional short form: Hong Kong

local long form: Heung Kong Takpit Hangching Ku (Eitel/Dyer-Ball)

local short form: Heung Kong (Eitel/Dyer-Ball)

abbreviation: HK

etymology: probably an imprecise phonetic rendering of the Cantonese name meaning "fragrant harbor"

DEPENDENCY STATUS:
special administrative region of the People's Republic of China

GOVERNMENT TYPE:
presidential limited democracy; a special administrative region of the People's Republic of China

ADMINISTRATIVE DIVISIONS:
none (special administrative region of the People's Republic of China)

INDEPENDENCE:
none (special administrative region of China)

NATIONAL HOLIDAY:
National Day (Anniversary of the Founding of the People's Republic of China), 1 October (1949); note - 1 July (1997) is celebrated as Hong Kong Special Administrative Region Establishment Day

CONSTITUTION:
history: several previous (governance documents while under British authority); latest drafted April 1988 to February 1989, approved March 1990, effective 1 July 1997 (Basic Law of the Hong Kong Special Administrative Region of the People's Republic of China serves as the constitution); note - since 1990, China's National People's Congress has interpreted specific articles of the Basic Law

amendments: proposed by the Standing Committee of the National People's Congress (NPC), the People's

Republic of China State Council, and the Special Administrative Region of Hong Kong; submittal of proposals to the NPC requires two-thirds majority vote by the Legislative Council of Hong Kong, approval by two thirds of Hong Kong's deputies to the NPC, and approval by the Hong Kong chief executive; final passage requires approval by the NPC

LEGAL SYSTEM:

mixed legal system of common law based on the English model and Chinese customary law (in matters of family and land tenure)

CITIZENSHIP:

see China

SUFFRAGE:

18 years of age in direct elections for half of the Legislative Council seats and all of the seats in 18 district councils; universal for permanent residents living in the territory of Hong Kong for the past 7 years; note - in indirect elections, suffrage is limited to about 220,000 members of functional constituencies for the other half of the legislature and a 1,200-member election committee for the chief executive drawn from broad sectoral groupings, central government bodies, municipal organizations, and elected Hong Kong officials

EXECUTIVE BRANCH:

chief of state: President of China XI Jinping (since 14 March 2013)

head of government: Chief Executive Carrie LAM (since 1 July 2017)

cabinet: Executive Council or ExCo appointed by the chief executive

elections/appointments: president indirectly elected by National People's Congress for a 5-year term (eligible for a second term); election last held on 17 March 2018 (next to be held in March 2023); chief executive indirectly elected by the Election Committee and appointed by the PRC Government for a 5-year term (eligible for a second term); election last held on 26 March 2017 (next to be held in 2022)

election results: Carrie LAM elected chief executive; Election Committee vote - Carrie LAM 777, John TSANG 365, WOO Kwok-hing 21, invalid 23

note: the Legislative Council voted in June 2010 to expand the Election Committee to 1,200 members

LEGISLATIVE BRANCH:

description: unicameral Legislative Council or LegCo (70 seats; 35 members directly elected in multi-seat constituencies by party-list proportional representation vote; 30 members indirectly elected by the approximately 220,000 members of various functional constituencies based on a variety of methods; 5 at large "super-seat" members directly elected by all of Hong Kong's eligible voters who do not participate in a functional constituency; members serve 4-year terms)

elections: last held on 4 September 2016; (next to be held in September 2020); note - byelection held on 11 March and 25 November 2018 to fill 5 seats left vacant after 5 legislators were removed from office

election results: percent of vote by block - pro-democracy 36%; pro-Beijing 40.2%, localist 19%, other 4.8%; seats by block/party - pro-Beijing 40 (DAB 12, BPA 7, FTU 5, Liberal Party 4, NPP 3, other 9); pro-democracy 23 (Democratic Party 7, Civic Party 6, PP-LSD 2, Professional Commons 2, Labor 1, NWSC 1, PTU 1, other democrats 3), localists 6 (ALLinHK 2, CP-PPI-HKRO 1, Demosisto 1, Democracy Groundwork 1, other localist 1), non-aligned independent 1; composition - men 59, women 11, percent of women 15.7%; note - 2 localists were barred from taking office in November 2016 and 4 pro-democracy legislators were removed in July 2017; two pan-democratic, two DAB, and one pro-establishment candidates won the byelections in 2018 to fill the seats vacated by the 5 legislators removed from office; one pro-democracy seat remains unfilled pending a court appeal; percent of vote by block as of March 2019 - pro-Beijing 62% pro-democracy 38%; seats by block/party as of March 2019 - pro-Beijing 43 (DAB 13, BPA 7, FTU 5, Liberal Party 4, NPP 3, other 11); pro-democracy 26 (Democratic Party 7, Civic Party 5, Professional Commons 2, Civic Passion 1, Labor 1 PTU 1, Council Front 6, independent 3); composition as of March 2019 - men 58, women 11; percent of women 15.7%

JUDICIAL BRANCH:

highest courts: Court of Final Appeal (consists of the chief justice, 3 permanent judges, and 20 non-permanent judges); note - a sitting bench consists of the chief justice, 3 permanent judges, and 1 non-permanent judge

judge selection and term of office: all judges appointed by the Hong Kong Chief Executive upon the recommendation of the Judicial Officers Recommendation Commission, an independent body consisting of the Secretary for Justice, other judges, and judicial and legal professionals; permanent judges serve until normal retirement at age 65, but term can be extended; non-permanent judges appointed for renewable 3-year terms without age limit

subordinate courts: High Court (consists of the Court of Appeal and Court of First Instance); District Courts (includes Family and Land Courts); magistrates' courts; specialized tribunals

POLITICAL PARTIES AND LEADERS:

parties:
ALLinHK (alliance of 6 localist groups)
Business and Professional Alliance or BPA [LO Wai-kwok]
Civic Party [Alvin YEUNG]
Civic Passion or CP [CHENG Chung-tai] (part of Civic Passion-Proletariat Political Institute-Hong Kong Resurgence Order alliance or CP-PPI-HKRO that dissolved after the 2016 election)
Democracy Groundwork [LAU Siu-lai]
Democratic Alliance for the Betterment and Progress of Hong Kong or DAB [Starry LEE Wai-king]
Democratic Party [WU Chi-wai]
Demosisto [Ivan LAM]
Federation of Trade Unions or FTU [Stanley NG Chau-pei]
Labor Party [Steven KWOK Wing-kin]
League of Social Democrats or LSD [Avery NG Man-yuen]
Liberal Party [Felix CHUNG Kwok-pan]
Neighborhood and Workers Service Center or NWSC [LEUNG Yui-chung]
New People's Party or NPP [Regina IP Lau Su-yee]
People Power or PP [Raymond CHAN]
Youngspiration [Sixtus "Baggio" LEUNG Chung-hang]

other:
Professional Commons [Charles Peter MOK] (think tank)
Professional Teachers Union or PTU

note: political blocks include: pro-democracy - Civic Party, Democratic Party, Labor Party, LSD, NWSC, PP, Professional Commons, PTU; pro-Beijing - DAB, FTU, Liberal Party,

NPP, BPA; localist - ALLinHK, CP, Democracy Groundwork, Demosisto; there is no political party ordinance, so there are no registered political parties; politically active groups register as societies or companies

INTERNATIONAL ORGANIZATION PARTICIPATION:

ADB, APEC, BIS, FATF, ICC (national committees), IHO, IMF, IMO (associate), Interpol (subbureau), IOC, ISO (correspondent), ITUC (NGOs), UNWTO (associate), UPU, WCO, WMO, WTO

DIPLOMATIC REPRESENTATION IN THE US:

none (Special Administrative Region of China); Hong Kong Economic and Trade Office (HKETO) carries out normal liaison activities and communication with the US Government and other US entities; Eddie MAK, JP (since 3 July 2018) is the Hong Kong Commissioner to the US Government of the Hong Kong Special Administrative Region; address: 1520 18th Street NW, Washington, DC 20036; telephone: [1] 202 331-8947; FAX: [1] 202 331-8958

HKETO offices: New York, San Francisco

DIPLOMATIC REPRESENTATION FROM THE US:

chief of mission: Consul General Hanscom SMITH (since July 2019); note - also accredited to Macau

telephone: [852] 2523-9011

embassy: U. S. Consulate General Hong Kong and Macau
26 Garden Road
Central, Hong Kong

mailing address: Unit 8000, Box 1, DPO AP 96521-0006

FAX: [852] 2845-1598

consulate(s) general: 26 Garden Road, Hong Kong

FLAG DESCRIPTION:

red with a stylized, white, five-petal Bauhinia flower in the center; each petal contains a small, red, five-pointed star in its middle; the red color is the same as that on the Chinese flag and represents the motherland; the fragrant Bauhinia - developed in Hong Kong the late 19th century - has come to symbolize the region; the five stars echo those on the flag of China

NATIONAL SYMBOL(S):

orchid tree flower; national colors: red, white

NATIONAL ANTHEM:

note: as a Special Administrative Region of China, "Yiyongjun Jinxingqu" is the official anthem (see China)

ECONOMY :: HONG KONG

ECONOMY - OVERVIEW:

Hong Kong has a free market economy, highly dependent on international trade and finance - the value of goods and services trade, including the sizable share of reexports, is about four times GDP. Hong Kong has no tariffs on imported goods, and it levies excise duties on only four commodities, whether imported or produced locally: hard alcohol, tobacco, oil, and methyl alcohol. There are no quotas or dumping laws. Hong Kong continues to link its currency closely to the US dollar, maintaining an arrangement established in 1983.

Excess liquidity, low interest rates and a tight housing supply have caused Hong Kong property prices to rise rapidly. The lower and middle-income segments of the population increasingly find housing unaffordable.

Hong Kong's open economy has left it exposed to the global economic situation. Its continued reliance on foreign trade and investment makes it vulnerable to renewed global financial market volatility or a slowdown in the global economy.

Mainland China has long been Hong Kong's largest trading partner, accounting for about half of Hong Kong's total trade by value. Hong Kong's natural resources are limited, and food and raw materials must be imported. As a result of China's easing of travel restrictions, the number of mainland tourists to the territory surged from 4.5 million in 2001 to 47.3 million in 2014, outnumbering visitors from all other countries combined. After peaking in 2014, overall tourist arrivals dropped 2.5% in 2015 and 4.5% in 2016. The tourism sector rebounded in 2017, with visitor arrivals rising 3.2% to 58.47 million. Travelers from Mainland China totaled 44.45 million, accounting for 76% of the total.

The Hong Kong Government is promoting the Special Administrative Region (SAR) as the preferred business hub for renminbi (RMB) internationalization. Hong Kong residents are allowed to establish RMB-denominated savings accounts, RMB-denominated corporate and Chinese government bonds have been issued in Hong Kong, RMB trade settlement is allowed, and investment schemes such as the Renminbi Qualified Foreign Institutional Investor (RQFII) Program was first launched in Hong Kong. Offshore RMB activities experienced a setback, however, after the People's Bank of China changed the way it set the central parity rate in August 2015. RMB deposits in Hong Kong fell from 1.0 trillion RMB at the end of 2014 to 559 billion RMB at the end of 2017, while RMB trade settlement handled by banks in Hong Kong also shrank from 6.8 trillion RMB in 2015 to 3.9 trillion RMB in 2017.

Hong Kong has also established itself as the premier stock market for Chinese firms seeking to list abroad. In 2015, mainland Chinese companies constituted about 50% of the firms listed on the Hong Kong Stock Exchange and accounted for about 66% of the exchange's market capitalization.

During the past decade, as Hong Kong's manufacturing industry moved to the mainland, its service industry has grown rapidly. In 2014, Hong Kong and China signed a new agreement on achieving basic liberalization of trade in services in Guangdong Province under the Closer Economic Partnership Agreement (CEPA), adopted in 2003 to forge closer ties between Hong Kong and the mainland. The new measures, which took effect in March 2015, cover a negative list and a most-favored treatment provision. On the basis of the Guangdong Agreement, the Agreement on Trade in Services signed in November 2015 further enhanced liberalization, including extending the implementation of the majority of Guangdong pilot liberalization measures to the whole Mainland, reducing the restrictive measures in the negative list, and adding measures in the positive lists for cross-border services as well as cultural and telecommunications services. In June 2017, the Investment Agreement and the Agreement on Economic and Technical Cooperation (Ecotech Agreement) were signed under the framework of CEPA.

Hong Kong's economic integration with the mainland continues to be most evident in the banking and finance sector. Initiatives like the Hong Kong-Shanghai Stock Connect, the Hong Kong- Shenzhen Stock Connect the Mutual Recognition of Funds, and the Bond Connect scheme are all important steps towards opening up the Mainland's capital markets and have reinforced Hong Kong's role as China's leading offshore RMB market. Additional connect schemes such as ETF Connect (for exchange-traded fund products) are also under exploration by Hong Kong authorities. In 2017, Chief Executive Carrie LAM announced plans to increase government spending on research and development, education, and technological innovation with the aim of spurring continued economic growth through greater sector diversification.

GDP (PURCHASING POWER PARITY):

$455.9 billion (2017 est.)

$439.2 billion (2016 est.)

$429.9 billion (2015 est.)

note: data are in 2017 dollars

country comparison to the world: 43

GDP (OFFICIAL EXCHANGE RATE):

$341.4 billion (2017 est.)

GDP - REAL GROWTH RATE:

3.8% (2017 est.)

2.2% (2016 est.)

2.4% (2015 est.)

country comparison to the world: 87

GDP - PER CAPITA (PPP):

$61,500 (2017 est.)

$59,500 (2016 est.)

$58,800 (2015 est.)

note: data are in 2017 dollars

country comparison to the world: 18

GROSS NATIONAL SAVING:

26.6% of GDP (2017 est.)

25.5% of GDP (2016 est.)

24.9% of GDP (2015 est.)

country comparison to the world: 47

GDP - COMPOSITION, BY END USE:

household consumption: 67% (2017 est.)

government consumption: 9.9% (2017 est.)

investment in fixed capital: 21.8% (2017 est.)

investment in inventories: 0.4% (2017 est.)

exports of goods and services: 188% (2017 est.)

imports of goods and services: -187.1% (2017 est.)

GDP - COMPOSITION, BY SECTOR OF ORIGIN:

agriculture: 0.1% (2017 est.)

industry: 7.6% (2017 est.)

services: 92.3% (2017 est.)

AGRICULTURE - PRODUCTS:

fresh vegetables and fruit; poultry, pork; fish

INDUSTRIES:

trading and logistics, financial services, professional services, tourism, cultural and creative, clothing and textiles, shipping, electronics, toys, clocks and watches

INDUSTRIAL PRODUCTION GROWTH RATE:

1.7% (2017 est.)

country comparison to the world: 139

LABOR FORCE:

3.965 million (2017 est.)

country comparison to the world: 94

LABOR FORCE - BY OCCUPATION:

agriculture: 3.8% (2013 est.)

industry: 2% (2016 est.)

services: 54.5% (2016 est.)

industry and services: 12.5% (2013 est.)

agriculture/fishing/forestry/mining: 10.1% (2013)

manufacturing: 17.1% (2013 est.)

note: above data exclude public sector

UNEMPLOYMENT RATE:

3.1% (2017 est.)

3.4% (2016 est.)

country comparison to the world: 38

POPULATION BELOW POVERTY LINE:

19.9% (2016 est.)

HOUSEHOLD INCOME OR CONSUMPTION BY PERCENTAGE SHARE:

lowest 10%: 1.8% NA

highest 10%: 38.1% NA (2016)

DISTRIBUTION OF FAMILY INCOME - GINI INDEX:

53.9 (2016)

53.7 (2011 est.)

country comparison to the world: 9

BUDGET:

revenues: 79.34 billion (2017 est.)

expenditures: 61.64 billion (2017 est.)

TAXES AND OTHER REVENUES:

23.2% (of GDP) (2017 est.)

country comparison to the world: 128

BUDGET SURPLUS (+) OR DEFICIT (-):

5.2% (of GDP) (2017 est.)

country comparison to the world: 6

PUBLIC DEBT:

0.1% of GDP (2017 est.)

0.1% of GDP (2016 est.)

country comparison to the world: 208

FISCAL YEAR:

1 April - 31 March

INFLATION RATE (CONSUMER PRICES):

1.5% (2017 est.)

2.4% (2016 est.)

country comparison to the world: 81

CENTRAL BANK DISCOUNT RATE:

1.75% (31 December 2017)

1% (31 December 2016)

country comparison to the world: 123

COMMERCIAL BANK PRIME LENDING RATE:

5% (31 December 2017 est.)

5% (31 December 2016 est.)

country comparison to the world: 150

STOCK OF NARROW MONEY:

$311.1 billion (31 December 2017 est.)

$285.5 billion (31 December 2016 est.)

country comparison to the world: 16

STOCK OF BROAD MONEY:

$311.1 billion (31 December 2017 est.)

$285.5 billion (31 December 2016 est.)

country comparison to the world: 16

STOCK OF DOMESTIC CREDIT:

$825.3 billion (31 December 2017 est.)

$676.5 billion (31 December 2016 est.)

country comparison to the world: 19

MARKET VALUE OF PUBLICLY TRADED SHARES:

$4.359 trillion (31 December 2017 est.)

$3.175 trillion (31 December 2016 est.)

$3.165 trillion (31 December 2015 est.)

country comparison to the world: 4
CURRENT ACCOUNT BALANCE:
$14.75 billion (2017 est.)
$12.71 billion (2016 est.)
country comparison to the world: 20
EXPORTS:
$537.8 billion (2017 est.)
$460 billion (2016 est.)
country comparison to the world: 8
EXPORTS - PARTNERS:
China 54.1%, US 7.7% (2017)
EXPORTS - COMMODITIES:
electrical machinery and appliances, textiles, apparel, watches and clocks, toys, "jewelry, goldsmiths' and silversmiths' wares, and other articles of precious or semi-precious materials"; Hong Kong plays an important role as entrepot to the Chinese mainland; in 2017, 58% of Hong Kong's re-exports originated in mainland China, and 54% were destined for the Chinese mainland
IMPORTS:
$561.8 billion (2017 est.)
$518.2 billion (2016 est.)
country comparison to the world: 7
IMPORTS - COMMODITIES:
raw materials and semi-manufactures, consumer goods, capital goods, foodstuffs, fuel (most is reexported)
IMPORTS - PARTNERS:
China 44.6%, Singapore 6.4%, Japan 6.1%, South Korea 5.5%, US 5.2% (2017)
RESERVES OF FOREIGN EXCHANGE AND GOLD:
$431.4 billion (31 December 2017 est.)
$386.2 billion (31 December 2016 est.)
country comparison to the world: 7
DEBT - EXTERNAL:
$633.6 billion (31 December 2017 est.)
$1.349 trillion (31 December 2016 est.)
country comparison to the world: 18
STOCK OF DIRECT FOREIGN INVESTMENT - AT HOME:
$2.2 trillion (31 December 2017 est.)
$1.616 trillion (31 December 2016 est.)
country comparison to the world: 3
STOCK OF DIRECT FOREIGN INVESTMENT - ABROAD:
$2.036 trillion (31 December 2017 est.)

$1.538 trillion (31 December 2016 est.)
country comparison to the world: 5
EXCHANGE RATES:
Hong Kong dollars (HKD) per US dollar -
7.82 (2017 est.)
7.76 (2016 est.)
7.762 (2015 est.)
7.752 (2014 est.)
7.754 (2013 est.)

ENERGY :: HONG KONG

ELECTRICITY ACCESS:
electrification - total population: 100% (2016)
ELECTRICITY - PRODUCTION:
35.97 billion kWh (2016 est.)
country comparison to the world: 60
ELECTRICITY - CONSUMPTION:
41.84 billion kWh (2016 est.)
country comparison to the world: 54
ELECTRICITY - EXPORTS:
1.205 billion kWh (2016 est.)
country comparison to the world: 55
ELECTRICITY - IMPORTS:
11.62 billion kWh (2016 est.)
country comparison to the world: 21
ELECTRICITY - INSTALLED GENERATING CAPACITY:
12.63 million kW (2016 est.)
country comparison to the world: 55
ELECTRICITY - FROM FOSSIL FUELS:
100% of total installed capacity (2016 est.)
country comparison to the world: 9
ELECTRICITY - FROM NUCLEAR FUELS:
0% of total installed capacity (2017 est.)
country comparison to the world: 108
ELECTRICITY - FROM HYDROELECTRIC PLANTS:
0% of total installed capacity (2017 est.)
country comparison to the world: 178
ELECTRICITY - FROM OTHER RENEWABLE SOURCES:
0% of total installed capacity (2017 est.)
country comparison to the world: 192
CRUDE OIL - PRODUCTION:

0 bbl/day (2018 est.)
country comparison to the world: 150
CRUDE OIL - EXPORTS:
0 bbl/day (2015 est.)
country comparison to the world: 138
CRUDE OIL - IMPORTS:
0 bbl/day (2015 est.)
country comparison to the world: 142
CRUDE OIL - PROVED RESERVES:
0 bbl (1 January 2018 est.)
country comparison to the world: 146
REFINED PETROLEUM PRODUCTS - PRODUCTION:
0 bbl/day (2015 est.)
country comparison to the world: 158
REFINED PETROLEUM PRODUCTS - CONSUMPTION:
403,100 bbl/day (2016 est.)
country comparison to the world: 38
REFINED PETROLEUM PRODUCTS - EXPORTS:
13,570 bbl/day (2015 est.)
country comparison to the world: 76
REFINED PETROLEUM PRODUCTS - IMPORTS:
402,100 bbl/day (2015 est.)
country comparison to the world: 22
NATURAL GAS - PRODUCTION:
0 cu m (2017 est.)
country comparison to the world: 147
NATURAL GAS - CONSUMPTION:
3.37 billion cu m (2017 est.)
country comparison to the world: 69
NATURAL GAS - EXPORTS:
0 cu m (2017 est.)
country comparison to the world: 122
NATURAL GAS - IMPORTS:
3.37 billion cu m (2017 est.)
country comparison to the world: 43
NATURAL GAS - PROVED RESERVES:
0 cu m (1 January 2016 est.)
country comparison to the world: 148
CARBON DIOXIDE EMISSIONS FROM CONSUMPTION OF ENERGY:
102.5 million Mt (2017 est.)
country comparison to the world: 43

COMMUNICATIONS :: HONG KONG

TELEPHONES - FIXED LINES:
total subscriptions: 4,266,837

subscriptions per 100 inhabitants: 59 (2017 est.)

country comparison to the world: 32

TELEPHONES - MOBILE CELLULAR:

total subscriptions: 18,340,347

subscriptions per 100 inhabitants: 255 (2017 est.)

country comparison to the world: 61

TELEPHONE SYSTEM:

general assessment: modern facilities provide excellent domestic and international services; some of the highest peak average broadband speeds in the world; HK aims to be among the earliest adopters of 5G mobile technology as early as 2020; almost all households have access to high-speed broadband connectivity; in the next five years the government has organized the development of 'smart cities' in six areas - "smart mobility", "smart living", "smart environment", "smart people", "smart government", and "smart economy" by 2022 (2018)

domestic: microwave radio relay links and extensive fiber-optic network; fixed-line is 59 per 100 and mobile-cellular is 255 per 100 (2018)

international: country code - 852; APG, ASE, EAC-C2C, HK-G, Bay-to-Bay Express Cable System, H2 Cable, HKA, SJC, SJC2, PLCN, SeaMeWe-3, TGN-IA, APCN-2, AAG, FLAG and FEA submarine cables provide connections to Asia, US, Australia, the Middle East, and Europe; satellite earth stations - 3 Intelsat (1 Pacific Ocean and 2 Indian Ocean); coaxial cable to Guangzhou, China (2019)

BROADCAST MEDIA:

4 commercial terrestrial TV networks each with multiple stations; multi-channel satellite and cable TV systems available; 3 licensed broadcasters of terrestrial radio, one of which is government funded, operate about 12 radio stations; note - 4 digital radio broadcasters operated in Hong Kong from 2010 to 2017, but all digital radio services were terminated in September 2017 due to weak market demand (2019)

INTERNET COUNTRY CODE:

.hk

INTERNET USERS:

total: 6.066 million

percent of population: 85% (July 2016 est.)

country comparison to the world: 68

BROADBAND - FIXED SUBSCRIPTIONS:

total: 2,645,752

subscriptions per 100 inhabitants: 37 (2017 est.)

country comparison to the world: 43

MILITARY AND SECURITY :: HONG KONG

MILITARY AND SECURITY FORCES:

no regular indigenous military forces; Hong Kong Police Force; Hong Kong garrison of China's People's Liberation Army (PLA) includes elements of the PLA Army, PLA Navy, and PLA Air Force; these forces are under the direct leadership of the Central Military Commission in Beijing and under administrative control of the adjacent Southern Theater Command (2019)

MILITARY - NOTE:

defense is the responsibility of China

TRANSPORTATION :: HONG KONG

NATIONAL AIR TRANSPORT SYSTEM:

number of registered air carriers: 7 (registered in China) (2015)

inventory of registered aircraft operated by air carriers: 253 (registered in China) (2015)

annual passenger traffic on registered air carriers: 41,867,157 (2015)

annual freight traffic on registered air carriers: 11.294 billion mt-km (2015)

CIVIL AIRCRAFT REGISTRATION COUNTRY CODE PREFIX:

B-H (2016)

AIRPORTS:

2 (2013)

country comparison to the world: 201

AIRPORTS - WITH PAVED RUNWAYS:

total: 2 (2017)

over 3,047 m: 1 (2017)

1,524 to 2,437 m: 1 (2017)

HELIPORTS:

9 (2013)

ROADWAYS:

total: 2,107 km (2017)

paved: 2,107 km (2017)

country comparison to the world: 166

MERCHANT MARINE:

total: 2,615

by type: bulk carrier 1143, container ship 499, general cargo 217, oil tanker 355, other 401 (2018)

country comparison to the world: 10

PORTS AND TERMINALS:

major seaport(s): Hong Kong

container port(s) (TEUs): Hong Kong (20,770,000) (2017)

TRANSNATIONAL ISSUES :: HONG KONG

DISPUTES - INTERNATIONAL:

Hong Kong plans to reduce its 2,800-hectare Frontier Closed Area (FCA) to 400 hectares by 2015; the FCA was established in 1951 as a buffer zone between Hong Kong and mainland China to prevent illegal migration from and the smuggling of goods

ILLICIT DRUGS:

despite strenuous law enforcement efforts, faces difficult challenges in controlling transit of heroin and methamphetamine to regional and world markets; modern banking system provides conduit for money laundering; rising indigenous use of synthetic drugs, especially among young people

EUROPE :: HUNGARY

INTRODUCTION :: HUNGARY

BACKGROUND:

Hungary became a Christian kingdom in A.D. 1000 and for many centuries served as a bulwark against Ottoman Turkish expansion in Europe. The kingdom eventually became part of the polyglot Austro-Hungarian Empire, which collapsed during World War I. The country fell under communist rule following World War II. In 1956, a revolt and an announced withdrawal from the Warsaw Pact were met with a massive military intervention by Moscow. Under the leadership of Janos KADAR in 1968, Hungary began liberalizing its economy, introducing so-called "Goulash Communism." Hungary held its first multiparty elections in 1990 and initiated a free market economy. It joined NATO in 1999 and the EU five years later.

GEOGRAPHY :: HUNGARY

LOCATION:
Central Europe, northwest of Romania

GEOGRAPHIC COORDINATES:
47 00 N, 20 00 E

MAP REFERENCES:
Europe

AREA:
total: 93,028 sq km

land: 89,608 sq km

water: 3,420 sq km

country comparison to the world: 111

AREA - COMPARATIVE:
slightly smaller than Virginia; about the same size as Indiana

LAND BOUNDARIES:
total: 2,106 km

border countries (7): Austria 321 km, Croatia 348 km, Romania 424 km, Serbia 164 km, Slovakia 627 km, Slovenia 94 km, Ukraine 128 km

COASTLINE:
0 km (landlocked)

MARITIME CLAIMS:
none (landlocked)

CLIMATE:
temperate; cold, cloudy, humid winters; warm summers

TERRAIN:
mostly flat to rolling plains; hills and low mountains on the Slovakian border

ELEVATION:
mean elevation: 143 m

lowest point: Tisza River 78 m

highest point: Kekes 1,014 m

NATURAL RESOURCES:
bauxite, coal, natural gas, fertile soils, arable land

LAND USE:
agricultural land: 58.9% (2011 est.)

arable land: 48.5% (2011 est.) / permanent crops: 2% (2011 est.) / permanent pasture: 8.4% (2011 est.)

forest: 22.5% (2011 est.)

other: 18.6% (2011 est.)

IRRIGATED LAND:
1,721 sq km (2012)

POPULATION DISTRIBUTION:
a fairly even distribution throughout most of the country, with urban areas attracting larger and denser populations

ENVIRONMENT - CURRENT ISSUES:
air and water pollution are some of Hungary's most serious environmental problems; water quality in the Hungarian part of the Danube has improved but is still plagued by pollutants from industry and large-scale agriculture; soil pollution

ENVIRONMENT - INTERNATIONAL AGREEMENTS:
party to: Air Pollution, Air Pollution-Nitrogen Oxides, Air Pollution-Persistent Organic Pollutants, Air Pollution-Sulfur 85, Air Pollution-Sulfur 94, Air Pollution-Volatile Organic Compounds, Antarctic Treaty, Biodiversity, Climate Change, Climate Change-Kyoto Protocol, Desertification, Endangered Species, Environmental Modification, Hazardous Wastes, Law of the Sea, Marine Dumping, Ozone Layer Protection, Ship Pollution, Wetlands, Whaling

signed, but not ratified: none of the selected agreements

GEOGRAPHY - NOTE:
landlocked; strategic location astride main land routes between Western Europe and Balkan Peninsula as well as between Ukraine and Mediterranean basin; the north-south flowing Duna (Danube) and Tisza Rivers divide the country into three large regions

PEOPLE AND SOCIETY :: HUNGARY

POPULATION:
9,825,704 (July 2018 est.)

country comparison to the world: 92

NATIONALITY:
noun: Hungarian(s)

adjective: Hungarian

ETHNIC GROUPS:

Hungarian 85.6%, Romani 3.2%, German 1.9%, other 2.6%, unspecified 14.1% (2011 est.)

note: percentages add up to more than 100% because respondents were able to identify more than one ethnic group; Romani populations are usually underestimated in official statistics and may represent 5-10% of Hungary's population

LANGUAGES:

Hungarian (official) 99.6%, English 16%, German 11.2%, Russian 1.6%, Romanian 1.3%, French 1.2%, other 4.2% (2011 est.)

note: shares sum to more than 100% because some respondents gave more than one answer on the census; Hungarian is the mother tongue of 98.9% of Hungarian speakers

RELIGIONS:

Roman Catholic 37.2%, Calvinist 11.6%, Lutheran 2.2%, Greek Catholic 1.8%, other 1.9%, none 18.2%, no response 27.2% (2011 est.)

AGE STRUCTURE:

0-14 years: 14.66% (male 741,624 /female 698,905)

15-24 years: 10.76% (male 546,437 /female 511,214)

25-54 years: 42.01% (male 2,077,449 /female 2,050,330)

55-64 years: 13.07% (male 593,250 /female 690,784)

65 years and over: 19.5% (male 725,728 /female 1,189,983) (2018 est.)

DEPENDENCY RATIOS:

total dependency ratio: 46.9 (2015 est.)

youth dependency ratio: 21.2 (2015 est.)

elderly dependency ratio: 25.7 (2015 est.)

potential support ratio: 3.9 (2015 est.)

MEDIAN AGE:

total: 42.7 years (2018 est.)

male: 40.8 years

female: 44.7 years

country comparison to the world: 25

POPULATION GROWTH RATE:

-0.26% (2018 est.)

country comparison to the world: 214

BIRTH RATE:

8.9 births/1,000 population (2018 est.)

country comparison to the world: 206

DEATH RATE:

12.8 deaths/1,000 population (2018 est.)

country comparison to the world: 12

NET MIGRATION RATE:

1.3 migrant(s)/1,000 population (2018 est.)

country comparison to the world: 58

POPULATION DISTRIBUTION:

a fairly even distribution throughout most of the country, with urban areas attracting larger and denser populations

URBANIZATION:

urban population: 71.6% of total population (2019)

rate of urbanization: 0.07% annual rate of change (2015-20 est.)

MAJOR URBAN AREAS - POPULATION:

1.764 million BUDAPEST (capital) (2019)

SEX RATIO:

at birth: 1.06 male(s)/female

0-14 years: 1.06 male(s)/female

15-24 years: 1.07 male(s)/female

25-54 years: 1.01 male(s)/female

55-64 years: 0.86 male(s)/female

65 years and over: 0.61 male(s)/female

total population: 0.91 male(s)/female (2018 est.)

MOTHER'S MEAN AGE AT FIRST BIRTH:

28.3 years (2014 est.)

MATERNAL MORTALITY RATE:

12 deaths/100,000 live births (2017 est.)

country comparison to the world: 139

INFANT MORTALITY RATE:

total: 4.8 deaths/1,000 live births (2018 est.)

male: 5.1 deaths/1,000 live births

female: 4.5 deaths/1,000 live births

country comparison to the world: 177

LIFE EXPECTANCY AT BIRTH:

total population: 76.3 years (2018 est.)

male: 72.6 years

female: 80.2 years

country comparison to the world: 88

TOTAL FERTILITY RATE:

1.45 children born/woman (2018 est.)

country comparison to the world: 205

CONTRACEPTIVE PREVALENCE RATE:

61.6% (2008/09)

note: percent of women aged 25-49

DRINKING WATER SOURCE:

improved:

urban: 100% of population

rural: 100% of population

total: 100% of population

unimproved:

urban: 0% of population

rural: 0% of population

total: 0% of population (2015 est.)

CURRENT HEALTH EXPENDITURE:

7.4% (2016)

PHYSICIANS DENSITY:

3.23 physicians/1,000 population (2016)

HOSPITAL BED DENSITY:

7 beds/1,000 population (2013)

SANITATION FACILITY ACCESS:

improved:

urban: 97.8% of population (2015 est.)

rural: 98.6% of population (2015 est.)

total: 98% of population (2015 est.)

unimproved:

urban: 2.2% of population (2015 est.)

rural: 1.4% of population (2015 est.)

total: 2% of population (2015 est.)

HIV/AIDS - ADULT PREVALENCE RATE:

<.1% (2018 est.)

HIV/AIDS - PEOPLE LIVING WITH HIV/AIDS:

3,700 (2018 est.)

country comparison to the world: 124

HIV/AIDS - DEATHS:

<100 (2018 est.)

MAJOR INFECTIOUS DISEASES:

degree of risk: intermediate (2016)

vectorborne diseases: tickborne encephalitis (2016)

OBESITY - ADULT PREVALENCE RATE:

26.4% (2016)

country comparison to the world: 41

EDUCATION EXPENDITURES:

4.6% of GDP (2015)

country comparison to the world: 84

LITERACY:

definition: age 15 and over can read and write

total population: 99.1%

male: 99.1%

female: 99% (2015 est.)

SCHOOL LIFE EXPECTANCY (PRIMARY TO TERTIARY EDUCATION):

total: 15 years

male: 15 years

female: 15 years (2016)

UNEMPLOYMENT, YOUTH AGES 15-24:

total: 10.7%

male: 9.7%

female: 12.1% (2017 est.)

country comparison to the world: 123

GOVERNMENT :: HUNGARY

COUNTRY NAME:

conventional long form: none

conventional short form: Hungary

local long form: none

local short form: Magyarorszag

former: Kingdom of Hungary, Hungarian People's Republic, Hungarian Soviet Republic, Hungarian Republic

etymology: the Byzantine Greeks refered to the tribes that arrived on the steppes of Eastern Europe in the 9th century as the "Oungroi," a name that was later Latinized to "Ungri" and which became "Hungari"; the name originally meant an "[alliance of] ten tribes"; the Hungarian name "Magyarorszag" means "Country of the Magyars"; the term may derive from the most prominent of the Hungarian tribes, the Megyer

GOVERNMENT TYPE:

parliamentary republic

CAPITAL:

name: Budapest

geographic coordinates: 47 30 N, 19 05 E

time difference: UTC+1 (6 hours ahead of Washington, DC, during Standard Time)

daylight saving time: +1hr, begins last Sunday in March; ends last Sunday in October

etymology: the Hungarian capital city was formed in 1873 from the merger of three cities on opposite banks of the Danube: Buda and Obuda (Old Buda) on the western shore and Pest on the eastern; the origins of the original names are obscure, but according to the second century A.D. geographer, Ptolemy, the settlement that would become Pest was called "Pession" in ancient times; "Buda" may derive from either a Slavic or Turkic personal name

ADMINISTRATIVE DIVISIONS:

19 counties (megyek, singular - megye), 23 cities with county rights (megyei jogu varosok, singular - megyei jogu varos), and 1 capital city (fovaros)

counties: Bacs-Kiskun, Baranya, Bekes, Borsod-Abauj-Zemplen, Csongrad, Fejer, Gyor-Moson-Sopron, Hajdu-Bihar, Heves, Jasz-Nagykun-Szolnok, Komarom-Esztergom, Nograd, Pest, Somogy, Szabolcs-Szatmar-Bereg, Tolna, Vas, Veszprem, Zala;

cities with county rights: Bekescsaba, Debrecen, Dunaujvaros, Eger, Erd, Gyor, Hodmezovasarhely, Kaposvar, Kecskemet, Miskolc, Nagykanizsa, Nyiregyhaza, Pecs, Salgotarjan, Sopron, Szeged, Szekesfehervar, Szekszard, Szolnok, Szombathely, Tatabanya, Veszprem, Zalaegerszeg;

capital city: Budapest

INDEPENDENCE:

16 November 1918 (republic proclaimed); notable earlier dates: 25 December 1000 (crowning of King STEPHEN I, traditional founding date); 30 March 1867 (Austro-Hungarian dual monarchy established)

NATIONAL HOLIDAY:

Saint Stephen's Day, 20 August (1083); note - commemorates his canonization and the transfer of his remains to Buda (now Budapest) in 1083

CONSTITUTION:

history: previous 1949 (heavily amended in 1989 following the collapse of communism); latest approved 18 April 2011, signed 25 April 2011, effective 1 January 2012

amendments: proposed by the president of the republic, by the government, by parliamentary committee, or by Parliament members; passage requires two-thirds majority vote of Parliament members and approval by the president; amended several times, last in 2018 (2019)

LEGAL SYSTEM:

civil legal system influenced by the German model

INTERNATIONAL LAW ORGANIZATION PARTICIPATION:

accepts compulsory ICJ jurisdiction with reservations; accepts ICCt jurisdiction

CITIZENSHIP:

citizenship by birth: no

citizenship by descent only: at least one parent must be a citizen of Hungary

dual citizenship recognized: yes

residency requirement for naturalization: 8 years

SUFFRAGE:

18 years of age, 16 if married and marriage is registered in Hungary; universal

EXECUTIVE BRANCH:

chief of state: President Janos ADER (since 10 May 2012)

head of government: Prime Minister Viktor ORBAN (since 29 May 2010)

cabinet: Cabinet of Ministers proposed by the prime minister and appointed by the president

elections/appointments: president indirectly elected by the National Assembly with two-thirds majority vote in first round or simple majority vote in second round for a 5-year term (eligible for a second term); election last held on 13 March 2017 (next to be held spring 2022); prime minister elected by the National Assembly on the recommendation of the president; election last held on 10 May 2018 (next to be held by spring 2022)

election results: Janos ADER (Fidesz) reelected president; National Assembly vote - 131 to 39; Viktor ORBAN (Fidesz) reelected prime minister; National Assembly vote - 134 to 28

LEGISLATIVE BRANCH:

description: unicameral National Assembly or Orszaggyules (199 seats; 106 members directly elected in single-member constituencies by simple majority vote and 93 members directly elected in a single nationwide constituency by party list proportional representation vote; members serve 4-year terms)

elections: last held on 8 April 2018 (next to be held in April 2022)

election results: percent of vote by party list - Fidesz-KDNP 49.3%, Jobbik 19.1%, MSZP-PM 11.9%, LMP 7.1%, DK 5.4%, Together 0.7%, LdU 0.5%, other 6%; seats by party - Fidesz 117, Jobbik 26, KDNP 16, MSZP 15, LMP 9, DK 9, PM 5, LdU 1, independent 1; composition - men 174, women 25, percent of women 12.6%

JUDICIAL BRANCH:

highest courts: Curia or Supreme Judicial Court (consists of the president, vice president, department heads, and approximately 91 judges and is organized into civil, criminal, and administrative-labor departments; Constitutional Court (consists of 15 judges, including the court president and vice president)

judge selection and term of office: Curia president elected by the National Assembly on the recommendation of the president of the republic; other Curia judges appointed by the president upon the recommendation of the National Judicial Council, a separate 15-member administrative body; judge tenure based on interim evaluations until normal retirement at age 62; Constitutional Court judges, including the president of the court, elected by the National Assembly; court vice president elected by the court itself; members serve 12-year terms with mandatory retirement at age 62

subordinate courts: 5 regional courts of appeal; 19 regional or county courts (including Budapest Metropolitan Court); 20 administrative-labor courts; 111 district or local courts

POLITICAL PARTIES AND LEADERS:

Christian Democratic People's Party or KDNP [Zsolt SEMJEN]
Democratic Coalition or DK [Ferenc GYURCSANY]
Dialogue for Hungary or PM [Gergely KARACSONY, Timea SZABO]
Fidesz-Hungarian Civic Alliance or Fidesz [Viktor ORBAN]
Hungarian Socialist Party or MSZP [Bertalan TOTH]
Momentum (Momentum Mozgalom) [Andras FEKETE-GYOR]
Movement for a Better Hungary or Jobbik [Tamas SNEIDER]
National Self-Government of Germans in Hungary or LdU [Olivia SCHUBERT]
Politics Can Be Different or LMP [Marta DEMETER, Laszlo LORANT-KERESZTES]

INTERNATIONAL ORGANIZATION PARTICIPATION:

Australia Group, BIS, CD, CE, CEI, CERN, EAPC, EBRD, ECB, EIB, ESA (cooperating state), EU, FAO, G-9, IAEA, IBRD, ICAO, ICC (national committees), ICCt, ICRM, IDA, IEA, IFAD, IFC, IFRCS, ILO, IMF, IMO, IMSO, Interpol, IOC, IOM, IPU, ISO, ITSO, ITU, ITUC (NGOs), MIGA, MINURSO, NATO, NEA, NSG, OAS (observer), OECD, OIF (observer), OPCW, OSCE, PCA, Schengen Convention, SELEC, UN, UNCTAD, UNESCO, UNFICYP, UNHCR, UNIDO, UNIFIL, UNWTO, UPU, WCO, WFTU (NGOs), WHO, WIPO, WMO, WTO, ZC

DIPLOMATIC REPRESENTATION IN THE US:

Ambassador Laszlo SZABO (since 8 September 2017)

chancery: 3910 Shoemaker Street NW, Washington, DC 20008

telephone: [1] (202) 362-6730

FAX: [1] (202) 966-8135

consulate(s) general: Chicago, Los Angeles, New York

DIPLOMATIC REPRESENTATION FROM THE US:

chief of mission: Ambassador David B. CORNSTEIN (since 25 June 2018)

telephone: [36] (1) 475-4400

embassy: Szabadsag ter 12, H-1054 Budapest

mailing address: pouch: American Embassy Budapest, 5270 Budapest Place, US Department of State, Washington, DC 20521-5270

FAX: [36] (1) 475-4248

FLAG DESCRIPTION:

three equal horizontal bands of red (top), white, and green; the flag dates to the national movement of the 18th and 19th centuries, and fuses the medieval colors of the Hungarian coat of arms with the revolutionary tricolor form of the French flag; folklore attributes virtues to the colors: red for strength, white for faithfulness, and green for hope; alternatively, the red is seen as being for the blood spilled in defense of the land, white for freedom, and green for the pasturelands that make up so much of the country

NATIONAL SYMBOL(S):

Holy Crown of Hungary (Crown of Saint Stephen); national colors: red, white, green

NATIONAL ANTHEM:

name: "Himnusz" (Hymn)

lyrics/music: Ferenc KOLCSEY/Ferenc ERKEL

note: adopted 1844

ECONOMY :: HUNGARY

ECONOMY - OVERVIEW:

Hungary has transitioned from a centrally planned to a market-driven economy with a per capita income approximately two-thirds of the EU-28 average; however, in recent years the government has become more involved in managing the economy. Budapest has implemented unorthodox economic policies to boost household consumption and has relied on EU-funded development projects to generate growth.

Following the fall of communism in 1990, Hungary experienced a drop-off in exports and financial assistance from the former Soviet Union. Hungary embarked on a series of economic reforms, including privatization of state-owned enterprises and reduction of social spending programs, to shift from a centrally planned to a market-driven economy, and to reorient its economy towards trade with the West. These efforts helped to spur growth, attract investment, and reduce Hungary's debt burden and fiscal deficits. Despite these reforms, living conditions for the average Hungarian initially deteriorated as inflation increased and unemployment reached double digits. Conditions slowly improved over the 1990s as the reforms came to fruition and export growth accelerated. Economic policies instituted during that decade helped position Hungary to join the European Union in 2004. Hungary has not yet joined the euro-zone. Hungary suffered a historic economic contraction as a result of the global economic slowdown in 2008-09 as export demand and domestic consumption dropped, prompting it to take an IMF-EU financial assistance package.

Since 2010, the government has backpedaled on many economic reforms and taken a more populist approach towards economic management. The government has favored national industries and government-linked businesses through legislation, regulation, and public procurements. In 2011 and 2014, Hungary nationalized private pension funds, which squeezed financial service providers out of the system, but also helped Hungary curb its public debt and lower its budget deficit to below 3% of GDP, as subsequent pension contributions have been channeled into the state-managed pension fund. Hungary's public debt (at 74.5% of GDP) is still high compared to EU peers in Central Europe. Real GDP growth has been robust in the past few years due to increased EU funding, higher EU demand for Hungarian exports, and a rebound in domestic household consumption. To further boost household consumption ahead of the 2018 election, the government embarked on a six-year phased increase to minimum wages and public sector salaries, decreased taxes on foodstuffs and services, cut the personal income tax from 16% to 15%, and implemented a uniform 9% business tax for small and medium-sized enterprises and large companies. Real GDP growth slowed in 2016 due to a cyclical decrease in EU funding, but increased to 3.8% in 2017 as the government pre-financed EU funded projects ahead of the 2018 election.

Systemic economic challenges include pervasive corruption, labor shortages driven by demographic declines and migration, widespread poverty in rural areas, vulnerabilities to changes in demand for exports, and a heavy reliance on Russian energy imports.

GDP (PURCHASING POWER PARITY):

$289.6 billion (2017 est.)

$278.5 billion (2016 est.)

$272.5 billion (2015 est.)

note: data are in 2017 dollars

country comparison to the world: 59

GDP (OFFICIAL EXCHANGE RATE):

$139.2 billion (2017 est.)

GDP - REAL GROWTH RATE:

4% (2017 est.)

2.2% (2016 est.)

3.4% (2015 est.)

country comparison to the world: 76

GDP - PER CAPITA (PPP):

$29,600 (2017 est.)

$28,300 (2016 est.)

$27,600 (2015 est.)

note: data are in 2017 dollars

country comparison to the world: 68

GROSS NATIONAL SAVING:

25.7% of GDP (2017 est.)

25.8% of GDP (2016 est.)

25.3% of GDP (2015 est.)

country comparison to the world: 54

GDP - COMPOSITION, BY END USE:

household consumption: 49.6% (2017 est.)

government consumption: 20% (2017 est.)

investment in fixed capital: 21.6% (2017 est.)

investment in inventories: 1% (2017 est.)

exports of goods and services: 90.2% (2017 est.)

imports of goods and services: -82.4% (2017 est.)

GDP - COMPOSITION, BY SECTOR OF ORIGIN:

agriculture: 3.9% (2017 est.)

industry: 31.3% (2017 est.)

services: 64.8% (2017 est.)

AGRICULTURE - PRODUCTS:

wheat, corn, sunflower seed, potatoes, sugar beets; pigs, cattle, poultry, dairy products

INDUSTRIES:

mining, metallurgy, construction materials, processed foods, textiles, chemicals (especially pharmaceuticals), motor vehicles

INDUSTRIAL PRODUCTION GROWTH RATE:

7.4% (2017 est.)

country comparison to the world: 29

LABOR FORCE:

4.599 million (2017 est.)

country comparison to the world: 87

LABOR FORCE - BY OCCUPATION:

agriculture: 4.9%

industry: 30.3%

services: 64.5% (2015 est.)

UNEMPLOYMENT RATE:

4.2% (2017 est.)

5.1% (2016 est.)

country comparison to the world: 54

POPULATION BELOW POVERTY LINE:

14.9% (2015 est.)

HOUSEHOLD INCOME OR CONSUMPTION BY PERCENTAGE SHARE:

lowest 10%: 3.3%

highest 10%: 22.4% (2015)

DISTRIBUTION OF FAMILY INCOME - GINI INDEX:

28.2 (2015 est.)

28.6 (2014)

country comparison to the world: 140

BUDGET:

revenues: 61.98 billion (2017 est.)

expenditures: 64.7 billion (2017 est.)

TAXES AND OTHER REVENUES:

44.5% (of GDP) (2017 est.)

country comparison to the world: 23

BUDGET SURPLUS (+) OR DEFICIT (-):

-2% (of GDP) (2017 est.)

note: Hungary has been under the EU Excessive Deficit Procedure since it joined the EU in 2004; in March 2012, the EU elevated its Excessive Deficit Procedure against Hungary and proposed freezing 30% of the country's Cohesion Funds because 2011 deficit reductions were not achieved in a sustainable manner; in June 2012, the EU lifted the freeze, recognizing that steps had been taken to reduce the deficit; the Hungarian deficit increased above 3% both in 2013 and in 2014 due to sluggish growth and the government's fiscal tightening

country comparison to the world: 104

PUBLIC DEBT:

73.6% of GDP (2017 est.)

76% of GDP (2016 est.)

note: general government gross debt is defined in the Maastricht Treaty as consolidated general government gross debt at nominal value, outstanding at the end of the year in the following categories of government liabilities: currency and deposits, securities other than shares excluding financial derivatives, and national, state, and local government and social security funds.

country comparison to the world: 43

FISCAL YEAR:

calendar year

INFLATION RATE (CONSUMER PRICES):

2.4% (2017 est.)

0.4% (2016 est.)

country comparison to the world: 119
CENTRAL BANK DISCOUNT RATE:
0.9% (31 December 2017)
0.9% (31 December 2016)
country comparison to the world: 134
COMMERCIAL BANK PRIME LENDING RATE:
1.48% (31 December 2017 est.)
2.09% (31 December 2016 est.)
country comparison to the world: 190
STOCK OF NARROW MONEY:
$74.77 billion (31 December 2017 est.)
$55.48 billion (31 December 2016 est.)
country comparison to the world: 46
STOCK OF BROAD MONEY:
$74.77 billion (31 December 2017 est.)
$55.48 billion (31 December 2016 est.)
country comparison to the world: 46
STOCK OF DOMESTIC CREDIT:
$86.22 billion (31 December 2017 est.)
$69.76 billion (31 December 2016 est.)
country comparison to the world: 56
MARKET VALUE OF PUBLICLY TRADED SHARES:
$27.7 billion (31 December 2017 est.)
$22.4 billion (31 December 2016 est.)
$17.69 billion (31 December 2015 est.)
country comparison to the world: 58
CURRENT ACCOUNT BALANCE:
$4.39 billion (2017 est.)
$7.597 billion (2016 est.)
country comparison to the world: 30
EXPORTS:
$98.74 billion (2017 est.)
$91.6 billion (2016 est.)
country comparison to the world: 38
EXPORTS - PARTNERS:
Germany 27.7%, Romania 5.4%, Italy 5.1%, Austria 5%, Slovakia 4.8%, France 4.4%, Czech Republic 4.4%, Poland 4.3% (2017)
EXPORTS - COMMODITIES:
machinery and equipment (55.8%), other manufactures (32.7%), food products (6.8%), raw materials (2.4%), fuels and electricity (2.3%) (2017 est.)
IMPORTS:
$96.3 billion (2017 est.)
$83.5 billion (2016 est.)
country comparison to the world: 35
IMPORTS - COMMODITIES:
machinery and equipment 45.4%, other manufactures 34.3%, fuels and electricity 12.6%, food products 5.3%, raw materials 2.5% (2012)
IMPORTS - PARTNERS:
Germany 26.2%, Austria 6.3%, China 5.9%, Poland 5.5%, Slovakia 5.3%, Netherlands 5%, Czech Republic 4.8%, Italy 4.7%, France 4% (2017)
RESERVES OF FOREIGN EXCHANGE AND GOLD:
$28 billion (31 December 2017 est.)
$25.82 billion (31 December 2016 est.)
country comparison to the world: 52
DEBT - EXTERNAL:
$138.1 billion (31 December 2017 est.)
$131.3 billion (31 December 2016 est.)
country comparison to the world: 43
STOCK OF DIRECT FOREIGN INVESTMENT - AT HOME:
$290 billion (31 December 2017 est.)
$298.2 billion (31 December 2016 est.)
country comparison to the world: 22
STOCK OF DIRECT FOREIGN INVESTMENT - ABROAD:
$212 billion (31 December 2017 est.)
$222.6 billion (31 December 2016 est.)
country comparison to the world: 27
EXCHANGE RATES:
forints (HUF) per US dollar -
279.5 (2017 est.)
281.52 (2016 est.)
281.52 (2015 est.)
279.33 (2014 est.)
232.6 (2013 est.)

ENERGY :: HUNGARY

ELECTRICITY ACCESS:
electrification - total population: 100% (2016)
ELECTRICITY - PRODUCTION:
30.22 billion kWh (2016 est.)
country comparison to the world: 64
ELECTRICITY - CONSUMPTION:
39.37 billion kWh (2016 est.)
country comparison to the world: 56
ELECTRICITY - EXPORTS:
5.24 billion kWh (2016 est.)
country comparison to the world: 34
ELECTRICITY - IMPORTS:
17.95 billion kWh (2016 est.)
country comparison to the world: 13
ELECTRICITY - INSTALLED GENERATING CAPACITY:
8.639 million kW (2016 est.)
country comparison to the world: 67
ELECTRICITY - FROM FOSSIL FUELS:
64% of total installed capacity (2016 est.)
country comparison to the world: 122
ELECTRICITY - FROM NUCLEAR FUELS:
22% of total installed capacity (2017 est.)
country comparison to the world: 5
ELECTRICITY - FROM HYDROELECTRIC PLANTS:
1% of total installed capacity (2017 est.)
country comparison to the world: 148
ELECTRICITY - FROM OTHER RENEWABLE SOURCES:
13% of total installed capacity (2017 est.)
country comparison to the world: 67
CRUDE OIL - PRODUCTION:
16,000 bbl/day (2018 est.)
country comparison to the world: 72
CRUDE OIL - EXPORTS:
2,713 bbl/day (2017 est.)
country comparison to the world: 69
CRUDE OIL - IMPORTS:
121,000 bbl/day (2017 est.)
country comparison to the world: 40
CRUDE OIL - PROVED RESERVES:
24 million bbl (1 January 2018 est.)
country comparison to the world: 82
REFINED PETROLEUM PRODUCTS - PRODUCTION:
152,400 bbl/day (2017 est.)
country comparison to the world: 59
REFINED PETROLEUM PRODUCTS - CONSUMPTION:
167,700 bbl/day (2017 est.)
country comparison to the world: 62
REFINED PETROLEUM PRODUCTS - EXPORTS:
58,720 bbl/day (2017 est.)
country comparison to the world: 50
REFINED PETROLEUM PRODUCTS - IMPORTS:
82,110 bbl/day (2017 est.)
country comparison to the world: 62
NATURAL GAS - PRODUCTION:
1.812 billion cu m (2017 est.)
country comparison to the world: 60

NATURAL GAS - CONSUMPTION:

10.39 billion cu m (2017 est.)

country comparison to the world: 46

NATURAL GAS - EXPORTS:

3.52 billion cu m (2017 est.)

country comparison to the world: 34

NATURAL GAS - IMPORTS:

13.37 billion cu m (2017 est.)

country comparison to the world: 24

NATURAL GAS - PROVED RESERVES:

6.598 billion cu m (1 January 2018 est.)

country comparison to the world: 83

CARBON DIOXIDE EMISSIONS FROM CONSUMPTION OF ENERGY:

51.28 million Mt (2017 est.)

country comparison to the world: 59

COMMUNICATIONS :: HUNGARY

TELEPHONES - FIXED LINES:

total subscriptions: 3,131,598

subscriptions per 100 inhabitants: 32 (2017 est.)

country comparison to the world: 44

TELEPHONES - MOBILE CELLULAR:

total subscriptions: 12,030,940

subscriptions per 100 inhabitants: 122 (2017 est.)

country comparison to the world: 75

TELEPHONE SYSTEM:

general assessment: modern telephone system is digital and highly automated; trunk services are carried by fiber-optic cable and digital microwave radio relay; regulator preps for 5G spectrum auction in 2019 (2018)

domestic: competition among mobile-cellular service providers has led to a sharp increase in the use of mobile-cellular phones, 122 per 100, and a decrease in the number of fixed-line connections, 32 per 100 persons (2018)

international: country code - 36; Hungary has fiber-optic cable connections with all neighboring countries; the international switch is in Budapest; satellite earth stations - 2 Intelsat (Atlantic Ocean and Indian Ocean regions), 1 Inmarsat, 1 very small aperture terminal (VSAT) system of ground terminals

BROADCAST MEDIA:

mixed system of state-supported public service broadcast media and private broadcasters; the 5 publicly owned TV channels and the 2 main privately owned TV stations are the major national broadcasters; a large number of special interest channels; highly developed market for satellite and cable TV services with about two-thirds of viewers utilizing their services; 4 state-supported public-service radio networks; a large number of local stations including commercial, public service, nonprofit, and community radio stations; digital transition completed at the end of 2013; government-linked businesses have greatly consolidated ownership in broadcast and print media

INTERNET COUNTRY CODE:

.hu

INTERNET USERS:

total: 7,826,695

percent of population: 79.3% (July 2016 est.)

country comparison to the world: 54

BROADBAND - FIXED SUBSCRIPTIONS:

total: 2,956,585

subscriptions per 100 inhabitants: 30 (2017 est.)

country comparison to the world: 41

MILITARY AND SECURITY :: HUNGARY

MILITARY EXPENDITURES:

1.08% of GDP (2018)

1.05% of GDP (2017)

1.02% of GDP (2016)

0.92% of GDP (2015)

0.87% of GDP (2014)

country comparison to the world: 113

MILITARY AND SECURITY FORCES:

Hungarian Defense Forces: Ground Forces and Hungarian Air Force. (2019)

Note: The Hungarian Defense Forces are organized into a joint force structure with ground, air, and logistic components.

MILITARY SERVICE AGE AND OBLIGATION:

18-25 years of age for voluntary military service; no conscription; 6-month service obligation (2012)

TRANSPORTATION :: HUNGARY

NATIONAL AIR TRANSPORT SYSTEM:

number of registered air carriers: 5 (2015)

inventory of registered aircraft operated by air carriers: 75 (2015)

annual passenger traffic on registered air carriers: 20,042,185 (2015)

annual freight traffic on registered air carriers: 0 mt-km (2015)

CIVIL AIRCRAFT REGISTRATION COUNTRY CODE PREFIX:

HA (2016)

AIRPORTS:

41 (2013)

country comparison to the world: 103

AIRPORTS - WITH PAVED RUNWAYS:

total: 20 (2017)

over 3,047 m: 2 (2017)

2,438 to 3,047 m: 6 (2017)

1,524 to 2,437 m: 6 (2017)

914 to 1,523 m: 5 (2017)

under 914 m: 1 (2017)

AIRPORTS - WITH UNPAVED RUNWAYS:

total: 21 (2013)

1,524 to 2,437 m: 2 (2013)

914 to 1,523 m: 8 (2013)

under 914 m: 11 (2013)

HELIPORTS:

3 (2013)

PIPELINES:

5874 km gas (high-pressure transmission system), 83732 km gas (low-pressure distribution network), 850 km oil, 1200 km refined products (2016)

RAILWAYS:

total: 8,049 km (2014)

standard gauge: 7,794 km 1.435-m gauge (2,889 km electrified) (2014)

narrow gauge: 219 km 0.760-m gauge (2014)

broad gauge: 36 km 1.524-m gauge (2014)

country comparison to the world: 28

ROADWAYS:

total: 203,601 km (2014)

paved: 77,087 km (includes 1,582 km of expressways) (2014)

unpaved: 126,514 km (2014)

country comparison to the world: 27

WATERWAYS:

1,622 km (most on Danube River) (2011)

country comparison to the world: 47

PORTS AND TERMINALS:

river port(s): Baja, Csepel (Budapest), Dunaujvaros, Gyor-Gonyu, Mohacs (Danube)

TRANSNATIONAL ISSUES :: HUNGARY

DISPUTES - INTERNATIONAL:

bilateral government, legal, technical and economic working group negotiations continue in 2006 with Slovakia over Hungary's failure to complete its portion of the Gabcikovo-Nagymaros hydroelectric dam project along the Danube; as a member state that forms part of the EU's external border, Hungary has implemented the strict Schengen border rules

REFUGEES AND INTERNALLY DISPLACED PERSONS:

refugees (country of origin): 5,950 applicants for forms of legal stay other than asylum (Ukraine) (2015)

stateless persons: 144 (2018)

note: 432,744 estimated refugee and migrant arrivals (January 2015-December 2018); Hungary is predominantly a transit country and hosts 137 migrants and asylum seekers as of the end of June 2018; 1,626 migrant arrivals in 2017

ILLICIT DRUGS:

transshipment point for Southwest Asian heroin and cannabis and for South American cocaine destined for Western Europe; limited producer of precursor chemicals, particularly for amphetamine and methamphetamine; efforts to counter money laundering, related to organized crime and drug trafficking are improving but remain vulnerable; significant consumer of ecstasy

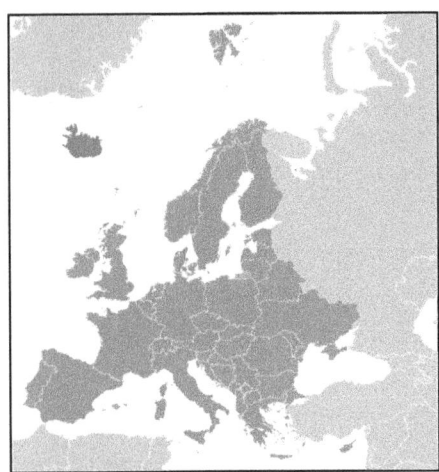

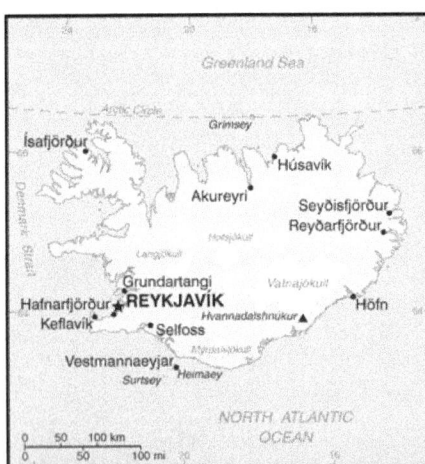

EUROPE :: ICELAND

INTRODUCTION :: ICELAND

BACKGROUND:

Settled by Norwegian and Celtic (Scottish and Irish) immigrants during the late 9th and 10th centuries A.D., Iceland boasts the world's oldest functioning legislative assembly, the Althingi, established in 930. Independent for over 300 years, Iceland was subsequently ruled by Norway and Denmark. Fallout from the Askja volcano of 1875 devastated the Icelandic economy and caused widespread famine. Over the next quarter century, 20% of the island's population emigrated, mostly to Canada and the US. Denmark granted limited home rule in 1874 and complete independence in 1944. The second half of the 20th century saw substantial economic growth driven primarily by the fishing industry. The economy diversified greatly after the country joined the European Economic Area in 1994, but Iceland was especially hard hit by the global financial crisis in the years following 2008. The economy is now on an upward trajectory, fueled primarily by a tourism and construction boom. Literacy, longevity, and social cohesion are first rate by world standards.

GEOGRAPHY :: ICELAND

LOCATION:

Northern Europe, island between the Greenland Sea and the North Atlantic Ocean, northwest of the United Kingdom

GEOGRAPHIC COORDINATES:

65 00 N, 18 00 W

MAP REFERENCES:

Arctic Region

AREA:

total: 103,000 sq km

land: 100,250 sq km

water: 2,750 sq km

country comparison to the world: 109

AREA - COMPARATIVE:

slightly smaller than Pennsylvania; about the same size as Kentucky

LAND BOUNDARIES:

0 km

COASTLINE:

4,970 km

MARITIME CLAIMS:

territorial sea: 12 nm

exclusive economic zone: 200 nm

continental shelf: 200 nm or to the edge of the continental margin

CLIMATE:

temperate; moderated by North Atlantic Current; mild, windy winters; damp, cool summers

TERRAIN:

mostly plateau interspersed with mountain peaks, icefields; coast deeply indented by bays and fiords

ELEVATION:

mean elevation: 557 m

lowest point: Atlantic Ocean 0 m

highest point: Hvannadalshnukur (at Vatnajokull Glacier) 2,110 m

NATURAL RESOURCES:

fish, hydropower, geothermal power, diatomite

LAND USE:

agricultural land: 18.7% (2011 est.)

arable land: 1.2% (2011 est.) / permanent crops: 0% (2011 est.) / permanent pasture: 17.5% (2011 est.)

forest: 0.3% (2011 est.)

other: 81% (2011 est.)

IRRIGATED LAND:

NA

POPULATION DISTRIBUTION:

Iceland is almost entirely urban with half of the population located in and around the capital of Reykjavik; smaller clusters are primarily found along the coast in the north and west

NATURAL HAZARDS:

earthquakes and volcanic activity

volcanism: Iceland, situated on top of a hotspot, experiences severe volcanic activity; Eyjafjallajokull (1,666 m) erupted in 2010, sending ash high into the atmosphere and seriously disrupting European air traffic; scientists continue to monitor nearby Katla (1,512 m), which has a high probability of eruption in the very near future, potentially disrupting air traffic; Grimsvoetn and Hekla are Iceland's most active volcanoes; other historically active volcanoes include Askja, Bardarbunga, Brennisteinsfjoll, Esjufjoll, Hengill, Krafla, Krisuvik, Kverkfjoll, Oraefajokull, Reykjanes, Torfajokull, and Vestmannaeyjar

ENVIRONMENT - CURRENT ISSUES:

water pollution from fertilizer runoff

ENVIRONMENT - INTERNATIONAL AGREEMENTS:

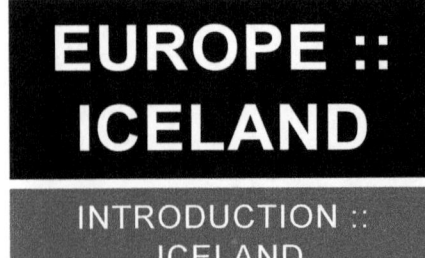

party to: Air Pollution, Air Pollution-Persistent Organic Pollutants, Biodiversity, Climate Change, Climate Change-Kyoto Protocol, Desertification, Endangered Species, Hazardous Wastes, Kyoto Protocol, Law of the Sea, Marine Dumping, Ozone Layer Protection, Ship Pollution, Transboundary Air Pollution, Wetlands, Whaling

signed, but not ratified: Environmental Modification, Marine Life Conservation

GEOGRAPHY - NOTE:

strategic location between Greenland and Europe; westernmost European country; Reykjavik is the northernmost national capital in the world; more land covered by glaciers than in all of continental Europe

PEOPLE AND SOCIETY :: ICELAND

POPULATION:

343,518 (July 2018 est.)

country comparison to the world: 178

NATIONALITY:

noun: Icelander(s)

adjective: Icelandic

ETHNIC GROUPS:

homogeneous mixture of descendants of Norse and Celts 81%, population with foreign background 19% (2018 est.)

note: population with foreign background includes immigrants and persons having at least one parent who was born abroad

LANGUAGES:

Icelandic, English, Nordic languages, German

RELIGIONS:

Evangelical Lutheran Church of Iceland (official) 67.2%, Roman Catholic 3.9%, Reykjavik Free Church 2.8%, Hafnarfjordur Free Church 2%, Asatru Association 1.2%, The Independent Congregation .9%, other religions 4% (includes Zuist and Pentecostal), none 6.7%, other or unspecified 11.3% (2018 est.)

AGE STRUCTURE:

0-14 years: 20.4% (male 35,812 /female 34,249)

15-24 years: 13.22% (male 22,952 /female 22,444)

25-54 years: 39.76% (male 69,177 /female 67,401)

55-64 years: 11.87% (male 20,350 /female 20,426)

65 years and over: 14.76% (male 23,822 /female 26,885) (2018 est.)

DEPENDENCY RATIOS:

total dependency ratio: 51.6 (2015 est.)

youth dependency ratio: 30.8 (2015 est.)

elderly dependency ratio: 20.8 (2015 est.)

potential support ratio: 4.8 (2015 est.)

MEDIAN AGE:

total: 36.7 years (2018 est.)

male: 36.1 years

female: 37.3 years

country comparison to the world: 73

POPULATION GROWTH RATE:

1.08% (2018 est.)

country comparison to the world: 103

BIRTH RATE:

13.6 births/1,000 population (2018 est.)

country comparison to the world: 140

DEATH RATE:

6.5 deaths/1,000 population (2018 est.)

country comparison to the world: 142

NET MIGRATION RATE:

3.7 migrant(s)/1,000 population (2018 est.)

country comparison to the world: 36

POPULATION DISTRIBUTION:

Iceland is almost entirely urban with half of the population located in and around the capital of Reykjavik; smaller clusters are primarily found along the coast in the north and west

URBANIZATION:

urban population: 93.9% of total population (2019)

rate of urbanization: 0.81% annual rate of change (2015-20 est.)

MAJOR URBAN AREAS - POPULATION:

216,000 REYKJAVIK (capital) (2018)

SEX RATIO:

at birth: 1.05 male(s)/female

0-14 years: 1.05 male(s)/female

15-24 years: 1.02 male(s)/female

25-54 years: 1.03 male(s)/female

55-64 years: 1 male(s)/female

65 years and over: 0.89 male(s)/female

total population: 1 male(s)/female (2018 est.)

MOTHER'S MEAN AGE AT FIRST BIRTH:

27.4 years (2015 est.)

MATERNAL MORTALITY RATE:

4 deaths/100,000 live births (2017 est.)

country comparison to the world: 173

INFANT MORTALITY RATE:

total: 2.1 deaths/1,000 live births (2018 est.)

male: 2.2 deaths/1,000 live births

female: 2 deaths/1,000 live births

country comparison to the world: 221

LIFE EXPECTANCY AT BIRTH:

total population: 83.1 years (2018 est.)

male: 80.9 years

female: 85.5 years

country comparison to the world: 7

TOTAL FERTILITY RATE:

1.99 children born/woman (2018 est.)

country comparison to the world: 120

DRINKING WATER SOURCE:

improved:

urban: 100% of population

rural: 100% of population

total: 100% of population

unimproved:

urban: 0% of population

rural: 0% of population

total: 0% of population (2015 est.)

CURRENT HEALTH EXPENDITURE:

8.3% (2016)

PHYSICIANS DENSITY:

3.97 physicians/1,000 population (2017)

HOSPITAL BED DENSITY:

3.4 beds/1,000 population (2015)

SANITATION FACILITY ACCESS:

improved:

urban: 98.7% of population (2015 est.)

rural: 100% of population (2015 est.)

total: 98.8% of population (2015 est.)

unimproved:

urban: 1.3% of population (2015 est.)

rural: 0% of population (2015 est.)

total: 1.2% of population (2015 est.)

HIV/AIDS - ADULT PREVALENCE RATE:

0.1% (2018)

country comparison to the world: 124

HIV/AIDS - PEOPLE LIVING WITH HIV/AIDS:

<500 (2018)

HIV/AIDS - DEATHS:

<100 (2018)

OBESITY - ADULT PREVALENCE RATE:

21.9% (2016)

country comparison to the world: 83

EDUCATION EXPENDITURES:

7.7% of GDP (2015)

country comparison to the world: 6

SCHOOL LIFE EXPECTANCY (PRIMARY TO TERTIARY EDUCATION):

total: 19 years

male: 18 years

female: 20 years (2016)

UNEMPLOYMENT, YOUTH AGES 15-24:

total: 7.9%

male: 8.6%

female: 7.1% (2017 est.)

country comparison to the world: 147

GOVERNMENT :: ICELAND

COUNTRY NAME:

conventional long form: Republic of Iceland

conventional short form: Iceland

local long form: Lydveldid Island

local short form: Island

etymology: Floki VILGERDARSON, an early explorer of the island (9th century), applied the name "Land of Ice" after spotting a fjord full of drift ice to the north and spending a bitter winter on the island; he eventually settled on the island, however, after he saw how it greened up in the summer and that it was, in fact, habitable

GOVERNMENT TYPE:

unitary parliamentary republic

CAPITAL:

name: Reykjavik

geographic coordinates: 64 09 N, 21 57 W

time difference: UTC 0 (5 hours ahead of Washington, DC, during Standard Time)

etymology: the name means "smoky bay" in Icelandic and refers to the steamy, smoke-like vapors discharged by hot springs in the area

ADMINISTRATIVE DIVISIONS:

74 municipalities (sveitarfelog, singular - sveitarfelagidh); Akrahreppur, Akraneskaupstadhur, Akureyrarkaupstadhur, Arneshreppur, Asahreppur, Blaskogabyggdh, Blonduosbaer, Bolungarvikurkaupstadhur, Borgarbyggdh, Borgarfjardharhreppur, Breidhdalshreppur, Dalabyggdh, Dalvikurbyggdh, Djupavogshreppur, Eyjafjardharsveit, Eyja-og Miklaholtshreppur, Fjallabyggdh, Fjardhabyggdh, Fljotsdalsheradh, Fljotsdalshreppur, Floahreppur, Gardhabaer, Grimsnes-og Grafningshreppur, Grindavikurbaer, Grundarfjardharbaer, Grytubakkahreppur, Hafnarfjardharkaupstadhur, Helgafellssveit, Horgarsveit, Hrunamannahreppur, Hunathing Vestra, Hunavatnshreppur, Hvalfjardharsveit, Hveragerdhisbaer, Isafjardharbaer, Kaldrananeshreppur, Kjosarhreppur, Kopavogsbaer, Langanesbyggdh, Mosfellsbaer, Myrdalshreppur, Nordhurthing, Rangarthing Eystra, Rangarthing Ytra, Reykholahreppur, Reykjanesbaer, Reykjavikurborg, Sandgerdhisbaer, Seltjarnarnesbaer, Seydhisfjardharkaupstadhur, Skaftarhreppur, Skagabyggdh, Skeidha-og Gnupverjahreppur, Skorradalshreppur, Skutustadhahreppur, Snaefellsbaer, Strandabyggdh, Stykkisholmsbaer, Sudhavikurhreppur, Svalbardhshreppur, Svalbardhsstrandarhreppur, Sveitarfelagidh Arborg, Sveitarfelagidh Gardhur, Sveitarfelagidh Hornafjordhur, Sveitarfelagidh Olfus, Sveitarfelagidh Skagafjordhur, Sveitarfelagidh Skagastrond, Sveitarfelagidh Vogar, Talknafjardharhreppur, Thingeyjarsveit, Tjorneshreppur, Vestmannaeyjabaer, Vesturbyggdh, Vopnafjardharhreppur

INDEPENDENCE:

1 December 1918 (became a sovereign state under the Danish Crown); 17 June 1944 (from Denmark; birthday of Jon SIGURDSSON, leader of Iceland's 19th Century independence movement)

NATIONAL HOLIDAY:

Independence Day, 17 June (1944)

CONSTITUTION:

history: several previous; latest ratified 16 June 1944, effective 17 June 1944 (at independence)

amendments: proposed by the Althingi; passage requires approval by the Althingi and by the next elected Althingi, and confirmation by the president of the republic; proposed amendments to Article 62 of the constitution – that the Evangelical Lutheran Church shall be the state church of Iceland – also require passage by referendum; amended many times, last in 2013 (2016)

LEGAL SYSTEM:

civil law system influenced by the Danish model

INTERNATIONAL LAW ORGANIZATION PARTICIPATION:

has not submitted an ICJ jurisdiction declaration; accepts ICCt jurisdiction

CITIZENSHIP:

citizenship by birth: no

citizenship by descent only: at least one parent must be a citizen of Iceland

dual citizenship recognized: yes

residency requirement for naturalization: 3 to 7 years

SUFFRAGE:

18 years of age; universal

EXECUTIVE BRANCH:

chief of state: President Gudni Thorlacius JOHANNESSON (since 1 August 2016)

head of government: Prime Minister Katrin JAKOBSDOTTIR (since 30 November 2017)

cabinet: Cabinet appointed by the president upon the recommendation of the prime minister

elections/appointments: president directly elected by simple majority popular vote for a 4-year term (no term limits); election last held on 25 June 2016 (next to be held in June 2020); following legislative elections, the leader of the majority party or majority coalition becomes prime minister

election results: Gudni Thorlacius JOHANNESSON elected president; percent of vote - Gudni Thorlacius

JOHANNESSON 39.1%, Halla TOMASDOTTIR 27.9%, Andri Snaer MAGNASON 14.3%, David ODDSSON 13.7%, Sturla JONSSON 3.5%, invalid 1.5%

LEGISLATIVE BRANCH:

description: unicameral Althingi or Parliament (63 seats; members directly elected in multi-seat constituencies by proportional representation vote to serve 4-year terms)

elections: last held on 28 October 2017 (next to be held in 2021)

election results: percent of vote by party - IP 25.2%, LGM 16.9%, SDA 12.1%, CP 10.9%, PP 10.7%, Pirate Party 9.2%, People's Party 6.9%, Reform Party 6.7%. other 1.5%; seats by party - IP 16, LGM 11, SDA 7, CP 7, PP 8, Pirate Party 6, Reform Party 4, People's Party 4

JUDICIAL BRANCH:

highest courts: Supreme Court or Haestirettur (consists of 9 judges)

judge selection and term of office: judges proposed by Ministry of Interior selection committee and appointed by the president; judges appointed for an indefinite period

subordinate courts: Appellate Court or Landsrettur; 8 district courts; Labor Court

POLITICAL PARTIES AND LEADERS:

Centrist Party (Midflokkurinn) or CP [Sigmundur David GUNNLAUGSSON]
Independence Party (Sjalfstaedisflokkurinn) or IP [Bjarni BENEDIKTSSON]
Left-Green Movement (Vinstrihreyfingin-graent frambod) or LGM [Katrin JAKOBSDOTTIR]
People's Party (Flokkur Folksins) [Inga SAELAND]
Pirate Party (Piratar) [rotating leadership]
Progressive Party (Framsoknarflokkurinn) or PP [Sigurdur Ingi JOHANNSSON]
Reform Party (Vidreisn) [Thorgerdur Katrin GUNNARSDOTTIR]
Social Democratic Alliance (Samfylkingin) or SDA [Logi Mar EINARSSON]

INTERNATIONAL ORGANIZATION PARTICIPATION:

Arctic Council, Australia Group, BIS, CBSS, CD, CE, EAPC, EBRD, EFTA, FAO, FATF, IAEA, IBRD, ICAO, ICC (national committees), ICCt, ICRM, IDA, IFAD, IFC, IFRCS, IHO, ILO, IMF, IMO, IMSO, Interpol, IOC, IOM, IPU, ISO, ITSO, ITU, ITUC (NGOs), MIGA, NATO, NC, NEA, NIB, NSG, OAS (observer), OECD, OPCW, OSCE, PCA, Schengen Convention, UN, UNCTAD, UNESCO, UPU, WCO, WHO, WIPO, WMO, WTO

DIPLOMATIC REPRESENTATION IN THE US:

Ambassador Geir Hilmar HAARDE (since 23 February 2015)

chancery: House of Sweden, 2900 K Street NW, #509, Washington, DC 20007

telephone: [1] (202) 265-6653

FAX: [1] (202) 265-6656

consulate(s) general: New York

DIPLOMATIC REPRESENTATION FROM THE US:

chief of mission: Ambassador Jeffrey Ross GUNTER (since 2 July 2019)

telephone: [354] 595-2200

embassy: Laufasvegur 21, 101 Reykjavik

mailing address: US Department of State, 5640 Reykjavik Place, Washington, D.C. 20521-5640

FAX: [354] 562-9118

FLAG DESCRIPTION:

blue with a red cross outlined in white extending to the edges of the flag; the vertical part of the cross is shifted to the hoist side in the style of the Dannebrog (Danish flag); the colors represent three of the elements that make up the island: red is for the island's volcanic fires, white recalls the snow and ice fields of the island, and blue is for the surrounding ocean

NATIONAL SYMBOL(S):

gyrfalcon; national colors: blue, white, red

NATIONAL ANTHEM:

name: "Lofsongur" (Song of Praise)

lyrics/music: Matthias JOCHUMSSON/Sveinbjorn SVEINBJORNSSON

note: adopted 1944; also known as "O, Gud vors lands" (O, God of Our Land), the anthem was originally written and performed in 1874

ECONOMY :: ICELAND

ECONOMY - OVERVIEW:

Iceland's economy combines a capitalist structure and free-market principles with an extensive welfare system. Except for a brief period during the 2008 crisis, Iceland has in recent years achieved high growth, low unemployment, and a remarkably even distribution of income. Iceland's economy has been diversifying into manufacturing and service industries in the last decade, particularly within the fields of tourism, software production, and biotechnology. Abundant geothermal and hydropower sources have attracted substantial foreign investment in the aluminum sector, boosted economic growth, and sparked some interest from high-tech firms looking to establish data centers using cheap green energy.

Tourism, aluminum smelting, and fishing are the pillars of the economy. For decades the Icelandic economy depended heavily on fisheries, but tourism has now surpassed fishing and aluminum as Iceland's main export industry. Tourism accounted for 8.6% of Iceland's GDP in 2016, and 39% of total exports of merchandise and services. From 2010 to 2017, the number of tourists visiting Iceland increased by nearly 400%. Since 2010, tourism has become a main driver of Icelandic economic growth, with the number of tourists reaching 4.5 times the Icelandic population in 2016. Iceland remains sensitive to fluctuations in world prices for its main exports, and to fluctuations in the exchange rate of the Icelandic Krona.

Following the privatization of the banking sector in the early 2000s, domestic banks expanded aggressively in foreign markets, and consumers and businesses borrowed heavily in foreign currencies. Worsening global financial conditions throughout 2008 resulted in a sharp depreciation of the krona vis-a-vis other major currencies. The foreign exposure of Icelandic banks, whose loans and other assets totaled nearly nine times the country's GDP, became unsustainable. Iceland's three largest banks collapsed in late 2008. GDP fell 6.8% in 2009, and unemployment peaked at 9.4% in February 2009. Three new banks were established to take over the domestic assets of the collapsed banks. Two of them have majority ownership by the state, which intends to re-privatize them.

Since the collapse of Iceland's financial sector, government economic priorities have included stabilizing the krona, implementing capital controls, reducing Iceland's high budget deficit, containing inflation, addressing high household debt, restructuring the financial sector, and diversifying the economy. Capital controls were lifted in March 2017, but some financial protections, such as reserve requirements for specified investments connected to new inflows of foreign currency, remain in place.

GDP (PURCHASING POWER PARITY):

$18.18 billion (2017 est.)

$17.48 billion (2016 est.)

$16.29 billion (2015 est.)

note: data are in 2017 dollars

country comparison to the world: 153

GDP (OFFICIAL EXCHANGE RATE):

$24.48 billion (2017 est.)

GDP - REAL GROWTH RATE:

4% (2017 est.)

7.4% (2016 est.)

4.5% (2015 est.)

country comparison to the world: 77

GDP - PER CAPITA (PPP):

$52,200 (2017 est.)

$51,700 (2016 est.)

$48,900 (2015 est.)

note: data are in 2017 dollars

country comparison to the world: 25

GROSS NATIONAL SAVING:

25.8% of GDP (2017 est.)

29.1% of GDP (2016 est.)

24.5% of GDP (2015 est.)

country comparison to the world: 52

GDP - COMPOSITION, BY END USE:

household consumption: 50.4% (2017 est.)

government consumption: 23.3% (2017 est.)

investment in fixed capital: 22.1% (2017 est.)

investment in inventories: 0% (2017 est.)

exports of goods and services: 47% (2017 est.)

imports of goods and services: -42.8% (2017 est.)

GDP - COMPOSITION, BY SECTOR OF ORIGIN:

agriculture: 5.8% (2017 est.)

industry: 19.7% (2017 est.)

services: 74.6% (2017 est.)

AGRICULTURE - PRODUCTS:

potatoes, carrots, green vegetables, tomatoes, cucumbers; mutton, chicken, pork, beef, dairy products; fish

INDUSTRIES:

tourism, fish processing; aluminum smelting;; geothermal power, hydropower; medical/pharmaceutical products

INDUSTRIAL PRODUCTION GROWTH RATE:

2.4% (2017 est.)

country comparison to the world: 120

LABOR FORCE:

198,700 (2017 est.)

country comparison to the world: 172

LABOR FORCE - BY OCCUPATION:

agriculture: 4.8%

industry: 22.2%

services: 73% (2008)

UNEMPLOYMENT RATE:

2.8% (2017 est.)

3% (2016 est.)

country comparison to the world: 30

POPULATION BELOW POVERTY LINE:

NA

note: 332,100 families (2011 est.)

HOUSEHOLD INCOME OR CONSUMPTION BY PERCENTAGE SHARE:

lowest 10%: NA

highest 10%: NA

DISTRIBUTION OF FAMILY INCOME - GINI INDEX:

28 (2006)

25 (2005)

country comparison to the world: 142

BUDGET:

revenues: 10.39 billion (2017 est.)

expenditures: 10.02 billion (2017 est.)

TAXES AND OTHER REVENUES:

42.4% (of GDP) (2017 est.)

country comparison to the world: 31

BUDGET SURPLUS (+) OR DEFICIT (-):

1.5% (of GDP) (2017 est.)

country comparison to the world: 22

PUBLIC DEBT:

40% of GDP (2017 est.)

51.7% of GDP (2016 est.)

country comparison to the world: 126

FISCAL YEAR:

calendar year

INFLATION RATE (CONSUMER PRICES):

1.8% (2017 est.)

1.7% (2016 est.)

country comparison to the world: 93

CENTRAL BANK DISCOUNT RATE:

5.4% (31 January 2012)

5.75% (31 December 2010)

country comparison to the world: 77

COMMERCIAL BANK PRIME LENDING RATE:

7.26% (31 December 2017 est.)

8.24% (31 December 2016 est.)

country comparison to the world: 116

STOCK OF NARROW MONEY:

$4.945 billion (31 December 2017 est.)

$4.251 billion (31 December 2016 est.)

country comparison to the world: 106

STOCK OF BROAD MONEY:

$4.945 billion (31 December 2016 est.)

$4.251 billion (31 December 2016 est.)

country comparison to the world: 110

STOCK OF DOMESTIC CREDIT:

$24.51 billion (31 December 2017 est.)

$21.18 billion (31 December 2016 est.)

country comparison to the world: 86

MARKET VALUE OF PUBLICLY TRADED SHARES:

$2.825 billion (31 December 2012 est.)

$2.021 billion (31 December 2011 est.)

$1.996 billion (31 December 2010 est.)

country comparison to the world: 94

CURRENT ACCOUNT BALANCE:

$857 million (2017 est.)

$1.556 billion (2016 est.)

country comparison to the world: 52

EXPORTS:

$4.957 billion (2017 est.)

$4.483 billion (2016 est.)

country comparison to the world: 109

EXPORTS - PARTNERS:

Netherlands 25.5%, Spain 13.6%, UK 9.4%, Germany 7.6%, US 7%, France 6.3%, Norway 4.9%

EXPORTS - COMMODITIES:

fish and fish products (42%), aluminum (38%), agricultural products, medicinal and medical products, ferro-silicon (2015)

IMPORTS:

$6.525 billion (2017 est.)

$5.315 billion (2016 est.)

country comparison to the world: 119

IMPORTS - COMMODITIES:

machinery and equipment, petroleum products, foodstuffs, textiles

IMPORTS - PARTNERS:

Germany 10.7%, Norway 9.2%, China 7%, Netherlands 6.7%, US 6.4%, Denmark 6.2%, UK 5.7%, Sweden 4.1%

RESERVES OF FOREIGN EXCHANGE AND GOLD:

$6.567 billion (31 December 2017 est.)

$7.226 billion (31 December 2016 est.)

country comparison to the world: 89

DEBT - EXTERNAL:

$21.7 billion (31 December 2017 est.)

$25.02 billion (31 December 2016 est.)

country comparison to the world: 91

STOCK OF DIRECT FOREIGN INVESTMENT - AT HOME:

$6.666 billion (31 December 2017 est.)

$13.89 billion (31 December 2016 est.)

country comparison to the world: 101

STOCK OF DIRECT FOREIGN INVESTMENT - ABROAD:

$11.24 billion (31 December 2017 est.)

$17.64 billion (31 December 2016 est.)

country comparison to the world: 63

EXCHANGE RATES:

Icelandic kronur (ISK) per US dollar -

111.7 (2017 est.)

120.81 (2016 est.)

120.81 (2015 est.)

131.92 (2014 est.)

116.77 (2013 est.)

ENERGY :: ICELAND

ELECTRICITY ACCESS:

electrification - total population: 100% (2016)

ELECTRICITY - PRODUCTION:

18.17 billion kWh (2016 est.)

country comparison to the world: 80

ELECTRICITY - CONSUMPTION:

17.68 billion kWh (2016 est.)

country comparison to the world: 73

ELECTRICITY - EXPORTS:

0 kWh (2016 est.)

country comparison to the world: 148

ELECTRICITY - IMPORTS:

0 kWh (2016 est.)

country comparison to the world: 160

ELECTRICITY - INSTALLED GENERATING CAPACITY:

2.772 million kW (2016 est.)

country comparison to the world: 100

ELECTRICITY - FROM FOSSIL FUELS:

4% of total installed capacity (2016 est.)

country comparison to the world: 206

ELECTRICITY - FROM NUCLEAR FUELS:

0% of total installed capacity (2017 est.)

country comparison to the world: 109

ELECTRICITY - FROM HYDROELECTRIC PLANTS:

71% of total installed capacity (2017 est.)

country comparison to the world: 16

ELECTRICITY - FROM OTHER RENEWABLE SOURCES:

25% of total installed capacity (2017 est.)

country comparison to the world: 29

CRUDE OIL - PRODUCTION:

0 bbl/day (2018 est.)

country comparison to the world: 151

CRUDE OIL - EXPORTS:

0 bbl/day (2017 est.)

country comparison to the world: 139

CRUDE OIL - IMPORTS:

0 bbl/day (2017 est.)

country comparison to the world: 143

CRUDE OIL - PROVED RESERVES:

0 bbl (1 January 2018 est.)

country comparison to the world: 147

REFINED PETROLEUM PRODUCTS - PRODUCTION:

0 bbl/day (2017 est.)

country comparison to the world: 159

REFINED PETROLEUM PRODUCTS - CONSUMPTION:

20,850 bbl/day (2017 est.)

country comparison to the world: 139

REFINED PETROLEUM PRODUCTS - EXPORTS:

2,530 bbl/day (2017 est.)

country comparison to the world: 101

REFINED PETROLEUM PRODUCTS - IMPORTS:

20,220 bbl/day (2017 est.)

country comparison to the world: 120

NATURAL GAS - PRODUCTION:

0 cu m (2017 est.)

country comparison to the world: 148

NATURAL GAS - CONSUMPTION:

0 cu m (2017 est.)

country comparison to the world: 160

NATURAL GAS - EXPORTS:

0 cu m (2017 est.)

country comparison to the world: 123

NATURAL GAS - IMPORTS:

0 cu m (2017 est.)

country comparison to the world: 140

NATURAL GAS - PROVED RESERVES:

0 cu m (1 January 2014 est.)

country comparison to the world: 149

CARBON DIOXIDE EMISSIONS FROM CONSUMPTION OF ENERGY:

3.228 million Mt (2017 est.)

country comparison to the world: 144

COMMUNICATIONS :: ICELAND

TELEPHONES - FIXED LINES:

total subscriptions: 146,213

subscriptions per 100 inhabitants: 43 (2017 est.)

country comparison to the world: 129

TELEPHONES - MOBILE CELLULAR:

total subscriptions: 410,662

subscriptions per 100 inhabitants: 121 (2017 est.)

country comparison to the world: 174

TELEPHONE SYSTEM:

general assessment: telecommunications infrastructure is modern and fully digitized, with satellite-earth stations, fiber-optic cables, and an extensive broadband network; LTE licenses providing 99% population coverage (2018)

domestic: liberalization of the telecommunications sector beginning in the late 1990s has led to increased competition especially in the mobile services segment of the market; 43 per 100 for fixed line and 121 per 100 for mobile-cellular subscriptions (2018)

international: country code - 354; the CANTAT-3, FARICE-1, Greenland Connect and DANICE submarine cable system provides connectivity to Canada, the Faroe Islands, Greenland, UK, Denmark, and Germany; satellite earth stations - 2 Intelsat (Atlantic

Ocean), 1 Inmarsat (Atlantic and Indian Ocean regions); note - Iceland shares the Inmarsat earth station with the other Nordic countries (Denmark, Finland, Norway, and Sweden) (2019)

BROADCAST MEDIA:

state-owned public TV broadcaster (RUV) operates 21 TV channels nationally (RUV and RUV 2, though RUV 2 is used less frequently); RUV broadcasts nationally, every household in Iceland is required to have RUV as it doubles as the emergency broadcast network; RUV also operates stringer offices in the north (Akureyri) and the east (Egilsstadir) but operations are all run out of RUV headquarters in Reykjavik; there are 3 privately owned TV stations; Stod 2 (Channel 2) is owned by Syn, following 365 Media and Vodafone merger, and is headquartered in Reykjavik; Syn also operates 4 sports channels under Stod 2; N4 is the only television station headquartered outside of Reykjavik, in Akureyri, with local programming for the north, south, and east of Iceland; Hringbraut is the newest station and is headquartered in Reykjavik; all of these television stations have nationwide penetration as 100% of households have multi-channel services though digital and/or fiber-optic connections

RUV operates 3 radio stations (RAS 1, RAS2, and Rondo) as well as 4 regional stations (but they mostly act as range extenders for RUV radio broadcasts nationwide); there is 1 privately owned radio conglomerate, Syn (4 stations), that broadcasts nationwide, and 3 other radio stations that broadcast to the most densely populated regions of the country. In addition there are upwards of 20 radio stations that operate regionally

(2019)

INTERNET COUNTRY CODE:

.is

INTERNET USERS:

total: 329,967

percent of population: 98.2% (July 2016 est.)

country comparison to the world: 155

BROADBAND - FIXED SUBSCRIPTIONS:

total: 133,574

subscriptions per 100 inhabitants: 39 (2017 est.)

country comparison to the world: 116

MILITARY AND SECURITY :: ICELAND

MILITARY EXPENDITURES:

0.3% of GDP (2018)

0.3% of GDP (2017)

0.3% of GDP (2016)

0.3% of GDP (2015)

0.5% of GDP (2014)

country comparison to the world: 154

MILITARY AND SECURITY FORCES:

no regular military forces; Icelandic Coast Guard; Icelandic National Police (2019)

MILITARY - NOTE:

Iceland is the only NATO member that has no standing military force; defense of Iceland remains a NATO commitment and NATO maintains an air policing presence in Icelandic airspace; Iceland participates in international peacekeeping missions with the civilian-manned Icelandic Crisis Response Unit (ICRU) (2019)

TRANSPORTATION :: ICELAND

NATIONAL AIR TRANSPORT SYSTEM:

number of registered air carriers: 5 (2015)

inventory of registered aircraft operated by air carriers: 43 (2015)

annual passenger traffic on registered air carriers: 3,413,950 (2015)

annual freight traffic on registered air carriers: 102,356,809 mt-km (2015)

CIVIL AIRCRAFT REGISTRATION COUNTRY CODE PREFIX:

TF (2016)

AIRPORTS:

96 (2013)

country comparison to the world: 59

AIRPORTS - WITH PAVED RUNWAYS:

total: 7 (2017)

over 3,047 m: 1 (2017)

1,524 to 2,437 m: 3 (2017)

914 to 1,523 m: 3 (2017)

AIRPORTS - WITH UNPAVED RUNWAYS:

total: 89 (2013)

1,524 to 2,437 m: 3 (2013)

914 to 1,523 m: 26 (2013)

under 914 m: 60 (2013)

ROADWAYS:

total: 12,898 km (2012)

paved/oiled gravel: 5,647 km (excludes urban roads) (2012)

unpaved: 7,251 km (2012)

country comparison to the world: 126

MERCHANT MARINE:

total: 33

by type: general cargo 5, oil tanker 1, other 27 (2018)

country comparison to the world: 122

PORTS AND TERMINALS:

major seaport(s): Grundartangi, Hafnarfjordur, Reykjavik

TRANSNATIONAL ISSUES :: ICELAND

DISPUTES - INTERNATIONAL:

Iceland, the UK, and Ireland dispute Denmark's claim that the Faroe Islands' continental shelf extends beyond 200 nm; the European Free Trade Association Surveillance Authority filed a suit against Iceland, claiming the country violated the Agreement on the European Economic Area in failing to pay minimum compensation to Icesave depositors

REFUGEES AND INTERNALLY DISPLACED PERSONS:

stateless persons: 69 (2018)

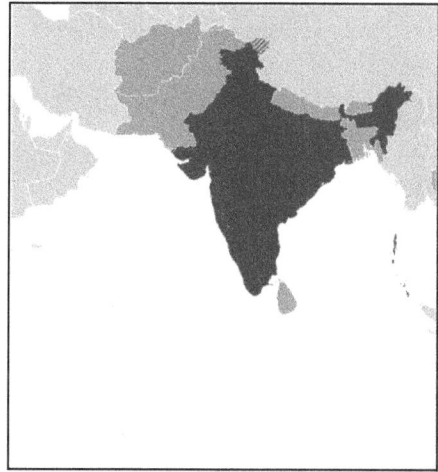

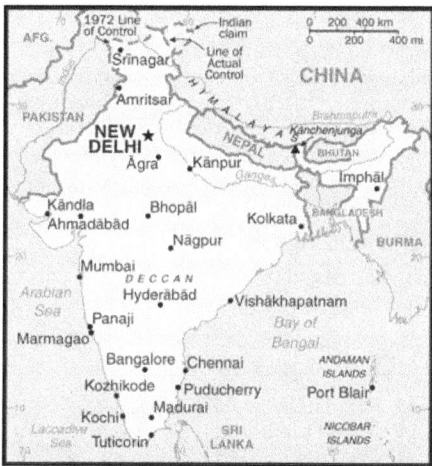

SOUTH ASIA :: INDIA

INTRODUCTION :: INDIA

BACKGROUND:

The Indus Valley civilization, one of the world's oldest, flourished during the 3rd and 2nd millennia B.C. and extended into northwestern India. Aryan tribes from the northwest infiltrated the Indian subcontinent about 1500 B.C.; their merger with the earlier Dravidian inhabitants created the classical Indian culture. The Maurya Empire of the 4th and 3rd centuries B.C. - which reached its zenith under ASHOKA - united much of South Asia. The Golden Age ushered in by the Gupta dynasty (4th to 6th centuries A.D.) saw a flowering of Indian science, art, and culture. Islam spread across the subcontinent over a period of 700 years. In the 10th and 11th centuries, Turks and Afghans invaded India and established the Delhi Sultanate. In the early 16th century, the Emperor BABUR established the Mughal Dynasty, which ruled India for more than three centuries. European explorers began establishing footholds in India during the 16th century.

By the 19th century, Great Britain had become the dominant political power on the subcontinent and India was seen as the "Jewel in the Crown" of the British Empire. The British Indian Army played a vital role in both World Wars. Years of nonviolent resistance to British rule, led by Mohandas GANDHI and Jawaharlal NEHRU, eventually resulted in Indian independence in 1947. Large-scale communal violence took place before and after the subcontinent partition into two separate states - India and Pakistan. The neighboring countries have fought three wars since independence, the last of which was in 1971 and resulted in East Pakistan becoming the separate nation of Bangladesh. India's nuclear weapons tests in 1998 emboldened Pakistan to conduct its own tests that same year. In November 2008, terrorists originating from Pakistan conducted a series of coordinated attacks in Mumbai, India's financial capital. India faces pressing problems such as environmental degradation, extensive poverty, and widespread corruption; however, economic growth following the launch of economic reforms in 1991, a massive youthful population, and a strategic geographic location are contributing to India's emergence as a regional and global power.

GEOGRAPHY :: INDIA

LOCATION:

Southern Asia, bordering the Arabian Sea and the Bay of Bengal, between Burma and Pakistan

GEOGRAPHIC COORDINATES:

20 00 N, 77 00 E

MAP REFERENCES:

Asia

AREA:

total: 3,287,263 sq km

land: 2,973,193 sq km

water: 314,070 sq km

country comparison to the world: 8

AREA - COMPARATIVE:

slightly more than one-third the size of the US

LAND BOUNDARIES:

total: 13,888 km

border countries (6): Bangladesh 4142 km, Bhutan 659 km, Burma 1468 km, China 2659 km, Nepal 1770 km, Pakistan 3190 km

COASTLINE:

7,000 km

MARITIME CLAIMS:

territorial sea: 12 nm

exclusive economic zone: 200 nm

contiguous zone: 24 nm

continental shelf: 200 nm or to the edge of the continental margin

CLIMATE:

varies from tropical monsoon in south to temperate in north

TERRAIN:

upland plain (Deccan Plateau) in south, flat to rolling plain along the Ganges, deserts in west, Himalayas in north

ELEVATION:

mean elevation: 160 m

lowest point: Indian Ocean 0 m

highest point: Kanchenjunga 8,586 m

NATURAL RESOURCES:

coal (fourth-largest reserves in the world), antimony, iron ore, lead, manganese, mica, bauxite, rare earth elements, titanium ore, chromite, natural gas, diamonds, petroleum, limestone, arable land

LAND USE:

agricultural land: 60.5% (2011 est.)

arable land: 52.8% (2011 est.) / permanent crops: 4.2% (2011 est.) / permanent pasture: 3.5% (2011 est.)

forest: 23.1% (2011 est.)

other: 16.4% (2011 est.)

IRRIGATED LAND:
667,000 sq km (2012)

POPULATION DISTRIBUTION:
with the notable exception of the deserts in the northwest, including the Thar Desert, and the mountain fringe in the north, a very high population density exists throughout most of the country; the core of the population is in the north along the banks of the Ganges, with other river valleys and southern coastal areas also having large population concentrations

NATURAL HAZARDS:
droughts; flash floods, as well as widespread and destructive flooding from monsoonal rains; severe thunderstorms; earthquakes

volcanism: Barren Island (354 m) in the Andaman Sea has been active in recent years

ENVIRONMENT - CURRENT ISSUES:
deforestation; soil erosion; overgrazing; desertification; air pollution from industrial effluents and vehicle emissions; water pollution from raw sewage and runoff of agricultural pesticides; tap water is not potable throughout the country; huge and growing population is overstraining natural resources; preservation and quality of forests; biodiversity loss

ENVIRONMENT - INTERNATIONAL AGREEMENTS:
party to: Antarctic-Environmental Protocol, Antarctic-Marine Living Resources, Antarctic Treaty, Biodiversity, Climate Change, Climate Change-Kyoto Protocol, Desertification, Endangered Species, Environmental Modification, Hazardous Wastes, Law of the Sea, Ozone Layer Protection, Ship Pollution, Tropical Timber 83, Tropical Timber 94, Wetlands, Whaling

signed, but not ratified: none of the selected agreements

GEOGRAPHY - NOTE:
dominates South Asian subcontinent; near important Indian Ocean trade routes; Kanchenjunga, third tallest mountain in the world, lies on the border with Nepal

PEOPLE AND SOCIETY :: INDIA

POPULATION:
1,296,834,042 (July 2018 est.)

country comparison to the world: 2

NATIONALITY:
noun: Indian(s)

adjective: Indian

ETHNIC GROUPS:
Indo-Aryan 72%, Dravidian 25%, Mongoloid and other 3% (2000)

LANGUAGES:
Hindi 43.6%, Bengali 8%, Marathi 6.9%, Telugu 6.7%, Tamil 5.7%, Gujarati 4.6%, Urdu 4.2%, Kannada 3.6%, Odia 3.1%, Malayalam 2.9%, Punjabi 2.7%, Assamese 1.3%, Maithili 1.1%, other 5.6% (2011 est.)

note: English enjoys the status of subsidiary official language but is the most important language for national, political, and commercial communication; there are 22 other officially recognized languages: Assamese, Bengali, Bodo, Dogri, Gujarati, Hindi, Kannada, Kashmiri, Konkani, Maithili, Malayalam, Manipuri, Nepali, Odia, Punjabi, Sanskrit, Santali, Sindhi, Tamil, Telugu, Urdu; Hindustani is a popular variant of Hindi/Urdu spoken widely throughout northern India but is not an official language

RELIGIONS:
Hindu 79.8%, Muslim 14.2%, Christian 2.3%, Sikh 1.7%, other and unspecified 2% (2011 est.)

AGE STRUCTURE:
0-14 years: 26.98% (male 185,736,879 /female 164,194,080)

15-24 years: 17.79% (male 122,573,662 /female 108,109,968)

25-54 years: 41.24% (male 276,283,581 /female 258,563,835)

55-64 years: 7.6% (male 49,334,703 /female 49,197,817)

65 years and over: 6.39% (male 39,184,523 /female 43,654,994) (2018 est.)

DEPENDENCY RATIOS:
total dependency ratio: 52.2 (2015 est.)

youth dependency ratio: 43.6 (2015 est.)

elderly dependency ratio: 8.6 (2015 est.)

potential support ratio: 11.7 (2015 est.)

MEDIAN AGE:
total: 28.1 years (2018 est.)

male: 27.5 years

female: 28.9 years

country comparison to the world: 142

POPULATION GROWTH RATE:
1.14% (2018 est.)

country comparison to the world: 94

BIRTH RATE:
18.7 births/1,000 population (2018 est.)

country comparison to the world: 88

DEATH RATE:
7.3 deaths/1,000 population (2018 est.)

country comparison to the world: 121

NET MIGRATION RATE:
0 migrant(s)/1,000 population (2018 est.)

country comparison to the world: 86

POPULATION DISTRIBUTION:
with the notable exception of the deserts in the northwest, including the Thar Desert, and the mountain fringe in the north, a very high population density exists throughout most of the country; the core of the population is in the north along the banks of the Ganges, with other river valleys and southern coastal areas also having large population concentrations

URBANIZATION:
urban population: 34.5% of total population (2019)

rate of urbanization: 2.37% annual rate of change (2015-20 est.)

MAJOR URBAN AREAS - POPULATION:
29.399 million NEW DELHI (capital), 20.185 million Mumbai, 14.755 million Kolkata, 11.883 million Bangalore, 10.711 million Chennai, 9.741 million Hyderabad (2019)

SEX RATIO:
at birth: 1.11 male(s)/female

0-14 years: 1.13 male(s)/female

15-24 years: 1.13 male(s)/female

25-54 years: 1.07 male(s)/female

55-64 years: 1 male(s)/female

65 years and over: 0.9 male(s)/female

total population: 1.08 male(s)/female (2018 est.)

MATERNAL MORTALITY RATE:
145 deaths/100,000 live births (2017 est.)

country comparison to the world: 57

INFANT MORTALITY RATE:
total: 37.8 deaths/1,000 live births (2018 est.)

male: 36.7 deaths/1,000 live births

female: 39.1 deaths/1,000 live births

country comparison to the world: 46

LIFE EXPECTANCY AT BIRTH:
total population: 69.1 years (2018 est.)

male: 67.8 years

female: 70.5 years

country comparison to the world: 163

TOTAL FERTILITY RATE:
2.4 children born/woman (2018 est.)

country comparison to the world: 81

CONTRACEPTIVE PREVALENCE RATE:
53.5% (2015/16)

DRINKING WATER SOURCE:
improved:

urban: 97.1% of population

rural: 92.6% of population

total: 94.1% of population

unimproved:

urban: 2.9% of population

rural: 7.4% of population

total: 5.9% of population (2015 est.)

CURRENT HEALTH EXPENDITURE:
3.7% (2016)

PHYSICIANS DENSITY:
0.78 physicians/1,000 population (2017)

HOSPITAL BED DENSITY:
0.7 beds/1,000 population (2011)

SANITATION FACILITY ACCESS:
improved:

urban: 62.6% of population (2015 est.)

rural: 28.5% of population (2015 est.)

total: 39.6% of population (2015 est.)

unimproved:

urban: 37.4% of population (2015 est.)

rural: 71.5% of population (2015 est.)

total: 60.4% of population (2015 est.)

HIV/AIDS - ADULT PREVALENCE RATE:
0.2% (2017 est.)

country comparison to the world: 99

HIV/AIDS - PEOPLE LIVING WITH HIV/AIDS:
2.1 million (2017 est.)

country comparison to the world: 3

HIV/AIDS - DEATHS:
69,000 (2017 est.)

country comparison to the world: 2

MAJOR INFECTIOUS DISEASES:
degree of risk: very high (2016)

food or waterborne diseases: bacterial diarrhea, hepatitis A and E, and typhoid fever (2016)

vectorborne diseases: dengue fever, Japanese encephalitis, and malaria (2016)

water contact diseases: leptospirosis (2016)

animal contact diseases: rabies (2016)

OBESITY - ADULT PREVALENCE RATE:
3.9% (2016)

country comparison to the world: 189

CHILDREN UNDER THE AGE OF 5 YEARS UNDERWEIGHT:
36.3% (2015)

country comparison to the world: 4

EDUCATION EXPENDITURES:
3.8% of GDP (2013)

country comparison to the world: 118

LITERACY:
definition: age 15 and over can read and write

total population: 71.2%

male: 81.3%

female: 60.6% (2015 est.)

SCHOOL LIFE EXPECTANCY (PRIMARY TO TERTIARY EDUCATION):
total: 12 years

male: 12 years

female: 13 years (2016)

UNEMPLOYMENT, YOUTH AGES 15-24:
total: 10.1%

male: 9.5%

female: 12% (2012 est.)

country comparison to the world: 129

GOVERNMENT :: INDIA

COUNTRY NAME:
conventional long form: Republic of India

conventional short form: India

local long form: Republic of India/Bharatiya Ganarajya

local short form: India/Bharat

etymology: the English name derives from the Indus River; the Indian name "Bharat" may derive from the "Bharatas" tribe mentioned in the Vedas of the second millennium B.C.; the name is also associated with Emperor Bharata, the legendary conqueror of all of India

GOVERNMENT TYPE:
federal parliamentary republic

CAPITAL:
name: New Delhi

geographic coordinates: 28 36 N, 77 12 E

time difference: UTC+5.5 (10.5 hours ahead of Washington, DC, during Standard Time)

etymology: the city's name is associated with various myths and legends; the original name for the city may have been Dhilli or Dhillika; alternatively, the name could be a corruption of the Hindustani words "dehleez" or "dehali" - both terms meaning "threshold" or "gateway" - and indicative of the city as a gateway to the Gangetic Plain; after the British decided to move the capital of their Indian Empire from Calcutta to Delhi in 1911, they created a new governmental district south of the latter designated as New Delhi; the new capital was not formally inaugurated until 1931

ADMINISTRATIVE DIVISIONS:
28 states and 9 union territories*; Andaman and Nicobar Islands*, Andhra Pradesh, Arunachal Pradesh, Assam, Bihar, Chandigarh*, Chhattisgarh, Dadra and Nagar Haveli*, Daman and Diu*, Delhi*, Goa, Gujarat, Haryana, Himachal Pradesh, Jammu and Kashmir*, Jharkhand, Karnataka, Kerala, Ladakh*, Lakshadweep*, Madhya Pradesh, Maharashtra, Manipur, Meghalaya, Mizoram, Nagaland, Odisha, Puducherry*, Punjab, Rajasthan, Sikkim, Tamil Nadu, Telangana, Tripura, Uttar Pradesh, Uttarakhand, West Bengal

note: although its status is that of a union territory, the official name of Delhi is National Capital Territory of Delhi

INDEPENDENCE:
15 August 1947 (from the UK)

NATIONAL HOLIDAY:
Republic Day, 26 January (1950)

CONSTITUTION:
history: previous 1935 (preindependence); latest draft completed 4 November 1949, adopted 26 November 1949, effective 26 January 1950

amendments: proposed by either the Council of States or the House of the People; passage requires majority participation of the total membership in each house and at least two-thirds majority of voting members of each house, followed by assent of the president of India; proposed amendments to the constitutional amendment procedures also must be ratified by at least one half of the India state legislatures before presidential assent; amended many times, last in 2019 (2019)

LEGAL SYSTEM:
common law system based on the English model; separate personal law codes apply to Muslims, Christians, and Hindus; judicial review of legislative acts

INTERNATIONAL LAW ORGANIZATION PARTICIPATION:
accepts compulsory ICJ jurisdiction with reservations; non-party state to the ICCt

CITIZENSHIP:
citizenship by birth: no

citizenship by descent only: at least one parent must be a citizen of India

dual citizenship recognized: no

residency requirement for naturalization: 5 years

SUFFRAGE:
18 years of age; universal

EXECUTIVE BRANCH:
chief of state: President Ram Nath KOVIND (since 25 July 2017); Vice President M. Venkaiah NAIDU (since 11 August 2017)

head of government: Prime Minister Narendra MODI (since 26 May 2014)

cabinet: Union Council of Ministers recommended by the prime minister, appointed by the president

elections/appointments: president indirectly elected by an electoral college consisting of elected members of both houses of Parliament for a 5-year term (no term limits); election last held on 17 July 2017 (next to be held in July 2022); vice president indirectly elected by an electoral college consisting of elected members of both houses of Parliament for a 5-year term (no term limits); election last held on 5 August 2017 (next to be held in August 2022); following legislative elections, the prime minister is elected by Lok Sabha members of the majority party

election results: Ram Nath KOVIND elected president; percent of electoral college vote - Ram Nath KOVIND (BJP) 65.7% Meira KUMAR (INC) 34.3%; M. Venkaiah NAIDU elected vice president; electoral college vote - M. Venkaiah NAIDU (BJP) 516, Gopalkrishna GANDHI (independent) 244

LEGISLATIVE BRANCH:
description: bicameral Parliament or Sansad consists of:
Council of States or Rajya Sabha (245 seats; 233 members indirectly elected by state and territorial assemblies by proportional representation vote and 12 members appointed by the president; members serve 6-year terms) House of the People or Lok Sabha (545 seats; 543 members directly elected in single-seat constituencies by simple majority vote and 2 appointed by the president; members serve 5-year terms)

elections: Council of States - last held by state and territorial assemblies at various dates in 2018

House of the People - last held April-May 2014 in 9 phases; (next to be held in 7 phases 11 April to 19 May 2019)

election results: Council of States - percent of vote by party - NA; seats by party - NA; composition - men 218, women 27, percent of women 11%

House of the People - percent of vote by party - BJP 31%, INC 19.3%, AITC 3.8%, SP 3.4%, AIADMK 3.3%, CPI(M) 3.3%, TDP 2.6%, YSRC 2.5%, AAP 2.1%, SAD 1.8%, BJD 1.7%, SS 1.7%, NCP 1.6%, RJD 1.3%, TRS 1.3%, LJP 0.4%, other 15.9%, independent 3%; seats by party - BJP 282, INC 44, AIADMK 37, AITC 34, BJD 20, SS 18, TDP 16, TRS 11, CPI(M) 9, YSRC 9, LJP 6, NCP 6, SP 5, AAP 4, RJD 4, SAD 4, other 33, independent 3; composition - men 483, women 62, percent of women 11.4%; note - total Parliament percent of women 11.3%

JUDICIAL BRANCH:
highest courts: Supreme Court (consists of 28 judges, including the chief justice)

judge selection and term of office: justices appointed by the president to serve until age 65

subordinate courts: High Courts; District Courts; Labour Court

note: in mid-2011, India's Cabinet approved the "National Mission for Justice Delivery and Legal Reform" to eliminate judicial corruption and reduce the backlog of cases

POLITICAL PARTIES AND LEADERS:
Aam Aadmi Party or AAP [Arvind KEJRIWAL]
All India Anna Dravida Munnetra Kazhagam or AIADMK [Edappadi PALANISWAMY, Occhaathevar PANNEERSELVAM]
All India Trinamool Congress or AITC [Mamata BANERJEE]
Bahujan Samaj Party or BSP [MAYAWATI]
Bharatiya Janata Party or BJP [Amit SHAH]
Biju Janata Dal or BJD [Naveen PATNAIK]
Communist Party of India-Marxist or CPI(M) [Sitaram YECHURY]
Indian National Congress or INC
Lok Janshakti Party (LJP) [Ram Vilas PASWAN]
Nationalist Congress Party or NCP [Sharad PAWAR]
Rashtriya Janata Dal or RJD [Lalu Prasad YADAV]
Samajwadi Party or SP [Akhilesh YADAV]
Shiromani Akali Dal or SAD [Sukhbir Singh BADAL]
Shiv Sena or SS [Uddhav THACKERAY]
Telegana Rashtra Samithi or TRS [K. Chandrashekar RAO]
Telugu Desam Party or TDP [Chandrababu NAIDU]
YSR Congress or YSRC [Jagan Mohan REDDY]

note: India has dozens of national and regional political parties

INTERNATIONAL ORGANIZATION PARTICIPATION:
ADB, AfDB (nonregional member), Arctic Council (observer), ARF, ASEAN (dialogue partner), BIMSTEC, BIS, BRICS, C, CD, CERN (observer), CICA, CP, EAS, FAO, FATF, G-15, G-20, G-24, G-5, G-77,

IAEA, IBRD, ICAO, ICC (national committees), ICRM, IDA, IFAD, IFC, IFRCS, IHO, ILO, IMF, IMO, IMSO, Interpol, IOC, IOM, IPU, ISO, ITSO, ITU, ITUC (NGOs), LAS (observer), MIGA, MINURSO, MONUSCO, NAM, OAS (observer), OECD, OPCW, Pacific Alliance (observer), PCA, PIF (partner), SAARC, SACEP, SCO (observer), UN, UNCTAD, UNDOF, UNESCO, UNHCR, UNIDO, UNIFIL, UNISFA, UNITAR, UNMISS, UNOCI, UNWTO, UPU, WCO, WFTU (NGOs), WHO, WIPO, WMO, WTO

DIPLOMATIC REPRESENTATION IN THE US:

Ambassador Harsh Vardhan SHRINGLA (since 11 January 2019)

chancery: 2107 Massachusetts Avenue NW, Washington, DC 20008; Consular Wing located at 2536 Massachusetts Avenue NW, Washington, DC 20008

telephone: [1] (202) 939-7000

FAX: [1] (202) 265-4351

consulate(s) general: Atlanta, Chicago, Houston, New York, San Francisco

DIPLOMATIC REPRESENTATION FROM THE US:

chief of mission: Ambassador Kenneth I. JUSTER (since 23 November 2017)

telephone: [91] (11) 2419-8000

embassy: Shantipath, Chanakyapuri, New Delhi 110021

mailing address: use embassy street address

FAX: [91] (11) 2419-0017

consulate(s) general: Chennai (Madras), Hyderabad, Kolkata (Calcutta), Mumbai (Bombay)

FLAG DESCRIPTION:

three equal horizontal bands of saffron (subdued orange) (top), white, and green, with a blue chakra (24-spoked wheel) centered in the white band; saffron represents courage, sacrifice, and the spirit of renunciation; white signifies purity and truth; green stands for faith and fertility; the blue chakra symbolizes the wheel of life in movement and death in stagnation

note: similar to the flag of Niger, which has a small orange disk centered in the white band

NATIONAL SYMBOL(S):

the Lion Capital of Ashoka, which depicts four Asiatic lions standing back to back mounted on a circular abacus, is the official emblem; Bengal tiger; lotus flower; national colors: saffron, white, green

NATIONAL ANTHEM:

name: "Jana-Gana-Mana" (Thou Art the Ruler of the Minds of All People)

lyrics/music: Rabindranath TAGORE

note: adopted 1950; Rabindranath TAGORE, a Nobel laureate, also wrote Bangladesh's national anthem

ECONOMY :: INDIA

ECONOMY - OVERVIEW:

India's diverse economy encompasses traditional village farming, modern agriculture, handicrafts, a wide range of modern industries, and a multitude of services. Slightly less than half of the workforce is in agriculture, but services are the major source of economic growth, accounting for nearly two-thirds of India's output but employing less than one-third of its labor force. India has capitalized on its large educated English-speaking population to become a major exporter of information technology services, business outsourcing services, and software workers. Nevertheless, per capita income remains below the world average. India is developing into an open-market economy, yet traces of its past autarkic policies remain. Economic liberalization measures, including industrial deregulation, privatization of state-owned enterprises, and reduced controls on foreign trade and investment, began in the early 1990s and served to accelerate the country's growth, which averaged nearly 7% per year from 1997 to 2017.

India's economic growth slowed in 2011 because of a decline in investment caused by high interest rates, rising inflation, and investor pessimism about the government's commitment to further economic reforms and about slow world growth. Investors' perceptions of India improved in early 2014, due to a reduction of the current account deficit and expectations of post-election economic reform, resulting in a surge of inbound capital flows and stabilization of the rupee. Growth rebounded in 2014 through 2016. Despite a high growth rate compared to the rest of the world, India's government-owned banks faced mounting bad debt, resulting in low credit growth. Rising macroeconomic imbalances in India and improving economic conditions in Western countries led investors to shift capital away from India, prompting a sharp depreciation of the rupee through 2016.

The economy slowed again in 2017, due to shocks of "demonetizaton" in 2016 and introduction of GST in 2017. Since the election, the government has passed an important goods and services tax bill and raised foreign direct investment caps in some sectors, but most economic reforms have focused on administrative and governance changes, largely because the ruling party remains a minority in India's upper house of Parliament, which must approve most bills.

India has a young population and corresponding low dependency ratio, healthy savings and investment rates, and is increasing integration into the global economy. However, long-term challenges remain significant, including: India's discrimination against women and girls, an inefficient power generation and distribution system, ineffective enforcement of intellectual property rights, decades-long civil litigation dockets, inadequate transport and agricultural infrastructure, limited non-agricultural employment opportunities, high spending and poorly targeted subsidies, inadequate availability of quality basic and higher education, and accommodating rural-to-urban migration.

GDP (PURCHASING POWER PARITY):

$9.474 trillion (2017 est.)

$8.88 trillion (2016 est.)

$8.291 trillion (2015 est.)

note: data are in 2017 dollars

country comparison to the world: 3

GDP (OFFICIAL EXCHANGE RATE):

$2.602 trillion (2017 est.)

GDP - REAL GROWTH RATE:

6.7% (2017 est.)

7.1% (2016 est.)

8.2% (2015 est.)

country comparison to the world: 27

GDP - PER CAPITA (PPP):

$7,200 (2017 est.)

$6,800 (2016 est.)

$6,500 (2015 est.)

note: data are in 2017 dollars

country comparison to the world: 156

GROSS NATIONAL SAVING:

28.8% of GDP (2017 est.)

29.7% of GDP (2016 est.)

30.7% of GDP (2015 est.)

country comparison to the world: 36

GDP - COMPOSITION, BY END USE:

household consumption: 59.1% (2017 est.)

government consumption: 11.5% (2017 est.)

investment in fixed capital: 28.5% (2017 est.)

investment in inventories: 3.9% (2017 est.)

exports of goods and services: 19.1% (2017 est.)

imports of goods and services: -22% (2017 est.)

GDP - COMPOSITION, BY SECTOR OF ORIGIN:

agriculture: 15.4% (2016 est.)

industry: 23% (2016 est.)

services: 61.5% (2016 est.)

AGRICULTURE - PRODUCTS:

rice, wheat, oilseed, cotton, jute, tea, sugarcane, lentils, onions, potatoes; dairy products, sheep, goats, poultry; fish

INDUSTRIES:

textiles, chemicals, food processing, steel, transportation equipment, cement, mining, petroleum, machinery, software, pharmaceuticals

INDUSTRIAL PRODUCTION GROWTH RATE:

5.5% (2017 est.)

country comparison to the world: 49

LABOR FORCE:

521.9 million (2017 est.)

country comparison to the world: 2

LABOR FORCE - BY OCCUPATION:

agriculture: 47%

industry: 22%

services: 31% (FY 2014 est.)

UNEMPLOYMENT RATE:

8.5% (2017 est.)

8.5% (2016 est.)

country comparison to the world: 122

POPULATION BELOW POVERTY LINE:

21.9% (2011 est.)

HOUSEHOLD INCOME OR CONSUMPTION BY PERCENTAGE SHARE:

lowest 10%: 3.6%

highest 10%: 29.8% (2011)

DISTRIBUTION OF FAMILY INCOME - GINI INDEX:

35.2 (2011)

37.8 (1997)

country comparison to the world: 96

BUDGET:

revenues: 238.2 billion (2017 est.)

expenditures: 329 billion (2017 est.)

TAXES AND OTHER REVENUES:

9.2% (of GDP) (2017 est.)

country comparison to the world: 215

BUDGET SURPLUS (+) OR DEFICIT (-):

-3.5% (of GDP) (2017 est.)

country comparison to the world: 146

PUBLIC DEBT:

71.2% of GDP (2017 est.)

69.5% of GDP (2016 est.)

note: data cover central government debt, and exclude debt instruments issued (or owned) by government entities other than the treasury; the data include treasury debt held by foreign entities; the data exclude debt issued by subnational entities, as well as intragovernmental debt; intragovernmental debt consists of treasury borrowings from surpluses in the social funds, such as for retirement, medical care, and unemployment; debt instruments for the social funds are not sold at public auctions

country comparison to the world: 47

FISCAL YEAR:

1 April - 31 March

INFLATION RATE (CONSUMER PRICES):

3.6% (2017 est.)

4.5% (2016 est.)

country comparison to the world: 143

CENTRAL BANK DISCOUNT RATE:

6% (31 December 2017)

6.25% (31 December 2016)

note: this is the Indian central bank's policy rate - the repurchase rate

country comparison to the world: 69

COMMERCIAL BANK PRIME LENDING RATE:

9.51% (31 December 2017 est.)

9.67% (31 December 2016 est.)

country comparison to the world: 88

STOCK OF NARROW MONEY:

$451.5 billion (31 December 2017 est.)

$293.5 billion (31 December 2016 est.)

country comparison to the world: 12

STOCK OF BROAD MONEY:

$451.5 billion (31 December 2017 est.)

$293.5 billion (31 December 2016 est.)

country comparison to the world: 12

STOCK OF DOMESTIC CREDIT:

$1.927 trillion (31 December 2017 est.)

$1.684 trillion (31 December 2016 est.)

country comparison to the world: 13

MARKET VALUE OF PUBLICLY TRADED SHARES:

$1.516 trillion (31 December 2015 est.)

$1.558 trillion (31 December 2014 est.)

$1.139 trillion (31 December 2013 est.)

country comparison to the world: 10

CURRENT ACCOUNT BALANCE:

-$48.66 billion (2017 est.)

-$14.35 billion (2016 est.)

country comparison to the world: 203

EXPORTS:

$304.1 billion (2017 est.)

$268.6 billion (2016 est.)

country comparison to the world: 19

EXPORTS - PARTNERS:

US 15.6%, UAE 10.2%, Hong Kong 4.9%, China 4.3% (2017)

EXPORTS - COMMODITIES:

petroleum products, precious stones, vehicles, machinery, iron and steel, chemicals, pharmaceutical products, cereals, apparel

IMPORTS:

$452.2 billion (2017 est.)

$376.1 billion (2016 est.)

country comparison to the world: 11

IMPORTS - COMMODITIES:

crude oil, precious stones, machinery, chemicals, fertilizer, plastics, iron and steel

IMPORTS - PARTNERS:

China 16.3%, US 5.5%, UAE 5.2%, Saudi Arabia 4.8%, Switzerland 4.7% (2017)

RESERVES OF FOREIGN EXCHANGE AND GOLD:

$409.8 billion (31 December 2017 est.)

$359.7 billion (31 December 2016 est.)

country comparison to the world: 8

DEBT - EXTERNAL:
$501.6 billion (31 December 2017 est.)
$456.4 billion (31 December 2016 est.)
country comparison to the world: 24

STOCK OF DIRECT FOREIGN INVESTMENT - AT HOME:
$377.5 billion (31 December 2017 est.)
$318.5 billion (31 December 2016 est.)
country comparison to the world: 20

STOCK OF DIRECT FOREIGN INVESTMENT - ABROAD:
$155.2 billion (31 December 2017 est.)
$144.1 billion (31 December 2016 est.)
country comparison to the world: 30

EXCHANGE RATES:
Indian rupees (INR) per US dollar -
65.17 (2017 est.)
67.195 (2016 est.)
67.195 (2015 est.)
64.152 (2014 est.)
61.03 (2013 est.)

ENERGY :: INDIA

ELECTRICITY ACCESS:
population without electricity: 168 million (2017)
electrification - total population: 84.5% (2016)
electrification - urban areas: 98.4% (2016)
electrification - rural areas: 77.6% (2016)

ELECTRICITY - PRODUCTION:
1.386 trillion kWh (2016 est.)
country comparison to the world: 3

ELECTRICITY - CONSUMPTION:
1.137 trillion kWh (2016 est.)
country comparison to the world: 3

ELECTRICITY - EXPORTS:
5.15 billion kWh (2015 est.)
country comparison to the world: 36

ELECTRICITY - IMPORTS:
5.617 billion kWh (2016 est.)
country comparison to the world: 35

ELECTRICITY - INSTALLED GENERATING CAPACITY:
367.8 million kW (2016 est.)
country comparison to the world: 3

ELECTRICITY - FROM FOSSIL FUELS:
71% of total installed capacity (2016 est.)
country comparison to the world: 104

ELECTRICITY - FROM NUCLEAR FUELS:
2% of total installed capacity (2017 est.)
country comparison to the world: 26

ELECTRICITY - FROM HYDROELECTRIC PLANTS:
12% of total installed capacity (2017 est.)
country comparison to the world: 111

ELECTRICITY - FROM OTHER RENEWABLE SOURCES:
16% of total installed capacity (2017 est.)
country comparison to the world: 53

CRUDE OIL - PRODUCTION:
709,000 bbl/day (2018 est.)
country comparison to the world: 25

CRUDE OIL - EXPORTS:
0 bbl/day (2015 est.)
country comparison to the world: 140

CRUDE OIL - IMPORTS:
4.057 million bbl/day (2015 est.)
country comparison to the world: 3

CRUDE OIL - PROVED RESERVES:
4.495 billion bbl (1 January 2018 est.)
country comparison to the world: 23

REFINED PETROLEUM PRODUCTS - PRODUCTION:
4.897 million bbl/day (2015 est.)
country comparison to the world: 4

REFINED PETROLEUM PRODUCTS - CONSUMPTION:
4.521 million bbl/day (2016 est.)
country comparison to the world: 3

REFINED PETROLEUM PRODUCTS - EXPORTS:
1.305 million bbl/day (2015 est.)
country comparison to the world: 7

REFINED PETROLEUM PRODUCTS - IMPORTS:
653,300 bbl/day (2015 est.)
country comparison to the world: 11

NATURAL GAS - PRODUCTION:
31.54 billion cu m (2017 est.)
country comparison to the world: 25

NATURAL GAS - CONSUMPTION:
55.43 billion cu m (2017 est.)
country comparison to the world: 14

NATURAL GAS - EXPORTS:
76.45 million cu m (2017 est.)
country comparison to the world: 50

NATURAL GAS - IMPORTS:
23.96 billion cu m (2017 est.)
country comparison to the world: 14

NATURAL GAS - PROVED RESERVES:
1.29 trillion cu m (1 January 2018 est.)
country comparison to the world: 22

CARBON DIOXIDE EMISSIONS FROM CONSUMPTION OF ENERGY:
2.383 billion Mt (2017 est.)
country comparison to the world: 3

COMMUNICATIONS :: INDIA

TELEPHONES - FIXED LINES:
total subscriptions: 23,234,687
subscriptions per 100 inhabitants: 2 (2017 est.)
country comparison to the world: 11

TELEPHONES - MOBILE CELLULAR:
total subscriptions: 1,168,902,277
subscriptions per 100 inhabitants: 91 (2017 est.)
country comparison to the world: 2

TELEPHONE SYSTEM:
general assessment: supported by deregulation and liberalization of telecommunications laws and policies, India has emerged as one of the fastest-growing telecom markets in the world; implementation of 4G/LTE services shift to data services across the country; steps taken towards 5G services; fixed broadband penetration is expected to grow at a moderate rate over the next five years to 2023 (2018)

domestic: fixed-line subscriptions stands at 2 per 100 and mobile-cellular at 91 per 100; mobile cellular service introduced in 1994 and organized nationwide into four metropolitan areas and 19 telecom circles, each with multiple private service providers and one or more state-owned service providers; in recent years significant trunk capacity added in the form of fiber-optic cable and one of the world's largest domestic satellite systems, the Indian National Satellite system (INSAT), with 6 satellites supporting 33,000 very small aperture terminals (VSAT) (2018)

international: country code - 91; a number of major international submarine cable systems, including SEA-ME-WE-3 & 4, AAE-1, BBG, EIG, FALCON, FEA, GBICS, MENA,

IMEWE, SEACOM/ Tata TGN-Eurasia, SAFE, WARF, Bharat Lanka Cable System, IOX, Chennai-Andaman & Nicobar Island Cable, SAEx2, Tata TGN-Tata Indicom and i2icn submarine cables to Europe, Africa, Asia, the Middle East, South East Asia, numerous Indian Ocean islands including Australia ; satellite earth stations - 8 Intelsat (Indian Ocean) and 1 Inmarsat (Indian Ocean region (2019)

BROADCAST MEDIA:

Doordarshan, India's public TV network, has a monopoly on terrestrial broadcasting and operates about 20 national, regional, and local services; a large and increasing number of privately owned TV stations are distributed by cable and satellite service providers; in 2015, more than 230 million homes had access to cable and satellite TV offering more than 700 TV channels; government controls AM radio with All India Radio operating domestic and external networks; news broadcasts via radio are limited to the All India Radio Network; since 2000, privately owned FM stations have been permitted and their numbers have increased rapidly

INTERNET COUNTRY CODE:

.in

INTERNET USERS:

total: 374,328,160

percent of population: 29.5% (July 2016 est.)

country comparison to the world: 2

BROADBAND - FIXED SUBSCRIPTIONS:

total: 17,856,024

subscriptions per 100 inhabitants: 1 (2017 est.)

country comparison to the world: 10

MILITARY AND SECURITY :: INDIA

MILITARY EXPENDITURES:

2.42% of GDP (2018)

2.51% of GDP (2017)

2.51% of GDP (2016)

2.41% of GDP (2015)

2.5% of GDP (2014)

country comparison to the world: 35

MILITARY AND SECURITY FORCES:

Indian Armed Forces: Army, Navy (includes marines), Air Force, Coast Guard; Defense Security Corps (paramilitary forces); Ministry of Home Affairs paramilitary forces: Central Armed Police Force (includes Assam Rifles, Border Security Force, Central Industrial Security Force, Central Reserve Police Force, Indo-Tibetan Border Police, National Security Guards, Sashastra Seema Bal) (2019)

MILITARY SERVICE AGE AND OBLIGATION:

16-18 years of age for voluntary military service (Army 17 1/2, Air Force 17, Navy 16 1/2); no conscription; women may join as officers, currently serve in combat roles as pilots, and under consideration for Army combat roles (2019)

TRANSPORTATION :: INDIA

NATIONAL AIR TRANSPORT SYSTEM:

number of registered air carriers: 20 (2015)

inventory of registered aircraft operated by air carriers: 485 (2015)

annual passenger traffic on registered air carriers: 98,927,860 (2015)

annual freight traffic on registered air carriers: 1,833,847,614 mt-km (2015)

CIVIL AIRCRAFT REGISTRATION COUNTRY CODE PREFIX:

VT (2016)

AIRPORTS:

346 (2013)

country comparison to the world: 21

AIRPORTS - WITH PAVED RUNWAYS:

total: 253 (2017)

over 3,047 m: 22 (2017)

2,438 to 3,047 m: 59 (2017)

1,524 to 2,437 m: 76 (2017)

914 to 1,523 m: 82 (2017)

under 914 m: 14 (2017)

AIRPORTS - WITH UNPAVED RUNWAYS:

total: 93 (2013)

over 3,047 m: 1 (2013)

2,438 to 3,047 m: 3 (2013)

1,524 to 2,437 m: 6 (2013)

914 to 1,523 m: 38 (2013)

under 914 m: 45 (2013)

HELIPORTS:

45 (2013)

PIPELINES:

9 km condensate/gas, 13581 km gas, 2054 km liquid petroleum gas, 8943 km oil, 20 km oil/gas/water, 11069 km refined products (2013)

RAILWAYS:

total: 68,525 km (2014)

narrow gauge: 9,499 km 1.000-m gauge (2014)

broad gauge: 58,404 km 1.676-m gauge (23,654 electrified) (2014)

622 0.762-m gauge

country comparison to the world: 5

ROADWAYS:

total: 4,699,024 km (2015)

note: includes 96,214 km of national highways and expressways, 147,800 km of state highways, and 4,455,010 km of other roads

country comparison to the world: 3

WATERWAYS:

14,500 km (5,200 km on major rivers and 485 km on canals suitable for mechanized vessels) (2012)

country comparison to the world: 9

MERCHANT MARINE:

total: 1,719

by type: bulk carrier 75, container ship 22, general cargo 582, oil tanker 133, other 907 (2018)

country comparison to the world: 14

PORTS AND TERMINALS:

major seaport(s): Chennai, Jawaharal Nehru Port, Kandla, Kolkata (Calcutta), Mumbai (Bombay), Sikka, Vishakhapatnam

container port(s) (TEUs): Chennai (1,549,457), Jawaharal Nehru Port (4,833,397), Mundra (4,240,260) (2017)

LNG terminal(s) (import): Dabhol, Dahej, Hazira

TERRORISM :: INDIA

TERRORIST GROUPS - HOME BASED:

Hizbul Mujahideen (HM): aim(s): annex the state of Jammu and Kashmir to Pakistan

area(s) of operation: HM is an indigenous Kashmiri militant group that operates in Jammu and Kashmir (2018)

Indian Mujahedeen (IM): aim(s): establish Islamic rule in India and, ultimately, convert all non-Muslims to Islam; stated goal is to carry out terrorist attacks against Indians for perceived atrocities against Indian Muslims
area(s) of operation: formerly based in the western state of Maharashtra, India's third-largest and second-most populous state, and now probably operates mostly outside India, particularly Nepal (2018)

TERRORIST GROUPS - FOREIGN BASED:

al-Qa'ida (AQ):
aim(s): overthrow the Indian Government and, ultimately, establish a pan-Islamic caliphate under a strict Salafi Muslim interpretation of sharia
area(s) of operation: maintains an operational presence as al-Qa'ida in the Indian Subcontinent (2018)

al-Qa'ida in the Indian Subcontinent (AQIS): aim(s): establish an Islamic caliphate in the Indian subcontinent
area(s) of operation: targets primarily military and security personnel, especially in the states of Assam, Gujarat, and Jammu and Kashmir; present in large cities, including Delhi (2018)

Harakat ul-Mujahidin (HUM): aim(s): enhance its networks and paramilitary training in India and, ultimately, annex Kashmir into Pakistan and establish an Islamic state in Kashmir
area(s) of operation: conducts attacks against Indian troops and civilians in Kashmir (2018)

Harakat ul-Jihad-i-Islami (HUJI): aim(s): enhance its networks and operational capabilities in India
area(s) of operation: maintains an operational presence, especially in the south, including in Bangalore and Hubli (2018)

Harakat ul-Jihad-i-Islami/Bangladesh (HUJI-B): aim(s): enhance its networks in India and, ultimately, install an Islamic state in Bangladesh
area(s) of operation: maintains a low-profile presence (2018)

Islamic State of Iraq and ash-Sham-Khorasan (ISIS-K): aim(s): spread the ISIS caliphate by eliminating the Indian Government and, ultimately, unite Kashmir with Pakistan
area(s) of operation: maintains a recruitment presence in major cities (2018)

Jaish-e-Mohammed (JEM): aim(s): annex Jammu and Kashmir to Pakistan
area(s) of operation: operates primarily in Jammu and Kashmir State (2018)

Lashkar-e Tayyiba (LT): aim(s): annex Jammu and Kashmir State to Pakistan and, ultimately, install Islamic rule throughout South Asia
area(s) of operation: operational throughout India, especially in the north in Jammu and Kashmir State, since at least 1993
note: continues to be one of the largest and most deadly of the anti-India-focused armed groups (2018)

Liberation Tigers of Tamil Eelam (LTTE): aim(s): enhance its networks in India and, ultimately, revive the movement to establish a Tamil homeland
area(s) of operation: maintains safe havens, transit routes, human trafficking, and an operational presence in an effort to revive the movement and conduct attacks (2018)

TRANSNATIONAL ISSUES :: INDIA

DISPUTES - INTERNATIONAL:

since China and India launched a security and foreign policy dialogue in 2005, consolidated discussions related to the dispute over most of their rugged, militarized boundary, regional nuclear proliferation, Indian claims that China transferred missiles to Pakistan, and other matters continue; Kashmir remains the site of the world's largest and most militarized territorial dispute with portions under the de facto administration of China (Aksai Chin), India (Jammu and Kashmir), and Pakistan (Azad Kashmir and Northern Areas); India and Pakistan resumed bilateral dialogue in February 2011 after a two-year hiatus, have maintained the 2003 cease-fire in Kashmir, and continue to have disputes over water sharing of the Indus River and its tributaries; UN Military Observer Group in India and Pakistan has maintained a small group of peacekeepers since 1949; India does not recognize Pakistan's ceding historic Kashmir lands to China in 1964; to defuse tensions and prepare for discussions on a maritime boundary, India and Pakistan seek technical resolution of the disputed boundary in Sir Creek estuary at the mouth of the Rann of Kutch in the Arabian Sea; Pakistani maps continue to show its Junagadh claim in Indian Gujarat State; Prime Minister Singh's September 2011 visit to Bangladesh resulted in the signing of a Protocol to the 1974 Land Boundary Agreement between India and Bangladesh, which had called for the settlement of longstanding boundary disputes over undemarcated areas and the exchange of territorial enclaves, but which had never been implemented; Bangladesh referred its maritime boundary claims with Burma and India to the International Tribunal on the Law of the Sea; Joint Border Committee with Nepal continues to examine contested boundary sections, including the 400 sq km dispute over the source of the Kalapani River; India maintains a strict border regime to keep out Maoist insurgents and control illegal cross-border activities from Nepal

REFUGEES AND INTERNALLY DISPLACED PERSONS:

refugees (country of origin): 108,008 (Tibet/China), 60,802 (Sri Lanka), 18,813 (Burma), 6,984 (Afghanistan) (2018)

IDPs: 479,000 (armed conflict and intercommunal violence) (2018)

ILLICIT DRUGS:

world's largest producer of licit opium for the pharmaceutical trade, but an undetermined quantity of opium is diverted to illicit international drug markets; transit point for illicit narcotics produced in neighboring countries and throughout Southwest Asia; illicit producer of methaqualone; vulnerable to narcotics money laundering through the hawala system; licit ketamine and precursor production

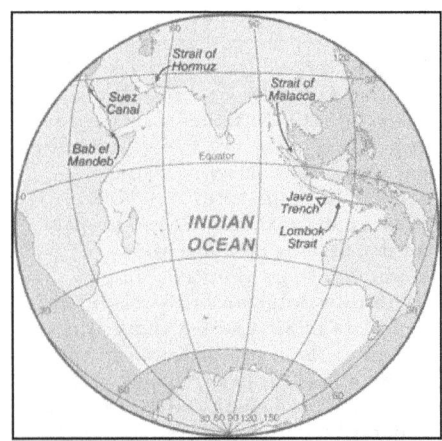

OCEANS :: INDIAN OCEAN

INTRODUCTION :: INDIAN OCEAN

BACKGROUND:

The Indian Ocean is the third largest of the world's five oceans (after the Pacific Ocean and Atlantic Ocean, but larger than the Southern Ocean and Arctic Ocean). Four critically important access waterways are the Suez Canal (Egypt), Bab el Mandeb (Djibouti-Yemen), Strait of Hormuz (Iran-Oman), and Strait of Malacca (Indonesia-Malaysia). The decision by the International Hydrographic Organization in the spring of 2000 to delimit a fifth ocean, the Southern Ocean, removed the portion of the Indian Ocean south of 60 degrees south latitude.

GEOGRAPHY :: INDIAN OCEAN

LOCATION:
body of water between Africa, the Southern Ocean, Asia, and Australia

GEOGRAPHIC COORDINATES:
20 00 S, 80 00 E

MAP REFERENCES:
Political Map of the World

AREA:
total: 68.556 million sq km

note: includes Andaman Sea, Arabian Sea, Bay of Bengal, Flores Sea, Great Australian Bight, Gulf of Aden, Gulf of Oman, Java Sea, Mozambique Channel, Persian Gulf, Red Sea, Savu Sea, Strait of Malacca, Timor Sea, and other tributary water bodies

AREA - COMPARATIVE:
almost 7 times the size of the US

COASTLINE:
66,526 km

CLIMATE:
northeast monsoon (December to April), southwest monsoon (June to October); tropical cyclones occur during May/June and October/November in the northern Indian Ocean and January/February in the southern Indian Ocean

TERRAIN:
surface dominated by a major gyre (broad, circular system of currents) in the southern Indian Ocean and a unique reversal of surface currents in the northern Indian Ocean; ocean floor is dominated by the Mid-Indian Ocean Ridge and subdivided by the Southeast Indian Ocean Ridge, Southwest Indian Ocean Ridge, and Ninetyeast Ridge

major surface currents: the counterclockwise Indian Ocean Gyre comprised of the southward flowing warm Agulhas and East Madagascar Currents in the west, the eastward flowing South Indian Current in the south, the northward flowing cold West Australian Current in the east, and the westward flowing South Equatorial Current in the north; a distinctive annual reversal of surface currents occurs in the northern Indian Ocean; low atmospheric pressure over southwest Asia from hot, rising, summer air results in the southwest monsoon and southwest-to-northeast winds and clockwise currents, while high pressure over northern Asia from cold, falling, winter air results in the northeast monsoon and northeast-to-southwest winds and counterclockwise currents

ELEVATION:
mean depth: -3,741 m

lowest point: Java Trench -7,258 m

highest point: sea level

NATURAL RESOURCES:
oil and gas fields, fish, shrimp, sand and gravel aggregates, placer deposits, polymetallic nodules

NATURAL HAZARDS:
occasional icebergs pose navigational hazard in southern reaches

ENVIRONMENT - CURRENT ISSUES:
marine pollution caused by ocean dumping, waste disposal, and oil spills; deep sea mining; oil pollution in Arabian Sea, Persian Gulf, and Red Sea; coral reefs threatened due climate change, direct human pressures, and inadequate governance, awareness, and political will; loss of biodiversity; endangered marine species include the dugong, seals, turtles, and whales

GEOGRAPHY - NOTE:
major chokepoints include Bab el Mandeb, Strait of Hormuz, Strait of Malacca, southern access to the Suez Canal, and the Lombok Strait

GOVERNMENT :: INDIAN OCEAN

COUNTRY NAME:
etymology: named for the country of India, which makes up much of its northern border

ECONOMY :: INDIAN OCEAN

ECONOMY - OVERVIEW:
The Indian Ocean provides major sea routes connecting the Middle East, Africa, and East Asia with Europe and the Americas. It carries a particularly heavy traffic of petroleum and petroleum products from the oilfields of the Persian Gulf and Indonesia. Its fish are of great and growing importance to the bordering countries for domestic consumption and export. Fishing fleets from Russia, Japan, South Korea, and Taiwan also exploit the Indian Ocean, mainly for shrimp and tuna. Large reserves of hydrocarbons are being tapped in the offshore areas of Saudi Arabia, Iran, India, and western Australia. An estimated 40% of the world's offshore oil production comes from the Indian Ocean. Beach sands rich in heavy minerals and offshore placer deposits are actively exploited by bordering countries, particularly India, South Africa, Indonesia, Sri Lanka, and Thailand.

MARINE FISHERIES:
the Indian Ocean fisheries are the third most important in the world accounting for 14%, or 11,318,783 mt of the global catch in 2016; tuna, small pelagic fish, and shrimp are important species in these regions; the Food and Agriculture Organization delineated two fishing regions in the Indian Ocean:

Eastern Indian Ocean region (Region 57) is the most important region and the fourth largest producing region in the world with 8%, or 6,387,659 mt, of the global catch in 2016; the region encompasses the waters north of 55º South latitude and east of 80º East longitude including the Bay of Bengal and Andaman Sea with the major producers including Indonesia (1,405,401 mt), India (1,382,504 mt), Burma (1,185,610 mt), Bangladesh (626,528mt), and Sri Lanka (445,842 mt); the principal catches include shad, Skipjack tuna, mackerel, shrimp, and sardinellas

Western Indian Ocean region (Region 51) is the world's sixth largest producing region with 6% or 4,931,124 mt of the global catch; this region encompasses the waters north of 40º South latitude and west of 80º East longitude including the western Indian Ocean, Arabian Sea, Persian Gulf, and Red Sea as well as the waters along the east coast of Africa and Madagascar, the south coast of the Arabian Peninsula, and the west coast of India with major producers including India (2,217,189 mt), Pakistan (376,266 mt), Oman (279,606 mt), and Mozambique (203,449 mt); the principal catches include Skipjack and Yellowfin tuna, mackerel, sardines, shrimp, and cephalopods

MILITARY AND SECURITY :: INDIAN OCEAN

MARITIME THREATS:
the International Maritime Bureau continues to report the territorial waters of littoral states and offshore waters as high risk for piracy and armed robbery against ships, particularly in the Gulf of Aden, along the east coast of Africa, the Bay of Bengal, and the Strait of Malacca; the presence of several naval task forces in the Gulf of Aden and additional anti-piracy measures on the part of ship operators, including the use of on-board armed security teams, have reduced incidents of piracy; in response, Somali-based pirates, using hijacked fishing trawlers as "mother ships" to extend their range, shifted operations as far south as the Mozambique Channel, eastward to the vicinity of the Maldives, and northeastward to the Strait of Hormuz; 2018 saw a slight decrease in attacks over 2017, with one incident in the Gulf of Aden, none in the Red Sea, and two off the coast of Somalia; Operation Ocean Shield, the NATO naval task force established in 2009 to combat Somali piracy, concluded its operations in December 2016 as a result of the drop in reported incidents over the last few years; the EU naval mission, Operation ATALANTA, continues its operations in the Gulf of Aden and Indian Ocean through 2020; naval units from Japan, India, and China also operate in conjunction with EU forces; China has established a logistical base in Djibouti to support its deployed naval units in the Horn of Africa

the Maritime Administration of the US Department of Transportation has issued a Maritime Advisory (2019-012-Persian Gulf, Strait of Hormuz, Gulf of Oman, Arabian Sea, Red Sea-Threats to US and International Shipping from Iran) effective 7 August 2019, which states in part that "heightened military activities and increased political tensions in this region continue to present risk to commercial shipping...there is a continued possibility that Iran and/or its regional proxies could take actions against US and partner interests in the region;" at present, Iran has seized two foreign-flagged tankers in the Persian Gulf; the US and UK navies have established Operation Sentinel to provide escorts for commercial shipping transiting the Persian Gulf, Strait of Hormuz, and Gulf of Oman

TRANSPORTATION :: INDIAN OCEAN

ROADWAYS:
PORTS AND TERMINALS:

major seaport(s): Chennai (Madras, India); Colombo (Sri Lanka); Durban (South Africa); Jakarta (Indonesia); Kolkata (Calcutta, India); Melbourne (Australia); Mumbai (Bombay, India); Richards Bay (South Africa)

TRANSNATIONAL ISSUES :: INDIAN OCEAN

DISPUTES - INTERNATIONAL:
some maritime disputes (see littoral states)

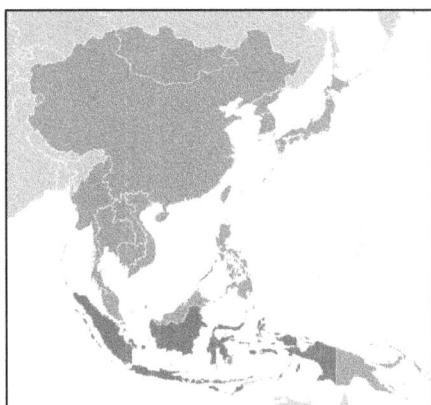

EAST ASIA / SOUTHEAST ASIA :: INDONESIA

INTRODUCTION :: INDONESIA

BACKGROUND:

The Dutch began to colonize Indonesia in the early 17th century; Japan occupied the islands from 1942 to 1945. Indonesia declared its independence shortly before Japan's surrender, but it required four years of sometimes brutal fighting, intermittent negotiations, and UN mediation before the Netherlands agreed to transfer sovereignty in 1949. A period of sometimes unruly parliamentary democracy ended in 1957 when President SOEKARNO declared martial law and instituted "Guided Democracy." After an abortive coup in 1965 by alleged communist sympathizers, SOEKARNO was gradually eased from power. From 1967 until 1998, President SUHARTO ruled Indonesia with his "New Order" government. After street protests toppled SUHARTO in 1998, free and fair legislative elections took place in 1999. Indonesia is now the world's third most populous democracy, the world's largest archipelagic state, and the world's largest Muslim-majority nation. Current issues include: alleviating poverty, improving education, preventing terrorism, consolidating democracy after four decades of authoritarianism, implementing economic and financial reforms, stemming corruption, reforming the criminal justice system, addressing climate change, and controlling infectious diseases, particularly those of global and regional importance. In 2005, Indonesia reached a historic peace agreement with armed separatists in Aceh, which led to democratic elections in Aceh in December 2006. Indonesia continues to face low intensity armed resistance in Papua by the separatist Free Papua Movement.

GEOGRAPHY :: INDONESIA

LOCATION:
Southeastern Asia, archipelago between the Indian Ocean and the Pacific Ocean

GEOGRAPHIC COORDINATES:
5 00 S, 120 00 E

MAP REFERENCES:
Southeast Asia

AREA:
total: 1,904,569 sq km

land: 1,811,569 sq km

water: 93,000 sq km

country comparison to the world: 16

AREA - COMPARATIVE:
slightly less than three times the size of Texas

LAND BOUNDARIES:
total: 2,958 km

border countries (3): Malaysia 1881 km, Papua New Guinea 824 km, Timor-Leste 253 km

COASTLINE:
54,716 km

MARITIME CLAIMS:
territorial sea: 12 nm

exclusive economic zone: 200 nm

measured from claimed archipelagic straight baselines

CLIMATE:
tropical; hot, humid; more moderate in highlands

TERRAIN:
mostly coastal lowlands; larger islands have interior mountains

ELEVATION:
mean elevation: 367 m

lowest point: Indian Ocean 0 m

highest point: Puncak Jaya 4,884 m

NATURAL RESOURCES:
petroleum, tin, natural gas, nickel, timber, bauxite, copper, fertile soils, coal, gold, silver

LAND USE:
agricultural land: 31.2% (2011 est.)

arable land: 13% (2011 est.) / permanent crops: 12.1% (2011 est.) / permanent pasture: 6.1% (2011 est.)

forest: 51.7% (2011 est.)

other: 17.1% (2011 est.)

IRRIGATED LAND:
67,220 sq km (2012)

POPULATION DISTRIBUTION:
major concentration on the island of Java, which is considered one of the most densely populated places on earth; of the outer islands (those surrounding Java and Bali), Sumatra contains some of the most significant clusters, particularly in the south near the Selat Sunda, and along the northeastern coast near Medan; the cities of Makasar (Sulawesi), Banjarmasin (Kalimantan) are also heavily populated

NATURAL HAZARDS:
occasional floods; severe droughts; tsunamis; earthquakes; volcanoes; forest fires

volcanism: Indonesia contains the most volcanoes of any country in the world - some 76 are historically active; significant volcanic activity occurs on Java, Sumatra, the Sunda Islands, Halmahera Island, Sulawesi Island, Sangihe Island, and in the Banda Sea; Merapi (2,968 m), Indonesia's most active volcano and in eruption since 2010, has been deemed a Decade Volcano by the International Association of Volcanology and Chemistry of the Earth's Interior, worthy of study due to its explosive history and close proximity to human populations; other notable historically active volcanoes include Agung, Awu, Karangetang, Krakatau (Krakatoa), Makian, Raung, and Tambora; see note 2 under "Geography - note"

ENVIRONMENT - CURRENT ISSUES:

large-scale deforestation (much of it illegal) and related wildfires cause heavy smog; over-exploitation of marine resources; environmental problems associated with rapid urbanization and economic development, including air pollution, traffic congestion, garbage management, and reliable water and waste water services; water pollution from industrial wastes, sewage

ENVIRONMENT - INTERNATIONAL AGREEMENTS:

party to: Biodiversity, Climate Change, Climate Change-Kyoto Protocol, Desertification, Endangered Species, Hazardous Wastes, Law of the Sea, Ozone Layer Protection, Ship Pollution, Tropical Timber 83, Tropical Timber 94, Wetlands

signed, but not ratified: Marine Life Conservation

GEOGRAPHY - NOTE:

note 1: according to Indonesia's National Coordinating Agency for Survey and Mapping, the total number of islands in the archipelago is 13,466, of which 922 are permanently inhabited (Indonesia is the world's largest country comprised solely of islands); the country straddles the equator and occupies a strategic location astride or along major sea lanes from the Indian Ocean to the Pacific Ocean

note 2: Indonesia is one of the countries along the Ring of Fire, a belt of active volcanoes and earthquake epicenters bordering the Pacific Ocean; up to 90% of the world's earthquakes and some 75% of the world's volcanoes occur within the Ring of Fire

note 3: despite having the fourth largest population in the world, Indonesia is the most heavily forested region on earth after the Amazon

PEOPLE AND SOCIETY :: INDONESIA

POPULATION:
262,787,403 (July 2018 est.)

country comparison to the world: 4

NATIONALITY:

noun: Indonesian(s)

adjective: Indonesian

ETHNIC GROUPS:

Javanese 40.1%, Sundanese 15.5%, Malay 3.7%, Batak 3.6%, Madurese 3%, Betawi 2.9%, Minangkabau 2.7%, Buginese 2.7%, Bantenese 2%, Banjarese 1.7%, Balinese 1.7%, Acehnese 1.4%, Dayak 1.4%, Sasak 1.3%, Chinese 1.2%, other 15% (2010 est.)

LANGUAGES:

Bahasa Indonesia (official, modified form of Malay), English, Dutch, local dialects (of which the most widely spoken is Javanese)

note: more than 700 languages are used in Indonesia

RELIGIONS:

Muslim 87.2%, Protestant 7%, Roman Catholic 2.9%, Hindu 1.7%, other 0.9% (includes Buddhist and Confucian), unspecified 0.4% (2010 est.)

AGE STRUCTURE:

0-14 years: 24.63% (male 32,967,727 /female 31,757,882)

15-24 years: 16.94% (male 22,661,264 /female 21,852,006)

25-54 years: 42.44% (male 57,097,131 /female 54,433,239)

55-64 years: 8.73% (male 10,447,365 /female 12,494,036)

65 years and over: 7.26% (male 8,326,858 /female 10,749,895) (2018 est.)

DEPENDENCY RATIOS:

total dependency ratio: 49.2 (2015 est.)

youth dependency ratio: 41.6 (2015 est.)

elderly dependency ratio: 7.6 (2015 est.)

potential support ratio: 13.2 (2015 est.)

MEDIAN AGE:

total: 30.5 years (2018 est.)

male: 29.9 years

female: 31.1 years

country comparison to the world: 116

POPULATION GROWTH RATE:

0.83% (2018 est.)

country comparison to the world: 127

BIRTH RATE:

15.9 births/1,000 population (2018 est.)

country comparison to the world: 113

DEATH RATE:

6.5 deaths/1,000 population (2018 est.)

country comparison to the world: 143

NET MIGRATION RATE:

-1.1 migrant(s)/1,000 population (2018 est.)

country comparison to the world: 143

POPULATION DISTRIBUTION:

major concentration on the island of Java, which is considered one of the most densely populated places on earth; of the outer islands (those surrounding Java and Bali), Sumatra contains some of the most significant clusters, particularly in the south near the Selat Sunda, and along the northeastern coast near Medan; the cities of Makasar (Sulawesi), Banjarmasin (Kalimantan) are also heavily populated

URBANIZATION:

urban population: 56% of total population (2019)

rate of urbanization: 2.27% annual rate of change (2015-20 est.)

MAJOR URBAN AREAS - POPULATION:

10.639 million JAKARTA (capital), 3.277 million Bekasi, 2.922 million Surabaya, 2.558 million Bandung, 2.311 million Medan, 2.28 million Tangerang (2019)

SEX RATIO:

at birth: 1.05 male(s)/female

0-14 years: 1.04 male(s)/female

15-24 years: 1.04 male(s)/female

25-54 years: 1.05 male(s)/female

55-64 years: 0.84 male(s)/female

65 years and over: 0.77 male(s)/female

total population: 1 male(s)/female (2018 est.)

MOTHER'S MEAN AGE AT FIRST BIRTH:

22.8 years (2012 est.)

note: median age at first birth among women 25-29

MATERNAL MORTALITY RATE:

177 deaths/100,000 live births (2017 est.)

country comparison to the world: 52

INFANT MORTALITY RATE:

total: 21.9 deaths/1,000 live births (2018 est.)

male: 25.7 deaths/1,000 live births

female: 17.9 deaths/1,000 live births

country comparison to the world: 73

LIFE EXPECTANCY AT BIRTH:

total population: 73.2 years (2018 est.)

male: 70.6 years

female: 76 years

country comparison to the world: 142

TOTAL FERTILITY RATE:

2.08 children born/woman (2018 est.)

country comparison to the world: 104

CONTRACEPTIVE PREVALENCE RATE:

61% (2016/17)

DRINKING WATER SOURCE:

improved:

urban: 94.2% of population

rural: 79.5% of population

total: 87.4% of population

unimproved:

urban: 5.8% of population

rural: 20.5% of population

total: 12.6% of population (2015 est.)

CURRENT HEALTH EXPENDITURE:

3.1% (2016)

PHYSICIANS DENSITY:

0.38 physicians/1,000 population (2017)

HOSPITAL BED DENSITY:

1.2 beds/1,000 population (2015)

SANITATION FACILITY ACCESS:

improved:

urban: 72.3% of population (2015 est.)

rural: 47.5% of population (2015 est.)

total: 60.8% of population (2015 est.)

unimproved:

urban: 27.7% of population (2015 est.)

rural: 52.5% of population (2015 est.)

total: 39.2% of population (2015 est.)

HIV/AIDS - ADULT PREVALENCE RATE:

0.4% (2018 est.)

country comparison to the world: 81

HIV/AIDS - PEOPLE LIVING WITH HIV/AIDS:

640,000 (2018 est.)

country comparison to the world: 14

HIV/AIDS - DEATHS:

38,000 (2018 est.)

country comparison to the world: 5

MAJOR INFECTIOUS DISEASES:

degree of risk: very high (2016)

food or waterborne diseases: bacterial diarrhea, hepatitis A, and typhoid fever (2016)

vectorborne diseases: dengue fever and malaria (2016)

OBESITY - ADULT PREVALENCE RATE:

6.9% (2016)

country comparison to the world: 162

CHILDREN UNDER THE AGE OF 5 YEARS UNDERWEIGHT:

19.9% (2013)

country comparison to the world: 28

EDUCATION EXPENDITURES:

3.6% of GDP (2015)

country comparison to the world: 123

LITERACY:

definition: age 15 and over can read and write

total population: 95.4%

male: 97.2%

female: 93.6% (2016 est.)

SCHOOL LIFE EXPECTANCY (PRIMARY TO TERTIARY EDUCATION):

total: 13 years

male: 13 years

female: 13 years (2017)

UNEMPLOYMENT, YOUTH AGES 15-24:

total: 15.6%

male: 15.6%

female: 15.6% (2017 est.)

country comparison to the world: 86

GOVERNMENT :: INDONESIA

COUNTRY NAME:

conventional long form: Republic of Indonesia

conventional short form: Indonesia

local long form: Republik Indonesia

local short form: Indonesia

former: Netherlands East Indies, Dutch East Indies

etymology: the name is an 18th-century construct of two Greek words, "Indos" (India) and "nesoi" (islands), meaning "Indian islands"

GOVERNMENT TYPE:

presidential republic

CAPITAL:

name: Jakarta

geographic coordinates: 6 10 S, 106 49 E

time difference: UTC+7 (12 hours ahead of Washington, DC, during Standard Time)

note: Indonesia has three time zones

etymology: "Jakarta" derives from the Sanscrit "Jayakarta" meaning "victorious city" and refers to a successful defeat and expulsion of the Portuguese in 1527; previously the port had been named "Sunda Kelapa"

ADMINISTRATIVE DIVISIONS:

31 provinces (provinsi-provinsi, singular - provinsi), 1 autonomous province*, 1 special region** (daerah-daerah istimewa, singular - daerah istimewa), and 1 national capital district*** (daerah khusus ibukota); Aceh*, Bali, Banten, Bengkulu, Gorontalo, Jakarta***, Jambi, Jawa Barat (West Java), Jawa Tengah (Central Java), Jawa Timur (East Java), Kalimantan Barat (West Kalimantan), Kalimantan Selatan (South Kalimantan), Kalimantan Tengah (Central Kalimantan), Kalimantan Timur (East Kalimantan), Kalimantan Utara (North Kalimantan), Kepulauan Bangka Belitung (Bangka Belitung Islands), Kepulauan Riau (Riau Islands), Lampung, Maluku, Maluku Utara (North Maluku), Nusa Tenggara Barat (West Nusa Tenggara), Nusa Tenggara Timur (East Nusa Tenggara), Papua, Papua Barat (West Papua), Riau, Sulawesi Barat (West Sulawesi), Sulawesi Selatan (South Sulawesi), Sulawesi Tengah (Central Sulawesi),

Sulawesi Tenggara (Southeast Sulawesi), Sulawesi Utara (North Sulawesi), Sumatera Barat (West Sumatra), Sumatera Selatan (South Sumatra), Sumatera Utara (North Sumatra), Yogyakarta**

note: following the implementation of decentralization beginning on 1 January 2001, regencies and municipalities have become the key administrative units responsible for providing most government services

INDEPENDENCE:

17 August 1945 (declared independence from the Netherlands)

NATIONAL HOLIDAY:

Independence Day, 17 August (1945)

CONSTITUTION:

history: drafted July to August 1945, effective 18 August 1945, abrogated by 1949 and 1950 constitutions; 1945 constitution restored 5 July 1959

amendments: proposed by the People's Consultative Assembly, with at least two thirds of its members present; passage requires simple majority vote by the Assembly membership; constitutional articles on the unitary form of the state cannot be amended; amended several times, last in 2002 (2017)

LEGAL SYSTEM:

civil law system based on the Roman-Dutch model and influenced by customary law

INTERNATIONAL LAW ORGANIZATION PARTICIPATION:

has not submitted an ICJ jurisdiction declaration; non-party state to the ICCt

CITIZENSHIP:

citizenship by birth: no

citizenship by descent only: at least one parent must be a citizen of Indonesia

dual citizenship recognized: no

residency requirement for naturalization: 5 continuous years

SUFFRAGE:

17 years of age; universal and married persons regardless of age

EXECUTIVE BRANCH:

chief of state: President Joko WIDODO (since 20 October 2014, reelected 17 April 2019, inauguration 19 October 2019); Vice President Jusuf KALLA (since 20 October 2014); note - the president is both chief of state and head of government (2019)

head of government: President Joko WIDODO (since 20 October 2014); Vice President Jusuf KALLA (since 20 October 2014) (2019)

cabinet: Cabinet appointed by the president

elections/appointments: president and vice president directly elected by absolute majority popular vote for a 5-year term (eligible for a second term); election last held on 17 April 2019 (next election 2024)

election results: Joko WIDODO elected president; percent of vote - Joko WIDODO (PDI-P) 55.5%, PRABOWO Subianto (GERINDRA) 44.5%

LEGISLATIVE BRANCH:

description: bicameral People's Consultative Assembly or Majelis Permusyawaratan Rakyat consists of: Regional Representative Council or Dewan Perwakilan Daerah (132 seats; non-partisan members directly elected in multi-seat constituencies - 4 each from the country's 33 electoral districts - by proportional representation vote to serve 5-year terms); note - the Regional Representative Council has no legislative authority
House of Representatives or Dewan Perwakilan Rakyat (560 seats; members directly elected in multi-seat constituencies by single non-transferable vote to serve 5-year terms) (2019)

elections: Regional Representative Council - last held 17 April 2019 (next to be held 2024)
House of Representatives - last held on 17 April 2019 (next to be held 2024) (2019)

election results: Regional Representative Council - all seats elected on a non-partisan basis
House of Representatives - percent of vote by party - PDI-P 19.3%, Gerindra 12.6%, Golkar 12.3%, PKB 9.7%, Nasdem 9.1%, PKS 8.2%, PD 7.8%, PAN 6.8%, PPP 4.5%, other 9.6%; seats by party - PDI-P 109, Golkar 91, Gerindra 73, PD 61, PAN 49, PKB 47, PKS 40, PPP 39, Nasdem 35, Hanura 16; composition - men 475, women 100, percent of women 17.9%; total People's Consultative Assembly percent of women 28% (2019)

JUDICIAL BRANCH:

highest courts: Supreme Court or Mahkamah Agung (51 judges divided into 8 chambers); Constitutional Court or Mahkamah Konstitusi (consists of 9 judges)

judge selection and term of office: Supreme Court judges nominated by Judicial Commission, appointed by president with concurrence of parliament; judges serve until retirement at age 65; Constitutional Court judges - 3 nominated by president, 3 by Supreme Court, and 3 by parliament; judges appointed by the president; judges serve until mandatory retirement at age 70

subordinate courts: High Courts of Appeal, district courts, religious courts

POLITICAL PARTIES AND LEADERS:

Democrat Party or PD [Susilo Bambang YUDHOYONO]
Functional Groups Party or GOLKAR [Airlangga HARTARTO]
Great Indonesia Movement Party or GERINDRA [PRABOWO Subianto Djojohadikusumo]
Indonesia Democratic Party-Struggle or PDI-P [MEGAWATI Sukarnoputri]
National Awakening Party or PKB [Muhaiman ISKANDAR]
National Democratic Party or NasDem [Surya PALOH]
National Mandate Party or PAN [Zulkifli HASAN]
Party of the Functional Groups or Golkar [Airlangga HARTARTO]
People's Conscience Party or HANURA [Oesman Sapta ODANG]
Prosperous Justice Party or PKS [Muhammad Sohibul IMAN]
United Development Party or PPP [Muhammad ROMAHURMUZIY] (2019)

INTERNATIONAL ORGANIZATION PARTICIPATION:

ADB, APEC, ARF, ASEAN, BIS, CD, CICA (observer), CP, D-8, EAS, EITI (compliant country), FAO, G-11, G-15, G-20, G-77, IAEA, IBRD, ICAO, ICC (national committees), ICRM, IDA, IDB, IFAD, IFC, IFRCS, IHO, ILO, IMF, IMO, IMSO, Interpol, IOC, IOM (observer), IORA, IPU, ISO, ITSO, ITU, ITUC (NGOs), MIGA, MINURSO, MINUSTAH, MONUSCO, MSG (associate member), NAM, OECD (enhanced engagement), OIC, OPCW, PIF (partner), UN, UNAMID, UNCTAD, UNESCO, UNIDO, UNIFIL, UNISFA, UNMIL, UNWTO, UPU,

WCO, WFTU (NGOs), WHO, WIPO, WMO, WTO

DIPLOMATIC REPRESENTATION IN THE US:

Ambassador Mahendra SIREGAR (since 8 April 2019)

chancery: 2020 Massachusetts Avenue NW, Washington, DC 20036

telephone: [1] (202) 775-5200

FAX: [1] (202) 775-5365

consulate(s) general: Chicago, Houston, Los Angeles, New York, San Francisco

DIPLOMATIC REPRESENTATION FROM THE US:

chief of mission: Ambassador Joseph R. DONOVAN, Jr. (since 12 January 2017)

telephone: [62] (21) 5083-1000 (2018)

embassy: Jalan Medan Merdeka Selatan 3-5, Jakarta 10110

mailing address: Unit 8129, Box 1, FPO AP 96520

FAX: [62] (21) 2395-1697 (2018)

consulate(s) general: Surabaya

consulate(s): Medan

FLAG DESCRIPTION:

two equal horizontal bands of red (top) and white; the colors derive from the banner of the Majapahit Empire of the 13th-15th centuries; red symbolizes courage, white represents purity

note: similar to the flag of Monaco, which is shorter; also similar to the flag of Poland, which is white (top) and red

NATIONAL SYMBOL(S):

garuda (mythical bird); national colors: red, white

NATIONAL ANTHEM:

name: "Indonesia Raya" (Great Indonesia)

lyrics/music: Wage Rudolf SOEPRATMAN

note: adopted 1945

ECONOMY :: INDONESIA

ECONOMY - OVERVIEW:

Indonesia, the largest economy in Southeast Asia, has seen a slowdown in growth since 2012, mostly due to the end of the commodities export boom. During the global financial crisis, Indonesia outperformed its regional neighbors and joined China and India as the only G20 members posting growth. Indonesia's annual budget deficit is capped at 3% of GDP, and the Government of Indonesia lowered its debt-to-GDP ratio from a peak of 100% shortly after the Asian financial crisis in 1999 to 34% today. In May 2017 Standard & Poor's became the last major ratings agency to upgrade Indonesia's sovereign credit rating to investment grade.

Poverty and unemployment, inadequate infrastructure, corruption, a complex regulatory environment, and unequal resource distribution among its regions are still part of Indonesia's economic landscape. President Joko WIDODO - elected in July 2014 – seeks to develop Indonesia's maritime resources and pursue other infrastructure development, including significantly increasing its electrical power generation capacity. Fuel subsidies were significantly reduced in early 2015, a move which has helped the government redirect its spending to development priorities. Indonesia, with the nine other ASEAN members, will continue to move towards participation in the ASEAN Economic Community, though full implementation of economic integration has not yet materialized.

GDP (PURCHASING POWER PARITY):

$3.25 trillion (2017 est.)

$3.093 trillion (2016 est.)

$2.945 trillion (2015 est.)

note: data are in 2017 dollars

country comparison to the world: 7

GDP (OFFICIAL EXCHANGE RATE):

$1.015 trillion (2017 est.)

GDP - REAL GROWTH RATE:

5.1% (2017 est.)

5% (2016 est.)

4.9% (2015 est.)

country comparison to the world: 47

GDP - PER CAPITA (PPP):

$12,400 (2017 est.)

$12,000 (2016 est.)

$11,500 (2015 est.)

note: data are in 2017 dollars

country comparison to the world: 127

GROSS NATIONAL SAVING:

31.7% of GDP (2017 est.)

32% of GDP (2016 est.)

32% of GDP (2015 est.)

country comparison to the world: 27

GDP - COMPOSITION, BY END USE:

household consumption: 57.3% (2017 est.)

government consumption: 9.1% (2017 est.)

investment in fixed capital: 32.1% (2017 est.)

investment in inventories: 0.3% (2017 est.)

exports of goods and services: 20.4% (2017 est.)

imports of goods and services: -19.2% (2017 est.)

GDP - COMPOSITION, BY SECTOR OF ORIGIN:

agriculture: 13.7% (2017 est.)

industry: 41% (2017 est.)

services: 45.4% (2017 est.)

AGRICULTURE - PRODUCTS:

rubber and similar products, palm oil, poultry, beef, forest products, shrimp, cocoa, coffee, medicinal herbs, essential oil, fish and its similar products, and spices

INDUSTRIES:

petroleum and natural gas, textiles, automotive, electrical appliances, apparel, footwear, mining, cement, medical instruments and appliances, handicrafts, chemical fertilizers, plywood, rubber, processed food, jewelry, and tourism

INDUSTRIAL PRODUCTION GROWTH RATE:

4.1% (2017 est.)

country comparison to the world: 73

LABOR FORCE:

125 million (2016 est.)

country comparison to the world: 4

LABOR FORCE - BY OCCUPATION:

agriculture: 32%

industry: 21%

services: 47% (2016 est.)

UNEMPLOYMENT RATE:

5.4% (2017 est.)

5.6% (2016 est.)

country comparison to the world: 79

POPULATION BELOW POVERTY LINE:

10.9% (2016 est.)

HOUSEHOLD INCOME OR CONSUMPTION BY PERCENTAGE SHARE:

lowest 10%: 3.4%

highest 10%: 28.2% (2010)

DISTRIBUTION OF FAMILY INCOME - GINI INDEX:

36.8 (2009)

39.4 (2005)

country comparison to the world: 84

BUDGET:

revenues: 131.7 billion (2017 est.)

expenditures: 159.6 billion (2017 est.)

TAXES AND OTHER REVENUES:

13% (of GDP) (2017 est.)

country comparison to the world: 208

BUDGET SURPLUS (+) OR DEFICIT (-):

-2.7% (of GDP) (2017 est.)

country comparison to the world: 121

PUBLIC DEBT:

28.8% of GDP (2017 est.)

28.3% of GDP (2016 est.)

country comparison to the world: 166

FISCAL YEAR:

calendar year

INFLATION RATE (CONSUMER PRICES):

3.8% (2017 est.)

3.5% (2016 est.)

country comparison to the world: 150

CENTRAL BANK DISCOUNT RATE:

6.37% (31 December 2010)

6.46% (31 December 2009)

note: this figure represents the 3-month SBI rate; the Bank of Indonesia has not employed the one-month SBI since September 2010

country comparison to the world: 65

COMMERCIAL BANK PRIME LENDING RATE:

11.07% (31 December 2017 est.)

11.89% (31 December 2016 est.)

note: these figures represent the average annualized rate on working capital loans

country comparison to the world: 74

STOCK OF NARROW MONEY:

$102.7 billion (31 December 2017 est.)

$92.11 billion (31 December 2016 est.)

country comparison to the world: 40

STOCK OF BROAD MONEY:

$102.7 billion (31 December 2017 est.)

$92.11 billion (31 December 2016 est.)

country comparison to the world: 40

STOCK OF DOMESTIC CREDIT:

$422.4 billion (31 December 2017 est.)

$397.7 billion (31 December 2016 est.)

country comparison to the world: 29

MARKET VALUE OF PUBLICLY TRADED SHARES:

$523.8 billion (31 December 2017 est.)

$426 billion (31 December 2016 est.)

$353.3 billion (31 December 2015 est.)

country comparison to the world: 22

CURRENT ACCOUNT BALANCE:

-$17.33 billion (2017 est.)

-$16.95 billion (2016 est.)

country comparison to the world: 197

EXPORTS:

$168.9 billion (2017 est.)

$144.4 billion (2016 est.)

country comparison to the world: 29

EXPORTS - PARTNERS:

China 13.6%, US 10.6%, Japan 10.5%, India 8.4%, Singapore 7.6%, Malaysia 5.1%, South Korea 4.8% (2017)

EXPORTS - COMMODITIES:

mineral fuels, animal or vegetable fats (includes palm oil), electrical machinery, rubber, machinery and mechanical appliance parts

IMPORTS:

$150.1 billion (2017 est.)

$129.2 billion (2016 est.)

country comparison to the world: 31

IMPORTS - COMMODITIES:

mineral fuels, boilers, machinery, and mechanical parts, electric machinery, iron and steel, foodstuffs

IMPORTS - PARTNERS:

China 23.2%, Singapore 10.9%, Japan 10%, Thailand 6%, Malaysia 5.6%, South Korea 5.3%, US 5.2% (2017)

RESERVES OF FOREIGN EXCHANGE AND GOLD:

$130.2 billion (31 December 2017 est.)

country comparison to the world: 19

DEBT - EXTERNAL:

$344.4 billion (31 December 2017 est.)

country comparison to the world: 30

STOCK OF DIRECT FOREIGN INVESTMENT - AT HOME:

$251.5 billion (31 December 2017 est.)

$229.1 billion (31 December 2016 est.)

country comparison to the world: 26

STOCK OF DIRECT FOREIGN INVESTMENT - ABROAD:

$20.5 billion (31 December 2017 est.)

$18.42 billion (31 December 2016 est.)

country comparison to the world: 53

EXCHANGE RATES:

Indonesian rupiah (IDR) per US dollar -

13,385 (2017 est.)

13,308.3 (2016 est.)

13,308.3 (2015 est.)

13,389.4 (2014 est.)

11,865.2 (2013 est.)

ENERGY :: INDONESIA

ELECTRICITY ACCESS:

population without electricity: 14 million (2017)

electrification - total population: 97.6% (2016)

electrification - urban areas: 100% (2016)

electrification - rural areas: 94.8% (2016)

ELECTRICITY - PRODUCTION:

235.4 billion kWh (2016 est.)

country comparison to the world: 20

ELECTRICITY - CONSUMPTION:

213.4 billion kWh (2016 est.)

country comparison to the world: 20

ELECTRICITY - EXPORTS:

0 kWh (2017 est.)

country comparison to the world: 149

ELECTRICITY - IMPORTS:

693 million kWh (2016 est.)

country comparison to the world: 76

ELECTRICITY - INSTALLED GENERATING CAPACITY:

61.43 million kW (2016 est.)

country comparison to the world: 19

ELECTRICITY - FROM FOSSIL FUELS:

85% of total installed capacity (2016 est.)

country comparison to the world: 71

ELECTRICITY - FROM NUCLEAR FUELS:

0% of total installed capacity (2017 est.)

country comparison to the world: 110

ELECTRICITY - FROM HYDROELECTRIC PLANTS:

9% of total installed capacity (2017 est.)

country comparison to the world: 118

ELECTRICITY - FROM OTHER RENEWABLE SOURCES:

6% of total installed capacity (2017 est.)

country comparison to the world: 99

CRUDE OIL - PRODUCTION:

772,000 bbl/day (2018 est.)

country comparison to the world: 24

CRUDE OIL - EXPORTS:

302,300 bbl/day (2015 est.)

country comparison to the world: 27

CRUDE OIL - IMPORTS:

498,500 bbl/day (2015 est.)

country comparison to the world: 18

CRUDE OIL - PROVED RESERVES:

3.31 billion bbl (1 January 2018 est.)

country comparison to the world: 28

REFINED PETROLEUM PRODUCTS - PRODUCTION:

950,000 bbl/day (2015 est.)

country comparison to the world: 18

REFINED PETROLEUM PRODUCTS - CONSUMPTION:

1.601 million bbl/day (2016 est.)

country comparison to the world: 14

REFINED PETROLEUM PRODUCTS - EXPORTS:

79,930 bbl/day (2015 est.)

country comparison to the world: 47

REFINED PETROLEUM PRODUCTS - IMPORTS:

591,500 bbl/day (2015 est.)

country comparison to the world: 15

NATURAL GAS - PRODUCTION:

72.09 billion cu m (2017 est.)

country comparison to the world: 12

NATURAL GAS - CONSUMPTION:

42.32 billion cu m (2017 est.)

country comparison to the world: 23

NATURAL GAS - EXPORTS:

29.78 billion cu m (2017 est.)

country comparison to the world: 12

NATURAL GAS - IMPORTS:

0 cu m (2017 est.)

country comparison to the world: 141

NATURAL GAS - PROVED RESERVES:

2.866 trillion cu m (1 January 2018 est.)

country comparison to the world: 12

CARBON DIOXIDE EMISSIONS FROM CONSUMPTION OF ENERGY:

540.7 million Mt (2017 est.)

country comparison to the world: 12

COMMUNICATIONS :: INDONESIA

TELEPHONES - FIXED LINES:

total subscriptions: 11,172,021

subscriptions per 100 inhabitants: 4 (2017 est.)

country comparison to the world: 18

TELEPHONES - MOBILE CELLULAR:

total subscriptions: 458,923,202

subscriptions per 100 inhabitants: 176 (2017 est.)

country comparison to the world: 3

TELEPHONE SYSTEM:

general assessment: domestic service includes an interisland microwave system, an HF radio police net, and a domestic satellite communications system; international service good; Indonesia has very low fixed line and fixed broadband penetration, high mobile penetration and moderate mobile broadband penetration (2018)

domestic: fixed-line 4 per 100 and mobile-cellular 175 per 100 persons; coverage provided by existing network has been expanded by use of over 200,000 telephone kiosks many located in remote areas; mobile-cellular subscribership growing rapidly (2018)

international: country code - 62; landing points for the SEA-ME-WE-3 & 5, DAMAI, JASUKA, BDM, Dumai-Melaka Cable System, IGG, JIBA, Link 1, 3, 4, & 5, PGASCOM, B3J2, Tanjung Pandam-Sungai Kakap Cable System, JAKABARE, JAYABAYA, INDIGO-West, Matrix Cable System, ASC, SJJK, Jaka2LaDeMa, S-U-B Cable System, JBCS, MKCS, BALOK, Palapa Ring East, West and Middle, SMPCS Packet-1 and 2, LTCS, TSCS, SEA-US and Kamal Domestic Submarine Cable System, 35 submarine cable networks that provide links throughout Asia, the Middle East, Australia, Southeast Asia, Africa and Europe; satellite earth stations - 2 Intelsat (1 Indian Ocean and 1 Pacific Ocean) (2019)

BROADCAST MEDIA:

mixture of about a dozen national TV networks - 1 public broadcaster, the remainder private broadcasters - each with multiple transmitters; more than 100 local TV stations; widespread use of satellite and cable TV systems; public radio broadcaster operates 6 national networks, as well as regional and local stations; overall, more than 700 radio stations with more than 650 privately operated (2019)

INTERNET COUNTRY CODE:

.id

INTERNET USERS:

total: 65,525,226

percent of population: 25.4% (July 2016 est.)

country comparison to the world: 9

BROADBAND - FIXED SUBSCRIPTIONS:

total: 6,044,712

subscriptions per 100 inhabitants: 2 (2017 est.)

country comparison to the world: 25

MILITARY AND SECURITY :: INDONESIA

MILITARY EXPENDITURES:

0.72% of GDP (2018)

0.84% of GDP (2017)

0.88% of GDP (2016)

0.89% of GDP (2015)

0.78% of GDP (2014)

country comparison to the world: 135

MILITARY AND SECURITY FORCES:

Indonesian National Armed Forces (Tentara Nasional Indonesia, TNI): Army (TNI-Angkatan Darat (TNI-AD)), Navy (TNI-Angkatan Laut (TNI-AL), includes marines (Korps Marinir, KorMar), naval air arm), Air Force (TNI-Angkatan Udara (TNI-AU)), National Air Defense Command (Komando Pertahanan Udara Nasional (Kohanudnas)), Armed Forces Special Operations Command (Koopssus), Strategic Reserve Command (Kostrad) (2019)

MILITARY SERVICE AGE AND OBLIGATION:

18-45 years of age for voluntary military service, with selective conscription authorized; 2-year service obligation, with reserve obligation to age 45 (officers); Indonesian citizens only (2013)

MARITIME THREATS:

The International Maritime Bureau continues to report the territorial and offshore waters in the Strait of Malacca and South China Sea as high risk for piracy and armed robbery against ships; attacks declined for the third year in a row from 43 incidents in 2016 to 36 in 2018 due to aggressive maritime patrolling by regional authorities; in 2018, 29 commercial vessels were boarded and three crew members were taken hostage; hijacked vessels are often disguised and cargo diverted to ports in East Asia (2018)

TRANSPORTATION :: INDONESIA

NATIONAL AIR TRANSPORT SYSTEM:

number of registered air carriers: 29 (2015)

inventory of registered aircraft operated by air carriers: 550 (2015)

annual passenger traffic on registered air carriers: 88,685,767 (2015)

annual freight traffic on registered air carriers: 747,473,207 mt-km (2015)

CIVIL AIRCRAFT REGISTRATION COUNTRY CODE PREFIX:

PK (2016)

AIRPORTS:

673 (2013)

country comparison to the world: 10

AIRPORTS - WITH PAVED RUNWAYS:

total: 186 (2017)

over 3,047 m: 5 (2017)

2,438 to 3,047 m: 21 (2017)

1,524 to 2,437 m: 51 (2017)

914 to 1,523 m: 72 (2017)

under 914 m: 37 (2017)

AIRPORTS - WITH UNPAVED RUNWAYS:

total: 487 (2013)

1,524 to 2,437 m: 4 (2013)

914 to 1,523 m: 23 (2013)

under 914 m: 460 (2013)

HELIPORTS:

76 (2013)

PIPELINES:

1064 km condensate, 150 km condensate/gas, 11702 km gas, 119 km liquid petroleum gas, 7767 km oil, 77 km oil/gas/water, 728 km refined products, 53 km unknown, 44 km water (2013)

RAILWAYS:

total: 8,159 km (2014)

narrow gauge: 8,159 km 1.067-m gauge (565 km electrified) (2014)

note: 4,816 km operational

country comparison to the world: 27

ROADWAYS:

total: 496,607 km (2011)

paved: 283,102 km (2011)

unpaved: 213,505 km (2011)

country comparison to the world: 14

WATERWAYS:

21,579 km (2011)

country comparison to the world: 7

MERCHANT MARINE:

total: 9,053

by type: bulk carrier 97, container ship 205, general cargo 2203, oil tanker 567, other 5981 (2018)

country comparison to the world: 1

PORTS AND TERMINALS:

major seaport(s): Banjarmasin, Belawan, Kotabaru, Krueg Geukueh, Palembang, Panjang, Sungai Pakning, Tanjung Perak, Tanjung Priok

container port(s) (TEUs): Tanjung Perak (3,553,370), Tanjung Priok (6,090,000) (2017)

LNG terminal(s) (export): Bontang, Tangguh

LNG terminal(s) (import): Arun, Lampung, West Java

TERRORISM :: INDONESIA

TERRORIST GROUPS - HOME BASED:

ISIS-associated Jemaah Anshorut Daulah (JAD): aim(s): establish an Islamic caliphate in Indonesia
area(s) of operation: an ISIS-aligned coalition of cells located throughout the country (2018)

Islamic State of Iraq and ash-Sham (ISIS) network in Indonesia: aim(s): replace the Indonesian Government with an Islamic state and implement ISIS's strict interpretation of sharia
area(s) of operation: maintains a covert operational presence (2018)

Jemaah Islamiyah (JI): aim(s): overthrow the Indonesian Government and, ultimately, establish a pan-Islamic state across Southeast Asia
area(s) of operation: Indonesia (2018)

TRANSNATIONAL ISSUES :: INDONESIA

DISPUTES - INTERNATIONAL:

Indonesia has a stated foreign policy objective of establishing stable fixed land and maritime boundaries with all of its neighbors; three stretches of land borders with Timor-Leste have yet to be delimited, two of which are in the Oecussi exclave area, and no maritime or Exclusive Economic Zone (EEZ) boundaries have been established between the countries; all borders between Indonesia and Australia have been agreed upon bilaterally, but a 1997 treaty that would settle the last of their maritime and EEZ boundary has yet to be ratified by Indonesia's legislature; Indonesian groups challenge Australia's claim to Ashmore Reef; Australia has closed parts of the Ashmore and Cartier Reserve to Indonesian traditional fishing and placed restrictions on certain catches; land and maritime negotiations with Malaysia are ongoing, and disputed areas include the controversial Tanjung Datu and Camar Wulan border area in Borneo and the maritime boundary in the Ambalat oil block in the Celebes Sea; Indonesia and Singapore continue to work on finalizing their 1973 maritime boundary agreement by defining unresolved areas north of Indonesia's Batam Island; Indonesian secessionists, squatters, and illegal migrants create repatriation problems for Papua New Guinea; maritime delimitation talks continue with Palau; EEZ negotiations with Vietnam are ongoing, and the two countries in Fall 2011 agreed to work together to reduce illegal fishing along their maritime boundary

REFUGEES AND INTERNALLY DISPLACED PERSONS:

refugees (country of origin): 6,098 (Afghanistan) (2018)

IDPs: 16,000 (inter-communal, inter-faith, and separatist violence between 1998 and 2004 in Aceh and Papua; religious attacks and land conflicts in 2012 and 2013; most IDPs in Aceh, Maluku, East Nusa Tengarra) (2018)

ILLICIT DRUGS:

illicit producer of cannabis largely for domestic use; producer of methamphetamine and ecstasy; President WIDODO's war on drugs has led to an increase in death sentences and executions, particularly of foreign drug traffickers

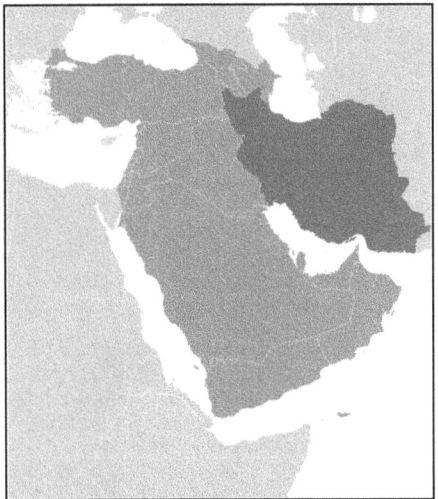

MIDDLE EAST :: IRAN

INTRODUCTION :: IRAN

BACKGROUND:

Known as Persia until 1935, Iran became an Islamic republic in 1979 after the ruling monarchy was overthrown and Shah Mohammad Reza PAHLAVI was forced into exile. Conservative clerical forces led by Ayatollah Ruhollah KHOMEINI established a theocratic system of government with ultimate political authority vested in a learned religious scholar referred to commonly as the Supreme Leader who, according to the constitution, is accountable only to the Assembly of Experts (AOE) - a popularly elected 88-member body of clerics. US-Iranian relations became strained when a group of Iranian students seized the US Embassy in Tehran in November 1979 and held embassy personnel hostages until mid-January 1981. The US cut off diplomatic relations with Iran in April 1980. During the period 1980-88, Iran fought a bloody, indecisive war with Iraq that eventually expanded into the Persian Gulf and led to clashes between US Navy and Iranian military forces. Iran has been designated a state sponsor of terrorism for its activities in Lebanon and elsewhere in the world and remains subject to US, UN, and EU economic sanctions and export controls because of its continued involvement in terrorism and concerns over possible military dimensions of its nuclear program. Following the election of reformer Hojjat ol-Eslam Mohammad KHATAMI as president in 1997 and a reformist Majles (legislature) in 2000, a campaign to foster political reform in response to popular dissatisfaction was initiated. The movement floundered as conservative politicians, supported by the Supreme Leader, unelected institutions of authority like the Council of Guardians, and the security services reversed and blocked reform measures while increasing security repression.

Starting with nationwide municipal elections in 2003 and continuing through Majles elections in 2004, conservatives reestablished control over Iran's elected government institutions, which culminated with the August 2005 inauguration of hardliner Mahmud AHMADINEZHAD as president. His controversial reelection in June 2009 sparked nationwide protests over allegations of electoral fraud, but the protests were quickly suppressed. Deteriorating economic conditions due primarily to government mismanagement and international sanctions prompted at least two major economically based protests in July and October 2012, but Iran's internal security situation remained stable. President AHMADINEZHAD's independent streak angered regime establishment figures, including the Supreme Leader, leading to conservative opposition to his agenda for the last year of his presidency, and an alienation of his political supporters. In June 2013 Iranians elected a centrist cleric Dr. Hasan Fereidun ROHANI to the presidency. He is a longtime senior member in the regime, but has made promises of reforming society and Iran's foreign policy. The UN Security Council has passed a number of resolutions calling for Iran to suspend its uranium enrichment and reprocessing activities and comply with its IAEA obligations and responsibilities, and in July 2015 Iran and the five permanent members, plus Germany (P5+1) signed the Joint Comprehensive Plan of Action (JCPOA) under which Iran agreed to restrictions on its nuclear program in exchange for sanctions relief. Iran held elections in 2016 for the AOE and Majles, resulting in a conservative-controlled AOE and a Majles that many Iranians perceive as more supportive of the ROHANI administration than the previous, conservative-dominated body. RUHANI was reelected president in May 2017. Economic concerns once again led to nationwide protests in December 2017 and January 2018 but they were contained by Iran's security services. In May 2018, the US withdrew from the JCPOA and reinstituted economic sanctions on Iran in November.

GEOGRAPHY :: IRAN

LOCATION:

Middle East, bordering the Gulf of Oman, the Persian Gulf, and the Caspian Sea, between Iraq and Pakistan

GEOGRAPHIC COORDINATES:

32 00 N, 53 00 E

MAP REFERENCES:

Middle East

AREA:

total: 1,648,195 sq km

land: 1,531,595 sq km

water: 116,600 sq km

country comparison to the world: 19

AREA - COMPARATIVE:

almost 2.5 times the size of Texas; slightly smaller than Alaska

LAND BOUNDARIES:

total: 5,894 km

border countries (7): Afghanistan 921 km, Armenia 44 km, Azerbaijan 689 km, Iraq 1599 km, Pakistan 959 km, Turkey 534 km, Turkmenistan 1148 km

COASTLINE:

2,440 km - note: Iran also borders the Caspian Sea (740 km)

MARITIME CLAIMS:

territorial sea: 12 nm

exclusive economic zone: bilateral agreements or median lines in the Persian Gulf

contiguous zone: 24 nm

continental shelf: natural prolongation

CLIMATE:

mostly arid or semiarid, subtropical along Caspian coast

TERRAIN:

rugged, mountainous rim; high, central basin with deserts, mountains; small, discontinuous plains along both coasts

ELEVATION:

mean elevation: 1,305 m

lowest point: Caspian Sea -28 m

highest point: Kuh-e Damavand 5,625 m

NATURAL RESOURCES:

petroleum, natural gas, coal, chromium, copper, iron ore, lead, manganese, zinc, sulfur

LAND USE:

agricultural land: 30.1% (2011 est.)

arable land: 10.8% (2011 est.) / permanent crops: 1.2% (2011 est.) / permanent pasture: 18.1% (2011 est.)

forest: 6.8% (2011 est.)

other: 63.1% (2011 est.)

IRRIGATED LAND:

95,530 sq km (2012)

POPULATION DISTRIBUTION:

population is concentrated in the north, northwest, and west, reflecting the position of the Zagros and Elburz Mountains; the vast dry areas in the center and eastern parts of the country, around the deserts of the Dasht-e Kavir and Dasht-e Lut, have a much lower population density

NATURAL HAZARDS:

periodic droughts, floods; dust storms, sandstorms; earthquakes

ENVIRONMENT - CURRENT ISSUES:

air pollution, especially in urban areas, from vehicle emissions, refinery operations, and industrial effluents; deforestation; overgrazing; desertification; oil pollution in the Persian Gulf; wetland losses from drought; soil degradation (salination); inadequate supplies of potable water; water pollution from raw sewage and industrial waste; urbanization

ENVIRONMENT - INTERNATIONAL AGREEMENTS:

party to: Biodiversity, Climate Change, Climate Change-Kyoto Protocol, Desertification, Endangered Species, Hazardous Wastes, Marine Dumping, Ozone Layer Protection, Ship Pollution, Wetlands

signed, but not ratified: Environmental Modification, Law of the Sea, Marine Life Conservation

GEOGRAPHY - NOTE:

strategic location on the Persian Gulf and Strait of Hormuz, which are vital maritime pathways for crude oil transport

PEOPLE AND SOCIETY :: IRAN

POPULATION:

83,024,745 (July 2018 est.)

country comparison to the world: 17

NATIONALITY:

noun: Iranian(s)

adjective: Iranian

ETHNIC GROUPS:

Persian, Azeri, Kurd, Lur, Baloch, Arab, Turkmen and Turkic tribes

LANGUAGES:

Persian (official), Azeri Turkic and Turkic dialects, Kurdish, Gilaki and Mazandarani, Luri, Balochi, Arabic

RELIGIONS:

Muslim (official) 99.4% (Shia 90-95%, Sunni 5-10%), other (includes Zoroastrian, Jewish, and Christian) 0.3%, unspecified 0.4% (2011 est.)

AGE STRUCTURE:

0-14 years: 24.23% (male 10,291,493 /female 9,823,838)

15-24 years: 14.05% (male 5,973,320 /female 5,689,501)

25-54 years: 48.86% (male 20,698,748 /female 19,863,223)

55-64 years: 7.39% (male 3,022,134 /female 3,113,443)

65 years and over: 5.48% (male 2,111,390 /female 2,437,655) (2018 est.)

DEPENDENCY RATIOS:

total dependency ratio: 40.2 (2015 est.)

youth dependency ratio: 33.1 (2015 est.)

elderly dependency ratio: 7.1 (2015 est.)

potential support ratio: 14.2 (2015 est.)

MEDIAN AGE:

total: 30.8 years (2018 est.)

male: 30.5 years

female: 31 years

country comparison to the world: 114

POPULATION GROWTH RATE:

1.19% (2018 est.)

country comparison to the world: 92

BIRTH RATE:

17.4 births/1,000 population (2018 est.)

country comparison to the world: 102

DEATH RATE:

5.3 deaths/1,000 population (2018 est.)

country comparison to the world: 186

NET MIGRATION RATE:

-0.2 migrant(s)/1,000 population (2018 est.)

country comparison to the world: 108

POPULATION DISTRIBUTION:

population is concentrated in the north, northwest, and west, reflecting the position of the Zagros and Elburz Mountains; the vast dry areas in the center and eastern parts of the country, around the deserts of the Dasht-e Kavir and Dasht-e Lut, have a much lower population density

URBANIZATION:

urban population: 75.4% of total population (2019)

rate of urbanization: 1.71% annual rate of change (2015-20 est.)

MAJOR URBAN AREAS - POPULATION:

9.014 million TEHRAN (capital), 3.152 million Mashhad, 2.086 million Esfahan, 1.628 million Shiraz, 1.581

million Karaj, 1.596 million Tabriz (2019)

SEX RATIO:
at birth: 1.05 male(s)/female

0-14 years: 1.05 male(s)/female

15-24 years: 1.05 male(s)/female

25-54 years: 1.04 male(s)/female

55-64 years: 0.97 male(s)/female

65 years and over: 0.87 male(s)/female

total population: 1.03 male(s)/female (2018 est.)

MATERNAL MORTALITY RATE:
16 deaths/100,000 live births (2017 est.)

country comparison to the world: 135

INFANT MORTALITY RATE:
total: 15.5 deaths/1,000 live births (2018 est.)

male: 16.6 deaths/1,000 live births

female: 14.4 deaths/1,000 live births

country comparison to the world: 98

LIFE EXPECTANCY AT BIRTH:
total population: 74.2 years (2018 est.)

male: 72.8 years

female: 75.6 years

country comparison to the world: 127

TOTAL FERTILITY RATE:
1.96 children born/woman (2018 est.)

country comparison to the world: 124

CONTRACEPTIVE PREVALENCE RATE:
77.4% (2010/11)

DRINKING WATER SOURCE:
improved:

urban: 97.7% of population

rural: 92.1% of population

total: 96.2% of population

unimproved:

urban: 2.3% of population

rural: 7.9% of population

total: 3.8% of population (2015 est.)

CURRENT HEALTH EXPENDITURE:
8.1% (2016)

PHYSICIANS DENSITY:
1.14 physicians/1,000 population (2015)

HOSPITAL BED DENSITY:
0.2 beds/1,000 population (2014)

SANITATION FACILITY ACCESS:
improved:

urban: 92.8% of population (2015 est.)

rural: 82.3% of population (2015 est.)

total: 90% of population (2015 est.)

unimproved:

urban: 7.2% of population (2015 est.)

rural: 17.7% of population (2015 est.)

total: 10% of population (2015 est.)

HIV/AIDS - ADULT PREVALENCE RATE:
0.1% (2018 est.)

country comparison to the world: 125

HIV/AIDS - PEOPLE LIVING WITH HIV/AIDS:
61,000 (2018 est.)

country comparison to the world: 57

HIV/AIDS - DEATHS:
2,600 (2018 est.)

country comparison to the world: 40

MAJOR INFECTIOUS DISEASES:
degree of risk: intermediate (2016)

food or waterborne diseases: bacterial diarrhea (2016)

vectorborne diseases: Crimean-Congo hemorrhagic fever (2016)

OBESITY - ADULT PREVALENCE RATE:
25.8% (2016)

country comparison to the world: 47

CHILDREN UNDER THE AGE OF 5 YEARS UNDERWEIGHT:
4.1% (2011)

country comparison to the world: 88

EDUCATION EXPENDITURES:
3.8% of GDP (2017)

country comparison to the world: 119

LITERACY:
definition: age 15 and over can read and write

total population: 85.5%

male: 90.4%

female: 80.8% (2016 est.)

SCHOOL LIFE EXPECTANCY (PRIMARY TO TERTIARY EDUCATION):
total: 15 years

male: 15 years

female: 15 years (2015)

UNEMPLOYMENT, YOUTH AGES 15-24:
total: 28.4%

male: 24.2%

female: 43.7% (2017 est.)

country comparison to the world: 39

GOVERNMENT :: IRAN

COUNTRY NAME:
conventional long form: Islamic Republic of Iran

conventional short form: Iran

local long form: Jomhuri-ye Eslami-ye Iran

local short form: Iran

former: Persia

etymology: name derives from the Avestan term "aryanam" meaning "Land of the Noble [Ones]"

GOVERNMENT TYPE:
theocratic republic

CAPITAL:
name: Tehran

geographic coordinates: 35 42 N, 51 25 E

time difference: UTC+3.5 (8.5 hours ahead of Washington, DC, during Standard Time)

daylight saving time: +1hr, begins fourth Wednesday in March; ends fourth Friday in September

ADMINISTRATIVE DIVISIONS:
31 provinces (ostanha, singular - ostan); Alborz, Ardabil, Azarbayjan-e Gharbi (West Azerbaijan), Azarbayjan-e Sharqi (East Azerbaijan), Bushehr, Chahar Mahal va Bakhtiari, Esfahan, Fars, Gilan, Golestan, Hamadan, Hormozgan, Ilam, Kerman, Kermanshah, Khorasan-e Jonubi (South Khorasan), Khorasan-e Razavi (Razavi Khorasan), Khorasan-e Shomali (North Khorasan), Khuzestan, Kohgiluyeh va Bowyer Ahmad, Kordestan, Lorestan, Markazi, Mazandaran, Qazvin, Qom, Semnan, Sistan va Baluchestan, Tehran, Yazd, Zanjan

INDEPENDENCE:
1 April 1979 (Islamic Republic of Iran proclaimed); notable earlier dates: ca. 550 B.C. (Achaemenid (Persian) Empire established); A.D. 1501 (Iran reunified under the Safavid Dynasty); 1794 (beginning of Qajar Dynasty); 12 December 1925 (modern Iran established under the PAHLAVI Dynasty)

NATIONAL HOLIDAY:

Republic Day, 1 April (1979)

CONSTITUTION:

history: previous 1906; latest adopted 24 October 1979, effective 3 December 1979

amendments: proposed by the supreme leader – after consultation with the Exigency Council – and submitted as an edict to the "Council for Revision of the Constitution," a body consisting of various executive, legislative, judicial, and academic leaders and members; passage requires absolute majority vote in a referendum and approval of the supreme leader; articles including Iran's political system, its religious basis, and its form of government cannot be amended; amended 1989 (2016)

LEGAL SYSTEM:

religious legal system based on secular and Islamic law

INTERNATIONAL LAW ORGANIZATION PARTICIPATION:

has not submitted an ICJ jurisdiction declaration; non-party state to the ICCt

CITIZENSHIP:

citizenship by birth: no

citizenship by descent only: the father must be a citizen of Iran

dual citizenship recognized: no

residency requirement for naturalization: 5 years

SUFFRAGE:

18 years of age; universal

EXECUTIVE BRANCH:

chief of state: Supreme Leader Ali Hoseini-KHAMENEI (since 4 June 1989)

head of government: President Hasan Fereidun ROHANI (since 3 August 2013); First Vice President Eshagh JAHANGIRI (since 5 August 2013)

cabinet: Council of Ministers selected by the president with legislative approval; the supreme leader has some control over appointments to several ministries

elections/appointments: supreme leader appointed for life by Assembly of Experts; president directly elected by absolute majority popular vote in 2 rounds if needed for a 4-year term (eligible for a second term and an additional nonconsecutive term); election last held on 19 May 2017 (next to be held in 2021)

election results: Hasan Fereidun ROHANI reelected president; percent of vote - Hasan Fereidun ROHANI (Moderation and Development Party) 58.8%, Ebrahim RAI'SI (Combat Clergy Association) 39.4% , Mostafa MIR-SALIM Islamic Coalition Party) 1.2%, Mostafa HASHEMITABA(Executives of Construction Party) 0.5%

note: 3 oversight bodies are also considered part of the executive branch of government

LEGISLATIVE BRANCH:

description: unicameral Islamic Consultative Assembly or Majles-e Shura-ye Eslami or Majles (290 seats; 285 members directly elected in single- and multi-seat constituencies by 2-round vote, and 1 seat each for Zoroastrians, Jews, Assyrian and Chaldean Christians, Armenians in the north of the country and Armenians in the south; members serve 4-year terms); note - all candidates to the Majles must be approved by the Council of Guardians, a 12-member group of which 6 are appointed by the supreme leader and 6 are jurists nominated by the judiciary and elected by the Majles

elections: first round held on 26 February 2016 and second round for 68 remaining seats held on 29 April 2016; (next full Majles election to be held in 2020)

election results: percent of vote by coalition - List of Hope 37.2%, Principlists Grand Coalition 25.9%, People's Voice Coalition 4.5%, joint Hope/People's Voice 4.1%, joint People's Voice/Principlist 0.3%, religious minorities 1.7%, independent 26.4%; seats by coalition - List of Hope 108, Principlists Grand Coalition 75, People's Voice Coalition 13, joint Hope/People's Voice 12, joint People's Voice/Principlist 1, religious minorities 5, independent 76; composition - men 273, women 17, percent of women 5.9%

JUDICIAL BRANCH:

highest courts: Supreme Court (consists of the president and NA judges)

judge selection and term of office: Supreme Court president appointed by the head of the High Judicial Council (HJC), a 5-member body to include the Supreme Court chief justice, the prosecutor general, and 3 clergy, in consultation with judges of the Supreme Court; president appointed for a single, renewable 5-year term; other judges appointed by the HJC; judge tenure NA

subordinate courts: Penal Courts I and II; Islamic Revolutionary Courts; Courts of Peace; Special Clerical Court (functions outside the judicial system and handles cases involving clerics); military courts

POLITICAL PARTIES AND LEADERS:

Combatant Clergy Association
Council for Coordinating the Reforms Front
Executives of Construction Party
Followers of the Guardianship of the Jurisprudent [Ali LARIJANI]
Front of Islamic Revolutionary Stability [Morteza AGHA-TEHRANI, general secretary]
Islamic Coalition Party
Islamic Iran Participation Front [associated with former President Mohammed KHATAMI]
Militant Clerics Society
Moderation and Development Party
National Trust Party
National Unity Party
Pervasive Coalition of Reformists [Ali SUFI, chairman] (includes Council for Coordinating the Reforms Front, National Trust Party, Union of Islamic Iran People Party, Moderation and Development Party)
Principlists Grand Coalition [Ali Reza ZAKANI] (includes Combatant Clergy Association and Islamic Coalition Party, Society of Devotees and Pathseekers of the Islamic Revolution, Front of Islamic Revolution Stability)
Progress, Welfare, and Justice Front
Progress and Justice Population of Islamic Iran or PJP [Hosein GHORBANZADEH, general secretary]
Resistance Front of Islamic Iran [Yadollah HABIBI, general secretary]
Steadfastness Front
Union of Islamic Iran People's Party
Wayfarers of the Islamic Revolution

INTERNATIONAL ORGANIZATION PARTICIPATION:

CICA, CP, D-8, ECO, FAO, G-15, G-24, G-77, IAEA, IBRD, ICAO, ICC (national committees), ICRM, IDA, IDB, IFAD, IFC, IFRCS, IHO, ILO, IMF, IMO, IMSO, Interpol, IOC, IOM, IPU, ISO, ITSO, ITU, MIGA, NAM, OIC, OPCW, OPEC, PCA, SAARC (observer), SCO (observer), UN, UNAMID, UNCTAD, UNESCO, UNHCR, UNIDO, UNITAR, UNWTO, UPU, WCO, WFTU

(NGOs), WHO, WIPO, WMO, WTO (observer)

DIPLOMATIC REPRESENTATION IN THE US:

none; Iran has an Interests Section in the Pakistani Embassy; address: Iranian Interests Section, Pakistani Embassy, 2209 Wisconsin Avenue NW, Washington, DC 20007; telephone: [1] (202) 965-4990; FAX [1] (202) 965-1073

DIPLOMATIC REPRESENTATION FROM THE US:

none; the US Interests Section is located in the Embassy of Switzerland, No. 39 Shahid Mousavi (Golestan 5th), Pasdaran Ave., Tehran, Iran; telephone [98] 21 2254 2178/2256 5273; FAX [98] 21 2258 0432

FLAG DESCRIPTION:

three equal horizontal bands of green (top), white, and red; the national emblem (a stylized representation of the word Allah in the shape of a tulip, a symbol of martyrdom) in red is centered in the white band; ALLAH AKBAR (God is Great) in white Arabic script is repeated 11 times along the bottom edge of the green band and 11 times along the top edge of the red band; green is the color of Islam and also represents growth, white symbolizes honesty and peace, red stands for bravery and martyrdom

NATIONAL SYMBOL(S):

lion; national colors: green, white, red

NATIONAL ANTHEM:

name: "Soroud-e Melli-ye Jomhouri-ye Eslami-ye Iran" (National Anthem of the Islamic Republic of Iran)

lyrics/music: multiple authors/Hassan RIAHI

note 1: adopted 1990; Iran has had six national anthems; the first, entitled Salam-e Shah (Royal Salute) was in use from 1873-1909; next came Salamati-ye Dowlat-e Elliye-ye Iran (Salute of the Sublime State of Persia, 1909-1933); it was followed by Sorud-e melli (The Imperial Anthem of Iran; 1933-1979), which chronicled the exploits of the Pahlavi Dynasty; Ey Iran (Oh Iran) functioned unofficially as the national anthem for a brief period between the ouster of the Shah in 1979 and the early days of the Islamic Republic in 1980; Payandeh Bada Iran (Long Live Iran) was used between 1980 and 1990 during the time of Ayatollah KHOMEINI

note 2: a recording of the current Iranian national anthem is unavailable since the US Navy Band does not record anthems for countries from which the US does not anticipate official visits; the US does not have diplomatic relations with Iran

ECONOMY :: IRAN

ECONOMY - OVERVIEW:

Iran's economy is marked by statist policies, inefficiencies, and reliance on oil and gas exports, but Iran also possesses significant agricultural, industrial, and service sectors. The Iranian government directly owns and operates hundreds of state-owned enterprises and indirectly controls many companies affiliated with the country's security forces. Distortions - including corruption, price controls, subsidies, and a banking system holding billions of dollars of non-performing loans - weigh down the economy, undermining the potential for private-sector-led growth.

Private sector activity includes small-scale workshops, farming, some manufacturing, and services, in addition to medium-scale construction, cement production, mining, and metalworking. Significant informal market activity flourishes and corruption is widespread.

The lifting of most nuclear-related sanctions under the Joint Comprehensive Plan of Action (JCPOA) in January 2016 sparked a restoration of Iran's oil production and revenue that drove rapid GDP growth, but economic growth declined in 2017 as oil production plateaued. The economy continues to suffer from low levels of investment and declines in productivity since before the JCPOA, and from high levels of unemployment, especially among women and college-educated Iranian youth.

In May 2017, the re-election of President Hasan RUHANI generated widespread public expectations that the economic benefits of the JCPOA would expand and reach all levels of society. RUHANI will need to implement structural reforms that strengthen the banking sector and improve Iran's business climate to attract foreign investment and encourage the growth of the private sector. Sanctions that are not related to Iran's nuclear program remain in effect, and these—plus fears over the possible re-imposition of nuclear-related sanctions—will continue to deter foreign investors from engaging with Iran.

GDP (PURCHASING POWER PARITY):

$1.64 trillion (2017 est.)

$1.581 trillion (2016 est.)

$1.405 trillion (2015 est.)

note: data are in 2017 dollars

country comparison to the world: 18

GDP (OFFICIAL EXCHANGE RATE):

$430.7 billion (2017 est.)

GDP - REAL GROWTH RATE:

3.7% (2017 est.)

12.5% (2016 est.)

-1.6% (2015 est.)

country comparison to the world: 89

GDP - PER CAPITA (PPP):

$20,100 (2017 est.)

$19,600 (2016 est.)

$17,700 (2015 est.)

note: data are in 2017 dollars

country comparison to the world: 89

GROSS NATIONAL SAVING:

37.9% of GDP (2017 est.)

37.6% of GDP (2016 est.)

35.2% of GDP (2015 est.)

country comparison to the world: 12

GDP - COMPOSITION, BY END USE:

household consumption: 49.7% (2017 est.)

government consumption: 14% (2017 est.)

investment in fixed capital: 20.6% (2017 est.)

investment in inventories: 14.5% (2017 est.)

exports of goods and services: 26% (2017 est.)

imports of goods and services: -24.9% (2017 est.)

GDP - COMPOSITION, BY SECTOR OF ORIGIN:

agriculture: 9.6% (2016 est.)

industry: 35.3% (2016 est.)

services: 55% (2017 est.)

AGRICULTURE - PRODUCTS:

wheat, rice, other grains, sugar beets, sugarcane, fruits, nuts, cotton; dairy products, wool; caviar

INDUSTRIES:

petroleum, petrochemicals, gas, fertilizer, caustic soda, textiles, cement and other construction materials, food processing (particularly sugar refining and vegetable oil production), ferrous and nonferrous metal fabrication, armaments

INDUSTRIAL PRODUCTION GROWTH RATE:
3% (2017 est.)

country comparison to the world: 103

LABOR FORCE:
30.5 million (2017 est.)

note: shortage of skilled labor

country comparison to the world: 21

LABOR FORCE - BY OCCUPATION:
agriculture: 16.3%

industry: 35.1%

services: 48.6% (2013 est.)

UNEMPLOYMENT RATE:
11.8% (2017 est.)

12.4% (2016 est.)

note: data are Iranian Government numbers

country comparison to the world: 157

POPULATION BELOW POVERTY LINE:
18.7% (2007 est.)

HOUSEHOLD INCOME OR CONSUMPTION BY PERCENTAGE SHARE:
lowest 10%: 2.6%

highest 10%: 29.6% (2005)

DISTRIBUTION OF FAMILY INCOME - GINI INDEX:
44.5 (2006)

country comparison to the world: 43

BUDGET:
revenues: 74.4 billion (2017 est.)

expenditures: 84.45 billion (2017 est.)

TAXES AND OTHER REVENUES:
17.3% (of GDP) (2017 est.)

country comparison to the world: 170

BUDGET SURPLUS (+) OR DEFICIT (-):
-2.3% (of GDP) (2017 est.)

country comparison to the world: 110

PUBLIC DEBT:
39.5% of GDP (2017 est.)

47.5% of GDP (2016 est.)

note: includes publicly guaranteed debt

country comparison to the world: 132

FISCAL YEAR:
21 March - 20 March

INFLATION RATE (CONSUMER PRICES):
9.6% (2017 est.)

9.1% (2016 est.)

note: official Iranian estimate

country comparison to the world: 202

CENTRAL BANK DISCOUNT RATE:
NA

COMMERCIAL BANK PRIME LENDING RATE:
18% (31 December 2017 est.)

18% (31 December 2016 est.)

country comparison to the world: 21

STOCK OF NARROW MONEY:
$48.08 billion (31 December 2017 est.)

$47.59 billion (31 December 2016 est.)

country comparison to the world: 54

STOCK OF BROAD MONEY:
$48.08 billion (31 December 2017 est.)

$47.59 billion (31 December 2016 est.)

country comparison to the world: 54

STOCK OF DOMESTIC CREDIT:
$348.2 billion (31 December 2017 est.)

$315.4 billion (31 December 2016 est.)

country comparison to the world: 33

MARKET VALUE OF PUBLICLY TRADED SHARES:
$89.43 billion (31 December 2015 est.)

$116.6 billion (31 December 2014 est.)

$345.8 billion (31 December 2013 est.)

country comparison to the world: 42

CURRENT ACCOUNT BALANCE:
$9.491 billion (2017 est.)

$16.28 billion (2016 est.)

country comparison to the world: 23

EXPORTS:
$101.4 billion (2017 est.)

$83.98 billion (2016 est.)

country comparison to the world: 37

EXPORTS - PARTNERS:
China 27.5%, India 15.1%, South Korea 11.4%, Turkey 11.1%, Italy 5.7%, Japan 5.3% (2017)

EXPORTS - COMMODITIES:
petroleum 60%, chemical and petrochemical products, fruits and nuts, carpets, cement, ore

IMPORTS:
$76.39 billion (2017 est.)

$63.14 billion (2016 est.)

country comparison to the world: 44

IMPORTS - COMMODITIES:
industrial supplies, capital goods, foodstuffs and other consumer goods, technical services

IMPORTS - PARTNERS:
UAE 29.8%, China 12.7%, Turkey 4.4%, South Korea 4%, Germany 4% (2017)

RESERVES OF FOREIGN EXCHANGE AND GOLD:
$120.6 billion (31 December 2017 est.)

$133.7 billion (31 December 2016 est.)

country comparison to the world: 21

DEBT - EXTERNAL:
$7.995 billion (31 December 2017 est.)

$8.196 billion (31 December 2016 est.)

country comparison to the world: 122

STOCK OF DIRECT FOREIGN INVESTMENT - AT HOME:
$50.33 billion (31 December 2017 est.)

$46.02 billion (31 December 2016 est.)

country comparison to the world: 58

STOCK OF DIRECT FOREIGN INVESTMENT - ABROAD:
$5.226 billion (31 December 2017 est.)

$4.656 billion (31 December 2016 est.)

country comparison to the world: 76

EXCHANGE RATES:
Iranian rials (IRR) per US dollar -

32,769.7 (2017 est.)

30,914.9 (2016 est.)

30,914.9 (2015 est.)

29,011.5 (2014 est.)

25,912 (2013 est.)

ENERGY :: IRAN

ELECTRICITY ACCESS:
electrification - total population: 100% (2016)

ELECTRICITY - PRODUCTION:
272.3 billion kWh (2016 est.)

country comparison to the world: 15

ELECTRICITY - CONSUMPTION:
236.3 billion kWh (2016 est.)

country comparison to the world: 17

ELECTRICITY - EXPORTS:
6.822 billion kWh (2015 est.)

country comparison to the world: 28

ELECTRICITY - IMPORTS:
4.221 billion kWh (2016 est.)

country comparison to the world: 44

ELECTRICITY - INSTALLED GENERATING CAPACITY:

77.6 million kW (2016 est.)

country comparison to the world: 16

ELECTRICITY - FROM FOSSIL FUELS:

84% of total installed capacity (2016 est.)

country comparison to the world: 75

ELECTRICITY - FROM NUCLEAR FUELS:

1% of total installed capacity (2017 est.)

country comparison to the world: 29

ELECTRICITY - FROM HYDROELECTRIC PLANTS:

15% of total installed capacity (2017 est.)

country comparison to the world: 103

ELECTRICITY - FROM OTHER RENEWABLE SOURCES:

0% of total installed capacity (2017 est.)

country comparison to the world: 193

CRUDE OIL - PRODUCTION:

4.251 million bbl/day (2018 est.)

country comparison to the world: 6

CRUDE OIL - EXPORTS:

750,200 bbl/day (2015 est.)

country comparison to the world: 16

CRUDE OIL - IMPORTS:

0 bbl/day (2015 est.)

country comparison to the world: 144

CRUDE OIL - PROVED RESERVES:

157.2 billion bbl (1 January 2018 est.)

country comparison to the world: 4

REFINED PETROLEUM PRODUCTS - PRODUCTION:

1.764 million bbl/day (2015 est.)

country comparison to the world: 11

REFINED PETROLEUM PRODUCTS - CONSUMPTION:

1.804 million bbl/day (2016 est.)

country comparison to the world: 12

REFINED PETROLEUM PRODUCTS - EXPORTS:

397,200 bbl/day (2015 est.)

country comparison to the world: 21

REFINED PETROLEUM PRODUCTS - IMPORTS:

64,160 bbl/day (2015 est.)

country comparison to the world: 72

NATURAL GAS - PRODUCTION:

214.5 billion cu m (2017 est.)

country comparison to the world: 3

NATURAL GAS - CONSUMPTION:

206.9 billion cu m (2017 est.)

country comparison to the world: 4

NATURAL GAS - EXPORTS:

11.64 billion cu m (2017 est.)

country comparison to the world: 18

NATURAL GAS - IMPORTS:

3.993 billion cu m (2017 est.)

country comparison to the world: 40

NATURAL GAS - PROVED RESERVES:

33.72 trillion cu m (1 January 2018 est.)

country comparison to the world: 2

CARBON DIOXIDE EMISSIONS FROM CONSUMPTION OF ENERGY:

638.3 million Mt (2017 est.)

country comparison to the world: 10

COMMUNICATIONS :: IRAN

TELEPHONES - FIXED LINES:

total subscriptions: 31,182,812

subscriptions per 100 inhabitants: 38 (2017 est.)

country comparison to the world: 9

TELEPHONES - MOBILE CELLULAR:

total subscriptions: 87,106,508

subscriptions per 100 inhabitants: 106 (2017 est.)

country comparison to the world: 18

TELEPHONE SYSTEM:

general assessment: opportunities for telecoms growth, but the disadvantage of lack of significant investment; one of the largest populations in the Middle East with a huge demand for services; mobile penetration is high with over 125% accessing 2G & 3G; 4G LTE becoming available; Iranian-net, is currently expanding a fiber network to have 8 million customers by 2020 (2018)

domestic: 38 per 100 for fixed-line and 106 per 100 for mobile-cellular subscriptions; heavy investment by Iran's state-owned telecom company has greatly improved and expanded both the fixed-line and mobile cellular networks; a huge percentage of the cell phones in the market have been smuggled into the country (2018)

international: country code - 98; landing points for Kuwait-Iran, GBICS & MENA, FALCON, OMRAN/3PEG Cable System, POI and UAE-Iran submarine fiber-optic cable to the Middle East, Africa and India; Trans-Asia-Europe (TAE) fiber-optic line runs from Azerbaijan through the northern portion of Iran to Turkmenistan with expansion to Georgia and Azerbaijan; HF radio and microwave radio relay to Turkey, Azerbaijan, Pakistan, Afghanistan, Turkmenistan, Syria, Kuwait, Tajikistan, and Uzbekistan; satellite earth stations - 13 (9 Intelsat and 4 Inmarsat) (2019)

BROADCAST MEDIA:

state-run broadcast media with no private, independent broadcasters; Islamic Republic of Iran Broadcasting (IRIB), the state-run TV broadcaster, operates 19 nationwide channels including a news channel, about 34 provincial channels, and several international channels; about 20 foreign Persian-language TV stations broadcasting on satellite TV are capable of being seen in Iran; satellite dishes are illegal and, while their use is subjectively tolerated, authorities confiscate satellite dishes from time to time; IRIB operates 16 nationwide radio networks, a number of provincial stations, and an external service; most major international broadcasters transmit to Iran (2019)

INTERNET COUNTRY CODE:

.ir

INTERNET USERS:

total: 36.07 million

percent of population: 44.1% (July 2016 est.)

country comparison to the world: 20

BROADBAND - FIXED SUBSCRIPTIONS:

total: 10,057,769

subscriptions per 100 inhabitants: 12 (2017 est.)

country comparison to the world: 17

MILITARY AND SECURITY :: IRAN

MILITARY EXPENDITURES:

2.67% of GDP (2018)

3.11% of GDP (2017)

2.97% of GDP (2016)

2.76% of GDP (2015)

2.28% of GDP (2014)

(Estimates)

country comparison to the world: 29

MILITARY AND SECURITY FORCES:

Islamic Republic of Iran Regular Forces (Artesh): Ground Forces, Navy (includes marines), Air Force, Air Defense Command; Islamic Revolutionary Guard Corps (Sepah, IRGC): Ground Forces, Navy (includes marines), Aerospace Force (controls strategic missile force), Qods Force (special operations), Cyber Command, Basij Paramilitary Forces (Popular Mobilization Army); Law Enforcement Forces (border and security troops, assigned to the armed forces in wartime) (2019)

MILITARY SERVICE AGE AND OBLIGATION:

18 years of age for compulsory military service; 16 years of age for volunteers; 17 years of age for Law Enforcement Forces; 15 years of age for Basij Forces (Popular Mobilization Army); conscript military service obligation is 18-24 months; women exempt from military service (2019)

MARITIME THREATS:

the Maritime Administration of the US Department of Transportation has issued a Maritime Advisory (2019-012-Persian Gulf, Strait of Hormuz, Gulf of Oman, Arabian Sea, Red Sea-Threats to US and International Shipping from Iran) effective 7 August 2019, which states in part that "heightened military activities and increased political tensions in this region continue to present risk to commercial shipping...there is a continued possibility that Iran and/or its regional proxies could take actions against US and partner interests in the region;" at present, Iran has seized two foreign-flagged tankers in the Persian Gulf; the US and UK navies have established Operation Sentinel to provide escorts for commercial shipping transiting the Persian Gulf, Strait of Hormuz, and Gulf of Oman

TRANSPORTATION :: IRAN

NATIONAL AIR TRANSPORT SYSTEM:

number of registered air carriers: 15 (2015)

inventory of registered aircraft operated by air carriers: 228 (2015)

annual passenger traffic on registered air carriers: 15,003,958 (2015)

annual freight traffic on registered air carriers: 107,184,869 mt-km (2015)

CIVIL AIRCRAFT REGISTRATION COUNTRY CODE PREFIX:

EP (2016)

AIRPORTS:

319 (2013)

country comparison to the world: 22

AIRPORTS - WITH PAVED RUNWAYS:

total: 140 (2017)

over 3,047 m: 42 (2017)

2,438 to 3,047 m: 29 (2017)

1,524 to 2,437 m: 26 (2017)

914 to 1,523 m: 36 (2017)

under 914 m: 7 (2017)

AIRPORTS - WITH UNPAVED RUNWAYS:

total: 179 (2013)

over 3,047 m: 1 (2013)

2,438 to 3,047 m: 2 (2013)

1,524 to 2,437 m: 9 (2013)

914 to 1,523 m: 135 (2013)

under 914 m: 32 (2013)

HELIPORTS:

26 (2013)

PIPELINES:

7 km condensate, 973 km condensate/gas, 20794 km gas, 570 km liquid petroleum gas, 8625 km oil, 7937 km refined products (2013)

RAILWAYS:

total: 8,484 km (2014)

standard gauge: 8,389.5 km 1.435-m gauge (189.5 km electrified) (2014)

broad gauge: 94 km 1.676-m gauge (2014)

country comparison to the world: 25

ROADWAYS:

total: 223,485 km (2018)

paved: 195,485 km (2018)

unpaved: 28,000 km (2018)

country comparison to the world: 23

WATERWAYS:

850 km (on Karun River; some navigation on Lake Urmia) (2012)

country comparison to the world: 69

MERCHANT MARINE:

total: 720

by type: bulk carrier 31, container ship 25, general cargo 336, oil tanker 17, other 311 (2018)

country comparison to the world: 30

PORTS AND TERMINALS:

major seaport(s): Bandar-e Asaluyeh, Bandar Abbas, Bandar Emam

container port(s) (TEUs): Bandar Abbas (2,607,000) (2017)

TERRORISM :: IRAN

TERRORIST GROUPS - HOME BASED:

Islamic Revolutionary Guard Corps (IRGC):

aim(s): protect Iran's Islamic Revolution; spread Shia influence; internal security, including border control, law enforcement, and suppressing domestic opposition; controls country's missiles and rockets; influence Iran's politics and economy

area of operation(s): headquartered in Tehran, throughout Iran

(2019)

Islamic Revolutionary Guard Corps - Qods Force (IRGC-QF):

aim(s): protect Iran's Islamic Revolution; spread Shia influence; conduct clandestine overseas operations, often supporting other terrorist organizations (including Sunni groups like the Taliban when their goals align) with significant funding, logistics, training, or weaponry to commit terror attacks, either directly or through proxies; recruit, train, and equip foreign Islamic revolutionary groups throughout the Middle East

area(s) of operations: headquartered in Tehran

(2019)

Jaysh al Adl:

note(s): formerly known as Jundallah

TERRORIST GROUPS - FOREIGN BASED:

al-Qa'ida (AQ): aim(s): unite the worldwide Muslim community, overthrow governments perceived as un-Islamic, and, ultimately, establish a pan-Islamic caliphate under a strict Salafi Muslim interpretation of sharia (2018)

Kurdistan Workers' Party (PKK):
aim(s): advance Kurdish autonomy, political, and cultural rights in Iran,

Turkey, Iraq, and Syria

area(s) of operation: operational in the northwest; majority of members inside Iran are Iranian Kurds, along with Kurds from Iraq, Syria, and Turkey (2018)

TRANSNATIONAL ISSUES :: IRAN

DISPUTES - INTERNATIONAL:

Iran protests Afghanistan's limiting flow of dammed Helmand River tributaries during drought; Iraq's lack of a maritime boundary with Iran prompts jurisdiction disputes beyond the mouth of the Shatt al Arab in the Persian Gulf; Iran and UAE dispute Tunb Islands and Abu Musa Island, which are occupied by Iran; Azerbaijan, Kazakhstan, and Russia ratified Caspian seabed delimitation treaties based on equidistance, while Iran continues to insist on a one-fifth slice of the sea; Afghan and Iranian commissioners have discussed boundary monument densification and resurvey

REFUGEES AND INTERNALLY DISPLACED PERSONS:

refugees (country of origin): 2.5-3.0 (1 million registered, 1.5-2.0 million undocumented) (Afghanistan) (2017); 28,268 (Iraq) (2018)

TRAFFICKING IN PERSONS:

current situation: Iran is a source, transit, and destination country for men, women, and children subjected to sex trafficking and forced labor; organized groups sex traffic Iranian women and children in Iran and to the UAE and Europe; the transport of girls from and through Iran en route to the Gulf for sexual exploitation or forced marriages is on the rise; Iranian children are also forced to work as beggars, street vendors, and in domestic workshops; Afghan boys forced to work in construction or agriculture are vulnerable to sexual abuse by their employers; Pakistani and Afghan migrants being smuggled to Europe often are subjected to forced labor, including debt bondage

tier rating: Tier 3 – Iran does not comply with the minimum standards for the elimination of trafficking, and is not making significant efforts to do so; the government does not share information on its anti-trafficking efforts, but publically available information from NGOs, the media, and international organizations indicates that Iran is not taking adequate measures to address its trafficking problems, particularly protecting victims; Iranian law does not prohibit all forms of human trafficking; female victims find it extremely difficult to get justice because Iranian courts accord women's testimony half the weight of men's, and female victims of sexual abuse, including trafficking, are likely to be prosecuted for adultery; the government did not identify or provide protection services to any victims and continued to punish victims for unlawful acts committed as a direct result of being trafficked; the government made some effort to cooperate with neighboring governments and an international organization to combat human trafficking and other crimes (2015)

ILLICIT DRUGS:

despite substantial interdiction efforts and considerable control measures along the border with Afghanistan, Iran remains one of the primary transshipment routes for Southwest Asian heroin to Europe; suffers one of the highest opiate addiction rates in the world, and has an increasing problem with synthetic drugs; regularly enforces the death penalty for drug offences; lacks anti-money laundering laws; has reached out to neighboring countries to share counter-drug intelligence

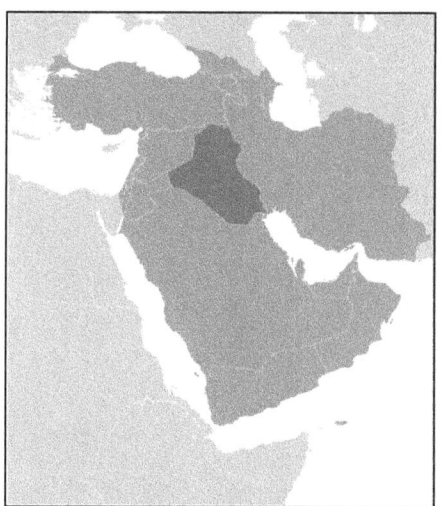

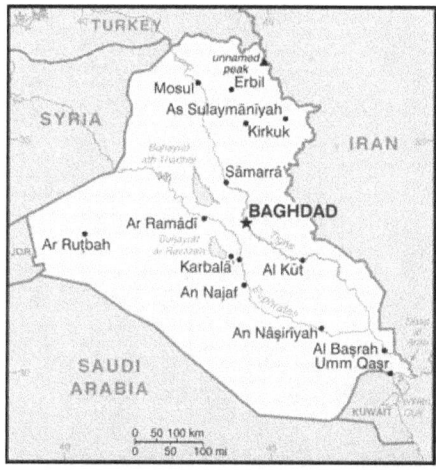

BACKGROUND:

Formerly part of the Ottoman Empire, Iraq was occupied by the United Kingdom during World War I and was declared a League of Nations mandate under UK administration in 1920. Iraq attained its independence as a kingdom in 1932. It was proclaimed a "republic" in 1958 after a coup overthrew the monarchy, but in actuality, a series of strongmen ruled the country until 2003. The last was SADDAM Husayn from 1979 to 2003. Territorial disputes with Iran led to an inconclusive and costly eight-year war (1980-88). In August 1990, Iraq seized Kuwait but was expelled by US-led UN coalition forces during the Gulf War of January-February 1991. After Iraq's expulsion, the UN Security Council (UNSC) required Iraq to scrap all weapons of mass destruction and long-range missiles and to allow UN verification inspections. Continued Iraqi noncompliance with UNSC resolutions led to the Second Gulf War in March 2003 and the ouster of the SADDAM Husayn regime by US-led forces.

In October 2005, Iraqis approved a constitution in a national referendum and, pursuant to this document, elected a 275-member Council of Representatives (COR) in December 2005. The COR approved most cabinet ministers in May 2006, marking the transition to Iraq's first constitutional government in nearly a half century. Iraq held elections for provincial councils in all governorates in January 2009 and April 2013 and postponed the next provincial elections, originally planned for April 2017, until 2019. Iraq has held three national legislative elections since 2005, most recently in May 2018 when 329 legislators were elected to the COR. Adil ABD AL-MAHDI assumed the premiership in October 2018 as a consensus and independent candidate - the first prime minister who is not an active member of a major political bloc. His cabinet has been hailed as one of the most technocratic since 2005.

Between 2014 and 2017, Iraq was engaged in a military campaign against the Islamic State of Iraq and ash-Sham (ISIS) to recapture territory lost in the western and northern portion of the country. Iraqi and allied forces recaptured Mosul, the country's second-largest city, in 2017 and drove ISIS out of its other urban strongholds. In December 2017, then-Prime Minister Haydar al-ABADI publicly declared victory against ISIS while continuing operations against the group's residual presence in rural areas. Also in late 2017, ABADI responded to an independence referendum held by the Kurdish Regional Government by ordering Iraqi forces to take control of disputed territories across central and northern Iraq that were previously occupied and governed by Kurdish forces.

GEOGRAPHY :: IRAQ

LOCATION:

Middle East, bordering the Persian Gulf, between Iran and Kuwait

GEOGRAPHIC COORDINATES:

33 00 N, 44 00 E

MAP REFERENCES:

Middle East

AREA:

total: 438,317 sq km

land: 437,367 sq km

water: 950 sq km

country comparison to the world: 60

AREA - COMPARATIVE:

slightly more than three times the size of New York state

LAND BOUNDARIES:

total: 3,809 km

border countries (6): Iran 1599 km, Jordan 179 km, Kuwait 254 km, Saudi Arabia 811 km, Syria 599 km, Turkey 367 km

COASTLINE:

58 km

MARITIME CLAIMS:

territorial sea: 12 nm

continental shelf: not specified

CLIMATE:

mostly desert; mild to cool winters with dry, hot, cloudless summers; northern mountainous regions along Iranian and Turkish borders experience cold winters with occasionally heavy snows that melt in early spring, sometimes causing extensive flooding in central and southern Iraq

TERRAIN:

mostly broad plains; reedy marshes along Iranian border in south with large flooded areas; mountains along borders with Iran and Turkey

ELEVATION:

mean elevation: 312 m

lowest point: Persian Gulf 0 m

highest point: Cheekha Dar (Kurdish for "Black Tent") 3,611 m

NATURAL RESOURCES:

petroleum, natural gas, phosphates, sulfur

LAND USE:

agricultural land: 18.1% (2011 est.)

arable land: 8.4% (2011 est.) / permanent crops: 0.5% (2011 est.) / permanent pasture: 9.2% (2011 est.)

forest: 1.9% (2011 est.)

other: 80% (2011 est.)

IRRIGATED LAND:

35,250 sq km (2012)

POPULATION DISTRIBUTION:

population is concentrated in the north, center, and eastern parts of the country, with many of the larger urban agglomerations found along extensive parts of the Tigris and Euphrates Rivers; much of the western and southern areas are either lightly populated or uninhabited

NATURAL HAZARDS:

dust storms; sandstorms; floods

ENVIRONMENT - CURRENT ISSUES:

government water control projects drained most of the inhabited marsh areas east of An Nasiriyah by drying up or diverting the feeder streams and rivers; a once sizable population of Marsh Arabs, who inhabited these areas for thousands of years, has been displaced; furthermore, the destruction of the natural habitat poses serious threats to the area's wildlife populations; inadequate supplies of potable water; soil degradation (salination) and erosion; desertification; military and industrial infrastructure has released heavy metals and other hazardous substances into the air, soil, and groundwater; major sources of environmental damage are effluents from oil refineries, factory and sewage discharges into rivers, fertilizer and chemical contamination of the soil, and industrial air pollution in urban areas

ENVIRONMENT - INTERNATIONAL AGREEMENTS:

party to: Biodiversity, Hazardous Wastes, Law of the Sea, Ozone Layer Protection

signed, but not ratified: Environmental Modification

GEOGRAPHY - NOTE:

strategic location on Shatt al Arab waterway and at the head of the Persian Gulf

PEOPLE AND SOCIETY :: IRAQ

POPULATION:

40,194,216 (July 2018 est.)

country comparison to the world: 36

NATIONALITY:

noun: Iraqi(s)

adjective: Iraqi

ETHNIC GROUPS:

Arab 75-80%, Kurdish 15-20%, other 5% (includes Turkmen, Yezidi, Shabak, Kaka'i, Bedouin, Romani, Assyrian, Circassian, Sabaean-Mandaean, Persian)

note: data is a 1987 government estimate; no more recent reliable numbers are available

LANGUAGES:

Arabic (official), Kurdish (official), Turkmen (a Turkish dialect), Syriac (Neo-Aramaic), and Armenian are official in areas where native speakers of these languages constitute a majority of the population

RELIGIONS:

Muslim (official) 95-98% (Shia 64-69%, Sunni 29-34%), Christian 1% (includes Catholic, Orthodox, Protestant, Assyrian Church of the East), other 1-4% (2015 est.)

note: while there has been voluntary relocation of many Christian families to northern Iraq, the overall Christian population has decreased at least 50% and perhaps as high as 90% since the fall of the SADDAM Husayn regime in 2003, according to US Embassy estimates, with many fleeing to Syria, Jordan, and Lebanon

AGE STRUCTURE:

0-14 years: 39.01% (male 8,005,327 /female 7,674,802)

15-24 years: 19.42% (male 3,976,085 /female 3,829,086)

25-54 years: 33.97% (male 6,900,984 /female 6,752,797)

55-64 years: 4.05% (male 788,602 /female 839,291)

65 years and over: 3.55% (male 632,753 /female 794,489) (2018 est.)

DEPENDENCY RATIOS:

total dependency ratio: 77.7 (2015 est.)

youth dependency ratio: 72.3 (2015 est.)

elderly dependency ratio: 5.5 (2015 est.)

potential support ratio: 18.3 (2015 est.)

MEDIAN AGE:

total: 20.2 years (2018 est.)

male: 20 years

female: 20.5 years

country comparison to the world: 189

POPULATION GROWTH RATE:

2.5% (2018 est.)

country comparison to the world: 22

BIRTH RATE:

30 births/1,000 population (2018 est.)

country comparison to the world: 37

DEATH RATE:

3.8 deaths/1,000 population (2018 est.)

country comparison to the world: 212

NET MIGRATION RATE:

-1.1 migrant(s)/1,000 population (2018 est.)

country comparison to the world: 144

POPULATION DISTRIBUTION:

population is concentrated in the north, center, and eastern parts of the country, with many of the larger urban agglomerations found along extensive parts of the Tigris and Euphrates Rivers; much of the western and southern areas are either lightly populated or uninhabited

URBANIZATION:

urban population: 70.7% of total population (2019)

rate of urbanization: 3.06% annual rate of change (2015-20 est.)

MAJOR URBAN AREAS - POPULATION:

6.974 million BAGHDAD (capital), 1.578 million Mosul, 1.325 million Basra, 996,000 Kirkuk, 833,000 Erbil, 847,000 Najaf (2019)

SEX RATIO:

at birth: 1.05 male(s)/female

0-14 years: 1.04 male(s)/female

15-24 years: 1.04 male(s)/female

25-54 years: 1.02 male(s)/female

55-64 years: 0.94 male(s)/female

65 years and over: 0.8 male(s)/female

total population: 1.02 male(s)/female (2018 est.)

MATERNAL MORTALITY RATE:

79 deaths/100,000 live births (2017 est.)

country comparison to the world: 80

INFANT MORTALITY RATE:

total: 37.5 deaths/1,000 live births (2018 est.)

male: 40.6 deaths/1,000 live births

female: 34.2 deaths/1,000 live births

country comparison to the world: 47

LIFE EXPECTANCY AT BIRTH:

total population: 74.9 years (2018 est.)

male: 72.6 years

female: 77.2 years

country comparison to the world: 117

TOTAL FERTILITY RATE:

3.94 children born/woman (2018 est.)

country comparison to the world: 36

CONTRACEPTIVE PREVALENCE RATE:

52.8% (2018)

DRINKING WATER SOURCE:

improved:

urban: 93.8% of population

rural: 70.1% of population

total: 86.6% of population

unimproved:

urban: 6.2% of population

rural: 29.9% of population

total: 13.4% of population (2015 est.)

CURRENT HEALTH EXPENDITURE:

3.3% (2016)

PHYSICIANS DENSITY:

0.82 physicians/1,000 population (2017)

HOSPITAL BED DENSITY:

1.4 beds/1,000 population (2014)

SANITATION FACILITY ACCESS:

improved:

urban: 86.4% of population (2015 est.)

rural: 83.8% of population (2015 est.)

total: 85.6% of population (2015 est.)

unimproved:

urban: 13.6% of population (2015 est.)

rural: 16.2% of population (2015 est.)

total: 14.4% of population (2015 est.)

HIV/AIDS - ADULT PREVALENCE RATE:

NA

HIV/AIDS - PEOPLE LIVING WITH HIV/AIDS:

NA

HIV/AIDS - DEATHS:

NA

MAJOR INFECTIOUS DISEASES:

degree of risk: intermediate (2016)

food or waterborne diseases: bacterial diarrhea, hepatitis A, and typhoid fever (2016)

OBESITY - ADULT PREVALENCE RATE:

30.4% (2016)

country comparison to the world: 23

CHILDREN UNDER THE AGE OF 5 YEARS UNDERWEIGHT:

7.2% (2011)

country comparison to the world: 72

EDUCATION EXPENDITURES:

NA

LITERACY:

definition: age 15 and over can read and write

total population: 79.7%

male: 85.7%

female: 73.7% (2015 est.)

UNEMPLOYMENT, YOUTH AGES 15-24:

total: 25.6%

male: 22%

female: 63.3% (2017)

country comparison to the world: 47

GOVERNMENT :: IRAQ

COUNTRY NAME:

conventional long form: Republic of Iraq

conventional short form: Iraq

local long form: Jumhuriyat al-Iraq/Komar-i Eraq

local short form: Al Iraq/Eraq

former: Mesopotamia, Mandatory Iraq, Hashemite Kingdom of Iraq

etymology: the name probably derives from "Uruk" (Biblical "Erech"), the ancient Sumerian and Babylonian city on the Euphrates River

GOVERNMENT TYPE:

federal parliamentary republic

CAPITAL:

name: Baghdad

geographic coordinates: 33 20 N, 44 24 E

time difference: UTC+3 (8 hours ahead of Washington, DC, during Standard Time)

although the origin of the name is disputed, it likely has compound Persian roots with "bagh" and "dad" meaning "god" and "given" respectively to create the meaning of "bestowed by God"

ADMINISTRATIVE DIVISIONS:

18 governorates (muhafazat, singular - muhafazah (Arabic); parezgakan, singular - parezga (Kurdish)) and 1 region*; Al Anbar; Al Basrah; Al Muthanna; Al Qadisiyah (Ad Diwaniyah); An Najaf; Arbil (Erbil) (Arabic), Hewler (Kurdish); As Sulaymaniyah (Arabic), Slemani (Kurdish); Babil; Baghdad; Dahuk (Arabic), Dihok (Kurdish); Dhi Qar; Diyala; Karbala'; Kirkuk; Kurdistan Regional Government*; Maysan; Ninawa; Salah ad Din; Wasit

INDEPENDENCE:

3 October 1932 (from League of Nations mandate under British administration); note - on 28 June 2004 the Coalition Provisional Authority transferred sovereignty to the Iraqi Interim Government

NATIONAL HOLIDAY:

Independence Day, 3 October (1932); Republic Day, 14 July (1958)

CONSTITUTION:

history: several previous; latest adopted by referendum 15 October 2005

amendments: proposed by the president of the republic and the Council of Minsters collectively, or by one fifth of the Council of Representatives members; passage requires at least two-thirds majority vote by the Council of Representatives, approval by referendum, and ratification by the president; passage of amendments to articles on citizen rights and liberties requires two-thirds majority vote of Council of Representatives members after two successive electoral terms, approval in a referendum, and ratification by the president (2016)

LEGAL SYSTEM:
mixed legal system of civil and Islamic law

INTERNATIONAL LAW ORGANIZATION PARTICIPATION:
has not submitted an ICJ jurisdiction declaration; non-party state to the ICCt

CITIZENSHIP:
citizenship by birth: no

citizenship by descent only: at least one parent must be a citizen of Iraq

dual citizenship recognized: yes

residency requirement for naturalization: 10 years

SUFFRAGE:
18 years of age; universal

EXECUTIVE BRANCH:
chief of state: President Barham SALIH (since 2 October 2018); vice presidents (vacant)

head of government: Prime Minister Adil ABD AL-MAHDI (since 24 October 2018)

cabinet: Council of Ministers proposed by the prime minister, approved by Council of Representatives

elections/appointments: president indirectly elected by Council of Representatives (COR) to serve a 4-year term (eligible for a second term); COR election last held on 12 May 2018 (next to be held in 2022); prime minister nominated by the largest COR bloc or by consensus and submission of COR minister nominees for majority COR approval; disapproval requires designation of a new prime minister candidate

election results:

COR vote in first round - Barham SALIH (PUK) 165, Fuad HUSAYN (KDP) 90; Barham SALIH elected president in second round - Barham SALIH 219, Fuad HUSAYN 22; note - the COR vote on 1 October 2018 failed due to a lack of quorum, and a new session was held on 2 October

LEGISLATIVE BRANCH:
description: unicameral Council of Representatives or Majlis an-Nuwwab al-Iraqiyy (329 seats; 320 members directly elected in multi-seat constituencies by open-list proportional representation vote and 9 seats at the national level reserved for minorities - 5 for Christians, 1 each for Sabaean-Mandaeans, Yazidis, Shabaks, Fayli Kurds; 25% of seats allocated to women; members serve 4-year terms); note - Iraq's constitution calls for the establishment of an upper house, the Federation Council, but it has not been instituted

elections: last held on 12 May 2018 (next to be held in 2022)

election results: percent of vote by party/coalition - NA; seats by party/coalition - Al Sa'irun Alliance 54, Al Fatah Alliance 48, Al Nasir Alliance 42, KDP 25, State of Law Coalition 25, Wataniyah 21, National Wisdom Trend 19, PUK 18, Iraqi Decision Alliance 14, Anbar Our Identity 6, Goran Movement 5, New Generation 4, other 48; composition - men 245, women 84, percent of women 25.5%

JUDICIAL BRANCH:
highest courts: Federal Supreme Court or FSC (consists of 9 judges); note - court jurisdiction limited to constitutional issues and disputes between regions or governorates and the central government; Court of Cassation (consists of a court president, 5 vice presidents, and at least 24 judges)

judge selection and term of office: Federal Supreme Court and Court of Cassation judges selected by the president of the republic from nominees selected by the Supreme Judicial Council (SJC), a 25-member committee of judicial officials that manages the judiciary and prosecutors; FSC members appointed for life; Court of Cassation judges appointed by the SJC and confirmed by the Council of Representatives to serve until retirement nominally at age 63

subordinate courts: Courts of Appeal (governorate level); civil courts, including first instance, personal status, labor, and customs; criminal courts including felony, misdemeanor, investigative, major crimes, juvenile, and traffic; religious courts

POLITICAL PARTIES AND LEADERS:

Al Fatah Alliance [Hadi al-AMIRI]
Al Nasr Alliance [Haydar al-ABADI]
Al Sadiqun Bloc [Adnan al-DULAYMI]
Al Sa'irun Alliance [Muqtda al-SADR]
Badr Organization [Hadi al-AMIRI]
Da`wa Party [Nuri al-MALIKI]
Fadilah Party [Muhammad al-YAQUBI]
Goran Movement [Omar SAYYID ALI]
Iraqi Communist Party [Hamid Majid MUSA]
Iraq Decision Alliance [Khamis al-KHANJAR, Usama al-NUJAYFI]
Islamic Supreme Council of Iraq or ISCI [Humam HAMMUDI]
Kurdistan Democratic Party or KDP [Masoud BARZANI]
National Wisdom Trend [Ammar al-HAKIM]
New Generation Movement [SHASWAR Abd al-Wahid Qadir]
Our Identity [Muhammad al-HALBUSI]
Patriotic Union of Kurdistan or PUK [KOSRAT Rasul Ali, acting]
State of Law Coalition [Nuri al MALIKI
Wataniyah coalition [Ayad ALLAWI]
numerous smaller religious, local, tribal, and minority parties

INTERNATIONAL ORGANIZATION PARTICIPATION:
ABEDA, AFESD, AMF, CAEU, CICA, EITI (compliant country), FAO, G-77, IAEA, IBRD, ICAO, ICRM, IDA, IDB, IFAD, IFC, IFRCS, ILO, IMF, IMO, IMSO, Interpol, IOC, IPU, ISO, ITSO, ITU, LAS, MIGA, NAM, OAPEC, OIC, OPCW, OPEC, PCA, UN, UNCTAD, UNESCO, UNIDO, UNWTO, UPU, WCO, WFTU (NGOs), WHO, WIPO, WMO, WTO (observer)

DIPLOMATIC REPRESENTATION IN THE US:
Ambassador Farid YASIN (since 18 January 2017)

chancery: 3421 Massachusetts Avenue, NW, Washington, DC 20007

telephone: [1] (202) 742-1600

FAX: [1] (202) 333-1129

consulate(s) general: Detroit, Los Angeles

DIPLOMATIC REPRESENTATION FROM THE US:
chief of mission: Ambassador Matthew TUELLER (since 9 June 2019)

telephone: 0760-030-3000

embassy: Al-Kindi Street, International Zone, Baghdad; note - consulate in Al Basrah closed as of 28 September 2018

mailing address: APO AE 09316

FAX: NA

FLAG DESCRIPTION:
three equal horizontal bands of red (top), white, and black; the Takbir (Arabic expression meaning "God is great") in green Arabic script is

centered in the white band; the band colors derive from the Arab Liberation flag and represent oppression (black), overcome through bloody struggle (red), to be replaced by a bright future (white); the Council of Representatives approved this flag in 2008 as a compromise replacement for the Ba'thist SADDAM-era flag

note: similar to the flag of Syria, which has two stars but no script; Yemen, which has a plain white band; and that of Egypt, which has a golden Eagle of Saladin centered in the white band

NATIONAL SYMBOL(S):

golden eagle; national colors: red, white, black

NATIONAL ANTHEM:

name: "Mawtini" (My Homeland)

lyrics/music: Ibrahim TOUQAN/Mohammad FLAYFEL

note: adopted 2004; following the ouster of SADDAM Husayn, Iraq adopted "Mawtini," a popular folk song throughout the Arab world; also serves as an unofficial anthem of the Palestinian people

ECONOMY :: IRAQ

ECONOMY - OVERVIEW:

Iraq's GDP growth slowed to 1.1% in 2017, a marked decline compared to the previous two years as domestic consumption and investment fell because of civil violence and a sluggish oil market. The Iraqi Government received its third tranche of funding from its 2016 Stand-By Arrangement (SBA) with the IMF in August 2017, which is intended to stabilize its finances by encouraging improved fiscal management, needed economic reform, and expenditure reduction. Additionally, in late 2017 Iraq received more than $1.4 billion in financing from international lenders, part of which was generated by issuing a $1 billion bond for reconstruction and rehabilitation in areas liberated from ISIL. Investment and key sector diversification are crucial components to Iraq's long-term economic development and require a strengthened business climate with enhanced legal and regulatory oversight to bolster private-sector engagement. The overall standard of living depends on global oil prices, the central government passage of major policy reforms, a stable security environment post-ISIS, and the resolution of civil discord with the Kurdish Regional Government (KRG).

Iraq's largely state-run economy is dominated by the oil sector, which provides roughly 85% of government revenue and 80% of foreign exchange earnings, and is a major determinant of the economy's fortunes. Iraq's contracts with major oil companies have the potential to further expand oil exports and revenues, but Iraq will need to make significant upgrades to its oil processing, pipeline, and export infrastructure to enable these deals to reach their economic potential.

In 2017, Iraqi oil exports from northern fields were disrupted following a KRG referendum that resulted in the Iraqi Government reasserting federal control over disputed oil fields and energy infrastructure in Kirkuk. The Iraqi government and the KRG dispute the role of federal and regional authorities in the development and export of natural resources. In 2007, the KRG passed an oil law to develop IKR oil and gas reserves independent of the federal government. The KRG has signed about 50 contracts with foreign energy companies to develop its reserves, some of which lie in territories taken by Baghdad in October 2017. The KRG is able to unilaterally export oil from the fields it retains control of through its own pipeline to Turkey, which Baghdad claims is illegal. In the absence of a national hydrocarbons law, the two sides have entered into five provisional oil- and revenue-sharing deals since 2009, all of which collapsed.

Iraq is making slow progress enacting laws and developing the institutions needed to implement economic policy, and political reforms are still needed to assuage investors' concerns regarding the uncertain business climate. The Government of Iraq is eager to attract additional foreign direct investment, but it faces a number of obstacles, including a tenuous political system and concerns about security and societal stability. Rampant corruption, outdated infrastructure, insufficient essential services, skilled labor shortages, and antiquated commercial laws stifle investment and continue to constrain growth of private, nonoil sectors. Under the Iraqi constitution, some competencies relevant to the overall investment climate are either shared by the federal government and the regions or are devolved entirely to local governments. Investment in the IKR operates within the framework of the Kurdistan Region Investment Law (Law 4 of 2006) and the Kurdistan Board of Investment, which is designed to provide incentives to help economic development in areas under the authority of the KRG.

Inflation has remained under control since 2006. However, Iraqi leaders remain hard-pressed to translate macroeconomic gains into an improved standard of living for the Iraqi populace. Unemployment remains a problem throughout the country despite a bloated public sector. Overregulation has made it difficult for Iraqi citizens and foreign investors to start new businesses. Corruption and lack of economic reforms - such as restructuring banks and developing the private sector – have inhibited the growth of the private sector.

GDP (PURCHASING POWER PARITY):

$649.3 billion (2017 est.)

$662.9 billion (2016 est.)

$586.3 billion (2015 est.)

note: data are in 2017 dollars

country comparison to the world: 34

GDP (OFFICIAL EXCHANGE RATE):

$192.4 billion (2017 est.)

GDP - REAL GROWTH RATE:

-2.1% (2017 est.)

13.1% (2016 est.)

2.5% (2015 est.)

country comparison to the world: 206

GDP - PER CAPITA (PPP):

$16,700 (2017 est.)

$17,500 (2016 est.)

$15,900 (2015 est.)

note: data are in 2017 dollars

country comparison to the world: 107

GROSS NATIONAL SAVING:

19% of GDP (2017 est.)

13.1% of GDP (2016 est.)

18.4% of GDP (2015 est.)

country comparison to the world: 103

GDP - COMPOSITION, BY END USE:

household consumption: 50.4% (2013 est.)

government consumption: 22.9% (2016 est.)

investment in fixed capital: 20.6% (2016 est.)

investment in inventories: 0% (2016 est.)

exports of goods and services: 32.5% (2016 est.)

imports of goods and services: -40.9% (2016 est.)

GDP - COMPOSITION, BY SECTOR OF ORIGIN:

agriculture: 3.3% (2017 est.)

industry: 51% (2017 est.)

services: 45.8% (2017 est.)

AGRICULTURE - PRODUCTS:

wheat, barley, rice, vegetables, dates, cotton; cattle, sheep, poultry

INDUSTRIES:

petroleum, chemicals, textiles, leather, construction materials, food processing, fertilizer, metal fabrication/processing

INDUSTRIAL PRODUCTION GROWTH RATE:

0.7% (2017 est.)

country comparison to the world: 163

LABOR FORCE:

8.9 million (2010 est.)

country comparison to the world: 57

LABOR FORCE - BY OCCUPATION:

agriculture: 21.6%

industry: 18.7%

services: 59.8% (2008 est.)

UNEMPLOYMENT RATE:

16% (2012 est.)

15% (2010 est.)

country comparison to the world: 175

POPULATION BELOW POVERTY LINE:

23% (2014 est.)

HOUSEHOLD INCOME OR CONSUMPTION BY PERCENTAGE SHARE:

lowest 10%: 3.6%

highest 10%: 25.7% (2007 est.)

BUDGET:

revenues: 68.71 billion (2017 est.)

expenditures: 76.82 billion (2017 est.)

TAXES AND OTHER REVENUES:

35.7% (of GDP) (2017 est.)

country comparison to the world: 59

BUDGET SURPLUS (+) OR DEFICIT (-):

-4.2% (of GDP) (2017 est.)

country comparison to the world: 160

PUBLIC DEBT:

59.7% of GDP (2017 est.)

66% of GDP (2016 est.)

country comparison to the world: 74

FISCAL YEAR:

calendar year

INFLATION RATE (CONSUMER PRICES):

0.1% (2017 est.)

0.5% (2016 est.)

country comparison to the world: 14

CENTRAL BANK DISCOUNT RATE:

6% (2016)

6% (2015)

country comparison to the world: 70

COMMERCIAL BANK PRIME LENDING RATE:

12.7% (31 December 2017 est.)

12.7% (31 December 2016 est.)

country comparison to the world: 65

STOCK OF NARROW MONEY:

$60.1 billion (31 December 2017 est.)

$59.84 billion (31 December 2016 est.)

country comparison to the world: 50

STOCK OF BROAD MONEY:

$60.1 billion (31 December 2017 est.)

$59.84 billion (31 December 2016 est.)

country comparison to the world: 50

STOCK OF DOMESTIC CREDIT:

$34.61 billion (31 December 2017 est.)

$31.93 billion (31 December 2016 est.)

country comparison to the world: 76

MARKET VALUE OF PUBLICLY TRADED SHARES:

$4 billion (9 December 2011)

$2.6 billion (31 July 2010)

$2 billion (31 July 2009 est.)

country comparison to the world: 89

CURRENT ACCOUNT BALANCE:

$4.344 billion (2017 est.)

-$13.38 billion (2016 est.)

country comparison to the world: 31

EXPORTS:

$61.4 billion (2017 est.)

$41.72 billion (2016 est.)

country comparison to the world: 46

EXPORTS - PARTNERS:

India 21.2%, China 20.2%, US 15.8%, South Korea 9.4%, Greece 5.3%, Netherlands 4.8%, Italy 4.7% (2017)

EXPORTS - COMMODITIES:

crude oil 99%, crude materials excluding fuels, food, live animals

IMPORTS:

$39.47 billion (2017 est.)

$19.57 billion (2016 est.)

country comparison to the world: 61

IMPORTS - COMMODITIES:

food, medicine, manufactures

IMPORTS - PARTNERS:

Turkey 27.8%, China 25.7%, South Korea 4.7%, Russia 4.3% (2017)

RESERVES OF FOREIGN EXCHANGE AND GOLD:

$48.88 billion (31 December 2017 est.)

$45.36 billion (31 December 2016 est.)

country comparison to the world: 41

DEBT - EXTERNAL:

$73.02 billion (31 December 2017 est.)

$64.16 billion (31 December 2016 est.)

country comparison to the world: 59

STOCK OF DIRECT FOREIGN INVESTMENT - AT HOME:

$26.63 billion (2015 est.)

$23.16 billion (2014 est.)

country comparison to the world: 74

STOCK OF DIRECT FOREIGN INVESTMENT - ABROAD:

$2.109 billion (2015 est.)

$1.956 billion (2014 est.)

country comparison to the world: 82

EXCHANGE RATES:

Iraqi dinars (IQD) per US dollar -

1,184 (2017 est.)

1,182 (2016 est.)

1,182 (2015 est.)

1,167.63 (2014 est.)

1,213.72 (2013 est.)

ENERGY :: IRAQ

ELECTRICITY ACCESS:

electrification - total population: 100% (2016)

ELECTRICITY - PRODUCTION:

75.45 billion kWh (2016 est.)

country comparison to the world: 40

ELECTRICITY - CONSUMPTION:

38.46 billion kWh (2016 est.)

country comparison to the world: 57

ELECTRICITY - EXPORTS:

0 kWh (2016 est.)

country comparison to the world: 150

ELECTRICITY - IMPORTS:

11.97 billion kWh (2016 est.)

country comparison to the world: 20

ELECTRICITY - INSTALLED GENERATING CAPACITY:

27.09 million kW (2016 est.)

country comparison to the world: 34

ELECTRICITY - FROM FOSSIL FUELS:

91% of total installed capacity (2016 est.)

country comparison to the world: 55

ELECTRICITY - FROM NUCLEAR FUELS:

0% of total installed capacity (2017 est.)

country comparison to the world: 111

ELECTRICITY - FROM HYDROELECTRIC PLANTS:

9% of total installed capacity (2017 est.)

country comparison to the world: 119

ELECTRICITY - FROM OTHER RENEWABLE SOURCES:

0% of total installed capacity (2017 est.)

country comparison to the world: 194

CRUDE OIL - PRODUCTION:

4.613 million bbl/day (2018 est.)

country comparison to the world: 4

CRUDE OIL - EXPORTS:

3.092 million bbl/day (2015 est.)

country comparison to the world: 3

CRUDE OIL - IMPORTS:

0 bbl/day (2015 est.)

country comparison to the world: 145

CRUDE OIL - PROVED RESERVES:

148.8 billion bbl (1 January 2018 est.)

country comparison to the world: 5

REFINED PETROLEUM PRODUCTS - PRODUCTION:

398,000 bbl/day (2015 est.)

country comparison to the world: 37

REFINED PETROLEUM PRODUCTS - CONSUMPTION:

826,000 bbl/day (2016 est.)

country comparison to the world: 26

REFINED PETROLEUM PRODUCTS - EXPORTS:

8,284 bbl/day (2015 est.)

country comparison to the world: 86

REFINED PETROLEUM PRODUCTS - IMPORTS:

255,100 bbl/day (2015 est.)

country comparison to the world: 28

NATURAL GAS - PRODUCTION:

1.274 billion cu m (2017 est.)

country comparison to the world: 63

NATURAL GAS - CONSUMPTION:

2.633 billion cu m (2017 est.)

country comparison to the world: 76

NATURAL GAS - EXPORTS:

0 cu m (2017 est.)

country comparison to the world: 124

NATURAL GAS - IMPORTS:

1.359 billion cu m (2017 est.)

country comparison to the world: 56

NATURAL GAS - PROVED RESERVES:

3.82 trillion cu m (1 January 2018 est.)

country comparison to the world: 11

CARBON DIOXIDE EMISSIONS FROM CONSUMPTION OF ENERGY:

117.9 million Mt (2017 est.)

country comparison to the world: 37

COMMUNICATIONS :: IRAQ

TELEPHONES - FIXED LINES:

total subscriptions: 2,918,396

subscriptions per 100 inhabitants: 7 (2017 est.)

country comparison to the world: 48

TELEPHONES - MOBILE CELLULAR:

total subscriptions: 33,335,316

subscriptions per 100 inhabitants: 85 (2017 est.)

country comparison to the world: 40

TELEPHONE SYSTEM:

general assessment: the 2003 liberation of Iraq severely disrupted telecommunications throughout Iraq; widespread government efforts to rebuild domestic and international communications have slowed due to political unrest; 2018 showed signs of stability and installations of new fibre-optic cables and growth in mobile broadband subscribers; the most popular plans are pre-paid (2018)

domestic: the mobile cellular market continues to expand; 3G services offered by three major mobile operators; 4G offered by one operator in Iraqi Kurdistan Region; conflict has destroyed infrastructure in areas; 7 per 100 for fixed-line and 85 per 100 for mobile-cellular subscriptions (2018)

international: country code - 964; landing points for FALCON, and GBICS/MENA submarine cables providing connections to the Middle East, Africa and India; satellite earth stations - 4 (2 Intelsat - 1 Atlantic Ocean and 1 Indian Ocean, 1 Intersputnik - Atlantic Ocean region, and 1 Arabsat (inoperative)); local microwave radio relay connects border regions to Jordan, Kuwait, Syria, and Turkey (2019)

BROADCAST MEDIA:

the number of private radio and TV stations has increased rapidly since 2003; government-owned TV and radio stations are operated by the publicly funded Iraqi Media Network; private broadcast media are mostly linked to political, ethnic, or religious groups; satellite TV is available to an estimated 70% of viewers and many of the broadcasters are based abroad; transmissions of multiple international radio broadcasters are accessible (2019)

INTERNET COUNTRY CODE:

.iq

INTERNET USERS:

total: 8,098,401

percent of population: 21.2% (July 2016 est.)

country comparison to the world: 53

MILITARY AND SECURITY :: IRAQ

MILITARY EXPENDITURES:

2.73% of GDP (2018)

3.84% of GDP (2017)

3.63% of GDP (2016)

5.35% of GDP (2015)

2.95% of GDP (2014)

country comparison to the world: 28

MILITARY AND SECURITY FORCES:

Ministry of Defense: Iraqi Army (includes Army Aviation Command), Iraqi Navy, Iraqi Air Force; National-Level Security Forces: Iraqi Counterterrorism Service, Prime Minister's Special Forces Division, Presidential Brigades; Ministry of Interior: Federal Police Forces Command, Border Guard Forces Command, Federal Intelligence and Investigations Agency, Emergency Response Division, Facilities Protection Directorate, and Energy Police Directorate; Popular

Mobilization Commission and Affiliated Forces; Peshmerga Ministry (Kurdistan Regional Government) (2019)

MILITARY SERVICE AGE AND OBLIGATION:

18-40 years of age for voluntary military service; no conscription (2017)

TRANSPORTATION :: IRAQ

NATIONAL AIR TRANSPORT SYSTEM:

number of registered air carriers: 4 (2015)

inventory of registered aircraft operated by air carriers: 39 (2015)

annual passenger traffic on registered air carriers: 484,803 (2015)

annual freight traffic on registered air carriers: 10,758,230 mt-km (2015)

CIVIL AIRCRAFT REGISTRATION COUNTRY CODE PREFIX:

YI (2016)

AIRPORTS:

102 (2013)

country comparison to the world: 55

AIRPORTS - WITH PAVED RUNWAYS:

total: 72 (2017)

over 3,047 m: 20 (2017)

2,438 to 3,047 m: 34 (2017)

1,524 to 2,437 m: 4 (2017)

914 to 1,523 m: 7 (2017)

under 914 m: 7 (2017)

AIRPORTS - WITH UNPAVED RUNWAYS:

total: 30 (2013)

over 3,047 m: 3 (2013)

2,438 to 3,047 m: 5 (2013)

1,524 to 2,437 m: 3 (2013)

914 to 1,523 m: 13 (2013)

under 914 m: 6 (2013)

HELIPORTS:

16 (2013)

PIPELINES:

2455 km gas, 913 km liquid petroleum gas, 5432 km oil, 1637 km refined products (2013)

RAILWAYS:

total: 2,272 km (2014)

standard gauge: 2,272 km 1.435-m gauge (2014)

country comparison to the world: 69

ROADWAYS:

total: 59,623 km (2012)

paved: 59,623 km (includes Kurdistan region) (2012)

country comparison to the world: 76

WATERWAYS:

5,279 km (the Euphrates River (2,815 km), Tigris River (1,899 km), and Third River (565 km) are the principal waterways) (2012)

country comparison to the world: 22

MERCHANT MARINE:

total: 80

by type: general cargo 1, oil tanker 6, other 73 (2018)

country comparison to the world: 98

PORTS AND TERMINALS:

river port(s): Al Basrah (Shatt al Arab); Khawr az Zubayr, Umm Qasr (Khawr az Zubayr waterway)

TERRORISM :: IRAQ

TERRORIST GROUPS - HOME BASED:

Ansar al-Islam (AAI): aim(s): expel western interests from Iraq and, ultimately, establish an independent Iraqi state operating according to its interpretation of sharia
area(s) of operation: headquartered in northern Iraq with its largest presence in Kirkuk, Tikrit, and Mosul; active in the western and central regions of the country
note: majority of members are Iraqi Kurds or Iraqi Arabs who are Sunni Muslim (2018)

Jaysh Rijal al-Tariq al-Naqshabandi (JRTN): aim(s): end external influence in Iraq and, ultimately, overthrow the Government of Iraq to install a secular Ba'athist state within the internationally recognized borders of Iraq
area(s) of operation: attacks separatist Kurdish groups, Iraqi Government military and security forces and facilities, and foreign military personnel (2018)

Kata'ib Hizballah (KH): aim(s): counter US influence and, ultimately, overthrow the Iraqi Government to install a government based on Shia Muslim laws and precepts
area(s) of operation: headquartered in the Shia Muslim areas of Baghdad, with fighters active in Ninawa, Al Anbar, and Babil governorates (2018)

Kurdistan Workers' Party (PKK): aim(s): advance Kurdish autonomy and security goals in Iraq, Turkey, Iran, and Syria
area(s) of operation: operational in the north and east, with its stronghold in the Qandil Mountains; majority of members inside Iraq are Iraqi, Turkish, and Iranian Kurds, along with Kurds from Syria (2018)

TERRORIST GROUPS - FOREIGN BASED:

Islamic Revolutionary Guard Corps -- Qods Force (IRGC-QF):

aim(s): back Iraq's pro-government Shia militias by supplying two battalions of IRGC forces to jointly engage in combat against ISIS; provide weapons and munitions to Shia militants targeting US forces
area(s) of operations: Baghdad, Basrah, Karbala, Mosul, Samarra, Tikrit

(2019)

Islamic State of Iraq and ash-Sham (ISIS): aim(s): replace the world order with a global Islamic state based in Iraq and Syria; expand its branches and networks in other countries; rule according to ISIS's strict interpretation of Islamic law
area(s) of operation: operational in the rural and desert areas of central and northern Iraq, primarily within and near Sunni populations, with some presence in major population areas (2018)

TRANSNATIONAL ISSUES :: IRAQ

DISPUTES - INTERNATIONAL:

Iraq's lack of a maritime boundary with Iran prompts jurisdiction disputes beyond the mouth of the Shatt al Arab in the Persian Gulf; Turkey has expressed concern over the autonomous status of Kurds in Iraq

REFUGEES AND INTERNALLY DISPLACED PERSONS:

refugees (country of origin): 15,405 (Turkey), 7,944 (West Bank and Gaza Strip), 7,026 (Iran) (2018); 231,006 (Syria) (2019)

IDPs: 2,507,042 (includes displacement between 2006 and 2008 due to ethno-sectarian violence and displacement in central and northern Iraq since January 2014) (2019)

stateless persons: 47,515 (2018); note - in the 1970s and 1980s under SADDAM Husayn's regime, thousands of Iraq's Faili Kurds, followers of Shia Islam, were stripped of their Iraqi citizenship, had their property seized by the government, and many were deported; some Faili Kurds had their citizenship reinstated under the 2,006 Iraqi Nationality Law, but others lack the documentation to prove their Iraqi origins; some Palestinian refugees persecuted by the SADDAM regime remain stateless

note: estimate revised to reflect the reduction of statelessness in line with Law 26 of 2006, which allows stateless persons to apply for nationality in certain circumstances; more accurate studies of statelessness in Iraq are pending (2015)

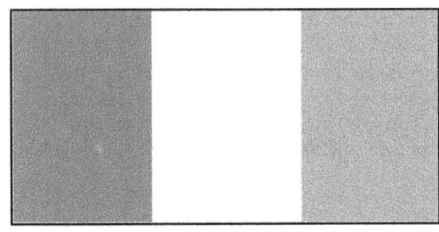

EUROPE :: IRELAND

INTRODUCTION :: IRELAND

BACKGROUND:

Celtic tribes arrived on the island between 600 and 150 B.C. Invasions by Norsemen that began in the late 8th century were finally ended when King Brian BORU defeated the Danes in 1014. Norman invasions began in the 12th century and set off more than seven centuries of Anglo-Irish struggle marked by fierce rebellions and harsh repressions. The Irish famine of the mid-19th century was responsible for a drop in the island's population by more than one quarter through starvation, disease, and emigration. For more than a century afterward, the population of the island continued to fall only to begin growing again in the 1960s. Over the last 50 years, Ireland's high birthrate has made it demographically one of the youngest populations in the EU.

The modern Irish state traces its origins to the failed 1916 Easter Monday Uprising that touched off several years of guerrilla warfare resulting in independence from the UK in 1921 for 26 southern counties; six northern (Ulster) counties remained part of the UK. Deep sectarian divides between the Catholic and Protestant populations and systemic discrimination in Northern Ireland erupted into years of violence known as the "Troubles" that began in the 1960s. The Government of Ireland was part of a process along with the UK and US Governments that helped broker the Good Friday Agreement in Northern Ireland in 1998. This initiated a new phase of cooperation between the Irish and British Governments. Ireland was neutral in World War II and continues its policy of military neutrality. Ireland joined the European Community in 1973 and the euro-zone currency union in 1999. The economic boom years of the Celtic Tiger (1995-2007) saw rapid economic growth, which came to an abrupt end in 2008 with the meltdown of the Irish banking system. Today the economy is recovering, fueled by large and growing foreign direct investment, especially from US multi-nationals.

GEOGRAPHY :: IRELAND

LOCATION:
Western Europe, occupying five-sixths of the island of Ireland in the North Atlantic Ocean, west of Great Britain

GEOGRAPHIC COORDINATES:
53 00 N, 8 00 W

MAP REFERENCES:
Europe

AREA:
total: 70,273 sq km

land: 68,883 sq km

water: 1,390 sq km

country comparison to the world: 121

AREA - COMPARATIVE:
slightly larger than West Virginia

LAND BOUNDARIES:
total: 490 km

border countries (1): UK 490 km

COASTLINE:
1,448 km

MARITIME CLAIMS:
territorial sea: 12 nm

exclusive fishing zone: 200 nm

CLIMATE:
temperate maritime; modified by North Atlantic Current; mild winters, cool summers; consistently humid; overcast about half the time

TERRAIN:
mostly flat to rolling interior plain surrounded by rugged hills and low mountains; sea cliffs on west coast

ELEVATION:
mean elevation: 118 m

lowest point: Atlantic Ocean 0 m

highest point: Carrauntoohil 1,041 m

NATURAL RESOURCES:
natural gas, peat, copper, lead, zinc, silver, barite, gypsum, limestone, dolomite

LAND USE:
agricultural land: 66.1% (2011 est.)

arable land: 15.4% (2011 est.) / permanent crops: 0% (2011 est.) / permanent pasture: 50.7% (2011 est.)

forest: 10.9% (2011 est.)

other: 23% (2011 est.)

IRRIGATED LAND:
0 sq km (2012)

POPULATION DISTRIBUTION:
population distribution is weighted to the eastern side of the island, with the largest concentration being in and around Dublin; populations in the west are small due to mountainous land, poorer soil, lack of good transport routes, and fewer job opportunities

NATURAL HAZARDS:
rare extreme weather events

ENVIRONMENT - CURRENT ISSUES:

water pollution, especially of lakes, from agricultural runoff; acid rain kills plants, destroys soil fertility, and contributes to deforestation

ENVIRONMENT - INTERNATIONAL AGREEMENTS:

party to: Air Pollution, Air Pollution-Nitrogen Oxides, Air Pollution-Sulfur 94, Biodiversity, Climate Change, Climate Change-Kyoto Protocol, Desertification, Endangered Species, Environmental Modification, Hazardous Wastes, Law of the Sea, Marine Dumping, Ozone Layer Protection, Ship Pollution, Tropical Timber 83, Tropical Timber 94, Wetlands, Whaling

signed, but not ratified: Air Pollution-Persistent Organic Pollutants, Marine Life Conservation

GEOGRAPHY - NOTE:

strategic location on major air and sea routes between North America and northern Europe; over 40% of the population resides within 100 km of Dublin

PEOPLE AND SOCIETY :: IRELAND

POPULATION:

5,068,050 (July 2018 est.)

country comparison to the world: 121

NATIONALITY:

noun: Irishman(men), Irishwoman(women), Irish (collective plural)

adjective: Irish

ETHNIC GROUPS:

Irish 82.2%, Irish travelers 0.7%, other white 9.5%, Asian 2.1%, black 1.4%, other 1.5%, unspecified 2.6% (2016 est.)

LANGUAGES:

English (official, the language generally used), Irish (Gaelic or Gaeilge) (official, spoken by approximately 39.8% of the population as of 2016; mainly spoken in areas along Ireland's western coast known as gaeltachtai, which are officially recognized regions where Irish is the predominant language)

RELIGIONS:

Roman Catholic 78.3%, Church of Ireland 2.7%, other Christian 1.6%, Orthodox 1.3%, Muslim 1.3%, other 2.4%, none 9.8%, unspecified 2.6% (2016 est.)

AGE STRUCTURE:

0-14 years: 21.37% (male 554,110 /female 529,067)

15-24 years: 11.92% (male 306,052 /female 297,890)

25-54 years: 42.86% (male 1,091,495 /female 1,080,594)

55-64 years: 10.53% (male 267,255 /female 266,438)

65 years and over: 13.32% (male 312,694 /female 362,455) (2018 est.)

DEPENDENCY RATIOS:

total dependency ratio: 53.8 (2015 est.)

youth dependency ratio: 33.4 (2015 est.)

elderly dependency ratio: 20.3 (2015 est.)

potential support ratio: 4.9 (2015 est.)

MEDIAN AGE:

total: 37.1 years (2018 est.)

male: 36.8 years

female: 37.5 years

country comparison to the world: 70

POPULATION GROWTH RATE:

1.11% (2018 est.)

country comparison to the world: 98

BIRTH RATE:

13.8 births/1,000 population (2018 est.)

country comparison to the world: 137

DEATH RATE:

6.6 deaths/1,000 population (2018 est.)

country comparison to the world: 140

NET MIGRATION RATE:

4 migrant(s)/1,000 population (2018 est.)

country comparison to the world: 33

POPULATION DISTRIBUTION:

population distribution is weighted to the eastern side of the island, with the largest concentration being in and around Dublin; populations in the west are small due to mountainous land, poorer soil, lack of good transport routes, and fewer job opportunities

URBANIZATION:

urban population: 63.4% of total population (2019)

rate of urbanization: 1.14% annual rate of change (2015-20 est.)

MAJOR URBAN AREAS - POPULATION:

1.215 million DUBLIN (capital) (2019)

SEX RATIO:

at birth: 1.06 male(s)/female

0-14 years: 1.05 male(s)/female

15-24 years: 1.03 male(s)/female

25-54 years: 1.01 male(s)/female

55-64 years: 1 male(s)/female

65 years and over: 0.86 male(s)/female

total population: 1 male(s)/female (2018 est.)

MOTHER'S MEAN AGE AT FIRST BIRTH:

30.7 years (2015 est.)

MATERNAL MORTALITY RATE:

5 deaths/100,000 live births (2017 est.)

country comparison to the world: 165

INFANT MORTALITY RATE:

total: 3.6 deaths/1,000 live births (2018 est.)

male: 4 deaths/1,000 live births

female: 3.2 deaths/1,000 live births

country comparison to the world: 197

LIFE EXPECTANCY AT BIRTH:

total population: 81 years (2018 est.)

male: 78.7 years

female: 83.5 years

country comparison to the world: 35

TOTAL FERTILITY RATE:

1.96 children born/woman (2018 est.)

country comparison to the world: 125

CONTRACEPTIVE PREVALENCE RATE:

73.3% (2010)

note: percent of women aged 18-45

DRINKING WATER SOURCE:

improved:

urban: 97.9% of population

rural: 97.8% of population

total: 97.9% of population

unimproved:

urban: 2.1% of population

rural: 2.2% of population

total: 2.1% of population (2015 est.)

CURRENT HEALTH EXPENDITURE:

7.4% (2016)

PHYSICIANS DENSITY:

3.09 physicians/1,000 population (2017)

HOSPITAL BED DENSITY:

2.8 beds/1,000 population (2013)

SANITATION FACILITY ACCESS:

improved:

urban: 89.1% of population (2015 est.)

rural: 92.9% of population (2015 est.)

total: 90.5% of population (2015 est.)

unimproved:

urban: 10.9% of population (2015 est.)

rural: 7.1% of population (2015 est.)

total: 9.5% of population (2015 est.)

HIV/AIDS - ADULT PREVALENCE RATE:

0.2% (2018 est.)

country comparison to the world: 100

HIV/AIDS - PEOPLE LIVING WITH HIV/AIDS:

7,200 (2018 est.)

country comparison to the world: 114

HIV/AIDS - DEATHS:

<100 (2018 est.)

OBESITY - ADULT PREVALENCE RATE:

25.3% (2016)

country comparison to the world: 51

EDUCATION EXPENDITURES:

3.8% of GDP (2015)

country comparison to the world: 120

SCHOOL LIFE EXPECTANCY (PRIMARY TO TERTIARY EDUCATION):

total: 19 years

male: 19 years

female: 19 years (2016)

UNEMPLOYMENT, YOUTH AGES 15-24:

total: 14.4%

male: 16%

female: 12.6% (2017 est.)

country comparison to the world: 99

GOVERNMENT :: IRELAND

COUNTRY NAME:

conventional long form: none

conventional short form: Ireland

local long form: none

local short form: Eire

etymology: the modern Irish name "Eire" evolved from the Gaelic "Eriu," the name of the matron goddess of Ireland (goddess of the land); the names "Ireland" in English and "Eire" in Irish are direct translations of each other

GOVERNMENT TYPE:

parliamentary republic

CAPITAL:

name: Dublin

geographic coordinates: 53 19 N, 6 14 W

time difference: UTC 0 (5 hours ahead of Washington, DC, during Standard Time)

daylight saving time: +1hr, begins last Sunday in March; ends last Sunday in October

etymology: derived from Irish "dubh" and "lind" meaning respectively "black, dark" and "pool" and which referred to the dark tidal pool where the River Poddle entered the River Liffey; today the area is the site of the castle gardens behind Dublin Castle

ADMINISTRATIVE DIVISIONS:

28 counties and 3 cities*; Carlow, Cavan, Clare, Cork, Cork*, Donegal, Dublin*, Dun Laoghaire-Rathdown, Fingal, Galway, Galway*, Kerry, Kildare, Kilkenny, Laois, Leitrim, Limerick, Longford, Louth, Mayo, Meath, Monaghan, Offaly, Roscommon, Sligo, South Dublin, Tipperary, Waterford, Westmeath, Wexford, Wicklow

INDEPENDENCE:

6 December 1921 (from the UK by the Anglo-Irish Treaty, which ended British rule); 6 December 1922 (Irish Free State established); 18 April 1949 (Republic of Ireland Act enabled)

NATIONAL HOLIDAY:

Saint Patrick's Day, 17 March; note - marks the traditional death date of Saint Patrick, patron saint of Ireland, during the latter half of the fifth century A.D. (most commonly cited years are c. 461 and c. 493); although Saint Patrick's feast day was celebrated in Ireland as early as the ninth century, it only became an official public holiday in Ireland in 1903

CONSTITUTION:

history: previous 1922; latest drafted 14 June 1937, adopted by plebiscite 1 July 1937, effective 29 December 1937

amendments: proposed as bills by Parliament; passage requires majority vote by both the Senate and House of Representatives, majority vote in a referendum, and presidential signature; amended many times, last in 2019 (2019)

LEGAL SYSTEM:

common law system based on the English model but substantially modified by customary law; judicial review of legislative acts by Supreme Court

INTERNATIONAL LAW ORGANIZATION PARTICIPATION:

accepts compulsory ICJ jurisdiction with reservations; accepts ICCt jurisdiction

CITIZENSHIP:

citizenship by birth: no, unless a parent of a child born in Ireland has been legally resident in Ireland for at least three of the four years prior to the birth of the child

citizenship by descent only: yes

dual citizenship recognized: yes

residency requirement for naturalization: 4 of the previous 8 years

SUFFRAGE:

18 years of age; universal

EXECUTIVE BRANCH:

chief of state: President Michael D. HIGGINS (since 11 November 2011)

head of government: Taoiseach (Prime Minister) Leo VARADKAR (since 14 June 2017)

cabinet: Cabinet nominated by the prime minister, appointed by the president, approved by the Dali Eireann (lower house of Parliament)

elections/appointments: president directly elected by majority popular vote for a 7-year term (eligible for a second term); election last held on 26 October 2018 (next to be held no later than November 2025); taoiseach (prime minister) nominated by the House of Representatives (Dail Eireann), appointed by the president

election results: Michael D. HIGGINS reelected president; percent of vote - Michael D. HIGGINS (independent) 55.8%, Peter CASEY (independent) 23.3%, Sean GALLAGHER (independent) 6.4%, Liadh NI RIADA (Sinn Fein) 6.4%, Joan FREEMAN (independent) 6%, Gavin DUFFY (independent) 2.2%

LEGISLATIVE BRANCH:

description: bicameral Parliament or Oireachtas consists of:
Senate or Seanad Eireann (60 seats; 43 members indirectly elected from 5 vocational panels of nominees by an electoral college consisting of members from the House of Representatives, outgoing Senate members, and city and county council members, 11 appointed by the prime minister, and 6 elected by 2 university constituencies - 3 each from the University of Dublin (Trinity College) and the National University of Ireland)
House of Representatives or Dail Eireann (158 seats; members directly elected in multi-seat constituencies by proportional representation vote; all Parliament members serve 5-year terms)

elections:
Senate - last held in April and May 2016 (next to be held no later than 2021)
House of Representatives - last held on 26 February 2016 (next to be held no later than 2021)

election results:
Senate - percent of vote by party - NA; seats by party - Fine Gael 19, Fianna Fail 14, Sinn Fein 7, Labor Party 5, Green Party 1, independent 14; composition - men 42, women 18, percent of women 30%
House of Representatives - percent of vote by party - Fine Gael 25.5%, Fianna Fail 24.4%, Sinn Fein 13.8%, Labor Party 6.6%, AAA-PBD 4.0%, Social Democrats 3.0%, Green Party 2.7%, Renua Ireland 2.2% independent 17.8%; seats by party - Fine Gael 50, Fianna Fail 44, Sinn Fein 23, Labor Party 7, AAA-PBP 6, Social Democrats 3, Green Party 2, independent 23; composition - men 123, women 35, percent of women 22.2%; note - total Parliament percent of women 24.3%

JUDICIAL BRANCH:

highest courts: Supreme Court of Ireland (consists of the chief justice, 9 judges, 2 ex-officio members - the presidents of the High Court and Court of Appeal - and organized in 3-, 5-, or 7-judge panels, depending on the importance or complexity of an issue of law)

judge selection and term of office: judges nominated by the prime minister and Cabinet and appointed by the president; chief justice serves in the position for 7 years; judges can serve until age 70

subordinate courts: High Court, Court of Appeal; circuit and district courts; criminal courts

POLITICAL PARTIES AND LEADERS:

Solidarity-People Before Profit or AAAS-PBP [collective leadership]
Fianna Fail [Micheal MARTIN]
Fine Gael [Leo VARADKAR]
Green Party [Eamon RYAN]
Labor (Labour) Party [Brendan HOWLIN]
Renua Ireland (vacant)
Sinn Fein [Mary Lou MCDONALD]
Social Democrats [Catherine MURPHY, Roisin SHORTALL]
Socialist Party [collective leadership]
The Workers' Party [Michael DONNELLY]

INTERNATIONAL ORGANIZATION PARTICIPATION:

ADB (nonregional member), Australia Group, BIS, CD, CE, EAPC, EBRD, ECB, EIB, EMU, ESA, EU, FAO, FATF, IAEA, IBRD, ICAO, ICC (national committees), ICCt, ICRM, IDA, IEA, IFAD, IFC, IFRCS, IGAD (partners), IHO, ILO, IMF, IMO, Interpol, IOC, IOM, IPU, ISO, ITSO, ITU, ITUC (NGOs), MIGA, MINURSO, MONUSCO, NEA, NSG, OAS (observer), OECD, OPCW, OSCE, Paris Club, PCA, PFP, UN, UNCTAD, UNDOF, UNESCO, UNHCR, UNIDO, UNIFIL, UNOCI, UNRWA, UNTSO, UPU, WCO, WHO, WIPO, WMO, WTO, ZC

DIPLOMATIC REPRESENTATION IN THE US:

Ambassador Daniel Gerard MULHALL (since 8 September 2017)

chancery: 2234 Massachusetts Avenue NW, Washington, DC 20008

telephone: [1] (202) 462-3939

FAX: [1] (202) 232-5993

consulate(s) general: Atlanta, Austin (TX), Boston, Chicago, New York, San Francisco

DIPLOMATIC REPRESENTATION FROM THE US:

chief of mission: Ambassador Edward F. CRAWFORD (since 1 July 2019)

telephone: [353] (1) 630-6200

embassy: 42 Elgin Road, Ballsbridge, Dublin 4

mailing address: use embassy street address

FAX: [353] (1) 688-9946

FLAG DESCRIPTION:

three equal vertical bands of green (hoist side), white, and orange; officially the flag colors have no meaning, but a common interpretation is that the green represents the Irish nationalist (Gaelic) tradition of Ireland; orange represents the Orange tradition (minority supporters of William of Orange); white symbolizes peace (or a lasting truce) between the green and the orange

note: similar to the flag of Cote d'Ivoire, which is shorter and has the colors reversed - orange (hoist side), white, and green; also similar to the flag of Italy, which is shorter and has colors of green (hoist side), white, and red

NATIONAL SYMBOL(S):

harp, shamrock (trefoil); national colors: blue, green

NATIONAL ANTHEM:

name: "Amhran na bhFiann" (The Soldier's Song)

lyrics/music: Peadar KEARNEY [English], Liam O RINN [Irish]/Patrick HEENEY and Peadar KEARNEY

note: adopted 1926; instead of "Amhran na bhFiann," the song "Ireland's Call" is often used at athletic events where citizens of Ireland and Northern Ireland compete as a unified team

ECONOMY :: IRELAND

ECONOMY - OVERVIEW:

Ireland is a small, modern, trade-dependent economy. It was among the initial group of 12 EU nations that began circulating the euro on 1 January 2002. GDP growth averaged 6% in 1995-2007, but economic activity dropped sharply during the world financial crisis and the subsequent collapse of its domestic property market and construction industry during 2008-11. Faced with sharply reduced revenues and a burgeoning budget deficit from efforts to stabilize its fragile banking sector, the Irish Government introduced the first in a series of draconian budgets in 2009. These measures were not sufficient to stabilize Ireland's public finances. In 2010, the budget deficit reached 32.4% of GDP - the world's largest deficit, as a percentage of GDP. In late 2010, the former COWEN government agreed to a $92 billion loan package from the EU and IMF to help Dublin recapitalize Ireland's banking sector and avoid defaulting on its sovereign debt. In March 2011, the KENNY government intensified austerity measures to meet the deficit targets under Ireland's EU-IMF bailout program.

In late 2013, Ireland formally exited its EU-IMF bailout program, benefiting from its strict adherence to deficit-reduction targets and success in refinancing a large amount of banking-related debt. In 2014, the economy rapidly picked up. In late 2014, the government introduced a fiscally neutral budget, marking the end of the austerity program. Continued growth of tax receipts has allowed the government to lower some taxes and increase public spending while keeping to its deficit-reduction targets. In 2015, GDP growth exceeded 26%. The magnitude of the increase reflected one-off statistical revisions, multinational corporate restructurings in intellectual property, and the aircraft leasing sector, rather than real gains in the domestic economy, which was still growing. Growth moderated to around 4.1% in 2017, but the recovering economy assisted lowering the deficit to 0.6% of GDP.

In the wake of the collapse of the construction sector and the downturn in consumer spending and business investment during the 2008-11 economic crisis, the export sector, dominated by foreign multinationals, has become an even more important component of Ireland's economy. Ireland's low corporation tax of 12.5% and a talented pool of high-tech laborers have been some of the key factors in encouraging business investment. Loose tax residency requirements made Ireland a common destination for international firms seeking to pay less tax or, in the case of U.S. multinationals, defer taxation owed to the United States. In 2014, amid growing international pressure, the Irish government announced it would phase in more stringent tax laws, effectively closing a commonly used loophole. The Irish economy continued to grow in 2017 and is forecast to do so through 2019, supported by a strong export sector, robust job growth, and low inflation, to the point that the Government must now address concerns about overheating and potential loss of competitiveness. The greatest risks to the economy are the UK's scheduled departure from the European Union ("Brexit") in March 2019, possible changes to international taxation policies that could affect Ireland's revenues, and global trade pressures.

GDP (PURCHASING POWER PARITY):
$353.3 billion (2017 est.)

$329.5 billion (2016 est.)

$314.1 billion (2015 est.)

note: data are in 2017 dollars

country comparison to the world: 51

GDP (OFFICIAL EXCHANGE RATE):
$331.5 billion (2017 est.)

GDP - REAL GROWTH RATE:
7.2% (2017 est.)

4.9% (2016 est.)

25% (2015 est.)

country comparison to the world: 17

GDP - PER CAPITA (PPP):
$73,200 (2017 est.)

$69,100 (2016 est.)

$66,600 (2015 est.)

note: data are in 2017 dollars

country comparison to the world: 10

GROSS NATIONAL SAVING:
33.1% of GDP (2017 est.)

33.7% of GDP (2016 est.)

29% of GDP (2015 est.)

country comparison to the world: 23

GDP - COMPOSITION, BY END USE:
household consumption: 34% (2017 est.)

government consumption: 10.1% (2017 est.)

investment in fixed capital: 23.4% (2017 est.)

investment in inventories: 1.2% (2017 est.)

exports of goods and services: 119.9% (2017 est.)

imports of goods and services: -89.7% (2017 est.)

GDP - COMPOSITION, BY SECTOR OF ORIGIN:
agriculture: 1.2% (2017 est.)

industry: 38.6% (2017 est.)

services: 60.2% (2017 est.)

AGRICULTURE - PRODUCTS:
barley, potatoes, wheat; beef, dairy products

INDUSTRIES:
pharmaceuticals, chemicals, computer hardware and software, food products, beverages and brewing; medical devices

INDUSTRIAL PRODUCTION GROWTH RATE:
7.8% (2017 est.)

country comparison to the world: 25

LABOR FORCE:
2.226 million (2017 est.)

country comparison to the world: 122

LABOR FORCE - BY OCCUPATION:
agriculture: 5%

industry: 11%

services: 84% (2015 est.)

UNEMPLOYMENT RATE:
6.7% (2017 est.)

8.4% (2016 est.)

country comparison to the world: 100

POPULATION BELOW POVERTY LINE:
8.2% (2013 est.)

HOUSEHOLD INCOME OR CONSUMPTION BY PERCENTAGE SHARE:
lowest 10%: 2.9%

highest 10%: 27.2% (2000)

DISTRIBUTION OF FAMILY INCOME - GINI INDEX:
31.3 (2013 est.)

35.9 (1987 est.)

country comparison to the world: 126

BUDGET:
revenues: 86.04 billion (2017 est.)

expenditures: 87.19 billion (2017 est.)

TAXES AND OTHER REVENUES:
26% (of GDP) (2017 est.)

country comparison to the world: 115

BUDGET SURPLUS (+) OR DEFICIT (-):
-0.3% (of GDP) (2017 est.)

country comparison to the world: 53

PUBLIC DEBT:
68.6% of GDP (2017 est.)

73.6% of GDP (2016 est.)

note: data cover general government debt and include debt instruments issued (or owned) by government entities other than the treasury; the data include treasury debt held by foreign entities; the data include debt issued by subnational entities, as well as intragovernmental debt; intragovernmental debt consists of treasury borrowings from surpluses in the social funds, such as for retirement, medical care, and unemployment; debt instruments for the social funds are not sold at public auctions

country comparison to the world: 53

FISCAL YEAR:

calendar year

INFLATION RATE (CONSUMER PRICES):

0.3% (2017 est.)

-0.2% (2016 est.)

country comparison to the world: 20

CENTRAL BANK DISCOUNT RATE:

0.05% (31 December 2015)

0.15% (31 August 2014)

note: this is the European Central Bank's rate on the marginal lending facility, which offers overnight credit to banks in the euro area

country comparison to the world: 145

COMMERCIAL BANK PRIME LENDING RATE:

4.08% (31 December 2017 est.)

3.48% (31 December 2016 est.)

country comparison to the world: 166

STOCK OF NARROW MONEY:

$191.9 billion (31 December 2017 est.)

$156.2 billion (31 December 2016 est.)

note: see entry for the European Union for money supply for the entire euro area; the European Central Bank (ECB) controls monetary policy for the 18 members of the Economic and Monetary Union (EMU); individual members of the EMU do not control the quantity of money circulating within their own borders

country comparison to the world: 26

STOCK OF BROAD MONEY:

$191.9 billion (31 December 2017 est.)

$156.2 billion (31 December 2016 est.)

country comparison to the world: 26

STOCK OF DOMESTIC CREDIT:

$299.1 billion (31 December 2017 est.)

$287.1 billion (31 December 2016 est.)

country comparison to the world: 37

MARKET VALUE OF PUBLICLY TRADED SHARES:

$128 billion (31 December 2015 est.)

$143.5 billion (31 December 2014 est.)

$170.1 billion (31 December 2013 est.)

country comparison to the world: 39

CURRENT ACCOUNT BALANCE:

$28.14 billion (2017 est.)

-$12.59 billion (2016 est.)

country comparison to the world: 12

EXPORTS:

$219.7 billion (2017 est.)

$206 billion (2016 est.)

country comparison to the world: 25

EXPORTS - PARTNERS:

US 27.1%, UK 13.4%, Belgium 11%, Germany 8.1%, Switzerland 5.1%, Netherlands 4.9%, France 4.3% (2017)

EXPORTS - COMMODITIES:

machinery and equipment, computers, chemicals, medical devices, pharmaceuticals; foodstuffs, animal products

IMPORTS:

$98.13 billion (2017 est.)

$92.09 billion (2016 est.)

country comparison to the world: 34

IMPORTS - COMMODITIES:

data processing equipment, other machinery and equipment, chemicals, petroleum and petroleum products, textiles, clothing

IMPORTS - PARTNERS:

UK 29%, US 18.9%, France 12.1%, Germany 9.6%, Netherlands 4.1% (2017)

RESERVES OF FOREIGN EXCHANGE AND GOLD:

$4.412 billion (31 December 2017 est.)

$2.203 billion (31 December 2015 est.)

country comparison to the world: 99

DEBT - EXTERNAL:

$2.47 trillion (31 March 2016 est.)

$2.35 trillion (31 March 2015 est.)

country comparison to the world: 8

STOCK OF DIRECT FOREIGN INVESTMENT - AT HOME:

$1.54 trillion (31 December 2017 est.)

$1.411 trillion (31 December 2016 est.)

country comparison to the world: 6

STOCK OF DIRECT FOREIGN INVESTMENT - ABROAD:

$1.56 trillion (31 December 2017 est.)

$1.404 trillion (31 December 2016 est.)

country comparison to the world: 7

EXCHANGE RATES:

euros (EUR) per US dollar -

0.885 (2017 est.)

0.903 (2016 est.)

0.9214 (2015 est.)

0.885 (2014 est.)

0.7634 (2013 est.)

ENERGY :: IRELAND

ELECTRICITY ACCESS:

electrification - total population: 100% (2016)

ELECTRICITY - PRODUCTION:

28.53 billion kWh (2016 est.)

country comparison to the world: 69

ELECTRICITY - CONSUMPTION:

25.68 billion kWh (2016 est.)

country comparison to the world: 68

ELECTRICITY - EXPORTS:

1.583 billion kWh (2016 est.)

country comparison to the world: 48

ELECTRICITY - IMPORTS:

871 million kWh (2016 est.)

country comparison to the world: 71

ELECTRICITY - INSTALLED GENERATING CAPACITY:

9.945 million kW (2016 est.)

country comparison to the world: 61

ELECTRICITY - FROM FOSSIL FUELS:

65% of total installed capacity (2016 est.)

country comparison to the world: 117

ELECTRICITY - FROM NUCLEAR FUELS:

0% of total installed capacity (2017 est.)

country comparison to the world: 112

ELECTRICITY - FROM HYDROELECTRIC PLANTS:

2% of total installed capacity (2017 est.)

country comparison to the world: 138

ELECTRICITY - FROM OTHER RENEWABLE SOURCES:

33% of total installed capacity (2017 est.)

country comparison to the world: 12

CRUDE OIL - PRODUCTION:

0 bbl/day (2018 est.)

country comparison to the world: 152

CRUDE OIL - EXPORTS:

5,900 bbl/day (2017 est.)

country comparison to the world: 64

CRUDE OIL - IMPORTS:

66,210 bbl/day (2017 est.)

country comparison to the world: 50

CRUDE OIL - PROVED RESERVES:

0 bbl (1 January 2018 est.)

country comparison to the world: 148

REFINED PETROLEUM PRODUCTS - PRODUCTION:

64,970 bbl/day (2017 est.)

country comparison to the world: 76

REFINED PETROLEUM PRODUCTS - CONSUMPTION:

153,700 bbl/day (2017 est.)

country comparison to the world: 66

REFINED PETROLEUM PRODUCTS - EXPORTS:

37,040 bbl/day (2017 est.)

country comparison to the world: 59

REFINED PETROLEUM PRODUCTS - IMPORTS:

126,600 bbl/day (2017 est.)

country comparison to the world: 47

NATURAL GAS - PRODUCTION:

3.511 billion cu m (2017 est.)

country comparison to the world: 54

NATURAL GAS - CONSUMPTION:

5.238 billion cu m (2017 est.)

country comparison to the world: 55

NATURAL GAS - EXPORTS:

0 cu m (2017 est.)

country comparison to the world: 125

NATURAL GAS - IMPORTS:

1.642 billion cu m (2017 est.)

country comparison to the world: 55

NATURAL GAS - PROVED RESERVES:

9.911 billion cu m (1 January 2018 est.)

country comparison to the world: 79

CARBON DIOXIDE EMISSIONS FROM CONSUMPTION OF ENERGY:

36.91 million Mt (2017 est.)

country comparison to the world: 71

COMMUNICATIONS :: IRELAND

TELEPHONES - FIXED LINES:

total subscriptions: 1,842,026

subscriptions per 100 inhabitants: 37 (2017 est.)

country comparison to the world: 59

TELEPHONES - MOBILE CELLULAR:

total subscriptions: 4,898,872

subscriptions per 100 inhabitants: 98 (2017 est.)

country comparison to the world: 121

TELEPHONE SYSTEM:

general assessment: modern digital system using cable and microwave radio relay; previous depressed economic climate has changed to one with Ireland having one of the highest GDP growth rates in Europe which translates to mean spending among telecom consumers; introduction of flat-rate plans; upgraded LTE technologies in rural areas; government intends to spend millions on the National Broadband Plan (NBP) initiative to change the broadband landscape (2018)

domestic: increasing levels of broadband access particularly in urban areas; fixed-line 37 per 100 and mobile-cellular 98 per 100 subscriptions (2018)

international: country code - 353; landing point for the AEConnect -1, Celtic-Norse, Havfrue/AEC-2, GTT Express, Cleltic, ESAT-1, IFC-1, Solas, Pan European Crossing, ESAT-2, CeltixConnect -1 & 2, GTT Atlantic, Sirius South, Emerald Bridge Fibres and Geo Eirgrid submarine cable with links to the US, Canada, Norway, Isle of Man and UK; satellite earth stations - 81 (2019)

BROADCAST MEDIA:

publicly owned broadcaster Radio Telefis Eireann (RTE) operates 4 TV stations; commercial TV stations are available; about 75% of households utilize multi-channel satellite and TV services that provide access to a wide range of stations; RTE operates 4 national radio stations and has launched digital audio broadcasts on several stations; a number of commercial broadcast stations operate at the national, regional, and local levels (2019)

INTERNET COUNTRY CODE:

.ie

INTERNET USERS:

total: 4,069,432

percent of population: 82.2% (July 2016 est.)

country comparison to the world: 87

BROADBAND - FIXED SUBSCRIPTIONS:

total: 1,401,356

subscriptions per 100 inhabitants: 28 (2017 est.)

country comparison to the world: 63

MILITARY AND SECURITY :: IRELAND

MILITARY EXPENDITURES:

0.33% of GDP (2018)

0.4% of GDP (2017)

0.34% of GDP (2016)

0.35% of GDP (2015)

0.47% of GDP (2014)

country comparison to the world: 153

MILITARY AND SECURITY FORCES:

Irish Defence Forces (Oglaigh na h-Eireannn): Army (includes Army Reserve), Naval Service (includes Naval Service Reserves), Air Corps (2019)

MILITARY SERVICE AGE AND OBLIGATION:

18-25 years of age for male and female voluntary military service recruits to the Defence Forces (18-27 years of age for the Naval Service); 18-26 for cadetship (officer) applicants; 12-year service (5 active, 7 reserves); Irish citizen, European Economic Area citizenship, or refugee status (2019)

TRANSPORTATION :: IRELAND

NATIONAL AIR TRANSPORT SYSTEM:

number of registered air carriers: 6 (2015)

inventory of registered aircraft operated by air carriers: 431 (2015)

annual passenger traffic on registered air carriers: 113,144,501 (2015)

annual freight traffic on registered air carriers: 138.58 million mt-km (2015)

CIVIL AIRCRAFT REGISTRATION COUNTRY CODE PREFIX:

EI (2016)

AIRPORTS:

40 (2013)

country comparison to the world: 105

AIRPORTS - WITH PAVED RUNWAYS:

total: 16 (2017)

over 3,047 m: 1 (2017)

2,438 to 3,047 m: 1 (2017)

1,524 to 2,437 m: 4 (2017)

914 to 1,523 m: 5 (2017)

under 914 m: 5 (2017)

AIRPORTS - WITH UNPAVED RUNWAYS:

total: 24 (2013)

2,438 to 3,047 m: 1 (2013)

914 to 1,523 m: 2 (2013)

under 914 m: 21 (2013)

PIPELINES:

2,427 km gas (2017)

RAILWAYS:

total: 4,301 km (2018)

narrow gauge: 1,930 km 0.914-m gauge (operated by the Irish Peat Board to transport peat to power stations and briquetting plants) (2018)

broad gauge: 2,371 km 1.600-m gauge (53 km electrified) (2018)

country comparison to the world: 44

ROADWAYS:

total: 99,830 km (2018)

paved: 99,830 km (includes 2,717 km of expressways) (2018)

country comparison to the world: 48

WATERWAYS:

956 km (pleasure craft only) (2010)

country comparison to the world: 67

MERCHANT MARINE:

total: 88

by type: bulk carrier 8, general cargo 34, oil tanker 1, other 45 (2018)

country comparison to the world: 91

PORTS AND TERMINALS:

major seaport(s): Dublin, Shannon Foynes

cruise port(s): Cork, Dublin

container port(s) (TEUs): Dublin (529,563) (2016)

river port(s): Cork (Lee), Waterford (Suir)

TERRORISM :: IRELAND

TERRORIST GROUPS - FOREIGN BASED:

Continuity Irish Republican Army (CIRA): aim(s): to bring about a united Ireland
area(s) of operation: maintains an operational presence (2018)

New Irish Republican Army (NIRA): aim(s): to bring about a united Ireland
area(s) of operation: maintains an operational presence

note: formerly known as the Real Irish Republican Army (RIRA) (2018)

TRANSNATIONAL ISSUES :: IRELAND

DISPUTES - INTERNATIONAL:

Ireland, Iceland, and the UK dispute Denmark's claim that the Faroe Islands' continental shelf extends beyond 200 nm

REFUGEES AND INTERNALLY DISPLACED PERSONS:

stateless persons: 99 (2018)

ILLICIT DRUGS:

transshipment point for and consumer of hashish from North Africa to the UK and Netherlands and of European-produced synthetic drugs; increasing consumption of South American cocaine; minor transshipment point for heroin and cocaine destined for Western Europe; despite recent legislation, narcotics-related money laundering - using bureaux de change, trusts, and shell companies involving the offshore financial community - remains a concern

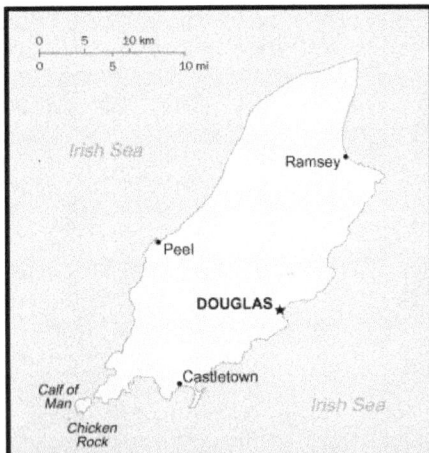

EUROPE :: ISLE OF MAN

INTRODUCTION :: ISLE OF MAN

BACKGROUND:
Part of the Norwegian Kingdom of the Hebrides until the 13th century when it was ceded to Scotland, the isle came under the British crown in 1765. Current concerns include reviving the almost extinct Manx Gaelic language. The Isle of Man is a crown dependency, which makes it a self-governing possession of the British crown that is not part of the UK. The UK Government, however, remains constitutionally responsible for its defense and international representation.

GEOGRAPHY :: ISLE OF MAN

LOCATION:
Western Europe, island in the Irish Sea, between Great Britain and Ireland

GEOGRAPHIC COORDINATES:
54 15 N, 4 30 W

MAP REFERENCES:
Europe

AREA:
total: 572 sq km
land: 572 sq km
water: 0 sq km
country comparison to the world: 194

AREA - COMPARATIVE:
slightly more than three times the size of Washington, DC

LAND BOUNDARIES:
0 km

COASTLINE:
160 km

MARITIME CLAIMS:
territorial sea: 12 nm
exclusive fishing zone: 12 nm

CLIMATE:
temperate; cool summers and mild winters; overcast about a third of the time

TERRAIN:
hills in north and south bisected by central valley

ELEVATION:
lowest point: Irish Sea 0 m
highest point: Snaefell 621 m

NATURAL RESOURCES:
none

LAND USE:
agricultural land: 74.7% (2011 est.)
arable land: 43.8% (2011 est.) / permanent crops: 0% (2011 est.) / permanent pasture: 30.9% (2011 est.)
forest: 6.1% (2011 est.)
other: 19.2% (2011 est.)

IRRIGATED LAND:
0 sq km (2012)

POPULATION DISTRIBUTION:
most people concentrated in cities and large towns of which Douglas, in the southeast, is the largest

NATURAL HAZARDS:
occasional high winds and rough seas

ENVIRONMENT - CURRENT ISSUES:
air pollution, marine pollution; waste disposal (both household and industrial)

GEOGRAPHY - NOTE:
one small islet, the Calf of Man, lies to the southwest and is a bird sanctuary

PEOPLE AND SOCIETY :: ISLE OF MAN

POPULATION:
89,407 (July 2018 est.)
country comparison to the world: 199

NATIONALITY:
noun: Manxman(men), Manxwoman(women)
adjective: Manx

ETHNIC GROUPS:
white 96.5%, Asian/Asian British 1.9%, other 1.5% (2011 est.)

LANGUAGES:
English, Manx Gaelic (about 2% of the population has some knowledge)

RELIGIONS:
Protestant (Anglican, Methodist, Baptist, Presbyterian, Society of Friends), Roman Catholic

AGE STRUCTURE:
0-14 years: 16.27% (male 7,587 /female 6,960)
15-24 years: 11.3% (male 5,354 /female 4,750)
25-54 years: 38.48% (male 17,191 /female 17,217)
55-64 years: 13.34% (male 6,012 /female 5,919)

65 years and over: 20.6% (male 8,661/female 9,756) (2018 est.)

MEDIAN AGE:

total: 44.4 years (2018 est.)

male: 43.4 years

female: 45.2 years

country comparison to the world: 11

POPULATION GROWTH RATE:

0.65% (2018 est.)

country comparison to the world: 146

BIRTH RATE:

10.9 births/1,000 population (2018 est.)

country comparison to the world: 180

DEATH RATE:

10.2 deaths/1,000 population (2018 est.)

country comparison to the world: 31

NET MIGRATION RATE:

5.8 migrant(s)/1,000 population (2018 est.)

country comparison to the world: 19

POPULATION DISTRIBUTION:

most people concentrated in cities and large towns of which Douglas, in the southeast, is the largest

URBANIZATION:

urban population: 52.7% of total population (2019)

rate of urbanization: 0.89% annual rate of change (2015-20 est.)

MAJOR URBAN AREAS - POPULATION:

27,000 DOUGLAS (capital) (2018)

SEX RATIO:

at birth: 1.08 male(s)/female

0-14 years: 1.09 male(s)/female

15-24 years: 1.13 male(s)/female

25-54 years: 1 male(s)/female

55-64 years: 1.02 male(s)/female

65 years and over: 0.89 male(s)/female

total population: 1 male(s)/female (2018 est.)

INFANT MORTALITY RATE:

total: 4 deaths/1,000 live births (2018 est.)

male: 4 deaths/1,000 live births

female: 4 deaths/1,000 live births

country comparison to the world: 191

LIFE EXPECTANCY AT BIRTH:

total population: 81.4 years (2018 est.)

male: 79.6 years

female: 83.3 years

country comparison to the world: 29

TOTAL FERTILITY RATE:

1.92 children born/woman (2018 est.)

country comparison to the world: 129

HIV/AIDS - ADULT PREVALENCE RATE:

NA

HIV/AIDS - PEOPLE LIVING WITH HIV/AIDS:

NA

HIV/AIDS - DEATHS:

NA

EDUCATION EXPENDITURES:

NA

UNEMPLOYMENT, YOUTH AGES 15-24:

total: 10.1%

male: 11.8%

female: 8.2% (2011 est.)

country comparison to the world: 130

GOVERNMENT :: ISLE OF MAN

COUNTRY NAME:

conventional long form: none

conventional short form: Isle of Man

abbreviation: I.O.M.

etymology: the name "man" may be derived from the Celtic word for "mountain"

DEPENDENCY STATUS:

British crown dependency

GOVERNMENT TYPE:

parliamentary democracy (Tynwald); a crown dependency of the UK

CAPITAL:

name: Douglas

geographic coordinates: 54 09 N, 4 29 W

time difference: UTC 0 (5 hours ahead of Washington, DC, during Standard Time)

daylight saving time: +1hr, begins last Sunday in March; ends last Sunday in October

etymology: name derives from the Dhoo and Glass Rivers, which flow through the valley in which the town is located and which in Manx mean the "dark" and the "light" rivers respectively

ADMINISTRATIVE DIVISIONS:

none; there are no first-order administrative divisions as defined by the US Government, but there are 24 local authorities each with its own elections

INDEPENDENCE:

none (British Crown dependency)

NATIONAL HOLIDAY:

Tynwald Day, 5 July (1417); date Tynwald Day was first recorded

CONSTITUTION:

history: development of the Isle of Man constitution dates to at least the 14th century

amendments: proposed as a bill in the House of Keys, by the "Government," by a "Member of the House," or through petition to the House or Legislative Council; passage normally requires three separate readings and approval of at least 13 House members; following both House and Council agreement, assent is required by the lieutenant governor on behalf of the Crown; the constitution has been expanded and amended many times, last in 2015 (2016)

LEGAL SYSTEM:

the laws of the UK apply where applicable and include Manx statutes

CITIZENSHIP:

see United Kingdom

SUFFRAGE:

16 years of age; universal

EXECUTIVE BRANCH:

chief of state: Lord of Mann Queen ELIZABETH II (since 6 February 1952); represented by Lieutenant Governor Sir Richard GOZNEY (since 27 May 2016)

head of government: Chief Minister Howard QUAYLE (since 4 October 2016)

cabinet: Council of Ministers appointed by the lieutenant governor

elections/appointments: the monarchy is hereditary; lieutenant governor appointed by the monarch; chief minister indirectly elected by the Tynwald for a 5-year term (eligible for second term); election last held on 4 October 2016 (next to be held in 2021)

election results: Howard QUAYLE (independent) elected chief minister; Tynwald vote - 21 of 33

LEGISLATIVE BRANCH:

description: bicameral Tynwald or the High Court of Tynwald consists of: Legislative Council (11 seats; includes the President of Tynwald, 2 ex-officio members - the Lord Bishop of Sodor and Man and the attorney general (non-voting) - and 8 members indirectly elected by the House of Keys with renewal of 4 members every 2 years; elected members serve 4-year terms)
House of Keys (24 seats; 2 members directly elected by simple majority vote from 12 constituencies to serve 5-year terms)

elections: Legislative Council - last held 28 February 2018 (next to be held NA)
House of Keys - last held on 22 September 2016 (next to be held in September 2021)

election results: Legislative Council - composition - men 6, women 5, percent of women 45.5%
House of Keys - percent of vote by party - Liberal Vannin 6.4%, independent 92.3%, other 1.3%; seats by party - Liberal Vannin 3, independent 21; composition - men 19, women 5, percent of women 20.8%; note - total Tynwald percent of women 28.6%

note: as of January 2019, seats by party - Liberal Vannin 2, independent 22

JUDICIAL BRANCH:

highest courts: Isle of Man High Court of Justice (consists of 3 permanent judges or "deemsters" and 1 judge of appeal; organized into the Staff of Government Division or Court of Appeal and the Civil Division); the Court of General Gaol Delivery is not formally part of the High Court but is administered as though part of the High Court and deals with serious criminal cases; note - appeals beyond the Court of Appeal are referred to the Judicial Committee of the Privy Council (in London)

judge selection and term of office: deemsters appointed by the Lord Chancellor of England on the nomination of the lieutenant governor; deemsters can serve until age 70

subordinate courts: High Court; Court of Summary Gaol Delivery; Summary Courts; Magistrate's Court; specialized courts

POLITICAL PARTIES AND LEADERS:

Liberal Vannin Party [Kate BEECROFT]
Manx Labor Party
Mec Vannin [Mark KERMODE] (sometimes referred to as the Manx Nationalist Party)

note: most members sit as independents

INTERNATIONAL ORGANIZATION PARTICIPATION:

UPU

DIPLOMATIC REPRESENTATION IN THE US:

none (British crown dependency)

DIPLOMATIC REPRESENTATION FROM THE US:

none (British crown dependency)

FLAG DESCRIPTION:

red with the Three Legs of Man emblem (triskelion), in the center; the three legs are joined at the thigh and bent at the knee; in order to have the toes pointing clockwise on both sides of the flag, a two-sided emblem is used; the flag is based on the coat of arms of the last recognized Norse King of Mann, Magnus III (r. 1252-65); the triskelion has its roots in an early Celtic sun symbol

NATIONAL SYMBOL(S):

triskelion (a motif of three legs); national colors: red, white

NATIONAL ANTHEM:

name: "Arrane Ashoonagh dy Vannin" (O Land of Our Birth)

lyrics/music: William Henry GILL [English], John J. KNEEN [Manx]/traditional

note: adopted 2003, in use since 1907; serves as a local anthem; as a British Crown dependency, "God Save the Queen" is official (see United Kingdom) and is played when the sovereign, members of the royal family, or the lieutenant governor are present

ECONOMY :: ISLE OF MAN

ECONOMY - OVERVIEW:

Financial services, manufacturing, and tourism are key sectors of the economy. The government offers low taxes and other incentives to high-technology companies and financial institutions to locate on the island; this has paid off in expanding employment opportunities in high-income industries. As a result, agriculture and fishing, once the mainstays of the economy, have declined in their contributions to GDP. The Isle of Man also attracts online gambling sites and the film industry. Online gambling sites provided about 10% of the islands income in 2014. The Isle of Man currently enjoys free access to EU markets and trade is mostly with the UK. The Isle of Man's trade relationship with the EU derives from the United Kingdom's EU membership and will need to be renegotiated in light of the United Kingdom's decision to withdraw from the bloc. A transition period is expected to allow the free movement of goods and agricultural products to the EU until the end of 2020 or until a new settlement is negotiated.

GDP (PURCHASING POWER PARITY):

$6.792 billion (2015 est.)

$7.428 billion (2014 est.)

$6.298 billion (2013 est.)

note: data are in 2014 US dollars

country comparison to the world: 169

GDP (OFFICIAL EXCHANGE RATE):

$6.792 billion (2015 est.) (2015 est.)

GDP - REAL GROWTH RATE:

-8.6% (2015 est.)

17.9% (2014 est.)

2.1% (2010 est.)

country comparison to the world: 221

GDP - PER CAPITA (PPP):

$84,600 (2014 est.)

$86,200 (2013 est.)

$73,700 (2012 est.)

country comparison to the world: 8

GDP - COMPOSITION, BY SECTOR OF ORIGIN:

agriculture: 1% (FY12/13 est.)

industry: 13% (FY12/13 est.)

services: 86% (FY12/13 est.)

AGRICULTURE - PRODUCTS:

cereals, vegetables; cattle, sheep, pigs, poultry

INDUSTRIES:

financial services, light manufacturing, tourism

LABOR FORCE:

41,790 (2006)

country comparison to the world: 195

LABOR FORCE - BY OCCUPATION:

manufacturing: 5% (2006 est.)

construction: 8% (2006 est.)

tourism: 1% (2006 est.)

transport and communications: 9% (2006 est.)

agriculture, forestry, and fishing: 2% (2006 est.)

gas, electricity, and water: 1% (2006 est.)

wholesale and retail distribution: 11% (2006 est.)

professional and scientific services: 20% (2006 est.)

public administration: 7% (2006 est.)

banking and finance: 23% (2006 est.)

entertainment and catering: 5% (2006 est.)

miscellaneous services: 8% (2006 est.)

UNEMPLOYMENT RATE:

1.1% (2017 est.)

2% (April 2011 est.)

country comparison to the world: 10

POPULATION BELOW POVERTY LINE:

NA

HOUSEHOLD INCOME OR CONSUMPTION BY PERCENTAGE SHARE:

lowest 10%: NA

highest 10%: NA

BUDGET:

revenues: 965 million (FY05/06 est.)

expenditures: 943 million (FY05/06 est.)

TAXES AND OTHER REVENUES:

14.2% (of GDP) (FY05/06 est.)

country comparison to the world: 201

BUDGET SURPLUS (+) OR DEFICIT (-):

0.3% (of GDP) (FY05/06 est.)

country comparison to the world: 40

FISCAL YEAR:

1 April - 31 March

INFLATION RATE (CONSUMER PRICES):

4.1% (2017 est.)

1% (2016 est.)

country comparison to the world: 160

MARKET VALUE OF PUBLICLY TRADED SHARES:

NA

EXPORTS:

NA

EXPORTS - COMMODITIES:

tweeds, herring, processed shellfish, beef, lamb

IMPORTS:

NA

IMPORTS - COMMODITIES:

timber, fertilizers, fish

DEBT - EXTERNAL:

NA

EXCHANGE RATES:

Manx pounds (IMP) per US dollar -

0.7836 (2017 est.)

0.738 (2016 est.)

0.738 (2015)

0.6542 (2014)

0.6472 (2013 est.)

ENERGY :: ISLE OF MAN

ELECTRICITY ACCESS:

electrification - total population: 100% (2016)

COMMUNICATIONS :: ISLE OF MAN

TELEPHONE SYSTEM:

domestic: landline, telefax, mobile cellular telephone system

international: country code - 44; fiber-optic cable, microwave radio relay, satellite earth station, submarine cable

BROADCAST MEDIA:

national public radio broadcasts over 3 FM stations and 1 AM station; 2 commercial broadcasters operating with 1 having multiple FM stations; receives radio and TV services via relays from British TV and radio broadcasters

INTERNET COUNTRY CODE:

.im

MILITARY AND SECURITY :: ISLE OF MAN

MILITARY - NOTE:

defense is the responsibility of the UK

TRANSPORTATION :: ISLE OF MAN

CIVIL AIRCRAFT REGISTRATION COUNTRY CODE PREFIX:

M (2016)

AIRPORTS:

1 (2013)

country comparison to the world: 224

AIRPORTS - WITH PAVED RUNWAYS:

total: 1 (2017)

1,524 to 2,437 m: 1 (2017)

RAILWAYS:

total: 63 km (2008)

narrow gauge: 6 km 1.076-m gauge (6 km electrified) (2008)

57 0.914-m gauge (29 km electrified)
note: primarily summer tourist attractions

country comparison to the world: 130

ROADWAYS:

total: 500 km (2008)

country comparison to the world: 190

PORTS AND TERMINALS:

major seaport(s): Douglas, Ramsey

TRANSNATIONAL ISSUES :: ISLE OF MAN

DISPUTES - INTERNATIONAL:

none

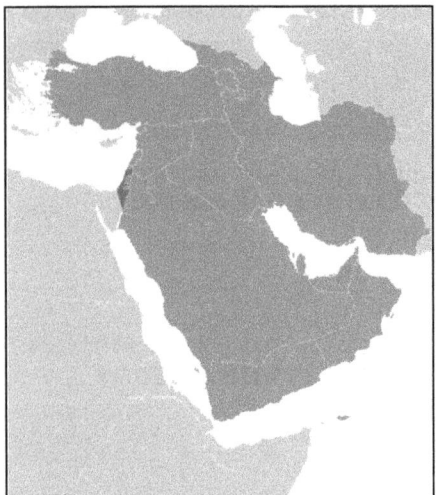

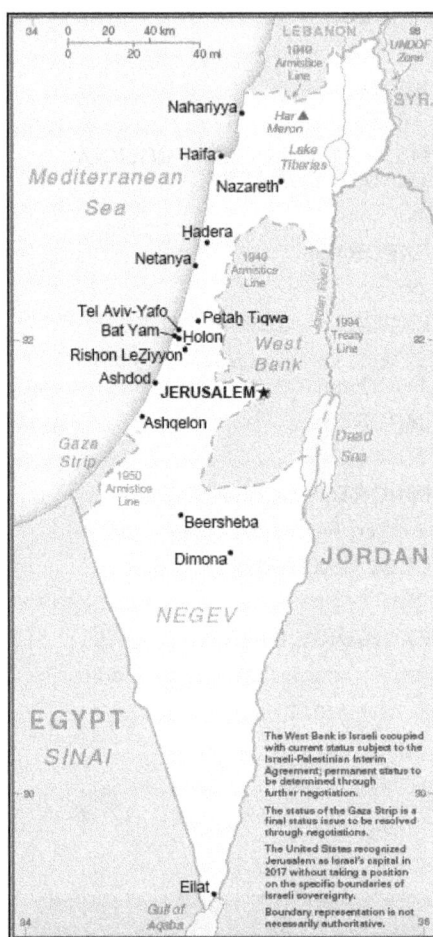

MIDDLE EAST :: ISRAEL

INTRODUCTION :: ISRAEL

BACKGROUND:

The State of Israel was declared in 1948, after Britain withdrew from its mandate of Palestine. The UN proposed partitioning the area into Arab and Jewish states, and Arab armies that rejected the UN plan were defeated. Israel was admitted as a member of the UN in 1949 and saw rapid population growth, primarily due to migration from Europe and the Middle East, over the following years. Israel fought wars against its Arab neighbors in 1967 and 1973, followed by peace treaties with Egypt in 1979 and Jordan in 1994. Israel took control of the West Bank and Gaza Strip in the 1967 war, and subsequently administered those territories through military authorities. Israel and Palestinian officials signed a number of interim agreements in the 1990s that created an interim period of Palestinian self-rule in the West Bank and Gaza. Israel withdrew from Gaza in 2005. While the most recent formal efforts to negotiate final status issues occurred in 2013-2014, the US continues its efforts to advance peace. Immigration to Israel continues, with 28,600 new immigrants, mostly Jewish, in 2016. The Israeli economy has undergone a dramatic transformation in the last 25 years, led by cutting-edge, high-tech sectors. Offshore gas discoveries in the Mediterranean, most notably in the Tamar and Leviathan gas fields, place Israel at the center of a potential regional natural gas market. However, longer-term structural issues such as low labor force participation among minority populations, low workforce productivity, high costs for housing and consumer staples, and a lack of competition, remain a concern for many Israelis and an important consideration for Israeli politicians. Prime Minister Benjamin NETANYAHU has led the Israeli Government since 2009; he formed a center-right coalition following the 2015 elections. In December 2018 the Knesset voted to dissolve itself, leading to an election in April 2019. When that election failed to result in formation of a government, the Knesset voted to dissolve itself again. A new election was held in September 2019.

GEOGRAPHY :: ISRAEL

LOCATION:
Middle East, bordering the Mediterranean Sea, between Egypt and Lebanon

GEOGRAPHIC COORDINATES:
31 30 N, 34 45 E

MAP REFERENCES:
Middle East

AREA:
total: 21,937 sq km
land: 21,497 sq km
water: 440 sq km
country comparison to the world: 153

AREA - COMPARATIVE:
slightly larger than New Jersey

LAND BOUNDARIES:
total: 1,065 km

border countries (6): Egypt 206 km, Gaza Strip 59 km, Jordan 336 km (20 km are within the Dead Sea), Lebanon 107 km, Syria 79 km, West Bank 278 km

COASTLINE:
273 km

MARITIME CLAIMS:
territorial sea: 12 nm

continental shelf: to depth of exploitation

CLIMATE:
temperate; hot and dry in southern and eastern desert areas

TERRAIN:
Negev desert in the south; low coastal plain; central mountains; Jordan Rift Valley

ELEVATION:
mean elevation: 508 m note - does not include elevation data from the Golan Heights

lowest point: Dead Sea -431 m

highest point: Mitspe Shlagim 2,224 m; note - this is the highest named point, the actual highest point is an unnamed dome slightly to the west of Mitspe Shlagim at 2,236 m; both points are on the northeastern border of Israel, along the southern end of the Anti-Lebanon mountain range

NATURAL RESOURCES:
timber, potash, copper ore, natural gas, phosphate rock, magnesium bromide, clays, sand

LAND USE:
agricultural land: 23.8% (2011 est.)

arable land: 13.7% (2011 est.) / permanent crops: 3.8% (2011 est.) / permanent pasture: 6.3% (2011 est.)

forest: 7.1% (2011 est.)

other: 69.1% (2011 est.)

IRRIGATED LAND:
2,250 sq km (2012)

POPULATION DISTRIBUTION:
population concentrated in and around Tel-Aviv, as well as around the Sea of Galilee; the south remains sparsely populated with the exception of the shore of the Gulf of Aqaba

NATURAL HAZARDS:
sandstorms may occur during spring and summer; droughts; periodic earthquakes

ENVIRONMENT - CURRENT ISSUES:
limited arable land and restricted natural freshwater resources; desertification; air pollution from industrial and vehicle emissions; groundwater pollution from industrial and domestic waste, chemical fertilizers, and pesticides

ENVIRONMENT - INTERNATIONAL AGREEMENTS:
party to: Biodiversity, Climate Change, Climate Change-Kyoto Protocol, Desertification, Endangered Species, Hazardous Wastes, Ozone Layer Protection, Ship Pollution, Wetlands, Whaling

signed, but not ratified: Marine Life Conservation

GEOGRAPHY - NOTE:
note 1: Lake Tiberias (Sea of Galilee) is an important freshwater source; the Dead Sea is the second saltiest body of water in the world (after Lake Assal in Djibouti)

note 2: the Malham Cave in Mount Sodom is the world's longest salt cave at 10 km (6 mi); its survey is not complete and its length will undoubtedly increase; Mount Sodom is actually a hill some 220 m (722 ft) high that is 80% salt (multiple salt layers covered by a veneer of rock)

note 3: in March 2019, there were 380 Israeli settlements, to include 213 settlements and 132 outposts in the West Bank, and 35 settlements in East Jerusalem; there are no Israeli settlements in the Gaza Strip, as all were evacuated in 2005 (2019)

PEOPLE AND SOCIETY :: ISRAEL

POPULATION:
8,424,904 (includes populations of the Golan Heights or Golan Sub-District and also East Jerusalem, which was annexed by Israel after 1967) (July 2018 est.)

note: approximately 22,000 Israeli settlers live in the Golan Heights (2016); approximately 201,000 Israeli settlers live in East Jerusalem (2014)

country comparison to the world: 98

NATIONALITY:
noun: Israeli(s)

adjective: Israeli

ETHNIC GROUPS:
Jewish 74.4% (of which Israel-born 76.9%, Europe/America/Oceania-born 15.9%, Africa-born 4.6%, Asia-born 2.6%), Arab 20.9%, other 4.7% (2018 est.)

LANGUAGES:
Hebrew (official), Arabic (used officially for Arab minority), English (most commonly used foreign language)

RELIGIONS:
Jewish 74.7%, Muslim 17.7%, Christian 2%, Druze 1.6%, other 4% (2016 est.)

AGE STRUCTURE:
0-14 years: 27.26% (male 1,175,106 /female 1,121,309)

15-24 years: 15.58% (male 670,121 /female 642,155)

25-54 years: 37.19% (male 1,601,516 /female 1,531,849)

55-64 years: 8.42% (male 350,050 /female 359,578)

65 years and over: 11.55% (male 437,511 /female 535,709) (2018 est.)

DEPENDENCY RATIOS:
total dependency ratio: 64.2 (2015 est.)

youth dependency ratio: 45.7 (2015 est.)

elderly dependency ratio: 18.4 (2015 est.)

potential support ratio: 5.4 (2015 est.)

MEDIAN AGE:
total: 30.1 years (2018 est.)

male: 29.5 years

female: 30.7 years

country comparison to the world: 119

POPULATION GROWTH RATE:
1.49% (2018 est.)

country comparison to the world: 73

BIRTH RATE:
17.9 births/1,000 population (2018 est.)

country comparison to the world: 94

DEATH RATE:
5.2 deaths/1,000 population (2018 est.)

country comparison to the world: 189

NET MIGRATION RATE:
2.1 migrant(s)/1,000 population (2018 est.)

country comparison to the world: 50

POPULATION DISTRIBUTION:

population concentrated in and around Tel-Aviv, as well as around the Sea of Galilee; the south remains sparsely populated with the exception of the shore of the Gulf of Aqaba

URBANIZATION:

urban population: 92.5% of total population (2019)

rate of urbanization: 1.64% annual rate of change (2015-20 est.)

MAJOR URBAN AREAS - POPULATION:

4.097 million Tel Aviv-Yafo, 1.141 million Haifa, 919,000 JERUSALEM (capital) (2019)

SEX RATIO:

at birth: 1.05 male(s)/female

0-14 years: 1.05 male(s)/female

15-24 years: 1.04 male(s)/female

25-54 years: 1.05 male(s)/female

55-64 years: 0.97 male(s)/female

65 years and over: 0.82 male(s)/female

total population: 1.01 male(s)/female (2018 est.)

MOTHER'S MEAN AGE AT FIRST BIRTH:

27.6 years (2015 est.)

MATERNAL MORTALITY RATE:

3 deaths/100,000 live births (2017 est.)

country comparison to the world: 179

INFANT MORTALITY RATE:

total: 3.4 deaths/1,000 live births (2018 est.)

male: 3.4 deaths/1,000 live births

female: 3.4 deaths/1,000 live births

country comparison to the world: 204

LIFE EXPECTANCY AT BIRTH:

total population: 82.7 years (2018 est.)

male: 80.8 years

female: 84.7 years

country comparison to the world: 10

TOTAL FERTILITY RATE:

2.63 children born/woman (2018 est.)

country comparison to the world: 69

DRINKING WATER SOURCE:

improved:

urban: 100% of population

rural: 100% of population

total: 100% of population

unimproved:

urban: 0% of population

rural: 0% of population

total: 0% of population (2015 est.)

CURRENT HEALTH EXPENDITURE:

7.3% (2016)

PHYSICIANS DENSITY:

3.22 physicians/1,000 population (2016)

HOSPITAL BED DENSITY:

3.1 beds/1,000 population (2013)

SANITATION FACILITY ACCESS:

improved:

urban: 100% of population (2015 est.)

rural: 100% of population (2015 est.)

total: 100% of population (2015 est.)

unimproved:

urban: 0% of population (2015 est.)

rural: 0% of population (2015 est.)

total: 0% of population (2015 est.)

HIV/AIDS - ADULT PREVALENCE RATE:

0.2% (2018)

country comparison to the world: 101

HIV/AIDS - PEOPLE LIVING WITH HIV/AIDS:

9,000 (2018)

country comparison to the world: 104

HIV/AIDS - DEATHS:

<100 (2018)

OBESITY - ADULT PREVALENCE RATE:

26.1% (2016)

country comparison to the world: 44

EDUCATION EXPENDITURES:

5.9% of GDP (2015)

country comparison to the world: 36

LITERACY:

definition: age 15 and over can read and write

total population: 97.8%

male: 98.7%

female: 96.8% (2011 est.)

SCHOOL LIFE EXPECTANCY (PRIMARY TO TERTIARY EDUCATION):

total: 16 years

male: 15 years

female: 17 years (2016)

UNEMPLOYMENT, YOUTH AGES 15-24:

total: 7.3%

male: 6.7%

female: 7.8% (2017 est.)

country comparison to the world: 153

GOVERNMENT :: ISRAEL

COUNTRY NAME:

conventional long form: State of Israel

conventional short form: Israel

local long form: Medinat Yisra'el

local short form: Yisra'el

etymology: named after the ancient Kingdom of Israel; according to Biblical tradition, the Jewish patriarch Jacob received the name "Israel" ("He who struggles with God") after he wrestled an entire night with an angel of the Lord; Jacob's 12 sons became the ancestors of the Israelites, also known as the Twelve Tribes of Israel, who formed the Kingdom of Israel

GOVERNMENT TYPE:

parliamentary democracy

CAPITAL:

name: Jerusalem; note - the US recognized Jerusalem as Israel's capital in December 2017 without taking a position on the specific boundaries of Israeli sovereignty

geographic coordinates: 31 46 N, 35 14 E

time difference: UTC+2 (7 hours ahead of Washington, DC, during Standard Time)

daylight saving time: +1hr, Friday before the last Sunday in March; ends the last Sunday in October

etymology: Jerusalem's settlement may date back to 2800 B.C.; it is named Urushalim in Egyptian texts of the 14th century B.C.; "uru-shalim" likely means "foundation of [by] the god Shalim", and derives from Hebrew/Semitic "yry", "to found or lay a cornerstone", and Shalim, the Canaanite god of dusk and the nether world; Shalim was associated with sunset and peace and the name is based on the same S-L-M root from which Semitic words for "peace" are derived (Salam or Shalom in modern Arabic and Hebrew); this confluence has thus led to naming interpretations such as "The City of Peace" or "The Abode of Peace"

ADMINISTRATIVE DIVISIONS:

6 districts (mehozot, singular - mehoz); Central, Haifa, Jerusalem, Northern, Southern, Tel Aviv

INDEPENDENCE:

14 May 1948 (following League of Nations mandate under British administration)

NATIONAL HOLIDAY:

Independence Day, 14 May (1948); note - Israel declared independence on 14 May 1948, but the Jewish calendar is lunar and the holiday may occur in April or May

CONSTITUTION:

history: no formal constitution; some functions of a constitution are filled by the Declaration of Establishment (1948), the Basic Laws, and the Law of Return (as amended)

amendments: proposed by Government of Israel ministers or by the Knesset; passage requires a majority vote of Knesset members and subject to Supreme Court judicial review; 11 of the 13 Basic Laws have been amended at least once, latest in 2018 (2018)

LEGAL SYSTEM:

mixed legal system of English common law, British Mandate regulations, and Jewish, Christian, and Muslim religious laws

INTERNATIONAL LAW ORGANIZATION PARTICIPATION:

has not submitted an ICJ jurisdiction declaration; withdrew acceptance of ICCt jurisdiction in 2002

CITIZENSHIP:

citizenship by birth: no

citizenship by descent only: at least one parent must be a citizen of Israel

dual citizenship recognized: yes, but naturalized citizens are not allowed to maintain dual citizenship

residency requirement for naturalization: 3 out of the 5 years preceding the application for naturalization

note: Israeli law (Law of Return, 5 July 1950) provides for the granting of citizenship to any Jew - defined as a person being born to a Jewish mother or having converted to Judaism while renouncing any other religion - who immigrates to and expresses a desire to settle in Israel on the basis of the Right of aliyah; the 1970 amendment of this act extended the right to family members including the spouse of a Jew, any child or grandchild, and the spouses of children and grandchildren

SUFFRAGE:

18 years of age; universal; 17 years of age for municipal elections

EXECUTIVE BRANCH:

chief of state: President Reuben RIVLIN (since 27 July 2014)

head of government: Prime Minister Binyamin NETANYAHU (since 31 March 2009); note - on 23 October 2019, following the inconclusive 25 September Knesset election, President RIVLIN tasked Benny GANTZ with forming a new government after Prime Minister NETANYAHU was unable to do so

cabinet: Cabinet selected by prime minister and approved by the Knesset

elections/appointments: president indirectly elected by the Knesset for a 7-year term (limited to 1 term); election last held on 10 June 2014 (next to be held on 9 April 2019); following legislative elections, the president, in consultation with party leaders, tasks a Knesset member (usually the member of the largest party) with forming a government

election results: Reuven RIVLIN elected president in second round; Knesset vote - Reuven RIVLIN (Likud) 63, Meir SHEETRIT (The Movement) 53, other/invalid 4

LEGISLATIVE BRANCH:

description: unicameral Knesset (120 seats; members directly elected in a single nationwide constituency by closed-list proportional representation vote, with a 3.25% threshold to gain representation; members serve 4-year terms)

elections: last held on 17 September 2019 (next to be held in 2023)

election results: percent by party - Blue and White 26%, Likud 25.1%, Joint List 10.6%, Shas 7.4%, Yisrael Beiteinu 7%, United Torah Judaism 6.1%, Yamina 5.9%, Labor-Gesher 4.8%, Democratic Union 4.3%, other 2.8%; seats by party - Blue and White 33, Likud 32, Joint List 13, Shas 9, Yisrael Beiteinu 8, United Torah Judaism 7, Yamina 7, Labor-Gesher 6, Democratic Union 5; composition - men 92, women 28, percent of women 23%

JUDICIAL BRANCH:

highest courts: Supreme Court (consists of the chief justice and 14 judges)

judge selection and term of office: judges selected by the Judicial Selection Committee, consisting of 3 Supreme Court judges, 2 Cabinet members including the Minister of Justice as chairman, 2 Knesset members, and 2 representatives from the Israel Bar Association; judges can serve up to mandatory retirement at age 70

subordinate courts: Court for Administrative Matters; district and magistrate courts; national and regional labor courts; special and religious courts

POLITICAL PARTIES AND LEADERS:

Democratic Union [Nitzan HOROWITZ] (alliance includes Democratic Israel, Meretz, Green Movement)
Joint List [Ayman ODEH] (alliance includes Hadash, Ta'al, United Arab List, Balad)
Kahol Lavan [Benny GANTZ] (alliance includes Israeli Resilience, Yesh Atid, Telem)
Labor-Gesher [Amir PERETZ]
Likud [Binyamin NETANYAHU]
Otzma Yehudit [Itamar BEN-GVIR]
SHAS [Arye DERI]
United Torah Judaism, or UTJ [Yaakov LITZMAN] (alliance includes Agudat Israel and Degel HaTorah)
Yamina [Ayelet SHAKED]
Yisrael Beiteinu [Avigdor LIEBERMAN]
Zehut [Moshe FEIGLIN]

INTERNATIONAL ORGANIZATION PARTICIPATION:

BIS, BSEC (observer), CE (observer), CERN, CICA, EBRD, FAO, IADB, IAEA, IBRD, ICAO, ICC (national committees), ICRM, IDA, IFAD, IFC, IFRCS, ILO, IMF, IMO, IMSO, Interpol, IOC, IOM, IPU, ISO, ITSO, ITU, ITUC (NGOs), MIGA, OAS (observer), OECD, OPCW (signatory), OSCE (partner), Pacific Alliance (observer), Paris Club, PCA, SELEC (observer), UN, UNCTAD, UNESCO, UNHCR, UNIDO, UNWTO, UPU, WCO, WHO, WIPO, WMO, WTO

DIPLOMATIC REPRESENTATION IN THE US:

Ambassador Ron DERMER (since 3 December 2013)

chancery: 3514 International Drive NW, Washington, DC 20008

telephone: [1] (202) 364-5500

FAX: [1] (202) 364-5607

consulate(s) general: Atlanta, Boston, Chicago, Houston, Los Angeles, Miami, New York, Philadelphia, San Francisco

DIPLOMATIC REPRESENTATION FROM THE US:

chief of mission: Ambassador David M. FRIEDMAN (since 23 May 2017)

telephone: [972] (2) 630-4000

embassy: David Flusser St.14, Jerusalem, 9378322

FAX: NA

note: on 14 May 2018, the US Embassy relocated to Jerusalem from Tel Aviv; on 4 March 2019, Consulate General Jerusalem merged into US Embassy Jerusalem to form a single diplomatic mission

FLAG DESCRIPTION:

white with a blue hexagram (six-pointed linear star) known as the Magen David (Star of David or Shield of David) centered between two equal horizontal blue bands near the top and bottom edges of the flag; the basic design resembles a traditional Jewish prayer shawl (tallit), which is white with blue stripes; the hexagram as a Jewish symbol dates back to medieval times

note: the Israeli flag proclamation states that the flag colors are sky blue and white, but the exact shade of blue has never been set and can vary from a light to a dark blue

NATIONAL SYMBOL(S):

Star of David (Magen David), menorah (seven-branched lampstand); national colors: blue, white

NATIONAL ANTHEM:

name: "Hatikvah" (The Hope)

lyrics/music: Naftali Herz IMBER/traditional, arranged by Samuel COHEN

note: adopted 2004, unofficial since 1948; used as the anthem of the Zionist movement since 1897; the 1888 arrangement by Samuel COHEN is thought to be based on the Romanian folk song "Carul cu boi" (The Ox Driven Cart)

ECONOMY :: ISRAEL

ECONOMY - OVERVIEW:

Israel has a technologically advanced free market economy. Cut diamonds, high-technology equipment, and pharmaceuticals are among its leading exports. Its major imports include crude oil, grains, raw materials, and military equipment. Israel usually posts sizable trade deficits, which are offset by tourism and other service exports, as well as significant foreign investment inflows.

Between 2004 and 2013, growth averaged nearly 5% per year, led by exports. The global financial crisis of 2008-09 spurred a brief recession in Israel, but the country entered the crisis with solid fundamentals, following years of prudent fiscal policy and a resilient banking sector. Israel's economy also weathered the 2011 Arab Spring because strong trade ties outside the Middle East insulated the economy from spillover effects.

Slowing domestic and international demand and decreased investment resulting from Israel's uncertain security situation reduced GDP growth to an average of roughly 2.8% per year during the period 2014-17. Natural gas fields discovered off Israel's coast since 2009 have brightened Israel's energy security outlook. The Tamar and Leviathan fields were some of the world's largest offshore natural gas finds in the last decade. Political and regulatory issues have delayed the development of the massive Leviathan field, but production from Tamar provided a 0.8% boost to Israel's GDP in 2013 and a 0.3% boost in 2014. One of the most carbon intense OECD countries, Israel generates about 57% of its power from coal and only 2.6% from renewable sources.

Income inequality and high housing and commodity prices continue to be a concern for many Israelis. Israel's income inequality and poverty rates are among the highest of OECD countries, and there is a broad perception among the public that a small number of "tycoons" have a cartel-like grip over the major parts of the economy. Government officials have called for reforms to boost the housing supply and to increase competition in the banking sector to address these public grievances. Despite calls for reforms, the restricted housing supply continues to impact younger Israelis seeking to purchase homes. Tariffs and non-tariff barriers, coupled with guaranteed prices and customs tariffs for farmers kept food prices high in 2016. Private consumption is expected to drive growth through 2018, with consumers benefitting from low inflation and a strong currency.

In the long term, Israel faces structural issues including low labor participation rates for its fastest growing social segments - the ultraorthodox and Arab-Israeli communities. Also, Israel's progressive, globally competitive, knowledge-based technology sector employs only about 8% of the workforce, with the rest mostly employed in manufacturing and services - sectors which face downward wage pressures from global competition. Expenditures on educational institutions remain low compared to most other OECD countries with similar GDP per capita.

GDP (PURCHASING POWER PARITY):

$317.1 billion (2017 est.)

$307 billion (2016 est.)

$295.3 billion (2015 est.)

note: data are in 2017 dollars

country comparison to the world: 54

GDP (OFFICIAL EXCHANGE RATE):

$350.7 billion (2017 est.)

GDP - REAL GROWTH RATE:

3.3% (2017 est.)

4% (2016 est.)

2.6% (2015 est.)

country comparison to the world: 105

GDP - PER CAPITA (PPP):

$36,400 (2017 est.)

$35,900 (2016 est.)

$35,200 (2015 est.)

note: data are in 2017 dollars

country comparison to the world: 55

GROSS NATIONAL SAVING:

23.6% of GDP (2017 est.)

24.2% of GDP (2016 est.)

25% of GDP (2015 est.)

country comparison to the world: 72

GDP - COMPOSITION, BY END USE:

household consumption: 55.1% (2017 est.)

government consumption: 22.8% (2017 est.)

investment in fixed capital: 20.1% (2017 est.)

investment in inventories: 0.7% (2017 est.)

exports of goods and services: 28.9% (2017 est.)

imports of goods and services: -27.5% (2017 est.)

GDP - COMPOSITION, BY SECTOR OF ORIGIN:
agriculture: 2.4% (2017 est.)

industry: 26.5% (2017 est.)

services: 69.5% (2017 est.)

AGRICULTURE - PRODUCTS:
citrus, vegetables, cotton; beef, poultry, dairy products

INDUSTRIES:
high-technology products (including aviation, communications, computer-aided design and manufactures, medical electronics, fiber optics), wood and paper products, potash and phosphates, food, beverages, and tobacco, caustic soda, cement, pharmaceuticals, construction, metal products, chemical products, plastics, cut diamonds, textiles, footwear

INDUSTRIAL PRODUCTION GROWTH RATE:
3.5% (2017 est.)

country comparison to the world: 86

LABOR FORCE:
4.021 million (2017 est.)

country comparison to the world: 93

LABOR FORCE - BY OCCUPATION:
agriculture: 1.1%

industry: 17.3%

services: 81.6% (2015 est.)

UNEMPLOYMENT RATE:
4.2% (2017 est.)

4.8% (2016 est.)

country comparison to the world: 55

POPULATION BELOW POVERTY LINE:
22% (2014 est.) (2014 est.)

note: Israel's poverty line is $7.30 per person per day

HOUSEHOLD INCOME OR CONSUMPTION BY PERCENTAGE SHARE:
lowest 10%: 1.7%

highest 10%: 31.3% (2010)

DISTRIBUTION OF FAMILY INCOME - GINI INDEX:
42.8 (2013)

39.2 (2008)

country comparison to the world: 49

BUDGET:
revenues: 93.11 billion (2017 est.)

expenditures: 100.2 billion (2017 est.)

TAXES AND OTHER REVENUES:
26.5% (of GDP) (2017 est.)

country comparison to the world: 110

BUDGET SURPLUS (+) OR DEFICIT (-):
-2% (of GDP) (2017 est.)

country comparison to the world: 105

PUBLIC DEBT:
60.9% of GDP (2017 est.)

62.3% of GDP (2016 est.)

country comparison to the world: 73

FISCAL YEAR:
calendar year

INFLATION RATE (CONSUMER PRICES):
0.2% (2017 est.)

-0.5% (2016 est.)

country comparison to the world: 17

CENTRAL BANK DISCOUNT RATE:
0.1% (15 December 2015)

0.25% (31 December 2014)

country comparison to the world: 142

COMMERCIAL BANK PRIME LENDING RATE:
3.5% (31 December 2017 est.)

3.42% (31 December 2016 est.)

country comparison to the world: 169

STOCK OF NARROW MONEY:
$100.4 billion (31 December 2017 est.)

$79.58 billion (31 December 2016 est.)

country comparison to the world: 41

STOCK OF BROAD MONEY:
$100.4 billion (31 December 2017 est.)

$79.58 billion (31 December 2016 est.)

country comparison to the world: 41

STOCK OF DOMESTIC CREDIT:
$290.7 billion (31 December 2017 est.)

$257.4 billion (31 December 2016 est.)

country comparison to the world: 39

MARKET VALUE OF PUBLICLY TRADED SHARES:
$243.9 billion (31 December 2015 est.)

$200.5 billion (31 December 2014 est.)

$203.3 billion (31 December 2013 est.)

country comparison to the world: 31

CURRENT ACCOUNT BALANCE:
$10.12 billion (2017 est.)

$11.94 billion (2016 est.)

country comparison to the world: 22

EXPORTS:
$58.67 billion (2017 est.)

$56.17 billion (2016 est.)

country comparison to the world: 48

EXPORTS - PARTNERS:
US 28.8%, UK 8.2%, Hong Kong 7%, China 5.4%, Belgium 4.5% (2017)

EXPORTS - COMMODITIES:
machinery and equipment, software, cut diamonds, agricultural products, chemicals, textiles and apparel

IMPORTS:
$68.61 billion (2017 est.)

$63.9 billion (2016 est.)

country comparison to the world: 46

IMPORTS - COMMODITIES:
raw materials, military equipment, investment goods, rough diamonds, fuels, grain, consumer goods

IMPORTS - PARTNERS:
US 11.7%, China 9.5%, Switzerland 8%, Germany 6.8%, UK 6.2%, Belgium 5.9%, Netherlands 4.2%, Turkey 4.2%, Italy 4% (2017)

RESERVES OF FOREIGN EXCHANGE AND GOLD:
$113 billion (31 December 2017 est.)

$95.45 billion (31 December 2016 est.)

country comparison to the world: 23

DEBT - EXTERNAL:
$88.66 billion (31 December 2017 est.)

$87.96 billion (31 December 2016 est.)

country comparison to the world: 54

STOCK OF DIRECT FOREIGN INVESTMENT - AT HOME:
$129.1 billion (31 December 2017 est.)

$107.3 billion (31 December 2016 est.)

country comparison to the world: 43

STOCK OF DIRECT FOREIGN INVESTMENT - ABROAD:
$100.3 billion (31 December 2017 est.)

$98.11 billion (31 December 2016 est.)

country comparison to the world: 35

EXCHANGE RATES:
new Israeli shekels (ILS) per US dollar -

3.606 (2017 est.)

3.8406 (2016 est.)

3.8406 (2015 est.)

3.8869 (2014 est.)

3.5779 (2013 est.)

ENERGY :: ISRAEL

ELECTRICITY ACCESS:

electrification - total population: 100% (2016)

ELECTRICITY - PRODUCTION:

63.09 billion kWh (2016 est.)

country comparison to the world: 46

ELECTRICITY - CONSUMPTION:

55 billion kWh (2016 est.)

country comparison to the world: 47

ELECTRICITY - EXPORTS:

5.2 billion kWh (2016 est.)

country comparison to the world: 35

ELECTRICITY - IMPORTS:

0 kWh (2016 est.)

country comparison to the world: 161

ELECTRICITY - INSTALLED GENERATING CAPACITY:

17.59 million kW (2016 est.)

country comparison to the world: 48

ELECTRICITY - FROM FOSSIL FUELS:

95% of total installed capacity (2016 est.)

country comparison to the world: 44

ELECTRICITY - FROM NUCLEAR FUELS:

0% of total installed capacity (2017 est.)

country comparison to the world: 113

ELECTRICITY - FROM HYDROELECTRIC PLANTS:

0% of total installed capacity (2017 est.)

country comparison to the world: 179

ELECTRICITY - FROM OTHER RENEWABLE SOURCES:

5% of total installed capacity (2017 est.)

country comparison to the world: 107

CRUDE OIL - PRODUCTION:

390 bbl/day (2018 est.)

country comparison to the world: 94

CRUDE OIL - EXPORTS:

0 bbl/day (2017 est.)

country comparison to the world: 141

CRUDE OIL - IMPORTS:

231,600 bbl/day (2017 est.)

country comparison to the world: 28

CRUDE OIL - PROVED RESERVES:

12.73 million bbl (1 January 2018 est.)

country comparison to the world: 87

REFINED PETROLEUM PRODUCTS - PRODUCTION:

294,300 bbl/day (2017 est.)

country comparison to the world: 42

REFINED PETROLEUM PRODUCTS - CONSUMPTION:

242,200 bbl/day (2017 est.)

country comparison to the world: 52

REFINED PETROLEUM PRODUCTS - EXPORTS:

111,700 bbl/day (2017 est.)

country comparison to the world: 39

REFINED PETROLEUM PRODUCTS - IMPORTS:

98,860 bbl/day (2017 est.)

country comparison to the world: 54

NATURAL GAS - PRODUCTION:

9.826 billion cu m (2017 est.)

country comparison to the world: 42

NATURAL GAS - CONSUMPTION:

9.995 billion cu m (2017 est.)

country comparison to the world: 49

NATURAL GAS - EXPORTS:

0 cu m (2017 est.)

country comparison to the world: 126

NATURAL GAS - IMPORTS:

509.7 million cu m (2017 est.)

country comparison to the world: 66

NATURAL GAS - PROVED RESERVES:

176 billion cu m (1 January 2018 est.)

country comparison to the world: 45

CARBON DIOXIDE EMISSIONS FROM CONSUMPTION OF ENERGY:

73.82 million Mt (2017 est.)

country comparison to the world: 49

COMMUNICATIONS :: ISRAEL

TELEPHONES - FIXED LINES:

total subscriptions: 3.24 million

subscriptions per 100 inhabitants: 39 (2017 est.)

country comparison to the world: 42

TELEPHONES - MOBILE CELLULAR:

total subscriptions: 10.54 million

subscriptions per 100 inhabitants: 127 (2017 est.)

country comparison to the world: 82

TELEPHONE SYSTEM:

general assessment: most highly developed system in the Middle East; mobile broadband 100% population penetration; consumers enjoy inexpensive 3G services; 4G cellular service; fixed broadband available to 99% of all households (2019)

domestic: good system of coaxial cable and microwave radio relay; all systems are digital; competition among both fixed-line and mobile cellular providers results in good coverage countrywide; fixed-line 39 per 100 and 127 per 100 for mobile-cellular subscriptions (2019)

international: country code - 972; landing points for the MedNautilus Submarine System, Tameres North, Jonah and Lev Submarine System submarine cables provide links to Europe, Cyprus, and parts of the Middle East; satellite earth stations - 3 Intelsat (2 Atlantic Ocean and 1 Indian Ocean) (2019)

BROADCAST MEDIA:

the Israel Broadcasting Corporation (est 2015) broadcasts on 3 channels, two in Hebrew and the other in Arabic; multi-channel satellite and cable TV packages provide access to foreign channels; the Israeli Broadcasting Corporation broadcasts on 8 radio networks with multiple repeaters and Israel Defense Forces Radio broadcasts over multiple stations; about 15 privately owned radio stations; overall more than 100 stations and repeater stations (2019)

INTERNET COUNTRY CODE:

.il

INTERNET USERS:

total: 6,521,539

percent of population: 79.8% (July 2016 est.)

country comparison to the world: 64

BROADBAND - FIXED SUBSCRIPTIONS:

total: 2.342 million

subscriptions per 100 inhabitants: 28 (2017 est.)

country comparison to the world: 49

MILITARY AND SECURITY :: ISRAEL

MILITARY EXPENDITURES:

5.1% of GDP (2017)

5.3% of GDP (2016)

5.3% of GDP (2015)

5.6% of GDP (2014)

5.6% of GDP (2013)

country comparison to the world: 5

MILITARY AND SECURITY FORCES:

Israel Defense Forces (IDF); Ground Forces, Israel Naval Force (IN, includes commandos), Israel Air Force (IAF, includes air defense) (2019)

MILITARY SERVICE AGE AND OBLIGATION:

18 years of age for compulsory (Jews, Druze) military service; 17 years of age for voluntary (Christians, Muslims, Circassians) military service; both sexes are obligated to military service; conscript service obligation - 32 months for enlisted men and about 24 months for enlisted women (varies based on military occupation), 48 months for officers; pilots commit to 9-year service; reserve obligation to age 41-51 (men), age 24 (women) (2015)

TRANSPORTATION :: ISRAEL

NATIONAL AIR TRANSPORT SYSTEM:

number of registered air carriers: 6 (2015)

inventory of registered aircraft operated by air carriers: 60 (2015)

annual passenger traffic on registered air carriers: 6,064,478 (2015)

annual freight traffic on registered air carriers: 758,633,996 mt-km (2015)

CIVIL AIRCRAFT REGISTRATION COUNTRY CODE PREFIX:

4X (2016)

AIRPORTS:

47 (2013)

country comparison to the world: 92

AIRPORTS - WITH PAVED RUNWAYS:

total: 29 (2017)

over 3,047 m: 2 (2017)

2,438 to 3,047 m: 5 (2017)

1,524 to 2,437 m: 6 (2017)

914 to 1,523 m: 11 (2017)

under 914 m: 5 (2017)

AIRPORTS - WITH UNPAVED RUNWAYS:

total: 18 (2013)

1,524 to 2,437 m: 1 (2013)

914 to 1,523 m: 3 (2013)

under 914 m: 14 (2013)

HELIPORTS:

3 (2013)

PIPELINES:

763 km gas, 442 km oil, 261 km refined products (2013)

RAILWAYS:

total: 1,384 km (2014)

standard gauge: 1,384 km 1.435-m gauge (2014)

country comparison to the world: 83

ROADWAYS:

total: 19,555 km (2017)

paved: 19,555 km (includes 449 km of expressways) (2017)

country comparison to the world: 114

MERCHANT MARINE:

total: 42

by type: container ship 5, general cargo 5, oil tanker 3, other 29 (2018)

country comparison to the world: 119

PORTS AND TERMINALS:

major seaport(s): Ashdod, Elat (Eilat), Hadera, Haifa

container port(s) (TEUs): Ashdod (1,443,000) (2016)

TERRORISM :: ISRAEL

TERRORIST GROUPS - HOME BASED:

Kahane Chai (Kach): aim(s): expel Arabs from Israel's biblical lands and, ultimately, restore the biblical state of Israel

area(s) of operation: Israel and West Bank settlements

note: considered to be operationally inactive in recent years (2018)

TERRORIST GROUPS - FOREIGN BASED:

TRANSNATIONAL ISSUES :: ISRAEL

DISPUTES - INTERNATIONAL:

West Bank and Gaza Strip are Israeli-occupied with current status subject to the Israeli-Palestinian Interim Agreement - permanent status to be determined through further negotiation; Israel continues construction of a "seam line" separation barrier along parts of the Green Line and within the West Bank; Israel withdrew its settlers and military from the Gaza Strip and from four settlements in the West Bank in August 2005; Golan Heights is Israeli-controlled (Lebanon claims the Shab'a Farms area of Golan Heights); since 1948, about 350 peacekeepers from the UN Truce Supervision Organization headquartered in Jerusalem monitor ceasefires, supervise armistice agreements, prevent isolated incidents from escalating, and assist other UN personnel in the region

REFUGEES AND INTERNALLY DISPLACED PERSONS:

refugees (country of origin): 14,516 (Eritrea) (2018), 7,857 (Ukraine) (2019)

stateless persons: 42 (2018)

ILLICIT DRUGS:

increasingly concerned about ecstasy, cocaine, and heroin abuse; drugs arrive in country from Lebanon and, increasingly, from Jordan; money-laundering center

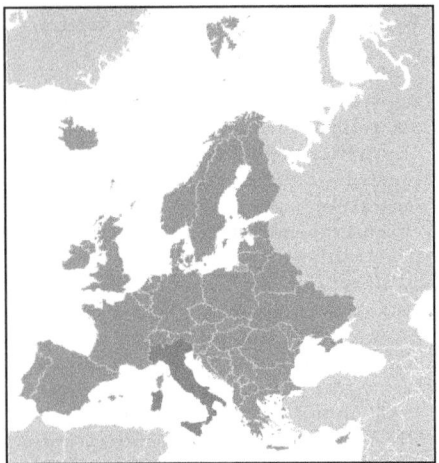

EUROPE :: ITALY

INTRODUCTION :: ITALY

BACKGROUND:
Italy became a nation-state in 1861 when the regional states of the peninsula, along with Sardinia and Sicily, were united under King Victor EMMANUEL II. An era of parliamentary government came to a close in the early 1920s when Benito MUSSOLINI established a Fascist dictatorship. His alliance with Nazi Germany led to Italy's defeat in World War II. A democratic republic replaced the monarchy in 1946 and economic revival followed. Italy is a charter member of NATO and the European Economic Community (EEC) and its subsequent successors the EC and the EU. It has been at the forefront of European economic and political unification, joining the Economic and Monetary Union in 1999. Persistent problems include sluggish economic growth, high youth and female unemployment, organized crime, corruption, and economic disparities between southern Italy and the more prosperous north.

GEOGRAPHY :: ITALY

LOCATION:
Southern Europe, a peninsula extending into the central Mediterranean Sea, northeast of Tunisia

GEOGRAPHIC COORDINATES:
42 50 N, 12 50 E

MAP REFERENCES:
Europe

AREA:
total: 301,340 sq km
land: 294,140 sq km
water: 7,200 sq km
note: includes Sardinia and Sicily
country comparison to the world: 73

AREA - COMPARATIVE:
almost twice the size of Georgia; slightly larger than Arizona

LAND BOUNDARIES:
total: 1,836.4 km
border countries (6): Austria 404 km, France 476 km, Holy See (Vatican City) 3.4 km, San Marino 37 km, Slovenia 218 km, Switzerland 698 km

COASTLINE:
7,600 km

MARITIME CLAIMS:
territorial sea: 12 nm
continental shelf: 200-m depth or to the depth of exploitation

CLIMATE
predominantly Mediterranean; alpine in far north; hot, dry in south

TERRAIN:
mostly rugged and mountainous; some plains, coastal lowlands

ELEVATION:
mean elevation: 538 m
lowest point: Mediterranean Sea 0 m
highest point: Mont Blanc (Monte Bianco) de Courmayeur (a secondary peak of Mont Blanc) 4,748 m

NATURAL RESOURCES:
coal, antimony, mercury, zinc, potash, marble, barite, asbestos, pumice, fluorspar, feldspar, pyrite (sulfur), natural gas and crude oil reserves, fish, arable land

LAND USE:
agricultural land: 47.1% (2011 est.)
arable land: 22.8% (2011 est.) / permanent crops: 8.6% (2011 est.) / permanent pasture: 15.7% (2011 est.)
forest: 31.4% (2011 est.)
other: 21.5% (2011 est.)

IRRIGATED LAND:
39,500 sq km (2012)

POPULATION DISTRIBUTION:
despite a distinctive pattern with an industrial north and an agrarian south, a fairly even population distribution exists throughout most of the country, with coastal areas, the Po River Valley, and urban centers (particularly Milan, Rome, and Naples), attracting larger and denser populations

NATURAL HAZARDS:
regional risks include landslides, mudflows, avalanches, earthquakes, volcanic eruptions, flooding; land subsidence in Venice

volcanism: significant volcanic activity; Etna (3,330 m), which is in eruption as of 2010, is Europe's most active volcano; flank eruptions pose a threat to nearby Sicilian villages; Etna, along with the famous Vesuvius, which remains a threat to the millions of nearby residents in the Bay of Naples area, have both been deemed Decade Volcanoes by the International Association of Volcanology and Chemistry of the Earth's Interior, worthy of study due to their explosive history and close proximity to human populations; Stromboli, on its namesake island, has also been continuously active with moderate volcanic activity; other historically active volcanoes include Campi Flegrei, Ischia, Larderello, Pantelleria, Vulcano, and Vulsini

ENVIRONMENT - CURRENT ISSUES:

air pollution from industrial emissions such as sulfur dioxide; coastal and inland rivers polluted from industrial and agricultural effluents; acid rain damaging lakes; inadequate industrial waste treatment and disposal facilities

ENVIRONMENT - INTERNATIONAL AGREEMENTS:

party to: Air Pollution, Air Pollution-Nitrogen Oxides, Air Pollution-Persistent Organic Pollutants, Air Pollution-Sulfur 85, Air Pollution-Sulfur 94, Air Pollution-Volatile Organic Compounds, Antarctic-Environmental Protocol, Antarctic-Marine Living Resources, Antarctic Seals, Antarctic Treaty, Biodiversity, Climate Change, Climate Change-Kyoto Protocol, Desertification, Endangered Species, Environmental Modification, Hazardous Wastes, Law of the Sea, Marine Dumping, Ozone Layer Protection, Ship Pollution, Tropical Timber 83, Tropical Timber 94, Wetlands, Whaling

signed, but not ratified: none of the selected agreements

GEOGRAPHY - NOTE:

strategic location dominating central Mediterranean as well as southern sea and air approaches to Western Europe

PEOPLE AND SOCIETY :: ITALY

POPULATION:

62,246,674 (July 2018 est.)

country comparison to the world: 23

NATIONALITY:

noun: Italian(s)

adjective: Italian

ETHNIC GROUPS:

Italian (includes small clusters of German-, French-, and Slovene-Italians in the north and Albanian-Italians and Greek-Italians in the south)

LANGUAGES:

Italian (official), German (parts of Trentino-Alto Adige region are predominantly German speaking), French (small French-speaking minority in Valle d'Aosta region), Slovene (Slovene-speaking minority in the Trieste-Gorizia area)

RELIGIONS:

Christian 83.3% (overwhelmingly Roman Catholic with very small groups of Jehovah's Witnesses and Protestants), Muslim 3.7%, unaffiliated 12.4%, other 0.6% (2010 est.)

AGE STRUCTURE:

0-14 years: 13.6% (male 4,326,862 /female 4,136,562)

15-24 years: 9.61% (male 2,994,651 /female 2,984,172)

25-54 years: 41.82% (male 12,845,442 /female 13,183,240)

55-64 years: 13.29% (male 4,012,640 /female 4,261,956)

65 years and over: 21.69% (male 5,817,819 /female 7,683,330) (2018 est.)

DEPENDENCY RATIOS:

total dependency ratio: 56.5 (2015 est.)

youth dependency ratio: 21.5 (2015 est.)

elderly dependency ratio: 35 (2015 est.)

potential support ratio: 2.9 (2015 est.)

MEDIAN AGE:

total: 45.8 years (2018 est.)

male: 44.7 years

female: 46.9 years

country comparison to the world: 5

POPULATION GROWTH RATE:

0.16% (2018 est.)

country comparison to the world: 183

BIRTH RATE:

8.5 births/1,000 population (2018 est.)

country comparison to the world: 216

DEATH RATE:

10.5 deaths/1,000 population (2018 est.)

country comparison to the world: 28

NET MIGRATION RATE:

3.6 migrant(s)/1,000 population (2018 est.)

country comparison to the world: 37

POPULATION DISTRIBUTION:

despite a distinctive pattern with an industrial north and an agrarian south, a fairly even population distribution exists throughout most of the country, with coastal areas, the Po River Valley, and urban centers (particularly Milan, Rome, and Naples), attracting larger and denser populations

URBANIZATION:

urban population: 70.7% of total population (2019)

rate of urbanization: 0.29% annual rate of change (2015-20 est.)

MAJOR URBAN AREAS - POPULATION:

4.234 million ROME (capital), 3.136 million Milan, 2.192 million Naples, 1.789 million Turin, 883,000 Bergamo, 852,000 Palermo (2019)

SEX RATIO:

at birth: 1.06 male(s)/female

0-14 years: 1.05 male(s)/female

15-24 years: 1 male(s)/female

25-54 years: 0.97 male(s)/female

55-64 years: 0.94 male(s)/female

65 years and over: 0.76 male(s)/female

total population: 0.93 male(s)/female (2018 est.)

MOTHER'S MEAN AGE AT FIRST BIRTH:

30.7 years (2014 est.)

MATERNAL MORTALITY RATE:

2 deaths/100,000 live births (2017 est.)

country comparison to the world: 182

INFANT MORTALITY RATE:

total: 3.2 deaths/1,000 live births (2018 est.)

male: 3.4 deaths/1,000 live births

female: 3 deaths/1,000 live births

country comparison to the world: 210

LIFE EXPECTANCY AT BIRTH:

total population: 82.4 years (2018 est.)

male: 79.7 years

female: 85.2 years

country comparison to the world: 15

TOTAL FERTILITY RATE:

1.45 children born/woman (2018 est.)

country comparison to the world: 206

CONTRACEPTIVE PREVALENCE RATE:

65.1% (2013)

note: percent of women aged 18-49

DRINKING WATER SOURCE:

improved:

urban: 100% of population

rural: 100% of population

total: 100% of population

unimproved:

urban: 0% of population

rural: 0% of population

total: 0% of population (2015 est.)

CURRENT HEALTH EXPENDITURE:

8.9% (2016)

PHYSICIANS DENSITY:

4.09 physicians/1,000 population (2017)

HOSPITAL BED DENSITY:

3.4 beds/1,000 population (2012)

SANITATION FACILITY ACCESS:

improved:

urban: 99.5% of population (2015 est.)

rural: 99.6% of population (2015 est.)

total: 99.5% of population (2015 est.)

unimproved:

urban: 0.5% of population (2015 est.)

rural: 0.4% of population (2015 est.)

total: 0.5% of population (2015 est.)

HIV/AIDS - ADULT PREVALENCE RATE:

0.3% (2018 est.)

country comparison to the world: 89

HIV/AIDS - PEOPLE LIVING WITH HIV/AIDS:

130,000 (2018 est.)

country comparison to the world: 38

HIV/AIDS - DEATHS:

<1000 (2018 est.)

OBESITY - ADULT PREVALENCE RATE:

19.9% (2016)

country comparison to the world: 108

EDUCATION EXPENDITURES:

4.1% of GDP (2015)

country comparison to the world: 104

LITERACY:

definition: age 15 and over can read and write

total population: 99.2%

male: 99.4%

female: 99% (2015 est.)

SCHOOL LIFE EXPECTANCY (PRIMARY TO TERTIARY EDUCATION):

total: 16 years

male: 16 years

female: 17 years (2016)

UNEMPLOYMENT, YOUTH AGES 15-24:

total: 34.7%

male: 33%

female: 37.3% (2017 est.)

country comparison to the world: 22

GOVERNMENT :: ITALY

COUNTRY NAME:

conventional long form: Italian Republic

conventional short form: Italy

local long form: Repubblica Italiana

local short form: Italia

former: Kingdom of Italy

etymology: derivation is unclear, but the Latin "Italia" may come from the Oscan "Viteliu" meaning "[Land] of Young Cattle" (the bull was a symbol of southern Italic tribes)

GOVERNMENT TYPE:

parliamentary republic

CAPITAL:

name: Rome

geographic coordinates: 41 54 N, 12 29 E

time difference: UTC+1 (6 hours ahead of Washington, DC, during Standard Time)

daylight saving time: +1hr, begins last Sunday in March; ends last Sunday in October

etymology: by tradition, named after Romulus, one of the legendary founders of the city and its first king

ADMINISTRATIVE DIVISIONS:

15 regions (regioni, singular - regione) and 5 autonomous regions (regioni autonome, singular - regione autonoma)

regions: Abruzzo, Basilicata, Calabria, Campania, Emilia-Romagna, Lazio (Latium), Liguria, Lombardia, Marche, Molise, Piemonte (Piedmont), Puglia (Apulia), Toscana (Tuscany), Umbria, Veneto;

autonomous regions: Friuli Venezia Giulia; Sardegna (Sardinia); Sicilia (Sicily); Trentino-Alto Adige (Trentino-South Tyrol) or Trentino-Suedtirol (German); Valle d'Aosta (Aosta Valley) or Vallee d'Aoste (French)

INDEPENDENCE:

17 March 1861 (Kingdom of Italy proclaimed; Italy was not finally unified until 1871)

NATIONAL HOLIDAY:

Republic Day, 2 June (1946)

CONSTITUTION:

history: previous 1848 (originally for the Kingdom of Sardinia and adopted by the Kingdom of Italy in 1861); latest enacted 22 December 1947, adopted 27 December 1947, entered into force 1 January 1948

amendments: proposed by both houses of Parliament; passage requires two successive debates and approval by absolute majority of each house on the second vote; a referendum is only required when requested by one fifth of the members of either house, by voter petition, or by five Regional Councils (elected legislative assemblies of the 15 first-level administrative regions and 5 autonomous regions of Italy); referendum not required if an amendment has been approved by a two-thirds majority in each house in the second vote; amended many times, last in 2012; note - a referendum held on 4 December 2016 on constitutional amendments was defeated (2017)

LEGAL SYSTEM:

civil law system; judicial review of legislation under certain conditions in Constitutional Court

INTERNATIONAL LAW ORGANIZATION PARTICIPATION:

accepts compulsory ICJ jurisdiction with reservations; accepts ICCt jurisdiction

CITIZENSHIP:

citizenship by birth: no

citizenship by descent only: at least one parent must be a citizen of Italy

dual citizenship recognized: yes

residency requirement for naturalization: 4 years for EU nationals, 5 years for refugees and specified exceptions, 10 years for all others

SUFFRAGE:

18 years of age; universal except in senatorial elections, where minimum age is 25

EXECUTIVE BRANCH:

chief of state: President Sergio MATTARELLA (since 3 February 2015)

head of government: Prime Minister Giuseppe CONTE (since 1 June 2018); the prime minister's official title is President of the Council of Ministers; note - CONTE resigned on 20 August

2019 but returned as prime minister after PD and M5S agreed to form a new coalition government on 28 August 2019

cabinet: Council of Ministers proposed by the prime minister, known officially as the President of the Council of Ministers and locally as the Premier; nominated by the president; the current deputy prime ministers, known officially as vice-presidents of the Council of Ministers, are Matteo Salvini (L) and Luigi Di Maio (M5S) (since 1 June 2018)

elections/appointments: president indirectly elected by an electoral college consisting of both houses of Parliament and 58 regional representatives for a 7-year term (no term limits); election last held on 31 January 2015 (next to be held in 2022); prime minister appointed by the president, confirmed by parliament

election results: Sergio MATTARELLA (independent) elected president; electoral college vote count in fourth round - 665 out of 1,009 (505-vote threshold)

LEGISLATIVE BRANCH:

description: bicameral Parliament or Parlamento consists of:
Senate or Senato della Repubblica (321 seats; 116 members directly elected in single-seat constituencies by simple majority vote, 193 members in multi-seat constituencies and 6 members in multi-seat constituencies abroad directly elected by party-list proportional representation vote to serve 5-year terms and 6 ex-officio members appointed by the president of the Republic to serve for life)
Chamber of Deputies or Camera dei Deputati (630 seats; 629 members directly elected in single- and multi-seat constituencies by proportional representation vote and 1 member from Valle d'Aosta elected by simple majority vote; members serve 5-year terms)

elections:
Senate - last held on 4 March 2018 (next to be held in March 2023)
Chamber of Deputies - last held on 4 March 2018 (next to be held in March 2023)

election results:
Senate - percent of vote by party - center-right coalition 37.5% (L 17.6%, FI 14.4%, FdI 4.3%, UdC 1.2%), M5S 32.2%, center-left coalition (PD 19.1%, +E 2.3%, I 0.5%, CP 0.5%, SVP-PATT 0.4%), LeU 3.3%; seats by party - center-right coalition 77(L 37, FI 33, FdI 7), M5S 68, center-left coalition 44(PD 43, SVP-PATT 1), LeU 4; composition - men 208, women 113, percent of women 35.2%

Chamber of Deputies - percent of vote by party - center-right coalition 37% (L 17.4%, FI 14%, FdI 4.4%, UdC 1.3%), M5S 33%, center-left coalition 22.9% (PD 18.8%, E+ 2.6%, I 0.6%, CP 0.5%, SVP-PATT 0.4%); seats by party - center-right coalition 151 (L73, FI 59, FdI 19), M5S 133, center-left coalition 88 (PD 86, SVP 2), LeU 14; composition - men 405, women 225, percent of women 35.7%; note - total Parliament percent of women 35.5%

Note: in October 2019, Italy's Parliament voted to reduce the number of Senate seats from 315 to 200 and the number of Chamber of Deputies seats from 630 to 400; changes will be effective for the 2023 election

JUDICIAL BRANCH:

highest courts: Supreme Court of Cassation or Corte Suprema di Cassazione (consists of the first president (chief justice), deputy president, 54 justices presiding over 6 civil and 7 criminal divisions, and 288 judges; an additional 30 judges of lower courts serve as supporting judges; cases normally heard by 5-judge panels; more complex cases heard by 9-judge panels); Constitutional Court or Corte Costituzionale (consists of the court president and 14 judges)

judge selection and term of office: Supreme Court judges appointed by the High Council of the Judiciary, headed by the president of the republic; judges may serve for life; Constitutional Court judges - 5 appointed by the president, 5 elected by Parliament, 5 elected by select higher courts; judges serve up to 9 years

subordinate courts: various lower civil and criminal courts (primary and secondary tribunals and courts of appeal)

POLITICAL PARTIES AND LEADERS:

Governing Coalition :
Northern League (Lega Nord) or Lega [Matteo SALVINI]
Five Star Movement or M5S [Luigi DI MAIO]

Left-center-right opposition:
Democratic Party or PD [Nicola ZINGARETTI]
Forza Italia or FI [Silvio BERLUSCONI]
Brothers of Italy [Giorgia MELONI]
Free and Equal (Liberi e Uguali) or LeU [Pietro GRASSO]
More Europe or +EU [Emma BONINO]
Popular Civic List or CP [Beatrice LORENZIN]

Other parties and parliamentary groups:
Possible [Beatrice BRIGNONE]
Us with Italy [Raffaele FITTO]
South Tyrolean People's Party or SVP [Philipp ACHAMMER]
Trentino Tyrolean Autonomist Party (Partito Autonomista Trentino Tirolese) or PATT [Franco PANIZZA, secretary]
Article One or Art.1-MDP [Roberto SPERANZA]

INTERNATIONAL ORGANIZATION PARTICIPATION:

ADB (nonregional member), AfDB (nonregional member), Arctic Council (observer), Australia Group, BIS, BSEC (observer), CBSS (observer), CD, CDB, CE, CEI, CERN, EAPC, EBRD, ECB, EIB, EITI (implementing country), EMU, ESA, EU, FAO, FATF, G-7, G-8, G-10, G-20, IADB, IAEA, IBRD, ICAO, ICC (national committees), ICCt, ICRM, IDA, IEA, IFAD, IFC, IFRCS, IGAD (partners), IHO, ILO, IMF, IMO, IMSO, Interpol, IOC, IOM, IPU, ISO, ITSO, ITU, ITUC (NGOs), LAIA (observer), MIGA, MINURSO, MINUSMA, NATO, NEA, NSG, OAS (observer), OECD, OPCW, OSCE, Pacific Alliance (observer), Paris Club, PCA, PIF (partner), Schengen Convention, SELEC (observer), SICA (observer), UN, UNCTAD, UNESCO, UNHCR, UNIDO, UNIFIL, Union Latina, UNMOGIP, UNRWA, UNTSO, UNWTO, UPU, WCO, WHO, WIPO, WMO, WTO, ZC

DIPLOMATIC REPRESENTATION IN THE US:

Ambassador Armando VARRICCHIO (since 2 March 2016)

chancery: 3000 Whitehaven Street NW, Washington, DC 20008

telephone: [1] (202) 612-4400

FAX: [1] (202) 518-2151

consulate(s) general: Boston, Chicago, Detroit, Houston, Miami, New York, Los Angeles, Philadelphia, San Francisco

consulate(s): Charlotte (NC), Cleveland (OH), Detroit (MI),

Hattiesburg (MS), Honolulu (HI), New Orleans, Newark (NJ), Norfolk (VA), Pittsburgh (PA), Portland (OR), Seattle

DIPLOMATIC REPRESENTATION FROM THE US:

chief of mission: Ambassador Lewis EISENBERG (since 4 October 2017); note - also accredited to San Marino

telephone: [39] 06-4674-1

embassy: Via Vittorio Veneto 121, 00187-Rome

mailing address: PSC 59, Box 100, APO AE 09624

FAX: [39] 06-488-2672

consulate(s) general: Florence, Milan, Naples

FLAG DESCRIPTION:

three equal vertical bands of green (hoist side), white, and red; design inspired by the French flag brought to Italy by Napoleon in 1797; colors are those of Milan (red and white) combined with the green uniform color of the Milanese civic guard

note: similar to the flag of Mexico, which is longer, uses darker shades of green and red, and has its coat of arms centered on the white band; Ireland, which is longer and is green (hoist side), white, and orange; also similar to the flag of the Cote d'Ivoire, which has the colors reversed - orange (hoist side), white, and green

NATIONAL SYMBOL(S):

white, five-pointed star (Stella d'Italia); national colors: red, white, green

NATIONAL ANTHEM:

name: "Il Canto degli Italiani" (The Song of the Italians)

lyrics/music: Goffredo MAMELI/Michele NOVARO

note: adopted 1946; the anthem, originally written in 1847, is also known as "L'Inno di Mameli" (Mameli's Hymn), and "Fratelli D'Italia" (Brothers of Italy)

ECONOMY :: ITALY

ECONOMY - OVERVIEW:

Italy's economy comprises a developed industrial north, dominated by private companies, and a less-developed, highly subsidized, agricultural south, with a legacy of unemployment and underdevelopment. The Italian economy is driven in large part by the manufacture of high-quality consumer goods produced by small and medium-sized enterprises, many of them family-owned. Italy also has a sizable underground economy, which by some estimates accounts for as much as 17% of GDP. These activities are most common within the agriculture, construction, and service sectors.

Italy is the third-largest economy in the euro zone, but its exceptionally high public debt and structural impediments to growth have rendered it vulnerable to scrutiny by financial markets. Public debt has increased steadily since 2007, reaching 131% of GDP in 2017. Investor concerns about Italy and the broader euro-zone crisis eased in 2013, bringing down Italy's borrowing costs on sovereign government debt from euro-era records. The government still faces pressure from investors and European partners to sustain its efforts to address Italy's longstanding structural economic problems, including labor market inefficiencies, a sluggish judicial system, and a weak banking sector. Italy's economy returned to modest growth in late 2014 for the first time since 2011. In 2015-16, Italy's economy grew at about 1% each year, and in 2017 growth accelerated to 1.5% of GDP. In 2017, overall unemployment was 11.4%, but youth unemployment remained high at 37.1%. GDP growth is projected to slow slightly in 2018.

GDP (PURCHASING POWER PARITY):

$2.317 trillion (2017 est.)

$2.282 trillion (2016 est.)

$2.263 trillion (2015 est.)

note: data are in 2017 dollars

country comparison to the world: 12

GDP (OFFICIAL EXCHANGE RATE):

$1.939 trillion (2017 est.)

GDP - REAL GROWTH RATE:

1.5% (2017 est.)

0.9% (2016 est.)

1% (2015 est.)

country comparison to the world: 171

GDP - PER CAPITA (PPP):

$38,200 (2017 est.)

$37,600 (2016 est.)

$37,200 (2015 est.)

note: data are in 2017 dollars

country comparison to the world: 50

GROSS NATIONAL SAVING:

20.3% of GDP (2017 est.)

19.7% of GDP (2016 est.)

18.8% of GDP (2015 est.)

country comparison to the world: 95

GDP - COMPOSITION, BY END USE:

household consumption: 61% (2017 est.)

government consumption: 18.6% (2017 est.)

investment in fixed capital: 17.5% (2017 est.)

investment in inventories: -0.2% (2017 est.)

exports of goods and services: 31.4% (2017 est.)

imports of goods and services: -28.3% (2017 est.)

GDP - COMPOSITION, BY SECTOR OF ORIGIN:

agriculture: 2.1% (2017 est.)

industry: 23.9% (2017 est.)

services: 73.9% (2017 est.)

AGRICULTURE - PRODUCTS:

fruits, vegetables, grapes, potatoes, sugar beets, soybeans, grain, olives; beef, dairy products; fish

INDUSTRIES:

tourism, machinery, iron and steel, chemicals, food processing, textiles, motor vehicles, clothing, footwear, ceramics

INDUSTRIAL PRODUCTION GROWTH RATE:

2.1% (2017 est.)

country comparison to the world: 128

LABOR FORCE:

25.94 million (2017 est.)

country comparison to the world: 24

LABOR FORCE - BY OCCUPATION:

agriculture: 3.9%

industry: 28.3%

services: 67.8% (2011)

UNEMPLOYMENT RATE:

11.3% (2017 est.)

11.7% (2016 est.)

country comparison to the world: 153

POPULATION BELOW POVERTY LINE:

29.9% (2012 est.)

HOUSEHOLD INCOME OR CONSUMPTION BY PERCENTAGE SHARE:

lowest 10%: 2.3%

highest 10%: 26.8% (2000)

DISTRIBUTION OF FAMILY INCOME - GINI INDEX:
31.9 (2012 est.)

27.3 (1995)

country comparison to the world: 121

BUDGET:
revenues: 903.3 billion (2017 est.)

expenditures: 948.1 billion (2017 est.)

TAXES AND OTHER REVENUES:
46.6% (of GDP) (2017 est.)

country comparison to the world: 20

BUDGET SURPLUS (+) OR DEFICIT (-):
-2.3% (of GDP) (2017 est.)

country comparison to the world: 111

PUBLIC DEBT:
131.8% of GDP (2017 est.)

132% of GDP (2016 est.)

note: Italy reports its data on public debt according to guidelines set out in the Maastricht Treaty; general government gross debt is defined in the Maastricht Treaty as consolidated general government gross debt at nominal value, outstanding at the end of the year, in the following categories of government liabilities (as defined in ESA95): currency and deposits (AF.2), securities other than shares excluding financial derivatives (AF.3, excluding AF.34), and loans (AF.4); the general government sector comprises central, state, and local government and social security funds

country comparison to the world: 5

FISCAL YEAR:
calendar year

INFLATION RATE (CONSUMER PRICES):
1.3% (2017 est.)

-0.1% (2016 est.)

country comparison to the world: 68

CENTRAL BANK DISCOUNT RATE:
0.25% (31 December 2013)

0.75% (31 December 2012)

note: this is the European Central Bank's rate on the marginal lending facility, which offers overnight credit to banks in the euro area

country comparison to the world: 139

COMMERCIAL BANK PRIME LENDING RATE:
3% (31 December 2017 est.)

3.5% (31 December 2016 est.)

country comparison to the world: 174

STOCK OF NARROW MONEY:
$1.347 trillion (31 December 2017 est.)

$1.101 trillion (31 December 2016 est.)

note: see entry for the European Union for money supply for the entire euro area; the European Central Bank (ECB) controls monetary policy for the 18 members of the Economic and Monetary Union (EMU); individual members of the EMU do not control the quantity of money circulating within their own borders

country comparison to the world: 6

STOCK OF BROAD MONEY:
$1.347 trillion (31 December 2017 est.)

$1.101 trillion (31 December 2016 est.)

country comparison to the world: 6

STOCK OF DOMESTIC CREDIT:
$3.422 trillion (31 December 2017 est.)

$3.024 trillion (31 December 2016 est.)

country comparison to the world: 6

MARKET VALUE OF PUBLICLY TRADED SHARES:
$587.3 billion (31 December 2014 est.)

$615.5 billion (31 December 2013 est.)

$480.5 billion (31 December 2012 est.)

country comparison to the world: 20

CURRENT ACCOUNT BALANCE:
$53.42 billion (2017 est.)

$47.64 billion (2016 est.)

country comparison to the world: 9

EXPORTS:
$496.3 billion (2017 est.)

$454.1 billion (2016 est.)

country comparison to the world: 9

EXPORTS - PARTNERS:
Germany 12.5%, France 10.3%, US 9%, Spain 5.2%, UK 5.2%, Switzerland 4.6% (2017)

EXPORTS - COMMODITIES:
engineering products, textiles and clothing, production machinery, motor vehicles, transport equipment, chemicals; foodstuffs, beverages, and tobacco; minerals, nonferrous metals

IMPORTS:
$432.9 billion (2017 est.)

$389.8 billion (2016 est.)

country comparison to the world: 13

IMPORTS - COMMODITIES:
engineering products, chemicals, transport equipment, energy products, minerals and nonferrous metals, textiles and clothing; food, beverages, tobacco

IMPORTS - PARTNERS:
Germany 16.3%, France 8.8%, China 7.1%, Netherlands 5.6%, Spain 5.3%, Belgium 4.5% (2017)

RESERVES OF FOREIGN EXCHANGE AND GOLD:
$151.2 billion (31 December 2017 est.)

$130.6 billion (31 December 2015 est.)

country comparison to the world: 16

DEBT - EXTERNAL:
$2.444 trillion (31 March 2016 est.)

$2.3 trillion (31 March 2015 est.)

country comparison to the world: 9

STOCK OF DIRECT FOREIGN INVESTMENT - AT HOME:
$552.1 billion (31 December 2017 est.)

$471.7 billion (31 December 2016 est.)

country comparison to the world: 17

STOCK OF DIRECT FOREIGN INVESTMENT - ABROAD:
$671.8 billion (31 December 2017 est.)

$584.1 billion (31 December 2016 est.)

country comparison to the world: 15

EXCHANGE RATES:
euros (EUR) per US dollar -

0.885 (2017 est.)

0.903 (2016 est.)

0.9214 (2015 est.)

0.885 (2014 est.)

0.7634 (2013 est.)

ENERGY :: ITALY

ELECTRICITY ACCESS:
electrification - total population: 100% (2016)

ELECTRICITY - PRODUCTION:
275.3 billion kWh (2016 est.)

country comparison to the world: 14

ELECTRICITY - CONSUMPTION:
293.5 billion kWh (2016 est.)

country comparison to the world: 13

ELECTRICITY - EXPORTS:
6.155 billion kWh (2016 est.)

country comparison to the world: 30

ELECTRICITY - IMPORTS:

43.18 billion kWh (2016 est.)

country comparison to the world: 2

ELECTRICITY - INSTALLED GENERATING CAPACITY:

114.2 million kW (2016 est.)

country comparison to the world: 10

ELECTRICITY - FROM FOSSIL FUELS:

54% of total installed capacity (2016 est.)

country comparison to the world: 143

ELECTRICITY - FROM NUCLEAR FUELS:

0% of total installed capacity (2017 est.)

country comparison to the world: 114

ELECTRICITY - FROM HYDROELECTRIC PLANTS:

14% of total installed capacity (2017 est.)

country comparison to the world: 106

ELECTRICITY - FROM OTHER RENEWABLE SOURCES:

32% of total installed capacity (2017 est.)

country comparison to the world: 14

CRUDE OIL - PRODUCTION:

90,000 bbl/day (2018 est.)

country comparison to the world: 44

CRUDE OIL - EXPORTS:

13,790 bbl/day (2017 est.)

country comparison to the world: 57

CRUDE OIL - IMPORTS:

1.341 million bbl/day (2017 est.)

country comparison to the world: 7

CRUDE OIL - PROVED RESERVES:

487.8 million bbl (1 January 2018 est.)

country comparison to the world: 45

REFINED PETROLEUM PRODUCTS - PRODUCTION:

1.607 million bbl/day (2017 est.)

country comparison to the world: 12

REFINED PETROLEUM PRODUCTS - CONSUMPTION:

1.236 million bbl/day (2017 est.)

country comparison to the world: 19

REFINED PETROLEUM PRODUCTS - EXPORTS:

615,900 bbl/day (2017 est.)

country comparison to the world: 13

REFINED PETROLEUM PRODUCTS - IMPORTS:

422,500 bbl/day (2017 est.)

country comparison to the world: 19

NATURAL GAS - PRODUCTION:

5.55 billion cu m (2017 est.)

country comparison to the world: 50

NATURAL GAS - CONSUMPTION:

75.15 billion cu m (2017 est.)

country comparison to the world: 11

NATURAL GAS - EXPORTS:

271.8 million cu m (2017 est.)

country comparison to the world: 44

NATURAL GAS - IMPORTS:

69.66 billion cu m (2017 est.)

country comparison to the world: 5

NATURAL GAS - PROVED RESERVES:

38.11 billion cu m (1 January 2018 est.)

country comparison to the world: 65

CARBON DIOXIDE EMISSIONS FROM CONSUMPTION OF ENERGY:

351 million Mt (2017 est.)

country comparison to the world: 20

COMMUNICATIONS :: ITALY

TELEPHONES - FIXED LINES:

total subscriptions: 20,700,659

subscriptions per 100 inhabitants: 33 (2017 est.)

country comparison to the world: 12

TELEPHONES - MOBILE CELLULAR:

total subscriptions: 83,871,543

subscriptions per 100 inhabitants: 135 (2017 est.)

country comparison to the world: 19

TELEPHONE SYSTEM:

general assessment: modern, well-developed, fast; fully automated telephone, telex, and data services; highest mobile penetration rates in Europe; leading edge of development with 5G; Rome, Turin and Naples have 5G commercially for users (2018)

domestic: high-capacity cable and microwave radio relay trunks; 33 per 100 for fixed-line and 135 per 100 for mobile-cellular subscriptions (2018)

international: country code - 39; landing points for Italy-Monaco, Italy-Libya, Italy-Malta, Italy-Greece-1, Italy-Croatia, BlueMed, Janna, FEA, SeaMeWe-3 & 4 & 5, Trapani-Kelibia, Columbus-III, Didon, GO-1, HANNIBAL System, MENA, Bridge International, Malta-Italy Interconnector, Melita1, IMEWE, VMSCS, AAE-1, and OTEGLOBE, submarine cables provide links to Asia, the Middle East, Europe, North Africa, Southeast Asia, Australia and US; satellite earth stations - 3 Intelsat (with a total of 5 antennas - 3 for Atlantic Ocean and 2 for Indian Ocean) (2019)

BROADCAST MEDIA:

two Italian media giants dominate - the publicly owned Radiotelevisione Italiana (RAI) with 3 national terrestrial stations and privately owned Mediaset with 3 national terrestrial stations; a large number of private stations and Sky Italia - a satellite TV network; RAI operates 3 AM/FM nationwide radio stations; about 1,300 commercial radio stations

INTERNET COUNTRY CODE:

.it

INTERNET USERS:

total: 38,025,661

percent of population: 61.3% (July 2016 est.)

country comparison to the world: 19

BROADBAND - FIXED SUBSCRIPTIONS:

total: 16,586,376

subscriptions per 100 inhabitants: 27 (2017 est.)

country comparison to the world: 12

MILITARY AND SECURITY :: ITALY

MILITARY EXPENDITURES:

1.33% of GDP (2018)

1.37% of GDP (2017)

1.34% of GDP (2016)

1.21% of GDP (2015)

1.29% of GDP (2014)

country comparison to the world: 88

MILITARY AND SECURITY FORCES:

Italian Armed Forces: Army (Esercito Italiano, EI), Navy (Marina Militare Italiana, MMI; includes aviation, marines), Italian Air Force (Aeronautica Militare Italiana, AMI), Carabinieri Corps (Arma dei Carabinieri, CC). (2019)

The Financial Guard (Guardia di Finanza) under the Ministry of Economy and Finance is a force with military status and nationwide remit for financial crime investigations, including narcotics trafficking, smuggling, and illegal immigration.

MILITARY SERVICE AGE AND OBLIGATION:

18-25 years of age for voluntary military service; women may serve in any military branch; Italian citizenship required; 1-year service obligation (2013)

MILITARY - NOTE:

Italy has established a Joint Special Operations Command and a Joint Headquarters Cyber Operations (Comando Interforze per le Operazioni Cibernetiche (CIOC) (2019)

TRANSPORTATION :: ITALY

NATIONAL AIR TRANSPORT SYSTEM:

number of registered air carriers: 9 (2015)

inventory of registered aircraft operated by air carriers: 382 (2015)

annual passenger traffic on registered air carriers: 26,036,010 (2015)

annual freight traffic on registered air carriers: 945,433,732 mt-km (2015)

CIVIL AIRCRAFT REGISTRATION COUNTRY CODE PREFIX:

I (2016)

AIRPORTS:

129 (2013)

country comparison to the world: 45

AIRPORTS - WITH PAVED RUNWAYS:

total: 98 (2017)

over 3,047 m: 9 (2017)

2,438 to 3,047 m: 31 (2017)

1,524 to 2,437 m: 18 (2017)

914 to 1,523 m: 29 (2017)

under 914 m: 11 (2017)

AIRPORTS - WITH UNPAVED RUNWAYS:

total: 31 (2013)

1,524 to 2,437 m: 1 (2013)

914 to 1,523 m: 10 (2013)

under 914 m: 20 (2013)

HELIPORTS:

5 (2013)

PIPELINES:

20223 km gas, 1393 km oil, 1574 km refined products (2013)

RAILWAYS:

total: 20,182 km (2014)

standard gauge: 18,770.1 km 1.435-m gauge (12,893.6 km electrified) (2014)

narrow gauge: 122.3 km 1.000-m gauge (122.3 km electrified) (2014)

1289.3 0.950-m gauge (151.3 km electrified)

country comparison to the world: 15

ROADWAYS:

total: 487,700 km (2007)

paved: 487,700 km (includes 6,700 km of expressways) (2007)

country comparison to the world: 15

WATERWAYS:

2,400 km (used for commercial traffic; of limited overall value compared to road and rail) (2012)

country comparison to the world: 36

MERCHANT MARINE:

total: 1,405

by type: bulk carrier 59, container ship 10, general cargo 142, oil tanker 128, other 1066 (2018)

country comparison to the world: 20

PORTS AND TERMINALS:

major seaport(s): Augusta, Cagliari, Genoa, Livorno, Taranto, Trieste, Venice

oil terminal(s): Melilli (Santa Panagia) oil terminal, Sarroch oil terminal

container port(s) (TEUs): Genoa (2,622,200), Gioia Tauro (2,448,600) (2017)

LNG terminal(s) (import): La Spezia, Panigaglia, Porto Levante

TRANSNATIONAL ISSUES :: ITALY

DISPUTES - INTERNATIONAL:

Italy's long coastline and developed economy entices tens of thousands of illegal immigrants from southeastern Europe and northern Africa

REFUGEES AND INTERNALLY DISPLACED PERSONS:

refugees (country of origin): 22,319 (Nigeria), 18,249 (Pakistan), 16,941 (Afghanistan), 15,003 (Mali), 13,373 (Somalia), 12,549 (Gambia), 13,525 (Ukraine), 7,644 (Senegal), 7,174 (Cote d'Ivoire), 6,975 (Eritrea) (2018); note - estimate for Ukraine represents asylum applicants since the beginning of the Ukraine crisis in 2014 to July 2018

stateless persons: 732 (2018)

note: 489,114 estimated refugee and migrant arrivals by sea (January 2015-December 2019); hosts an estimated 108,924 migrants and asylum seekers as of the end of June 2019; 23,370 arrivals in 2018

ILLICIT DRUGS:

important gateway for and consumer of Latin American cocaine and Southwest Asian heroin entering the European market; money laundering by organized crime and from smuggling

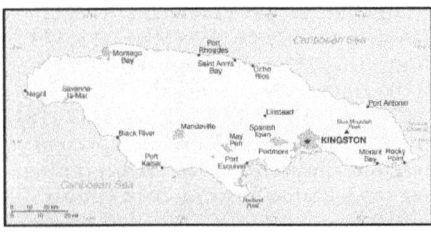

CENTRAL AMERICA :: JAMAICA

INTRODUCTION :: JAMAICA

BACKGROUND:

The island - discovered by Christopher COLUMBUS in 1494 - was settled by the Spanish early in the 16th century. The native Taino, who had inhabited Jamaica for centuries, were gradually exterminated and replaced by African slaves. England seized the island in 1655 and established a plantation economy based on sugar, cocoa, and coffee. The abolition of slavery in 1834 freed a quarter million slaves, many of whom became small farmers. Jamaica gradually increased its independence from Britain. In 1958 it joined other British Caribbean colonies in forming the Federation of the West Indies. Jamaica withdrew from the Federation in 1961 and gained full independence in 1962. Deteriorating economic conditions during the 1970s led to recurrent violence as rival gangs affiliated with the major political parties evolved into powerful organized crime networks involved in international drug smuggling and money laundering. Violent crime, drug trafficking, and poverty pose significant challenges to the government today. Nonetheless, many rural and resort areas remain relatively safe and contribute substantially to the economy.

GEOGRAPHY :: JAMAICA

LOCATION:

Caribbean, island in the Caribbean Sea, south of Cuba

GEOGRAPHIC COORDINATES:

18 15 N, 77 30 W

MAP REFERENCES:

Central America and the Caribbean

AREA:

total: 10,991 sq km

land: 10,831 sq km

water: 160 sq km

country comparison to the world: 167

AREA - COMPARATIVE:

about half the size of New Jersey; slightly smaller than Connecticut

LAND BOUNDARIES:

0 km

COASTLINE:

1,022 km

MARITIME CLAIMS:

territorial sea: 12 nm

exclusive economic zone: 200 nm

contiguous zone: 24 nm

continental shelf: 200 nm or to edge of the continental margin

measured from claimed archipelagic straight baselines

CLIMATE:

tropical; hot, humid; temperate interior

TERRAIN:

mostly mountains, with narrow, discontinuous coastal plain

ELEVATION:

mean elevation: 18 m

lowest point: Caribbean Sea 0 m

highest point: Blue Mountain Peak 2,256 m

NATURAL RESOURCES:

bauxite, alumina, gypsum, limestone

LAND USE:

agricultural land: 41.4% (2011 est.)

arable land: 11.1% (2011 est.) / permanent crops: 9.2% (2011 est.) / permanent pasture: 21.1% (2011 est.)

forest: 31.1% (2011 est.)

other: 27.5% (2011 est.)

IRRIGATED LAND:

250 sq km (2012)

POPULATION DISTRIBUTION:

population density is high throughout, but increases in and around Kingston, Montego Bay, and Port Esquivel

NATURAL HAZARDS:

hurricanes (especially July to November)

ENVIRONMENT - CURRENT ISSUES:

heavy rates of deforestation; coastal waters polluted by industrial waste, sewage, and oil spills; damage to coral reefs; air pollution in Kingston from vehicle emissions; land erosion

ENVIRONMENT - INTERNATIONAL AGREEMENTS:

party to: Biodiversity, Climate Change, Climate Change-Kyoto Protocol, Desertification, Endangered Species, Hazardous Wastes, Law of the Sea, Marine Dumping, Marine Life Conservation, Ozone Layer Protection, Ship Pollution, Wetlands

signed, but not ratified: none of the selected agreements

GEOGRAPHY - NOTE:

third largest island in the Caribbean (after Cuba and Hispaniola); strategic location between Cayman Trench and Jamaica Channel, the main sea lanes for the Panama Canal

PEOPLE AND SOCIETY :: JAMAICA

POPULATION:

2,812,090 (July 2018 est.)

country comparison to the world: 139

NATIONALITY:

noun: Jamaican(s)

adjective: Jamaican

ETHNIC GROUPS:

black 92.1%, mixed 6.1%, East Indian 0.8%, other 0.4%, unspecified 0.7% (2011 est.)

LANGUAGES:
English, English patois

RELIGIONS:
Protestant 64.8% (includes Seventh Day Adventist 12.0%, Pentecostal 11.0%, Other Church of God 9.2%, New Testament Church of God 7.2%, Baptist 6.7%, Church of God in Jamaica 4.8%, Church of God of Prophecy 4.5%, Anglican 2.8%, United Church 2.1%, Methodist 1.6%, Revived 1.4%, Brethren 0.9%, and Moravian 0.7%), Roman Catholic 2.2%, Jehovah's Witness 1.9%, Rastafarian 1.1%, other 6.5%, none 21.3%, unspecified 2.3% (2011 est.)

AGE STRUCTURE:
0-14 years: 26.01% (male 372,158 /female 359,388)

15-24 years: 18.36% (male 261,012 /female 255,223)

25-54 years: 38.03% (male 518,984 /female 550,412)

55-64 years: 8.89% (male 123,769 /female 126,350)

65 years and over: 8.71% (male 115,573 /female 129,221) (2018 est.)

DEPENDENCY RATIOS:
total dependency ratio: 48.7 (2015 est.)

youth dependency ratio: 34.9 (2015 est.)

elderly dependency ratio: 13.8 (2015 est.)

potential support ratio: 7.2 (2015 est.)

MEDIAN AGE:
total: 28.6 years (2018 est.)

male: 27.8 years

female: 29.3 years

country comparison to the world: 133

POPULATION GROWTH RATE:
-0.05% (2018 est.)

country comparison to the world: 201

BIRTH RATE:
16.5 births/1,000 population (2018 est.)

country comparison to the world: 110

DEATH RATE:
7.6 deaths/1,000 population (2018 est.)

country comparison to the world: 104

NET MIGRATION RATE:
-9.4 migrant(s)/1,000 population (2018 est.)

country comparison to the world: 216

POPULATION DISTRIBUTION:
population density is high throughout, but increases in and around Kingston, Montego Bay, and Port Esquivel

URBANIZATION:
urban population: 56% of total population (2019)

rate of urbanization: 0.82% annual rate of change (2015-20 est.)

MAJOR URBAN AREAS - POPULATION:
590,000 KINGSTON (capital) (2019)

SEX RATIO:
at birth: 1.05 male(s)/female

0-14 years: 1.04 male(s)/female

15-24 years: 1.02 male(s)/female

25-54 years: 0.94 male(s)/female

55-64 years: 0.98 male(s)/female

65 years and over: 0.89 male(s)/female

total population: 0.98 male(s)/female (2018 est.)

MOTHER'S MEAN AGE AT FIRST BIRTH:
21.2 years (2008 est.)

note: median age at first birth among women 25-29

MATERNAL MORTALITY RATE:
80 deaths/100,000 live births (2017 est.)

country comparison to the world: 79

INFANT MORTALITY RATE:
total: 12.4 deaths/1,000 live births (2018 est.)

male: 13.9 deaths/1,000 live births

female: 10.8 deaths/1,000 live births

country comparison to the world: 108

LIFE EXPECTANCY AT BIRTH:
total population: 74.5 years (2018 est.)

male: 72.7 years

female: 76.5 years

country comparison to the world: 123

TOTAL FERTILITY RATE:
2.09 children born/woman (2018 est.)

country comparison to the world: 102

CONTRACEPTIVE PREVALENCE RATE:
72.5% (2008/09)

DRINKING WATER SOURCE:
improved:

urban: 97.5% of population

rural: 89.4% of population

total: 93.8% of population

unimproved:

urban: 2.5% of population

rural: 10.6% of population

total: 6.2% of population (2015 est.)

CURRENT HEALTH EXPENDITURE:
6.1% (2016)

PHYSICIANS DENSITY:
1.32 physicians/1,000 population (2017)

HOSPITAL BED DENSITY:
1.7 beds/1,000 population (2013)

SANITATION FACILITY ACCESS:
improved:

urban: 79.9% of population (2015 est.)

rural: 84.1% of population (2015 est.)

total: 81.8% of population (2015 est.)

unimproved:

urban: 20.1% of population (2015 est.)

rural: 15.9% of population (2015 est.)

total: 18.2% of population (2015 est.)

HIV/AIDS - ADULT PREVALENCE RATE:
1.9% (2018 est.)

country comparison to the world: 27

HIV/AIDS - PEOPLE LIVING WITH HIV/AIDS:
40,000 (2018 est.)

country comparison to the world: 67

HIV/AIDS - DEATHS:
1,500 (2018 est.)

country comparison to the world: 52

MAJOR INFECTIOUS DISEASES:
note: active local transmission of Zika virus by Aedes species mosquitoes has been identified in this country (as of August 2016); it poses an important risk (a large number of cases possible) among US citizens if bitten by an infective mosquito; other less common ways to get Zika are through sex, via blood transfusion, or during pregnancy, in which the pregnant woman passes Zika virus to her fetus

OBESITY - ADULT PREVALENCE RATE:
24.7% (2016)

country comparison to the world: 55

CHILDREN UNDER THE AGE OF 5 YEARS UNDERWEIGHT:
2.2% (2014)

country comparison to the world: 110

EDUCATION EXPENDITURES:
5.3% of GDP (2017)

country comparison to the world: 50

LITERACY:
definition: age 15 and over has ever attended school

total population: 88.7%

male: 84%

female: 93.1% (2015 est.)

UNEMPLOYMENT, YOUTH AGES 15-24:
total: 24.1%

male: 20.1%

female: 29.2% (2018 est.)

country comparison to the world: 53

GOVERNMENT :: JAMAICA

COUNTRY NAME:
conventional long form: none

conventional short form: Jamaica

etymology: from the native Taino word "haymaca" meaning "Land of Wood and Water" or possibly "Land of Springs"

GOVERNMENT TYPE:
parliamentary democracy (Parliament) under a constitutional monarchy; a Commonwealth realm

CAPITAL:
name: Kingston

geographic coordinates: 18 00 N, 76 48 W

time difference: UTC-5 (same time as Washington, DC, during Standard Time)

etymology: the name is a blending of the words "king's" and "town"; the English king at the time of the city's founding in 1692 was William III

ADMINISTRATIVE DIVISIONS:
14 parishes; Clarendon, Hanover, Kingston, Manchester, Portland, Saint Andrew, Saint Ann, Saint Catherine, Saint Elizabeth, Saint James, Saint Mary, Saint Thomas, Trelawny, Westmoreland

note: for local government purposes, Kingston and Saint Andrew were amalgamated in 1923 into the present single corporate body known as the Kingston and Saint Andrew Corporation

INDEPENDENCE:
6 August 1962 (from the UK)

NATIONAL HOLIDAY:
Independence Day, 6 August (1962)

CONSTITUTION:
history: several previous (preindependence); latest drafted 1961-62, submitted to British Parliament 24 July 1962, entered into force 6 August 1962 (at independence)

amendments: proposed by Parliament; passage of amendments to "non-entrenched" constitutional sections, such as lowering the voting age, requires majority vote by the Parliament membership; passage of amendments to "entrenched" sections, such as fundamental rights and freedoms, requires two-thirds majority vote of Parliament; passage of amendments to "specially entrenched" sections such as the dissolution of Parliament or the executive authority of the monarch requires two-thirds approval by Parliament and approval in a referendum; amended many times, last in 2017 (2018)

LEGAL SYSTEM:
common law system based on the English model

INTERNATIONAL LAW ORGANIZATION PARTICIPATION:
has not submitted an ICJ jurisdiction declaration; non-party state to the ICCt

CITIZENSHIP:
citizenship by birth: yes

citizenship by descent only: yes

dual citizenship recognized: yes

residency requirement for naturalization: 4 out of the previous 5 years

SUFFRAGE:
18 years of age; universal

EXECUTIVE BRANCH:
chief of state: Queen ELIZABETH II (since 6 February 1952); represented by Governor General Sir Patrick L. ALLEN (since 26 February 2009)

head of government: Prime Minister Andrew HOLNESS (since 3 March 2016)

cabinet: Cabinet appointed by the governor general on the advice of the prime minister

elections/appointments: the monarchy is hereditary; governor general appointed by the monarch on the recommendation of the prime minister; following legislative elections, the leader of the majority party or majority coalition in the House of Representatives is appointed prime minister by the governor general

LEGISLATIVE BRANCH:
description: bicameral Parliament consists of:
Senate (21 seats; members appointed by the governor general on the recommendation of the prime minister and the opposition leader, 13 seats allocated to the ruling party, and 8 seats allocated to the opposition party; members serve 5-year terms or until Parliament is dissolved)
House of Representatives (63 seats; members directly elected in single-seat constituencies by simple majority vote to serve 5-year terms or until Parliament is dissolved)

elections: Senate - last full slate of appointments on 10 March 2016 (next no later than February 2021)
House of Representatives - last held on 25 February 2016; by-election for 5 seats held on 30 October 2017 (3 seats), 5 March 2018, and 4 April 2019 (next to be held no later than February 2021)

election results: Senate - percent by party - NA; seats by party - NA; composition - men 16, women 5, percent of women 23.8%
House of Representatives - percent of vote by party - JLP 50.1%, PNP 49.7%, other 0.2%; seats by party - JLP 32, PNP 31; note - as of June 2019, by-elections have changed House seats to JLP 34, PNP 29; composition - men 51, women 12, percent of women 19%; note - total Parliament percent of women 20%

JUDICIAL BRANCH:
highest courts: Court of Appeal (consists of president of the court and a minimum of 4 judges); Supreme Court (40 judges organized in specialized divisions); note - appeals beyond Jamaica's highest courts are referred to the Judicial Committee of the Privy Council (in London) rather than to the Caribbean Court of Justice (the appellate court for member states of the Caribbean Community)

judge selection and term of office: chief justice of the Supreme Court and president of the Court of Appeal appointed by the governor-general on the advice of the prime minister; other judges of both courts appointed by the governor-general on the advice of the Judicial Service Commission; judges of both courts serve till age 70

subordinate courts: resident magistrate courts, district courts, and petty sessions courts

POLITICAL PARTIES AND LEADERS:

Jamaica Labor Party or JLP [Andrew Michael HOLNESS]
People's National Party or PNP [Dr. Peter David PHILLIPS]
National Democratic Movement or NDM [Peter TOWNSEND]

INTERNATIONAL ORGANIZATION PARTICIPATION:

ACP, AOSIS, C, Caricom, CDB, CELAC, FAO, G-15, G-77, IADB, IAEA, IBRD, ICAO, ICC (NGOs), ICRM, IDA, IFAD, IFC, IFRCS, IHO, ILO, IMF, IMO, Interpol, IOC, IOM, ISO, ITSO, ITU, LAES, MIGA, NAM, OAS, OPANAL, OPCW, Petrocaribe, UN, UNCTAD, UNESCO, UNIDO, UNITAR, UNWTO, UPU, WCO, WFTU (NGOs), WHO, WIPO, WMO, WTO

DIPLOMATIC REPRESENTATION IN THE US:

Ambassador Audrey Patrice MARKS (since 18 January 2017)

chancery: 1520 New Hampshire Avenue NW, Washington, DC 20036

telephone: [1] (202) 452-0660

FAX: [1] (202) 452-0036

consulate(s) general: Miami, New York

consulate(s): Atlanta, Boston, Chicago, Concord (MA), Houston, Los Angeles, Philadelphia, Richmond (VA), San Francisco, Seattle

DIPLOMATIC REPRESENTATION FROM THE US:

chief of mission: Ambassador Designate Donald R. TAPIA (confirmed by US Senate on 18 July 2019)

telephone: [1] (876) 702-6000 (2018)

embassy: 142 Old Hope Road, Kingston 6

mailing address: P.O. Box 541, Kingston 5

FAX: [1] (876) 702-6001 (2018)

FLAG DESCRIPTION:

diagonal yellow cross divides the flag into four triangles - green (top and bottom) and black (hoist side and fly side); green represents hope, vegetation, and agriculture, black reflects hardships overcome and to be faced, and yellow recalls golden sunshine and the island's natural resources

NATIONAL SYMBOL(S):

green-and-black streamertail (bird), Guaiacum officinale (Guaiacwood); national colors: green, yellow, black

NATIONAL ANTHEM:

name: Jamaica, Land We Love

lyrics/music: Hugh Braham SHERLOCK/Robert Charles LIGHTBOURNE

note: adopted 1962

ECONOMY :: JAMAICA

ECONOMY - OVERVIEW:

The Jamaican economy is heavily dependent on services, which accounts for more than 70% of GDP. The country derives most of its foreign exchange from tourism, remittances, and bauxite/alumina. Earnings from remittances and tourism each account for 14% and 20% of GDP, while bauxite/alumina exports have declined to less than 5% of GDP.

Jamaica's economy has grown on average less than 1% a year for the last three decades and many impediments remain to growth: a bloated public sector which crowds out spending on important projects; high crime and corruption; red-tape; and a high debt-to-GDP ratio. Jamaica, however, has made steady progress in reducing its debt-to-GDP ratio from a high of almost 150% in 2012 to less than 110% in 2017, in close collaboration with the International Monetary Fund (IMF). The current IMF Stand-By Agreement requires Jamaica to produce an annual primary surplus of 7%, in an attempt to reduce its debt burden below 60% by 2025.

Economic growth reached 1.6% in 2016, but declined to 0.9% in 2017 after intense rainfall, demonstrating the vulnerability of the economy to weather-related events. The HOLNESS administration therefore faces the difficult prospect of maintaining fiscal discipline to reduce the debt load while simultaneously implementing growth inducing policies and attacking a serious crime problem. High unemployment exacerbates the crime problem, including gang violence fueled by advanced fee fraud (lottery scamming) and the drug trade.

GDP (PURCHASING POWER PARITY):

$26.06 billion (2017 est.)

$25.89 billion (2016 est.)

$25.51 billion (2015 est.)

note: data are in 2017 dollars

country comparison to the world: 140

GDP (OFFICIAL EXCHANGE RATE):

$14.77 billion (2017 est.)

GDP - REAL GROWTH RATE:

0.7% (2017 est.)

1.5% (2016 est.)

0.9% (2015 est.)

country comparison to the world: 189

GDP - PER CAPITA (PPP):

$9,200 (2017 est.)

$9,200 (2016 est.)

$9,100 (2015 est.)

note: data are in 2017 dollars

country comparison to the world: 143

GROSS NATIONAL SAVING:

18.3% of GDP (2017 est.)

20.6% of GDP (2016 est.)

18% of GDP (2015 est.)

country comparison to the world: 109

GDP - COMPOSITION, BY END USE:

household consumption: 81.9% (2017 est.)

government consumption: 13.7% (2017 est.)

investment in fixed capital: 21.3% (2017 est.)

investment in inventories: 0.1% (2017 est.)

exports of goods and services: 30.1% (2017 est.)

imports of goods and services: -47.1% (2017 est.)

GDP - COMPOSITION, BY SECTOR OF ORIGIN:

agriculture: 7% (2017 est.)

industry: 21.1% (2017 est.)

services: 71.9% (2017 est.)

AGRICULTURE - PRODUCTS:

sugar cane, bananas, coffee, citrus, yams, ackees, vegetables; poultry, goats, milk; shellfish

INDUSTRIES:

agriculture, mining, manufacture, construction, financial and insurance services, tourism, telecommunications

INDUSTRIAL PRODUCTION GROWTH RATE:

0.9% (2017 est.)

country comparison to the world: 162

LABOR FORCE:

1.348 million (2017 est.)

country comparison to the world: 135

LABOR FORCE - BY OCCUPATION:

agriculture: 16.1%

industry: 16%

services: 67.9% (2017)

UNEMPLOYMENT RATE:

12.2% (2017 est.)

12.8% (2016 est.)

country comparison to the world: 162

POPULATION BELOW POVERTY LINE:

17.1% (2016 est.)

HOUSEHOLD INCOME OR CONSUMPTION BY PERCENTAGE SHARE:

lowest 10%: 2.6%

highest 10%: 29.3% (2015)

DISTRIBUTION OF FAMILY INCOME - GINI INDEX:

35 (2016)

38 (2015)

country comparison to the world: 97

BUDGET:

revenues: 4.382 billion (2017 est.)

expenditures: 4.314 billion (2017 est.)

TAXES AND OTHER REVENUES:

29.7% (of GDP) (2017 est.)

country comparison to the world: 81

BUDGET SURPLUS (+) OR DEFICIT (-):

0.5% (of GDP) (2017 est.)

country comparison to the world: 37

PUBLIC DEBT:

101% of GDP (2017 est.)

113.6% of GDP (2016 est.)

country comparison to the world: 16

FISCAL YEAR:

1 April - 31 March

INFLATION RATE (CONSUMER PRICES):

4.4% (2017 est.)

2.3% (2016 est.)

country comparison to the world: 166

CENTRAL BANK DISCOUNT RATE:

3.25% (31 December 2017)

3% (31 December 2016)

country comparison to the world: 105

COMMERCIAL BANK PRIME LENDING RATE:

14.91% (31 December 2017 est.)

16.49% (31 December 2016 est.)

country comparison to the world: 41

STOCK OF NARROW MONEY:

$3.55 billion (31 December 2017 est.)

$3.427 billion (31 December 2016 est.)

country comparison to the world: 115

STOCK OF BROAD MONEY:

$3.55 billion (31 December 2017 est.)

$3.427 billion (31 December 2016 est.)

country comparison to the world: 121

STOCK OF DOMESTIC CREDIT:

$7.326 billion (31 December 2017 est.)

$7.382 billion (31 December 2016 est.)

country comparison to the world: 118

MARKET VALUE OF PUBLICLY TRADED SHARES:

$8.393 billion (31 December 2017 est.)

$5.715 billion (31 December 2016 est.)

$5.38 billion (31 December 2015 est.)

country comparison to the world: 76

CURRENT ACCOUNT BALANCE:

-$679 million (2017 est.)

-$381 million (2016 est.)

country comparison to the world: 126

EXPORTS:

$1.296 billion (2017 est.)

$1.195 billion (2016 est.)

country comparison to the world: 152

EXPORTS - PARTNERS:

US 39.1%, Netherlands 12.3%, Canada 8.4% (2017)

EXPORTS - COMMODITIES:

alumina, bauxite, chemicals, coffee, mineral fuels, waste and scrap metals, sugar, yams

IMPORTS:

$5.151 billion (2017 est.)

$4.169 billion (2016 est.)

country comparison to the world: 126

IMPORTS - COMMODITIES:

food and other consumer goods, industrial supplies, fuel, parts and accessories of capital goods, machinery and transport equipment, construction materials

IMPORTS - PARTNERS:

US 40.6%, Colombia 6.8%, Japan 5.8%, China 5.8%, Trinidad and Tobago 4.7% (2017)

RESERVES OF FOREIGN EXCHANGE AND GOLD:

$3.781 billion (31 December 2017 est.)

$2.719 billion (31 December 2016 est.)

country comparison to the world: 100

DEBT - EXTERNAL:

$14.94 billion (31 December 2017 est.)

$10.24 billion (31 December 2016 est.)

country comparison to the world: 103

STOCK OF DIRECT FOREIGN INVESTMENT - AT HOME:

$15.03 billion (2016)

$10.86 billion (2010)

country comparison to the world: 90

STOCK OF DIRECT FOREIGN INVESTMENT - ABROAD:

$604 million (2016)

$176 million (2010)

country comparison to the world: 96

EXCHANGE RATES:

Jamaican dollars (JMD) per US dollar -

128.36 (2017 est.)

125.14 (2016 est.)

125.126 (2015 est.)

116.898 (2014 est.)

110.935 (2013 est.)

ENERGY :: JAMAICA

ELECTRICITY ACCESS:

electrification - total population: 98.2% (2016)

electrification - urban areas: 100% (2016)

electrification - rural areas: 96% (2016)

ELECTRICITY - PRODUCTION:

4.007 billion kWh (2016 est.)

country comparison to the world: 128

ELECTRICITY - CONSUMPTION:

2.847 billion kWh (2016 est.)

country comparison to the world: 137

ELECTRICITY - EXPORTS:

0 kWh (2016 est.)

country comparison to the world: 151

ELECTRICITY - IMPORTS:

0 kWh (2016 est.)

country comparison to the world: 162

ELECTRICITY - INSTALLED GENERATING CAPACITY:

1.078 million kW (2016 est.)

country comparison to the world: 126

ELECTRICITY - FROM FOSSIL FUELS:

83% of total installed capacity (2016 est.)

country comparison to the world: 76

ELECTRICITY - FROM NUCLEAR FUELS:

0% of total installed capacity (2017 est.)

country comparison to the world: 115

ELECTRICITY - FROM HYDROELECTRIC PLANTS:

3% of total installed capacity (2017 est.)

country comparison to the world: 134

ELECTRICITY - FROM OTHER RENEWABLE SOURCES:

15% of total installed capacity (2017 est.)

country comparison to the world: 59

CRUDE OIL - PRODUCTION:

0 bbl/day (2018 est.)

country comparison to the world: 153

CRUDE OIL - EXPORTS:

0 bbl/day (2015 est.)

country comparison to the world: 142

CRUDE OIL - IMPORTS:

24,360 bbl/day (2015 est.)

country comparison to the world: 61

CRUDE OIL - PROVED RESERVES:

0 bbl (1 January 2018 est.)

country comparison to the world: 149

REFINED PETROLEUM PRODUCTS - PRODUCTION:

24,250 bbl/day (2017 est.)

country comparison to the world: 87

REFINED PETROLEUM PRODUCTS - CONSUMPTION:

55,000 bbl/day (2016 est.)

country comparison to the world: 99

REFINED PETROLEUM PRODUCTS - EXPORTS:

823 bbl/day (2015 est.)

country comparison to the world: 109

REFINED PETROLEUM PRODUCTS - IMPORTS:

30,580 bbl/day (2015 est.)

country comparison to the world: 100

NATURAL GAS - PRODUCTION:

0 cu m (2017 est.)

country comparison to the world: 149

NATURAL GAS - CONSUMPTION:

198.2 million cu m (2017 est.)

country comparison to the world: 104

NATURAL GAS - EXPORTS:

0 cu m (2017 est.)

country comparison to the world: 127

NATURAL GAS - IMPORTS:

198.2 million cu m (2017 est.)

country comparison to the world: 71

NATURAL GAS - PROVED RESERVES:

0 cu m (1 January 2014 est.)

country comparison to the world: 150

CARBON DIOXIDE EMISSIONS FROM CONSUMPTION OF ENERGY:

8.9 million Mt (2017 est.)

country comparison to the world: 112

COMMUNICATIONS :: JAMAICA

TELEPHONES - FIXED LINES:

total subscriptions: 297,027

subscriptions per 100 inhabitants: 10 (2017 est.)

country comparison to the world: 113

TELEPHONES - MOBILE CELLULAR:

total subscriptions: 3,091,222

subscriptions per 100 inhabitants: 103 (2017 est.)

country comparison to the world: 140

TELEPHONE SYSTEM:

general assessment: fully automatic domestic telephone network; LTE networks providing coverage to 90% of the island population (2018)

domestic: the 1999 agreement to open the market for telecommunications services resulted in rapid growth in mobile-cellular telephone usage, 103 per 100 subscriptions, while the number of fixed-lines, 10 per 100, subscriptions has declined (2018)

international: country code - 1-876 and 1-658; landing points for the ALBA-1, CFX-1, Fibralink, East-West, and Cayman-Jamaican Fiber System submarine cables providing connections to South America, parts of the Caribbean, Central America and the US; satellite earth stations - 2 Intelsat (Atlantic Ocean) (2019)

BROADCAST MEDIA:

3 free-to-air TV stations, subscription cable services, and roughly 30 radio stations (2019)

INTERNET COUNTRY CODE:

.jm

INTERNET USERS:

total: 1,336,653

percent of population: 45% (July 2016 est.)

country comparison to the world: 124

BROADBAND - FIXED SUBSCRIPTIONS:

total: 239,120

subscriptions per 100 inhabitants: 8 (2017 est.)

country comparison to the world: 103

MILITARY AND SECURITY :: JAMAICA

MILITARY EXPENDITURES:

1.35% of GDP (2018)

0.98% of GDP (2017)

0.96% of GDP (2016)

0.87% of GDP (2015)

0.87% of GDP (2014)

country comparison to the world: 87

MILITARY AND SECURITY FORCES:

Jamaica Defense Force (JDF): Ground Forces, Coast Guard, Air Wing (2019)

MILITARY SERVICE AGE AND OBLIGATION:

17 1/2 is the legal minimum age for voluntary military service; no conscription (2012)

TRANSPORTATION :: JAMAICA

NATIONAL AIR TRANSPORT SYSTEM:

number of registered air carriers: 2 (2015)

inventory of registered aircraft operated by air carriers: 5 (2015)

annual passenger traffic on registered air carriers: 92,836 (2015)

annual freight traffic on registered air carriers: 0 mt-km (2015)

CIVIL AIRCRAFT REGISTRATION COUNTRY CODE PREFIX:

6Y (2016)

AIRPORTS:

28 (2013)

country comparison to the world: 122

AIRPORTS - WITH PAVED RUNWAYS:

total: 11 (2017)

2,438 to 3,047 m: 2 (2017)

914 to 1,523 m: 4 (2017)

under 914 m: 5 (2017)

AIRPORTS - WITH UNPAVED RUNWAYS:

total: 17 (2013)

914 to 1,523 m: 1 (2013)

under 914 m: 16 (2013)

ROADWAYS:

total: 22,121 km (includes 44 km of expressways) (2011)

paved: 16,148 km (2011)

unpaved: 5,973 km (2011)

country comparison to the world: 108

MERCHANT MARINE:

total: 43

by type: bulk carrier 1, container ship 8, general cargo 10, oil tanker 1, other 23 (2018)

country comparison to the world: 118

PORTS AND TERMINALS:

major seaport(s): Discovery Bay (Port Rhoades), Kingston, Montego Bay, Port Antonio, Port Esquivel, Port Kaiser, Rocky Point

container port(s) (TEUs): Kingston (1,681,706) (2017)

TRANSNATIONAL ISSUES :: JAMAICA

DISPUTES - INTERNATIONAL:

none

TRAFFICKING IN PERSONS:

current situation: Jamaica is a source and destination country for children and adults subjected to sex trafficking and forced labor; sex trafficking of children and adults occurs on the street, in night clubs, bars, massage parlors, and private homes; child sex tourism is a problem in resort areas; Jamaicans have been subjected to sexual exploitation or forced labor in the Caribbean, Canada, the US, and the UK, while foreigners have endured conditions of forced labor in Jamaica or aboard foreign-flagged fishing vessels operating in Jamaican waters; a high number of Jamaican children are reported missing

tier rating: Tier 2 Watch List – Jamaica does not fully comply with the minimum standards for the elimination of trafficking; however, it is making significant efforts to do so; in 2014, the government made significant efforts to raise public awareness of human trafficking, and named a national trafficking-in-persons rapporteur – the first in the region; authorities initiated more new trafficking investigations than in 2013 and concluded a trafficking case in the Supreme Court, but chronic delays impeded prosecutions and no offenders were convicted for the sixth consecutive year; more adult trafficking victims were identified than in previous years, but only one child victim was identified, which was exceptionally low relative to the number of vulnerable children (2015)

ILLICIT DRUGS:

transshipment point for cocaine from South America to North America and Europe; illicit cultivation and consumption of cannabis; government has an active manual cannabis eradication program; corruption is a major concern; substantial money-laundering activity; Colombian narcotics traffickers favor Jamaica for illicit financial transactions

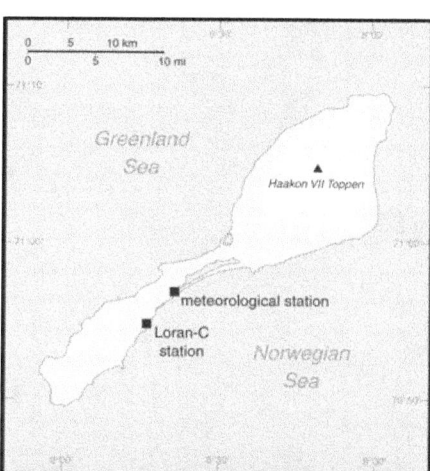

EUROPE :: JAN MAYEN

INTRODUCTION :: JAN MAYEN

BACKGROUND:

This desolate, arctic, mountainous island was named after a Dutch whaling captain who indisputably discovered it in 1614 (earlier claims are inconclusive). Visited only occasionally by seal hunters and trappers over the following centuries, the island came under Norwegian sovereignty in 1929. The long dormant Beerenberg volcano, the northernmost active volcano on earth, resumed activity in 1970 and the most recent eruption occurred in 1985.

GEOGRAPHY :: JAN MAYEN

LOCATION:
Northern Europe, island between the Greenland Sea and the Norwegian Sea, northeast of Iceland

GEOGRAPHIC COORDINATES:
71 00 N, 8 00 W

MAP REFERENCES:
Arctic Region

AREA:
total: 377 sq km

land: 377 sq km

water: 0 sq km

country comparison to the world: 206

AREA - COMPARATIVE:
slightly more than twice the size of Washington, DC

LAND BOUNDARIES:
0 km

COASTLINE:
124.1 km

MARITIME CLAIMS:
territorial sea: 12 nm

exclusive economic zone: 200 nm

contiguous zone: 24 nm

continental shelf: 200-m depth or to the depth of exploitation

CLIMATE:
arctic maritime with frequent storms and persistent fog

TERRAIN:
volcanic island, partly covered by glaciers

ELEVATION:
lowest point: Norwegian Sea 0 m

highest point: Haakon VII Toppen on Beerenberg 2,277

note: Beerenberg volcano has numerous peaks; the highest point on the volcano rim is named Haakon VII Toppen, after Norway's first king following the reestablishment of Norwegian independence in 1905

NATURAL RESOURCES:
none

LAND USE:
agricultural land: 0% (2011 est.)

arable land: 0% (2011 est.) / permanent crops: 0% (2011 est.) / permanent pasture: 0% (2011 est.)

forest: 0% (2011 est.)

other: 100% (2011 est.)

IRRIGATED LAND:
0 sq km (2012)

NATURAL HAZARDS:
dominated by the volcano Beerenberg

volcanism: Beerenberg (2,227 m) is Norway's only active volcano; volcanic activity resumed in 1970; the most recent eruption occurred in 1985

ENVIRONMENT - CURRENT ISSUES:
pollutants transported from southerly latitudes by winds, ocean currents, and rivers accumulate in the food chains of native animals; climate change

GEOGRAPHY - NOTE:
barren volcanic spoon-shaped island with some moss and grass flora; island consists of two parts: a larger northeast Nord-Jan (the spoon "bowl") and the smaller Sor-Jan (the "handle"), linked by a 2.5 km-wide isthmus (the "stem") with two large lakes, Sorlaguna (South Lagoon) and Nordlaguna (North Lagoon)

PEOPLE AND SOCIETY :: JAN MAYEN

POPULATION:
no indigenous inhabitants

note: military personnel operate the the weather and coastal services radio station

GOVERNMENT :: JAN MAYEN

COUNTRY NAME:
conventional long form: none

conventional short form: Jan Mayen

etymology: named after Dutch Captain Jan Jacobszoon MAY, one of the first explorers to reach the island in 1614

DEPENDENCY STATUS:

territory of Norway; since August 1994, administered from Oslo through the county governor (fylkesmann) of Nordland; however, authority has been delegated to a station commander of the Norwegian Defense Communication Service; in 2010, Norway designated the majority of Jan Mayen as a nature reserve

LEGAL SYSTEM:

the laws of Norway apply where applicable

FLAG DESCRIPTION:

the flag of Norway is used

ECONOMY :: JAN MAYEN

ECONOMY - OVERVIEW:

Jan Mayen is a volcanic island with no exploitable natural resources, although surrounding waters contain substantial fish stocks and potential untapped petroleum resources. Economic activity is limited to providing services for employees of Norway's radio and meteorological stations on the island.

COMMUNICATIONS :: JAN MAYEN

BROADCAST MEDIA:

a coastal radio station has been remotely operated since 1994

MILITARY AND SECURITY :: JAN MAYEN

MILITARY - NOTE:

defense is the responsibility of Norway

TRANSPORTATION :: JAN MAYEN

AIRPORTS:

1 (2013)

country comparison to the world: 225

AIRPORTS - WITH UNPAVED RUNWAYS:

total: 1 (2013)

1,524 to 2,437 m: 1 (2013)

ROADWAYS:

PORTS AND TERMINALS:

none; offshore anchorage only

TRANSNATIONAL ISSUES :: JAN MAYEN

DISPUTES - INTERNATIONAL:

none

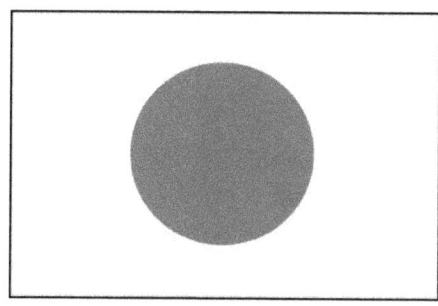

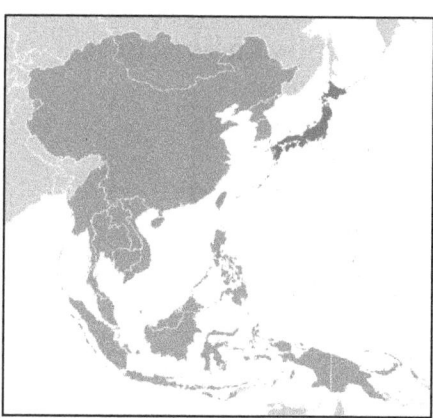

EAST ASIA / SOUTHEAST ASIA :: JAPAN

INTRODUCTION :: JAPAN

BACKGROUND:
In 1603, after decades of civil warfare, the Tokugawa shogunate (a military-led, dynastic government) ushered in a long period of relative political stability and isolation from foreign influence. For more than two centuries this policy enabled Japan to enjoy a flowering of its indigenous culture. Japan opened its ports after signing the Treaty of Kanagawa with the US in 1854 and began to intensively modernize and industrialize. During the late 19th and early 20th centuries, Japan became a regional power that was able to defeat the forces of both China and Russia. It occupied Korea, Formosa (Taiwan), and southern Sakhalin Island. In 1931-32 Japan occupied Manchuria, and in 1937 it launched a full-scale invasion of China. Japan attacked US forces in 1941 - triggering America's entry into World War II - and soon occupied much of East and Southeast Asia. After its defeat in World War II, Japan recovered to become an economic power and an ally of the US. While the emperor retains his throne as a symbol of national unity, elected politicians hold actual decision-making power. Following three decades of unprecedented growth, Japan's economy experienced a major slowdown starting in the 1990s, but the country remains an economic power. In March 2011, Japan's strongest-ever earthquake, and an accompanying tsunami, devastated the northeast part of Honshu island, killed thousands, and damaged several nuclear power plants. The catastrophe hobbled the country's economy and its energy infrastructure, and tested its ability to deal with humanitarian disasters. Prime Minister Shinzo ABE was reelected to office in December 2012, and has since embarked on ambitious economic and security reforms to improve Japan's economy and bolster the country's international standing.

GEOGRAPHY :: JAPAN

LOCATION:
Eastern Asia, island chain between the North Pacific Ocean and the Sea of Japan, east of the Korean Peninsula

GEOGRAPHIC COORDINATES:
36 00 N, 138 00 E

MAP REFERENCES:
Asia

AREA:
total: 377,915 sq km

land: 364,485 sq km

water: 13,430 sq km

note: includes Bonin Islands (Ogasawara-gunto), Daito-shoto, Minami-jima, Okino-tori-shima, Ryukyu Islands (Nansei-shoto), and Volcano Islands (Kazan-retto)

country comparison to the world: 63

AREA - COMPARATIVE:
slightly smaller than California

LAND BOUNDARIES:
0 km

COASTLINE:
29,751 km

MARITIME CLAIMS:
territorial sea: 12 nm; between 3 nm and 12 nm in the international straits - La Perouse or Soya, Tsugaru, Osumi, and Eastern and Western Channels of the Korea or Tsushima Strait

exclusive economic zone: 200 nm

contiguous zone: 24 nm

CLIMATE:
varies from tropical in south to cool temperate in north

TERRAIN:
mostly rugged and mountainous

ELEVATION:
mean elevation: 438 m

lowest point: Hachiro-gata -4 m

highest point: Mount Fuji 3,776 m

NATURAL RESOURCES:
negligible mineral resources, fish, note, with virtually no natural energy resources, Japan is the world's largest importer of coal and liquefied natural gas, as well as the second largest importer of oil

LAND USE:
agricultural land: 12.5% (2011 est.)

arable land: 11.7% (2011 est.) / permanent crops: 0.8% (2011 est.) / permanent pasture: 0% (2011 est.)

forest: 68.5% (2011 est.)

other: 19% (2011 est.)

IRRIGATED LAND:
24,690 sq km (2012)

POPULATION DISTRIBUTION:
all primary and secondary regions of high population density lie on the coast; one-third of the population

resides in and around Tokyo on the central plain (Kanto Plain)

NATURAL HAZARDS:

many dormant and some active volcanoes; about 1,500 seismic occurrences (mostly tremors but occasional severe earthquakes) every year; tsunamis; typhoons

volcanism: both Unzen (1,500 m) and Sakura-jima (1,117 m), which lies near the densely populated city of Kagoshima, have been deemed Decade Volcanoes by the International Association of Volcanology and Chemistry of the Earth's Interior, worthy of study due to their explosive history and close proximity to human populations; other notable historically active volcanoes include Asama, Honshu Island's most active volcano, Aso, Bandai, Fuji, Iwo-Jima, Kikai, Kirishima, Komaga-take, Oshima, Suwanosejima, Tokachi, Yake-dake, and Usu; see note 2 under "Geography - note"

ENVIRONMENT - CURRENT ISSUES:

air pollution from power plant emissions results in acid rain; acidification of lakes and reservoirs degrading water quality and threatening aquatic life; Japan is one of the largest consumers of fish and tropical timber, contributing to the depletion of these resources in Asia and elsewhere; following the 2011 Fukushima nuclear disaster, Japan originally planned to phase out nuclear power, but it has now implemented a new policy of seeking to restart nuclear power plants that meet strict new safety standards; waste management is an ongoing issue; Japanese municipal facilities used to burn high volumes of trash, but air pollution issues forced the government to adopt an aggressive recycling policy

ENVIRONMENT - INTERNATIONAL AGREEMENTS:

party to: Antarctic-Environmental Protocol, Antarctic-Marine Living Resources, Antarctic Seals, Antarctic Treaty, Biodiversity, Climate Change, Climate Change-Kyoto Protocol, Desertification, Endangered Species, Environmental Modification, Hazardous Wastes, Law of the Sea, Marine Dumping, Ozone Layer Protection, Ship Pollution, Tropical Timber 83, Tropical Timber 94, Wetlands, Whaling

signed, but not ratified: none of the selected agreements

GEOGRAPHY - NOTE:

note 1: strategic location in northeast Asia; composed of four main islands - from north: Hokkaido, Honshu (the largest and most populous), Shikoku, and Kyushu (the "Home Islands") - and 6,848 smaller islands and islets

note 2: Japan annually records the most earthquakes in the world; it is one of the countries along the Ring of Fire, a belt of active volcanoes and earthquake epicenters bordering the Pacific Ocean; up to 90% of the world's earthquakes and some 75% of the world's volcanoes occur within the Ring of Fire

PEOPLE AND SOCIETY :: JAPAN

POPULATION:
126,168,156 (July 2018 est.)

country comparison to the world: 10

NATIONALITY:

noun: Japanese (singular and plural)

adjective: Japanese

ETHNIC GROUPS:

Japanese 98.1%, Chinese 0.5%, Korean 0.4%, other 1% (includes Filipino, Vietnamese, and Brazilian) (2016 est.)

note: data represent population by nationality; up to 230,000 Brazilians of Japanese origin migrated to Japan in the 1990s to work in industries; some have returned to Brazil

LANGUAGES:

Japanese

RELIGIONS:

Shintoism 70.4%, Buddhism 69.8%, Christianity 1.5%, other 6.9% (2015 est.)

note: total adherents exceeds 100% because many people practice both Shintoism and Buddhism

AGE STRUCTURE:

0-14 years: 12.71% (male 8,251,336 /female 7,787,234)

15-24 years: 9.63% (male 6,397,995 /female 5,746,140)

25-54 years: 37.28% (male 23,246,562 /female 23,784,273)

55-64 years: 12.01% (male 7,588,597 /female 7,563,245)

65 years and over: 28.38% (male 15,655,860 /female 20,146,914) (2018 est.)

DEPENDENCY RATIOS:

total dependency ratio: 64 (2015 est.)

youth dependency ratio: 21.3 (2015 est.)

elderly dependency ratio: 42.7 (2015 est.)

potential support ratio: 2.3 (2015 est.)

MEDIAN AGE:

total: 47.7 years (2018 est.)

male: 46.4 years

female: 49.2 years

country comparison to the world: 2

POPULATION GROWTH RATE:

-0.24% (2018 est.)

country comparison to the world: 212

BIRTH RATE:

7.5 births/1,000 population (2018 est.)

country comparison to the world: 223

DEATH RATE:

9.9 deaths/1,000 population (2018 est.)

country comparison to the world: 37

NET MIGRATION RATE:

0 migrant(s)/1,000 population (2018 est.)

country comparison to the world: 87

POPULATION DISTRIBUTION:

all primary and secondary regions of high population density lie on the coast; one-third of the population resides in and around Tokyo on the central plain (Kanto Plain)

URBANIZATION:

urban population: 91.7% of total population (2019)

rate of urbanization: -0.14% annual rate of change (2015-20 est.)

MAJOR URBAN AREAS - POPULATION:

37.435 million TOKYO (capital), 19.223 million Osaka, 9.532 million Nagoya, 5.54 million Kitakyushu-Fukuoka, 2.912 million Shizuoka-Hamamatsu, 2.668 million Sapporo (2019)

SEX RATIO:

at birth: 1.06 male(s)/female

0-14 years: 1.06 male(s)/female

15-24 years: 1.11 male(s)/female

25-54 years: 0.98 male(s)/female

55-64 years: 1 male(s)/female

65 years and over: 0.78 male(s)/female

total population: 0.94 male(s)/female (2018 est.)

MOTHER'S MEAN AGE AT FIRST BIRTH:

30.7 years (2015 est.)

MATERNAL MORTALITY RATE:

5 deaths/100,000 live births (2017 est.)

country comparison to the world: 166

INFANT MORTALITY RATE:

total: 2 deaths/1,000 live births (2018 est.)

male: 2.2 deaths/1,000 live births

female: 1.7 deaths/1,000 live births

country comparison to the world: 222

LIFE EXPECTANCY AT BIRTH:

total population: 85.5 years (2018 est.)

male: 82.2 years

female: 89 years

country comparison to the world: 2

TOTAL FERTILITY RATE:

1.42 children born/woman (2018 est.)

country comparison to the world: 209

CONTRACEPTIVE PREVALENCE RATE:

39.8% (2015)

note: percent of women aged 20-49

DRINKING WATER SOURCE:

improved:

urban: 100% of population

rural: 100% of population

total: 100% of population

unimproved:

urban: 0% of population

rural: 0% of population

total: 0% of population (2015 est.)

CURRENT HEALTH EXPENDITURE:

10.9% (2016)

PHYSICIANS DENSITY:

2.41 physicians/1,000 population (2016)

HOSPITAL BED DENSITY:

13.4 beds/1,000 population (2012)

SANITATION FACILITY ACCESS:

improved:

urban: 100% of population (2015 est.)

rural: 100% of population (2015 est.)

total: 100% of population (2015 est.)

unimproved:

urban: 0% of population (2015 est.)

rural: 0% of population (2015 est.)

total: 0% of population (2015 est.)

HIV/AIDS - ADULT PREVALENCE RATE:

<.1% (2018 est.)

HIV/AIDS - PEOPLE LIVING WITH HIV/AIDS:

30,000 (2018 est.)

country comparison to the world: 72

HIV/AIDS - DEATHS:

<200 (2017 est.)

OBESITY - ADULT PREVALENCE RATE:

4.3% (2016)

country comparison to the world: 186

CHILDREN UNDER THE AGE OF 5 YEARS UNDERWEIGHT:

3.4% (2010)

country comparison to the world: 95

EDUCATION EXPENDITURES:

3.5% of GDP (2016)

country comparison to the world: 126

SCHOOL LIFE EXPECTANCY (PRIMARY TO TERTIARY EDUCATION):

total: 15 years

male: 15 years

female: 15 years (2016)

UNEMPLOYMENT, YOUTH AGES 15-24:

total: 3.6%

male: 4.1%

female: 3.1% (2018 est.)

country comparison to the world: 171

GOVERNMENT :: JAPAN

COUNTRY NAME:

conventional long form: none

conventional short form: Japan

local long form: Nihon-koku/Nippon-koku

local short form: Nihon/Nippon

etymology: the English word for Japan comes via the Chinese name for the country "Cipangu"; both Nihon and Nippon mean "where the sun originates" and are frequently translated as "Land of the Rising Sun"

GOVERNMENT TYPE:

parliamentary constitutional monarchy

CAPITAL:

name: Tokyo

geographic coordinates: 35 41 N, 139 45 E

time difference: UTC+9 (14 hours ahead of Washington, DC, during Standard Time)

etymology: originally known as Edo, meaning "estuary" in Japanese, the name was changed to Tokyo, meaning "eastern capital," in 1868

ADMINISTRATIVE DIVISIONS:

47 prefectures; Aichi, Akita, Aomori, Chiba, Ehime, Fukui, Fukuoka, Fukushima, Gifu, Gunma, Hiroshima, Hokkaido, Hyogo, Ibaraki, Ishikawa, Iwate, Kagawa, Kagoshima, Kanagawa, Kochi, Kumamoto, Kyoto, Mie, Miyagi, Miyazaki, Nagano, Nagasaki, Nara, Niigata, Oita, Okayama, Okinawa, Osaka, Saga, Saitama, Shiga, Shimane, Shizuoka, Tochigi, Tokushima, Tokyo, Tottori, Toyama, Wakayama, Yamagata, Yamaguchi, Yamanashi

INDEPENDENCE:

3 May 1947 (current constitution adopted as amendment to Meiji Constitution); notable earlier dates: 11 February 660 B.C. (mythological date of the founding of the nation by Emperor JIMMU); 29 November 1890 (Meiji Constitution provides for constitutional monarchy)

NATIONAL HOLIDAY:

Birthday of Emperor NARUHITO, 23 February (1960); note - celebrates the birthday of the current emperor

CONSTITUTION:

history: previous 1890; latest approved 6 October 1946, adopted 3 November 1946, effective 3 May 1947

amendments: proposed by the Diet; passage requires approval by at least two-thirds majority of both houses of the Diet and approval by majority in a referendum; note - the constitution has not been amended since its enactment in 1947 (2017)

LEGAL SYSTEM:

civil law system based on German model; system also reflects Anglo-American influence and Japanese traditions; judicial review of legislative acts in the Supreme Court

INTERNATIONAL LAW ORGANIZATION PARTICIPATION:

accepts compulsory ICJ jurisdiction with reservations; accepts ICCt jurisdiction

CITIZENSHIP:

citizenship by birth: no

citizenship by descent only: at least one parent must be a citizen of Japan

dual citizenship recognized: no

residency requirement for naturalization: 5 years

SUFFRAGE:

18 years of age; universal

EXECUTIVE BRANCH:

chief of state: Emperor NARUHITO (since 1 May 2019); note - succeeds his father who abdicated on 30 April 2019

head of government: Prime Minister Shinzo ABE (since 26 December 2012); Deputy Prime Minister Taro ASO (since 26 December 2012)

cabinet: Cabinet appointed by the prime minister

elections/appointments: the monarchy is hereditary; the leader of the majority party or majority coalition in the House of Representatives usually becomes prime minister

LEGISLATIVE BRANCH:

description: bicameral Diet or Kokkai consists of:
House of Councillors or Sangi-in (242 seats; 146 members directly elected in multi-seat districts by simple majority vote and 96 directly elected in a single national constituency by proportional representation vote; members serve 6-year terms with half the membership renewed every 3 years)
House of Representatives or Shugi-in (465 seats; 289 members directly elected in single-seat districts by simple majority vote and 176 directly elected in multi-seat districts by party-list proportional representation vote; members serve 4-year terms)

elections:
House of Councillors - last held on 10 July 2016 (next to be held in July 2019)
House of Representatives - last held on 22 October 2017 (next to be held by 21 October 2021)

election results:
House of Councillors - percent of vote by party - NA; seats by party - LDP 55, DP 32, Komeito 14, JCP 6, Osaka Ishin no Kai (Initiatives from Osaka) 7, PLPTYF 1, SDP 1, independent 5
House of Representatives - percent of vote by party - NA; seats by party - LDP 284, CDP 55, Party of Hope 50, Komeito 29, JCP 12, JIP 11, SDP 2, independent 22

note: the Diet in June 2017 redrew Japan's electoral district boundaries and reduced from 475 to 465 seats in the House of Representatives; the amended electoral law, which cuts 6 seats in single-seat districts and 4 in multi-seat districts, was reportedly intended to reduce voting disparities between densely and sparsely populated voting districts

JUDICIAL BRANCH:

highest courts: Supreme Court or Saiko saibansho (consists of the chief justice and 14 associate justices); note - the Supreme Court has jurisdiction in constitutional issues

judge selection and term of office: Supreme Court chief justice designated by the Cabinet and appointed by the monarch; associate justices appointed by the Cabinet and confirmed by the monarch; all justices are reviewed in a popular referendum at the first general election of the House of Representatives following each judge's appointment and every 10 years afterward

subordinate courts: 8 High Courts (Koto-saiban-sho), each with a Family Court (Katei-saiban-sho); 50 District Courts (Chiho saibansho), with 203 additional branches; 438 Summary Courts (Kani saibansho)

POLITICAL PARTIES AND LEADERS:

Constitutional Democratic Party of Japan or CDP [Yukio EDANO]
Democratic Party of Japan or DPJ [Kohei OTSUKA]
Group of Reformists [Sakihito OZAWA]
Initiatives from Osaka (Osaka Ishin no kai) [Ichiro MATSUI]
Japan Communist Party or JCP [Kazuo SHII]
Japan Innovation Party or JIP [Ichiro MATSUI]
Party of Hope or Kibo no To [Yuichiro TAMAKI]
Komeito [Natsuo YAMAGUCHI]
Liberal Democratic Party or LDP [Shinzo ABE]
Liberal Party [Ichiro OZAWA] (formerly People's Life Party & Taro Yamamoto and Friends or PLPTYF)New Renaissance Party [Hiroyuki ARAI]
Party for Japanese Kokoro or PJK [Masashi NAKANO]Social Democratic Party or SDP [Tadatomo YOSHIDA]The Assembly to Energize Japan and the Independents [Kota MATSUDA]

INTERNATIONAL ORGANIZATION PARTICIPATION:

ADB, AfDB (nonregional member), APEC, Arctic Council (observer), ARF, ASEAN (dialogue partner), Australia Group, BIS, CD, CE (observer), CERN (observer), CICA (observer), CP, CPLP (associate), EAS, EBRD, EITI (implementing country), FAO, FATF, G-5, G-7, G-8, G-10, G-20, IADB, IAEA, IBRD, ICAO, ICC (national committees), ICCt, ICRM, IDA, IEA, IFAD, IFC, IFRCS, IGAD (partners), IHO, ILO, IMF, IMO, IMSO, Interpol, IOC, IOM, IPU, ISO, ITSO, ITU, ITUC (NGOs), LAIA (observer), MIGA, NEA, NSG, OAS (observer), OECD, OPCW, OSCE (partner), Pacific Alliance (observer), Paris Club, PCA, PIF (partner), SAARC (observer), SELEC (observer), SICA (observer), UN, UNCTAD, UNESCO, UNHCR, UNIDO, UNMISS, UNRWA, UNWTO, UPU, WCO, WFTU (NGOs), WHO, WIPO, WMO, WTO, ZC

DIPLOMATIC REPRESENTATION IN THE US:

Ambassador Shinsuke SUGIYAMA (since 28 March 2018) (2018)

chancery: 2520 Massachusetts Avenue NW, Washington, DC 20008

telephone: [1] (202) 238-6700

FAX: [1] (202) 328-2187

consulate(s) general: Anchorage (AK), Atlanta, Boston, Chicago, Dallas, Denver (CO), Detroit (MI), Honolulu, Houston, Las Vegas (NV), Los Angeles, Miami, Nashville (TN), New Orleans, New York, Oklahoma City (OK), Orlando (FL), Philadelphia, Phoenix (AZ), Portland (OR), San Francisco, Seattle, Saipan (Northern Mariana Islands), Tamuning (Guam)

DIPLOMATIC REPRESENTATION FROM THE US:

chief of mission: Ambassador (vacant); Charge d'Affaires Joseph M. YOUNG (since 20 July 2019)

telephone: [81] (03) 3224-5000

embassy: 1-10-5 Akasaka, Minato-ku, Tokyo 107-8420

mailing address: Unit 9800, Box 300, APO AP 96303-0300

FAX: [81] (03) 3505-1862

consulate(s) general: Naha (Okinawa), Osaka-Kobe, Sapporo

consulate(s): Fukuoka, Nagoya

FLAG DESCRIPTION:

white with a large red disk (representing the sun without rays) in the center

NATIONAL SYMBOL(S):

red sun disc, chrysanthemum; national colors: red, white

NATIONAL ANTHEM:

name: "Kimigayo" (The Emperor"s Reign)

lyrics/music: unknown/Hiromori HAYASHI

note: adopted 1999; unofficial national anthem since 1883; oldest anthem lyrics in the world, dating to the 10th century or earlier; there is some opposition to the anthem because of its association with militarism and worship of the emperor

ECONOMY :: JAPAN

ECONOMY - OVERVIEW:

Over the past 70 years, government-industry cooperation, a strong work ethic, mastery of high technology, and a comparatively small defense allocation (slightly less than 1% of GDP) have helped Japan develop an advanced economy. Two notable characteristics of the post-World War II economy were the close interlocking structures of manufacturers, suppliers, and distributors, known as keiretsu, and the guarantee of lifetime employment for a substantial portion of the urban labor force. Both features have significantly eroded under the dual pressures of global competition and domestic demographic change.

Measured on a purchasing power parity basis that adjusts for price differences, Japan in 2017 stood as the fourth-largest economy in the world after first-place China, which surpassed Japan in 2001, and third-place India, which edged out Japan in 2012. For three postwar decades, overall real economic growth was impressive - averaging 10% in the 1960s, 5% in the 1970s, and 4% in the 1980s. Growth slowed markedly in the 1990s, averaging just 1.7%, largely because of the aftereffects of inefficient investment and the collapse of an asset price bubble in the late 1980s, which resulted in several years of economic stagnation as firms sought to reduce excess debt, capital, and labor. Modest economic growth continued after 2000, but the economy has fallen into recession four times since 2008.

Japan enjoyed an uptick in growth since 2013, supported by Prime Minister Shinzo ABE's "Three Arrows" economic revitalization agenda - dubbed "Abenomics" - of monetary easing, "flexible" fiscal policy, and structural reform. Led by the Bank of Japan's aggressive monetary easing, Japan is making modest progress in ending deflation, but demographic decline – a low birthrate and an aging, shrinking population – poses a major long-term challenge for the economy. The government currently faces the quandary of balancing its efforts to stimulate growth and institute economic reforms with the need to address its sizable public debt, which stands at 235% of GDP. To help raise government revenue, Japan adopted legislation in 2012 to gradually raise the consumption tax rate. However, the first such increase, in April 2014, led to a sharp contraction, so Prime Minister ABE has twice postponed the next increase, which is now scheduled for October 2019. Structural reforms to unlock productivity are seen as central to strengthening the economy in the long-run.

Scarce in critical natural resources, Japan has long been dependent on imported energy and raw materials. After the complete shutdown of Japan's nuclear reactors following the earthquake and tsunami disaster in 2011, Japan's industrial sector has become even more dependent than before on imported fossil fuels. However, ABE's government is seeking to restart nuclear power plants that meet strict new safety standards and is emphasizing nuclear energy's importance as a base-load electricity source. In August 2015, Japan successfully restarted one nuclear reactor at the Sendai Nuclear Power Plant in Kagoshima prefecture, and several other reactors around the country have since resumed operations; however, opposition from local governments has delayed several more restarts that remain pending. Reforms of the electricity and gas sectors, including full liberalization of Japan's energy market in April 2016 and gas market in April 2017, constitute an important part of Prime Minister Abe's economic program.

Under the Abe Administration, Japan's government sought to open the country's economy to greater foreign competition and create new export opportunities for Japanese businesses, including by joining 11 trading partners in the Trans-Pacific Partnership (TPP). Japan became the first country to ratify the TPP in December 2016, but the United States signaled its withdrawal from the agreement in January 2017. In November 2017 the remaining 11 countries agreed on the core elements of a modified agreement, which they renamed the Comprehensive and Progressive Agreement for Trans-Pacific Partnership (CPTPP). Japan also reached agreement with the European Union on an Economic Partnership Agreement in July 2017, and is likely seek to ratify both agreements in the Diet this year.

GDP (PURCHASING POWER PARITY):

$5.443 trillion (2017 est.)

$5.35 trillion (2016 est.)

$5.299 trillion (2015 est.)

note: data are in 2017 dollars

country comparison to the world: 4

GDP (OFFICIAL EXCHANGE RATE):

$4.873 trillion (2017 est.)

GDP - REAL GROWTH RATE:

1.7% (2017 est.)

1% (2016 est.)

1.4% (2015 est.)

country comparison to the world: 164

GDP - PER CAPITA (PPP):

$42,900 (2017 est.)

$42,100 (2016 est.)

$41,700 (2015 est.)

note: data are in 2017 dollars

country comparison to the world: 42

GROSS NATIONAL SAVING:

28% of GDP (2017 est.)

27.5% of GDP (2016 est.)

27.1% of GDP (2015 est.)

country comparison to the world: 41

GDP - COMPOSITION, BY END USE:

household consumption: 55.5% (2017 est.)

government consumption: 19.6% (2017 est.)

investment in fixed capital: 24% (2017 est.)

investment in inventories: 0% (2017 est.)

exports of goods and services: 17.7% (2017 est.)

imports of goods and services: -16.8% (2017 est.)

GDP - COMPOSITION, BY SECTOR OF ORIGIN:
- agriculture: 1.1% (2017 est.)
- industry: 30.1% (2017 est.)
- services: 68.7% (2017 est.)

AGRICULTURE - PRODUCTS:
vegetables, rice, fish, poultry, fruit, dairy products, pork, beef, flowers, potatoes/taros/yams, sugarcane, tea, legumes, wheat and barley

INDUSTRIES:
among world's largest and most technologically advanced producers of motor vehicles, electronic equipment, machine tools, steel and nonferrous metals, ships, chemicals, textiles, processed foods

INDUSTRIAL PRODUCTION GROWTH RATE:
1.4% (2017 est.)

country comparison to the world: 145

LABOR FORCE:
65.01 million (2017 est.)

country comparison to the world: 8

LABOR FORCE - BY OCCUPATION:
- agriculture: 2.9%
- industry: 26.2%
- services: 70.9% (February 2015 est.)

UNEMPLOYMENT RATE:
2.9% (2017 est.)
3.1% (2016 est.)

country comparison to the world: 34

POPULATION BELOW POVERTY LINE:
16.1% (2013 est.)

HOUSEHOLD INCOME OR CONSUMPTION BY PERCENTAGE SHARE:
- lowest 10%: 2.7%
- highest 10%: 24.8% (2008)

DISTRIBUTION OF FAMILY INCOME - GINI INDEX:
37.9 (2011)
24.9 (1993)

country comparison to the world: 79

BUDGET:
- revenues: 1.714 trillion (2017 est.)
- expenditures: 1.885 trillion (2017 est.)

TAXES AND OTHER REVENUES:
35.2% (of GDP) (2017 est.)

country comparison to the world: 63

BUDGET SURPLUS (+) OR DEFICIT (-):
-3.5% (of GDP) (2017 est.)

country comparison to the world: 147

PUBLIC DEBT:
237.6% of GDP (2017 est.)
235.6% of GDP (2016 est.)

country comparison to the world: 1

FISCAL YEAR:
1 April - 31 March

INFLATION RATE (CONSUMER PRICES):
0.5% (2017 est.)
-0.1% (2016 est.)

country comparison to the world: 27

CENTRAL BANK DISCOUNT RATE:
0.3% (31 December 2015)
0.3% (31 December 2014)

country comparison to the world: 138

COMMERCIAL BANK PRIME LENDING RATE:
1.48% (31 December 2017 est.)
1.48% (31 December 2016 est.)

country comparison to the world: 191

STOCK OF NARROW MONEY:
$6.317 trillion (31 December 2017 est.)
$5.65 trillion (31 December 2016 est.)

country comparison to the world: 2

STOCK OF BROAD MONEY:
$6.317 trillion (31 December 2017 est.)
$5.65 trillion (31 December 2016 est.)

country comparison to the world: 2

STOCK OF DOMESTIC CREDIT:
$13.07 trillion (31 December 2017 est.)
$12.18 trillion (31 December 2016 est.)

country comparison to the world: 3

MARKET VALUE OF PUBLICLY TRADED SHARES:
$4.895 trillion (31 December 2015 est.)
$4.378 trillion (31 December 2014 est.)
$4.543 trillion (31 December 2013 est.)

country comparison to the world: 3

CURRENT ACCOUNT BALANCE:
$196.1 billion (2017 est.)
$194.9 billion (2016 est.)

country comparison to the world: 2

EXPORTS:
$688.9 billion (2017 est.)
$634.9 billion (2016 est.)

country comparison to the world: 4

EXPORTS - PARTNERS:
US 19.4%, China 19%, South Korea 7.6%, Hong Kong 5.1%, Thailand 4.2% (2017)

EXPORTS - COMMODITIES:
14.9 motor vehicles5.4 iron and steel products5 semiconductors4.8 auto parts3.5 power generating machinery3.3 plastic materials (2014 est.)

IMPORTS:
$644.7 billion (2017 est.)
$584.7 billion (2016 est.)

country comparison to the world: 4

IMPORTS - COMMODITIES:
16.1 petroleum9.1 liquid natural gas3.8 clothing3.3 semiconductors2.4 coal1.4 audio and visual apparatus (2014 est.)

IMPORTS - PARTNERS:
China 24.5%, US 11%, Australia 5.8%, South Korea 4.2%, Saudi Arabia 4.1% (2017)

RESERVES OF FOREIGN EXCHANGE AND GOLD:
$1.264 trillion (31 December 2017 est.)
$1.233 trillion (31 December 2015 est.)

country comparison to the world: 2

DEBT - EXTERNAL:
$3.24 trillion (31 March 2016 est.)
$2.83 trillion (31 March 2015 est.)

country comparison to the world: 7

STOCK OF DIRECT FOREIGN INVESTMENT - AT HOME:
$252.9 billion (31 December 2017 est.)
$238.4 billion (31 December 2016 est.)

country comparison to the world: 25

STOCK OF DIRECT FOREIGN INVESTMENT - ABROAD:
$1.547 trillion (31 December 2017 est.)
$1.363 trillion (31 December 2016 est.)

country comparison to the world: 8

EXCHANGE RATES:
yen (JPY) per US dollar -
111.1 (2017 est.)
108.76 (2016 est.)
108.76 (2015 est.)
121.02 (2014 est.)

97.44 (2013 est.)

ENERGY :: JAPAN

ELECTRICITY ACCESS:

electrification - total population: 100% (2016)

ELECTRICITY - PRODUCTION:

989.3 billion kWh (2016 est.)

country comparison to the world: 5

ELECTRICITY - CONSUMPTION:

943.7 billion kWh (2016 est.)

country comparison to the world: 4

ELECTRICITY - EXPORTS:

0 kWh (2016 est.)

country comparison to the world: 152

ELECTRICITY - IMPORTS:

0 kWh (2016 est.)

country comparison to the world: 163

ELECTRICITY - INSTALLED GENERATING CAPACITY:

295.9 million kW (2016 est.)

country comparison to the world: 4

ELECTRICITY - FROM FOSSIL FUELS:

71% of total installed capacity (2016 est.)

country comparison to the world: 105

ELECTRICITY - FROM NUCLEAR FUELS:

1% of total installed capacity (2017 est.)

country comparison to the world: 30

ELECTRICITY - FROM HYDROELECTRIC PLANTS:

8% of total installed capacity (2017 est.)

country comparison to the world: 121

ELECTRICITY - FROM OTHER RENEWABLE SOURCES:

20% of total installed capacity (2017 est.)

country comparison to the world: 38

CRUDE OIL - PRODUCTION:

3,200 bbl/day (2018 est.)

country comparison to the world: 82

CRUDE OIL - EXPORTS:

0 bbl/day (2017 est.)

country comparison to the world: 143

CRUDE OIL - IMPORTS:

3.208 million bbl/day (2017 est.)

country comparison to the world: 4

CRUDE OIL - PROVED RESERVES:

44.12 million bbl (1 January 2018 est.)

country comparison to the world: 77

REFINED PETROLEUM PRODUCTS - PRODUCTION:

3.467 million bbl/day (2017 est.)

country comparison to the world: 5

REFINED PETROLEUM PRODUCTS - CONSUMPTION:

3.894 million bbl/day (2017 est.)

country comparison to the world: 4

REFINED PETROLEUM PRODUCTS - EXPORTS:

370,900 bbl/day (2017 est.)

country comparison to the world: 24

REFINED PETROLEUM PRODUCTS - IMPORTS:

1.1 million bbl/day (2017 est.)

country comparison to the world: 5

NATURAL GAS - PRODUCTION:

3.058 billion cu m (2017 est.)

country comparison to the world: 57

NATURAL GAS - CONSUMPTION:

127.2 billion cu m (2017 est.)

country comparison to the world: 5

NATURAL GAS - EXPORTS:

169.9 million cu m (2017 est.)

country comparison to the world: 47

NATURAL GAS - IMPORTS:

116.6 billion cu m (2017 est.)

country comparison to the world: 2

NATURAL GAS - PROVED RESERVES:

20.9 billion cu m (1 January 2018 est.)

country comparison to the world: 74

CARBON DIOXIDE EMISSIONS FROM CONSUMPTION OF ENERGY:

1.268 billion Mt (2017 est.)

country comparison to the world: 5

COMMUNICATIONS :: JAPAN

TELEPHONES - FIXED LINES:

total subscriptions: 63,941,094

subscriptions per 100 inhabitants: 51 (2017 est.)

country comparison to the world: 3

TELEPHONES - MOBILE CELLULAR:

total subscriptions: 170,128,499

subscriptions per 100 inhabitants: 135 (2017 est.)

country comparison to the world: 7

TELEPHONE SYSTEM:

general assessment: excellent domestic and international service; Japan has exceedingly high mobile, mobile broadband and fixed broadband penetration; one of Japan's largest e-commerce companies planning to build its own nationwide stand-alone 5G mobile network; in 2019, Japan govt released spectrum for 5G services to be commercially available in 2020 (2018)

domestic: high level of modern technology and excellent service of every kind; 51 per 100 for fixed-line and 135 per 100 for mobile-cellular subscriptions (2018)

international: country code - 81; numerous submarine cables with landing points for HSCS, JIH, RJCN, APCN-2, JUS, EAC-C2C, PC-1, Tata TGN-Pacific, FLAG North Asia Loop/REACH North Asia Loop, APCN-2, FASTER, SJC, SJC2, Unity/EAC-Pacific, JGA-N, APG, ASE, AJC, JUPITER, MOC, Okinawa Cellular Cable, KJCN, GOKI, KJCN, and SeaMeWE-3, submarine cables provide links throughout Asia, Australia, the Middle East, Europe, Southeast Asia, Africa and US; satellite earth stations - 7 Intelsat (Pacific and Indian Oceans), 1 Intersputnik (Indian Ocean region), 2 Inmarsat (Pacific and Indian Ocean regions), and 8 SkyPerfect JSAT (2019)

BROADCAST MEDIA:

a mixture of public and commercial broadcast TV and radio stations; 6 national terrestrial TV networks including 1 public broadcaster; the large number of radio and TV stations available provide a wide range of choices; satellite and cable services provide access to international channels (2019)

INTERNET COUNTRY CODE:

.jp

INTERNET USERS:

total: 116,565,962

percent of population: 92% (July 2016 est.)

country comparison to the world: 5

BROADBAND - FIXED SUBSCRIPTIONS:

total: 40,390,640

subscriptions per 100 inhabitants: 32 (2017 est.)

country comparison to the world: 3

MILITARY AND SECURITY :: JAPAN

MILITARY EXPENDITURES:
0.93% of GDP (2018)
0.93% of GDP (2017)
0.94% of GDP (2016)
0.94% of GDP (2015)
0.97% of GDP (2014)

country comparison to the world: 124

MILITARY AND SECURITY FORCES:
Japanese Ministry of Defense (MOD): Ground Self-Defense Force (Rikujou Jieitai, GSDF; includes aviation), Maritime Self-Defense Force (Kaijou Jieitai, MSDF; includes naval aviation), Air Self-Defense Force (Koukuu Jieitai, ASDF); Japan Coast Guard (Ministry of Land, Transport, Infrastructure and Tourism) (2019)

MILITARY SERVICE AGE AND OBLIGATION:
18 years of age for voluntary military service; no conscription; mandatory retirement at age 53 for senior enlisted personnel and at 62 years for senior service officers (2012)

TRANSPORTATION :: JAPAN

NATIONAL AIR TRANSPORT SYSTEM:
number of registered air carriers: 23 (2015)

inventory of registered aircraft operated by air carriers: 627 (2015)

annual passenger traffic on registered air carriers: 113.762 million (2015)

annual freight traffic on registered air carriers: 8,868,745,000 mt-km (2015)

CIVIL AIRCRAFT REGISTRATION COUNTRY CODE PREFIX:
JA (2016)

AIRPORTS:
175 (2013)

country comparison to the world: 33

AIRPORTS - WITH PAVED RUNWAYS:
total: 142 (2017)

over 3,047 m: 6 (2017)

2,438 to 3,047 m: 45 (2017)

1,524 to 2,437 m: 38 (2017)

914 to 1,523 m: 28 (2017)

under 914 m: 25 (2017)

AIRPORTS - WITH UNPAVED RUNWAYS:
total: 33 (2013)

914 to 1,523 m: 5 (2013)

under 914 m: 28 (2013)

HELIPORTS:
16 (2013)

PIPELINES:
4456 km gas, 174 km oil, 104 km oil/gas/water (2013)

RAILWAYS:
total: 27,311 km (2015)

standard gauge: 4,800 km 1.435-m gauge (4,800 km electrified) (2015)

narrow gauge: 124 km 1.372-m gauge (124 km electrified) (2015)

dual gauge: 132 km 1.435-1.067-m gauge (132 km electrified) (2015)

22,207 km 1.067-m gauge (15,430 km electrified)
48 km 0.762-m gauge (48 km electrified)

country comparison to the world: 11

ROADWAYS:
total: 1,218,772 km (2015)

paved: 992,835 km (includes 8,428 km of expressways) (2015)

unpaved: 225,937 km (2015)

country comparison to the world: 6

WATERWAYS:
1,770 km (seagoing vessels use inland seas) (2010)

country comparison to the world: 44

MERCHANT MARINE:
total: 5,299

by type: bulk carrier 158, container ship 29, general cargo 1942, oil tanker 703, other 2467 (2018)

country comparison to the world: 3

PORTS AND TERMINALS:
major seaport(s): Chiba, Kawasaki, Kobe, Mizushima, Moji, Nagoya, Osaka, Tokyo, Tomakomai, Yokohama

container port(s) (TEUs): Kobe (2,924,179), Nagoya (2,784,109), Osaka (2,326,852), Tokyo (4,500,156), Yokohama (2,926,698) (2017)

LNG terminal(s) (import): Chita, Fukwoke, Futtsu, Hachinone, Hakodate, Hatsukaichi, Higashi Ohgishima, Higashi Niigata, Himeiji, Joetsu, Kagoshima, Kawagoe, Kita Kyushu, Mizushima, Nagasaki, Naoetsu, Negishi, Ohgishima, Oita, Sakai, Sakaide, Senboku, Shimizu, Shin Minato, Sodegaura, Tobata, Yanai, Yokkaichi

Okinawa - Nakagusuku

TERRORISM :: JAPAN

TERRORIST GROUPS - HOME BASED:
Aum Shinrikyo (AUM):

aim(s): attract new members seeking religious guidance and exhibiting a willingness to financially support the organization; historically, leaders sought to overthrow the Japanese Government and to spark a nuclear war between Japan and the US to create a global Armageddon, 'cleansing' the world so its members could achieve salvation

area(s) of operation: headquartered in the north in Hokkaido; also operates in Russia

note: in November 2017, Japanese police raided the offices of a "successor" group to AUM; AUM leader Shoko ASAHARA was executed in July 2018

(2019)

TRANSNATIONAL ISSUES :: JAPAN

DISPUTES - INTERNATIONAL:
the sovereignty dispute over the islands of Etorofu, Kunashiri, and Shikotan, and the Habomai group, known in Japan as the "Northern Territories" and in Russia as the "Southern Kuril Islands," occupied by the Soviet Union in 1945, now administered by Russia and claimed by Japan, remains the primary sticking point to signing a peace treaty formally ending World War II hostilities; Japan and South Korea claim Liancourt Rocks (Takeshima/Tok-do) occupied by South Korea since 1954; the Japanese-administered Senkaku Islands are also claimed by China and Taiwan

REFUGEES AND INTERNALLY DISPLACED PERSONS:
stateless persons: 709 (2018)

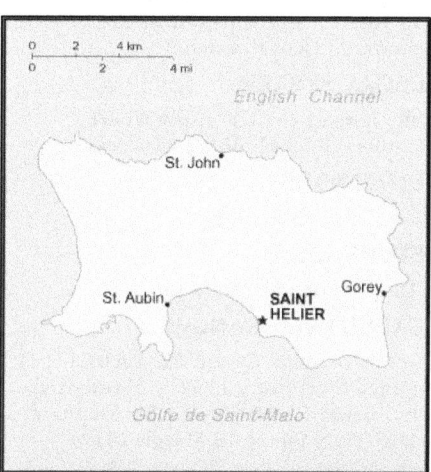

EUROPE :: JERSEY

INTRODUCTION :: JERSEY

BACKGROUND:

Jersey and the other Channel Islands represent the last remnants of the medieval Duchy of Normandy that held sway in both France and England. These islands were the only British soil occupied by German troops in World War II. The Bailiwick of Jersey is a British crown dependency, which means that it is not part of the UK but is rather a self-governing possession of the British crown. However, the UK Government is constitutionally responsible for its defense and international representation.

GEOGRAPHY :: JERSEY

LOCATION:
Western Europe, island in the English Channel, northwest of France

GEOGRAPHIC COORDINATES:
49 15 N, 2 10 W

MAP REFERENCES:
Europe

AREA:
total: 116 sq km
land: 116 sq km
water: 0 sq km
country comparison to the world: 225

AREA - COMPARATIVE:
about two-thirds the size of Washington, DC

LAND BOUNDARIES:
0 km

COASTLINE:
70 km

MARITIME CLAIMS:
territorial sea: 12 nm
exclusive fishing zone: 12 nm

CLIMATE:
temperate; mild winters and cool summers

TERRAIN:
gently rolling plain with low, rugged hills along north coast

ELEVATION:
lowest point: English Channel 0 m
highest point: Les Platons 136 m

NATURAL RESOURCES:
arable land

LAND USE:
agricultural land: 66% (2011 est.)
arable land: 66% (2011 est.) / permanent crops: 0% (2011 est.) / permanent pasture: 0% (2011 est.)
forest: 0% (2011 est.)
other: 34% (2011 est.)

IRRIGATED LAND:
NA

POPULATION DISTRIBUTION:
fairly even distribution; no notable trends

NATURAL HAZARDS:
very large tidal variation can be hazardous to navigation

ENVIRONMENT - CURRENT ISSUES:
habitat and species depletion due to human encroachment; water pollution; improper solid waste disposal

GEOGRAPHY - NOTE:
largest and southernmost of Channel Islands; about 30% of population concentrated in Saint Helier

PEOPLE AND SOCIETY :: JERSEY

POPULATION:
99,602 (July 2018 est.)
country comparison to the world: 196

NATIONALITY:
noun: Channel Islander(s)
adjective: Channel Islander

ETHNIC GROUPS:
Jersey 46.4%, British 32.7%, Portuguese/Madeiran 8.2%, Polish 3.3%, Irish, French, and other white 7.1%, other 2.4% (2011 est.)

LANGUAGES:
English 94.5% (official), Portuguese 4.6%, other 0.9% (2001 census)

RELIGIONS:
Protestant (Anglican, Baptist, Congregational New Church, Methodist, Presbyterian), Roman Catholic

AGE STRUCTURE:
0-14 years: 16.37% (male 8,430 /female 7,870)
15-24 years: 13.63% (male 7,004 /female 6,572)
25-54 years: 40.71% (male 20,392 /female 20,160)
55-64 years: 12.73% (male 6,187 /female 6,497)
65 years and over: 16.56% (male 7,015 /female 9,475) (2018 est.)

DEPENDENCY RATIOS:
total dependency ratio: 47.1 (2015 est.)

youth dependency ratio: 21.6 (2015 est.)

elderly dependency ratio: 25.4 (2015 est.)

potential support ratio: 3.9 (2015 est.)

note: data represent the Guernsey and Jersey

MEDIAN AGE:

total: 37.7 years (2018 est.)

male: 35.9 years

female: 40.2 years

country comparison to the world: 65

POPULATION GROWTH RATE:

0.76% (2018 est.)

country comparison to the world: 134

BIRTH RATE:

12.5 births/1,000 population (2018 est.)

country comparison to the world: 154

DEATH RATE:

7.8 deaths/1,000 population (2018 est.)

country comparison to the world: 96

NET MIGRATION RATE:

2.9 migrant(s)/1,000 population (2018 est.)

country comparison to the world: 40

POPULATION DISTRIBUTION:

fairly even distribution; no notable trends

URBANIZATION:

urban population: 30.9% of total population (2019)

rate of urbanization: 0.46% annual rate of change (2015-20 est.)

note: data represent Guernsey and Jersey

MAJOR URBAN AREAS - POPULATION:

34,000 SAINT HELIER (capital) (2018)

SEX RATIO:

at birth: 1.06 male(s)/female

0-14 years: 1.07 male(s)/female

15-24 years: 1.07 male(s)/female

25-54 years: 1.01 male(s)/female

55-64 years: 0.95 male(s)/female

65 years and over: 0.74 male(s)/female

total population: 0.97 male(s)/female (2018 est.)

INFANT MORTALITY RATE:

total: 3.7 deaths/1,000 live births (2018 est.)

male: 3.9 deaths/1,000 live births

female: 3.5 deaths/1,000 live births

country comparison to the world: 194

LIFE EXPECTANCY AT BIRTH:

total population: 82 years (2018 est.)

male: 79.5 years

female: 84.7 years

country comparison to the world: 20

TOTAL FERTILITY RATE:

1.66 children born/woman (2018 est.)

country comparison to the world: 176

HIV/AIDS - ADULT PREVALENCE RATE:

NA

HIV/AIDS - PEOPLE LIVING WITH HIV/AIDS:

NA

HIV/AIDS - DEATHS:

NA

EDUCATION EXPENDITURES:

NA

GOVERNMENT :: JERSEY

COUNTRY NAME:

conventional long form: Bailiwick of Jersey

conventional short form: Jersey

former: Norman Isles

etymology: the name is of Old Norse origin, but the meaning of the root "Jer(s)" is uncertain; the "-ey" ending means "island"

DEPENDENCY STATUS:

British crown dependency

GOVERNMENT TYPE:

parliamentary democracy (Assembly of the States of Jersey); a crown dependency of the UK

CAPITAL:

name: Saint Helier

geographic coordinates: 49 11 N, 2 06 W

time difference: UTC 0 (5 hours ahead of Washington, DC, during Standard Time)

daylight saving time: +1hr, begins last Sunday in March; ends last Sunday in October

etymology: named after Saint Helier, the patron saint of Jersey, who was reputedly martyred on the island in A.D. 555

ADMINISTRATIVE DIVISIONS:

none (British crown dependency); there are no first-order administrative divisions as defined by the US Government, but there are 12 parishes; Grouville, Saint Brelade, Saint Clement, Saint Helier, Saint John, Saint Lawrence, Saint Martin, Saint Mary, Saint Ouen, Saint Peter, Saint Saviour, and Trinity

INDEPENDENCE:

none (British crown dependency)

NATIONAL HOLIDAY:

Liberation Day, 9 May (1945)

CONSTITUTION:

history: unwritten; partly statutes, partly common law and practice

amendments: proposed by a government minister to the Assembly of the States of Jersey, by an Assembly member, or by an elected parish head; passage requires several Assembly readings, a majority vote by the Assembly, review by the UK Ministry of Justice, and approval of the British monarch (Royal Assent)

LEGAL SYSTEM:

the laws of the UK apply where applicable; includes local statutes

CITIZENSHIP:

see United Kingdom

SUFFRAGE:

16 years of age; universal

EXECUTIVE BRANCH:

chief of state: Queen ELIZABETH II (since 6 February 1952); represented by Lieutenant Governor Sir Stephen DALTON (since 13 March 2017)

head of government: Chief Minister John LE FONDRE (since 8 June 2018); Bailiff William BAILHACHE (since 29 January 2015)

cabinet: Council of Ministers appointed individually by the states

elections/appointments: the monarchy is hereditary; Council of Ministers, including the chief minister, indirectly elected by the Assembly of States; lieutenant governor and bailiff appointed by the monarch

LEGISLATIVE BRANCH:

description: unicameral Assembly of the States of Jersey (49 elected members; 8 senators to serve 4-year terms, and 29 deputies and 12 connetables, or heads of parishes, to serve 4-year terms; 5 non-voting members appointed by the monarch include the bailiff, lieutenant governor, dean of Jersey, attorney general, and the solicitor general)

elections: last held on 16 May 2018 (next to be held on 16 May 2022)

election results: percent of vote - NA; seats - independents 49; composition - men 36, women 13, percent of 26.5%

JUDICIAL BRANCH:

highest courts: Jersey Court of Appeal (consists of the bailiff, deputy bailiff, and 12 judges); Royal Court (consists of the bailiff, deputy bailiff, 6 commissioners and lay people referred to as jurats, and is organized into Heritage, Family, Probate, and Samedi Divisions); appeals beyond the Court of Appeal are heard by the Judicial Committee of the Privy Council (in London)

judge selection and term of office: Jersey Court of Appeal bailiffs and judges appointed by the Crown upon the advice of the Secretary of State for Justice; bailiffs and judges appointed for "extent of good behavior;" Royal Court bailiffs appointed by the Crown upon the advice of the Secretary of State for Justice; commissioners appointed by the bailiff; jurats appointed by the Electoral College; bailiffs and commissioners appointed for "extent of good behavior;" jurats appointed until retirement at age 72

subordinate courts: Magistrate's Court; Youth Court; Petty Debts Court; Parish Hall Enquires (a process of preliminary investigation into youth and minor adult offenses to determine need for presentation before a court)

POLITICAL PARTIES AND LEADERS:

one registered party: Reform Jersey [Sam MEZEC]

note: most senators and deputies sit as independents

INTERNATIONAL ORGANIZATION PARTICIPATION:

UPU

DIPLOMATIC REPRESENTATION IN THE US:

none (British crown dependency)

DIPLOMATIC REPRESENTATION FROM THE US:

none (British crown dependency)

FLAG DESCRIPTION:

white with a diagonal red cross extending to the corners of the flag; in the upper quadrant, surmounted by a yellow crown, a red shield with three lions in yellow; according to tradition, the ships of Jersey - in an attempt to differentiate themselves from English ships flying the horizontal cross of St. George - rotated the cross to the "X" (saltire) configuration; because this arrangement still resembled the Irish cross of St. Patrick, the yellow Plantagenet crown and Jersey coat of arms were added

NATIONAL SYMBOL(S):

Jersey cow; national colors: red, white

NATIONAL ANTHEM:

name: "Isle de Siez Nous" (Island Home)

lyrics/music: Gerard LE FEUVRE

note: adopted 2008; serves as a local anthem; as a British Crown dependency, "God Save the Queen" is official (see United Kingdom)

ECONOMY :: JERSEY

ECONOMY - OVERVIEW:

Jersey's economy is based on international financial services, agriculture, and tourism. In 2016, the financial services sector accounted for about 41% of the island's output. Agriculture represented about 1% of Jersey's economy in 2016. Potatoes are an important export crop, shipped mostly to the UK. The Jersey breed of dairy cattle originated on the island and is known worldwide. The dairy industry remains important to the island with approximately $8.8 million gallons of milk produced in 2015. Tourism accounts for a significant portion of Jersey's economy, with more than 700,000 total visitors in 2015. Living standards come close to those of the UK. All raw material and energy requirements are imported as well as a large share of Jersey's food needs. Light taxes and death duties make the island a popular offshore financial center. Jersey maintains its relationship with the EU through the UK. Therefore, in light of the UK's decision to leave the EU, Jersey will also need to renegotiate its ties to the EU.

GDP (PURCHASING POWER PARITY):

$5.569 billion (2016 est.)

$5.514 billion (2015 est.)

$4.98 billion (2014)

note: data are in 2015 US dollars

country comparison to the world: 175

GDP (OFFICIAL EXCHANGE RATE):

$5.004 billion (2015 est.) (2015 est.)

GDP - REAL GROWTH RATE:

1% (2016 est.)

10.7% (2015 est.)

country comparison to the world: 184

GDP - PER CAPITA (PPP):

$56,600 (2016 est.)

$49,500 (2015 est.)

country comparison to the world: 21

GDP - COMPOSITION, BY SECTOR OF ORIGIN:

agriculture: 2% (2010)

industry: 2% (2010)

services: 96% (2010)

AGRICULTURE - PRODUCTS:

potatoes, cauliflower, tomatoes; beef, dairy products

INDUSTRIES:

tourism, banking and finance, dairy, electronics

INDUSTRIAL PRODUCTION GROWTH RATE:

NA

LABOR FORCE:

59,950 (2017 est.)

country comparison to the world: 187

LABOR FORCE - BY OCCUPATION:

agriculture: 3%

industry: 12%

services: 85% (2014 est.)

UNEMPLOYMENT RATE:

4% (2015 est.)

4.6% (2014 est.)

country comparison to the world: 52

POPULATION BELOW POVERTY LINE:

NA

HOUSEHOLD INCOME OR CONSUMPTION BY PERCENTAGE SHARE:

lowest 10%: NA

highest 10%: NA

DISTRIBUTION OF FAMILY INCOME - GINI INDEX:

0.3 (2014 est.)

0.3 (2013 est.)

country comparison to the world: 158

BUDGET:

revenues: 829 million (2005)

expenditures: 851 million (2005)

TAXES AND OTHER REVENUES:

16.6% (of GDP) (2005)

country comparison to the world: 179

BUDGET SURPLUS (+) OR DEFICIT (-):

-0.4% (of GDP) (2005)

country comparison to the world: 57

FISCAL YEAR:

1 April - 31 March

INFLATION RATE (CONSUMER PRICES):

3.7% (2006)

country comparison to the world: 146

MARKET VALUE OF PUBLICLY TRADED SHARES:

NA

EXPORTS:

NA

EXPORTS - COMMODITIES:

light industrial and electrical goods, dairy cattle, foodstuffs, textiles, flowers

IMPORTS:

NA

IMPORTS - COMMODITIES:

machinery and transport equipment, manufactured goods, foodstuffs, mineral fuels, chemicals

DEBT - EXTERNAL:

NA

STOCK OF DIRECT FOREIGN INVESTMENT - AT HOME:

(31 December 2009 est.)

EXCHANGE RATES:

Jersey pounds (JEP) per US dollar

0.7836 (2017 est.)

0.738 (2016 est.)

0.738 (2015)

0.6542 (2012)

0.6391 (2011 est.)

ENERGY :: JERSEY

ELECTRICITY ACCESS:

electrification - total population: 100% (2016)

ELECTRICITY - PRODUCTION:

NA (2017)

ELECTRICITY - CONSUMPTION:

630.1 million kWh (2004 est.)

country comparison to the world: 163

CARBON DIOXIDE EMISSIONS FROM CONSUMPTION OF ENERGY:

450,000 Mt (2012 est.)

country comparison to the world: 185

COMMUNICATIONS :: JERSEY

TELEPHONES - FIXED LINES:

total subscriptions: 55,938

subscriptions per 100 inhabitants: 58 (July 2016 est.)

country comparison to the world: 157

TELEPHONES - MOBILE CELLULAR:

total subscriptions: 122,668

subscriptions per 100 inhabitants: 119 (July 2016 est.)

country comparison to the world: 189

TELEPHONE SYSTEM:

general assessment: modern system with broadband access (2018)

domestic: fixed-line and mobile-cellular services widely available; fixed-line 58 per 100 and mobile-cellular 119 per 100 subscriptions (2018)

international: country code - 44; landing points for the INGRID, UK-Channel Islands-8, and Guernsey-Jersey-4, submarine cable connectivity to Guernsey, the UK, and France (2019)

BROADCAST MEDIA:

multiple UK terrestrial TV broadcasts are received via a transmitter in Jersey; satellite packages available; BBC Radio Jersey and 1 other radio station operating

INTERNET COUNTRY CODE:

.je

INTERNET USERS:

total: 58,000

percent of population: 59.6% (July 2016 est.)

country comparison to the world: 188

MILITARY AND SECURITY :: JERSEY

MILITARY - NOTE:

defense is the responsibility of the UK

TRANSPORTATION :: JERSEY

NATIONAL AIR TRANSPORT SYSTEM:

number of registered air carriers: 2 (registered in UK) (2015)

inventory of registered aircraft operated by air carriers: 11 (registered in UK) (2015)

AIRPORTS:

1 (2013)

country comparison to the world: 226

AIRPORTS - WITH PAVED RUNWAYS:

total: 1 (2017)

1,524 to 2,437 m: 1 (2017)

ROADWAYS:

total: 576 km (2010)

country comparison to the world: 186

PORTS AND TERMINALS:

major seaport(s): Gorey, Saint Aubin, Saint Helier

TRANSNATIONAL ISSUES :: JERSEY

DISPUTES - INTERNATIONAL:

none

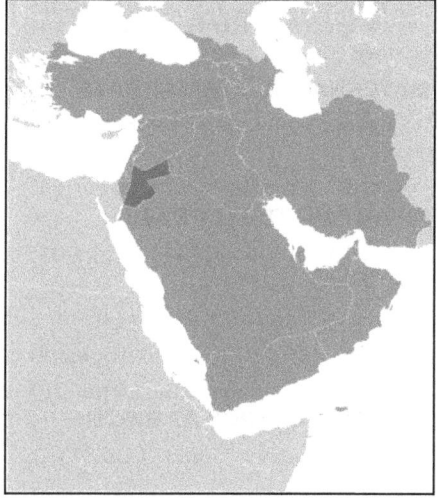

MIDDLE EAST :: JORDAN

INTRODUCTION :: JORDAN

BACKGROUND:

Following World War I and the dissolution of the Ottoman Empire, the League of Nations awarded Britain the mandate to govern much of the Middle East. Britain demarcated a semi-autonomous region of Transjordan from Palestine in the early 1920s. The area gained its independence in 1946 and thereafter became The Hashemite Kingdom of Jordan. The country's long-time ruler, King HUSSEIN (1953-99), successfully navigated competing pressures from the major powers (US, USSR, and UK), various Arab states, Israel, and a large internal Palestinian population. Jordan lost the West Bank to Israel in the 1967 Six-Day War. King HUSSEIN in 1988 permanently relinquished Jordanian claims to the West Bank; in 1994 he signed a peace treaty with Israel. King ABDALLAH II, King HUSSEIN's eldest son, assumed the throne following his father's death in 1999. He has implemented modest political reforms, including the passage of a new electoral law in early 2016 and an effort to devolve some authority to governorate- and municipal-level councils following subnational elections in 2017. In 2016, the Islamic Action Front, which is the political arm of the Jordanian Muslim Brotherhood, returned to the National Assembly with 15 seats after boycotting the previous two elections in 2010 and 2013.

GEOGRAPHY :: JORDAN

LOCATION:
Middle East, northwest of Saudi Arabia, between Israel (to the west) and Iraq

GEOGRAPHIC COORDINATES:
31 00 N, 36 00 E

MAP REFERENCES:
Middle East

AREA:
total: 89,342 sq km

land: 88,802 sq km

water: 540 sq km

country comparison to the world: 113

AREA - COMPARATIVE:
about three-quarters the size of Pennsylvania; slightly smaller than Indiana

LAND BOUNDARIES:
total: 1,744 km

border countries (5): Iraq 179 km, Israel 307 km, Saudi Arabia 731 km, Syria 379 km, West Bank 148 km

COASTLINE:
26 km

MARITIME CLAIMS:
territorial sea: 3 nm

CLIMATE:
mostly arid desert; rainy season in west (November to April)

TERRAIN:
mostly arid desert plateau; a great north-south geological rift along the west of the country is the dominant topographical feature and includes the Jordan River Valley, the Dead Sea, and the Jordanian Highlands

ELEVATION:
mean elevation: 812 m

lowest point: Dead Sea -431 m

highest point: Jabal Umm ad Dami 1,854 m

NATURAL RESOURCES:
phosphates, potash, shale oil

LAND USE:
agricultural land: 11.4% (2011 est.)

arable land: 2% (2011 est.) / permanent crops: 1% (2011 est.) / permanent pasture: 8.4% (2011 est.)

forest: 1.1% (2011 est.)

other: 87.5% (2011 est.)

IRRIGATED LAND:
964 sq km (2012)

POPULATION DISTRIBUTION:
population heavily concentrated in the west, and particularly the northwest, in and around the capital of Amman; a sizeable, but smaller population is located in the southwest along the shore of the Gulf of Aqaba

NATURAL HAZARDS:
droughts; periodic earthquakes; flash floods

ENVIRONMENT - CURRENT ISSUES:
limited natural freshwater resources; declining water table; salinity; deforestation; overgrazing; soil erosion; desertification; biodiversity and ecosystem damage/loss

ENVIRONMENT - INTERNATIONAL AGREEMENTS:
party to: Biodiversity, Climate Change, Climate Change-Kyoto Protocol, Desertification, Endangered Species, Hazardous Wastes, Law of the

Sea, Marine Dumping, Ozone Layer Protection, Wetlands

signed, but not ratified: none of the selected agreements

GEOGRAPHY - NOTE:

strategic location at the head of the Gulf of Aqaba and as the Arab country that shares the longest border with Israel and the occupied West Bank; the Dead Sea, the lowest point in Asia and the second saltiest body of water in the world (after Lac Assal in Djibouti), lies on Jordan's western border with Israel and the West Bank; Jordan is almost landlocked but does have a 26 km southwestern coastline with a single port, Al 'Aqabah (Aqaba)

PEOPLE AND SOCIETY :: JORDAN

POPULATION:

10,458,413 (July 2018 est.)

note: increased estimate reflects revised assumptions about the net migration rate due to the increased flow of Syrian refugees

country comparison to the world: 86

NATIONALITY:

noun: Jordanian(s)

adjective: Jordanian

ETHNIC GROUPS:

Jordanian 69.3%, Syrian 13.3%, Palestinian 6.7%, Egyptian 6.7%, Iraqi 1.4%, other 2.6% (includes Armenian, Circassian) (2015 est.)

note: data represent population by self-identified nationality

LANGUAGES:

Arabic (official), English (widely understood among upper and middle classes)

RELIGIONS:

Muslim 97.2% (official; predominantly Sunni), Christian 2.2% (majority Greek Orthodox, but some Greek and Roman Catholics, Syrian Orthodox, Coptic Orthodox, Armenian Orthodox, and Protestant denominations), Buddhist 0.4%, Hindu 0.1%, Jewish <0.1, folk <0.1, unaffiliated <0.1, other <0.1 (2010 est.)

AGE STRUCTURE:

0-14 years: 34.14% (male 1,835,094 /female 1,735,773)

15-24 years: 19.98% (male 1,114,783 /female 975,086)

25-54 years: 37.72% (male 2,137,424 /female 1,807,573)

55-64 years: 4.64% (male 253,029 /female 232,652)

65 years and over: 3.51% (male 180,652 /female 186,347) (2018 est.)

DEPENDENCY RATIOS:

total dependency ratio: 66.1 (2015 est.)

youth dependency ratio: 59.8 (2015 est.)

elderly dependency ratio: 6.2 (2015 est.)

potential support ratio: 16 (2015 est.)

MEDIAN AGE:

total: 22.8 years (2018 est.)

male: 23.2 years

female: 22.3 years

country comparison to the world: 177

POPULATION GROWTH RATE:

2.02% (2018 est.)

country comparison to the world: 46

BIRTH RATE:

23.6 births/1,000 population (2018 est.)

country comparison to the world: 56

DEATH RATE:

3.4 deaths/1,000 population (2018 est.)

country comparison to the world: 218

NET MIGRATION RATE:

0 migrant(s)/1,000 population (2018 est.)

country comparison to the world: 88

POPULATION DISTRIBUTION:

population heavily concentrated in the west, and particularly the northwest, in and around the capital of Amman; a sizeable, but smaller population is located in the southwest along the shore of the Gulf of Aqaba

URBANIZATION:

urban population: 91.2% of total population (2019)

rate of urbanization: 2.43% annual rate of change (2015-20 est.)

MAJOR URBAN AREAS - POPULATION:

2.109 million AMMAN (capital) (2019)

SEX RATIO:

at birth: 1.06 male(s)/female

0-14 years: 1.06 male(s)/female

15-24 years: 1.14 male(s)/female

25-54 years: 1.18 male(s)/female

55-64 years: 1.09 male(s)/female

65 years and over: 0.97 male(s)/female

total population: 1.12 male(s)/female (2018 est.)

MOTHER'S MEAN AGE AT FIRST BIRTH:

24.8 years (2017/18 est.)

note: median age at first birth among women 30-34

MATERNAL MORTALITY RATE:

46 deaths/100,000 live births (2017 est.)

country comparison to the world: 96

INFANT MORTALITY RATE:

total: 13.7 deaths/1,000 live births (2018 est.)

male: 14.5 deaths/1,000 live births

female: 12.9 deaths/1,000 live births

country comparison to the world: 103

LIFE EXPECTANCY AT BIRTH:

total population: 75 years (2018 est.)

male: 73.6 years

female: 76.6 years

country comparison to the world: 116

TOTAL FERTILITY RATE:

3.14 children born/woman (2018 est.)

country comparison to the world: 49

CONTRACEPTIVE PREVALENCE RATE:

51.8% (2017/18)

DRINKING WATER SOURCE:

improved:

urban: 97.8% of population

rural: 92.3% of population

total: 96.9% of population

unimproved:

urban: 2.2% of population

rural: 7.7% of population

total: 3.1% of population (2015 est.)

CURRENT HEALTH EXPENDITURE:

5.5% (2016)

PHYSICIANS DENSITY:

2.34 physicians/1,000 population (2017)

HOSPITAL BED DENSITY:

1.4 beds/1,000 population (2015)

SANITATION FACILITY ACCESS:

improved:

urban: 98.6% of population (2015 est.)

rural: 98.9% of population (2015 est.)

total: 98.6% of population (2015 est.)

unimproved:

urban: 1.4% of population (2015 est.)

rural: 1.1% of population (2015 est.)

total: 1.4% of population (2015 est.)

HIV/AIDS - ADULT PREVALENCE RATE:

<.1% (2018 est.)

HIV/AIDS - PEOPLE LIVING WITH HIV/AIDS:

<500 (2018 est.)

HIV/AIDS - DEATHS:

<100 (2018 est.)

OBESITY - ADULT PREVALENCE RATE:

35.5% (2016)

country comparison to the world: 13

CHILDREN UNDER THE AGE OF 5 YEARS UNDERWEIGHT:

3% (2012)

country comparison to the world: 100

EDUCATION EXPENDITURES:

3.6% of GDP (2017)

country comparison to the world: 124

LITERACY:

definition: age 15 and over can read and write

total population: 95.4%

male: 97.7%

female: 92.9% (2015 est.)

SCHOOL LIFE EXPECTANCY (PRIMARY TO TERTIARY EDUCATION):

total: 13 years

male: 12 years

female: 13 years (2012)

UNEMPLOYMENT, YOUTH AGES 15-24:

total: 35.6%

male: 31.5%

female: 57% (2016 est.)

country comparison to the world: 21

GOVERNMENT :: JORDAN

COUNTRY NAME:

conventional long form: Hashemite Kingdom of Jordan

conventional short form: Jordan

local long form: Al Mamlakah al Urduniyah al Hashimiyah

local short form: Al Urdun

former: Transjordan

etymology: named for the Jordan River, which makes up part of Jordan's northwest border

GOVERNMENT TYPE:

parliamentary constitutional monarchy

CAPITAL:

name: Amman

geographic coordinates: 31 57 N, 35 56 E

time difference: UTC+2 (7 hours ahead of Washington, DC, during Standard Time)

daylight saving time: +1hr, begins last Friday in March; ends last Friday in October

etymology: in the 13th century B.C., the Ammonites named their main city "Rabbath Ammon"; "rabbath" designated "capital" so the name meant "The Capital of [the] Ammon[ites]"; over time, the "Rabbath" came to be dropped and the city became known simply as "Ammon" and then "Amman"

ADMINISTRATIVE DIVISIONS:

12 governorates (muhafazat, singular - muhafazah); 'Ajlun, Al 'Aqabah, Al Balqa', Al Karak, Al Mafraq, Al 'Asimah (Amman), At Tafilah, Az Zarqa', Irbid, Jarash, Ma'an, Madaba

INDEPENDENCE:

25 May 1946 (from League of Nations mandate under British administration)

NATIONAL HOLIDAY:

Independence Day, 25 May (1946)

CONSTITUTION:

history: previous 1928 (preindependence); latest initially adopted 28 November 1947, revised and ratified 1 January 1952

amendments: constitutional amendments require at least a two-thirds majority vote of both the Senate and the House and ratification by the king; no amendment of the constitution affecting the rights of the king and the succession to the throne is permitted during the regency period; amended several times, last in 2016 (2016)

LEGAL SYSTEM:

mixed system developed from codes instituted by the Ottoman Empire (based on French law), British common law, and Islamic law

INTERNATIONAL LAW ORGANIZATION PARTICIPATION:

has not submitted an ICJ jurisdiction declaration; accepts ICCt jurisdiction

CITIZENSHIP:

citizenship by birth: no

citizenship by descent only: the father must be a citizen of Jordan

dual citizenship recognized: yes

residency requirement for naturalization: 15 years

SUFFRAGE:

18 years of age; universal

EXECUTIVE BRANCH:

chief of state: King ABDALLAH II (since 7 February 1999); Crown Prince HUSSEIN (born 28 June 1994), eldest son of King ABDALLAH II

head of government: Prime Minister Omar al-RAZZAZ (since 4 June 2018)

cabinet: Cabinet appointed by the prime minister in consultation with the monarch

elections/appointments: the monarchy is hereditary; prime minister appointed by the monarch

LEGISLATIVE BRANCH:

description: bicameral National Assembly or Majlis al-'Umma consists of:
Senate or the House of Notables or Majlis al-Ayan (65 seats; members appointed by the monarch to serve 4-year terms)
Chamber of Deputies or House of Representatives or Majlis al-Nuwaab (130 seats; 115 members directly elected in single- and multi-seat constituencies by open-list proportional representation vote and 15 seats for women; 12 of the 115 seats reserved for Christian, Chechen, and Circassian candidates; members serve 4-year terms)

elections:
Chamber of Deputies - last held on 20 September 2016 (next to be held in 2020)

election results:
Chamber of Deputies - percent of vote by party - NA; seats by party - NA

JUDICIAL BRANCH:

highest courts: Court of Cassation or Supreme Court (consists of 15 members, including the chief justice);

Constitutional Court (consists of 9 members)

judge selection and term of office: Supreme Court chief justice appointed by the king; other judges nominated by the Judicial Council, an 11-member judicial policymaking body consisting of high-level judicial officials and judges, and approved by the king; judge tenure generally not limited; Constitutional Court members appointed by the king for 6-year non-renewable terms with one-third of the membership renewed every 2 years

subordinate courts: Courts of Appeal; Great Felonies Court; religious courts; military courts; juvenile courts; Land Settlement Courts; Income Tax Court; Higher Administrative Court; Customs Court; special courts including the State Security Court

POLITICAL PARTIES AND LEADERS:

Ahrar al-Urdun (Free People of Jordan) Party [Samir al-ZU'BI]
Al-Awn al-Watani (National Aid) Party [Faysal al-AWAR]
Al-Balad al-Amin Party [Khalil al-SAYED]
Al-Itijah al-Watani (National Trend Party) [Ahmad al-KAYED]
Al-Mustaqbal (Future) Party [Salah al-QUDAH]
Al-Nida' Party [Abd-al-Majid ABU-KHALID]
Al-Rayah Party (Flag Party) [Bilal DHEISAT]
Al-Shahama Party [Mashhour ZREIQAT]
Al-Shura Party [Firas al-ABBADI]
Arab Socialist Ba'th Party [Zyad AL-HOMSI]
Conservatives Party [Hasan RASHID]
Democratic Popular Unity Party [Sa'eed DHIYAB]
Democratic Sha'b Party (HASHD) [Abla ABU-OLBEH]
Freedom and Equality Party [Hamad Abu ZEID]
Islamic Action Front [Murad AL-ADAYLAH]
Islamic Centrist Party [Madallah AL-TARAWNEH]
Jordanian Al-Ansar Party [Awni al-RJOUB]
Jordanian Al-Hayah Party [Abd-al-Fattah al-KILANI]
Jordanian Communist Party [Faraj ITMIZYEH]
Jordanian Democratic Socialist Party [Jamil al-NIMRI]
Jordanian Democratic Tabiy'ah (Nature) Party [Ali ASFOUR]
Jordanian Equality Party [Zuhair al-SHURAFA]
Jordanian Fursan (Cavaliers Party) [Ali al-DHWEIB]
Jordanian Justice and Development Party [Ali al-SHURAFA]
Jordanian National Action Party [Abd-al-Hadi al-MAHARMAH]
Jordanian National Constitutional Party [Ahmad al-SHUNNAQ]
Jordanian National Democratic Grouping Party [Shakir al-ABBADI]
Jordanian National Party [Muna ABU-BAKR]
Jordanian National Union Party [Zeid ABU-ZEID]
Jordanian Progressive Ba'th Party [Fu'ad DABBOUR]
Jordanian Promise Party [Mahmoud al-KHALILI]
Jordanian Reform Party [Eid DHAYYAT]
Jordanian Social Justice Party [Abd-al-Fattah al-NSOUR]
Jordanian Wafa' (Loyalty) Party [Mazin al-QADI]
Justice and Reform Party [Sa'eed Nathir ARABIYAT]
Modernity and Change Party [Nayef al-HAMAYDEH]
National Congress Party [Irhayil GHARAYBEH] (formerly the Zamzam party)
National Renaissance Front Party [Isma'il KHATATBEH]
National Unity Party [Muhammad al-ZBOUN]
Pan Arab Movement Party [Dayfallah FARRAJ]
Partnership and Salvation Party [Muhammad al-HAMMOURI]
Reform and Renewal Party [Mazin RYAL]
Risalah Party [Hazim QASHOU']
Stronger Jordan Party [Rula al-HROUB]
Unified Jordanian Front Party [Farouq AL-ABBADI]

INTERNATIONAL ORGANIZATION PARTICIPATION:

ABEDA, AFESD, AMF, CAEU, CD, CICA, EBRD, FAO, G-11, G-77, IAEA, IBRD, ICAO, ICC (national committees), ICCt, ICRM, IDA, IDB, IFAD, IFC, IFRCS, ILO, IMF, IMO, IMSO, Interpol, IOC, IOM, IPU, ISO, ITSO, ITU, ITUC (NGOs), LAS, MIGA, MINUSTAH, MINUSMA, MONUSCO, NAM, OIC, OPCW, OSCE (partner), PCA, UN, UNAMID, UNCTAD, UNESCO, UNHCR, UNIDO, UNMIL, UNMISS, UNOCI, UNRWA, UNWTO, UPU, WCO, WFTU (NGOs), WHO, WIPO, WMO, WTO

DIPLOMATIC REPRESENTATION IN THE US:

Ambassador Dina Khalil Tawiq KAWAR (since 27 June 2016)

chancery: 3504 International Drive NW, Washington, DC 20008

telephone: [1] (202) 966-2664

FAX: [1] (202) 966-3110

DIPLOMATIC REPRESENTATION FROM THE US:

chief of mission: Ambassador (vacant); Charge d'Affaires Karen SASAHARA (since March 2019)

telephone: [962] (6) 590-6000

embassy: Abdoun, Al-Umawyeen St., Amman

mailing address: P. O. Box 354, Amman 11118 Jordan; Unit 70200, Box 5, DPO AE 09892-0200

FAX: [962] (6) 592-0163

FLAG DESCRIPTION:

three equal horizontal bands of black (top), representing the Abbassid Caliphate, white, representing the Ummayyad Caliphate, and green, representing the Fatimid Caliphate; a red isosceles triangle on the hoist side, representing the Great Arab Revolt of 1916, and bearing a small white seven-pointed star symbolizing the seven verses of the opening Sura (Al-Fatiha) of the Holy Koran; the seven points on the star represent faith in One God, humanity, national spirit, humility, social justice, virtue, and aspirations; design is based on the Arab Revolt flag of World War I

NATIONAL SYMBOL(S):

eagle; national colors: black, white, green, red

NATIONAL ANTHEM:

name: "As-salam al-malaki al-urdoni" (Long Live the King of Jordan)

lyrics/music: Abdul-Mone'm al-RIFAI'/Abdul-Qader al-TANEER

note: adopted 1946; the shortened version of the anthem is used most commonly, while the full version is reserved for special occasions

ECONOMY :: JORDAN

ECONOMY - OVERVIEW:

Jordan's economy is among the smallest in the Middle East, with insufficient supplies of water, oil, and other natural resources, underlying the government's heavy reliance on foreign assistance. Other economic challenges for the government include chronic high rates of unemployment and underemployment, budget and current account deficits, and government debt.

King ABDALLAH, during the first decade of the 2000s, implemented significant economic reforms, such as expanding foreign trade and privatizing state-owned companies that attracted foreign investment and contributed to average annual economic growth of 8% for 2004 through 2008. The global economic slowdown and regional turmoil contributed to slower growth from 2010 to 2017 - with growth averaging about 2.5% per year - and hurt export-oriented sectors, construction/real estate, and tourism. Since the onset of the civil war in Syria and resulting refugee crisis, one of Jordan's most pressing socioeconomic challenges has been managing the influx of approximately 660,000 UN-registered refugees, more than 80% of whom live in Jordan's urban areas. Jordan's own official census estimated the refugee number at 1.3 million Syrians as of early 2016.

Jordan is nearly completely dependent on imported energy—mostly natural gas—and energy consistently makes up 25-30% of Jordan's imports. To diversify its energy mix, Jordan has secured several contracts for liquefied and pipeline natural gas, developed several major renewables projects, and is currently exploring nuclear power generation and exploitation of abundant oil shale reserves. In August 2016, Jordan and the IMF agreed to a $723 million Extended Fund Facility that aims to build on the three-year, $2.1 billion IMF program that ended in August 2015 with the goal of helping Jordan correct budgetary and balance of payments imbalances.

GDP (PURCHASING POWER PARITY):

$89 billion (2017 est.)

$87.28 billion (2016 est.)

$85.56 billion (2015 est.)

note: data are in 2017 dollars

country comparison to the world: 90

GDP (OFFICIAL EXCHANGE RATE):

$40.13 billion (2017 est.)

GDP - REAL GROWTH RATE:

2% (2017 est.)

2% (2016 est.)

2.4% (2015 est.)

country comparison to the world: 151

GDP - PER CAPITA (PPP):

$9,200 (2017 est.)

$9,200 (2016 est.)

$9,300 (2015 est.)

note: data are in 2017 dollars

country comparison to the world: 144

GROSS NATIONAL SAVING:

9.1% of GDP (2017 est.)

9.3% of GDP (2016 est.)

10.2% of GDP (2015 est.)

country comparison to the world: 165

GDP - COMPOSITION, BY END USE:

household consumption: 80.5% (2017 est.)

government consumption: 19.8% (2017 est.)

investment in fixed capital: 22.8% (2017 est.)

investment in inventories: 0.7% (2017 est.)

exports of goods and services: 34.2% (2017 est.)

imports of goods and services: -58% (2017 est.)

GDP - COMPOSITION, BY SECTOR OF ORIGIN:

agriculture: 4.5% (2017 est.)

industry: 28.8% (2017 est.)

services: 66.6% (2017 est.)

AGRICULTURE - PRODUCTS:

citrus, tomatoes, cucumbers, olives, strawberries, stone fruits; sheep, poultry, dairy

INDUSTRIES:

tourism, information technology, clothing, fertilizer, potash, phosphate mining, pharmaceuticals, petroleum refining, cement, inorganic chemicals, light manufacturing

INDUSTRIAL PRODUCTION GROWTH RATE:

1.4% (2017 est.)

country comparison to the world: 146

LABOR FORCE:

2.295 million (2017 est.)

country comparison to the world: 117

LABOR FORCE - BY OCCUPATION:

agriculture: 2%

industry: 20%

services: 78% (2013 est.)

UNEMPLOYMENT RATE:

18.3% (2017 est.)

15.3% (2016 est.)

note: official rate; unofficial rate is approximately 30%

country comparison to the world: 181

POPULATION BELOW POVERTY LINE:

14.2% (2002 est.)

HOUSEHOLD INCOME OR CONSUMPTION BY PERCENTAGE SHARE:

lowest 10%: 3.4%

highest 10%: 28.7% (2010 est.)

DISTRIBUTION OF FAMILY INCOME - GINI INDEX:

39.7 (2007)

36.4 (1997)

country comparison to the world: 69

BUDGET:

revenues: 9.462 billion (2017 est.)

expenditures: 11.51 billion (2017 est.)

TAXES AND OTHER REVENUES:

23.6% (of GDP) (2017 est.)

country comparison to the world: 124

BUDGET SURPLUS (+) OR DEFICIT (-):

-5.1% (of GDP) (2017 est.)

country comparison to the world: 170

PUBLIC DEBT:

95.9% of GDP (2017 est.)

95.1% of GDP (2016 est.)

note: data cover central government debt and include debt instruments issued (or owned) by government entities other than the treasury; the data include treasury debt held by foreign entities; the data exclude debt issued by subnational entities, as well as intragovernmental debt; intragovernmental debt consists of treasury borrowings from surpluses in the social funds, such as for retirement, medical care, and unemployment; debt instruments for the social funds are not sold at public auctions

country comparison to the world: 22

FISCAL YEAR:

calendar year

INFLATION RATE (CONSUMER PRICES):

3.3% (2017 est.)

-0.8% (2016 est.)

country comparison to the world: 138

CENTRAL BANK DISCOUNT RATE:

3.75% (31 December 2015)

0.3% (31 December 2010)

country comparison to the world: 100

COMMERCIAL BANK PRIME LENDING RATE:

8.65% (31 December 2017 est.)

7.83% (31 December 2016 est.)

country comparison to the world: 97

STOCK OF NARROW MONEY:

$14.64 billion (31 December 2017 est.)

$14.63 billion (31 December 2016 est.)

country comparison to the world: 74

STOCK OF BROAD MONEY:

$14.64 billion (31 December 2017 est.)

$14.63 billion (31 December 2016 est.)

country comparison to the world: 75

STOCK OF DOMESTIC CREDIT:

$42.7 billion (31 December 2017 est.)

$41.87 billion (31 December 2016 est.)

country comparison to the world: 68

MARKET VALUE OF PUBLICLY TRADED SHARES:

$24.25 billion (31 December 2016 est.)

$25.45 billion (31 December 2015 est.)

$25.55 billion (31 December 2014 est.)

country comparison to the world: 61

CURRENT ACCOUNT BALANCE:

-$4.257 billion (2017 est.)

-$3.693 billion (2016 est.)

country comparison to the world: 180

EXPORTS:

$7.511 billion (2017 est.)

$7.509 billion (2016 est.)

country comparison to the world: 99

EXPORTS - PARTNERS:

US 24.9%, Saudi Arabia 12.8%, India 8.2%, Iraq 8.2%, Kuwait 5.4%, UAE 4.6% (2017)

EXPORTS - COMMODITIES:

textiles, fertilizers, potash, phosphates, vegetables, pharmaceuticals

IMPORTS:

$18.21 billion (2017 est.)

$17.14 billion (2016 est.)

country comparison to the world: 82

IMPORTS - COMMODITIES:

crude oil, refined petroleum products, machinery, transport equipment, iron, cereals

IMPORTS - PARTNERS:

China 13.6%, Saudi Arabia 13.6%, US 9.9%, UAE 4.9%, Germany 4.4% (2017)

RESERVES OF FOREIGN EXCHANGE AND GOLD:

$15.56 billion (31 December 2017 est.)

$15.54 billion (31 December 2016 est.)

country comparison to the world: 67

DEBT - EXTERNAL:

$29.34 billion (31 December 2017 est.)

$26.38 billion (31 December 2016 est.)

country comparison to the world: 82

STOCK OF DIRECT FOREIGN INVESTMENT - AT HOME:

$33.83 billion (31 December 2017 est.)

$32.15 billion (31 December 2016 est.)

country comparison to the world: 69

STOCK OF DIRECT FOREIGN INVESTMENT - ABROAD:

$646.5 million (31 December 2017 est.)

$612.5 million (31 December 2016 est.)

country comparison to the world: 95

EXCHANGE RATES:

Jordanian dinars (JOD) per US dollar -

0.71 (2017 est.)

0.71 (2016 est.)

0.71 (2015 est.)

0.71 (2014 est.)

0.71 (2013 est.)

ENERGY :: JORDAN

ELECTRICITY ACCESS:

electrification - total population: 100% (2016)

ELECTRICITY - PRODUCTION:

18.6 billion kWh (2016 est.)

country comparison to the world: 77

ELECTRICITY - CONSUMPTION:

16.82 billion kWh (2016 est.)

country comparison to the world: 74

ELECTRICITY - EXPORTS:

50 million kWh (2015 est.)

country comparison to the world: 88

ELECTRICITY - IMPORTS:

334 million kWh (2016 est.)

country comparison to the world: 86

ELECTRICITY - INSTALLED GENERATING CAPACITY:

4.764 million kW (2016 est.)

country comparison to the world: 82

ELECTRICITY - FROM FOSSIL FUELS:

87% of total installed capacity (2016 est.)

country comparison to the world: 62

ELECTRICITY - FROM NUCLEAR FUELS:

0% of total installed capacity (2017 est.)

country comparison to the world: 116

ELECTRICITY - FROM HYDROELECTRIC PLANTS:

0% of total installed capacity (2017 est.)

country comparison to the world: 180

ELECTRICITY - FROM OTHER RENEWABLE SOURCES:

12% of total installed capacity (2017 est.)

country comparison to the world: 74

CRUDE OIL - PRODUCTION:

22 bbl/day (2018 est.)

country comparison to the world: 99

CRUDE OIL - EXPORTS:

0 bbl/day (2015 est.)

country comparison to the world: 144

CRUDE OIL - IMPORTS:

67,980 bbl/day (2015 est.)

country comparison to the world: 49

CRUDE OIL - PROVED RESERVES:

1 million bbl (1 January 2018 est.)

country comparison to the world: 96

REFINED PETROLEUM PRODUCTS - PRODUCTION:

67,240 bbl/day (2015 est.)

country comparison to the world: 73

REFINED PETROLEUM PRODUCTS - CONSUMPTION:

139,000 bbl/day (2016 est.)

country comparison to the world: 69

REFINED PETROLEUM PRODUCTS - EXPORTS:

0 bbl/day (2015 est.)

country comparison to the world: 166

REFINED PETROLEUM PRODUCTS - IMPORTS:

68,460 bbl/day (2015 est.)

country comparison to the world: 68

NATURAL GAS - PRODUCTION:

121.8 million cu m (2017 est.)

country comparison to the world: 80

NATURAL GAS - CONSUMPTION:

5.238 billion cu m (2017 est.)

country comparison to the world: 56

NATURAL GAS - EXPORTS:

1.359 billion cu m (2017 est.)

country comparison to the world: 38

NATURAL GAS - IMPORTS:

6.456 billion cu m (2017 est.)

country comparison to the world: 31

NATURAL GAS - PROVED RESERVES:

6.031 billion cu m (1 January 2018 est.)

country comparison to the world: 87

CARBON DIOXIDE EMISSIONS FROM CONSUMPTION OF ENERGY:

27.39 million Mt (2017 est.)

country comparison to the world: 76

COMMUNICATIONS :: JORDAN

TELEPHONES - FIXED LINES:

total subscriptions: 404,112

subscriptions per 100 inhabitants: 4 (July 2016 est.)

country comparison to the world: 103

TELEPHONES - MOBILE CELLULAR:

total subscriptions: 9,818,446

subscriptions per 100 inhabitants: 96 (July 2016 est.)

country comparison to the world: 86

TELEPHONE SYSTEM:

general assessment: microwave radio relay transmission and coaxial and fiber-optic cable are employed on trunk lines; growing mobile-cellular usage in both urban and rural areas is reducing use of fixed-line services; recent influx of refugees putting burden on country's econmy, infrastructure and society; mobile broadband area of growth with 4G services (2018)

domestic: 1995 telecommunications law opened all non-fixed-line services to private competition; in 2005, monopoly over fixed-line services terminated and the entire telecommunications sector was opened to competition; currently multiple mobile-cellular providers with subscribership up to 96 per 100 persons; fixed-line 4 per 100 persons (2018)

international: country code - 962; landing point for the FEA and Taba-Aqaba submarine cable networks providing connectivity to Europe, the Middle East, Southeast Asia and Asia; satellite earth stations - 33 (3 Intelsat, 1 Arabsat, and 29 land and maritime Inmarsat terminals (2019)

BROADCAST MEDIA:

radio and TV dominated by the government-owned Jordan Radio and Television Corporation (JRTV) that operates a main network, a sports network, a film network, and a satellite channel; first independent TV broadcaster aired in 2007; international satellite TV and Israeli and Syrian TV broadcasts are available; roughly 30 radio stations with JRTV operating the main government-owned station; transmissions of multiple international radio broadcasters are available

INTERNET COUNTRY CODE:

.jo

INTERNET USERS:

total: 5,099,674

percent of population: 62.3% (July 2016 est.)

country comparison to the world: 76

BROADBAND - FIXED SUBSCRIPTIONS:

total: 456,610

subscriptions per 100 inhabitants: 4 (2017 est.)

country comparison to the world: 82

MILITARY AND SECURITY :: JORDAN

MILITARY EXPENDITURES:

4.68% of GDP (2018)

4.8% of GDP (2017)

4.58% of GDP (2016)

4.31% of GDP (2015)

4.32% of GDP (2014)

country comparison to the world: 8

MILITARY AND SECURITY FORCES:

Jordanian Armed Forces (JAF): Royal Jordanian Army (includes Special Operations Forces, Border Guards, Royal Guard), Royal Jordanian Navy, Royal Jordanian Air Force (2019)

MILITARY SERVICE AGE AND OBLIGATION:

17 years of age for voluntary male military service; initial service term 2 years, with option to reenlist for 18 years; conscription at age 18 suspended in 1999; women are not conscripted, but can volunteer to serve in noncombat military positions in the Royal Jordanian Arab Army Women's Corps and RJAF (2013)

MILITARY - NOTE:

Ministry of Interior: General Directorate of Gendarmerie Forces, Public Security Directorate (2019)

TRANSPORTATION :: JORDAN

NATIONAL AIR TRANSPORT SYSTEM:

number of registered air carriers: 7 (2015)

inventory of registered aircraft operated by air carriers: 40 (2015)

annual passenger traffic on registered air carriers: 3,065,145 (2015)

annual freight traffic on registered air carriers: 169.105 million mt-km (2015)

CIVIL AIRCRAFT REGISTRATION COUNTRY CODE PREFIX:

JY (2016)

AIRPORTS:

18 (2013)

country comparison to the world: 141

AIRPORTS - WITH PAVED RUNWAYS:

total: 16 (2017)

over 3,047 m: 8 (2017)

2,438 to 3,047 m: 5 (2017)

1,524 to 2,437 m: 2 (2017)

914 to 1,523 m: 1 (2017)

AIRPORTS - WITH UNPAVED RUNWAYS:

total: 2 (2013)

under 914 m: 2 (2013)

HELIPORTS:

1 (2012)

PIPELINES:

473 km gas, 49 km oil (2013)

RAILWAYS:

total: 509 km (2014)

narrow gauge: 509 km 1.050-m gauge (2014)

country comparison to the world: 113

ROADWAYS:

total: 7,203 km (2011)

paved: 7,203 km (2011)

country comparison to the world: 136

MERCHANT MARINE:

total: 32

by type: general cargo 8, oil tanker 1, other 23 (2018)

country comparison to the world: 124

PORTS AND TERMINALS:

major seaport(s): Al 'Aqabah

TRANSNATIONAL ISSUES :: JORDAN

DISPUTES - INTERNATIONAL:

2004 Agreement settles border dispute with Syria pending demarcation

REFUGEES AND INTERNALLY DISPLACED PERSONS:

refugees (country of origin): 2,242,579 (Palestinian refugees), 654,192 (Syria), 67,266 (Iraq), 14,730 (Yemen), 6,116 Sudan (2019)

CENTRAL ASIA :: KAZAKHSTAN

INTRODUCTION :: KAZAKHSTAN

BACKGROUND:

Ethnic Kazakhs, a mix of Turkic and Mongol nomadic tribes with additional Persian cultural influences, migrated to the region by the 13th century. The area was conquered by Russia in the 18th century, and Kazakhstan became a Soviet Republic in 1936. Repression and starvation associated with forced agricultural collectivization led to a massive number of deaths in the 1930s. During the 1950s and 1960s, the agricultural "Virgin Lands" program led to an influx of immigrants (mostly ethnic Russians, but also other nationalities) and at the time of Kazakhstan's independence in 1991, ethnic Kazakhs were a minority. Non-Muslim ethnic minorities departed Kazakhstan in large numbers from the mid-1990s through the mid-2000s and a national program has repatriated about a million ethnic Kazakhs back to Kazakhstan. As a result of this shift, the ethnic Kazakh share of the population now exceeds two-thirds.

Kazakhstan's economy is the largest in the Central Asian states, mainly due to the country's vast natural resources. Current issues include: diversifying the economy, obtaining membership in global and regional international economic institutions, enhancing Kazakhstan's economic competitiveness, and strengthening relations with neighboring states and foreign powers.

GEOGRAPHY :: KAZAKHSTAN

LOCATION:
Central Asia, northwest of China; a small portion west of the Ural (Zhayyq) River in easternmost Europe

GEOGRAPHIC COORDINATES:
48 00 N, 68 00 E

MAP REFERENCES:
Asia

AREA:
total: 2,724,900 sq km

land: 2,699,700 sq km

water: 25,200 sq km

country comparison to the world: 10

AREA - COMPARATIVE:
slightly less than four times the size of Texas

LAND BOUNDARIES:
total: 13,364 km

border countries (5): China 1765 km, Kyrgyzstan 1212 km, Russia 7644 km, Turkmenistan 413 km, Uzbekistan 2330 km

COASTLINE:
0 km (landlocked); note - Kazakhstan borders the Aral Sea, now split into two bodies of water (1,070 km), and the Caspian Sea (1,894 km)

MARITIME CLAIMS:
none (landlocked)

CLIMATE:
continental, cold winters and hot summers, arid and semiarid

TERRAIN:
vast flat steppe extending from the Volga in the west to the Altai Mountains in the east and from the plains of western Siberia in the north to oases and deserts of Central Asia in the south

ELEVATION:
mean elevation: 387 m

lowest point: Vpadina Kaundy -132 m

highest point: Khan Tangiri Shyngy (Pik Khan-Tengri) 6,995 m

NATURAL RESOURCES:
major deposits of petroleum, natural gas, coal, iron ore, manganese, chrome ore, nickel, cobalt, copper, molybdenum, lead, zinc, bauxite, gold, uranium

LAND USE:
agricultural land: 77.4% (2011 est.)

arable land: 8.9% (2011 est.) / permanent crops: 0% (2011 est.) / permanent pasture: 68.5% (2011 est.)

forest: 1.2% (2011 est.)

other: 21.4% (2011 est.)

IRRIGATED LAND:
20,660 sq km (2012)

POPULATION DISTRIBUTION:
most of the country displays a low population density, particularly the interior; population clusters appear in urban agglomerations in the far northern and southern portions of the country

NATURAL HAZARDS:
earthquakes in the south; mudslides around Almaty

ENVIRONMENT - CURRENT ISSUES:
radioactive or toxic chemical sites associated with former defense industries and test ranges scattered throughout the country pose health risks for humans and animals; industrial pollution is severe in some cities; because the two main rivers that flowed into the Aral Sea have been diverted for irrigation, it is drying up and leaving behind a harmful layer of chemical pesticides and natural salts; these substances are then picked up by the wind and blown into noxious dust storms; pollution in the Caspian Sea; desertification; soil pollution from overuse of agricultural chemicals and

salination from poor infrastructure and wasteful irrigation practices

ENVIRONMENT - INTERNATIONAL AGREEMENTS:

party to: Air Pollution, Biodiversity, Climate Change, Desertification, Endangered Species, Environmental Modification, Hazardous Wastes, Ozone Layer Protection, Ship Pollution, Wetlands

signed, but not ratified: Climate Change-Kyoto Protocol

GEOGRAPHY - NOTE:

world's largest landlocked country and one of only two landlocked countries in the world that extends into two continents (the other is Azerbaijan); Russia leases approximately 6,000 sq km of territory enclosing the Baykonur Cosmodrome; in January 2004, Kazakhstan and Russia extended the lease to 2050

PEOPLE AND SOCIETY :: KAZAKHSTAN

POPULATION:

18,744,548 (July 2018 est.)

country comparison to the world: 63

NATIONALITY:

noun: Kazakhstani(s)

adjective: Kazakhstani

ETHNIC GROUPS:

Kazakh (Qazaq) 68%, Russian 19.3%, Uzbek 3.2%, Ukrainian 1.5%, Uighur 1.5%, Tatar 1.1%, German 1%, other 4.4% (2019 est.)

LANGUAGES:

Kazakh (official, Qazaq) 83.1% (understand spoken language) and trilingual (Kazakh, Russian, English) 22.3% (2017 est.); Russian (official, used in everyday business, designated the "language of interethnic communication") 94.4% (understand spoken language) (2009 est.)

RELIGIONS:

Muslim 70.2%, Christian 26.2% (mainly Russian Orthodox), other 0.2%, atheist 2.8%, unspecified 0.5% (2009 est.)

AGE STRUCTURE:

0-14 years: 26.09% (male 2,406,397 /female 2,483,562)

15-24 years: 13.55% (male 1,295,882 /female 1,244,540)

25-54 years: 42.32% (male 3,884,454 /female 4,049,072)

55-64 years: 10.14% (male 831,872 /female 1,068,651)

65 years and over: 7.9% (male 517,471 /female 962,647) (2018 est.)

DEPENDENCY RATIOS:

total dependency ratio: 50.4 (2015 est.)

youth dependency ratio: 40.3 (2015 est.)

elderly dependency ratio: 10.2 (2015 est.)

potential support ratio: 9.8 (2015 est.)

MEDIAN AGE:

total: 30.9 years (2018 est.)

male: 29.7 years

female: 32.2 years

country comparison to the world: 112

POPULATION GROWTH RATE:

0.98% (2018 est.)

country comparison to the world: 111

BIRTH RATE:

17.5 births/1,000 population (2018 est.)

country comparison to the world: 99

DEATH RATE:

8.2 deaths/1,000 population (2018 est.)

country comparison to the world: 84

NET MIGRATION RATE:

0.4 migrant(s)/1,000 population (2018 est.)

country comparison to the world: 70

POPULATION DISTRIBUTION:

most of the country displays a low population density, particularly the interior; population clusters appear in urban agglomerations in the far northern and southern portions of the country

URBANIZATION:

urban population: 57.5% of total population (2019)

rate of urbanization: 1.29% annual rate of change (2015-20 est.)

MAJOR URBAN AREAS - POPULATION:

1.863 million Almaty, 1.118 million NUR-SULTAN (capital), 1.021 million Shimkent (2019)

SEX RATIO:

at birth: 0.94 male(s)/female

0-14 years: 0.97 male(s)/female

15-24 years: 1.04 male(s)/female

25-54 years: 0.96 male(s)/female

55-64 years: 0.78 male(s)/female

65 years and over: 0.54 male(s)/female

total population: 0.91 male(s)/female (2018 est.)

MOTHER'S MEAN AGE AT FIRST BIRTH:

25 years (2014 est.)

MATERNAL MORTALITY RATE:

10 deaths/100,000 live births (2017 est.)

country comparison to the world: 146

INFANT MORTALITY RATE:

total: 19 deaths/1,000 live births (2018 est.)

male: 21.6 deaths/1,000 live births

female: 16.6 deaths/1,000 live births

country comparison to the world: 82

LIFE EXPECTANCY AT BIRTH:

total population: 71.4 years (2018 est.)

male: 66.2 years

female: 76.3 years

country comparison to the world: 150

TOTAL FERTILITY RATE:

2.22 children born/woman (2018 est.)

country comparison to the world: 93

CONTRACEPTIVE PREVALENCE RATE:

54.8% (2018)

note: percent of women aged 18-49

DRINKING WATER SOURCE:

improved:

urban: 99.4% of population

rural: 85.6% of population

total: 92.9% of population

unimproved:

urban: 0.6% of population

rural: 14.4% of population

total: 7.1% of population (2015 est.)

CURRENT HEALTH EXPENDITURE:

3.5% (2016)

PHYSICIANS DENSITY:

3.25 physicians/1,000 population (2014)

HOSPITAL BED DENSITY:

6.7 beds/1,000 population (2013)

SANITATION FACILITY ACCESS:

improved:

urban: 97% of population (2015 est.)

rural: 98.1% of population (2015 est.)

total: 97.5% of population (2015 est.)

unimproved:

urban: 3% of population (2015 est.)

rural: 1.9% of population (2015 est.)

total: 2.5% of population (2015 est.)

HIV/AIDS - ADULT PREVALENCE RATE:

0.2% (2018 est.)

country comparison to the world: 102

HIV/AIDS - PEOPLE LIVING WITH HIV/AIDS:

26,000 (2018 est.)

country comparison to the world: 77

HIV/AIDS - DEATHS:

<500 (2018 est.)

OBESITY - ADULT PREVALENCE RATE:

21% (2016)

country comparison to the world: 94

CHILDREN UNDER THE AGE OF 5 YEARS UNDERWEIGHT:

2% (2015)

country comparison to the world: 112

EDUCATION EXPENDITURES:

2.9% of GDP (2017)

country comparison to the world: 144

LITERACY:

definition: age 15 and over can read and write

total population: 99.8%

male: 99.8%

female: 99.8% (2015 est.)

SCHOOL LIFE EXPECTANCY (PRIMARY TO TERTIARY EDUCATION):

total: 15 years

male: 15 years

female: 16 years (2017)

UNEMPLOYMENT, YOUTH AGES 15-24:

total: 3.9%

male: 3.6%

female: 4.3% (2013 est.)

country comparison to the world: 167

GOVERNMENT :: KAZAKHSTAN

COUNTRY NAME:

conventional long form: Republic of Kazakhstan

conventional short form: Kazakhstan

local long form: Qazaqstan Respublikasy

local short form: Qazaqstan

former: Kazakh Soviet Socialist Republic

etymology: the name "Kazakh" derives from the Turkic word "kaz" meaning "to wander," recalling the Kazakh's nomadic lifestyle; the Persian suffix "-stan" means "place of" or "country," so the word Kazakhstan literally means "Land of the Wanderers"

GOVERNMENT TYPE:

presidential republic

CAPITAL:

name: Nur-Sultan

geographic coordinates: 51 10 N, 71 25 E

time difference: UTC+6 (11 hours ahead of Washington, DC, during Standard Time)

note 1: Kazakhstan has two time zones

note 2: on 20 March 2019, Kazakhstan changed the name of its capital city from Astana to Nur-Sultan in honor of its long-serving, recently retired president, Nursultan NAZARBAYEV; this was not the first time the city had its name changed; founded in 1830 as Akmoly, it became Akmolinsk in 1832, Tselinograd in 1961, Akmola (Aqmola) in 1992, and Astana in 1998

ADMINISTRATIVE DIVISIONS:

14 provinces (oblyslar, singular - oblys) and 4 cities* (qalalar, singular - qala); Almaty (Taldyqorghan), Almaty*, Aqmola (Kokshetau), Aqtobe, Astana*, Atyrau, Batys Qazaqstan [West Kazakhstan] (Oral), Bayqongyr*, Mangghystau (Aqtau), Pavlodar, Qaraghandy, Qostanay, Qyzylorda, Shyghys Qazaqstan [East Kazakhstan] (Oskemen), Shymkent*, Soltustik Qazaqstan [North Kazakhstan] (Petropavl), Turkistan, Zhambyl (Taraz)

note: administrative divisions have the same names as their administrative centers (exceptions have the administrative center name following in parentheses); in 1995, the Governments of Kazakhstan and Russia entered into an agreement whereby Russia would lease for a period of 20 years an area of 6,000 sq km enclosing the Baikonur space launch facilities and the city of Bayqongyr (Baikonur, formerly Leninsk); in 2004, a new agreement extended the lease to 2050

INDEPENDENCE:

16 December 1991 (from the Soviet Union)

NATIONAL HOLIDAY:

Independence Day, 16 December (1991)

CONSTITUTION:

history: previous 1937, 1978 (preindependence), 1993; latest approved by referendum 30 August 1995, effective 5 September 1995

amendments: introduced by a referendum initiated by the president of the republic, on the recommendation of Parliament, or by the government; the president has the option of submitting draft amendments to Parliament or directly to a referendum; passage of amendments by Parliament requires four-fifths majority vote of both houses and the signature of the president; passage by referendum requires absolute majority vote by more than one half of the voters in at least two thirds of the oblasts, major cities, and the capital, followed by the signature of the president; amended several times, last in 2019 (2019)

LEGAL SYSTEM:

civil law system influenced by Roman-Germanic law and by the theory and practice of the Russian Federation

INTERNATIONAL LAW ORGANIZATION PARTICIPATION:

has not submitted an ICJ jurisdiction declaration; non-party state to the ICCt

CITIZENSHIP:

citizenship by birth: no

citizenship by descent only: at least one parent must be a citizen of Kazakhstan

dual citizenship recognized: no

residency requirement for naturalization: 5 years

SUFFRAGE:

18 years of age; universal

EXECUTIVE BRANCH:

chief of state: President Kassym-Jomart TOKAYEV (since 20 March 2019); note - Nursultan NAZARBAYEV, who was president since 24 April 1990 (and in power since 22 June 1989 under the Soviet period), resigned on 20 March 2019; NAZARBAYEV retained the title and powers of "First President"; TOKAYEV completed NAZARBAYEV's term, which was shortened due to the early election of 9 June 2019, and then continued as president following his election victory

head of government: Prime Minister Askar MAMIN (since 25 February 2019); First Deputy Prime Minister Alikhan SMAILOV (since 25 February 2019); Deputy Prime Ministers Zhenis KASSYMBEK and Gulshara ABDYKALIKOVA (since 25 February 2019)

cabinet: Council of Ministers appointed by the president

elections/appointments: president directly elected by simple majority popular vote for a 5-year term (eligible for a second consecutive term); election last held on 9 June 2019 (next to be held in 2024); prime minister and deputy prime ministers appointed by the president, approved by the Mazhilis

election results: Kassym-Jomart TOKAYEV elected president; percent of vote - Kassym-Jomart TOKAYEV (Nur Otan) 71%, Amirzhan KOSANOV (Ult Tagdyry) 16.2%, Daniya YESPAYEVA (Ak Zhol) 5.1%, other 7.7%

LEGISLATIVE BRANCH:

description: bicameral Parliament consists of:
Senate (49 seats; 34 members indirectly elected by majority 2-round vote by the oblast-level assemblies and 15 members appointed by decree of the president; members serve 6-year terms, with one-half of the membership renewed every 3 years)
Mazhilis (107 seats; 98 members directly elected in a single national constituency by proportional representation vote to serve 5-year terms and 9 indirectly elected by the Assembly of People of Kazakhstan, a 350-member, presidentially appointed advisory body designed to represent the country's ethnic minorities)

elections:
Senate - last held on 28 June 2017 (next to be held in 2020)
Mazhilis - last held on 20 March 2016 (next to be held by 2021)

election results:
Senate - percent of vote by party - NA; seats by party - NA; composition - men 42, women 5, percent of women 10.6%
Mazhilis - percent of vote by party - Nur Otan 82.2%, Ak Zhol 7.2%, Communist People's Party 7.1%, other 3.5%; seats by party - Nur Otan 84, Ak Zhol 7, Communist People's Party 7; composition - men 78, women 29, percent of women 27.1%; note - total Parliament percent of women 22.1%

JUDICIAL BRANCH:

highest courts: Supreme Court of the Republic (consists of 44 members); Constitutional Council (consists of the chairman and 6 members)

judge selection and term of office: Supreme Court judges proposed by the president of the republic on recommendation of the Supreme Judicial Council and confirmed by the Senate; judges normally serve until age 65 but can be extended to age 70; Constitutional Council - the president of the republic, the Senate chairperson, and the Mazhilis chairperson each appoints 2 members for a 6-year term; chairman of the Constitutional Council appointed by the president for a 6-year term

subordinate courts: regional and local courts

POLITICAL PARTIES AND LEADERS:

Ak Zhol (Bright Path) Party or Democratic Party of Kazakhstan Ak Zhol [Azat PERUASHEV]
Birlik (Unity) Party [Serik SULTANGALI]
Communist People's Party of Kazakhstan [informal leader Aikyn KONUROV]
National Social Democratic Party or NSDP [Zharmakhan TUYAKBAY]
Nur Otan (Radiant Fatherland) Democratic People's Party [Nursultan NAZARBAYEV]
People's Democratic (Patriotic) Party "Auyl" [Ali BEKTAYEV]
Ult Tagdyry (Conscience of the Nation)

INTERNATIONAL ORGANIZATION PARTICIPATION:

ADB, CICA, CIS, CSTO, EAEU, EAPC, EBRD, ECO, EITI (compliant country), FAO, GCTU, IAEA, IBRD, ICAO, ICC (NGOs), ICRM, IDA, IDB, IFAD, IFC, IFRCS, ILO, IMF, IMO, Interpol, IOC, IOM, IPU, ISO, ITSO, ITU, MIGA, MINURSO, NAM (observer), NSG, OAS (observer), OIC, OPCW, OSCE, PFP, SCO, UN, UNCTAD, UNESCO, UNIDO, UN Security Council (temporary), UNWTO, UPU, WCO, WFTU (NGOs), WHO, WIPO, WMO, WTO (observer), ZC

DIPLOMATIC REPRESENTATION IN THE US:

Ambassador Yerzhan KAZYKHANOV (since 24 April 2017)

chancery: 1401 16th Street NW, Washington, DC 20036

telephone: [1] (202) 232-5488

FAX: [1] (202) 232-5845

consulate(s) general: New York

DIPLOMATIC REPRESENTATION FROM THE US:

chief of mission: Ambassador William MOSER (since 27 March 2019)

telephone: [7] (7172) 70-21-00

embassy: Rakhymzhan Koshkarbayev Ave. No 3, Astana 010010

mailing address: use embassy street address

FAX: [7] (7172) 54-09-14

consulate(s) general: Almaty

FLAG DESCRIPTION:

a gold sun with 32 rays above a soaring golden steppe eagle, both centered on a sky blue background; the hoist side displays a national ornamental pattern "koshkar-muiz" (the horns of the ram) in gold; the blue color is of religious significance to the Turkic peoples of the country, and so symbolizes cultural and ethnic unity; it also represents the endless sky as well as water; the sun, a source of life and energy, exemplifies wealth and plenitude; the sun's rays are shaped like grain, which is the basis of abundance and prosperity; the eagle has appeared on the flags of Kazakh tribes for centuries and represents freedom, power, and the flight to the future

NATIONAL SYMBOL(S):

golden eagle; national colors: blue, yellow

NATIONAL ANTHEM:

name: "Menin Qazaqstanim" (My Kazakhstan)

lyrics/music: Zhumeken NAZHIMEDENOV and Nursultan NAZARBAYEV/Shamshi KALDAYAKOV

note: adopted 2006; President Nursultan NAZARBAYEV played a role in revising the lyrics

ECONOMY :: KAZAKHSTAN

ECONOMY - OVERVIEW:

Kazakhstan's vast hydrocarbon and mineral reserves form the backbone of its economy. Geographically the largest of the former Soviet republics, excluding Russia, Kazakhstan, g possesses substantial fossil fuel reserves and other minerals and metals, such as uranium, copper, and zinc. It also has a large agricultural sector featuring livestock and grain. The government realizes that its economy suffers from an overreliance on oil and extractive industries and has made initial attempts to diversify its economy by targeting sectors like transport, pharmaceuticals, telecommunications, petrochemicals and food processing for greater development and investment. It also adopted a Subsoil Code in December 2017 with the aim of increasing exploration and investment in the hydrocarbon, and particularly mining, sectors.

Kazakhstan's oil production and potential is expanding rapidly. A $36.8 billion expansion of Kazakhstan's premiere Tengiz oil field by Chevron-led Tengizchevroil should be complete in 2022. Meanwhile, the super-giant Kashagan field finally launched production in October 2016 after years of delay and an estimated $55 billion in development costs. Kazakhstan's total oil production in 2017 climbed 10.5%.

Kazakhstan is landlocked and depends on Russia to export its oil to Europe. It also exports oil directly to China. In 2010, Kazakhstan joined Russia and Belarus to establish a Customs Union in an effort to boost foreign investment and improve trade. The Customs Union evolved into a Single Economic Space in 2012 and the Eurasian Economic Union (EAEU) in January 2015. Supported by rising commodity prices, Kazakhstan's exports to EAEU countries increased 30.2% in 2017. Imports from EAEU countries grew by 24.1%.

The economic downturn of its EAEU partner, Russia, and the decline in global commodity prices from 2014 to 2016 contributed to an economic slowdown in Kazakhstan. In 2014, Kazakhstan devalued its currency, the tenge, and announced a stimulus package to cope with its economic challenges. In the face of further decline in the ruble, oil prices, and the regional economy, Kazakhstan announced in 2015 it would replace its currency band with a floating exchange rate, leading to a sharp fall in the value of the tenge. Since reaching a low of 391 to the dollar in January 2016, the tenge has modestly appreciated, helped by somewhat higher oil prices. While growth slowed to about 1% in both 2015 and 2016, a moderate recovery in oil prices, relatively stable inflation and foreign exchange rates, and the start of production at Kashagan helped push 2017 GDP growth to 4%.

Despite some positive institutional and legislative changes in the last several years, investors remain concerned about corruption, bureaucracy, and arbitrary law enforcement, especially at the regional and municipal levels. An additional concern is the condition of the country's banking sector, which suffers from poor asset quality and a lack of transparency. Investors also question the potentially negative effects on the economy of a contested presidential succession as Kazakhstan's first president, Nursultan NAZARBAYEV, turned 77 in 2017.

GDP (PURCHASING POWER PARITY):

$478.6 billion (2017 est.)

$460.3 billion (2016 est.)

$455.3 billion (2015 est.)

  note: data are in 2017 dollars

  country comparison to the world: 42

GDP (OFFICIAL EXCHANGE RATE):

$159.4 billion (2017 est.)

GDP - REAL GROWTH RATE:

4% (2017 est.)

1.1% (2016 est.)

1.2% (2015 est.)

  country comparison to the world: 78

GDP - PER CAPITA (PPP):

$26,300 (2017 est.)

$25,700 (2016 est.)

$25,800 (2015 est.)

  note: data are in 2017 dollars

  country comparison to the world: 79

GROSS NATIONAL SAVING:

23.7% of GDP (2017 est.)

21.4% of GDP (2016 est.)

25.1% of GDP (2015 est.)

  country comparison to the world: 71

GDP - COMPOSITION, BY END USE:

  household consumption: 53.2% (2017 est.)

  government consumption: 11.1% (2017 est.)

  investment in fixed capital: 22.5% (2017 est.)

  investment in inventories: 4.8% (2017 est.)

  exports of goods and services: 35.4% (2017 est.)

  imports of goods and services: -27.1% (2017 est.)

GDP - COMPOSITION, BY SECTOR OF ORIGIN:

  agriculture: 4.7% (2017 est.)

  industry: 34.1% (2017 est.)

  services: 61.2% (2017 est.)

AGRICULTURE - PRODUCTS:

grain (mostly spring wheat and barley), potatoes, vegetables, melons; livestock

INDUSTRIES:

oil, coal, iron ore, manganese, chromite, lead, zinc, copper, titanium, bauxite, gold, silver, phosphates, sulfur, uranium, iron and steel; tractors and other agricultural machinery, electric motors, construction materials

INDUSTRIAL PRODUCTION GROWTH RATE:

5.8% (2017 est.)

  country comparison to the world: 45

LABOR FORCE:

8.97 million (2017 est.)

  country comparison to the world: 53

LABOR FORCE - BY OCCUPATION:

  agriculture: 18.1%

  industry: 20.4%

  services: 61.6% (2017 est.)

UNEMPLOYMENT RATE:

5% (2017 est.)

5% (2016 est.)

  country comparison to the world: 74

POPULATION BELOW POVERTY LINE:

2.6% (2016 est.)

HOUSEHOLD INCOME OR CONSUMPTION BY PERCENTAGE SHARE:

  lowest 10%: 4.2%

  highest 10%: 23.3% (2016)

DISTRIBUTION OF FAMILY INCOME - GINI INDEX:

26.3 (2013)

31.5 (2003)

  country comparison to the world: 149

BUDGET:

  revenues: 35.48 billion (2017 est.)

  expenditures: 38.3 billion (2017 est.)

TAXES AND OTHER REVENUES:
22.3% (of GDP) (2017 est.)

country comparison to the world: 134

BUDGET SURPLUS (+) OR DEFICIT (-):
-1.8% (of GDP) (2017 est.)

country comparison to the world: 98

PUBLIC DEBT:
20.8% of GDP (2017 est.)
19.7% of GDP (2016 est.)

country comparison to the world: 187

FISCAL YEAR:
calendar year

INFLATION RATE (CONSUMER PRICES):
7.4% (2017 est.)
14.6% (2016 est.)

country comparison to the world: 194

CENTRAL BANK DISCOUNT RATE:
11% (10 April 2017)
12% (9 January 2017)

country comparison to the world: 18

COMMERCIAL BANK PRIME LENDING RATE:
14.17% (31 December 2017 est.)
15.34% (31 December 2016 est.)

country comparison to the world: 48

STOCK OF NARROW MONEY:
$14.99 billion (31 December 2017 est.)
$13.77 billion (31 December 2016 est.)

country comparison to the world: 72

STOCK OF BROAD MONEY:
$14.99 billion (31 December 2017 est.)
$13.77 billion (31 December 2016 est.)

country comparison to the world: 73

STOCK OF DOMESTIC CREDIT:
$54.92 billion (31 December 2017 est.)
$55.1 billion (31 December 2016 est.)

country comparison to the world: 64

MARKET VALUE OF PUBLICLY TRADED SHARES:
$741.7 million (31 December 2016 est.)
$4.737 billion (31 December 2015 est.)
$26.23 billion (31 December 2013 est.)

country comparison to the world: 107

CURRENT ACCOUNT BALANCE:
-$5.353 billion (2017 est.)
-$8.874 billion (2016 est.)

country comparison to the world: 185

EXPORTS:
$49.29 billion (2017 est.)
$37.26 billion (2016 est.)

country comparison to the world: 51

EXPORTS - PARTNERS:
Italy 17.9%, China 11.9%, Netherlands 9.8%, Russia 9.3%, Switzerland 6.4%, France 5.9% (2017)

EXPORTS - COMMODITIES:
oil and oil products, natural gas, ferrous metals, chemicals, machinery, grain, wool, meat, coal

IMPORTS:
$31.85 billion (2017 est.)
$28.07 billion (2016 est.)

country comparison to the world: 64

IMPORTS - COMMODITIES:
machinery and equipment, metal products, foodstuffs

IMPORTS - PARTNERS:
Russia 38.9%, China 16.1%, Germany 5.1%, US 4.3% (2017)

RESERVES OF FOREIGN EXCHANGE AND GOLD:
$30.75 billion (31 December 2017 est.)
$29.53 billion (31 December 2016 est.)

country comparison to the world: 50

DEBT - EXTERNAL:
$167.5 billion (31 December 2017 est.)
$163.6 billion (31 December 2016 est.)

country comparison to the world: 40

STOCK OF DIRECT FOREIGN INVESTMENT - AT HOME:
$161.6 billion (31 December 2017 est.)
$143.2 billion (31 December 2016 est.)

country comparison to the world: 37

STOCK OF DIRECT FOREIGN INVESTMENT - ABROAD:
$35.04 billion (31 December 2017 est.)
$32.74 billion (31 December 2016 est.)

country comparison to the world: 48

EXCHANGE RATES:
tenge (KZT) per US dollar -
326.3 (2017 est.)
342.13 (2016 est.)
342.13 (2015 est.)
221.73 (2014 est.)
179.19 (2013 est.)

ENERGY :: KAZAKHSTAN

ELECTRICITY ACCESS:
electrification - total population: 100% (2016)

ELECTRICITY - PRODUCTION:
100.8 billion kWh (2016 est.)

country comparison to the world: 35

ELECTRICITY - CONSUMPTION:
94.23 billion kWh (2016 est.)

country comparison to the world: 33

ELECTRICITY - EXPORTS:
5.1 billion kWh (2017 est.)

country comparison to the world: 37

ELECTRICITY - IMPORTS:
1.318 billion kWh (2016 est.)

country comparison to the world: 64

ELECTRICITY - INSTALLED GENERATING CAPACITY:
20.15 million kW (2016 est.)

country comparison to the world: 44

ELECTRICITY - FROM FOSSIL FUELS:
86% of total installed capacity (2016 est.)

country comparison to the world: 66

ELECTRICITY - FROM NUCLEAR FUELS:
0% of total installed capacity (2017 est.)

country comparison to the world: 117

ELECTRICITY - FROM HYDROELECTRIC PLANTS:
14% of total installed capacity (2017 est.)

country comparison to the world: 107

ELECTRICITY - FROM OTHER RENEWABLE SOURCES:
1% of total installed capacity (2017 est.)

country comparison to the world: 155

CRUDE OIL - PRODUCTION:
1.856 million bbl/day (2018 est.)

country comparison to the world: 12

CRUDE OIL - EXPORTS:
1.409 million bbl/day (2015 est.)

country comparison to the world: 9

CRUDE OIL - IMPORTS:
1,480 bbl/day (2015 est.)

country comparison to the world: 79

CRUDE OIL - PROVED RESERVES:
30 billion bbl (1 January 2018 est.)

country comparison to the world: 11

REFINED PETROLEUM PRODUCTS - PRODUCTION:
290,700 bbl/day (2015 est.)

country comparison to the world: 44

REFINED PETROLEUM PRODUCTS - CONSUMPTION:
274,000 bbl/day (2016 est.)

country comparison to the world: 46
REFINED PETROLEUM PRODUCTS - EXPORTS:
105,900 bbl/day (2015 est.)

country comparison to the world: 41
REFINED PETROLEUM PRODUCTS - IMPORTS:
39,120 bbl/day (2015 est.)

country comparison to the world: 90
NATURAL GAS - PRODUCTION:
22.41 billion cu m (2017 est.)

country comparison to the world: 30
NATURAL GAS - CONSUMPTION:
15.37 billion cu m (2017 est.)

country comparison to the world: 43
NATURAL GAS - EXPORTS:
12.8 billion cu m (2017 est.)

country comparison to the world: 17
NATURAL GAS - IMPORTS:
5.748 billion cu m (2017 est.)

country comparison to the world: 34
NATURAL GAS - PROVED RESERVES:
2.407 trillion cu m (1 January 2018 est.)

country comparison to the world: 14
CARBON DIOXIDE EMISSIONS FROM CONSUMPTION OF ENERGY:
304.6 million Mt (2017 est.)

country comparison to the world: 23

COMMUNICATIONS :: KAZAKHSTAN

TELEPHONES - FIXED LINES:
total subscriptions: 3,697,300

subscriptions per 100 inhabitants: 20 (2017 est.)

country comparison to the world: 37

TELEPHONES - MOBILE CELLULAR:
total subscriptions: 26.473 million

subscriptions per 100 inhabitants: 143 (2017 est.)

country comparison to the world: 48

TELEPHONE SYSTEM:
general assessment: one of the most progressive telecoms sectors in Central Asia; vast 4G network; low fixed-line and fixed-broadband penetration, moderate mobile broadband penetration and high mobile penetration (2018)

domestic: intercity by landline and microwave radio relay; number of fixed-line connections is 20 per 100 persons; mobile-cellular usage increased rapidly and the subscriber base approaches 143 per 100 persons (2018)

international: country code - 7; international traffic with other former Soviet republics and China carried by landline and microwave radio relay and with other countries by satellite and by the Trans-Asia-Europe (TAE) fiber-optic cable; satellite earth stations - 2 Intelsat

BROADCAST MEDIA:
the state owns nearly all radio and TV transmission facilities and operates national TV and radio networks; there are 96 TV channels, many of which are owned by the government, and 4 state-run radio stations; some former state-owned media outlets have been privatized; households with satellite dishes have access to foreign media; a small number of commercial radio stations operate along with state-run radio stations; recent legislation requires all media outlets to register with the government and all TV providers to broadcast in digital format by 2018; broadcasts reach some 99% of the population as well as neighboring countries

INTERNET COUNTRY CODE:
.kz

INTERNET USERS:
total: 14,100,751

percent of population: 76.8% (July 2016 est.)

country comparison to the world: 41

BROADBAND - FIXED SUBSCRIPTIONS:
total: 2,573,500

subscriptions per 100 inhabitants: 14 (2017 est.)

country comparison to the world: 45

MILITARY AND SECURITY :: KAZAKHSTAN

MILITARY EXPENDITURES:
0.95% of GDP (2018)

0.84% of GDP (2017)

0.96% of GDP (2016)

1.1% of GDP (2015)

1.04% of GDP (2014)

country comparison to the world: 122

MILITARY AND SECURITY FORCES:
Armed Forces of Kazakhstan : Land Forces, Navy, Air Defense Force (2019)

MILITARY SERVICE AGE AND OBLIGATION:
All men 18-27 are required to serve in the military for at least one year. (2019)

MILITARY - NOTE:
Ministry of Internal Affairs: National Guard, Border Service (2019)

TRANSPORTATION :: KAZAKHSTAN

NATIONAL AIR TRANSPORT SYSTEM:
number of registered air carriers: 10 (2015)

inventory of registered aircraft operated by air carriers: 71 (2015)

annual passenger traffic on registered air carriers: 5,081,631 (2015)

annual freight traffic on registered air carriers: 37,669,008 mt-km (2015)

CIVIL AIRCRAFT REGISTRATION COUNTRY CODE PREFIX:
UP (2016)

AIRPORTS:
96 (2013)

country comparison to the world: 60

AIRPORTS - WITH PAVED RUNWAYS:
total: 63 (2017)

over 3,047 m: 10 (2017)

2,438 to 3,047 m: 25 (2017)

1,524 to 2,437 m: 15 (2017)

914 to 1,523 m: 5 (2017)

under 914 m: 8 (2017)

AIRPORTS - WITH UNPAVED RUNWAYS:
total: 33 (2013)

over 3,047 m: 5 (2013)

2,438 to 3,047 m: 7 (2013)

1,524 to 2,437 m: 3 (2013)

914 to 1,523 m: 5 (2013)

under 914 m: 13 (2013)

HELIPORTS:
3 (2013)

PIPELINES:
658 km condensate, 15,256 km gas (2017), 8,013 km oil (2017), 1,095 km refined products, 1,975 km water (2016) (2017)

RAILWAYS:
total: 16,614 km (2017)

broad gauge: 16,614 km 1.520-m gauge (4,200 km electrified) (2017)

country comparison to the world: 18

ROADWAYS:
total: 95,409 km (2017)

paved: 81,814 km (2017)

unpaved: 13,595 km (2017)

country comparison to the world: 51

WATERWAYS:
4,000 km (on the Ertis (Irtysh) River (80%) and Syr Darya (Syrdariya) River) (2010)

country comparison to the world: 25

MERCHANT MARINE:
total: 121

by type: general cargo 3, oil tanker 10, other 108 (2018)

country comparison to the world: 77

PORTS AND TERMINALS:
major seaport(s): Caspian Sea - Aqtau (Shevchenko), Atyrau (Gur'yev)

river port(s): Oskemen (Ust-Kamenogorsk), Pavlodar, Semey (Semipalatinsk) (Irtysh River)

TRANSNATIONAL ISSUES :: KAZAKHSTAN

DISPUTES - INTERNATIONAL:
in January 2019, the Kyrgyz Republic ratified the demarcation agreement of the Kazakh-Kyrgyz border; the demarcation of the Kazakh-Uzbek borders is ongoing; the ongoing demarcation with Russia began in 2007; demarcation with China completed in 2002

REFUGEES AND INTERNALLY DISPLACED PERSONS:
stateless persons: 7,690 (2018)

ILLICIT DRUGS:
significant illicit cultivation of cannabis for CIS markets, as well as limited cultivation of opium poppy and ephedra (for the drug ephedrine); limited government eradication of illicit crops; transit point for Southwest Asian narcotics bound for Russia and the rest of Europe; significant consumer of opiates

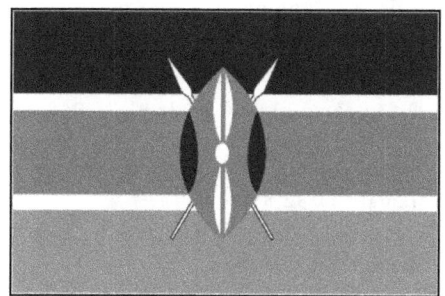

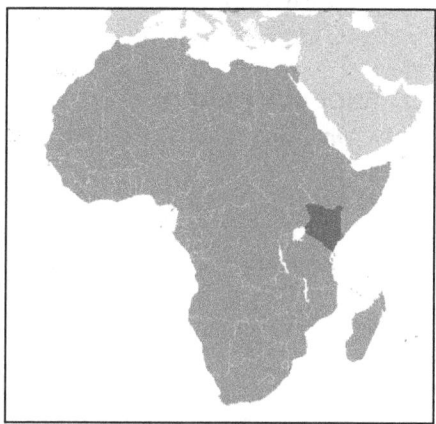

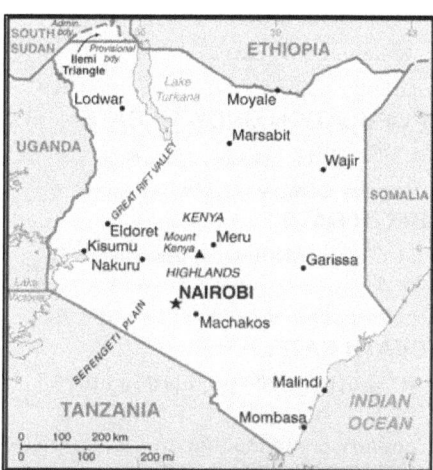

AFRICA :: KENYA

INTRODUCTION :: KENYA

BACKGROUND:

Founding president and liberation struggle icon Jomo KENYATTA led Kenya from independence in 1963 until his death in 1978, when Vice President Daniel Arap MOI took power in a constitutional succession. The country was a de facto one-party state from 1969 until 1982, after which time the ruling Kenya African National Union (KANU) changed the constitution to make itself the sole legal party in Kenya. MOI acceded to internal and external pressure for political liberalization in late 1991. The ethnically fractured opposition failed to dislodge KANU from power in elections in 1992 and 1997, which were marred by violence and fraud. President MOI stepped down in December 2002 following fair and peaceful elections. Mwai KIBAKI, running as the candidate of the multiethnic, united opposition group, the National Rainbow Coalition (NARC), defeated KANU candidate Uhuru KENYATTA, the son of founding president Jomo KENYATTA, and assumed the presidency following a campaign centered on an anticorruption platform.

KIBAKI's reelection in December 2007 brought charges of vote rigging from Orange Democratic Movement (ODM) candidate Raila ODINGA and unleashed two months of violence in which approximately 1,100 people died. African Union-sponsored mediation led by former UN Secretary General Kofi ANNAN in late February 2008 resulted in a power-sharing accord bringing ODINGA into the government in the restored position of prime minister. The power sharing accord included a broad reform agenda, the centerpiece of which was constitutional reform. In August 2010, Kenyans overwhelmingly adopted a new constitution in a national referendum. The new constitution introduced additional checks and balances to executive power and devolved power and resources to 47 newly created counties. It also eliminated the position of prime minister. Uhuru KENYATTA won the first presidential election under the new constitution in March 2013, and was sworn into office the following month; he began a second term in November 2017 following a contentious, repeat election.

GEOGRAPHY :: KENYA

LOCATION:

Eastern Africa, bordering the Indian Ocean, between Somalia and Tanzania

GEOGRAPHIC COORDINATES:

1 00 N, 38 00 E

MAP REFERENCES:

Africa

AREA:

total: 580,367 sq km

land: 569,140 sq km

water: 11,227 sq km

country comparison to the world: 50

AREA - COMPARATIVE:

five times the size of Ohio; slightly more than twice the size of Nevada

LAND BOUNDARIES:

total: 3,457 km

border countries (5): Ethiopia 867 km, Somalia 684 km, South Sudan 317 km, Tanzania 775 km, Uganda 814 km

COASTLINE:

536 km

MARITIME CLAIMS:

territorial sea: 12 nm

exclusive economic zone: 200 nm

continental shelf: 200-m depth or to the depth of exploitation

CLIMATE:

varies from tropical along coast to arid in interior

TERRAIN:

low plains rise to central highlands bisected by Great Rift Valley; fertile plateau in west

ELEVATION:

mean elevation: 762 m

lowest point: Indian Ocean 0 m

highest point: Mount Kenya 5,199 m

NATURAL RESOURCES:

limestone, soda ash, salt, gemstones, fluorspar, zinc, diatomite, gypsum, wildlife, hydropower

LAND USE:

agricultural land: 48.1% (2011 est.)

arable land: 9.8% (2011 est.) / permanent crops: 0.9% (2011 est.) / permanent pasture: 37.4% (2011 est.)

forest: 6.1% (2011 est.)

other: 45.8% (2011 est.)

IRRIGATED LAND:

1,030 sq km (2012)

POPULATION DISTRIBUTION:

population heavily concentrated in the west along the shore of Lake Victoria; other areas of high density include the

capital of Nairobi, and in the southeast along the Indian Ocean coast

NATURAL HAZARDS:

recurring drought; flooding during rainy seasons

volcanism: limited volcanic activity; the Barrier (1,032 m) last erupted in 1921; South Island is the only other historically active volcano

ENVIRONMENT - CURRENT ISSUES:

water pollution from urban and industrial wastes; water shortage and degraded water quality from increased use of pesticides and fertilizers; flooding; water hyacinth infestation in Lake Victoria; deforestation; soil erosion; desertification; poaching

ENVIRONMENT - INTERNATIONAL AGREEMENTS:

party to: Biodiversity, Climate Change, Climate Change-Kyoto Protocol, Desertification, Endangered Species, Hazardous Wastes, Law of the Sea, Marine Dumping, Marine Life Conservation, Ozone Layer Protection, Ship Pollution, Wetlands, Whaling

signed, but not ratified: none of the selected agreements

GEOGRAPHY - NOTE:

the Kenyan Highlands comprise one of the most successful agricultural production regions in Africa; glaciers are found on Mount Kenya, Africa's second highest peak; unique physiography supports abundant and varied wildlife of scientific and economic value; Lake Victoria, the world's largest tropical lake and the second largest fresh water lake, is shared among three countries: Kenya, Tanzania, and Uganda

PEOPLE AND SOCIETY :: KENYA

POPULATION:

48,397,527 (July 2018 est.)

note: estimates for this country explicitly take into account the effects of excess mortality due to AIDS; this can result in lower life expectancy, higher infant mortality, higher death rates, lower population growth rates, and changes in the distribution of population by age and sex than would otherwise be expected

country comparison to the world: 29

NATIONALITY:

noun: Kenyan(s)

adjective: Kenyan

ETHNIC GROUPS:

Kikuyu 17.2%, Luhya 13.8%, Kalejin 12.9%, Luo 10.5%, Kamba 10.1%, Somali 6.2%, Kisii 5.7%, Mijikenda 5.1%, Meru 4.3%, Turkana 2.6%, Masai 2.2%, other 9.4% (2014 est.)

LANGUAGES:

English (official), Kiswahili (official), numerous indigenous languages

RELIGIONS:

Christian 83% (Protestant 47.7%, Catholic 23.4%, other Christian 11.9%), Muslim 11.2%, Traditionalists 1.7%, other 1.6%, none 2.4%, unspecified 0.2% (2009 est.)

DEMOGRAPHIC PROFILE:

Kenya has experienced dramatic population growth since the mid-20th century as a result of its high birth rate and its declining mortality rate. More than 40% of Kenyans are under the age of 15 because of sustained high fertility, early marriage and childbearing, and an unmet need for family planning. Kenya's persistent rapid population growth strains the labor market, social services, arable land, and natural resources. Although Kenya in 1967 was the first sub-Saharan country to launch a nationwide family planning program, progress in reducing the birth rate has largely stalled since the late 1990s, when the government decreased its support for family planning to focus on the HIV epidemic. Government commitment and international technical support spurred Kenyan contraceptive use, decreasing the fertility rate (children per woman) from about 8 in the late 1970s to less than 5 children twenty years later, but it has plateaued at just over 3 children today.

Kenya is a source of emigrants and a host country for refugees. In the 1960s and 1970s, Kenyans pursued higher education in the UK because of colonial ties, but as British immigration rules tightened, the US, the then Soviet Union, and Canada became attractive study destinations. Kenya's stagnant economy and political problems during the 1980s and 1990s led to an outpouring of Kenyan students and professionals seeking permanent opportunities in the West and southern Africa. Nevertheless, Kenya's relative stability since its independence in 1963 has attracted hundreds of thousands of refugees escaping violent conflicts in neighboring countries; Kenya shelters more than 300,000 Somali refugees as of April 2017.

AGE STRUCTURE:

0-14 years: 39.03% (male 9,474,968 /female 9,416,609)

15-24 years: 19.61% (male 4,737,647 /female 4,752,896)

25-54 years: 34.27% (male 8,393,673 /female 8,193,800)

55-64 years: 4% (male 894,371 /female 1,040,883)

65 years and over: 3.08% (male 640,005 /female 852,675) (2018 est.)

DEPENDENCY RATIOS:

total dependency ratio: 78.3 (2015 est.)

youth dependency ratio: 73.7 (2015 est.)

elderly dependency ratio: 4.6 (2015 est.)

potential support ratio: 21.7 (2015 est.)

MEDIAN AGE:

total: 20 years (2018 est.)

male: 19.9 years

female: 20.2 years

country comparison to the world: 191

POPULATION GROWTH RATE:

1.57% (2018 est.)

country comparison to the world: 67

BIRTH RATE:

22.6 births/1,000 population (2018 est.)

country comparison to the world: 66

DEATH RATE:

6.7 deaths/1,000 population (2018 est.)

country comparison to the world: 137

NET MIGRATION RATE:

-0.2 migrant(s)/1,000 population (2018 est.)

country comparison to the world: 109

POPULATION DISTRIBUTION:

population heavily concentrated in the west along the shore of Lake Victoria; other areas of high density include the capital of Nairobi, and in the southeast along the Indian Ocean coast

URBANIZATION:

urban population: 27.5% of total population (2019)

rate of urbanization: 4.23% annual rate of change (2015-20 est.)

MAJOR URBAN AREAS - POPULATION:

4.556 million NAIROBI (capital), 1.254 million Mombassa (2019)

SEX RATIO:

at birth: 1.02 male(s)/female

0-14 years: 1.01 male(s)/female

15-24 years: 1 male(s)/female

25-54 years: 1.02 male(s)/female

55-64 years: 0.86 male(s)/female

65 years and over: 0.75 male(s)/female

total population: 1 male(s)/female (2018 est.)

MOTHER'S MEAN AGE AT FIRST BIRTH:

20.3 years (2014 est.)

note: median age at first birth among women 25-29

MATERNAL MORTALITY RATE:

342 deaths/100,000 live births (2017 est.)

country comparison to the world: 32

INFANT MORTALITY RATE:

total: 36.1 deaths/1,000 live births (2018 est.)

male: 40.3 deaths/1,000 live births

female: 31.7 deaths/1,000 live births

country comparison to the world: 48

LIFE EXPECTANCY AT BIRTH:

total population: 64.6 years (2018 est.)

male: 63.1 years

female: 66.1 years

country comparison to the world: 187

TOTAL FERTILITY RATE:

2.81 children born/woman (2018 est.)

country comparison to the world: 59

CONTRACEPTIVE PREVALENCE RATE:

60.5% (2017)

DRINKING WATER SOURCE:

improved:

urban: 81.6% of population

rural: 56.8% of population

total: 63.2% of population

unimproved:

urban: 18.4% of population

rural: 43.2% of population

total: 36.8% of population (2015 est.)

CURRENT HEALTH EXPENDITURE:

4.5% (2016)

PHYSICIANS DENSITY:

0.2 physicians/1,000 population (2014)

HOSPITAL BED DENSITY:

1.4 beds/1,000 population (2010)

SANITATION FACILITY ACCESS:

improved:

urban: 31.2% of population (2015 est.)

rural: 29.7% of population (2015 est.)

total: 30.1% of population (2015 est.)

unimproved:

urban: 68.8% of population (2015 est.)

rural: 70.3% of population (2015 est.)

total: 69.9% of population (2015 est.)

HIV/AIDS - ADULT PREVALENCE RATE:

4.7% (2018 est.)

country comparison to the world: 12

HIV/AIDS - PEOPLE LIVING WITH HIV/AIDS:

1.6 million (2018 est.)

country comparison to the world: 5

HIV/AIDS - DEATHS:

25,000 (2018 est.)

country comparison to the world: 6

MAJOR INFECTIOUS DISEASES:

degree of risk: very high (2016)

food or waterborne diseases: bacterial and protozoal diarrhea, hepatitis A, and typhoid fever (2016)

vectorborne diseases: malaria, dengue fever, and Rift Valley fever (2016)

water contact diseases: schistosomiasis (2016)

animal contact diseases: rabies (2016)

OBESITY - ADULT PREVALENCE RATE:

7.1% (2016)

country comparison to the world: 161

CHILDREN UNDER THE AGE OF 5 YEARS UNDERWEIGHT:

11.2% (2014)

country comparison to the world: 58

EDUCATION EXPENDITURES:

5.2% of GDP (2017)

country comparison to the world: 58

LITERACY:

definition: age 15 and over can read and write

total population: 78%

male: 81.1%

female: 74.9% (2015 est.)

SCHOOL LIFE EXPECTANCY (PRIMARY TO TERTIARY EDUCATION):

total: 11 years

male: 11 years

female: 11 years (2009)

GOVERNMENT :: KENYA

COUNTRY NAME:

conventional long form: Republic of Kenya

conventional short form: Kenya

local long form: Republic of Kenya/Jamhuri ya Kenya

local short form: Kenya

former: British East Africa

etymology: named for Mount Kenya; the meaning of the name is unclear but may derive from the Kikuyu, Embu, and Kamba words "kirinyaga," "kirenyaa," and "kiinyaa" - all of which mean "God's resting place"

GOVERNMENT TYPE:

presidential republic

CAPITAL:

name: Nairobi

geographic coordinates: 1 17 S, 36 49 E

time difference: UTC+3 (8 hours ahead of Washington, DC, during Standard Time)

etymology: the name derives from the Maasai expression meaning "cool waters" and refers to a cold water stream that flowed through the area in the late 19th century

ADMINISTRATIVE DIVISIONS:

47 counties; Baringo, Bomet, Bungoma, Busia, Elgeyo/Marakwet, Embu, Garissa, Homa Bay, Isiolo, Kajiado, Kakamega, Kericho, Kiambu, Kilifi, Kirinyaga, Kisii, Kisumu, Kitui, Kwale, Laikipia, Lamu, Machakos, Makueni, Mandera, Marsabit, Meru, Migori, Mombasa, Murang'a, Nairobi City, Nakuru, Nandi, Narok, Nyamira, Nyandarua, Nyeri, Samburu, Siaya, Taita/Taveta, Tana River, Tharaka-Nithi, Trans Nzoia, Turkana, Uasin Gishu, Vihiga, Wajir, West Pokot

INDEPENDENCE:

12 December 1963 (from the UK)

NATIONAL HOLIDAY:

Jamhuri Day (Independence Day), 12 December (1963); note - Madaraka Day, 1 June (1963) marks the day Kenya attained internal self-rule

CONSTITUTION:

history: previous 1963, 1969; latest drafted 6 May 2010, passed by referendum 4 August 2010, promulgated 27 August 2010

amendments: proposed by either house of Parliament or by petition of at least one million eligible voters; passage of amendments by Parliament requires approval by at least two-thirds majority vote of both houses in each of two readings, approval in a referendum by majority of votes cast by at least 20% of eligible voters in at least one half of Kenya's counties, and approval by the president; passage of amendments introduced by petition requires approval by a majority of county assemblies, approval by majority vote of both houses, and approval by the president (2017)

LEGAL SYSTEM:

mixed legal system of English common law, Islamic law, and customary law; judicial review in the new Supreme Court established by the new constitution

INTERNATIONAL LAW ORGANIZATION PARTICIPATION:

accepts compulsory ICJ jurisdiction with reservations; accepts ICCt jurisdiction

CITIZENSHIP:

citizenship by birth: no

citizenship by descent only: at least one parent must be a citizen of Kenya

dual citizenship recognized: yes

residency requirement for naturalization: 4 out of the previous 7 years

SUFFRAGE:

18 years of age; universal

EXECUTIVE BRANCH:

chief of state: President Uhuru KENYATTA (since 9 April 2013); Deputy President William RUTO (since 9 April 2013); note - the president is both chief of state and head of government

head of government: President Uhuru KENYATTA (since 9 April 2013); Deputy President William RUTO (since 9 April 2013); note - position of the prime minister was abolished after the March 2013 elections

cabinet: Cabinet appointed by the president, subject to confirmation by the National Assembly

elections/appointments: president and deputy president directly elected on the same ballot by qualified majority popular vote for a 5-year term (eligible for a second term); in addition to receiving an absolute majority popular vote, the presidential candidate must also win at least 25% of the votes cast in at least 24 of the 47 counties to avoid a runoff; election last held on 26 October 2017 (next to be held in 2022)

election results: Uhuru KENYATTA reelected president; percent of vote - Uhuru KENYATTA (Jubilee Party) 98.3%, Raila ODINGA (ODM) 1%, other 0.7%; note - Kenya held a previous presidential election on 8 August 2017, but Kenya's Supreme Court on 1 September 2017 nullified the results, citing irregularities; the political opposition boycotted the October vote

LEGISLATIVE BRANCH:

description: bicameral Parliament consists of:
Senate (67 seats; 47 members directly elected in single-seat constituencies by simple majority vote and 20 directly elected by proportional representation vote - 16 women, 2 representing youth, and 2 representing the disabled; members serve 5-year terms)
National Assembly (349 seats; 290 members directly elected in single-seat constituencies by simple majority vote, 47 women in single-seat constituencies elected by simple majority vote, and 12 members nominated by the National Assembly - 6 representing youth and 6 representing the disabled; members serve 5-year terms)

elections: Senate - last held on 8 August 2017 (next to be held in August 2022)
National Assembly - last held on 8 August 2017 (next to be held in August 2022)

election results: Senate - percent of vote by party/coalition - NA; seats by party/coalition - Jubilee Party 24; National Super Alliance 28, other 14, independent 1; composition - men 46, women 41, percent of women is 31.3%

National Assembly - percent of vote by party/coalition - NA; seats by party/coalition - Jubilee Party 165, National Super Alliance 119, other 51, independent 13; composition - men 273, women 76, percent of women 21.8%; note - total Parliament percent of women is 23%

JUDICIAL BRANCH:

highest courts: Supreme Court (consists of chief and deputy chief justices and 5 judges)

judge selection and term of office: chief and deputy chief justices nominated by Judicial Service Commission (JSC) and appointed by the president with approval of the National Assembly; other judges nominated by the JSC and appointed by president; chief justice serves a nonrenewable 10-year term or until age 70, whichever comes first; other judges serve until age 70

subordinate courts: High Court; Court of Appeal; military courts; magistrates' courts; religious courts

POLITICAL PARTIES AND LEADERS:

Alliance Party of Kenya or APK [Kiraitu MURUNGI]
Amani National Congress or ANC [Musalia MUDAVADI]
Federal Party of Kenya or FPK [Cyrus JIRONGA]
Forum for the Restoration of Democracy-Kenya or FORD-K [Moses WETANGULA]
Forum for the Restoration of Democracy-People or FORD-P [Henry OBWOCHA]
Jubilee Party [Uhuru KENYATTA]
Kenya African National Union or KANU [Gideon MOI]
National Rainbow Coalition or NARC [Charity NGILU]
Orange Democratic Movement Party of Kenya or ODM [Raila ODINGA]
Wiper Democratic Movement-K or WDM-K (formerly Orange Democratic Movement-Kenya or ODM-K) [Kalonzo MUSYOKA]

INTERNATIONAL ORGANIZATION PARTICIPATION:

ACP, AfDB, AU, C, CD, COMESA, EAC, EADB, FAO, G-15, G-77, IAEA, IBRD, ICAO, ICCt, ICRM, IDA, IFAD, IFC, IFRCS, IGAD, ILO, IMF, IMO, IMSO, Interpol, IOC, IOM, IPU, ISO, ITSO, ITU, ITUC (NGOs), MIGA, MINUSMA, MONUSCO, NAM, OPCW, PCA, UN, UNAMID, UNCTAD, UNESCO, UNHCR, UNIDO, UNIFIL, UNMIL, UNMISS, UNWTO, UPU, WCO, WHO, WMO, WTO

DIPLOMATIC REPRESENTATION IN THE US:

Ambassador Robinson Njeru GITHAE (since 18 November 2014)

chancery: 2249 R Street NW, Washington, DC 20008

telephone: [1] (202) 387-6101

FAX: [1] (202) 462-3829

consulate(s) general: Los Angeles

consulate(s): New York

DIPLOMATIC REPRESENTATION FROM THE US:

chief of mission: Ambassador Kyle MCCARTER (since 12 March 2019)

telephone: [254] (20) 363-6000

embassy: United Nations Avenue, Nairobi; P.O. Box 606 Village Market, Nairobi 00621

mailing address: American Embassy Nairobi, U.S. Department of State, Washington, DC 20521-8900

FAX: [254] (20) 363-6157

FLAG DESCRIPTION:

three equal horizontal bands of black (top), red, and green; the red band is edged in white; a large Maasai warrior's shield covering crossed spears is superimposed at the center; black symbolizes the majority population, red the blood shed in the struggle for freedom, green stands for natural wealth, and white for peace; the shield and crossed spears symbolize the defense of freedom

NATIONAL SYMBOL(S):

lion; national colors: black, red, green, white

NATIONAL ANTHEM:

name: "Ee Mungu Nguvu Yetu" (Oh God of All Creation)

lyrics/music: Graham HYSLOP, Thomas KALUME, Peter KIBUKOSYA, Washington OMONDI, and George W. SENOGA-ZAKE/traditional, adapted by Graham HYSLOP, Thomas KALUME, Peter KIBUKOSYA, Washington OMONDI, and George W. SENOGA-ZAKE

note: adopted 1963; based on a traditional Kenyan folk song

ECONOMY :: KENYA

ECONOMY - OVERVIEW:

Kenya is the economic, financial, and transport hub of East Africa. Kenya's real GDP growth has averaged over 5% for the last decade. Since 2014, Kenya has been ranked as a lower middle income country because its per capita GDP crossed a World Bank threshold. While Kenya has a growing entrepreneurial middle class and steady growth, its economic development has been impaired by weak governance and corruption. Although reliable numbers are hard to find, unemployment and underemployment are extremely high, and could be near 40% of the population. In 2013, the country adopted a devolved system of government with the creation of 47 counties, and is in the process of devolving state revenues and responsibilities to the counties.

Agriculture remains the backbone of the Kenyan economy, contributing one-third of GDP. About 75% of Kenya's population of roughly 48.5 million work at least part-time in the agricultural sector, including livestock and pastoral activities. Over 75% of agricultural output is from small-scale, rain-fed farming or livestock production. Tourism also holds a significant place in Kenya's economy. In spite of political turmoil throughout the second half of 2017, tourism was up 20%, showcasing the strength of this sector. Kenya has long been a target of terrorist activity and has struggled with instability along its northeastern borders. Some high visibility terrorist attacks during 2013-2015 (e.g., at Nairobi's Westgate Mall and Garissa University) affected the tourism industry severely, but the sector rebounded strongly in 2016-2017 and appears poised to continue growing.

Inadequate infrastructure continues to hamper Kenya's efforts to improve its annual growth so that it can meaningfully address poverty and unemployment. The KENYATTA administration has been successful in courting external investment for infrastructure development. International financial institutions and donors remain important to Kenya's growth and development, but Kenya has also successfully raised capital in the global bond market issuing its first sovereign bond offering in mid-2014, with a second occurring in February 2018. The first phase of a Chinese-financed and constructed standard gauge railway connecting Mombasa and Nairobi opened in May 2017.

In 2016 the government was forced to take over three small and undercapitalized banks when underlying weaknesses were exposed. The government also enacted legislation that limits interest rates banks can charge on loans and set a rate that banks must pay their depositors. This measure led to a sharp shrinkage of credit in the economy. A prolonged election cycle in 2017 hurt the economy, drained government resources, and slowed GDP growth. Drought-like conditions in parts of the country pushed 2017 inflation above 8%, but the rate had fallen to 4.5% in February 2018.

The economy, however, is well placed to resume its decade-long 5%-6% growth rate. While fiscal deficits continue to pose risks in the medium term, other economic indicators, including foreign exchange reserves, interest rates, current account deficits, remittances and FDI are positive. The credit and drought-related impediments were temporary. Now In his second term, President KENYATTA has pledged to make economic growth and development a centerpiece of his second administration, focusing on his "Big Four" initiatives of universal healthcare, food security, affordable housing, and expansion of manufacturing.

GDP (PURCHASING POWER PARITY):

$163.7 billion (2017 est.)

$156 billion (2016 est.)

$147.4 billion (2015 est.)

note: data are in 2017 dollars

country comparison to the world: 74

GDP (OFFICIAL EXCHANGE RATE):

$79.22 billion (2017 est.)

GDP - REAL GROWTH RATE:

4.9% (2017 est.)

5.9% (2016 est.)

5.7% (2015 est.)

country comparison to the world: 53

GDP - PER CAPITA (PPP):

$3,500 (2017 est.)

$3,400 (2016 est.)

$3,300 (2015 est.)

note: data are in 2017 dollars

country comparison to the world: 187

GROSS NATIONAL SAVING:

10.4% of GDP (2017 est.)

11% of GDP (2016 est.)

11.4% of GDP (2015 est.)

country comparison to the world: 162

GDP - COMPOSITION, BY END USE:

household consumption: 79.5% (2017 est.)

government consumption: 14.3% (2017 est.)

investment in fixed capital: 18.9% (2017 est.)

investment in inventories: -1% (2017 est.)

exports of goods and services: 13.9% (2017 est.)

imports of goods and services: -25.5% (2017 est.)

GDP - COMPOSITION, BY SECTOR OF ORIGIN:

agriculture: 34.5% (2017 est.)

industry: 17.8% (2017 est.)

services: 47.5% (2017 est.)

AGRICULTURE - PRODUCTS:

tea, coffee, corn, wheat, sugarcane, fruit, vegetables; dairy products, beef, fish, pork, poultry, eggs

INDUSTRIES:

small-scale consumer goods (plastic, furniture, batteries, textiles, clothing, soap, cigarettes, flour), agricultural products, horticulture, oil refining; aluminum, steel, lead; cement, commercial ship repair, tourism, information technology

INDUSTRIAL PRODUCTION GROWTH RATE:

3.6% (2017 est.)

country comparison to the world: 82

LABOR FORCE:

19.6 million (2017 est.)

country comparison to the world: 30

LABOR FORCE - BY OCCUPATION:

agriculture: 61.1%

industry: 6.7%

services: 32.2% (2005 est.)

UNEMPLOYMENT RATE:

40% (2013 est.)

40% (2001 est.)

country comparison to the world: 214

POPULATION BELOW POVERTY LINE:

36.1% (2016 est.)

HOUSEHOLD INCOME OR CONSUMPTION BY PERCENTAGE SHARE:

lowest 10%: 1.8%

highest 10%: 37.8% (2005)

DISTRIBUTION OF FAMILY INCOME - GINI INDEX:

48.5 (2016 est.)

42.5 (2008 est.)

country comparison to the world: 23

BUDGET:

revenues: 13.95 billion (2017 est.)

expenditures: 19.24 billion (2017 est.)

TAXES AND OTHER REVENUES:

17.6% (of GDP) (2017 est.)

country comparison to the world: 168

BUDGET SURPLUS (+) OR DEFICIT (-):

-6.7% (of GDP) (2017 est.)

country comparison to the world: 190

PUBLIC DEBT:

54.2% of GDP (2017 est.)

53.2% of GDP (2016 est.)

country comparison to the world: 84

FISCAL YEAR:

1 July - 30 June

INFLATION RATE (CONSUMER PRICES):

8% (2017 est.)

6.3% (2016 est.)

country comparison to the world: 197

CENTRAL BANK DISCOUNT RATE:

10% (1 January 2017)

11.5% (1 January 2016)

country comparison to the world: 21

COMMERCIAL BANK PRIME LENDING RATE:

13.67% (31 December 2017 est.)

16.56% (31 December 2016 est.)

country comparison to the world: 53

STOCK OF NARROW MONEY:

$14.07 billion (31 December 2017 est.)

$12.77 billion (31 December 2016 est.)

country comparison to the world: 76

STOCK OF BROAD MONEY:

$14.07 billion (31 December 2017 est.)

$12.77 billion (31 December 2016 est.)

country comparison to the world: 77

STOCK OF DOMESTIC CREDIT:

$32 billion (31 December 2017 est.)

$29.88 billion (31 December 2016 est.)

country comparison to the world: 79

MARKET VALUE OF PUBLICLY TRADED SHARES:

$19.33 billion (31 December 2016 est.)

$26.48 billion (31 December 2015 est.)

$26.16 billion (31 December 2014 est.)

country comparison to the world: 63

CURRENT ACCOUNT BALANCE:

-$5.021 billion (2017 est.)

-$3.697 billion (2016 est.)

country comparison to the world: 183

EXPORTS:

$5.792 billion (2017 est.)

$5.695 billion (2016 est.)

country comparison to the world: 105

EXPORTS - PARTNERS:

Uganda 10.8%, Pakistan 10.6%, US 8.1%, Netherlands 7.3%, UK 6.4%, Tanzania 4.8%, UAE 4.4% (2017)

EXPORTS - COMMODITIES:

tea, horticultural products, coffee, petroleum products, fish, cement, apparel

IMPORTS:

$15.99 billion (2017 est.)

$13.41 billion (2016 est.)

country comparison to the world: 86

IMPORTS - COMMODITIES:

machinery and transportation equipment, oil, petroleum products, motor vehicles, iron and steel, resins and plastics

IMPORTS - PARTNERS:

China 22.5%, India 9.9%, UAE 8.7%, Saudi Arabia 5.1%, Japan 4.5% (2017)

RESERVES OF FOREIGN EXCHANGE AND GOLD:

$7.354 billion (31 December 2017 est.)

$7.256 billion (31 December 2016 est.)

country comparison to the world: 83

DEBT - EXTERNAL:

$27.59 billion (31 December 2017 est.)

$37.7 billion (31 December 2016 est.)

country comparison to the world: 85

STOCK OF DIRECT FOREIGN INVESTMENT - AT HOME:

$8.738 billion (31 December 2017 est.)

$5.317 billion (31 December 2016 est.)

country comparison to the world: 97

STOCK OF DIRECT FOREIGN INVESTMENT - ABROAD:

$1.545 billion (31 December 2017 est.)

$335.5 million (31 December 2016 est.)

country comparison to the world: 86

EXCHANGE RATES:

Kenyan shillings (KES) per US dollar -

102.1 (2017 est.)

101.5 (2016 est.)

101.504 (2015 est.)

98.179 (2014 est.)

87.921 (2013 est.)

ENERGY :: KENYA

ELECTRICITY ACCESS:

population without electricity: 13 million (2017)

electrification - total population: 56% (2016)

electrification - urban areas: 77.6% (2016)

electrification - rural areas: 39.3% (2016)

ELECTRICITY - PRODUCTION:

9.634 billion kWh (2016 est.)

country comparison to the world: 105

ELECTRICITY - CONSUMPTION:

7.863 billion kWh (2016 est.)

country comparison to the world: 104

ELECTRICITY - EXPORTS:

39.1 million kWh (2016 est.)

country comparison to the world: 89

ELECTRICITY - IMPORTS:

184 million kWh (2016 est.)

country comparison to the world: 95

ELECTRICITY - INSTALLED GENERATING CAPACITY:

2.401 million kW (2016 est.)

country comparison to the world: 109

ELECTRICITY - FROM FOSSIL FUELS:

33% of total installed capacity (2016 est.)

country comparison to the world: 183

ELECTRICITY - FROM NUCLEAR FUELS:

0% of total installed capacity (2017 est.)

country comparison to the world: 118

ELECTRICITY - FROM HYDROELECTRIC PLANTS:

34% of total installed capacity (2017 est.)

country comparison to the world: 62

ELECTRICITY - FROM OTHER RENEWABLE SOURCES:

33% of total installed capacity (2017 est.)

country comparison to the world: 13

CRUDE OIL - PRODUCTION:

0 bbl/day (2018 est.)

country comparison to the world: 154

CRUDE OIL - EXPORTS:

0 bbl/day (2015 est.)

country comparison to the world: 145

CRUDE OIL - IMPORTS:

12,550 bbl/day (2015 est.)

country comparison to the world: 71

CRUDE OIL - PROVED RESERVES:

0 bbl (1 January 2018 est.)

country comparison to the world: 150

REFINED PETROLEUM PRODUCTS - PRODUCTION:

13,960 bbl/day (2015 est.)

country comparison to the world: 96

REFINED PETROLEUM PRODUCTS - CONSUMPTION:

109,000 bbl/day (2016 est.)

country comparison to the world: 76

REFINED PETROLEUM PRODUCTS - EXPORTS:

173 bbl/day (2015 est.)

country comparison to the world: 118

REFINED PETROLEUM PRODUCTS - IMPORTS:

90,620 bbl/day (2015 est.)

country comparison to the world: 57

NATURAL GAS - PRODUCTION:

0 cu m (2017 est.)

country comparison to the world: 150

NATURAL GAS - CONSUMPTION:

0 cu m (2017 est.)

country comparison to the world: 161

NATURAL GAS - EXPORTS:

0 cu m (2017 est.)

country comparison to the world: 128

NATURAL GAS - IMPORTS:

0 cu m (2017 est.)

country comparison to the world: 142

NATURAL GAS - PROVED RESERVES:

0 cu m (1 January 2014 est.)

country comparison to the world: 151

CARBON DIOXIDE EMISSIONS FROM CONSUMPTION OF ENERGY:

17.98 million Mt (2017 est.)

country comparison to the world: 88

COMMUNICATIONS :: KENYA

TELEPHONES - FIXED LINES:

total subscriptions: 69,861

subscriptions per 100 inhabitants: less than 1 (2017 est.)

country comparison to the world: 149

TELEPHONES - MOBILE CELLULAR:

total subscriptions: 42,815,109

subscriptions per 100 inhabitants: 90 (2017 est.)

country comparison to the world: 33

TELEPHONE SYSTEM:

general assessment:

the mobile-cellular system is generally good, especially in urban areas; fixed-line telephone system is small and inefficient; trunks are primarily microwave radio relay; to encourage advancement of the LTE services the govt. has fostered an open-access approach; govt. progresses with national broadband strategy; more licensing being awarded has led to competition which is good for growth

(2018)

domestic: multiple providers in the mobile-cellular segment of the market fostering a boom in mobile-cellular telephone usage with teledensity reaching 90 per 100 persons; fixed-line subscriptions stand at less than 1 per 100 persons (2018)

international: country code - 254; landing point for the EASSy, TEAMS, LION2, DARE1, PEACE Cable, and SEACOM fiber-optic submarine cable systems covering East, North and South Africa, Europe, the Middle East, and Asia; satellite earth stations - 4 Intelsat; launched first micro satellites (2019)

BROADCAST MEDIA:

about a half-dozen large-scale privately owned media companies with TV and radio stations, as well as a state-owned TV broadcaster, provide service nationwide; satellite and cable TV subscription services available; state-owned radio broadcaster operates 2 national radio channels and provides regional and local radio services in multiple languages; many private radio stations broadcast on a national level along with over 100 private and non-profit regional stations broadcasting in local languages; TV transmissions of all major international broadcasters available, mostly via paid subscriptions; direct radio frequency modulation transmissions available for several foreign government-owned broadcasters (2019)

INTERNET COUNTRY CODE:

.ke

INTERNET USERS:

total: 12,165,597

percent of population: 26% (July 2016 est.)

country comparison to the world: 45

BROADBAND - FIXED SUBSCRIPTIONS:

total: 288,303

subscriptions per 100 inhabitants: less than 1 (2017 est.)

country comparison to the world: 97

MILITARY AND SECURITY :: KENYA

MILITARY EXPENDITURES:

1.3% of GDP (2019)

1.22% of GDP (2018)

1.32% of GDP (2017)

1.32% of GDP (2016)

1.32% of GDP (2015)

country comparison to the world: 91

MILITARY AND SECURITY FORCES:

Kenya Defence Forces: Kenya Army, Kenya Navy, Kenya Air Force (2019)

MILITARY SERVICE AGE AND OBLIGATION:

18-26 years of age for male and female voluntary service (under 18 with parental consent), with a 9-year obligation (7 years for Kenyan Navy) and subsequent 3-year reenlistments; applicants must be Kenyan citizens and provide a national identity card (obtained at age 18) and a school-leaving certificate, and undergo a series of mental and physical examinations; women serve under the same terms and conditions as men; mandatory retirement at age 55 but personnel leaving before this age remain in a reserve status until they reach age 55 unless they were removed for disciplinary reasons; there is no active military reserve, although the Ministry of Defence has stated its desire to create one as recently as 2017 (2019)

MARITIME THREATS:

The International Maritime Bureau reports that shipping in territorial and offshore waters in the Indian Ocean remain at risk for piracy and armed robbery against ships, especially as Somali-based pirates extend their activities south; numerous commercial vessels have been attacked and hijacked both at anchor and while underway; crews have been robbed and stores or cargoes stolen.

MILITARY - NOTE:

The Kenya Coast Guard Service (established 2018) is separate from the Defence Forces, but led by a military officer and comprised of personnel from the military, as well as the National Police Service, intelligence services, and other government agencies. (2019)

TRANSPORTATION :: KENYA

NATIONAL AIR TRANSPORT SYSTEM:

number of registered air carriers: 16 (2015)

inventory of registered aircraft operated by air carriers: 106 (2015)

annual passenger traffic on registered air carriers: 4,874,590 (2015)

annual freight traffic on registered air carriers: 286,414,683 mt-km (2015)

CIVIL AIRCRAFT REGISTRATION COUNTRY CODE PREFIX:

5Y (2016)

AIRPORTS:

197 (2013)

country comparison to the world: 28

AIRPORTS - WITH PAVED RUNWAYS:

total: 16 (2017)

over 3,047 m: 5 (2017)

2,438 to 3,047 m: 2 (2017)

1,524 to 2,437 m: 2 (2017)

914 to 1,523 m: 6 (2017)

under 914 m: 1 (2017)

AIRPORTS - WITH UNPAVED RUNWAYS:

total: 181 (2013)

1,524 to 2,437 m: 14 (2013)

914 to 1,523 m: 107 (2013)

under 914 m: 60 (2013)

PIPELINES:

4 km oil, 1,432 km refined products (2018)

RAILWAYS:

total: 3,819 km (2018)

standard gauge: 485 km 1.435-m gauge (2018)

narrow gauge: 3,334 km 1.000-m gauge (2018)

country comparison to the world: 52

ROADWAYS:

total: 177,800 km (2018)

paved: 14,420 km (8,500 km highways, 1,872 urban roads, and 4,048 rural roads) (2017)

unpaved: 147,032 km (2017)

country comparison to the world: 31

WATERWAYS:

none specifically; the only significant inland waterway is the part of Lake Victoria within the boundaries of Kenya; Kisumu is the main port and has ferry connections to Uganda and Tanzania (2011)

MERCHANT MARINE:

total: 22

by type: general cargo 1, oil tanker 2, other 19 (2018)

country comparison to the world: 137

PORTS AND TERMINALS:

major seaport(s): Kisumu, Mombasa

LNG terminal(s) (import): Mombasa

TERRORISM :: KENYA

TERRORIST GROUPS - FOREIGN BASED:

al-Shabaab: aim(s): establish Islamic rule in Kenya's northeastern border region and coast; avenge Kenya's past intervention in Somalia against al-Shabaab and its ongoing participation in the African Union mission; compel Kenya to withdraw troops from Somalia; attract Kenyan recruits to support operations in Somalia

area(s) of operation: maintains an operational and recruitment presence, mostly along the coast and the northeastern border region (2018)

TRANSNATIONAL ISSUES :: KENYA

DISPUTES - INTERNATIONAL:

Kenya served as an important mediator in brokering Sudan's north-south separation in February 2005; as of March 2019, Kenya provides shelter to nearly 475,000 refugees and asylum seekers, including Ugandans who flee across the border periodically to seek protection from Lord's Resistance Army rebels; Kenya works hard to prevent the clan and militia fighting in Somalia from spreading across the border, which has long been open to nomadic pastoralists; the boundary that separates Kenya's and Sudan's sovereignty is unclear in the "Ilemi

Triangle," which Kenya has administered since colonial times

REFUGEES AND INTERNALLY DISPLACED PERSONS:

refugees (country of origin): 260,683 (Somalia) (refugees and asylum seekers), 119,110 (South Sudan) (refugees and asylum seekers), 43,517 (Democratic Republic of the Congo) (refugees and asylum seekers), 27,989 (Ethiopia) (refugees and asylum seekers), 14,674 (Burundi) (refugees and asylum seekers), 10,011 (Sudan) (refugees and asylum seekers) (2019)

IDPs: 162,000 (election-related violence, intercommunal violence, resource conflicts, al-Shabaab attacks in 2017 and 2018) (2018)

stateless persons: 18,500 (2018); note - the stateless population consists of Nubians, Kenyan Somalis, and coastal Arabs; the Nubians are descendants of Sudanese soldiers recruited by the British to fight for them in East Africa more than a century ago; Nubians did not receive Kenyan citizenship when the country became independent in 1963; only recently have Nubians become a formally recognized tribe and had less trouble obtaining national IDs; Galjeel and other Somalis who have lived in Kenya for decades are included with more recent Somali refugees and denied ID cards

ILLICIT DRUGS:

widespread harvesting of small plots of marijuana; transit country for South Asian heroin destined for Europe and North America; Indian methaqualone also transits on way to South Africa; significant potential for money-laundering activity given the country's status as a regional financial center; massive corruption, and relatively high levels of narcotics-associated activities

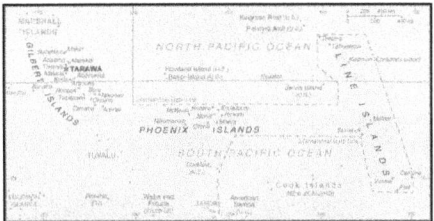

AUSTRALIA - OCEANIA :: KIRIBATI

INTRODUCTION :: KIRIBATI

BACKGROUND:

The Gilbert Islands became a British protectorate in 1892 and a colony in 1915; they were captured by the Japanese in the Pacific War in 1941. The islands of Makin and Tarawa were the sites of major US amphibious victories over entrenched Japanese garrisons in 1943. The Gilbert Islands were granted self-rule by the UK in 1971 and complete independence in 1979 under the new name of Kiribati. The US relinquished all claims to the sparsely inhabited Phoenix and Line Island groups in a 1979 treaty of friendship with Kiribati. Kiribati joined the UN in 1999 and has been an active participant in international efforts to combat climate change.

GEOGRAPHY :: KIRIBATI

LOCATION:
Oceania, group of 32 coral atolls and one raised coral island in the Pacific Ocean, straddling the Equator; the capital Tarawa is about halfway between Hawaii and Australia

GEOGRAPHIC COORDINATES:
1 25 N, 173 00 E

MAP REFERENCES:
Oceania

AREA:
total: 811 sq km

land: 811 sq km

water: 0 sq km

note: includes three island groups - Gilbert Islands, Line Islands, and Phoenix Islands - dispersed over about 3.5 million sq km (1.35 million sq mi)

country comparison to the world: 187

AREA - COMPARATIVE:
four times the size of Washington, DC

LAND BOUNDARIES:
0 km

COASTLINE:
1,143 km

MARITIME CLAIMS:
territorial sea: 12 nm

exclusive economic zone: 200 nm

CLIMATE:
tropical; marine, hot and humid, moderated by trade winds

TERRAIN:
mostly low-lying coral atolls surrounded by extensive reefs

ELEVATION:
mean elevation: 2 m

lowest point: Pacific Ocean 0 m

highest point: unnamed elevation on Banaba 81 m m

NATURAL RESOURCES:
phosphate (production discontinued in 1979), coconuts (copra), fish

LAND USE:
agricultural land: 42% (2011 est.)

arable land: 2.5% (2011 est.) / permanent crops: 39.5% (2011 est.) / permanent pasture: 0% (2011 est.)

forest: 15% (2011 est.)

other: 43% (2011 est.)

IRRIGATED LAND:
0 sq km (2012)

POPULATION DISTRIBUTION:
consists of three achipelagos spread out over an area roughly the size of India; the eastern Line Islands and central Phoenix Islands are sparsely populated, but the western Gilbert Islands are some of the most densely settled places on earth, with the main island of South Tarawa boasting a population density similar to Tokyo or Hong Kong

NATURAL HAZARDS:
typhoons can occur any time, but usually November to March; occasional tornadoes; low level of some of the islands make them sensitive to changes in sea level

ENVIRONMENT - CURRENT ISSUES:
heavy pollution in lagoon of south Tarawa atoll due to overcrowding mixed with traditional practices such as lagoon latrines and open-pit dumping; ground water at risk; potential for water shortages, disease; coastal erosion

ENVIRONMENT - INTERNATIONAL AGREEMENTS:
party to: Biodiversity, Climate Change, Climate Change-Kyoto Protocol, Desertification, Hazardous Wastes, Law of the Sea, Marine Dumping, Ozone Layer Protection, Whaling

signed, but not ratified: none of the selected agreements

GEOGRAPHY - NOTE:
21 of the 33 islands are inhabited; Banaba (Ocean Island) in Kiribati is one of the three great phosphate rock islands in the Pacific Ocean - the others are Makatea in French Polynesia, and Nauru; Kiribati is the only country in the world to fall into all four hemispheres (northern, southern, eastern, and western)

PEOPLE AND SOCIETY :: KIRIBATI

POPULATION:
109,367 (July 2018 est.)

country comparison to the world: 191

NATIONALITY:
noun: I-Kiribati (singular and plural)

adjective: I-Kiribati

ETHNIC GROUPS:

I-Kiribati 96.2%, I-Kiribati/mixed 1.8%, Tuvaluan 0.2%, other 1.8% (2015 est.)

LANGUAGES:

I-Kiribati, English (official)

RELIGIONS:

Roman Catholic 57.3%, Kiribati Uniting Church 31.3%, Mormon 5.3%, Baha'i 2.1%, Seventh Day Adventist 1.9%, other 2.1% (2015 est.)

AGE STRUCTURE:

0-14 years: 29.27% (male 16,316 /female 15,693)

15-24 years: 20.74% (male 11,213 /female 11,466)

25-54 years: 39.43% (male 20,756 /female 22,363)

55-64 years: 6.23% (male 3,071 /female 3,747)

65 years and over: 4.34% (male 1,863 /female 2,879) (2018 est.)

DEPENDENCY RATIOS:

total dependency ratio: 63 (2015 est.)

youth dependency ratio: 57 (2015 est.)

elderly dependency ratio: 6 (2015 est.)

potential support ratio: 16.6 (2015 est.)

MEDIAN AGE:

total: 25 years (2018 est.)

male: 24.1 years

female: 25.8 years

country comparison to the world: 157

POPULATION GROWTH RATE:

1.12% (2018 est.)

country comparison to the world: 96

BIRTH RATE:

21 births/1,000 population (2018 est.)

country comparison to the world: 75

DEATH RATE:

7 deaths/1,000 population (2018 est.)

country comparison to the world: 129

NET MIGRATION RATE:

-2.8 migrant(s)/1,000 population (2018 est.)

country comparison to the world: 175

POPULATION DISTRIBUTION:

consists of three achipelagos spread out over an area roughly the size of India; the eastern Line Islands and central Phoenix Islands are sparsely populated, but the western Gilbert Islands are some of the most densely settled places on earth, with the main island of South Tarawa boasting a population density similar to Tokyo or Hong Kong

URBANIZATION:

urban population: 54.8% of total population (2019)

rate of urbanization: 3.19% annual rate of change (2015-20 est.)

MAJOR URBAN AREAS - POPULATION:

64,000 TARAWA (capital) (2018)

SEX RATIO:

at birth: 1.05 male(s)/female

0-14 years: 1.04 male(s)/female

15-24 years: 0.98 male(s)/female

25-54 years: 0.93 male(s)/female

55-64 years: 0.82 male(s)/female

65 years and over: 0.65 male(s)/female

total population: 0.95 male(s)/female (2018 est.)

MOTHER'S MEAN AGE AT FIRST BIRTH:

23.1 years (2009 est.)

note: median age at first birth among women 25-29

MATERNAL MORTALITY RATE:

92 deaths/100,000 live births (2017 est.)

country comparison to the world: 73

INFANT MORTALITY RATE:

total: 31.1 deaths/1,000 live births (2018 est.)

male: 32.3 deaths/1,000 live births

female: 29.9 deaths/1,000 live births

country comparison to the world: 58

LIFE EXPECTANCY AT BIRTH:

total population: 66.9 years (2018 est.)

male: 64.3 years

female: 69.5 years

country comparison to the world: 174

TOTAL FERTILITY RATE:

2.34 children born/woman (2018 est.)

country comparison to the world: 86

CONTRACEPTIVE PREVALENCE RATE:

22.3% (2009)

DRINKING WATER SOURCE:

improved:

urban: 87.3% of population

rural: 50.6% of population

total: 66.9% of population

unimproved:

urban: 12.7% of population

rural: 49.4% of population

total: 33.1% of population (2015 est.)

CURRENT HEALTH EXPENDITURE:

11.9% (2016)

PHYSICIANS DENSITY:

0.2 physicians/1,000 population (2013)

HOSPITAL BED DENSITY:

1.9 beds/1,000 population (2015)

SANITATION FACILITY ACCESS:

improved:

urban: 51.2% of population (2015 est.)

rural: 30.6% of population (2015 est.)

total: 39.7% of population (2015 est.)

unimproved:

urban: 48.8% of population (2015 est.)

rural: 69.4% of population (2015 est.)

total: 60.3% of population (2015 est.)

HIV/AIDS - ADULT PREVALENCE RATE:

NA

HIV/AIDS - PEOPLE LIVING WITH HIV/AIDS:

NA

HIV/AIDS - DEATHS:

NA

OBESITY - ADULT PREVALENCE RATE:

46% (2016)

country comparison to the world: 9

CHILDREN UNDER THE AGE OF 5 YEARS UNDERWEIGHT:

14.9% (2009)

country comparison to the world: 43

EDUCATION EXPENDITURES:

NA

SCHOOL LIFE EXPECTANCY (PRIMARY TO TERTIARY EDUCATION):

total: 12 years

male: 11 years

female: 12 years (2008)

UNEMPLOYMENT, YOUTH AGES 15-24:

total: 17.1%

male: 22.2%

female: 7.4% (2015 est.)

country comparison to the world: 80

GOVERNMENT :: KIRIBATI

COUNTRY NAME:

conventional long form: Republic of Kiribati

conventional short form: Kiribati

local long form: Republic of Kiribati

local short form: Kiribati

former: Gilbert Islands

etymology: the name is the local pronunciation of "Gilberts," the former designation of the islands; originally named after explorer Thomas GILBERT, who mapped many of the islands in 1788

note: pronounced keer-ree-bahss

GOVERNMENT TYPE:

presidential republic

CAPITAL:

name: Tarawa

geographic coordinates: 1 21 N, 173 02 E

time difference: UTC+12 (17 hours ahead of Washington, DC, during Standard Time)

note: Kiribati has three time zones: the Gilbert Islands group at UTC+12, the Phoenix Islands at UTC+13, and the Line Islands at UTC+14

etymology: in Kiribati creation mythology, "tarawa" was what the spider Nareau named the land to distinguish it from "karawa" (the sky) and "marawa" (the ocean)

ADMINISTRATIVE DIVISIONS:

3 geographical units: Gilbert Islands, Line Islands, Phoenix Islands; note - there are no first-order administrative divisions, but there are 6 districts (Banaba, Central Gilberts, Line Islands, Northern Gilberts, Southern Gilberts, Tarawa) and 21 island councils - one for each of the inhabited islands (Abaiang, Abemama, Aranuka, Arorae, Banaba, Beru, Butaritari, Kanton, Kiritimati, Kuria, Maiana, Makin, Marakei, Nikunau, Nonouti, Onotoa, Tabiteuea, Tabuaeran, Tamana, Tarawa, Teraina)

INDEPENDENCE:

12 July 1979 (from the UK)

NATIONAL HOLIDAY:

Independence Day, 12 July (1979)

CONSTITUTION:

history: The Gilbert and Ellice Islands Order in Council 1915, The Gilbert Islands Order in Council 1975 (preindependence); latest promulgated 12 July 1979 (at independence)

amendments: proposed by the House of Assembly; passage requires two-thirds majority vote by the Assembly membership; passage of amendments affecting the constitutional section on amendment procedures and parts of the constitutional chapter on citizenship requires deferral of the proposal to the next Assembly meeting where approval is required by at least two-thirds majority vote of the Assembly membership and support of the nominated or elected Banaban member of the Assembly; amendments affecting the protection of fundamental rights and freedoms also requires approval by at least two-thirds majority in a referendum; amended 1995, 2013 (2017)

LEGAL SYSTEM:

English common law supplemented by customary law

INTERNATIONAL LAW ORGANIZATION PARTICIPATION:

has not submitted an ICJ jurisdiction declaration; non-party state to the ICCt

CITIZENSHIP:

citizenship by birth: no

citizenship by descent only: at least one parent must be a native-born citizen of Kiribati

dual citizenship recognized: no

residency requirement for naturalization: 7 years

SUFFRAGE:

18 years of age; universal

EXECUTIVE BRANCH:

chief of state: President Taneti MAAMAU (since 11 March 2016); Vice President Kourabi NENEM (since 17 March 2016); note - the president is both chief of state and head of government

head of government: President Taneti MAAMAU (since 11 March 2016); Vice President Kourabi NENEM (since 17 March 2016)

cabinet: Cabinet appointed by the president from among House of Assembly members

elections/appointments: president directly elected by simple majority popular vote following nomination of candidates from among House of Assembly members; term is 4 years (eligible for 2 additional terms); election last held on 9 March 2016 (next to be held in 2020); vice president appointed by the president

election results: Taneti MAAMAU elected president; percent of vote - Taneti MAAMAU 60%, Rimeta BENIAMINA (BTK) 38.6%, Taneti IOANE (BTK) 1.4%

LEGISLATIVE BRANCH:

description: unicameral House of Assembly or Maneaba Ni Maungatabu (46 seats; 44 members directly elected in single- and multi-seat constituencies by absolute majority vote in two-rounds if needed; 1 member appointed by the Rabi Council of Leaders - representing Banaba Island, and 1 ex officio member - the attorney general; members serve 4-year terms)

elections: legislative elections were held in two rounds - the first on 30 December 2015 and the second on 7 January 2016 (next to be held in 2019)

election results: percent of vote by party - NA; seats by party - BTK 26, KTK and MKP 19, other 2 (includes attorney general); composition - men 43, women 3, percent of women 6.5%

JUDICIAL BRANCH:

highest courts: High Court (consists of a chief justice and other judges as prescribed by the president); note - the High Court has jurisdiction on constitutional issues

judge selection and term of office: chief justice appointed by the president on the advice of the cabinet in consultation with the Public Service Commission (PSC); other judges appointed by the president on the advice of the chief justice along with the PSC

subordinate courts: Court of Appeal; magistrates' courts

POLITICAL PARTIES AND LEADERS:

Boutokaan Te Koaua Party or BTK or Pillars of Truth [Anote TONG]
Kamaeuraoan Te I-Kiribati Party or KTK [Tetaua TAITAI]
Maurin Kiribati Pati or MKP [Rimeta BENIAMINA]
Tobwaan Kiribati Party or TKP [Taneti MAAMAU]

note: there is no tradition of formally organized political parties in Kiribati; they more closely resemble factions or interest groups because they have no party headquarters, formal platforms, or party structures

INTERNATIONAL ORGANIZATION PARTICIPATION:

ABEDA, ACP, ADB, AOSIS, C, FAO, IBRD, ICAO, ICRM, IDA, IFAD, IFC, IFRCS, ILO, IMF, IMO, IOC, ITU, ITUC (NGOs), OPCW, PIF, Sparteca, SPC, UN, UNCTAD, UNESCO, UPU, WHO, WIPO, WMO

DIPLOMATIC REPRESENTATION IN THE US:

none; the Kiribati Permanent Mission to the UN serves as the embassy; it is headed by Teburoro TITO (since 13 September 2017); address: 800 Second Avenue, Suite 400A, New York, NY 10017; telephone: [1](212)867-3310; FAX: [1](212)867-3320

DIPLOMATIC REPRESENTATION FROM THE US:

the US does not have an embassy in Kiribati; the US Ambassador to Fiji is accredited to Kiribati

FLAG DESCRIPTION:

the upper half is red with a yellow frigatebird flying over a yellow rising sun, and the lower half is blue with three horizontal wavy white stripes to represent the Pacific ocean; the white stripes represent the three island groups - the Gilbert, Line, and Phoenix Islands; the 17 rays of the sun represent the 16 Gilbert Islands and Banaba (formerly Ocean Island); the frigatebird symbolizes authority and freedom

NATIONAL SYMBOL(S):

frigatebird; national colors: red, white, blue, yellow

NATIONAL ANTHEM:

name: "Teirake kaini Kiribati" (Stand Up, Kiribati)

lyrics/music: Urium Tamuera IOTEBA

note: adopted 1979

ECONOMY :: KIRIBATI

ECONOMY - OVERVIEW:

A remote country of 33 scattered coral atolls, Kiribati has few natural resources and is one of the least developed Pacific Island countries. Commercially viable phosphate deposits were exhausted by the time of independence from the United Kingdom in 1979. Earnings from fishing licenses and seafarer remittances are important sources of income. Although the number of seafarers employed declined due to changes in global shipping demands, remittances are expected to improve with more overseas temporary and seasonal work opportunities for Kiribati nationals.

Economic development is constrained by a shortage of skilled workers, weak infrastructure, and remoteness from international markets. The public sector dominates economic activity, with ongoing capital projects in infrastructure including road rehabilitation, water and sanitation projects, and renovations to the international airport, spurring some growth. Public debt increased from 23% of GDP at the end of 2015 to 25.8% in 2016.

Kiribati is dependent on foreign aid, which was estimated to have contributed over 32.7% in 2016 to the government's finances. The country's sovereign fund, the Revenue Equalization Reserve Fund (RERF), which is held offshore, had an estimated balance of $855.5 million in late July 2016. The RERF seeks to avoid exchange rate risk by holding investments in more than 20 currencies, including the Australian dollar, US dollar, the Japanese yen, and the Euro. Drawdowns from the RERF helped finance the government's annual budget.

GDP (PURCHASING POWER PARITY):

$227 million (2017 est.)

$220.2 million (2016 est.)

$217.7 million (2015 est.)

note: data are in 2017 dollars

country comparison to the world: 219

GDP (OFFICIAL EXCHANGE RATE):

$197 million (2017 est.)

GDP - REAL GROWTH RATE:

3.1% (2017 est.)

1.1% (2016 est.)

10.3% (2015 est.)

country comparison to the world: 108

GDP - PER CAPITA (PPP):

$2,000 (2017 est.)

$2,000 (2016 est.)

$2,000 (2015 est.)

note: data are in 2017 dollars

country comparison to the world: 210

GDP - COMPOSITION, BY SECTOR OF ORIGIN:

agriculture: 23% (2016 est.)

industry: 7% (2016 est.)

services: 70% (2016 est.)

AGRICULTURE - PRODUCTS:

copra, breadfruit, fish

INDUSTRIES:

fishing, handicrafts

INDUSTRIAL PRODUCTION GROWTH RATE:

1.1% (2012 est.)

country comparison to the world: 153

LABOR FORCE:

39,000 (2010 est.)

note: economically active, not including subsistence farmers

country comparison to the world: 198

LABOR FORCE - BY OCCUPATION:

agriculture: 15%

industry: 10%

services: 75% (2010)

UNEMPLOYMENT RATE:

30.6% (2010 est.)

6.1% (2005)

country comparison to the world: 209

POPULATION BELOW POVERTY LINE:

NA

HOUSEHOLD INCOME OR CONSUMPTION BY PERCENTAGE SHARE:

lowest 10%: NA

highest 10%: NA

BUDGET:

revenues: 151.2 million (2017 est.)

expenditures: 277.5 million (2017 est.)

TAXES AND OTHER REVENUES:

76.8% (of GDP) (2017 est.)

country comparison to the world: 4

BUDGET SURPLUS (+) OR DEFICIT (-):

-64.1% (of GDP) (2017 est.)

country comparison to the world: 221

PUBLIC DEBT:

26.3% of GDP (2017 est.)

22.9% of GDP (2016 est.)

country comparison to the world: 172

FISCAL YEAR:

NA

INFLATION RATE (CONSUMER PRICES):

0.4% (2017 est.)

1.9% (2016 est.)

country comparison to the world: 24

MARKET VALUE OF PUBLICLY TRADED SHARES:

NA

CURRENT ACCOUNT BALANCE:

$18 million (2017 est.)

$35 million (2016 est.)

country comparison to the world: 62

EXPORTS:

$84.75 million (2013 est.)

$62.31 million (2012 est.)

country comparison to the world: 199

EXPORTS - PARTNERS:

Philippines 50.8%, Malaysia 17.2%, US 11.4%, Bangladesh 5.8%, Fiji 5.4% (2017)

EXPORTS - COMMODITIES:

fish, coconut products

IMPORTS:

$107.1 million (2016 est.)

$182.2 million (2013 est.)

country comparison to the world: 215

IMPORTS - COMMODITIES:

food, machinery and equipment, miscellaneous manufactured goods, fuel

IMPORTS - PARTNERS:

Australia 29.3%, Fiji 17.3%, NZ 10.7%, China 5.8%, US 5.8%, Singapore 5.1%, Japan 4.6%, Thailand 4.1% (2017)

RESERVES OF FOREIGN EXCHANGE AND GOLD:

$0 (31 December 2017 est.)

$8.37 million (31 December 2010 est.)

country comparison to the world: 192

DEBT - EXTERNAL:

$40.9 million (2016 est.)

$32.3 million (2015 est.)

country comparison to the world: 196

STOCK OF DIRECT FOREIGN INVESTMENT - AT HOME:

NA

EXCHANGE RATES:

Australian dollars (AUD) per US dollar -

1.31 (2017 est.)

1.34 (2016 est.)

1.34 (2015 est.)

1.33 (2014 est.)

1.11 (2013 est.)

note: the Australian dollar circulates as legal tender

ENERGY :: KIRIBATI

ELECTRICITY ACCESS:

electrification - total population: 84.9% (2016)

electrification - urban areas: 88.4% (2016)

electrification - rural areas: 82.2% (2016)

ELECTRICITY - PRODUCTION:

29 million kWh (2016 est.)

country comparison to the world: 210

ELECTRICITY - CONSUMPTION:

26.97 million kWh (2016 est.)

country comparison to the world: 210

ELECTRICITY - EXPORTS:

0 kWh (2016 est.)

country comparison to the world: 153

ELECTRICITY - IMPORTS:

0 kWh (2016 est.)

country comparison to the world: 164

ELECTRICITY - INSTALLED GENERATING CAPACITY:

11,000 kW (2016 est.)

country comparison to the world: 209

ELECTRICITY - FROM FOSSIL FUELS:

73% of total installed capacity (2016 est.)

country comparison to the world: 99

ELECTRICITY - FROM NUCLEAR FUELS:

0% of total installed capacity (2017 est.)

country comparison to the world: 119

ELECTRICITY - FROM HYDROELECTRIC PLANTS:

0% of total installed capacity (2017 est.)

country comparison to the world: 181

ELECTRICITY - FROM OTHER RENEWABLE SOURCES:

27% of total installed capacity (2017 est.)

country comparison to the world: 25

CRUDE OIL - PRODUCTION:

0 bbl/day (2018 est.)

country comparison to the world: 155

CRUDE OIL - EXPORTS:

0 bbl/day (2015 est.)

country comparison to the world: 146

CRUDE OIL - IMPORTS:

0 bbl/day (2015 est.)

country comparison to the world: 146

CRUDE OIL - PROVED RESERVES:

0 bbl (1 January 2018 est.)

country comparison to the world: 151

REFINED PETROLEUM PRODUCTS - PRODUCTION:

0 bbl/day (2015 est.)

country comparison to the world: 160

REFINED PETROLEUM PRODUCTS - CONSUMPTION:

400 bbl/day (2016 est.)

country comparison to the world: 211

REFINED PETROLEUM PRODUCTS - EXPORTS:

0 bbl/day (2015 est.)

country comparison to the world: 167

REFINED PETROLEUM PRODUCTS - IMPORTS:

420 bbl/day (2015 est.)

country comparison to the world: 207

NATURAL GAS - PRODUCTION:

0 cu m (2017 est.)

country comparison to the world: 151

NATURAL GAS - CONSUMPTION:

0 cu m (2017 est.)

country comparison to the world: 162

NATURAL GAS - EXPORTS:

0 cu m (2017 est.)

country comparison to the world: 129

NATURAL GAS - IMPORTS:

0 cu m (2017 est.)

country comparison to the world: 143

NATURAL GAS - PROVED RESERVES:

0 cu m (1 January 2014 est.)

country comparison to the world: 152

CARBON DIOXIDE EMISSIONS FROM CONSUMPTION OF ENERGY:

58,850 Mt (2017 est.)

country comparison to the world: 209

COMMUNICATIONS :: KIRIBATI

TELEPHONES - FIXED LINES:

total subscriptions: 765

subscriptions per 100 inhabitants: 1 (2017 est.)

country comparison to the world: 216

TELEPHONES - MOBILE CELLULAR:

total subscriptions: 46,123

subscriptions per 100 inhabitants: 43 (2017 est.)

country comparison to the world: 202

TELEPHONE SYSTEM:

general assessment: generally good quality national and international service; wireline service available on Tarawa and Kiritimati (Christmas Island); connections to outer islands by HF/VHF radiotelephone; recently formed mobile network operator (MNO) is implementing the first phase of improvements with 3G and 4G upgrades on some islands; islands are connected to each other and the rest of the world via satellite

domestic: fixed-line 1 per 100 and mobile-cellular 43 per 100 subscriptions

international: country code - 686; landing point for the Southern Cross NEXT submarine cable system from Australia, 7 Pacific Ocean island countries to the US; satellite earth station - 1 Intelsat (Pacific Ocean) (2019)

BROADCAST MEDIA:

multi-channel TV packages provide access to Australian and US stations; 1 government-operated radio station broadcasts on AM, FM, and shortwave (2017)

INTERNET COUNTRY CODE:

.ki

INTERNET USERS:

total: 14,649

percent of population: 13.7% (July 2016 est.)

country comparison to the world: 208

BROADBAND - FIXED SUBSCRIPTIONS:

total: 76

subscriptions per 100 inhabitants: less than 1 (2017 est.)

country comparison to the world: 197

MILITARY AND SECURITY :: KIRIBATI

MILITARY AND SECURITY FORCES:

no regular military forces (establishment prevented by the constitution); Police Force (2011)

MILITARY - NOTE:

Kiribati does not have military forces; defense assistance is provided by Australia and NZ

TRANSPORTATION :: KIRIBATI

CIVIL AIRCRAFT REGISTRATION COUNTRY CODE PREFIX:

T3 (2016)

AIRPORTS:

19 (2013)

country comparison to the world: 137

AIRPORTS - WITH PAVED RUNWAYS:

total: 4 (2017)

1,524 to 2,437 m: 4 (2017)

AIRPORTS - WITH UNPAVED RUNWAYS:

total: 15 (2013)

914 to 1,523 m: 10 (2013)

under 914 m: 5 (2013)

ROADWAYS:

total: 670 km (2017)

country comparison to the world: 184

WATERWAYS:

5 km (small network of canals in Line Islands) (2012)

country comparison to the world: 107

MERCHANT MARINE:

total: 111

by type: bulk carrier 3, general cargo 46, oil tanker 16, other 46 (2018)

country comparison to the world: 80

PORTS AND TERMINALS:

major seaport(s): Betio (Tarawa Atoll), Canton Island, English Harbor

TRANSNATIONAL ISSUES :: KIRIBATI

DISPUTES - INTERNATIONAL:

none

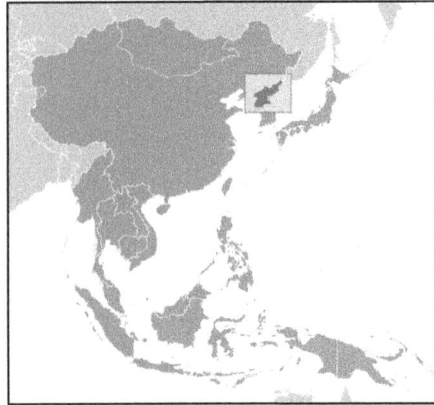

EAST ASIA / SOUTHEAST ASIA :: KOREA, NORTH

INTRODUCTION :: KOREA, NORTH

BACKGROUND:

An independent kingdom for much of its long history, Korea was occupied by Japan beginning in 1905 following the Russo-Japanese War. Five years later, Japan formally annexed the entire peninsula. Following World War II, Korea was split with the northern half coming under Soviet-sponsored communist control. After failing in the Korean War (1950-53) to conquer the US-backed Republic of Korea (ROK) in the southern portion by force, North Korea (DPRK), under its founder President KIM Il Sung, adopted a policy of ostensible diplomatic and economic "self-reliance" as a check against outside influence. The DPRK demonized the US as the ultimate threat to its social system through state-funded propaganda, and molded political, economic, and military policies around the core ideological objective of eventual unification of Korea under Pyongyang's control. KIM Il Sung's son, KIM Jong Il, was officially designated as his father's successor in 1980, assuming a growing political and managerial role until the elder KIM's death in 1994. Under KIM Jong Il's rein, the DPRK developed nuclear weapons and ballistic missiles. KIM Jong Un was publicly unveiled as his father's successor in 2010.

Following KIM Jong Il's death in 2011, KIM Jong Un quickly assumed power and has since occupied the regime's highest political and military posts. After decades of economic mismanagement and resource misallocation, the DPRK since the mid-1990s has faced chronic food shortages. In recent years, the North's domestic agricultural production has increased, but still falls far short of producing sufficient food to provide for its entire population. The DPRK began to ease restrictions to allow semi-private markets, starting in 2002, but has made few other efforts to meet its goal of improving the overall standard of living. North Korea's history of regional military provocations; proliferation of military-related items; long-range missile development; WMD programs including tests of nuclear devices in 2006, 2009, 2013, 2016, and 2017; and massive conventional armed forces are of major concern to the international community and have limited the DPRK's international engagement, particularly economically. In 2013, the DPRK declared a policy of simultaneous development of its nuclear weapons program and economy. In 2018, KIM Jong Un declared the North's nuclear weapons development complete, announced economic development as a leading priority, and increased diplomatic engagement. He participated in three 2018 inter-Korean summits with ROK President Moon Jae-in and in two with US President TRUMP (in 2018 and 2019).

GEOGRAPHY :: KOREA, NORTH

LOCATION:
Eastern Asia, northern half of the Korean Peninsula bordering the Korea Bay and the Sea of Japan, between China and South Korea

GEOGRAPHIC COORDINATES:
40 00 N, 127 00 E

MAP REFERENCES:
Asia

AREA:
total: 120,538 sq km

land: 120,408 sq km

water: 130 sq km

country comparison to the world: 100

AREA - COMPARATIVE:
slightly larger than Virginia; slightly smaller than Mississippi

LAND BOUNDARIES:
total: 1,607 km

border countries (3): China 1352 km, South Korea 237 km, Russia 18 km

COASTLINE:
2,495 km

MARITIME CLAIMS:
territorial sea: 12 nm

exclusive economic zone: 200 nm

note: military boundary line 50 nm in the Sea of Japan and the exclusive economic zone limit in the Yellow Sea where all foreign vessels and aircraft without permission are banned

CLIMATE:
temperate, with rainfall concentrated in summer; long, bitter winters

TERRAIN:

mostly hills and mountains separated by deep, narrow valleys; wide coastal plains in west, discontinuous in east

ELEVATION:

mean elevation: 600 m

lowest point: Sea of Japan 0 m

highest point: Paektu-san 2,744 m

NATURAL RESOURCES:

coal, iron ore, limestone, magnesite, graphite, copper, zinc, lead, precious metals, hydropower

LAND USE:

agricultural land: 21.8% (2011 est.)

arable land: 19.5% (2011 est.) / permanent crops: 1.9% (2011 est.) / permanent pasture: 0.4% (2011 est.)

forest: 46% (2011 est.)

other: 32.2% (2011 est.)

IRRIGATED LAND:

14,600 sq km (2012)

POPULATION DISTRIBUTION:

population concentrated in the plains and lowlands; least populated regions are the mountainous provinces adjacent to the Chinese border; largest concentrations are in the western provinces, particularly the municipal district of Pyongyang, and around Hungnam and Wonsan in the east

NATURAL HAZARDS:

late spring droughts often followed by severe flooding; occasional typhoons during the early fall

volcanism: Changbaishan (2,744 m) (also known as Baitoushan, Baegdu or P'aektu-san), on the Chinese border, is considered historically active

ENVIRONMENT - CURRENT ISSUES:

water pollution; inadequate supplies of potable water; waterborne disease; deforestation; soil erosion and degradation

ENVIRONMENT - INTERNATIONAL AGREEMENTS:

party to: Antarctic Treaty, Biodiversity, Climate Change, Climate Change-Kyoto Protocol, Desertification, Environmental Modification, Hazardous Wastes, Ozone Layer Protection, Ship Pollution

signed, but not ratified: Law of the Sea

GEOGRAPHY - NOTE:

strategic location bordering China, South Korea, and Russia; mountainous interior is isolated and sparsely populated

PEOPLE AND SOCIETY :: KOREA, NORTH

POPULATION:

25,381,085 (July 2018 est.)

country comparison to the world: 54

NATIONALITY:

noun: Korean(s)

adjective: Korean

ETHNIC GROUPS:

racially homogeneous; there is a small Chinese community and a few ethnic Japanese

LANGUAGES:

Korean

RELIGIONS:

traditionally Buddhist and Confucianist, some Christian and syncretic Chondogyo (Religion of the Heavenly Way)

note: autonomous religious activities now almost nonexistent; government-sponsored religious groups exist to provide illusion of religious freedom

AGE STRUCTURE:

0-14 years: 20.65% (male 2,669,357/female 2,571,195)

15-24 years: 15.35% (male 1,959,440/female 1,935,607)

25-54 years: 44.17% (male 5,627,175/female 5,583,008)

55-64 years: 10.34% (male 1,241,473/female 1,383,444)

65 years and over: 9.5% (male 826,101/female 1,584,285) (2018 est.)

DEPENDENCY RATIOS:

total dependency ratio: 44.5 (2015 est.)

youth dependency ratio: 30.5 (2015 est.)

elderly dependency ratio: 14 (2015 est.)

potential support ratio: 7.1 (2015 est.)

MEDIAN AGE:

total: 34.2 years (2018 est.)

male: 32.7 years

female: 35.8 years

country comparison to the world: 86

POPULATION GROWTH RATE:

0.52% (2018 est.)

country comparison to the world: 152

BIRTH RATE:

14.6 births/1,000 population (2018 est.)

country comparison to the world: 130

DEATH RATE:

9.3 deaths/1,000 population (2018 est.)

country comparison to the world: 56

NET MIGRATION RATE:

0 migrant(s)/1,000 population (2018 est.)

country comparison to the world: 89

POPULATION DISTRIBUTION:

population concentrated in the plains and lowlands; least populated regions are the mountainous provinces adjacent to the Chinese border; largest concentrations are in the western provinces, particularly the municipal district of Pyongyang, and around Hungnam and Wonsan in the east

URBANIZATION:

urban population: 62.1% of total population (2019)

rate of urbanization: 0.82% annual rate of change (2015-20 est.)

MAJOR URBAN AREAS - POPULATION:

3.061 million PYONGYANG (capital) (2019)

SEX RATIO:

at birth: 1.06 male(s)/female

0-14 years: 1.04 male(s)/female

15-24 years: 1.01 male(s)/female

25-54 years: 1.01 male(s)/female

55-64 years: 0.9 male(s)/female

65 years and over: 0.52 male(s)/female

total population: 0.94 male(s)/female (2018 est.)

MATERNAL MORTALITY RATE:

89 deaths/100,000 live births (2017 est.)

country comparison to the world: 74

INFANT MORTALITY RATE:

total: 21.4 deaths/1,000 live births (2018 est.)

male: 23.8 deaths/1,000 live births

female: 18.9 deaths/1,000 live births

country comparison to the world: 75

LIFE EXPECTANCY AT BIRTH:

total population: 71 years (2018 est.)

male: 67.2 years

female: 75 years

country comparison to the world: 158

TOTAL FERTILITY RATE:

1.94 children born/woman (2018 est.)

country comparison to the world: 127

CONTRACEPTIVE PREVALENCE RATE:

78.2% (2014)

note: percent of women aged 20-49

DRINKING WATER SOURCE:

improved:

urban: 99.9% of population

rural: 99.4% of population

total: 99.7% of population

unimproved:

urban: 0.1% of population

rural: 0.6% of population

total: 0.3% of population (2015 est.)

PHYSICIANS DENSITY:

3.67 physicians/1,000 population (2017)

HOSPITAL BED DENSITY:

13.2 beds/1,000 population (2012)

SANITATION FACILITY ACCESS:

improved:

urban: 87.9% of population (2015 est.)

rural: 72.5% of population (2015 est.)

total: 81.9% of population (2015 est.)

unimproved:

urban: 12.1% of population (2015 est.)

rural: 27.5% of population (2015 est.)

total: 18.1% of population (2015 est.)

HIV/AIDS - ADULT PREVALENCE RATE:

NA

HIV/AIDS - PEOPLE LIVING WITH HIV/AIDS:

NA

HIV/AIDS - DEATHS:

NA

OBESITY - ADULT PREVALENCE RATE:

6.8% (2016)

country comparison to the world: 163

CHILDREN UNDER THE AGE OF 5 YEARS UNDERWEIGHT:

9.3% (2017)

country comparison to the world: 67

EDUCATION EXPENDITURES:

NA

LITERACY:

definition: age 15 and over can read and write

total population: 100%

male: 100%

female: 100% (2015 est.)

SCHOOL LIFE EXPECTANCY (PRIMARY TO TERTIARY EDUCATION):

total: 11 years

male: 11 years

female: 11 years (2015)

GOVERNMENT :: KOREA, NORTH

COUNTRY NAME:

conventional long form: Democratic People's Republic of Korea

conventional short form: North Korea

local long form: Choson-minjujuui-inmin-konghwaguk

local short form: Choson

abbreviation: DPRK

etymology: derived from the Chinese name for Goryeo, which was the Korean dynasty that united the peninsula in the 10th century A.D.; the North Korean name "Choson" means "[Land of the] Morning Calm"

GOVERNMENT TYPE:

dictatorship, single-party state; official state ideology of "Juche" or "national self-reliance

CAPITAL:

name: Pyongyang

geographic coordinates: 39 01 N, 125 45 E

time difference: UTC+9 (14 hours ahead of Washington, DC, during Standard Time)

note: on 5 May 2018, North Korea reverted to UTC+9, the same time zone as South Korea

etymology: the name translates as "flat land" in Korean

ADMINISTRATIVE DIVISIONS:

9 provinces (do, singular and plural) and 3 cities (si, singular and plural)

provinces: Chagang, Hambuk (North Hamgyong), Hamnam (South Hamgyong), Hwangbuk (North Hwanghae), Hwangnam (South Hwanghae), Kangwon, P'yongbuk (North Pyongan), P'yongnam (South Pyongan), Ryanggang;

cities: Namp'o, P'yongyang, Rason

note: Namp'o is sometimes designated as a metropolitan city, P'yongyang as a directly controlled city, and Rason as a city

INDEPENDENCE:

15 August 1945 (from Japan)

NATIONAL HOLIDAY:

Founding of the Democratic People's Republic of Korea (DPRK), 9 September (1948)

CONSTITUTION:

history: previous 1948, 1972; latest adopted 1998 (during KIM Jong Il era)

amendments: proposed by the Supreme People's Assembly (SPA); passage requires more than two-thirds majority vote of the total SPA membership; revised 2009, 2012, 2013, 2016 (2019)

LEGAL SYSTEM:

civil law system based on the Prussian model; system influenced by Japanese traditions and Communist legal theory

INTERNATIONAL LAW ORGANIZATION PARTICIPATION:

has not submitted an ICJ jurisdiction declaration; non-party state to the ICCt

CITIZENSHIP:

citizenship by birth: no

citizenship by descent only: at least one parent must be a citizen of North Korea

dual citizenship recognized: no

residency requirement for naturalization: unknown

SUFFRAGE:

17 years of age; universal and compulsory

EXECUTIVE BRANCH:

chief of state: Supreme People's Assembly President CHOE Ryong Hae (since 11 April 2019); note - functions as the technical head of state and performs related duties, such as receiving ambassadors' credentials

head of government: State Affairs Commission Chairman KIM Jong Un (since 17 December 2011); note - functions as the commander-in-chief and chief executive cabinet: Cabinet or Naegak members appointed by the Supreme People's Assembly except the Minister of People's Armed Forces

elections/appointments: chief of state and premier indirectly elected by the Supreme People's Assembly; election last held on 9 March 2014 (next election NA)

election results: KIM Jong Un reelected unopposed

note: the Korean Workers' Party continues to list deceased leaders KIM Il Sung and KIM Jong Il as Eternal President and Eternal General Secretary respectively

LEGISLATIVE BRANCH:

description: unicameral Supreme People's Assembly or Ch'oego Inmin Hoeui (687 seats; members directly elected by majority vote in 2 rounds if needed to serve 5-year terms); note - the Korean Workers' Party selects all candidates

elections: last held on 10 March 2019 (next to be held March 2024)

election results: percent of vote by party - NA; seats by party - KWP 607, KSDP 50, Chondoist Chongu Party 22, General Association of Korean Residents in Japan (Chongryon) 5, religious associations 3; ruling party approves a list of candidates who are elected without opposition; composition - men 575, women 112, percent of women 16.3%

note: KWP, KSDP, Chondoist Chongu Party, and Chongryon are under the KWP's control; a token number of seats reserved for minor parties

JUDICIAL BRANCH:

highest courts: Supreme Court or Central Court (consists of one judge and 2 "People's Assessors" or, for some cases, 3 judges)

judge selection and term of office: judges elected by the Supreme People's Assembly for 5-year terms

subordinate courts: lower provincial courts as determined by the Supreme People's Assembly

POLITICAL PARTIES AND LEADERS:

major parties:
Korean Workers' Party or KWP [KIM Jong Un]
General Association of Korean Residents in Japan (Chongryon)
minor parties:
Chondoist Chongu Party (under KWP control)
Social Democratic Party or KSDP [KIM Yong Dae] (under KWP control)

INTERNATIONAL ORGANIZATION PARTICIPATION:

ARF, FAO, G-77, ICAO, ICRM, IFAD, IFRCS, IHO, IMO, IMSO, IOC, IPU, ISO, ITSO, ITU, NAM, UN, UNCTAD, UNESCO, UNIDO, UNWTO, UPU, WFTU (NGOs), WHO, WIPO, WMO

DIPLOMATIC REPRESENTATION IN THE US:

none; North Korea has a Permanent Mission to the UN in New York

DIPLOMATIC REPRESENTATION FROM THE US:

none; the Swedish Embassy in Pyongyang represents the US as consular protecting power

FLAG DESCRIPTION:

three horizontal bands of blue (top), red (triple width), and blue; the red band is edged in white; on the hoist side of the red band is a white disk with a red five-pointed star; the broad red band symbolizes revolutionary traditions; the narrow white bands stand for purity, strength, and dignity; the blue bands signify sovereignty, peace, and friendship; the red star represents socialism

NATIONAL SYMBOL(S):

red star, chollima (winged horse); national colors: red, white, blue

NATIONAL ANTHEM:

name: "Aegukka" (Patriotic Song)

lyrics/music: PAK Se Yong/KIM Won Gyun

note: adopted 1947; both North Korea's and South Korea's anthems share the same name and have a vaguely similar melody but have different lyrics; the North Korean anthem is also known as "Ach'imun pinnara" (Let Morning Shine)

ECONOMY :: KOREA, NORTH

ECONOMY - OVERVIEW:

North Korea, one of the world's most centrally directed and least open economies, faces chronic economic problems. Industrial capital stock is nearly beyond repair as a result of years of underinvestment, shortages of spare parts, and poor maintenance. Large-scale military spending and development of its ballistic missile and nuclear program severely draws off resources needed for investment and civilian consumption. Industrial and power outputs have stagnated for years at a fraction of pre-1990 levels. Frequent weather-related crop failures aggravated chronic food shortages caused by on-going systemic problems, including a lack of arable land, collective farming practices, poor soil quality, insufficient fertilization, and persistent shortages of tractors and fuel.

The mid 1990s through mid-2000s were marked by severe famine and widespread starvation. Significant food aid was provided by the international community through 2009. Since that time, food assistance has declined significantly. In the last few years, domestic corn and rice production has improved, although domestic production does not fully satisfy demand. A large portion of the population continues to suffer from prolonged malnutrition and poor living conditions. Since 2002, the government has allowed semi-private markets to begin selling a wider range of goods, allowing North Koreans to partially make up for diminished public distribution system rations. It also implemented changes in the management process of communal farms in an effort to boost agricultural output.

In December 2009, North Korea carried out a redenomination of its currency, capping the amount of North Korean won that could be exchanged for the new notes, and limiting the exchange to a one-week window. A concurrent crackdown on markets and foreign currency use yielded severe shortages and inflation, forcing Pyongyang to ease the restrictions by February 2010. In response to the sinking of the South Korean warship Cheonan and the shelling of Yeonpyeong Island in 2010, South Korea's government cut off most aid, trade, and bilateral cooperation activities. In February 2016, South Korea ceased its remaining bilateral economic activity by closing the Kaesong Industrial Complex in response to North Korea's fourth nuclear test a month earlier. This nuclear test and another in September 2016 resulted in two United Nations Security Council Resolutions that targeted North Korea's foreign currency earnings, particularly coal and other mineral exports. Throughout 2017, North Korea's continued nuclear and missile tests led to a tightening of UN sanctions, resulting in full sectoral bans on DPRK exports and drastically limited key imports. Over the last decade, China has been North Korea's primary trading partner.

The North Korean Government continues to stress its goal of improving the overall standard of living, but has taken few steps to make that goal a reality for its populace. In 2016, the regime used two mass mobilizations — one totaling 70 days and another 200 days — to spur the population to increase production and complete construction projects quickly. The regime released a five-year economic development strategy in May 2016 that outlined plans for promoting growth across sectors. Firm political control remains the government's overriding concern, which likely will inhibit formal changes to North Korea's current economic system.

GDP (PURCHASING POWER PARITY):
$40 billion (2015 est.)

$40 billion (2014 est.)

$40 billion (2013 est.)

note: data are in 2015 US dollars North Korea does not publish reliable National Income Accounts data; the data shown are derived from purchasing power parity (PPP) GDP estimates that were made by Angus MADDISON in a study conducted for the OECD; his figure for 1999 was extrapolated to 2015 using estimated real growth rates for North Korea's GDP and an inflation factor based on the US GDP deflator; the results were rounded to the nearest $10 billion.

country comparison to the world: 117

GDP (OFFICIAL EXCHANGE RATE):
$28 billion (2013 est.) (2013 est.)

GDP - REAL GROWTH RATE:
-1.1% (2015 est.)

1% (2014 est.)

1.1% (2013 est.)

country comparison to the world: 204

GDP - PER CAPITA (PPP):
$1,700 (2015 est.)

$1,800 (2014 est.)

$1,800 (2013 est.)

note: data are in 2015 US dollars

country comparison to the world: 214

GROSS NATIONAL SAVING:
NA

GDP - COMPOSITION, BY END USE:
household consumption: NA (2014 est.)

government consumption: NA (2014 est.)

investment in fixed capital: NA (2014 est.)

investment in inventories: NA (2014 est.)

exports of goods and services: 5.9% (2016 est.)

imports of goods and services: -11.1% (2016 est.)

GDP - COMPOSITION, BY SECTOR OF ORIGIN:
agriculture: 22.5% (2017 est.)

industry: 47.6% (2017 est.)

services: 29.9% (2017 est.)

AGRICULTURE - PRODUCTS:
rice, corn, potatoes, wheat, soybeans, pulses, beef, pork, eggs, fruit, nuts

INDUSTRIES:
military products; machine building, electric power, chemicals; mining (coal, iron ore, limestone, magnesite, graphite, copper, zinc, lead, and precious metals), metallurgy; textiles, food processing; tourism

INDUSTRIAL PRODUCTION GROWTH RATE:
1% (2017 est.)

country comparison to the world: 156

LABOR FORCE:
14 million (2014 est.)

note: estimates vary widely

country comparison to the world: 41

LABOR FORCE - BY OCCUPATION:
agriculture: 37%

industry: 63% (2008 est.)

UNEMPLOYMENT RATE:
25.6% (2013 est.)

25.5% (2012 est.)

country comparison to the world: 197

POPULATION BELOW POVERTY LINE:
NA

HOUSEHOLD INCOME OR CONSUMPTION BY PERCENTAGE SHARE:
lowest 10%: NA

highest 10%: NA

BUDGET:
revenues: 3.2 billion (2007 est.)

expenditures: 3.3 billion (2007 est.)

TAXES AND OTHER REVENUES:
11.4% (of GDP) (2007 est.)

note: excludes earnings from state-operated enterprises

country comparison to the world: 209

BUDGET SURPLUS (+) OR DEFICIT (-):
-0.4% (of GDP) (2007 est.)

country comparison to the world: 58

FISCAL YEAR:
calendar year

INFLATION RATE (CONSUMER PRICES):
NA

EXPORTS:
$45.82 billion (2017 est.)

$2.908 billion (2015 est.)

country comparison to the world: 53

EXPORTS - PARTNERS:
China 86.3% (2017)

EXPORTS - COMMODITIES:
minerals, metallurgical products, manufactures (including armaments), textiles, agricultural and fishery products

IMPORTS:
$43.75 billion (2018 est.)

$3.86 billion (2016 est.)

country comparison to the world: 58

IMPORTS - COMMODITIES:
petroleum, coking coal, machinery and equipment, textiles, grain

IMPORTS - PARTNERS:
China 91.9% (2017)

DEBT - EXTERNAL:
$5 billion (2013 est.)

country comparison to the world: 132

STOCK OF DIRECT FOREIGN INVESTMENT - AT HOME:
$1.878 billion (31 December 2015 est.)

$1.9 billion (31 December 2013 est.)

country comparison to the world: 120

EXCHANGE RATES:
North Korean won (KPW) per US dollar (average market rate)

135 (2017 est.)

130 (2016 est.)

130 (2015 est.)

98.5 (2013 est.)

155.5 (2012 est.)

ENERGY :: KOREA, NORTH

ELECTRICITY ACCESS:

population without electricity: 19 million (2017)

electrification - total population: 26% (2016)

electrification - urban areas: 36% (2016)

electrification - rural areas: 11% (2016)

ELECTRICITY - PRODUCTION:

16.57 billion kWh (2016 est.)

country comparison to the world: 87

ELECTRICITY - CONSUMPTION:

13.89 billion kWh (2016 est.)

country comparison to the world: 83

ELECTRICITY - EXPORTS:

0 kWh (2016 est.)

country comparison to the world: 154

ELECTRICITY - IMPORTS:

0 kWh (2016 est.)

country comparison to the world: 165

ELECTRICITY - INSTALLED GENERATING CAPACITY:

10.01 million kW (2016 est.)

country comparison to the world: 60

ELECTRICITY - FROM FOSSIL FUELS:

45% of total installed capacity (2016 est.)

country comparison to the world: 161

ELECTRICITY - FROM NUCLEAR FUELS:

0% of total installed capacity (2017 est.)

country comparison to the world: 120

ELECTRICITY - FROM HYDROELECTRIC PLANTS:

55% of total installed capacity (2017 est.)

country comparison to the world: 31

ELECTRICITY - FROM OTHER RENEWABLE SOURCES:

0% of total installed capacity (2017 est.)

country comparison to the world: 195

CRUDE OIL - PRODUCTION:

0 bbl/day (2018 est.)

country comparison to the world: 156

CRUDE OIL - EXPORTS:

0 bbl/day (2015 est.)

country comparison to the world: 147

CRUDE OIL - IMPORTS:

10,640 bbl/day (2015 est.)

country comparison to the world: 72

CRUDE OIL - PROVED RESERVES:

0 bbl (1 January 2018 est.)

country comparison to the world: 152

REFINED PETROLEUM PRODUCTS - PRODUCTION:

11,270 bbl/day (2015 est.)

country comparison to the world: 99

REFINED PETROLEUM PRODUCTS - CONSUMPTION:

18,000 bbl/day (2016 est.)

country comparison to the world: 145

REFINED PETROLEUM PRODUCTS - EXPORTS:

0 bbl/day (2015 est.)

country comparison to the world: 168

REFINED PETROLEUM PRODUCTS - IMPORTS:

8,260 bbl/day (2015 est.)

country comparison to the world: 151

NATURAL GAS - PRODUCTION:

0 cu m (2017 est.)

country comparison to the world: 152

NATURAL GAS - CONSUMPTION:

0 cu m (2017 est.)

country comparison to the world: 163

NATURAL GAS - EXPORTS:

0 cu m (2017 est.)

country comparison to the world: 130

NATURAL GAS - IMPORTS:

0 cu m (2017 est.)

country comparison to the world: 144

NATURAL GAS - PROVED RESERVES:

0 cu m (1 January 2014 est.)

country comparison to the world: 153

CARBON DIOXIDE EMISSIONS FROM CONSUMPTION OF ENERGY:

27.83 million Mt (2017 est.)

country comparison to the world: 74

COMMUNICATIONS :: KOREA, NORTH

TELEPHONES - FIXED LINES:

total subscriptions: 1.18 million

subscriptions per 100 inhabitants: 5 (July 2016 est.)

country comparison to the world: 71

TELEPHONES - MOBILE CELLULAR:

total subscriptions: 3.606 million

subscriptions per 100 inhabitants: 14 (July 2016 est.)

country comparison to the world: 133

TELEPHONE SYSTEM:

general assessment: nationwide fiber-optic network; mobile-cellular service expanded beyond Pyongyang; infrastructure underdeveloped yet growing mobile penetration by means of foreign investment; low broadband penetration; mobile penetration in North Korea believed to stay well below other Asian nations due to govt restrictions; 3G network deployed among universal population coverage (2018)

domestic: fiber-optic links installed down to the county level; telephone directories unavailable; mobile service launched in late 2008 for the Pyongyang area and considerable progress in expanding to other parts of the country since; fixed-lines are 5 per 100 and mobile-cellular 14 per 100 persons (2018)

international: country code - 850; satellite earth stations - 2 (1 Intelsat - Indian Ocean, 1 Russian - Indian Ocean region); other international connections through Moscow and Beijing

BROADCAST MEDIA:

no independent media; radios and TVs are pre-tuned to government stations; 4 government-owned TV stations; the Korean Workers' Party owns and operates the Korean Central Broadcasting Station, and the state-run Voice of Korea operates an external broadcast service; the government prohibits listening to and jams foreign broadcasts (2019)

INTERNET COUNTRY CODE:

.kp

MILITARY AND SECURITY :: KOREA, NORTH

MILITARY AND SECURITY FORCES:

Korean People's Army (KPA): KPA Ground Forces, KPA Navy, KPA Air Force (includes air defense), KPA Strategic Force (missile forces); Guard Command (protects the Kim family, other senior North Korean leadership figures, and government facilities in Pyongyang); Ministry of Public Security: Border Guards, civil security forces (2018)

MILITARY SERVICE AGE AND OBLIGATION:

17 years of age for compulsory male and female military service; service obligation 10 years for men, to age 23 for women (2015)

TRANSPORTATION :: KOREA, NORTH

NATIONAL AIR TRANSPORT SYSTEM:

number of registered air carriers: 1 (2015)

inventory of registered aircraft operated by air carriers: 17 (2015)

annual passenger traffic on registered air carriers: 223,418 (2015)

annual freight traffic on registered air carriers: 1,574,719 mt-km (2015)

CIVIL AIRCRAFT REGISTRATION COUNTRY CODE PREFIX:

P (2016)

AIRPORTS:

82 (2013)

country comparison to the world: 67

AIRPORTS - WITH PAVED RUNWAYS:

total: 39 (2017)

over 3,047 m: 3 (2017)

2,438 to 3,047 m: 22 (2017)

1,524 to 2,437 m: 8 (2017)

914 to 1,523 m: 2 (2017)

under 914 m: 4 (2017)

AIRPORTS - WITH UNPAVED RUNWAYS:

total: 43 (2013)

2,438 to 3,047 m: 3 (2013)

1,524 to 2,437 m: 17 (2013)

914 to 1,523 m: 15 (2013)

under 914 m: 8 (2013)

HELIPORTS:

23 (2013)

PIPELINES:

6 km oil (2013)

RAILWAYS:

total: 7,435 km (2014)

standard gauge: 7,435 km 1.435-m gauge (5,400 km electrified) (2014)

note: figures are approximate; some narrow-gauge railway also exists

country comparison to the world: 29

ROADWAYS:

total: 25,554 km (2006)

paved: 724 km (2006)

unpaved: 24,830 km (2006)

country comparison to the world: 102

WATERWAYS:

2,250 km (most navigable only by small craft) (2011)

country comparison to the world: 37

MERCHANT MARINE:

total: 274

by type: bulk carrier 8, container ship 5, general cargo 198, oil tanker 31, other 32 (2018)

country comparison to the world: 52

PORTS AND TERMINALS:

major seaport(s): Ch'ongjin, Haeju, Hungnam, Namp'o, Songnim, Sonbong (formerly Unggi), Wonsan

TRANSNATIONAL ISSUES :: KOREA, NORTH

DISPUTES - INTERNATIONAL:

risking arrest, imprisonment, and deportation, tens of thousands of North Koreans cross into China to escape famine, economic privation, and political oppression; North Korea and China dispute the sovereignty of certain islands in Yalu and Tumen Rivers; Military Demarcation Line within the 4-km-wide Demilitarized Zone has separated North from South Korea since 1953; periodic incidents in the Yellow Sea with South Korea which claims the Northern Limiting Line as a maritime boundary; North Korea supports South Korea in rejecting Japan's claim to Liancourt Rocks (Tok-do/Take-shima)

REFUGEES AND INTERNALLY DISPLACED PERSONS:

IDPs: undetermined (periodic flooding and famine during mid-1990s) (2017)

TRAFFICKING IN PERSONS:

current situation: North Korea is a source country for men, women, and children who are subjected to forced labor and sex trafficking; many North Korean workers recruited to work abroad under bilateral contracts with foreign governments, most often Russia and China, are subjected to forced labor and do not have a choice in the work the government assigns them, are not free to change jobs, and face government reprisals if they try to escape or complain to outsiders; tens of thousands of North Koreans, including children, held in prison camps are subjected to forced labor, including logging, mining, and farming; many North Korean women and girls, lured by promises of food, jobs, and freedom, have migrated to China illegally to escape poor social and economic conditions only to be forced into prostitution, domestic service, or agricultural work through forced marriages

tier rating: Tier 3 - North Korea does not fully comply with minimum standards for the elimination of trafficking and is not making significant efforts to do so; the government continued to participate in human trafficking through its use of domestic forced labor camps and the provision of forced labor to foreign governments through bilateral contracts; officials did not demonstrate any efforts to address human trafficking through prosecution, protection, or prevention measures; no known investigations, prosecutions, or convictions of trafficking offenders or officials complicit in trafficking-related offenses were conducted; the government also made no efforts to identify or protect trafficking victims and did not permit NGOs to assist victims (2015)

ILLICIT DRUGS:

at present there is insufficient information to determine the current level of involvement of government officials in the production or trafficking of illicit drugs, but for years, from the 1970s into the 2000s, citizens of the Democratic People's Republic of (North) Korea (DPRK), many of them diplomatic employees of the government, were apprehended abroad while trafficking in narcotics; police investigations in Taiwan and Japan in recent years have linked North Korea to large illicit shipments of heroin and methamphetamine

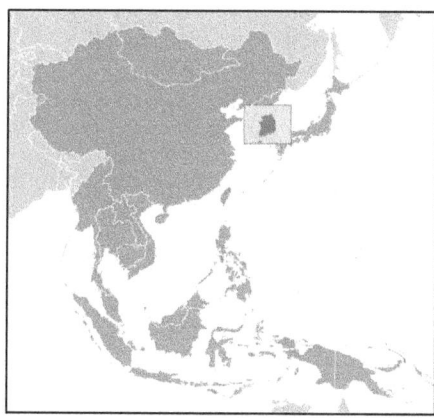

EAST ASIA / SOUTHEAST ASIA :: KOREA, SOUTH

INTRODUCTION :: KOREA, SOUTH

BACKGROUND:

An independent kingdom for much of its long history, Korea was occupied by Japan beginning in 1905 following the Russo-Japanese War. In 1910, Tokyo formally annexed the entire Peninsula. Korea regained its independence following Japan's surrender to the US in 1945. After World War II, a democratic government (Republic of Korea, ROK) was set up in the southern half of the Korean Peninsula while a communist-style government was installed in the north (Democratic People's Republic of Korea, DPRK). During the Korean War (1950-53), US troops and UN forces fought alongside ROK soldiers to defend South Korea from a DPRK invasion supported by communist China and the Soviet Union. A 1953 armistice split the Peninsula along a demilitarized zone at about the 38th parallel. PARK Chung-hee took over leadership of the country in a 1961 coup. During his regime, from 1961 to 1979, South Korea achieved rapid economic growth, with per capita income rising to roughly 17 times the level of North Korea in 1979.

South Korea held its first free presidential election under a revised democratic constitution in 1987, with former ROK Army general ROH Tae-woo winning a close race. In 1993, KIM Young-sam (1993-98) became the first civilian president of South Korea's new democratic era. President KIM Dae-jung (1998-2003) won the Nobel Peace Prize in 2000 for his contributions to South Korean democracy and his "Sunshine" policy of engagement with North Korea. President PARK Geun-hye, daughter of former ROK President PARK Chung-hee, took office in February 2013 as South Korea's first female leader. In December 2016, the National Assembly passed an impeachment motion against President PARK over her alleged involvement in a corruption and influence-peddling scandal, immediately suspending her presidential authorities. The impeachment was upheld in March 2017, triggering an early presidential election in May 2017 won by MOON Jae-in. South Korea hosted the Winter Olympic and Paralympic Games in February 2018, in which North Korea also participated. Discord with North Korea has permeated inter-Korean relations for much of the past decade, highlighted by the North's attacks on a South Korean ship and island in 2010, the exchange of artillery fire across the DMZ in 2015, and multiple nuclear and missile tests in 2016 and 2017. North Korea's participation in the Winter Olympics, dispatch of a senior delegation to Seoul, and three inter-Korean summits in 2018 appear to have ushered in a temporary period of respite, buoyed by the historic US-DPRK summits in 2018 and 2019.

GEOGRAPHY :: KOREA, SOUTH

LOCATION:

Eastern Asia, southern half of the Korean Peninsula bordering the Sea of Japan and the Yellow Sea

GEOGRAPHIC COORDINATES:

37 00 N, 127 30 E

MAP REFERENCES:

Asia

AREA:

total: 99,720 sq km

land: 96,920 sq km

water: 2,800 sq km

country comparison to the world: 110

AREA - COMPARATIVE:

slightly smaller than Pennsylvania; slightly larger than Indiana

LAND BOUNDARIES:

total: 237 km

border countries (1): North Korea 237 km

COASTLINE:

2,413 km

MARITIME CLAIMS:

territorial sea: 12 nm; between 3 nm and 12 nm in the Korea Strait

exclusive economic zone: 200 nm

contiguous zone: 24 nm

continental shelf: not specified

CLIMATE:

temperate, with rainfall heavier in summer than winter; cold winters

TERRAIN:

mostly hills and mountains; wide coastal plains in west and south

ELEVATION:

mean elevation: 282 m

lowest point: Sea of Japan 0 m

highest point: Halla-san 1,950 m

NATURAL RESOURCES:

coal, tungsten, graphite, molybdenum, lead, hydropower potential

LAND USE:

agricultural land: 18.1% (2011 est.)

arable land: 15.3% (2011 est.) / permanent crops: 2.2% (2011 est.) / permanent pasture: 0.6% (2011 est.)

forest: 63.9% (2011 est.)

other: 18% (2011 est.)

IRRIGATED LAND:

7,780 sq km (2012)

POPULATION DISTRIBUTION:

with approximately 70% of the country considered mountainous, the country's population is primarily concentrated in the lowland areas, where density is quite high; Gyeonggi Province in the northwest, which surrounds the capital of Seoul and contains the port of Incheon, is the most densely populated province; Gangwon in the northeast is the least populated

NATURAL HAZARDS:

occasional typhoons bring high winds and floods; low-level seismic activity common in southwest

volcanism: Halla (1,950 m) is considered historically active although it has not erupted in many centuries

ENVIRONMENT - CURRENT ISSUES:

air pollution in large cities; acid rain; water pollution from the discharge of sewage and industrial effluents; drift net fishing; solid waste disposal; transboundary pollution

ENVIRONMENT - INTERNATIONAL AGREEMENTS:

party to: Antarctic-Environmental Protocol, Antarctic-Marine Living Resources, Antarctic Treaty, Biodiversity, Climate Change, Climate Change-Kyoto Protocol, Desertification, Endangered Species, Environmental Modification, Hazardous Wastes, Law of the Sea, Marine Dumping, Ozone Layer Protection, Ship Pollution, Tropical Timber 83, Tropical Timber 94, Wetlands, Whaling

signed, but not ratified: none of the selected agreements

GEOGRAPHY - NOTE:

strategic location on Korea Strait; about 3,000 mostly small and uninhabited islands lie off the western and southern coasts

PEOPLE AND SOCIETY :: KOREA, SOUTH

POPULATION:

51,418,097 (July 2018 est.)

country comparison to the world: 27

NATIONALITY:

noun: Korean(s)

adjective: Korean

ETHNIC GROUPS:

homogeneous

LANGUAGES:

Korean, English (widely taught in elementary, junior high, and high school)

RELIGIONS:

Protestant 19.7%, Buddhist 15.5%, Catholic 7.9%, none 56.9% (2015 est.)

note: many people also carry on at least some Confucian traditions and practices

AGE STRUCTURE:

0-14 years: 13.03% (male 3,448,627 /female 3,251,786)

15-24 years: 12.19% (male 3,295,814 /female 2,970,439)

25-54 years: 45.13% (male 11,986,760 /female 11,220,268)

55-64 years: 15.09% (male 3,825,127 /female 3,935,700)

65 years and over: 14.55% (male 3,202,232 /female 4,281,344) (2018 est.)

DEPENDENCY RATIOS:

total dependency ratio: 36.7 (2015 est.)

youth dependency ratio: 19 (2015 est.)

elderly dependency ratio: 17.7 (2015 est.)

potential support ratio: 5.6 (2015 est.)

MEDIAN AGE:

total: 42.3 years (2018 est.)

male: 40.6 years

female: 44 years

country comparison to the world: 33

POPULATION GROWTH RATE:

0.44% (2018 est.)

country comparison to the world: 157

BIRTH RATE:

8.3 births/1,000 population (2018 est.)

country comparison to the world: 219

DEATH RATE:

6.3 deaths/1,000 population (2018 est.)

country comparison to the world: 151

NET MIGRATION RATE:

2.4 migrant(s)/1,000 population (2018 est.)

country comparison to the world: 43

POPULATION DISTRIBUTION:

with approximately 70% of the country considered mountainous, the country's population is primarily concentrated in the lowland areas, where density is quite high; Gyeonggi Province in the northwest, which surrounds the capital of Seoul and contains the port of Incheon, is the most densely populated province; Gangwon in the northeast is the least populated

URBANIZATION:

urban population: 81.4% of total population (2019)

rate of urbanization: 0.3% annual rate of change (2015-20 est.)

MAJOR URBAN AREAS - POPULATION:

9.962 million SEOUL (capital), 3.466 million Busan, 2.783 million Incheon, 2.209 million Daegu (Taegu), 1.562 million Daejon (Taejon), 1.519 million Gwangju (Kwangju) (2019)

SEX RATIO:

at birth: 1.05 male(s)/female

0-14 years: 1.06 male(s)/female

15-24 years: 1.11 male(s)/female

25-54 years: 1.07 male(s)/female

55-64 years: 0.97 male(s)/female

65 years and over: 0.75 male(s)/female

total population: 1 male(s)/female (2018 est.)

MOTHER'S MEAN AGE AT FIRST BIRTH:

31 years (2014 est.)

MATERNAL MORTALITY RATE:

11 deaths/100,000 live births (2017 est.)

country comparison to the world: 142

INFANT MORTALITY RATE:

total: 3 deaths/1,000 live births (2018 est.)

male: 3.2 deaths/1,000 live births

female: 2.8 deaths/1,000 live births

LIFE EXPECTANCY AT BIRTH:

total population: 82.5 years (2018 est.)

male: 79.4 years

female: 85.8 years

country comparison to the world: 13

TOTAL FERTILITY RATE:

1.27 children born/woman (2018 est.)

country comparison to the world: 219

CONTRACEPTIVE PREVALENCE RATE:

79.6% (2015)

note: percent of women aged 20-49

DRINKING WATER SOURCE:

improved:

urban: 99.7% of population

rural: 87.9% of population

total: 97.8% of population

unimproved:

urban: 0.3% of population

rural: 12.1% of population

total: 2.2% of population (2012 est.)

CURRENT HEALTH EXPENDITURE:

7.3% (2016)

PHYSICIANS DENSITY:

2.37 physicians/1,000 population (2017)

HOSPITAL BED DENSITY:

11.5 beds/1,000 population (2015)

SANITATION FACILITY ACCESS:

improved:

urban: 100% of population (2015 est.)

rural: 100% of population (2015 est.)

total: 100% of population (2015 est.)

unimproved:

urban: 0% of population (2015 est.)

rural: 0% of population (2015 est.)

total: 0% of population (2015 est.)

HIV/AIDS - ADULT PREVALENCE RATE:

NA

HIV/AIDS - PEOPLE LIVING WITH HIV/AIDS:

NA

HIV/AIDS - DEATHS:

NA

OBESITY - ADULT PREVALENCE RATE:

4.7% (2016)

country comparison to the world: 184

CHILDREN UNDER THE AGE OF 5 YEARS UNDERWEIGHT:

0.7% (2010)

country comparison to the world: 124

EDUCATION EXPENDITURES:

5.3% of GDP (2015)

country comparison to the world: 51

SCHOOL LIFE EXPECTANCY (PRIMARY TO TERTIARY EDUCATION):

total: 17 years

male: 17 years

female: 16 years (2013)

UNEMPLOYMENT, YOUTH AGES 15-24:

total: 10.4%

male: 11.3%

female: 9.7% (2017 est.)

country comparison to the world: 126

GOVERNMENT :: KOREA, SOUTH

COUNTRY NAME:

conventional long form: Republic of Korea

conventional short form: South Korea

local long form: Taehan-min'guk

local short form: Han'guk

abbreviation: ROK

etymology: derived from the Chinese name for Goryeo, which was the Korean dynasty that united the peninsula in the 10th century A.D.; the South Korean name "Han'guk" derives from the long form, "Taehan-min'guk," which is itself a derivation from "Daehan-je'guk," which means "the Great Empire of the Han"; "Han" refers to the "Sam'han" or the "Three Han Kingdoms" (Goguryeo, Baekje, and Silla from the Three Kingdoms Era, 1st-7th centuries A.D.)

GOVERNMENT TYPE:

presidential republic

CAPITAL:

name: Seoul; note - Sejong, located some 120 km (75 mi) south of Seoul, is being developed as a new capital

geographic coordinates: 37 33 N, 126 59 E

time difference: UTC+9 (14 hours ahead of Washington, DC, during Standard Time)

etymology: the name originates from the Korean word meaning "capital city" and which is believed to be derived from Seorabeol, the name of the capital of the ancient Korean Kingdom of Silla

ADMINISTRATIVE DIVISIONS:

9 provinces (do, singular and plural), 6 metropolitan cities (gwangyeoksi, singular and plural), 1 special city (teugbyeolsi), and 1 special self-governing city (teukbyeoljachisi)

provinces: Chungbuk (North Chungcheong), Chungnam (South Chungcheong), Gangwon, Gyeongbuk (North Gyeongsang), Gyeonggi, Gyeongnam (South Gyeongsang), Jeju, Jeonbuk (North Jeolla), Jeonnam (South Jeolla);

metropolitan cities: Busan (Pusan), Daegu (Taegu), Daejeon (Taejon), Gwangju (Kwangju), Incheon (Inch'on), Ulsan;

special city: Seoul;

special self-governing city: Sejong

INDEPENDENCE:

15 August 1945 (from Japan)

NATIONAL HOLIDAY:

Liberation Day, 15 August (1945)

CONSTITUTION:

history: several previous; latest passed by National Assembly 12 October 1987, approved in referendum 28 October 1987, effective 25 February 1988

amendments: proposed by the president or by majority support of the National Assembly membership; passage requires at least two-thirds majority vote by the Assembly membership, approval in a referendum by more than one half of the votes by more than one half of eligible voters, and promulgation by the president; amended several times, last in 1987; note - an amendment proposed in March 2018 that would change the presidential term to 4 years and increase the term limit to 2 failed in the National Assembly vote in June 2018 (2018)

LEGAL SYSTEM:

mixed legal system combining European civil law, Anglo-American law, and Chinese classical thought

INTERNATIONAL LAW ORGANIZATION PARTICIPATION:

has not submitted an ICJ jurisdiction declaration; accepts ICCt jurisdiction

CITIZENSHIP:

citizenship by birth: no

citizenship by descent only: at least one parent must be a citizen of South Korea

dual citizenship recognized: no

residency requirement for naturalization: 5 years

SUFFRAGE:

19 years of age; universal

EXECUTIVE BRANCH:

chief of state: President MOON Jae-in (since 10 May 2017); note - President PARK Geun-hye (since 25 February 2013) was impeached by the National Assembly on 9 December 2016; PARK's impeachment was upheld by the Constitutional Court and she was removed from office on 9 March 2017

head of government: Prime Minister LEE Nak-yon (since 1 June 2017); Deputy Prime Ministers KIM Dong-yeon (since 9 June 2017), KIM Sang-kon (since 4 July 2017)

cabinet: State Council appointed by the president on the prime minister's recommendation

elections/appointments: president directly elected by simple majority popular vote for a single 5-year term; election last held on 9 May 2017 (next to be held in 2022); prime minister appointed by president with consent of National Assembly

election results: MOON Jae-in elected president; percent of vote - MOON Jae-in (DP) 41.1%, HONG Joon-pyo (LKP) 25.5%, AHN Cheol-soo (PP) 21.4%, other 12%

LEGISLATIVE BRANCH:

description: unicameral National Assembly or Kuk Hoe (300 seats statutory, 299 for current term); 253 members directly elected in single-seat constituencies by simple majority vote and 47 directly elected in a single national constituency by proportional representation vote; members serve 4-year terms)

elections: last held on 13 April 2016 (next to be held on 15 April 2020)

election results: percent of vote by party - NFP 33.5%, PP 26.7%, MPK 25.5%, JP 7.2%, other 7.1%; seats by party - MPK 123, NFP 122, PP 38, JP 6, independent 11

note: as of October 2019, seats by party - DP 128, LKP 110, BFP 28, JP 6, PDP 4, ORP 2, MP 1, independent 18

JUDICIAL BRANCH:

highest courts: Supreme Court of South Korea (consists of a chief justice and 13 justices); Constitutional Court (consists of a court head and 8 justices)

judge selection and term of office: Supreme Court chief justice appointed by the president with the consent of the National Assembly; other justices appointed by the president upon the recommendation of the chief justice and consent of the National Assembly; position of the chief justice is a 6-year nonrenewable term; other justices serve 6-year renewable terms; Constitutional Court justices appointed - 3 by the president, 3 by the National Assembly, and 3 by the Supreme Court chief justice; court head serves until retirement at age 70, while other justices serve 6-year renewable terms with mandatory retirement at age 65

subordinate courts: High Courts; District Courts; Branch Courts (organized under the District Courts); specialized courts for family and administrative issues

POLITICAL PARTIES AND LEADERS:

Bareun Future Party or BFP [PARK Joo-sun] (merger of Bareun Party and People's Party)
Democratic Party or DP [CHOO Mi-ae] (renamed from Minjoo Party of Korea or MPK in October 2016; formerly New Politics Alliance for Democracy or NPAD, which was a merger of the Democratic Party or DP (formerly DUP) [KIM Han-gil] and the New Political Vision Party or NPVP [AHN Cheol-soo] in March 2014)
Justice Party or JP [LEE Jeong-mi]
Liberty Korea Party or LKP (formerly the New Frontier Party (NFP) or Saenuri, previously the Grand National Party [HONG Jueen-Pyo])
Minjung Party or MP (formed from the merger of the New People's Party (formerly the New People's Political Party or NPP) and the People's United Party or PUP)
Our Republic Party [CHO Won-jin and HONG Moon-jong] (formerly Korean Patriots' Party or KPP)
Parliamentary Group for Peace and Justice [ROH Hoe-chan] (parliamentary group made up of PDP and JP)
Party for Democracy and Peace or PDP [CHO Bae-sook]
People's Party or PP [AHN Cheol-soo]

INTERNATIONAL ORGANIZATION PARTICIPATION:

ADB, AfDB (nonregional member), APEC, Arctic Council (observer), ARF, ASEAN (dialogue partner), Australia Group, BIS, CD, CICA, CP, EAS, EBRD, FAO, FATF, G-20, IADB, IAEA, IBRD, ICAO, ICC (national committees), ICCt, ICRM, IDA, IEA, IFAD, IFC, IFRCS, IHO, ILO, IMF, IMO, IMSO, Interpol, IOC, IOM, IPU, ISO, ITSO, ITU, ITUC (NGOs), LAIA (observer), MIGA, MINURSO, MINUSTAH, NEA, NSG, OAS (observer), OECD, OPCW, OSCE (partner), Pacific Alliance (observer), Paris Club (associate), PCA, PIF (partner), SAARC (observer), SICA (observer), UN, UNAMID, UNCTAD, UNESCO, UNHCR, UNIDO, UNIFIL, UNMIL, UNMISS, UNMOGIP, UNOCI, UNWTO, UPU, WCO, WHO, WIPO, WMO, WTO, ZC

DIPLOMATIC REPRESENTATION IN THE US:

Ambassador CHO Yoon-je (since 29 November 2017)

chancery: 2450 Massachusetts Avenue NW, Washington, DC 20008

telephone: [1] (202) 939-5600

FAX: [1] (202) 797-0595

consulate(s) general: Agana (Guam), Anchorage (AK), Atlanta, Boston, Chicago, Honolulu, Houston, Los Angeles, New York, San Francisco, Seattle

DIPLOMATIC REPRESENTATION FROM THE US:

chief of mission: Ambassador Harry HARRIS (since 10 July 2018)

telephone: [82] (2) 397-4114

embassy: 188 Sejong-daero, Jongno-gu, Seoul 03141

mailing address: US Embassy Seoul, 9600 Seoul Place Washington, D.C., 20521-9600

FAX: [82] (2) 725-0152

FLAG DESCRIPTION:

white with a red (top) and blue yin-yang symbol in the center; there is a different black trigram from the ancient I Ching (Book of Changes) in each corner of the white field; the South Korean national flag is called Taegukki; white is a traditional Korean color and represents peace and purity; the blue section represents the negative cosmic forces of the yin, while the red symbolizes the opposite positive forces of the yang; each trigram (kwae) denotes one of the four universal elements, which together express the principle of movement and harmony

NATIONAL SYMBOL(S):

taegeuk (yin yang symbol), Hibiscus syriacus (Rose of Sharon), Siberian tiger; national colors: red, white, blue, black

NATIONAL ANTHEM:

name: "Aegukga" (Patriotic Song)

lyrics/music: YUN Ch'i-Ho or AN Ch'ang-Ho/AHN Eaktay

note: adopted 1948, well-known by 1910; both North Korea's and South Korea's anthems share the same name and have a vaguely similar melody but have different lyrics

ECONOMY :: KOREA, SOUTH

ECONOMY - OVERVIEW:

After emerging from the 1950-53 war with North Korea, South Korea emerged as one of the 20th century's most remarkable economic success stories, becoming a developed, globally connected, high-technology society within decades. In the 1960s, GDP per capita was comparable with levels in the poorest countries in the world. In 2004, South Korea's GDP surpassed one trillion dollars.

Beginning in the 1960s under President PARK Chung-hee, the government promoted the import of raw materials and technology, encouraged saving and investment over consumption, kept wages low, and directed resources to export-oriented industries that remain important to the economy to this day. Growth surged under these policies, and frequently reached double-digits in the 1960s and 1970s. Growth gradually moderated in the 1990s as the economy matured, but remained strong enough to propel South Korea into the ranks of the advanced economies of the OECD by 1997. These policies also led to the emergence of family-owned chaebol conglomerates such as Daewoo, Hyundai, and Samsung, which retained their dominant positions even as the government loosened its grip on the economy amid the political changes of the 1980s and 1990s.

The Asian financial crisis of 1997-98 hit South Korea's companies hard because of their excessive reliance on short-term borrowing, and GDP ultimately plunged by 7% in 1998. South Korea tackled difficult economic reforms following the crisis, including restructuring some chaebols, increasing labor market flexibility, and opening up to more foreign investment and imports. These steps lead to a relatively rapid economic recovery. South Korea also began expanding its network of free trade agreements to help bolster exports, and has since implemented 16 free trade agreements covering 58 countries—including the United State and China—that collectively cover more than three-quarters of global GDP.

In 2017, the election of President MOON Jae-in brought a surge in consumer confidence, in part, because of his successful efforts to increase wages and government spending. These factors combined with an uptick in export growth to drive real GDP growth to more than 3%, despite disruptions in South Korea's trade with China over the deployment of a US missile defense system in South Korea.

In 2018 and beyond, South Korea will contend with gradually slowing economic growth - in the 2-3% range - not uncommon for advanced economies. This could be partially offset by efforts to address challenges arising from its rapidly aging population, inflexible labor market, continued dominance of the chaebols, and heavy reliance on exports rather than domestic consumption. Socioeconomic problems also persist, and include rising inequality, poverty among the elderly, high youth unemployment, long working hours, low worker productivity, and corruption.

GDP (PURCHASING POWER PARITY):

$2.035 trillion (2017 est.)

$1.974 trillion (2016 est.)

$1.918 trillion (2015 est.)

note: data are in 2017 dollars

country comparison to the world: 14

GDP (OFFICIAL EXCHANGE RATE):

$1.54 trillion (2017 est.)

GDP - REAL GROWTH RATE:

3.1% (2017 est.)

2.9% (2016 est.)

2.8% (2015 est.)

country comparison to the world: 109

GDP - PER CAPITA (PPP):

$39,500 (2017 est.)

$38,500 (2016 est.)

$37,600 (2015 est.)

note: data are in 2017 dollars

country comparison to the world: 46

GROSS NATIONAL SAVING:

36.6% of GDP (2017 est.)

36.3% of GDP (2016 est.)

36.6% of GDP (2015 est.)

country comparison to the world: 15

GDP - COMPOSITION, BY END USE:

household consumption: 48.1% (2017 est.)

government consumption: 15.3% (2017 est.)

investment in fixed capital: 31.1% (2017 est.)

investment in inventories: 0% (2017 est.)

exports of goods and services: 43.1% (2017 est.)

imports of goods and services: -37.7% (2017 est.)

GDP - COMPOSITION, BY SECTOR OF ORIGIN:

agriculture: 2.2% (2017 est.)

industry: 39.3% (2017 est.)

services: 58.3% (2017 est.)

AGRICULTURE - PRODUCTS:

rice, root crops, barley, vegetables, fruit, cattle, pigs, chickens, milk, eggs, fish

INDUSTRIES:

electronics, telecommunications, automobile production, chemicals, shipbuilding, steel

INDUSTRIAL PRODUCTION GROWTH RATE:

4.6% (2017 est.)

country comparison to the world: 63

LABOR FORCE:

27.75 million (2017 est.)

country comparison to the world: 23

LABOR FORCE - BY OCCUPATION:

agriculture: 4.8%

industry: 24.6%

services: 70.6% (2017 est.)

UNEMPLOYMENT RATE:

3.7% (2017 est.)

3.7% (2016 est.)

country comparison to the world: 45

POPULATION BELOW POVERTY LINE:

14.4% (2016 est.)

HOUSEHOLD INCOME OR CONSUMPTION BY PERCENTAGE SHARE:

lowest 10%: 6.8%

highest 10%: 48.5% (2015 est.)

DISTRIBUTION OF FAMILY INCOME - GINI INDEX:

35.7 (2016 est.)

35.4 (2015 est.)

country comparison to the world: 94

BUDGET:

revenues: 357.1 billion (2017 est.)

expenditures: 335.8 billion (2017 est.)

TAXES AND OTHER REVENUES:

23.2% (of GDP) (2017 est.)

country comparison to the world: 129

BUDGET SURPLUS (+) OR DEFICIT (-):

1.4% (of GDP) (2017 est.)

country comparison to the world: 24

PUBLIC DEBT:

39.5% of GDP (2017 est.)

39.9% of GDP (2016 est.)

country comparison to the world: 133

FISCAL YEAR:

calendar year

INFLATION RATE (CONSUMER PRICES):

1.9% (2017 est.)

1% (2016 est.)

country comparison to the world: 97

CENTRAL BANK DISCOUNT RATE:

1.5% (31 December 2017 est.)

1.25% (31 December 2016 est.)

country comparison to the world: 126

COMMERCIAL BANK PRIME LENDING RATE:

3.48% (31 December 2017 est.)

3.37% (31 December 2016 est.)

country comparison to the world: 170

STOCK OF NARROW MONEY:

$793.9 billion (31 December 2017 est.)

$658.7 billion (31 December 2016 est.)

country comparison to the world: 8

STOCK OF BROAD MONEY:

$793.9 billion (31 December 2017 est.)

$658.7 billion (31 December 2016 est.)

country comparison to the world: 8

STOCK OF DOMESTIC CREDIT:

$2.986 trillion (31 December 2017 est.)

$2.515 trillion (31 December 2016 est.)

country comparison to the world: 9

MARKET VALUE OF PUBLICLY TRADED SHARES:

$1.305 trillion (31 December 2016 est.)

$1.28 trillion (31 December 2015 est.)

$1.269 trillion (31 December 2014 est.)

country comparison to the world: 11

CURRENT ACCOUNT BALANCE:

$78.46 billion (2017 est.)

$99.24 billion (2016 est.)

country comparison to the world: 6

EXPORTS:

$577.4 billion (2017 est.)

$512 billion (2016 est.)

country comparison to the world: 5

EXPORTS - PARTNERS:

China 25.1%, US 12.2%, Vietnam 8.2%, Hong Kong 6.9%, Japan 4.7% (2017)

EXPORTS - COMMODITIES:

semiconductors, petrochemicals, automobile/auto parts, ships, wireless communication equipment, flat displays, steel, electronics, plastics, computers

IMPORTS:

$457.5 billion (2017 est.)

$393.1 billion (2016 est.)

country comparison to the world: 9

IMPORTS - COMMODITIES:

crude oil/petroleum products, semiconductors, natural gas, coal, steel, computers, wireless communication equipment, automobiles, fine chemicals, textiles

IMPORTS - PARTNERS:

China 20.5%, Japan 11.5%, US 10.5%, Germany 4.2%, Saudi Arabia 4.1% (2017)

RESERVES OF FOREIGN EXCHANGE AND GOLD:

$389.2 billion (31 December 2017 est.)

$371.1 billion (31 December 2016 est.)

country comparison to the world: 9

DEBT - EXTERNAL:

$384.6 billion (31 December 2017 est.)

$384.1 billion (31 December 2016 est.)

country comparison to the world: 29

STOCK OF DIRECT FOREIGN INVESTMENT - AT HOME:

$230.6 billion (31 December 2017 est.)

$180.1 billion (31 December 2016 est.)

country comparison to the world: 29

STOCK OF DIRECT FOREIGN INVESTMENT - ABROAD:

$344.7 billion (31 December 2017 est.)

$358 billion (31 December 2016 est.)

country comparison to the world: 20

EXCHANGE RATES:

South Korean won (KRW) per US dollar -

1,130.48 (2017 est.)

1,160.41 (2016 est.)

1,160.77 (2015 est.)

1,130.95 (2014 est.)

1,052.96 (2013 est.)

ENERGY :: KOREA, SOUTH

ELECTRICITY ACCESS:

electrification - total population: 100% (2016)

ELECTRICITY - PRODUCTION:

526 billion kWh (2016 est.)

country comparison to the world: 10

ELECTRICITY - CONSUMPTION:

507.6 billion kWh (2016 est.)

country comparison to the world: 9

ELECTRICITY - EXPORTS:

0 kWh (2016 est.)

country comparison to the world: 155

ELECTRICITY - IMPORTS:

0 kWh (2016 est.)

country comparison to the world: 166

ELECTRICITY - INSTALLED GENERATING CAPACITY:

111.2 million kW (2016 est.)

country comparison to the world: 11

ELECTRICITY - FROM FOSSIL FUELS:

70% of total installed capacity (2016 est.)

country comparison to the world: 109

ELECTRICITY - FROM NUCLEAR FUELS:

21% of total installed capacity (2017 est.)

country comparison to the world: 7
ELECTRICITY - FROM HYDROELECTRIC PLANTS:
2% of total installed capacity (2017 est.)

country comparison to the world: 139
ELECTRICITY - FROM OTHER RENEWABLE SOURCES:
8% of total installed capacity (2017 est.)

country comparison to the world: 86
CRUDE OIL - PRODUCTION:
0 bbl/day (2018 est.)

country comparison to the world: 157
CRUDE OIL - EXPORTS:
0 bbl/day (2017 est.)

country comparison to the world: 148
CRUDE OIL - IMPORTS:
3.057 million bbl/day (2017 est.)

country comparison to the world: 5
CRUDE OIL - PROVED RESERVES:
NA (1 January 2017 est.)

REFINED PETROLEUM PRODUCTS - PRODUCTION:
3.302 million bbl/day (2017 est.)

country comparison to the world: 6
REFINED PETROLEUM PRODUCTS - CONSUMPTION:
2.584 million bbl/day (2017 est.)

country comparison to the world: 8
REFINED PETROLEUM PRODUCTS - EXPORTS:
1.396 million bbl/day (2017 est.)

country comparison to the world: 6
REFINED PETROLEUM PRODUCTS - IMPORTS:
908,800 bbl/day (2017 est.)

country comparison to the world: 6
NATURAL GAS - PRODUCTION:
339.8 million cu m (2017 est.)

country comparison to the world: 76
NATURAL GAS - CONSUMPTION:
45.28 billion cu m (2017 est.)

country comparison to the world: 18
NATURAL GAS - EXPORTS:
0 cu m (2017 est.)

country comparison to the world: 131
NATURAL GAS - IMPORTS:
48.65 billion cu m (2017 est.)

country comparison to the world: 9
NATURAL GAS - PROVED RESERVES:
7.079 billion cu m (1 January 2018 est.)

country comparison to the world: 82
CARBON DIOXIDE EMISSIONS FROM CONSUMPTION OF ENERGY:
778.4 million Mt (2017 est.)

country comparison to the world: 7

COMMUNICATIONS :: KOREA, SOUTH

TELEPHONES - FIXED LINES:
total subscriptions: 26,842,952
subscriptions per 100 inhabitants: 52 (2017 est.)

country comparison to the world: 10
TELEPHONES - MOBILE CELLULAR:
total subscriptions: 63,658,688
subscriptions per 100 inhabitants: 124 (2017 est.)

country comparison to the world: 23
TELEPHONE SYSTEM:
general assessment: excellent domestic and international services featuring rapid incorporation of new technologies; ranked 1st out of 34 Asian telecoms; exceedingly high mobile and mobile broadband penetration and very high fixed broadband penetration; strong support from govt, savvy population has catapulted the nation into one of the world's most active telecommunication markets; 5G services to go live for enterprise customers in 2019; slower growth predicted over the next five years to 2023; Chinese telecommunications company Huawei has partnered with other MNOs in South Korea (2018)

domestic: fixed-line 52 per 100 and mobile-cellular services 124 per 100 persons widely available; rapid assimilation of a full range of telecommunications technologies leading to a boom in e-commerce (2018)

international: country code - 82; landing points for EAC-C2C, FEA, SeaMeWe-3, TPE, APCN-2, APG, FLAG North Asia Loop/REACH North Asia Loop, KJCN, NCP, and SJC2 submarine cables providing links throughout Asia, Australia, the Middle East, Africa, Europe, Southeast Asia and US; satellite earth stations - 66 (2019)

BROADCAST MEDIA:
multiple national TV networks with 2 of the 3 largest networks publicly operated; the largest privately owned network, Seoul Broadcasting Service (SBS), has ties with other commercial TV networks; cable and satellite TV subscription services available; publicly operated radio broadcast networks and many privately owned radio broadcasting networks, each with multiple affiliates, and independent local stations

INTERNET COUNTRY CODE:
.kr

INTERNET USERS:
total: 44.153 million
percent of population: 89.9% (July 2016 est.)

country comparison to the world: 16
BROADBAND - FIXED SUBSCRIPTIONS:
total: 21,195,918
subscriptions per 100 inhabitants: 41 (2017 est.)

country comparison to the world: 9

MILITARY AND SECURITY :: KOREA, SOUTH

MILITARY EXPENDITURES:
2.62% of GDP (2018)
2.7% of GDP (2017)
2.3% of GDP (2016)
2.3% of GDP (2015)
2.64% of GDP (2014)

country comparison to the world: 30
MILITARY AND SECURITY FORCES:
Republic of Korea Army (ROKA), Navy (ROKN, includes Marine Corps, ROKMC), Air Force (ROKAF); Military reserves include Mobilization Reserve Forces (First Combat Forces) and Homeland Defense Forces (Regional Combat Forces); Korea Coast Guard (Ministry of Maritime Affairs and Fisheries) (2019)

MILITARY SERVICE AGE AND OBLIGATION:
18-28 years of age for compulsory military service; minimum conscript service obligation varies by service- 21 months (Army, Marines), 23 months (Navy), 24 months (Air Force); 18-26 years of age for voluntary military service; women, in service since 1950, are able to serve in all branches (2019)

Note: South Korea intends to reduce the length of military service to 18 – 22 months by 2022

TRANSPORTATION :: KOREA, SOUTH

NATIONAL AIR TRANSPORT SYSTEM:
number of registered air carriers: 12 (2015)

inventory of registered aircraft operated by air carriers: 348 (2015)

annual passenger traffic on registered air carriers: 65,482,307 (2015)

annual freight traffic on registered air carriers: 11.297 billion mt-km (2015)

CIVIL AIRCRAFT REGISTRATION COUNTRY CODE PREFIX:
HL (2016)

AIRPORTS:
111 (2013)

country comparison to the world: 53

AIRPORTS - WITH PAVED RUNWAYS:
total: 71 (2017)

over 3,047 m: 4 (2017)

2,438 to 3,047 m: 19 (2017)

1,524 to 2,437 m: 12 (2017)

914 to 1,523 m: 13 (2017)

under 914 m: 23 (2017)

AIRPORTS - WITH UNPAVED RUNWAYS:
total: 40 (2013)

914 to 1,523 m: 2 (2013)

under 914 m: 38 (2013)

HELIPORTS:
466 (2013)

PIPELINES:
3790 km gas, 16 km oil, 889 km refined products (2017)

RAILWAYS:
total: 3,979 km (2016)

standard gauge: 3,979 km 1.435-m gauge (2,727 km electrified) (2016)

country comparison to the world: 49

ROADWAYS:
total: 100,428 km (2016)

paved: 92,795 km (includes 4,193 km of expressways) (2016)

unpaved: 7,633 km (2016)

country comparison to the world: 47

WATERWAYS:
1,600 km (most navigable only by small craft) (2011)

country comparison to the world: 49

MERCHANT MARINE:
total: 1,897

by type: bulk carrier 95, container ship 86, general cargo 379, oil tanker 196, other 1141 (2018)

country comparison to the world: 12

PORTS AND TERMINALS:
major seaport(s): Busan, Incheon, Gunsan, Kwangyang, Mokpo, Pohang, Ulsan, Yeosu

container port(s) (TEUs): Busan (20,493,000), Incheon (3,050,000), Kwangyang (2,230,000) (2017)

LNG terminal(s) (import): Incheon, Kwangyang, Pyeongtaek, Samcheok, Tongyeong, Yeosu

TRANSNATIONAL ISSUES :: KOREA, SOUTH

DISPUTES - INTERNATIONAL:
Military Demarcation Line within the 4-km-wide Demilitarized Zone has separated North from South Korea since 1953; periodic incidents with North Korea in the Yellow Sea over the Northern Limit Line, which South Korea claims as a maritime boundary; South Korea and Japan claim Liancourt Rocks (Tok-do/Take-shima), occupied by South Korea since 1954

REFUGEES AND INTERNALLY DISPLACED PERSONS:
stateless persons: 197 (2018)

EUROPE :: KOSOVO

INTRODUCTION :: KOSOVO

BACKGROUND:

The central Balkans were part of the Roman and Byzantine Empires before ethnic Serbs migrated to the territories of modern Kosovo in the 7th century. During the medieval period, Kosovo became the center of a Serbian Empire and saw the construction of many important Serb religious sites, including many architecturally significant Serbian Orthodox monasteries. The defeat of Serbian forces at the Battle of Kosovo in 1389 led to five centuries of Ottoman rule during which large numbers of Turks and Albanians moved to Kosovo. By the end of the 19th century, Albanians replaced Serbs as the dominant ethnic group in Kosovo. Serbia reacquired control over the region from the Ottoman Empire during the First Balkan War of 1912. After World War II, Kosovo's present-day boundaries were established when Kosovo became an autonomous province of Serbia in the Socialist Federal Republic of Yugoslavia (S.F.R.Y.). Despite legislative concessions, Albanian nationalism increased in the 1980s, which led to riots and calls for Kosovo's independence. The Serbs - many of whom viewed Kosovo as their cultural heartland - instituted a new constitution in 1989 revoking Kosovo's autonomous status. Kosovo's Albanian leaders responded in 1991 by organizing a referendum declaring Kosovo independent. Serbia undertook repressive measures against the Kosovar Albanians in the 1990s, provoking a Kosovar Albanian insurgency.

Beginning in 1998, Serbia conducted a brutal counterinsurgency campaign that resulted in massacres and massive expulsions of ethnic Albanians (some 800,000 ethnic Albanians were forced from their homes in Kosovo). After international attempts to mediate the conflict failed, a three-month NATO military operation against Serbia beginning in March 1999 forced the Serbs to agree to withdraw their military and police forces from Kosovo. UN Security Council Resolution 1244 (1999) placed Kosovo under a transitional administration, the UN Interim Administration Mission in Kosovo (UNMIK), pending a determination of Kosovo's future status. A UN-led process began in late 2005 to determine Kosovo's final status. The 2006-07 negotiations ended without agreement between Belgrade and Pristina, though the UN issued a comprehensive report on Kosovo's final status that endorsed independence. On 17 February 2008, the Kosovo Assembly declared Kosovo independent. Since then, over 100 countries have recognized Kosovo, and it has joined numerous international organizations. In October 2008, Serbia sought an advisory opinion from the International Court of Justice (ICJ) on the legality under international law of Kosovo's declaration of independence. The ICJ released the advisory opinion in July 2010 affirming that Kosovo's declaration of independence did not violate general principles of international law, UN Security Council Resolution 1244, or the Constitutive Framework. The opinion was closely tailored to Kosovo's unique history and circumstances.

Demonstrating Kosovo's development into a sovereign, multi-ethnic, democratic country the international community ended the period of Supervised Independence in 2012. Kosovo held its most recent national and municipal elections in 2017. Serbia continues to reject Kosovo's independence, but the two countries agreed in April 2013 to normalize their relations through EU-facilitated talks, which produced several subsequent agreements the parties are engaged in implementing, though they have not yet reached a comprehensive normalization of relations. Kosovo seeks full integration into the international community, and has pursued bilateral recognitions and memberships in international organizations. Kosovo signed a Stabilization and Association Agreement with the EU in 2015, and was named by a 2018 EU report as one of six Western Balkan countries that will be able to join the organization once it meets the criteria to accede. Kosovo also seeks memberships in the UN and in NATO.

GEOGRAPHY :: KOSOVO

LOCATION:

Southeast Europe, between Serbia and Macedonia

GEOGRAPHIC COORDINATES:

42 35 N, 21 00 E

MAP REFERENCES:

Europe

AREA:

total: 10,887 sq km

land: 10,887 sq km

water: 0 sq km

country comparison to the world: 168

AREA - COMPARATIVE:

slightly larger than Delaware

LAND BOUNDARIES:

total: 714 km

border countries (4): Albania 112 km, Macedonia 160 km, Montenegro 76 km, Serbia 366 km

COASTLINE:

0 km (landlocked)

MARITIME CLAIMS:

none (landlocked)

CLIMATE:

influenced by continental air masses resulting in relatively cold winters with heavy snowfall and hot, dry summers and autumns; Mediterranean and alpine influences create regional variation; maximum rainfall between October and December

TERRAIN:

flat fluvial basin at an elevation of 400-700 m above sea level surrounded by several high mountain ranges with elevations of 2,000 to 2,500 m

ELEVATION:

mean elevation: 450 m

lowest point: Drini i Bardhe/Beli Drim (located on the border with Albania) 297 m

highest point: Gjeravica/Deravica 2,656 m

NATURAL RESOURCES:

nickel, lead, zinc, magnesium, lignite, kaolin, chrome, bauxite

LAND USE:

agricultural land: 52.8% (2001 est.)

arable land: 27.4% (2001 est.) / permanent crops: 1.9% (2001 est.) / permanent pasture: 23.5% (2001 est.)

forest: 41.7% (2001 est.)

other: 5.5% (2001 est.)

IRRIGATED LAND:

NA

POPULATION DISTRIBUTION:

population clusters exist throughout the country, the largest being in the east in and around the capital of Pristina

ENVIRONMENT - CURRENT ISSUES:

air pollution (pollution from power plants and nearby lignite mines take a toll on people's health); water scarcity and pollution; land degradation

GEOGRAPHY - NOTE:

the 41-km long Nerodimka River divides into two branches each of which flows into a different sea: the northern branch flows into the Sitnica River, which via the Ibar, Morava, and Danube Rivers ultimately flows into the Black Sea; the southern branch flows via the Lepenac and Vardar Rivers into the Aegean Sea

PEOPLE AND SOCIETY :: KOSOVO

POPULATION:

1,907,592 (July 2018 est.)

country comparison to the world: 151

NATIONALITY:

noun: Kosovar (Albanian), Kosovac (Serbian)

adjective: Kosovar (Albanian), Kosovski (Serbian)

note: Kosovan, a neutral term, is sometimes also used as a noun or adjective

ETHNIC GROUPS:

Albanians 92.9%, Bosniaks 1.6%, Serbs 1.5%, Turk 1.1%, Ashkali 0.9%, Egyptian 0.7%, Gorani 0.6%, Romani 0.5%, other/unspecified 0.2% (2011 est.)

note: these estimates may under-represent Serb, Romani, and some other ethnic minorities because they are based on the 2011 Kosovo national census, which excluded northern Kosovo (a largely Serb-inhabited region) and was partially boycotted by Serb and Romani communities in southern Kosovo

LANGUAGES:

Albanian (official) 94.5%, Bosnian 1.7%, Serbian (official) 1.6%, Turkish 1.1%, other 0.9% (includes Romani), unspecified 0.1% (2011 est.)

note: in municipalities where a community's mother tongue is not one of Kosovo's official languages, the language of that community may be given official status according to the 2006 Law on the Use of Languages

RELIGIONS:

Muslim 95.6%, Roman Catholic 2.2%, Orthodox 1.5%, other 0.1%, none 0.1%, unspecified 0.6% (2011 est.)

AGE STRUCTURE:

0-14 years: 24.74% (male 245,188 /female 226,766)

15-24 years: 17.12% (male 170,448 /female 156,199)

25-54 years: 42.52% (male 428,030 /female 383,045)

55-64 years: 8.19% (male 79,415 /female 76,743)

65 years and over: 7.43% (male 59,830 /female 81,928) (2018 est.)

MEDIAN AGE:

total: 29.6 years (2018 est.)

male: 29.3 years

female: 29.9 years

country comparison to the world: 122

NET MIGRATION RATE:

-2.6 migrant(s)/1,000 population (2018 est.)

country comparison to the world: 171

POPULATION DISTRIBUTION:

population clusters exist throughout the country, the largest being in the east in and around the capital of Pristina

MAJOR URBAN AREAS - POPULATION:

207,062 PRISTINA (capital) (2014)

SEX RATIO:

at birth: 1.08 male(s)/female

0-14 years: 1.08 male(s)/female

15-24 years: 1.09 male(s)/female

25-54 years: 1.12 male(s)/female

55-64 years: 1.03 male(s)/female

65 years and over: 0.73 male(s)/female

total population: 1.06 male(s)/female (2018 est.)

HIV/AIDS - ADULT PREVALENCE RATE:

NA

HIV/AIDS - DEATHS:

NA

EDUCATION EXPENDITURES:

NA

UNEMPLOYMENT, YOUTH AGES 15-24:

total: 52.4%

male: 47.3%

female: 65.4% (2016 est.)

country comparison to the world: 3

GOVERNMENT :: KOSOVO

COUNTRY NAME:

conventional long form: Republic of Kosovo

conventional short form: Kosovo

local long form: Republika e Kosoves (Republika Kosovo)

local short form: Kosove (Kosovo)

etymology: name derives from the Serbian "kos" meaning "blackbird," an ellipsis (linguistic omission) for "kosove polje" or "field of the blackbirds"

GOVERNMENT TYPE:

parliamentary republic

CAPITAL:

name: Pristina (Prishtine, Prishtina)

geographic coordinates: 42 40 N, 21 10 E

time difference: UTC+1 (6 hours ahead of Washington, DC, during Standard Time)

daylight saving time: +1hr, begins last Sunday in March; ends last Sunday in October

etymology: the name may derive from a Proto-Slavic word reconstructed as "pryshchina," meaning "spring (of water)"

ADMINISTRATIVE DIVISIONS:

38 municipalities (komunat, singular - komuna (Albanian); opstine, singular - opstina (Serbian)); Decan (Decani), Dragash (Dragas), Ferizaj (Urosevac), Fushe Kosove (Kosovo Polje), Gjakove (Dakovica), Gjilan (Gnjilane), Gllogovc (Glogovac), Gracanice (Gracanica), Hani i Elezit (Deneral Jankovic), Istog (Istok), Junik, Kacanik, Kamenice (Kamenica), Kline (Klina), Kllokot (Klokot), Leposaviq (Leposavic), Lipjan (Lipljan), Malisheve (Malisevo), Mamushe (Mamusa), Mitrovice e Jugut (Juzna Mitrovica) [South Mitrovica], Mitrovice e Veriut (Severna Mitrovica) [North Mitrovica], Novoberde (Novo Brdo), Obiliq (Obilic), Partesh (Partes), Peje (Pec), Podujeve (Podujevo), Prishtine (Pristina), Prizren, Rahovec (Orahovac), Ranillug (Ranilug), Shterpce (Strpce), Shtime (Stimlje), Skenderaj (Srbica), Suhareke (Suva Reka), Viti (Vitina), Vushtrri (Vucitrn), Zubin Potok, Zvecan

INDEPENDENCE:

17 February 2008 (from Serbia)

NATIONAL HOLIDAY:

Independence Day, 17 February (2008)

CONSTITUTION:

history: previous 1974, 1990; latest (postindependence) draft finalized 2 April 2008, signed 7 April 2008, ratified 9 April 2008, entered into force 15 June 2008; note - amendment 24, passed by the Assembly in August 2015, established the Kosovo Relocated Specialist Institution, referred to as the Kosovo Specialist Chamber or "Specialist Court," to try war crimes allegedly committed by members of the Kosovo Liberation Army in the late 1990s

amendments: proposed by the government, by the president of the republic, or by one fourth of Assembly deputies; passage requires two-thirds majority vote of the Assembly, including two-thirds majority vote of deputies representing non-majority communities, followed by a favorable Constitutional Court assessment; amended several times, last in 2016 (2016)

LEGAL SYSTEM:

civil law system; note - the European Union Rule of Law Mission (EULEX) retained limited executive powers within the Kosovo judiciary for complex cases from 2008 to 2018

INTERNATIONAL LAW ORGANIZATION PARTICIPATION:

has not submitted an ICJ jurisdiction declaration; non-party state to the ICCt

CITIZENSHIP:

citizenship by birth: no

citizenship by descent only: at least one parent must be a citizen of Kosovo

dual citizenship recognized: yes

residency requirement for naturalization: 5 years

SUFFRAGE:

18 years of age; universal

EXECUTIVE BRANCH:

chief of state: President Hashim THACI (since 7 April 2016)

head of government: Prime Minister (vacant); note - Prime Minister Ramush HARADINAJ (since 9 September 2017) resigned on 19 July 2019

cabinet: Cabinet elected by the Assembly

elections/appointments: president indirectly elected by at least two-thirds majority vote of the Assembly for a 5-year term; if a candidate does not attain a two-thirds threshold in the first two ballots, the candidate winning a simple majority vote in the third ballot is elected (eligible for a second term); election last held on 26 February 2016 (next to be held in 2021); prime minister indirectly elected by the Assembly

election results: Hashim THACI elected president in the third ballot; Assembly vote - Hashim THACI (PDK) 71, Rafet RAMA (PDK) 0, invalid 10; Ramush HARADINAJ nominated prime minister by the president and elected by the Assembly, receiving 61 votes out of 62 (1 abstention)

LEGISLATIVE BRANCH:

description: unicameral Assembly or Kuvendi i Kosoves/Skupstina Kosova (120 seats; 100 members directly elected by open-list proportional representation vote with 20 seats reserved for ethnic minorities - 10 for Serbs and 10 for other ethnic minorities; members serve 4-year terms)

elections: last held on 6 October 2019 (next to be held in 2023); note - early elections were held on 6 October 2019 following the dissolution of parliament on 22 August 2019, as a result of political deadlock since the resignation of Prime Minister HARADINAJ on 19 July 2019

election results: percent of vote by party/coalition - VV 25.5%, LDK 24.8%, PDK 21.2%, AAK-PSD 11.6%, Serb List 6.6%, other 10.3%; seats by party/coalition - VV 31, LDK 30, PDK 25, AAK-PSD 14, Serb List 10, Vakat 2, KDTP 2, other 6; composition - men NA, women NA, percent of women NA%

JUDICIAL BRANCH:

highest courts: Supreme Court (consists of the court president and 18 judges and organized into Appeals Panel of the Kosovo Property Agency and Special Chamber); Constitutional Court (consists of the court president, vice president, and 7 judges)

judge selection and term of office: Supreme Court judges nominated by the Kosovo Judicial Council, a 13-member independent body staffed by judges and lay members, and also responsible for overall administration of Kosovo's judicial system; judges appointed by the president of the Republic of Kosovo; judges appointed until mandatory retirement age; Constitutional Court judges nominated by the Kosovo Assembly and appointed by the president of the republic to serve single, 9-year terms subordinate courts: Court of Appeals (organized into 4 departments: General, Serious Crime, Commercial Matters, and Administrative Matters); Basic Court (located in 7 municipalities, each with several branches)

note: in August 2015, the Kosovo Assembly approved a constitutional amendment that establishes the Kosovo Relocated Specialist Judicial Institution, also referred to as the Kosovo Specialist Chambers or "Special Court"; the court, located at the Hague in the Netherlands, began operating in late 2016 and has jurisdiction to try crimes against humanity, war crimes, and other crimes under Kosovo law that occurred in the 1998-2000 period

POLITICAL PARTIES AND LEADERS:

Alliance for the Future of Kosovo or AAK [Ramush HARADINAJ]
Alternativa [Mimoza KUSARI-LILA]
Democratic League of Kosovo or LDK [Isa MUSTAFA]
Democratic Party of Kosovo or PDK [Kadri VESELI]
Independent Liberal Party or SLS [Slobodan PETROVIC]
Initiative for Kosovo or NISMA [Fatmir LIMAJ]
Movement for Self-Determination (Vetevendosje) or VV [Albin KURTI]
New Kosovo Alliance or AKR [Behgjet PACOLLI]
Serb List [Goran RAKIC]
Social Democratic Party of Kosovo or PSD [Shpend AHMETI]
Turkish Democratic Party of Kosovo or KDTP [Mahir YAGCILAR]
Vakat Coalition or VAKAT [Rasim DEMIRI]

INTERNATIONAL ORGANIZATION PARTICIPATION:

IBRD, IDA, IFC, IMF, ITUC (NGOs), MIGA, OIF (observer)

DIPLOMATIC REPRESENTATION IN THE US:

Ambassador Vlora CITAKU (since 17 September 2015)

chancery: 2175 K Street NW, Suite 300, Washington, DC 20037

telephone: [1] (202) 450-2130

FAX: [1] (202) 735-0609

consulate(s) general: New York

consulate(s): Des Moines (IA)

DIPLOMATIC REPRESENTATION FROM THE US:

chief of mission: Ambassador Philip KOSNETT (since 3 December 2018)

telephone: [383] 38 59 59 3000

embassy: Arberia/Dragodan, Nazim Hikmet 30, Pristina, Kosovo

mailing address: use embassy street address

FAX: [383] 38 549 890

FLAG DESCRIPTION:

centered on a dark blue field is a gold-colored silhouette of Kosovo surmounted by six white, five-pointed stars arrayed in a slight arc; each star represents one of the major ethnic groups of Kosovo: Albanians, Serbs, Turks, Gorani, Roma, and Bosniaks

note: one of only two national flags that uses a map as a design element; the flag of Cyprus is the other

NATIONAL SYMBOL(S):

six, five-pointed, white stars; national colors: blue, gold, white

NATIONAL ANTHEM:

name: Europe

lyrics/music: no lyrics/Mendi MENGJIQI

note: adopted 2008; Kosovo chose to exclude lyrics in its anthem so as not to offend the country's minority ethnic groups

ECONOMY :: KOSOVO

ECONOMY - OVERVIEW:

Kosovo's economy has shown progress in transitioning to a market-based system and maintaining macroeconomic stability, but it is still highly dependent on the international community and the diaspora for financial and technical assistance. Remittances from the diaspora - located mainly in Germany, Switzerland, and the Nordic countries - are estimated to account for about 17% of GDP and international donor assistance accounts for approximately 10% of GDP. With international assistance, Kosovo has been able to privatize a majority of its state-owned enterprises.

Kosovo's citizens are the second poorest in Europe, after Moldova, with a per capita GDP (PPP) of $10,400 in 2017. An unemployment rate of 33%, and a youth unemployment rate near 60%, in a country where the average age is 26, encourages emigration and fuels a significant informal, unreported economy. Most of Kosovo's population lives in rural towns outside of the capital, Pristina. Inefficient, near-subsistence farming is common - the result of small plots, limited mechanization, and a lack of technical expertise. Kosovo enjoys lower labor costs than the rest of the region. However, high levels of corruption, little contract enforcement, and unreliable electricity supply have discouraged potential investors. The official currency of Kosovo is the euro, but the Serbian dinar is also used illegally in Serb majority communities. Kosovo's tie to the euro has helped keep core inflation low.

Minerals and metals production - including lignite, lead, zinc, nickel, chrome, aluminum, magnesium, and a wide variety of construction materials - once the backbone of industry, has declined because of aging equipment and insufficient investment, problems exacerbated by competing and unresolved ownership claims of Kosovo's largest mines. A limited and unreliable electricity supply is a major impediment to economic development. The US Government is cooperating with the Ministry of Economic Development (MED) and the World Bank to conclude a commercial tender for the construction of Kosovo C, a new lignite-fired power plant that would leverage Kosovo's large lignite reserves. MED also has plans for the rehabilitation of an older bituminous-fired power plant, Kosovo B, and the development of a coal mine that could supply both plants.

In June 2009, Kosovo joined the World Bank and International Monetary Fund, the Central Europe Free Trade Area (CEFTA) in 2006, the European Bank for Reconstruction and Development in 2012, and the Council of Europe Development Bank in 2013. In 2016, Kosovo implemented the Stabilization and Association Agreement (SAA) negotiations with the EU, focused on trade liberalization. In 2014, nearly 60% of customs duty-eligible imports into Kosovo were EU goods. In August 2015, as part of its EU-facilitated normalization process with Serbia, Kosovo signed agreements on telecommunications and energy distribution, but disagreements over who owns economic assets, such as the Trepca mining conglomerate, within Kosovo continue.

Kosovo experienced its first federal budget deficit in 2012, when government expenditures climbed sharply. In May 2014, the government introduced a 25% salary increase for public sector employees and an equal increase in certain social benefits. Central revenues could not sustain these increases, and the government was forced to reduce its planned capital investments. The government, led by Prime Minister MUSTAFA - a trained economist - recently made several changes to its fiscal policy, expanding the list of duty-free imports, decreasing the Value Added Tax (VAT) for basic food items and public utilities, and increasing the VAT for all other goods.

While Kosovo's economy continued to make progress, unemployment has not been reduced, nor living standards raised, due to lack of economic reforms and investment.

GDP (PURCHASING POWER PARITY):

$19.6 billion (2017 est.)

$18.89 billion (2016 est.)

$18.16 billion (2015 est.)

note: data are in 2017 dollars

country comparison to the world: 151

GDP (OFFICIAL EXCHANGE RATE):

$7.094 billion (2017 est.)

GDP - REAL GROWTH RATE:

3.7% (2017 est.)

4.1% (2016 est.)

4.1% (2015 est.)

country comparison to the world: 90

GDP - PER CAPITA (PPP):

$10,900 (2017 est.)

$10,600 (2016 est.)

$10,200 (2015 est.)

note: data are in 2016 US dollars

country comparison to the world: 137

GROSS NATIONAL SAVING:

17.3% of GDP (2017 est.)

13.2% of GDP (2016 est.)

15.1% of GDP (2015 est.)

country comparison to the world: 118

GDP - COMPOSITION, BY END USE:

household consumption: 84.3% (2017 est.)

government consumption: 13.6% (2017 est.)

investment in fixed capital: 29% (2017 est.)

investment in inventories: 0% (2016 est.)

exports of goods and services: 27% (2017 est.)

imports of goods and services: -53.8% (2017 est.)

GDP - COMPOSITION, BY SECTOR OF ORIGIN:

agriculture: 11.9% (2017 est.)

industry: 17.7% (2017 est.)

services: 70.4% (2017 est.)

AGRICULTURE - PRODUCTS:

wheat, corn, berries, potatoes, peppers, fruit; dairy, livestock; fish

INDUSTRIES:

mineral mining, construction materials, base metals, leather, machinery, appliances, foodstuffs and beverages, textiles

INDUSTRIAL PRODUCTION GROWTH RATE:

1.2% (2016 est.)

country comparison to the world: 149

LABOR FORCE:

500,300 (2017 est.)

note: includes those estimated to be employed in the gray economy

country comparison to the world: 156

LABOR FORCE - BY OCCUPATION:

agriculture: 4.4%

industry: 17.4%

services: 78.2% (2017 est.)

UNEMPLOYMENT RATE:

30.5% (2017 est.)

27.5% (2016 est.)

note: Kosovo has a large informal sector that may not be reflected in these data

country comparison to the world: 208

POPULATION BELOW POVERTY LINE:

17.6% (2015 est.)

HOUSEHOLD INCOME OR CONSUMPTION BY PERCENTAGE SHARE:

lowest 10%: 3.8%

highest 10%: 22% (2015 est.)

DISTRIBUTION OF FAMILY INCOME - GINI INDEX:

23.2 (2015 est.)

24.1 (2014 est.)

country comparison to the world: 156

BUDGET:

revenues: 2.054 billion (2017 est.)

expenditures: 2.203 billion (2017 est.)

TAXES AND OTHER REVENUES:

29% (of GDP) (2017 est.)

country comparison to the world: 87

BUDGET SURPLUS (+) OR DEFICIT (-):

-2.1% (of GDP) (2017 est.)

country comparison to the world: 108

PUBLIC DEBT:

21.2% of GDP (2017 est.)

19.4% of GDP (2016 est.)

country comparison to the world: 186

INFLATION RATE (CONSUMER PRICES):

1.5% (2017 est.)

0.3% (2016 est.)

country comparison to the world: 82

COMMERCIAL BANK PRIME LENDING RATE:

6.83% (31 December 2017 est.)

7.47% (31 December 2016 est.)

country comparison to the world: 122

STOCK OF BROAD MONEY:

$3.11 billion (2016 est.)

$2.855 billion (2015 est.)

country comparison to the world: 126

STOCK OF DOMESTIC CREDIT:

$2.02 billion (2014 est.)

$2.505 billion (2013 est.)

country comparison to the world: 150

CURRENT ACCOUNT BALANCE:

-$467 million (2017 est.)

-$533 million (2016 est.)

country comparison to the world: 117

EXPORTS:

$428 million (2017 est.)

$340 million (2016 est.)

country comparison to the world: 180

EXPORTS - PARTNERS:

Albania 16%, India 14%, Macedonia, The Former Yugo Rep of 12.1%, Serbia 10.6%, Switzerland 5.6%, Germany 5.4% (2017)

EXPORTS - COMMODITIES:

mining and processed metal products, scrap metals, leather products, machinery, appliances, prepared foodstuffs, beverages and tobacco, vegetable products, textiles and apparel

IMPORTS:

$3.223 billion (2017 est.)

$2.876 billion (2016 est.)

country comparison to the world: 146

IMPORTS - COMMODITIES:

foodstuffs, livestock, wood, petroleum, chemicals, machinery, minerals, textiles, stone, ceramic and glass products, electrical equipment

IMPORTS - PARTNERS:

Germany 12.4%, Serbia 12.3%, Turkey 9.6%, China 9.1%, Italy 6.4%, Macedonia, The Former Yugo Rep of 5.1%, Albania 5%, Greece 4.4% (2017)

RESERVES OF FOREIGN EXCHANGE AND GOLD:

$683.9 million (31 December 2016 est.)

$708.7 million (31 December 2015 est.)

country comparison to the world: 142

DEBT - EXTERNAL:

$506 million (31 December 2017 est.)

$448 million (31 December 2016 est.)

country comparison to the world: 179

STOCK OF DIRECT FOREIGN INVESTMENT - AT HOME:

$3.59 billion (31 December 2017 est.)

$39.02 billion (31 December 2016 est.)

country comparison to the world: 113

STOCK OF DIRECT FOREIGN INVESTMENT - ABROAD:

$275 million (31 December 2017 est.)

$230 million (31 December 2016 est.)

country comparison to the world: 105

EXCHANGE RATES:

euros (EUR) per US dollar -

0.885 (2017 est.)

0.903 (2016 est.)

0.9214 (2015 est.)

0.885 (2014 est.)

0.7634 (2013 est.)

ENERGY :: KOSOVO

ELECTRICITY ACCESS:

electrification - total population: 100% (2016)

ELECTRICITY - PRODUCTION:

5.638 billion kWh (2016 est.)

country comparison to the world: 117

ELECTRICITY - CONSUMPTION:

3.957 billion kWh (2016 est.)

country comparison to the world: 127

ELECTRICITY - EXPORTS:

885.7 million kWh (2017 est.)

country comparison to the world: 60

ELECTRICITY - IMPORTS:

557 million kWh (2016 est.)

country comparison to the world: 78

ELECTRICITY - INSTALLED GENERATING CAPACITY:

1.573 million kW (2016 est.)

country comparison to the world: 121

ELECTRICITY - FROM FOSSIL FUELS:

97% of total installed capacity (2016 est.)

country comparison to the world: 35

ELECTRICITY - FROM NUCLEAR FUELS:

0% of total installed capacity (2017 est.)

country comparison to the world: 121

ELECTRICITY - FROM HYDROELECTRIC PLANTS:

3% of total installed capacity (2017 est.)

country comparison to the world: 135

ELECTRICITY - FROM OTHER RENEWABLE SOURCES:

1% of total installed capacity (2017 est.)

country comparison to the world: 156

CRUDE OIL - PRODUCTION:

0 bbl/day (2017 est.)

country comparison to the world: 158

CRUDE OIL - EXPORTS:

0 bbl/day (2015 est.)

country comparison to the world: 149

CRUDE OIL - IMPORTS:

0 bbl/day (2015 est.)

country comparison to the world: 147

CRUDE OIL - PROVED RESERVES:

0 bbl NA (2017 est.)

country comparison to the world: 153

REFINED PETROLEUM PRODUCTS - PRODUCTION:

0 bbl/day (2015 est.)

country comparison to the world: 161

REFINED PETROLEUM PRODUCTS - CONSUMPTION:

14,000 bbl/day (2016 est.)

country comparison to the world: 155

REFINED PETROLEUM PRODUCTS - EXPORTS:

192 bbl/day (2015 est.)

country comparison to the world: 117

REFINED PETROLEUM PRODUCTS - IMPORTS:

14,040 bbl/day (2015 est.)

country comparison to the world: 139

NATURAL GAS - PRODUCTION:

0 cu m (2017 est.)

country comparison to the world: 153

NATURAL GAS - CONSUMPTION:

0 cu m (2017 est.)

country comparison to the world: 164

NATURAL GAS - EXPORTS:

0 cu m (2017 est.)

country comparison to the world: 132

NATURAL GAS - IMPORTS:

0 cu m (2017 est.)

country comparison to the world: 145

NATURAL GAS - PROVED RESERVES:

0 cu m NA (2017 est.)

country comparison to the world: 154

CARBON DIOXIDE EMISSIONS FROM CONSUMPTION OF ENERGY:

10.05 million Mt (2017 est.)

country comparison to the world: 106

COMMUNICATIONS :: KOSOVO

TELEPHONES - FIXED LINES:

total subscriptions: 831,470

subscriptions per 100 inhabitants: 45 (July 2016 est.)

country comparison to the world: 80

TELEPHONES - MOBILE CELLULAR:

total subscriptions: 562,000

subscriptions per 100 inhabitants: 31 (July 2016 est.)

country comparison to the world: 168

TELEPHONE SYSTEM:

general assessment: Kosovo being part of the EU pre-accession process has helped with their progress in the telecom industry, following a regulatory framework, European standards, and a market of new players encourages development in its telecommunications; 2 MNOs dominate the sector; poor telecom infrastructure means low fixed-line penetration (2018)

domestic: fixed-line stands at 45 per 100 and mobile-cellular 31 per 100 persons (2018)

international: country code - 383

INTERNET COUNTRY CODE:

.xk

note: assigned as a temporary code under UN Security Council resolution 1244/99

MILITARY AND SECURITY :: KOSOVO

MILITARY EXPENDITURES:

0.8% of GDP (2018)

0.8% of GDP (2017)

0.77% of GDP (2016)

0.78% of GDP (2015)

0.73% of GDP (2014)

country comparison to the world: 130

MILITARY AND SECURITY FORCES:

in December 2018, Kosovo adopted a legislative package to initiate a ten-year transition of the Kosovo Security Force (KSF) into a professional multi-ethnic force with a limited territorial defense mandate (2019)

TRANSPORTATION :: KOSOVO

CIVIL AIRCRAFT REGISTRATION COUNTRY CODE PREFIX:

Z6 (2016)

AIRPORTS:

6 (2013)

country comparison to the world: 172

AIRPORTS - WITH PAVED RUNWAYS:

total: 3 (2017)

2,438 to 3,047 m: 1 (2017)

1,524 to 2,437 m: 1 (2017)

under 914 m: 1 (2017)

AIRPORTS - WITH UNPAVED RUNWAYS:

total: 3 (2013)

under 914 m: 3 (2013)

HELIPORTS:

2 (2013)

RAILWAYS:

total: 333 km (2015)

standard gauge: 333 km 1.435-m gauge (2015)

country comparison to the world: 120

ROADWAYS:

total: 2,012 km (2015)

paved: 1,921 km (includes 78 km of expressways) (2015)

unpaved: 91 km (2015)

country comparison to the world: 168

TRANSNATIONAL ISSUES :: KOSOVO

DISPUTES - INTERNATIONAL:

Serbia with several other states protest the US and other states' recognition of Kosovo's declaration of its status as a sovereign and independent state in February 2008; ethnic Serbian municipalities along Kosovo's northern border challenge final status of Kosovo-Serbia boundary; NATO-led Kosovo Force peacekeepers under UN Interim Administration Mission in Kosovo authority continue to ensure a safe and secure environment and freedom of movement for all Kosovo citizens; Kosovo and North Macedonia completed demarcation of their boundary in September 2008; Kosovo ratified the border demarcation agreement with Montenegro in March 2018, but the actual demarcation has not been completed

REFUGEES AND INTERNALLY DISPLACED PERSONS:

IDPs: 16,000 (primarily ethnic Serbs displaced during the 1998-1999 war fearing reprisals from the majority ethnic-Albanian population; a smaller number of ethnic Serbs, Roma, Ashkali, and Egyptians fled their homes in 2,004 as a result of violence) (2018)

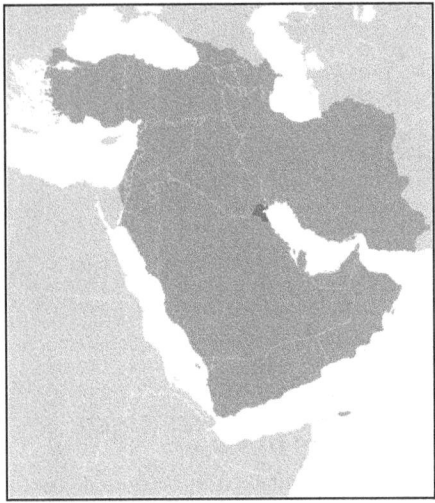

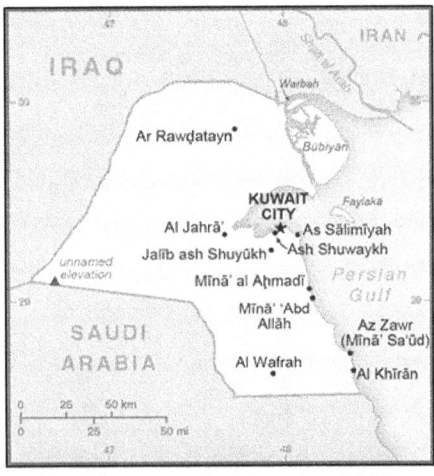

MIDDLE EAST :: KUWAIT

INTRODUCTION :: KUWAIT

BACKGROUND:

Kuwait has been ruled by the AL-SABAH dynasty since the 18th century. The threat of Ottoman invasion in 1899 prompted Amir Mubarak AL-SABAH to seek protection from Britain, ceding foreign and defense responsibility to Britain until 1961, when the country attained its independence. Kuwait was attacked and overrun by Iraq in August 1990. Following several weeks of aerial bombardment, a US-led UN coalition began a ground assault in February 1991 that liberated Kuwait in four days. In 1992, the Amir reconstituted the parliament that he had dissolved in 1986. Amid the 2010-11 uprisings and protests across the Arab world, stateless Arabs, known as Bidoon, staged small protests in early 2011 demanding citizenship, jobs, and other benefits available to Kuwaiti nationals. Other demographic groups, notably Islamists and Kuwaitis from tribal backgrounds, soon joined the growing protest movements, which culminated in late 2011 with the resignation of the prime minister amidst allegations of corruption. Demonstrations renewed in late 2012 in response to an amiri decree amending the electoral law that lessened the voting power of the tribal blocs.

An opposition coalition of Sunni Islamists, tribal populists, and some liberals, largely boycotted legislative elections in 2012 and 2013, which ushered in a legislature more amenable to the government's agenda. Faced with the prospect of painful subsidy cuts, oppositionists and independents actively participated in the November 2016 election, winning nearly half of the seats but a cohesive opposition alliance largely ceased to exist with the 2016 election and the opposition became increasingly factionalized. Since coming to power in 2006, the Amir has dissolved the National Assembly on seven occasions (the Constitutional Court annulled the Assembly elections in June 2012 and again in June 2013) and shuffled the cabinet over a dozen times, usually citing political stagnation and gridlock between the legislature and the government.

GEOGRAPHY :: KUWAIT

LOCATION:

Middle East, bordering the Persian Gulf, between Iraq and Saudi Arabia

GEOGRAPHIC COORDINATES:

29 30 N, 45 45 E

MAP REFERENCES:

Middle East

AREA:

total: 17,818 sq km

land: 17,818 sq km

water: 0 sq km

country comparison to the world: 158

AREA - COMPARATIVE:

slightly smaller than New Jersey

LAND BOUNDARIES:

total: 475 km

border countries (2): Iraq 254 km, Saudi Arabia 221 km

COASTLINE:

499 km

MARITIME CLAIMS:

territorial sea: 12 nm

CLIMATE:

dry desert; intensely hot summers; short, cool winters

TERRAIN:

flat to slightly undulating desert plain

ELEVATION:

mean elevation: 108 m

lowest point: Persian Gulf 0 m

highest point: 3.6 km W. of Al-Salmi Border Post 300 m

NATURAL RESOURCES:

petroleum, fish, shrimp, natural gas

LAND USE:

agricultural land: 8.5% (2011 est.)

arable land: 0.6% (2011 est.) / permanent crops: 0.3% (2011 est.) / permanent pasture: 7.6% (2011 est.)

forest: 0.4% (2011 est.)

other: 91.1% (2011 est.)

IRRIGATED LAND:

105 sq km (2012)

POPULATION DISTRIBUTION:

densest settlement is along the Persian Gulf, particularly in Kuwait City and on Bubiyan Island; significant population threads extend south and west along highways that radiate from the capital, particularly in the southern half of the country

NATURAL HAZARDS:

sudden cloudbursts are common from October to April and bring heavy rain, which can damage roads and houses; sandstorms and dust storms occur throughout the year but are most common between March and August

ENVIRONMENT - CURRENT ISSUES:

limited natural freshwater resources; some of world's largest and most sophisticated desalination facilities provide much of the water; air and water pollution; desertification; loss of biodiversity

ENVIRONMENT - INTERNATIONAL AGREEMENTS:

party to: Biodiversity, Climate Change, Climate Change-Kyoto Protocol, Desertification, Endangered Species, Environmental Modification, Hazardous Wastes, Law of the Sea, Ozone Layer Protection

signed, but not ratified: Marine Dumping

GEOGRAPHY - NOTE:

strategic location at head of Persian Gulf

PEOPLE AND SOCIETY :: KUWAIT

POPULATION:

2,916,467 (July 2017 est.) (July 2018 est.)

note: Kuwait's Public Authority for Civil Information estimates the country's total population to be 4,437,590 for 2017, with immigrants accounting for more than 69.5%

country comparison to the world: 138

NATIONALITY:

noun: Kuwaiti(s)

adjective: Kuwaiti

ETHNIC GROUPS:

Kuwaiti 30.4%, other Arab 27.4%, Asian 40.3%, African 1%, other .9% (includes European, North American, South American, and Australian) (2018 est.)

LANGUAGES:

Arabic (official), English widely spoken

RELIGIONS:

Muslim (official) 74.6%, Christian 18.2%, other and unspecified 7.2% (2013 est.)

note: data represent the total population; about 69% of the population consists of immigrants

AGE STRUCTURE:

0-14 years: 24.81% (male 376,652/female 347,019)

15-24 years: 15.04% (male 240,638/female 197,946)

25-54 years: 52.3% (male 961,205/female 563,979)

55-64 years: 5.2% (male 85,146/female 66,373)

65 years and over: 2.66% (male 35,117/female 42,392) (2018 est.)

DEPENDENCY RATIOS:

total dependency ratio: 29.8 (2015 est.)

youth dependency ratio: 27.1 (2015 est.)

elderly dependency ratio: 2.7 (2015 est.)

potential support ratio: 37.3 (2015 est.)

MEDIAN AGE:

total: 29.4 years (2018 est.)

male: 30.5 years

female: 27.6 years

country comparison to the world: 124

POPULATION GROWTH RATE:

1.38% (2018 est.)

country comparison to the world: 81

BIRTH RATE:

18.8 births/1,000 population (2018 est.)

country comparison to the world: 86

DEATH RATE:

2.3 deaths/1,000 population (2018 est.)

country comparison to the world: 224

NET MIGRATION RATE:

-2.8 migrant(s)/1,000 population (2018 est.)

country comparison to the world: 176

POPULATION DISTRIBUTION:

densest settlement is along the Persian Gulf, particularly in Kuwait City and on Bubiyan Island; significant population threads extend south and west along highways that radiate from the capital, particularly in the southern half of the country

URBANIZATION:

urban population: 100% of total population (2019)

rate of urbanization: 1.78% annual rate of change (2015-20 est.)

MAJOR URBAN AREAS - POPULATION:

3.052 million KUWAIT (capital) (2019)

SEX RATIO:

at birth: 1.05 male(s)/female

0-14 years: 1.09 male(s)/female

15-24 years: 1.22 male(s)/female

25-54 years: 1.7 male(s)/female

55-64 years: 1.28 male(s)/female

65 years and over: 0.83 male(s)/female

total population: 1.4 male(s)/female (2018 est.)

MATERNAL MORTALITY RATE:

12 deaths/100,000 live births (2017 est.)

country comparison to the world: 140

INFANT MORTALITY RATE:

total: 6.8 deaths/1,000 live births (2018 est.)

male: 6.6 deaths/1,000 live births

female: 7 deaths/1,000 live births

country comparison to the world: 161

LIFE EXPECTANCY AT BIRTH:

total population: 78.3 years (2018 est.)

male: 76.9 years

female: 79.8 years

country comparison to the world: 63

TOTAL FERTILITY RATE:

2.35 children born/woman (2018 est.)

country comparison to the world: 84

DRINKING WATER SOURCE:

improved:

urban: 99% of population

rural: 99% of population

total: 99% of population

unimproved:

urban: 1% of population

rural: 1% of population

total: 1% of population (2015 est.)

CURRENT HEALTH EXPENDITURE:

3.9% (2016)

PHYSICIANS DENSITY:

2.58 physicians/1,000 population (2015)

HOSPITAL BED DENSITY:

2 beds/1,000 population (2014)

SANITATION FACILITY ACCESS:

improved:

urban: 100% of population (2015 est.)

rural: 100% of population (2015 est.)

total: 100% of population (2015 est.)

unimproved:

urban: 0% of population (2015 est.)

rural: 0% of population (2015 est.)

total: 0% of population (2015 est.)

HIV/AIDS - ADULT PREVALENCE RATE:

<.1% (2018 est.)

HIV/AIDS - PEOPLE LIVING WITH HIV/AIDS:

<1000 (2018 est.)

HIV/AIDS - DEATHS:

<100 (2018 est.)

OBESITY - ADULT PREVALENCE RATE:

37.9% (2016)

country comparison to the world: 11

CHILDREN UNDER THE AGE OF 5 YEARS UNDERWEIGHT:

3% (2014)

country comparison to the world: 101

EDUCATION EXPENDITURES:

NA

LITERACY:

definition: age 15 and over can read and write

total population: 96%

male: 96.7%

female: 94.8% (2017 est.)

SCHOOL LIFE EXPECTANCY (PRIMARY TO TERTIARY EDUCATION):

total: 14 years

male: 13 years

female: 14 years (2013)

UNEMPLOYMENT, YOUTH AGES 15-24:

total: 15.4%

male: 9.4% N/A

female: 30% N/A (2016 est.)

country comparison to the world: 88

GOVERNMENT :: KUWAIT

COUNTRY NAME:

conventional long form: State of Kuwait

conventional short form: Kuwait

local long form: Dawlat al Kuwayt

local short form: Al Kuwayt

etymology: the name derives from the capital city, which is from Arabic "al-Kuwayt" a diminutive of "kut" meaning "fortress," possibly a reference to a small castle built on the current location of Kuwait City by the Beni Khaled tribe in the 17th century

GOVERNMENT TYPE:

constitutional monarchy (emirate)

CAPITAL:

name: Kuwait City

geographic coordinates: 29 22 N, 47 58 E

time difference: UTC+3 (8 hours ahead of Washington, DC, during Standard Time)

etymology: the name derives from Arabic "al-Kuwayt" a diminutive of "kut" meaning "fortress," possibly a reference to a small castle built on the current location of Kuwait City by the Beni Khaled tribe in the 17th century

ADMINISTRATIVE DIVISIONS:

6 governorates (muhafazat, singular - muhafazah); Al Ahmadi, Al 'Asimah, Al Farwaniyah, Al Jahra', Hawalli, Mubarak al Kabir

INDEPENDENCE:

19 June 1961 (from the UK)

NATIONAL HOLIDAY:

National Day, 25 February (1950)

CONSTITUTION:

history: approved and promulgated 11 November 1962

amendments: proposed by the amir or supported by at least one third of the National Assembly; passage requires two-thirds consent of the Assembly membership and promulgation by the amir; constitutional articles on the initiation, approval, and promulgation of general legislation cannot be amended (2016)

LEGAL SYSTEM:

mixed legal system consisting of English common law, French civil law, and Islamic sharia law

INTERNATIONAL LAW ORGANIZATION PARTICIPATION:

has not submitted an ICJ jurisdiction declaration; non-party state to the ICCt

CITIZENSHIP:

citizenship by birth: no

citizenship by descent only: at least one parent must be a citizen of Kuwait

dual citizenship recognized: no

residency requirement for naturalization: not specified

SUFFRAGE:

21 years of age and at least 20-year citizenship

EXECUTIVE BRANCH:

chief of state: Amir SABAH al-Ahmad al-Jabir al-Sabah (since 29 January 2006); Crown Prince NAWAF al-Ahmad al-Jabir al-Sabah

head of government: Prime Minister JABIR AL-MUBARAK al-Hamad al-Sabah (since 30 November 2011); First Deputy Prime Minister NASIR Sabah al-Ahmad al-Sabah (since 11 December 2017); Deputy Prime Ministers SABAH KHALID al-Hamid al-Sabah (since 13 December 2011), KHALID al-Jarrah al-Sabah (since 4 August 2013), Anas Khalid al-SALEH (since 4 August 2013); note - on 14 November 2019, the government of Prime Minister JABIR AL-MUBARAK al-Hamad al-Sabah resigned

cabinet: Council of Ministers appointed by the prime minister, approved by the amir

elections/appointments: amir chosen from within the ruling family, confirmed by the National Assembly; prime minister and deputy prime ministers appointed by the amir; crown prince appointed by the amir and approved by the National Assembly

LEGISLATIVE BRANCH:

description: unicameral National Assembly or Majlis al-Umma (65 seats; 50 members directly elected from 5 multi-seat constituencies by simple majority vote and 15 ex-officio members (cabinet ministers) appointed by the amir; members serve 4-year terms)

elections: last held on 26 November 2016 (next to be held in 2020)

election results: seats won - oppositionists and independents, including populists, Islamists, and liberals 26, pro-government loyalists 24; composition for elected members only - men 49, women 1, percent of women 1.5%

note: seats as of May 2019 - oppositionists and independents, including populists, Islamists, and liberals 25, pro-government loyalists 25; composition as of May 2019 for elected members only - men 49, women 1, percent of women 2%

JUDICIAL BRANCH:

highest courts: Constitutional Court (consists of 5 judges); Supreme Court or Court of Cassation (organized into several circuits, each with 5 judges)

judge selection and term of office: all Kuwaiti judges appointed by the Amir upon recommendation of the Supreme Judicial Council, a consultative body comprised of Kuwaiti judges and Ministry of Justice officials

subordinate courts: High Court of Appeal; Court of First Instance; Summary Court

POLITICAL PARTIES AND LEADERS:

none; the government does not recognize any political parties or allow their formation, although no formal law bans political parties

INTERNATIONAL ORGANIZATION PARTICIPATION:

ABEDA, AfDB (nonregional member), AFESD, AMF, BDEAC, CAEU, CD, FAO, G-77, GCC, IAEA, IBRD, ICAO, ICC (national committees), ICRM, IDA, IDB, IFAD, IFC, IFRCS, IHO, ILO, IMF, IMO, IMSO, Interpol, IOC, IPU, ISO, ITSO, ITU, ITUC (NGOs), LAS, MIGA, NAM, OAPEC, OIC, OPCW, OPEC, Paris Club (associate), PCA, UN, UNCTAD, UNESCO, UNIDO, UNRWA, UN Security Council (temporary), UNWTO, UPU, WCO, WFTU (NGOs), WHO, WIPO, WMO, WTO

DIPLOMATIC REPRESENTATION IN THE US:

Ambassador SALIM al-Abdallah al-Jabir al-Sabah (since 10 October 2001)

chancery: 2940 Tilden Street NW, Washington, DC 20008

telephone: [1] (202) 966-0702

FAX: [1] (202) 966-8468

consulate(s) general: New York City

consulate(s): Lost Angeles

DIPLOMATIC REPRESENTATION FROM THE US:

chief of mission: Ambassador Lawrence R. SILVERMAN (since 5 October 2016)

telephone: [965] 2259-1001

embassy: P.O. Box 77, Safat 13001

mailing address: P. O. Box 77 Safat 13001 Kuwait; or PSC 1280 APO AE 09880-9000

FAX: [965] 2538-6562

FLAG DESCRIPTION:

three equal horizontal bands of green (top), white, and red with a black trapezoid based on the hoist side; colors and design are based on the Arab Revolt flag of World War I; green represents fertile fields, white stands for purity, red denotes blood on Kuwaiti swords, black signifies the defeat of the enemy

NATIONAL SYMBOL(S):

golden falcon; national colors: green, white, red, black

NATIONAL ANTHEM:

name: "Al-Nasheed Al-Watani" (National Anthem)

lyrics/music: Ahmad MUSHARI al-Adwani/Ibrahim Nasir al-SOULA

note: adopted 1978; the anthem is only used on formal occasions

ECONOMY :: KUWAIT

ECONOMY - OVERVIEW:

Kuwait has a geographically small, but wealthy, relatively open economy with crude oil reserves of about 102 billion barrels - more than 6% of world reserves. Kuwaiti officials plan to increase production to 4 million barrels of oil equivalent per day by 2020. Petroleum accounts for over half of GDP, 92% of export revenues, and 90% of government income.

With world oil prices declining, Kuwait realized a budget deficit in 2015 for the first time more than a decade; in 2016, the deficit grew to 16.5% of GDP. Kuwaiti authorities announced cuts to fuel subsidies in August 2016, provoking outrage among the public and National Assembly, and the Amir dissolved the government for the seventh time in ten years. In 2017 the deficit was reduced to 7.2% of GDP, and the government raised $8 billion by issuing international bonds. Despite Kuwait's dependence on oil, the government has cushioned itself against the impact of lower oil prices, by saving annually at least 10% of government revenue in the Fund for Future Generations.

Kuwait has failed to diversify its economy or bolster the private sector, because of a poor business climate, a large public sector that employs about 74% of citizens, and an acrimonious relationship between the National Assembly and the executive branch that has stymied most economic reforms. The Kuwaiti Government has made little progress on its long-term economic development plan first passed in 2010. While the government planned to spend up to $104 billion over four years to diversify the economy, attract more investment, and boost private sector participation in the economy, many of the projects did not materialize because of an uncertain political situation or delays in awarding contracts. To increase non-oil revenues, the Kuwaiti Government in August 2017 approved draft bills supporting a Gulf Cooperation Council-wide value added tax scheduled to take effect in 2018.

GDP (PURCHASING POWER PARITY):

$289.7 billion (2017 est.)

$299.7 billion (2016 est.)

$293.2 billion (2015 est.)

note: data are in 2017 dollars

country comparison to the world: 58

GDP (OFFICIAL EXCHANGE RATE):

$120.7 billion (2017 est.)

GDP - REAL GROWTH RATE:

-3.3% (2017 est.)

2.2% (2016 est.)

-1% (2015 est.)

country comparison to the world: 214

GDP - PER CAPITA (PPP):

$65,800 (2017 est.)

$69,900 (2016 est.)

$69,200 (2015 est.)

note: data are in 2017 dollars

country comparison to the world: 15

GROSS NATIONAL SAVING:

35.4% of GDP (2017 est.)

32.9% of GDP (2016 est.)

37.1% of GDP (2015 est.)

country comparison to the world: 16

GDP - COMPOSITION, BY END USE:

household consumption: 43.1% (2017 est.)

government consumption: 24.5% (2017 est.)

investment in fixed capital: 26.5% (2017 est.)

investment in inventories: 3.5% (2017 est.)

exports of goods and services: 49.4% (2017 est.)

imports of goods and services: -47% (2017 est.)

GDP - COMPOSITION, BY SECTOR OF ORIGIN:
agriculture: 0.4% (2017 est.)
industry: 58.7% (2017 est.)
services: 40.9% (2017 est.)

AGRICULTURE - PRODUCTS:
fish

INDUSTRIES:
petroleum, petrochemicals, cement, shipbuilding and repair, water desalination, food processing, construction materials

INDUSTRIAL PRODUCTION GROWTH RATE:
2.8% (2017 est.)
country comparison to the world: 109

LABOR FORCE:
2.695 million (2017 est.)
note: non-Kuwaitis represent about 60% of the labor force
country comparison to the world: 112

LABOR FORCE - BY OCCUPATION:
agriculture: NA
industry: NA
services: NA

UNEMPLOYMENT RATE:
1.1% (2017 est.)
1.1% (2016 est.)
country comparison to the world: 11

POPULATION BELOW POVERTY LINE:
NA

HOUSEHOLD INCOME OR CONSUMPTION BY PERCENTAGE SHARE:
lowest 10%: NA
highest 10%: NA

BUDGET:
revenues: 50.5 billion (2017 est.)
expenditures: 62.6 billion (2017 est.)

TAXES AND OTHER REVENUES:
41.8% (of GDP) (2017 est.)
country comparison to the world: 32

BUDGET SURPLUS (+) OR DEFICIT (-):
-10% (of GDP) (2017 est.)
country comparison to the world: 210

PUBLIC DEBT:
20.6% of GDP (2017 est.)
9.9% of GDP (2016 est.)
country comparison to the world: 188

FISCAL YEAR:
1 April - 31 March

INFLATION RATE (CONSUMER PRICES):
1.5% (2017 est.)
3.5% (2016 est.)
country comparison to the world: 83

CENTRAL BANK DISCOUNT RATE:
2.75% (18 December 2017)
2.5% (31 December 2016)
country comparison to the world: 113

COMMERCIAL BANK PRIME LENDING RATE:
4.68% (31 December 2017 est.)
4.5% (31 December 2016 est.)
country comparison to the world: 154

STOCK OF NARROW MONEY:
$33.68 billion (31 December 2017 est.)
$31.86 billion (31 December 2016 est.)
country comparison to the world: 60

STOCK OF BROAD MONEY:
$33.68 billion (31 December 2017 est.)
$31.86 billion (31 December 2016 est.)
country comparison to the world: 60

STOCK OF DOMESTIC CREDIT:
$111.2 billion (31 December 2017 est.)
$103.4 billion (31 December 2016 est.)
country comparison to the world: 53

MARKET VALUE OF PUBLICLY TRADED SHARES:
$81.78 billion (31 December 2016 est.)
$83.13 billion (31 December 2015 est.)
$99.77 billion (31 December 2014 est.)
country comparison to the world: 45

CURRENT ACCOUNT BALANCE:
$7.127 billion (2017 est.)
-$5.056 billion (2016 est.)
country comparison to the world: 26

EXPORTS:
$55.17 billion (2017 est.)
$46.26 billion (2016 est.)
country comparison to the world: 50

EXPORTS - PARTNERS:
South Korea 18.3%, China 17.4%, Japan 11.5%, India 11.2%, Singapore 6.3%, US 5.7% (2017)

EXPORTS - COMMODITIES:
oil and refined products, fertilizers

IMPORTS:
$29.53 billion (2017 est.)
$26.56 billion (2016 est.)
country comparison to the world: 70

IMPORTS - COMMODITIES:
food, construction materials, vehicles and parts, clothing

IMPORTS - PARTNERS:
China 13.5%, US 13.3%, UAE 9.5%, Saudi Arabia 5.8%, Germany 5.4%, Japan 5%, India 4.7%, Italy 4.5% (2017)

RESERVES OF FOREIGN EXCHANGE AND GOLD:
$33.7 billion (31 December 2017 est.)
$31.13 billion (31 December 2016 est.)
country comparison to the world: 48

DEBT - EXTERNAL:
$47.24 billion (31 December 2017 est.)
$38.34 billion (31 December 2016 est.)
country comparison to the world: 68

STOCK OF DIRECT FOREIGN INVESTMENT - AT HOME:
$12.9 billion (31 December 2017 est.)
$12.62 billion (31 December 2016 est.)
country comparison to the world: 92

STOCK OF DIRECT FOREIGN INVESTMENT - ABROAD:
$82.35 billion (31 December 2017 est.)
$74.13 billion (31 December 2016 est.)
country comparison to the world: 37

EXCHANGE RATES:
Kuwaiti dinars (KD) per US dollar -
0.3041 (2017 est.)
0.3022 (2016 est.)
0.3022 (2015 est.)
0.3009 (2014 est.)
0.2845 (2013 est.)

ENERGY :: KUWAIT

ELECTRICITY ACCESS:
electrification - total population: 100% (2016)

ELECTRICITY - PRODUCTION:
65.95 billion kWh (2016 est.)
country comparison to the world: 44

ELECTRICITY - CONSUMPTION:
57.78 billion kWh (2016 est.)
country comparison to the world: 44

ELECTRICITY - EXPORTS:
0 kWh (2016 est.)
country comparison to the world: 156

ELECTRICITY - IMPORTS:

0 kWh (2016 est.)

country comparison to the world: 167

ELECTRICITY - INSTALLED GENERATING CAPACITY:

18.89 million kW (2016 est.)

country comparison to the world: 47

ELECTRICITY - FROM FOSSIL FUELS:

100% of total installed capacity (2016 est.)

country comparison to the world: 10

ELECTRICITY - FROM NUCLEAR FUELS:

0% of total installed capacity (2017 est.)

country comparison to the world: 122

ELECTRICITY - FROM HYDROELECTRIC PLANTS:

0% of total installed capacity (2017 est.)

country comparison to the world: 182

ELECTRICITY - FROM OTHER RENEWABLE SOURCES:

0% of total installed capacity (2017 est.)

country comparison to the world: 196

CRUDE OIL - PRODUCTION:

2.807 million bbl/day (2018 est.)

country comparison to the world: 9

CRUDE OIL - EXPORTS:

479,700 bbl/day (2015 est.)

country comparison to the world: 21

CRUDE OIL - IMPORTS:

0 bbl/day (2015 est.)

country comparison to the world: 148

CRUDE OIL - PROVED RESERVES:

101.5 billion bbl (1 January 2018 est.)

country comparison to the world: 6

REFINED PETROLEUM PRODUCTS - PRODUCTION:

915,800 bbl/day (2015 est.)

country comparison to the world: 22

REFINED PETROLEUM PRODUCTS - CONSUMPTION:

446,000 bbl/day (2016 est.)

country comparison to the world: 34

REFINED PETROLEUM PRODUCTS - EXPORTS:

705,500 bbl/day (2015 est.)

country comparison to the world: 11

REFINED PETROLEUM PRODUCTS - IMPORTS:

0 bbl/day (2015 est.)

country comparison to the world: 212

NATURAL GAS - PRODUCTION:

17.1 billion cu m (2017 est.)

country comparison to the world: 34

NATURAL GAS - CONSUMPTION:

21.72 billion cu m (2017 est.)

country comparison to the world: 36

NATURAL GAS - EXPORTS:

0 cu m (2017 est.)

country comparison to the world: 133

NATURAL GAS - IMPORTS:

5.125 billion cu m (2017 est.)

country comparison to the world: 35

NATURAL GAS - PROVED RESERVES:

1.784 trillion cu m (1 January 2018 est.)

country comparison to the world: 19

CARBON DIOXIDE EMISSIONS FROM CONSUMPTION OF ENERGY:

106.5 million Mt (2017 est.)

country comparison to the world: 41

COMMUNICATIONS :: KUWAIT

TELEPHONES - FIXED LINES:

total subscriptions: 542,082

subscriptions per 100 inhabitants: 19 (2017 est.)

country comparison to the world: 93

TELEPHONES - MOBILE CELLULAR:

total subscriptions: 5,136,384

subscriptions per 100 inhabitants: 179 (2017 est.)

country comparison to the world: 118

TELEPHONE SYSTEM:

general assessment: the quality of service is excellent; new telephone exchanges provide a large capacity for new subscribers; trunk traffic is carried by microwave radio relay, coaxial cable, and open-wire and fiber-optic cable; a 4G LTE mobile-cellular telephone system operates throughout Kuwai; Internet access is available via 4G LTE connections for fixed and mobile users; high ownership of smart phone in Kuwait; one of the highest mobile penetration rates in the world (2018)

domestic: fixed-line subscriptions are 19 per 100 and mobile-cellular stands at 179 per 100 subscriptions (2018)

international: country code - 965; landing points for the FOG, GBICS, MENA, Kuwait-Iran, and FALCON submarine cables linking Africa, the Middle East, and Asia; microwave radio relay to Saudi Arabia; satellite earth stations - 6 (3 Intelsat - 1 Atlantic Ocean and 2 Indian Ocean, 1 Inmarsat - Atlantic Ocean, and 2 Arabsat) (2019)

BROADCAST MEDIA:

state-owned TV broadcaster operates 4 networks and a satellite channel; several private TV broadcasters have emerged; satellite TV available and pan-Arab TV stations are especially popular; state-owned Radio Kuwait broadcasts on a number of channels in Arabic and English; first private radio station emerged in 2005; transmissions of at least 2 international radio broadcasters are available (2019)

INTERNET COUNTRY CODE:

.kw

INTERNET USERS:

total: 2,219,972

percent of population: 78.4% (July 2016 est.)

country comparison to the world: 108

BROADBAND - FIXED SUBSCRIPTIONS:

total: 113,427

subscriptions per 100 inhabitants: 4 (2017 est.)

country comparison to the world: 118

MILITARY AND SECURITY :: KUWAIT

MILITARY EXPENDITURES:

5.06% of GDP (2018)

5.64% of GDP (2017)

5.81% of GDP (2016)

5.01% of GDP (2015)

3.59% of GDP (2014)

country comparison to the world: 6

MILITARY AND SECURITY FORCES:

Kuwaiti Armed Forces: Kuwaiti Land Forces (KLF), Kuwaiti Navy (includes Coast Guard), Kuwaiti Air Force (Al-Quwwat al-Jawwiya al-Kuwaitiya; includes Kuwaiti Air Defense Force, KADF), Kuwaiti National Guard (KNG) (2019)

MILITARY SERVICE AGE AND OBLIGATION:

17-21 years of age for voluntary military service; Kuwait reintroduced one-year mandatory service for men aged 18-35 in May 2017 after having suspended conscription in 2001; service is divided in two phases – four months for training and eight months for military service. (2018)

TRANSPORTATION :: KUWAIT

NATIONAL AIR TRANSPORT SYSTEM:
number of registered air carriers: 3 (2015)

inventory of registered aircraft operated by air carriers: 31 (2015)

annual passenger traffic on registered air carriers: 3,655,366 (2015)

annual freight traffic on registered air carriers: 275,777,666 mt-km (2015)

CIVIL AIRCRAFT REGISTRATION COUNTRY CODE PREFIX:
9K (2016)

AIRPORTS:
7 (2013)

country comparison to the world: 168

AIRPORTS - WITH PAVED RUNWAYS:
total: 4 (2017)

over 3,047 m: 1 (2017)

2,438 to 3,047 m: 2 (2017)

914 to 1,523 m: 1 (2017)

AIRPORTS - WITH UNPAVED RUNWAYS:
total: 3 (2013)

1,524 to 2,437 m: 1 (2013)

under 914 m: 2 (2013)

HELIPORTS:
4 (2013)

PIPELINES:
261 km gas, 540 km oil, 57 km refined products (2013)

ROADWAYS:
total: 5,749 km (2018)

paved: 4,887 km (2018)

unpaved: 862 km (2018)

country comparison to the world: 141

MERCHANT MARINE:
total: 158

by type: general cargo 18, oil tanker 26, other 114 (2018)

country comparison to the world: 69

PORTS AND TERMINALS:
major seaport(s): Ash Shu'aybah, Ash Shuwaykh, Az Zawr (Mina' Sa'ud), Mina' 'Abd Allah, Mina' al Ahmadi

TRANSNATIONAL ISSUES :: KUWAIT

DISPUTES - INTERNATIONAL:
Kuwait and Saudi Arabia continue negotiating a joint maritime boundary with Iran; no maritime boundary exists with Iraq in the Persian Gulf

REFUGEES AND INTERNALLY DISPLACED PERSONS:
stateless persons: 92,000 (2018); note - Kuwait's 1959 Nationality Law defined citizens as persons who settled in the country before 1920 and who had maintained normal residence since then; one-third of the population, descendants of Bedouin tribes, missed the window of opportunity to register for nationality rights after Kuwait became independent in 1961 and were classified as bidun (meaning "without"); since the 1980s Kuwait's bidun have progressively lost their rights, including opportunities for employment and education, amid official claims that they are nationals of other countries who have destroyed their identification documents in hopes of gaining Kuwaiti citizenship; Kuwaiti authorities have delayed processing citizenship applications and labeled biduns as "illegal residents," denying them access to civil documentation, such as birth and marriage certificates

TRAFFICKING IN PERSONS:
current situation: Kuwait is a destination country for men and women subjected to forced labor and, to a lesser degree, forced prostitution; men and women migrate from South and Southeast Asia, Egypt, the Middle East, and increasingly Africa to work in Kuwait, most of them in the domestic service, construction, and sanitation sectors; although most of these migrants enter Kuwait voluntarily, upon arrival some are subjected to conditions of forced labor by their sponsors and labor agents, including debt bondage; Kuwait's sponsorship law restricts workers' movements and penalizes them for running away from abusive workplaces, making domestic workers particularly vulnerable to forced labor in private homes

tier rating: Tier 3 - Kuwait does not fully comply with the minimum standards for the elimination of trafficking and is not making sufficient efforts to do so; although investigations into visa fraud rings lead to the referral of hundreds of people for prosecution, including complicit officials, the government has not prosecuted or convicted any suspected traffickers; authorities made no effort to enforce the prohibition against withholding workers' passports, as mandated under Kuwaiti law; punishment of forced labor cases was limited to shutting down labor recruitment firms, assessing fines, and ordering the return of withheld passports and the paying of back-wages; the government made progress in victims' protection by opening a high-capacity shelter for runaway domestic workers but still lacks formal procedures to identify and refer victims to care services (2015)

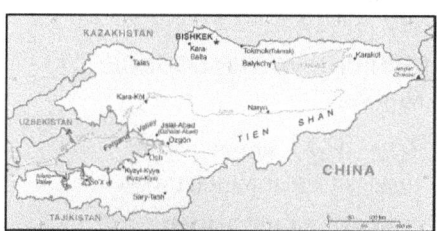

CENTRAL ASIA :: KYRGYZSTAN

INTRODUCTION :: KYRGYZSTAN

BACKGROUND:

A Central Asian country of incredible natural beauty and proud nomadic traditions, most of the territory of the present-day Kyrgyz Republic was formally annexed to the Russian Empire in 1876. The Kyrgyz staged a major revolt against the Tsarist Empire in 1916 in which almost one-sixth of the Kyrgyz population was killed. The Kyrgyz Republic became a Soviet republic in 1936 and achieved independence in 1991 when the USSR dissolved. Nationwide demonstrations in 2005 and 2010 resulted in the ouster of the country's first two presidents, Askar AKAEV and Kurmanbek BAKIEV. Interim President Roza OTUNBAEVA led a transitional government and following a nation-wide election, President Almazbek ATAMBAEV was sworn in as president in 2011. In 2017, ATAMBAEV became the first Kyrgyz president to step down after serving one full six-year term as required in the country's constitution. Former prime minister and ruling Social-Democratic Party of Kyrgyzstan member Sooronbai JEENBEKOV replaced him after winning an October 2017 presidential election that was the most competitive in the country's history, although international and local election observers noted cases of vote buying and abuse of public resources. The president holds substantial powers as head of state even though the prime minister oversees the Kyrgyz Government and selects most cabinet members. The president represents the country internationally and can sign or veto laws, call for new elections, and nominate Supreme Court judges, cabinet members for posts related to security or defense, and numerous other high-level positions. Continuing concerns for the Kyrgyz Republic include the trajectory of democratization, endemic corruption, a history of tense, and at times violent, interethnic relations, border security vulnerabilities, and potential terrorist threats.

GEOGRAPHY :: KYRGYZSTAN

LOCATION:
Central Asia, west of China, south of Kazakhstan

GEOGRAPHIC COORDINATES:
41 00 N, 75 00 E

MAP REFERENCES:
Asia

AREA:
total: 199,951 sq km

land: 191,801 sq km

water: 8,150 sq km

country comparison to the world: 88

AREA - COMPARATIVE:
slightly smaller than South Dakota

LAND BOUNDARIES:
total: 4,573 km

border countries (4): China 1063 km, Kazakhstan 1212 km, Tajikistan 984 km, Uzbekistan 1314 km

COASTLINE:
0 km (landlocked)

MARITIME CLAIMS:
none (landlocked)

CLIMATE:
dry continental to polar in high Tien Shan Mountains; subtropical in southwest (Fergana Valley); temperate in northern foothill zone

TERRAIN:
peaks of the Tien Shan mountain range and associated valleys and basins encompass the entire country

ELEVATION:
mean elevation: 2,988 m

lowest point: Kara-Daryya (Karadar'ya) 132 m

highest point: Jengish Chokusu (Pik Pobedy) 7,439 m

NATURAL RESOURCES:
abundant hydropower; gold, rare earth metals; locally exploitable coal, oil, and natural gas; other deposits of nepheline, mercury, bismuth, lead, and zinc

LAND USE:
agricultural land: 55.4% (2011 est.)

arable land: 6.7% (2011 est.) / permanent crops: 0.4% (2011 est.) / permanent pasture: 48.3% (2011 est.)

forest: 5.1% (2011 est.)

other: 39.5% (2011 est.)

IRRIGATED LAND:
10,233 sq km (2012)

POPULATION DISTRIBUTION:
the vast majority of Kyrgyzstanis live in rural areas; densest population settlement is to the north in and around the capital, Bishkek, followed by Osh in the west; the least densely populated area is the east, southeast in the Tien Shan mountains

NATURAL HAZARDS:
major flooding during snow melt; prone to earthquakes

ENVIRONMENT - CURRENT ISSUES:
water pollution; many people get their water directly from contaminated

streams and wells; as a result, water-borne diseases are prevalent; increasing soil salinity from faulty irrigation practices; air pollution due to rapid increase of traffic

ENVIRONMENT - INTERNATIONAL AGREEMENTS:

party to: Air Pollution, Biodiversity, Climate Change, Climate Change-Kyoto Protocol, Desertification, Hazardous Wastes, Ozone Layer Protection, Wetlands

signed, but not ratified: none of the selected agreements

GEOGRAPHY - NOTE:

landlocked; entirely mountainous, dominated by the Tien Shan range; 94% of the country is 1,000 m above sea level with an average elevation of 2,750 m; many tall peaks, glaciers, and high-altitude lakes

PEOPLE AND SOCIETY :: KYRGYZSTAN

POPULATION:

5,849,296 (July 2018 est.)

country comparison to the world: 114

NATIONALITY:

noun: Kyrgyzstani(s)

adjective: Kyrgyzstani

ETHNIC GROUPS:

Kyrgyz 73.5%, Uzbek 14.7%, Russian 5.5%, Dungan 1.1%, other 5.2% (includes Uyghur, Tajik, Turk, Kazakh, Tatar, Ukrainian, Korean, German) (2019 est.)

LANGUAGES:

Kyrgyz (official) 71.4%, Uzbek 14.4%, Russian (official) 9%, other 5.2% (2009 est.)

RELIGIONS:

Muslim 90% (majority Sunni), Christian 7% (Russian Orthodox 3%), other 3% (includes Jewish, Buddhist, Baha'i) (2017 est.)

AGE STRUCTURE:

0-14 years: 30.4% (male 912,455 /female 865,910)

15-24 years: 16.28% (male 483,799 /female 468,653)

25-54 years: 39.94% (male 1,146,221 /female 1,189,763)

55-64 years: 7.95% (male 202,754 /female 262,412)

65 years and over: 5.43% (male 121,221 /female 196,108) (2018 est.)

DEPENDENCY RATIOS:

total dependency ratio: 54.7 (2015 est.)

youth dependency ratio: 48.1 (2015 est.)

elderly dependency ratio: 6.6 (2015 est.)

potential support ratio: 15.1 (2015 est.)

MEDIAN AGE:

total: 26.8 years (2018 est.)

male: 25.7 years

female: 27.9 years

country comparison to the world: 147

POPULATION GROWTH RATE:

1.02% (2018 est.)

country comparison to the world: 106

BIRTH RATE:

21.6 births/1,000 population (2018 est.)

country comparison to the world: 72

DEATH RATE:

6.4 deaths/1,000 population (2018 est.)

country comparison to the world: 146

NET MIGRATION RATE:

-5.1 migrant(s)/1,000 population (2018 est.)

country comparison to the world: 195

POPULATION DISTRIBUTION:

the vast majority of Kyrgyzstanis live in rural areas; densest population settlement is to the north in and around the capital, Bishkek, followed by Osh in the west; the least densely populated area is the east, southeast in the Tien Shan mountains

URBANIZATION:

urban population: 36.6% of total population (2019)

rate of urbanization: 2.03% annual rate of change (2015-20 est.)

MAJOR URBAN AREAS - POPULATION:

1.017 million BISHKEK (capital) (2019)

SEX RATIO:

at birth: 1.07 male(s)/female

0-14 years: 1.05 male(s)/female

15-24 years: 1.03 male(s)/female

25-54 years: 0.96 male(s)/female

55-64 years: 0.77 male(s)/female

65 years and over: 0.62 male(s)/female

total population: 0.96 male(s)/female (2018 est.)

MOTHER'S MEAN AGE AT FIRST BIRTH:

23.2 years (2014 est.)

MATERNAL MORTALITY RATE:

60 deaths/100,000 live births (2017 est.)

country comparison to the world: 89

INFANT MORTALITY RATE:

total: 25 deaths/1,000 live births (2018 est.)

male: 29 deaths/1,000 live births

female: 20.7 deaths/1,000 live births

country comparison to the world: 68

LIFE EXPECTANCY AT BIRTH:

total population: 71.2 years (2018 est.)

male: 67.1 years

female: 75.6 years

country comparison to the world: 156

TOTAL FERTILITY RATE:

2.59 children born/woman (2018 est.)

country comparison to the world: 71

CONTRACEPTIVE PREVALENCE RATE:

42% (2014)

DRINKING WATER SOURCE:

improved:

urban: 96.7% of population

rural: 86.2% of population

total: 90% of population

unimproved:

urban: 3.3% of population

rural: 13.8% of population

total: 10% of population (2015 est.)

CURRENT HEALTH EXPENDITURE:

6.6% (2016)

PHYSICIANS DENSITY:

1.88 physicians/1,000 population (2014)

HOSPITAL BED DENSITY:

4.5 beds/1,000 population (2013)

SANITATION FACILITY ACCESS:

improved:

urban: 89.1% of population (2015 est.)

rural: 95.6% of population (2015 est.)

total: 93.3% of population (2015 est.)

unimproved:

urban: 10.9% of population (2015 est.)

rural: 4.4% of population (2015 est.)

total: 6.7% of population (2015 est.)

HIV/AIDS - ADULT PREVALENCE RATE:
0.2% (2018 est.)

country comparison to the world: 103

HIV/AIDS - PEOPLE LIVING WITH HIV/AIDS:
8,500 (2018 est.)

country comparison to the world: 106

HIV/AIDS - DEATHS:
<200 (2018 est.)

OBESITY - ADULT PREVALENCE RATE:
16.6% (2016)

country comparison to the world: 121

CHILDREN UNDER THE AGE OF 5 YEARS UNDERWEIGHT:
2.8% (2014)

country comparison to the world: 104

EDUCATION EXPENDITURES:
7.2% of GDP (2017)

country comparison to the world: 13

LITERACY:
definition: age 15 and over can read and write

total population: 99.5%

male: 99.6%

female: 99.4% (2015 est.)

SCHOOL LIFE EXPECTANCY (PRIMARY TO TERTIARY EDUCATION):
total: 13 years

male: 13 years

female: 14 years (2017)

UNEMPLOYMENT, YOUTH AGES 15-24:
total: 14.8%

male: 11.7%

female: 21% (2017 est.)

country comparison to the world: 93

GOVERNMENT :: KYRGYZSTAN

COUNTRY NAME:
conventional long form: Kyrgyz Republic

conventional short form: Kyrgyzstan

local long form: Kyrgyz Respublikasy

local short form: Kyrgyzstan

former: Kirghiz Soviet Socialist Republic

etymology: a combination of the Turkic words "kyrg" (forty) and "-yz" (tribes) with the Persian suffix "-stan" (country) creating the meaning "Land of the Forty Tribes"; the name refers to the 40 clans united by the legendary Kyrgyz hero, MANAS

GOVERNMENT TYPE:
parliamentary republic

CAPITAL:
name: Bishkek

geographic coordinates: 42 52 N, 74 36 E

time difference: UTC+6 (11 hours ahead of Washington, DC, during Standard Time)

etymology: founded in 1868 as a Russian settlement on the site of a previously destroyed fortress named "Pishpek"; the name was retained and overtime became "Bishkek"

ADMINISTRATIVE DIVISIONS:
7 provinces (oblustar, singular - oblus) and 2 cities* (shaarlar, singular - shaar); Batken Oblusu, Bishkek Shaary*, Chuy Oblusu (Bishkek), Jalal-Abad Oblusu, Naryn Oblusu, Osh Oblusu, Osh Shaary*, Talas Oblusu, Ysyk-Kol Oblusu (Karakol)

note: administrative divisions have the same names as their administrative centers (exceptions have the administrative center name following in parentheses)

INDEPENDENCE:
31 August 1991 (from the Soviet Union)

NATIONAL HOLIDAY:
Independence Day, 31 August (1991)

CONSTITUTION:
history: previous 1993; latest adopted by referendum 27 June 2010, effective 2 July 2010; note - constitutional amendments that bolstered some presidential powers and transferred others from the president to the prime minister passed in a referendum in December 2016, effective December 2017

amendments: proposed as a draft law by the majority of the Supreme Council membership or by petition of 300,000 voters; passage requires at least two-thirds majority vote of the Council membership in each of at least three readings of the draft two months apart; the draft may be submitted to a referendum if approved by two thirds of the Council membership; adoption requires the signature of the president; amended 2017 (2018)

LEGAL SYSTEM:
civil law system, which includes features of French civil law and Russian Federation laws

INTERNATIONAL LAW ORGANIZATION PARTICIPATION:
has not submitted an ICJ jurisdiction declaration; non-party state to the ICCt

CITIZENSHIP:
citizenship by birth: no

citizenship by descent only: at least one parent must be a citizen of Kyrgyzstan

dual citizenship recognized: yes, but only if a mutual treaty on dual citizenship is in force

residency requirement for naturalization: 5 years

SUFFRAGE:
18 years of age; universal

EXECUTIVE BRANCH:
chief of state: President Sooronbay JEENBEKOV (since 24 November 2017)

head of government: Prime Minister Mukhammedkalyy ABYL-GAZIEV (since 20 April 2018); First Deputy Prime Minister Kubatbek BORONOV (since 20 April 2018); Deputy Prime Ministers Jenish RAZAKOV (since 20 April 2018), Altynay OMURBEKOVA (since 20 April 2018), Zamirbek ASKAROV (since 20 April 2018)

cabinet: Cabinet of Ministers proposed by the prime minister, appointed by the president upon approval by the Supreme Council; defense and security committee chairs appointed by the president

elections/appointments: president directly elected by absolute majority popular vote in 2 rounds if needed for a single 6-year term; election last held on 15 October 2017 (next to be held in October 2023); prime minister nominated by the majority party or majority coalition in the Supreme Council, appointed by the president upon approval by the Supreme Council

election results: Sooronbay JEENBEKOV elected president in first round; percent of vote - Sooronbay JEENBEKOV (SDPK) 54.2%, Omurbek BABANOV (Respublika)

33.5%, Adakhan MADUMAROV (Butun Kyrgyzstan) 6.6%, Temir SARIYEV (Akshumar) 2.5%, other 3.2%

LEGISLATIVE BRANCH:

description: unicameral Supreme Council or Jogorku Kengesh (120 seats; parties directly elected in a single nationwide constituency by closed party-list proportional representation vote; members selected from party lists to serve 5-year terms)

elections: last held on 4 October 2015 (next to be held in 2020)

election results: percent of vote by party - SDPK 27.4%, Respublika-Ata-Jurt 20.1%, Kyrgyzstan Party 12.9%, Onuguu-Progress 9.3%, Bir Bol 8.5%, Ata-Meken 7.7%, other 14.1%; seats by party - SDPK 38, Respublika-Ata-Jurt 28, Kyrgyzstan Party 18, Onuguu-Progress 13, Bir Bol 12, Ata-Meken 11; composition - men 97, women 23, percent of women 19.2%

JUDICIAL BRANCH:

highest courts: Supreme Court (consists of 25 judges); Constitutional Chamber of the Supreme Court (consists of the chairperson, deputy chairperson, and 9 judges)

judge selection and term of office: Supreme Court and Constitutional Court judges appointed by the Supreme Council on the recommendation of the president; Supreme Court judges serve for 10 years, Constitutional Court judges serve for 15 years; mandatory retirement at age 70 for judges of both courts

subordinate courts: Higher Court of Arbitration; oblast (provincial) and city courts

POLITICAL PARTIES AND LEADERS:

Ata-Meken (Fatherland) [Almambet SHYKMAMATOV]
Bir Bol (Stay United) [Altynbek SULAYMANOV]
Kyrgyzstan Party [Almazbek BAATYRBEKOV]
Onuguu-Progress (Development-Progress) [Bakyt TOROBAEV]
Respublika-Ata-Jurt (Republic-Homeland) [Jyrgalbek TURUSKULOV] (parliamentary faction)
Social-Democratic Party of Kyrgyzstan or SDPK [Almazbek ATAMBAEV, Isa OMURKULOV]

INTERNATIONAL ORGANIZATION PARTICIPATION:

ADB, CICA, CIS, CSTO, EAEC, EAEU, EAPC, EBRD, ECO, EITI (compliant country), FAO, GCTU, IAEA, IBRD, ICAO, ICC (NGOs), ICRM, IDA, IDB, IFAD, IFC, IFRCS, ILO, IMF, Interpol, IOC, IOM, IPU, ISO (correspondent), ITSO, ITU, MIGA, NAM (observer), OIC, OPCW, OSCE, PCA, PFP, SCO, UN, UNAMID, UNCTAD, UNESCO, UNIDO, UNISFA, UNMIL, UNMISS, UNWTO, UPU, WCO, WFTU (NGOs), WHO, WIPO, WMO, WTO

DIPLOMATIC REPRESENTATION IN THE US:

Ambassador Bolot I. OTUNBAEV (since 8 April 2018)

chancery: 2360 Massachusetts Avenue NW, Washington, DC 20008

telephone: [1] (202) 449-9822

FAX: [1] (202) 449-8275

honorary consulate(s): Maple Valley (WA)

DIPLOMATIC REPRESENTATION FROM THE US:

chief of mission: Ambassador Donald LU (since 18 September 2018)

telephone: [996] (312) 597-000

embassy: 171 Prospect Mira, Bishkek 720016

mailing address: use embassy street address

FAX: [996] (312) 597-744

FLAG DESCRIPTION:

red field with a yellow sun in the center having 40 rays representing the 40 Kyrgyz tribes; on the obverse side the rays run counterclockwise, on the reverse, clockwise; in the center of the sun is a red ring crossed by two sets of three lines, a stylized representation of a "tunduk" - the crown of a traditional Kyrgyz yurt; red symbolizes bravery and valor, the sun evinces peace and wealth

NATIONAL SYMBOL(S):

white falcon; national colors: red, yellow

NATIONAL ANTHEM:

name: "Kyrgyz Respublikasynyn Mamlekettik Gimni" (National Anthem of the Kyrgyz Republic)

lyrics/music: Djamil SADYKOV and Eshmambet KULUEV/Nasyr DAVLESOV and Kalyi MOLDOBASANOV

note: adopted 1992

ECONOMY :: KYRGYZSTAN

ECONOMY - OVERVIEW:

Kyrgyzstan is a landlocked, mountainous, lower middle income country with an economy dominated by minerals extraction, agriculture, and reliance on remittances from citizens working abroad. Cotton, wool, and meat are the main agricultural products, although only cotton is exported in any quantity. Other exports include gold, mercury, uranium, natural gas, and - in some years - electricity. The country has sought to attract foreign investment to expand its export base, including construction of hydroelectric dams, but a difficult investment climate and an ongoing legal battle with a Canadian firm over the joint ownership structure of the nation's largest gold mine deter potential investors. Remittances from Kyrgyz migrant workers, predominantly in Russia and Kazakhstan, are equivalent to more than one-quarter of Kyrgyzstan's GDP.

Following independence, Kyrgyzstan rapidly implemented market reforms, such as improving the regulatory system and instituting land reform. In 1998, Kyrgyzstan was the first Commonwealth of Independent States country to be accepted into the World Trade Organization. The government has privatized much of its ownership shares in public enterprises. Despite these reforms, the country suffered a severe drop in production in the early 1990s and has again faced slow growth in recent years as the global financial crisis and declining oil prices have dampened economies across Central Asia. The Kyrgyz government remains dependent on foreign donor support to finance its annual budget deficit of approximately 3 to 5% of GDP.

Kyrgyz leaders hope the country's August 2015 accession to the Eurasian Economic Union (EAEU) will bolster trade and investment, but slowing economies in Russia and China and low commodity prices continue to hamper economic growth. Large-scale trade and investment pledged by Kyrgyz leaders has been slow to develop. Many Kyrgyz entrepreneurs and politicians complain that non-tariff measures imposed by other EAEU member states are hurting certain sectors of the Kyrgyz economy, such as meat and dairy production, in which they have comparative advantage. Since acceding to the EAEU, the Kyrgyz Republic has continued harmonizing its laws and regulations to meet EAEU standards, though many local entrepreneurs believe this process as disjointed and incomplete. Kyrgyzstan's economic development continues to be hampered by corruption, lack of administrative transparency, lack of diversity in domestic industries, and difficulty attracting foreign aid and investment.

GDP (PURCHASING POWER PARITY):

$23.15 billion (2017 est.)

$22.14 billion (2016 est.)

$21.22 billion (2015 est.)

note: data are in 2017 dollars

country comparison to the world: 144

GDP (OFFICIAL EXCHANGE RATE):

$7.565 billion (2017 est.)

GDP - REAL GROWTH RATE:

4.6% (2017 est.)

4.3% (2016 est.)

3.9% (2015 est.)

country comparison to the world: 63

GDP - PER CAPITA (PPP):

$3,700 (2017 est.)

$3,600 (2016 est.)

$3,500 (2015 est.)

note: data are in 2017 dollars

country comparison to the world: 183

GROSS NATIONAL SAVING:

27.3% of GDP (2017 est.)

20.1% of GDP (2016 est.)

18.3% of GDP (2015 est.)

country comparison to the world: 42

GDP - COMPOSITION, BY END USE:

household consumption: 85.4% (2017 est.)

government consumption: 18.9% (2017 est.)

investment in fixed capital: 33.2% (2017 est.)

investment in inventories: 1.8% (2017 est.)

exports of goods and services: 39.7% (2017 est.)

imports of goods and services: -79% (2017 est.)

GDP - COMPOSITION, BY SECTOR OF ORIGIN:

agriculture: 14.6% (2017 est.)

industry: 31.2% (2017 est.)

services: 54.2% (2017 est.)

AGRICULTURE - PRODUCTS:

cotton, potatoes, vegetables, grapes, fruits and berries; sheep, goats, cattle, wool

INDUSTRIES:

small machinery, textiles, food processing, cement, shoes, lumber, refrigerators, furniture, electric motors, gold, rare earth metals

INDUSTRIAL PRODUCTION GROWTH RATE:

10.9% (2017 est.)

country comparison to the world: 10

LABOR FORCE:

2.841 million (2017 est.)

country comparison to the world: 107

LABOR FORCE - BY OCCUPATION:

agriculture: 48%

industry: 12.5%

services: 39.5% (2005 est.)

UNEMPLOYMENT RATE:

7.1% (2017 est.)

7.2% (2016 est.)

country comparison to the world: 109

POPULATION BELOW POVERTY LINE:

32.1% (2015 est.)

HOUSEHOLD INCOME OR CONSUMPTION BY PERCENTAGE SHARE:

lowest 10%: 4.4%

highest 10%: 22.9% (2014 est.)

DISTRIBUTION OF FAMILY INCOME - GINI INDEX:

33.4 (2007)

29 (2001)

country comparison to the world: 113

BUDGET:

revenues: 2.169 billion (2017 est.)

expenditures: 2.409 billion (2017 est.)

TAXES AND OTHER REVENUES:

28.7% (of GDP) (2017 est.)

country comparison to the world: 92

BUDGET SURPLUS (+) OR DEFICIT (-):

-3.2% (of GDP) (2017 est.)

country comparison to the world: 140

PUBLIC DEBT:

56% of GDP (2017 est.)

55.9% of GDP (2016 est.)

country comparison to the world: 79

FISCAL YEAR:

calendar year

INFLATION RATE (CONSUMER PRICES):

3.2% (2017 est.)

0.4% (2016 est.)

country comparison to the world: 135

CENTRAL BANK DISCOUNT RATE:

5% (31 December 2016)

8% (31 December 2015)

country comparison to the world: 81

COMMERCIAL BANK PRIME LENDING RATE:

18.49% (31 December 2017 est.)

22.23% (31 December 2016 est.)

country comparison to the world: 19

STOCK OF NARROW MONEY:

$1.698 billion (31 December 2017 est.)

$1.411 billion (31 December 2016 est.)

country comparison to the world: 139

STOCK OF BROAD MONEY:

$1.698 billion (31 December 2017 est.)

$1.411 billion (31 December 2016 est.)

country comparison to the world: 147

STOCK OF DOMESTIC CREDIT:

$1.856 billion (31 December 2017 est.)

$1.444 billion (31 December 2016 est.)

country comparison to the world: 155

MARKET VALUE OF PUBLICLY TRADED SHARES:

$165 million (31 December 2012 est.)

$165 million (31 December 2011 est.)

$79 million (31 December 2010 est.)

country comparison to the world: 120

CURRENT ACCOUNT BALANCE:

-$306 million (2017 est.)

-$792 million (2016 est.)

country comparison to the world: 105

EXPORTS:

$1.84 billion (2017 est.)

$1.544 billion (2016 est.)

country comparison to the world: 145

EXPORTS - PARTNERS:

Switzerland 59.1%, Uzbekistan 9.4%, Kazakhstan 5.1%, Russia 4.9%, UK 4% (2017)

EXPORTS - COMMODITIES:

gold, cotton, wool, garments, meat; mercury, uranium, electricity; machinery; shoes

IMPORTS:

$4.187 billion (2017 est.)

$3.709 billion (2016 est.)

country comparison to the world: 138

IMPORTS - COMMODITIES:

oil and gas, machinery and equipment, chemicals, foodstuffs

IMPORTS - PARTNERS:

China 32.6%, Russia 24.8%, Kazakhstan 16.4%, Turkey 4.8%, US 4.2% (2017)

RESERVES OF FOREIGN EXCHANGE AND GOLD:

$2.177 billion (31 December 2017 est.)

$1.97 billion (31 December 2016 est.)

country comparison to the world: 120

DEBT - EXTERNAL:

$8.164 billion (31 December 2017 est.)

$8.182 billion (31 December 2016 est.)

country comparison to the world: 121

STOCK OF DIRECT FOREIGN INVESTMENT - AT HOME:

$6.003 billion (31 December 2017 est.)

$5.21 billion (31 December 2016 est.)

country comparison to the world: 105

STOCK OF DIRECT FOREIGN INVESTMENT - ABROAD:

$709.3 million (31 December 2017 est.)

$655.5 million (31 December 2016 est.)

country comparison to the world: 91

EXCHANGE RATES:

soms (KGS) per US dollar -

68.35 (2017 est.)

69.914 (2016 est.)

69.914 (2015 est.)

64.462 (2014 est.)

53.654 (2013 est.)

ENERGY :: KYRGYZSTAN

ELECTRICITY ACCESS:

electrification - total population: 100% (2016)

ELECTRICITY - PRODUCTION:

13.04 billion kWh (2016 est.)

country comparison to the world: 93

ELECTRICITY - CONSUMPTION:

10.52 billion kWh (2016 est.)

country comparison to the world: 94

ELECTRICITY - EXPORTS:

184 million kWh (2015 est.)

country comparison to the world: 77

ELECTRICITY - IMPORTS:

331 million kWh (2016 est.)

country comparison to the world: 87

ELECTRICITY - INSTALLED GENERATING CAPACITY:

4.046 million kW (2016 est.)

country comparison to the world: 87

ELECTRICITY - FROM FOSSIL FUELS:

24% of total installed capacity (2016 est.)

country comparison to the world: 190

ELECTRICITY - FROM NUCLEAR FUELS:

0% of total installed capacity (2017 est.)

country comparison to the world: 123

ELECTRICITY - FROM HYDROELECTRIC PLANTS:

76% of total installed capacity (2017 est.)

country comparison to the world: 13

ELECTRICITY - FROM OTHER RENEWABLE SOURCES:

0% of total installed capacity (2017 est.)

country comparison to the world: 197

CRUDE OIL - PRODUCTION:

1,000 bbl/day (2018 est.)

country comparison to the world: 92

CRUDE OIL - EXPORTS:

0 bbl/day (2015 est.)

country comparison to the world: 150

CRUDE OIL - IMPORTS:

4,480 bbl/day (2015 est.)

country comparison to the world: 77

CRUDE OIL - PROVED RESERVES:

40 million bbl (1 January 2018 est.)

country comparison to the world: 79

REFINED PETROLEUM PRODUCTS - PRODUCTION:

6,996 bbl/day (2015 est.)

country comparison to the world: 102

REFINED PETROLEUM PRODUCTS - CONSUMPTION:

37,000 bbl/day (2016 est.)

country comparison to the world: 114

REFINED PETROLEUM PRODUCTS - EXPORTS:

2,290 bbl/day (2015 est.)

country comparison to the world: 103

REFINED PETROLEUM PRODUCTS - IMPORTS:

34,280 bbl/day (2015 est.)

country comparison to the world: 96

NATURAL GAS - PRODUCTION:

28.32 million cu m (2017 est.)

country comparison to the world: 88

NATURAL GAS - CONSUMPTION:

186.9 million cu m (2017 est.)

country comparison to the world: 106

NATURAL GAS - EXPORTS:

0 cu m (2017 est.)

country comparison to the world: 134

NATURAL GAS - IMPORTS:

169.9 million cu m (2017 est.)

country comparison to the world: 74

NATURAL GAS - PROVED RESERVES:

5.663 billion cu m (1 January 2018 est.)

country comparison to the world: 89

CARBON DIOXIDE EMISSIONS FROM CONSUMPTION OF ENERGY:

10.02 million Mt (2017 est.)

country comparison to the world: 108

COMMUNICATIONS :: KYRGYZSTAN

TELEPHONES - FIXED LINES:

total subscriptions: 362,288

subscriptions per 100 inhabitants: 6 (2017 est.)

country comparison to the world: 106

TELEPHONES - MOBILE CELLULAR:

total subscriptions: 7,369,927

subscriptions per 100 inhabitants: 127 (2017 est.)

country comparison to the world: 103

TELEPHONE SYSTEM:

general assessment: digital radio-relay stations, and fiber-optic links; low fixed-line and fixed-broadband penetration and low to moderate mobile broadband penetration; international connectivity continues to grow; 4 mobile networks in operation; 4G networks cover over 50% of the nation, eventually 5G networks will be available (2018)

domestic: fixed-line penetration 6 per 100 persons remains low and concentrated in urban areas; mobile-cellular subscribership up to over 127 per 100 persons (2018) international: country code - 996; connections with other CIS countries by landline or microwave radio relay and with other countries by leased connections with Moscow international gateway switch and by satellite; satellite earth stations - 2 (1 Intersputnik, 1 Intelsat) (2019)

BROADCAST MEDIA:

state-funded public TV broadcaster KTRK has nationwide coverage; also operates Ala-Too 24 news channel which broadcasts 24/7 and 4 other educational, cultural, and sports channels; ELTR and Channel 5 are state-owned stations with national reach; the switchover to digital TV in 2017 resulted in private TV station growth; approximately 20 stations are struggling to increase their own content up to 50% of airtime, as required by law, instead of rebroadcasting primarily programs from Russian channels or airing unlicensed movies and music; 3 Russian TV stations also broadcast; state-funded radio stations and about 10 significant private radio stations also exist (2019)

INTERNET COUNTRY CODE:

.kg

INTERNET USERS:

total: 1,976,006

percent of population: 34.5% (July 2016 est.)

country comparison to the world: 113

BROADBAND - FIXED SUBSCRIPTIONS:

total: 258,013

subscriptions per 100 inhabitants: 4 (2017 est.)

country comparison to the world: 100

MILITARY AND SECURITY :: KYRGYZSTAN

MILITARY EXPENDITURES:

1.57% of GDP (2018)
1.67% of GDP (2017)
1.77% of GDP (2016)
1.75% of GDP (2015)
1.71% of GDP (2014)

country comparison to the world: 73

MILITARY AND SECURITY FORCES:

Kyrgyz Armed Forces: Land Forces, Air Defense Forces, National Guard, State Border Service, and State Committee on Defense Affairs (GKDO) (2018)

MILITARY SERVICE AGE AND OBLIGATION:

18-27 years of age for compulsory or voluntary male military service in the Armed Forces or Interior Ministry; 1-year service obligation (9 months for university graduates), with optional fee-based 3-year service in the call-up mobilization reserve; women may volunteer at age 19; 16-17 years of age for military cadets, who cannot take part in military operations (2013)

TRANSPORTATION :: KYRGYZSTAN

NATIONAL AIR TRANSPORT SYSTEM:

number of registered air carriers: 3 (2015)

inventory of registered aircraft operated by air carriers: 10 (2015)

annual passenger traffic on registered air carriers: 625,294 (2015)

annual freight traffic on registered air carriers: 69,290 mt-km (2015)

CIVIL AIRCRAFT REGISTRATION COUNTRY CODE PREFIX:

EX (2016)

AIRPORTS:

28 (2013)

country comparison to the world: 123

AIRPORTS - WITH PAVED RUNWAYS:

total: 18 (2017)

over 3,047 m: 1 (2017)

2,438 to 3,047 m: 3 (2017)

1,524 to 2,437 m: 11 (2017)

under 914 m: 3 (2017)

AIRPORTS - WITH UNPAVED RUNWAYS:

total: 10 (2013)

1,524 to 2,437 m: 1 (2013)

914 to 1,523 m: 1 (2013)

under 914 m: 8 (2013)

PIPELINES:

3566 km gas (2018), 16 km oil (2013)

RAILWAYS:

total: 424 km (2018)

broad gauge: 424 km 1.520-m gauge (2018)

country comparison to the world: 118

ROADWAYS:

total: 34,000 km (2018)

country comparison to the world: 93

WATERWAYS:

600 km (2010)

country comparison to the world: 78

PORTS AND TERMINALS:

lake port(s): Balykchy (Ysyk-Kol or Rybach'ye)(Lake Ysyk-Kol)

TRANSNATIONAL ISSUES :: KYRGYZSTAN

DISPUTES - INTERNATIONAL:

disputes in Isfara Valley delay completion of delimitation with Tajikistan; delimitation of approximately 15% or 200 km of border with Uzbekistan is hampered by serious disputes over enclaves and other areas

ILLICIT DRUGS:

limited illicit cultivation of cannabis and opium poppy for CIS markets; limited government eradication of illicit crops; transit point for Southwest Asian narcotics bound for Russia and the rest of Europe; major consumer of opiates

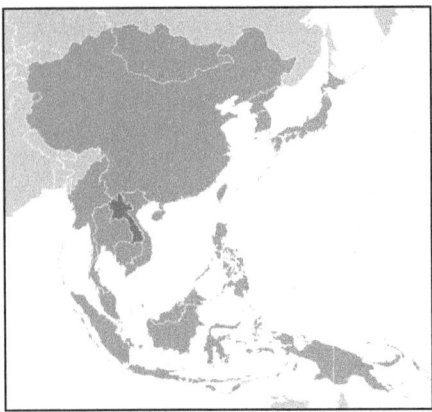

EAST ASIA / SOUTHEAST ASIA :: LAOS

INTRODUCTION :: LAOS

BACKGROUND:

Modern-day Laos has its roots in the ancient Lao kingdom of Lan Xang, established in the 14th century under King FA NGUM. For 300 years Lan Xang had influence reaching into present-day Cambodia and Thailand, as well as over all of what is now Laos. After centuries of gradual decline, Laos came under the domination of Siam (Thailand) from the late 18th century until the late 19th century, when it became part of French Indochina. The Franco-Siamese Treaty of 1907 defined the current Lao border with Thailand. In 1975, the communist Pathet Lao took control of the government, ending a six-century-old monarchy and instituting a strict socialist regime closely aligned to Vietnam. A gradual, limited return to private enterprise and the liberalization of foreign investment laws began in 1988. Laos became a member of ASEAN in 1997 and the WTO in 2013.

GEOGRAPHY :: LAOS

LOCATION:

Southeastern Asia, northeast of Thailand, west of Vietnam

GEOGRAPHIC COORDINATES:

18 00 N, 105 00 E

MAP REFERENCES:

Southeast Asia

AREA:

total: 236,800 sq km

land: 230,800 sq km

water: 6,000 sq km

country comparison to the world: 85

AREA - COMPARATIVE:

about twice the size of Pennsylvania; slightly larger than Utah

LAND BOUNDARIES:

total: 5,274 km

border countries (5): Burma 238 km, Cambodia 555 km, China 475 km, Thailand 1845 km, Vietnam 2161 km

COASTLINE:

0 km (landlocked)

MARITIME CLAIMS:

none (landlocked)

CLIMATE:

tropical monsoon; rainy season (May to November); dry season (December to April)

TERRAIN:

mostly rugged mountains; some plains and plateaus

ELEVATION:

mean elevation: 710 m

lowest point: Mekong River 70 m

highest point: Phu Bia 2,817 m

NATURAL RESOURCES:

timber, hydropower, gypsum, tin, gold, gemstones

LAND USE:

agricultural land: 10.6% (2011 est.)

arable land: 6.2% (2011 est.) / permanent crops: 0.7% (2011 est.) / permanent pasture: 3.7% (2011 est.)

forest: 67.9% (2011 est.)

other: 21.5% (2011 est.)

IRRIGATED LAND:

3,100 sq km (2012)

POPULATION DISTRIBUTION:

most densely populated area is in and around the capital city of Vientiane; large communities are primarily found along the Mekong River along the southwestern border; overall density is considered one of the lowest in Southeast Asia

NATURAL HAZARDS:

floods, droughts

ENVIRONMENT - CURRENT ISSUES:

unexploded ordnance; deforestation; soil erosion; loss of biodiversity; water pollution, most of the population does not have access to potable water

ENVIRONMENT - INTERNATIONAL AGREEMENTS:

party to: Biodiversity, Climate Change, Climate Change-Kyoto Protocol, Desertification, Endangered Species, Environmental Modification, Hazardous Wastes, Law of the Sea, Ozone Layer Protection

signed, but not ratified: none of the selected agreements

GEOGRAPHY - NOTE:

landlocked; most of the country is mountainous and thickly forested; the Mekong River forms a large part of the western boundary with Thailand

PEOPLE AND SOCIETY :: LAOS

POPULATION:

7,234,171 (July 2018 est.)

country comparison to the world: 101

NATIONALITY:
noun: Lao(s) or Laotian(s)

adjective: Lao or Laotian

ETHNIC GROUPS:
Lao 53.2%, Khmou 11%, Hmong 9.2%, Phouthay 3.4%, Tai 3.1%, Makong 2.5%, Katong 2.2%, Lue 2%, Akha 1.8%, other 11.6% (2015 est.)

note: the Laos Government officially recognizes 49 ethnic groups, but the total number of ethnic groups is estimated to be well over 200

LANGUAGES:
Lao (official), French, English, various ethnic languages

RELIGIONS:
Buddhist 64.7%, Christian 1.7%, none 31.4%, other/not stated 2.1% (2015 est.)

AGE STRUCTURE:
0-14 years: 32.19% (male 1,177,639 /female 1,151,134)

15-24 years: 21% (male 754,198 /female 764,673)

25-54 years: 37.29% (male 1,332,231 /female 1,365,715)

55-64 years: 5.57% (male 196,509 /female 206,613)

65 years and over: 3.95% (male 129,336 /female 156,123) (2018 est.)

DEPENDENCY RATIOS:
total dependency ratio: 60.2 (2015 est.)

youth dependency ratio: 54 (2015 est.)

elderly dependency ratio: 6.2 (2015 est.)

potential support ratio: 16.1 (2015 est.)

MEDIAN AGE:
total: 23.4 years (2018 est.)

male: 23 years

female: 23.7 years

country comparison to the world: 170

POPULATION GROWTH RATE:
1.48% (2018 est.)

country comparison to the world: 76

BIRTH RATE:
23.2 births/1,000 population (2018 est.)

country comparison to the world: 61

DEATH RATE:
7.3 deaths/1,000 population (2018 est.)

country comparison to the world: 122

NET MIGRATION RATE:
-1 migrant(s)/1,000 population (2018 est.)

country comparison to the world: 140

POPULATION DISTRIBUTION:
most densely populated area is in and around the capital city of Vientiane; large communities are primarily found along the Mekong River along the southwestern border; overall density is considered one of the lowest in Southeast Asia

URBANIZATION:
urban population: 35.6% of total population (2019)

rate of urbanization: 3.28% annual rate of change (2015-20 est.)

MAJOR URBAN AREAS - POPULATION:
673,000 VIENTIANE (capital) (2019)

SEX RATIO:
at birth: 1.04 male(s)/female

0-14 years: 1.02 male(s)/female

15-24 years: 0.99 male(s)/female

25-54 years: 0.98 male(s)/female

55-64 years: 0.95 male(s)/female

65 years and over: 0.83 male(s)/female

total population: 0.99 male(s)/female (2018 est.)

MATERNAL MORTALITY RATE:
185 deaths/100,000 live births (2017 est.)

country comparison to the world: 50

INFANT MORTALITY RATE:
total: 48.4 deaths/1,000 live births (2018 est.)

male: 53.6 deaths/1,000 live births

female: 43 deaths/1,000 live births

country comparison to the world: 30

LIFE EXPECTANCY AT BIRTH:
total population: 65 years (2018 est.)

male: 62.9 years

female: 67.1 years

country comparison to the world: 184

TOTAL FERTILITY RATE:
2.65 children born/woman (2018 est.)

country comparison to the world: 66

CONTRACEPTIVE PREVALENCE RATE:
54.1% (2017)

DRINKING WATER SOURCE:
improved:

urban: 85.6% of population

rural: 69.4% of population

total: 75.7% of population

unimproved:

urban: 14.4% of population

rural: 30.6% of population

total: 24.3% of population (2015 est.)

CURRENT HEALTH EXPENDITURE:
2.4% (2016)

PHYSICIANS DENSITY:
0.5 physicians/1,000 population (2014)

HOSPITAL BED DENSITY:
1.5 beds/1,000 population (2012)

SANITATION FACILITY ACCESS:
improved:

urban: 94.5% of population (2015 est.)

rural: 56% of population (2015 est.)

total: 70.9% of population (2015 est.)

unimproved:

urban: 5.5% of population (2015 est.)

rural: 44% of population (2015 est.)

total: 29.1% of population (2015 est.)

HIV/AIDS - ADULT PREVALENCE RATE:
0.3% (2018 est.)

country comparison to the world: 90

HIV/AIDS - PEOPLE LIVING WITH HIV/AIDS:
12,000 (2018 est.)

country comparison to the world: 96

HIV/AIDS - DEATHS:
<500 (2018 est.)

MAJOR INFECTIOUS DISEASES:
degree of risk: very high (2016)

food or waterborne diseases: bacterial and protozoal diarrhea, hepatitis A, and typhoid fever (2016)

vectorborne diseases: dengue fever and malaria (2016)

OBESITY - ADULT PREVALENCE RATE:
5.3% (2016)

country comparison to the world: 179

CHILDREN UNDER THE AGE OF 5 YEARS UNDERWEIGHT:
26.9% (2011)

country comparison to the world: 16

EDUCATION EXPENDITURES:

2.9% of GDP (2014)

country comparison to the world: 145

LITERACY:

definition: age 15 and over can read and write

total population: 84.7%

male: 90%

female: 79.4% (2015 est.)

SCHOOL LIFE EXPECTANCY (PRIMARY TO TERTIARY EDUCATION):

total: 11 years

male: 11 years

female: 11 years (2017)

UNEMPLOYMENT, YOUTH AGES 15-24:

total: 18.2%

male: 20.8%

female: 15.5% (2017 est.)

country comparison to the world: 75

GOVERNMENT :: LAOS

COUNTRY NAME:

conventional long form: Lao People's Democratic Republic

conventional short form: Laos

local long form: Sathalanalat Paxathipatai Paxaxon Lao

local short form: Mueang Lao (unofficial)

etymology: name means "Land of the Lao [people]"

GOVERNMENT TYPE:

communist state

CAPITAL:

name: Vientiane (Viangchan)

geographic coordinates: 17 58 N, 102 36 E

time difference: UTC+7 (12 hours ahead of Washington, DC, during Standard Time)

etymology: the meaning in Pali, a Buddhist liturgical language, is "city of sandalwood"

ADMINISTRATIVE DIVISIONS:

17 provinces (khoueng, singular and plural) and 1 prefecture* (kampheng nakhon); Attapu, Bokeo, Bolikhamxai, Champasak, Houaphan, Khammouan, Louangnamtha, Louangphabang, Oudomxai, Phongsali, Salavan, Savannakhet, Viangchan (Vientiane)*, Viangchan, Xaignabouli, Xaisomboun, Xekong, Xiangkhouang

INDEPENDENCE:

19 July 1949 (from France by the Franco-Lao General Convention); 22 October 1953 (Franco-Lao Treaty recognizes full independence)

NATIONAL HOLIDAY:

Republic Day (National Day), 2 December (1975)

CONSTITUTION:

history: previous 1947 (preindependence); latest promulgated 13-15 August 1991

amendments: proposed by the National Assembly; passage requires at least two-thirds majority vote of the Assembly membership and promulgation by the president of the republic; amended 2003, 2015 (2018)

LEGAL SYSTEM:

civil law system similar in form to the French system

INTERNATIONAL LAW ORGANIZATION PARTICIPATION:

has not submitted an ICJ jurisdiction declaration; non-party state to the ICCt

CITIZENSHIP:

citizenship by birth: no

citizenship by descent only: at least one parent must be a citizen of Laos

dual citizenship recognized: no

residency requirement for naturalization: 10 years

SUFFRAGE:

18 years of age; universal

EXECUTIVE BRANCH:

chief of state: President BOUNNYANG Vorachit (since 20 April 2016); Vice President PHANKHAM Viphavan (since 20 April 2016)

head of government: Prime Minister THONGLOUN Sisoulit (since 20 April 2016); Deputy Prime Ministers BOUNTHONG Chitmani, SONXAI Siphandon, SOMDI Douangdi (since 20 April 2016)

cabinet: Council of Ministers appointed by the president, approved by the National Assembly

elections/appointments: president and vice president indirectly elected by the National Assembly for a 5-year term (no term limits); election last held on 20 April 2016 (next to be held in 2021); prime minister nominated by the president, elected by the National Assembly for 5-year term

election results: BOUNNYANG Vorachit (LPRP) elected president; PHANKHAM Viphavan (LPRP) elected vice president; percent of National Assembly vote - NA; THONGLOUN Sisoulit (LPRP) elected prime minister; percent of National Assembly vote - NA

LEGISLATIVE BRANCH:

description: unicameral National Assembly or Sapha Heng Xat (149 seats; members directly elected in multi-seat constituencies by simple majority vote from candidate lists provided by the Lao People's Revolutionary Party; members serve 5-year terms)

elections: last held on 20 March 2016 (next to be held in 2021)

election results: percent of vote by party - NA; seats by party - LPRP 144, independent 5; composition - men 108, women 41, percent of women 27.5%

JUDICIAL BRANCH:

highest courts: People's Supreme Court (consists of the court president and organized into criminal, civil, administrative, commercial, family, and juvenile chambers, each with a vice president and several judges)

judge selection and term of office: president of People's Supreme Court appointed by the National Assembly upon the recommendation of the president of the republic for a 5-year term; vice presidents of the People's Supreme Court appointed by the president of the republic upon the recommendation of the National Assembly; appointment of chamber judges NA; tenure of court vice presidents and chamber judges NA

subordinate courts: appellate courts; provincial, municipal, district, and military courts

POLITICAL PARTIES AND LEADERS:

Lao People's Revolutionary Party or LPRP [BOUNNYANG Vorachit]

note: other parties proscribed

INTERNATIONAL ORGANIZATION PARTICIPATION:

ADB, ARF, ASEAN, CP, EAS, FAO, G-77, IAEA, IBRD, ICAO, ICRM, IDA, IFAD, IFC, IFRCS, ILO, IMF, Interpol, IOC, IPU, ISO (subscriber), ITU, MIGA, NAM, OIF, OPCW, PCA, UN, UNCTAD, UNESCO,

UNIDO, UNWTO, UPU, WCO, WFTU (NGOs), WHO, WIPO, WMO, WTO

DIPLOMATIC REPRESENTATION IN THE US:

Ambassador MAI Xaignavong (since 3 August 2015)

chancery: 2222 S Street NW, Washington, DC 20008

telephone: [1] (202) 332-6416

FAX: [1] (202) 332-4923

consulate(s): New York

DIPLOMATIC REPRESENTATION FROM THE US:

chief of mission: Ambassador Rena BITTER (since 2 November 2016)

telephone: [856] 21-48-7000

embassy: Thadeua Road, Kilometer 9, Ban Somvang Tai, Hatsayfong District, Vientiane

mailing address: American Embassy Vientiane, Unit 46222, APO AP 96546-6222

FAX: [856] 21-48-7190

FLAG DESCRIPTION:

three horizontal bands of red (top), blue (double width), and red with a large white disk centered in the blue band; the red bands recall the blood shed for liberation; the blue band represents the Mekong River and prosperity; the white disk symbolizes the full moon against the Mekong River, but also signifies the unity of the people under the Lao People's Revolutionary Party, as well as the country's bright future

NATIONAL SYMBOL(S):

elephant; national colors: red, white, blue

NATIONAL ANTHEM:

name: "Pheng Xat Lao" (Hymn of the Lao People)

lyrics/music: SISANA Sisane/THONGDY Sounthonevichit

note: music adopted 1945, lyrics adopted 1975; the anthem's lyrics were changed following the 1975 Communist revolution that overthrew the monarchy

ECONOMY :: LAOS

ECONOMY - OVERVIEW:

The government of Laos, one of the few remaining one-party communist states, began decentralizing control and encouraging private enterprise in 1986. Economic growth averaged more than 6% per year in the period 1988-2008, and Laos' growth has more recently been amongst the fastest in Asia, averaging more than 7% per year for most of the last decade.

Nevertheless, Laos remains a country with an underdeveloped infrastructure, particularly in rural areas. It has a basic, but improving, road system, and limited external and internal land-line telecommunications. Electricity is available to 83% of the population. Agriculture, dominated by rice cultivation in lowland areas, accounts for about 20% of GDP and 73% of total employment. Recently, the country has faced a persistent current account deficit, falling foreign currency reserves, and growing public debt.

Laos' economy is heavily dependent on capital-intensive natural resource exports. The economy has benefited from high-profile foreign direct investment in hydropower dams along the Mekong River, copper and gold mining, logging, and construction, although some projects in these industries have drawn criticism for their environmental impacts.

Laos gained Normal Trade Relations status with the US in 2004 and applied for Generalized System of Preferences trade benefits in 2013 after being admitted to the World Trade Organization earlier in the year. Laos held the chairmanship of ASEAN in 2016. Laos is in the process of implementing a value-added tax system. The government appears committed to raising the country's profile among foreign investors and has developed special economic zones replete with generous tax incentives, but a limited labor pool, a small domestic market, and corruption remain impediments to investment. Laos also has ongoing problems with the business environment, including onerous registration requirements, a gap between legislation and implementation, and unclear or conflicting regulations.

GDP (PURCHASING POWER PARITY):

$49.34 billion (2017 est.)

$46.16 billion (2016 est.)

$43.13 billion (2015 est.)

note: data are in 2017 dollars

country comparison to the world: 111

GDP (OFFICIAL EXCHANGE RATE):

$16.97 billion (2017 est.)

GDP - REAL GROWTH RATE:

6.9% (2017 est.)

7% (2016 est.)

7.3% (2015 est.)

country comparison to the world: 22

GDP - PER CAPITA (PPP):

$7,400 (2017 est.)

$7,000 (2016 est.)

$6,600 (2015 est.)

note: data are in 2017 dollars

country comparison to the world: 155

GROSS NATIONAL SAVING:

22.7% of GDP (2017 est.)

21.3% of GDP (2016 est.)

15.8% of GDP (2015 est.)

country comparison to the world: 79

GDP - COMPOSITION, BY END USE:

household consumption: 63.7% (2017 est.)

government consumption: 14.1% (2017 est.)

investment in fixed capital: 30.9% (2017 est.)

investment in inventories: 3.1% (2017 est.)

exports of goods and services: 34.6% (2017 est.)

imports of goods and services: -43.2% (2017 est.)

GDP - COMPOSITION, BY SECTOR OF ORIGIN:

agriculture: 20.9% (2017 est.)

industry: 33.2% (2017 est.)

services: 45.9% (2017 est.)

AGRICULTURE - PRODUCTS:

sweet potatoes, vegetables, corn, coffee, sugarcane, tobacco, cotton, tea, peanuts, rice; cassava (manioc, tapioca), water buffalo, pigs, cattle, poultry

INDUSTRIES:

mining (copper, tin, gold, gypsum); timber, electric power, agricultural processing, rubber, construction, garments, cement, tourism

INDUSTRIAL PRODUCTION GROWTH RATE:

8% (2017 est.)

country comparison to the world: 23

LABOR FORCE:

3.582 million (2017 est.)

country comparison to the world: 100

LABOR FORCE - BY OCCUPATION:

agriculture: 73.1%

industry: 6.1%

services: 20.6% (2012 est.)

UNEMPLOYMENT RATE:

0.7% (2017 est.)

0.7% (2016 est.)

country comparison to the world: 4

POPULATION BELOW POVERTY LINE:

22% (2013 est.)

HOUSEHOLD INCOME OR CONSUMPTION BY PERCENTAGE SHARE:

lowest 10%: 3.3%

highest 10%: 30.3% (2008)

DISTRIBUTION OF FAMILY INCOME - GINI INDEX:

36.7 (2008)

34.6 (2002)

country comparison to the world: 87

BUDGET:

revenues: 3.099 billion (2017 est.)

expenditures: 4.038 billion (2017 est.)

TAXES AND OTHER REVENUES:

18.3% (of GDP) (2017 est.)

country comparison to the world: 161

BUDGET SURPLUS (+) OR DEFICIT (-):

-5.5% (of GDP) (2017 est.)

country comparison to the world: 172

PUBLIC DEBT:

63.6% of GDP (2017 est.)

58.4% of GDP (2016 est.)

country comparison to the world: 64

FISCAL YEAR:

1 October - 30 September

INFLATION RATE (CONSUMER PRICES):

0.8% (2017 est.)

1.6% (2016 est.)

country comparison to the world: 42

CENTRAL BANK DISCOUNT RATE:

4.3% (31 December 2010)

4% (31 December 2009)

country comparison to the world: 86

COMMERCIAL BANK PRIME LENDING RATE:

18.5% (31 December 2017 est.)

18% (31 December 2016 est.)

country comparison to the world: 18

STOCK OF NARROW MONEY:

$1.131 billion (31 December 2017 est.)

$1.1 billion (31 December 2016 est.)

country comparison to the world: 155

STOCK OF BROAD MONEY:

$1.131 billion (31 December 2017 est.)

$1.1 billion (31 December 2016 est.)

country comparison to the world: 160

STOCK OF DOMESTIC CREDIT:

$9.3 billion (31 December 2017 est.)

$8.623 billion (31 December 2016 est.)

country comparison to the world: 108

MARKET VALUE OF PUBLICLY TRADED SHARES:

$1.012 billion (2012 est.)

$576.8 million (2011 est.)

country comparison to the world: 105

CURRENT ACCOUNT BALANCE:

-$2.057 billion (2017 est.)

-$2.07 billion (2016 est.)

country comparison to the world: 165

EXPORTS:

$3.654 billion (2017 est.)

$2.705 billion (2016 est.)

country comparison to the world: 121

EXPORTS - PARTNERS:

Thailand 42.6%, China 28.7%, Vietnam 10.4%, India 4.4% (2017)

EXPORTS - COMMODITIES:

wood products, coffee, electricity, tin, copper, gold, cassava

IMPORTS:

$4.976 billion (2017 est.)

$4.739 billion (2016 est.)

country comparison to the world: 131

IMPORTS - COMMODITIES:

machinery and equipment, vehicles, fuel, consumer goods

IMPORTS - PARTNERS:

Thailand 59.1%, China 21.5%, Vietnam 9.8% (2017)

RESERVES OF FOREIGN EXCHANGE AND GOLD:

$1.27 billion (31 December 2017 est.)

$940.1 million (31 December 2016 est.)

country comparison to the world: 128

DEBT - EXTERNAL:

$14.9 billion (31 December 2017 est.)

$12.9 billion (31 December 2016 est.)

country comparison to the world: 104

STOCK OF DIRECT FOREIGN INVESTMENT - AT HOME:

$15.14 billion (31 December 2012 est.)

$12.44 billion (31 December 2011 est.)

country comparison to the world: 89

EXCHANGE RATES:

kips (LAK) per US dollar -

8,231.1 (2017 est.)

8,129.1 (2016 est.)

8,129.1 (2015 est.)

8,147.9 (2014 est.)

8,049 (2013 est.)

ENERGY :: LAOS

ELECTRICITY ACCESS:

electrification - total population: 87.1% (2016)

electrification - urban areas: 97.4% (2016)

electrification - rural areas: 80.3% (2016)

ELECTRICITY - PRODUCTION:

29.74 billion kWh (2016 est.)

country comparison to the world: 66

ELECTRICITY - CONSUMPTION:

5.471 billion kWh (2016 est.)

country comparison to the world: 120

ELECTRICITY - EXPORTS:

8.469 billion kWh (2015 est.)

country comparison to the world: 24

ELECTRICITY - IMPORTS:

2.5 billion kWh (2016 est.)

country comparison to the world: 53

ELECTRICITY - INSTALLED GENERATING CAPACITY:

6.94 million kW (2016 est.)

country comparison to the world: 75

ELECTRICITY - FROM FOSSIL FUELS:

28% of total installed capacity (2016 est.)

country comparison to the world: 186

ELECTRICITY - FROM NUCLEAR FUELS:

0% of total installed capacity (2017 est.)

country comparison to the world: 124

ELECTRICITY - FROM HYDROELECTRIC PLANTS:

72% of total installed capacity (2017 est.)

country comparison to the world: 15

ELECTRICITY - FROM OTHER RENEWABLE SOURCES:

1% of total installed capacity (2017 est.)

country comparison to the world: 157

CRUDE OIL - PRODUCTION:

0 bbl/day (2018 est.)

country comparison to the world: 159

CRUDE OIL - EXPORTS:

0 bbl/day (2015 est.)

country comparison to the world: 151

CRUDE OIL - IMPORTS:

0 bbl/day (2015 est.)

country comparison to the world: 149

CRUDE OIL - PROVED RESERVES:

0 bbl (1 January 2018 est.)

country comparison to the world: 154

REFINED PETROLEUM PRODUCTS - PRODUCTION:

0 bbl/day (2015 est.)

country comparison to the world: 162

REFINED PETROLEUM PRODUCTS - CONSUMPTION:

18,000 bbl/day (2016 est.)

country comparison to the world: 146

REFINED PETROLEUM PRODUCTS - EXPORTS:

0 bbl/day (2015 est.)

country comparison to the world: 169

REFINED PETROLEUM PRODUCTS - IMPORTS:

17,460 bbl/day (2015 est.)

country comparison to the world: 132

NATURAL GAS - PRODUCTION:

0 cu m (2017 est.)

country comparison to the world: 154

NATURAL GAS - CONSUMPTION:

0 cu m (2017 est.)

country comparison to the world: 165

NATURAL GAS - EXPORTS:

0 cu m (2017 est.)

country comparison to the world: 135

NATURAL GAS - IMPORTS:

0 cu m (2017 est.)

country comparison to the world: 146

NATURAL GAS - PROVED RESERVES:

0 cu m (1 January 2014 est.)

country comparison to the world: 155

CARBON DIOXIDE EMISSIONS FROM CONSUMPTION OF ENERGY:

10.42 million Mt (2017 est.)

country comparison to the world: 105

COMMUNICATIONS :: LAOS

TELEPHONES - FIXED LINES:

total subscriptions: 1,125,469

subscriptions per 100 inhabitants: 16 (2017 est.)

country comparison to the world: 75

TELEPHONES - MOBILE CELLULAR:

total subscriptions: 3,711,813

subscriptions per 100 inhabitants: 52 (2017 est.)

country comparison to the world: 131

TELEPHONE SYSTEM:

general assessment: service to public is generally improving; the government relies on a radiotelephone network to communicate with remote areas; regulatory reform below industry standards; low fixed-broadband penetration due to dominance of mobile platforms; strong boost in mobile broadband penetration but still low compared to other Asian markets; development of mobile broadband Internet services given the expansion of 4G services (2018)

domestic: fixed-line 16 per 100 and 52 per 100 for mobile-cellular subscriptions (2018)

international: country code - 856; satellite earth station - 1 Intersputnik (Indian Ocean region) and a second to be developed by China

BROADCAST MEDIA:

6 TV stations operating out of Vientiane - 3 government-operated and the others commercial; 17 provincial stations operating with nearly all programming relayed via satellite from the government-operated stations in Vientiane; Chinese and Vietnamese programming relayed via satellite from Lao National TV; broadcasts available from stations in Thailand and Vietnam in border areas; multi-channel satellite and cable TV systems provide access to a wide range of foreign stations; state-controlled radio with state-operated Lao National Radio (LNR) broadcasting on 5 frequencies - 1 AM, 1 SW, and 3 FM; LNR's AM and FM programs are relayed via satellite constituting a large part of the programming schedules of the provincial radio stations; Thai radio broadcasts available in border areas and transmissions of multiple international broadcasters are also accessible

INTERNET COUNTRY CODE:

.la

INTERNET USERS:

total: 1.258 million

percent of population: 18.2% (July 2016 est.)

country comparison to the world: 128

BROADBAND - FIXED SUBSCRIPTIONS:

total: 27,217

subscriptions per 100 inhabitants: less than 1 (2017 est.)

country comparison to the world: 143

MILITARY AND SECURITY :: LAOS

MILITARY EXPENDITURES:

0.19% of GDP (2013)

0.2% of GDP (2012)

0.21% of GDP (2011)

country comparison to the world: 156

MILITARY AND SECURITY FORCES:

Lao People's Armed Forces (LPAF): Lao People's Army (LPA, includes Riverine Force), Air Force (2019)

MILITARY SERVICE AGE AND OBLIGATION:

18 years of age for compulsory or voluntary military service; conscript service obligation - minimum 18 months (2015)

TRANSPORTATION :: LAOS

NATIONAL AIR TRANSPORT SYSTEM:

number of registered air carriers: 1 (2015)

inventory of registered aircraft operated by air carriers: 11 (2015)

annual passenger traffic on registered air carriers: 1,181,187 (2015)

annual freight traffic on registered air carriers: 1,356,497 mt-km (2015)

CIVIL AIRCRAFT REGISTRATION COUNTRY CODE PREFIX:

RDPL (2016)

AIRPORTS:

41 (2013)

country comparison to the world: 104

AIRPORTS - WITH PAVED RUNWAYS:

total: 8 (2017)

2,438 to 3,047 m: 3 (2017)

1,524 to 2,437 m: 4 (2017)

914 to 1,523 m: 1 (2017)

AIRPORTS - WITH UNPAVED RUNWAYS:

total: 33 (2013)

1,524 to 2,437 m: 2 (2013)

914 to 1,523 m: 9 (2013)

under 914 m: 22 (2013)

PIPELINES:

540 km refined products (2013)

ROADWAYS:

total: 39,586 km (2009)

paved: 5,415 km (2009)

unpaved: 34,171 km (2009)

country comparison to the world: 89

WATERWAYS:

4,600 km (primarily on the Mekong River and its tributaries; 2,900 additional km are intermittently navigable by craft drawing less than 0.5 m) (2012)

country comparison to the world: 23

MERCHANT MARINE:

total: 1

by type: general cargo 1 (2017)

country comparison to the world: 172

TRANSNATIONAL ISSUES :: LAOS

DISPUTES - INTERNATIONAL:

southeast Asian states have enhanced border surveillance to check the spread of avian flu; talks continue on completion of demarcation with Thailand but disputes remain over islands in the Mekong River; Cambodia and Laos have a longstanding border demarcation dispute; concern among Mekong River Commission members that China's construction of eight dams on the Upper Mekong River and construction of more dams on its tributaries will affect water levels, sediment flows, and fisheries; Cambodia and Vietnam are concerned about Laos' extensive plans for upstream dam construction for the same reasons

TRAFFICKING IN PERSONS:

current situation: Laos is a source and, to a lesser extent, transit and destination country for men, women, and children subjected to forced labor and sex trafficking; Lao economic migrants may encounter conditions of forced labor or sexual exploitation in destination countries, most often Thailand; Lao women and girls are exploited in Thailand's commercial sex trade, domestic service, factories, and agriculture; a small, possibly growing, number of Lao women and girls are sold as brides in China and South Korea and subsequently sex trafficked; Lao men and boys are victims of forced labor in the Thai fishing, construction, and agriculture industries; some Lao children, as well as Vietnamese and Chinese women and girls, are subjected to sex trafficking in Laos; other Vietnamese and Chinese, and possibly Burmese, adults and girls transit Laos for sexual and labor exploitation in neighboring countries, particularly Thailand

tier rating: Tier 2 Watch List – Laos does not fully comply with the minimum standards for the elimination of trafficking; however, it is making significant efforts to do so; authorities sustained moderate efforts to investigate, prosecute, and convict trafficking offenders; the government failed to make progress in proactively identifying victims exploited within the country or among those deported from abroad; the government continues to rely almost entirely on local and international organizations to provide and fund services to trafficking victims; although Lao men and boys are trafficked, most protective services are only available to women and girls, and long-term support is lacking; modest prevention efforts include the promotion of anti-trafficking awareness on state-controlled media (2015)

ILLICIT DRUGS:

estimated opium poppy cultivation in 2015 was estimated to be 5,700 hectares, compared with 6,200 hectares in 2014; estimated potential production of between 84 and 176 mt of raw opium; unsubstantiated reports of domestic methamphetamine production; growing domestic methamphetamine problem

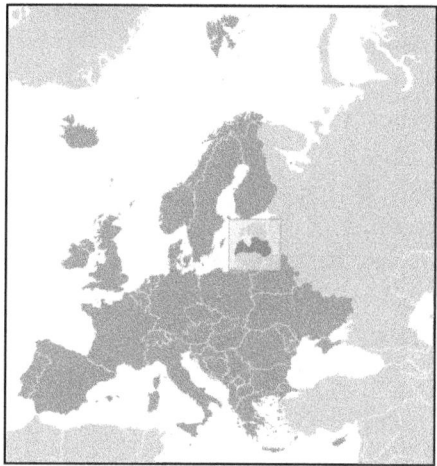

EUROPE :: LATVIA

INTRODUCTION :: LATVIA

BACKGROUND:
Several eastern Baltic tribes merged in medieval times to form the ethnic core of the Latvian people (ca. 8th-12th centuries A.D.). The region subsequently came under the control of Germans, Poles, Swedes, and finally, Russians. A Latvian republic emerged following World War I, but it was annexed by the USSR in 1940 - an action never recognized by the US and many other countries. Latvia reestablished its independence in 1991 following the breakup of the Soviet Union. Although the last Russian troops left in 1994, the status of the Russian minority (some 26% of the population) remains of concern to Moscow. Latvia acceded to both NATO and the EU in the spring of 2004; it joined the euro zone in 2014 and the OECD in 2016. A dual citizenship law was adopted in 2013, easing naturalization for non-citizen children.

GEOGRAPHY :: LATVIA

LOCATION:
Eastern Europe, bordering the Baltic Sea, between Estonia and Lithuania

GEOGRAPHIC COORDINATES:
57 00 N, 25 00 E

MAP REFERENCES:
Europe

AREA:
total: 64,589 sq km

land: 62,249 sq km

water: 2,340 sq km

country comparison to the world: 125

AREA - COMPARATIVE:
slightly larger than West Virginia

LAND BOUNDARIES:
total: 1,370 km

border countries (4): Belarus 161 km, Estonia 333 km, Lithuania 544 km, Russia 332 km

COASTLINE:
498 km

MARITIME CLAIMS:
territorial sea: 12 nm

exclusive economic zone: limits as agreed to by Estonia, Finland, Latvia, Sweden, and Russia

continental shelf: 200 m depth or to the depth of exploitation

CLIMATE:
maritime; wet, moderate winters

TERRAIN:
low plain

ELEVATION:
mean elevation: 87 m

lowest point: Baltic Sea 0 m

highest point: Gaizina Kalns 312 m

NATURAL RESOURCES:
peat, limestone, dolomite, amber, hydropower, timber, arable land

LAND USE:
agricultural land: 29.2% (2011 est.)

arable land: 18.6% (2011 est.) / permanent crops: 0.1% (2011 est.) / permanent pasture: 10.5% (2011 est.)

forest: 54.1% (2011 est.)

other: 16.7% (2011 est.)

IRRIGATED LAND:
12 sq km (2012)

note: land in Latvia is often too wet and in need of drainage not irrigation; approximately 16,000 sq km or 85% of agricultural land has been improved by drainage

POPULATION DISTRIBUTION:
largest concentration of people is found in and around the port and capital city of Riga; small agglomerations are scattered throughout the country

NATURAL HAZARDS:
large percentage of agricultural fields can become waterlogged and require drainage

ENVIRONMENT - CURRENT ISSUES:
while land, water, and air pollution are evident, Latvia's environment has benefited from a shift to service industries after the country regained independence; improvements have occurred in drinking water quality, sewage treatment, household and hazardous waste management, as well as reduction of air pollution; concerns include nature protection and the management of water resources and the protection of the Baltic Sea

ENVIRONMENT - INTERNATIONAL AGREEMENTS:
party to: Air Pollution, Air Pollution-Persistent Organic Pollutants, Biodiversity, Climate Change, Climate Change-Kyoto Protocol, Desertification, Endangered Species, Hazardous Wastes, Law of the Sea, Ozone Layer Protection, Ship Pollution, Wetlands

signed, but not ratified: none of the selected agreements

GEOGRAPHY - NOTE:
most of the country is composed of fertile low-lying plains with some hills in the east

PEOPLE AND SOCIETY :: LATVIA

POPULATION:
1,923,559 (July 2018 est.)

country comparison to the world: 150

NATIONALITY:

noun: Latvian(s)

adjective: Latvian

ETHNIC GROUPS:

Latvian 62.2%, Russian 25.2%, Belarusian 3.2%, Ukrainian 2.2%, Polish 2.1%, Lithuanian 1.2%, other 1.5%, unspecified 2.3% (2018 est.)

LANGUAGES:

Latvian (official) 56.3%, Russian 33.8%, other 0.6% (includes Polish, Ukrainian, and Belarusian), unspecified 9.4% (2011 est.)

note: data represent language usually spoken at home

RELIGIONS:

Lutheran 36.2%, Roman Catholic 19.5%, Orthodox 19.1%, other Christian 1.6%, other 0.1%, unspecified/none 23.5% (2017 est.)

AGE STRUCTURE:

0-14 years: 15.24% (male 150,514 /female 142,580)

15-24 years: 9.16% (male 90,980 /female 85,302)

25-54 years: 41.36% (male 396,677 /female 398,972)

55-64 years: 14.38% (male 123,611 /female 153,007)

65 years and over: 19.85% (male 125,709 /female 256,207) (2018 est.)

DEPENDENCY RATIOS:

total dependency ratio: 52.5 (2015 est.)

youth dependency ratio: 23.1 (2015 est.)

elderly dependency ratio: 29.4 (2015 est.)

potential support ratio: 3.4 (2015 est.)

MEDIAN AGE:

total: 43.9 years (2018 est.)

male: 40 years

female: 47.3 years

country comparison to the world: 16

POPULATION GROWTH RATE:

-1.1% (2018 est.)

country comparison to the world: 227

BIRTH RATE:

9.6 births/1,000 population (2018 est.)

country comparison to the world: 197

DEATH RATE:

14.5 deaths/1,000 population (2018 est.)

country comparison to the world: 5

NET MIGRATION RATE:

-6 migrant(s)/1,000 population (2018 est.)

country comparison to the world: 202

POPULATION DISTRIBUTION:

largest concentration of people is found in and around the port and capital city of Riga; small agglomerations are scattered throughout the country

URBANIZATION:

urban population: 68.2% of total population (2019)

rate of urbanization: -0.93% annual rate of change (2015-20 est.)

MAJOR URBAN AREAS - POPULATION:

634,000 RIGA (capital) (2019)

SEX RATIO:

at birth: 1.05 male(s)/female

0-14 years: 1.06 male(s)/female

15-24 years: 1.07 male(s)/female

25-54 years: 0.99 male(s)/female

55-64 years: 0.81 male(s)/female

65 years and over: 0.49 male(s)/female

total population: 0.86 male(s)/female (2018 est.)

MOTHER'S MEAN AGE AT FIRST BIRTH:

27.2 years (2014 est.)

MATERNAL MORTALITY RATE:

19 deaths/100,000 live births (2017 est.)

country comparison to the world: 124

INFANT MORTALITY RATE:

total: 5.1 deaths/1,000 live births (2018 est.)

male: 5.5 deaths/1,000 live births

female: 4.7 deaths/1,000 live births

country comparison to the world: 175

LIFE EXPECTANCY AT BIRTH:

total population: 74.9 years (2018 est.)

male: 70.4 years

female: 79.7 years

country comparison to the world: 118

TOTAL FERTILITY RATE:

1.52 children born/woman (2018 est.)

country comparison to the world: 193

DRINKING WATER SOURCE:

improved:

urban: 99.8% of population

rural: 98.3% of population

total: 99.3% of population

unimproved:

urban: 0.2% of population

rural: 1.7% of population

total: 0.7% of population (2015 est.)

CURRENT HEALTH EXPENDITURE:

6.2% (2016)

PHYSICIANS DENSITY:

3.19 physicians/1,000 population (2016)

HOSPITAL BED DENSITY:

5.8 beds/1,000 population (2013)

SANITATION FACILITY ACCESS:

improved:

urban: 90.8% of population (2015 est.)

rural: 81.5% of population (2015 est.)

total: 87.8% of population (2015 est.)

unimproved:

urban: 9.2% of population (2015 est.)

rural: 18.5% of population (2015 est.)

total: 12.2% of population (2015 est.)

HIV/AIDS - ADULT PREVALENCE RATE:

0.4% (2018 est.)

country comparison to the world: 82

HIV/AIDS - PEOPLE LIVING WITH HIV/AIDS:

5,300 (2018 est.)

country comparison to the world: 120

HIV/AIDS - DEATHS:

<100 (2018 est.)

MAJOR INFECTIOUS DISEASES:

degree of risk: intermediate (2016)

vectorborne diseases: tickborne encephalitis (2016)

OBESITY - ADULT PREVALENCE RATE:

23.6% (2016)

country comparison to the world: 65

EDUCATION EXPENDITURES:

5.3% of GDP (2015)

country comparison to the world: 52

LITERACY:

definition: age 15 and over can read and write

total population: 99.9%

male: 99.9%

female: 99.9% (2015 est.)

SCHOOL LIFE EXPECTANCY (PRIMARY TO TERTIARY EDUCATION):

total: 16 years

male: 15 years

female: 17 years (2016)

UNEMPLOYMENT, YOUTH AGES 15-24:

total: 17%

male: 18.3%

female: 15.4% (2017 est.)

country comparison to the world: 81

GOVERNMENT :: LATVIA

COUNTRY NAME:

conventional long form: Republic of Latvia

conventional short form: Latvia

local long form: Latvijas Republika

local short form: Latvija

former: Latvian Soviet Socialist Republic

etymology: the name "Latvia" originates from the ancient Latgalians, one of four eastern Baltic tribes that formed the ethnic core of the Latvian people (ca. 8th-12th centuries A.D.)

GOVERNMENT TYPE:

parliamentary republic

CAPITAL:

name: Riga

geographic coordinates: 56 57 N, 24 06 E

time difference: UTC+2 (7 hours ahead of Washington, DC, during Standard Time)

daylight saving time: +1hr, begins last Sunday in March; ends last Sunday in October

etymology: of the several theories explaining the name's origin, the one relating to the city's role in Baltic and North Sea commerce is the most probable; the name is likely related to the Latvian word "rija," meaning "warehouse," where the 'j' became a 'g' under the heavy German influence in the city from the late Middle Ages to the early 20th century

ADMINISTRATIVE DIVISIONS:

110 municipalities (novadi, singular - novads) and 9 cities

municipalities: Adazu Novads, Aglonas Novads, Aizkraukles Novads, Aizputes Novads, Aknistes Novads, Alojas Novads, Alsungas Novads, Aluksnes Novads, Amatas Novads, Apes Novads, Auces Novads, Babites Novads, Baldones Novads, Baltinavas Novads, Balvu Novads, Bauskas Novads, Beverinas Novads, Brocenu Novads, Burtnieku Novads, Carnikavas Novads, Cesu Novads, Cesvaines Novads, Ciblas Novads, Dagdas Novads, Daugavpils Novads, Dobeles Novads, Dundagas Novads, Durbes Novads, Engures Novads, Erglu Novads, Garkalnes Novads, Grobinas Novads, Gulbenes Novads, Iecavas Novads, Ikskiles Novads, Ilukstes Novads, Incukalna Novads, Jaunjelgavas Novads, Jaunpiebalgas Novads, Jaunpils Novads, Jekabpils Novads, Jelgavas Novads, Kandavas Novads, Karsavas Novads, Keguma Novads, Kekavas Novads, Kocenu Novads, Kokneses Novads, Kraslavas Novads, Krimuldas Novads, Krustpils Novads, Kuldigas Novads, Lielvardes Novads, Ligatnes Novads, Limbazu Novads, Livanu Novads, Lubanas Novads, Ludzas Novads, Madonas Novads, Malpils Novads, Marupes Novads, Mazsalacas Novads, Mersraga Novads, Nauksenu Novads, Neretas Novads, Nicas Novads, Ogres Novads, Olaines Novads, Ozolnieku Novads, Pargaujas Novads, Pavilostas Novads, Plavinu Novads, Preilu Novads, Priekules Novads, Priekulu Novads, Raunas Novads, Rezeknes Novads, Riebinu Novads, Rojas Novads, Ropazu Novads, Rucavas Novads, Rugaju Novads, Rujienas Novads, Rundales Novads, Salacgrivas Novads, Salas Novads, Salaspils Novads, Saldus Novads, Saulkrastu Novads, Sejas Novads, Siguldas Novads, Skriveru Novads, Skrundas Novads, Smiltenes Novads, Stopinu Novads, Strencu Novads, Talsu Novads, Tervetes Novads, Tukuma Novads, Vainodes Novads, Valkas Novads, Varaklanu Novads, Varkavas Novads, Vecpiebalgas Novads, Vecumnieku Novads, Ventspils Novads, Viesites Novads, Vilakas Novads, Vilanu Novads, Zilupes Novads;

cities: Daugavpils, Jekabpils, Jelgava, Jurmala, Liepaja, Rezekne, Riga, Valmiera, Ventspils

INDEPENDENCE:

4 May 1990 (declared independence from the Soviet Union); 6 September 1991 (recognized by the Soviet Union)

NATIONAL HOLIDAY:

Independence Day (Republic of Latvia Proclamation Day), 18 November (1918); note - 18 November 1918 was the date Latvia established its statehood and its concomitant independence from Soviet Russia; 4 May 1990 was the date it declared the restoration of Latvian statehood and its concomitant independence from the Soviet Union

CONSTITUTION:

history: several previous (pre-1991 independence); note - following the restoration of independence in 1991, parts of the 1922 constitution were reintroduced 4 May 1990 and fully reintroduced 6 July 1993

amendments: proposed by two thirds of Parliament members or by petition of one tenth of qualified voters submitted through the president; passage requires at least two-thirds majority vote of Parliament in each of three readings; amendment of constitutional articles, including national sovereignty, language, the parliamentary electoral system, and constitutional amendment procedures, requires passage in a referendum by majority vote of at least one half of the electorate; amended several times, last in 2019 (2019)

LEGAL SYSTEM:

civil law system with traces of socialist legal traditions and practices

INTERNATIONAL LAW ORGANIZATION PARTICIPATION:

has not submitted an ICJ jurisdiction declaration; accepts ICCt jurisdiction

CITIZENSHIP:

citizenship by birth: no

citizenship by descent only: at least one parent must be a citizen of Latvia

dual citizenship recognized: no

residency requirement for naturalization: 5 years

SUFFRAGE:

18 years of age; universal

EXECUTIVE BRANCH:

chief of state: President Egils LEVITS (since 8 July 2019)

head of government: Prime Minister Krisjanis KARINS (since 23 January 2019)

cabinet: Cabinet of Ministers nominated by the prime minister, appointed by Parliament

elections/appointments: president indirectly elected by Parliament for a 4-year term (eligible for a second term); election last held on 29 May 2019 (next to be held in 2023); prime minister appointed by the president, confirmed by Parliament

election results: Egils LEVITS elected president; Parliament vote - Egils LEVITS 61 votes, Didzis SMITS 24, Juris JANSONS 8; Krisjanis KARINS confirmed prime minister 61-39

LEGISLATIVE BRANCH:

description: unicameral Parliament or Saeima (100 seats; members directly elected in multi-seat constituencies by party list proportional representation vote; members serve 4-year terms)

elections: last held on 6 October 2018 (next to be held in October 2022)

election results: percent of vote by party - SDPS 19.8%, KPV LV 14.3%, JKP 13.6%, AP! 12%, NA 11%, ZZS 9.9%, V 6.7%, other 12.7%; seats by party - SDPS 23, KPV LV 16, JKP 16, AP! 13, NA 13, ZZS 11, V 8; composition - men 69, women 31, percent of women 31%

note: since the October 2018 elections, several efforts to form a government around a new prime minister have proved unsuccessful

JUDICIAL BRANCH:

highest courts: Supreme Court (consists of the Senate with 36 judges); Constitutional Court (consists of 7 judges)

judge selection and term of office: Supreme Court judges nominated by chief justice and confirmed by the Saeima; judges serve until age 70, but term can be extended 2 years; Constitutional Court judges - 3 nominated by Saeima members, 2 by Cabinet ministers, and 2 by plenum of Supreme Court; all judges confirmed by Saeima majority vote; Constitutional Court president and vice president serve in their positions for 3 years; all judges serve 10-year terms; mandatory retirement at age 70

subordinate courts: district (city) and regional courts

POLITICAL PARTIES AND LEADERS:

Development/For! or AP! [Daniels PAVLUTS, Juris PUCE]
National Alliance "All For Latvia!"-"For Fatherland and Freedom/LNNK" or NA [Raivis DZINTARS] New Conservative Party or JKP [Janis BORDANS]
Social Democratic Party "Harmony" or SDPS [Nils USAKOVS] Union of Greens and Farmers or ZZS [Armands KRAUZE] Unity or V [Arvils ASERADENS]
Who Owns the State? or KPV LV [Artuss KAIMINS]

INTERNATIONAL ORGANIZATION PARTICIPATION:

Australia Group, BA, BIS, CBSS, CD, CE, EAPC, EBRD, ECB, EIB, EMU, ESA (cooperating state), EU, FAO, IAEA, IBRD, ICAO, ICC (NGOs), ICCt, ICRM, IDA, IFC, IFRCS, IHO, ILO, IMF, IMO, IMSO, Interpol, IOC, IOM, IPU, ISO (correspondent), ITU, ITUC (NGOs), MIGA, NATO, NIB, NSG, OAS (observer), OIF (observer), OPCW, OSCE, PCA, Schengen Convention, UN, UNCTAD, UNESCO, UNHCR, UNWTO, UPU, WCO, WHO, WIPO, WMO, WTO

DIPLOMATIC REPRESENTATION IN THE US:

Ambassador Andris TEIKMANIS (since 16 September 2016)

chancery: 2306 Massachusetts Avenue NW, Washington, DC 20008

telephone: [1] (202) 328-2840

FAX: [1] (202) 328-2860

DIPLOMATIC REPRESENTATION FROM THE US:

chief of mission: Ambassador John Leslie CARWILE (since 5 November 2019)

telephone: [371] 6710-7000

embassy: 1 Samnera Velsa St, Riga LV-1510

mailing address: Embassy of the United States of America, 1 Samnera Velsa St, Riga, LV-1510, Latvia

FAX: [371] 6710-7050

FLAG DESCRIPTION:

three horizontal bands of maroon (top), white (half-width), and maroon; the flag is one of the older banners in the world; a medieval chronicle mentions a red standard with a white stripe being used by Latvian tribes in about 1280

NATIONAL SYMBOL(S):

white wagtail (bird); national colors: maroon, white

NATIONAL ANTHEM:

name: "Dievs, sveti Latviju!" (God Bless Latvia)

lyrics/music: Karlis BAUMANIS

note: adopted 1920, restored 1990; first performed in 1873 while Latvia was a part of Russia; banned during the Soviet occupation from 1940 to 1990

ECONOMY :: LATVIA

ECONOMY - OVERVIEW:

Latvia is a small, open economy with exports contributing more than half of GDP. Due to its geographical location, transit services are highly-developed, along with timber and wood-processing, agriculture and food products, and manufacturing of machinery and electronics industries. Corruption continues to be an impediment to attracting foreign direct investment and Latvia's low birth rate and decreasing population are major challenges to its long-term economic vitality.

Latvia's economy experienced GDP growth of more than 10% per year during 2006-07, but entered a severe recession in 2008 as a result of an unsustainable current account deficit and large debt exposure amid the slowing world economy. Triggered by the collapse of the second largest bank, GDP plunged by more than 14% in 2009 and, despite strong growth since 2011, the economy took until 2017 return to pre-crisis levels in real terms. Strong investment and consumption, the latter stoked by rising wages, helped the economy grow by more than 4% in 2017, while inflation rose to 3%. Continued gains in competitiveness and investment will be key to maintaining economic growth, especially in light of unfavorable demographic trends, including the emigration of skilled workers, and one of the highest levels of income inequality in the EU.

In the wake of the 2008-09 crisis, the IMF, EU, and other international donors provided substantial financial assistance to Latvia as part of an agreement to defend the currency's peg to the euro in exchange for the government's commitment to stringent austerity measures. The IMF/EU program successfully concluded in December 2011, although, the austerity measures imposed large social costs. The majority of companies, banks, and real estate have been privatized, although the state still holds sizable stakes in a few large enterprises, including 80% ownership of the Latvian national airline. Latvia officially joined the World Trade Organization in February 1999 and the EU in May 2004. Latvia also joined the euro zone in 2014 and the OECD in 2016.

GDP (PURCHASING POWER PARITY):

$54.02 billion (2017 est.)

$51.67 billion (2016 est.)

$50.55 billion (2015 est.)

note: data are in 2017 dollars

country comparison to the world: 108

GDP (OFFICIAL EXCHANGE RATE):

$30.33 billion (2017 est.)

GDP - REAL GROWTH RATE:

4.5% (2017 est.)

2.2% (2016 est.)

3% (2015 est.)

country comparison to the world: 64

GDP - PER CAPITA (PPP):

$27,700 (2017 est.)

$26,200 (2016 est.)

$25,500 (2015 est.)

note: data are in 2017 dollars

country comparison to the world: 76

GROSS NATIONAL SAVING:

20.7% of GDP (2017 est.)

21% of GDP (2016 est.)

21.8% of GDP (2015 est.)

country comparison to the world: 91

GDP - COMPOSITION, BY END USE:

household consumption: 61.8% (2017 est.)

government consumption: 18.2% (2017 est.)

investment in fixed capital: 19.9% (2017 est.)

investment in inventories: 1.5% (2017 est.)

exports of goods and services: 60.6% (2017 est.)

imports of goods and services: -61.9% (2017 est.)

GDP - COMPOSITION, BY SECTOR OF ORIGIN:

agriculture: 3.9% (2017 est.)

industry: 22.4% (2017 est.)

services: 73.7% (2017 est.)

AGRICULTURE - PRODUCTS:

grain, rapeseed, potatoes, vegetables; pork, poultry, milk, eggs; fish

INDUSTRIES:

processed foods, processed wood products, textiles, processed metals, pharmaceuticals, railroad cars, synthetic fibers, electronics

INDUSTRIAL PRODUCTION GROWTH RATE:

10.6% (2017 est.)

country comparison to the world: 12

LABOR FORCE:

990,000 (2017 est.)

country comparison to the world: 144

LABOR FORCE - BY OCCUPATION:

agriculture: 7.7%

industry: 24.1%

services: 68.1% (2016 est.)

UNEMPLOYMENT RATE:

8.7% (2017 est.)

9.6% (2016 est.)

country comparison to the world: 124

POPULATION BELOW POVERTY LINE:

25.5% (2015)

HOUSEHOLD INCOME OR CONSUMPTION BY PERCENTAGE SHARE:

lowest 10%: 2.2%

highest 10%: 26.3% (2015)

DISTRIBUTION OF FAMILY INCOME - GINI INDEX:

34.5 (2015)

35.4 (2014)

country comparison to the world: 102

BUDGET:

revenues: 11.39 billion (2017 est.)

expenditures: 11.53 billion (2017 est.)

TAXES AND OTHER REVENUES:

37.5% (of GDP) (2017 est.)

country comparison to the world: 54

BUDGET SURPLUS (+) OR DEFICIT (-):

-0.5% (of GDP) (2017 est.)

country comparison to the world: 62

PUBLIC DEBT:

36.3% of GDP (2017 est.)

37.4% of GDP (2016 est.)

note: data cover general government debt, and includes debt instruments issued (or owned) by government entities, including sub-sectors of central government, state government, local government, and social security funds

country comparison to the world: 147

FISCAL YEAR:

calendar year

INFLATION RATE (CONSUMER PRICES):

2.9% (2017 est.)

0.1% (2016 est.)

country comparison to the world: 130

CENTRAL BANK DISCOUNT RATE:

0% (31 December 2017 est.)

0.05% (31 December 2015 est.)

country comparison to the world: 155

COMMERCIAL BANK PRIME LENDING RATE:

2.58% (31 December 2017 est.)

2.61% (31 December 2016 est.)

country comparison to the world: 181

STOCK OF NARROW MONEY:

$12.91 billion (31 December 2017 est.)

$10.71 billion (31 December 2016 est.)

country comparison to the world: 78

STOCK OF BROAD MONEY:

$12.91 billion (31 December 2017 est.)

$10.71 billion (31 December 2016 est.)

country comparison to the world: 79

STOCK OF DOMESTIC CREDIT:

$17.27 billion (31 December 2017 est.)

$15.11 billion (31 December 2016 est.)

country comparison to the world: 94

MARKET VALUE OF PUBLICLY TRADED SHARES:

$6.76 billion (31 December 2016 est.)

$6.799 billion (31 December 2015 est.)

$7.127 billion (31 December 2014 est.)

country comparison to the world: 80

CURRENT ACCOUNT BALANCE:

-$231 million (2017 est.)

$378 million (2016 est.)

country comparison to the world: 99

EXPORTS:

$12.84 billion (2017 est.)

$11.35 billion (2016 est.)

country comparison to the world: 82

EXPORTS - PARTNERS:

Lithuania 15.8%, Russia 14%, Estonia 10.9%, Germany 6.9%, Sweden 5.7%, UK 4.9%, Poland 4.3%, Denmark 4.1% (2017)

EXPORTS - COMMODITIES:

foodstuffs, wood and wood products, metals, machinery and equipment, textiles

IMPORTS:

$15.79 billion (2017 est.)

$13.61 billion (2016 est.)

country comparison to the world: 87

IMPORTS - COMMODITIES:

machinery and equipment, consumer goods, chemicals, fuels, vehicles

IMPORTS - PARTNERS:

Lithuania 17.6%, Germany 11.7%, Poland 8.7%, Estonia 7.6%, Russia 7.1%, Netherlands 4.2%, Finland 4.2%, Italy 4% (2017)

RESERVES OF FOREIGN EXCHANGE AND GOLD:

$4.614 billion (31 December 2017 est.)

$3.514 billion (31 December 2016 est.)

country comparison to the world: 97

DEBT - EXTERNAL:

$40.02 billion (31 March 2016 est.)

$38.19 billion (31 March 2015 est.)

country comparison to the world: 74

STOCK OF DIRECT FOREIGN INVESTMENT - AT HOME:

$18.84 billion (31 December 2017 est.)

$15.36 billion (31 December 2016 est.)

country comparison to the world: 82

STOCK OF DIRECT FOREIGN INVESTMENT - ABROAD:

$3.402 billion (31 December 2017 est.)

$2.485 billion (31 December 2016 est.)

country comparison to the world: 80

EXCHANGE RATES:

euros (EUR) per US dollar -

0.885 (2017 est.)

0.903 (2016 est.)

0.9214 (2015 est.)
0.885 (2014 est.)
0.7634 (2013 est.)

ENERGY :: LATVIA

ELECTRICITY ACCESS:

electrification - total population: 100% (2016)

ELECTRICITY - PRODUCTION:

6.241 billion kWh (2016 est.)

country comparison to the world: 115

ELECTRICITY - CONSUMPTION:

6.798 billion kWh (2016 est.)

country comparison to the world: 109

ELECTRICITY - EXPORTS:

3.795 billion kWh (2016 est.)

country comparison to the world: 38

ELECTRICITY - IMPORTS:

4.828 billion kWh (2016 est.)

country comparison to the world: 39

ELECTRICITY - INSTALLED GENERATING CAPACITY:

2.932 million kW (2016 est.)

country comparison to the world: 98

ELECTRICITY - FROM FOSSIL FUELS:

39% of total installed capacity (2016 est.)

country comparison to the world: 173

ELECTRICITY - FROM NUCLEAR FUELS:

0% of total installed capacity (2017 est.)

country comparison to the world: 125

ELECTRICITY - FROM HYDROELECTRIC PLANTS:

53% of total installed capacity (2017 est.)

country comparison to the world: 33

ELECTRICITY - FROM OTHER RENEWABLE SOURCES:

8% of total installed capacity (2017 est.)

country comparison to the world: 87

CRUDE OIL - PRODUCTION:

0 bbl/day (2018 est.)

country comparison to the world: 160

CRUDE OIL - EXPORTS:

0 bbl/day (2017 est.)

country comparison to the world: 152

CRUDE OIL - IMPORTS:

0 bbl/day (2017 est.)

country comparison to the world: 150

CRUDE OIL - PROVED RESERVES:

0 bbl (1 January 2018 est.)

country comparison to the world: 155

REFINED PETROLEUM PRODUCTS - PRODUCTION:

0 bbl/day (2017 est.)

country comparison to the world: 163

REFINED PETROLEUM PRODUCTS - CONSUMPTION:

44,600 bbl/day (2017 est.)

country comparison to the world: 111

REFINED PETROLEUM PRODUCTS - EXPORTS:

16,180 bbl/day (2017 est.)

country comparison to the world: 72

REFINED PETROLEUM PRODUCTS - IMPORTS:

54,370 bbl/day (2017 est.)

country comparison to the world: 77

NATURAL GAS - PRODUCTION:

0 cu m (2017 est.)

country comparison to the world: 155

NATURAL GAS - CONSUMPTION:

1.218 billion cu m (2017 est.)

country comparison to the world: 88

NATURAL GAS - EXPORTS:

0 cu m (2017 est.)

country comparison to the world: 136

NATURAL GAS - IMPORTS:

1.246 billion cu m (2017 est.)

country comparison to the world: 58

NATURAL GAS - PROVED RESERVES:

0 cu m (2014 est.)

country comparison to the world: 156

CARBON DIOXIDE EMISSIONS FROM CONSUMPTION OF ENERGY:

8.632 million Mt (2017 est.)

country comparison to the world: 114

COMMUNICATIONS :: LATVIA

TELEPHONES - FIXED LINES:

total subscriptions: 342,097

subscriptions per 100 inhabitants: 18 (2017 est.)

country comparison to the world: 109

TELEPHONES - MOBILE CELLULAR:

total subscriptions: 2,464,122

subscriptions per 100 inhabitants: 127 (2017 est.)

country comparison to the world: 144

TELEPHONE SYSTEM:

general assessment: recent efforts focused on bringing competition to the telecommunications sector; the number of fixed lines is decreasing as mobile-cellular telephone service expands; EU regulatory policies, and framework provide guidelines for growth; govt. adopted measures to build a national fiber broadband network, part-funded by European Commission; commercial 5G services coming in 2019 (2018)

domestic: fixed-line 18 per 100 and mobile-cellular 127 per 100 subscriptions (2018)

international: country code - 371; the Latvian network is now connected via fiber-optic cable to Estonia, Finland, and Sweden

BROADCAST MEDIA:

several national and regional commercial TV stations are foreign-owned, 2 national TV stations are publicly owned; system supplemented by privately owned regional and local TV stations; cable and satellite multi-channel TV services with domestic and foreign broadcasts available; publicly owned broadcaster operates 4 radio networks with dozens of stations throughout the country; dozens of private broadcasters also operate radio stations

INTERNET COUNTRY CODE:

.lv

INTERNET USERS:

total: 1,570,374

percent of population: 79.9% (July 2016 est.)

country comparison to the world: 119

BROADBAND - FIXED SUBSCRIPTIONS:

total: 525,679

subscriptions per 100 inhabitants: 27 (2017 est.)

country comparison to the world: 80

MILITARY AND SECURITY :: LATVIA

MILITARY EXPENDITURES:

1.98% of GDP (2018)
1.68% of GDP (2017)
1.47% of GDP (2016)
1.05% of GDP (2015)
0.94% of GDP (2014)

country comparison to the world: 50

MILITARY AND SECURITY FORCES:

National Armed Forces (Nacionalie Brunotie Speki): Land Forces (Latvijas Sauszemes Speki), Naval Force (Latvijas Juras Speki, includes Coast Guard (Latvijas Kara Flote)), Air Force

(Latvijas Gaisa Speki), National Guard (2019)

MILITARY SERVICE AGE AND OBLIGATION:

18 years of age for voluntary male and female military service; no conscription; under current law, every citizen is entitled to serve in the armed forces for life (2017)

TRANSPORTATION :: LATVIA

NATIONAL AIR TRANSPORT SYSTEM:

number of registered air carriers: 3 (2015)

inventory of registered aircraft operated by air carriers: 47 (2015)

annual passenger traffic on registered air carriers: 2,527,368 (2015)

annual freight traffic on registered air carriers: 2,277,996 mt-km (2015)

CIVIL AIRCRAFT REGISTRATION COUNTRY CODE PREFIX:

YL (2016)

AIRPORTS:

42 (2013)

country comparison to the world: 101

AIRPORTS - WITH PAVED RUNWAYS:

total: 18 (2017)

over 3,047 m: 1 (2017)

2,438 to 3,047 m: 3 (2017)

1,524 to 2,437 m: 4 (2017)

914 to 1,523 m: 3 (2017)

under 914 m: 7 (2017)

AIRPORTS - WITH UNPAVED RUNWAYS:

total: 24 (2013)

under 914 m: 24 (2013)

HELIPORTS:

1 (2013)

PIPELINES:

1,213 km gas, 417 km refined products (2018)

RAILWAYS:

total: 1,860 km (2018)

narrow gauge: 34 km 0.750-m gauge (2018)

broad gauge: 1,826 km 1.520-m gauge (2018)

country comparison to the world: 75

ROADWAYS:

total: 70,244 km (2018)

paved: 15,158 km (2018)

unpaved: 55,086 km (2018)

country comparison to the world: 69

WATERWAYS:

300 km (navigable year-round) (2010)

country comparison to the world: 92

MERCHANT MARINE:

total: 68

by type: general cargo 18, oil tanker 8, other 42 (2018)

country comparison to the world: 102

PORTS AND TERMINALS:

major seaport(s): Riga, Ventspils

TRANSNATIONAL ISSUES :: LATVIA

DISPUTES - INTERNATIONAL:

Russia demands better Latvian treatment of ethnic Russians in Latvia; boundary demarcated with Latvia and Lithuania; the Latvian parliament has not ratified its 1998 maritime boundary treaty with Lithuania, primarily due to concerns over oil exploration rights; as a member state that forms part of the EU's external border, Latvia has implemented the strict Schengen border rules with Russia

REFUGEES AND INTERNALLY DISPLACED PERSONS:

stateless persons: 224,844 (2018); note - individuals who were Latvian citizens prior to the 1940 Soviet occupation and their descendants were recognized as Latvian citizens when the country's independence was restored in 1991; citizens of the former Soviet Union residing in Latvia who have neither Latvian nor other citizenship are considered non-citizens (officially there is no statelessness in Latvia) and are entitled to non-citizen passports; children born after Latvian independence to stateless parents are entitled to Latvian citizenship upon their parents' request; non-citizens cannot vote or hold certain government jobs and are exempt from military service but can travel visa-free in the EU under the Schengen accord like Latvian citizens; non-citizens can obtain naturalization if they have been permanent residents of Latvia for at least five years, pass tests in Latvian language and history, and know the words of the Latvian national anthem

ILLICIT DRUGS:

transshipment and destination point for cocaine, synthetic drugs, opiates, and cannabis from Southwest Asia, Western Europe, Latin America, and neighboring Baltic countries; despite improved legislation, vulnerable to money laundering due to nascent enforcement capabilities and comparatively weak regulation of offshore companies and the gaming industry; CIS organized crime (including counterfeiting, corruption, extortion, stolen cars, and prostitution) accounts for most laundered proceeds

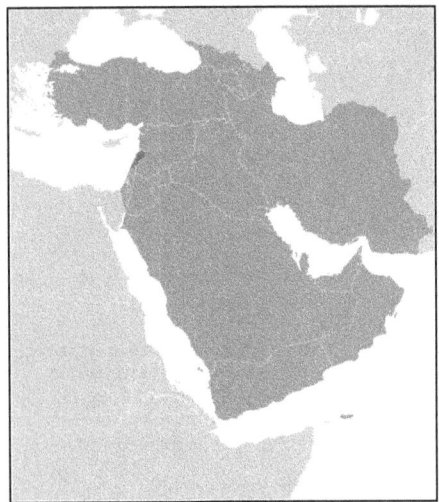

MIDDLE EAST :: LEBANON

INTRODUCTION :: LEBANON

BACKGROUND:
Following World War I, France acquired a mandate over the northern portion of the former Ottoman Empire province of Syria. The French demarcated the region of Lebanon in 1920 and granted this area independence in 1943. Since independence, the country has been marked by periods of political turmoil interspersed with prosperity built on its position as a regional center for finance and trade. The country's 1975-90 civil war, which resulted in an estimated 120,000 fatalities, was followed by years of social and political instability. Sectarianism is a key element of Lebanese political life. Neighboring Syria has historically influenced Lebanon's foreign policy and internal policies, and its military occupied Lebanon from 1976 until 2005. The Lebanon-based Hizballah militia and Israel continued attacks and counterattacks against each other after Syria's withdrawal, and fought a brief war in 2006. Lebanon's borders with Syria and Israel remain unresolved.

GEOGRAPHY :: LEBANON

LOCATION:
Middle East, bordering the Mediterranean Sea, between Israel and Syria

GEOGRAPHIC COORDINATES:
33 50 N, 35 50 E

MAP REFERENCES:
Middle East

AREA:
total: 10,400 sq km

land: 10,230 sq km

water: 170 sq km

country comparison to the world: 169

AREA - COMPARATIVE:
about one-third the size of Maryland

LAND BOUNDARIES:
total: 484 km

border countries (2): Israel 81 km, Syria 403 km

COASTLINE:
225 km

MARITIME CLAIMS:
territorial sea: 12 nm

CLIMATE:
Mediterranean; mild to cool, wet winters with hot, dry summers; the Lebanon Mountains experience heavy winter snows

TERRAIN:
narrow coastal plain; El Beqaa (Bekaa Valley) separates Lebanon and Anti-Lebanon Mountains

ELEVATION:
mean elevation: 1,250 m

lowest point: Mediterranean Sea 0 m

highest point: Qornet es Saouda 3,088 m

NATURAL RESOURCES:
limestone, iron ore, salt, water-surplus state in a water-deficit region, arable land

LAND USE:
agricultural land: 63.3% (2011 est.)

arable land: 11.9% (2011 est.) / permanent crops: 12.3% (2011 est.) / permanent pasture: 39.1% (2011 est.)

forest: 13.4% (2011 est.)

other: 23.3% (2011 est.)

IRRIGATED LAND:
1,040 sq km (2012)

POPULATION DISTRIBUTION:
the majority of the people live on or near the Mediterranean coast, and of these most live in and around the capital, Beirut; favorable growing conditions in the Bekaa Valley, on the southeastern side of the Lebanon Mountains, have attracted farmers and thus the area exhibits a smaller population density

NATURAL HAZARDS:
earthquakes; dust storms, sandstorms

ENVIRONMENT - CURRENT ISSUES:
deforestation; soil deterioration, erosion; desertification; species loss; air pollution in Beirut from vehicular traffic and the burning of industrial wastes; pollution of coastal waters from raw sewage and oil spills; waste-water management

ENVIRONMENT - INTERNATIONAL AGREEMENTS:
party to: Biodiversity, Climate Change, Climate Change-Kyoto Protocol, Desertification, Hazardous Wastes, Law of the Sea, Ozone Layer Protection, Ship Pollution, Wetlands

signed, but not ratified: Environmental Modification, Marine Life Conservation

GEOGRAPHY - NOTE:

smallest country in continental Asia; Nahr el Litani is the only major river in Near East not crossing an international boundary; rugged terrain historically helped isolate, protect, and develop numerous factional groups based on religion, clan, and ethnicity

PEOPLE AND SOCIETY :: LEBANON

POPULATION:
6,100,075 (July 2018 est.)

country comparison to the world: 110

NATIONALITY:
noun: Lebanese (singular and plural)

adjective: Lebanese

ETHNIC GROUPS:
Arab 95%, Armenian 4%, other 1%

note: many Christian Lebanese do not identify themselves as Arab but rather as descendants of the ancient Canaanites and prefer to be called Phoenicians

LANGUAGES:
Arabic (official), French, English, Armenian

RELIGIONS:
Muslim 57.7% (28.7% Sunni, 28.4% Shia, smaller percentages of Alawites and Ismailis), Christian 36.2% (Maronite Catholics are the largest Christian group), Druze 5.2%, very small numbers of Jews, Baha'is, Buddhists, and Hindus (2017 est.)

note: data represent the religious affiliation of the citizen population (data do not include Lebanon's sizable Syrian and Palestinian refugee populations); 18 religious sects recognized

AGE STRUCTURE:
0-14 years: 23.32% (male 728,025 /female 694,453)

15-24 years: 16.04% (male 500,592 /female 477,784)

25-54 years: 45.27% (male 1,398,087 /female 1,363,386)

55-64 years: 8.34% (male 241,206 /female 267,747)

65 years and over: 7.03% (male 185,780 /female 243,015) (2018 est.)

DEPENDENCY RATIOS:
total dependency ratio: 47.3 (2015 est.)

youth dependency ratio: 35.3 (2015 est.)

elderly dependency ratio: 12 (2015 est.)

potential support ratio: 8.3 (2015 est.)

MEDIAN AGE:
total: 31.3 years (2018 est.)

male: 30.7 years

female: 31.9 years

country comparison to the world: 111

POPULATION GROWTH RATE:
-3.13% (2018 est.)

country comparison to the world: 234

BIRTH RATE:
14.1 births/1,000 population (2018 est.)

country comparison to the world: 134

DEATH RATE:
5.1 deaths/1,000 population (2018 est.)

country comparison to the world: 193

NET MIGRATION RATE:
-40.3 migrant(s)/1,000 population (2018 est.)

country comparison to the world: 228

POPULATION DISTRIBUTION:
the majority of the people live on or near the Mediterranean coast, and of these most live in and around the capital, Beirut; favorable growing conditions in the Bekaa Valley, on the southeastern side of the Lebanon Mountains, have attracted farmers and thus the area exhibits a smaller population density

URBANIZATION:
urban population: 88.8% of total population (2019)

rate of urbanization: 0.75% annual rate of change (2015-20 est.)

MAJOR URBAN AREAS - POPULATION:
2.407 million BEIRUT (capital) (2019)

SEX RATIO:
at birth: 1.05 male(s)/female

0-14 years: 1.05 male(s)/female

15-24 years: 1.05 male(s)/female

25-54 years: 1.03 male(s)/female

55-64 years: 0.9 male(s)/female

65 years and over: 0.76 male(s)/female

total population: 1 male(s)/female (2018 est.)

MATERNAL MORTALITY RATE:
29 deaths/100,000 live births (2017 est.)

country comparison to the world: 112

INFANT MORTALITY RATE:
total: 7.2 deaths/1,000 live births (2018 est.)

male: 7.6 deaths/1,000 live births

female: 6.8 deaths/1,000 live births

country comparison to the world: 160

LIFE EXPECTANCY AT BIRTH:
total population: 77.9 years (2018 est.)

male: 76.6 years

female: 79.3 years

country comparison to the world: 66

TOTAL FERTILITY RATE:
1.72 children born/woman (2018 est.)

country comparison to the world: 167

CONTRACEPTIVE PREVALENCE RATE:
54.5% (2009)

DRINKING WATER SOURCE:
improved:

urban: 99% of population

rural: 99% of population

total: 99% of population

unimproved:

urban: 1% of population

rural: 1% of population

total: 1% of population (2015 est.)

CURRENT HEALTH EXPENDITURE:
8% (2016)

PHYSICIANS DENSITY:
2.27 physicians/1,000 population (2017)

HOSPITAL BED DENSITY:
2.9 beds/1,000 population (2014)

SANITATION FACILITY ACCESS:
improved:

urban: 80.7% of population (2015 est.)

rural: 80.7% of population (2015 est.)

total: 80.7% of population (2015 est.)

unimproved:

urban: 19.3% of population (2015 est.)

rural: 19.3% of population (2015 est.)

total: 19.3% of population (2015 est.)

HIV/AIDS - ADULT PREVALENCE RATE:
<.1% (2018 est.)

HIV/AIDS - PEOPLE LIVING WITH HIV/AIDS:
2,500 (2018 est.)

country comparison to the world: 134

HIV/AIDS - DEATHS:
<100 (2018 est.)

OBESITY - ADULT PREVALENCE RATE:

32% (2016)

country comparison to the world: 19

EDUCATION EXPENDITURES:

2.5% of GDP (2013)

country comparison to the world: 161

LITERACY:

definition: age 15 and over can read and write

total population: 93.9%

male: 96%

female: 91.8% (2015 est.)

SCHOOL LIFE EXPECTANCY (PRIMARY TO TERTIARY EDUCATION):

total: 11 years

male: 12 years

female: 11 years (2014)

GOVERNMENT :: LEBANON

COUNTRY NAME:

conventional long form: Lebanese Republic

conventional short form: Lebanon

local long form: Al Jumhuriyah al Lubnaniyah

local short form: Lubnan

former: Greater Lebanon

etymology: derives from the Semitic root "lbn" meaning "white" and refers to snow-capped Mount Lebanon

GOVERNMENT TYPE:

parliamentary republic

CAPITAL:

name: Beirut

geographic coordinates: 33 52 N, 35 30 E

time difference: UTC+2 (7 hours ahead of Washington, DC, during Standard Time)

daylight saving time: +1hr, begins last Sunday in March; ends last Sunday in October

etymology: derived from the Canaanite or Phoenician word "ber'ot," meaning "the wells" or "fountain," which referred to the site's accessible water table

ADMINISTRATIVE DIVISIONS:

8 governorates (mohafazat, singular - mohafazah); Aakkar, Baalbek-Hermel, Beqaa (Bekaa), Beyrouth (Beirut), Liban-Nord (North Lebanon), Liban-Sud (South Lebanon), Mont-Liban (Mount Lebanon), Nabatiye

INDEPENDENCE:

22 November 1943 (from League of Nations mandate under French administration)

NATIONAL HOLIDAY:

Independence Day, 22 November (1943)

CONSTITUTION:

history: drafted 15 May 1926, adopted 23 May 1926

amendments: proposed by the president of the republic and introduced as a government bill to the National Assembly or proposed by at least 10 members of the Assembly and agreed upon by two thirds of its members; if proposed by the National Assembly, review and approval by two-thirds majority of the Cabinet is required; if approved, the proposal is next submitted to the Cabinet for drafting as an amendment; Cabinet approval requires at least two-thirds majority, followed by submission to the National Assembly for discussion and vote; passage requires at least two-thirds majority vote of a required two-thirds quorum of the Assembly membership and promulgation by the president; amended several times, last in 2004 (2019)

LEGAL SYSTEM:

mixed legal system of civil law based on the French civil code, Ottoman legal tradition, and religious laws covering personal status, marriage, divorce, and other family relations of the Jewish, Islamic, and Christian communities

INTERNATIONAL LAW ORGANIZATION PARTICIPATION:

has not submitted an ICJ jurisdiction declaration; non-party state to the ICCt

CITIZENSHIP:

citizenship by birth: no

citizenship by descent only: the father must be a citizen of Lebanon

dual citizenship recognized: yes

residency requirement for naturalization: unknown

SUFFRAGE:

21 years of age; authorized for all men and women regardless of religion; excludes persons convicted of felonies and other crimes or those imprisoned; excludes all military and security service personnel regardless of rank

EXECUTIVE BRANCH:

chief of state: President Michel AWN (since 31 October 2016)

head of government: Prime Minister Saad al-HARIRI (since 24 May 2018); resigned on 30 October 2019, and President AWN requested the Cabinet continue in caretaker status until a new government is formed

cabinet: Cabinet chosen by the prime minister in consultation with the president and National Assembly

elections/appointments: president indirectly elected by the National Assembly with two-thirds majority vote in the first round and if needed absolute majority vote in a second round for a 6-year term (eligible for non-consecutive terms); last held on 31 October 2016 (next to be held in 2022); prime minister appointed by the president in consultation with the National Assembly; deputy prime minister determined during cabinet formation

election results: Michel AWN elected president in second round; National Assembly vote - Michel AWN (FPM) 83; note - in the initial election held on 23 April 2014, no candidate received the required two-thirds vote, and subsequent attempts failed because the Assembly lacked the necessary quorum to hold a vote; the president was finally elected in its 46th attempt on 31 October 2016

LEGISLATIVE BRANCH:

description: unicameral National Assembly or Majlis al-Nuwab in Arabic or Assemblee Nationale in French (128 seats; members directly elected in multi-seat constituencies by proportional representation vote; members serve 4-year terms); in 2017, the Assembly changed the electoral system from majoritarian to proporional representation

elections: last held on 6 May 2018 (next to be held in 2022)

election results:

percent of vote by coalition - NA; seats by coalition – Strong Lebanon Bloc (Free Patriotic Movement-led) 25; Future Bloc (Future Movement-led) 20; Development and Liberation Bloc (Amal Movement-led) 16; Loyalty to the Resistance Bloc (Hizballah-led) 15; Strong Republic Bloc (Lebanese Forces-led) 15; Democratic Gathering (Progressive Socialist Party-led) 9; Independent Centre Bloc (Mikati-led) 4; National Bloc (Marada Movement-led) 3; Syrian Social Nationalist Party 3; Tashnaq 3; Kata'ib 3; other 8; independent 4; composition - men 122, women 6, percent of women 4.6%

note: Lebanon's constitution states the National Assembly cannot conduct regular business until it elects a president when the position is vacant

JUDICIAL BRANCH:

highest courts: Court of Cassation or Supreme Court (organized into 8 chambers, each with a presiding judge and 2 associate judges); Constitutional Council (consists of 10 members)

judge selection and term of office: Court of Cassation judges appointed by Supreme Judicial Council, a 10-member body headed by the chief justice, and includes other judicial officials; judge tenure NA; Constitutional Council members appointed - 5 by the Council of Ministers and 5 by parliament; members serve 5-year terms

subordinate courts: Courts of Appeal; Courts of First Instance; specialized tribunals, religious courts; military courts

POLITICAL PARTIES AND LEADERS:

Al-Ahbash or Association of Islamic Charitable Projects [Adnan TARABULSI]
Amal Movement [Nabih BERRI]
Azm Movement [Najib MIQATI]
Ba'th Arab Socialist Party of Lebanon [Fayiz SHUKR]
Free Patriotic Movement or FPM [Gibran BASSIL]
Future Movement Bloc [Sa'ad al-HARIRI]
Hizballah [Hassan NASRALLAH]
Islamic Actions Front [Sheikh Zuhayr al-JU'AYD]
Kata'ib Party [Sami GEMAYEL]
Lebanese Democratic Party [Talal ARSLAN]
Lebanese Forces or LF [Samir JA'JA]
Marada Movement [Sulayman FRANJIEH]
Progressive Socialist Party or PSP [Walid JUNBLATT]
Social Democrat Hunshaqian Party [Sabuh KALPAKIAN]Syrian Social Nationalist Party [Ali QANSO]
Syrian Social Nationalist Party [Hanna al-NASHIF]
Tashnaq or Armenian Revolutionary Federation [Hagop PAKRADOUNIAN]

INTERNATIONAL ORGANIZATION PARTICIPATION:

ABEDA, AFESD, AMF, CAEU, FAO, G-24, G-77, IAEA, IBRD, ICAO, ICC (national committees), ICRM, IDA, IDB, IFAD, IFC, IFRCS, ILO, IMF, IMO, IMSO, Interpol, IOC, IPU, ISO, ITSO, ITU, LAS, MIGA, NAM, OAS (observer), OIC, OIF, OPCW, PCA, UN, UNCTAD, UNESCO, UNHCR, UNIDO, UNRWA, UNWTO, UPU, WCO, WFTU (NGOs), WHO, WIPO, WMO, WTO (observer)

DIPLOMATIC REPRESENTATION IN THE US:

Ambassador Gabriel ISSA (since 24 January 2018)

chancery: 2560 28th Street NW, Washington, DC 20008

telephone: [1] (202) 939-6300

FAX: [1] (202) 939-6324

consulate(s) general: Detroit, New York, Los Angeles

DIPLOMATIC REPRESENTATION FROM THE US:

chief of mission: Ambassador Elizabeth H. RICHARD (since 17 May 2016)

telephone: [961] (4) 542600, 543600

embassy: Awkar, Lebanon (Awkar facing the Municipality), Main Street

mailing address: P. O. Box 70-840, Antelias, Lebanon; from US: US Embassy Beirut, 6070 Beirut Place, Washington, DC 20521-6070

FAX: [961] (4) 544136

FLAG DESCRIPTION:

three horizontal bands consisting of red (top), white (middle, double width), and red (bottom) with a green cedar tree centered in the white band; the red bands symbolize blood shed for liberation, the white band denotes peace, the snow of the mountains, and purity; the green cedar tree is the symbol of Lebanon and represents eternity, steadiness, happiness, and prosperity

NATIONAL SYMBOL(S):

cedar tree; national colors: red, white, green

NATIONAL ANTHEM:

name: "Kulluna lil-watan" (All Of Us, For Our Country!)

lyrics/music: Rachid NAKHLE/Wadih SABRA

note: adopted 1927; chosen following a nationwide competition

ECONOMY :: LEBANON

ECONOMY - OVERVIEW:

Lebanon has a free-market economy and a strong laissez-faire commercial tradition. The government does not restrict foreign investment; however, the investment climate suffers from red tape, corruption, arbitrary licensing decisions, complex customs procedures, high taxes, tariffs, and fees, archaic legislation, and inadequate intellectual property rights protection. The Lebanese economy is service-oriented; main growth sectors include banking and tourism.

The 1975-90 civil war seriously damaged Lebanon's economic infrastructure, cut national output by half, and derailed Lebanon's position as a Middle Eastern banking hub. Following the civil war, Lebanon rebuilt much of its war-torn physical and financial infrastructure by borrowing heavily, mostly from domestic banks, which saddled the government with a huge debt burden. Pledges of economic and financial reforms made at separate international donor conferences during the 2000s have mostly gone unfulfilled, including those made during the Paris III Donor Conference in 2007, following the July 2006 war. The "CEDRE" investment event hosted by France in April 2018 again rallied the international community to assist Lebanon with concessional financing and some grants for capital infrastructure improvements, conditioned upon long-delayed structural economic reforms in fiscal management, electricity tariffs, and transparent public procurement, among many others.

The Syria conflict cut off one of Lebanon's major markets and a transport corridor through the Levant. The influx of nearly one million registered and an estimated 300,000 unregistered Syrian refugees has increased social tensions and heightened competition for low-skill jobs and public services. Lebanon continues to face several long-term structural weaknesses that predate the Syria crisis, notably, weak infrastructure, poor service delivery, institutionalized corruption, and bureaucratic over-regulation. Chronic fiscal deficits have increased Lebanon's debt-to-GDP ratio, the third highest in the world; most of the debt is held internally by Lebanese banks. These factors combined to slow economic growth to the 1-2% range in 2011-17, after four years of averaging 8% growth. Weak economic growth limits tax revenues, while the largest government expenditures remain debt servicing, salaries for government workers, and transfers to the electricity sector. These limitations constrain other government spending, limiting its ability to invest in necessary infrastructure improvements, such as water, electricity, and transportation. In early 2018, the Lebanese government signed long-awaited contract agreements with an international consortium for petroleum exploration and production as part of the country's first offshore licensing round. Exploration is expected to begin in 2019.

GDP (PURCHASING POWER PARITY):

$88.25 billion (2017 est.)

$86.94 billion (2016 est.)

$85.45 billion (2015 est.)

note: data are in 2017 dollars

country comparison to the world: 92

GDP (OFFICIAL EXCHANGE RATE):

$54.18 billion (2017 est.)

GDP - REAL GROWTH RATE:

1.5% (2017 est.)

1.7% (2016 est.)

0.2% (2015 est.)

country comparison to the world: 172

GDP - PER CAPITA (PPP):

$19,600 (2017 est.)

$19,500 (2016 est.)

$19,300 (2015 est.)

note: data are in 2017 dollars

country comparison to the world: 91

GROSS NATIONAL SAVING:

-0.7% of GDP (2017 est.)

0.7% of GDP (2016 est.)

4.5% of GDP (2015 est.)

country comparison to the world: 181

GDP - COMPOSITION, BY END USE:

household consumption: 87.6% (2017 est.)

government consumption: 13.3% (2017 est.)

investment in fixed capital: 21.8% (2017 est.)

investment in inventories: 0.5% (2017 est.)

exports of goods and services: 23.6% (2017 est.)

imports of goods and services: -46.4% (2017 est.)

GDP - COMPOSITION, BY SECTOR OF ORIGIN:

agriculture: 3.9% (2017 est.)

industry: 13.1% (2017 est.)

services: 83% (2017 est.)

AGRICULTURE - PRODUCTS:

citrus, grapes, tomatoes, apples, vegetables, potatoes, olives, tobacco; sheep, goats

INDUSTRIES:

banking, tourism, real estate and construction, food processing, wine, jewelry, cement, textiles, mineral and chemical products, wood and furniture products, oil refining, metal fabricating

INDUSTRIAL PRODUCTION GROWTH RATE:

-21.1% (2017 est.)

country comparison to the world: 201

LABOR FORCE:

2.166 million (2016 est.)

note: excludes as many as 1 million foreign workers and refugees

country comparison to the world: 123

LABOR FORCE - BY OCCUPATION:

agriculture: 39% NA (2009 est.)

industry: NA

services: NA

UNEMPLOYMENT RATE:

9.7% (2007)

country comparison to the world: 138

POPULATION BELOW POVERTY LINE:

28.6% (2004 est.)

HOUSEHOLD INCOME OR CONSUMPTION BY PERCENTAGE SHARE:

lowest 10%: NA

highest 10%: NA

BUDGET:

revenues: 11.62 billion (2017 est.)

expenditures: 15.38 billion (2017 est.)

TAXES AND OTHER REVENUES:

21.5% (of GDP) (2017 est.)

country comparison to the world: 136

BUDGET SURPLUS (+) OR DEFICIT (-):

-6.9% (of GDP) (2017 est.)

country comparison to the world: 193

PUBLIC DEBT:

146.8% of GDP (2017 est.)

145.5% of GDP (2016 est.)

note: data cover central government debt and exclude debt instruments issued (or owned) by government entities other than the treasury; the data include treasury debt held by foreign entities; the data include debt issued by subnational entities, as well as intragovernmental debt; intragovernmental debt consists of treasury borrowings from surpluses in the social funds, such as for retirement, medical care, and unemployment

country comparison to the world: 4

FISCAL YEAR:

calendar year

INFLATION RATE (CONSUMER PRICES):

4.5% (2017 est.)

-0.8% (2016 est.)

country comparison to the world: 167

CENTRAL BANK DISCOUNT RATE:

10% (31 December 2017)

10% (31 December 2016)

country comparison to the world: 22

COMMERCIAL BANK PRIME LENDING RATE:

8.29% (31 December 2017 est.)

8.35% (31 December 2016 est.)

country comparison to the world: 103

STOCK OF NARROW MONEY:

$7.047 billion (31 December 2017 est.)

$6.739 billion (31 December 2016 est.)

country comparison to the world: 90

STOCK OF BROAD MONEY:

$7.047 billion (31 December 2017 est.)

$6.739 billion (31 December 2016 est.)

country comparison to the world: 92

STOCK OF DOMESTIC CREDIT:

$108.2 billion (31 December 2017 est.)

$104 billion (31 December 2016 est.)

country comparison to the world: 55

MARKET VALUE OF PUBLICLY TRADED SHARES:

$11.22 billion (30 December 2014 est.)

$10.54 billion (30 December 2013 est.)

$10.42 billion (28 December 2012 est.)

country comparison to the world: 73

CURRENT ACCOUNT BALANCE:

-$12.37 billion (2017 est.)

-$11.18 billion (2016 est.)

country comparison to the world: 193

EXPORTS:

$3.524 billion (2017 est.)

$3.689 billion (2016 est.)

country comparison to the world: 123

EXPORTS - PARTNERS:

China 13%, UAE 9.9%, South Africa 7.5%, Saudi Arabia 6.5%, Syria 6.5%, Iraq 5.8%, Turkey 4.6% (2017)

EXPORTS - COMMODITIES:

jewelry, base metals, chemicals, consumer goods, fruit and vegetables, tobacco, construction minerals, electric power machinery and switchgear, textile fibers, paper

IMPORTS:

$18.34 billion (2017 est.)

$17.71 billion (2016 est.)

country comparison to the world: 81

IMPORTS - COMMODITIES:

petroleum products, cars, medicinal products, clothing, meat and live animals, consumer goods, paper, textile fabrics, tobacco, electrical machinery and equipment, chemicals

IMPORTS - PARTNERS:

China 10.2%, Italy 8.9%, Greece 7%, Germany 6.6%, US 6.3%, Turkey 4.5%, Egypt 4.2% (2017)

RESERVES OF FOREIGN EXCHANGE AND GOLD:
$55.42 billion (31 December 2017 est.)

$54.04 billion (31 December 2016 est.)

country comparison to the world: 37

DEBT - EXTERNAL:
$39.3 billion (31 December 2017 est.)

$36.6 billion (31 December 2016 est.)

country comparison to the world: 76

STOCK OF DIRECT FOREIGN INVESTMENT - AT HOME:
$61.02 billion (2016)

$58.46 billion (2015)

country comparison to the world: 56

STOCK OF DIRECT FOREIGN INVESTMENT - ABROAD:
$13.46 billion (2016)

$12.69 billion (2015)

country comparison to the world: 61

EXCHANGE RATES:
Lebanese pounds (LBP) per US dollar -

1,507.5 (2017 est.)

1,507.5 (2016 est.)

1,507.5 (2015 est.)

1,507.5 (2014 est.)

1,507.5 (2013 est.)

ENERGY :: LEBANON

ELECTRICITY ACCESS:
electrification - total population: 100% (2016)

ELECTRICITY - PRODUCTION:
17.59 billion kWh (2016 est.)

country comparison to the world: 82

ELECTRICITY - CONSUMPTION:
15.71 billion kWh (2016 est.)

country comparison to the world: 77

ELECTRICITY - EXPORTS:
0 kWh (2016 est.)

country comparison to the world: 157

ELECTRICITY - IMPORTS:
69 million kWh (2016 est.)

country comparison to the world: 104

ELECTRICITY - INSTALLED GENERATING CAPACITY:
2.346 million kW (2016 est.)

country comparison to the world: 110

ELECTRICITY - FROM FOSSIL FUELS:
88% of total installed capacity (2016 est.)

country comparison to the world: 59

ELECTRICITY - FROM NUCLEAR FUELS:
0% of total installed capacity (2017 est.)

country comparison to the world: 126

ELECTRICITY - FROM HYDROELECTRIC PLANTS:
11% of total installed capacity (2017 est.)

country comparison to the world: 114

ELECTRICITY - FROM OTHER RENEWABLE SOURCES:
1% of total installed capacity (2017 est.)

country comparison to the world: 158

CRUDE OIL - PRODUCTION:
0 bbl/day (2018 est.)

country comparison to the world: 161

CRUDE OIL - EXPORTS:
0 bbl/day (2015 est.)

country comparison to the world: 153

CRUDE OIL - IMPORTS:
0 bbl/day (2015 est.)

country comparison to the world: 151

CRUDE OIL - PROVED RESERVES:
0 bbl (1 January 2018 est.)

country comparison to the world: 156

REFINED PETROLEUM PRODUCTS - PRODUCTION:
0 bbl/day (2015 est.)

country comparison to the world: 164

REFINED PETROLEUM PRODUCTS - CONSUMPTION:
154,000 bbl/day (2016 est.)

country comparison to the world: 65

REFINED PETROLEUM PRODUCTS - EXPORTS:
0 bbl/day (2015 est.)

country comparison to the world: 170

REFINED PETROLEUM PRODUCTS - IMPORTS:
151,100 bbl/day (2015 est.)

country comparison to the world: 41

NATURAL GAS - PRODUCTION:
0 cu m (2017 est.)

country comparison to the world: 156

NATURAL GAS - CONSUMPTION:
0 cu m (2017 est.)

country comparison to the world: 166

NATURAL GAS - EXPORTS:
0 cu m (2017 est.)

country comparison to the world: 137

NATURAL GAS - IMPORTS:
0 cu m (2017 est.)

country comparison to the world: 147

NATURAL GAS - PROVED RESERVES:
0 cu m (1 January 2014 est.)

country comparison to the world: 157

CARBON DIOXIDE EMISSIONS FROM CONSUMPTION OF ENERGY:
23.36 million Mt (2017 est.)

country comparison to the world: 83

COMMUNICATIONS :: LEBANON

TELEPHONES - FIXED LINES:
total subscriptions: 1,816,262

subscriptions per 100 inhabitants: 17 (July 2016 est.)

country comparison to the world: 60

TELEPHONES - MOBILE CELLULAR:
total subscriptions: 4,890,534

subscriptions per 100 inhabitants: 79 (July 2016 est.)

country comparison to the world: 122

TELEPHONE SYSTEM:
general assessment: new landlines and fiber-optic networks installed along with faster DSL in 2017; two mobile-cellular networks provide good service, with 4G LTE services; preparing for 5G service; future improvements to fiber-optic infrastructure for total nation coverage in 2020 (2018)

domestic: fixed-line 17 per 100 and 79 per 100 for mobile-cellular subscriptions (2018)

international: country code - 961; landing points for the IMEWE, BERYTAR AND CADMOS submarine cable links to Europe, Africa, the Middle East and Asia; satellite earth stations - 2 Intelsat (1 Indian Ocean and 1 Atlantic Ocean) (2019)

BROADCAST MEDIA:
7 TV stations, 1 of which is state owned; more than 30 radio stations, 1 of which is state owned; satellite and cable TV services available; transmissions of at least 2 international broadcasters are accessible through partner stations (2019)

INTERNET COUNTRY CODE:
.lb

INTERNET USERS:
total: 4,747,542

percent of population: 76.1% (July 2016 est.)

country comparison to the world: 79

BROADBAND - FIXED SUBSCRIPTIONS:

total: 1.3 million

subscriptions per 100 inhabitants: 21 (2017 est.)

country comparison to the world: 65

MILITARY AND SECURITY :: LEBANON

MILITARY EXPENDITURES:

4.99% of GDP (2018)

4.6% of GDP (2017)

5.17% of GDP (2016)

4.53% of GDP (2015)

4.75% of GDP (2014)

country comparison to the world: 7

MILITARY AND SECURITY FORCES:

Lebanese Armed Forces (LAF): Army Command (includes Presidential Guard Brigade, Land Border Regiments), Naval Forces, Air Forces; Ministry of Interior: Lebanese Internal Security Forces Directorate (includes Mobile Gendarmerie) (2019)

MILITARY SERVICE AGE AND OBLIGATION:

17-25 years of age for voluntary military service (including women); no conscription (2019)

MILITARY - NOTE:

the United Nations Interim Force In Lebanon (UNIFIL) has operated in the country since 1978, originally under UNSCRs 425 and 426 to confirm Israeli withdrawal from Lebanon, restore international peace and security and assist the Lebanese Government in restoring its effective authority in the area; following the July-August 2006 war, the UN Security Council adopted resolution 1701 enhancing UNIFIL and deciding that in addition to the original mandate, it would, among other things, monitor the cessation of hostilities; accompany and support the Lebanese Armed Forces (LAF) as they deploy throughout the south of Lebanon; and extend its assistance to help ensure humanitarian access to civilian populations and the voluntary and safe return of displaced persons; UNIFIL had about 10,250 personnel deployed in the country as of September 2019 (2019)

TRANSPORTATION :: LEBANON

NATIONAL AIR TRANSPORT SYSTEM:

number of registered air carriers: 2 (2015)

inventory of registered aircraft operated by air carriers: 21 (2015)

annual passenger traffic on registered air carriers: 2,583,274 (2015)

annual freight traffic on registered air carriers: 53,902,026 mt-km (2015)

CIVIL AIRCRAFT REGISTRATION COUNTRY CODE PREFIX:

OD (2016)

AIRPORTS:

8 (2013)

country comparison to the world: 161

AIRPORTS - WITH PAVED RUNWAYS:

total: 5 (2017)

over 3,047 m: 1 (2017)

2,438 to 3,047 m: 2 (2017)

1,524 to 2,437 m: 1 (2017)

under 914 m: 1 (2017)

AIRPORTS - WITH UNPAVED RUNWAYS:

total: 3 (2013)

914 to 1,523 m: 2 (2013)

under 914 m: 1 (2013)

HELIPORTS:

1 (2013)

PIPELINES:

88 km gas (2013)

RAILWAYS:

total: 401 km (2017)

standard gauge: 319 km 1.435-m gauge (2017)

narrow gauge: 82 km 1.050-m gauge (2017)

note: rail system is still unusable due to damage sustained from fighting in the 1980s and in 2006

country comparison to the world: 119

ROADWAYS:

total: 21,705 km (2017)

country comparison to the world: 109

MERCHANT MARINE:

total: 55

by type: bulk carrier 1, container ship 1, general cargo 40, oil tanker 1, other 12 (2018)

country comparison to the world: 112

PORTS AND TERMINALS:

major seaport(s): Beirut, Tripoli

container port(s) (TEUs): Beirut (1,305,038) (2017)

TERRORISM :: LEBANON

TERRORIST GROUPS - HOME BASED:

Abdallah Azzam Brigades (AAB): aim(s): enhance its networks in Lebanon to combat Shia Muslim influence in the country; seeks to disrupt Israel's economy and its efforts to establish security; attack Western interests in the Middle East
area(s) of operation: headquartered in the Ayn al-Hilwah Palestinian refugee camp near Sidon in the south (2018)

Asbat al-Ansar (AAA): aim(s): overthrow the Lebanese Government, rid Lebanon of Western influences, destroy the state of Israel to seize Jerusalem and, ultimately, establish an Islamic state in the Levant region
area(s) of operation: headquartered in the Ayn al-Hilwah Palestinian refugee camp near Sidon in the south (2018)

Hizballah: aim(s): accrue military resources and political power and defend its position of strength in Lebanon; destroy the state of Israel; counter the West; provide paramilitary support to Syrian President Bashar al-ASAD's regime
area(s) of operation: headquartered in Beirut with a significant presence in the Bekaa Valley and Southern Lebanon
note: remains the most capable armed group in the country, enjoying support among many Lebanese Shia and some Christians; receives considerable support from Iran (2018)

Islamic State of Iraq and ash-Sham (ISIS) network in Lebanon: aim(s): replace the Lebanese Government with an Islamic state and implement ISIS's strict interpretation of sharia
area(s) of operation: operational primarily in the east along the border with Syria; also maintains a presence in Ayn al-Hilweh refugee camp (2018)

TERRORIST GROUPS - FOREIGN BASED:

al-Aqsa Martyrs Brigade (AAMB): aim(s): bolster its recruitment presence in Lebanon and, ultimately, establish a Palestinian state comprising the West Bank, Gaza Strip, and Jerusalem
area(s) of operation: recruits youths in Palestinian refugee camps (2018)

al-Nusrah Front/al-Qa'ida: aim(s): bolster networks in Lebanon and, ultimately, establish a regional Islamic caliphate
area(s) of operation: in the east in the Bekaa Valley and along the Lebanon-Syria border; targets Lebanese Government institutions, security forces, and Lebanese civilians (2018)

Islamic Revolutionary Guard Corps -- Qods Force (IRGC-QF):

aim(s): support Lebanon's Hezbollah movement to advance Shia agenda through funding, training, and weapons area(s) of operations: Beirut, Bekaa Valley, southern Lebanon

(2019)

Palestine Liberation Front (PLF):
aim(s): enhance its networks in Lebanon and, ultimately, destroy the state of Israel to establish a secular, Marxist Palestinian state with Jerusalem as its capital
area(s) of operation: maintains a recruitment and training presence in many refugee camps (2018)

PFLP-General Command (PFLP-GC):
aim(s): enhance recruitment and operational networks in Lebanon
area(s) of operation: recruits young men living in Palestinian refugee camps, including camps in the Bekaa Valley (2018)

Popular Front for the Liberation of Palestine (PFLP): aim(s): enhance its recruitment network in Lebanon and, ultimately, establish a secular, Marxist Palestinian state
area(s) of operation: recruits youths residing in the country's Palestinian refugee camps (2018)

TRANSNATIONAL ISSUES :: LEBANON

DISPUTES - INTERNATIONAL:

lacking a treaty or other documentation describing the boundary, portions of the Lebanon-Syria boundary are unclear with several sections in dispute; since 2000, Lebanon has claimed Shab'a Farms area in the Israeli-controlled Golan Heights; the roughly 2,000-strong UN Interim Force in Lebanon has been in place since 1978

REFUGEES AND INTERNALLY DISPLACED PERSONS:

refugees (country of origin): 918,974 (Syria), 475,075 (Palestinian refugees) (2019)

IDPs: 11,000 (2007 Lebanese security forces' destruction of Palestinian refugee camp) (2018)

stateless persons: undetermined (2016); note - tens of thousands of persons are stateless in Lebanon, including many Palestinian refugees and their descendants, Syrian Kurds denaturalized in Syria in 1962, children born to Lebanese women married to foreign or stateless men; most babies born to Syrian refugees, and Lebanese children whose births are unregistered

TRAFFICKING IN PERSONS:

current situation: Lebanon is a source and destination country for women and children subjected to forced labor and sex trafficking and a transit point for Eastern European women and children subjected to sex trafficking in other Middle Eastern countries; women and girls from South and Southeast Asia and an increasing number from East and West Africa are recruited by agencies to work in domestic service but are subject to conditions of forced labor; under Lebanon's artiste visa program, women from Eastern Europe, North Africa, and the Dominican Republic enter Lebanon to work in the adult entertainment industry but are often forced into the sex trade; Lebanese children are reportedly forced into street begging and commercial sexual exploitation, with small numbers of Lebanese girls sex trafficked in other Arab countries; Syrian refugees are vulnerable to forced labor and prostitution

tier rating: Tier 2 Watch List – Lebanon does not fully comply with the minimum standards for the elimination of trafficking; however, it is making significant efforts to do so; in 2014, Lebanon was granted a waiver from an otherwise required downgrade to Tier 3 because its government has a written plan that, if implemented would constitute making significant efforts to bring itself into compliance with the minimum standards for the elimination of trafficking; law enforcement efforts in 2014 were uneven; the number of convicted traffickers increased, but judges lack of familiarity with anti-trafficking law meant that many offenders were not brought to justice; the government relied heavily on an NGO to identify and provide service to trafficking victims; and its lack of thoroughly implemented victim identification procedures resulted in victims continuing to be arrested, detained, and deported for crimes committed as a direct result of being trafficked (2015)

ILLICIT DRUGS:

Lebanon is a transit country for hashish, cocaine, heroin, and fenethylene; fenethylene, cannabis, hashish, and some opium are produced in the Bekaa Valley; small amounts of Latin American cocaine and Southwest Asian heroin transit country on way to European markets and for Middle Eastern consumption; money laundering of drug proceeds fuels concern that extremists are benefiting from drug trafficking

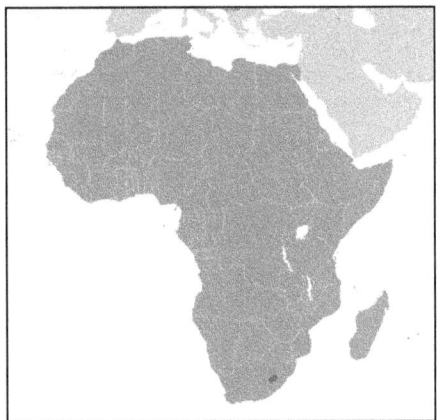

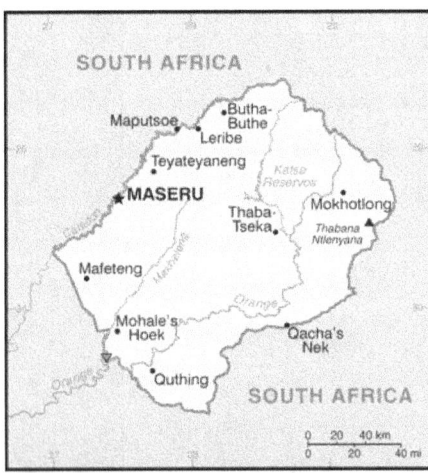

AFRICA :: LESOTHO

INTRODUCTION :: LESOTHO

BACKGROUND:

Basutoland was renamed the Kingdom of Lesotho upon independence from the UK in 1966. The Basotho National Party ruled the country during its first two decades. King MOSHOESHOE II was exiled in 1990, but returned to Lesotho in 1992 and was reinstated in 1995 and subsequently succeeded by his son, King LETSIE III, in 1996. Constitutional government was restored in 1993 after seven years of military rule. In 1998, violent protests and a military mutiny following a contentious election prompted a brief but bloody intervention by South African and Botswana military forces under the aegis of the Southern African Development Community. Subsequent constitutional reforms restored relative political stability. Peaceful parliamentary elections were held in 2002, but the National Assembly elections in 2007 were hotly contested and aggrieved parties disputed how the electoral law was applied to award proportional seats in the Assembly. In 2012, competitive elections involving 18 parties saw Prime Minister Motsoahae Thomas THABANE form a coalition government - the first in the country's history - that ousted the 14-year incumbent, Pakalitha MOSISILI, who peacefully transferred power the following month. MOSISILI returned to power in snap elections in February 2015 after the collapse of THABANE's coalition government and an alleged attempted military coup. In June 2017, THABANE returned to become prime minister.

GEOGRAPHY :: LESOTHO

LOCATION:
Southern Africa, an enclave of South Africa

GEOGRAPHIC COORDINATES:
29 30 S, 28 30 E

MAP REFERENCES:
Africa

AREA:
total: 30,355 sq km

land: 30,355 sq km

water: 0 sq km

country comparison to the world: 142

AREA - COMPARATIVE:
slightly smaller than Maryland

LAND BOUNDARIES:
total: 1,106 km

border countries (1): South Africa 1106 km

COASTLINE:
0 km (landlocked)

MARITIME CLAIMS:
none (landlocked)

CLIMATE:
temperate; cool to cold, dry winters; hot, wet summers

TERRAIN:
mostly highland with plateaus, hills, and mountains

ELEVATION:
mean elevation: 2,161 m

lowest point: junction of the Orange and Makhaleng Rivers 1,400 m

highest point: Thabana Ntlenyana 3,482 m

NATURAL RESOURCES:
water, agricultural and grazing land, diamonds, sand, clay, building stone

LAND USE:
agricultural land: 76.1% (2011 est.)

arable land: 10.1% (2011 est.) / permanent crops: 0.1% (2011 est.) / permanent pasture: 65.9% (2011 est.)

forest: 1.5% (2011 est.)

other: 22.4% (2011 est.)

IRRIGATED LAND:
30 sq km (2012)

POPULATION DISTRIBUTION:
relatively higher population density in the western half of the nation, with the capital of Maseru, and the smaller cities of Mafeteng, Teyateyaneng, and Leribe attracting the most people

NATURAL HAZARDS:
periodic droughts

ENVIRONMENT - CURRENT ISSUES:
population pressure forcing settlement in marginal areas results in overgrazing, severe soil erosion, and soil exhaustion; desertification; Highlands Water Project controls, stores, and redirects water to South Africa

ENVIRONMENT - INTERNATIONAL AGREEMENTS:
party to: Biodiversity, Climate Change, Climate Change-Kyoto Protocol, Desertification, Endangered Species, Hazardous Wastes, Law of the Sea, Marine Life Conservation, Ozone Layer Protection, Wetlands

signed, but not ratified: none of the selected agreements

GEOGRAPHY - NOTE:

landlocked, an enclave of (completely surrounded by) South Africa; mountainous, more than 80% of the country is 1,800 m above sea level

PEOPLE AND SOCIETY :: LESOTHO

POPULATION:
1,962,461 (July 2018 est.)

note: estimates for this country explicitly take into account the effects of excess mortality due to AIDS; this can result in lower life expectancy, higher infant mortality, higher death rates, lower population growth rates, and changes in the distribution of population by age and sex than would otherwise be expected

country comparison to the world: 149

NATIONALITY:
noun: Mosotho (singular), Basotho (plural)

adjective: Basotho

ETHNIC GROUPS:
Sotho 99.7%, Europeans, Asians, and other 0.3%

LANGUAGES:
Sesotho (official) (southern Sotho), English (official), Zulu, Xhosa

RELIGIONS:
Protestant 47.8% (Pentecostal 23.1%, Lesotho Evangelical 17.3%, Anglican 7.4%), Roman Catholic 39.3%, other Christian 9.1%, non-Christian 1.4%, none 2.3% (2014 est.)

DEMOGRAPHIC PROFILE:
Lesotho faces great socioeconomic challenges. More than half of its population lives below the property line, and the country's HIV/AIDS prevalence rate is the second highest in the world. In addition, Lesotho is a small, mountainous, landlocked country with little arable land, leaving its population vulnerable to food shortages and reliant on remittances. Lesotho's persistently high infant, child, and maternal mortality rates have been increasing during the last decade, according to the last two Demographic and Health Surveys. Despite these significant shortcomings, Lesotho has made good progress in education; it is on-track to achieve universal primary education and has one of the highest adult literacy rates in Africa.

Lesotho's migration history is linked to its unique geography; it is surrounded by South Africa with which it shares linguistic and cultural traits. Lesotho at one time had more of its workforce employed outside its borders than any other country. Today remittances equal about 17% of its GDP. With few job options at home, a high rate of poverty, and higher wages available across the border, labor migration to South Africa replaced agriculture as the prevailing Basotho source of income decades ago. The majority of Basotho migrants were single men contracted to work as gold miners in South Africa. However, migration trends changed in the 1990s, and fewer men found mining jobs in South Africa because of declining gold prices, stricter immigration policies, and a preference for South African workers.

Although men still dominate cross-border labor migration, more women are working in South Africa, mostly as domestics, because they are widows or their husbands are unemployed. Internal rural-urban flows have also become more frequent, with more women migrating within the country to take up jobs in the garment industry or moving to care for loved ones with HIV/AIDS. Lesotho's small population of immigrants is increasingly composed of Taiwanese and Chinese migrants who are involved in the textile industry and small retail businesses.

AGE STRUCTURE:
0-14 years: 31.84% (male 314,155 /female 310,772)

15-24 years: 19.34% (male 181,332 /female 198,236)

25-54 years: 38.27% (male 366,652 /female 384,333)

55-64 years: 5.02% (male 52,490 /female 46,016)

65 years and over: 5.53% (male 55,804 /female 52,671) (2018 est.)

DEPENDENCY RATIOS:
total dependency ratio: 66.9 (2015 est.)

youth dependency ratio: 59.5 (2015 est.)

elderly dependency ratio: 7.4 (2015 est.)

potential support ratio: 13.5 (2015 est.)

MEDIAN AGE:
total: 24.4 years (2018 est.)

male: 24.4 years

female: 24.3 years

country comparison to the world: 164

POPULATION GROWTH RATE:
0.24% (2018 est.)

country comparison to the world: 178

BIRTH RATE:
24.2 births/1,000 population (2018 est.)

country comparison to the world: 52

DEATH RATE:
15.1 deaths/1,000 population (2018 est.)

country comparison to the world: 2

NET MIGRATION RATE:
-6.6 migrant(s)/1,000 population (2018 est.)

country comparison to the world: 205

POPULATION DISTRIBUTION:
relatively higher population density in the western half of the nation, with the capital of Maseru, and the smaller cities of Mafeteng, Teyateyaneng, and Leribe attracting the most people

URBANIZATION:
urban population: 28.6% of total population (2019)

rate of urbanization: 2.83% annual rate of change (2015-20 est.)

MAJOR URBAN AREAS - POPULATION:
202,000 MASERU (capital) (2018)

SEX RATIO:
at birth: 1.03 male(s)/female

0-14 years: 1.01 male(s)/female

15-24 years: 0.91 male(s)/female

25-54 years: 0.95 male(s)/female

55-64 years: 1.14 male(s)/female

65 years and over: 1.06 male(s)/female

total population: 0.98 male(s)/female (2018 est.)

MOTHER'S MEAN AGE AT FIRST BIRTH:
21 years (2014 est.)

note: median age at first birth among women 25-29

MATERNAL MORTALITY RATE:
544 deaths/100,000 live births (2017 est.)

country comparison to the world: 17

INFANT MORTALITY RATE:
total: 44.6 deaths/1,000 live births (2018 est.)

male: 48.1 deaths/1,000 live births

female: 40.9 deaths/1,000 live births

country comparison to the world: 36

LIFE EXPECTANCY AT BIRTH:

total population: 53 years (2018 est.)

male: 53 years

female: 53.1 years

country comparison to the world: 221

TOTAL FERTILITY RATE:

2.59 children born/woman (2018 est.)

country comparison to the world: 72

CONTRACEPTIVE PREVALENCE RATE:

60.2% (2014)

DRINKING WATER SOURCE:

improved:

urban: 94.6% of population

rural: 77% of population

total: 81.8% of population

unimproved:

urban: 5.4% of population

rural: 23% of population

total: 18.2% of population (2015 est.)

CURRENT HEALTH EXPENDITURE:

8.1% (2016)

PHYSICIANS DENSITY:

0.07 physicians/1,000 population (2010)

SANITATION FACILITY ACCESS:

improved:

urban: 37.3% of population (2015 est.)

rural: 27.6% of population (2015 est.)

total: 30.3% of population (2015 est.)

unimproved:

urban: 62.7% of population (2015 est.)

rural: 72.4% of population (2015 est.)

total: 69.7% of population (2015 est.)

HIV/AIDS - ADULT PREVALENCE RATE:

23.6% (2018 est.)

country comparison to the world: 2

HIV/AIDS - PEOPLE LIVING WITH HIV/AIDS:

340,000 (2018 est.)

country comparison to the world: 20

HIV/AIDS - DEATHS:

6,100 (2018 est.)

country comparison to the world: 24

OBESITY - ADULT PREVALENCE RATE:

16.6% (2016)

country comparison to the world: 122

CHILDREN UNDER THE AGE OF 5 YEARS UNDERWEIGHT:

10.5% (2014)

country comparison to the world: 60

EDUCATION EXPENDITURES:

6.4% of GDP (2018)

country comparison to the world: 25

LITERACY:

definition: age 15 and over can read and write

total population: 79.4%

male: 70.1%

female: 88.3% (2015 est.)

SCHOOL LIFE EXPECTANCY (PRIMARY TO TERTIARY EDUCATION):

total: 11 years

male: 10 years

female: 11 years (2015)

UNEMPLOYMENT, YOUTH AGES 15-24:

total: 34.4%

male: NA

female: NA (2013 est.)

country comparison to the world: 24

GOVERNMENT :: LESOTHO

COUNTRY NAME:

conventional long form: Kingdom of Lesotho

conventional short form: Lesotho

local long form: Kingdom of Lesotho

local short form: Lesotho

former: Basutoland

etymology: the name translates as "Land of the Sesotho Speakers"

GOVERNMENT TYPE:

parliamentary constitutional monarchy

CAPITAL:

name: Maseru

geographic coordinates: 29 19 S, 27 29 E

time difference: UTC+2 (7 hours ahead of Washington, DC, during Standard Time)

etymology: in the Sesotho language the name means "[place of] red sandstones"

ADMINISTRATIVE DIVISIONS:

10 districts; Berea, Butha-Buthe, Leribe, Mafeteng, Maseru, Mohale's Hoek, Mokhotlong, Qacha's Nek, Quthing, Thaba-Tseka

INDEPENDENCE:

4 October 1966 (from the UK)

NATIONAL HOLIDAY:

Independence Day, 4 October (1966)

CONSTITUTION:

history: previous 1959, 1967; latest adopted 2 April 1993 (effectively restoring the 1967 version)

amendments: proposed by Parliament; passage of amendments affecting constitutional provisions, including fundamental rights and freedoms, sovereignty of the kingdom, the office of the king, and powers of Parliament, requires a majority vote by the National Assembly, approval by the Senate, approval in a referendum by a majority of qualified voters, and assent of the king; passage of amendments other than those specified provisions requires at least a two-thirds majority vote in both houses of Parliament; amended several times, last in 2011 (2017)

LEGAL SYSTEM:

mixed legal system of English common law and Roman-Dutch law; judicial review of legislative acts in High Court and Court of Appeal

INTERNATIONAL LAW ORGANIZATION PARTICIPATION:

accepts compulsory ICJ jurisdiction with reservations; accepts ICCt jurisdiction

CITIZENSHIP:

citizenship by birth: yes

citizenship by descent only: yes

dual citizenship recognized: no

residency requirement for naturalization: 5 years

SUFFRAGE:

18 years of age; universal

EXECUTIVE BRANCH:

chief of state: King LETSIE III (since 7 February 1996); note - King LETSIE III formerly occupied the throne from November 1990 to February 1995 while his father was in exile

head of government: Prime Minister Thomas Motsoahae THABANE (since

16 June 2017)

cabinet: consists of the prime minister, appointed by the King on the advice of the Council of State, the deputy prime minister, and 26 other ministers

elections/appointments: the monarchy is hereditary, but under the terms of the constitution that came into effect after the March 1993 election, the monarch is a "living symbol of national unity" with no executive or legislative powers; under traditional law, the college of chiefs has the power to depose the monarch, to determine next in line of succession, or to serve as regent in the event that a successor is not of mature age; following legislative elections, the leader of the majority party or majority coalition in the Assembly automatically becomes prime minister

LEGISLATIVE BRANCH:

description: bicameral Parliament consists of:
Senate (33 seats; 22 principal chiefs and 11 other senators nominated by the king with the advice of the Council of State, a 13-member body of key government and non-government officials; members serve 5-year terms)
National Assembly (120 seats; 80 members directly elected in single-seat constituencies by simple majority vote and 40 elected through proportional representation; members serve 5-year terms)

elections: Senate - last nominated by the king 11 July 2017 (next NA)
National Assembly - last held on 3 June 2017 (next to be held in 2022)

election results: Senate - percent of votes by party - NA, seats by party - NA; composition - men 25, women 8, percent of women 24.2%
National Assembly - percent of votes by party - ABC 40.5%, DC 25.8%, LCD 9%, AD 7.3%, MEC 5.1%, BNP 4.1, PFD 2.3%, other 5.9%; seats by party - ABC 51, DC 30, LCD 11, AD 9, MEC 6, BNP 5, PFD 3, other 5; composition - men 95, women 27, percent of women 22.5%; note - total Parliament percent of women 22.9%

JUDICIAL BRANCH:

highest courts: Court of Appeal (consists of the court president, such number of justices of appeal as set by Parliament, and the Chief Justice and the puisne judges of the High Court ex officio); High Court (consists of the chief justice and such number of puisne judges as set by Parliament); note - both the Court of Appeal and the High Court have jurisdiction in constitutional issues

judge selection and term of office: Court of Appeal president and High Court chief justice appointed by the monarch on the advice of the prime minister; puisne judges appointed by the monarch on advice of the Judicial Service Commission, an independent body of judicial officers and officials designated by the monarch; judges of both courts can serve until age 75

subordinate courts: Magistrate Courts; customary or traditional courts; military courts

POLITICAL PARTIES AND LEADERS:

All Basotho Convention or ABC [Thomas Motsoahae THABANE]
Alliance of Democrats or AD [Monyane MOLELEKI]
Basotho Congress Party or BCP [Thulo MAHLAKENG]
Basotho National Party or BNP [Thesele MASERIBANE]
Democratic Congress or DC [Pakalitha MOSISILI]
Democratic Party of Lesotho or DPL [Limpho TAU]
Lesotho Congress for Democracy or LCD [Mothetjoa METSING]
Movement of Economic Change or MEC [Selibe MOCHOBOROANE]
National Independent Party or NIP [Kimetso MATHABA]
Popular Front for Democracy of PFD [Lekhetho RAKUOANE]
Reformed Congress of Lesotho or RCL [Keketso RANTSO]

INTERNATIONAL ORGANIZATION PARTICIPATION:

ACP, AfDB, AU, C, CD, FAO, G-77, IAEA, IBRD, ICAO, ICCt, ICRM, IDA, IFAD, IFC, IFRCS, ILO, IMF, Interpol, IOC, IOM, IPU, ISO (correspondent), ITU, MIGA, NAM, OPCW, SACU, SADC, UN, UNAMID, UNCTAD, UNESCO, UNHCR, UNIDO, UNWTO, UPU, WCO, WFTU (NGOs), WHO, WIPO, WMO, WTO

DIPLOMATIC REPRESENTATION IN THE US:

Ambassador Sankatana Gabriel MAJA (since 22 June 2018)

chancery: 2511 Massachusetts Avenue NW, Washington, DC 20008

telephone: [1] (202) 797-5533

FAX: [1] (202) 234-6815

DIPLOMATIC REPRESENTATION FROM THE US:

chief of mission: Ambassador Rebecca E. GONZALES (since 8 February 2018)

telephone: [266] 22 312 666

embassy: 254 Kingsway Road, Maseru West

mailing address: P.O. Box 333, Maseru 100, Lesotho

FAX: [266] 22 310 116

FLAG DESCRIPTION:

three horizontal stripes of blue (top), white, and green in the proportions of 3:4:3; the colors represent rain, peace, and prosperity respectively; centered in the white stripe is a black Basotho hat representing the indigenous people; the flag was unfurled in October 2006 to celebrate 40 years of independence

NATIONAL SYMBOL(S):

mokorotio (Basotho hat); national colors: blue, white, green, black

NATIONAL ANTHEM:

name: "Lesotho fatse la bo ntat'a rona" (Lesotho, Land of Our Fathers)

lyrics/music: Francois COILLARD/Ferdinand-Samuel LAUR

note: adopted 1967; music derives from an 1823 Swiss songbook

ECONOMY :: LESOTHO

ECONOMY - OVERVIEW:

Small, mountainous, and completely landlocked by South Africa, Lesotho depends on a narrow economic base of textile manufacturing, agriculture, remittances, and regional customs revenue. About three-fourths of the people live in rural areas and engage in animal herding and subsistence agriculture, although Lesotho produces less than 20% of the nation's demand for food. Agriculture is vulnerable to weather and climate variability.

Lesotho relies on South Africa for much of its economic activity; Lesotho imports 85% of the goods it consumes from South Africa, including most agricultural inputs. Households depend heavily on remittances from family members working in South Africa in mines, on farms, and as domestic workers, though mining employment has declined substantially since the 1990s. Lesotho is a member of the Southern Africa Customs Union (SACU), and revenues from SACU accounted for roughly 26% of total

GDP in 2016; however, SACU revenues are volatile and expected to decline over the next 5 years. Lesotho also gains royalties from the South African Government for water transferred to South Africa from a dam and reservoir system in Lesotho. However, the government continues to strengthen its tax system to reduce dependency on customs duties and other transfers.

The government maintains a large presence in the economy - government consumption accounted for about 26% of GDP in 2017. The government remains Lesotho's largest employer; in 2016, the government wage bill rose to 23% of GDP – the largest in sub-Saharan Africa. Lesotho's largest private employer is the textile and garment industry - approximately 36,000 Basotho, mainly women, work in factories producing garments for export to South Africa and the US. Diamond mining in Lesotho has grown in recent years and accounted for nearly 35% of total exports in 2015. Lesotho managed steady GDP growth at an average of 4.5% from 2010 to 2014, dropping to about 2.5% in 2015-16, but poverty remains widespread around 57% of the total population.

GDP (PURCHASING POWER PARITY):

$6.656 billion (2017 est.)

$6.762 billion (2016 est.)

$6.561 billion (2015 est.)

note: data are in 2017 dollars

country comparison to the world: 170

GDP (OFFICIAL EXCHANGE RATE):

$2.749 billion (2017 est.)

GDP - REAL GROWTH RATE:

-1.6% (2017 est.)

3.1% (2016 est.)

2.5% (2015 est.)

country comparison to the world: 205

GDP - PER CAPITA (PPP):

$3,300 (2017 est.)

$3,400 (2016 est.)

$3,300 (2015 est.)

note: data are in 2017 dollars

country comparison to the world: 190

GROSS NATIONAL SAVING:

20.3% of GDP (2017 est.)

19.7% of GDP (2016 est.)

24.7% of GDP (2015 est.)

country comparison to the world: 96

GDP - COMPOSITION, BY END USE:

household consumption: 69.2% (2017 est.)

government consumption: 26.4% (2017 est.)

investment in fixed capital: 31.4% (2017 est.)

investment in inventories: -13.4% (2017 est.)

exports of goods and services: 40.8% (2017 est.)

imports of goods and services: -54.4% (2017 est.)

GDP - COMPOSITION, BY SECTOR OF ORIGIN:

agriculture: 5.8% (2016 est.)

industry: 39.2% (2016 est.)

services: 54.9% (2017 est.)

AGRICULTURE - PRODUCTS:

corn, wheat, pulses, sorghum, barley; livestock

INDUSTRIES:

food, beverages, textiles, apparel assembly, handicrafts, construction, tourism

INDUSTRIAL PRODUCTION GROWTH RATE:

12.5% (2017 est.)

country comparison to the world: 6

LABOR FORCE:

930,800 (2017 est.)

country comparison to the world: 148

LABOR FORCE - BY OCCUPATION:

agriculture: 86%

industry and services: 14% (2002 est.)

note: most of the resident population is engaged in subsistence agriculture; roughly 35% of the active male wage earners work in South Africa

UNEMPLOYMENT RATE:

28.1% (2014 est.)

25% (2008 est.)

country comparison to the world: 205

POPULATION BELOW POVERTY LINE:

57% (2016 est.)

HOUSEHOLD INCOME OR CONSUMPTION BY PERCENTAGE SHARE:

lowest 10%: 1%

highest 10%: 39.4% (2003)

DISTRIBUTION OF FAMILY INCOME - GINI INDEX:

63.2 (1995)

56 (1986-87)

country comparison to the world: 1

BUDGET:

revenues: 1.09 billion (2017 est.)

expenditures: 1.255 billion (2017 est.)

TAXES AND OTHER REVENUES:

39.7% (of GDP) (2017 est.)

country comparison to the world: 43

BUDGET SURPLUS (+) OR DEFICIT (-):

-6% (of GDP) (2017 est.)

country comparison to the world: 184

PUBLIC DEBT:

33.7% of GDP (2017 est.)

36.2% of GDP (2016 est.)

country comparison to the world: 155

FISCAL YEAR:

1 April - 31 March

INFLATION RATE (CONSUMER PRICES):

5.3% (2017 est.)

6.2% (2016 est.)

country comparison to the world: 173

CENTRAL BANK DISCOUNT RATE:

6.75% (2 February 2016)

6.25% (31 December 2015)

country comparison to the world: 53

COMMERCIAL BANK PRIME LENDING RATE:

11.58% (31 December 2017 est.)

11.58% (31 December 2016 est.)

country comparison to the world: 69

STOCK OF NARROW MONEY:

$420.8 million (31 December 2017 est.)

$356.3 million (31 December 2016 est.)

country comparison to the world: 175

STOCK OF BROAD MONEY:

$420.8 million (31 December 2017 est.)

$356.3 million (31 December 2016 est.)

country comparison to the world: 179

STOCK OF DOMESTIC CREDIT:

$442.3 million (31 December 2017 est.)

$230.9 million (31 December 2016 est.)

country comparison to the world: 180

CURRENT ACCOUNT BALANCE:

-$102 million (2017 est.)

-$201 million (2016 est.)

country comparison to the world: 86

EXPORTS:

$1.028 billion (2017 est.)

$894 million (2016 est.)

country comparison to the world: 160

EXPORTS - PARTNERS:

South Africa 57%, US 33.5% (2017)

EXPORTS - COMMODITIES:

manufactures (clothing, footwear), wool and mohair, food and live animals, electricity, water, diamonds

IMPORTS:

$1.826 billion (2017 est.)

$1.613 billion (2016 est.)

country comparison to the world: 172

IMPORTS - COMMODITIES:

food; building materials, vehicles, machinery, medicines, petroleum products

IMPORTS - PARTNERS:

South Africa 87.2% (2017)

RESERVES OF FOREIGN EXCHANGE AND GOLD:

$657.7 million (31 December 2017 est.)

$925.2 million (31 December 2016 est.)

country comparison to the world: 143

DEBT - EXTERNAL:

$934.6 million (31 December 2017 est.)

$921.3 million (31 December 2016 est.)

country comparison to the world: 167

STOCK OF DIRECT FOREIGN INVESTMENT - AT HOME:

$497.7 million (31 December 2017 est.)

$456.5 million (31 December 2016 est.)

country comparison to the world: 129

STOCK OF DIRECT FOREIGN INVESTMENT - ABROAD:

$122 million (31 December 2017 est.)

$206.9 million (31 December 2016 est.)

country comparison to the world: 109

EXCHANGE RATES:

maloti (LSL) per US dollar -

14.48 (2017 est.)

14.71 (2016 est.)

14.71 (2015 est.)

12.76 (2014 est.)

10.85 (2013 est.)

ENERGY :: LESOTHO

ELECTRICITY ACCESS:

population without electricity: 1 million (2017)

electrification - total population: 29.7% (2016)

electrification - urban areas: 66% (2016)

electrification - rural areas: 15.7% (2016)

ELECTRICITY - PRODUCTION:

510 million kWh (2016 est.)

country comparison to the world: 165

ELECTRICITY - CONSUMPTION:

847.3 million kWh (2016 est.)

country comparison to the world: 160

ELECTRICITY - EXPORTS:

0 kWh (2016 est.)

country comparison to the world: 158

ELECTRICITY - IMPORTS:

373 million kWh (2016 est.)

country comparison to the world: 84

ELECTRICITY - INSTALLED GENERATING CAPACITY:

80,400 kW (2016 est.)

country comparison to the world: 184

ELECTRICITY - FROM FOSSIL FUELS:

0% of total installed capacity (2016 est.)

country comparison to the world: 213

ELECTRICITY - FROM NUCLEAR FUELS:

0% of total installed capacity (2017 est.)

country comparison to the world: 127

ELECTRICITY - FROM HYDROELECTRIC PLANTS:

100% of total installed capacity (2017 est.)

country comparison to the world: 1

ELECTRICITY - FROM OTHER RENEWABLE SOURCES:

1% of total installed capacity (2017 est.)

country comparison to the world: 159

CRUDE OIL - PRODUCTION:

0 bbl/day (2018 est.)

country comparison to the world: 162

CRUDE OIL - EXPORTS:

0 bbl/day (2015 est.)

country comparison to the world: 154

CRUDE OIL - IMPORTS:

0 bbl/day (2015 est.)

country comparison to the world: 152

CRUDE OIL - PROVED RESERVES:

0 bbl (1 January 2018 est.)

country comparison to the world: 157

REFINED PETROLEUM PRODUCTS - PRODUCTION:

0 bbl/day (2015 est.)

country comparison to the world: 165

REFINED PETROLEUM PRODUCTS - CONSUMPTION:

5,000 bbl/day (2016 est.)

country comparison to the world: 179

REFINED PETROLEUM PRODUCTS - EXPORTS:

0 bbl/day (2015 est.)

country comparison to the world: 171

REFINED PETROLEUM PRODUCTS - IMPORTS:

5,118 bbl/day (2015 est.)

country comparison to the world: 170

NATURAL GAS - PRODUCTION:

0 cu m (2017 est.)

country comparison to the world: 157

NATURAL GAS - CONSUMPTION:

0 cu m (2017 est.)

country comparison to the world: 167

NATURAL GAS - EXPORTS:

0 cu m (2017 est.)

country comparison to the world: 138

NATURAL GAS - IMPORTS:

0 cu m (2017 est.)

country comparison to the world: 148

NATURAL GAS - PROVED RESERVES:

0 cu m (1 January 2014 est.)

country comparison to the world: 158

CARBON DIOXIDE EMISSIONS FROM CONSUMPTION OF ENERGY:

711,100 Mt (2017 est.)

country comparison to the world: 177

COMMUNICATIONS :: LESOTHO

TELEPHONES - FIXED LINES:

total subscriptions: 10,637

subscriptions per 100 inhabitants: 1 (2017 est.)

country comparison to the world: 194

TELEPHONES - MOBILE CELLULAR:

total subscriptions: 2,380,804

subscriptions per 100 inhabitants: 122 (2017 est.)

country comparison to the world: 146

TELEPHONE SYSTEM:

general assessment: rudimentary system consisting of a modest number of landlines, a small microwave radio relay system, and a small radiotelephone communication system; fixed-line teledensity is low; mobile-cellular telephone system is expanding; commercial services with LTE technology (2018)

domestic: mobile-cellular service dominates the market with a subscribership now over 122 per 100 persons; fixed-line is 1 per 100 subscriptions (2018)

international: country code - 266; satellite earth station - 1 Intelsat (Atlantic Ocean); Internet accessibility has improved with several submarine fibre optic cables that land on African east and west coasts, but the country's land locked position makes access prices expensive (2019)

BROADCAST MEDIA:

1 state-owned TV station and 2 state-owned radio stations; government controls most private broadcast media; satellite TV subscription service available; transmissions of multiple international broadcasters obtainable (2019)

INTERNET COUNTRY CODE:

.ls

INTERNET USERS:

total: 534,360

percent of population: 27.4% (July 2016 est.)

country comparison to the world: 148

BROADBAND - FIXED SUBSCRIPTIONS:

total: 4,984

subscriptions per 100 inhabitants: less than 1 (2017 est.)

country comparison to the world: 176

MILITARY AND SECURITY :: LESOTHO

MILITARY EXPENDITURES:

1.81% of GDP (2018)

2.01% of GDP (2017)

1.83% of GDP (2016)

1.85% of GDP (2015)

1.84% of GDP (2014)

country comparison to the world: 61

MILITARY AND SECURITY FORCES:

Lesotho Defense Force (LDF): Army (includes Air Wing) (2012)

MILITARY SERVICE AGE AND OBLIGATION:

18-24 years of age for voluntary military service; no conscription; women serve as commissioned officers (2012)

MILITARY - NOTE:

Lesotho's declared policy for its military is the maintenance of the country's sovereignty and the preservation of internal security; in practice, external security is guaranteed by South Africa

TRANSPORTATION :: LESOTHO

CIVIL AIRCRAFT REGISTRATION COUNTRY CODE PREFIX:

7P (2016)

AIRPORTS:

24 (2013)

country comparison to the world: 131

AIRPORTS - WITH PAVED RUNWAYS:

total: 3 (2017)

over 3,047 m: 1 (2017)

914 to 1,523 m: 1 (2017)

under 914 m: 1 (2017)

AIRPORTS - WITH UNPAVED RUNWAYS:

total: 21 (2013)

914 to 1,523 m: 5 (2013)

under 914 m: 16 (2013)

ROADWAYS:

total: 5,940 km (2011)

paved: 1,069 km (2011)

unpaved: 4,871 km (2011)

country comparison to the world: 140

TRANSNATIONAL ISSUES :: LESOTHO

DISPUTES - INTERNATIONAL:

South Africa has placed military units to assist police operations along the border of Lesotho, Zimbabwe, and Mozambique to control smuggling, poaching, and illegal migration

TRAFFICKING IN PERSONS:

current situation: Lesotho is a source, transit, and destination country for women and children subjected to forced labor and sex trafficking and for men subjected to forced labor; in Lesotho and South Africa, Basotho women and children are subjected to domestic servitude, and Basotho children increasingly endure commercial sexual exploitation; some Basotho men who voluntarily migrate to South Africa for work become victims of forced labor in agriculture and mining or are coerced into committing crimes; foreign nationals continue to traffic fellow citizens in Lesotho

tier rating: Tier 2 Watch List – Lesotho does not fully comply with the minimum standards for the elimination of trafficking; however, it is making significant efforts to do so; in 2014, Lesotho was granted a waiver from an otherwise required downgrade to Tier 3 because its government has a written plan that, if implemented would constitute making significant efforts to bring itself into compliance with the minimum standards for the elimination of trafficking; the government failed to initiate any prosecutions against alleged traffickers and has not convicted any offenders under the 2011 anti-trafficking act, which remains unimplemented for a fifth year; authorities did not develop formal victim identification and referral procedures, did not establish victim care centers, as required under the 2011 anti-trafficking act, and did not support NGOs offering victims protective services (2015)

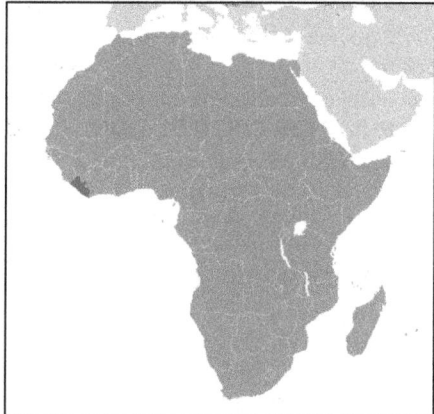

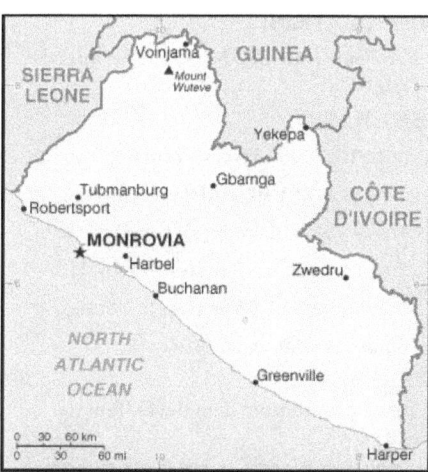

AFRICA :: LIBERIA

INTRODUCTION :: LIBERIA

BACKGROUND:

Settlement of freed slaves from the US in what is today Liberia began in 1822; by 1847, the Americo-Liberians were able to establish a republic. William TUBMAN, president from 1944-71, did much to promote foreign investment and to bridge the economic, social, and political gaps between the descendants of the original settlers and the inhabitants of the interior. In 1980, a military coup led by Samuel DOE ushered in a decade of authoritarian rule. In December 1989, Charles TAYLOR launched a rebellion against DOE's regime that led to a prolonged civil war in which DOE was killed. A period of relative peace in 1997 allowed for an election that brought TAYLOR to power, but major fighting resumed in 2000. An August 2003 peace agreement ended the war and prompted the resignation of former president Charles TAYLOR, who was convicted by the UN-backed Special Court for Sierra Leone in The Hague for his involvement in Sierra Leone's civil war. After two years of rule by a transitional government, democratic elections in late 2005 brought President Ellen JOHNSON SIRLEAF to power. She subsequently won reelection in 2011 but was challenged to rebuild Liberia's economy, particularly following the 2014-15 Ebola epidemic, and to reconcile a nation still recovering from 14 years of fighting. Constitutional term limits barred President JOHNSON SIRLEAF from running for re-election. Legal challenges delayed the 2017 presidential runoff election, which was eventually won by George WEAH. In March 2018, the UN completed its 15-year peacekeeping mission in Liberia.

GEOGRAPHY :: LIBERIA

LOCATION:
Western Africa, bordering the North Atlantic Ocean, between Cote d'Ivoire and Sierra Leone

GEOGRAPHIC COORDINATES:
6 30 N, 9 30 W

MAP REFERENCES:
Africa

AREA:
total: 111,369 sq km

land: 96,320 sq km

water: 15,049 sq km

country comparison to the world: 105

AREA - COMPARATIVE:
slightly larger than Virginia

LAND BOUNDARIES:
total: 1,667 km

border countries (3): Guinea 590 km, Cote d'Ivoire 778 km, Sierra Leone 299 km

COASTLINE:
579 km

MARITIME CLAIMS:
territorial sea: 200 nm

CLIMATE:
tropical; hot, humid; dry winters with hot days and cool to cold nights; wet, cloudy summers with frequent heavy showers

TERRAIN:
mostly flat to rolling coastal plains rising to rolling plateau and low mountains in northeast

ELEVATION:
mean elevation: 243 m

lowest point: Atlantic Ocean 0 m

highest point: Mount Wuteve 1,447 m

NATURAL RESOURCES:
iron ore, timber, diamonds, gold, hydropower

LAND USE:
agricultural land: 28.1% (2011 est.)

arable land: 5.2% (2011 est.) / permanent crops: 2.1% (2011 est.) / permanent pasture: 20.8% (2011 est.)

forest: 44.6% (2011 est.)

other: 27.3% (2011 est.)

IRRIGATED LAND:
30 sq km (2012)

POPULATION DISTRIBUTION:
more than half of the population lives in urban areas, with approximately one-third living within an 80-km radius of Monrovia

NATURAL HAZARDS:
dust-laden harmattan winds blow from the Sahara (December to March)

ENVIRONMENT - CURRENT ISSUES:
tropical rain forest deforestation; soil erosion; loss of biodiversity; hunting of endangered species for bushmeat; pollution of coastal waters from oil residue and raw sewage; pollution of rivers from industrial run-off; burning and dumping of household waste

ENVIRONMENT - INTERNATIONAL AGREEMENTS:
party to: Biodiversity, Climate Change, Climate Change-Kyoto Protocol, Desertification, Endangered Species, Hazardous Wastes, Law of the Sea, Ozone Layer Protection, Ship

Pollution, Tropical Timber 83, Tropical Timber 94, Wetlands

signed, but not ratified: Environmental Modification, Marine Life Conservation

GEOGRAPHY - NOTE:

facing the Atlantic Ocean, the coastline is characterized by lagoons, mangrove swamps, and river-deposited sandbars; the inland grassy plateau supports limited agriculture

PEOPLE AND SOCIETY :: LIBERIA

POPULATION:

4,809,768 (July 2018 est.)

country comparison to the world: 124

NATIONALITY:

noun: Liberian(s)

adjective: Liberian

ETHNIC GROUPS:

Kpelle 20.3%, Bassa 13.4%, Grebo 10%, Gio 8%, Mano 7.9%, Kru 6%, Lorma 5.1%, Kissi 4.8%, Gola 4.4%, Krahn 4%, Vai 4%, Mandingo 3.2%, Gbandi 3%, Mende 1.3%, Sapo 1.3%, other Liberian 1.7%, other African 1.4%, non-African .1% (2008 est.)

LANGUAGES:

English 20% (official), some 20 ethnic group languages few of which can be written or used in correspondence

RELIGIONS:

Christian 85.6%, Muslim 12.2%, Traditional 0.6%, other 0.2%, none 1.5% (2008 est.)

DEMOGRAPHIC PROFILE:

Liberia's high fertility rate of nearly 5 children per woman and large youth cohort – more than 60% of the population is under the age of 25 – will sustain a high dependency ratio for many years to come. Significant progress has been made in preventing child deaths, despite a lack of health care workers and infrastructure. Infant and child mortality have dropped nearly 70% since 1990; the annual reduction rate of about 5.4% is the highest in Africa.

Nevertheless, Liberia's high maternal mortality rate remains among the world's worst; it reflects a high unmet need for family planning services, frequency of early childbearing, lack of quality obstetric care, high adolescent fertility, and a low proportion of births attended by a medical professional. Female mortality is also increased by the prevalence of female genital cutting (FGC), which is practiced by 10 of Liberia's 16 tribes and affects more than two-thirds of women and girls. FGC is an initiation ritual performed in rural bush schools, which teach traditional beliefs on marriage and motherhood and are an obstacle to formal classroom education for Liberian girls.

Liberia has been both a source and a destination for refugees. During Liberia's 14-year civil war (1989-2003), more than 250,000 people became refugees and another half million were internally displaced. Between 2004 and the cessation of refugee status for Liberians in June 2012, the UNHCR helped more than 155,000 Liberians to voluntarily repatriate, while others returned home on their own. Some Liberian refugees spent more than two decades living in other West African countries. Liberia hosted more than 125,000 Ivoirian refugees escaping post-election violence in 2010-11; as of mid-2017, about 12,000 Ivoirian refugees were still living in Liberia as of October 2017 because of instability.

AGE STRUCTURE:

0-14 years: 43.72% (male 1,062,766 /female 1,040,211)

15-24 years: 19.9% (male 478,041 /female 478,999)

25-54 years: 30.1% (male 711,963 /female 735,878)

55-64 years: 3.43% (male 84,474 /female 80,410)

65 years and over: 2.85% (male 67,229 /female 69,797) (2018 est.)

DEPENDENCY RATIOS:

total dependency ratio: 83.2 (2015 est.)

youth dependency ratio: 77.6 (2015 est.)

elderly dependency ratio: 5.5 (2015 est.)

potential support ratio: 18.1 (2015 est.)

MEDIAN AGE:

total: 17.8 years (2018 est.)

male: 17.6 years

female: 18.1 years

country comparison to the world: 217

POPULATION GROWTH RATE:

2.59% (2018 est.)

country comparison to the world: 19

BIRTH RATE:

37.9 births/1,000 population (2018 est.)

country comparison to the world: 10

DEATH RATE:

7.4 deaths/1,000 population (2018 est.)

country comparison to the world: 116

NET MIGRATION RATE:

-4.7 migrant(s)/1,000 population (2018 est.)

country comparison to the world: 192

POPULATION DISTRIBUTION:

more than half of the population lives in urban areas, with approximately one-third living within an 80-km radius of Monrovia

URBANIZATION:

urban population: 51.6% of total population (2019)

rate of urbanization: 3.41% annual rate of change (2015-20 est.)

MAJOR URBAN AREAS - POPULATION:

1.467 million MONROVIA (capital) (2019)

SEX RATIO:

at birth: 1.03 male(s)/female

0-14 years: 1.02 male(s)/female

15-24 years: 1 male(s)/female

25-54 years: 0.97 male(s)/female

55-64 years: 1.05 male(s)/female

65 years and over: 0.96 male(s)/female

total population: 1 male(s)/female (2018 est.)

MOTHER'S MEAN AGE AT FIRST BIRTH:

19.2 years (2013 est.)

note: median age at first birth among women 25-29

MATERNAL MORTALITY RATE:

661 deaths/100,000 live births (2017 est.)

country comparison to the world: 10

INFANT MORTALITY RATE:

total: 50.6 deaths/1,000 live births (2018 est.)

male: 55 deaths/1,000 live births

female: 46 deaths/1,000 live births

country comparison to the world: 25

LIFE EXPECTANCY AT BIRTH:

total population: 63.8 years (2018 est.)

male: 61.6 years

female: 66 years

country comparison to the world: 193

TOTAL FERTILITY RATE:

5 children born/woman (2018 est.)

country comparison to the world: 13

CONTRACEPTIVE PREVALENCE RATE:

31.2% (2016)

DRINKING WATER SOURCE:

improved:

urban: 88.6% of population

rural: 62.6% of population

total: 75.6% of population

unimproved:

urban: 11.4% of population

rural: 37.4% of population

total: 24.4% of population (2015 est.)

CURRENT HEALTH EXPENDITURE:

9.6% (2016)

PHYSICIANS DENSITY:

0.04 physicians/1,000 population (2015)

HOSPITAL BED DENSITY:

0.8 beds/1,000 population (2010)

SANITATION FACILITY ACCESS:

improved:

urban: 28% of population (2015 est.)

rural: 5.9% of population (2015 est.)

total: 16.9% of population (2015 est.)

unimproved:

urban: 72% of population (2015 est.)

rural: 94.1% of population (2015 est.)

total: 83.1% of population (2015 est.)

HIV/AIDS - ADULT PREVALENCE RATE:

1.3% (2018 est.)

country comparison to the world: 39

HIV/AIDS - PEOPLE LIVING WITH HIV/AIDS:

39,000 (2018 est.)

country comparison to the world: 68

HIV/AIDS - DEATHS:

1,800 (2018 est.)

country comparison to the world: 49

MAJOR INFECTIOUS DISEASES:

degree of risk: very high (2016)

food or waterborne diseases: bacterial and protozoal diarrhea, hepatitis A, and typhoid fever (2016)

vectorborne diseases: malaria, dengue fever, and yellow fever (2016)

water contact diseases: schistosomiasis (2016)

animal contact diseases: rabies (2016)

aerosolized dust or soil contact diseases: Lassa fever (2016)

OBESITY - ADULT PREVALENCE RATE:

9.9% (2016)

country comparison to the world: 141

CHILDREN UNDER THE AGE OF 5 YEARS UNDERWEIGHT:

15.3% (2013)

country comparison to the world: 42

EDUCATION EXPENDITURES:

3.8% of GDP (2017)

country comparison to the world: 121

LITERACY:

definition: age 15 and over can read and write

total population: 47.6%

male: 62.4%

female: 32.8% (2015 est.)

UNEMPLOYMENT, YOUTH AGES 15-24:

total: 2.3%

male: 2.4%

female: 2.2% (2016 est.)

country comparison to the world: 174

GOVERNMENT :: LIBERIA

COUNTRY NAME:

conventional long form: Republic of Liberia

conventional short form: Liberia

etymology: name derives from the Latin word "liber" meaning "free"; so named because the nation was created as a homeland for liberated African-American slaves

GOVERNMENT TYPE:

presidential republic

CAPITAL:

name: Monrovia

geographic coordinates: 6 18 N, 10 48 W

time difference: UTC 0 (5 hours ahead of Washington, DC, during Standard Time)

etymology: named after James Monroe (1758-1831), the fifth president of the United States and supporter of the colonization of Liberia by freed slaves; one of two national capitals named for a US president, the other is Washington, D.C.

ADMINISTRATIVE DIVISIONS:

15 counties; Bomi, Bong, Gbarpolu, Grand Bassa, Grand Cape Mount, Grand Gedeh, Grand Kru, Lofa, Margibi, Maryland, Montserrado, Nimba, River Cess, River Gee, Sinoe

INDEPENDENCE:

26 July 1847

NATIONAL HOLIDAY:

Independence Day, 26 July (1847)

CONSTITUTION:

history: previous 1847 (at independence); latest drafted 19 October 1983, revised version adopted by referendum 3 July 1984, effective 6 January 1986

amendments: proposed by agreement of at least two thirds of both National Assembly houses or by petition of at least 10,000 citizens; passage requires at least two-thirds majority approval of both houses and approval in a referendum by at least two-thirds majority of registered voters; amended 2011 (2018)

LEGAL SYSTEM:

mixed legal system of common law, based on Anglo-American law, and customary law

INTERNATIONAL LAW ORGANIZATION PARTICIPATION:

accepts compulsory ICJ jurisdiction with reservations; accepts ICCt jurisdiction

CITIZENSHIP:

citizenship by birth: no

citizenship by descent only: at least one parent must be a citizen of Liberia

dual citizenship recognized: no

residency requirement for naturalization: 2 years

SUFFRAGE:

18 years of age; universal

EXECUTIVE BRANCH:

chief of state: President George WEAH (since 22 January 2018); Vice President Jewel HOWARD-TAYLOR (since 22 January 2018); note - the president is both chief of state and head of government

head of government: President George WEAH (since 22 January 2018); Vice President Jewel HOWARD-TAYLOR (since 22 January 2018)

cabinet: Cabinet appointed by the president, confirmed by the Senate

elections/appointments: president directly elected by absolute majority popular vote in 2 rounds if needed for a 6-year term (eligible for a second term); election last held on 10 October 2017 with a run-off on 26 December 2017); the runoff originally scheduled for 7 November 2017 was delayed due to allegations of fraud in the first round, which the Supreme Court dismissed

election results: George WEAH elected president in second round; percent of vote in first round - George WEAH (Coalition for Democratic Change) 38.4%, Joseph BOAKAI (UP) 28.8%, Charles BRUMSKINE (LP) 9.6%, Prince JOHNSON (MDR) 8.2%, Alexander B. CUMMINGS (ANC) 7.2%, other 7.8%; percentage of vote in second round - George WEAH 61.5%, Joseph BOAKAI 38.5%

LEGISLATIVE BRANCH:

description: bicameral National Assembly consists of:
The Liberian Senate (30 seats; members directly elected in 15 2-seat districts by simple majority vote to serve 9-year staggered terms; each district elects 1 senator and elects the second senator 3 years later, followed by a 6-year hiatus, after which the first Senate seat is up for election)
House of Representatives (73 seats; members directly elected in single-seat districts by simple majority vote to serve 6-year terms; eligible for a second term)

elections: Senate - last held on 20 December 2014 (originally scheduled for 14 October 2014 but postponed due to Ebola-virus epidemic; next to be held in October 2020); by-elections to fill the senate seats vacated by WEAH and HOWARD-TAYLOR was held on 31 July 2018
House of Representatives - last held on 10 October 2017 (next to be held in October 2023)

election results: Senate - percent of vote by party - CDC 29.8%, UP 10.3%, LP 11.5%, NPP 6.1%, PUP 4.9%, ANC 4.2%, NDC 1.3%, other 7.6%, independent 24.3%; seats by party - UP 4, CDC 2, LP 2, ANC 1, NDC 1, NPP 1, PUP 1, independent 3; composition - men 27, women 3, percent of women 10%

House of Representatives - percent of vote by party/coalition - Coalition for Democratic Change 15.6%, UP 14%, LP 8.7%, ANC 6.1%, PUP 5.9%, ALP 5.1%, MDR 3.4%, other 41.2%; seats by coalition/party - Coalition for Democratic Change 21, UP 20, PUP 5, LP 3, ALP 3, MDR 2, independent 13, other 6; composition - men 64, women 9, percent of women 12.3%; total Parliament percent of women 11.7%

JUDICIAL BRANCH:

highest courts: Supreme Court (consists of a chief justice and 4 associate justices); note - the Supreme Court has jurisdiction for all constitutional cases

judge selection and term of office: chief justice and associate justices appointed by the president of Liberia with consent of the Senate; judges can serve until age 70

subordinate courts: judicial circuit courts; special courts, including criminal, civil, labor, traffic; magistrate and traditional or customary courts

POLITICAL PARTIES AND LEADERS:

Alliance for Peace and Democracy or APD [Marcus S. G. DAHN]
All Liberian Party or ALP [Benoi UREY]
Alternative National Congress or ANC [Orishil GOULD]
Coalition for Democratic Change [George WEAH] (includes CDC, NPP, and LPDP)Congress for Democratic Change or CDC [George WEAH]
Liberia Destiny Party or LDP [Nathaniel BARNES]
Liberia National Union or LINU [Nathaniel BLAMA]
Liberia Transformation Party or LTP [Julius SUKU]
Liberian People Democratic Party or LPDP [Alex J. TYLER]
Liberian People's Party or LPP
Liberty Party or LP [J. Fonati KOFFA]
Movement for Democracy and Reconstruction or MDR [Prince Y. JOHNSON]
Movement for Economic Empowerment [J. Mill JONES, Dr.]
Movement for Progressive Change or MPC [Simeon FREEMAN]
National Democratic Coalition or NDC [Dew MAYSON]
National Democratic Party of Liberia or NDPL [D. Nyandeh SIEH]
National Patriotic Party or NPP [Jewel HOWARD TAYLOR]
National Reformist Party or NRP [Maximillian T. W. DIABE]
National Union for Democratic Progress or NUDP [Victor BARNEY]
People's Unification Party or PUP [Isobe GBORKORKOLLIE]
Unity Party or UP [Varney SHERMAN]
United People's Party [MacDonald WENTO]
Victory for Change Party [Marcus R. JONES]

INTERNATIONAL ORGANIZATION PARTICIPATION:

ACP, AfDB, AU, ECOWAS, EITI (compliant country), FAO, G-77, IAEA, IBRD, ICAO, ICC (NGOs), ICCt, ICRM, IDA, IFAD, IFC, IFRCS, ILO, IMF, IMO, IMSO, Interpol, IOC, IOM, ISO (correspondent), ITU, ITUC (NGOs), MIGA, MINUSMA, NAM, OPCW, UN, UNCTAD, UNESCO, UNIDO, UNWTO, UPU, WCO, WFTU (NGOs), WHO, WIPO, WMO, WTO (observer)

DIPLOMATIC REPRESENTATION IN THE US:

Ambassador George PATTEN (since 11 January 2019)

chancery: 5201 16th Street NW, Washington, DC 20011

telephone: [1] (202) 723-0437

FAX: [1] (202) 723-0436

consulate(s) general: New York

DIPLOMATIC REPRESENTATION FROM THE US:

chief of mission: Ambassador Christine A. ELDER (since 23 June 2016)

telephone: [231] 77-677-7000

embassy: U.S. Embassy, 502 Benson Street, Monrovia

mailing address: P.O. Box 98, Monrovia

FAX: [231] 77-677-7370

FLAG DESCRIPTION:

11 equal horizontal stripes of red (top and bottom) alternating with white; a white five-pointed star appears on a blue square in the upper hoist-side corner; the stripes symbolize the signatories of the Liberian Declaration of Independence; the blue square represents the African mainland, and the star represents the freedom granted to the ex-slaves; according to the constitution, the blue color signifies liberty, justice, and fidelity, the white color purity, cleanliness, and guilelessness, and the red color steadfastness, valor, and fervor

note: the design is based on the US flag

NATIONAL SYMBOL(S):

white star; national colors: red, white, blue

NATIONAL ANTHEM:

name: All Hail, Liberia Hail!

lyrics/music: Daniel Bashiel WARNER/Olmstead LUCA

note: lyrics adopted 1847, music adopted 1860; the anthem's author later became the third president of Liberia

ECONOMY :: LIBERIA

ECONOMY - OVERVIEW:

Liberia is a low-income country that relies heavily on foreign assistance and remittances from the diaspora. It is richly endowed with water, mineral resources, forests, and a climate favorable to agriculture. Its principal exports are iron ore, rubber, diamonds, and gold. Palm oil and cocoa are emerging as new export products. The government has attempted to revive raw timber extraction and is encouraging oil exploration.

In the 1990s and early 2000s, civil war and government mismanagement destroyed much of Liberia's economy, especially infrastructure in and around the capital. Much of the conflict was fueled by control over Liberia's natural resources. With the conclusion of fighting and the installation of a democratically elected government in 2006, businesses that had fled the country began to return. The country achieved high growth during the period 2010-13 due to favorable world prices for its commodities. However, during the 2014-2015 Ebola crisis, the economy declined and many foreign-owned businesses departed with their capital and expertise. The epidemic forced the government to divert scarce resources to combat the spread of the virus, reducing funds available for needed public investment. The cost of addressing the Ebola epidemic coincided with decreased economic activity reducing government revenue, although higher donor support significantly offset this loss. During the same period, global commodities prices for key exports fell and have yet to recover to pre-Ebola levels.

In 2017, gold was a key driver of growth, as a new mining project began its first full year of production; iron ore exports are also increased as Arcelor Mittal opened new mines at Mount Gangra. The completion of the rehabilitation of the Mount Coffee Hydroelectric Dam increased electricity production to support ongoing and future economic activity, although electricity tariffs remain high relative to other countries in the region and transmission infrastructure is limited. Presidential and legislative elections in October 2017 generated election-related spending pressures.

Revitalizing the economy in the future will depend on economic diversification, increasing investment and trade, higher global commodity prices, sustained foreign aid and remittances, development of infrastructure and institutions, combating corruption, and maintaining political stability and security.

GDP (PURCHASING POWER PARITY):

$6.112 billion (2017 est.)

$5.965 billion (2016 est.)

$6.064 billion (2015 est.)

note: data are in 2017 dollars

country comparison to the world: 173

GDP (OFFICIAL EXCHANGE RATE):

$3.285 billion (2017 est.)

GDP - REAL GROWTH RATE:

2.5% (2017 est.)

-1.6% (2016 est.)

0% (2015 est.)

country comparison to the world: 129

GDP - PER CAPITA (PPP):

$1,300 (2017 est.)

$1,300 (2016 est.)

$1,300 (2015 est.)

note: data are in 2017 dollars

country comparison to the world: 221

GROSS NATIONAL SAVING:

NA% (2017)

-21.9% of GDP (2016 est.)

1.9% of GDP (2016 est.)

country comparison to the world: 184

GDP - COMPOSITION, BY END USE:

household consumption: 128.8% (2016 est.)

government consumption: 16.7% (2016 est.)

investment in fixed capital: 19.5% (2016 est.)

investment in inventories: 6.7% (2016 est.)

exports of goods and services: 17.5% (2016 est.)

imports of goods and services: -89.2% (2016 est.)

GDP - COMPOSITION, BY SECTOR OF ORIGIN:

agriculture: 34% (2017 est.)

industry: 13.8% (2017 est.)

services: 52.2% (2017 est.)

AGRICULTURE - PRODUCTS:

rubber, coffee, cocoa, rice, cassava (manioc, tapioca), palm oil, sugarcane, bananas; sheep, goats; timber

INDUSTRIES:

mining (iron ore and gold), rubber processing, palm oil processing, diamonds

INDUSTRIAL PRODUCTION GROWTH RATE:

9% (2017 est.)

country comparison to the world: 19

LABOR FORCE:

1.677 million (2017 est.)

country comparison to the world: 128

LABOR FORCE - BY OCCUPATION:

agriculture: 70%

industry: 8%

services: 22% (2000 est.)

UNEMPLOYMENT RATE:

2.8% (2014 est.)

country comparison to the world: 31

POPULATION BELOW POVERTY LINE:

54.1% (2014 est.)

HOUSEHOLD INCOME OR CONSUMPTION BY PERCENTAGE SHARE:

lowest 10%: 2.4%

highest 10%: 30.1% (2007)

DISTRIBUTION OF FAMILY INCOME - GINI INDEX:

32 (2014)

38.2 (2007)

country comparison to the world: 120

BUDGET:

revenues: 553.6 million (2017 est.)

expenditures: 693.8 million (2017 est.)

TAXES AND OTHER REVENUES:

16.9% (of GDP) (2017 est.)

country comparison to the world: 174

BUDGET SURPLUS (+) OR DEFICIT (-):

-4.3% (of GDP) (2017 est.)

country comparison to the world: 161

PUBLIC DEBT:

34.4% of GDP (2017 est.)

28.3% of GDP (2016 est.)

country comparison to the world: 154

FISCAL YEAR:

calendar year

INFLATION RATE (CONSUMER PRICES):

12.4% (2017 est.)

8.8% (2016 est.)

country comparison to the world: 207

CENTRAL BANK DISCOUNT RATE:

3.2% (2016)

country comparison to the world: 107

COMMERCIAL BANK PRIME LENDING RATE:

13.3% (31 December 2017 est.)

13.59% (31 December 2016 est.)

country comparison to the world: 56

STOCK OF NARROW MONEY:

$423 million (31 December 2017 est.)

$438.3 million (31 December 2016 est.)

country comparison to the world: 174

STOCK OF BROAD MONEY:

$423 million (31 December 2017 est.)

$438.3 million (31 December 2016 est.)

country comparison to the world: 178

STOCK OF DOMESTIC CREDIT:

$792.3 million (31 December 2017 est.)

$789.4 million (31 December 2016 est.)

country comparison to the world: 170

MARKET VALUE OF PUBLICLY TRADED SHARES:

NA

CURRENT ACCOUNT BALANCE:

-$627 million (2017 est.)

-$464 million (2016 est.)

country comparison to the world: 125

EXPORTS:

$260.6 million (2017 est.)

$169.8 million (2016 est.)

country comparison to the world: 186

EXPORTS - PARTNERS:

Germany 36.2%, Switzerland 14.2%, UAE 8.8%, US 6.8%, Indonesia 4.7% (2017)

EXPORTS - COMMODITIES:

rubber, timber, iron, diamonds, cocoa, coffee

IMPORTS:

$1.166 billion (2017 est.)

$1.296 billion (2016 est.)

country comparison to the world: 179

IMPORTS - COMMODITIES:

fuels, chemicals, machinery, transportation equipment, manufactured goods; foodstuffs

IMPORTS - PARTNERS:

Singapore 29.8%, China 24.4%, South Korea 17.5%, Japan 9.4% (2017)

RESERVES OF FOREIGN EXCHANGE AND GOLD:

$459.8 million (31 December 2017 est.)

$528.7 million (31 December 2016 est.)

country comparison to the world: 154

DEBT - EXTERNAL:

$1.036 billion (31 December 2017 est.)

$938.9 million (31 December 2016 est.)

country comparison to the world: 165

STOCK OF DIRECT FOREIGN INVESTMENT - AT HOME:

$17.01 billion (31 December 2015 est.)

$16.56 billion (31 December 2014 est.)

country comparison to the world: 86

STOCK OF DIRECT FOREIGN INVESTMENT - ABROAD:

$201 million (31 December 2013 est.)

$201 million (31 December 2012 est.)

country comparison to the world: 108

EXCHANGE RATES:

Liberian dollars (LRD) per US dollar -

109.4 (2017 est.)

93.4 (2016 est.)

93.4 (2015 est.)

85.3 (2014 est.)

83.893 (2013 est.)

ENERGY :: LIBERIA

ELECTRICITY ACCESS:

population without electricity: 4 million (2017)

electrification - total population: 19.8% (2016)

electrification - urban areas: 34% (2016)

electrification - rural areas: 1.3% (2016)

ELECTRICITY - PRODUCTION:

300 million kWh (2016 est.)

note: according to a 2014 household survey, only 4.5% of Liberians use Liberia Electricity Corporation (LEC) power, 4.9% use a community generator, 4.4% have their own generator, 3.9% use vehicle batteries, and 0.8% use other sources of electricity, and 81.3% have no access to electricity; LEC accounts for roughly 70 million kWh of ouput.

country comparison to the world: 184

ELECTRICITY - CONSUMPTION:

279 million kWh (2016 est.)

country comparison to the world: 187

ELECTRICITY - EXPORTS:

0 kWh (2016 est.)

country comparison to the world: 159

ELECTRICITY - IMPORTS:

0 kWh (2016 est.)

country comparison to the world: 168

ELECTRICITY - INSTALLED GENERATING CAPACITY:

151,000 kW (2016 est.)

country comparison to the world: 173

ELECTRICITY - FROM FOSSIL FUELS:

57% of total installed capacity (2016 est.)

country comparison to the world: 138

ELECTRICITY - FROM NUCLEAR FUELS:

0% of total installed capacity (2017 est.)

country comparison to the world: 128

ELECTRICITY - FROM HYDROELECTRIC PLANTS:

43% of total installed capacity (2017 est.)

country comparison to the world: 46

ELECTRICITY - FROM OTHER RENEWABLE SOURCES:

0% of total installed capacity (2017 est.)

country comparison to the world: 198

CRUDE OIL - PRODUCTION:

0 bbl/day (2018 est.)

country comparison to the world: 163

CRUDE OIL - EXPORTS:

0 bbl/day (2015 est.)

country comparison to the world: 155

CRUDE OIL - IMPORTS:

0 bbl/day (2015 est.)

country comparison to the world: 153

CRUDE OIL - PROVED RESERVES:

0 bbl (1 January 2018 est.)

country comparison to the world: 158

REFINED PETROLEUM PRODUCTS - PRODUCTION:

0 bbl/day (2017 est.)

country comparison to the world: 166

REFINED PETROLEUM PRODUCTS - CONSUMPTION:

8,000 bbl/day (2016 est.)

country comparison to the world: 164

REFINED PETROLEUM PRODUCTS - EXPORTS:

0 bbl/day (2015 est.)

country comparison to the world: 172

REFINED PETROLEUM PRODUCTS - IMPORTS:

8,181 bbl/day (2015 est.)

country comparison to the world: 152

NATURAL GAS - PRODUCTION:

0 cu m (2017 est.)

country comparison to the world: 158

NATURAL GAS - CONSUMPTION:

0 cu m (2017 est.)

country comparison to the world: 168

NATURAL GAS - EXPORTS:

0 cu m (2017 est.)

country comparison to the world: 139

NATURAL GAS - IMPORTS:

0 cu m (2017 est.)

country comparison to the world: 149

NATURAL GAS - PROVED RESERVES:

0 cu m (1 January 2014 est.)

country comparison to the world: 159

CARBON DIOXIDE EMISSIONS FROM CONSUMPTION OF ENERGY:

1.163 million Mt (2017 est.)

country comparison to the world: 164

COMMUNICATIONS :: LIBERIA

TELEPHONES - FIXED LINES:

total subscriptions: 8,000

subscriptions per 100 inhabitants: less than 1 (July 2016 est.)

country comparison to the world: 198

TELEPHONES - MOBILE CELLULAR:

total subscriptions: 3,117,002

subscriptions per 100 inhabitants: 66 (July 2016 est.)

country comparison to the world: 139

TELEPHONE SYSTEM:

general assessment: the limited services available are found almost exclusively in the capital, Monrovia; fixed-line service stagnant and extremely limited; telephone coverage extended to a number of other towns and rural areas by four mobile-cellular network operators; almost entirely wireless telecommunications market; mobile market penetration is low compared to others in the region; number of operators avoid paying dues and operate despite regulations (2018)

domestic: fixed-line less than 1 per 100; mobile-cellular subscription base growing and teledensity approached 66 per 100 persons (2018)

international: country code - 231; landing point for the ACE submarine cable linking 20 West African countries and Europe; satellite earth station - 1 Intelsat (Atlantic Ocean) (2019)

BROADCAST MEDIA:

8 private and 1 government-owned TV station; satellite TV service available; 1 state-owned radio station; approximately 20 independent radio stations broadcasting in Monrovia, with approximately 80 more local stations operating in other areas; transmissions of 4 international (including the British Broadcasting Corporation and Radio France Internationale) broadcasters are available (2019)

INTERNET COUNTRY CODE:

.lr

INTERNET USERS:

total: 314,717

percent of population: 7.3% (July 2016 est.)

country comparison to the world: 158

BROADBAND - FIXED SUBSCRIPTIONS:

total: 8,000

subscriptions per 100 inhabitants: less than 1 (2017 est.)

country comparison to the world: 172

MILITARY AND SECURITY :: LIBERIA

MILITARY EXPENDITURES:

0.77% of GDP (2018)

0.73% of GDP (2017)

0.7% of GDP (2016)

0.73% of GDP (2015)

0.72% of GDP (2014)

country comparison to the world: 133

MILITARY AND SECURITY FORCES:

Armed Forces of Liberia (AFL): Army, Liberia Air Wing, Liberian Coast Guard (2019)

MILITARY SERVICE AGE AND OBLIGATION:

18 years of age for voluntary military service; no conscription (2012)

TRANSPORTATION :: LIBERIA

CIVIL AIRCRAFT REGISTRATION COUNTRY CODE PREFIX:

A8 (2016)

AIRPORTS:

29 (2013)

country comparison to the world: 117

AIRPORTS - WITH PAVED RUNWAYS:

total: 2 (2017)

over 3,047 m: 1 (2017)

1,524 to 2,437 m: 1 (2017)

AIRPORTS - WITH UNPAVED RUNWAYS:

total: 27 (2013)

1,524 to 2,437 m: 5 (2013)

914 to 1,523 m: 8 (2013)

under 914 m: 14 (2013)

PIPELINES:

4 km oil (2013)

RAILWAYS:

total: 429 km (2008)

standard gauge: 345 km 1.435-m gauge (2008)

narrow gauge: 84 km 1.067-m gauge (2008)

note: most sections of the railways inoperable due to damage sustained during the civil wars from 1980 to 2003, but many are being rebuilt

country comparison to the world: 117

ROADWAYS:
total: 10,600 km (2018)
paved: 657 km (2018)
unpaved: 9,943 km (2018)
country comparison to the world: 130

MERCHANT MARINE:
total: 3,321
by type: bulk carrier 1086, container ship 834, general cargo 130, oil tanker 723, other 548 (2018)
country comparison to the world: 8

PORTS AND TERMINALS:
major seaport(s): Buchanan, Monrovia

TRANSNATIONAL ISSUES :: LIBERIA

DISPUTES - INTERNATIONAL:
as the UN Mission in Liberia (UNMIL) continues to drawdown prior to the 1 March 2018 closure date, the peacekeeping force is being reduced to 434 soldiers and two police units; some Liberian refugees still remain in Guinea, Cote d'Ivoire, Sierra Leone, and Ghana; Liberia shelters 8,804 Ivoirian refugees, as of 2019

REFUGEES AND INTERNALLY DISPLACED PERSONS:
refugees (country of origin): 8,551 (Cote d'Ivoire) (2019)

ILLICIT DRUGS:
transshipment point for Southeast and Southwest Asian heroin and South American cocaine for the European and US markets; corruption, criminal activity, arms-dealing, and diamond trade provide significant potential for money laundering, but the lack of well-developed financial system limits the country's utility as a major money-laundering center

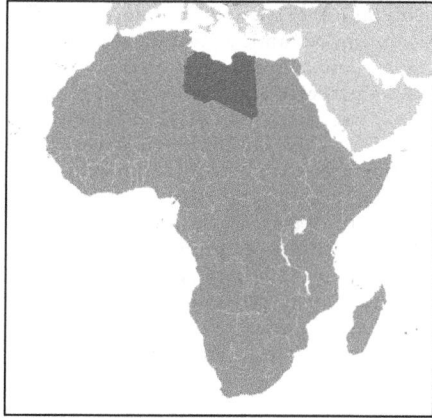

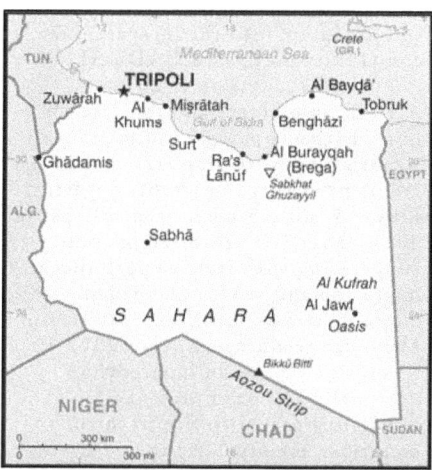

AFRICA :: LIBYA

INTRODUCTION :: LIBYA

BACKGROUND:

The Italians supplanted the Ottoman Turks in the area around Tripoli in 1911 and did not relinquish their hold until 1943 when they were defeated in World War II. Libya then passed to UN administration and achieved independence in 1951. Following a 1969 military coup, Col. Muammar al-QADHAFI assumed leadership and began to espouse his political system at home, which was a combination of socialism and Islam. During the 1970s, QADHAFI used oil revenues to promote his ideology outside Libya, supporting subversive and terrorist activities that included the downing of two airliners - one over Scotland, another in Northern Africa - and a discotheque bombing in Berlin. UN sanctions in 1992 isolated QADHAFI politically and economically following the attacks; sanctions were lifted in 2003 following Libyan acceptance of responsibility for the bombings and agreement to claimant compensation. QADHAFI also agreed to end Libya's program to develop weapons of mass destruction, and he made significant strides in normalizing relations with Western nations.

Unrest that began in several Middle Eastern and North African countries in late 2010 erupted in Libyan cities in early 2011. QADHAFI's brutal crackdown on protesters spawned a civil war that triggered UN authorization of air and naval intervention by the international community. After months of seesaw fighting between government and opposition forces, the QADHAFI regime was toppled in mid-2011 and replaced by a transitional government known as the National Transitional Council (NTC). In 2012, the NTC handed power to an elected parliament, the General National Congress (GNC). Voters chose a new parliament to replace the GNC in June 2014 - the House of Representatives (HoR), which relocated to the eastern city of Tobruk after fighting broke out in Tripoli and Benghazi in July 2014.

In October 2015, the UN brokered an agreement among a broad array of Libyan political parties and social groups - known as the Libyan Political Agreement (LPA). Members of the Libyan Political Dialogue, including representatives of the HoR and defunct-GNC, signed the LPA in December 2015. The LPA called for the formation of an interim Government of National Accord or GNA, with a nine-member Presidency Council, the HoR, and an advisory High Council of State that most ex-GNC members joined. The LPA's roadmap for a transition to a new constitution and elected government was subsequently endorsed by UN Security Council Resolution 2259, which also called upon member states to cease official contact with parallel institutions. In January 2016, the HoR voted to approve the LPA, including the Presidency Council, while voting against a controversial provision on security leadership positions and the Presidency Council's proposed cabinet of ministers. In March 2016, the GNA Presidency Council seated itself in Tripoli. In 2016, the GNA twice announced a slate of ministers who operate in an acting capacity, but the HoR did not endorse the ministerial list. HoR and defunct-GNC-affiliated political hardliners continued to oppose the GNA and hamper the LPA's implementation. In September 2017, UN Special Representative Ghassan SALAME announced a new roadmap for national political reconciliation. SALAME's plan called for amendments to the LPA, a national conference of Libyan leaders, and a constitutional referendum and general elections. In November 2018, the international partners supported SALAME's recalibrated Action Plan for Libya that aimed to break the political deadlock by holding a National Conference in Libya in 2019 on a timeline for political transition. The National Conference was delayed following a failure of the parties to implement an agreement mediated by SALAME in Abu Dhabi on February 27, and the subsequent military action by Khalifa HAFTAR's "Libya National Army" against GNA forces in Tripoli that began April 3.

GEOGRAPHY :: LIBYA

LOCATION:
Northern Africa, bordering the Mediterranean Sea, between Egypt, Tunisia, and Algeria

GEOGRAPHIC COORDINATES:
25 00 N, 17 00 E

MAP REFERENCES:
Africa

AREA:
total: 1,759,540 sq km
land: 1,759,540 sq km
water: 0 sq km
country comparison to the world: 18

AREA - COMPARATIVE:
about 2.5 times the size of Texas; slightly larger than Alaska

LAND BOUNDARIES:

total: 4,339 km

border countries (6): Algeria 989 km, Chad 1050 km, Egypt 1115 km, Niger 342 km, Sudan 382 km, Tunisia 461 km

COASTLINE:
1,770 km

MARITIME CLAIMS:
territorial sea: 12 nm

exclusive fishing zone: 62 nm

note: Gulf of Sidra closing line - 32 degrees, 30 minutes north

CLIMATE:
Mediterranean along coast; dry, extreme desert interior

TERRAIN:
mostly barren, flat to undulating plains, plateaus, depressions

ELEVATION:
mean elevation: 423 m

lowest point: Sabkhat Ghuzayyil -47 m

highest point: Bikku Bitti 2,267 m

NATURAL RESOURCES:
petroleum, natural gas, gypsum

LAND USE:
agricultural land: 8.8% (2011 est.)

arable land: 1% (2011 est.) / permanent crops: 0.2% (2011 est.) / permanent pasture: 7.6% (2011 est.)

forest: 0.1% (2011 est.)

other: 91.1% (2011 est.)

IRRIGATED LAND:
4,700 sq km (2012)

POPULATION DISTRIBUTION:
well over 90% of the population lives along the Mediterranean coast in and between Tripoli to the west and Al Bayda to the east; the interior remains vastly underpopulated due to the Sahara and lack of surface water

NATURAL HAZARDS:
hot, dry, dust-laden ghibli is a southern wind lasting one to four days in spring and fall; dust storms, sandstorms

ENVIRONMENT - CURRENT ISSUES:
desertification; limited natural freshwater resources; the Great Manmade River Project, the largest water development scheme in the world, brings water from large aquifers under the Sahara to coastal cities; water pollution is a significant problem; the combined impact of sewage, oil byproducts, and industrial waste threatens Libya's coast and the Mediterranean Sea

ENVIRONMENT - INTERNATIONAL AGREEMENTS:
party to: Biodiversity, Climate Change, Climate Change-Kyoto Protocol, Desertification, Endangered Species, Hazardous Wastes, Marine Dumping, Ozone Layer Protection, Ship Pollution, Wetlands

signed, but not ratified: Law of the Sea

GEOGRAPHY - NOTE:
note 1: more than 90% of the country is desert or semidesert

note 2: the volcano Waw an Namus lies in south central Libya in the middle of the Sahara; the caldera is an oasis - the name means "oasis of mosquitoes" - containing several small lakes surrounded by vegetation and hosting various insects and a large diversity of birds

PEOPLE AND SOCIETY :: LIBYA

POPULATION:
6,754,507 (July 2018 est.)

note: immigrants make up just over 12% of the total population, according to UN data (2017)

country comparison to the world: 107

NATIONALITY:
noun: Libyan(s)

adjective: Libyan

ETHNIC GROUPS:
Berber and Arab 97%, other 3% (includes Greeks, Maltese, Italians, Egyptians, Pakistanis, Turks, Indians, and Tunisians)

LANGUAGES:
Arabic (official), Italian, English (all widely understood in the major cities); Berber (Nafusi, Ghadamis, Suknah, Awjilah, Tamasheq)

RELIGIONS:
Muslim (official; virtually all Sunni) 96.6%, Christian 2.7%, Buddhist 0.3%, Hindu <0.1, Jewish <0.1, folk religion <0.1, unaffilliated 0.2%, other <0.1 (2010 est.)

note: non-Sunni Muslims include native Ibadhi Muslims (<1% of the population) and foreign Muslims

DEMOGRAPHIC PROFILE:

Despite continuing unrest, Libya remains a destination country for economic migrants. It is also a hub for transit migration to Europe because of its proximity to southern Europe and its lax border controls. Labor migrants have been drawn to Libya since the development of its oil sector in the 1960s. Until the latter part of the 1990s, most migrants to Libya were Arab (primarily Egyptians and Sudanese). However, international isolation stemming from Libya's involvement in international terrorism and a perceived lack of support from Arab countries led QADHAFI in 1998 to adopt a decade-long pan-African policy that enabled large numbers of sub-Saharan migrants to enter Libya without visas to work in the construction and agricultural industries. Although sub-Saharan Africans provided a cheap labor source, they were poorly treated and were subjected to periodic mass expulsions.

By the mid-2000s, domestic animosity toward African migrants and a desire to reintegrate into the international community motivated QADHAFI to impose entry visas on Arab and African immigrants and to agree to joint maritime patrols and migrant repatriations with Italy, the main recipient of illegal migrants departing Libya. As his regime neared collapse in 2011, QADHAFI reversed his policy of cooperating with Italy to curb illegal migration and sent boats loaded with migrants and asylum seekers to strain European resources. Libya's 2011 revolution decreased immigration drastically and prompted nearly 800,000 migrants to flee to third countries, mainly Tunisia and Egypt, or to their countries of origin. The inflow of migrants declined in 2012 but returned to normal levels by 2013, despite continued hostility toward sub-Saharan Africans and a less-inviting job market.

While Libya is not an appealing destination for migrants, since 2014, transiting migrants – primarily from East and West Africa – continue to exploit its political instability and weak border controls and use it as a primary departure area to migrate across the central Mediterranean to Europe in growing numbers. In addition, more than 200,000 people were displaced internally as of August 2017 by fighting between armed groups in eastern and western Libya and, to a lesser extent, by inter-tribal clashes in the country's south.

AGE STRUCTURE:
0-14 years: 25.53% (male 882,099 /female 842,320)

15-24 years: 16.81% (male 582,247 /female 553,004)

25-54 years: 47.47% (male 1,684,019 /female 1,522,027)

55-64 years: 5.77% (male 197,196 /female 192,320)

65 years and over: 4.43% (male 147,168 /female 152,107) (2018 est.)

DEPENDENCY RATIOS:
total dependency ratio: 49.1 (2015 est.)

youth dependency ratio: 42.6 (2015 est.)

elderly dependency ratio: 6.4 (2015 est.)

potential support ratio: 15.5 (2015 est.)

MEDIAN AGE:
total: 29.4 years (2018 est.)

male: 29.5 years

female: 29.2 years

country comparison to the world: 125

POPULATION GROWTH RATE:
1.45% (2018 est.)

country comparison to the world: 77

BIRTH RATE:
17.2 births/1,000 population (2018 est.)

country comparison to the world: 104

DEATH RATE:
3.7 deaths/1,000 population (2018 est.)

country comparison to the world: 215

NET MIGRATION RATE:
0.9 migrant(s)/1,000 population (2018 est.)

country comparison to the world: 63

POPULATION DISTRIBUTION:
well over 90% of the population lives along the Mediterranean coast in and between Tripoli to the west and Al Bayda to the east; the interior remains vastly underpopulated due to the Sahara and lack of surface water

URBANIZATION:
urban population: 80.4% of total population (2019)

rate of urbanization: 1.68% annual rate of change (2015-20 est.)

MAJOR URBAN AREAS - POPULATION:
1.161 million TRIPOLI (capital), 841,000 Misratah, 811,000 Benghazi (2019)

SEX RATIO:
at birth: 1.05 male(s)/female

0-14 years: 1.05 male(s)/female

15-24 years: 1.05 male(s)/female

25-54 years: 1.11 male(s)/female

55-64 years: 1.03 male(s)/female

65 years and over: 0.97 male(s)/female

total population: 1.07 male(s)/female (2018 est.)

MATERNAL MORTALITY RATE:
72 deaths/100,000 live births (2017 est.)

country comparison to the world: 81

INFANT MORTALITY RATE:
total: 10.5 deaths/1,000 live births (2018 est.)

male: 11.3 deaths/1,000 live births

female: 9.6 deaths/1,000 live births

country comparison to the world: 130

LIFE EXPECTANCY AT BIRTH:
total population: 76.9 years (2018 est.)

male: 75.1 years

female: 78.7 years

country comparison to the world: 83

TOTAL FERTILITY RATE:
2.03 children born/woman (2018 est.)

country comparison to the world: 115

CONTRACEPTIVE PREVALENCE RATE:
27.7% (2014)

DRINKING WATER SOURCE:
improved:

urban: 54.2% of population

rural: 54.9% of population

total: 54.4% of population

unimproved:

urban: 45.8% of population

rural: 45.1% of population

total: 45.6% of population (2001 est.)

PHYSICIANS DENSITY:
2.16 physicians/1,000 population (2017)

HOSPITAL BED DENSITY:
3.7 beds/1,000 population (2014)

SANITATION FACILITY ACCESS:
improved:

urban: 96.8% of population (2015 est.)

rural: 95.7% of population (2015 est.)

total: 96.6% of population (2015 est.)

unimproved:

urban: 3.2% of population (2015 est.)

rural: 4.3% of population (2015 est.)

total: 3.4% of population (2015 est.)

HIV/AIDS - ADULT PREVALENCE RATE:
0.2% (2018)

country comparison to the world: 104

HIV/AIDS - PEOPLE LIVING WITH HIV/AIDS:
9,200 (2018)

country comparison to the world: 103

HIV/AIDS - DEATHS:
<200 (2018)

OBESITY - ADULT PREVALENCE RATE:
32.5% (2016)

country comparison to the world: 16

EDUCATION EXPENDITURES:
NA

LITERACY:
definition: age 15 and over can read and write

total population: 91%

male: 96.7%

female: 85.6% (2015 est.)

UNEMPLOYMENT, YOUTH AGES 15-24:
total: 48.7%

male: 40.8%

female: 67.8% (2012 est.)

country comparison to the world: 4

GOVERNMENT :: LIBYA

COUNTRY NAME:
conventional long form: State of Libya

conventional short form: Libya

local long form: Dawiat Libiya

local short form: Libiya

etymology: name derives from the Libu, an ancient Libyan tribe first mentioned in texts from the 13th century B.C.

GOVERNMENT TYPE:
in transition

CAPITAL:

name: Tripoli (Tarabulus)

geographic coordinates: 32 53 N, 13 10 E

time difference: UTC+2 (7 hours ahead of Washington, DC, during Standard Time)

etymology: originally founded by the Phoenicians as Oea in the 7th century B.C., the city changed rulers many times over the successive centuries; by the beginning of the 3rd century A.D. the region around the city was referred to as Regio Tripolitana by the Romans, meaning "region of the three cities" - namely Oea (i.e., modern Tripoli), Sabratha (to the west), and Leptis Magna (to the east); over time, the shortened name of "Tripoli" came to refer to just Oea, which derives from the Greek words "tria" and "polis" meaning "three cities"

ADMINISTRATIVE DIVISIONS:

22 governorates (muhafazah, singular - muhafazat); Al Butnan, Al Jabal al Akhdar, Al Jabal al Gharbi, Al Jafarah, Al Jufrah, Al Kufrah, Al Marj, Al Marqab, Al Wahat, An Nuqat al Khams, Az Zawiyah, Banghazi (Benghazi), Darnah, Ghat, Misratah, Murzuq, Nalut, Sabha, Surt, Tarabulus (Tripoli), Wadi al Hayat, Wadi ash Shati

INDEPENDENCE:

24 December 1951 (from UN trusteeship)

NATIONAL HOLIDAY:

Liberation Day, 23 October (2011)

CONSTITUTION:

history: previous 1951, 1977; in July 2017, the Constitutional Assembly completed and approved a draft of a new permanent constitution; in September 2018, the House of Representatives passed a constitutional referendum law in a session with contested reports of the quorum needed to pass the vote, and submitted it to the High National Elections Commission in December to begin preparations for a constitutional referendum

LEGAL SYSTEM:

Libya's post-revolution legal system is in flux and driven by state and non-state entities

INTERNATIONAL LAW ORGANIZATION PARTICIPATION:

has not submitted an ICJ jurisdiction declaration; non-party state to the ICCt

CITIZENSHIP:

citizenship by birth: no

citizenship by descent only: at least one parent or grandparent must be a citizen of Libya

dual citizenship recognized: no

residency requirement for naturalization: varies from 3 to 5 years

SUFFRAGE:

18 years of age, universal

EXECUTIVE BRANCH:

chief of state: Chairman, Presidential Council, Fayiz al-SARAJ (since December 2015)

head of government: Prime Minister Fayiz al-SARAJ (since December 2015)

cabinet: GNA Presidency Council (pending approval by the House of Representatives - as of December 2018)

elections/appointments:

direct presidential election to be held pending election-related legislation and constitutional referendum law

election results: NA

LEGISLATIVE BRANCH:

description: unicameral House of Representatives (Majlis Al Nuwab) or HoR (200 seats including 32 reserved for women; members directly elected by majority vote; member term NA); note - the High Council of State serves as an advisory group for the HoR

elections: last held on 25 June 2014 (parliamentary election to be held pending election-related legislation); note - the Libyan Supreme Court in November 2014 declared the HoR election unconstitutional, but the HoR and the international community rejected the ruling

election results: percent of vote by party - NA; seats by party - NA; composition - men 158, women 30, percent of women 16%; note - only 188 of the 200 seats were filled in the June 2014 election because of boycotts and lack of security at some polling stations; some elected members of the HoR also boycotted the election

JUDICIAL BRANCH:

NA; note - government is in transition

POLITICAL PARTIES AND LEADERS:

NA

INTERNATIONAL ORGANIZATION PARTICIPATION:

ABEDA, AfDB, AFESD, AMF, AMU, AU, BDEAC, CAEU, COMESA, FAO, G-77, IAEA, IBRD, ICAO, ICC (NGOs), ICRM, IDA, IDB, IFAD, IFC, IFRCS, ILO, IMF, IMO, IMSO, Interpol, IOC, IOM, IPU, ISO, ITSO, ITU, LAS, MIGA, NAM, OAPEC, OIC, OPCW, OPEC, PCA, UN, UNCTAD, UNESCO, UNIDO, UNWTO, UPU, WCO, WFTU (NGOs), WHO, WIPO, WMO, WTO (observer)

DIPLOMATIC REPRESENTATION IN THE US:

Ambassador Wafa M.T. BUGHAIGHIS (since 29 November 2017)

chancery:

1460 Dahlia Street NW, Washington, DC

telephone: [1] (202) 944-9601

FAX: [1] (202) 944-9606

DIPLOMATIC REPRESENTATION FROM THE US:

chief of mission: Ambassador Richard B. NORLAND (since 22 August 2019)

telephone: [218] (0) 91-220-3239

embassy: Sidi Slim Area/Walie Al-Ahed Road, Tripoli (temporarily closed)

mailing address: US Embassy, 8850 Tripoli Place, Washington, DC 20521-8850

note: the US Embassy in Tripoli closed in July 2014 due to fighting near the embassy related to Libyan civil unrest; embassy staff and operations temporarily first relocated to Valetta, Malta and currently are temporarily relocated to Tunis, Tunisia

FLAG DESCRIPTION:

three horizontal bands of red (top), black (double width), and green with a white crescent and star centered on the black stripe; the National Transitional Council reintroduced this flag design of the former Kingdom of Libya (1951-1969) on 27 February 2011; it replaced the former all-green banner promulgated by the QADHAFI regime in 1977; the colors represent the three major regions of the country: red stands for Fezzan, black symbolizes Cyrenaica, and green denotes Tripolitania; the crescent and star represent Islam, the main religion of the country

NATIONAL SYMBOL(S):

star and crescent, hawk; national colors: red, black, green

NATIONAL ANTHEM:

name: Libya, Libya, Libya

lyrics/music: Al Bashir AL AREBI/Mohamad Abdel WAHAB

note: also known as "Ya Beladi" or "Oh, My Country!"; adopted 1951; readopted 2011 with some modification to the lyrics; during the QADHAFI years between 1969 and 2011, the anthem was "Allahu Akbar," (God is Great) a marching song of the Egyptian Army in the 1956 Suez War

ECONOMY :: LIBYA

ECONOMY - OVERVIEW:

Libya's economy, almost entirely dependent on oil and gas exports, has struggled since 2014 given security and political instability, disruptions in oil production, and decline in global oil prices. The Libyan dinar has lost much of its value since 2014 and the resulting gap between official and black market exchange rates has spurred the growth of a shadow economy and contributed to inflation. The country suffers from widespread power outages, caused by shortages of fuel for power generation. Living conditions, including access to clean drinking water, medical services, and safe housing have all declined since 2011. Oil production in 2017 reached a five-year high, driving GDP growth, with daily average production rising to 879,000 barrels per day. However, oil production levels remain below the average pre-Revolution highs of 1.6 million barrels per day.

The Central Bank of Libya continued to pay government salaries to a majority of the Libyan workforce and to fund subsidies for fuel and food, resulting in an estimated budget deficit of about 17% of GDP in 2017. Low consumer confidence in the banking sector and the economy as a whole has driven a severe liquidity shortage.

GDP (PURCHASING POWER PARITY):

$61.97 billion (2017 est.)

$37.78 billion (2016 est.)

$40.8 billion (2015 est.)

note: data are in 2017 dollars

country comparison to the world: 106

GDP (OFFICIAL EXCHANGE RATE):

$30.57 billion (2017 est.)

GDP - REAL GROWTH RATE:

64% (2017 est.)

-7.4% (2016 est.)

-13% (2015 est.)

country comparison to the world: 1

GDP - PER CAPITA (PPP):

$9,600 (2017 est.)

$5,900 (2016 est.)

$6,500 (2015 est.)

note: data are in 2017 dollars

country comparison to the world: 141

GROSS NATIONAL SAVING:

5% of GDP (2017 est.)

-9% of GDP (2016 est.)

-25.1% of GDP (2015 est.)

country comparison to the world: 177

GDP - COMPOSITION, BY END USE:

household consumption: 71.6% (2017 est.)

government consumption: 19.4% (2017 est.)

investment in fixed capital: 2.7% (2017 est.)

investment in inventories: 1.3% (2016 est.)

exports of goods and services: 38.8% (2017 est.)

imports of goods and services: -33.8% (2017 est.)

GDP - COMPOSITION, BY SECTOR OF ORIGIN:

agriculture: 1.3% (2017 est.)

industry: 52.3% (2017 est.)

services: 46.4% (2017 est.)

AGRICULTURE - PRODUCTS:

wheat, barley, olives, dates, citrus, vegetables, peanuts, soybeans; cattle

INDUSTRIES:

petroleum, petrochemicals, aluminum, iron and steel, food processing, textiles, handicrafts, cement

INDUSTRIAL PRODUCTION GROWTH RATE:

60.3% (2017 est.)

country comparison to the world: 1

LABOR FORCE:

1.114 million (2017 est.)

country comparison to the world: 143

LABOR FORCE - BY OCCUPATION:

agriculture: 17%

industry: 23%

services: 59% (2004 est.)

UNEMPLOYMENT RATE:

30% (2004 est.)

country comparison to the world: 207

POPULATION BELOW POVERTY LINE:

note: about one-third of Libyans live at or below the national poverty line

HOUSEHOLD INCOME OR CONSUMPTION BY PERCENTAGE SHARE:

lowest 10%: NA

highest 10%: NA

BUDGET:

revenues: 15.78 billion (2017 est.)

expenditures: 23.46 billion (2017 est.)

TAXES AND OTHER REVENUES:

51.6% (of GDP) (2017 est.)

country comparison to the world: 14

BUDGET SURPLUS (+) OR DEFICIT (-):

-25.1% (of GDP) (2017 est.)

country comparison to the world: 219

PUBLIC DEBT:

4.7% of GDP (2017 est.)

7.5% of GDP (2016 est.)

country comparison to the world: 205

FISCAL YEAR:

calendar year

INFLATION RATE (CONSUMER PRICES):

28.5% (2017 est.)

25.9% (2016 est.)

country comparison to the world: 221

CENTRAL BANK DISCOUNT RATE:

9.52% (31 December 2010)

3% (31 December 2009)

country comparison to the world: 27

COMMERCIAL BANK PRIME LENDING RATE:

7.3% (31 December 2017 est.)

6% (31 December 2016 est.)

country comparison to the world: 115

STOCK OF NARROW MONEY:

$76.21 billion (31 December 2017 est.)

$62.57 billion (31 December 2016 est.)

country comparison to the world: 45

STOCK OF BROAD MONEY:

$76.21 billion (31 December 2017 est.)

$62.57 billion (31 December 2016 est.)

country comparison to the world: 45

STOCK OF DOMESTIC CREDIT:

$21 billion (31 December 2017 est.)

$14.14 billion (31 December 2016 est.)

country comparison to the world: 90

MARKET VALUE OF PUBLICLY TRADED SHARES:

NA

CURRENT ACCOUNT BALANCE:

$2.574 billion (2017 est.)

-$4.575 billion (2016 est.)

country comparison to the world: 35

EXPORTS:

$18.38 billion (2017 est.)

$11.99 billion (2016 est.)

country comparison to the world: 72

EXPORTS - PARTNERS:

Italy 19%, Spain 12.5%, France 11%, Egypt 8.6%, Germany 8.6%, China 8.3%, US 4.9%, UK 4.6%, Netherlands 4.5% (2017)

EXPORTS - COMMODITIES:

crude oil, refined petroleum products, natural gas, chemicals

IMPORTS:

$11.36 billion (2017 est.)

$8.667 billion (2016 est.)

country comparison to the world: 95

IMPORTS - COMMODITIES:

machinery, semi-finished goods, food, transport equipment, consumer products

IMPORTS - PARTNERS:

China 13.5%, Turkey 11.3%, Italy 6.9%, South Korea 5.9%, Spain 4.8% (2017)

RESERVES OF FOREIGN EXCHANGE AND GOLD:

$74.71 billion (31 December 2017 est.)

$66.05 billion (31 December 2016 est.)

country comparison to the world: 31

DEBT - EXTERNAL:

$3.02 billion (31 December 2017 est.)

$3.116 billion (31 December 2016 est.)

country comparison to the world: 143

STOCK OF DIRECT FOREIGN INVESTMENT - AT HOME:

$20.21 billion (31 December 2017 est.)

$18.96 billion (31 December 2016 est.)

country comparison to the world: 78

STOCK OF DIRECT FOREIGN INVESTMENT - ABROAD:

$20.97 billion (31 December 2017 est.)

$22.19 billion (31 December 2016 est.)

country comparison to the world: 52

EXCHANGE RATES:

Libyan dinars (LYD) per US dollar -

1.413 (2017 est.)

1.3904 (2016 est.)

1.3904 (2015 est.)

1.379 (2014 est.)

1.2724 (2013 est.)

ENERGY :: LIBYA

ELECTRICITY ACCESS:

electrification - total population: 98.5% (2016)

electrification - urban areas: 99.1% (2016)

electrification - rural areas: 96.4% (2016)

ELECTRICITY - PRODUCTION:

34.24 billion kWh (2016 est.)

note: persistent electricity shortages have contributed to the ongoing instability throughout the country

country comparison to the world: 61

ELECTRICITY - CONSUMPTION:

27.3 billion kWh (2016 est.)

country comparison to the world: 65

ELECTRICITY - EXPORTS:

0 kWh (2015 est.)

country comparison to the world: 160

ELECTRICITY - IMPORTS:

376 million kWh (2016 est.)

country comparison to the world: 83

ELECTRICITY - INSTALLED GENERATING CAPACITY:

9.46 million kW (2016 est.)

country comparison to the world: 62

ELECTRICITY - FROM FOSSIL FUELS:

100% of total installed capacity (2016 est.)

country comparison to the world: 11

ELECTRICITY - FROM NUCLEAR FUELS:

0% of total installed capacity (2017 est.)

country comparison to the world: 129

ELECTRICITY - FROM HYDROELECTRIC PLANTS:

0% of total installed capacity (2017 est.)

country comparison to the world: 183

ELECTRICITY - FROM OTHER RENEWABLE SOURCES:

0% of total installed capacity (2017 est.)

country comparison to the world: 199

CRUDE OIL - PRODUCTION:

1.039 million bbl/day (2018 est.)

country comparison to the world: 19

CRUDE OIL - EXPORTS:

337,800 bbl/day (2015 est.)

note: Libyan crude oil export values are highly volatile because of continuing protests and other disruptions across the country

country comparison to the world: 23

CRUDE OIL - IMPORTS:

0 bbl/day (2015 est.)

country comparison to the world: 154

CRUDE OIL - PROVED RESERVES:

48.36 billion bbl (1 January 2018 est.)

country comparison to the world: 9

REFINED PETROLEUM PRODUCTS - PRODUCTION:

89,620 bbl/day (2015 est.)

country comparison to the world: 69

REFINED PETROLEUM PRODUCTS - CONSUMPTION:

260,000 bbl/day (2016 est.)

country comparison to the world: 49

REFINED PETROLEUM PRODUCTS - EXPORTS:

16,880 bbl/day (2015 est.)

country comparison to the world: 71

REFINED PETROLEUM PRODUCTS - IMPORTS:

168,200 bbl/day (2015 est.)

country comparison to the world: 36

NATURAL GAS - PRODUCTION:

9.089 billion cu m (2017 est.)

country comparison to the world: 43

NATURAL GAS - CONSUMPTION:

4.446 billion cu m (2017 est.)

country comparison to the world: 64

NATURAL GAS - EXPORTS:

4.644 billion cu m (2017 est.)

country comparison to the world: 31

NATURAL GAS - IMPORTS:

0 cu m (2017 est.)

country comparison to the world: 150

NATURAL GAS - PROVED RESERVES:

1.505 trillion cu m (1 January 2018 est.)

country comparison to the world: 21

CARBON DIOXIDE EMISSIONS FROM CONSUMPTION OF ENERGY:

46.48 million Mt (2017 est.)

country comparison to the world: 62

COMMUNICATIONS :: LIBYA

TELEPHONES - FIXED LINES:
total subscriptions: 1,374,408

subscriptions per 100 inhabitants: 21 (July 2016 est.)

country comparison to the world: 65

TELEPHONES - MOBILE CELLULAR:
total subscriptions: 7,660,068

subscriptions per 100 inhabitants: 115 (July 2016 est.)

country comparison to the world: 101

TELEPHONE SYSTEM:
general assessment: political and security instability in Libya has disrupted its telecommunications sector, but much of its infrastructure remains superior to that in most other African countries; registering a SIM card now requires proof of ID; govt. established new independent regulatory authority; LTE-based fixed broadband network launched (2018)

domestic: 21 per 100 fixed-line and 115 per 100 mobile-cellular subscriptions; service generally adequate, but pressure to rebuild damaged infrastructure growing (2018)

international: country code - 218; landing points for LFON, EIG, Italy-Libya, Silphium and Tobrok-Emasaed submarine cable system connecting Europe, Africa, the Middle East and Asia; satellite earth stations - 4 Intelsat, NA Arabsat, and NA Intersputnik; microwave radio relay to Tunisia and Egypt; tropospheric scatter to Greece; participant in Medarabtel (2019)

BROADCAST MEDIA:
state-funded and private TV stations; some provinces operate local TV stations; pan-Arab satellite TV stations are available; state-funded radio (2019)

INTERNET COUNTRY CODE:
.ly

INTERNET USERS:
total: 1,326,194

percent of population: 20.3% (July 2016 est.)

country comparison to the world: 125

BROADBAND - FIXED SUBSCRIPTIONS:
total: 168,920

subscriptions per 100 inhabitants: 3 (2017 est.)

country comparison to the world: 112

MILITARY AND SECURITY :: LIBYA

MILITARY AND SECURITY FORCES:
note - in transition; Government of National Accord (GNA) has various ground, air, naval, and coast guard forces under its command; the ground forces are comprised of a mix of semi-regular military units, tribal militias, and civilian volunteers (2019)

TRANSPORTATION :: LIBYA

NATIONAL AIR TRANSPORT SYSTEM:
number of registered air carriers: 8 (2015)

inventory of registered aircraft operated by air carriers: 23 (2015)

annual passenger traffic on registered air carriers: 2,566,465 (2015)

annual freight traffic on registered air carriers: 3,833,542 mt-km (2015)

CIVIL AIRCRAFT REGISTRATION COUNTRY CODE PREFIX:
5A (2016)

AIRPORTS:
146 (2013)

country comparison to the world: 41

AIRPORTS - WITH PAVED RUNWAYS:
total: 68 (2017)

over 3,047 m: 23 (2017)

2,438 to 3,047 m: 7 (2017)

1,524 to 2,437 m: 30 (2017)

914 to 1,523 m: 7 (2017)

under 914 m: 1 (2017)

AIRPORTS - WITH UNPAVED RUNWAYS:
total: 78 (2013)

over 3,047 m: 2 (2013)

2,438 to 3,047 m: 5 (2013)

1,524 to 2,437 m: 14 (2013)

914 to 1,523 m: 37 (2013)

under 914 m: 20 (2013)

HELIPORTS:
2 (2013)

PIPELINES:
882 km condensate, 3743 km gas, 7005 km oil (2013)

ROADWAYS:
total: 37,000 km (2010)

paved: 34,000 km (2010)

unpaved: 3,000 km (2010)

country comparison to the world: 91

MERCHANT MARINE:
total: 98

by type: general cargo 2, oil tanker 16, other 80 (2018)

country comparison to the world: 88

PORTS AND TERMINALS:
major seaport(s): Marsa al Burayqah (Marsa el Brega), Tripoli

oil terminal(s): Az Zawiyah, Ra's Lanuf

LNG terminal(s) (export): Marsa el Brega

TERRORISM :: LIBYA

TERRORIST GROUPS - HOME BASED:
al-Qa'ida in the Islamic Maghreb (AQIM): aim(s): overthrow various African regimes and replace them with one ruled by sharia; establish a regional Islamic caliphate across all of North and West Africa
area(s) of operation: leadership headquartered in Algeria; operates in Tunisia and Libya (2018)

Ansar al-Sharia groups: aim(s): implement sharia in Libya
area(s) of operation: in the east, mostly in Benghazi and Darnah
note: officially disbanded in June 2017, but fighters and local elements remain; operated as a member of the Benghazi Revolutionaries Shura Council and Darnah Mujahidin Shura Council, a coalition of jihadist groups combating the Libyan House of Representatives-aligned forces (2018)

Islamic State of Iraq and ash-Sham (ISIS)-Libya: aim(s): prevent the formation of a reunified Libyan state, secure control over the country's critical resources and, ultimately, establish an Islamic caliphate in Libya
area(s) of operation: based in Libya since circa 2015, with its original headquarters in Sirte; no longer controls territory in Libya but does maintain a low-profile presence

throughout much of the country (2018)

TERRORIST GROUPS - FOREIGN BASED:

al-Mulathamun Battalion: aim(s): replace several African governments, including Libya's transitional government, with an Islamic state area(s) of operation: maintains an operational presence; engages in kidnappings for ransom (2018)

TRANSNATIONAL ISSUES :: LIBYA

DISPUTES - INTERNATIONAL:

dormant disputes include Libyan claims of about 32,000 sq km still reflected on its maps of southeastern Algeria and the FLN's assertions of a claim to Chirac Pastures in southeastern Morocco; various Chadian rebels from the Aozou region reside in southern Libya

REFUGEES AND INTERNALLY DISPLACED PERSONS:

refugees (country of origin): 16,820 (Syria) (refugees and asylum seekers), 12,220 (Sudan) (refugees and asylum seekers), 5,899 (Eritrea) (refugees and asylum seekers) (2019)

IDPs: 301,407 (conflict between pro-QADHAFI and anti-QADHAFI forces in 2011; post-QADHAFI tribal clashes 2014) (2019)

TRAFFICKING IN PERSONS:

current situation: Libya is a destination and transit country for men and women from sub-Saharan Africa and Asia subjected to forced labor and forced prostitution; migrants who seek employment in Libya as laborers and domestic workers or who transit Libya en route to Europe are vulnerable to forced labor; private employers also exploit migrants from detention centers as forced laborers on farms and construction sites, returning them to detention when they are no longer needed; some sub-Saharan women are reportedly forced to work in Libyan brothels, particularly in the country's south; since 2013, militia groups and other informal armed groups, including some affiliated with the government, are reported to conscript Libyan children under the age of 18; large-scale violence driven by militias, civil unrest, and increased lawlessness increased in 2014, making it more difficult to obtain information on human trafficking

tier rating: Tier 3 - the Libyan Government does not fully comply with the minimum standards for the elimination of trafficking and is not making significant efforts to do so; in 2014, the government's capacity to address human trafficking was hampered by the ongoing power struggle and violence; the judicial system was not functioning, preventing any efforts to investigate, prosecute, or convict traffickers, complicit detention camp guards or government officials, or militias or armed groups that used child soldiers; the government failed to identify or provide protection to trafficking victims, including child conscripts, and continued to punish victims for unlawful acts committed as a direct result of being trafficked; no public anti-trafficking awareness campaigns were conducted (2015)

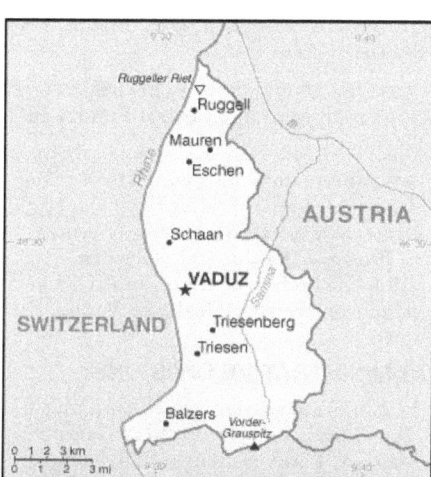

EUROPE :: LIECHTENSTEIN

INTRODUCTION :: LIECHTENSTEIN

BACKGROUND:

The Principality of Liechtenstein was established within the Holy Roman Empire in 1719. Occupied by both French and Russian troops during the Napoleonic Wars, it became a sovereign state in 1806 and joined the German Confederation in 1815. Liechtenstein became fully independent in 1866 when the Confederation dissolved. Until the end of World War I, it was closely tied to Austria, but the economic devastation caused by that conflict forced Liechtenstein to enter into a customs and monetary union with Switzerland. Since World War II (in which Liechtenstein remained neutral), the country's low taxes have spurred outstanding economic growth. In 2000, shortcomings in banking regulatory oversight resulted in concerns about the use of financial institutions for money laundering. However, Liechtenstein implemented anti-money laundering legislation and a Mutual Legal Assistance Treaty with the US that went into effect in 2003.

GEOGRAPHY :: LIECHTENSTEIN

LOCATION:
Central Europe, between Austria and Switzerland

GEOGRAPHIC COORDINATES:
47 16 N, 9 32 E

MAP REFERENCES:
Europe

AREA:
total: 160 sq km

land: 160 sq km

water: 0 sq km

country comparison to the world: 219

AREA - COMPARATIVE:
about 0.9 times the size of Washington, DC

LAND BOUNDARIES:
total: 75 km

border countries (2): Austria 34 km, Switzerland 41 km

COASTLINE:
0 km (doubly landlocked)

MARITIME CLAIMS:
none (landlocked)

CLIMATE:
continental; cold, cloudy winters with frequent snow or rain; cool to moderately warm, cloudy, humid summers

TERRAIN:
mostly mountainous (Alps) with Rhine Valley in western third

ELEVATION:
lowest point: Ruggeller Riet 430 m

highest point: Vorder-Grauspitz 2,599 m

NATURAL RESOURCES:
hydroelectric potential, arable land

LAND USE:
agricultural land: 37.6% (2011 est.)

arable land: 18.8% (2011 est.) / permanent crops: 0% (2011 est.) / permanent pasture: 18.8% (2011 est.)

forest: 43.1% (2011 est.)

other: 19.3% (2011 est.)

IRRIGATED LAND:
0 sq km (2012)

POPULATION DISTRIBUTION:
most of the population is found in the western half of the country along the Rhine River

NATURAL HAZARDS:
avalanches, landslides

ENVIRONMENT - CURRENT ISSUES:
some air pollution generated locally, some transferred from surrounding countries

ENVIRONMENT - INTERNATIONAL AGREEMENTS:
party to: Air Pollution, Air Pollution-Nitrogen Oxides, Air Pollution-Persistent Organic Pollutants, Air Pollution-Sulfur 85, Air Pollution-Sulfur 94, Air Pollution-Volatile Organic Compounds, Biodiversity, Climate Change, Climate Change-Kyoto Protocol, Desertification, Endangered Species, Hazardous Wastes, Ozone Layer Protection, Wetlands

signed, but not ratified: Law of the Sea

GEOGRAPHY - NOTE:
along with Uzbekistan, one of only two doubly landlocked countries in the world; variety of microclimatic variations based on elevation

PEOPLE AND SOCIETY :: LIECHTENSTEIN

POPULATION:
38,547 (July 2018 est.)

note: immigrants make up 65% of the total population, according to UN data (2017)

country comparison to the world: 213

NATIONALITY:

noun: Liechtensteiner(s)

adjective: Liechtenstein

ETHNIC GROUPS:

Liechtensteiner 66%, Swiss 9.6%, Austrian 5.8%, German 4.3%, Italian 3.1%, other 11.2% (2017 est.)

note: data represent population by nationality

LANGUAGES:

German 91.5% (official) (Alemannic is the main dialect), Italian 1.5%, Turkish 1.3%, Portuguese 1.1%, other 4.6% (2015 est.)

RELIGIONS:

Roman Catholic (official) 73.4%, Protestant Reformed 6.3%, Muslim 5.9%, Christian Orthodox 1.3%, Lutheran 1.2%, other Protestant .7%, other Christian .3%, other .8%, none 7%, unspecified 3.3% (2015 est.)

AGE STRUCTURE:

0-14 years: 15.23% (male 3,179 /female 2,692)

15-24 years: 11.53% (male 2,256 /female 2,190)

25-54 years: 41.18% (male 7,923 /female 7,951)

55-64 years: 14.14% (male 2,640 /female 2,811)

65 years and over: 17.91% (male 3,171 /female 3,734) (2018 est.)

MEDIAN AGE:

total: 43.4 years (2018 est.)

male: 41.8 years

female: 44.8 years

country comparison to the world: 19

POPULATION GROWTH RATE:

0.78% (2018 est.)

country comparison to the world: 132

BIRTH RATE:

10.4 births/1,000 population (2018 est.)

country comparison to the world: 188

DEATH RATE:

7.6 deaths/1,000 population (2018 est.)

country comparison to the world: 105

NET MIGRATION RATE:

5 migrant(s)/1,000 population (2018 est.)

country comparison to the world: 27

POPULATION DISTRIBUTION:

most of the population is found in the western half of the country along the Rhine River

URBANIZATION:

urban population: 14.4% of total population (2019)

rate of urbanization: 0.81% annual rate of change (2015-20 est.)

MAJOR URBAN AREAS - POPULATION:

5,000 VADUZ (capital) (2018)

SEX RATIO:

at birth: 1.26 male(s)/female

0-14 years: 1.18 male(s)/female

15-24 years: 1.03 male(s)/female

25-54 years: 1 male(s)/female

55-64 years: 0.94 male(s)/female

65 years and over: 0.85 male(s)/female

total population: 0.99 male(s)/female (2018 est.)

INFANT MORTALITY RATE:

total: 4.2 deaths/1,000 live births (2018 est.)

male: 4.5 deaths/1,000 live births

female: 3.8 deaths/1,000 live births

country comparison to the world: 189

LIFE EXPECTANCY AT BIRTH:

total population: 82 years (2018 est.)

male: 79.8 years

female: 84.8 years

country comparison to the world: 21

TOTAL FERTILITY RATE:

1.69 children born/woman (2018 est.)

country comparison to the world: 174

HIV/AIDS - ADULT PREVALENCE RATE:

NA

HIV/AIDS - PEOPLE LIVING WITH HIV/AIDS:

NA

HIV/AIDS - DEATHS:

NA

EDUCATION EXPENDITURES:

2.6% of GDP (2011)

country comparison to the world: 157

SCHOOL LIFE EXPECTANCY (PRIMARY TO TERTIARY EDUCATION):

total: 15 years

male: 16 years

female: 13 years (2016)

GOVERNMENT :: LIECHTENSTEIN

COUNTRY NAME:

conventional long form: Principality of Liechtenstein

conventional short form: Liechtenstein

local long form: Fuerstentum Liechtenstein

local short form: Liechtenstein

etymology: named after the Liechtenstein dynasty that purchased and united the counties of Schellenburg and Vaduz and that was allowed by the Holy Roman Emperor in 1719 to rename the new property after their family; the name in German means "light (bright) stone"

GOVERNMENT TYPE:

constitutional monarchy

CAPITAL:

name: Vaduz

geographic coordinates: 47 08 N, 9 31 E

time difference: UTC+1 (6 hours ahead of Washington, DC, during Standard Time)

daylight saving time: +1hr, begins last Sunday in March; ends last Sunday in October

etymology: may be a conflation from the Latin "vallis" (valley) and the High German "diutisk" (meaning "German") to produce "Valdutsch" (German valley), which over time simplified and came to refer specifically to Vaduz, the town

ADMINISTRATIVE DIVISIONS:

11 communes (Gemeinden, singular - Gemeinde); Balzers, Eschen, Gamprin, Mauren, Planken, Ruggell, Schaan, Schellenberg, Triesen, Triesenberg, Vaduz

INDEPENDENCE:

23 January 1719 (Principality of Liechtenstein established); 12 July 1806 (independence from the Holy Roman Empire); 24 August 1866 (independence from the German Confederation)

NATIONAL HOLIDAY:

National Day, 15 August (1940); note - a National Day was originally established in 1940 to combine celebrations for the Feast of the Assumption (15 August) with those honoring the birthday of former Prince FRANZ JOSEF II (1906-1989) whose birth fell on 16 August; after the prince's death, National Day became the official national holiday by law in 1990

CONSTITUTION:

history: previous 1862; latest adopted 5 October 1921

amendments: proposed by Parliament, by the reigning prince (in the form of "Government" proposals), by petition of at least 1,500 qualified voters, or by at least four communes; passage requires unanimous approval of Parliament members in one sitting or three-quarters majority vote in two successive sittings; referendum required only if petitioned by at least 1,500 voters or by at least four communes; passage by referendum requires absolute majority of votes cast; amended several times, last in 2011 (2019)

LEGAL SYSTEM:

civil law system influenced by Swiss, Austrian, and German law

INTERNATIONAL LAW ORGANIZATION PARTICIPATION:

accepts compulsory ICJ jurisdiction with reservations; accepts ICCt jurisdiction

CITIZENSHIP:

citizenship by birth: no

citizenship by descent only: the father must be a citizen of Liechtenstein; in the case of a child born out of wedlock, the mother must be a citizen

dual citizenship recognized: no

residency requirement for naturalization: 5 years

SUFFRAGE:

18 years of age; universal

EXECUTIVE BRANCH:

chief of state: Prince HANS-ADAM II (since 13 November 1989, assumed executive powers on 26 August 1984); Heir Apparent and Regent of Liechtenstein Prince ALOIS (son of the monarch, born 11 June 1968); note - 15 August 2004, HANS-ADAM II transferred the official duties of the ruling prince to ALOIS, but HANS-ADAM II retains status of chief of state

head of government: Prime Minister Adrian HASLER (since 27 March 2013)

cabinet: Cabinet elected by the Parliament, confirmed by the monarch

elections/appointments: the monarchy is hereditary; following legislative elections, the leader of the majority party in the Parliament usually appointed the head of government by the monarch, and the leader of the largest minority party in the Landtag usually appointed the deputy head of government by the monarch if there is a coalition government

LEGISLATIVE BRANCH:

description: unicameral Parliament or Landtag (25 seats; members directly elected in 2 multi-seat constituencies by proportional representation vote to serve 4-year terms)

elections: last held on 5 February 2017 (next to be held in February 2021)

election results: percent of vote by party - FBP 35.2%, VU 33.7%, DU 18.4% FL 12.6%; seats by party - FBP 9, VU 8, DU 5, FL 3; composition - men 22, women 3, percent of women 12%

JUDICIAL BRANCH:

highest courts: Supreme Court or Oberster Gerichtshof (consists of 5 judges); Constitutional Court or Verfassungsgericht (consists of 5 judges and 5 alternates)

judge selection and term of office: judges of both courts elected by the Landtag and appointed by the monarch; Supreme Court judges serve 4-year renewable terms; Constitutional Court judges appointed for renewable 5-year terms

subordinate courts: Court of Appeal or Obergericht (second instance), Court of Justice (first instance), Administrative Court, county courts

POLITICAL PARTIES AND LEADERS:

Fatherland Union (Vaterlaendische Union) or VU [Guenther FRITZ]
Progressive Citizens' Party (Fortschrittliche Buergerpartei) or FBP [Thomas BANZER]
The Free List (Die Freie Liste) or FL [Pepo FRICK and Conny BUECHEL BRUEHWILER]
The Independents (Die Unabhaengigen) or DU [Harry QUADERER]

INTERNATIONAL ORGANIZATION PARTICIPATION:

CD, CE, EBRD, EFTA, IAEA, ICCt, ICRM, IFRCS, Interpol, IOC, IPU, ITSO, ITU, ITUC (NGOs), OAS (observer), OPCW, OSCE, PCA, Schengen Convention, UN, UNCTAD, UPU, WIPO, WTO

DIPLOMATIC REPRESENTATION IN THE US:

Ambassador Kurt JAEGER (since 16 September 2016)

chancery: 2900 K Street NW, Suite 602B, Washington, DC 20007

telephone: [1] (202) 331-0590

FAX: [1] (202) 331-3221

DIPLOMATIC REPRESENTATION FROM THE US:

the US does not have an embassy in Liechtenstein; the US Ambassador to Switzerland is accredited to Liechtenstein

FLAG DESCRIPTION:

two equal horizontal bands of blue (top) and red with a gold crown on the hoist side of the blue band; the colors may derive from the blue and red livery design used in the principality's household in the 18th century; the prince's crown was introduced in 1937 to distinguish the flag from that of Haiti

NATIONAL SYMBOL(S):

princely hat (crown); national colors: blue, red

NATIONAL ANTHEM:

name: "Oben am jungen Rhein" (High Above the Young Rhine)

lyrics/music: Jakob Joseph JAUCH/Josef FROMMELT

note: adopted 1850, revised 1963; uses the tune of "God Save the Queen"

ECONOMY :: LIECHTENSTEIN

ECONOMY - OVERVIEW:

Despite its small size and lack of natural resources, Liechtenstein has developed into a prosperous, highly industrialized, free-enterprise economy with a vital financial services sector and one of the highest per capita income levels in the world. The Liechtenstein economy is widely diversified with a large number of small and medium-sized businesses, particularly in the services sector. Low business taxes - a flat tax of 12.5% on income is applied - and easy incorporation rules have induced many holding companies to establish nominal offices in Liechtenstein, providing 30% of state revenues.

The country participates in a customs union with Switzerland and uses the Swiss franc as its national currency. It imports more than 90% of its energy requirements. Liechtenstein has been a member of the European Economic Area (an organization serving as a bridge between the European Free Trade Association and the EU) since May 1995. The government is working to harmonize its economic policies with those of an integrated EU. As of 2015, 54% of Liechtenstein's workforce consisted of cross-border commuters, largely from Austria, Germany, and Switzerland.

Since 2008, Liechtenstein has faced renewed international pressure - particularly from Germany and the US - to improve transparency in its banking and tax systems. In December 2008, Liechtenstein signed a Tax Information Exchange Agreement with the US. Upon Liechtenstein's conclusion of 12 bilateral information-sharing agreements, the OECD in October 2009 removed the principality from its "grey list" of countries that had yet to implement the organization's Model Tax Convention. By the end of 2010, Liechtenstein had signed 25 Tax Information Exchange Agreements or Double Tax Agreements. In 2011, Liechtenstein joined the Schengen area, which allows passport-free travel across 26 European countries. In 2015, Liechtenstein and the EU agreed to clamp down on tax fraud and evasion and in 2018 will start automatically exchanging information on the bank accounts of each other's residents.

GDP (PURCHASING POWER PARITY):

$4.978 billion (2014 est.)

$3.2 billion (2009 est.)

$3.216 billion (2008 est.)

country comparison to the world: 179

GDP (OFFICIAL EXCHANGE RATE):

$6.672 billion (2014 est.) (2014 est.)

GDP - REAL GROWTH RATE:

1.8% (2012 est.)

-0.5% (2011 est.)

3.1% (2007 est.)

country comparison to the world: 161

GDP - PER CAPITA (PPP):

$139,100 (2009 est.)

$90,100 (2008 est.)

$91,300 (2007 est.)

country comparison to the world: 1

GDP - COMPOSITION, BY SECTOR OF ORIGIN:

agriculture: 7% (2014)

industry: 41% (2014)

services: 52% (2014)

AGRICULTURE - PRODUCTS:

wheat, barley, corn, potatoes; livestock, dairy products

INDUSTRIES:

electronics, metal manufacturing, dental products, ceramics, pharmaceuticals, food products, precision instruments, tourism, optical instruments

INDUSTRIAL PRODUCTION GROWTH RATE:

NA

LABOR FORCE:

38,520 (2012) (2015 est.)

note: 51% of the labor force in Liechtenstein commute daily from Austria, Switzerland, and Germany

country comparison to the world: 199

LABOR FORCE - BY OCCUPATION:

agriculture: 0.8%

industry: 36.9%

services: 62.3% (2015)

UNEMPLOYMENT RATE:

2.4% (2015)

2.4% (2014)

country comparison to the world: 24

POPULATION BELOW POVERTY LINE:

NA

HOUSEHOLD INCOME OR CONSUMPTION BY PERCENTAGE SHARE:

lowest 10%: NA

highest 10%: NA

BUDGET:

revenues: 995.3 million (2012 est.)

expenditures: 890.4 million (2011 est.)

TAXES AND OTHER REVENUES:

14.9% (of GDP) (2012 est.)

country comparison to the world: 195

BUDGET SURPLUS (+) OR DEFICIT (-):

1.6% (of GDP) (2012 est.)

country comparison to the world: 20

FISCAL YEAR:

calendar year

INFLATION RATE (CONSUMER PRICES):

-0.4% (2016 est.)

-0.2% (2013)

country comparison to the world: 7

MARKET VALUE OF PUBLICLY TRADED SHARES:

NA

EXPORTS:

$3.217 billion (2015 est.)

$3.774 billion (2014 est.)

note: trade data exclude trade with Switzerland

country comparison to the world: 128

EXPORTS - COMMODITIES:

small specialty machinery, connectors for audio and video, parts for motor vehicles, dental products, hardware, prepared foodstuffs, electronic equipment, optical products

IMPORTS:

NA (2015 est.)

$2.23 billion (2014 est.)

note: trade data exclude trade with Switzerland

country comparison to the world: 163

IMPORTS - COMMODITIES:

agricultural products, raw materials, energy products, machinery, metal goods, textiles, foodstuffs, motor vehicles

DEBT - EXTERNAL:

$0 (2015 est.)

note: public external debt only; private external debt unavailable

country comparison to the world: 206

EXCHANGE RATES:

Swiss francs (CHF) per US dollar -

0.9875 (2017 est.)

0.9852 (2016 est.)

0.9852 (2015 est.)

0.9627 (2014 est.)

0.9152 (2013 est.)

ENERGY :: LIECHTENSTEIN

ELECTRICITY ACCESS:

electrification - total population: 100% (2016)

ELECTRICITY - PRODUCTION:

68.43 million kWh (2015 est.)

country comparison to the world: 202

ELECTRICITY - CONSUMPTION:

393.6 million kWh (2015 est.)

country comparison to the world: 174

ELECTRICITY - EXPORTS:

0 kWh (2015 est.) (2015 est.)

country comparison to the world: 161

ELECTRICITY - IMPORTS:

325.2 million kWh (2015 est.)

country comparison to the world: 88

COMMUNICATIONS :: LIECHTENSTEIN

TELEPHONES - FIXED LINES:

total subscriptions: 15,852

subscriptions per 100 inhabitants: 41 (2017 est.)

country comparison to the world: 187

TELEPHONES - MOBILE CELLULAR:

total subscriptions: 46,625

subscriptions per 100 inhabitants: 122 (2017 est.)

country comparison to the world: 201

TELEPHONE SYSTEM:

general assessment: automatic telephone system; 44 Internet service providers in Liechtenstein and Switzerland combined (2018)

domestic: fixed-line 41 per 100 and mobile-cellular services 122 per 100; widely available (2018)

international: country code - 423; linked to Swiss networks by cable and microwave radio relay

BROADCAST MEDIA:

relies on foreign terrestrial and satellite broadcasters for most broadcast media services; first Liechtenstein-based TV station established August 2008; Radio Liechtenstein operates multiple radio stations; a Swiss-based broadcaster operates one radio station in Liechtenstein

INTERNET COUNTRY CODE:

.li

INTERNET USERS:

total: 37,214

percent of population: 98.1% (July 2016 est.)

country comparison to the world: 200

BROADBAND - FIXED SUBSCRIPTIONS:

total: 15,935

subscriptions per 100 inhabitants: 42 (2017 est.)

country comparison to the world: 159

MILITARY AND SECURITY :: LIECHTENSTEIN

MILITARY AND SECURITY FORCES:

no regular military forces; National Police maintain close relations with neighboring forces (2019)

MILITARY - NOTE:

Liechtenstein has no military forces, but the modern National Police maintain close relations with neighboring forces (2013)

TRANSPORTATION :: LIECHTENSTEIN

CIVIL AIRCRAFT REGISTRATION COUNTRY CODE PREFIX:

HB (2016)

PIPELINES:

434.5 km gas (2018)

RAILWAYS:

total: 9 km (2018)

standard gauge: 9 km 1.435-m gauge (electrified) (2018)

note: belongs to the Austrian Railway System connecting Austria and Switzerland

country comparison to the world: 136

ROADWAYS:

total: 630 km (2019)

country comparison to the world: 185

WATERWAYS:

28 km (2010)

country comparison to the world: 105

TRANSNATIONAL ISSUES :: LIECHTENSTEIN

DISPUTES - INTERNATIONAL:

none

ILLICIT DRUGS:

has strengthened money laundering controls, but money laundering remains a concern due to Liechtenstein's sophisticated offshore financial services sector

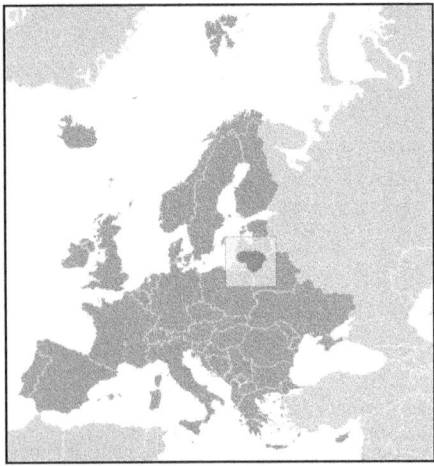

EUROPE :: LITHUANIA

INTRODUCTION :: LITHUANIA

BACKGROUND:

Lithuanian lands were united under MINDAUGAS in 1236; over the next century, through alliances and conquest, Lithuania extended its territory to include most of present-day Belarus and Ukraine. By the end of the 14th century Lithuania was the largest state in Europe. An alliance with Poland in 1386 led the two countries into a union through the person of a common ruler. In 1569, Lithuania and Poland formally united into a single dual state, the Polish-Lithuanian Commonwealth. This entity survived until 1795 when its remnants were partitioned by surrounding countries. Lithuania regained its independence following World War I but was annexed by the USSR in 1940 - an action never recognized by the US and many other countries. On 11 March 1990, Lithuania became the first of the Soviet republics to declare its independence, but Moscow did not recognize this proclamation until September of 1991 (following the abortive coup in Moscow). The last Russian troops withdrew in 1993. Lithuania subsequently restructured its economy for integration into Western European institutions; it joined both NATO and the EU in the spring of 2004. In 2015, Lithuania joined the euro zone, and it joined the Organization for Economic Cooperation and Development in 2018.

GEOGRAPHY :: LITHUANIA

LOCATION:
Eastern Europe, bordering the Baltic Sea, between Latvia and Russia, west of Belarus

GEOGRAPHIC COORDINATES:
56 00 N, 24 00 E

MAP REFERENCES:
Europe

AREA:
total: 65,300 sq km
land: 62,680 sq km
water: 2,620 sq km
country comparison to the world: 124

AREA - COMPARATIVE:
slightly larger than West Virginia

LAND BOUNDARIES:
total: 1,549 km
border countries (4): Belarus 640 km, Latvia 544 km, Poland 104 km, Russia (Kaliningrad) 261 km

COASTLINE:
90 km

MARITIME CLAIMS:
territorial sea: 12 nm

CLIMATE:
transitional, between maritime and continental; wet, moderate winters and summers

TERRAIN:
lowland, many scattered small lakes, fertile soil

ELEVATION:
mean elevation: 110 m
lowest point: Baltic Sea 0 m
highest point: Aukstojas 294 m

NATURAL RESOURCES:
peat, arable land, amber

LAND USE:
agricultural land: 44.8% (2011 est.)
arable land: 34.9% (2011 est.) / permanent crops: 0.5% (2011 est.) / permanent pasture: 9.4% (2011 est.)
forest: 34.6% (2011 est.)
other: 20.6% (2011 est.)

IRRIGATED LAND:
44 sq km (2012)

POPULATION DISTRIBUTION:
fairly even population distribution throughout the country, but somewhat greater concentrations in the southern cities of Vilnius and Kaunas, and the western port of Klaipeda

NATURAL HAZARDS:
occasional floods, droughts

ENVIRONMENT - CURRENT ISSUES:
water pollution; air pollution; deforestation; threatened animal and plant species; chemicals and waste materials released into the environment contaminate soil and groundwater; soil degradation and erosion

ENVIRONMENT - INTERNATIONAL AGREEMENTS:
party to: Air Pollution, Air Pollution-Nitrogen Oxides, Air Pollution-Persistent Organic Pollutants, Air Pollution-Sulphur 85, Air Pollution-Sulphur 94, Air Pollution-Volatile Organic Compounds, Biodiversity, Climate Change, Climate Change-Kyoto Protocol, Desertification, Endangered Species, Environmental Modification, Hazardous Wastes, Law

of the Sea, Ozone Layer Protection, Ship Pollution, Wetlands

signed, but not ratified: none of the selected agreements

GEOGRAPHY - NOTE:
fertile central plains are separated by hilly uplands that are ancient glacial deposits

PEOPLE AND SOCIETY :: LITHUANIA

POPULATION:
2,793,284 (July 2018 est.)

country comparison to the world: 141

NATIONALITY:
noun: Lithuanian(s)

adjective: Lithuanian

ETHNIC GROUPS:
Lithuanian 84.1%, Polish 6.6%, Russian 5.8%, Belarusian 1.2%, other 1.1%, unspecified 1.2% (2011 est.)

LANGUAGES:
Lithuanian (official) 82%, Russian 8%, Polish 5.6%, other 0.9%, unspecified 3.5% (2011 est.)

RELIGIONS:
Roman Catholic 77.2%, Russian Orthodox 4.1%, Old Believer 0.8%, Evangelical Lutheran 0.6%, Evangelical Reformist 0.2%, other (including Sunni Muslim, Jewish, Greek Catholic, and Karaite) 0.8%, none 6.1%, unspecified 10.1% (2011 est.)

AGE STRUCTURE:
0-14 years: 15.11% (male 216,519 /female 205,624)

15-24 years: 10.7% (male 154,708 /female 144,244)

25-54 years: 39.72% (male 548,586 /female 561,007)

55-64 years: 14.55% (male 180,294 /female 226,250)

65 years and over: 19.91% (male 188,269 /female 367,783) (2018 est.)

DEPENDENCY RATIOS:
total dependency ratio: 49.9 (2015 est.)

youth dependency ratio: 21.9 (2015 est.)

elderly dependency ratio: 28 (2015 est.)

potential support ratio: 3.6 (2015 est.)

MEDIAN AGE:
total: 44 years (2018 est.)

male: 39.8 years

female: 47.4 years

country comparison to the world: 15

POPULATION GROWTH RATE:
-1.1% (2018 est.)

country comparison to the world: 228

BIRTH RATE:
9.8 births/1,000 population (2018 est.)

country comparison to the world: 195

DEATH RATE:
14.8 deaths/1,000 population (2018 est.)

country comparison to the world: 3

NET MIGRATION RATE:
-6.1 migrant(s)/1,000 population (2018 est.)

country comparison to the world: 203

POPULATION DISTRIBUTION:
fairly even population distribution throughout the country, but somewhat greater concentrations in the southern cities of Vilnius and Kaunas, and the western port of Klaipeda

URBANIZATION:
urban population: 67.9% of total population (2019)

rate of urbanization: -0.31% annual rate of change (2015-20 est.)

MAJOR URBAN AREAS - POPULATION:
538,000 VILNIUS (capital) (2019)

SEX RATIO:
at birth: 1.06 male(s)/female

0-14 years: 1.05 male(s)/female

15-24 years: 1.07 male(s)/female

25-54 years: 0.98 male(s)/female

55-64 years: 0.8 male(s)/female

65 years and over: 0.51 male(s)/female

total population: 0.86 male(s)/female (2018 est.)

MOTHER'S MEAN AGE AT FIRST BIRTH:
27 years (2014 est.)

MATERNAL MORTALITY RATE:
5 deaths/100,000 live births (2017 est.)

country comparison to the world: 167

INFANT MORTALITY RATE:
total: 3.8 deaths/1,000 live births (2018 est.)

male: 4.2 deaths/1,000 live births

female: 3.3 deaths/1,000 live births

country comparison to the world: 193

LIFE EXPECTANCY AT BIRTH:
total population: 75.2 years (2018 est.)

male: 69.9 years

female: 80.8 years

country comparison to the world: 110

TOTAL FERTILITY RATE:
1.6 children born/woman (2018 est.)

country comparison to the world: 183

DRINKING WATER SOURCE:
improved:

urban: 99.7% of population

rural: 90.4% of population

total: 96.6% of population

unimproved:

urban: 0.3% of population

rural: 9.6% of population

total: 3.4% of population (2015 est.)

CURRENT HEALTH EXPENDITURE:
6.7% (2016)

PHYSICIANS DENSITY:
4.34 physicians/1,000 population (2016)

HOSPITAL BED DENSITY:
7.3 beds/1,000 population (2013)

SANITATION FACILITY ACCESS:
improved:

urban: 97.2% of population (2015 est.)

rural: 82.8% of population (2015 est.)

total: 92.4% of population (2015 est.)

unimproved:

urban: 2.8% of population (2015 est.)

rural: 17.2% of population (2015 est.)

total: 7.6% of population (2015 est.)

HIV/AIDS - ADULT PREVALENCE RATE:
0.2% (2017 est.)

country comparison to the world: 105

HIV/AIDS - PEOPLE LIVING WITH HIV/AIDS:
2,800 (2017 est.)

country comparison to the world: 132

HIV/AIDS - DEATHS:
<100 (2017 est.)

MAJOR INFECTIOUS DISEASES:
degree of risk: intermediate (2016)

vectorborne diseases: tickborne encephalitis (2016)

OBESITY - ADULT PREVALENCE RATE:
26.3% (2016)

country comparison to the world: 43

EDUCATION EXPENDITURES:
4.2% of GDP (2015)

country comparison to the world: 102

LITERACY:
definition: age 15 and over can read and write

total population: 99.8%

male: 99.8%

female: 99.8% (2015 est.)

SCHOOL LIFE EXPECTANCY (PRIMARY TO TERTIARY EDUCATION):
total: 16 years

male: 16 years

female: 17 years (2016)

UNEMPLOYMENT, YOUTH AGES 15-24:
total: 13.3%

male: 14.6%

female: 11.7% (2017 est.)

country comparison to the world: 105

GOVERNMENT :: LITHUANIA

COUNTRY NAME:
conventional long form: Republic of Lithuania

conventional short form: Lithuania

local long form: Lietuvos Respublika

local short form: Lietuva

former: Lithuanian Soviet Socialist Republic

etymology: meaning of the name "Lietuva" remains unclear; it may derive from the Lietava, a stream in east central Lithuania

GOVERNMENT TYPE:
semi-presidential republic

CAPITAL:
name: Vilnius

geographic coordinates: 54 41 N, 25 19 E

time difference: UTC+2 (7 hours ahead of Washington, DC, during Standard Time)

daylight saving time: +1hr, begins last Sunday in March; ends last Sunday in October

etymology: named after the Vilnia River, which flows into the Neris River at Vilnius; the river name derives from the Lithuanian word "vilnis" meaning "a surge"

ADMINISTRATIVE DIVISIONS:
60 municipalities (savivaldybe, singular - savivaldybe); Akmene, Alytaus Miestas, Alytus, Anksciai, Birstono, Birzai, Druskininkai, Elektrenai, Ignalina, Jonava, Joniskis, Jurbarkas, Kaisiadorys, Kalvarijos, Kauno Miestas, Kaunas, Kazlu Rudos, Kedainiai, Kelme, Klaipedos Miestas, Klaipeda, Kretinga, Kupiskis, Lazdijai, Marijampole, Mazeikiai, Moletai, Neringa, Pagegiai, Pakruojis, Palangos Miestas, Panevezio Miestas, Panevezys, Pasvalys, Plunge, Prienai, Radviliskis, Raseiniai, Rietavo, Rokiskis, Sakiai, Salcininkai, Siauliu Miestas, Siauliai, Silale, Silute, Sirvintos, Skuodas, Svencionys, Taurage, Telsiai, Trakai, Ukmerge, Utena, Varena, Vilkaviskis, Vilniaus Miestas, Vilnius, Visaginas, Zarasai

INDEPENDENCE:
11 March 1990 (declared independence from the Soviet Union); 6 September 1991 (recognized by the Soviet Union); notable earlier dates: 6 July 1253 (coronation of MINDAUGAS, traditional founding date); 1 July 1569 (Polish-Lithuanian Commonwealth created); 16 February 1918 (independence from Soviet Russia and Germany)

NATIONAL HOLIDAY:
Independence Day (or National Day), 16 February (1918); note - 16 February 1918 was the date Lithuania established its statehood and its concomitant independence from Soviet Russia and Germany; 11 March 1990 was the date it declared the restoration of Lithuanian statehood and its concomitant independence from the Soviet Union

CONSTITUTION:
history: several previous; latest adopted by referendum 25 October 1992, entered into force 2 November 1992

amendments: proposed by at least one fourth of all Parliament members or by petition of at least 300,000 voters; passage requires two-thirds majority vote of Parliament in each of two readings three months apart and a presidential signature; amendments to constitutional articles on national sovereignty and constitutional amendment procedure also require three-fourths voter approval in a referendum; amended 1996, 2003, 2006 (2016)

LEGAL SYSTEM:
civil law system; legislative acts can be appealed to the Constitutional Court

INTERNATIONAL LAW ORGANIZATION PARTICIPATION:
accepts compulsory ICJ jurisdiction with reservations; accepts ICCt jurisdiction

CITIZENSHIP:
citizenship by birth: no

citizenship by descent only: at least one parent must be a citizen of Lithuania

dual citizenship recognized: no

residency requirement for naturalization: 10 years

SUFFRAGE:
18 years of age; universal

EXECUTIVE BRANCH:
chief of state: President Gitanas NAUSEDA (since 12 July 2019)

head of government: Prime Minister Saulius SKVERNELIS (since 13 December 2016)

cabinet: Council of Ministers nominated by the prime minister, appointed by the president, and approved by Parliament

elections/appointments: president directly elected by absolute majority popular vote in 2 rounds if needed for a 5-year term (eligible for a second term); election last held on 12 and 26 May 2019 (next to be held in May 2024); prime minister appointed by the president, approved by Parliament

election results: Gitanas NAUSEDA elected president in second round; percent of vote - Gitanas NAUSEDA (independent) 66.7%, Ingrida SIMONYTE (independent) 33.3%; Saulius SKVERNELIS (LVZS) approved as prime minister by Parliament vote - 90 to 4

LEGISLATIVE BRANCH:
description: unicameral Parliament or Seimas (141 seats; 71 members directly elected in single-seat constituencies by absolute majority vote and 70 directly elected in a single nationwide constituency by proportional representation vote; members serve 4-year terms)

elections: last held on 9 and 23 October 2016 (next to be held in October 2020)

election results: percent of vote by party - TS-LKD 22.6%, LVLS 22.5%, LSDP 15%, LS 9.5%, LCP-LPP 6.3%, LLRA 5.7%, TT 5.6%, DP 4.9%, LZP 2%, Lithuanian List 1.8%, other 4.1%; seats by party - LVLS 54, TS-LKD 31, LSDP 17, LS 14, LLRA 8, TT 8, DP 2, LCP-LPP 1, LZP 1, Lithuanian List 1, independent 4; composition - men 111, women 30, percent of women 21.3%

JUDICIAL BRANCH:

highest courts: Supreme Court (consists of 37 judges); Constitutional Court (consists of 9 judges)

judge selection and term of office: Supreme Court judges nominated by the president and appointed by the Seimas; judges serve 5-year renewable terms; Constitutional Court judges appointed by the Seimas from nominations - 3 each by the president of the republic, the Seimas chairperson, and the Supreme Court president; judges serve 9-year, nonrenewable terms; one-third of membership reconstituted every 3 years

subordinate courts: Court of Appeals; district and local courts

POLITICAL PARTIES AND LEADERS:

Electoral Action of Lithuanian Poles or LLRA [Valdemar TOMASEVSKI]
Farmers and Greens Union or LVZS [Ramunas KARBAUSKIS]
Homeland Union-Lithuanian Christian Democrats or TS-LKD [Gabrielius LANDSBERGIS]
Labor Party or LP [Viktor USPASKICH]
Lithuanian Center Party or LCP [Naglis PUTEIKIS]
Lithuanian Green Party or LZP [Linas BALSYS]
Lithuanian Liberal Movement or LS or LRLS (Eugenijus GENTVILAS)
Lithuanian List or LL [Darius KUOLYS]
Lithuanian Social Democratic Party or LSDP [Gintautas PALUCKAS]
Lithuanian Social Democratic Labor Party [Gediminas KIRKILAS]
Order and Justice Party or TT [Remigijus ZEMAITAITIS]

INTERNATIONAL ORGANIZATION PARTICIPATION:

Australia Group, BA, BIS, CBSS, CD, CE, EAPC, EBRD, ECB, EIB, EU, FAO, IAEA, IBRD, ICAO, ICC (national committees), ICCt, ICRM, IDA, IFC, IFRCS, ILO, IMF, IMO, Interpol, IOC, IOM, IPU, ISO, ITU, ITUC (NGOs), MIGA, NATO, NIB, NSG, OAS (observer), OECD, OIF (observer), OPCW, OSCE, PCA, Schengen Convention, UN, UNCTAD, UNESCO, UNIDO, UNWTO, UPU, WCO, WHO, WIPO, WMO, WTO

DIPLOMATIC REPRESENTATION IN THE US:

Ambassador Rolandas KRISCIUNAS (since 17 September 2015)

chancery: 2622 16th Street NW, Washington, DC 20009

telephone: [1] (202) 234-5860

FAX: [1] (202) 328-0466

consulate(s) general: Chicago, Los Angeles, New York

DIPLOMATIC REPRESENTATION FROM THE US:

chief of mission: Ambassador (vacant); Charge d'Affaires Marcus MICHELI (since July 2019)

telephone: [370] (5) 266-5500

embassy: Akmenu gatve 6, Vilnius, LT-03106

mailing address: American Embassy, Akmenu Gatve 6, Vilnius LT-03106

FAX: [370] (5) 266-5510

FLAG DESCRIPTION:

three equal horizontal bands of yellow (top), green, and red; yellow symbolizes golden fields, as well as the sun, light, and goodness; green represents the forests of the countryside, in addition to nature, freedom, and hope; red stands for courage and the blood spilled in defense of the homeland

NATIONAL SYMBOL(S):

mounted knight known as Vytis (the Chaser), white stork; national colors: yellow, green, red

NATIONAL ANTHEM:

name: "Tautiska giesme" (The National Song)

lyrics/music: Vincas KUDIRKA

note: adopted 1918, restored 1990; written in 1898 while Lithuania was a part of Russia; banned during the Soviet occupation from 1940 to 1990

ECONOMY :: LITHUANIA

ECONOMY - OVERVIEW:

After the country declared independence from the Soviet Union in 1990, Lithuania faced an initial dislocation that is typical during transitions from a planned economy to a free-market economy. Macroeconomic stabilization policies, including privatization of most state-owned enterprises, and a strong commitment to a currency board arrangement led to an open and rapidly growing economy and rising consumer demand. Foreign investment and EU funding aided in the transition. Lithuania joined the WTO in May 2001, the EU in May 2004, and the euro zone in January 2015, and is now working to complete the OECD accession roadmap it received in July 2015. In 2017, joined the OECD Working Group on Bribery, an important step in the OECD accession process.

The Lithuanian economy was severely hit by the 2008-09 global financial crisis, but it has rebounded and become one of the fastest growing in the EU. Increases in exports, investment, and wage growth that supported consumption helped the economy grow by 3.6% in 2017. In 2015, Russia was Lithuania's largest trading partner, followed by Poland, Germany, and Latvia; goods and services trade between the US and Lithuania totaled $2.2 billion. Lithuania opened a self-financed liquefied natural gas terminal in January 2015, providing the first non-Russian supply of natural gas to the Baltic States and reducing Lithuania's dependence on Russian gas from 100% to approximately 30% in 2016.

Lithuania's ongoing recovery hinges on improving the business environment, especially by liberalizing labor laws, and improving competitiveness and export growth, the latter hampered by economic slowdowns in the EU and Russia. In addition, a steady outflow of young and highly educated people is causing a shortage of skilled labor, which, combined with a rapidly aging population, could stress public finances and constrain long-term growth.

GDP (PURCHASING POWER PARITY):

$91.47 billion (2017 est.)

$88.07 billion (2016 est.)

$86.05 billion (2015 est.)

note: data are in 2017 dollars

country comparison to the world: 87

GDP (OFFICIAL EXCHANGE RATE):

$47.26 billion (2017 est.)

GDP - REAL GROWTH RATE:

3.9% (2017 est.)

2.3% (2016 est.)

2% (2015 est.)

country comparison to the world: 82

GDP - PER CAPITA (PPP):

$32,400 (2017 est.)

$30,700 (2016 est.)

$29,600 (2015 est.)

note: data are in 2017 dollars

country comparison to the world: 63

GROSS NATIONAL SAVING:

18% of GDP (2017 est.)

16.2% of GDP (2016 est.)

17.8% of GDP (2015 est.)

country comparison to the world: 111

GDP - COMPOSITION, BY END USE:

household consumption: 63.9% (2017 est.)

government consumption: 16.6% (2017 est.)

investment in fixed capital: 18.8% (2017 est.)

investment in inventories: -1.3% (2017 est.)

exports of goods and services: 81.6% (2017 est.)

imports of goods and services: -79.3% (2017 est.)

GDP - COMPOSITION, BY SECTOR OF ORIGIN:

agriculture: 3.5% (2017 est.)

industry: 29.4% (2017 est.)

services: 67.2% (2017 est.)

AGRICULTURE - PRODUCTS:

grain, potatoes, sugar beets, flax, vegetables; beef, milk, eggs, pork, cheese; fish

INDUSTRIES:

metal-cutting machine tools, electric motors, televisions, refrigerators and freezers, petroleum refining, shipbuilding (small ships), furniture, textiles, food processing, fertilizer, agricultural machinery, optical equipment, lasers, electronic components, computers, amber jewelry, information technology, video game development, app/software development, biotechnology

INDUSTRIAL PRODUCTION GROWTH RATE:

5.9% (2017 est.)

country comparison to the world: 43

LABOR FORCE:

1.467 million (2017 est.)

country comparison to the world: 132

LABOR FORCE - BY OCCUPATION:

agriculture: 9.1%

industry: 25.2%

services: 65.8% (2015 est.)

UNEMPLOYMENT RATE:

7.1% (2017 est.)

7.9% (2016 est.)

country comparison to the world: 110

POPULATION BELOW POVERTY LINE:

22.2% (2015 est.)

HOUSEHOLD INCOME OR CONSUMPTION BY PERCENTAGE SHARE:

lowest 10%: 2.2%

highest 10%: 28.8% (2015)

DISTRIBUTION OF FAMILY INCOME - GINI INDEX:

37.9 (2015)

35 (2014)

country comparison to the world: 80

BUDGET:

revenues: 15.92 billion (2017 est.)

expenditures: 15.7 billion (2017 est.)

TAXES AND OTHER REVENUES:

33.7% (of GDP) (2017 est.)

country comparison to the world: 65

BUDGET SURPLUS (+) OR DEFICIT (-):

0.5% (of GDP) (2017 est.)

country comparison to the world: 38

PUBLIC DEBT:

39.7% of GDP (2017 est.)

40.1% of GDP (2016 est.)

note: official data; data cover general government debt and include debt instruments issued (or owned) by government entities other than the treasury; the data include treasury debt held by foreign entities, debt issued by subnational entities, as well as intragovernmental debt; intragovernmental debt consists of treasury borrowings from surpluses in the social funds, such as for retirement, medical care, and unemployment; debt instruments for the social funds are sold at public auctions

country comparison to the world: 129

FISCAL YEAR:

calendar year

INFLATION RATE (CONSUMER PRICES):

3.7% (2017 est.)

0.7% (2016 est.)

country comparison to the world: 147

CENTRAL BANK DISCOUNT RATE:

0% (31 December 2017 est.)

0.05% (31 December 2015 est.)

country comparison to the world: 156

COMMERCIAL BANK PRIME LENDING RATE:

2.8% (31 December 2017 est.)

2.83% (31 December 2016 est.)

country comparison to the world: 177

STOCK OF NARROW MONEY:

$25.61 billion (31 December 2017 est.)

$20.93 billion (31 December 2016 est.)

country comparison to the world: 65

STOCK OF BROAD MONEY:

$25.61 billion (31 December 2017 est.)

$20.93 billion (31 December 2016 est.)

country comparison to the world: 65

STOCK OF DOMESTIC CREDIT:

$36.91 billion (31 December 2017 est.)

$28.55 billion (31 December 2016 est.)

country comparison to the world: 72

MARKET VALUE OF PUBLICLY TRADED SHARES:

$6.76 billion (31 December 2016 est.)

$6.799 billion (31 December 2015 est.)

$7.127 billion (31 December 2014 est.)

country comparison to the world: 81

CURRENT ACCOUNT BALANCE:

$364 million (2017 est.)

-$479 million (2016 est.)

country comparison to the world: 56

EXPORTS:

$29.12 billion (2017 est.)

$24.23 billion (2016 est.)

country comparison to the world: 65

EXPORTS - PARTNERS:

Russia 15%, Latvia 9.9%, Poland 8.1%, Germany 7.3%, US 5.2%, Estonia 5%, Sweden 4.8% (2017)

EXPORTS - COMMODITIES:

refined fuel, machinery and equipment, chemicals, textiles, foodstuffs, plastics

IMPORTS:

$31.56 billion (2017 est.)

$26.21 billion (2016 est.)

country comparison to the world: 66
IMPORTS - COMMODITIES:
oil, natural gas, machinery and equipment, transport equipment, chemicals, textiles and clothing, metals

IMPORTS - PARTNERS:
Russia 13%, Germany 12.3%, Poland 10.6%, Latvia 7.1%, Italy 5.2%, Netherlands 5.1%, Sweden 4% (2017)

RESERVES OF FOREIGN EXCHANGE AND GOLD:
$4.45 billion (31 December 2017 est.)
$1.697 billion (31 December 2015 est.)
country comparison to the world: 98

DEBT - EXTERNAL:
$34.48 billion (31 March 2016 est.)
$31.6 billion (31 March 2015 est.)
country comparison to the world: 78

STOCK OF DIRECT FOREIGN INVESTMENT - AT HOME:
$20.43 billion (31 December 2017 est.)
$15.87 billion (31 December 2016 est.)
country comparison to the world: 77

STOCK OF DIRECT FOREIGN INVESTMENT - ABROAD:
$6.268 billion (31 December 2017 est.)
$4.48 billion (31 December 2016 est.)
country comparison to the world: 72

EXCHANGE RATES:
litai (LTL) per US dollar -
0.884 (2017 est.)
0.9037 (2016 est.)
0.9037 (2015 est.)
0.9012 (2014 est.)
0.7525 (2013 est.)

ENERGY :: LITHUANIA

ELECTRICITY ACCESS:
electrification - total population: 100% (2016)

ELECTRICITY - PRODUCTION:
3.131 billion kWh (2016 est.)
country comparison to the world: 131

ELECTRICITY - CONSUMPTION:
10.5 billion kWh (2016 est.)
country comparison to the world: 95

ELECTRICITY - EXPORTS:
730 million kWh (2015 est.)
country comparison to the world: 62

ELECTRICITY - IMPORTS:
11.11 billion kWh (2016 est.)
country comparison to the world: 22

ELECTRICITY - INSTALLED GENERATING CAPACITY:
3.71 million kW (2016 est.)
country comparison to the world: 93

ELECTRICITY - FROM FOSSIL FUELS:
73% of total installed capacity (2016 est.)
country comparison to the world: 100

ELECTRICITY - FROM NUCLEAR FUELS:
0% of total installed capacity (2017 est.)
country comparison to the world: 130

ELECTRICITY - FROM HYDROELECTRIC PLANTS:
4% of total installed capacity (2017 est.)
country comparison to the world: 132

ELECTRICITY - FROM OTHER RENEWABLE SOURCES:
23% of total installed capacity (2017 est.)
country comparison to the world: 31

CRUDE OIL - PRODUCTION:
2,000 bbl/day (2018 est.)
country comparison to the world: 87

CRUDE OIL - EXPORTS:
1,002 bbl/day (2015 est.)
country comparison to the world: 75

CRUDE OIL - IMPORTS:
182,900 bbl/day (2015 est.)
country comparison to the world: 32

CRUDE OIL - PROVED RESERVES:
12 million bbl (1 January 2018 est.)
country comparison to the world: 88

REFINED PETROLEUM PRODUCTS - PRODUCTION:
196,500 bbl/day (2015 est.)
country comparison to the world: 51

REFINED PETROLEUM PRODUCTS - CONSUMPTION:
58,000 bbl/day (2016 est.)
country comparison to the world: 98

REFINED PETROLEUM PRODUCTS - EXPORTS:
174,800 bbl/day (2015 est.)
country comparison to the world: 32

REFINED PETROLEUM PRODUCTS - IMPORTS:
42,490 bbl/day (2015 est.)
country comparison to the world: 87

NATURAL GAS - PRODUCTION:
0 cu m (2017 est.)
country comparison to the world: 159

NATURAL GAS - CONSUMPTION:
2.492 billion cu m (2017 est.)
country comparison to the world: 79

NATURAL GAS - EXPORTS:
0 cu m (2017 est.)
country comparison to the world: 140

NATURAL GAS - IMPORTS:
2.492 billion cu m (2017 est.)
country comparison to the world: 47

NATURAL GAS - PROVED RESERVES:
0 cu m (2016 est.)
country comparison to the world: 160

CARBON DIOXIDE EMISSIONS FROM CONSUMPTION OF ENERGY:
13.49 million Mt (2017 est.)
country comparison to the world: 97

COMMUNICATIONS :: LITHUANIA

TELEPHONES - FIXED LINES:
total subscriptions: 486,895
subscriptions per 100 inhabitants: 17 (2017 est.)
country comparison to the world: 97

TELEPHONES - MOBILE CELLULAR:
total subscriptions: 4,361,329
subscriptions per 100 inhabitants: 154 (2017 est.)
country comparison to the world: 124

TELEPHONE SYSTEM:
general assessment: adequate; being modernized to provide improved international capability and better residential access; SIM card penetration is high for the region; prepaid sector accounts for most subscribers; postpaid subscribers is increasing; LTE networks available to more than 99% of the population; Lithuanian FttP (fiber to the home cable connections for Internet) penetration ranked third highest in Europe (2018)

domestic: 17 per 100 for fixed-line subscriptions; rapid expansion of mobile-cellular services has resulted in a steady decline in the number of fixed-line connections; mobile-cellular teledensity stands at about 154 per 100 persons (2018)

international: country code - 370; landing points for the BCS East, BCS East-West Interlink and NordBalt connecting Lithuania to Sweden, and

Latvia ; further transmission by satellite; landline connections to Latvia and Poland (2019)

BROADCAST MEDIA:

public broadcaster operates 3 channels with the third channel - a satellite channel - introduced in 2007; various privately owned commercial TV broadcasters operate national and multiple regional channels; many privately owned local TV stations; multi-channel cable and satellite TV services available; publicly owned broadcaster operates 3 radio networks; many privately owned commercial broadcasters, with repeater stations in various regions throughout the country

INTERNET COUNTRY CODE:

.lt

INTERNET USERS:

total: 2,122,884

percent of population: 74.4% (July 2016 est.)

country comparison to the world: 110

BROADBAND - FIXED SUBSCRIPTIONS:

total: 798,769

subscriptions per 100 inhabitants: 28 (2017 est.)

country comparison to the world: 72

MILITARY AND SECURITY :: LITHUANIA

MILITARY EXPENDITURES:

1.96% of GDP (2018)

1.72% of GDP (2017)

1.48% of GDP (2016)

1.14% of GDP (2015)

0.88% of GDP (2014)

country comparison to the world: 52

MILITARY AND SECURITY FORCES:

Lithuanian Armed Forces (Lietuvos Ginkluotosios Pajegos): Land Forces (Sausumos Pajegos), Naval Forces (Karines Juru Pajegos), Air Forces (Karines Oro Pajegos), Special Operations Forces (Specialiuju Operaciju Pajegos); National Defense Volunteer Forces (Savanoriu Pajegos) (2019)

MILITARY SERVICE AGE AND OBLIGATION:

19-26 years of age for conscripted military service (males); 9-month service obligation; in 2015, Lithuania reinstated conscription after having converted to a professional military in 2008; 18-38 for voluntary service (male and female) (2019)

TRANSPORTATION :: LITHUANIA

NATIONAL AIR TRANSPORT SYSTEM:

number of registered air carriers: 2 (2015)

inventory of registered aircraft operated by air carriers: 52 (2015)

annual passenger traffic on registered air carriers: 1,363,950 (2015)

annual freight traffic on registered air carriers: 565,642 mt-km (2015)

CIVIL AIRCRAFT REGISTRATION COUNTRY CODE PREFIX:

LY (2016)

AIRPORTS:

61 (2013)

country comparison to the world: 80

AIRPORTS - WITH PAVED RUNWAYS:

total: 22 (2017)

over 3,047 m: 3 (2017)

2,438 to 3,047 m: 1 (2017)

1,524 to 2,437 m: 7 (2017)

914 to 1,523 m: 2 (2017)

under 914 m: 9 (2017)

AIRPORTS - WITH UNPAVED RUNWAYS:

total: 39 (2013)

over 3,047 m: 1 (2013)

914 to 1,523 m: 2 (2013)

under 914 m: 36 (2013)

PIPELINES:

1921 km gas, 121 km refined products (2013)

RAILWAYS:

total: 1,768 km (2014)

standard gauge: 22 km 1.435-m gauge (2014)

broad gauge: 1,746 km 1.520-m gauge (122 km electrified) (2014)

country comparison to the world: 79

ROADWAYS:

total: 84,166 km (2012)

paved: 72,297 km (includes 312 km of expressways) (2012)

unpaved: 11,869 km (2012)

country comparison to the world: 59

WATERWAYS:

441 km (navigable year-round) (2007)

country comparison to the world: 86

MERCHANT MARINE:

total: 61

by type: container ship 3, general cargo 28, oil tanker 2, other 28 (2018)

country comparison to the world: 106

PORTS AND TERMINALS:

major seaport(s): Klaipeda

oil terminal(s): Butinge oil terminal

LNG terminal(s) (import): Klaipeda

TRANSNATIONAL ISSUES :: LITHUANIA

DISPUTES - INTERNATIONAL:

Lithuania and Russia committed to demarcating their boundary in 2006 in accordance with the land and maritime treaty ratified by Russia in May 2003 and by Lithuania in 1999; Lithuania operates a simplified transit regime for Russian nationals traveling from the Kaliningrad coastal exclave into Russia, while still conforming, as a EU member state having an external border with a non-EU member, to strict Schengen border rules; boundary demarcated with Latvia and Lithuania; as of January 2007, ground demarcation of the boundary with Belarus was complete and mapped with final ratification documents in preparation

REFUGEES AND INTERNALLY DISPLACED PERSONS:

stateless persons: 3,039 (2018)

ILLICIT DRUGS:

transshipment and destination point for cannabis, cocaine, ecstasy, and opiates from Southwest Asia, Latin America, Western Europe, and neighboring Baltic countries; growing production of high-quality amphetamines, but limited production of cannabis, methamphetamines; susceptible to money laundering despite changes to banking legislation

EUROPE :: LUXEMBOURG

INTRODUCTION :: LUXEMBOURG

BACKGROUND:

Founded in 963, Luxembourg became a grand duchy in 1815 and an independent state under the Netherlands. It lost more than half of its territory to Belgium in 1839 but gained a larger measure of autonomy. In 1867, Luxembourg attained full independence under the condition that it promise perpetual neutrality. Overrun by Germany in both world wars, it ended its neutrality in 1948 when it entered into the Benelux Customs Union and when it joined NATO the following year. In 1957, Luxembourg became one of the six founding countries of the EEC (later the EU), and in 1999 it joined the euro currency zone.

GEOGRAPHY :: LUXEMBOURG

LOCATION:
Western Europe, between France and Germany

GEOGRAPHIC COORDINATES:
49 45 N, 6 10 E

MAP REFERENCES:
Europe

AREA:
total: 2,586 sq km
land: 2,586 sq km
water: 0 sq km
country comparison to the world: 179

AREA - COMPARATIVE:
slightly smaller than Rhode Island; about half the size of Delaware

LAND BOUNDARIES:
total: 327 km
border countries (3): Belgium 130 km, France 69 km, Germany 128 km

COASTLINE:
0 km (landlocked)

MARITIME CLAIMS:
none (landlocked)

CLIMATE:
modified continental with mild winters, cool summers

TERRAIN:
mostly gently rolling uplands with broad, shallow valleys; uplands to slightly mountainous in the north; steep slope down to Moselle flood plain in the southeast

ELEVATION:
mean elevation: 325 m
lowest point: Moselle River 133 m
highest point: Buurgplaatz 559 m

NATURAL RESOURCES:
iron ore (no longer exploited), arable land

LAND USE:
agricultural land: 50.7% (2011 est.)
arable land: 24% (2011 est.) / permanent crops: 0.6% (2011 est.) / permanent pasture: 26.1% (2011 est.)
forest: 33.5% (2011 est.)
other: 15.8% (2011 est.)

IRRIGATED LAND:
0 sq km (2012)

POPULATION DISTRIBUTION:
most people live in the south, on or near the border with France

NATURAL HAZARDS:
occasional flooding

ENVIRONMENT - CURRENT ISSUES:
air and water pollution in urban areas, soil pollution of farmland; unsustainable patterns of consumption (transport, energy, recreation, space) threaten biodiversity and landscapes

ENVIRONMENT - INTERNATIONAL AGREEMENTS:
party to: Air Pollution, Air Pollution-Nitrogen Oxides, Air Pollution-Persistent Organic Pollutants, Air Pollution-Sulfur 85, Air Pollution-Sulfur 94, Air Pollution-Volatile Organic Compounds, Biodiversity, Climate Change, Climate Change-Kyoto Protocol, Desertification, Endangered Species, Hazardous Wastes, Law of the Sea, Marine Dumping, Ozone Layer Protection, Ship Pollution, Tropical Timber 83, Tropical Timber 94, Wetlands
signed, but not ratified: Environmental Modification

GEOGRAPHY - NOTE:
landlocked; the only grand duchy in the world

PEOPLE AND SOCIETY :: LUXEMBOURG

POPULATION:
605,764 (July 2018 est.)
country comparison to the world: 171

NATIONALITY:
noun: Luxembourger(s)
adjective: Luxembourg

ETHNIC GROUPS:

Luxembourger 51.1%, Portuguese 15.7%, French 7.5%, Italian 3.6%, Belgian 3.3%, German 2.1%, Spanish 1.1%, British 1%, other 14.6% (2019 est.)

note: data represent population by nationality

LANGUAGES:

Luxembourgish (official administrative and judicial language and national language (spoken vernacular)) 55.8%, Portuguese 15.7%, French (official administrative, judicial, and legislative language) 12.1%, German (official administrative and judicial language) 3.1%, Italian 2.9%, English 2.1%, other 8.4% (2011 est.)

RELIGIONS:

Christian (predominantly Roman Catholic) 70.4%, Muslim 2.3%, other (includes Buddhist, folk religions, Hindu, Jewish) 0.5%, none 26.8% (2010 est.)

AGE STRUCTURE:

0-14 years: 16.74% (male 52,243 /female 49,183)

15-24 years: 12.06% (male 37,391 /female 35,650)

25-54 years: 44.18% (male 137,381 /female 130,252)

55-64 years: 11.9% (male 36,670 /female 35,442)

65 years and over: 15.11% (male 41,002 /female 50,550) (2018 est.)

DEPENDENCY RATIOS:

total dependency ratio: 43.6 (2015 est.)

youth dependency ratio: 23.5 (2015 est.)

elderly dependency ratio: 20.1 (2015 est.)

potential support ratio: 5 (2015 est.)

MEDIAN AGE:

total: 39.3 years (2018 est.)

male: 38.7 years

female: 39.9 years

country comparison to the world: 54

POPULATION GROWTH RATE:

1.9% (2018 est.)

country comparison to the world: 53

BIRTH RATE:

11.6 births/1,000 population (2018 est.)

country comparison to the world: 170

DEATH RATE:

7.3 deaths/1,000 population (2018 est.)

country comparison to the world: 123

NET MIGRATION RATE:

14.8 migrant(s)/1,000 population (2018 est.)

country comparison to the world: 3

POPULATION DISTRIBUTION:

most people live in the south, on or near the border with France

URBANIZATION:

urban population: 91.2% of total population (2019)

rate of urbanization: 1.55% annual rate of change (2015-20 est.)

MAJOR URBAN AREAS - POPULATION:

120,000 LUXEMBOURG (capital) (2018)

SEX RATIO:

at birth: 1.06 male(s)/female

0-14 years: 1.06 male(s)/female

15-24 years: 1.05 male(s)/female

25-54 years: 1.05 male(s)/female

55-64 years: 1.03 male(s)/female

65 years and over: 0.81 male(s)/female

total population: 1.01 male(s)/female (2018 est.)

MOTHER'S MEAN AGE AT FIRST BIRTH:

30.1 years (2015 est.)

MATERNAL MORTALITY RATE:

5 deaths/100,000 live births (2017 est.)

country comparison to the world: 168

INFANT MORTALITY RATE:

total: 3.4 deaths/1,000 live births (2018 est.)

male: 3.8 deaths/1,000 live births

female: 3 deaths/1,000 live births

country comparison to the world: 205

LIFE EXPECTANCY AT BIRTH:

total population: 82.4 years (2018 est.)

male: 79.9 years

female: 85 years

country comparison to the world: 16

TOTAL FERTILITY RATE:

1.62 children born/woman (2018 est.)

country comparison to the world: 178

DRINKING WATER SOURCE:

improved:

urban: 100% of population

rural: 100% of population

total: 100% of population

unimproved:

urban: 0% of population

rural: 0% of population

total: 0% of population (2015 est.)

CURRENT HEALTH EXPENDITURE:

6.2% (2016)

PHYSICIANS DENSITY:

3.03 physicians/1,000 population (2017)

HOSPITAL BED DENSITY:

4.9 beds/1,000 population (2014)

SANITATION FACILITY ACCESS:

improved:

urban: 97.5% of population (2015 est.)

rural: 98.5% of population (2015 est.)

total: 97.6% of population (2015 est.)

unimproved:

urban: 2.5% of population (2015 est.)

rural: 1.5% of population (2015 est.)

total: 2.4% of population (2015 est.)

HIV/AIDS - ADULT PREVALENCE RATE:

0.3% (2018 est.)

country comparison to the world: 91

HIV/AIDS - PEOPLE LIVING WITH HIV/AIDS:

1,200 (2018 est.)

country comparison to the world: 139

HIV/AIDS - DEATHS:

<100 (2018 est.)

OBESITY - ADULT PREVALENCE RATE:

22.6% (2016)

country comparison to the world: 74

EDUCATION EXPENDITURES:

3.9% of GDP (2015)

country comparison to the world: 113

SCHOOL LIFE EXPECTANCY (PRIMARY TO TERTIARY EDUCATION):

total: 14 years

male: 14 years

female: 14 years (2016)

UNEMPLOYMENT, YOUTH AGES 15-24:

total: 15.4%

male: 17.2%

female: 13.2% (2017 est.)

country comparison to the world: 89

GOVERNMENT :: LUXEMBOURG

COUNTRY NAME:
conventional long form: Grand Duchy of Luxembourg

conventional short form: Luxembourg

local long form: Grand Duche de Luxembourg

local short form: Luxembourg

etymology: the name derives from the Celtic "lucilem" (little) and the German "burg" (castle or fortress) to produce the meaning of the "little castle"; the name is actually ironic, since for centuries the Fortress of Luxembourg was one of Europe's most formidable fortifications; the name passed to the surrounding city and then to the country itself

GOVERNMENT TYPE:
constitutional monarchy

CAPITAL:
name: Luxembourg

geographic coordinates: 49 36 N, 6 07 E

time difference: UTC+1 (6 hours ahead of Washington, DC, during Standard Time)

daylight saving time: +1hr, begins last Sunday in March; ends last Sunday in October

etymology: the name derives from the Celtic "lucilem" (little) and the German "burg" (castle or fortress) to produce the meaning of the "little castle"; the name is actually ironic, since for centuries the Fortress of Luxembourg was one of Europe's most formidable fortifications; the name passed to the city that grew around the fortress

ADMINISTRATIVE DIVISIONS:
12 cantons (cantons, singular - canton); Capellen, Clervaux, Diekirch, Echternach, Esch-sur-Alzette, Grevenmacher, Luxembourg, Mersch, Redange, Remich, Vianden, Wiltz

INDEPENDENCE:
1839 (from the Netherlands)

NATIONAL HOLIDAY:
National Day (birthday of Grand Duke HENRI), 23 June; note - this date of birth is not the true date of birth for any of the Royals, but the national festivities were shifted in 1962 to allow observance during a more favorable time of year

CONSTITUTION:
history: previous 1842 (heavily amended 1848, 1856); latest effective 17 October 1868

amendments: proposed by the Chamber of Deputies or by the monarch to the Chamber; passage requires at least two-thirds majority vote by the Chamber in two successive readings three months apart; a referendum can be substituted for the second reading if approved by more than a quarter of the Chamber members or by 25,000 valid voters; adoption by referendum requires a majority of all valid voters; amended many times, last in 2009 (2016)

LEGAL SYSTEM:
civil law system

INTERNATIONAL LAW ORGANIZATION PARTICIPATION:
accepts compulsory ICJ jurisdiction; accepts ICCt jurisdiction

CITIZENSHIP:
citizenship by birth: limited to situations where the parents are either unknown, stateless, or when the nationality law of the parents' state of origin does not permit acquisition of citizenship by descent when the birth occurs outside of national territory

citizenship by descent only: at least one parent must be a citizen of Luxembourg

dual citizenship recognized: yes

residency requirement for naturalization: 7 years

SUFFRAGE:
18 years of age; universal and compulsory

EXECUTIVE BRANCH:
chief of state: Grand Duke HENRI (since 7 October 2000); Heir Apparent Prince GUILLAUME (son of the monarch, born 11 November 1981)

head of government: Prime Minister Xavier BETTEL (since 4 December 2013); Deputy Prime Minister Etienne SCHNEIDER (since 4 December 2013); Deputy Prime Minister Felix BRAZ (since 5 December 2018)

cabinet: Council of Ministers recommended by the prime minister, appointed by the monarch

elections/appointments: the monarchy is hereditary; following elections to the Chamber of Deputies, the leader of the majority party or majority coalition usually appointed prime minister by the monarch; deputy prime minister appointed by the monarch; prime minister and deputy prime minister are responsible to the Chamber of Deputies

LEGISLATIVE BRANCH:
description: unicameral Chamber of Deputies or Chambre des Deputes (60 seats; members directly elected in multi-seat constituencies by party-list proportional representation vote; members serve 5-year terms); note - a 21-member Council of State appointed by the Grand Duke on the advice of the prime minister serves as an advisory body to the Chamber of Deputies

elections: last held on 14 October 2018 (next to be held by October 2023)

election results: percent of vote by party - CSV 28.3%, LSAP 17.6%, DP 16.9%, Green Party 15.1%, ADR 8.3%, Pirate Party 6.4%, The Left 5.5%, other 1.9%; seats by party - CSV 21, DP 12, LSAP 10, Green Party 9, ADR 4, Pirate Party 2, The Left 2; composition - men 46, women 14, percent of women 23.3%

JUDICIAL BRANCH:
highest courts: Supreme Court of Justice includes Court of Appeal and Court of Cassation (consists of 27 judges on 9 benches); Constitutional Court (consists of 9 members)

judge selection and term of office: judges of both courts appointed by the monarch for life

subordinate courts: Court of Accounts; district and local tribunals and courts

POLITICAL PARTIES AND LEADERS:
Alternative Democratic Reform Party or ADR [Jean SCHOOS]
Christian Social People's Party or CSV [Marc SPAUTZ]
Democratic Party or DP [Corinne CAHEN]
Green Party [Francoise FOLMER, Christian KMIOTEK]
Luxembourg Socialist Workers' Party or LSAP [Claude HAAGEN]
The Left (dei Lenk/la Gauche) [collective leadership, Central Committee]
other minor parties

INTERNATIONAL ORGANIZATION PARTICIPATION:

ADB (nonregional member), Australia Group, Benelux, BIS, CD, CE, EAPC, EBRD, ECB, EIB, EMU, ESA, EU, FAO, FATF, IAEA, IBRD, ICAO, ICC (national committees), ICCt, ICRM, IDA, IEA, IFAD, IFC, IFRCS, ILO, IMF, IMO, Interpol, IOC, IOM, IPU, ISO, ITSO, ITU, ITUC (NGOs), MIGA, NATO, NEA, NSG, OAS (observer), OECD, OIF, OPCW, OSCE, PCA, Schengen Convention, UN, UNCTAD, UNESCO, UNHCR, UNIDO, UNRWA, UPU, WCO, WHO, WIPO, WMO, WTO, ZC

DIPLOMATIC REPRESENTATION IN THE US:

Ambassador Sylvie LUCAS (since 16 September 2016)

chancery: 2200 Massachusetts Avenue NW, Washington, DC 20008

telephone: [1] (202) 265-4171

FAX: [1] (202) 328-8270

consulate(s) general: New York, San Francisco

DIPLOMATIC REPRESENTATION FROM THE US:

chief of mission: Ambassador James Randolph "Randy" EVANS (since 19 June 2018)

telephone: [352] 46-01-23 00

embassy: 22 Boulevard Emmanuel Servais, L-2535 Luxembourg City

mailing address: Unit 3560, APO AE 09126-3560 (official mail)

FAX: [352] 46-14-01

FLAG DESCRIPTION:

three equal horizontal bands of red (top), white, and light blue; similar to the flag of the Netherlands, which uses a darker blue and is shorter; the coloring is derived from the Grand Duke's coat of arms (a red lion on a white and blue striped field)

NATIONAL SYMBOL(S):

red, rampant lion; national colors: red, white, light blue

NATIONAL ANTHEM:

name: "Ons Heemecht" (Our Motherland); "De Wilhelmus" (The William)

lyrics/music: Michel LENTZ/Jean-Antoine ZINNEN; Nikolaus WELTER/unknown

note: "Ons Heemecht," adopted 1864, is the national anthem, while "De Wilhelmus," adopted 1919, serves as a royal anthem for use when members of the grand ducal family enter or exit a ceremony in Luxembourg

ECONOMY :: LUXEMBOURG

ECONOMY - OVERVIEW:

This small, stable, high-income economy has historically featured solid growth, low inflation, and low unemployment. Luxembourg, the only Grand Duchy in the world, is a landlocked country in northwestern Europe surrounded by Belgium, France, and Germany. Despite its small landmass and small population, Luxembourg is the fifth-wealthiest country in the world when measured on a gross domestic product (PPP) per capita basis. Luxembourg has one of the highest current account surpluses as a share of GDP in the euro zone, and it maintains a healthy budgetary position, with a 2017 surplus of 0.5% of GDP, and the lowest public debt level in the region.

Since 2002, Luxembourg's government has proactively implemented policies and programs to support economic diversification and to attract foreign direct investment. The government focused on key innovative industries that showed promise for supporting economic growth: logistics, information and communications technology (ICT); health technologies, including biotechnology and biomedical research; clean energy technologies, and more recently, space technology and financial services technologies. The economy has evolved and flourished, posting strong GDP growth of 3.4% in 2017, far outpacing the European average of 1.8%.

Luxembourg remains a financial powerhouse – the financial sector accounts for more than 35% of GDP - because of the exponential growth of the investment fund sector through the launch and development of cross-border funds (UCITS) in the 1990s. Luxembourg is the world's second-largest investment fund asset domicile, after the US, with $4 trillion of assets in custody in financial institutions.

Luxembourg has lost some of its advantage as a favorable tax location because of OECD and EU pressure, as well as the "LuxLeaks" scandal, which revealed advantageous tax treatments offered to foreign corporations. In 2015, the government's compliance with EU requirements to implement automatic exchange of tax information on savings accounts - thus ending banking secrecy - has constricted banking activity. Likewise, changes to the way EU members collect taxes from e-commerce has cut Luxembourg's sales tax revenues, requiring the government to raise additional levies and to reduce some direct social benefits as part of the tax reform package of 2017. The tax reform package also included reductions in the corporate tax rate and increases in deductions for families, both intended to increase purchasing power and increase competitiveness.

GDP (PURCHASING POWER PARITY):

$62.11 billion (2017 est.)

$60.71 billion (2016 est.)

$58.9 billion (2015 est.)

note: data are in 2017 dollars

country comparison to the world: 105

GDP (OFFICIAL EXCHANGE RATE):

$62.53 billion (2017 est.)

GDP - REAL GROWTH RATE:

2.3% (2017 est.)

3.1% (2016 est.)

2.9% (2015 est.)

country comparison to the world: 142

GDP - PER CAPITA (PPP):

$105,100 (2017 est.)

$105,400 (2016 est.)

$104,600 (2015 est.)

note: data are in 2017 dollars

country comparison to the world: 5

GROSS NATIONAL SAVING:

22.3% of GDP (2017 est.)

23% of GDP (2016 est.)

23.2% of GDP (2015 est.)

country comparison to the world: 82

GDP - COMPOSITION, BY END USE:

household consumption: 30.2% (2017 est.)

government consumption: 16.5% (2017 est.)

investment in fixed capital: 16.2% (2017 est.)

investment in inventories: 1.1% (2017 est.)

exports of goods and services: 230% (2017 est.)

imports of goods and services: -194% (2017 est.)

GDP - COMPOSITION, BY SECTOR OF ORIGIN:

agriculture: 0.3% (2017 est.)

industry: 12.8% (2017 est.)

services: 86.9% (2017 est.)

AGRICULTURE - PRODUCTS:

grapes, barley, oats, potatoes, wheat, fruits; dairy and livestock products

INDUSTRIES:

banking and financial services, construction, real estate services, iron, metals, and steel, information technology, telecommunications, cargo transportation and logistics, chemicals, engineering, tires, glass, aluminum, tourism, biotechnology

INDUSTRIAL PRODUCTION GROWTH RATE:

1.9% (2017 est.)

country comparison to the world: 134

LABOR FORCE:

282,800 (2017 est.)

note: data exclude foreign workers; in addition to the figure for domestic labor force, about 150,000 workers commute daily from France, Belgium, and Germany

country comparison to the world: 165

LABOR FORCE - BY OCCUPATION:

agriculture: 1.1%

industry: 20%

services: 78.9% (2013 est.)

UNEMPLOYMENT RATE:

5.8% (2017 est.)

6.3% (2016 est.)

country comparison to the world: 89

POPULATION BELOW POVERTY LINE:

NA

HOUSEHOLD INCOME OR CONSUMPTION BY PERCENTAGE SHARE:

lowest 10%: 3.5%

highest 10%: 23.8% (2000)

DISTRIBUTION OF FAMILY INCOME - GINI INDEX:

30.4 (2013 est.)

26 (2005 est.)

country comparison to the world: 132

BUDGET:

revenues: 27.75 billion (2017 est.)

expenditures: 26.8 billion (2017 est.)

TAXES AND OTHER REVENUES:

44.4% (of GDP) (2017 est.)

country comparison to the world: 24

BUDGET SURPLUS (+) OR DEFICIT (-):

1.5% (of GDP) (2017 est.)

country comparison to the world: 23

PUBLIC DEBT:

23% of GDP (2017 est.)

20.8% of GDP (2016 est.)

note: data cover general government debt and include debt instruments issued (or owned) by government entities other than the treasury; the data include treasury debt held by foreign entities; the data include debt issued by subnational entities, as well as intragovernmental debt; intragovernmental debt consists of treasury borrowings from surpluses in the social funds, such as for retirement, medical care, and unemployment; debt instruments for the social funds are not sold at public auctions

country comparison to the world: 183

FISCAL YEAR:

calendar year

INFLATION RATE (CONSUMER PRICES):

2.1% (2017 est.)

0% (2016 est.)

country comparison to the world: 109

CENTRAL BANK DISCOUNT RATE:

0% (31 December 2017)

0% (31 December 2010)

note: this is the European Central Bank's rate on the marginal lending facility, which offers overnight credit to banks in the euro area

country comparison to the world: 157

COMMERCIAL BANK PRIME LENDING RATE:

1.9% (31 December 2017 est.)

1.98% (31 December 2016 est.)

country comparison to the world: 186

STOCK OF NARROW MONEY:

$275.6 billion (31 December 2017 est.)

$229.2 billion (31 December 2016 est.)

note: see entry for the EU for money supply for the entire euro area; the European Central Bank (ECB) controls monetary policy for the 18 members of the Economic and Monetary Union (EMU); individual members of the EMU do not control the quantity of money circulating within their own borders

country comparison to the world: 18

STOCK OF BROAD MONEY:

$275.6 billion (31 December 2017 est.)

$229.2 billion (31 December 2016 est.)

country comparison to the world: 18

STOCK OF DOMESTIC CREDIT:

$128.5 billion (31 December 2017 est.)

$109.9 billion (31 December 2016 est.)

country comparison to the world: 51

MARKET VALUE OF PUBLICLY TRADED SHARES:

$47.13 billion (31 December 2015 est.)

$63.17 billion (31 December 2014 est.)

$78.64 billion (31 December 2013 est.)

country comparison to the world: 52

CURRENT ACCOUNT BALANCE:

$3.112 billion (2017 est.)

$2.988 billion (2016 est.)

country comparison to the world: 34

EXPORTS:

$15.99 billion (2017 est.)

$16.37 billion (2016 est.)

country comparison to the world: 73

EXPORTS - PARTNERS:

Germany 25.6%, Belgium 17.6%, France 14%, Netherlands 5.1%, Italy 4.1%, UK 4.1% (2017)

EXPORTS - COMMODITIES:

machinery and equipment, steel products, chemicals, rubber products, glass

IMPORTS:

$20.66 billion (2017 est.)

$20.41 billion (2016 est.)

country comparison to the world: 76

IMPORTS - COMMODITIES:

commercial aircraft, minerals, chemicals, metals, foodstuffs, luxury consumer goods

IMPORTS - PARTNERS:

Belgium 32%, Germany 24.9%, France 11.1%, US 5.7%, Netherlands 4.9% (2017)

RESERVES OF FOREIGN EXCHANGE AND GOLD:

$878 million (31 December 2017 est.)

$974 million (31 December 2016 est.)

country comparison to the world: 137

DEBT - EXTERNAL:

$3.781 trillion (31 March 2016 est.)

$3.806 trillion (31 March 2015 est.)

country comparison to the world: 6

STOCK OF DIRECT FOREIGN INVESTMENT - AT HOME:

$11.21 billion (31 December 2008 est.)

country comparison to the world: 95

STOCK OF DIRECT FOREIGN INVESTMENT - ABROAD:

NA

EXCHANGE RATES:

euros (EUR) per US dollar -

0.885 (2017 est.)

0.903 (2016 est.)

0.9214 (2015 est.)

0.885 (2014 est.)

0.7634 (2013 est.)

ENERGY :: LUXEMBOURG

ELECTRICITY ACCESS:

electrification - total population: 100% (2016)

ELECTRICITY - PRODUCTION:

334.5 million kWh (2016 est.)

country comparison to the world: 178

ELECTRICITY - CONSUMPTION:

6.475 billion kWh (2016 est.)

country comparison to the world: 111

ELECTRICITY - EXPORTS:

1.42 billion kWh (2016 est.)

country comparison to the world: 51

ELECTRICITY - IMPORTS:

7.718 billion kWh (2016 est.)

country comparison to the world: 30

ELECTRICITY - INSTALLED GENERATING CAPACITY:

1.709 million kW (2016 est.)

country comparison to the world: 118

ELECTRICITY - FROM FOSSIL FUELS:

25% of total installed capacity (2016 est.)

country comparison to the world: 189

ELECTRICITY - FROM NUCLEAR FUELS:

0% of total installed capacity (2017 est.)

country comparison to the world: 131

ELECTRICITY - FROM HYDROELECTRIC PLANTS:

8% of total installed capacity (2017 est.)

country comparison to the world: 122

ELECTRICITY - FROM OTHER RENEWABLE SOURCES:

67% of total installed capacity (2017 est.)

country comparison to the world: 2

CRUDE OIL - PRODUCTION:

0 bbl/day (2018 est.)

country comparison to the world: 164

CRUDE OIL - EXPORTS:

0 bbl/day (2017 est.)

country comparison to the world: 156

CRUDE OIL - IMPORTS:

0 bbl/day (2017 est.)

country comparison to the world: 155

CRUDE OIL - PROVED RESERVES:

0 bbl (1 January 2018 est.)

country comparison to the world: 159

REFINED PETROLEUM PRODUCTS - PRODUCTION:

0 bbl/day (2017 est.)

country comparison to the world: 167

REFINED PETROLEUM PRODUCTS - CONSUMPTION:

59,850 bbl/day (2017 est.)

country comparison to the world: 96

REFINED PETROLEUM PRODUCTS - EXPORTS:

0 bbl/day (2017 est.)

country comparison to the world: 173

REFINED PETROLEUM PRODUCTS - IMPORTS:

59,020 bbl/day (2017 est.)

country comparison to the world: 73

NATURAL GAS - PRODUCTION:

0 cu m (2017 est.)

country comparison to the world: 160

NATURAL GAS - CONSUMPTION:

792.8 million cu m (2017 est.)

country comparison to the world: 96

NATURAL GAS - EXPORTS:

0 cu m (2017 est.)

country comparison to the world: 141

NATURAL GAS - IMPORTS:

792.8 million cu m (2017 est.)

country comparison to the world: 63

NATURAL GAS - PROVED RESERVES:

0 cu m (1 January 2014 est.)

country comparison to the world: 161

CARBON DIOXIDE EMISSIONS FROM CONSUMPTION OF ENERGY:

10.72 million Mt (2017 est.)

country comparison to the world: 103

COMMUNICATIONS :: LUXEMBOURG

TELEPHONES - FIXED LINES:

total subscriptions: 275,300

subscriptions per 100 inhabitants: 46 (2017 est.)

country comparison to the world: 118

TELEPHONES - MOBILE CELLULAR:

total subscriptions: 794,000

subscriptions per 100 inhabitants: 134 (2017 est.)

country comparison to the world: 163

TELEPHONE SYSTEM:

general assessment: highly developed, completely automated and efficient system; by 2020 the government's program is to provide a 1Gb/s service to all citizens, and to make Luxembourg the first fully fibred country in Europe; new law requiring SIM cards be registered has slowed down growth for mobile subscribers; 5G launch by 2020 (2018)

domestic: fixed-line teledensity about 46 per 100 persons; nationwide mobile-cellular telephone system with market for mobile-cellular phones virtually saturated with 134 per 100 mobile-cellular (2018)

international: country code - 352

BROADCAST MEDIA:

Luxembourg has a long tradition of operating radio and TV services for pan-European audiences and is home to Europe's largest privately owned broadcast media group, the RTL Group, which operates 46 TV stations and 29 radio stations in Europe; also home to Europe's largest satellite operator, Societe Europeenne des Satellites (SES); domestically, the RTL Group operates TV and radio networks; other domestic private radio and TV operators and French and German stations available; satellite and cable TV services available

INTERNET COUNTRY CODE:

.lu

INTERNET USERS:

total: 567,698

percent of population: 97.5% (July 2016 est.)

country comparison to the world: 147

BROADBAND - FIXED SUBSCRIPTIONS:

total: 212,900

subscriptions per 100 inhabitants: 36 (2017 est.)

country comparison to the world: 107

MILITARY AND SECURITY :: LUXEMBOURG

MILITARY EXPENDITURES:
0.55% of GDP (2018)

0.52% of GDP (2017)

0.4% of GDP (2016)

0.43% of GDP (2015)

0.42% of GDP (2014)

country comparison to the world: 145

MILITARY AND SECURITY FORCES:
Luxembourg Army (l'Armée Luxembourgeoise) (2019)

MILITARY SERVICE AGE AND OBLIGATION:
18-26 years of age for male and female voluntary military service; no conscription; Luxembourg citizen or EU citizen with 3-year residence in Luxembourg (2019)

TRANSPORTATION :: LUXEMBOURG

NATIONAL AIR TRANSPORT SYSTEM:
number of registered air carriers: 3 (2015)

inventory of registered aircraft operated by air carriers: 119 (2015)

annual passenger traffic on registered air carriers: 1,830,972 (2015)

annual freight traffic on registered air carriers: 6,309,473,324 mt-km (2015)

CIVIL AIRCRAFT REGISTRATION COUNTRY CODE PREFIX:
LX (2016)

AIRPORTS:
2 (2013)

country comparison to the world: 202

AIRPORTS - WITH PAVED RUNWAYS:
total: 1 (2017)

over 3,047 m: 1 (2017)

AIRPORTS - WITH UNPAVED RUNWAYS:
total: 1 (2013)

under 914 m: 1 (2013)

HELIPORTS:
1 (2013)

PIPELINES:
142 km gas, 27 km refined products (2013)

RAILWAYS:
total: 275 km (2014)

standard gauge: 275 km 1.435-m gauge (275 km electrified) (2014)

country comparison to the world: 124

ROADWAYS:
total: 2,875 km (2019)

country comparison to the world: 161

WATERWAYS:
37 km (on Moselle River) (2010)

country comparison to the world: 104

MERCHANT MARINE:
total: 152

by type: bulk carrier 4, container ship 9, general cargo 6, oil tanker 2, other 131 (2018)

country comparison to the world: 70

PORTS AND TERMINALS:
river port(s): Mertert (Moselle)

TRANSNATIONAL ISSUES :: LUXEMBOURG

DISPUTES - INTERNATIONAL:
none

REFUGEES AND INTERNALLY DISPLACED PERSONS:
stateless persons: 83 (2018)

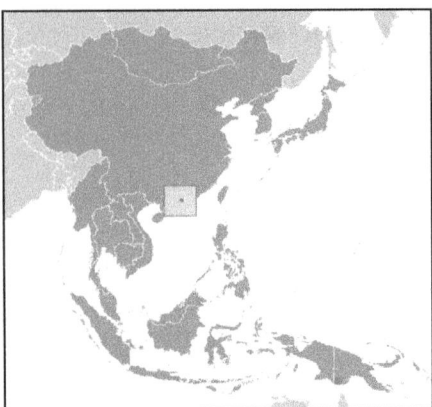

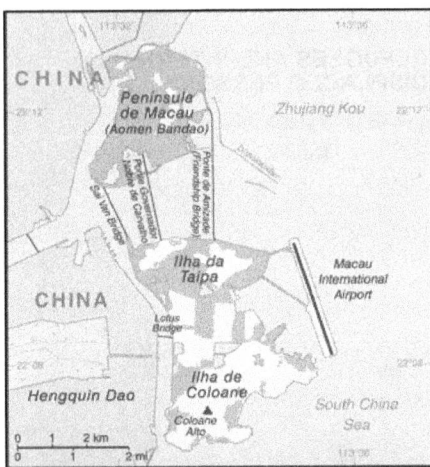

EAST ASIA / SOUTHEAST ASIA :: MACAU

INTRODUCTION :: MACAU

BACKGROUND:
Colonized by the Portuguese in the 16th century, Macau was the first European settlement in the Far East. Pursuant to an agreement signed by China and Portugal on 13 April 1987, Macau became the Macau Special Administrative Region of the People's Republic of China on 20 December 1999. In this agreement, China promised that, under its "one country, two systems" formula, China's political and economic system would not be imposed on Macau, and that Macau would enjoy a "high degree of autonomy" in all matters except foreign affairs and defense for the subsequent 50 years.

GEOGRAPHY :: MACAU

LOCATION:
Eastern Asia, bordering the South China Sea and China

GEOGRAPHIC COORDINATES:
22 10 N, 113 33 E

MAP REFERENCES:
Southeast Asia

AREA:
total: 28.2 sq km
land: 28.2 sq km
water: 0 sq km
country comparison to the world: 237

AREA - COMPARATIVE:
less than one-sixth the size of Washington, DC

LAND BOUNDARIES:
total: 3 km
regional borders (1): China 3 km

COASTLINE:
41 km

MARITIME CLAIMS:
not specified

CLIMATE:
subtropical; marine with cool winters, warm summers

TERRAIN:
generally flat

ELEVATION:
lowest point: South China Sea 0 m
highest point: Alto Coloane 172 m

NATURAL RESOURCES:
NEGL

LAND USE:
agricultural land: 0% (2011 est.)
arable land: 0% (2011 est.) / permanent crops: 0% (2011 est.) / permanent pasture: 0% (2011 est.)
forest: 0% (2011 est.)
other: 100% (2011 est.)

IRRIGATED LAND:
0 sq km (2012)

POPULATION DISTRIBUTION:
population fairly equally distributed

NATURAL HAZARDS:
typhoons

ENVIRONMENT - CURRENT ISSUES:
air pollution; coastal waters pollution; insufficient policies in reducing and recycling solid wastes; increasing population density worsening noise pollution

ENVIRONMENT - INTERNATIONAL AGREEMENTS:
party to: Marine Dumping (associate member), Ship Pollution (associate member)

GEOGRAPHY - NOTE:
essentially urban; an area of land reclaimed from the sea measuring 5.2 sq km and known as Cotai now connects the islands of Coloane and Taipa; the island area is connected to the mainland peninsula by three bridges

PEOPLE AND SOCIETY :: MACAU

POPULATION:
606,340 (July 2018 est.)
note: Macau's statistical agency estimated the total population to be approximately 648,550 as of September 2017
country comparison to the world: 170

NATIONALITY:
noun: Chinese
adjective: Chinese

ETHNIC GROUPS:
Chinese 88.7%, Portuguese 1.1%, mixed 1.1%, other 9.2% (includes Macanese - mixed Portuguese and Asian ancestry) (2016 est.)

LANGUAGES:
Cantonese 80.1%, Mandarin 5.5%, other Chinese dialects 5.3%, Tagalog 3%, English 2.8%, Portuguese 0.6%, other 2.8% (2016 est.)

note: Chinese and Portuguese are official languages

RELIGIONS:
folk religionist 58.9%, Buddhist 17.3%, Christian 7.2%, other 1.2%, none 15.4% (2010 est.)

AGE STRUCTURE:
0-14 years: 13.92% (male 43,730 /female 40,651)

15-24 years: 11.22% (male 35,874 /female 32,146)

25-54 years: 49.75% (male 134,301 /female 167,359)

55-64 years: 13.95% (male 42,409 /female 42,174)

65 years and over: 11.16% (male 31,689 /female 36,007) (2018 est.)

DEPENDENCY RATIOS:
total dependency ratio: 26.6 (2015 est.)

youth dependency ratio: 15.7 (2015 est.)

elderly dependency ratio: 10.9 (2015 est.)

potential support ratio: 9.2 (2015 est.)

MEDIAN AGE:
total: 39.8 years (2018 est.)

male: 39.9 years

female: 39.7 years

country comparison to the world: 51

POPULATION GROWTH RATE:
0.71% (2018 est.)

country comparison to the world: 141

BIRTH RATE:
8.4 births/1,000 population (2018 est.)

country comparison to the world: 217

DEATH RATE:
4.6 deaths/1,000 population (2018 est.)

country comparison to the world: 203

NET MIGRATION RATE:
3.3 migrant(s)/1,000 population (2018 est.)

country comparison to the world: 38

POPULATION DISTRIBUTION:
population fairly equally distributed

URBANIZATION:
urban population: 100% of total population (2019)

rate of urbanization: 1.63% annual rate of change (2015-20 est.)

SEX RATIO:
at birth: 1.05 male(s)/female

0-14 years: 1.08 male(s)/female

15-24 years: 1.12 male(s)/female

25-54 years: 0.8 male(s)/female

55-64 years: 1.01 male(s)/female

65 years and over: 0.88 male(s)/female

total population: 0.9 male(s)/female (2018 est.)

INFANT MORTALITY RATE:
total: 3.1 deaths/1,000 live births (2018 est.)

male: 3.2 deaths/1,000 live births

female: 2.9 deaths/1,000 live births

country comparison to the world: 211

LIFE EXPECTANCY AT BIRTH:
total population: 84.6 years (2018 est.)

male: 81.6 years

female: 87.7 years

country comparison to the world: 4

TOTAL FERTILITY RATE:
0.95 children born/woman (2018 est.)

country comparison to the world: 223

PHYSICIANS DENSITY:
2.41 physicians/1,000 population (2010)

HIV/AIDS - ADULT PREVALENCE RATE:
NA

HIV/AIDS - PEOPLE LIVING WITH HIV/AIDS:
NA

HIV/AIDS - DEATHS:
NA

EDUCATION EXPENDITURES:
3.1% of GDP (2016)

country comparison to the world: 137

LITERACY:
definition: age 15 and over can read and write

total population: 96.5%

male: 98.2%

female: 95% (2016 est.)

SCHOOL LIFE EXPECTANCY (PRIMARY TO TERTIARY EDUCATION):
total: 16 years

male: 15 years

female: 16 years (2017)

UNEMPLOYMENT, YOUTH AGES 15-24:
total: 5.3%

male: 6.7%

female: 3.9% (2017 est.)

country comparison to the world: 163

GOVERNMENT :: MACAU

COUNTRY NAME:
conventional long form: Macau Special Administrative Region

conventional short form: Macau

official long form: Aomen Tebie Xingzhengqu (Chinese); Regiao Administrativa Especial de Macau (Portuguese)

official short form: Aomen (Chinese); Macau (Portuguese)

etymology: name is thought to derive from the A-Ma Temple - built in 1488 and dedicated to Mazu, the goddess of seafarers and fishermen - which is referred to locally as "Maa Gok" - and in Portuguese became "Macau"; the Chinese name Aomen means "inlet gates"

DEPENDENCY STATUS:
special administrative region of the People's Republic of China

GOVERNMENT TYPE:
executive-led limited democracy; a special administrative region of the People's Republic of China

ADMINISTRATIVE DIVISIONS:
none (special administrative region of the People's Republic of China)

INDEPENDENCE:
none (special administrative region of China)

NATIONAL HOLIDAY:
National Day (anniversary of the Founding of the People's Republic of China), 1 October (1949); note - 20 December (1999) is celebrated as Macau Special Administrative Region Establishment Day

CONSTITUTION:
history: previous 1976 (Organic Statute of Macau, under Portuguese authority); latest adopted 31 March 1993, effective 20 December 1999 (Basic Law of the Macau Special Administrative Region of the People's Republic of China serves as Macau's constitution)

amendments: proposed by the Standing Committee of the National People's Congress (NPC), the People's Republic of China State Council, and the Macau Special Administrative Region; submittal of proposals to the NPC requires two-thirds majority vote by the Legislative Assembly of Macau, approval by two thirds of Macau's deputies to the NPC, and consent of the Macau chief executive; final passage requires approval by the NPC; amended 2005, 2012 (2018)

LEGAL SYSTEM:

civil law system based on the Portuguese model

CITIZENSHIP:

see China

SUFFRAGE:

18 years of age in direct elections for some legislative positions, universal for permanent residents living in Macau for the past 7 years; note - indirect elections are limited to organizations registered as "corporate voters" and an election committee for the chief executive drawn from broad regional groupings, municipal organizations, central government bodies, and elected Macau officials

EXECUTIVE BRANCH:

chief of state: President of China XI Jinping (since 14 March 2013)

head of government: Chief Executive Fernando CHUI Sai On (since 20 December 2009)

cabinet: Executive Council appointed by the chief executive

elections/appointments: president indirectly elected by National People's Congress for a 5-year term (eligible for a second term); election last held on 17 March 2018 (next to be held in March 2023);chief executive chosen by a 400-member Election Committee for a 5-year term (eligible for a second term); election last held on 25 August 2019 (next to be held in 2024)

election results: Fernando CHUI Sai On reelected chief executive; Election Committee vote - 380 of 396; note - HO Iat Seng was elected chief executive (receiving 392 out of 400 votes) on 24 August 2019 and will take office on 20 December 2019

LEGISLATIVE BRANCH:

description: unicameral Legislative Assembly or Regiao Administrativa Especial de Macau (33 seats; 14 members directly elected by proportional representation vote, 12 indirectly elected by an electoral college of professional and commercial interest groups, and 7 appointed by the chief executive; members serve 4-year terms)

elections: last held on 17 September 2017 (next to be held in 2021)

election results: percent of vote - UMG 10%, UPD 9.7%, ACUM 8.6%, NE 8.3%, UPP 7.2, ANMD 6.6%, NUDM 6.1%, ACDM 5.9%, APMD 5.8%, Civic Watch 5.6%, ABL 5.5%, ANPM 5.3%, other 15.4%; seats by political group - UMG 2, UPD 2, ABL 1, ACDM 1, ACUM 1, ANMD 1, ANPM 1, APMD 1, Civic Watch 1, NE 1, NUDM 1, UPP 1; 12 seats filled by professional and business groups; 7 members appointed by the chief executive; composition - men 27, women 6, percent of women 18.6%

JUDICIAL BRANCH:

highest courts: Court of Final Appeal of Macau Special Administrative Region (consists of the court president and 2 associate justices)

judge selection and term of office: justices appointed by the Macau chief executive upon the recommendation of an independent commission of judges, lawyers, and "eminent" persons; judge tenure NA

subordinate courts: Court of Second Instance; Court of First instance; Lower Court; Administrative Court

POLITICAL PARTIES AND LEADERS:

Alliance for Change or APM [Melinda CHAN Mei-yi]
Alliance for a Happy Home or ABL [WONG Kit-cheng] (an electoral list of UPP)
Civic Watch or Civico [Agnes LAM Iok-fong]
Macau-Guangdong Union or UMG [MAK Soi-kun]
Macau Citizens' Development Association or ACDM [Becky SONG Pek-kei] (an electoral list of ACUM)New Democratic Macau Association or ANMD [AU Kam-san]
New Hope or NE [Jose Maria Pereira COUTINHO]
New Macau Association (New Macau Progressives) or AMN or ANPM [Sulu SOU Ka-hou]
New Union for Macau's Development or NUDM [Angela LEONG On-kei]
Prosperous Democratic Macau Association or APMD (an electoral list of AMN)
Union for Development or UPD [Ella LEI Cheng-I]
Union for Promoting Progress or UPP [HO Ion-sang]
United Citizens Association of Macau or ACUM [CHAN Meng-kam]

note: there is no political party ordinance, so there are no registered political parties; politically active groups register as societies or companies

INTERNATIONAL ORGANIZATION PARTICIPATION:

ICC (national committees), IHO, IMF, IMO (associate), Interpol (subbureau), ISO (correspondent), UNESCO (associate), UNWTO (associate), UPU, WCO, WMO, WTO

DIPLOMATIC REPRESENTATION IN THE US:

none (Special Administrative Region of China)

DIPLOMATIC REPRESENTATION FROM THE US:

the US has no offices in Macau; US Consulate General in Hong Kong is accredited to Macau

FLAG DESCRIPTION:

green with a lotus flower above a stylized bridge and water in white, beneath an arc of five gold, five-pointed stars: one large in the center of the arc and two smaller on either side; the lotus is the floral emblem of Macau, the three petals represent the peninsula and two islands that make up Macau; the five stars echo those on the flag of China

NATIONAL SYMBOL(S):

lotus blossom; national colors: green, white, yellow

NATIONAL ANTHEM:

note: as a Special Administrative Region of China, "Yiyongjun Jinxingqu" is the official anthem (see China)

ECONOMY :: MACAU

ECONOMY - OVERVIEW:

Since opening up its locally-controlled casino industry to foreign competition in 2001, Macau has attracted tens of billions of dollars in foreign investment, transforming the territory into one of the world's largest gaming centers. Macau's gaming and tourism businesses were fueled by China's decision to relax travel restrictions on Chinese citizens wishing to visit Macau. In 2016, Macau's gaming-related taxes accounted for more than 76% of total government revenue.

Macau's economy slowed dramatically in 2009 as a result of the global economic slowdown, but strong growth resumed in the 2010-13 period, largely on the back of tourism from mainland China and the gaming sectors. In 2015, this city of 646,800 hosted nearly 30.7 million visitors. Almost 67% came from mainland China. Macau's traditional manufacturing industry has slowed greatly since the termination of the Multi-Fiber Agreement in 2005. Services export — primarily gaming — increasingly has driven Macau's economic performance. Mainland China's anti-corruption campaign brought Macau's gambling boom to a halt in 2014, with spending in casinos contracting 34.3% in 2015. As a result, Macau's inflation-adjusted GDP contracted 21.5% in 2015 and another 2.1% in 2016 - down from double-digit expansion rates in the period 2010-13 - but the economy recovered handsomely in 2017.

Macau continues to face the challenges of managing its growing casino industry, risks from money-laundering activities, and the need to diversify the economy away from heavy dependence on gaming revenues. Macau's currency, the pataca, is closely tied to the Hong Kong dollar, which is also freely accepted in the territory.

GDP (PURCHASING POWER PARITY):
$71.82 billion (2017 est.)

$65.84 billion (2016 est.)

$66.41 billion (2015 est.)

note: data are in 2017 dollars

country comparison to the world: 98

GDP (OFFICIAL EXCHANGE RATE):
$50.36 billion (2017 est.)

GDP - REAL GROWTH RATE:
9.1% (2017 est.)

-0.9% (2016 est.)

-21.6% (2015 est.)

country comparison to the world: 6

GDP - PER CAPITA (PPP):
$110,000 (2017 est.)

$102,100 (2016 est.)

$102,600 (2015 est.)

country comparison to the world: 4

GDP - COMPOSITION, BY END USE:
household consumption: 24.2% (2017 est.)

government consumption: 9.9% (2017 est.)

investment in fixed capital: 18.5% (2017 est.)

investment in inventories: 0.8% (2017 est.)

exports of goods and services: 79.4% (2017 est.)

imports of goods and services: -32% (2017 est.)

GDP - COMPOSITION, BY SECTOR OF ORIGIN:
agriculture: 0% (2016 est.)

industry: 6.3% (2017 est.)

services: 93.7% (2017 est.)

AGRICULTURE - PRODUCTS:
only 2% of land area is cultivated, mainly by vegetable growers; fishing, mostly for crustaceans, is important; some of the catch is exported to Hong Kong

INDUSTRIES:
tourism, gambling, clothing, textiles, electronics, footwear, toys

INDUSTRIAL PRODUCTION GROWTH RATE:
2% (2017 est.)

country comparison to the world: 131

LABOR FORCE:
400,000 (2017 est.)

country comparison to the world: 159

LABOR FORCE - BY OCCUPATION:
agriculture: 2.5%

industry: 9.8%

services: 4.4%

industry and services: 12.4%

agriculture/fishing/forestry/mining: 15%

manufacturing: 25.9%

construction: 7.1%

transportation and utilities: 2.6%

commerce: 20.3% (2013 est.)

UNEMPLOYMENT RATE:
2% (2017 est.)

1.9% (2016 est.)

country comparison to the world: 18

POPULATION BELOW POVERTY LINE:
NA

HOUSEHOLD INCOME OR CONSUMPTION BY PERCENTAGE SHARE:
lowest 10%: NA

highest 10%: NA

DISTRIBUTION OF FAMILY INCOME - GINI INDEX:
35 (2013)

38 (2008)

country comparison to the world: 98

BUDGET:
revenues: 14.71 billion (2017 est.)

expenditures: 9.684 billion (2017 est.)

TAXES AND OTHER REVENUES:
29.2% (of GDP) (2017 est.)

country comparison to the world: 85

BUDGET SURPLUS (+) OR DEFICIT (-):
10% (of GDP) (2017 est.)

country comparison to the world: 2

PUBLIC DEBT:
0% of GDP (2017 est.)

0% of GDP (2016 est.)

country comparison to the world: 210

FISCAL YEAR:
calendar year

INFLATION RATE (CONSUMER PRICES):
1.2% (2017 est.)

2.4% (2016 est.)

country comparison to the world: 65

COMMERCIAL BANK PRIME LENDING RATE:
5.25% (31 December 2017 est.)

5.25% (31 December 2016 est.)

country comparison to the world: 145

STOCK OF NARROW MONEY:
$8.866 billion (31 December 2017 est.)

$7.858 billion (31 December 2016 est.)

country comparison to the world: 86

STOCK OF BROAD MONEY:
$8.866 billion (31 December 2017 est.)

$7.858 billion (31 December 2016 est.)

country comparison to the world: 88

STOCK OF DOMESTIC CREDIT:
$18.24 billion (31 December 2017 est.)

$17.16 billion (31 December 2016 est.)

country comparison to the world: 93

MARKET VALUE OF PUBLICLY TRADED SHARES:
$85.5 billion (2 March 2012 est.)

$2.3 billion (31 December 2008 est.)

$46.1 billion (31 est.)

country comparison to the world: 44

CURRENT ACCOUNT BALANCE:
$16.75 billion (2017 est.)

$12.22 billion (2016 est.)

country comparison to the world: 18

EXPORTS:

$1.45 billion (2018)

note: includes reexports

country comparison to the world: 149

EXPORTS - PARTNERS:

Hong Kong 47.9%, China 12.6%, Japan 1% (2018)

EXPORTS - COMMODITIES:

clothing, textiles, footwear, toys, electronics, machinery and parts

IMPORTS:

$9.7 billion (2017 est.)

country comparison to the world: 102

IMPORTS - COMMODITIES:

raw materials and semi-manufactured goods, consumer goods (foodstuffs, beverages, tobacco, garments and footwear, motor vehicles), capital goods, mineral fuels and oils

IMPORTS - PARTNERS:

China 33.9%, Italy 9.3%, Hong Kong 9%, France 7.5%, Switzerland 7.4%, Japan 7.2%, US 4.4% (2017)

RESERVES OF FOREIGN EXCHANGE AND GOLD:

$20.17 billion (31 December 2017 est.)

$18.89 billion (31 December 2015 est.)

note: the Fiscal Reserves Act that came into force on 1 January 2012 requires the fiscal reserves to be separated from the foreign exchange reserves and to be managed separately; the transfer of assets took place in February 2012

country comparison to the world: 59

DEBT - EXTERNAL:

$0 (31 December 2013)

$0 (31 December 2012)

country comparison to the world: 207

STOCK OF DIRECT FOREIGN INVESTMENT - AT HOME:

$18.91 billion (31 December 2011 est.)

$14.91 billion (31 December 2011 est.)

country comparison to the world: 81

STOCK OF DIRECT FOREIGN INVESTMENT - ABROAD:

$1.166 billion (2012 est.)

$667.8 million (2011 est.)

country comparison to the world: 89

EXCHANGE RATES:

patacas (MOP) per US dollar -

8 (2017 est.)

7.9951 (2016 est.)

7.9951 (2015 est.)

7.985 (2014 est.)

7.9871 (2013 est.)

ENERGY :: MACAU

ELECTRICITY ACCESS:

electrification - total population: 100% (2016)

ELECTRICITY - PRODUCTION:

929 million kWh (2016 est.)

country comparison to the world: 154

ELECTRICITY - CONSUMPTION:

5.077 billion kWh (2016 est.)

country comparison to the world: 123

ELECTRICITY - EXPORTS:

0 kWh (2016 est.)

country comparison to the world: 162

ELECTRICITY - IMPORTS:

4.306 billion kWh (2016 est.)

country comparison to the world: 43

ELECTRICITY - INSTALLED GENERATING CAPACITY:

472,000 kW (2016 est.)

country comparison to the world: 150

ELECTRICITY - FROM FOSSIL FUELS:

100% of total installed capacity (2016 est.)

country comparison to the world: 12

ELECTRICITY - FROM NUCLEAR FUELS:

0% of total installed capacity (2017 est.)

country comparison to the world: 132

ELECTRICITY - FROM HYDROELECTRIC PLANTS:

0% of total installed capacity (2017 est.)

country comparison to the world: 184

ELECTRICITY - FROM OTHER RENEWABLE SOURCES:

0% of total installed capacity (2017 est.)

country comparison to the world: 200

CRUDE OIL - PRODUCTION:

0 bbl/day (2018 est.)

country comparison to the world: 165

CRUDE OIL - EXPORTS:

0 bbl/day (2015 est.)

country comparison to the world: 157

CRUDE OIL - IMPORTS:

0 bbl/day (2015 est.)

country comparison to the world: 156

CRUDE OIL - PROVED RESERVES:

0 bbl (1 January 2018 est.)

country comparison to the world: 160

REFINED PETROLEUM PRODUCTS - PRODUCTION:

0 bbl/day (2015 est.)

country comparison to the world: 168

REFINED PETROLEUM PRODUCTS - CONSUMPTION:

12,700 bbl/day (2016 est.)

country comparison to the world: 158

REFINED PETROLEUM PRODUCTS - EXPORTS:

0 bbl/day (2015 est.)

country comparison to the world: 174

REFINED PETROLEUM PRODUCTS - IMPORTS:

14,180 bbl/day (2015 est.)

country comparison to the world: 137

NATURAL GAS - PRODUCTION:

0 cu m (2017 est.)

country comparison to the world: 161

NATURAL GAS - CONSUMPTION:

178.2 million cu m (2017 est.)

country comparison to the world: 107

NATURAL GAS - EXPORTS:

0 cu m (2017 est.)

country comparison to the world: 142

NATURAL GAS - IMPORTS:

175.5 million cu m (2017 est.)

country comparison to the world: 73

NATURAL GAS - PROVED RESERVES:

0 cu m (1 January 2014 est.)

country comparison to the world: 162

CARBON DIOXIDE EMISSIONS FROM CONSUMPTION OF ENERGY:

2.563 million Mt (2017 est.)

country comparison to the world: 153

COMMUNICATIONS :: MACAU

TELEPHONES - FIXED LINES:

total subscriptions: 142,000

subscriptions per 100 inhabitants: 24 (July 2016 est.)

country comparison to the world: 131

TELEPHONES - MOBILE CELLULAR:

total subscriptions: 1,969,972

subscriptions per 100 inhabitants: 327 (July 2016 est.)

country comparison to the world: 150

TELEPHONE SYSTEM:

general assessment: modern communication facilities maintained for domestic and international services; high mobile subscriber numbers and mobile penetration with 4 network operators and a mobile virtual network operator (MNVO), offering 4 G and LTE services; 5G wireless technology for commercial use in 2020, possible synchronizing with neighbouring regions (2018)

domestic: fixed-line 20 per 100 and mobile-celluar 344 per 100 persons (2018)

international: country code - 853; landing point for the SEA-ME-WE-3 submarine cable network that provides links to Asia, Africa, Australia, the Middle East, and Europe; HF radiotelephone communication facility; satellite earth station - 1 Intelsat (Indian Ocean) (2019)

BROADCAST MEDIA:

local government dominates broadcast media; 2 television stations operated by the government with one broadcasting in Portuguese and the other in Cantonese and Mandarin; 1 cable TV and 4 satellite TV services available; 3 radio stations broadcasting, of which 2 are government-operated (2019)

INTERNET COUNTRY CODE:

.mo

INTERNET USERS:

total: 460,000

percent of population: 77.6% (July 2016 est.)

country comparison to the world: 149

BROADBAND - FIXED SUBSCRIPTIONS:

total: 177,959

subscriptions per 100 inhabitants: 30 (2017 est.)

country comparison to the world: 111

MILITARY AND SECURITY :: MACAU

MILITARY AND SECURITY FORCES:

no regular indigenous military forces

MILITARY - NOTE:

defense is the responsibility of China and the Chinese People's Liberation Army (PLA) maintains a garrison in Macau.

TRANSPORTATION :: MACAU

NATIONAL AIR TRANSPORT SYSTEM:

number of registered air carriers: 1 (registered in China) (2015)

inventory of registered aircraft operated by air carriers: 17 (registered in China) (2015)

annual passenger traffic on registered air carriers: 2,276,436 (2015)

annual freight traffic on registered air carriers: 25.435 million mt-km (2015)

CIVIL AIRCRAFT REGISTRATION COUNTRY CODE PREFIX:

B-M (2016)

AIRPORTS:

1 (2013)

country comparison to the world: 227

AIRPORTS - WITH PAVED RUNWAYS:

total: 1 (2017)

over 3,047 m: 1 (2017)

HELIPORTS:

2 (2013)

ROADWAYS:

total: 428 km (2017)

paved: 428 km (2017)

country comparison to the world: 193

MERCHANT MARINE:

total: 1

by type: other 1 (2018)

country comparison to the world: 173

PORTS AND TERMINALS:

major seaport(s): Macau

TRANSNATIONAL ISSUES :: MACAU

DISPUTES - INTERNATIONAL:

none

ILLICIT DRUGS:

transshipment point for drugs going into mainland China; consumer of opiates and amphetamines

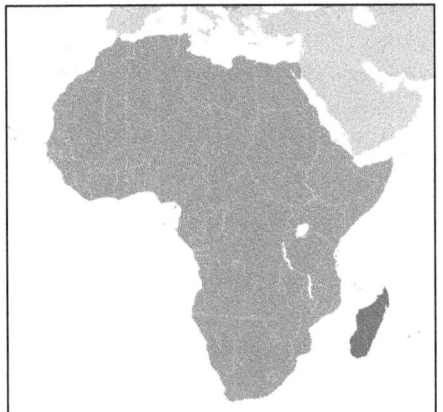

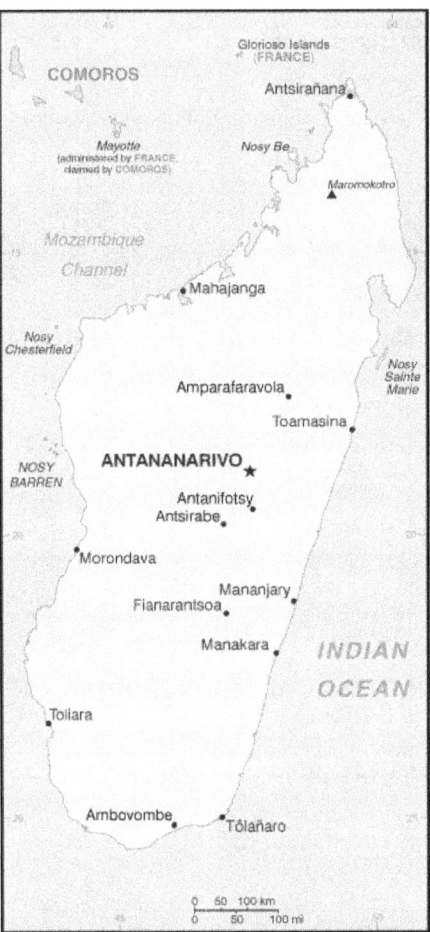

AFRICA :: MADAGASCAR

INTRODUCTION :: MADAGASCAR

BACKGROUND:

Madagascar was one of the last major habitable landmasses on earth settled by humans. While some transient visits to the island may have occurred in the centuries B.C., large-scale settlement began between A.D. 350 and 550 with settlers from present-day Indonesia. The island attracted Arab and Persian traders as early as the 7th century, and migrants from Africa arrived around A.D. 1000. Madagascar was a pirate stronghold during the late 17th and early 18th centuries, and served as a slave trading center into the 19th century. From the 16th to the late 19th century, a native Merina Kingdom dominated much of Madagascar. The island was conquered by the French in 1896 who made it a colony; independence was regained in 1960.

During 1992-93, free presidential and National Assembly elections were held ending 17 years of single-party rule. In 1997, in the second presidential race, Didier RATSIRAKA, the leader during the 1970s and 1980s, returned to the presidency. The 2001 presidential election was contested between the followers of Didier RATSIRAKA and Marc RAVALOMANANA, nearly causing secession of half of the country. In 2002, the High Constitutional Court announced RAVALOMANANA the winner. RAVALOMANANA won a second term in 2006 but, following protests in 2009, handed over power to the military, which then conferred the presidency on the mayor of Antananarivo, Andry RAJOELINA, in what amounted to a coup d'etat. Following a lengthy mediation process led by the Southern African Development Community, Madagascar held UN-supported presidential and parliamentary elections in 2013. Former de facto finance minister Hery RAJAONARIMAMPIANINA won a runoff election in December 2013 and was inaugurated in January 2014. In January 2019, RAJOELINA was declared the winner of a runoff election against RAVALOMANANA; both RATSIRAKA and RAJAONARIMAMPIANINA also ran in the first round of the election, which took place in November 2018.

GEOGRAPHY :: MADAGASCAR

LOCATION:
Southern Africa, island in the Indian Ocean, east of Mozambique

GEOGRAPHIC COORDINATES:
20 00 S, 47 00 E

MAP REFERENCES:
Africa

AREA:
total: 587,041 sq km

land: 581,540 sq km

water: 5,501 sq km

country comparison to the world: 48

AREA - COMPARATIVE:
almost four times the size of Georgia; slightly less than twice the size of

Arizona

LAND BOUNDARIES:

0 km

COASTLINE:

4,828 km

MARITIME CLAIMS:

territorial sea: 12 nm

exclusive economic zone: 200 nm

contiguous zone: 24 nm

continental shelf: 200 nm or 100 nm from the 2,500-m isobath

CLIMATE:

tropical along coast, temperate inland, arid in south

TERRAIN:

narrow coastal plain, high plateau and mountains in center

ELEVATION:

mean elevation: 615 m

lowest point: Indian Ocean 0 m

highest point: Maromokotro 2,876 m

NATURAL RESOURCES:

graphite, chromite, coal, bauxite, rare earth elements, salt, quartz, tar sands, semiprecious stones, mica, fish, hydropower

LAND USE:

agricultural land: 71.1% (2011 est.)

arable land: 6% (2011 est.) / permanent crops: 1% (2011 est.) / permanent pasture: 64.1% (2011 est.)

forest: 21.5% (2011 est.)

other: 7.4% (2011 est.)

IRRIGATED LAND:

10,860 sq km (2012)

POPULATION DISTRIBUTION:

most of population lives on the eastern half of the island; significant clustering is found in the central highlands and eastern coastline

NATURAL HAZARDS:

periodic cyclones; drought; and locust infestation

volcanism: Madagascar's volcanoes have not erupted in historical times

ENVIRONMENT - CURRENT ISSUES:

erosion and soil degradation results from deforestation and overgrazing; desertification; agricultural fires; surface water contaminated with raw sewage and other organic wastes; wildlife preservation (endangered species of flora and fauna unique to the island)

ENVIRONMENT - INTERNATIONAL AGREEMENTS:

party to: Biodiversity, Climate Change, Climate Change-Kyoto Protocol, Desertification, Endangered Species, Hazardous Wastes, Law of the Sea, Marine Life Conservation, Ozone Layer Protection, Ship Pollution, Wetlands

signed, but not ratified: none of the selected agreements

GEOGRAPHY - NOTE:

world's fourth-largest island; strategic location along Mozambique Channel; despite Madagascar's close proximity to the African continent, ocean currents isolate the island resulting in high rates of endemic plant and animal species; approximately 90% of the flora and fauna on the island are found nowhere else

PEOPLE AND SOCIETY :: MADAGASCAR

POPULATION:

25,683,610 (July 2018 est.)

country comparison to the world: 52

NATIONALITY:

noun: Malagasy (singular and plural)

adjective: Malagasy

ETHNIC GROUPS:

Malayo-Indonesian (Merina and related Betsileo), Cotiers (mixed African, Malayo-Indonesian, and Arab ancestry - Betsimisaraka, Tsimihety, Antaisaka, Sakalava), French, Indian, Creole, Comoran

LANGUAGES:

French (official), Malagasy (official), English

RELIGIONS:

Christian, indigenous, Muslim

DEMOGRAPHIC PROFILE:

Madagascar's youthful population – just over 60% are under the age of 25 – and high total fertility rate of more than 4 children per women ensures that the Malagasy population will continue its rapid growth trajectory for the foreseeable future. The population is predominantly rural and poor; chronic malnutrition is prevalent, and large families are the norm. Many young Malagasy girls are withdrawn from school, marry early (often pressured to do so by their parents), and soon begin having children. Early childbearing, coupled with Madagascar's widespread poverty and lack of access to skilled health care providers during delivery, increases the risk of death and serious health problems for young mothers and their babies.

Child marriage perpetuates gender inequality and is prevalent among the poor, the uneducated, and rural households – as of 2013, of Malagasy women aged 20 to 24, more than 40% were married and more than a third had given birth by the age of 18. Although the legal age for marriage is 18, parental consent is often given for earlier marriages or the law is flouted, especially in rural areas that make up nearly 65% of the country. Forms of arranged marriage whereby young girls are married to older men in exchange for oxen or money are traditional. If a union does not work out, a girl can be placed in another marriage, but the dowry paid to her family diminishes with each unsuccessful marriage.

Madagascar's population consists of 18 main ethnic groups, all of whom speak the same Malagasy language. Most Malagasy are multi-ethnic, however, reflecting the island's diversity of settlers and historical contacts (see Background). Madagascar's legacy of hierarchical societies practicing domestic slavery (most notably the Merina Kingdom of the 16th to the 19th century) is evident today in persistent class tension, with some ethnic groups maintaining a caste system. Slave descendants are vulnerable to unequal access to education and jobs, despite Madagascar's constitutional guarantee of free compulsory primary education and its being party to several international conventions on human rights. Historical distinctions also remain between central highlanders and coastal people.

AGE STRUCTURE:

0-14 years: 39.55% (male 5,119,804 /female 5,037,438)

15-24 years: 20.23% (male 2,608,996 /female 2,587,745)

25-54 years: 32.42% (male 4,160,278 /female 4,166,538)

55-64 years: 4.45% (male 560,072 /female 581,963)

65 years and over: 3.35% (male 390,094 /female 470,682) (2018 est.)

DEPENDENCY RATIOS:

total dependency ratio: 80.1 (2015 est.)

youth dependency ratio: 75 (2015 est.)

elderly dependency ratio: 5.1 (2015 est.)

potential support ratio: 19.6 (2015 est.)

MEDIAN AGE:

total: 19.9 years (2018 est.)

male: 19.7 years

female: 20.1 years

country comparison to the world: 195

POPULATION GROWTH RATE:

2.46% (2018 est.)

country comparison to the world: 24

BIRTH RATE:

31 births/1,000 population (2018 est.)

country comparison to the world: 33

DEATH RATE:

6.4 deaths/1,000 population (2018 est.)

country comparison to the world: 147

NET MIGRATION RATE:

0 migrant(s)/1,000 population (2018 est.)

country comparison to the world: 90

POPULATION DISTRIBUTION:

most of population lives on the eastern half of the island; significant clustering is found in the central highlands and eastern coastline

URBANIZATION:

urban population: 37.9% of total population (2019)

rate of urbanization: 4.48% annual rate of change (2015-20 est.)

MAJOR URBAN AREAS - POPULATION:

3.21 million ANTANANARIVO (capital) (2019)

SEX RATIO:

at birth: 1.03 male(s)/female

0-14 years: 1.02 male(s)/female

15-24 years: 1.01 male(s)/female

25-54 years: 1 male(s)/female

55-64 years: 0.96 male(s)/female

65 years and over: 0.83 male(s)/female

total population: 1 male(s)/female (2018 est.)

MOTHER'S MEAN AGE AT FIRST BIRTH:

19.5 years (2008/09 est.)

note: median age at first birth among women 25-29

MATERNAL MORTALITY RATE:

335 deaths/100,000 live births (2017 est.)

country comparison to the world: 33

INFANT MORTALITY RATE:

total: 40.1 deaths/1,000 live births (2018 est.)

male: 43.8 deaths/1,000 live births

female: 36.2 deaths/1,000 live births

country comparison to the world: 44

LIFE EXPECTANCY AT BIRTH:

total population: 66.6 years (2018 est.)

male: 65.1 years

female: 68.2 years

country comparison to the world: 175

TOTAL FERTILITY RATE:

3.95 children born/woman (2018 est.)

country comparison to the world: 35

CONTRACEPTIVE PREVALENCE RATE:

47.9% (2017)

DRINKING WATER SOURCE:

improved:

urban: 81.6% of population

rural: 35.3% of population

total: 51.5% of population

unimproved:

urban: 18.4% of population

rural: 64.7% of population

total: 48.5% of population (2015 est.)

CURRENT HEALTH EXPENDITURE:

6% (2016)

PHYSICIANS DENSITY:

0.18 physicians/1,000 population (2014)

HOSPITAL BED DENSITY:

0.2 beds/1,000 population (2010)

SANITATION FACILITY ACCESS:

improved:

urban: 18% of population (2015 est.)

rural: 8.7% of population (2015 est.)

total: 12% of population (2015 est.)

unimproved:

urban: 82% of population (2015 est.)

rural: 91.3% of population (2015 est.)

total: 88% of population (2015 est.)

HIV/AIDS - ADULT PREVALENCE RATE:

0.3% (2018 est.)

country comparison to the world: 92

HIV/AIDS - PEOPLE LIVING WITH HIV/AIDS:

39,000 (2018 est.)

country comparison to the world: 69

HIV/AIDS - DEATHS:

1,700 (2018 est.)

country comparison to the world: 51

MAJOR INFECTIOUS DISEASES:

degree of risk: very high (2016)

food or waterborne diseases: bacterial diarrhea, hepatitis A, and typhoid fever (2016)

vectorborne diseases: malaria and dengue fever (2016)

water contact diseases: schistosomiasis (2016)

animal contact diseases: rabies (2016)

OBESITY - ADULT PREVALENCE RATE:

5.3% (2016)

country comparison to the world: 180

CHILDREN UNDER THE AGE OF 5 YEARS UNDERWEIGHT:

32.9% (2013)

country comparison to the world: 6

EDUCATION EXPENDITURES:

2.8% of GDP (2014)

country comparison to the world: 150

LITERACY:

definition: age 15 and over can read and write

total population: 64.7%

male: 66.7%

female: 62.6% (2015 est.)

SCHOOL LIFE EXPECTANCY (PRIMARY TO TERTIARY EDUCATION):

total: 10 years

male: 10 years

female: 10 years (2016)

UNEMPLOYMENT, YOUTH AGES 15-24:

total: 1%

male: 1%

female: 1% (2012 est.)

country comparison to the world: 179

GOVERNMENT :: MADAGASCAR

COUNTRY NAME:

conventional long form: Republic of Madagascar

conventional short form: Madagascar

local long form: Republique de Madagascar/Repoblikan'i Madagasikara

local short form: Madagascar/Madagasikara

former: Malagasy Republic

etymology: the name "Madageiscar" was first used by the 13th-century Venetian explorer Marco POLO, as a corrupted transliteration of Mogadishu, the Somali port with which POLO confused the island

GOVERNMENT TYPE:

semi-presidential republic

CAPITAL:

name: Antananarivo

geographic coordinates: 18 55 S, 47 31 E

time difference: UTC+3 (8 hours ahead of Washington, DC, during Standard Time)

etymology: the name, which means "City of the Thousand," was bestowed by 17th century King Adrianjakaking to honor the soldiers assigned to guard the city

ADMINISTRATIVE DIVISIONS:

6 provinces (faritany); Antananarivo, Antsiranana, Fianarantsoa, Mahajanga, Toamasina, Toliara

INDEPENDENCE:

26 June 1960 (from France)

NATIONAL HOLIDAY:

Independence Day, 26 June (1960)

CONSTITUTION:

history: previous 1992; latest passed by referendum 17 November 2010, promulgated 11 December 2010

amendments: proposed by the president of the republic in consultation with the cabinet or supported by a least two thirds of both the Senate and National Assembly membership; passage requires at least three-fourths approval of both the Senate and National Assembly and approval in a referendum; constitutional articles, including the form and powers of government, the sovereignty of the state, and the autonomy of Madagascar's collectivities, cannot be amended (2017)

LEGAL SYSTEM:

civil law system based on the old French civil code and customary law in matters of marriage, family, and obligation

INTERNATIONAL LAW ORGANIZATION PARTICIPATION:

accepts compulsory ICJ jurisdiction with reservations; accepts ICCt jurisdiction

CITIZENSHIP:

citizenship by birth: no

citizenship by descent only: the father must be a citizen of Madagascar; in the case of a child born out of wedlock, the mother must be a citizen

dual citizenship recognized: no

residency requirement for naturalization: unknown

SUFFRAGE:

18 years of age; universal

EXECUTIVE BRANCH:

chief of state: President Andry RAJOELINA (since 21 January 2019) (2019)

head of government: Prime Minister Christian NTSAY (since 6 June 2018 and re-appointed 19 July 2019)

cabinet: Council of Ministers appointed by the prime minister

elections/appointments: president directly elected by absolute majority popular vote in 2 rounds if needed for a 5-year term (eligible for a second term); election last held on 7 November and 19 December 2018 (next to be held in 2023); prime minister nominated by the National Assembly, appointed by the president

election results: Andry RAJOELINA elected President in second round; percent of vote - Andry RAJOELINA (TGV) 55.7%, Marc RAVALOMANANA 44.3% (TIM)

LEGISLATIVE BRANCH:

description:
bicameral Parliament consists of: Senate or Antenimieran-Doholona (reestablished on 22 January 2016, following the December 2015 senatorial election) (63 seats; 42 members indirectly elected by an electoral college of municipal, communal, regional, and provincial leaders and 21 appointed by the president of the republic; members serve 5-year terms)
National Assembly or Antenimierampirenena (151 seats; 87 members directly elected in single-seat constituencies by simple majority vote and 64 directly elected in multi-seat constituencies by closed-list proportional representation vote; members serve 5-year terms)

elections: Senate - last held 29 December 2015 (next to be held in 2021)
National Assembly - last held on 27 May 2019

election results: Senate - percent of vote by party - NA; seats by party - HVM 34, TIM 3, MAPAR 2, LEADER-Fanilo 1, independent 2, appointed by the president 21; composition - men 51, women 12, percent of women 19%
National Assembly - percent of vote by party -Independent Pro-HVM 18%, MAPAR 17%, MAPAR pro-HVM 16%, VPM-MMM 10%, VERTS 3%, LEADER FANILO 3%, HIARAKA ISIKA 3%, GPS/ARD 7%, INDEPENDENT 9%, TAMBATRA 1%, TIM 13%; composition - men 120, women 31, percent of women 20.5%; note - total National Assembly percent of women 20.1%

JUDICIAL BRANCH:

highest courts: Supreme Court or Cour Supreme (consists of 11 members; addresses judicial administration issues only); High Constitutional Court or Haute Cour Constitutionnelle (consists of 9 members); note - the judiciary includes a High Court of Justice responsible for adjudicating crimes and misdemeanors by government officials, including the president

judge selection and term of office: Supreme Court heads elected by the president and judiciary officials to serve 3-year, single renewable terms; High Constitutional Court members appointed - 3 each by the president, by both legislative bodies, and by the Council of Magistrates; members serve single, 7-year terms

subordinate courts: Courts of Appeal; Courts of First Instance

POLITICAL PARTIES AND LEADERS:

Economic liberalism and democratic action for national recovery or LEADER FANILO [Jean Max RAKOTOMAMONJY]
FOMBA [Ny Rado RAFALIMANANA]

Gideons fighting against poverty in Madagascar (Gedeona Miady amin'ny Fahantrana eto Madagascar) or GFFM [Andre Christian Dieu Donne MAILHOL]
Green party or VERTS (Antoko Maintso) [Alexandre GEORGET]
I Love Madagascar (Tiako I Madagasikara) or TIM [Marc RAVALOMANANA]
Malagasy aware (Malagasy Tonga Saina) or MTS [Roland RATSIRAKA]
Malagasy raising together (Malagasy Miara-Miainga) or MMM [Hajo ANDRIANAINARIVELO]
New Force for Madagascar (Hery Vaovao ho an'ny Madagasikara) or HVM [Hery Martial RAJAONARIMAMPIANINA Rakotoarimanana]
Total Refoundation of Madagascar (Refondation Totale de Madagascar) or RTM [Joseph Martin RANDRIAMAMPIONONA]
Vanguard for the renovation of Madagascar (Avant-Garde pour la renovation de Madagascar) or AREMA [Didier RATSIRAKA]
Young Malagasies Determined (Malagasy: Tanora malaGasy Vonona) or TGV [Andry RAJOELINA]and MAPAR [Andry RAJOELINA], and IRD (We are all with Andy Rajoelina) [Andry RAJOELINA]

INTERNATIONAL ORGANIZATION PARTICIPATION:

ACP, AfDB, AU, CD, COMESA, EITI (candidate country), FAO, G-77, IAEA, IBRD, ICAO, ICC (NGOs), ICCt, ICRM, IDA, IFAD, IFC, IFRCS, ILO, IMF, IMO, InOC, Interpol, IOC, IOM, IPU, ISO (correspondent), ITSO, ITU, ITUC (NGOs), MIGA, NAM, OIF, OPCW, PCA, SADC, UN, UNCTAD, UNESCO, UNHCR, UNIDO, UNWTO, UPU, WCO, WFTU (NGOs), WHO, WIPO, WMO, WTO

DIPLOMATIC REPRESENTATION IN THE US:

(vacant)

chancery: 2374 Massachusetts Avenue NW, Washington, DC 20008

telephone: [1] (202) 265-5525

FAX: [1] (202) 265-3034

consulate(s) general: New York

DIPLOMATIC REPRESENTATION FROM THE US:

chief of mission: Ambassador Michael PELLETIER (since 14 February 2019)

telephone: [261] 20 23 480 00

embassy: Lot 207A, Point Liberty, Andranoro, Antehiroka, 105 Antananarivo

mailing address: B.P. 620, Antsahavola, Antananarivo

FAX: [261] 20 23 480 35 or [261] 33 44 328 17

FLAG DESCRIPTION:

two equal horizontal bands of red (top) and green with a vertical white band of the same width on hoist side; by tradition, red stands for sovereignty, green for hope, white for purity

NATIONAL SYMBOL(S):

traveller's palm, zebu; national colors: red, green, white

NATIONAL ANTHEM:

name: "Ry Tanindraza nay malala o" (Oh, Our Beloved Fatherland)

lyrics/music: Pasteur RAHAJASON/Norbert RAHARISOA

note: adopted 1959

ECONOMY :: MADAGASCAR

ECONOMY - OVERVIEW:

Madagascar is a mostly unregulated economy with many untapped natural resources, but no capital markets, a weak judicial system, poorly enforced contracts, and rampant government corruption. The country faces challenges to improve education, healthcare, and the environment to boost long-term economic growth. Agriculture, including fishing and forestry, is a mainstay of the economy, accounting for more than one-fourth of GDP and employing roughly 80% of the population. Deforestation and erosion, aggravated by bushfires, slash-and-burn clearing techniques, and the use of firewood as the primary source of fuel, are serious concerns to the agriculture dependent economy.

After discarding socialist economic policies in the mid-1990s, Madagascar followed a World Bank- and IMF-led policy of privatization and liberalization until a 2009 coup d'état led many nations, including the United States, to suspend non-humanitarian aid until a democratically-elected president was inaugurated in 2014. The pre-coup strategy had placed the country on a slow and steady growth path from an extremely low starting point. Exports of apparel boomed after gaining duty-free access to the US market in 2000 under the African Growth and Opportunity Act (AGOA); however, Madagascar's failure to comply with the requirements of the AGOA led to the termination of the country's duty-free access in January 2010, a sharp fall in textile production, a loss of more than 100,000 jobs, and a GDP drop of nearly 11%.

Madagascar regained AGOA access in January 2015 and ensuing growth has been slow and fragile. Madagascar produces around 80% of the world's vanilla and its reliance on this commodity for most of its foreign exchange is a significant source of vulnerability. Economic reforms have been modest and the country's financial sector remains weak, limiting the use of monetary policy to control inflation. An ongoing IMF program aims to strengthen financial and investment management capacity.

GDP (PURCHASING POWER PARITY):

$39.85 billion (2017 est.)

$38.25 billion (2016 est.)

$36.72 billion (2015 est.)

note: data are in 2017 dollars

country comparison to the world: 119

GDP (OFFICIAL EXCHANGE RATE):

$11.5 billion (2017 est.)

GDP - REAL GROWTH RATE:

4.2% (2017 est.)

4.2% (2016 est.)

3.1% (2015 est.)

country comparison to the world: 72

GDP - PER CAPITA (PPP):

$1,600 (2017 est.)

$1,500 (2016 est.)

$1,500 (2015 est.)

note: data are in 2017 dollars

country comparison to the world: 218

GROSS NATIONAL SAVING:

14.8% of GDP (2017 est.)

15.4% of GDP (2016 est.)

11.2% of GDP (2015 est.)

country comparison to the world: 138

GDP - COMPOSITION, BY END USE:

household consumption: 67.1% (2017 est.)

government consumption: 11.2% (2017 est.)

investment in fixed capital: 15.1% (2017 est.)

investment in inventories: 8.8% (2017 est.)

exports of goods and services: 31.5% (2017 est.)

imports of goods and services: -33.7% (2017 est.)

GDP - COMPOSITION, BY SECTOR OF ORIGIN:

agriculture: 24% (2017 est.)

industry: 19.5% (2017 est.)

services: 56.4% (2017 est.)

AGRICULTURE - PRODUCTS:

coffee, vanilla, sugarcane, cloves, cocoa, rice, cassava (manioc, tapioca), beans, bananas, peanuts; livestock products

INDUSTRIES:

meat processing, seafood, soap, beer, leather, sugar, textiles, glassware, cement, automobile assembly plant, paper, petroleum, tourism, mining

INDUSTRIAL PRODUCTION GROWTH RATE:

5.2% (2017 est.)

country comparison to the world: 54

LABOR FORCE:

13.4 million (2017 est.)

country comparison to the world: 43

UNEMPLOYMENT RATE:

1.8% (2017 est.)

1.8% (2016 est.)

country comparison to the world: 17

POPULATION BELOW POVERTY LINE:

70.7% (2012 est.)

HOUSEHOLD INCOME OR CONSUMPTION BY PERCENTAGE SHARE:

lowest 10%: 2.2%

highest 10%: 34.7% (2010 est.)

DISTRIBUTION OF FAMILY INCOME - GINI INDEX:

41 (2012)

42.7 (2010)

country comparison to the world: 59

BUDGET:

revenues: 1.828 billion (2017 est.)

expenditures: 2.136 billion (2017 est.)

TAXES AND OTHER REVENUES:

15.9% (of GDP) (2017 est.)

country comparison to the world: 185

BUDGET SURPLUS (+) OR DEFICIT (-):

-2.7% (of GDP) (2017 est.)

country comparison to the world: 123

PUBLIC DEBT:

36% of GDP (2017 est.)

38.4% of GDP (2016 est.)

country comparison to the world: 148

FISCAL YEAR:

calendar year

INFLATION RATE (CONSUMER PRICES):

8.3% (2017 est.)

6.7% (2016 est.)

country comparison to the world: 199

CENTRAL BANK DISCOUNT RATE:

9.5% (31 December 2017)

8.3% (31 December 2016)

country comparison to the world: 28

COMMERCIAL BANK PRIME LENDING RATE:

60% (31 December 2017 est.)

60% (31 December 2016 est.)

country comparison to the world: 1

STOCK OF NARROW MONEY:

$1.045 billion (31 December 2017 est.)

$849.1 million (31 December 2016 est.)

country comparison to the world: 156

STOCK OF BROAD MONEY:

$1.045 billion (31 December 2017 est.)

$849.1 million (31 December 2016 est.)

country comparison to the world: 161

STOCK OF DOMESTIC CREDIT:

$2.345 billion (31 December 2017 est.)

$1.746 billion (31 December 2016 est.)

country comparison to the world: 145

MARKET VALUE OF PUBLICLY TRADED SHARES:

NA

CURRENT ACCOUNT BALANCE:

-$35 million (2017 est.)

$57 million (2016 est.)

country comparison to the world: 77

EXPORTS:

$2.29 billion (2017 est.)

$2.26 billion (2016 est.)

country comparison to the world: 137

EXPORTS - PARTNERS:

France 24.8%, US 16.5%, China 6.7%, Germany 6.5%, Japan 6%, Netherlands 4.7% (2017)

EXPORTS - COMMODITIES:

coffee, vanilla, shellfish, sugar, cotton cloth, clothing, chromite, petroleum products, gems, ilmenite, cobalt, nickel

IMPORTS:

$2.738 billion (2017 est.)

$2.427 billion (2016 est.)

country comparison to the world: 153

IMPORTS - COMMODITIES:

capital goods, petroleum, consumer goods, food

IMPORTS - PARTNERS:

China 18.7%, India 9.3%, France 6.4%, South Africa 5.6%, UAE 5.3% (2017)

RESERVES OF FOREIGN EXCHANGE AND GOLD:

$1.6 billion (31 December 2017 est.)

$1.076 billion (31 December 2016 est.)

country comparison to the world: 124

DEBT - EXTERNAL:

$4.089 billion (31 December 2017 est.)

$3.425 billion (31 December 2016 est.)

country comparison to the world: 139

STOCK OF DIRECT FOREIGN INVESTMENT - AT HOME:

$6.461 billion (2014 est.)

$6.462 billion (2013 est.)

country comparison to the world: 102

STOCK OF DIRECT FOREIGN INVESTMENT - ABROAD:

NA

EXCHANGE RATES:

Malagasy ariary (MGA) per US dollar -

3,116.1 (2017 est.)

3,176.5 (2016 est.)

3,176.5 (2015 est.)

2,933.5 (2014 est.)

2,414.8 (2013 est.)

ENERGY :: MADAGASCAR

ELECTRICITY ACCESS:

population without electricity: 20 million (2017)

electrification - total population: 22.9% (2016)

electrification - urban areas: 67.3% (2016)

electrification - rural areas: 17.3% (2016)

ELECTRICITY - PRODUCTION:

1.706 billion kWh (2016 est.)

country comparison to the world: 142

ELECTRICITY - CONSUMPTION:

1.587 billion kWh (2016 est.)

country comparison to the world: 147

ELECTRICITY - EXPORTS:

0 kWh (2016 est.)

country comparison to the world: 163

ELECTRICITY - IMPORTS:

0 kWh (2016 est.)

country comparison to the world: 169

ELECTRICITY - INSTALLED GENERATING CAPACITY:

675,400 kW (2016 est.)

country comparison to the world: 136

ELECTRICITY - FROM FOSSIL FUELS:

74% of total installed capacity (2016 est.)

country comparison to the world: 97

ELECTRICITY - FROM NUCLEAR FUELS:

0% of total installed capacity (2017 est.)

country comparison to the world: 134

ELECTRICITY - FROM HYDROELECTRIC PLANTS:

24% of total installed capacity (2017 est.)

country comparison to the world: 80

ELECTRICITY - FROM OTHER RENEWABLE SOURCES:

2% of total installed capacity (2017 est.)

country comparison to the world: 141

CRUDE OIL - PRODUCTION:

0 bbl/day (2018 est.)

country comparison to the world: 167

CRUDE OIL - EXPORTS:

0 bbl/day (2015 est.)

country comparison to the world: 158

CRUDE OIL - IMPORTS:

0 bbl/day (2015 est.)

country comparison to the world: 158

CRUDE OIL - PROVED RESERVES:

0 bbl (1 January 2018 est.)

country comparison to the world: 162

REFINED PETROLEUM PRODUCTS - PRODUCTION:

0 bbl/day (2015 est.)

country comparison to the world: 170

REFINED PETROLEUM PRODUCTS - CONSUMPTION:

18,000 bbl/day (2016 est.)

country comparison to the world: 147

REFINED PETROLEUM PRODUCTS - EXPORTS:

0 bbl/day (2015 est.)

country comparison to the world: 175

REFINED PETROLEUM PRODUCTS - IMPORTS:

18,880 bbl/day (2015 est.)

country comparison to the world: 125

NATURAL GAS - PRODUCTION:

0 cu m (2017 est.)

country comparison to the world: 163

NATURAL GAS - CONSUMPTION:

0 cu m (2017 est.)

country comparison to the world: 169

NATURAL GAS - EXPORTS:

0 cu m (2017 est.)

country comparison to the world: 144

NATURAL GAS - IMPORTS:

0 cu m (2017 est.)

country comparison to the world: 151

NATURAL GAS - PROVED RESERVES:

0 cu m (1 January 2012 est.)

country comparison to the world: 164

CARBON DIOXIDE EMISSIONS FROM CONSUMPTION OF ENERGY:

4.021 million Mt (2017 est.)

country comparison to the world: 138

COMMUNICATIONS :: MADAGASCAR

TELEPHONES - FIXED LINES:

total subscriptions: 68,792

subscriptions per 100 inhabitants: less than 1 (2017 est.)

country comparison to the world: 150

TELEPHONES - MOBILE CELLULAR:

total subscriptions: 8,730,499

subscriptions per 100 inhabitants: 35 (2017 est.)

country comparison to the world: 93

TELEPHONE SYSTEM:

general assessment: system is above average for the region; competition among the four mobile service providers has spurred recent growth in the mobile market and helped the service to be less expensive for the consumer; LTE services available (2018)

domestic: less than 1 per 100 for fixed-line and mobile-cellular teledensity about 35 per 100 persons (2018)

international: country code - 261; landing points for the EASSy, METISS, and LION fiber-optic submarine cable systems connecting to numerous Indian Ocean Islands, South Africa, and Eastern African countries; satellite earth stations - 2 (1 Intelsat - Indian Ocean, 1 Intersputnik - Atlantic Ocean region) (2019)

BROADCAST MEDIA:

state-owned Radio Nationale Malagasy (RNM) and Television Malagasy (TVM) have an extensive national network reach; privately owned radio and TV broadcasters in cities and major towns; state-run radio dominates in rural areas; relays of 2 international broadcasters are available in Antananarivo (2019)

INTERNET COUNTRY CODE:

.mg

INTERNET USERS:

total: 1,151,563

percent of population: 4.7% (July 2016 est.)

country comparison to the world: 130

BROADBAND - FIXED SUBSCRIPTIONS:

total: 25,062

subscriptions per 100 inhabitants: less than 1 (2017 est.)

country comparison to the world: 144

MILITARY AND SECURITY :: MADAGASCAR

MILITARY EXPENDITURES:

0.6% of GDP (2018)

0.58% of GDP (2017)

0.59% of GDP (2016)

0.6% of GDP (2015)

0.65% of GDP (2014)

country comparison to the world: 142

MILITARY AND SECURITY FORCES:

People's Armed Forces: Intervention Force, Development Force, Navy, Air Force (2018)

MILITARY SERVICE AGE AND OBLIGATION:

Madagascar has an all-volunteer military; 18-25 years of age for males; service obligation 18 months; women are permitted to serve in all branches (2018)

TRANSPORTATION :: MADAGASCAR

NATIONAL AIR TRANSPORT SYSTEM:

number of registered air carriers: 3 (2015)

inventory of registered aircraft operated by air carriers: 11 (2015)

annual passenger traffic on registered air carriers: 546,946 (2015)

annual freight traffic on registered air carriers: 30,512,607 mt-km (2015)

CIVIL AIRCRAFT REGISTRATION COUNTRY CODE PREFIX:

5R (2016)

AIRPORTS:

83 (2013)

country comparison to the world: 66

AIRPORTS - WITH PAVED RUNWAYS:

total: 26 (2017)

over 3,047 m: 1 (2017)

2,438 to 3,047 m: 2 (2017)

1,524 to 2,437 m: 6 (2017)

914 to 1,523 m: 16 (2017)

under 914 m: 1 (2017)

AIRPORTS - WITH UNPAVED RUNWAYS:

total: 57 (2013)

1,524 to 2,437 m: 1 (2013)

914 to 1,523 m: 38 (2013)

under 914 m: 18 (2013)

RAILWAYS:

total: 836 km (2018)

narrow gauge: 836 km 1.000-m gauge (2018)

country comparison to the world: 96

ROADWAYS:

total: 31,640 km (2018)

country comparison to the world: 95

WATERWAYS:

600 km (432 km navigable) (2011)

country comparison to the world: 79

MERCHANT MARINE:

total: 28

by type: general cargo 15, oil tanker 3, other 10 (2018)

country comparison to the world: 128

PORTS AND TERMINALS:

major seaport(s): Antsiranana (Diego Suarez), Mahajanga, Toamasina, Toliara (Tulear)

TRANSNATIONAL ISSUES :: MADAGASCAR

DISPUTES - INTERNATIONAL:

claims Bassas da India, Europa Island, Glorioso Islands, and Juan de Nova Island (all administered by France); the vegetated drying cays of Banc du Geyser, which were claimed by Madagascar in 1976, also fall within the EEZ claims of the Comoros and France (Glorioso Islands, part of the French Southern and Antarctic Lands)

ILLICIT DRUGS:

illicit producer of cannabis (cultivated and wild varieties) used mostly for domestic consumption; transshipment point for heroin

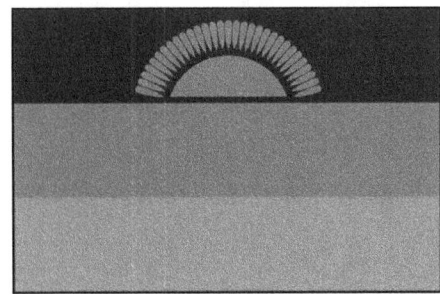
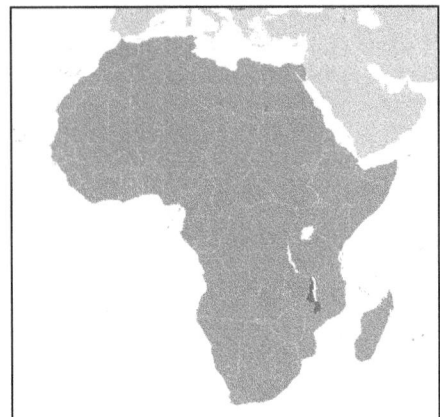
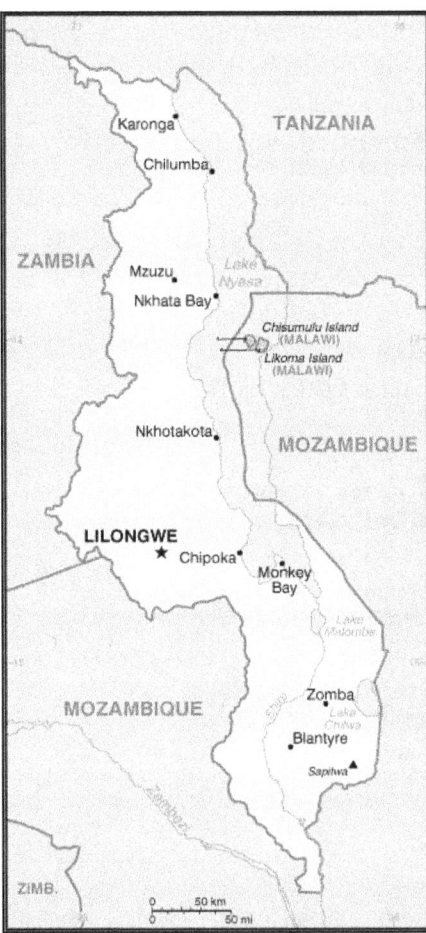

AFRICA :: MALAWI

INTRODUCTION :: MALAWI

BACKGROUND:

Established in 1891, the British protectorate of Nyasaland became the independent nation of Malawi in 1964. After three decades of one-party rule under President Hastings Kamuzu BANDA, the country held multiparty presidential and parliamentary elections in 1994, under a provisional constitution that came into full effect the following year. Bakili MULUZI became the first freely elected president of Malawi when he won the presidency in 1994; he won re-election in 1999. President Bingu wa MUTHARIKA, elected in 2004 after a failed attempt by the previous president to amend the constitution to permit another term, struggled to assert his authority against his predecessor and subsequently started his own party, the Democratic Progressive Party in 2005. MUTHARIKA was reelected to a second term in 2009. He oversaw some economic improvement in his first term, but was accused of economic mismanagement and poor governance in his second term. He died abruptly in 2012 and was succeeded by vice president, Joyce BANDA, who had earlier started her own party, the People's Party. MUTHARIKA's brother, Peter MUTHARIKA, defeated BANDA in the 2014 election. Population growth, increasing pressure on agricultural lands, corruption, and the scourge of HIV/AIDS pose major problems for Malawi.

GEOGRAPHY :: MALAWI

LOCATION:
Southern Africa, east of Zambia, west and north of Mozambique

GEOGRAPHIC COORDINATES:
13 30 S, 34 00 E

MAP REFERENCES:
Africa

AREA:
total: 118,484 sq km

land: 94,080 sq km

water: 24,404 sq km

country comparison to the world: 101

AREA - COMPARATIVE:
slightly smaller than Pennsylvania

LAND BOUNDARIES:
total: 2,857 km

border countries (3): Mozambique 1498 km, Tanzania 512 km, Zambia 847 km

COASTLINE:
0 km (landlocked)

MARITIME CLAIMS:
none (landlocked)

CLIMATE:
sub-tropical; rainy season (November to May); dry season (May to November)

TERRAIN:
narrow elongated plateau with rolling plains, rounded hills, some mountains

ELEVATION:
mean elevation: 779 m

lowest point: junction of the Shire River and international boundary with Mozambique 37 m

highest point: Sapitwa (Mount Mlanje) 3,002 m

NATURAL RESOURCES:
limestone, arable land, hydropower, unexploited deposits of uranium, coal, and bauxite

LAND USE:
agricultural land: 59.2% (2011 est.)

arable land: 38.2% (2011 est.) / **permanent crops:** 1.4% (2011 est.) / **permanent pasture:** 19.6% (2011 est.)

forest: 34% (2011 est.)

other: 6.8% (2011 est.)

IRRIGATED LAND:
740 sq km (2012)

POPULATION DISTRIBUTION:
population density is highest south of Lake Nyasa

NATURAL HAZARDS:
flooding; droughts; earthquakes

ENVIRONMENT - CURRENT ISSUES:
deforestation; land degradation; water pollution from agricultural runoff, sewage, industrial wastes; siltation of spawning grounds endangers fish populations; negative effects of climate change (extreme high temperatures, changing precipatation pattens)

ENVIRONMENT - INTERNATIONAL AGREEMENTS:
party to: Biodiversity, Climate Change, Climate Change-Kyoto Protocol, Desertification, Endangered Species, Environmental Modification, Hazardous Wastes, Marine Life Conservation, Ozone Layer Protection, Ship Pollution, Wetlands

signed, but not ratified: Law of the Sea

GEOGRAPHY - NOTE:
landlocked; Lake Nyasa, some 580 km long, is the country's most prominent physical feature; it contains more fish species than any other lake on earth

PEOPLE AND SOCIETY :: MALAWI

POPULATION:
19,842,560 (July 2018 est.)

note: estimates for this country explicitly take into account the effects of excess mortality due to AIDS; this can result in lower life expectancy, higher infant mortality, higher death rates, lower population growth rates, and changes in the distribution of population by age and sex than would otherwise be expected

country comparison to the world: 60

NATIONALITY:
noun: Malawian(s)

adjective: Malawian

ETHNIC GROUPS:
Chewa 34.3%, Lomwe 18.8%, Yao 13.2%, Ngoni 10.4%, Tumbuka 9.2%, Sena 3.8%, Mang'anja 3.2%, Tonga 1.8%, Nyanja 1.8%, Nkhonde 1%, other 2.2%, foreign .3% (2018 est.)

LANGUAGES:
English (official), Chichewa (common), Chinyanja, Chiyao, Chitumbuka, Chilomwe, Chinkhonde, Chingoni, Chisena, Chitonga, Chinyakyusa, Chilambya

RELIGIONS:
Protestant 33.5% (includes Church of Central Africa Presbyterian 14.2%, Seventh Day Adventist/Baptist 9.4%, Pentecostal 7.6%, Anglican 2.3%), Roman Catholic 17.2%, other Christian 26.6%, Muslim 13.8%, traditionalist 1.1%, other 5.6%, none 2.1% (2018 est.)

DEMOGRAPHIC PROFILE:
Malawi has made great improvements in maternal and child health, but has made less progress in reducing its high fertility rate. In both rural and urban areas, very high proportions of mothers are receiving prenatal care and skilled birth assistance, and most children are being vaccinated. Malawi's fertility rate, however, has only declined slowly, decreasing from more than 7 children per woman in the 1980s to about 5.5 today. Nonetheless, Malawians prefer smaller families than in the past, and women are increasingly using contraceptives to prevent or space pregnancies. Rapid population growth and high population density is putting pressure on Malawi's land, water, and forest resources. Reduced plot sizes and increasing vulnerability to climate change, further threaten the sustainability of Malawi's agriculturally based economy and will worsen food shortages. About 80% of the population is employed in agriculture.

Historically, Malawians migrated abroad in search of work, primarily to South Africa and present-day Zimbabwe, but international migration became uncommon after the 1970s, and most migration in recent years has been internal. During the colonial period, Malawians regularly migrated to southern Africa as contract farm laborers, miners, and domestic servants. In the decade and a half after independence in 1964, the Malawian Government sought to transform its economy from one dependent on small-scale farms to one based on estate agriculture. The resulting demand for wage labor induced more than 300,000 Malawians to return home between the mid-1960s and the mid-1970s. In recent times, internal migration has generally been local, motivated more by marriage than economic reasons.

AGE STRUCTURE:
0-14 years: 46.17% (male 4,560,940 /female 4,600,184)

15-24 years: 20.58% (male 2,023,182 /female 2,059,765)

25-54 years: 27.57% (male 2,717,613 /female 2,752,983)

55-64 years: 3% (male 284,187 /female 310,393)

65 years and over: 2.69% (male 234,776 /female 298,537) (2018 est.)

DEPENDENCY RATIOS:
total dependency ratio: 91 (2015 est.)

youth dependency ratio: 85.3 (2015 est.)

elderly dependency ratio: 5.7 (2015 est.)

potential support ratio: 17.4 (2015 est.)

MEDIAN AGE:
total: 16.6 years (2018 est.)

male: 16.5 years

female: 16.8 years

country comparison to the world: 223

POPULATION GROWTH RATE:
3.31% (2018 est.)

country comparison to the world: 3

BIRTH RATE:
40.7 births/1,000 population (2018 est.)

country comparison to the world: 8

DEATH RATE:
7.7 deaths/1,000 population (2018 est.)

country comparison to the world: 100

NET MIGRATION RATE:
0 migrant(s)/1,000 population (2018 est.)

country comparison to the world: 91

POPULATION DISTRIBUTION:
population density is highest south of Lake Nyasa

URBANIZATION:
urban population: 17.2% of total population (2019)

rate of urbanization: 4.19% annual rate of change (2015-20 est.)

MAJOR URBAN AREAS - POPULATION:

1.075 million LILONGWE (capital), 905,000 Blantyre-Limbe (2019)

SEX RATIO:
at birth: 1.02 male(s)/female

0-14 years: 0.99 male(s)/female

15-24 years: 0.98 male(s)/female

25-54 years: 0.99 male(s)/female

55-64 years: 0.92 male(s)/female

65 years and over: 0.79 male(s)/female

total population: 0.98 male(s)/female (2018 est.)

MOTHER'S MEAN AGE AT FIRST BIRTH:
18.9 years (2015/16 est.)

note: median age at first birth among women 25-29

MATERNAL MORTALITY RATE:
349 deaths/100,000 live births (2017 est.)

country comparison to the world: 31

INFANT MORTALITY RATE:
total: 42.1 deaths/1,000 live births (2018 est.)

male: 48.6 deaths/1,000 live births

female: 35.5 deaths/1,000 live births

country comparison to the world: 42

LIFE EXPECTANCY AT BIRTH:
total population: 62.2 years (2018 est.)

male: 60.2 years

female: 64.3 years

country comparison to the world: 200

TOTAL FERTILITY RATE:
5.43 children born/woman (2018 est.)

country comparison to the world: 9

CONTRACEPTIVE PREVALENCE RATE:
59.2% (2015/16)

DRINKING WATER SOURCE:
improved:

urban: 95.7% of population

rural: 89.1% of population

total: 90.2% of population

unimproved:

urban: 4.3% of population

rural: 10.9% of population

total: 9.8% of population (2015 est.)

CURRENT HEALTH EXPENDITURE:
9.8% (2016)

PHYSICIANS DENSITY:
0.02 physicians/1,000 population (2016)

HOSPITAL BED DENSITY:
1.3 beds/1,000 population (2011)

SANITATION FACILITY ACCESS:
improved:

urban: 47.3% of population (2015 est.)

rural: 39.8% of population (2015 est.)

total: 41% of population (2015 est.)

unimproved:

urban: 52.7% of population (2015 est.)

rural: 60.2% of population (2015 est.)

total: 59% of population (2015 est.)

HIV/AIDS - ADULT PREVALENCE RATE:
9.2% (2018 est.)

country comparison to the world: 9

HIV/AIDS - PEOPLE LIVING WITH HIV/AIDS:
1 million (2018 est.)

country comparison to the world: 10

HIV/AIDS - DEATHS:
13,000 (2018 est.)

country comparison to the world: 18

MAJOR INFECTIOUS DISEASES:
degree of risk: very high (2016)

food or waterborne diseases: bacterial and protozoal diarrhea, hepatitis A, and typhoid fever (2016)

vectorborne diseases: malaria and dengue fever (2016)

water contact diseases: schistosomiasis (2016)

animal contact diseases: rabies (2016)

OBESITY - ADULT PREVALENCE RATE:
5.8% (2016)

country comparison to the world: 173

CHILDREN UNDER THE AGE OF 5 YEARS UNDERWEIGHT:
11.8% (2015)

country comparison to the world: 56

EDUCATION EXPENDITURES:
4% of GDP (2017)

country comparison to the world: 110

LITERACY:
definition: age 15 and over can read and write

total population: 62.1%

male: 69.8%

female: 55.2% (2015 est.)

SCHOOL LIFE EXPECTANCY (PRIMARY TO TERTIARY EDUCATION):
total: 11 years

male: 11 years

female: 11 years (2011)

UNEMPLOYMENT, YOUTH AGES 15-24:
total: 8.5%

male: 6.7%

female: 10.6% (2017 est.)

country comparison to the world: 140

GOVERNMENT :: MALAWI

COUNTRY NAME:
conventional long form: Republic of Malawi

conventional short form: Malawi

local long form: Dziko la Malawi

local short form: Malawi

former: British Central African Protectorate, Nyasaland Protectorate, Nyasaland

etymology: named for the East African Maravi Kingdom of the 16th century; the word "maravi" means "fire flames"

GOVERNMENT TYPE:
presidential republic

CAPITAL:
name: Lilongwe

geographic coordinates: 13 58 S, 33 47 E

time difference: UTC+2 (7 hours ahead of Washington, DC, during Standard Time)

etymology: named after the Lilongwe River that flows through the city

ADMINISTRATIVE DIVISIONS:
28 districts; Balaka, Blantyre, Chikwawa, Chiradzulu, Chitipa, Dedza, Dowa, Karonga, Kasungu, Likoma, Lilongwe, Machinga, Mangochi, Mchinji, Mulanje, Mwanza, Mzimba, Neno, Ntcheu, Nkhata Bay, Nkhotakota, Nsanje, Ntchisi, Phalombe, Rumphi, Salima, Thyolo, Zomba

INDEPENDENCE:
6 July 1964 (from the UK)

NATIONAL HOLIDAY:
Independence Day, 6 July (1964); note - also called Republic Day since 6 July 1966

CONSTITUTION:
history: previous 1953 (preindependence), 1966; latest drafted January to May 1994,

approved 16 May 1994, entered into force 18 May 1995

amendments: proposed by the National Assembly; passage of amendments affecting constitutional articles, including the sovereignty and territory of the state, fundamental constitutional principles, human rights, voting rights, and the judiciary, requires majority approval in a referendum and majority approval by the Assembly; passage of other amendments requires at least two-thirds majority vote of the Assembly; amended several times, last in 2017 (2018)

LEGAL SYSTEM:

mixed legal system of English common law and customary law; judicial review of legislative acts in the Supreme Court of Appeal

INTERNATIONAL LAW ORGANIZATION PARTICIPATION:

accepts compulsory ICJ jurisdiction with reservations; accepts ICCt jurisdiction

CITIZENSHIP:

citizenship by birth: no

citizenship by descent only: at least one parent must be a citizen of Malawi

dual citizenship recognized: no

residency requirement for naturalization: 7 years

SUFFRAGE:

18 years of age; universal

EXECUTIVE BRANCH:

chief of state: President Arthur Peter MUTHARIKA (since 31 May 2014); Vice President Everton CHIMULIRENJI (since 28 May 2019; note - the president is both chief of state and head of government

head of government: President Arthur Peter MUTHARIKA (since 31 May 2014); Vice President Everton CHIMULIRENJI (since 28 May 2019)

cabinet: Cabinet named by the president

elections/appointments: president directly elected by simple majority popular vote for a 5-year term (eligible for a second term); election last held on 21 May 2019 (next to be held in May 2024)

election results: Peter MUTHARIKA elected president; percent of vote - Peter MUTHARIKA (DPP) 38.6%, Lazarus CHAKWERA (MCP) 35.4%, Saulos CHILIMA (UTM) 20.2%, Atupele MULUZI (UDF) 4.7%, other 3.1%

LEGISLATIVE BRANCH:

description: unicameral National Assembly (193 seats; members directly elected in single-seat constituencies by simple majority vote to serve 5-year terms)

elections: last held on 21 May 2019 (next to be held in May 2024)

election results: percent of vote by party - n/a; seats by party - DPP 62, MCP 55, UDF 10, PP 5, other 5, independent 55, vacant 1; composition - men 161, women 32, percent of women 16.6%

JUDICIAL BRANCH:

highest courts: Supreme Court of Appeal (consists of the chief justice and at least 3 judges)

judge selection and term of office: Supreme Court chief justice appointed by the president and confirmed by the National Assembly; other judges appointed by the president upon the recommendation of the Judicial Service Commission, which regulates judicial officers; judges serve until age 65

subordinate courts: High Court; magistrate courts; Industrial Relations Court; district and city traditional or local courts

POLITICAL PARTIES AND LEADERS:

Democratic Progressive Party or DPP [Peter MUTHARIKA]
Malawi Congress Party or MCP [Lazarus CHAKWERA]
Peoples Party or PP [Joyce BANDA]
United Democratic Front or UDF [Atupele MULUZI]
United Transformation Movement or UTM [Saulos CHILIMA]

INTERNATIONAL ORGANIZATION PARTICIPATION:

ACP, AfDB, AU, C, CD, COMESA, FAO, G-77, IAEA, IBRD, ICAO, ICCt, ICRM, IDA, IFAD, IFC, IFRCS, ILO, IMF, IMO, Interpol, IOC, IOM, IPU, ISO (correspondent), ITSO, ITU, ITUC (NGOs), MIGA, MINURSO, MONUSCO, NAM, OPCW, SADC, UN, UNCTAD, UNESCO, UNIDO, UNISFA, UNOCI, UNWTO, UPU, WCO, WFTU (NGOs), WHO, WIPO, WMO, WTO

DIPLOMATIC REPRESENTATION IN THE US:

Ambassador Edward Yakobe SAWERENGERA (since 16 September 2016)

chancery: 2408 Massachusetts Avenue NW, Washington, DC 20008

telephone: [1] (202) 721-0270

FAX: [1] (202) 721-0288

DIPLOMATIC REPRESENTATION FROM THE US:

chief of mission: Ambassador Robert SCOTT (since 6 August 2019)

telephone: 265 (0) 1773166

embassy: 16 Jomo Kenyatta Road, Lilongwe 3

mailing address: P.O. Box 30016, Lilongwe 3, Malawi

FAX: 265 (0) 1770471

FLAG DESCRIPTION:

three equal horizontal bands of black (top), red, and green with a radiant, rising, red sun centered on the black band; black represents the native peoples, red the blood shed in their struggle for freedom, and green the color of nature; the rising sun represents the hope of freedom for the continent of Africa

NATIONAL SYMBOL(S):

lion; national colors: black, red, green

NATIONAL ANTHEM:

name: "Mulungu dalitsa Malawi" (Oh God Bless Our Land of Malawi)

lyrics/music: Michael-Fredrick Paul SAUKA

note: adopted 1964

ECONOMY :: MALAWI

ECONOMY - OVERVIEW:

Landlocked Malawi ranks among the world's least developed countries. The country's economic performance has historically been constrained by policy inconsistency, macroeconomic instability, poor infrastructure, rampant corruption, high population growth, and poor health and education outcomes that limit labor productivity. The economy is predominately agricultural with about 80% of the population living in rural areas. Agriculture accounts for about one-third of GDP and 80% of export revenues. The performance of the tobacco sector is key to short-term growth as tobacco accounts for more than half of exports, although Malawi is looking to diversify away from tobacco to other cash crops.

The economy depends on substantial inflows of economic assistance from the IMF, the World Bank, and individual donor nations. Donors halted direct budget support from 2013 to 2016 because of concerns about corruption and fiscal carelessness, but the World Bank resumed budget support in May 2017. In 2006, Malawi was approved for relief under the Heavily Indebted Poor Countries (HIPC) program but recent increases in domestic borrowing mean that debt servicing in 2016 exceeded the levels prior to HIPC debt relief.

Heavily dependent on rain-fed agriculture, with corn being the staple crop, Malawi's economy was hit hard by the El Nino-driven drought in 2015 and 2016, and now faces threat from the fall armyworm. The drought also slowed economic activity, led to two consecutive years of declining economic growth, and contributed to high inflation rates. Depressed food prices over 2017 led to a significant drop in inflation (from an average of 21.7% in 2016 to 12.3% in 2017), with a similar drop in interest rates.

GDP (PURCHASING POWER PARITY):
$22.42 billion (2017 est.)

$21.56 billion (2016 est.)

$21.08 billion (2015 est.)

note: data are in 2017 dollars

country comparison to the world: 145

GDP (OFFICIAL EXCHANGE RATE):
$6.24 billion (2017 est.)

GDP - REAL GROWTH RATE:
4% (2017 est.)

2.3% (2016 est.)

3% (2015 est.)

country comparison to the world: 79

GDP - PER CAPITA (PPP):
$1,200 (2017 est.)

$1,200 (2016 est.)

$1,200 (2015 est.)

note: data are in 2017 dollars

country comparison to the world: 223

GROSS NATIONAL SAVING:
3.9% of GDP (2017 est.)

-2.8% of GDP (2016 est.)

2.8% of GDP (2015 est.)

country comparison to the world: 178

GDP - COMPOSITION, BY END USE:
household consumption: 84.3% (2017 est.)

government consumption: 16.3% (2017 est.)

investment in fixed capital: 15.3% (2017 est.)

investment in inventories: 0% (2017 est.)

exports of goods and services: 27.9% (2017 est.)

imports of goods and services: -43.8% (2017 est.)

GDP - COMPOSITION, BY SECTOR OF ORIGIN:
agriculture: 28.6% (2017 est.)

industry: 15.4% (2017 est.)

services: 56% (2017 est.)

AGRICULTURE - PRODUCTS:
tobacco, sugarcane, tea, corn, potatoes, sweet potatoes, cassava (manioc, tapioca), sorghum, pulses, cotton, groundnuts, macadamia nuts, coffee; cattle, goats

INDUSTRIES:
tobacco, tea, sugar, sawmill products, cement, consumer goods

INDUSTRIAL PRODUCTION GROWTH RATE:
1.2% (2017 est.)

country comparison to the world: 150

LABOR FORCE:
7 million (2013 est.)

country comparison to the world: 66

LABOR FORCE - BY OCCUPATION:
agriculture: 76.9%

industry: 4.1%

services: 19% (2013 est.)

UNEMPLOYMENT RATE:
20.4% (2013 est.)

country comparison to the world: 187

POPULATION BELOW POVERTY LINE:
50.7% (2010 est.)

HOUSEHOLD INCOME OR CONSUMPTION BY PERCENTAGE SHARE:
lowest 10%: 2.2%

highest 10%: 37.5% (2010 est.)

DISTRIBUTION OF FAMILY INCOME - GINI INDEX:
46.1 (2010)

39 (2004)

country comparison to the world: 33

BUDGET:
revenues: 1.356 billion (2017 est.)

expenditures: 1.567 billion (2017 est.)

TAXES AND OTHER REVENUES:
21.7% (of GDP) (2017 est.)

country comparison to the world: 135

BUDGET SURPLUS (+) OR DEFICIT (-):
-3.4% (of GDP) (2017 est.)

country comparison to the world: 144

PUBLIC DEBT:
59.2% of GDP (2017 est.)

60.3% of GDP (2016 est.)

country comparison to the world: 75

FISCAL YEAR:
1 July - 30 June

INFLATION RATE (CONSUMER PRICES):
12.2% (2017 est.)

21.7% (2016 est.)

country comparison to the world: 205

CENTRAL BANK DISCOUNT RATE:
16% (31 December 2017 est.)

24% (31 December 2016 est.)

country comparison to the world: 9

COMMERCIAL BANK PRIME LENDING RATE:
38.1% (31 December 2017 est.)

44.11% (31 December 2016 est.)

country comparison to the world: 3

STOCK OF NARROW MONEY:
$632.4 million (31 December 2017 est.)

$534 million (31 December 2016 est.)

country comparison to the world: 164

STOCK OF BROAD MONEY:
$632.4 million (31 December 2017 est.)

$534 million (31 December 2016 est.)

country comparison to the world: 168

STOCK OF DOMESTIC CREDIT:
$1.161 billion (31 December 2017 est.)

$1.049 billion (31 December 2016 est.)

country comparison to the world: 165

MARKET VALUE OF PUBLICLY TRADED SHARES:
$18.97 million (31 December 2017 est.)

$8.643 million (31 December 2016 est.)

$101.9 million (31 December 2015 est.)

country comparison to the world: 122

CURRENT ACCOUNT BALANCE:
-$591 million (2017 est.)

-$744 million (2016 est.)

country comparison to the world: 122

EXPORTS:
$1.42 billion (2017 est.)

$1.361 billion (2016 est.)

country comparison to the world: 151

EXPORTS - PARTNERS:
Zimbabwe 13.1%, Mozambique 11.8%, Belgium 10.7%, South Africa 6.3%, Netherlands 5%, UK 4.7%, Germany 4.3%, US 4.2% (2017)

EXPORTS - COMMODITIES:
tobacco (55%), dried legumes (8.8%), sugar (6.7%), tea (5.7%), cotton (2%), peanuts, coffee, soy (2015 est.)

IMPORTS:
$2.312 billion (2017 est.)
$2.277 billion (2016 est.)
country comparison to the world: 161

IMPORTS - COMMODITIES:
food, petroleum products, semi-manufactures, consumer goods, transportation equipment

IMPORTS - PARTNERS:
South Africa 20.7%, China 14.2%, India 11.6%, UAE 7%, Netherlands 4.4% (2017)

RESERVES OF FOREIGN EXCHANGE AND GOLD:
$780.2 million (31 December 2017 est.)
$585.7 million (31 December 2016 est.)
country comparison to the world: 140

DEBT - EXTERNAL:
$2.102 billion (31 December 2017 est.)
$1.5 billion (31 December 2016 est.)
country comparison to the world: 152

STOCK OF DIRECT FOREIGN INVESTMENT - AT HOME:
$142.5 million (2015 est.)
country comparison to the world: 136

STOCK OF DIRECT FOREIGN INVESTMENT - ABROAD:
NA

EXCHANGE RATES:
Malawian kwachas (MWK) per US dollar -
731.69 (2017 est.)
720.1 (2016 est.)
713.85 (2015 est.)
499.6 (2014 est.)
424.9 (2013 est.)

ENERGY :: MALAWI

ELECTRICITY ACCESS:
population without electricity: 17 million (2017)
electrification - total population: 11% (2016)
electrification - urban areas: 42% (2016)
electrification - rural areas: 4% (2016)

ELECTRICITY - PRODUCTION:
1.42 billion kWh (2016 est.)
country comparison to the world: 144

ELECTRICITY - CONSUMPTION:
1.321 billion kWh (2016 est.)
country comparison to the world: 150

ELECTRICITY - EXPORTS:
0 kWh (2016 est.)
country comparison to the world: 164

ELECTRICITY - IMPORTS:
0 kWh (2016 est.)
country comparison to the world: 170

ELECTRICITY - INSTALLED GENERATING CAPACITY:
375,000 kW (2016 est.)
country comparison to the world: 152

ELECTRICITY - FROM FOSSIL FUELS:
1% of total installed capacity (2016 est.)
country comparison to the world: 212

ELECTRICITY - FROM NUCLEAR FUELS:
0% of total installed capacity (2017 est.)
country comparison to the world: 135

ELECTRICITY - FROM HYDROELECTRIC PLANTS:
93% of total installed capacity (2017 est.)
country comparison to the world: 7

ELECTRICITY - FROM OTHER RENEWABLE SOURCES:
6% of total installed capacity (2017 est.)
country comparison to the world: 100

CRUDE OIL - PRODUCTION:
0 bbl/day (2018 est.)
country comparison to the world: 168

CRUDE OIL - EXPORTS:
0 bbl/day (2015 est.)
country comparison to the world: 159

CRUDE OIL - IMPORTS:
0 bbl/day (2015 est.)
country comparison to the world: 159

CRUDE OIL - PROVED RESERVES:
0 bbl (1 January 2018 est.)
country comparison to the world: 163

REFINED PETROLEUM PRODUCTS - PRODUCTION:
0 bbl/day (2015 est.)
country comparison to the world: 171

REFINED PETROLEUM PRODUCTS - CONSUMPTION:
6,000 bbl/day (2016 est.)
country comparison to the world: 171

REFINED PETROLEUM PRODUCTS - EXPORTS:
0 bbl/day (2015 est.)
country comparison to the world: 176

REFINED PETROLEUM PRODUCTS - IMPORTS:
4,769 bbl/day (2015 est.)
country comparison to the world: 173

NATURAL GAS - PRODUCTION:
0 cu m (2017 est.)
country comparison to the world: 164

NATURAL GAS - CONSUMPTION:
0 cu m (2017 est.)
country comparison to the world: 170

NATURAL GAS - EXPORTS:
0 cu m (2017 est.)
country comparison to the world: 145

NATURAL GAS - IMPORTS:
0 cu m (2017 est.)
country comparison to the world: 152

NATURAL GAS - PROVED RESERVES:
0 cu m (2017 est.)
country comparison to the world: 165

CARBON DIOXIDE EMISSIONS FROM CONSUMPTION OF ENERGY:
1.082 million Mt (2017 est.)
country comparison to the world: 167

COMMUNICATIONS :: MALAWI

TELEPHONES - FIXED LINES:
total subscriptions: 17,337
subscriptions per 100 inhabitants: less than 1 (2017 est.)
country comparison to the world: 181

TELEPHONES - MOBILE CELLULAR:
total subscriptions: 7,772,503
subscriptions per 100 inhabitants: 40 (2017 est.)
country comparison to the world: 100

TELEPHONE SYSTEM:
general assessment: rudimentary; 2 fixed-line and 3 mobile-cellular operators govern the market; some mobile services to rural areas; in a resolution to discourage crime the regulatory has imposed SIM card registration since 2018; 50 licensed ISPs; DSL services are available; LTE services are available (2018)

domestic: limited fixed-line subscribership less than 1 per 100 households; mobile-cellular services are expanding but network coverage is limited and is based around the main urban areas; mobile-cellular subscribership approaching 40 per 100 households (2018)

international: country code - 265; satellite earth stations - 2 Intelsat (1 Indian Ocean, 1 Atlantic Ocean) (2019)

BROADCAST MEDIA:

radio is the main broadcast medium; privately owned Zodiak radio has the widest national broadcasting reach, followed by state-run radio; numerous private and community radio stations broadcast in cities and towns around the country; the largest TV network is government-owned, but at least 4 private TV networks broadcast in urban areas; relays of multiple international broadcasters are available (2019)

INTERNET COUNTRY CODE:
.mw

INTERNET USERS:
total: 1,785,369

percent of population: 9.6% (July 2016 est.)

country comparison to the world: 116

BROADBAND - FIXED SUBSCRIPTIONS:
total: 9,220

subscriptions per 100 inhabitants: less than 1 (2017 est.)

country comparison to the world: 170

MILITARY AND SECURITY :: MALAWI

MILITARY EXPENDITURES:
0.85% of GDP (2018)

0.76% of GDP (2017)

0.64% of GDP (2016)

0.63% of GDP (2015)

0.82% of GDP (2014)

country comparison to the world: 129

MILITARY AND SECURITY FORCES:
Malawi Defense Force (MDF): Army (includes Air Wing, Marine Unit); note - a 2017 amendment to Malawi's Defense Force Act established a separate Army, Air Force, and Maritime Force within the MDF, but these services have yet to develop independent budgets, chains of command, and training institutions (2019)

MILITARY SERVICE AGE AND OBLIGATION:
18 years of age for voluntary military service; high school equivalent required for enlisted recruits and college equivalent for officer recruits; initial engagement is 7 years for enlisted personnel and 10 years for officers (2014)

TRANSPORTATION :: MALAWI

NATIONAL AIR TRANSPORT SYSTEM:
number of registered air carriers: 1 (2015)

inventory of registered aircraft operated by air carriers: 2 (2015)

annual passenger traffic on registered air carriers: 6,010 (2015)

annual freight traffic on registered air carriers: 5,467 mt-km (2015)

CIVIL AIRCRAFT REGISTRATION COUNTRY CODE PREFIX:
7Q (2016)

AIRPORTS:
32 (2013)

country comparison to the world: 113

AIRPORTS - WITH PAVED RUNWAYS:
total: 7 (2017)

over 3,047 m: 1 (2017)

1,524 to 2,437 m: 2 (2017)

914 to 1,523 m: 4 (2017)

AIRPORTS - WITH UNPAVED RUNWAYS:
total: 25 (2013)

1,524 to 2,437 m: 1 (2013)

914 to 1,523 m: 11 (2013)

under 914 m: 13 (2013)

RAILWAYS:
total: 767 km (2014)

narrow gauge: 767 km 1.067-m gauge (2014)

country comparison to the world: 99

ROADWAYS:
total: 15,452 km (2015)

paved: 4,074 km (2015)

unpaved: 11,378 km (2015)

country comparison to the world: 121

WATERWAYS:
700 km (on Lake Nyasa [Lake Malawi] and Shire River) (2010)

country comparison to the world: 75

PORTS AND TERMINALS:
lake port(s): Chipoka, Monkey Bay, Nkhata Bay, Nkhotakota, Chilumba (Lake Nyasa)

TRANSNATIONAL ISSUES :: MALAWI

DISPUTES - INTERNATIONAL:
dispute with Tanzania over the boundary in Lake Nyasa (Lake Malawi) and the meandering Songwe River; Malawi contends that the entire lake up to the Tanzanian shoreline is its territory, while Tanzania claims the border is in the center of the lake; the conflict was reignited in 2012 when Malawi awarded a license to a British company for oil exploration in the lake

REFUGEES AND INTERNALLY DISPLACED PERSONS:
refugees (country of origin): 27,168 (Democratic Republic of the Congo) (refugees and asylum seekers), 8,752 (Burundi) (refugees and asylum seekers), 6,606 (Rwanda) (refugees and asylum seekers) (2019)

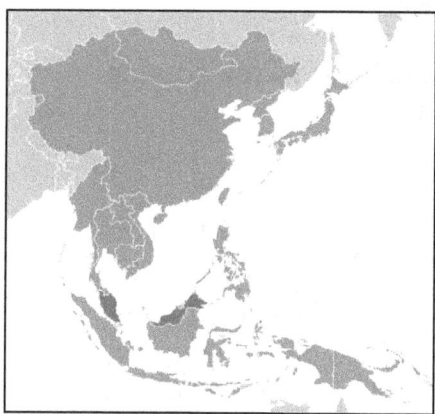

EAST ASIA / SOUTHEAST ASIA :: MALAYSIA

INTRODUCTION :: MALAYSIA

BACKGROUND:

During the late 18th and 19th centuries, Great Britain established colonies and protectorates in the area of current Malaysia; these were occupied by Japan from 1942 to 1945. In 1948, the British-ruled territories on the Malay Peninsula except Singapore formed the Federation of Malaya, which became independent in 1957. Malaysia was formed in 1963 when the former British colonies of Singapore, as well as Sabah and Sarawak on the northern coast of Borneo, joined the Federation. The first several years of the country's independence were marred by a communist insurgency, Indonesian confrontation with Malaysia, Philippine claims to Sabah, and Singapore's withdrawal in 1965. During the 22-year term of Prime Minister MAHATHIR bin Mohamad (1981-2003), Malaysia was successful in diversifying its economy from dependence on exports of raw materials to the development of manufacturing, services, and tourism. Prime Minister MAHATHIR and a newly-formed coalition of opposition parties defeated Prime Minister Mohamed NAJIB bin Abdul Razak in May 2018, ending over 60 years of uninterrupted rule by NAJIB's party.

GEOGRAPHY :: MALAYSIA

LOCATION:
Southeastern Asia, peninsula bordering Thailand and northern one-third of the island of Borneo, bordering Indonesia, Brunei, and the South China Sea, south of Vietnam

GEOGRAPHIC COORDINATES:
2 30 N, 112 30 E

MAP REFERENCES:
Southeast Asia

AREA:
total: 329,847 sq km
land: 328,657 sq km
water: 1,190 sq km
country comparison to the world: 68

AREA - COMPARATIVE:
slightly larger than New Mexico

LAND BOUNDARIES:
total: 2,742 km
border countries (3): Brunei 266 km, Indonesia 1881 km, Thailand 595 km

COASTLINE:
4,675 km (Peninsular Malaysia 2,068 km, East Malaysia 2,607 km)

MARITIME CLAIMS:
territorial sea: 12 nm
exclusive economic zone: 200 nm
continental shelf: 200-m depth or to the depth of exploitation; specified boundary in the South China Sea

CLIMATE:
tropical; annual southwest (April to October) and northeast (October to February) monsoons

TERRAIN:
coastal plains rising to hills and mountains

ELEVATION:
mean elevation: 419 m
lowest point: Indian Ocean 0 m
highest point: Gunung Kinabalu 4,095 m

NATURAL RESOURCES:
tin, petroleum, timber, copper, iron ore, natural gas, bauxite

LAND USE:
agricultural land: 23.2% (2011 est.)
arable land: 2.9% (2011 est.) / permanent crops: 19.4% (2011 est.) / permanent pasture: 0.9% (2011 est.)
forest: 62% (2011 est.)
other: 14.8% (2011 est.)

IRRIGATED LAND:
3,800 sq km (2012)

POPULATION DISTRIBUTION:
a highly uneven distribution with over 80% of the population residing on the Malay Peninsula

NATURAL HAZARDS:
flooding; landslides; forest fires

ENVIRONMENT - CURRENT ISSUES:
air pollution from industrial and vehicular emissions; water pollution from raw sewage; deforestation; smoke/haze from Indonesian forest fires; endangered species; coastal reclamation damaging mangroves and turtle nesting sites

ENVIRONMENT - INTERNATIONAL AGREEMENTS:
party to: Biodiversity, Climate Change, Climate Change-Kyoto Protocol, Desertification, Endangered Species, Hazardous Wastes, Law of the Sea, Marine Life Conservation, Ozone Layer Protection, Ship Pollution, Tropical Timber 83, Tropical Timber 94, Wetlands
signed, but not ratified: none of the selected agreements

GEOGRAPHY - NOTE:
strategic location along Strait of Malacca and southern South China Sea

PEOPLE AND SOCIETY :: MALAYSIA

POPULATION:
31,809,660 (July 2018 est.)

country comparison to the world: 42

NATIONALITY:
noun: Malaysian(s)

adjective: Malaysian

ETHNIC GROUPS:
Bumiputera 62% (Malays and indigenous peoples, including Orang Asli, Dayak, Anak Negeri), Chinese 20.6%, Indian 6.2%, other 0.9%, non-citizens 10.3% (2017 est.)

LANGUAGES:
Bahasa Malaysia (official), English, Chinese (Cantonese, Mandarin, Hokkien, Hakka, Hainan, Foochow), Tamil, Telugu, Malayalam, Panjabi, Thai

note: Malaysia has 134 living languages - 112 indigenous languages and 22 non-indigenous languages; in East Malaysia, there are several indigenous languages; the most widely spoken are Iban and Kadazan

RELIGIONS:
Muslim (official) 61.3%, Buddhist 19.8%, Christian 9.2%, Hindu 6.3%, Confucianism, Taoism, other traditional Chinese religions 1.3%, other 0.4%, none 0.8%, unspecified 1% (2010 est.)

AGE STRUCTURE:
0-14 years: 27.48% (male 4,498,796 /female 4,243,418)

15-24 years: 16.74% (male 2,704,318 /female 2,621,444)

25-54 years: 40.97% (male 6,587,529 /female 6,444,430)

55-64 years: 8.46% (male 1,364,858 /female 1,325,595)

65 years and over: 6.35% (male 957,841 /female 1,061,431) (2018 est.)

DEPENDENCY RATIOS:
total dependency ratio: 44.6 (2015 est.)

youth dependency ratio: 36.1 (2015 est.)

elderly dependency ratio: 8.5 (2015 est.)

potential support ratio: 11.8 (2015 est.)

MEDIAN AGE:
total: 28.7 years (2018 est.)

male: 28.4 years

female: 29 years

country comparison to the world: 130

POPULATION GROWTH RATE:
1.34% (2018 est.)

country comparison to the world: 82

BIRTH RATE:
18.8 births/1,000 population (2018 est.)

country comparison to the world: 87

DEATH RATE:
5.2 deaths/1,000 population (2018 est.)

country comparison to the world: 190

NET MIGRATION RATE:
-0.3 migrant(s)/1,000 population (2018 est.)

country comparison to the world: 117

POPULATION DISTRIBUTION:
a highly uneven distribution with over 80% of the population residing on the Malay Peninsula

URBANIZATION:
urban population: 76.6% of total population (2019)

rate of urbanization: 2.13% annual rate of change (2015-20 est.)

MAJOR URBAN AREAS - POPULATION:
7.78 million KUALA LUMPUR (capital), 1.003 million Johor Bahru, 800,000 Ipoh (2019)

SEX RATIO:
at birth: 1.07 male(s)/female

0-14 years: 1.06 male(s)/female

15-24 years: 1.03 male(s)/female

25-54 years: 1.02 male(s)/female

55-64 years: 1.03 male(s)/female

65 years and over: 0.9 male(s)/female

total population: 1.03 male(s)/female (2018 est.)

MATERNAL MORTALITY RATE:
29 deaths/100,000 live births (2017 est.)

country comparison to the world: 113

INFANT MORTALITY RATE:
total: 12.1 deaths/1,000 live births (2018 est.)

male: 14 deaths/1,000 live births

female: 10.1 deaths/1,000 live births

country comparison to the world: 112

LIFE EXPECTANCY AT BIRTH:
total population: 75.4 years (2018 est.)

male: 72.6 years

female: 78.4 years

country comparison to the world: 107

TOTAL FERTILITY RATE:
2.48 children born/woman (2018 est.)

country comparison to the world: 78

CONTRACEPTIVE PREVALENCE RATE:
52.2% (2014)

DRINKING WATER SOURCE:
improved:

urban: 100% of population

rural: 93% of population

total: 98.2% of population

unimproved:

urban: 0% of population

rural: 7% of population

total: 1.8% of population (2015 est.)

CURRENT HEALTH EXPENDITURE:
3.8% (2016)

PHYSICIANS DENSITY:
1.51 physicians/1,000 population (2015)

HOSPITAL BED DENSITY:
1.9 beds/1,000 population (2015)

SANITATION FACILITY ACCESS:
improved:

urban: 96.1% of population (2015 est.)

rural: 95.9% of population (2015 est.)

total: 96% of population (2015 est.)

unimproved:

urban: 3.9% of population (2015 est.)

rural: 4.1% of population (2015 est.)

total: 4% of population (2015 est.)

HIV/AIDS - ADULT PREVALENCE RATE:
0.4% (2018 est.)

country comparison to the world: 83

HIV/AIDS - PEOPLE LIVING WITH HIV/AIDS:
87,000 (2018 est.)

country comparison to the world: 47

HIV/AIDS - DEATHS:
2,600 (2018 est.)

country comparison to the world: 41

MAJOR INFECTIOUS DISEASES:
degree of risk: intermediate (2016)

food or waterborne diseases: bacterial diarrhea (2016)

vectorborne diseases: dengue fever (2016)

water contact diseases: leptospirosis (2016)

OBESITY - ADULT PREVALENCE RATE:
15.6% (2016)

country comparison to the world: 125

CHILDREN UNDER THE AGE OF 5 YEARS UNDERWEIGHT:
13.7% (2016)

country comparison to the world: 48

EDUCATION EXPENDITURES:
4.7% of GDP (2017)

country comparison to the world: 80

LITERACY:
definition: age 15 and over can read and write

total population: 94.6%

male: 96.2%

female: 93.2% (2015 est.)

SCHOOL LIFE EXPECTANCY (PRIMARY TO TERTIARY EDUCATION):
total: 13 years

male: 13 years

female: 14 years (2017)

UNEMPLOYMENT, YOUTH AGES 15-24:
total: 10.5%

male: 9.8%

female: 11.4% (2016 est.)

country comparison to the world: 125

GOVERNMENT :: MALAYSIA

COUNTRY NAME:
conventional long form: none

conventional short form: Malaysia

local long form: none

local short form: Malaysia

former: Federation of Malaya

etymology: the name means "Land of the Malays"

GOVERNMENT TYPE:
federal parliamentary constitutional monarchy

note: all Peninsular Malaysian states have hereditary rulers (commonly referred to as sultans) except Melaka (Malacca) and Pulau Pinang (Penang); those two states along with Sabah and Sarawak in East Malaysia have governors appointed by government; powers of state governments are limited by the federal constitution; under terms of federation, Sabah and Sarawak retain certain constitutional prerogatives (e.g., right to maintain their own immigration controls)

CAPITAL:
name: Kuala Lumpur; note - nearby Putrajaya is referred to as a federal government administrative center but not the capital; Parliament meets in Kuala Lumpur

geographic coordinates: 3 10 N, 101 42 E

time difference: UTC+8 (13 hours ahead of Washington, DC, during Standard Time)

etymology: the Malay word for "river junction or estuary" is "kuala" and "lumpur" means "mud"; together the words render the meaning of "muddy confluence"

ADMINISTRATIVE DIVISIONS:
13 states (negeri-negeri, singular - negeri); Johor, Kedah, Kelantan, Melaka, Negeri Sembilan, Pahang, Perak, Perlis, Pulau Pinang, Sabah, Sarawak, Selangor, Terengganu; and 1 federal territory (Wilayah Persekutuan) with 3 components, Kuala Lumpur, Labuan, and Putrajaya

INDEPENDENCE:
31 August 1957 (from the UK)

NATIONAL HOLIDAY:
Independence Day (or Merdeka Day), 31 August (1957) (independence of Malaya); Malaysia Day, 16 September (1963) (formation of Malaysia)

CONSTITUTION:
history: previous 1948; latest drafted 21 February 1957, effective 27 August 1957

amendments: proposed as a bill by Parliament; passage requires at least two-thirds majority vote by the Parliament membership in the bill's second and third readings; a number of constitutional sections are excluded from amendment or repeal; amended many times, last in 2010 (2017)

LEGAL SYSTEM:
mixed legal system of English common law, Islamic (sharia) law, and customary law; judicial review of legislative acts in the Federal Court at request of supreme head of the federation

INTERNATIONAL LAW ORGANIZATION PARTICIPATION:
has not submitted an ICJ jurisdiction declaration; non-party state to the ICCt

CITIZENSHIP:
citizenship by birth: no

citizenship by descent only: at least one parent must be a citizen of Malaysia

dual citizenship recognized: no

residency requirement for naturalization: 10 out 12 years preceding application

SUFFRAGE:
21 years of age; universal

EXECUTIVE BRANCH:
chief of state: King Sultan ABDULLAH Sultan Ahmad Shah (since 24 January 2019); note - King MUHAMMAD V (formerly known as Tuanku Muhammad Faris Petra) (selected on 14 October 2016; installed on 13 December 2016) resigned on 6 January 2019; the position of the king is primarily ceremonial, but he is the final arbiter on the appointment of the prime minister

head of government: Prime Minister MAHATHIR bin Mohamad (since 10 May 2018); Deputy Prime Minister WAN AZIZAH Wan Ismail (since 21 May 2018)

cabinet: Cabinet appointed by the prime minister from among members of Parliament with the consent of the king

elections/appointments: king elected by and from the hereditary rulers of 9 states for a 5-year term; election is on a rotational basis among rulers of the 9 states; election last held on 24 January 2019 (next to be held in 2024); prime minister designated from among members of the House of Representatives; following legislative elections, the leader who commands support of the majority of members in the House becomes prime minister

LEGISLATIVE BRANCH:
description: bicameral Parliament or Parlimen consists of:
Senate or Dewan Negara (70 seats; 44 members appointed by the king and 26 indirectly elected by 13 state legislatures; members serve 3-year terms)
House of Representatives or Dewan Rakyat (222 seats; members directly elected in single-seat constituencies by

simple majority vote to serve 5-year terms)

elections:
Senate - appointed
House of Representatives - last held on 9 May 2018 (next to be held no later than May 2023)

election results:
Senate - appointed; composition - men 54, women 14, percent of women 20.6%
House of Representatives - percent of vote by party/coalition - PH 45.6%, BN 33.8%, PAS 16.9%, WARISAN 2.3%, other 1.4%; seats by party/coalition - PH 113, BN 79, PAS 18, WARISAN 8, USA 1, independent 3; composition - men 199, women 23, percent of women 10.4%; note - total Parliament percent of women 12.8%

note: as of March 2019, seats by party - PH 129, BN 40, GS 18, GPS 18, WARISAN 9, GBS 3, UPKO 1, PSB 1, independent 3

JUDICIAL BRANCH:

highest courts: Federal Court (consists of the chief justice, president of the Court of Appeal, chief justice of the High Court of Malaya, chief judge of the High Court of Sabah and Sarawak, 8 judges, and 1 "additional" judge); note - Malaysia has a dual judicial hierarchy of civil and religious (sharia) courts

judge selection and term of office: Federal Court justices appointed by the monarch on advice of the prime minister; judges serve until mandatory retirement at age 66 with the possibility of a single 6-month extension

subordinate courts: Court of Appeal; High Court; Sessions Court; Magistrates' Court

POLITICAL PARTIES AND LEADERS:

National Front (Barisan Nasional) or BN:
Malaysian Chinese Association (Persatuan China Malaysia) or MCA [LIOW Tiong Lai]
Malaysian Indian Congress (Kongres India Malaysia) or MIC [S. SUBRAMANIAM]
United Malays National Organization or UMNO [MOHAMAD Hasan, acting]

Coalition of Hope (Pakatan Harapan) or PH (formerly the People's Alliance):
Democratic Action Party (Parti Tindakan Demokratik) or DAP [TAN Kok Wai]
Malaysian United Indigenous Party (Parti Pribumi Bersatu Malaysia) or PPBM [MAHATHIR bin Mohamad]
National Trust Party (Parti Amanah Negara) or AMANAH [Mohamad SABU]
People's Justice Party (Parti Keadilan Rakyat) or PKR [ANWAR Ibrahim]

Other:
Pan-Malaysian Islamic Party (Parti Islam se Malaysia) or PAS [Abdul HADI Awang]
Progressive Democratic Party or PDP [TIONG King Sing]
Sabah Heritage Party (Parti Warisan Sabah) or WARISAN [SHAFIE Apdal]
Sarawak Parties Alliance (Gabungan Parti Sarawak) or GPS [ABANG JOHARI Openg] (includes PBB, SUPP, PRS, PDP)
Sarawak People's Party (Parti Rakyat Sarawak) or PRS [James MASING]
Sarawak United People's Party (Parti Bersatu Rakyat Sarawak) or SUPP [Dr. SIM Kui Hian]
United Pasokmomogun Kadazandusun Murut Organization (Pertubuhan Pasko Momogun Kadazan Dusun Bersatu) or UPKO [Wilfred Madius TANGAU]
United Sabah Alliance or USA (Gabungan Sabah)
United Sabah Party (Parti Bersatu Sabah) or PBS [Maximus ONGKILI]
United Sabah People's (Party Parti Bersatu Rakyat Sabah) or PBRS [Joseph KURUP]
United Traditional Bumiputera Party (Parti Pesaka Bumiputera Bersata) or PBB; note - PBB is listed under GPS above

INTERNATIONAL ORGANIZATION PARTICIPATION:

ADB, APEC, ARF, ASEAN, BIS, C, CICA (observer), CP, D-8, EAS, FAO, G-15, G-77, IAEA, IBRD, ICAO, ICC (national committees), ICRM, IDA, IDB, IFAD, IFC, IFRCS, IHO, ILO, IMF, IMO, IMSO, Interpol, IOC, IPU, ISO, ITSO, ITU, ITUC (NGOs), MIGA, MINURSO, MONUSCO, NAM, OIC, OPCW, PCA, PIF (partner), UN, UNAMID, UNCTAD, UNESCO, UNIDO, UNIFIL, UNISFA, UNMIL, UNWTO, UPU, WCO, WFTU (NGOs), WHO, WIPO, WMO, WTO

DIPLOMATIC REPRESENTATION IN THE US:

Ambassador AZMIL Mohd Azbidi (since 8 April 2019)

chancery: 3516 International Court NW, Washington, DC 20008

telephone: [1] (202) 572-9700

FAX: [1] (202) 572-9882

consulate(s) general: Los Angeles, New York

DIPLOMATIC REPRESENTATION FROM THE US:

chief of mission: Ambassador Kamala Shirin LAKHDHIR (since 21 February 2017)

telephone: [60] (3) 2168-5000

embassy: 376 Jalan Tun Razak, 50400 Kuala Lumpur

mailing address: US Embassy Kuala Lumpur, APO AP 96535-8152

FAX: [60] (3) 2142-2207

FLAG DESCRIPTION:

14 equal horizontal stripes of red (top) alternating with white (bottom); there is a dark blue rectangle in the upper hoist-side corner bearing a yellow crescent and a yellow 14-pointed star; the flag is often referred to as Jalur Gemilang (Stripes of Glory); the 14 stripes stand for the equal status in the federation of the 13 member states and the federal government; the 14 points on the star represent the unity between these entities; the crescent is a traditional symbol of Islam; blue symbolizes the unity of the Malay people and yellow is the royal color of Malay rulers

note: the design is based on the flag of the US

NATIONAL SYMBOL(S):

tiger, hibiscus; national colors: gold, black

NATIONAL ANTHEM:

name: "Negaraku" (My Country)

lyrics/music: collective, led by Tunku ABDUL RAHMAN/Pierre Jean DE BERANGER

note: adopted 1957; full version only performed in the presence of the king; the tune, which was adopted from a popular French melody titled "La Rosalie," was originally the anthem of Perak, one of Malaysia's 13 states

ECONOMY :: MALAYSIA

ECONOMY - OVERVIEW:

Malaysia, an upper middle-income country, has transformed itself since the 1970s from a producer of raw materials into a multi-sector economy. Under current Prime Minister NAJIB, Malaysia is attempting to achieve high-income status by 2020 and to move further up the value-added production chain by attracting investments in high technology, knowledge-based industries and services. NAJIB's Economic Transformation Program is a series of projects and policy measures intended to accelerate the country's economic growth. The government has also taken steps to liberalize some services sub-sectors. Malaysia is vulnerable to a fall in world commodity prices or a general slowdown in global economic activity.

The NAJIB administration is continuing efforts to boost domestic demand and reduce the economy's dependence on exports. Domestic demand continues to anchor economic growth, supported mainly by private consumption, which accounts for 53% of GDP. Nevertheless, exports - particularly of electronics, oil and gas, and palm oil - remain a significant driver of the economy. In 2015, gross exports of goods and services were equivalent to 73% of GDP. The oil and gas sector supplied about 22% of government revenue in 2015, down significantly from prior years amid a decline in commodity prices and diversification of government revenues. Malaysia has embarked on a fiscal reform program aimed at achieving a balanced budget by 2020, including rationalization of subsidies and the 2015 introduction of a 6% value added tax. Sustained low commodity prices throughout the period not only strained government finances, but also shrunk Malaysia's current account surplus and weighed heavily on the Malaysian ringgit, which was among the region's worst performing currencies during 2013-17. The ringgit hit new lows following the US presidential election amid a broader selloff of emerging market assets.

Bank Negara Malaysia (the central bank) maintains adequate foreign exchange reserves; a well-developed regulatory regime has limited Malaysia's exposure to riskier financial instruments, although it remains vulnerable to volatile global capital flows. In order to increase Malaysia's competitiveness, Prime Minister NAJIB raised possible revisions to the special economic and social preferences accorded to ethnic Malays under the New Economic Policy of 1970, but retreated in 2013 after he encountered significant opposition from Malay nationalists and other vested interests. In September 2013 NAJIB launched the new Bumiputra Economic Empowerment Program, policies that favor and advance the economic condition of ethnic Malays.

Malaysia signed the 12-nation Trans-Pacific Partnership (TPP) free trade agreement in February 2016, although the future of the TPP remains unclear following the US withdrawal from the agreement. Along with nine other ASEAN members, Malaysia established the ASEAN Economic Community in 2015, which aims to advance regional economic integration.

GDP (PURCHASING POWER PARITY):

$933.3 billion (2017 est.)

$881.3 billion (2016 est.)

$845.6 billion (2015 est.)

note: data are in 2017 dollars

country comparison to the world: 26

GDP (OFFICIAL EXCHANGE RATE):

$312.4 billion (2017 est.)

GDP - REAL GROWTH RATE:

5.9% (2017 est.)

4.2% (2016 est.)

5.1% (2015 est.)

country comparison to the world: 37

GDP - PER CAPITA (PPP):

$29,100 (2017 est.)

$27,900 (2016 est.)

$27,100 (2015 est.)

note: data are in 2017 dollars

country comparison to the world: 71

GROSS NATIONAL SAVING:

28.5% of GDP (2017 est.)

28.3% of GDP (2016 est.)

28.2% of GDP (2015 est.)

country comparison to the world: 38

GDP - COMPOSITION, BY END USE:

household consumption: 55.3% (2017 est.)

government consumption: 12.2% (2017 est.)

investment in fixed capital: 25.3% (2017 est.)

investment in inventories: 0.3% (2017 est.)

exports of goods and services: 71.4% (2017 est.)

imports of goods and services: -64.4% (2017 est.)

GDP - COMPOSITION, BY SECTOR OF ORIGIN:

agriculture: 8.8% (2017 est.)

industry: 37.6% (2017 est.)

services: 53.6% (2017 est.)

AGRICULTURE - PRODUCTS:

Peninsular Malaysia - palm oil, rubber, cocoa, rice;Sabah - palm oil, subsistence crops; rubber, timber;Sarawak - palm oil, rubber, timber; pepper

INDUSTRIES:

Peninsular Malaysia - rubber and oil palm processing and manufacturing, petroleum and natural gas, light manufacturing, pharmaceuticals, medical technology, electronics and semiconductors, timber processing;Sabah - logging, petroleum and natural gas production;Sarawak - agriculture processing, petroleum and natural gas production, logging

INDUSTRIAL PRODUCTION GROWTH RATE:

5% (2017 est.)

country comparison to the world: 55

LABOR FORCE:

14.94 million (2017 est.)

country comparison to the world: 39

LABOR FORCE - BY OCCUPATION:

agriculture: 11%

industry: 36%

services: 53% (2012 est.)

UNEMPLOYMENT RATE:

3.4% (2017 est.)

3.5% (2016 est.)

country comparison to the world: 41

POPULATION BELOW POVERTY LINE:

3.8% (2009 est.)

HOUSEHOLD INCOME OR CONSUMPTION BY PERCENTAGE SHARE:

lowest 10%: 1.8%

highest 10%: 34.7% (2009 est.)

DISTRIBUTION OF FAMILY INCOME - GINI INDEX:

46.2 (2009)

49.2 (1997)

country comparison to the world: 32

BUDGET:

revenues: 51.25 billion (2017 est.)

expenditures: 60.63 billion (2017 est.)

TAXES AND OTHER REVENUES:

16.4% (of GDP) (2017 est.)

country comparison to the world: 180

BUDGET SURPLUS (+) OR DEFICIT (-):

-3% (of GDP) (2017 est.)

country comparison to the world: 133

PUBLIC DEBT:

54.1% of GDP (2017 est.)

56.2% of GDP (2016 est.)

note: this figure is based on the amount of federal government debt, RM501.6 billion ($167.2 billion) in 2012; this includes Malaysian Treasury bills and other government securities, as well as loans raised externally and bonds and notes issued overseas; this figure excludes debt issued by non-financial public enterprises and guaranteed by the federal government, which was an additional $47.7 billion in 2012

country comparison to the world: 86

FISCAL YEAR:

calendar year

INFLATION RATE (CONSUMER PRICES):

3.8% (2017 est.)

2.1% (2016 est.)

note: approximately 30% of goods are price-controlled

country comparison to the world: 151

CENTRAL BANK DISCOUNT RATE:

3% (31 December 2011)

2.83% (31 December 2010)

country comparison to the world: 111

COMMERCIAL BANK PRIME LENDING RATE:

4.61% (31 December 2017 est.)

4.52% (31 December 2016 est.)

country comparison to the world: 155

STOCK OF NARROW MONEY:

$107.5 billion (31 December 2017 est.)

$84.9 billion (31 December 2016 est.)

country comparison to the world: 37

STOCK OF BROAD MONEY:

$107.5 billion (31 December 2017 est.)

$84.9 billion (31 December 2016 est.)

country comparison to the world: 37

STOCK OF DOMESTIC CREDIT:

$482.7 billion (31 December 2017 est.)

$398.3 billion (31 December 2016 est.)

country comparison to the world: 26

MARKET VALUE OF PUBLICLY TRADED SHARES:

$383 billion (31 December 2015 est.)

$459 billion (31 December 2014 est.)

$500.4 billion (31 December 2013 est.)

country comparison to the world: 27

CURRENT ACCOUNT BALANCE:

$9.296 billion (2017 est.)

$7.236 billion (2016 est.)

country comparison to the world: 24

EXPORTS:

$187.9 billion (2017 est.)

$165.3 billion (2016 est.)

country comparison to the world: 28

EXPORTS - PARTNERS:

Singapore 15.1%, China 12.6%, US 9.4%, Japan 8.2%, Thailand 5.7%, Hong Kong 4.5% (2017)

EXPORTS - COMMODITIES:

semiconductors and electronic equipment, palm oil, petroleum and liquefied natural gas, wood and wood products, palm oil, rubber, textiles, chemicals, solar panels

IMPORTS:

$160.7 billion (2017 est.)

$141 billion (2016 est.)

country comparison to the world: 27

IMPORTS - COMMODITIES:

electronics, machinery, petroleum products, plastics, vehicles, iron and steel products, chemicals

IMPORTS - PARTNERS:

China 19.9%, Singapore 10.8%, US 8.4%, Japan 7.6%, Thailand 5.8%, South Korea 4.5%, Indonesia 4.4% (2017)

RESERVES OF FOREIGN EXCHANGE AND GOLD:

$102.4 billion (31 December 2017 est.)

$94.5 billion (31 December 2016 est.)

country comparison to the world: 25

DEBT - EXTERNAL:

$217.2 billion (31 December 2017 est.)

$195.3 billion (31 December 2016 est.)

country comparison to the world: 33

STOCK OF DIRECT FOREIGN INVESTMENT - AT HOME:

$139.5 billion (31 December 2017 est.)

$121.6 billion (31 December 2016 est.)

country comparison to the world: 39

STOCK OF DIRECT FOREIGN INVESTMENT - ABROAD:

$128.5 billion (31 December 2017 est.)

$126.9 billion (31 December 2016 est.)

country comparison to the world: 31

EXCHANGE RATES:

ringgits (MYR) per US dollar -

4.343 (2017 est.)

4.15 (2016 est.)

4.15 (2015 est.)

3.91 (2014 est.)

3.27 (2013 est.)

ENERGY :: MALAYSIA

ELECTRICITY ACCESS:

electrification - total population: 100% (2016)

ELECTRICITY - PRODUCTION:

148.3 billion kWh (2016 est.)

country comparison to the world: 28

ELECTRICITY - CONSUMPTION:

136.9 billion kWh (2016 est.)

country comparison to the world: 26

ELECTRICITY - EXPORTS:

3 million kWh (2015 est.)

country comparison to the world: 93

ELECTRICITY - IMPORTS:

33 million kWh (2016 est.)

country comparison to the world: 109

ELECTRICITY - INSTALLED GENERATING CAPACITY:

33 million kW (2016 est.)

country comparison to the world: 31

ELECTRICITY - FROM FOSSIL FUELS:

78% of total installed capacity (2016 est.)

country comparison to the world: 90

ELECTRICITY - FROM NUCLEAR FUELS:

0% of total installed capacity (2017 est.)

country comparison to the world: 136

ELECTRICITY - FROM HYDROELECTRIC PLANTS:

18% of total installed capacity (2017 est.)

country comparison to the world: 95

ELECTRICITY - FROM OTHER RENEWABLE SOURCES:

4% of total installed capacity (2017 est.)

country comparison to the world: 113

CRUDE OIL - PRODUCTION:

647,000 bbl/day (2018 est.)

country comparison to the world: 26

CRUDE OIL - EXPORTS:

326,200 bbl/day (2015 est.)

country comparison to the world: 24

CRUDE OIL - IMPORTS:

166,000 bbl/day (2015 est.)

country comparison to the world: 35

CRUDE OIL - PROVED RESERVES:

3.6 billion bbl (1 January 2018 est.)

country comparison to the world: 27

REFINED PETROLEUM PRODUCTS - PRODUCTION:

528,300 bbl/day (2015 est.)

country comparison to the world: 32

REFINED PETROLEUM PRODUCTS - CONSUMPTION:

704,000 bbl/day (2016 est.)

country comparison to the world: 28

REFINED PETROLEUM PRODUCTS - EXPORTS:

208,400 bbl/day (2015 est.)

country comparison to the world: 31

REFINED PETROLEUM PRODUCTS - IMPORTS:

304,600 bbl/day (2015 est.)

country comparison to the world: 24

NATURAL GAS - PRODUCTION:

69.49 billion cu m (2017 est.)

country comparison to the world: 13

NATURAL GAS - CONSUMPTION:

30.44 billion cu m (2017 est.)

country comparison to the world: 31

NATURAL GAS - EXPORTS:

38.23 billion cu m (2017 est.)

country comparison to the world: 9

NATURAL GAS - IMPORTS:

2.803 billion cu m (2017 est.)

country comparison to the world: 45

NATURAL GAS - PROVED RESERVES:

1.183 trillion cu m (1 January 2018 est.)

country comparison to the world: 23

CARBON DIOXIDE EMISSIONS FROM CONSUMPTION OF ENERGY:

226.8 million Mt (2017 est.)

country comparison to the world: 31

COMMUNICATIONS :: MALAYSIA

TELEPHONES - FIXED LINES:

total subscriptions: 6,578,200

subscriptions per 100 inhabitants: 21 (2017 est.)

country comparison to the world: 25

TELEPHONES - MOBILE CELLULAR:

total subscriptions: 42,338,500

subscriptions per 100 inhabitants: 135 (2017 est.)

country comparison to the world: 34

TELEPHONE SYSTEM:

general assessment: modern system featuring good intercity services mainly by microwave radio relay and an adequate intercity microwave radio relay network between Sabah and Sarawak via Brunei; international service excellent; one of the most advanced telecom networks; roll-out of a national broadband network (2018)

domestic: fixed-line 21 per 100 and mobile-cellular teledensity exceeds 135 per 100 persons; domestic satellite system with 2 earth stations (2018)

international: country code - 60; landing points for BBG, FEA, SAFE, SeaMeWe-3 & 4 & 5, AAE-1, JASUKA, BDM, Dumai-Melaka Cable System, BRCS, ACE, AAG, East-West Submarine Cable System, SEAX-1, SKR1M, APCN-2, APG, BtoBe, MCT, BaSICS, and Labuan-Brunei Submarine cable providing connectivity via international submarine cable networks to Asia, the Middle East, Southeast Asia, Australia and Europe; satellite earth stations - 2 Intelsat (1 Indian Ocean, 1 Pacific Ocean) (2019)

BROADCAST MEDIA:

state-owned TV broadcaster operates 2 TV networks with relays throughout the country, and the leading private commercial media group operates 4 TV stations with numerous relays throughout the country; satellite TV subscription service is available; state-owned radio broadcaster operates multiple national networks, as well as regional and local stations; many private commercial radio broadcasters and some subscription satellite radio services are available; about 55 radio stations overall (2019)

INTERNET COUNTRY CODE:

.my

INTERNET USERS:

total: 24,384,952

percent of population: 78.8% (July 2016 est.)

country comparison to the world: 29

BROADBAND - FIXED SUBSCRIPTIONS:

total: 2,687,800

subscriptions per 100 inhabitants: 9 (2017 est.)

country comparison to the world: 42

MILITARY AND SECURITY :: MALAYSIA

MILITARY EXPENDITURES:

0.98% of GDP (2018)

1.12% of GDP (2017)

1.41% of GDP (2016)

1.53% of GDP (2015)

1.46% of GDP (2014)

country comparison to the world: 119

MILITARY AND SECURITY FORCES:

Malaysian Armed Forces (Angkatan Tentera Malaysia, ATM): Malaysian Army (Tentera Darat Malaysia), Royal Malaysian Navy (Tentera Laut Diraja Malaysia, TLDM), Royal Malaysian Air Force (Tentera Udara Diraja Malaysia, TUDM) (2019)

Malaysia created a National Special Operations Force in 2016 for combating terrorism threats; the force is comprised of personnel from the Armed Forces, the Royal Malaysian Police (PDRM), and the Malaysian Maritime Enforcement Agency (Malaysian Coast Guard, MMEA)

MILITARY SERVICE AGE AND OBLIGATION:

17 years 6 months of age for voluntary military service (younger with parental consent and proof of age); mandatory retirement age 60; women serve in the Malaysian Armed Forces; no conscription (2017)

MARITIME THREATS:

the International Maritime Bureau reports that the territorial and offshore waters in the Strait of Malacca and South China Sea remain high risk for piracy and armed robbery against ships; in the past, commercial vessels have been attacked and hijacked both at anchor and while underway; hijacked vessels are often disguised and cargo diverted to ports in East Asia; crews have been murdered or cast adrift; 11 attacks were reported in 2018 including eight ships boarded and seven crew taken hostage

TRANSPORTATION :: MALAYSIA

NATIONAL AIR TRANSPORT SYSTEM:

number of registered air carriers: 12 (2015)

inventory of registered aircraft operated by air carriers: 263 (2015)

annual passenger traffic on registered air carriers: 50,347,149 (2015)

annual freight traffic on registered air carriers: 2,005,979,379 mt-km (2015)

CIVIL AIRCRAFT REGISTRATION COUNTRY CODE PREFIX:

9M (2016)

AIRPORTS:

114 (2013)

country comparison to the world: 51

AIRPORTS - WITH PAVED RUNWAYS:

total: 39 (2017)

over 3,047 m: 8 (2017)

2,438 to 3,047 m: 8 (2017)

1,524 to 2,437 m: 7 (2017)

914 to 1,523 m: 8 (2017)

under 914 m: 8 (2017)

AIRPORTS - WITH UNPAVED RUNWAYS:

total: 75 (2013)

914 to 1,523 m: 6 (2013)

under 914 m: 69 (2013)

HELIPORTS:

4 (2013)

PIPELINES:

354 km condensate, 6439 km gas, 155 km liquid petroleum gas, 1937 km oil, 43 km oil/gas/water, 114 km refined products, 26 km water (2013)

RAILWAYS:

total: 1,851 km (2014)

standard gauge: 59 km 1.435-m gauge (59 km electrified) (2014)

narrow gauge: 1,792 km 1.000-m gauge (339 km electrified) (2014)

country comparison to the world: 77

ROADWAYS:

total: 144,403 km (excludes local roads) (2010)

paved: 116,169 km (includes 1,821 km of expressways) (2010)

unpaved: 28,234 km (2010)

country comparison to the world: 35

WATERWAYS:

7,200 km (Peninsular Malaysia 3,200 km; Sabah 1,500 km; Sarawak 2,500 km) (2011)

country comparison to the world: 19

MERCHANT MARINE:

total: 1,704

by type: bulk carrier 15, container ship 22, general cargo 182, oil tanker 137, other 1348 (2018)

country comparison to the world: 15

PORTS AND TERMINALS:

major seaport(s): Bintulu, Johor Bahru, George Town (Penang), Port Kelang (Port Klang), Tanjung Pelepas

container port(s) (TEUs): Port Kelang (Port Klang) (11,978,000), Tanjung Pelepas (8,260,000) (2017)

LNG terminal(s) (export): Bintulu (Sarawak)

LNG terminal(s) (import): Sungei Udang

TERRORISM :: MALAYSIA

TERRORIST GROUPS - FOREIGN BASED:

Jemaah Islamiyah (JI): aim(s): enhance networks in Malaysia and, ultimately, overthrow the secular Malaysian Government and establish a pan-Islamic state across Southeast Asia area(s) of operation: maintains a recruitment and operational presence, primarily in major cities (2018)

TRANSNATIONAL ISSUES :: MALAYSIA

DISPUTES - INTERNATIONAL:

while the 2002 "Declaration on the Conduct of Parties in the South China Sea" has eased tensions over the Spratly Islands, it is not the legally binding "code of conduct" sought by some parties, which is currently being negotiated between China and ASEAN; Malaysia was not party to the March 2005 joint accord among the national oil companies of China, the Philippines, and Vietnam on conducting marine seismic activities in the Spratly Islands; disputes continue over deliveries of fresh water to Singapore, Singapore's land reclamation, bridge construction, and maritime boundaries in the Johor and Singapore Straits; in 2008, ICJ awarded sovereignty of Pedra Branca (Pulau Batu Puteh/Horsburgh Island) to Singapore, and Middle Rocks to Malaysia, but did not rule on maritime regimes, boundaries, or disposition of South Ledge; land and maritime negotiations with Indonesia are ongoing, and disputed areas include the controversial Tanjung Datu and Camar Wulan border area in Borneo and the maritime boundary in the Ambalat oil block in the Celebes Sea; separatist violence in Thailand's predominantly Muslim southern provinces prompts measures to close and monitor border with Malaysia to stem terrorist activities; Philippines retains a dormant claim to Malaysia's Sabah State in northern Borneo; per Letters of Exchange signed in 2009, Malaysia in 2010 ceded two hydrocarbon concession blocks to Brunei in exchange for Brunei's sultan dropping claims to the Limbang corridor, which divides Brunei; piracy remains a problem in the Malacca Strait

REFUGEES AND INTERNALLY DISPLACED PERSONS:

refugees (country of origin): 114,227 (Burma) (2018)

stateless persons: 9,631 (2018); note - Malaysia's stateless population consists of Rohingya refugees from Burma, ethnic Indians, and the children of Filipino and Indonesian illegal migrants; Burma stripped the Rohingya of their nationality in 1982; Filipino and Indonesian children who have not been registered for birth certificates by their parents or who received birth certificates stamped "foreigner" are not eligible to attend government schools; these children are vulnerable to statelessness should they not be able to apply to their parents' country of origin for passports

TRAFFICKING IN PERSONS:

current situation: Malaysia is a destination and, to a lesser extent, a source and transit country for men, women, and children subjected to forced labor and women and children subjected to sex trafficking; Malaysia is mainly a destination country for foreign workers who migrate willingly from countries, including Indonesia, Bangladesh, the Philippines, Nepal, Burma, and other Southeast Asian countries, but subsequently encounter forced labor or debt bondage in agriculture, construction, factories, and domestic service at the hands of employers, employment agents, and labor recruiters; women from Southeast Asia and, to a much lesser extent, Africa, are recruited for legal work in restaurants, hotels, and salons but are forced into prostitution; refugees, including Rohingya adults and children, are not legally permitted to work and are vulnerable to trafficking; a small number of

Malaysians are trafficked internally and subjected to sex trafficking abroad

tier rating: Tier 2 Watch list - Malaysia does not fully comply with the minimum standards for the elimination of trafficking; however, it is making significant efforts to do so; in 2014, amendments to strengthen existing anti-trafficking laws, including enabling victims to move freely and to work and for NGOs to run protective facilities, were drafted by the government and are pending approval from Parliament; authorities more than doubled investigations and prosecutions but convicted only three traffickers for forced labor and none for sex trafficking, a decline from 2013 and a disproportionately small number compared to the scale of the country's trafficking problem; NGOs provided the majority of victim rehabilitation and counseling services with no financial support from the government (2015)

ILLICIT DRUGS:

drug trafficking prosecuted vigorously, including enforcement of the death penalty; heroin still primary drug of abuse, but synthetic drug demand remains strong; continued ecstasy and methamphetamine producer for domestic users and, to a lesser extent, the regional drug market

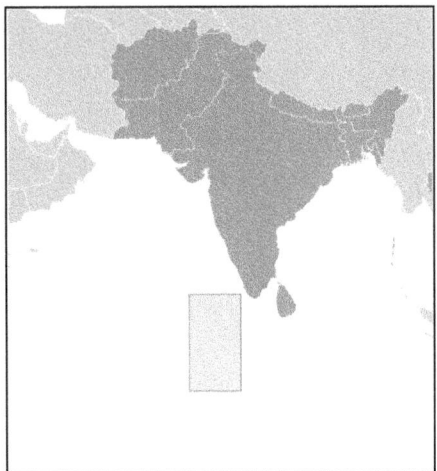

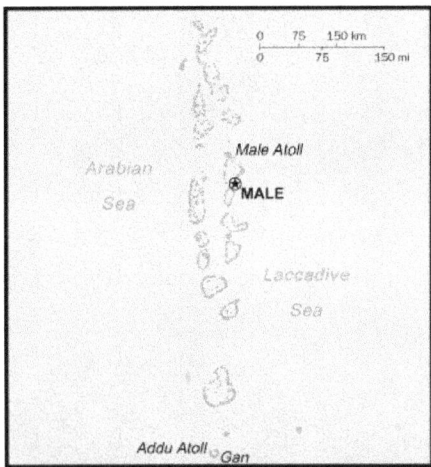

SOUTH ASIA :: MALDIVES

INTRODUCTION :: MALDIVES

BACKGROUND:

A sultanate since the 12th century, the Maldives became a British protectorate in 1887. The islands became a republic in 1968, three years after independence. President Maumoon Abdul GAYOOM dominated Maldives' political scene for 30 years, elected to six successive terms by single-party referendums. Following political demonstrations in the capital Male in August 2003, GAYOOM and his government pledged to embark upon a process of liberalization and democratic reforms, including a more representative political system and expanded political freedoms. Political parties were legalized in 2005.

In June 2008, a constituent assembly - termed the "Special Majlis" - finalized a new constitution ratified by GAYOOM in August 2008. The first-ever presidential elections under a multi-candidate, multi-party system were held in October 2008. GAYOOM was defeated in a runoff poll by Mohamed NASHEED, a political activist who had been jailed several years earlier by the GAYOOM regime. In early February 2012, after several weeks of street protests in response to his ordering the arrest of a top judge, NASHEED purportedly resigned the presidency and handed over power to Vice President Mohammed WAHEED Hassan Maniku. A government-appointed Commission of National Inquiry concluded there was no evidence of a coup, but NASHEED contends that police and military personnel forced him to resign. NASHEED, WAHEED, and Abdulla YAMEEN Abdul Gayoom ran in the 2013 elections with YAMEEN ultimately winning the presidency after three rounds of voting. As president, YAMEEN weakened democratic institutions, curtailed civil liberties, jailed his political opponents, restricted the press, and exerted control over the judiciary to strengthen his hold on power and limit dissent. In September 2018, YAMEEN lost his reelection bid to Ibrahim Mohamed SOLIH, a parliamentarian of the Maldivian Democratic Party (MDP), who had the support of a coalition of four parties that came together to defeat YAMEEN and restore democratic norms to Maldives. In April 2019, SOLIH's MDP won 65 of 87 seats in parliament.

GEOGRAPHY :: MALDIVES

LOCATION:

Southern Asia, group of atolls in the Indian Ocean, south-southwest of India

GEOGRAPHIC COORDINATES:

3 15 N, 73 00 E

MAP REFERENCES:

Asia

AREA:

total: 298 sq km

land: 298 sq km

water: 0 sq km

country comparison to the world: 210

AREA - COMPARATIVE:

about 1.7 times the size of Washington, DC

LAND BOUNDARIES:

0 km

COASTLINE:

644 km

MARITIME CLAIMS:

territorial sea: 12 nm

exclusive economic zone: 200 nm

contiguous zone: 24 nm

measured from claimed archipelagic straight baselines

CLIMATE:

tropical; hot, humid; dry, northeast monsoon (November to March); rainy, southwest monsoon (June to August)

TERRAIN:

flat, with white sandy beaches

ELEVATION:

mean elevation: 2 m

lowest point: Indian Ocean 0 m

highest point: 8th tee, golf course, Villingi Island 5 m

NATURAL RESOURCES:

fish

LAND USE:

agricultural land: 23.3% (2011 est.)

arable land: 10% (2011 est.) / permanent crops: 10% (2011 est.) / permanent pasture: 3.3% (2011 est.)

forest: 3% (2011 est.)

other: 73.7% (2011 est.)

IRRIGATED LAND:

0 sq km (2012)

POPULATION DISTRIBUTION:

about a third of the population lives in the centrally located capital city of Male and almost a tenth in southern

Addu City; the remainder of the populace is spread over the 200 or so populated islands of the archipelago

NATURAL HAZARDS:

tsunamis; low elevation of islands makes them sensitive to sea level rise

ENVIRONMENT - CURRENT ISSUES:

depletion of freshwater aquifers threatens water supplies; inadequate sewage treatment; coral reef bleaching

ENVIRONMENT - INTERNATIONAL AGREEMENTS:

party to: Biodiversity, Climate Change, Climate Change-Kyoto Protocol, Desertification, Hazardous Wastes, Law of the Sea, Ozone Layer Protection, Ship Pollution

signed, but not ratified: none of the selected agreements

GEOGRAPHY - NOTE:

smallest Asian country; archipelago of 1,190 coral islands grouped into 26 atolls (200 inhabited islands, plus 80 islands with tourist resorts); strategic location astride and along major sea lanes in Indian Ocean

PEOPLE AND SOCIETY :: MALDIVES

POPULATION:

392,473 (July 2018 est.)

country comparison to the world: 176

NATIONALITY:

noun: Maldivian(s)

adjective: Maldivian

ETHNIC GROUPS:

homogeneous mixture of Sinhalese, Dravidian, Arab, Australasian, and African resulting from historical changes in regional hegemony over marine trade routes

LANGUAGES:

Dhivehi (official, dialect of Sinhala, script derived from Arabic), English (spoken by most government officials)

RELIGIONS:

Sunni Muslim (official)

AGE STRUCTURE:

0-14 years: 21.62% (male 43,293 /female 41,563)

15-24 years: 19.15% (male 42,849 /female 32,326)

25-54 years: 48.47% (male 106,083 /female 84,160)

55-64 years: 6.22% (male 11,888 /female 12,540)

65 years and over: 4.53% (male 8,101 /female 9,670) (2018 est.)

DEPENDENCY RATIOS:

total dependency ratio: 38 (2015 est.)

youth dependency ratio: 32.3 (2015 est.)

elderly dependency ratio: 5.7 (2015 est.)

potential support ratio: 17.7 (2015 est.)

MEDIAN AGE:

total: 28.6 years (2018 est.)

male: 28.4 years

female: 28.8 years

country comparison to the world: 134

POPULATION GROWTH RATE:

-0.06% (2018 est.)

country comparison to the world: 202

BIRTH RATE:

16.1 births/1,000 population (2018 est.)

country comparison to the world: 112

DEATH RATE:

4 deaths/1,000 population (2018 est.)

country comparison to the world: 209

NET MIGRATION RATE:

-12.7 migrant(s)/1,000 population (2018 est.)

country comparison to the world: 219

POPULATION DISTRIBUTION:

about a third of the population lives in the centrally located capital city of Male and almost a tenth in southern Addu City; the remainder of the populace is spread over the 200 or so populated islands of the archipelago

URBANIZATION:

urban population: 40.2% of total population (2019)

rate of urbanization: 2.93% annual rate of change (2015-20 est.)

MAJOR URBAN AREAS - POPULATION:

177,000 MALE (capital) (2018)

SEX RATIO:

at birth: 1.05 male(s)/female

0-14 years: 1.04 male(s)/female

15-24 years: 1.33 male(s)/female

25-54 years: 1.26 male(s)/female

55-64 years: 0.95 male(s)/female

65 years and over: 0.84 male(s)/female

total population: 1.18 male(s)/female (2018 est.)

MOTHER'S MEAN AGE AT FIRST BIRTH:

24.5 years (2009 est.)

note: median age at first birth among women 25-29

MATERNAL MORTALITY RATE:

53 deaths/100,000 live births (2017 est.)

country comparison to the world: 92

INFANT MORTALITY RATE:

total: 21.3 deaths/1,000 live births (2018 est.)

male: 23.6 deaths/1,000 live births

female: 18.9 deaths/1,000 live births

country comparison to the world: 76

LIFE EXPECTANCY AT BIRTH:

total population: 76 years (2018 est.)

male: 73.7 years

female: 78.5 years

country comparison to the world: 94

TOTAL FERTILITY RATE:

1.72 children born/woman (2018 est.)

country comparison to the world: 168

CONTRACEPTIVE PREVALENCE RATE:

34.7% (2009)

DRINKING WATER SOURCE:

improved:

urban: 99.5% of population

rural: 97.9% of population

total: 98.6% of population

unimproved:

urban: 0.5% of population

rural: 2.1% of population

total: 1.4% of population (2015 est.)

CURRENT HEALTH EXPENDITURE:

10.6% (2016)

PHYSICIANS DENSITY:

1.04 physicians/1,000 population (2016)

HOSPITAL BED DENSITY:

4.3 beds/1,000 population (2009)

SANITATION FACILITY ACCESS:

improved:

urban: 97.5% of population (2015 est.)

rural: 98.3% of population (2015 est.)

total: 97.9% of population (2015 est.)

unimproved:

urban: 2.5% of population (2015 est.)

rural: 1.7% of population (2015 est.)

total: 2.1% of population (2015 est.)

HIV/AIDS - ADULT PREVALENCE RATE:

NA

HIV/AIDS - PEOPLE LIVING WITH HIV/AIDS:

NA

HIV/AIDS - DEATHS:

NA

OBESITY - ADULT PREVALENCE RATE:

8.6% (2016)

country comparison to the world: 148

CHILDREN UNDER THE AGE OF 5 YEARS UNDERWEIGHT:

17.7% (2009)

country comparison to the world: 33

EDUCATION EXPENDITURES:

4.3% of GDP (2016)

country comparison to the world: 97

LITERACY:

definition: age 15 and over can read and write

total population: 99.3%

male: 99.8%

female: 98.8% (2015 est.)

UNEMPLOYMENT, YOUTH AGES 15-24:

total: 15.9%

male: 19.1%

female: 12.1% (2016 est.)

country comparison to the world: 85

GOVERNMENT :: MALDIVES

COUNTRY NAME:

conventional long form: Republic of Maldives

conventional short form: Maldives

local long form: Dhivehi Raajjeyge Jumhooriyyaa

local short form: Dhivehi Raajje

etymology: archipelago apparently named after the main island (and capital) of Male; the word "Maldives" means "the islands (dives) of Male"; alternatively, the name may derive from the Sanskrit word "maladvipa" meaning "garland of islands"; Dhivehi Raajje in Dhivehi means "Kingdom of the Dhivehi people"

GOVERNMENT TYPE:

presidential republic

CAPITAL:

name: Male

geographic coordinates: 4 10 N, 73 30 E

time difference: UTC+5 (10 hours ahead of Washington, DC, during Standard Time)

etymology: derived from the Sanskrit word "mahaalay" meaning "big house"

ADMINISTRATIVE DIVISIONS:

21 administrative atolls (atholhuthah, singular - atholhu); Addu (Addu City), Ariatholhu Dhekunuburi (South Ari Atoll), Ariatholhu Uthuruburi (North Ari Atoll), Faadhippolhu, Felidhuatholhu (Felidhu Atoll), Fuvammulah, Hahdhunmathi, Huvadhuatholhu Dhekunuburi (South Huvadhu Atoll), Huvadhuatholhu Uthuruburi (North Huvadhu Atoll), Kolhumadulu, Maale (Male), Maaleatholhu (Male Atoll), Maalhosmadulu Dhekunuburi (South Maalhosmadulu), Maalhosmadulu Uthuruburi (North Maalhosmadulu), Miladhunmadulu Dhekunuburi (South Miladhunmadulu), Miladhunmadulu Uthuruburi (North Miladhunmadulu), Mulakatholhu (Mulaku Atoll), Nilandheatholhu Dhekunuburi (South Nilandhe Atoll), Nilandheatholhu Uthuruburi (North Nilandhe Atoll), Thiladhunmathee Dhekunuburi (South Thiladhunmathi), Thiladhunmathee Uthuruburi (North Thiladhunmathi)

INDEPENDENCE:

26 July 1965 (from the UK)

NATIONAL HOLIDAY:

Independence Day, 26 July (1965)

CONSTITUTION:

history: many previous; latest ratified 7 August 2008

amendments: proposed by Parliament; passage requires at least three-quarters majority vote by its membership and the signature of the president of the republic; passage of amendments to constitutional articles on rights and freedoms and the terms of office of Parliament and of the president also requires a majority vote in a referendum; amended 2015 (2018)

LEGAL SYSTEM:

Islamic (sharia) legal system with English common law influences, primarily in commercial matters

INTERNATIONAL LAW ORGANIZATION PARTICIPATION:

has not submitted an ICJ jurisdiction declaration; accepts ICCt jurisdiction

CITIZENSHIP:

citizenship by birth: no

citizenship by descent only: at least one parent must be a citizen of Maldives

dual citizenship recognized: yes

residency requirement for naturalization: unknown

SUFFRAGE:

18 years of age; universal

EXECUTIVE BRANCH:

chief of state: President Ibrahim "Ibu" Mohamed SOLIH (since 17 November 2018); Vice President Faisal NASEEM (since 17 November 2018); the president is both chief of state and head of government

head of government: President Ibrahim Mohamed SOLIH (since 17 November 2018); Vice President Faisal NASEEM (since 17 November 2018)

cabinet: Cabinet of Ministers appointed by the president, approved by Parliament

elections/appointments: president directly elected by absolute majority popular vote in 2 rounds if needed for a 5-year term (eligible for a second term); election last held on 23 September 2018 (next to be held in 2023)

election results: Ibrahim Mohamed SOLIH elected president (in 1 round); Ibrahim Mohamed SOLIH (MDP) 58.3%, Abdulla YAMEEN Abdul Gayoom (PPM) 41.7%

LEGISLATIVE BRANCH:

description: unicameral Parliament or People's Majlis (87 seats - includes 2 seats added by the Elections Commission in late 2018; members directly elected in single-seat constituencies by simple majority vote to serve 5-year terms)

elections: last held on 6 April 2019 (next to be held in 2023)

election results: percent of vote - MDP 44.7%, JP 10.8%, PPM 8.7%, PNC 6.4%, MDA 2.8%, other 5.6%, independent 21%; seats by party - MDP 65, JP 5, PPM 5, PNC 3, MDA

2, independent 7; composition - men 83, women 4, percent of women 4.6%

JUDICIAL BRANCH:

highest courts: Supreme Court (consists of the chief justice and 4 judges)

judge selection and term of office: Supreme Court judges appointed by the president in consultation with the Judicial Service Commission - a 10-member body of selected high government officials and the public - and upon confirmation by voting members of the People's Majlis; judges serve until mandatory retirement at age 70

subordinate courts: High Court; Criminal, Civil, Family, Juvenile, and Drug Courts; Magistrate Courts (on each of the inhabited islands)

POLITICAL PARTIES AND LEADERS:

Adhaalath (Justice) Party or AP [Sheikh Imran ABDULLA]
Maldives Development Alliance or MDA [Ahmed Shiyam MOHAMED]
Maldivian Democratic Party or MDP [Mohamed NASHEED]
Maldives Labor and Social Democratic Party or MLSDP [Ahmed SHIHAM]
Maldives Third Way Democrats or MTD [Ahmed ADEEB]
Maldives Reform Movement or MRM [Maumoon Abdul GAYOOM]
People's National Congress or PNC [Abdul Raheem ABDULLA] (formed in early 2019)
Progressive Party of Maldives or PPM [Abdulla YAMEEN]
Republican (Jumhooree) Party or JP [Qasim IBRAHIM] (2019)

INTERNATIONAL ORGANIZATION PARTICIPATION:

ADB, AOSIS, C, CP, FAO, G-77, IBRD, ICAO, ICC (NGOs), ICCt, IDA, IDB, IFAD, IFC, IFRCS, ILO, IMF, IMO, Interpol, IOC, IOM, IPU, ITU, MIGA, NAM, OIC, OPCW, SAARC, SACEP, UN, UNCTAD, UNESCO, UNIDO, UNWTO, UPU, WCO, WHO, WIPO, WMO, WTO

DIPLOMATIC REPRESENTATION IN THE US:

Ambassador THILMEEZA Hussain (since 8 July 2019)

chancery: 801 Second Avenue, Suite 400E, New York, NY 10017

telephone: [1] (212) 599-6194 and 599-6195

FAX: [1] (212) 661-6405

DIPLOMATIC REPRESENTATION FROM THE US:

the US does not have an embassy in Maldives; US Ambassador to Sri Lanka and Maldives, Alaina TEPLITZ (since 1 November 2018), is accredited to both countries

FLAG DESCRIPTION:

red with a large green rectangle in the center bearing a vertical white crescent moon; the closed side of the crescent is on the hoist side of the flag; red recalls those who have sacrificed their lives in defense of their country, the green rectangle represents peace and prosperity, and the white crescent signifies Islam

NATIONAL SYMBOL(S):

coconut palm, yellowfin tuna; national colors: red, green, white

NATIONAL ANTHEM:

name: "Gaumee Salaam" (National Salute)

lyrics/music: Mohamed Jameel DIDI/Wannakuwattawaduge DON AMARADEVA

note: lyrics adopted 1948, music adopted 1972; between 1948 and 1972, the lyrics were sung to the tune of "Auld Lang Syne"

ECONOMY :: MALDIVES

ECONOMY - OVERVIEW:

Maldives has quickly become a middle-income country, driven by the rapid growth of its tourism and fisheries sectors, but the country still contends with a large and growing fiscal deficit. Infrastructure projects, largely funded by China, could add significantly to debt levels. Political turmoil and the declaration of a state of emergency in February 2018 led to the issuance of travel warnings by several countries whose citizens visit Maldives in significant numbers, but the overall impact on tourism revenue was unclear.

In 2015, Maldives' Parliament passed a constitutional amendment legalizing foreign ownership of land; foreign land-buyers must reclaim at least 70% of the desired land from the ocean and invest at least $1 billion in a construction project approved by Parliament.

Diversifying the economy beyond tourism and fishing, reforming public finance, increasing employment opportunities, and combating corruption, cronyism, and a growing drug problem are near-term challenges facing the government. Over the longer term, Maldivian authorities worry about the impact of erosion and possible global warming on their low-lying country; 80% of the area is 1 meter or less above sea level.

GDP (PURCHASING POWER PARITY):

$6.901 billion (2017 est.)

$6.583 billion (2016 est.)

$6.3 billion (2015 est.)

note: data are in 2017 dollars

country comparison to the world: 168

GDP (OFFICIAL EXCHANGE RATE):

$4.505 billion (2017 est.)

GDP - REAL GROWTH RATE:

4.8% (2017 est.)

4.5% (2016 est.)

2.2% (2015 est.)

country comparison to the world: 57

GDP - PER CAPITA (PPP):

$19,200 (2017 est.)

$18,600 (2016 est.)

$18,100 (2015 est.)

note: data are in 2017 dollars

country comparison to the world: 93

GROSS NATIONAL SAVING:

0.5% of GDP (2017 est.)

-4.5% of GDP (2016 est.)

12.6% of GDP (2015 est.)

country comparison to the world: 180

GDP - COMPOSITION, BY END USE:

household consumption: NA (2016 est.)

government consumption: NA (2016 est.)

investment in fixed capital: NA (2016 est.)

investment in inventories: NA (2016 est.)

exports of goods and services: 93.6% (2016 est.)

imports of goods and services: 89% (2016 est.)

GDP - COMPOSITION, BY SECTOR OF ORIGIN:

agriculture: 3% (2015 est.)

industry: 16% (2015 est.)

services: 81% (2015 est.)

AGRICULTURE - PRODUCTS:

coconuts, corn, sweet potatoes; fish

INDUSTRIES:

tourism, fish processing, shipping, boat building, coconut processing, woven mats, rope, handicrafts, coral and sand mining

INDUSTRIAL PRODUCTION GROWTH RATE:

14% (2012 est.)

country comparison to the world: 4

LABOR FORCE:

222,200 (2017 est.)

country comparison to the world: 168

LABOR FORCE - BY OCCUPATION:

agriculture: 7.7%

industry: 22.8%

services: 69.5% (2017 est.)

UNEMPLOYMENT RATE:

2.9% (2017 est.)

3.2% (2016 est.)

country comparison to the world: 35

POPULATION BELOW POVERTY LINE:

15% (2009 est.)

HOUSEHOLD INCOME OR CONSUMPTION BY PERCENTAGE SHARE:

lowest 10%: 1.2%

highest 10%: 33.3% (FY09/10)

DISTRIBUTION OF FAMILY INCOME - GINI INDEX:

38.4 (2009 est.)

37.4 (2004 est.)

country comparison to the world: 77

BUDGET:

revenues: 1.19 billion (2016 est.)

expenditures: 1.643 billion (2016 est.)

TAXES AND OTHER REVENUES:

26.4% (of GDP) (2016 est.)

country comparison to the world: 111

BUDGET SURPLUS (+) OR DEFICIT (-):

-10.1% (of GDP) (2016 est.)

country comparison to the world: 212

PUBLIC DEBT:

63.9% of GDP (2017 est.)

61.7% of GDP (2016 est.)

country comparison to the world: 62

FISCAL YEAR:

calendar year

INFLATION RATE (CONSUMER PRICES):

2.3% (2017 est.)

0.8% (2016 est.)

country comparison to the world: 116

CENTRAL BANK DISCOUNT RATE:

7% (30 September 2017)

7% (30 September 2016)

country comparison to the world: 50

COMMERCIAL BANK PRIME LENDING RATE:

10.5% (31 December 2012 est.)

10.2% (31 December 2011 est.)

country comparison to the world: 82

STOCK OF NARROW MONEY:

$908.6 million (31 October 2017 est.)

$865.9 million (31 October 2016 est.)

country comparison to the world: 160

STOCK OF BROAD MONEY:

$1.982 billion (31 October 2017)

$2.043 billion (31 October 2016 est.)

country comparison to the world: 143

STOCK OF DOMESTIC CREDIT:

$1.559 billion (31 December 2012 est.)

$1.601 billion (31 December 2011 est.)

country comparison to the world: 160

MARKET VALUE OF PUBLICLY TRADED SHARES:

$555 million (31 December 2011 est.)

country comparison to the world: 112

CURRENT ACCOUNT BALANCE:

-$876 million (2017 est.)

-$1.033 billion (2016 est.)

country comparison to the world: 137

EXPORTS:

$256.2 million (2016 est.)

$239.8 million (2015 est.)

country comparison to the world: 188

EXPORTS - PARTNERS:

Thailand 42.8%, Sri Lanka 8.7%, Bangladesh 6.4%, France 6.2%, US 6.1%, Germany 5%, Ireland 4.6% (2017)

EXPORTS - COMMODITIES:

fish

IMPORTS:

$2.125 billion (2016 est.)

$1.896 billion (2015 est.)

country comparison to the world: 165

IMPORTS - COMMODITIES:

petroleum products, clothing, intermediate and capital goods

IMPORTS - PARTNERS:

UAE 17.1%, India 13.5%, Singapore 13.3%, China 10.8%, Sri Lanka 6.7%, Malaysia 6%, Thailand 4.5% (2017)

RESERVES OF FOREIGN EXCHANGE AND GOLD:

$477.9 million (31 December 2016 est.)

$575.8 million (31 December 2015 est.)

country comparison to the world: 153

DEBT - EXTERNAL:

$848.8 million (31 December 2016 est.)

$696.2 million (31 December 2015 est.)

country comparison to the world: 168

STOCK OF DIRECT FOREIGN INVESTMENT - AT HOME:

$324 million (31 December 2015)

$256 million (31 December 2013)

country comparison to the world: 133

STOCK OF DIRECT FOREIGN INVESTMENT - ABROAD:

$448 million (31 December 2016 est.)

$307.7 million (31 December 2015)

country comparison to the world: 98

EXCHANGE RATES:

rufiyaa (MVR) per US dollar -

15.42 (2017 est.)

15.35 (2016 est.)

ENERGY :: MALDIVES

ELECTRICITY ACCESS:

electrification - total population: 100% (2016)

ELECTRICITY - PRODUCTION:

402 million kWh (2016 est.)

country comparison to the world: 171

ELECTRICITY - CONSUMPTION:

373.9 million kWh (2016 est.)

country comparison to the world: 178

ELECTRICITY - EXPORTS:

0 kWh (2016 est.)

country comparison to the world: 165

ELECTRICITY - IMPORTS:

0 kWh (2016 est.)

country comparison to the world: 171

ELECTRICITY - INSTALLED GENERATING CAPACITY:

278,000 kW (2016 est.)

country comparison to the world: 161

ELECTRICITY - FROM FOSSIL FUELS:

96% of total installed capacity (2016 est.)

country comparison to the world: 40

ELECTRICITY - FROM NUCLEAR FUELS:

0% of total installed capacity (2017 est.)

country comparison to the world: 137

ELECTRICITY - FROM HYDROELECTRIC PLANTS:

0% of total installed capacity (2017 est.)

country comparison to the world: 185

ELECTRICITY - FROM OTHER RENEWABLE SOURCES:

4% of total installed capacity (2017 est.)

country comparison to the world: 114

CRUDE OIL - PRODUCTION:

0 bbl/day (2018 est.)

country comparison to the world: 169

CRUDE OIL - EXPORTS:

0 bbl/day (2015 est.)

country comparison to the world: 160

CRUDE OIL - IMPORTS:

0 bbl/day (2015 est.)

country comparison to the world: 160

CRUDE OIL - PROVED RESERVES:

0 bbl (1 January 2018 est.)

country comparison to the world: 164

REFINED PETROLEUM PRODUCTS - PRODUCTION:

0 bbl/day (2015 est.)

country comparison to the world: 172

REFINED PETROLEUM PRODUCTS - CONSUMPTION:

11,000 bbl/day (2016 est.)

country comparison to the world: 160

REFINED PETROLEUM PRODUCTS - EXPORTS:

0 bbl/day (2015 est.)

country comparison to the world: 177

REFINED PETROLEUM PRODUCTS - IMPORTS:

10,840 bbl/day (2015 est.)

country comparison to the world: 144

NATURAL GAS - PRODUCTION:

0 cu m (2017 est.)

country comparison to the world: 165

NATURAL GAS - CONSUMPTION:

0 cu m (2017 est.)

country comparison to the world: 171

NATURAL GAS - EXPORTS:

0 cu m (2017 est.)

country comparison to the world: 146

NATURAL GAS - IMPORTS:

0 cu m (2017 est.)

country comparison to the world: 153

NATURAL GAS - PROVED RESERVES:

0 cu m (1 January 2016 est.)

country comparison to the world: 166

CARBON DIOXIDE EMISSIONS FROM CONSUMPTION OF ENERGY:

1.648 million Mt (2017 est.)

country comparison to the world: 161

COMMUNICATIONS :: MALDIVES

TELEPHONES - FIXED LINES:

total subscriptions: 20,377

subscriptions per 100 inhabitants: 5 (2017 est.)

country comparison to the world: 176

TELEPHONES - MOBILE CELLULAR:

total subscriptions: 900,120

subscriptions per 100 inhabitants: 229 (2017 est.)

country comparison to the world: 161

TELEPHONE SYSTEM:

general assessment: all inhabited islands and resorts are connected with telephone and fax service; two mobile operators extend LTE coverage; tourism has strengthened the telecom market with investment; the unusually high mobile penetration rate is also helped by tourism; Internet bandwidth increased 37% in 2016; mobile penetration passes 250% (2018)

domestic: fixed-line is at 5 per 100 persons and high mobile-cellular subscriptions stands at 229 per 100 persons (2018)

international: country code - 960; landing points for Dhiraagu Cable Network, NaSCOM, Dhiraagu-SLT Submarine Cable Networks and WARF submarine cables providing connections to 8 points in Maldives, India, and Sri Lanka; satellite earth station - 3 Intelsat (Indian Ocean) (2019)

BROADCAST MEDIA:

state-owned radio and TV monopoly until recently; 4 state-operated and 7 privately owned TV stations and 4 state-operated and 7 privately owned radio stations (2019)

INTERNET COUNTRY CODE:

.mv

INTERNET USERS:

total: 232,210

percent of population: 59.1% (July 2016 est.)

country comparison to the world: 166

BROADBAND - FIXED SUBSCRIPTIONS:

total: 36,001

subscriptions per 100 inhabitants: 9 (2017 est.)

country comparison to the world: 135

MILITARY AND SECURITY :: MALDIVES

MILITARY AND SECURITY FORCES:

Maldives National Defense Force (MNDF): Marine Corps, Special Protection Group, Coast Guard (2018)

MILITARY SERVICE AGE AND OBLIGATION:

18-28 years of age for voluntary service; no conscription; 10th grade or equivalent education required; must not be a member of a political party

MILITARY - NOTE:

Maldives National Defense Force (MNDF), with its small size and with little serviceable equipment, is inadequate to prevent external aggression and is primarily tasked to reinforce Maldives Police Service (MPS) and ensure security in the exclusive economic zone (2015)

TRANSPORTATION :: MALDIVES

NATIONAL AIR TRANSPORT SYSTEM:

number of registered air carriers: 3 (2015)

inventory of registered aircraft operated by air carriers: 15 (2015)

CIVIL AIRCRAFT REGISTRATION COUNTRY CODE PREFIX:

8Q (2016)

AIRPORTS:

9 (2013)

country comparison to the world: 158

AIRPORTS - WITH PAVED RUNWAYS:

total: 7 (2017)

over 3,047 m: 1 (2017)

2,438 to 3,047 m: 1 (2017)

1,524 to 2,437 m: 1 (2017)

914 to 1,523 m: 4 (2017)

AIRPORTS - WITH UNPAVED RUNWAYS:

total: 2 (2013)

914 to 1,523 m: 2 (2013)

ROADWAYS:

total: 93 km (2018)

paved: 93 km - 60 km in Male; 16 km on Addu Atolis; 17 km on Laamu (2018)

note: island roads are mainly compacted coral

country comparison to the world: 208

MERCHANT MARINE:

total: 67

by type: bulk carrier 1, general cargo 27, oil tanker 15, other 24 (2018)

country comparison to the world: 103

PORTS AND TERMINALS:

major seaport(s): Male

TRANSNATIONAL ISSUES :: MALDIVES

DISPUTES - INTERNATIONAL:

none

TRAFFICKING IN PERSONS:

current situation: Maldives is a destination country for men, women, and children subjected to forced labor and sex trafficking and a source country for women and children subjected to labor and sex trafficking; primarily Bangladeshi and Indian migrants working both legally and illegally in the construction and service sectors face conditions of forced labor, including fraudulent recruitment, confiscation of identity and travel documents, nonpayment and withholding of wages, and debt bondage; a small number of women from Asia, Eastern Europe, and former Soviet states are trafficked to Maldives for sexual exploitation; Maldivian women may be subjected to sex trafficking domestically or in Sri Lanka; some Maldivian children are transported to the capital for domestic service, where they may also be victims of sexual abuse and forced labor

tier rating: Tier 2 Watch List – Maldives does not fully comply with the minimum standards for the elimination of trafficking; however, it is making significant efforts to do so; the government adopted a national action plan for 2015-19 and is continuing to develop victim identification, protection, and referral procedures, but overall its anti-trafficking efforts did not increase; only five trafficking investigations were conducted, no new prosecutions were initiated for the second consecutive year, and no convictions were made, down from one in 2013; some officials warned businesses in advance of planned raids for suspected trafficking offenses; victim protection deteriorated when the state-run shelter for female victims barred access to victims shortly after opening in January 2014, in part because of bureaucratic disputes, which dissuaded victims from pursuing charges against perpetrators; the government did not prosecute or hold accountable any employers or government officials for withholding passports (2015)

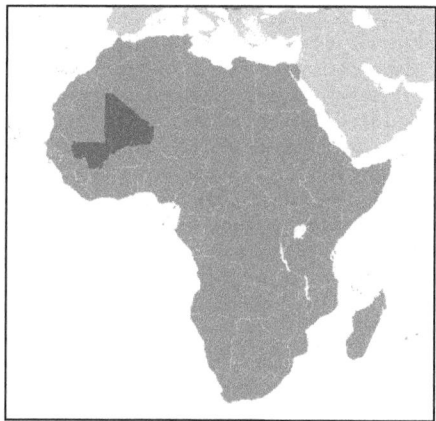

AFRICA :: MALI

INTRODUCTION :: MALI

BACKGROUND:

The Sudanese Republic and Senegal became independent of France in 1960 as the Mali Federation. When Senegal withdrew after only a few months, what formerly made up the Sudanese Republic was renamed Mali. Rule by dictatorship was brought to a close in 1991 by a military coup that ushered in a period of democratic rule. President Alpha Oumar KONARE won Mali's first two democratic presidential elections in 1992 and 1997. In keeping with Mali's two-term constitutional limit, he stepped down in 2002 and was succeeded by Amadou Toumani TOURE, who was elected to a second term in a 2007 election that was widely judged to be free and fair. Malian returnees from Libya in 2011 exacerbated tensions in northern Mali, and Tuareg ethnic militias rebelled in January 2012. Low- and mid-level soldiers, frustrated with the poor handling of the rebellion, overthrew TOURE on 22 March. Intensive mediation efforts led by the Economic Community of West African States (ECOWAS) returned power to a civilian administration in April with the appointment of Interim President Dioncounda TRAORE.

The post-coup chaos led to rebels expelling the Malian military from the country's three northern regions and allowed Islamic militants to set up strongholds. Hundreds of thousands of northern Malians fled the violence to southern Mali and neighboring countries, exacerbating regional food shortages in host communities. A French-led international military intervention to retake the three northern regions began in January 2013 and within a month, most of the north had been retaken. In a democratic presidential election conducted in July and August of 2013, Ibrahim Boubacar KEITA was elected president. The Malian Government and northern armed groups signed an internationally mediated peace accord in June 2015, however, the parties to the peace accord have made little progress in the accord's implementation, despite a June 2017 target for its completion. Furthermore, extremist groups outside the peace process made steady inroads into rural areas of central Mali following the consolidation of three major terrorist organizations in March 2017. In central and northern Mali, terrorist groups have exploited age-old ethnic rivalries between pastoralists and sedentary communities and inflicted serious losses on the Malian military. Intercommunal violence incidents such as targeted killings occur with increasing regularity. KEITA was reelected president in 2018 in an election that was deemed credible by international observers, despite some security and logistic shortfalls.

GEOGRAPHY :: MALI

LOCATION:
interior Western Africa, southwest of Algeria, north of Guinea, Cote d'Ivoire, and Burkina Faso, west of Niger

GEOGRAPHIC COORDINATES:
17 00 N, 4 00 W

MAP REFERENCES:
Africa

AREA:
total: 1,240,192 sq km

land: 1,220,190 sq km

water: 20,002 sq km

country comparison to the world: 25

AREA - COMPARATIVE:
slightly less than twice the size of Texas

LAND BOUNDARIES:
total: 7,908 km

border countries (7): Algeria 1359 km, Burkina Faso 1325 km, Cote d'Ivoire 599 km, Guinea 1062 km, Mauritania 2236 km, Niger 838 km, Senegal 489 km

COASTLINE:
0 km (landlocked)

MARITIME CLAIMS:
none (landlocked)

CLIMATE:
subtropical to arid; hot and dry (February to June); rainy, humid, and mild (June to November); cool and dry (November to February)

TERRAIN:
mostly flat to rolling northern plains covered by sand; savanna in south, rugged hills in northeast

ELEVATION:
mean elevation: 343 m

lowest point: Senegal River 23 m

highest point: Hombori Tondo 1,155 m

NATURAL RESOURCES:
gold, phosphates, kaolin, salt, limestone, uranium, gypsum, granite, hydropower, note, bauxite, iron ore, manganese, tin, and copper deposits are known but not exploited

LAND USE:

agricultural land: 34.1% (2011 est.)

arable land: 5.6% (2011 est.) / permanent crops: 0.1% (2011 est.) / permanent pasture: 28.4% (2011 est.)

forest: 10.2% (2011 est.)

other: 55.7% (2011 est.)

IRRIGATED LAND:

3,780 sq km (2012)

POPULATION DISTRIBUTION:

the overwhelming majority of the population lives in the southern half of the country, with greater density along the border with Burkina Faso

NATURAL HAZARDS:

hot, dust-laden harmattan haze common during dry seasons; recurring droughts; occasional Niger River flooding

ENVIRONMENT - CURRENT ISSUES:

deforestation; soil erosion; desertification; loss of pasture land; inadequate supplies of potable water

ENVIRONMENT - INTERNATIONAL AGREEMENTS:

party to: Biodiversity, Climate Change, Climate Change-Kyoto Protocol, Desertification, Endangered Species, Hazardous Wastes, Law of the Sea, Ozone Layer Protection, Wetlands, Whaling

signed, but not ratified: none of the selected agreements

GEOGRAPHY - NOTE:

landlocked; divided into three natural zones: the southern, cultivated Sudanese; the central, semiarid Sahelian; and the northern, arid Saharan

PEOPLE AND SOCIETY :: MALI

POPULATION:

18,429,893 (July 2018 est.)

country comparison to the world: 64

NATIONALITY:

noun: Malian(s)

adjective: Malian

ETHNIC GROUPS:

Bambara 33.3%, Fulani (Peuhl) 13.3%, Sarakole/Soninke/Marka 9.8%, Senufo/Manianka 9.6%, Malinke 8.8%, Dogon 8.7%, Sonrai 5.9%, Bobo 2.1%, Tuareg/Bella 1.7%, other Malian 6%, from member of Economic Community of West Africa .4%, other .3% (2018 est.)

LANGUAGES:

French (official), Bambara 46.3%, Peuhl/Foulfoulbe 9.4%, Dogon 7.2%, Maraka/Soninke 6.4%, Malinke 5.6%, Sonrhai/Djerma 5.6%, Minianka 4.3%, Tamacheq 3.5%, Senoufo 2.6%, Bobo 2.1%, unspecified 0.7%, other 6.3% (2009 est.)

note: Mali has 13 national languages in addition to its official language

RELIGIONS:

Muslim 93.9%, Christian 2.8%, Animist .7%, none 2.5% (2018 est.)

DEMOGRAPHIC PROFILE:

Mali's total population is expected to double by 2035; its capital Bamako is one of the fastest-growing cities in Africa. A young age structure, a declining mortality rate, and a sustained high total fertility rate of 6 children per woman – the third highest in the world – ensure continued rapid population growth for the foreseeable future. Significant outmigration only marginally tempers this growth. Despite decreases, Mali's infant, child, and maternal mortality rates remain among the highest in sub-Saharan Africa because of limited access to and adoption of family planning, early childbearing, short birth intervals, the prevalence of female genital cutting, infrequent use of skilled birth attendants, and a lack of emergency obstetrical and neonatal care.

Mali's high total fertility rate has been virtually unchanged for decades, as a result of the ongoing preference for large families, early childbearing, the lack of female education and empowerment, poverty, and extremely low contraceptive use. Slowing Mali's population growth by lowering its birth rate will be essential for poverty reduction, improving food security, and developing human capital and the economy.

Mali has a long history of seasonal migration and emigration driven by poverty, conflict, demographic pressure, unemployment, food insecurity, and droughts. Many Malians from rural areas migrate during the dry period to nearby villages and towns to do odd jobs or to adjoining countries to work in agriculture or mining. Pastoralists and nomads move seasonally to southern Mali or nearby coastal states. Others migrate long term to Mali's urban areas, Cote d'Ivoire, other neighboring countries, and in smaller numbers to France, Mali's former colonial ruler. Since the early 1990s, Mali's role has grown as a transit country for regional migration flows and illegal migration to Europe. Human smugglers and traffickers exploit the same regional routes used for moving contraband drugs, arms, and cigarettes.

Between early 2012 and 2013, renewed fighting in northern Mali between government forces and Tuareg secessionists and their Islamist allies, a French-led international military intervention, as well as chronic food shortages, caused the displacement of hundreds of thousands of Malians. Most of those displaced domestically sought shelter in urban areas of southern Mali, except for pastoralist and nomadic groups, who abandoned their traditional routes, gave away or sold their livestock, and dispersed into the deserts of northern Mali or crossed into neighboring countries. Almost all Malians who took refuge abroad (mostly Tuareg and Maure pastoralists) stayed in the region, largely in Mauritania, Niger, and Burkina Faso.

AGE STRUCTURE:

0-14 years: 48.03% (male 4,449,790 /female 4,402,076)

15-24 years: 18.89% (male 1,657,609 /female 1,823,453)

25-54 years: 26.36% (male 2,243,158 /female 2,615,695)

55-64 years: 3.7% (male 346,003 /female 335,733)

65 years and over: 3.02% (male 277,834 /female 278,542) (2018 est.)

DEPENDENCY RATIOS:

total dependency ratio: 101.9 (2015 est.)

youth dependency ratio: 96.8 (2015 est.)

elderly dependency ratio: 5.1 (2015 est.)

potential support ratio: 19.5 (2015 est.)

MEDIAN AGE:

total: 15.8 years (2018 est.)

male: 15.2 years

female: 16.5 years

country comparison to the world: 227

POPULATION GROWTH RATE:

2.98% (2018 est.)

country comparison to the world: 8

BIRTH RATE:

43.2 births/1,000 population (2018 est.)

country comparison to the world: 3

DEATH RATE:

9.6 deaths/1,000 population (2018 est.)

country comparison to the world: 45

NET MIGRATION RATE:

-3.9 migrant(s)/1,000 population (2018 est.)

country comparison to the world: 183

POPULATION DISTRIBUTION:

the overwhelming majority of the population lives in the southern half of the country, with greater density along the border with Burkina Faso

URBANIZATION:

urban population: 43.1% of total population (2019)

rate of urbanization: 4.86% annual rate of change (2015-20 est.)

MAJOR URBAN AREAS - POPULATION:

2.529 million BAMAKO (capital) (2019)

SEX RATIO:

at birth: 1.03 male(s)/female

0-14 years: 1.01 male(s)/female

15-24 years: 0.91 male(s)/female

25-54 years: 0.86 male(s)/female

55-64 years: 1.03 male(s)/female

65 years and over: 1 male(s)/female

total population: 0.95 male(s)/female (2018 est.)

MOTHER'S MEAN AGE AT FIRST BIRTH:

18.9 years (2018 est.)

note: median age at first birth among women 25-29

MATERNAL MORTALITY RATE:

562 deaths/100,000 live births (2017 est.)

country comparison to the world: 15

INFANT MORTALITY RATE:

total: 67.6 deaths/1,000 live births (2018 est.)

male: 73.3 deaths/1,000 live births

female: 61.7 deaths/1,000 live births

country comparison to the world: 7

LIFE EXPECTANCY AT BIRTH:

total population: 60.8 years (2018 est.)

male: 58.6 years

female: 63 years

country comparison to the world: 206

TOTAL FERTILITY RATE:

5.9 children born/woman (2018 est.)

country comparison to the world: 5

CONTRACEPTIVE PREVALENCE RATE:

15.6% (2015)

DRINKING WATER SOURCE:

improved:

urban: 96.5% of population

rural: 64.1% of population

total: 77% of population

unimproved:

urban: 3.5% of population

rural: 35.9% of population

total: 23% of population (2015 est.)

CURRENT HEALTH EXPENDITURE:

3.8% (2016)

PHYSICIANS DENSITY:

0.14 physicians/1,000 population (2016)

HOSPITAL BED DENSITY:

0.1 beds/1,000 population (2010)

SANITATION FACILITY ACCESS:

improved:

urban: 37.5% of population (2015 est.)

rural: 16.1% of population (2015 est.)

total: 24.7% of population (2015 est.)

unimproved:

urban: 62.5% of population (2015 est.)

rural: 83.9% of population (2015 est.)

total: 75.3% of population (2015 est.)

HIV/AIDS - ADULT PREVALENCE RATE:

1.4% (2018 est.)

country comparison to the world: 36

HIV/AIDS - PEOPLE LIVING WITH HIV/AIDS:

150,000 (2018 est.)

country comparison to the world: 35

HIV/AIDS - DEATHS:

6,500 (2018 est.)

country comparison to the world: 22

MAJOR INFECTIOUS DISEASES:

degree of risk: very high (2016)

food or waterborne diseases: bacterial and protozoal diarrhea, hepatitis A, and typhoid fever (2016)

vectorborne diseases: malaria and dengue fever (2016)

water contact diseases: schistosomiasis (2016)

animal contact diseases: rabies (2016)

respiratory diseases: meningococcal meningitis (2016)

OBESITY - ADULT PREVALENCE RATE:

8.6% (2016)

country comparison to the world: 149

CHILDREN UNDER THE AGE OF 5 YEARS UNDERWEIGHT:

25% (2015)

country comparison to the world: 18

EDUCATION EXPENDITURES:

3.1% of GDP (2016)

country comparison to the world: 138

LITERACY:

definition: age 15 and over can read and write

total population: 33.1%

male: 45.1%

female: 22.2% (2015 est.)

SCHOOL LIFE EXPECTANCY (PRIMARY TO TERTIARY EDUCATION):

total: 7 years

male: 8 years

female: 7 years (2015)

UNEMPLOYMENT, YOUTH AGES 15-24:

total: 2.3%

male: 2.5%

female: 2.2% (2016 est.)

country comparison to the world: 175

GOVERNMENT :: MALI

COUNTRY NAME:

conventional long form: Republic of Mali

conventional short form: Mali

local long form: Republique de Mali

local short form: Mali

former: French Sudan and Sudanese Republic

etymology: name derives from the West African Mali Empire of the 13th to 16th centuries A.D.

GOVERNMENT TYPE:
semi-presidential republic

CAPITAL:
name: Bamako

geographic coordinates: 12 39 N, 8 00 W

time difference: UTC 0 (5 hours ahead of Washington, DC, during Standard Time)

etymology: the name in the Bambara language can mean either "crocodile tail" or "crocodile river" and three crocodiles appear on the city seal

ADMINISTRATIVE DIVISIONS:
10 regions (regions, singular - region), 1 district*; District de Bamako*, Gao, Kayes, Kidal, Koulikoro, Menaka, Mopti, Segou, Sikasso, Taoudenni, Tombouctou (Timbuktu); note - Menaka and Taoudenni were legislated in 2016, but implementation has not been confirmed by the US Board on Geographic Names

INDEPENDENCE:
22 September 1960 (from France)

NATIONAL HOLIDAY:
Independence Day, 22 September (1960)

CONSTITUTION:
history: several previous; latest drafted August 1991, approved by referendum 12 January 1992, effective 25 February 1992, suspended briefly in 2012

amendments: proposed by the president of the republic or by members of the National Assembly; passage requires two-thirds majority vote by the Assembly and approval in a referendum; constitutional sections on the integrity of the state, its republican and secular form of government, and its multiparty system cannot be amended; amended 1999 (2017)

LEGAL SYSTEM:
civil law system based on the French civil law model and influenced by customary law; judicial review of legislative acts in the Constitutional Court

INTERNATIONAL LAW ORGANIZATION PARTICIPATION:
has not submitted an ICJ jurisdiction declaration; accepts ICCt jurisdiction

CITIZENSHIP:
citizenship by birth: no

citizenship by descent only: at least one parent must be a citizen of Mali

dual citizenship recognized: yes

residency requirement for naturalization: 5 years

SUFFRAGE:
18 years of age; universal

EXECUTIVE BRANCH:
chief of state: President Ibrahim Boubacar KEITA (since 4 September 2013)

head of government: Prime Minister Boubou CISSE (since 23 April 2019)

cabinet: Council of Ministers appointed by the prime minister

elections/appointments: president directly elected by absolute majority popular vote in 2 rounds if needed for a 5-year term (eligible for a second term); election last held on 29 July 2018 with a runoff on 12 August 2018; prime minister appointed by the president

election results: Ibrahim Boubacar KEITA elected president in second round; percent of vote - Ibrahim Boubacar KEITA (RPM) 77.6%, Soumaila CISSE (URD) 22.4%

LEGISLATIVE BRANCH:
description: unicameral National Assembly or Assemblee Nationale (147 seats; members directly elected in single and multi-seat constituencies by absolute majority vote in 2 rounds if needed; 13 seats reserved for citizens living abroad; members serve 5-year terms)

elections: last held on 24 November and 15 December 2013 (next originally scheduled for 25 November 2018, but postponed to 2019)

election results: percent of vote by party - RPM 29.4%, URD 22.6%, ADEMA 11.5, other 36.5%; seats by party - RPM 66, URD 17, ADEMA 16, FARE 6, CODEM 5, SADI 5, CNID 4, other 24, independent 4; composition - men 133, women 14, percent of women 9.5%

JUDICIAL BRANCH:
highest courts: Supreme Court or Cour Supreme (consists of 19 members organized into 3 civil chambers and a criminal chamber); Constitutional Court (consists of 9 members)

judge selection and term of office: Supreme Court members appointed by the Ministry of Justice to serve 5-year terms; Constitutional Court members selected - 3 each by the president, the National Assembly, and the Supreme Council of the Magistracy; members serve single renewable 7-year terms

subordinate courts: Court of Appeal; High Court of Justice (jurisdiction limited to cases of high treason or criminal offenses by the president or ministers while in office); magistrate courts; first instance courts; labor dispute courts; special court of state security

POLITICAL PARTIES AND LEADERS:
African Solidarity for Democracy and Independence or SADI [Oumar MARIKO]
Alliance for Democracy in Mali-Pan-African Party for Liberty, Solidarity, and Justice or ADEMA-PASJ [Tiemoko SANGARE]
Alliance for Democracy and Progress or ADP-Maliba [Amadou THIAM]
Alliance for the Solidarity of Mali-Convergence of Patriotic Forces or ASMA-CFP [Soumeylou Boubeye MAIGA]
Alternative Forces for Renewal and Emergence or FARE [Modibo SIDIBE]
Convergence for the Development of Mali or CODEM [Housseyni Amion GUINDO]
Economic and Social Development Party or PDES [Jamille BITTAR]
Front for Democracy and the Republic or FDR (coalition of smaller opposition parties)
National Congress for Democratic Initiative or CNID [Mountaga TALL]
Party for National Renewal or PARENA [Tiebile DRAME]
Patriotic Movement for Renewal or MPR [Choguel Kokalla MAIGA]
Rally for Mali or RPM [Boucary TRETA]
Union for Republic and Democracy or URD [Younoussi TOURE]

INTERNATIONAL ORGANIZATION PARTICIPATION:
ACP, AfDB, AU, CD, ECOWAS, EITI (compliant country), FAO, FZ, G-77, IAEA, IBRD, ICAO, ICCt, ICRM, IDA, IDB, IFAD, IFC, IFRCS, ILO, IMF, Interpol, IOC, IOM, IPU, ISO, ITSO, ITU, ITUC (NGOs), MIGA, MONUSCO, NAM, OIC, OIF, OPCW, UN, UNAMID, UNCTAD, UNESCO, UNIDO, UNISFA, UNMISS, UNWTO, UPU, WADB (regional), WAEMU, WCO, WFTU (NGOs), WHO, WIPO, WMO, WTO

DIPLOMATIC REPRESENTATION IN THE US:
Ambassador Mahamadou NIMAGA (since 22 June 2018)

chancery: 2130 R Street NW, Washington, DC 20008

telephone: [1] (202) 332-2249, 939-8950

FAX: [1] (202) 332-6603

DIPLOMATIC REPRESENTATION FROM THE US:

chief of mission: Ambassador Dennis B. HANKINS (since 15 March 2019)

telephone: [223] 2070-2300

embassy: located off the Roi Bin Fahad Aziz Bridge west of the Bamako central district; ACI 2000, Rue 243, Porte 297

mailing address: ACI 2000, Rue 243, Porte 297, Bamako

FAX: [223] 2070-2479

FLAG DESCRIPTION:

three equal vertical bands of green (hoist side), yellow, and red

note: uses the popular Pan-African colors of Ethiopia; the colors from left to right are the same as those of neighboring Senegal (which has an additional green central star) and the reverse of those on the flag of neighboring Guinea

NATIONAL SYMBOL(S):

Great Mosque of Djenne; national colors: green, yellow, red

NATIONAL ANTHEM:

name: "Le Mali" (Mali)

lyrics/music: Seydou Badian KOUYATE/Banzoumana SISSOKO

note: adopted 1962; also known as "Pour L'Afrique et pour toi, Mali" (For Africa and for You, Mali) and "A ton appel Mali" (At Your Call, Mali)

ECONOMY :: MALI

ECONOMY - OVERVIEW:

Among the 25 poorest countries in the world, landlocked Mali depends on gold mining and agricultural exports for revenue. The country's fiscal status fluctuates with gold and agricultural commodity prices and the harvest; cotton and gold exports make up around 80% of export earnings. Mali remains dependent on foreign aid.

Economic activity is largely confined to the riverine area irrigated by the Niger River; about 65% of Mali's land area is desert or semidesert. About 10% of the population is nomadic and about 80% of the labor force is engaged in farming and fishing.

Industrial activity is concentrated on processing farm commodities. The government subsidizes the production of cereals to decrease the country's dependence on imported foodstuffs and to reduce its vulnerability to food price shocks.

Mali is developing its iron ore extraction industry to diversify foreign exchange earnings away from gold, but the pace will depend on global price trends. Although the political coup in 2012 slowed Mali's growth, the economy has since bounced back, with GDP growth above 5% in 2014-17, although physical insecurity, high population growth, corruption, weak infrastructure, and low levels of human capital continue to constrain economic development. Higher rainfall helped to boost cotton output in 2017, and the country's 2017 budget increased spending more than 10%, much of which was devoted to infrastructure and agriculture. Corruption and political turmoil are strong downside risks in 2018 and beyond.

GDP (PURCHASING POWER PARITY):

$41.22 billion (2017 est.)

$39.1 billion (2016 est.)

$36.97 billion (2015 est.)

note: data are in 2017 dollars

country comparison to the world: 116

GDP (OFFICIAL EXCHANGE RATE):

$15.37 billion (2017 est.)

GDP - REAL GROWTH RATE:

5.4% (2017 est.)

5.8% (2016 est.)

6.2% (2015 est.)

country comparison to the world: 39

GDP - PER CAPITA (PPP):

$2,200 (2017 est.)

$2,100 (2016 est.)

$2,100 (2015 est.)

note: data are in 2017 dollars

country comparison to the world: 206

GROSS NATIONAL SAVING:

16.5% of GDP (2017 est.)

15.5% of GDP (2016 est.)

15.4% of GDP (2015 est.)

country comparison to the world: 126

GDP - COMPOSITION, BY END USE:

household consumption: 82.9% (2017 est.)

government consumption: 17.4% (2017 est.)

investment in fixed capital: 19.3% (2017 est.)

investment in inventories: -0.7% (2017 est.)

exports of goods and services: 22.1% (2017 est.)

imports of goods and services: -41.1% (2017 est.)

GDP - COMPOSITION, BY SECTOR OF ORIGIN:

agriculture: 41.8% (2017 est.)

industry: 18.1% (2017 est.)

services: 40.5% (2017 est.)

AGRICULTURE - PRODUCTS:

cotton, millet, rice, corn, vegetables, peanuts; cattle, sheep, goats

INDUSTRIES:

food processing; construction; phosphate and gold mining

INDUSTRIAL PRODUCTION GROWTH RATE:

6.3% (2017 est.)

country comparison to the world: 37

LABOR FORCE:

6.447 million (2017 est.)

country comparison to the world: 71

LABOR FORCE - BY OCCUPATION:

agriculture: 80%

industry and services: 20% (2005 est.)

UNEMPLOYMENT RATE:

7.9% (2017 est.)

7.8% (2016 est.)

country comparison to the world: 114

POPULATION BELOW POVERTY LINE:

36.1% (2005 est.)

HOUSEHOLD INCOME OR CONSUMPTION BY PERCENTAGE SHARE:

lowest 10%: 3.5%

highest 10%: 25.8% (2010 est.)

DISTRIBUTION OF FAMILY INCOME - GINI INDEX:

40.1 (2001)

50.5 (1994)

country comparison to the world: 67

BUDGET:

revenues: 3.075 billion (2017 est.)

expenditures: 3.513 billion (2017 est.)

TAXES AND OTHER REVENUES:

20% (of GDP) (2017 est.)

country comparison to the world: 153

BUDGET SURPLUS (+) OR DEFICIT (-):

-2.9% (of GDP) (2017 est.)

country comparison to the world: 128

PUBLIC DEBT:

35.4% of GDP (2017 est.)

36% of GDP (2016 est.)

country comparison to the world: 150

FISCAL YEAR:

calendar year

INFLATION RATE (CONSUMER PRICES):

1.8% (2017 est.)

-1.8% (2016 est.)

country comparison to the world: 94

CENTRAL BANK DISCOUNT RATE:

16% (31 December 2010)

4.25% (31 December 2009)

country comparison to the world: 10

COMMERCIAL BANK PRIME LENDING RATE:

5.2% (31 December 2017 est.)

5.3% (31 December 2016 est.)

country comparison to the world: 147

STOCK OF NARROW MONEY:

$3.04 billion (31 December 2017 est.)

$2.553 billion (31 December 2016 est.)

country comparison to the world: 122

STOCK OF BROAD MONEY:

$3.04 billion (31 December 2017 est.)

$2.553 billion (31 December 2016 est.)

country comparison to the world: 128

STOCK OF DOMESTIC CREDIT:

$5.972 billion (31 December 2017 est.)

$4.891 billion (31 December 2016 est.)

country comparison to the world: 126

MARKET VALUE OF PUBLICLY TRADED SHARES:

NA

CURRENT ACCOUNT BALANCE:

-$886 million (2017 est.)

-$1.015 billion (2016 est.)

country comparison to the world: 138

EXPORTS:

$3.06 billion (2017 est.)

$2.803 billion (2016 est.)

country comparison to the world: 130

EXPORTS - PARTNERS:

Switzerland 31.8%, UAE 15.4%, Burkina Faso 7.8%, Cote dIvoire 7.3%, South Africa 5%, Bangladesh 4.6% (2017)

EXPORTS - COMMODITIES:

cotton, gold, livestock

IMPORTS:

$3.644 billion (2017 est.)

$3.403 billion (2016 est.)

country comparison to the world: 143

IMPORTS - COMMODITIES:

petroleum, machinery and equipment, construction materials, foodstuffs, textiles

IMPORTS - PARTNERS:

Senegal 24.4%, China 13.2%, Cote dIvoire 9%, France 7.3% (2017)

RESERVES OF FOREIGN EXCHANGE AND GOLD:

$647.8 million (31 December 2017 est.)

$395.7 million (31 December 2016 est.)

country comparison to the world: 144

DEBT - EXTERNAL:

$4.192 billion (31 December 2017 est.)

$3.981 billion (31 December 2016 est.)

country comparison to the world: 137

STOCK OF DIRECT FOREIGN INVESTMENT - AT HOME:

$3.845 billion (31 December 2017 est.)

$3.266 billion (31 December 2016 est.)

country comparison to the world: 111

STOCK OF DIRECT FOREIGN INVESTMENT - ABROAD:

$286.2 million (31 December 2017 est.)

$62.2 million (31 December 2016 est.)

country comparison to the world: 103

EXCHANGE RATES:

Communaute Financiere Africaine francs (XOF) per US dollar -

605.3 (2017 est.)

593.01 (2016 est.)

593.01 (2015 est.)

591.45 (2014 est.)

494.42 (2013 est.)

ENERGY :: MALI

ELECTRICITY ACCESS:

population without electricity: 11 million (2017)

electrification - total population: 35.1% (2016)

electrification - urban areas: 83.6% (2016)

electrification - rural areas: 1.8% (2016)

ELECTRICITY - PRODUCTION:

2.489 billion kWh (2016 est.)

country comparison to the world: 136

ELECTRICITY - CONSUMPTION:

2.982 billion kWh (2016 est.)

country comparison to the world: 136

ELECTRICITY - EXPORTS:

0 kWh (2016 est.)

country comparison to the world: 166

ELECTRICITY - IMPORTS:

800 million kWh (2016 est.)

country comparison to the world: 73

ELECTRICITY - INSTALLED GENERATING CAPACITY:

590,000 kW (2016 est.)

country comparison to the world: 140

ELECTRICITY - FROM FOSSIL FUELS:

68% of total installed capacity (2016 est.)

country comparison to the world: 113

ELECTRICITY - FROM NUCLEAR FUELS:

0% of total installed capacity (2017 est.)

country comparison to the world: 138

ELECTRICITY - FROM HYDROELECTRIC PLANTS:

31% of total installed capacity (2017 est.)

country comparison to the world: 68

ELECTRICITY - FROM OTHER RENEWABLE SOURCES:

1% of total installed capacity (2017 est.)

country comparison to the world: 160

CRUDE OIL - PRODUCTION:

0 bbl/day (2018 est.)

country comparison to the world: 170

CRUDE OIL - EXPORTS:

0 bbl/day (2015 est.)

country comparison to the world: 161

CRUDE OIL - IMPORTS:

0 bbl/day (2015 est.)

country comparison to the world: 161

CRUDE OIL - PROVED RESERVES:

0 bbl (1 January 2018 est.)

country comparison to the world: 165

REFINED PETROLEUM PRODUCTS - PRODUCTION:

0 bbl/day (2015 est.)

country comparison to the world: 173

REFINED PETROLEUM PRODUCTS - CONSUMPTION:

22,000 bbl/day (2016 est.)

country comparison to the world: 134

REFINED PETROLEUM PRODUCTS - EXPORTS:

0 bbl/day (2015 est.)

country comparison to the world: 178

REFINED PETROLEUM PRODUCTS - IMPORTS:

20,610 bbl/day (2015 est.)

country comparison to the world: 119

NATURAL GAS - PRODUCTION:

0 cu m (2017 est.)

country comparison to the world: 166

NATURAL GAS - CONSUMPTION:

0 cu m (2017 est.)

country comparison to the world: 172

NATURAL GAS - EXPORTS:

0 cu m (2017 est.)

country comparison to the world: 147

NATURAL GAS - IMPORTS:

0 cu m (2017 est.)

country comparison to the world: 154

NATURAL GAS - PROVED RESERVES:

0 cu m (1 January 2014 est.)

country comparison to the world: 167

CARBON DIOXIDE EMISSIONS FROM CONSUMPTION OF ENERGY:

3.388 million Mt (2017 est.)

country comparison to the world: 143

COMMUNICATIONS :: MALI

TELEPHONES - FIXED LINES:

total subscriptions: 200,812

subscriptions per 100 inhabitants: 1 (July 2016 est.)

country comparison to the world: 124

TELEPHONES - MOBILE CELLULAR:

total subscriptions: 20,217,697

subscriptions per 100 inhabitants: 113 (July 2016 est.)

country comparison to the world: 56

TELEPHONE SYSTEM:

general assessment: domestic system improving; increasing use of local radio loops to extend network coverage to remote areas; geography a challenge for telecommunications; poverty, security, high illiteracy and low PC use has taken its toll; 4 mobile operators in market; potential for mobile broadband services; local plans for Internet Exchange Point (2018)

domestic: fixed-line subscribership remains less than 1 per 100 persons; mobile-cellular subscribership has increased sharply to over 113 per 100 persons (2018)

international: country code - 223; satellite communications center and fiber-optic links to neighboring countries; satellite earth stations - 2 Intelsat (1 Atlantic Ocean, 1 Indian Ocean); new competition with submarine fiber optic cables in the region

BROADCAST MEDIA:

national public TV broadcaster; 2 privately owned companies provide subscription services to foreign multi-channel TV packages; national public radio broadcaster supplemented by a large number of privately owned and community broadcast stations; transmissions of multiple international broadcasters are available (2019)

INTERNET COUNTRY CODE:

.ml

INTERNET USERS:

total: 1,940,978

percent of population: 11.1% (July 2016 est.)

country comparison to the world: 114

BROADBAND - FIXED SUBSCRIPTIONS:

total: 21,444

subscriptions per 100 inhabitants: less than 1 (2017 est.)

country comparison to the world: 151

MILITARY AND SECURITY :: MALI

MILITARY EXPENDITURES:

2.87% of GDP (2018)

3.01% of GDP (2017)

2.58% of GDP (2016)

2.36% of GDP (2015)

1.52% of GDP (2014)

country comparison to the world: 26

MILITARY AND SECURITY FORCES:

Malian Armed Forces (FAMa): Army (Armee de Terre), Republic of Mali Air Force (Force Aerienne de la Republique du Mali, FARM), National Guard (Garde National du Mali), Gendarmerie (2019)

Note: Mali planned to establish a border guard force in 2019

MILITARY SERVICE AGE AND OBLIGATION:

18 years of age for selective compulsory and voluntary military service (men and women); 2-year conscript service obligation (2014)

MILITARY - NOTE:

the United Nations Multidimensional Integrated Stabilization Mission in Mali (MINUSMA) has operated in the country since 2013; the Mission's responsibilities include providing security, rebuilding Malian security forces, supporting national political dialogue, and assisting in the reestablishment of Malian government authority; as of July 2019, MINUSMA had more than 16,000 military, police, and civilian personnel deployed (2019)

TRANSPORTATION :: MALI

NATIONAL AIR TRANSPORT SYSTEM:

number of registered air carriers: 1 (2015)

inventory of registered aircraft operated by air carriers: 2 (2015)

CIVIL AIRCRAFT REGISTRATION COUNTRY CODE PREFIX:

TZ, TT (2016)

AIRPORTS:

25 (2013)

country comparison to the world: 128

AIRPORTS - WITH PAVED RUNWAYS:

total: 8 (2017)

over 3,047 m: 1 (2017)

2,438 to 3,047 m: 4 (2017)

1,524 to 2,437 m: 2 (2017)

914 to 1,523 m: 1 (2017)

AIRPORTS - WITH UNPAVED RUNWAYS:

total: 17 (2013)

1,524 to 2,437 m: 3 (2013)

914 to 1,523 m: 9 (2013)

under 914 m: 5 (2013)

HELIPORTS:

2 (2013)

RAILWAYS:

total: 593 km (2014)

narrow gauge: 593 km 1.000-m gauge (2014)

country comparison to the world: 110

ROADWAYS:

total: 139,107 km (2018)

country comparison to the world: 38

WATERWAYS:

1,800 km (downstream of Koulikoro; low water levels on the River Niger cause problems in dry years; in the months before the rainy season the river is not navigable by commercial vessels) (2011)

country comparison to the world: 43

PORTS AND TERMINALS:

river port(s): Koulikoro (Niger)

TERRORISM :: MALI

TERRORIST GROUPS - HOME BASED:

al-Mulathamun Battalion: aim(s): implement ISIS's strict interpretation of Sharia; replace the Malian Government with an Islamic state
area(s) of operation: headquartered in the north; targets primarily international interests, especially Westerners and Western entities

(2018)

al-Qa'ida-affiliated Jama'at Nusrat al-Islam wal-Muslimin (JNIM): aim(s): establish an Islamic state centered in Mali
area(s) of operation: primarily based in northern and central Mali; targets Western and local interests in West Africa and Sahel; has claimed responsibility for attacks in Mali, Niger and Burkina Faso

note: pledged allegiance to al-Qa'ida and AQIM; holds Western hostages; wages attacks against security and peacekeeping forces in Mali (2018)

Islamic State of Iraq and ash-sham networks in the Greater Sahara (ISGS): aim(s): replace regional governments with an Islamic state
area(s) of operation: mostly concentrated along the Mali-Niger border region; targets primarily security forces (2018)

TRANSNATIONAL ISSUES :: MALI

DISPUTES - INTERNATIONAL:

demarcation is underway with Burkina Faso

REFUGEES AND INTERNALLY DISPLACED PERSONS:

refugees (country of origin): 15,319 (Mauritania), 8,457 (Burkina Faso) (2019)

IDPs: 199,385 (Tuareg rebellion since 2012) (2019)

TRAFFICKING IN PERSONS:

current situation: Mali is a source, transit, and destination country for men, women, and children subjected to forced labor and sex trafficking; internal trafficking is more prevalent than transnational trafficking, but foreign women and girls are forced into domestic servitude, agricultural labor, and support roles in gold mines, as well as subjected to sex trafficking; Malian boys are forced to work in agricultural settings, gold mines, the informal commercial sector and to beg within Mali and neighboring countries; Malians and other Africans who travel through Mali to Mauritania, Algeria, or Libya in hopes of reaching Europe are particularly at risk of becoming victims of human trafficking; men and boys, primarily of Songhai ethnicity, are subjected to debt bondage in the salt mines of Taoudenni in northern Mali; some members of Mali's Tamachek community are subjected to hereditary slavery-related practices; Malian women and girls are victims of sex trafficking in Gabon, Libya, Lebanon, and Tunisia; the recruitment of child soldiers by armed groups in northern Mali decreased

tier rating: Tier 2 Watch List - Mali does not fully comply with the minimum standards for the elimination of trafficking; however, it is making significant efforts to do so; in 2014, Mali was granted a waiver from an otherwise required downgrade to Tier 3 because its government has a written plan that, if implemented would constitute making significant efforts to bring itself into compliance with the minimum standards for the elimination of trafficking; officials failed to distribute the 2012 anti-trafficking law to judicial and law enforcement personnel, perpetuating a lack of understanding and awareness of the legislation; anti-trafficking law enforcement efforts decreased in 2014, with only one case investigated and no prosecutions or convictions; fewer victims were identified, and the government did not support the privately funded NGOs and international organizations it relied upon to provide victims with services; the government did not conduct any awareness-raising campaigns, workshops, or training sessions (2015)

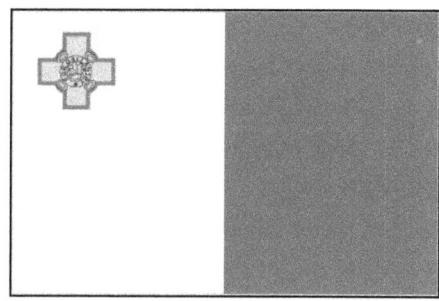

EUROPE :: MALTA

INTRODUCTION :: MALTA

BACKGROUND:
With a civilization that dates back thousands of years, Malta boasts some of the oldest megalithic sites in the world. Situated in the center of the Mediterranean, Malta's islands have long served as a strategic military asset, with the islands at various times having come under control of the Phoenicians, Carthaginians, Greeks, Romans, Byzantines, Moors, Normans, Sicilians, Spanish, Knights of St. John, and the French. Most recently a British colony (since 1814), Malta gained its independence in 1964 and declared itself a republic ten years later. While under British rule, the island staunchly supported the UK through both world wars. Since about the mid-1980s, the island has transformed itself into a freight transshipment point, a financial center, and a tourist destination while its key industries moved toward more service-oriented activities. Malta became an EU member in May 2004 and began using the euro as currency in 2008.

GEOGRAPHY :: MALTA

LOCATION:
Southern Europe, islands in the Mediterranean Sea, south of Sicily (Italy)

GEOGRAPHIC COORDINATES:
35 50 N, 14 35 E

MAP REFERENCES:
Europe

AREA:
total: 316 sq km

land: 316 sq km

water: 0 sq km

country comparison to the world: 209

AREA - COMPARATIVE:
slightly less than twice the size of Washington, DC

LAND BOUNDARIES:
0 km

COASTLINE:
196.8 km (excludes 56 km for the island of Gozo)

MARITIME CLAIMS:
territorial sea: 12 nm

contiguous zone: 24 nm

continental shelf: 200-m depth or to the depth of exploitation

exclusive fishing zone: 25 nm

CLIMATE:
Mediterranean; mild, rainy winters; hot, dry summers

TERRAIN:
mostly low, rocky, flat to dissected plains; many coastal cliffs

ELEVATION:
lowest point: Mediterranean Sea 0 m

highest point: Ta'Dmejrek on Dingli Cliffs 253 m

NATURAL RESOURCES:
limestone, salt, arable land

LAND USE:
agricultural land: 32.3% (2011 est.)

arable land: 28.4% (2011 est.) / permanent crops: 3.9% (2011 est.) / permanent pasture: 0% (2011 est.)

forest: 0.9% (2011 est.)

other: 66.8% (2011 est.)

IRRIGATED LAND:
35 sq km (2012)

POPULATION DISTRIBUTION:
most of the population lives on the eastern half of Malta, the largest of the three inhabited islands

NATURAL HAZARDS:
occasional droughts

ENVIRONMENT - CURRENT ISSUES:
limited natural freshwater resources; increasing reliance on desalination; deforestation; wildlife preservation

ENVIRONMENT - INTERNATIONAL AGREEMENTS:
party to: Air Pollution, Biodiversity, Climate Change, Climate Change-Kyoto Protocol, Desertification, Endangered Species, Hazardous Wastes, Law of the Sea, Marine Dumping, Ozone Layer Protection, Ship Pollution, Wetlands

signed, but not ratified: none of the selected agreements

GEOGRAPHY - NOTE:
the country comprises an archipelago, with only the three largest islands (Malta, Ghawdex or Gozo, and Kemmuna or Comino) inhabited; numerous bays provide good harbors; Malta and Tunisia are discussing oil exploration on the continental shelf between their countries, although no commercially viable reserves have been found as of 2017

PEOPLE AND SOCIETY :: MALTA

POPULATION:
449,043 (July 2018 est.)

country comparison to the world: 175

NATIONALITY:

noun: Maltese (singular and plural)

adjective: Maltese

ETHNIC GROUPS:
Maltese (descendants of ancient Carthaginians and Phoenicians with strong elements of Italian and other Mediterranean stock)

LANGUAGES:
Maltese (official) 90.1%, English (official) 6%, multilingual 3%, other 0.9% (2005 est.)

RELIGIONS:
Roman Catholic (official) more than 90% (2006 est.)

AGE STRUCTURE:

0-14 years: 14.29% (male 33,156 /female 31,012)

15-24 years: 11.03% (male 25,713 /female 23,815)

25-54 years: 40.92% (male 95,162 /female 88,602)

55-64 years: 13.25% (male 29,787 /female 29,703)

65 years and over: 20.51% (male 41,900 /female 50,193) (2018 est.)

DEPENDENCY RATIOS:

total dependency ratio: 48.8 (2015 est.)

youth dependency ratio: 21.4 (2015 est.)

elderly dependency ratio: 27.3 (2015 est.)

potential support ratio: 3.7 (2015 est.)

MEDIAN AGE:

total: 41.8 years (2018 est.)

male: 40.6 years

female: 43.1 years

country comparison to the world: 37

POPULATION GROWTH RATE:
0.99% (2018 est.)

country comparison to the world: 110

BIRTH RATE:
10 births/1,000 population (2018 est.)

country comparison to the world: 192

DEATH RATE:
7.9 deaths/1,000 population (2018 est.)

country comparison to the world: 93

NET MIGRATION RATE:
7.8 migrant(s)/1,000 population (2018 est.)

country comparison to the world: 12

POPULATION DISTRIBUTION:
most of the population lives on the eastern half of Malta, the largest of the three inhabited islands

URBANIZATION:

urban population: 94.7% of total population (2019)

rate of urbanization: 0.38% annual rate of change (2015-20 est.)

MAJOR URBAN AREAS - POPULATION:
213,000 VALLETTA (capital) (2018)

SEX RATIO:

at birth: 1.04 male(s)/female

0-14 years: 1.07 male(s)/female

15-24 years: 1.08 male(s)/female

25-54 years: 1.07 male(s)/female

55-64 years: 1 male(s)/female

65 years and over: 0.83 male(s)/female

total population: 1.01 male(s)/female (2018 est.)

MOTHER'S MEAN AGE AT FIRST BIRTH:
26.9 years (2010 est.)

note: data refer to the average of the different childbearing ages of first-order births

MATERNAL MORTALITY RATE:
6 deaths/100,000 live births (2017 est.)

country comparison to the world: 161

INFANT MORTALITY RATE:

total: 4.7 deaths/1,000 live births (2018 est.)

male: 4.6 deaths/1,000 live births

female: 4.9 deaths/1,000 live births

country comparison to the world: 178

LIFE EXPECTANCY AT BIRTH:

total population: 82.7 years (2018 est.)

male: 80.6 years

female: 84.8 years

country comparison to the world: 11

TOTAL FERTILITY RATE:
1.48 children born/woman (2018 est.)

country comparison to the world: 200

DRINKING WATER SOURCE:

improved:

urban: 100% of population

rural: 100% of population

total: 100% of population

unimproved:

urban: 0% of population

rural: 0% of population

total: 0% of population (2015 est.)

CURRENT HEALTH EXPENDITURE:
9.3% (2016)

PHYSICIANS DENSITY:
3.83 physicians/1,000 population (2015)

HOSPITAL BED DENSITY:
4.7 beds/1,000 population (2014)

SANITATION FACILITY ACCESS:

improved:

urban: 100% of population (2015 est.)

rural: 100% of population (2015 est.)

total: 100% of population (2015 est.)

unimproved:

urban: 0% of population (2015 est.)

rural: 0% of population (2015 est.)

total: 0% of population (2015 est.)

HIV/AIDS - ADULT PREVALENCE RATE:
0.1% (2016 est.)

country comparison to the world: 126

HIV/AIDS - PEOPLE LIVING WITH HIV/AIDS:
<500 (2016 est.)

HIV/AIDS - DEATHS:
<100 (2016 est.)

OBESITY - ADULT PREVALENCE RATE:
28.9% (2016)

country comparison to the world: 28

EDUCATION EXPENDITURES:
5.3% of GDP (2015)

country comparison to the world: 53

LITERACY:

definition: age 15 and over can read and write

total population: 94.4%

male: 93.1%

female: 95.8% (2015 est.)

SCHOOL LIFE EXPECTANCY (PRIMARY TO TERTIARY EDUCATION):

total: 16 years

male: 15 years

female: 16 years (2016)

UNEMPLOYMENT, YOUTH AGES 15-24:

total: 11.3%

male: 12.2%

female: 10.2% (2017 est.)

country comparison to the world: 115

GOVERNMENT :: MALTA

COUNTRY NAME:

conventional long form: Republic of Malta

conventional short form: Malta

local long form: Repubblika ta' Malta

local short form: Malta

etymology: the ancient Greeks called the island "Melite" meaning "honey-sweet" from the Greek word "meli" meaning "honey" and referring to the island's honey production

GOVERNMENT TYPE:

parliamentary republic

CAPITAL:

name: Valletta

geographic coordinates: 35 53 N, 14 30 E

time difference: UTC+1 (6 hours ahead of Washington, DC, during Standard Time)

daylight saving time: +1hr, begins last Sunday in March; ends last Sunday in October

etymology: named in honor of Jean de Valette, the Grand Master of the Order of Saint John (crusader knights), who successfully led a defense of the island from an Ottoman invasion in 1565

ADMINISTRATIVE DIVISIONS:

68 localities (Il-lokalita); Attard, Balzan, Birgu, Birkirkara, Birzebbuga, Bormla, Dingli, Fgura, Floriana, Fontana, Ghajnsielem, Gharb, Gharghur, Ghasri, Ghaxaq, Gudja, Gzira, Hamrun, Iklin, Imdina, Imgarr, Imqabba, Imsida, Imtarfa, Isla, Kalkara, Kercem, Kirkop, Lija, Luqa, Marsa, Marsaskala, Marsaxlokk, Mellieha, Mosta, Munxar, Nadur, Naxxar, Paola, Pembroke, Pieta, Qala, Qormi, Qrendi, Rabat, Rabat (Ghawdex), Safi, San Giljan/Saint Julian, San Gwann/Saint John, San Lawrenz/Saint Lawrence, Sannat, San Pawl il-Bahar/Saint Paul's Bay, Santa Lucija/Saint Lucia, Santa Venera/Saint Venera, Siggiewi, Sliema, Swieqi, Tarxien, Ta' Xbiex, Valletta, Xaghra, Xewkija, Xghajra, Zabbar, Zebbug, Zebbug (Ghawdex), Zejtun, Zurrieq

INDEPENDENCE:

21 September 1964 (from the UK)

NATIONAL HOLIDAY:

Independence Day, 21 September (1964); Republic Day, 13 December (1974)

CONSTITUTION:

history: many previous; latest adopted 21 September 1964

amendments: proposals (Acts of Parliament) require at least two-thirds majority vote by the House of Representatives; passage of Acts requires majority vote by referendum, followed by final majority vote by the House and assent of the president of the republic; amended many times, last in 2016 (2017)

LEGAL SYSTEM:

mixed legal system of English common law and civil law based on the Roman and Napoleonic civil codes; subject to European Union law

INTERNATIONAL LAW ORGANIZATION PARTICIPATION:

accepts compulsory ICJ jurisdiction with reservations; accepts ICCt jurisdiction

CITIZENSHIP:

citizenship by birth: no

citizenship by descent only: at least one parent must be a citizen of Malta

dual citizenship recognized: no

residency requirement for naturalization: 5 years

SUFFRAGE:

18 years of age (16 in local council elections); universal

EXECUTIVE BRANCH:

chief of state: President George VELLA (since 4 April 2019)

head of government: Prime Minister Joseph MUSCAT (since 11 March 2013)

cabinet: Cabinet appointed by the president on the advice of the prime minister

elections/appointments: president indirectly elected by the House of Representatives for a single 5-year term; election last held on 2 April 2019 (next to be held by April 2024); following legislative elections, the leader of the majority party or majority coalition usually appointed prime minister by the president for a 5-year term; deputy prime minister appointed by the president on the advice of the prime minister

election results: George VELLA (PL) elected president; House of Representatives vote - unanimous; Joseph MUSCAT (PL) reappointed prime minister

LEGISLATIVE BRANCH:

description: unicameral House of Representatives or Il-Kamra Tad-Deputati, a component of the Parliament of Malta (normally 65 seats but can include at-large members; members directly elected in 5 multi-seat constituencies by proportional representation vote; members serve 5-year terms); note - the parliament elected in 2013 had 69 seats; an additional two seats were added in 2016 by the Constitutional Court to correct for mistakes made in the 2013 vote-counting process

elections: last held on 3 June 2017 (next to be held in 2022); note - Prime Minister MUSCAT called for early elections amid corruption allegations

election results: percent of vote by party - PL 55%, PN 43.7%, other 1.3%; seats by party - PL 37 PN 30; note - PN was awarded two additional seats for a total of 30 in accordance with the proportionality provisions specified in the constitution; PD candidates ran under the PN list; composition - men 57, women 10, percent of women 14.9%

JUDICIAL BRANCH:

highest courts: Court of Appeal (consists of either 1 or 3 judges); Constitutional Court (consists of 3 judges); Court of Criminal Appeal (consists of either 1 or 3 judges)

judge selection and term of office: Court of Appeal and Constitutional Court judges appointed by the president, usually upon the advice of the prime minister; judges of both courts serve until age 65

subordinate courts: Civil Court (divided into the General Jurisdiction Section, Family Section, and Voluntary Section); Criminal Court; Court of Magistrates; Gozo Courts (for the islands of Gozo and Comino)

POLITICAL PARTIES AND LEADERS:

Democratic Party (Partit Demokratiku) or PD [Godfrey FARRUGIA]

Labor Party (Partit Laburista) or PL [Joseph MUSCAT]

Nationalist Party (Partit Nazzjonalista) or PN [Adrian DELIA]

INTERNATIONAL ORGANIZATION PARTICIPATION:

Australia Group, C, CD, CE, EAPC, EBRD, ECB, EIB, EMU, EU, FAO, IAEA, IBRD, ICAO, ICC (NGOs), ICCt, ICRM, IDA, IFAD, IFC, IFRCS, ILO, IMF, IMO, IMSO, Interpol, IOC, IOM, IPU, ISO, ITSO, ITU, ITUC (NGOs), MIGA, NSG, OAS (observer), OPCW, OSCE, PCA, PFP, Schengen Convention, UN, UNCTAD, UNESCO, UNIDO, Union Latina (observer), UNWTO, UPU, WCO, WHO, WIPO, WMO, WTO

DIPLOMATIC REPRESENTATION IN THE US:

Ambassador Keith AZZOPARDI (since 17 September 2018)

chancery: 2017 Connecticut Avenue NW, Washington, DC 20008

telephone: [1] (202) 462-3611 through 3612

FAX: [1] (202) 387-5470

DIPLOMATIC REPRESENTATION FROM THE US:

chief of mission: Ambassador (vacant); Charge d'Affaires Mark A. SCHAPIRO (since 29 September 2018)

telephone: [356] 2561-4000

embassy: Ta' Qali National Park, Attard, ATD 4000

mailing address: 5800 Valletta Place, Dulles, VA 20189

FAX: [356] 2561-4183

FLAG DESCRIPTION:

two equal vertical bands of white (hoist side) and red; in the upper hoist-side corner is a representation of the George Cross, edged in red; according to legend, the colors are taken from the red and white checkered banner of Count Roger of Sicily who removed a bi-colored corner and granted it to Malta in 1091; an uncontested explanation is that the colors are those of the Knights of Saint John who ruled Malta from 1530 to 1798; in 1942, King George VI of the UK awarded the George Cross to the islanders for their exceptional bravery and gallantry in World War II; since independence in 1964, the George Cross bordered in red has appeared directly on the white field

NATIONAL SYMBOL(S):

Maltese eight-pointed cross; national colors: red, white

NATIONAL ANTHEM:

name: "L-Innu Malti" (The Maltese Anthem)

lyrics/music: Dun Karm PSAILA/Robert SAMMUT

note: adopted 1945; written in the form of a prayer

ECONOMY :: MALTA

ECONOMY - OVERVIEW:

Malta's free market economy – the smallest economy in the euro-zone – relies heavily on trade in both goods and services, principally with Europe. Malta produces less than a quarter of its food needs, has limited fresh water supplies, and has few domestic energy sources. Malta's economy is dependent on foreign trade, manufacturing, and tourism. Malta joined the EU in 2004 and adopted the euro on 1 January 2008.

Malta has weathered the euro-zone crisis better than most EU member states due to a low debt-to-GDP ratio and financially sound banking sector. It maintains one of the lowest unemployment rates in Europe, and growth has fully recovered since the 2009 recession. In 2014 through 2016, Malta led the euro zone in growth, expanding more than 4.5% per year.

Malta's services sector continues to grow, with sustained growth in the financial services and online gaming sectors. Advantageous tax schemes remained attractive to foreign investors, though EU discussions of anti-tax avoidance measures have raised concerns among Malta's financial services and insurance providers, as the measures could have a significant impact on those sectors. The tourism sector also continued to grow, with 2016 showing record-breaking numbers of both air and cruise passenger arrivals.

Malta's GDP growth remains strong and is supported by a strong labor market. The government has implemented new programs, including free childcare, to encourage increased labor participation. The high cost of borrowing and small labor market remain potential constraints to future economic growth. Increasingly, other EU and European migrants are relocating to Malta for employment, though wages have remained low compared to other European countries. Inflation remains low.

GDP (PURCHASING POWER PARITY):

$19.26 billion (2017 est.)

$18.05 billion (2016 est.)

$17.16 billion (2015 est.)

note: data are in 2017 dollars

country comparison to the world: 152

GDP (OFFICIAL EXCHANGE RATE):

$12.58 billion (2017 est.)

GDP - REAL GROWTH RATE:

6.7% (2017 est.)

5.2% (2016 est.)

9.5% (2015 est.)

country comparison to the world: 28

GDP - PER CAPITA (PPP):

$41,900 (2017 est.)

$40,100 (2016 est.)

$39,000 (2015 est.)

note: data are in 2017 dollars

country comparison to the world: 43

GROSS NATIONAL SAVING:

33.5% of GDP (2017 est.)

31.8% of GDP (2016 est.)

31.2% of GDP (2015 est.)

country comparison to the world: 22

GDP - COMPOSITION, BY END USE:

household consumption: 45.2% (2017 est.)

government consumption: 15.3% (2017 est.)

investment in fixed capital: 21.1% (2017 est.)

investment in inventories: 0.3% (2017 est.)

exports of goods and services: 136.1% (2017 est.)

imports of goods and services: -117.9% (2017 est.)

GDP - COMPOSITION, BY SECTOR OF ORIGIN:

agriculture: 1.1% (2017 est.)

industry: 10.2% (2017 est.)

services: 88.7% (2017 est.)

AGRICULTURE - PRODUCTS:

potatoes, cauliflower, grapes, wheat, barley, tomatoes, citrus, cut flowers, green peppers; pork, milk, poultry, eggs

INDUSTRIES:

tourism, electronics, ship building and repair, construction, food and beverages, pharmaceuticals, footwear, clothing, tobacco, aviation services, financial services, information technology services

INDUSTRIAL PRODUCTION GROWTH RATE:

-3.3% (2016 est.)

country comparison to the world: 189

LABOR FORCE:

206,300 (2017 est.)

country comparison to the world: 169

LABOR FORCE - BY OCCUPATION:

agriculture: 1.6%

industry: 20.7%

services: 77.7% (2016 est.)

UNEMPLOYMENT RATE:

4.6% (2017 est.)

5.3% (2016 est.)

country comparison to the world: 67

POPULATION BELOW POVERTY LINE:

16.3% (2015 est.)

HOUSEHOLD INCOME OR CONSUMPTION BY PERCENTAGE SHARE:

lowest 10%: NA

highest 10%: NA

DISTRIBUTION OF FAMILY INCOME - GINI INDEX:

28.1 (2015)

27.7 (2014)

country comparison to the world: 141

BUDGET:

revenues: 5.076 billion (2017 est.)

expenditures: 4.583 billion (2017 est.)

TAXES AND OTHER REVENUES:

40.4% (of GDP) (2017 est.)

country comparison to the world: 38

BUDGET SURPLUS (+) OR DEFICIT (-):

3.9% (of GDP) (2017 est.)

country comparison to the world: 9

PUBLIC DEBT:

50.7% of GDP (2017 est.)

56.3% of GDP (2016 est.)

note: Malta reports public debt at nominal value outstanding at the end of the year, according to guidelines set out in the Maastricht Treaty for general government gross debt; the data include the following categories of government liabilities (as defined in ESA95): currency and deposits (AF.2), securities other than shares excluding financial derivatives (AF.3, excluding AF.34), and loans (AF.4); general government comprises the central, state, and local governments, and social security funds

country comparison to the world: 99

FISCAL YEAR:

calendar year

INFLATION RATE (CONSUMER PRICES):

1.3% (2017 est.)

0.9% (2016 est.)

country comparison to the world: 69

CENTRAL BANK DISCOUNT RATE:

-0.35% (31 December 2016 est.)

-0.2% (31 December 2015)

note: this is the European Central Bank's rate on the marginal lending facility, which offers overnight credit to banks in the euro area

country comparison to the world: 162

COMMERCIAL BANK PRIME LENDING RATE:

3.7% (31 December 2017 est.)

5.06% (31 December 2016 est.)

country comparison to the world: 167

STOCK OF NARROW MONEY:

$17.93 billion (31 December 2017 est.)

$14.28 billion (31 December 2016 est.)

note: see entry for the EU for money supply for the entire euro area; the European Central Bank controls monetary policy for the 18 members of the Economic and Monetary Union (EMU); individual members of the EMU do not control the quantity of money circulating within their own borders

country comparison to the world: 71

STOCK OF BROAD MONEY:

$17.93 billion (31 December 2017 est.)

$14.28 billion (31 December 2016 est.)

country comparison to the world: 72

STOCK OF DOMESTIC CREDIT:

$13.97 billion (31 December 2017 est.)

$11.99 billion (31 December 2016 est.)

country comparison to the world: 101

MARKET VALUE OF PUBLICLY TRADED SHARES:

$4.632 billion (31 December 2016 est.)

$4.468 billion (31 December 2015 est.)

$3.353 billion (31 December 2014 est.)

country comparison to the world: 84

CURRENT ACCOUNT BALANCE:

$1.712 billion (2017 est.)

$788 million (2016 est.)

country comparison to the world: 44

EXPORTS:

$3.272 billion (2017 est.)

$2.493 billion (2016 est.)

country comparison to the world: 126

EXPORTS - PARTNERS:

Germany 17.3%, France 10.2%, Italy 9.4%, Singapore 5.9%, Hong Kong 5.8%, US 5.7%, Japan 4.9%, Libya 4.5% (2017)

EXPORTS - COMMODITIES:

machinery and mechanical appliances; mineral fuels, oils and petroleum products; pharmaceutical products; books and newspapers; aircraft/spacecraft and parts; toys, games, and sports equipment

IMPORTS:

$4.996 billion (2017 est.)

$4.965 billion (2016 est.)

country comparison to the world: 129

IMPORTS - COMMODITIES:

mineral fuels, oils and products; electrical machinery; aircraft/spacecraft and parts thereof; machinery and mechanical appliances; plastic and other semi-manufactured goods; vehicles and parts

IMPORTS - PARTNERS:

Italy 23%, Germany 7.9%, UK 7.7%, Spain 5%, Canada 4.5%, US 4.3%, France 4.2% (2017)

RESERVES OF FOREIGN EXCHANGE AND GOLD:

$833 million (31 December 2017 est.)

$677.1 million (31 December 2016 est.)

country comparison to the world: 139

DEBT - EXTERNAL:

$90.98 billion (September 2016 est.)

$99.02 billion (31 December 2015 est.)

country comparison to the world: 53

STOCK OF DIRECT FOREIGN INVESTMENT - AT HOME:

$166.1 million (1 June 2016 est.)

$155.5 million (1 June 2015 est.)

country comparison to the world: 134

STOCK OF DIRECT FOREIGN INVESTMENT - ABROAD:

$65.49 million (June 2015 est.)

$64.77 million (31 June 2014 est.)

country comparison to the world: 112
EXCHANGE RATES:
euros (EUR) per US dollar -
0.885 (2017 est.)
0.903 (2016 est.)
0.9214 (2015 est.)
0.885 (2014 est.)
0.7634 (2013 est.)

ENERGY :: MALTA

ELECTRICITY ACCESS:
electrification - total population: 100% (2016)

ELECTRICITY - PRODUCTION:
813 million kWh (2016 est.)
country comparison to the world: 156

ELECTRICITY - CONSUMPTION:
2.122 billion kWh (2016 est.)
country comparison to the world: 142

ELECTRICITY - EXPORTS:
0 kWh (2016 est.)
country comparison to the world: 167

ELECTRICITY - IMPORTS:
1.525 billion kWh (2016 est.)
country comparison to the world: 61

ELECTRICITY - INSTALLED GENERATING CAPACITY:
575,100 kW (2016 est.)
country comparison to the world: 142

ELECTRICITY - FROM FOSSIL FUELS:
81% of total installed capacity (2016 est.)
country comparison to the world: 80

ELECTRICITY - FROM NUCLEAR FUELS:
0% of total installed capacity (2017 est.)
country comparison to the world: 139

ELECTRICITY - FROM HYDROELECTRIC PLANTS:
0% of total installed capacity (2017 est.)
country comparison to the world: 186

ELECTRICITY - FROM OTHER RENEWABLE SOURCES:
19% of total installed capacity (2017 est.)
country comparison to the world: 43

CRUDE OIL - PRODUCTION:
0 bbl/day (2018 est.)
country comparison to the world: 171

CRUDE OIL - EXPORTS:
0 bbl/day (2015 est.)
country comparison to the world: 162

CRUDE OIL - IMPORTS:
0 bbl/day (2015 est.)
country comparison to the world: 162

CRUDE OIL - PROVED RESERVES:
0 bbl (1 January 2018 est.)
country comparison to the world: 166

REFINED PETROLEUM PRODUCTS - PRODUCTION:
0 bbl/day (2017 est.)
country comparison to the world: 174

REFINED PETROLEUM PRODUCTS - CONSUMPTION:
45,000 bbl/day (2016 est.)
country comparison to the world: 110

REFINED PETROLEUM PRODUCTS - EXPORTS:
10,400 bbl/day (2015 est.)
country comparison to the world: 81

REFINED PETROLEUM PRODUCTS - IMPORTS:
52,290 bbl/day (2015 est.)
country comparison to the world: 79

NATURAL GAS - PRODUCTION:
0 cu m (2017 est.)
country comparison to the world: 167

NATURAL GAS - CONSUMPTION:
283.2 million cu m (2017 est.)
country comparison to the world: 102

NATURAL GAS - EXPORTS:
0 cu m (2017 est.)
country comparison to the world: 148

NATURAL GAS - IMPORTS:
311.5 million cu m (2017 est.)
country comparison to the world: 69

NATURAL GAS - PROVED RESERVES:
0 cu m (1 January 2014 est.)
country comparison to the world: 168

CARBON DIOXIDE EMISSIONS FROM CONSUMPTION OF ENERGY:
8.141 million Mt (2017 est.)
country comparison to the world: 116

COMMUNICATIONS :: MALTA

TELEPHONES - FIXED LINES:
total subscriptions: 240,280
subscriptions per 100 inhabitants: 58 (2017 est.)
country comparison to the world: 123

TELEPHONES - MOBILE CELLULAR:
total subscriptions: 560,010
subscriptions per 100 inhabitants: 135 (2017 est.)
country comparison to the world: 169

TELEPHONE SYSTEM:
general assessment: automatic system featuring submarine cable and microwave radio relay between islands; one of the most advanced telecoms in Europe, high penetration of mobile and broadband, and a way forward to expand e-commerce opportunities; '5G ready' and LTE network; regulatory system that encourages investors (2018)

domestic: fixed-line 58 per 100 persons and mobile-cellular subscribership 135 per 100 persons (2018)

international: country code - 356; landing points for the Malta-Gozo Cable, VMSCS, GO-1 Mediterranean Cable System, Malta Italy Interconnector, Melita-1, and the Italy-Malta submarine cable connections to Italy; satellite earth station - 1 Intelsat (Atlantic Ocean) (2019)

BROADCAST MEDIA:
2 publicly owned TV stations, Television Malta broadcasting nationally plus an educational channel; several privately owned national television stations, 2 of which are owned by political parties; Italian and British broadcast programs are available; multi-channel cable and satellite TV services are available; publicly owned radio broadcaster operates 3 stations; roughly 20 commercial radio stations (2019)

INTERNET COUNTRY CODE:
.mt

INTERNET USERS:
total: 320,902
percent of population: 77.3% (July 2016 est.)
country comparison to the world: 156

BROADBAND - FIXED SUBSCRIPTIONS:
total: 181,318
subscriptions per 100 inhabitants: 44 (2017 est.)
country comparison to the world: 110

MILITARY AND SECURITY :: MALTA

MILITARY EXPENDITURES:
0.49% of GDP (2018)

0.51% of GDP (2017)

0.54% of GDP (2016)

0.5% of GDP (2015)

0.5% of GDP (2014)

country comparison to the world: 148

MILITARY AND SECURITY FORCES:
Armed Forces of Malta (AFM, includes land, maritime, and air elements, plus a Volunteer Reserve Force) (2019)

MILITARY SERVICE AGE AND OBLIGATION:
18-30 years of age for voluntary military service; no conscription (2019)

TRANSPORTATION :: MALTA

NATIONAL AIR TRANSPORT SYSTEM:
number of registered air carriers: 9 (2015)

inventory of registered aircraft operated by air carriers: 28 (2015)

annual passenger traffic on registered air carriers: 1,583,046 (2015)

annual freight traffic on registered air carriers: 3.352 million mt-km (2015)

CIVIL AIRCRAFT REGISTRATION COUNTRY CODE PREFIX:
9H (2016)

AIRPORTS:
1 (2013)

country comparison to the world: 228

AIRPORTS - WITH PAVED RUNWAYS:
total: 1 (2017)

over 3,047 m: 1 (2017)

HELIPORTS:
2 (2013)

ROADWAYS:
total: 2,254 km (2001)

paved: 1,973 km (2001)

unpaved: 281 km (2001)

urban: 1,422 km (2001)

non-urban: 832 km (2001)

country comparison to the world: 165

MERCHANT MARINE:
total: 2,205

by type: bulk carrier 645, container ship 283, general cargo 288, oil tanker 391, other 598 (2018)

country comparison to the world: 11

PORTS AND TERMINALS:
major seaport(s): Marsaxlokk (Malta Freeport), Valletta

container port(s) (TEUs): Marsaxlokk (3,150,000) (2017)

TRANSNATIONAL ISSUES :: MALTA

DISPUTES - INTERNATIONAL:
none

REFUGEES AND INTERNALLY DISPLACED PERSONS:
stateless persons: 11 (2018)

note: 5,000 estimated refugee and migrant arrivals by sea (January 2015-December 2019)

ILLICIT DRUGS:
minor transshipment point for hashish from North Africa to Western Europe

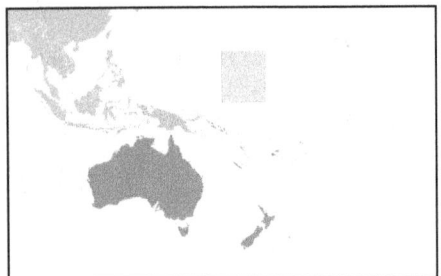

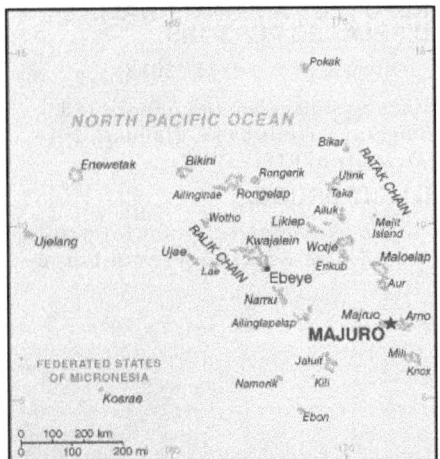

AUSTRALIA - OCEANIA :: MARSHALL ISLANDS

INTRODUCTION :: MARSHALL ISLANDS

BACKGROUND:
After almost four decades under US administration as the easternmost part of the UN Trust Territory of the Pacific Islands, the Marshall Islands attained independence in 1986 under a Compact of Free Association. Compensation claims continue as a result of US nuclear testing conducted on some of the atolls between 1947 and 1962 (67 tests total). The Marshall Islands hosts the US Army Kwajalein Atoll Reagan Missile Test Site, a key installation in the US missile defense network. Kwajalein also hosts one of four dedicated ground antennas that assist in the operation of the Global Positioning System (GPS) navigation system (the others are at Cape Canaveral, Florida (US), on Ascension (Saint Helena, Ascension, and Tristan da Cunha), and at Diego Garcia (British Indian Ocean Territory)).

GEOGRAPHY :: MARSHALL ISLANDS

LOCATION:
Oceania, consists of 29 atolls and five isolated islands in the North Pacific Ocean, about halfway between Hawaii and Australia; the atolls and islands are situated in two, almost-parallel island chains - the Ratak (Sunrise) group and the Ralik (Sunset) group; the total number of islands and islets is about 1,225; 22 of the atolls and four of the islands are uninhabited

GEOGRAPHIC COORDINATES:
9 00 N, 168 00 E

MAP REFERENCES:
Oceania

AREA:
total: 181 sq km

land: 181 sq km

water: 0 sq km

note: the archipelago includes 11,673 sq km of lagoon waters and encompasses the atolls of Bikini, Enewetak, Kwajalein, Majuro, Rongelap, and Utirik

country comparison to the world: 217

AREA - COMPARATIVE:
about the size of Washington, DC

LAND BOUNDARIES:
0 km

COASTLINE:
370.4 km

MARITIME CLAIMS:
territorial sea: 12 nm

exclusive economic zone: 200 nm

contiguous zone: 24 nm

CLIMATE:
tropical; hot and humid; wet season May to November; islands border typhoon belt

TERRAIN:
low coral limestone and sand islands

ELEVATION:
mean elevation: 2 m

lowest point: Pacific Ocean 0 m

highest point: East-central Airik Island, Maloelap Atoll 14 m

NATURAL RESOURCES:
coconut products, marine products, deep seabed minerals

LAND USE:
agricultural land: 50.7% (2011 est.)

arable land: 7.8% (2011 est.) / permanent crops: 31.2% (2011 est.) / permanent pasture: 11.7% (2011 est.)

forest: 49.3% (2011 est.)

other: 0% (2011 est.)

IRRIGATED LAND:
0 sq km (2012)

POPULATION DISTRIBUTION:
most people live in urban clusters found on many of the country's islands; more than two-thirds of the population lives on the atolls of Majuro and Ebeye

NATURAL HAZARDS:
infrequent typhoons

ENVIRONMENT - CURRENT ISSUES:
inadequate supplies of potable water; pollution of Majuro lagoon from household waste and discharges from fishing vessels; sea level rise

ENVIRONMENT - INTERNATIONAL AGREEMENTS:
party to: Biodiversity, Climate Change, Climate Change-Kyoto Protocol, Desertification, Hazardous Wastes, Law of the Sea, Ozone Layer Protection, Ship Pollution, Wetlands, Whaling

signed, but not ratified: none of the selected agreements

GEOGRAPHY - NOTE:
the islands of Bikini and Enewetak are former US nuclear test sites; Kwajalein atoll, famous as a World War II battleground, surrounds the world's largest lagoon and is used as a US missile test range; the island city of Ebeye is the second largest settlement in the Marshall Islands, after the capital of Majuro, and one of the most

densely populated locations in the Pacific

PEOPLE AND SOCIETY :: MARSHALL ISLANDS

POPULATION:
75,684 (July 2018 est.)

country comparison to the world: 201

NATIONALITY:
noun: Marshallese (singular and plural)

adjective: Marshallese

ETHNIC GROUPS:
Marshallese 92.1%, mixed Marshallese 5.9%, other 2% (2006)

LANGUAGES:
Marshallese (official) 98.2%, other languages 1.8% (1999 census)

note: English (official), widely spoken as a second language

RELIGIONS:
Protestant 80.5% (United Church of Christ 47%, Assembly of God 16.2%, Bukot Nan Jesus 5.4%, Full Gospel 3.3%, Reformed Congregational Church 3%, Salvation Army 1.9%, Seventh Day Adventist 1.4%, Meram in Jesus 1.2%, other Protestant 1.1%), Roman Catholic 8.5%, Mormon 7%, Jehovah's Witness 1.7%, other 1.2%, none 1.1% (2011 est.)

AGE STRUCTURE:
0-14 years: 34.26% (male 13,224 /female 12,706)

15-24 years: 18.49% (male 7,117 /female 6,875)

25-54 years: 37.15% (male 14,318 /female 13,800)

55-64 years: 5.86% (male 2,221 /female 2,215)

65 years and over: 4.24% (male 1,580 /female 1,628) (2018 est.)

MEDIAN AGE:
total: 23.1 years (2018 est.)

male: 23 years

female: 23.2 years

country comparison to the world: 176

POPULATION GROWTH RATE:
1.5% (2018 est.)

country comparison to the world: 72

BIRTH RATE:
23.8 births/1,000 population (2018 est.)

country comparison to the world: 53

DEATH RATE:
4.2 deaths/1,000 population (2018 est.)

country comparison to the world: 207

NET MIGRATION RATE:
-4.6 migrant(s)/1,000 population (2018 est.)

country comparison to the world: 190

POPULATION DISTRIBUTION:
most people live in urban clusters found on many of the country's islands; more than two-thirds of the population lives on the atolls of Majuro and Ebeye

URBANIZATION:
urban population: 77.4% of total population (2019)

rate of urbanization: 0.61% annual rate of change (2015-20 est.)

MAJOR URBAN AREAS - POPULATION:
31,000 MAJURO (capital) (2018)

SEX RATIO:
at birth: 1.05 male(s)/female

0-14 years: 1.04 male(s)/female

15-24 years: 1.04 male(s)/female

25-54 years: 1.04 male(s)/female

55-64 years: 1 male(s)/female

65 years and over: 0.97 male(s)/female

total population: 1.03 male(s)/female (2018 est.)

INFANT MORTALITY RATE:
total: 18.7 deaths/1,000 live births (2018 est.)

male: 21.1 deaths/1,000 live births

female: 16.1 deaths/1,000 live births

country comparison to the world: 84

LIFE EXPECTANCY AT BIRTH:
total population: 73.6 years (2018 est.)

male: 71.4 years

female: 76 years

country comparison to the world: 135

TOTAL FERTILITY RATE:
2.98 children born/woman (2018 est.)

country comparison to the world: 53

DRINKING WATER SOURCE:
improved:

urban: 93.5% of population

rural: 97.6% of population

total: 94.6% of population

unimproved:

urban: 6.5% of population

rural: 2.4% of population

total: 5.4% of population (2015 est.)

CURRENT HEALTH EXPENDITURE:
23.3% (2016)

PHYSICIANS DENSITY:
0.46 physicians/1,000 population (2012)

HOSPITAL BED DENSITY:
2.7 beds/1,000 population (2010)

SANITATION FACILITY ACCESS:
improved:

urban: 84.5% of population (2015 est.)

rural: 56.2% of population (2015 est.)

total: 76.9% of population (2015 est.)

unimproved:

urban: 15.5% of population (2015 est.)

rural: 43.8% of population (2015 est.)

total: 23.1% of population (2015 est.)

HIV/AIDS - ADULT PREVALENCE RATE:
NA

HIV/AIDS - PEOPLE LIVING WITH HIV/AIDS:
NA

HIV/AIDS - DEATHS:
NA

MAJOR INFECTIOUS DISEASES:
note: active local transmission of Zika virus by Aedes species mosquitoes has been identified in this country (as of August 2016); it poses an important risk (a large number of cases possible) among US citizens if bitten by an infective mosquito; other less common ways to get Zika are through sex, via blood transfusion, or during pregnancy, in which the pregnant woman passes Zika virus to her fetus

OBESITY - ADULT PREVALENCE RATE:
52.9% (2016)

country comparison to the world: 4

CHILDREN UNDER THE AGE OF 5 YEARS UNDERWEIGHT:
11.9% (2017)

country comparison to the world: 55

EDUCATION EXPENDITURES:
NA

LITERACY:

definition: age 15 and over can read and write

total population: 98.3%

male: 98.3%

female: 98.2% (2011 est.)

UNEMPLOYMENT, YOUTH AGES 15-24:

total: 11%

male: 12.2%

female: 8.7% (2010 est.)

country comparison to the world: 119

GOVERNMENT :: MARSHALL ISLANDS

COUNTRY NAME:

conventional long form: Republic of the Marshall Islands

conventional short form: Marshall Islands

local long form: Republic of the Marshall Islands

local short form: Marshall Islands

former: Trust Territory of the Pacific Islands, Marshall Islands District

abbreviation: RMI

etymology: named after British Captain John MARSHALL, who charted many of the islands in 1788

GOVERNMENT TYPE:

mixed presidential-parliamentary system in free association with the US

CAPITAL:

name: Majuro; note - the capital is an atoll of 64 islands; governmental buildings are housed on three fused islands: Djarrit, Uliga, and Delap

geographic coordinates: 7 06 N, 171 23 E

time difference: UTC+12 (17 hours ahead of Washington, DC, during Standard Time)

ADMINISTRATIVE DIVISIONS:

24 municipalities; Ailinglaplap, Ailuk, Arno, Aur, Bikini & Kili, Ebon, Enewetak & Ujelang, Jabat, Jaluit, Kwajalein, Lae, Lib, Likiep, Majuro, Maloelap, Mejit, Mili, Namorik, Namu, Rongelap, Ujae, Utrik, Wotho, Wotje

INDEPENDENCE:

21 October 1986 (from the US-administered UN trusteeship)

NATIONAL HOLIDAY:

Constitution Day, 1 May (1979)

CONSTITUTION:

history: effective 1 May 1979

amendments: proposed by the National Parliament or by a constitutional convention; passage by Parliament requires at least two-thirds majority vote of the total membership in each of two readings and approval by a majority of votes in a referendum; amendments submitted by a constitutional convention require approval of at least two thirds of votes in a referendum; amended several times, last in 1995 (2018)

LEGAL SYSTEM:

mixed legal system of US and English common law, customary law, and local statutes

INTERNATIONAL LAW ORGANIZATION PARTICIPATION:

accepts compulsory ICJ jurisdiction with reservations; accepts ICCt jurisdiction

CITIZENSHIP:

citizenship by birth: no

citizenship by descent only: at least one parent must be a citizen of the Marshall Islands

dual citizenship recognized: no

residency requirement for naturalization: 5 years

SUFFRAGE:

18 years of age; universal

EXECUTIVE BRANCH:

chief of state: President Hilda C. HEINE (since 28 January 2016); note - the president is both chief of state and head of government

head of government: President Hilda C. HEINE (since 28 January 2016)

cabinet: Cabinet nominated by the president from among members of the Nitijela, appointed by Nitijela speaker

elections/appointments: president indirectly elected by the Nitijela from among its members for a 4-year term (no term limits); election last held on 27 January 2016 (next to be held in 2020)

election results: Hilda C. HEINE elected president; Parliament vote - Hilda C. HEINE 24 votes, she was the only candidate

note: Hilda C. HEINE is the first female elected head of state of any Pacific island nation

LEGISLATIVE BRANCH:

description: bicameral National Parliament consists of: Council of Iroij, a 12-member group of tribal leaders advises the Presidential Cabinet and reviews legislation affecting customary law or any traditional practice); members appointed to serve 1-year terms Nitijela (33 seats; members in 19 single- and 5 multi-seat constituencies directly elected by simple majority vote to serve 4-year terms); note - legislative power resides in the Nitijela

elections: last held on 16 November 2015 (next to be held by November 2019)

election results: percent of vote by party - NA; seats by party - independent 33; composition - men 28, women 5, percent of women 15.2%

JUDICIAL BRANCH:

highest courts: Supreme Court (consists of the chief justice and 2 associate justices)

judge selection and term of office: judges appointed by the Cabinet upon the recommendation of the Judicial Service Commission (consists of the chief justice of the High Court, the attorney general and a private citizen selected by the Cabinet) and upon approval of the Nitijela; the current chief justice, appointed in 2013, serves for 10 years; Marshallese citizens appointed as justices serve until retirement at age 72

subordinate courts: High Court; District Courts; Traditional Rights Court; Community Courts

POLITICAL PARTIES AND LEADERS:

traditionally there have been no formally organized political parties; what has existed more closely resembles factions or interest groups because they do not have party headquarters, formal platforms, or party structures; the following two "groupings" have competed in legislative balloting in recent years - Aelon Kein Ad Party [Imata KABUA] and United Democratic Party or UDP [Litokwa TOMEING]

INTERNATIONAL ORGANIZATION PARTICIPATION:

ACP, ADB, AOSIS, FAO, G-77, IAEA, IBRD, ICAO, ICCt, IDA, IFAD, IFC, ILO, IMF, IMO, IMSO, Interpol, IOC, IOM, ITU, OPCW, PIF, Sparteca, SPC, UN, UNCTAD, UNESCO, WHO

DIPLOMATIC REPRESENTATION IN THE US:

Ambassador Gerald M. ZACKIOS (since 16 September 2016)

chancery: 2433 Massachusetts Avenue NW, 1st Floor, Washington, DC 20008

telephone: [1] (202) 234-5414

FAX: [1] (202) 232-3236

consulate(s) general: Honolulu, Springdale (AR)

consulate(s): Agana (Guam)

DIPLOMATIC REPRESENTATION FROM THE US:

chief of mission: Ambassador Karen Brevard STEWART (since 25 July 2016)

telephone: [692] 247-4011

embassy: Oceanside, Mejen Weto, Long Island, Majuro

mailing address: P. O. Box 1379, Majuro, Republic of the Marshall Islands 96960-1379

FAX: [692] 247-4012

FLAG DESCRIPTION:

blue with two stripes radiating from the lower hoist-side corner - orange (top) and white; a white star with four large rays and 20 small rays appears on the hoist side above the two stripes; blue represents the Pacific Ocean, the orange stripe signifies the Ralik Chain or sunset and courage, while the white stripe signifies the Ratak Chain or sunrise and peace; the star symbolizes the cross of Christianity, each of the 24 rays designates one of the electoral districts in the country and the four larger rays highlight the principal cultural centers of Majuro, Jaluit, Wotje, and Ebeye; the rising diagonal band can also be interpreted as representing the equator, with the star showing the archipelago's position just to the north

NATIONAL SYMBOL(S):

a 24-rayed star; national colors: blue, white, orange

NATIONAL ANTHEM:

name: Forever Marshall Islands

lyrics/music: Amata KABUA

note: adopted 1981

ECONOMY :: MARSHALL ISLANDS

ECONOMY - OVERVIEW:

US assistance and lease payments for the use of Kwajalein Atoll as a US military base are the mainstay of this small island country. Agricultural production, primarily subsistence, is concentrated on small farms; the most important commercial crops are coconuts and breadfruit. Industry is limited to handicrafts, tuna processing, and copra. Tourism holds some potential. The islands and atolls have few natural resources, and imports exceed exports.

The Marshall Islands received roughly $1 billion in aid from the US during the period 1986-2001 under the original Compact of Free Association (Compact). In 2002 and 2003, the US and the Marshall Islands renegotiated the Compact's financial package for a 20-year period, 2004 to 2024. Under the amended Compact, the Marshall Islands will receive roughly $1.5 billion in direct US assistance. Under the amended Compact, the US and Marshall Islands are also jointly funding a Trust Fund for the people of the Marshall Islands that will provide an income stream beyond 2024, when direct Compact aid ends.

GDP (PURCHASING POWER PARITY):

$196 million (2017 est.)

$191.3 million (2016 est.)

$184.6 million (2015 est.)

note: data are in 2017 dollars

country comparison to the world: 221

GDP (OFFICIAL EXCHANGE RATE):

$222 million (2017 est.)

GDP - REAL GROWTH RATE:

2.5% (2017 est.)

3.6% (2016 est.)

2% (2015 est.)

country comparison to the world: 130

GDP - PER CAPITA (PPP):

$3,600 (2017 est.)

$3,500 (2016 est.)

$3,400 (2015 est.)

note: data are in 2017 dollars

country comparison to the world: 186

GDP - COMPOSITION, BY END USE:

government consumption: 50% (2016 est.)

investment in fixed capital: 17.8% (2016 est.)

investment in inventories: 0.2% (2016 est.)

exports of goods and services: 52.9% (2016 est.)

imports of goods and services: -102.3% (2016 est.)

GDP - COMPOSITION, BY SECTOR OF ORIGIN:

agriculture: 4.4% (2013 est.)

industry: 9.9% (2013 est.)

services: 85.7% (2013 est.)

AGRICULTURE - PRODUCTS:

coconuts, tomatoes, melons, taro, breadfruit, fruits; pigs, chickens

INDUSTRIES:

copra, tuna processing, tourism, craft items (from seashells, wood, and pearls)

INDUSTRIAL PRODUCTION GROWTH RATE:

NA

LABOR FORCE:

10,670 (2013 est.)

country comparison to the world: 217

LABOR FORCE - BY OCCUPATION:

agriculture: 11%

industry: 16.3%

services: 72.7% (2011 est.)

UNEMPLOYMENT RATE:

36% (2006 est.)

30.9% (2000 est.)

country comparison to the world: 212

POPULATION BELOW POVERTY LINE:

NA

HOUSEHOLD INCOME OR CONSUMPTION BY PERCENTAGE SHARE:

lowest 10%: NA

highest 10%: NA

BUDGET:

revenues: 116.7 million (2013 est.)

expenditures: 113.9 million (2013 est.)

TAXES AND OTHER REVENUES:

52.6% (of GDP) (2013 est.)

country comparison to the world: 13

BUDGET SURPLUS (+) OR DEFICIT (-):

1.3% (of GDP) (2013 est.)

country comparison to the world: 26

PUBLIC DEBT:

25.5% of GDP (2017 est.)

30% of GDP (2016 est.)

country comparison to the world: 173

FISCAL YEAR:

1 October - 30 September

INFLATION RATE (CONSUMER PRICES):

0% (2017 est.)

-1.5% (2016 est.)

country comparison to the world: 11

CURRENT ACCOUNT BALANCE:

-$1 million (2017 est.)

$15 million (2016 est.)

country comparison to the world: 68

EXPORTS:

$0 (2013 est.)

country comparison to the world: 223

EXPORTS - COMMODITIES:

copra cake, coconut oil, handicrafts, fish

IMPORTS:

$103.8 million (2016 est.)

$133.7 million (2013 est.)

country comparison to the world: 216

IMPORTS - COMMODITIES:

foodstuffs, machinery and equipment, fuels, beverages, tobacco

DEBT - EXTERNAL:

$97.96 million (2013 est.)

$87 million (2008 est.)

country comparison to the world: 193

EXCHANGE RATES:

the US dollar is used

ENERGY :: MARSHALL ISLANDS

ELECTRICITY ACCESS:

electrification - total population: 93.1% (2016)

electrification - urban areas: 94.6% (2016)

electrification - rural areas: 89.1% (2016)

ELECTRICITY - PRODUCTION:

650 million kWh (2016 est.)

country comparison to the world: 161

ELECTRICITY - CONSUMPTION:

604.5 million kWh (2016 est.)

country comparison to the world: 167

ELECTRICITY - EXPORTS:

0 kWh (2016 est.)

country comparison to the world: 168

ELECTRICITY - IMPORTS:

0 kWh (2016 est.)

country comparison to the world: 172

ELECTRICITY - INSTALLED GENERATING CAPACITY:

52,000 kW (2016 est.)

country comparison to the world: 190

ELECTRICITY - FROM FOSSIL FUELS:

81% of total installed capacity (2016 est.)

country comparison to the world: 81

ELECTRICITY - FROM NUCLEAR FUELS:

0% of total installed capacity (2017 est.)

country comparison to the world: 140

ELECTRICITY - FROM HYDROELECTRIC PLANTS:

19% of total installed capacity (2017 est.)

country comparison to the world: 90

ELECTRICITY - FROM OTHER RENEWABLE SOURCES:

0% of total installed capacity (2017 est.)

country comparison to the world: 201

CRUDE OIL - PRODUCTION:

0 bbl/day (2017 est.)

country comparison to the world: 172

CRUDE OIL - EXPORTS:

0 bbl/day (2015 est.)

country comparison to the world: 163

CRUDE OIL - IMPORTS:

0 bbl/day (2015 est.)

country comparison to the world: 163

CRUDE OIL - PROVED RESERVES:

0 bbl (1 January 2018 est.)

country comparison to the world: 167

REFINED PETROLEUM PRODUCTS - PRODUCTION:

0 bbl/day (2015 est.)

country comparison to the world: 175

REFINED PETROLEUM PRODUCTS - CONSUMPTION:

2,000 bbl/day (2016 est.)

country comparison to the world: 195

REFINED PETROLEUM PRODUCTS - EXPORTS:

0 bbl/day (2015 est.)

country comparison to the world: 179

REFINED PETROLEUM PRODUCTS - IMPORTS:

2,060 bbl/day (2015 est.)

country comparison to the world: 190

NATURAL GAS - PRODUCTION:

0 cu m (2017 est.)

country comparison to the world: 168

NATURAL GAS - CONSUMPTION:

0 cu m (2017 est.)

country comparison to the world: 173

NATURAL GAS - EXPORTS:

0 cu m (2017 est.)

country comparison to the world: 149

NATURAL GAS - IMPORTS:

0 cu m (2017 est.)

country comparison to the world: 155

CARBON DIOXIDE EMISSIONS FROM CONSUMPTION OF ENERGY:

293,700 Mt (2017 est.)

country comparison to the world: 192

COMMUNICATIONS :: MARSHALL ISLANDS

TELEPHONES - FIXED LINES:

total subscriptions: 2,361

subscriptions per 100 inhabitants: 3 (July 2016 est.)

country comparison to the world: 211

TELEPHONES - MOBILE CELLULAR:

total subscriptions: 16,000

subscriptions per 100 inhabitants: 21 (July 2016 est.)

country comparison to the world: 210

TELEPHONE SYSTEM:

general assessment:

some telecom infrastructure improvements made in recent years; modern services include fiber optic cable service, cellular, Internet, international calling, caller ID, and leased data circuits; the US Government, World Bank, UN and International Telecommunication Union (ITU), have aided in improvements and monetary aid to the islands telecom; mobile penetrations is around 30%; radio communication is especially vital to remote islands

(2018)

domestic: Majuro Atoll and Ebeye and Kwajalein islands have regular, seven-digit, direct-dial telephones; other islands interconnected by high frequency radiotelephone (used mostly for government purposes) and mini-satellite telephones; fixed-line 3 per 100 persons and mobile-cellular is 21 per 100 persons (2018)

international: country code - 692; satellite earth stations - 2 Intelsat (Pacific Ocean); US Government satellite communications system on Kwajalein

BROADCAST MEDIA:

no TV broadcast station; a cable network is available on Majuro with programming via videotape replay and satellite relays; 4 radio broadcast stations; American Armed Forces Radio and Television Service (AFRTS) provides satellite radio and television service to Kwajalein Atoll (2019)

INTERNET COUNTRY CODE:

.mh

INTERNET USERS:

total: 21,857

percent of population: 29.8% (July 2016 est.)

country comparison to the world: 204

BROADBAND - FIXED SUBSCRIPTIONS:

total: 1,000

subscriptions per 100 inhabitants: 1 (2017 est.)

country comparison to the world: 192

COMMUNICATIONS - NOTE:

Kwajalein hosts one of four dedicated ground antennas that assist in the operation of the Global Positioning System (GPS) navigation system (the others are at Cape Canaveral, Florida (US), on Ascension (Saint Helena, Ascension, and Tristan da Cunha), and at Diego Garcia (British Indian Ocean Territory))

MILITARY AND SECURITY :: MARSHALL ISLANDS

MILITARY AND SECURITY FORCES:

no regular military forces; Marshall Islands Police Department (2019)

MILITARY - NOTE:

defense is the responsibility of the US

TRANSPORTATION :: MARSHALL ISLANDS

NATIONAL AIR TRANSPORT SYSTEM:

number of registered air carriers: 1 (2015)

inventory of registered aircraft operated by air carriers: 1 (2015)

annual passenger traffic on registered air carriers: 86,868 (2015)

annual freight traffic on registered air carriers: 0 mt-km (2015)

CIVIL AIRCRAFT REGISTRATION COUNTRY CODE PREFIX:

V7 (2016)

AIRPORTS:

15 (2013)

country comparison to the world: 147

AIRPORTS - WITH PAVED RUNWAYS:

total: 4 (2017)

1,524 to 2,437 m: 3 (2017)

914 to 1,523 m: 1 (2017)

AIRPORTS - WITH UNPAVED RUNWAYS:

total: 11 (2013)

914 to 1,523 m: 10 (2013)

under 914 m: 1 (2013)

ROADWAYS:

total: 2,028 km (2007)

paved: 75 km (2007)

unpaved: 1,953 km

country comparison to the world: 167

MERCHANT MARINE:

total: 3,419

by type: bulk carrier 1437, container ship 256, general cargo 68, oil tanker 837, other 821 (2018)

country comparison to the world: 7

PORTS AND TERMINALS:

major seaport(s): Enitwetak Island, Kwajalein, Majuro

TRANSNATIONAL ISSUES :: MARSHALL ISLANDS

DISPUTES - INTERNATIONAL:

claims US territory of Wake Island

TRAFFICKING IN PERSONS:

current situation: The Marshall Islands is a source and destination country for Marshallese women and girls and women from East Asia subjected to sex trafficking; Marshallese and foreign women are forced into prostitution in businesses frequented by crew members of fishing and transshipping vessels that dock in Majuro; some Chinese women are recruited to the Marshall Islands with promises of legitimate work and are subsequently forced into prostitution

tier rating: Tier 3 – The Marshall Islands do not fully comply with the minimum standards for the elimination of trafficking and is not making significant efforts to do so; the government made no anti-trafficking law enforcement efforts, including developing a written plan to combat trafficking; no new trafficking investigations were opened in 2014, and no prosecutions or convictions were made for the fourth consecutive year; no efforts were made to identify trafficking victims, especially among women in prostitution or men working on foreign fishing vessels in Marshallese waters, and no attempt was made to ensure their access to protective services; limited awareness-raising events were conducted by an international organization (2015)

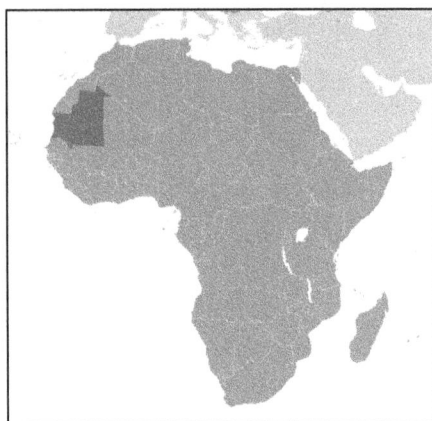

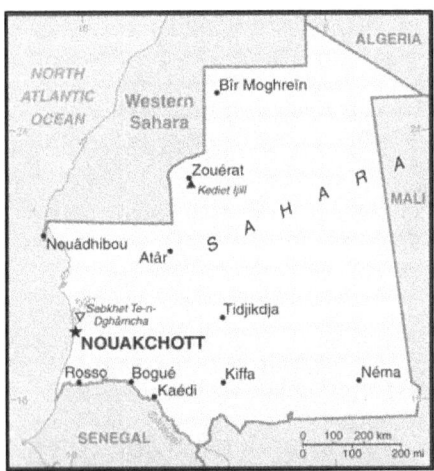

AFRICA :: MAURITANIA

INTRODUCTION :: MAURITANIA

BACKGROUND:

Independent from France in 1960, Mauritania annexed the southern third of the former Spanish Sahara (now Western Sahara) in 1976 but relinquished it after three years of raids by the Polisario guerrilla front seeking independence for the territory. Maaouya Ould Sid Ahmed TAYA seized power in a coup in 1984 and ruled Mauritania with a heavy hand for more than two decades. A series of presidential elections that he held were widely seen as flawed. A bloodless coup in August 2005 deposed President TAYA and ushered in a military council that oversaw a transition to democratic rule. Independent candidate Sidi Ould Cheikh ABDALLAHI was inaugurated in April 2007 as Mauritania's first freely and fairly elected president. His term ended prematurely in August 2008 when a military junta led by General Mohamed Ould Abdel AZIZ deposed him and installed a military council government. AZIZ was subsequently elected president in July 2009 and sworn in the following month. AZIZ sustained injuries from an accidental shooting by his own troops in October 2012 but has continued to maintain his authority. He was reelected in 2014 to a second and final term as president (according to the present constitution). AZIZ will be replaced through elections scheduled for June 2019. The country continues to experience ethnic tensions among three major groups: Arabic-speaking descendants of slaves (Haratines), Arabic-speaking "White Moors" (Beydane), and members of Sub-Saharan ethnic groups mostly originating in the Senegal River valley (Halpulaar, Soninke, and Wolof).

Al-Qaeda in the Islamic Maghreb (AQIM) launched a series of attacks in Mauritania between 2005 and 2011, murdering American and foreign tourists and aid workers, attacking diplomatic and government facilities, and ambushing Mauritanian soldiers and gendarmes. A successful strategy against terrorism that combines dialogue with the terrorists and military actions has prevented the country from further terrorist attacks since 2011. However, AQIM and similar groups remain active in neighboring Mali and elsewhere in the Sahel region and continue to pose a threat to Mauritanians and foreign visitors.

GEOGRAPHY :: MAURITANIA

LOCATION:
Western Africa, bordering the North Atlantic Ocean, between Senegal and Western Sahara

GEOGRAPHIC COORDINATES:
20 00 N, 12 00 W

MAP REFERENCES:
Africa

AREA:
total: 1,030,700 sq km

land: 1,030,700 sq km

water: 0 sq km

country comparison to the world: 30

AREA - COMPARATIVE:
slightly larger than three times the size of New Mexico; about six times the size of Florida

LAND BOUNDARIES:
total: 5,002 km

border countries (4): Algeria 460 km, Mali 2236 km, Senegal 742 km, Western Sahara 1564 km

COASTLINE:
754 km

MARITIME CLAIMS:
territorial sea: 12 nm

exclusive economic zone: 200 nm

contiguous zone: 24 nm

continental shelf: 200 nm or to the edge of the continental margin

CLIMATE:
desert; constantly hot, dry, dusty

TERRAIN:
mostly barren, flat plains of the Sahara; some central hills

ELEVATION:
mean elevation: 276 m

lowest point: Sebkhet Te-n-Dghamcha -5 m

highest point: Kediet Ijill 915 m

NATURAL RESOURCES:
iron ore, gypsum, copper, phosphate, diamonds, gold, oil, fish

LAND USE:
agricultural land: 38.5% (2011 est.)

arable land: 0.4% (2011 est.) / permanent crops: 0% (2011 est.) / permanent pasture: 38.1% (2011 est.)

forest: 0.2% (2011 est.)

other: 61.3% (2011 est.)

IRRIGATED LAND:

450 sq km (2012)

POPULATION DISTRIBUTION:

with most of the country being a desert, vast areas of the country, particularly in the central, northern, and eastern areas, are without sizeable population clusters; half the population lives in or around the coastal capital of Nouakchott; smaller clusters are found near the southern border with Mali and Senegal

NATURAL HAZARDS:

hot, dry, dust/sand-laden sirocco wind primarily in March and April; periodic droughts

ENVIRONMENT - CURRENT ISSUES:

overgrazing, deforestation, and soil erosion aggravated by drought are contributing to desertification; limited natural freshwater resources away from the Senegal, which is the only perennial river; locust infestation

ENVIRONMENT - INTERNATIONAL AGREEMENTS:

party to: Biodiversity, Climate Change, Climate Change-Kyoto Protocol, Desertification, Endangered Species, Hazardous Wastes, Law of the Sea, Ozone Layer Protection, Ship Pollution, Wetlands, Whaling

signed, but not ratified: none of the selected agreements

GEOGRAPHY - NOTE:

Mauritania is considered both a part of North Africa's Maghreb region and West Africa's Sahel region; most of the population is concentrated in the cities of Nouakchott and Nouadhibou and along the Senegal River in the southern part of the country

PEOPLE AND SOCIETY :: MAURITANIA

POPULATION:

3,840,429 (July 2018 est.)

country comparison to the world: 130

NATIONALITY:

noun: Mauritanian(s)

adjective: Mauritanian

ETHNIC GROUPS:

black Moors (Haratines - Arab-speaking slaves, former slaves, and their descendants of African origin, enslaved by white Moors) 40%, white Moors (of Arab-Berber descent, known as Beydane) 30%, sub-Saharan Mauritanians (non-Arabic speaking, largely resident in or originating from the Senegal River Valley, including Halpulaar, Fulani, Soninke, Wolof, and Bambara ethnic groups) 30%

LANGUAGES:

Arabic (official and national), Pular, Soninke, Wolof (all national languages), French

note: the spoken Arabic in Mauritania differs considerably from the modern standard Arabic used for official written purposes or in the media; the Mauritanian dialect, which incorporates many Berber words, is referred to as Hassaniya

RELIGIONS:

Muslim (official) 100%

DEMOGRAPHIC PROFILE:

With a sustained total fertility rate of about 4 children per woman and almost 60% of the population under the age of 25, Mauritania's population is likely to continue growing for the foreseeable future. Mauritania's large youth cohort is vital to its development prospects, but available schooling does not adequately prepare students for the workplace. Girls continue to be underrepresented in the classroom, educational quality remains poor, and the dropout rate is high. The literacy rate is only about 50%, even though access to primary education has improved since the mid-2000s. Women's restricted access to education and discriminatory laws maintain gender inequality - worsened by early and forced marriages and female genital cutting.

The denial of education to black Moors also helps to perpetuate slavery. Although Mauritania abolished slavery in 1981 (the last country in the world to do so) and made it a criminal offense in 2007, the millenniums-old practice persists largely because anti-slavery laws are rarely enforced and the custom is so ingrained. According to a 2018 nongovernmental organization's report, a little more than 2% of Mauritania's population is enslaved, which includes individuals sujbected to forced labor and forced marriage, although many thousands of individuals who are legally free contend with discrimination, poor education, and a lack of identity papers and, therefore, live in de facto slavery. The UN and international press outlets have claimed that up to 20% of Mauritania's population is enslaved, which would be the highest rate worldwide.

Drought, poverty, and unemployment have driven outmigration from Mauritania since the 1970s. Early flows were directed toward other West African countries, including Senegal, Mali, Cote d'Ivoire, and Gambia. The 1989 Mauritania-Senegal conflict forced thousands of black Mauritanians to take refuge in Senegal and pushed labor migrants toward the Gulf, Libya, and Europe in the late 1980s and early 1990s. Mauritania has accepted migrants from neighboring countries to fill labor shortages since its independence in 1960 and more recently has received refugees escaping civil wars, including tens of thousands of Tuaregs who fled Mali in 2012.

Mauritania was an important transit point for sub-Saharan migrants moving illegally to North Africa and Europe. In the mid-2000s, as border patrols increased in the Strait of Gibraltar, security increased around Spain's North African enclaves (Ceuta and Melilla), and Moroccan border controls intensified, illegal migration flows shifted from the Western Mediterranean to Spain's Canary Islands. In 2006, departure points moved southward along the West African coast from Morocco and Western Sahara to Mauritania's two key ports (Nouadhibou and the capital Nouakchott), and illegal migration to the Canaries peaked at almost 32,000. The numbers fell dramatically in the following years because of joint patrolling off the West African coast by Frontex (the EU's border protection agency), Spain, Mauritania, and Senegal; the expansion of Spain's border surveillance system; and the 2008 European economic downturn.

AGE STRUCTURE:

0-14 years: 38.24% (male 737,570 /female 730,969)

15-24 years: 19.78% (male 372,070 /female 387,375)

25-54 years: 33.44% (male 595,472 /female 688,620)

55-64 years: 4.74% (male 82,197 /female 99,734)

65 years and over: 3.81% (male 62,072 /female 84,350) (2018 est.)

DEPENDENCY RATIOS:

total dependency ratio: 76.5 (2015 est.)

youth dependency ratio: 71 (2015 est.)

elderly dependency ratio: 5.5 (2015 est.)

potential support ratio: 18.3 (2015 est.)

MEDIAN AGE:

total: 20.7 years (2018 est.)

male: 19.7 years

female: 21.6 years

country comparison to the world: 186

POPULATION GROWTH RATE:

2.14% (2018 est.)

country comparison to the world: 41

BIRTH RATE:

29.9 births/1,000 population (2018 est.)

country comparison to the world: 38

DEATH RATE:

7.8 deaths/1,000 population (2018 est.)

country comparison to the world: 97

NET MIGRATION RATE:

-0.8 migrant(s)/1,000 population (2018 est.)

country comparison to the world: 135

POPULATION DISTRIBUTION:

with most of the country being a desert, vast areas of the country, particularly in the central, northern, and eastern areas, are without sizeable population clusters; half the population lives in or around the coastal capital of Nouakchott; smaller clusters are found near the southern border with Mali and Senegal

URBANIZATION:

urban population: 54.5% of total population (2019)

rate of urbanization: 4.28% annual rate of change (2015-20 est.)

MAJOR URBAN AREAS - POPULATION:

1.259 million NOUAKCHOTT (capital) (2019)

SEX RATIO:

at birth: 1.03 male(s)/female

0-14 years: 1.01 male(s)/female

15-24 years: 0.96 male(s)/female

25-54 years: 0.86 male(s)/female

55-64 years: 0.82 male(s)/female

65 years and over: 0.74 male(s)/female

total population: 0.93 male(s)/female (2018 est.)

MATERNAL MORTALITY RATE:

766 deaths/100,000 live births (2017 est.)

country comparison to the world: 7

INFANT MORTALITY RATE:

total: 50.5 deaths/1,000 live births (2018 est.)

male: 55.3 deaths/1,000 live births

female: 45.6 deaths/1,000 live births

country comparison to the world: 26

LIFE EXPECTANCY AT BIRTH:

total population: 63.8 years (2018 est.)

male: 61.4 years

female: 66.2 years

country comparison to the world: 194

TOTAL FERTILITY RATE:

3.79 children born/woman (2018 est.)

country comparison to the world: 39

CONTRACEPTIVE PREVALENCE RATE:

17.8% (2015)

DRINKING WATER SOURCE:

improved:

urban: 58.4% of population

rural: 57.1% of population

total: 57.9% of population

unimproved:

urban: 41.6% of population

rural: 42.9% of population

total: 42.1% of population (2015 est.)

CURRENT HEALTH EXPENDITURE:

4.2% (2016)

PHYSICIANS DENSITY:

0.18 physicians/1,000 population (2017)

SANITATION FACILITY ACCESS:

improved:

urban: 57.5% of population (2015 est.)

rural: 13.8% of population (2015 est.)

total: 40% of population (2015 est.)

unimproved:

urban: 42.5% of population (2015 est.)

rural: 86.2% of population (2015 est.)

total: 60% of population (2015 est.)

HIV/AIDS - ADULT PREVALENCE RATE:

0.2% (2018 est.)

country comparison to the world: 106

HIV/AIDS - PEOPLE LIVING WITH HIV/AIDS:

5,600 (2018 est.)

country comparison to the world: 118

HIV/AIDS - DEATHS:

<500 (2018 est.)

MAJOR INFECTIOUS DISEASES:

degree of risk: very high (2016)

food or waterborne diseases: bacterial and protozoal diarrhea, hepatitis A, and typhoid fever (2016)

vectorborne diseases: malaria and dengue fever (2016)

animal contact diseases: rabies (2016)

respiratory diseases: meningococcal meningitis (2016)

OBESITY - ADULT PREVALENCE RATE:

12.7% (2016)

country comparison to the world: 132

CHILDREN UNDER THE AGE OF 5 YEARS UNDERWEIGHT:

24.9% (2015)

country comparison to the world: 19

EDUCATION EXPENDITURES:

2.6% of GDP (2016)

country comparison to the world: 158

LITERACY:

definition: age 15 and over can read and write

total population: 52.1%

male: 62.6%

female: 41.6% (2015 est.)

SCHOOL LIFE EXPECTANCY (PRIMARY TO TERTIARY EDUCATION):

total: 8 years

male: 8 years

female: 8 years (2017)

UNEMPLOYMENT, YOUTH AGES 15-24:

total: 15.2%

male: 14.1%

female: 17% (2012 est.)

country comparison to the world: 92

GOVERNMENT :: MAURITANIA

COUNTRY NAME:

conventional long form: Islamic Republic of Mauritania

conventional short form: Mauritania

local long form: Al Jumhuriyah al Islamiyah al Muritaniyah

local short form: Muritaniyah

etymology: named for the ancient kingdom of Mauretania (3rd century B.C. to 1st century A.D.), which existed further north in present-day Morocco; the name derives from the Mauri (Moors), the Berber-speaking peoples of northwest Africa

GOVERNMENT TYPE:
presidential republic

CAPITAL:
name: Nouakchott

geographic coordinates: 18 04 N, 15 58 W

time difference: UTC 0 (5 hours ahead of Washington, DC, during Standard Time)

etymology: may derive from the Berber "nawakshut" meaning "place of the winds"

ADMINISTRATIVE DIVISIONS:
15 regions (wilayas, singular - wilaya); Adrar, Assaba, Brakna, Dakhlet Nouadhibou, Gorgol, Guidimaka, Hodh ech Chargui, Hodh El Gharbi, Inchiri, Nouakchott Nord, Nouakchott Ouest, Nouakchott Sud, Tagant, Tiris Zemmour, Trarza

INDEPENDENCE:
28 November 1960 (from France)

NATIONAL HOLIDAY:
Independence Day, 28 November (1960)

CONSTITUTION:
history: previous 1964; latest adopted 12 July 1991

amendments: proposed by the president of the republic or by Parliament; consideration of amendments by Parliament requires approval of at least one third of the membership; a referendum is held only if the amendment is approved by two-thirds majority vote; passage by referendum requires simple majority vote by eligible voters; passage of amendments proposed by the president can bypass a referendum if approved by at least three-fifths majority vote by Parliament; amended many times, last in 2017 (by referendum) (2019)

LEGAL SYSTEM:
mixed legal system of Islamic and French civil law

INTERNATIONAL LAW ORGANIZATION PARTICIPATION:
has not submitted an ICJ jurisdiction declaration; non-party state to the ICCt

CITIZENSHIP:
citizenship by birth: no

citizenship by descent only: at least one parent must be a citizen of Mauritania

dual citizenship recognized: no

residency requirement for naturalization: 5 years

SUFFRAGE:
18 years of age; universal

EXECUTIVE BRANCH:
chief of state: President Mohamed Cheikh El GHAZOUANI (since 1 August 2019)

head of government: Prime Minister Ould Bedda Ould Cheikh SIDIYA (since 5 August 2019)

cabinet: Council of Ministers - nominees suggested by the prime minister, appointed by the president

elections/appointments: president directly elected by absolute majority popular vote in 2 rounds if needed for a 5-year term (eligible for a second term); election last held on 22 June 2019 (next scheduled for 22 June 2024); prime minister appointed by the president

election results: Mohamed Cheikh El GHAZOUANI elected president in first round; percent of vote - Mahamed Cheikh El GHAZOUANI (UPR) 52%, Biram Dah Ould ABEID (independent) 18.6%, Sidi Mohamed Ould BOUBACAR (independent) 17.9%, other 11.55%

LEGISLATIVE BRANCH:
description: unicameral Parliament or Barlamane consists of the National Assembly or Al Jamiya Al Wataniya (157 seats; 113 members in single- and multi-seat constituencies directly elected by a combination of plurality and proportional representation voting systems, 40 members in a single, nationwide constituency directly elected by proportional representation vote, and 4 members directly elected by the diaspora; all members serve 5-year terms)

elections: first held as the unicameral National Assembly in 2 rounds on 1 and 15 September 2018 (next to be held in 2023)

election results: National Assembly - percent of vote by party - NA; seats by party - NA; composition - NA

note: a referendum held in August 2017 approved a constitutional amendment to change the Parliament structure from bicameral to unicameral by abolishing the Senate and creating Regional Councils for local development

JUDICIAL BRANCH:
highest courts: Supreme Court or Cour Supreme (subdivided into 7 chambers: 2 civil, 2 labor, 1 commercial, 1 administrative, and 1 criminal, each with a chamber president and 2 councilors); Constitutional Council (consists of 6 members)

judge selection and term of office: Supreme Court president appointed by the president of the republic to serve a 5-year renewable term; Constitutional Council members appointed - 3 by the president of the republic, 2 by the president of the National Assembly, and 1 by the president of the Senate; members serve single, 9-year terms with one-third of membership renewed every 3 years

subordinate courts: Courts of Appeal; courts of first instance or wilya courts are established in the regions' headquarters and include commercial and labor courts, criminal courts, Moughataa (district) Courts, and informal/customary courts

POLITICAL PARTIES AND LEADERS:
Alliance for Justice and Democracy/Movement for Renewal or AJD/MR [Ibrahima Moctar SARR]
Burst of Youth for the Nation [Lalla Mint CHERIF]
Coalition of Majority Parties or CPM (includes UPR, UDP)
El Karama Party [Cheikhna Ould Mohamed Ould HAJBOU]
El Vadila Party [Ethmane Ould Ahmed ABOULMAALY]
National Forum for Democracy and Unity or FNDU [Mohamed Ould MAOLOUD] (coalition of hard-line opposition parties, includes RNRD-TAWASSOUL)
National Rally for Reform and Development or RNRD-TAWASSOUL [Mohamed Mahmoud Ould SEYIDI]
Party of Unity and Development or PUD [Mohamed BARO]
Popular Progressive Alliance or APP [Messaoud Ould BOULKHEIR]
Rally of Democratic Forces or RFD [Ahmed Ould DADDAH]
Ravah Party [Mohamed Ould VALL]
Republican Party for Democracy and Renewal or PRDR [Mintata Mint HEDEID]
Union for Democracy and Progress or UDP [Naha Mint MOUKNASS]
Union of Progress Forces [Mohamed

Ould MAOULOUD]
Union for the Republic or UPR [Seyidna Ali Ould MOHAMED KHOUNA]

INTERNATIONAL ORGANIZATION PARTICIPATION:

ABEDA, ACP, AfDB, AFESD, AMF, AMU, AU, CAEU (candidate), EITI (compliant country), FAO, G-77, IAEA, IBRD, ICAO, ICC (NGOs), ICRM, IDA, IDB, IFAD, IFC, IFRCS, IHO (pending member), ILO, IMF, IMO, Interpol, IOC, IOM, IPU, ISO (correspondent), ITSO, ITU, ITUC (NGOs), LAS, MIGA, MIUSMA, NAM, OIC, OIF, OPCW, UN, UNCTAD, UNESCO, UNIDO, UNWTO, UPU, WCO, WHO, WIPO, WMO, WTO

DIPLOMATIC REPRESENTATION IN THE US:

Ambassador Mohamedoun DADDAH (since 27 June 2016)

chancery: 2129 Leroy Place NW, Washington, DC 20008

telephone: [1] (202) 232-5700 through 5701

FAX: [1] (202) 319-2623

DIPLOMATIC REPRESENTATION FROM THE US:

chief of mission: Ambassador Michael J. DODMAN (since 5 January 2018)

telephone: [222] 4525-2660 or [222] 2660-2663

embassy: Avenue Al Quds, Nouadhibou, Nouadhibou Road, Nouakchott, Mauritania

mailing address: use embassy street address

FAX: [222] 4525-1592

FLAG DESCRIPTION:

green with a yellow, five-pointed star between the horns of a yellow, upward-pointing crescent moon; red stripes along the top and bottom edges; the crescent, star, and color green are traditional symbols of Islam; green also represents hope for a bright future; the yellow color stands for the sands of the Sahara; red symbolizes the blood shed in the struggle for independence

NATIONAL SYMBOL(S):

five-pointed star between the horns of a horizontal crescent moon; national colors: green, yellow

NATIONAL ANTHEM:

name: "Hymne National de la Republique Islamique de Mauritanie" (National Anthem of the Islamic Republic of Mauritania)

lyrics/music: Baba Ould CHEIKH/traditional, arranged by Tolia NIKIPROWETZKY

note: adopted 1960; the unique rhythm of the Mauritanian anthem makes it particularly challenging to sing; Mauritania in November 2017 adopted a new national anthem, "Bilada-l ubati-l hudati-l kiram" (The Country of Fatherhood is the Honorable Gift) composed by Rageh Daoud (sound file of the new anthem is forthcoming)

ECONOMY :: MAURITANIA

ECONOMY - OVERVIEW:

Mauritania's economy is dominated by extractive industries (oil and mines), fisheries, livestock, agriculture, and services. Half the population still depends on farming and raising livestock, even though many nomads and subsistence farmers were forced into the cities by recurrent droughts in the 1970s, 1980s, 2000s, and 2017. Recently, GDP growth has been driven largely by foreign investment in the mining and oil sectors.

Mauritania's extensive mineral resources include iron ore, gold, copper, gypsum, and phosphate rock, and exploration is ongoing for tantalum, uranium, crude oil, and natural gas. Extractive commodities make up about three-quarters of Mauritania's total exports, subjecting the economy to price swings in world commodity markets. Mining is also a growing source of government revenue, rising from 13% to 30% of total revenue from 2006 to 2014. The nation's coastal waters are among the richest fishing areas in the world, and fishing accounts for about 15% of budget revenues, 45% of foreign currency earnings. Mauritania processes a total of 1,800,000 tons of fish per year, but overexploitation by foreign and national fleets threaten the sustainability of this key source of revenue.

The economy is highly sensitive to international food and extractive commodity prices. Other risks to Mauritania's economy include its recurring droughts, dependence on foreign aid and investment, and insecurity in neighboring Mali, as well as significant shortages of infrastructure, institutional capacity, and human capital. In December 2017, Mauritania and the IMF agreed to a three year agreement under the Extended Credit Facility to foster economic growth, maintain macroeconomic stability, and reduce poverty. Investment in agriculture and infrastructure are the largest components of the country's public expenditures.

GDP (PURCHASING POWER PARITY):

$17.28 billion (2017 est.)

$16.7 billion (2016 est.)

$16.4 billion (2015 est.)

note: data are in 2017 dollars

country comparison to the world: 154

GDP (OFFICIAL EXCHANGE RATE):

$4.935 billion (2017 est.)

GDP - REAL GROWTH RATE:

3.5% (2017 est.)

1.8% (2016 est.)

0.4% (2015 est.)

country comparison to the world: 99

GDP - PER CAPITA (PPP):

$4,500 (2017 est.)

$4,400 (2016 est.)

$4,400 (2015 est.)

note: data are in 2017 dollars

country comparison to the world: 173

GROSS NATIONAL SAVING:

24.2% of GDP (2017 est.)

24.8% of GDP (2016 est.)

19% of GDP (2015 est.)

country comparison to the world: 68

GDP - COMPOSITION, BY END USE:

household consumption: 64.9% (2017 est.)

government consumption: 21.8% (2017 est.)

investment in fixed capital: 56.1% (2017 est.)

investment in inventories: -3.2% (2017 est.)

exports of goods and services: 39% (2017 est.)

imports of goods and services: -78.6% (2017 est.)

GDP - COMPOSITION, BY SECTOR OF ORIGIN:

agriculture: 27.8% (2017 est.)

industry: 29.3% (2017 est.)

services: 42.9% (2017 est.)

AGRICULTURE - PRODUCTS:

dates, millet, sorghum, rice, corn; cattle, camel and sheep

INDUSTRIES:

fish processing, oil production, mining (iron ore, gold, copper)

note: gypsum deposits have never been exploited

INDUSTRIAL PRODUCTION GROWTH RATE:

1% (2017 est.)

country comparison to the world: 157

LABOR FORCE:

1.437 million (2017 est.)

country comparison to the world: 133

LABOR FORCE - BY OCCUPATION:

agriculture: 50%

industry: 1.9%

services: 48.1% (2014 est.)

UNEMPLOYMENT RATE:

10.2% (2017 est.)

10.1% (2016 est.)

country comparison to the world: 142

POPULATION BELOW POVERTY LINE:

31% (2014 est.)

HOUSEHOLD INCOME OR CONSUMPTION BY PERCENTAGE SHARE:

lowest 10%: 2.5%

highest 10%: 29.5% (2000)

DISTRIBUTION OF FAMILY INCOME - GINI INDEX:

37 (2014)

39 (2006 est.)

country comparison to the world: 83

BUDGET:

revenues: 1.354 billion (2017 est.)

expenditures: 1.396 billion (2017 est.)

TAXES AND OTHER REVENUES:

27.4% (of GDP) (2017 est.)

country comparison to the world: 100

BUDGET SURPLUS (+) OR DEFICIT (-):

-0.8% (of GDP) (2017 est.)

country comparison to the world: 69

PUBLIC DEBT:

96.6% of GDP (2017 est.)

100% of GDP (2016 est.)

country comparison to the world: 21

FISCAL YEAR:

calendar year

INFLATION RATE (CONSUMER PRICES):

2.3% (2017 est.)

1.5% (2016 est.)

country comparison to the world: 117

CENTRAL BANK DISCOUNT RATE:

9% (31 December 2009)

12% (31 December 2007)

country comparison to the world: 32

COMMERCIAL BANK PRIME LENDING RATE:

17% (31 December 2017 est.)

17% (31 December 2016 est.)

country comparison to the world: 27

STOCK OF NARROW MONEY:

$1.296 billion (31 December 2017 est.)

$1.287 billion (31 December 2016 est.)

country comparison to the world: 149

STOCK OF BROAD MONEY:

$1.296 billion (31 December 2017 est.)

$1.287 billion (31 December 2016 est.)

country comparison to the world: 155

STOCK OF DOMESTIC CREDIT:

$2.364 billion (31 December 2017 est.)

$2.355 billion (31 December 2016 est.)

country comparison to the world: 144

MARKET VALUE OF PUBLICLY TRADED SHARES:

NA

CURRENT ACCOUNT BALANCE:

-$711 million (2017 est.)

-$707 million (2016 est.)

country comparison to the world: 129

EXPORTS:

$1.722 billion (2017 est.)

$1.401 billion (2016 est.)

country comparison to the world: 148

EXPORTS - PARTNERS:

China 31.2%, Switzerland 14.4%, Spain 10.1%, Germany 8.2%, Japan 8.1% (2017)

EXPORTS - COMMODITIES:

iron ore, fish and fish products, livestock, gold, copper, crude oil

IMPORTS:

$2.094 billion (2017 est.)

$1.9 billion (2016 est.)

country comparison to the world: 166

IMPORTS - COMMODITIES:

machinery and equipment, petroleum products, capital goods, foodstuffs, consumer goods

IMPORTS - PARTNERS:

Belgium 11.5%, UAE 11.3%, US 9.2%, China 7.5%, France 7.4%, Netherlands 6.1%, Morocco 6%, Slovenia 4.8%, Vanuatu 4.7%, Spain 4.7% (2017)

RESERVES OF FOREIGN EXCHANGE AND GOLD:

$875 million (31 December 2017 est.)

$849.3 million (31 December 2016 est.)

country comparison to the world: 138

DEBT - EXTERNAL:

$4.15 billion (31 December 2017 est.)

$3.899 billion (31 December 2016 est.)

country comparison to the world: 138

STOCK OF DIRECT FOREIGN INVESTMENT - AT HOME:

(31 December 2009 est.)

EXCHANGE RATES:

ouguiyas (MRO) per US dollar -

363.6 (2017 est.)

352.37 (2016 est.)

352.37 (2015 est.)

319.7 (2014 est.)

299.5 (2013 est.)

ENERGY :: MAURITANIA

ELECTRICITY ACCESS:

population without electricity: 3 million (2017)

electrification - total population: 41.7% (2016)

electrification - urban areas: 81% (2016)

electrification - rural areas: 2.3% (2016)

ELECTRICITY - PRODUCTION:

1.139 billion kWh (2016 est.)

country comparison to the world: 147

ELECTRICITY - CONSUMPTION:

1.059 billion kWh (2016 est.)

country comparison to the world: 154

ELECTRICITY - EXPORTS:

0 kWh (2016 est.)

country comparison to the world: 169

ELECTRICITY - IMPORTS:

0 kWh (2016 est.)

country comparison to the world: 173

ELECTRICITY - INSTALLED GENERATING CAPACITY:
558,000 kW (2016 est.)

country comparison to the world: 144

ELECTRICITY - FROM FOSSIL FUELS:
65% of total installed capacity (2016 est.)

country comparison to the world: 118

ELECTRICITY - FROM NUCLEAR FUELS:
0% of total installed capacity (2017 est.)

country comparison to the world: 141

ELECTRICITY - FROM HYDROELECTRIC PLANTS:
16% of total installed capacity (2017 est.)

country comparison to the world: 100

ELECTRICITY - FROM OTHER RENEWABLE SOURCES:
20% of total installed capacity (2017 est.)

country comparison to the world: 39

CRUDE OIL - PRODUCTION:
4,000 bbl/day (2018 est.)

country comparison to the world: 81

CRUDE OIL - EXPORTS:
5,333 bbl/day (2015 est.)

country comparison to the world: 65

CRUDE OIL - IMPORTS:
0 bbl/day (2015 est.)

country comparison to the world: 164

CRUDE OIL - PROVED RESERVES:
20 million bbl (1 January 2018 est.)

country comparison to the world: 83

REFINED PETROLEUM PRODUCTS - PRODUCTION:
0 bbl/day (2015 est.)

country comparison to the world: 176

REFINED PETROLEUM PRODUCTS - CONSUMPTION:
17,000 bbl/day (2016 est.)

country comparison to the world: 150

REFINED PETROLEUM PRODUCTS - EXPORTS:
0 bbl/day (2015 est.)

country comparison to the world: 180

REFINED PETROLEUM PRODUCTS - IMPORTS:
17,290 bbl/day (2015 est.)

country comparison to the world: 133

NATURAL GAS - PRODUCTION:
0 cu m (2017 est.)

country comparison to the world: 169

NATURAL GAS - CONSUMPTION:
0 cu m (2017 est.)

country comparison to the world: 174

NATURAL GAS - EXPORTS:
0 cu m (2017 est.)

country comparison to the world: 150

NATURAL GAS - IMPORTS:
0 cu m (2017 est.)

country comparison to the world: 156

NATURAL GAS - PROVED RESERVES:
28.32 billion cu m (1 January 2018 est.)

country comparison to the world: 70

CARBON DIOXIDE EMISSIONS FROM CONSUMPTION OF ENERGY:
2.615 million Mt (2017 est.)

country comparison to the world: 152

COMMUNICATIONS :: MAURITANIA

TELEPHONES - FIXED LINES:
total subscriptions: 57,057

subscriptions per 100 inhabitants: 2 (2017 est.)

country comparison to the world: 155

TELEPHONES - MOBILE CELLULAR:
total subscriptions: 4,074,157

subscriptions per 100 inhabitants: 108 (2017 est.)

country comparison to the world: 127

TELEPHONE SYSTEM:
general assessment: limited system of cable and open-wire lines, minor microwave radio relay links, and radiotelephone communications stations; mobile-cellular services expanding rapidly; 3 mobile network operators; 3G penetration high; mobile broadband speeds are low; World Bank and European Investment Bank support attempts to improve telecom and improve regulatory measures; efforts to improve backbone of network; auction for fourth mobile provider and 4G service in spring 2019 (2018)

domestic: fixed-line teledensity 2 per 100 persons; mobile-cellular network coverage extends mainly to urban areas with a teledensity of roughly 108 per 100 persons; mostly cable and open-wire lines; a domestic satellite telecommunications system links Nouakchott with regional capitals (2018)

international: country code - 222; landing point for the ACE submarine cable for connectivity for 19 West African countries and 2 European countries; satellite earth stations - 3 (1 Intelsat - Atlantic Ocean, 2 Arabsat) (2019)

BROADCAST MEDIA:
10 TV stations: 5 government-owned and 5 private; in October 2017, the government suspended all private TV stations due to non-payment of broadcasting fees; as of April 2018, only one private TV station was broadcasting, Al Mourabitoune, the official TV of the Mauritanian Islamist party, Tewassoul; the other stations are negotiating payment options with the government and hope to be back on the air soon; 18 radio broadcasters: 15 government-owned, 3 (Radio Nouakchott Libre, Radio Tenwir, Radio Kobeni) private; all 3 private radio stations broadcast from Nouakchott; of the 15 government stations, 3 broadcast from Nouakchott (Radio Mauritanie, Radio Jeunesse, Radio Koran) and the other 12 broadcast from each of the 12 regions outside Nouakchott; Radio Jeunesse and Radio Koran are now also being re-broadcast in the regions (2019)

INTERNET COUNTRY CODE:
.mr

INTERNET USERS:
total: 661,913

percent of population: 18% (July 2016 est.)

country comparison to the world: 143

BROADBAND - FIXED SUBSCRIPTIONS:
total: 12,637

subscriptions per 100 inhabitants: less than 1 (2017 est.)

country comparison to the world: 165

MILITARY AND SECURITY :: MAURITANIA

MILITARY EXPENDITURES:
3.02% of GDP (2018)

2.91% of GDP (2017)

2.91% of GDP (2016)

2.75% of GDP (2015)

2.7% of GDP (2014)

country comparison to the world: 22

MILITARY AND SECURITY FORCES:

Mauritanian Armed Forces: Army, Mauritanian Navy (Marine Mauritanienne), Islamic Republic of Mauritania Air Group (Groupement Aerienne Islamique de Mauritanie, GAIM); Ministry of Interior: Gendarmerie, National Guard (2019)

MILITARY SERVICE AGE AND OBLIGATION:

18 is the legal minimum age for voluntary military service; no conscription (2012)

TRANSPORTATION :: MAURITANIA

NATIONAL AIR TRANSPORT SYSTEM:

number of registered air carriers: 1 (2015)

inventory of registered aircraft operated by air carriers: 4 (2015)

annual passenger traffic on registered air carriers: 248,158 (2015)

annual freight traffic on registered air carriers: 0 mt-km (2015)

CIVIL AIRCRAFT REGISTRATION COUNTRY CODE PREFIX:

5T (2016)

AIRPORTS:

30 (2013)

country comparison to the world: 115

AIRPORTS - WITH PAVED RUNWAYS:

total: 9 (2017)

2,438 to 3,047 m: 5 (2017)

1,524 to 2,437 m: 4 (2017)

AIRPORTS - WITH UNPAVED RUNWAYS:

total: 21 (2013)

2,438 to 3,047 m: 1 (2013)

1,524 to 2,437 m: 10 (2013)

914 to 1,523 m: 8 (2013)

under 914 m: 2 (2013)

RAILWAYS:

total: 728 km (2014)

standard gauge: 728 km 1.435-m gauge (2014)

country comparison to the world: 100

ROADWAYS:

total: 12,253 km (2018)

paved: 3,988 km (2018)

unpaved: 8,265 km (2018)

country comparison to the world: 128

WATERWAYS:

(some navigation possible on the Senegal River) (2011)

MERCHANT MARINE:

total: 7

by type: bulk carrier 1, general cargo 2, oil tanker 1, other 3 (2018)

country comparison to the world: 159

PORTS AND TERMINALS:

major seaport(s): Nouadhibou, Nouakchott

TRANSNATIONAL ISSUES :: MAURITANIA

DISPUTES - INTERNATIONAL:

Mauritanian claims to Western Sahara remain dormant

REFUGEES AND INTERNALLY DISPLACED PERSONS:

refugees (country of origin): 26,001 (Western Saharan Sahrawis) (2018); 56,680 (Mali) (2019)

TRAFFICKING IN PERSONS:

current situation: Mauritania is a source and destination country for men, women, and children subjected to forced labor and sex trafficking; adults and children from traditional slave castes are subjected to slavery-related practices rooted in ancestral master-slave relationships; Mauritanian boy students called talibes are trafficked within the country by religious teachers for forced begging; Mauritanian girls, as well as girls from Mali, Senegal, The Gambia, and other West African countries, are forced into domestic servitude; Mauritanian women and girls are forced into prostitution domestically or transported to countries in the Middle East for the same purpose, sometimes through forced marriages

tier rating: Tier 3 - Mauritania does not fully comply with the minimum standards for the elimination of trafficking and is not making significant efforts to do so; anti-trafficking law enforcement efforts were negligible; one slavery case identified by an NGO was investigated, but no prosecutions or convictions were made, including among the 4,000 child labor cases NGOs referred to the police; the 2007 anti-slavery law remains ineffective because it requires slaves, most of whom are illiterate, to file their own legal complaint, and the government agency that can submit claims on them did not file any in 2014; authorities arrested, prosecuted, and convicted several anti-slavery activists; NGOs continued to provide the majority of protective services to trafficking victims without support from the government; some steps were taken to raise public awareness about human trafficking (2015)

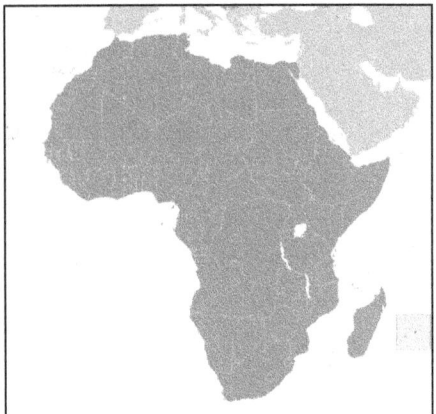

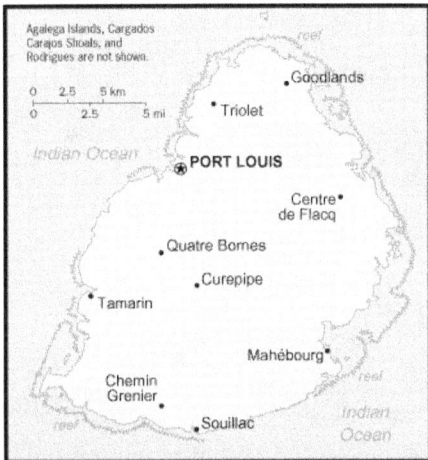

AFRICA :: MAURITIUS

INTRODUCTION :: MAURITIUS

BACKGROUND:
Although known to Arab and Malay sailors as early as the 10th century, Mauritius was first explored by the Portuguese in the 16th century and subsequently settled by the Dutch - who named it in honor of Prince Maurits van NASSAU - in the 17th century. The French assumed control in 1715, developing the island into an important naval base overseeing Indian Ocean trade, and establishing a plantation economy of sugar cane. The British captured the island in 1810, during the Napoleonic Wars. Mauritius remained a strategically important British naval base, and later an air station, playing an important role during World War II for anti-submarine and convoy operations, as well as the collection of signals intelligence. Independence from the UK was attained in 1968. A stable democracy with regular free elections and a positive human rights record, the country has attracted considerable foreign investment and has one of Africa's highest per capita incomes.

GEOGRAPHY :: MAURITIUS

LOCATION:
Southern Africa, island in the Indian Ocean, about 800 km (500 mi) east of Madagascar

GEOGRAPHIC COORDINATES:
20 17 S, 57 33 E

MAP REFERENCES:
Africa

AREA:
total: 2,040 sq km

land: 2,030 sq km

water: 10 sq km

note: includes Agalega Islands, Cargados Carajos Shoals (Saint Brandon), and Rodrigues

country comparison to the world: 181

AREA - COMPARATIVE:
almost 11 times the size of Washington, DC

LAND BOUNDARIES:
0 km

COASTLINE:
177 km

MARITIME CLAIMS:
territorial sea: 12 nm

exclusive economic zone: 200 nm

continental shelf: 200 nm or to the edge of the continental margin measured from claimed archipelagic straight baselines

CLIMATE:
tropical, modified by southeast trade winds; warm, dry winter (May to November); hot, wet, humid summer (November to May)

TERRAIN:
small coastal plain rising to discontinuous mountains encircling central plateau

ELEVATION:
lowest point: Indian Ocean 0 m

highest point: Mont Piton 828 m

NATURAL RESOURCES:
arable land, fish

LAND USE:
agricultural land: 43.8% (2011 est.)

arable land: 38.4% (2011 est.) / permanent crops: 2% (2011 est.) / permanent pasture: 3.4% (2011 est.)

forest: 17.3% (2011 est.)

other: 38.9% (2011 est.)

IRRIGATED LAND:
190 sq km (2012)

POPULATION DISTRIBUTION:
population density is one of the highest in the world; urban cluster are found throught the main island, with a greater density in and around Port Luis; population on Rodrigues Island is spread across the island with a slightly denser cluster on the north coast

NATURAL HAZARDS:
cyclones (November to April); almost completely surrounded by reefs that may pose maritime hazards

ENVIRONMENT - CURRENT ISSUES:
water pollution, degradation of coral reefs; soil erosion; wildlife preservation; solid waste disposal

ENVIRONMENT - INTERNATIONAL AGREEMENTS:
party to: Antarctic-Marine Living Resources, Biodiversity, Climate Change, Climate Change-Kyoto Protocol, Desertification, Endangered Species, Environmental Modification, Hazardous Wastes, Law of the Sea, Marine Life Conservation, Ozone Layer Protection, Ship Pollution, Wetlands

signed, but not ratified: none of the selected agreements

GEOGRAPHY - NOTE:

the main island, from which the country derives its name, is of volcanic origin and is almost entirely surrounded by coral reefs; former home of the dodo, a large flightless bird related to pigeons, driven to extinction by the end of the 17th century through a combination of hunting and the introduction of predatory species

PEOPLE AND SOCIETY :: MAURITIUS

POPULATION:

1,364,283 (July 2018 est.)

country comparison to the world: 155

NATIONALITY:

noun: Mauritian(s)

adjective: Mauritian

ETHNIC GROUPS:

Indo-Mauritian (compose approximately two thirds of the total population), Creole, Sino-Mauritian, Franco-Mauritian

note: Mauritius has not had a question on ethnicity on its national census since 1972

LANGUAGES:

Creole 86.5%, Bhojpuri 5.3%, French 4.1%, two languages 1.4%, other 2.6% (includes English, the official language of the National Assembly, which is spoken by less than 1% of the population), unspecified 0.1% (2011 est.)

RELIGIONS:

Hindu 48.5%, Roman Catholic 26.3%, Muslim 17.3%, other Christian 6.4%, other 0.6%, none 0.7%, unspecified 0.1% (2011 est.)

DEMOGRAPHIC PROFILE:

Mauritius has transitioned from a country of high fertility and high mortality rates in the 1950s and mid-1960s to one with among the lowest population growth rates in the developing world today. After World War II, Mauritius' population began to expand quickly due to increased fertility and a dramatic drop in mortality rates as a result of improved health care and the eradication of malaria. This period of heightened population growth – reaching about 3% a year – was followed by one of the world's most rapid birth rate declines.

The total fertility rate fell from 6.2 children per women in 1963 to 3.2 in 1972 – largely the result of improved educational attainment, especially among young women, accompanied by later marriage and the adoption of family planning methods. The family planning programs' success was due to support from the government and eventually the traditionally pronatalist religious communities, which both recognized that controlling population growth was necessary because of Mauritius' small size and limited resources. Mauritius' fertility rate has consistently been below replacement level since the late 1990s, a rate that is substantially lower than nearby countries in southern Africa.

With no indigenous population, Mauritius' ethnic mix is a product of more than two centuries of European colonialism and continued international labor migration. Sugar production relied on slave labor mainly from Madagascar, Mozambique, and East Africa from the early 18th century until its abolition in 1835, when slaves were replaced with indentured Indians. Most of the influx of indentured labor – peaking between the late 1830s and early 1860 – settled permanently creating massive population growth of more than 7% a year and reshaping the island's social and cultural composition. While Indians represented about 12% of Mauritius' population in 1837, they and their descendants accounted for roughly two-thirds by the end of the 19th century. Most were Hindus, but the majority of the free Indian traders were Muslims.

Mauritius again turned to overseas labor when its success in clothing and textile exports led to a labor shortage in the mid-1980s. Clothing manufacturers brought in contract workers (increasingly women) from China, India, and, to a lesser extent Bangladesh and Madagascar, who worked longer hours for lower wages under poor conditions and were viewed as more productive than locals. Downturns in the sugar and textile industries in the mid-2000s and a lack of highly qualified domestic workers for Mauritius' growing services sector led to the emigration of low-skilled workers and a reliance on skilled foreign labor. Since 2007, Mauritius has pursued a circular migration program to enable citizens to acquire new skills and savings abroad and then return home to start businesses and to invest in the country's development.

AGE STRUCTURE:

0-14 years: 19.9% (male 138,707 /female 132,774)

15-24 years: 14.52% (male 100,281 /female 97,836)

25-54 years: 43.6% (male 297,558 /female 297,243)

55-64 years: 11.81% (male 76,620 /female 84,554)

65 years and over: 10.17% (male 57,094 /female 81,616) (2018 est.)

DEPENDENCY RATIOS:

total dependency ratio: 41.6 (2015 est.)

youth dependency ratio: 27.5 (2015 est.)

elderly dependency ratio: 14.1 (2015 est.)

potential support ratio: 7.1 (2015 est.)

MEDIAN AGE:

total: 35.7 years (2018 est.)

male: 34.5 years

female: 36.7 years

country comparison to the world: 77

POPULATION GROWTH RATE:

0.57% (2018 est.)

country comparison to the world: 150

BIRTH RATE:

12.8 births/1,000 population (2018 est.)

country comparison to the world: 152

DEATH RATE:

7.1 deaths/1,000 population (2018 est.)

country comparison to the world: 127

NET MIGRATION RATE:

0 migrant(s)/1,000 population (2018 est.)

country comparison to the world: 92

POPULATION DISTRIBUTION:

population density is one of the highest in the world; urban cluster are found throught the main island, with a greater density in and around Port Luis; population on Rodrigues Island is spread across the island with a slightly denser cluster on the north coast

URBANIZATION:

urban population: 40.8% of total population (2019)

rate of urbanization: 0.11% annual rate of change (2015-20 est.)

MAJOR URBAN AREAS - POPULATION:

149,000 PORT LOUIS (capital) (2018)

SEX RATIO:

at birth: 1.05 male(s)/female

0-14 years: 1.04 male(s)/female

15-24 years: 1.02 male(s)/female

25-54 years: 1 male(s)/female

55-64 years: 0.91 male(s)/female

65 years and over: 0.7 male(s)/female

total population: 0.97 male(s)/female (2018 est.)

MATERNAL MORTALITY RATE:

61 deaths/100,000 live births (2017 est.)

country comparison to the world: 87

INFANT MORTALITY RATE:

total: 9.5 deaths/1,000 live births (2018 est.)

male: 11.3 deaths/1,000 live births

female: 7.7 deaths/1,000 live births

country comparison to the world: 139

LIFE EXPECTANCY AT BIRTH:

total population: 76 years (2018 est.)

male: 72.6 years

female: 79.7 years

country comparison to the world: 95

TOTAL FERTILITY RATE:

1.74 children born/woman (2018 est.)

country comparison to the world: 163

CONTRACEPTIVE PREVALENCE RATE:

63.8% (2014)

DRINKING WATER SOURCE:

improved:

urban: 99.9% of population

rural: 99.8% of population

total: 99.9% of population

unimproved:

urban: 0.1% of population

rural: 0.2% of population

total: 0.1% of population (2015 est.)

CURRENT HEALTH EXPENDITURE:

5.7% (2016)

PHYSICIANS DENSITY:

2.54 physicians/1,000 population (2018)

HOSPITAL BED DENSITY:

3.7 beds/1,000 population (2018)

SANITATION FACILITY ACCESS:

improved:

urban: 93.9% of population (2015 est.)

rural: 92.6% of population (2015 est.)

total: 93.1% of population (2015 est.)

unimproved:

urban: 6.1% of population (2015 est.)

rural: 7.4% of population (2015 est.)

total: 6.9% of population (2015 est.)

HIV/AIDS - ADULT PREVALENCE RATE:

1.3% (2018)

country comparison to the world: 40

HIV/AIDS - PEOPLE LIVING WITH HIV/AIDS:

13,000 (2018)

country comparison to the world: 94

HIV/AIDS - DEATHS:

<1000 (2018)

OBESITY - ADULT PREVALENCE RATE:

10.8% (2016)

country comparison to the world: 137

EDUCATION EXPENDITURES:

5% of GDP (2017)

country comparison to the world: 67

LITERACY:

definition: age 15 and over can read and write

total population: 93.2%

male: 95.4%

female: 91% (2016 est.)

SCHOOL LIFE EXPECTANCY (PRIMARY TO TERTIARY EDUCATION):

total: 15 years

male: 14 years

female: 16 years (2017)

UNEMPLOYMENT, YOUTH AGES 15-24:

total: 24%

male: 18.6%

female: 31% (2017 est.)

country comparison to the world: 54

GOVERNMENT :: MAURITIUS

COUNTRY NAME:

conventional long form: Republic of Mauritius

conventional short form: Mauritius

local long form: Republic of Mauritius

local short form: Mauritius

etymology: island named after Prince Maurice VAN NASSAU, stadtholder of the Dutch Republic, in 1598

note: pronounced mar-i-shus

GOVERNMENT TYPE:

parliamentary republic

CAPITAL:

name: Port Louis

geographic coordinates: 20 09 S, 57 29 E

time difference: UTC+4 (9 hours ahead of Washington, DC, during Standard Time)

etymology: named after Louis XV, who was king of France in 1736 when the port became the administrative center of Mauritius and a major reprovisioning stop for French ships traveling between Europe and Asia

ADMINISTRATIVE DIVISIONS:

9 districts and 3 dependencies*; Agalega Islands*, Black River, Cargados Carajos Shoals*, Flacq, Grand Port, Moka, Pamplemousses, Plaines Wilhems, Port Louis, Riviere du Rempart, Rodrigues*, Savanne

INDEPENDENCE:

12 March 1968 (from the UK)

NATIONAL HOLIDAY:

Independence and Republic Day, 12 March (1968 & 1992); note - became independent and a republic on the same date in 1968 and 1992 respectively

CONSTITUTION:

history: several previous; latest adopted 12 March 1968

amendments: proposed by the National Assembly; passage of amendments affecting constitutional articles, including the sovereignty of the state, fundamental rights and freedoms, citizenship, or the branches of government, requires approval in a referendum by at least three-fourths majority of voters followed by a unanimous vote by the Assembly; passage of other amendments requires only two-thirds majority vote by the Assembly; amended many times, last in 2016 (2017)

LEGAL SYSTEM:

civil legal system based on French civil law with some elements of English common law

INTERNATIONAL LAW ORGANIZATION PARTICIPATION:

accepts compulsory ICJ jurisdiction with reservations; accepts ICCt jurisdiction

CITIZENSHIP:

citizenship by birth: yes

citizenship by descent only: yes

dual citizenship recognized: yes

residency requirement for naturalization: 5 out of the previous 7 years including the last 12 months

SUFFRAGE:

18 years of age; universal

EXECUTIVE BRANCH:

chief of state: President Pradeep ROOPUN (since 2 December 2019); Vice President Marie Cyril Eddy Boissézon (2 December 2019) note - President Ameenah GURIB-FAKIM (since 5 June 2015) resigned on 23 March 2018 amid a credit card scandal

head of government: Prime Minister Pravind JUGNAUTH (since 23 January 2017, remains PM after parliamentary election 7 Nov 2019); note - Prime Minister Sir Aneerood JUGNAUTH (since 17 December 2014) stepped down on 23 January 2017 in favor of his son, Pravind Kumar JUGNAUTH, who was then appointed prime minister; 7 Nov 2019 Pravind Jugnauth remains prime minister and home affairs minister and also becomes defense minister (2019)

cabinet: Cabinet of Ministers (Council of Ministers) appointed by the president on the recommendation of the prime minister

elections/appointments: president and vice president indirectly elected by the National Assembly for 5-year renewable terms; election last held on 7 Nov 2019 (next to be held in 2024); prime minister and deputy prime minister appointed by the president, responsible to the National Assembly (2019)

election results: Ameenah GURIB-FAKIM (independent) elected president by the National Assembly - unanimous vote; note - GURIB-FAKIM, Mauritius'- first female president, resigned on 23 March 2018 (2018)

LEGISLATIVE BRANCH:

description: unicameral National Assembly or Assemblee Nationale (70 seats maximum; 62 members directly elected multi-seat constituencies by simple majority vote and up to 8 seats allocated to non-elected party candidates by the Office of Electoral Commissioner; members serve a 5-year term)

elections: last held on 7 November 2019 (next to be held by late 2024)

election results: percent of vote by party - MSM 61%, Labour Party 23%, MMM 13%, OPR 3%; elected seats by party - the Militant Socialist Movement (MSM) wins 38 seats, the Labour Party (PTR) or (MLP) 14, Mauritian Militant Movement (MMM) 8 and the Rodrigues People's Organization (OPR) 2 (2019)

JUDICIAL BRANCH:

highest courts: Supreme Court of Mauritius (consists of the chief justice, a senior puisne judge, and 18 puisne judges); note - the Judicial Committee of the Privy Council (in London) serves as the final court of appeal

judge selection and term of office: chief justice appointed by the president after consultation with the prime minister; senior puisne judge appointed by the president with the advice of the chief justice; other puisne judges appointed by the president with the advice of the Judicial and Legal Commission, a 4-member body of judicial officials including the chief justice; all judges serve until retirement at age 67

subordinate courts: lower regional courts known as District Courts, Court of Civil Appeal; Court of Criminal Appeal; Public Bodies Appeal Tribunal

POLITICAL PARTIES AND LEADERS:

Alliance Lepep (Alliance of the People) [Pravind JUGNAUTH] (coalition includes MSM and ML) Labor Party (Parti Travailliste) or PTR or MLP [Navinchandra RAMGOOLAM]
Mauritian Militant Movement (Mouvement Militant Mauricien) or MMM [Paul BERENGER]
Mauritian Social Democratic Party (Parti Mauricien Social Democrate) or PMSD [Xavier Luc DUVAL]
Mauritian Solidarity Front (Front Solidarite Mauricienne) or FSM [Cehl FAKEERMEEAH, aka Cehl MEEAH]
Militant Socialist Movement (Mouvement Socialist Mauricien) or MSM [Pravind JUGNAUTH]
Muvman Liberater or ML [Ivan COLLENDAVELLOO]
Patriotic Movement (Mouvement Patriotic) [Alan GANOO]
Rodrigues Peoples Organization (Organisation du Peuple Rodriguais) or OPR [Serge CLAIR]

INTERNATIONAL ORGANIZATION PARTICIPATION:

ACP, AfDB, AOSIS, AU, C, CD, COMESA, CPLP (associate), FAO, G-77, IAEA, IBRD, ICAO, ICC (NGOs), ICCt, ICRM, IDA, IFAD, IFC, IFRCS, IHO, ILO, IMF, IMO, IMSO, InOC, Interpol, IOC, IOM, IPU, ISO, ITSO, ITU, ITUC (NGOs), MIGA, NAM, OIF, OPCW, PCA, SAARC (observer), SADC, UN, UNCTAD, UNESCO, UNIDO, UNWTO, UPU, WCO, WFTU (NGOs), WHO, WIPO, WMO, WTO

DIPLOMATIC REPRESENTATION IN THE US:

Ambassador Sooroojdev PHOKEER (since 3 August 2015)

chancery: 1709 N Street NW, Washington, DC 20036; administrative offices at 3201 Connecticut Avenue NW, Suite 441, Washington, DC 20036

telephone: [1] (202) 244-1491 through 1492

FAX: [1] (202) 966-0983

DIPLOMATIC REPRESENTATION FROM THE US:

chief of mission: Ambassador David D. REIMER (since 10 January 2018); note - also accredited to Seychelles

telephone: [230] 202-4400

embassy: 4th Floor, Rogers House, John Kennedy Avenue, Port Louis

mailing address: international mail: P.O. Box 544, Port Louis; US mail: American Embassy, Port Louis, US Department of State, Washington, DC 20521-2450

FAX: [230] 208-9534

FLAG DESCRIPTION:

four equal horizontal bands of red (top), blue, yellow, and green; red represents self-determination and independence, blue the Indian Ocean surrounding the island, yellow has been interpreted as the new light of independence, golden sunshine, or the bright future, and green can symbolize either agriculture or the lush vegetation of the island

note: while many national flags consist of three - and in some cases five - horizontal bands of color, the flag of Mauritius is the world's only national flag to consist of four horizontal color bands

NATIONAL SYMBOL(S):

dodo bird, Trochetia Boutoniana flower; national colors: red, blue, yellow, green

NATIONAL ANTHEM:

name: Motherland

lyrics/music: Jean Georges PROSPER/Philippe GENTIL

note: adopted 1968

ECONOMY :: MAURITIUS

ECONOMY - OVERVIEW:

Since independence in 1968, Mauritius has undergone a remarkable economic transformation from a low-income, agriculturally based economy to a diversified, upper middle-income economy with growing industrial, financial, and tourist sectors. Mauritius has achieved steady growth over the last several decades, resulting in more equitable income distribution, increased life expectancy, lowered infant mortality, and a much-improved infrastructure.

The economy currently depends on sugar, tourism, textiles and apparel, and financial services, but is expanding into fish processing, information and communications technology, education, and hospitality and property development. Sugarcane is grown on about 90% of the cultivated land area but sugar makes up only around 3-4% of national GDP. Authorities plan to emphasize services and innovation in the coming years. After several years of slow growth, government policies now seek to stimulate economic growth in five areas: serving as a gateway for international investment into Africa; increasing the use of renewable energy; developing smart cities; growing the ocean economy; and upgrading and modernizing infrastructure, including public transportation, the port, and the airport.

Mauritius has attracted more than 32,000 offshore entities, many aimed at commerce in India, South Africa, and China. The Mauritius International Financial Center is under scrutiny by international bodies promoting fair tax competition and Mauritius has been cooperating with the European Union and the United states in the automatic exchange of account information. Mauritius is also a member of the OECD/G20's Inclusive Framework on Base Erosion and Profit Shifting and is under pressure to review its Double Taxation Avoidance Agreements. The offshore sector is vulnerable to changes in the tax framework and authorities have been working on a Financial Services Sector Blueprint to enable Mauritius to transition to a jurisdiction of higher value added. Mauritius' textile sector has taken advantage of the Africa Growth and Opportunity Act, a preferential trade program that allows duty free access to the US market, with Mauritian exports to the US growing by 35.6 % from 2000 to 2014. However, lack of local labor as well as rising labor costs eroding the competitiveness of textile firms in Mauritius.

Mauritius' sound economic policies and prudent banking practices helped mitigate negative effects of the global financial crisis in 2008-09. GDP grew in the 3-4% per year range in 2010-17, and the country continues to expand its trade and investment outreach around the globe. Growth in the US and Europe fostered goods and services exports, including tourism, while lower oil prices kept inflation low. Mauritius continues to rank as one of the most business-friendly environments on the continent and passed a Business Facilitation Act to improve competitiveness and long-term growth prospects. A new National Economic Development Board was set up in 2017-2018 to spearhead efforts to promote exports and attract inward investment.

GDP (PURCHASING POWER PARITY):

$28.27 billion (2017 est.)

$27.23 billion (2016 est.)

$26.23 billion (2015 est.)

note: data are in 2017 dollars

country comparison to the world: 137

GDP (OFFICIAL EXCHANGE RATE):

$13.33 billion (2017 est.)

GDP - REAL GROWTH RATE:

3.8% (2017 est.)

3.8% (2016 est.)

3.6% (2015 est.)

country comparison to the world: 88

GDP - PER CAPITA (PPP):

$22,300 (2017 est.)

$21,500 (2016 est.)

$20,800 (2015 est.)

note: data are in 2017 dollars

country comparison to the world: 86

GROSS NATIONAL SAVING:

16.9% of GDP (2017 est.)

15.8% of GDP (2016 est.)

15.2% of GDP (2015 est.)

country comparison to the world: 122

GDP - COMPOSITION, BY END USE:

household consumption: 81% (2017 est.)

government consumption: 15.1% (2017 est.)

investment in fixed capital: 17.3% (2017 est.)

investment in inventories: -0.4% (2017 est.)

exports of goods and services: 42.1% (2017 est.)

imports of goods and services: -55.1% (2017 est.)

GDP - COMPOSITION, BY SECTOR OF ORIGIN:

agriculture: 4% (2017 est.)

industry: 21.8% (2017 est.)

services: 74.1% (2017 est.)

AGRICULTURE - PRODUCTS:

sugarcane, tea, corn, potatoes, bananas, pulses; cattle, goats; fish

INDUSTRIES:

food processing (largely sugar milling), textiles, clothing, mining, chemicals, metal products, transport equipment, nonelectrical machinery, tourism

INDUSTRIAL PRODUCTION GROWTH RATE:

3.2% (2017 est.)

country comparison to the world: 98

LABOR FORCE:

633,900 (2017 est.)

country comparison to the world: 153

LABOR FORCE - BY OCCUPATION:

agriculture: 8%

industry: 29.8%

services: 62.2% (2014 est.)

UNEMPLOYMENT RATE:

7.1% (2017 est.)

7.3% (2016 est.)

country comparison to the world: 111

POPULATION BELOW POVERTY LINE:

8% (2006 est.)

HOUSEHOLD INCOME OR CONSUMPTION BY PERCENTAGE SHARE:

lowest 10%: NA

highest 10%: NA

DISTRIBUTION OF FAMILY INCOME - GINI INDEX:

35.9 (2012 est.)

39 (2006 est.)

country comparison to the world: 92

BUDGET:

revenues: 2.994 billion (2017 est.)

expenditures: 3.038 billion (2017 est.)

TAXES AND OTHER REVENUES:

22.5% (of GDP) (2017 est.)

country comparison to the world: 133

BUDGET SURPLUS (+) OR DEFICIT (-):

-0.3% (of GDP) (2017 est.)

country comparison to the world: 54

PUBLIC DEBT:

64% of GDP (2017 est.)

66.1% of GDP (2016 est.)

country comparison to the world: 60

FISCAL YEAR:

1 July - 30 June

INFLATION RATE (CONSUMER PRICES):

3.7% (2017 est.)

1% (2016 est.)

country comparison to the world: 148

CENTRAL BANK DISCOUNT RATE:

9% (31 December 2010)

country comparison to the world: 33

COMMERCIAL BANK PRIME LENDING RATE:

8.5% (31 December 2017 est.)

8.5% (31 December 2016 est.)

country comparison to the world: 98

STOCK OF NARROW MONEY:

$3.335 billion (31 December 2017 est.)

$2.833 billion (31 December 2016 est.)

country comparison to the world: 120

STOCK OF BROAD MONEY:

$3.335 billion (31 December 2017 est.)

$2.833 billion (31 December 2016 est.)

country comparison to the world: 125

STOCK OF DOMESTIC CREDIT:

$17.16 billion (31 December 2017 est.)

$13.7 billion (31 December 2016 est.)

country comparison to the world: 95

MARKET VALUE OF PUBLICLY TRADED SHARES:

$7.239 billion (31 December 2015 est.)

$8.751 billion (31 December 2014 est.)

$8.942 billion (31 December 2013 est.)

country comparison to the world: 78

CURRENT ACCOUNT BALANCE:

-$875 million (2017 est.)

-$531 million (2016 est.)

country comparison to the world: 136

EXPORTS:

$2.36 billion (2017 est.)

$2.359 billion (2016 est.)

country comparison to the world: 136

EXPORTS - PARTNERS:

France 16.7%, US 12.5%, UK 12%, South Africa 9%, Madagascar 6.7%, Italy 6.6%, Spain 5.2% (2017)

EXPORTS - COMMODITIES:

clothing and textiles, sugar, cut flowers, molasses, fish, primates (for research)

IMPORTS:

$4.986 billion (2017 est.)

$4.406 billion (2016 est.)

country comparison to the world: 130

IMPORTS - COMMODITIES:

manufactured goods, capital equipment, foodstuffs, petroleum products, chemicals

IMPORTS - PARTNERS:

India 17.9%, China 15.7%, France 11.1%, South Africa 9.7% (2017)

RESERVES OF FOREIGN EXCHANGE AND GOLD:

$5.984 billion (31 December 2017 est.)

$4.967 billion (31 December 2016 est.)

country comparison to the world: 92

DEBT - EXTERNAL:

$19.99 billion (31 December 2017 est.)

$14.34 billion (31 December 2016 est.)

country comparison to the world: 92

STOCK OF DIRECT FOREIGN INVESTMENT - AT HOME:

NA

STOCK OF DIRECT FOREIGN INVESTMENT - ABROAD:

NA

EXCHANGE RATES:

Mauritian rupees (MUR) per US dollar -

35.17 (2017 est.)

35.542 (2016 est.)

35.542 (2015 est.)

35.057 (2014 est.)

30.622 (2013 est.)

ENERGY :: MAURITIUS

ELECTRICITY ACCESS:

electrification - total population: 100% (2016)

ELECTRICITY - PRODUCTION:

2.898 billion kWh (2016 est.)

country comparison to the world: 134

ELECTRICITY - CONSUMPTION:

2.726 billion kWh (2016 est.)

country comparison to the world: 140

ELECTRICITY - EXPORTS:

0 kWh (2016 est.)

country comparison to the world: 170

ELECTRICITY - IMPORTS:

0 kWh (2016 est.)

country comparison to the world: 174

ELECTRICITY - INSTALLED GENERATING CAPACITY:

894,000 kW (2016 est.)

country comparison to the world: 132

ELECTRICITY - FROM FOSSIL FUELS:

79% of total installed capacity (2016 est.)

country comparison to the world: 86

ELECTRICITY - FROM NUCLEAR FUELS:

0% of total installed capacity (2017 est.)

country comparison to the world: 142

ELECTRICITY - FROM HYDROELECTRIC PLANTS:

7% of total installed capacity (2017 est.)

country comparison to the world: 126

ELECTRICITY - FROM OTHER RENEWABLE SOURCES:

14% of total installed capacity (2017 est.)

country comparison to the world: 62

CRUDE OIL - PRODUCTION:

0 bbl/day (2018 est.)

country comparison to the world: 173

CRUDE OIL - EXPORTS:

0 bbl/day (2015 est.)

country comparison to the world: 164
CRUDE OIL - IMPORTS:
0 bbl/day (2015 est.)

country comparison to the world: 165
CRUDE OIL - PROVED RESERVES:
0 bbl (1 January 2018 est.)

country comparison to the world: 168
REFINED PETROLEUM PRODUCTS - PRODUCTION:
0 bbl/day (2017 est.)

country comparison to the world: 177
REFINED PETROLEUM PRODUCTS - CONSUMPTION:
27,000 bbl/day (2016 est.)

country comparison to the world: 123
REFINED PETROLEUM PRODUCTS - EXPORTS:
0 bbl/day (2015 est.)

country comparison to the world: 181
REFINED PETROLEUM PRODUCTS - IMPORTS:
26,960 bbl/day (2015 est.)

country comparison to the world: 102
NATURAL GAS - PRODUCTION:
0 cu m (2017 est.)

country comparison to the world: 170
NATURAL GAS - CONSUMPTION:
0 cu m (2017 est.)

country comparison to the world: 175
NATURAL GAS - EXPORTS:
0 cu m (2017 est.)

country comparison to the world: 151
NATURAL GAS - IMPORTS:
0 cu m (2017 est.)

country comparison to the world: 157
NATURAL GAS - PROVED RESERVES:
0 cu m (1 January 2014 est.)

country comparison to the world: 169
CARBON DIOXIDE EMISSIONS FROM CONSUMPTION OF ENERGY:
6.429 million Mt (2017 est.)

country comparison to the world: 125

COMMUNICATIONS :: MAURITIUS

TELEPHONES - FIXED LINES:

total subscriptions: 413,100

subscriptions per 100 inhabitants: 30 (2017 est.)

country comparison to the world: 102
TELEPHONES - MOBILE CELLULAR:

total subscriptions: 1,839,500

subscriptions per 100 inhabitants: 136 (2017 est.)

country comparison to the world: 152
TELEPHONE SYSTEM:

general assessment: small system with good service; LTE and fiber broadband service are available; government building a national Wi-Fi network; partial privatization of biggest telecommunications company, open to competition (2018)

domestic: fixed-line teledensity roughly 30 per 100 persons; mobile-cellular services teledensity approaching 136 per 100 persons (2018)

international: country code - 230; landing points for the SAFE, MARS, IOX Cable System, METISS and LION submarine cable system that provides links to Asia, Africa, Southeast Asia, Indian Ocean Islands of Reunion, Madagascar, and Mauritius; satellite earth station - 1 Intelsat (Indian Ocean); new microwave link to Reunion; HF radiotelephone links to several countries (2019)

BROADCAST MEDIA:

the government maintains control over TV broadcasting through the Mauritius Broadcasting Corporation (MBC), which only operates digital TV stations since June 2015; MBC is a shareholder in a local company that operates 2 pay-TV stations; the state retains the largest radio broadcast network with multiple stations; several private radio broadcasters have entered the market since 2001; transmissions of at least 2 international broadcasters are available (2019)

INTERNET COUNTRY CODE:
.mu

INTERNET USERS:

total: 717,618

percent of population: 53.2% (July 2016 est.)

country comparison to the world: 140
BROADBAND - FIXED SUBSCRIPTIONS:

total: 246,000

subscriptions per 100 inhabitants: 18 (2017 est.)

country comparison to the world: 102

MILITARY AND SECURITY :: MAURITIUS

MILITARY EXPENDITURES:

0.16% of GDP (2018)

0.18% of GDP (2017)

0.19% of GDP (2016)

0.18% of GDP (2015)

0.15% of GDP (2014)

country comparison to the world: 158
MILITARY AND SECURITY FORCES:

no regular military forces; Mauritius Police Force includes a Special Mobile Force (a paramilitary force formed as a mobile infantry battalion) and the National Coast Guard (2019)

TRANSPORTATION :: MAURITIUS

NATIONAL AIR TRANSPORT SYSTEM:

number of registered air carriers: 1 (2015)

inventory of registered aircraft operated by air carriers: 13 (2015)

annual passenger traffic on registered air carriers: 1,466,527 (2015)

annual freight traffic on registered air carriers: 168.773 million mt-km (2015)

CIVIL AIRCRAFT REGISTRATION COUNTRY CODE PREFIX:

3B (2016)

AIRPORTS:

5 (2013)

country comparison to the world: 180
AIRPORTS - WITH PAVED RUNWAYS:

total: 2 (2017)

over 3,047 m: 1 (2017)

914 to 1,523 m: 1 (2017)

AIRPORTS - WITH UNPAVED RUNWAYS:

total: 3 (2013)

914 to 1,523 m: 2 (2013)

under 914 m: 1 (2013)

ROADWAYS:

total: 2,428 km (2015)

paved: 2,379 km (includes 99 km of expressways) (2015)

unpaved: 49 km (2015)

country comparison to the world: 164

MERCHANT MARINE:

total: 28

by type: general cargo 1, oil tanker 4, other 23 (2018)

country comparison to the world: 129

PORTS AND TERMINALS:

major seaport(s): Port Louis

TRANSNATIONAL ISSUES :: MAURITIUS

DISPUTES - INTERNATIONAL:

Mauritius and Seychelles claim the Chagos Islands; claims French-administered Tromelin Island

TRAFFICKING IN PERSONS:

current situation: Mauritius is a source, transit, and destination country for men, women, and children subjected to forced labor and sex trafficking; Mauritian girls are induced or sold into prostitution, often by peers, family members, or businessmen offering other forms of employment; Mauritian adults have been identified as labor trafficking victims in the UK, Belgium, and Canada, while Mauritian women from Rodrigues Island are also subject to domestic servitude in Mauritius; Malagasy women transit Mauritius en route to the Middle East for jobs as domestic servants and subsequently are subjected to forced labor; Cambodian men are victims of forced labor on foreign fishing vessels in Mauritius' territorial waters; other migrant workers from East and South Asia and Madagascar are also subject to forced labor in Mauritius' manufacturing and construction sectors

tier rating: Tier 2 Watch List – Mauritius does not fully comply with the minimum standards for the elimination of trafficking; however, it is making significant efforts to do so; in 2014, the government made modest efforts to address child sex trafficking but none related to adult forced labor; law enforcement lacks an understanding of trafficking crimes outside of child sex trafficking, despite increasing evidence of other forms of human trafficking; authorities made no trafficking prosecutions or convictions and made modest efforts to assist a couple of child sex trafficking victims; officials sustained an extensive public awareness campaign to prevent child sex trafficking, but no efforts were made to raise awareness or reduce demand for forced adult or child labor (2015)

ILLICIT DRUGS:

consumer and transshipment point for heroin from South Asia; small amounts of cannabis produced and consumed locally; significant offshore financial industry creates potential for money laundering, but corruption levels are relatively low and the government appears generally to be committed to regulating its banking industry

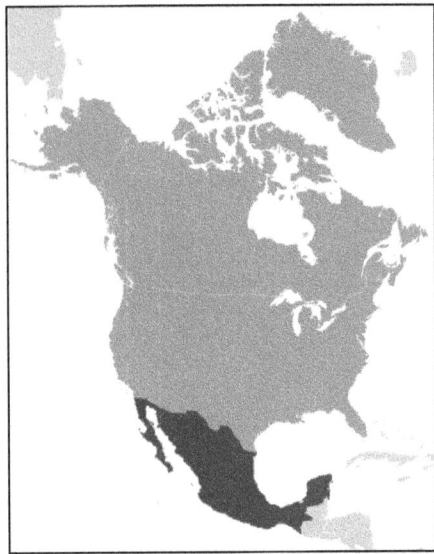

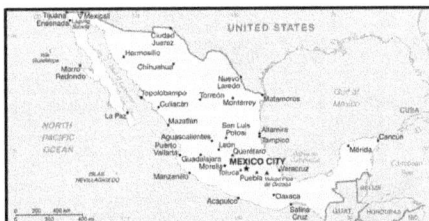

NORTH AMERICA :: MEXICO

INTRODUCTION :: MEXICO

BACKGROUND:

The site of several advanced Amerindian civilizations - including the Olmec, Toltec, Teotihuacan, Zapotec, Maya, and Aztec - Mexico was conquered and colonized by Spain in the early 16th century. Administered as the Viceroyalty of New Spain for three centuries, it achieved independence early in the 19th century. Elections held in 2000 marked the first time since the 1910 Mexican Revolution that an opposition candidate - Vicente FOX of the National Action Party (PAN) - defeated the party in government, the Institutional Revolutionary Party (PRI). He was succeeded in 2006 by another PAN candidate Felipe CALDERON, but Enrique PENA NIETO regained the presidency for the PRI in 2012. Left-leaning antiestablishment politician and former mayor of Mexico City (2000-05) Andres Manuel LOPEZ OBRADOR, from the National Regeneration Movement (MORENA), became president in December 2018.

The global financial crisis in late 2008 caused a massive economic downturn in Mexico the following year, although growth returned quickly in 2010. Ongoing economic and social concerns include low real wages, high underemployment, inequitable income distribution, and few advancement opportunities for the largely indigenous population in the impoverished southern states. Since 2007, Mexico's powerful drug-trafficking organizations have engaged in bloody feuding, resulting in tens of thousands of drug-related homicides.

GEOGRAPHY :: MEXICO

LOCATION:
North America, bordering the Caribbean Sea and the Gulf of Mexico, between Belize and the United States and bordering the North Pacific Ocean, between Guatemala and the United States

GEOGRAPHIC COORDINATES:
23 00 N, 102 00 W

MAP REFERENCES:
North America

AREA:
total: 1,964,375 sq km

land: 1,943,945 sq km

water: 20,430 sq km

country comparison to the world: 15

AREA - COMPARATIVE:
slightly less than three times the size of Texas

LAND BOUNDARIES:
total: 4,389 km

border countries (3): Belize 276 km, Guatemala 958 km, US 3155 km

COASTLINE:
9,330 km

MARITIME CLAIMS:
territorial sea: 12 nm

exclusive economic zone: 200 nm

contiguous zone: 24 nm

continental shelf: 200 nm or to the edge of the continental margin

CLIMATE:
varies from tropical to desert

TERRAIN:
high, rugged mountains; low coastal plains; high plateaus; desert

ELEVATION:
mean elevation: 1,111 m

lowest point: Laguna Salada -10 m

highest point: Volcan Pico de Orizaba 5,636 m

NATURAL RESOURCES:
petroleum, silver, antimony, copper, gold, lead, zinc, natural gas, timber

LAND USE:
agricultural land: 54.9% (2011 est.)

arable land: 11.8% (2011 est.) / permanent crops: 1.4% (2011 est.) / permanent pasture: 41.7% (2011 est.)

forest: 33.3% (2011 est.)

other: 11.8% (2011 est.)

IRRIGATED LAND:
65,000 sq km (2012)

POPULATION DISTRIBUTION:
most of the population is found in the middle of the country between the states of Jalisco and Veracruz; approximately a quarter of the population lives in and around Mexico City

NATURAL HAZARDS:
tsunamis along the Pacific coast, volcanoes and destructive earthquakes in the center and south, and hurricanes on the Pacific, Gulf of Mexico, and Caribbean coasts

volcanism: volcanic activity in the central-southern part of the country; the volcanoes in Baja California are mostly dormant; Colima (3,850 m), which erupted in 2010, is Mexico's most active volcano and is responsible for causing periodic evacuations of nearby villagers; it has been deemed a Decade Volcano by the International Association of Volcanology and Chemistry of the Earth's Interior, worthy of study due to its explosive history and close proximity to human populations; Popocatepetl (5,426 m) poses a threat to Mexico City; other historically active volcanoes include Barcena, Ceboruco, El Chichon, Michoacan-Guanajuato, Pico de Orizaba, San Martin, Socorro, and Tacana; see note 2 under "Geography - note"

ENVIRONMENT - CURRENT ISSUES:

scarcity of hazardous waste disposal facilities; rural to urban migration; natural freshwater resources scarce and polluted in north, inaccessible and poor quality in center and extreme southeast; raw sewage and industrial effluents polluting rivers in urban areas; deforestation; widespread erosion; desertification; deteriorating agricultural lands; serious air and water pollution in the national capital and urban centers along US-Mexico border; land subsidence in Valley of Mexico caused by groundwater depletion

note: the government considers the lack of clean water and deforestation national security issues

ENVIRONMENT - INTERNATIONAL AGREEMENTS:

party to: Biodiversity, Climate Change, Climate Change-Kyoto Protocol, Desertification, Endangered Species, Hazardous Wastes, Law of the Sea, Marine Dumping, Marine Life Conservation, Ozone Layer Protection, Ship Pollution, Wetlands, Whaling

signed, but not ratified: none of the selected agreements

GEOGRAPHY - NOTE:

note 1: strategic location on southern border of the US; Mexico is one of the countries along the Ring of Fire, a belt of active volcanoes and earthquake epicenters bordering the Pacific Ocean; up to 90% of the world's earthquakes and some 75% of the world's volcanoes occur within the Ring of Fire

note 2: the "Three Sisters" companion plants - winter squash, maize (corn), and climbing beans - served as the main agricultural crops for various North American Indian groups; all three apparently originated in Mexico but then were widely disseminated through much of North America; vanilla, the world's most popular aroma and flavor spice, also emanates from Mexico

note 3: the Sac Actun cave system at 348 km (216 mi) is the longest underwater cave in the world and the second longest cave worldwide, after Mammoth Cave in the United States (see "Geography - note" under United States)

note 4: the prominent Yucatan Peninsula that divides the Gulf of Mexico from the Caribbean Sea is shared by Mexico, Guatemala, and Belize; just on the northern coast of Yucatan, near the town of Chicxulub (pronounce cheek-sha-loob), lie the remnants of a massive crater (some 150 km in diameter and extending well out into the Gulf of Mexico); formed by an asteroid or comet when it struck the earth 66 million years ago, the impact is now widely accepted as initiating a worldwide climate disruption that caused a mass extinction of 75% of all the earth's plant and animal species - including the non-avian dinosaurs

PEOPLE AND SOCIETY :: MEXICO

POPULATION:

125,959,205 (July 2018 est.)

country comparison to the world: 11

NATIONALITY:

noun: Mexican(s)

adjective: Mexican

ETHNIC GROUPS:

mestizo (Amerindian-Spanish) 62%, predominantly Amerindian 21%, Amerindian 7%, other 10% (mostly European) (2012 est.)

note: Mexico does not collect census data on ethnicity

LANGUAGES:

Spanish only 92.7%, Spanish and indigenous languages 5.7%, indigenous only 0.8%, unspecified 0.8% (2005)

note: indigenous languages include various Mayan, Nahuatl, and other regional languages

RELIGIONS:

Roman Catholic 82.7%, Pentecostal 1.6%, Jehovah's Witness 1.4%, other Evangelical Churches 5%, other 1.9%, none 4.7%, unspecified 2.7% (2010 est.)

AGE STRUCTURE:

0-14 years: 26.61% (male 17,143,124 /female 16,378,309)

15-24 years: 17.35% (male 11,072,817 /female 10,779,029)

25-54 years: 40.91% (male 24,916,204 /female 26,612,272)

55-64 years: 7.87% (male 4,538,167 /female 5,375,867)

65 years and over: 7.26% (male 4,079,513 /female 5,063,903) (2018 est.)

DEPENDENCY RATIOS:

total dependency ratio: 51.4 (2015 est.)

youth dependency ratio: 41.6 (2015 est.)

elderly dependency ratio: 9.8 (2015 est.)

potential support ratio: 10.2 (2015 est.)

MEDIAN AGE:

total: 28.6 years (2018 est.)

male: 27.5 years

female: 29.7 years

country comparison to the world: 135

POPULATION GROWTH RATE:

1.09% (2018 est.)

country comparison to the world: 101

BIRTH RATE:

18.1 births/1,000 population (2018 est.)

country comparison to the world: 93

DEATH RATE:

5.4 deaths/1,000 population (2018 est.)

country comparison to the world: 180

NET MIGRATION RATE:

-1.8 migrant(s)/1,000 population (2018 est.)

country comparison to the world: 158

POPULATION DISTRIBUTION:

most of the population is found in the middle of the country between the states of Jalisco and Veracruz; approximately a quarter of the population lives in and around Mexico City

URBANIZATION:

urban population: 80.4% of total population (2019)

rate of urbanization: 1.59% annual rate of change (2015-20 est.)

MAJOR URBAN AREAS - POPULATION:

21.672 million MEXICO CITY (capital), 5.101 million Guadalajara, 4.793 million Monterrey, 3.145 million Puebla, 2.411 million Toluca de Lerdo, 2.099 million Tijuana (2019)

SEX RATIO:

at birth: 1.05 male(s)/female

0-14 years: 1.05 male(s)/female

15-24 years: 1.03 male(s)/female

25-54 years: 0.94 male(s)/female

55-64 years: 0.84 male(s)/female

65 years and over: 0.81 male(s)/female

total population: 0.96 male(s)/female (2018 est.)

MOTHER'S MEAN AGE AT FIRST BIRTH:

21.3 years (2008 est.)

MATERNAL MORTALITY RATE:

33 deaths/100,000 live births (2017 est.)

country comparison to the world: 108

INFANT MORTALITY RATE:

total: 11.3 deaths/1,000 live births (2018 est.)

male: 12.6 deaths/1,000 live births

female: 9.8 deaths/1,000 live births

country comparison to the world: 125

LIFE EXPECTANCY AT BIRTH:

total population: 76.3 years (2018 est.)

male: 73.5 years

female: 79.2 years

country comparison to the world: 89

TOTAL FERTILITY RATE:

2.22 children born/woman (2018 est.)

country comparison to the world: 94

CONTRACEPTIVE PREVALENCE RATE:

66.9% (2015)

DRINKING WATER SOURCE:

improved:

urban: 97.2% of population

rural: 92.1% of population

total: 96.1% of population

unimproved:

urban: 2.8% of population

rural: 7.9% of population

total: 3.9% of population (2015 est.)

CURRENT HEALTH EXPENDITURE:

5.5% (2016)

PHYSICIANS DENSITY:

2.25 physicians/1,000 population (2016)

HOSPITAL BED DENSITY:

1.5 beds/1,000 population (2015)

SANITATION FACILITY ACCESS:

improved:

urban: 88% of population (2015 est.)

rural: 74.5% of population (2015 est.)

total: 85.2% of population (2015 est.)

unimproved:

urban: 12% of population (2015 est.)

rural: 25.5% of population (2015 est.)

total: 14.8% of population (2015 est.)

HIV/AIDS - ADULT PREVALENCE RATE:

0.2% (2018 est.)

country comparison to the world: 107

HIV/AIDS - PEOPLE LIVING WITH HIV/AIDS:

230,000 (2018 est.)

country comparison to the world: 25

HIV/AIDS - DEATHS:

4,000 (2017 est.)

country comparison to the world: 32

MAJOR INFECTIOUS DISEASES:

degree of risk: intermediate (2016)

food or waterborne diseases: bacterial diarrhea and hepatitis A (2016)

vectorborne diseases: dengue fever (2016)

note: active local transmission of Zika virus by Aedes species mosquitoes has been identified in this country (as of August 2016); it poses an important risk (a large number of cases possible) among US citizens if bitten by an infective mosquito; other less common ways to get Zika are through sex, via blood transfusion, or during pregnancy, in which the pregnant woman passes Zika virus to her fetus

OBESITY - ADULT PREVALENCE RATE:

28.9% (2016)

country comparison to the world: 29

CHILDREN UNDER THE AGE OF 5 YEARS UNDERWEIGHT:

4.2% (2016)

country comparison to the world: 87

EDUCATION EXPENDITURES:

5.2% of GDP (2015)

country comparison to the world: 59

LITERACY:

definition: age 15 and over can read and write

total population: 94.9%

male: 95.8%

female: 94% (2016 est.)

SCHOOL LIFE EXPECTANCY (PRIMARY TO TERTIARY EDUCATION):

total: 14 years

male: 14 years

female: 14 years (2016)

UNEMPLOYMENT, YOUTH AGES 15-24:

total: 6.9%

male: 6.5%

female: 7.6% (2018 est.)

country comparison to the world: 157

GOVERNMENT :: MEXICO

COUNTRY NAME:

conventional long form: United Mexican States

conventional short form: Mexico

local long form: Estados Unidos Mexicanos

local short form: Mexico

etymology: named after the capital city, whose name stems from the Mexica, the largest and most powerful branch of the Aztecs; the meaning of the name is uncertain

GOVERNMENT TYPE:

federal presidential republic

CAPITAL:

name: Mexico City (Ciudad de Mexico)

geographic coordinates: 19 26 N, 99 08 W

time difference: UTC-6 (1 hour behind Washington, DC, during Standard Time)

daylight saving time: +1hr, begins first Sunday in April; ends last Sunday in October

note: Mexico has four time zones

etymology: named after the Mexica, the largest and most powerful branch of the Aztecs; the meaning of the name is uncertain

ADMINISTRATIVE DIVISIONS:

32 states (estados, singular - estado); Aguascalientes, Baja California, Baja California Sur, Campeche, Chiapas, Chihuahua, Coahuila, Colima, Cuidad de Mexico, Durango, Guanajuato, Guerrero, Hidalgo, Jalisco, Mexico, Michoacan, Morelos, Nayarit, Nuevo Leon, Oaxaca, Puebla, Queretaro, Quintana Roo, San Luis Potosi, Sinaloa, Sonora, Tabasco, Tamaulipas, Tlaxcala, Veracruz, Yucatan, Zacatecas

INDEPENDENCE:
16 September 1810 (declared independence from Spain); 27 September 1821 (recognized by Spain)

NATIONAL HOLIDAY:
Independence Day, 16 September (1810)

CONSTITUTION:
history: several previous; latest approved 5 February 1917

amendments: proposed by the Congress of the Union; passage requires approval by at least two thirds of the members present and approval by a majority of the state legislatures; amended many times, last in 2019 (2019)

LEGAL SYSTEM:
civil law system with US constitutional law influence; judicial review of legislative acts

INTERNATIONAL LAW ORGANIZATION PARTICIPATION:
accepts compulsory ICJ jurisdiction with reservations; accepts ICCt jurisdiction

CITIZENSHIP:
citizenship by birth: yes

citizenship by descent only: yes

dual citizenship recognized: not specified

residency requirement for naturalization: 5 years

SUFFRAGE:
18 years of age; universal and compulsory

EXECUTIVE BRANCH:
chief of state: President Andres Manuel LOPEZ OBRADOR (since 1 December 2018); note - the president is both chief of state and head of government

head of government: President Andres Manuel LOPEZ OBRADOR (since 1 December 2018)

cabinet: Cabinet appointed by the president; note - appointment of attorney general, the head of the Bank of Mexico, and senior treasury officials require consent of the Senate

elections/appointments: president directly elected by simple majority popular vote for a single 6-year term; election last held on 1 July 2018 (next to be held in July 2024)

election results: Andres Manuel LOPEZ OBRADOR elected president; percent of vote - Andres Manuel LOPEZ OBRADOR (MORENA) 53.2%, Ricardo ANAYA (PAN) 22.3%, Jose Antonio MEADE Kuribrena (PRI) 16.4%, Jaime RODRIGUEZ Calderon 5.2% (independent), other 2.9%

LEGISLATIVE BRANCH:
description: bicameral National Congress or Congreso de la Union consists of:
Senate or Camara de Senadores (128 seats; 96 members directly elected in multi-seat constituencies by simple majority vote and 32 directly elected in a single, nationwide constituency by proportional representation vote; members serve 6-year terms)
Chamber of Deputies or Camara de Diputados (500 seats; 300 members directly elected in single-seat constituencies by simple majority vote and 200 directly elected in a single, nationwide constituency by proportional representation vote; members serve 3-year terms)

elections:
Senate - last held on 1 July 2018 (next to be held on 1 July 2024)
Chamber of Deputies - last held on 1 July 2018 (next to be held on 1 July 2021)

election results:
Senate - percent of vote by party - percent of vote by party - NA; seats by party - MORENA 58, PAN 22, PRI 14, PRD 9, MC 7, PT 7, PES 5, PVEM 5, PNA/PANAL 1; composition - men 65, women 63, percent of women 49.3%
Chamber of Deputies - percent of vote by party - NA; seats by party - MORENA 193, PAN 79, PT 61, PES 58, PRI 42, MC 26, PRD 23, PVEM 17, PNA/PANAL 1; composition - men 259, women 241, percent of women 48.2%; note - total National Congress percent of women 48.4%

note: for the 2018 election, senators will be eligible for a second term and deputies up to 4 consecutive terms

JUDICIAL BRANCH:

highest courts: Supreme Court of Justice or Suprema Corte de Justicia de la Nacion (consists of the chief justice and 11 justices and organized into civil, criminal, administrative, and labor panels) and the Electoral Tribunal of the Federal Judiciary (organized into the superior court, with 7 judges including the court president, and 5 regional courts, each with 3 judges)

judge selection and term of office: Supreme Court justices nominated by the president of the republic and approved by two-thirds vote of the members present in the Senate; justices serve 15-year terms; Electoral Tribunal superior and regional court judges nominated by the Supreme Court and elected by two-thirds vote of members present in the Senate; superior court president elected from among its members to hold office for a 4-year term; other judges of the superior and regional courts serve staggered, 9-year terms

subordinate courts: federal level includes circuit, collegiate, and unitary courts; state and district level courts

POLITICAL PARTIES AND LEADERS:
Citizen's Movement (Movimiento Ciudadano) or MC [Clemente CASTANEDA]
Institutional Revolutionary Party (Partido Revolucionario Institucional) or PRI [Claudia RUIZ Massieu]
Labor Party (Partido del Trabajo) or PT [Alberto ANAYA Gutierrez]
Mexican Green Ecological Party (Partido Verde Ecologista de Mexico) or PVEM [Carlos Alberto PUENTE Salas]
Movement for National Regeneration (Movimiento Regeneracion Nacional) or MORENA [Andres Manuel LOPEZ Obrador]
National Action Party (Partido Accion Nacional) or PAN [Damian ZEPEDA Vidales]
Party of the Democratic Revolution (Partido de la Revolucion Democratica) or PRD [Manuel GRANADOS]

INTERNATIONAL ORGANIZATION PARTICIPATION:
APEC, Australia Group, BCIE, BIS, CAN (observer), Caricom (observer), CD, CDB, CE (observer), CELAC, CSN (observer), EBRD, FAO, FATF, G-3, G-15, G-20, G-24, G-5, IADB, IAEA, IBRD, ICAO, ICC (national committees), ICCt, ICRM, IDA, IFAD, IFC, IFRCS, IHO, ILO, IMF,

IMO, IMSO, Interpol, IOC, IOM, IPU, ISO, ITSO, ITU, ITUC (NGOs), LAES, LAIA, MIGA, NAFTA, NAM (observer), NEA, NSG, OAS, OECD, OPANAL, OPCW, Pacific Alliance, Paris Club (associate), PCA, SICA (observer), UN, UNASUR (observer), UNCTAD, UNESCO, UNHCR, UNIDO, Union Latina (observer), UNWTO, UPU, WCO, WFTU (NGOs), WHO, WIPO, WMO, WTO

DIPLOMATIC REPRESENTATION IN THE US:

Ambassador Martha BARCENA Coqui (since 11 January 2019); note - Ambassador BARCENA Coqui is Mexico'a first-ever female ambassador to the US

chancery: 1911 Pennsylvania Avenue NW, Washington, DC 20006

telephone: [1] (202) 728-1600

FAX: [1] (202) 728-1698

consulate(s) general: Atlanta, Austin, Boston, Chicago, Dallas, Denver, El Paso (TX), Houston, Laredo (TX), Los Angeles, Miami, New York, Nogales (AZ), Phoenix, Sacramento (CA), San Antonio (TX), San Diego, San Francisco, San Jose (CA), San Juan (Puerto Rico), Saint Paul (MN)

consulate(s): Albuquerque (NM), Anchorage (AK), Boise (ID), Brownsville (TX), Calexico (CA), Del Rio (TX), Detroit, Douglas (AZ), Eagle Pass (TX), Fresno (CA), Indianapolis (IN), Kansas City (MO), Las Vegas, Little Rock (AR), McAllen (TX), Minneapolis (MN), New Orleans, Omaha (NE), Orlando (FL), Oxnard (CA), Philadelphia, Portland (OR), Presidio (TX), Raleigh (NC), Salt Lake City, San Bernardino (CA), Santa Ana (CA), Seattle, Tucson (AZ), Yuma (AZ); note - Washington DC Consular Section is located in a separate building from the Mexican Embassy and has jurisdiction over DC, parts of Virginia, Maryland, and West Virginia

DIPLOMATIC REPRESENTATION FROM THE US:

chief of mission: Ambassador Christopher LANDAU (since 26 August 2019)

telephone: (011) 52-55-5080-2000

embassy: Paseo de la Reforma 305, Colonia Cuauhtemoc, 06500 Mexico, Distrito Federal

mailing address: P. O. Box 9000, Brownsville, TX 78520-9000

FAX: (011) 52-55-5080-2005

consulate(s) general: Ciudad Juarez, Guadalajara, Hermosillo, Matamoros, Merida, Monterrey, Nogales, Nuevo Laredo, Tijuana

FLAG DESCRIPTION:

three equal vertical bands of green (hoist side), white, and red; Mexico's coat of arms (an eagle with a snake in its beak perched on a cactus) is centered in the white band; green signifies hope, joy, and love; white represents peace and honesty; red stands for hardiness, bravery, strength, and valor; the coat of arms is derived from a legend that the wandering Aztec people were to settle at a location where they would see an eagle on a cactus eating a snake; the city they founded, Tenochtitlan, is now Mexico City

note: similar to the flag of Italy, which is shorter, uses lighter shades of green and red, and does not display anything in its white band

NATIONAL SYMBOL(S):

golden eagle; national colors: green, white, red

NATIONAL ANTHEM:

name: "Himno Nacional Mexicano" (National Anthem of Mexico)

lyrics/music: Francisco Gonzalez BOCANEGRA/Jaime Nuno ROCA

note: adopted 1943, in use since 1854; also known as "Mexicanos, al grito de Guerra" (Mexicans, to the War Cry); according to tradition, Francisco Gonzalez BOCANEGRA, an accomplished poet, was uninterested in submitting lyrics to a national anthem contest; his fiancee locked him in a room and refused to release him until the lyrics were completed

ECONOMY :: MEXICO

ECONOMY - OVERVIEW:

Mexico's $2.4 trillion economy – 11th largest in the world - has become increasingly oriented toward manufacturing since the North American Free Trade Agreement (NAFTA) entered into force in 1994. Per capita income is roughly one-third that of the US; income distribution remains highly unequal.

Mexico has become the US' second-largest export market and third-largest source of imports. In 2017, two-way trade in goods and services exceeded $623 billion. Mexico has free trade agreements with 46 countries, putting more than 90% of its trade under free trade agreements. In 2012, Mexico formed the Pacific Alliance with Peru, Colombia, and Chile.

Mexico's current government, led by President Enrique PENA NIETO, has emphasized economic reforms, passing and implementing sweeping energy, financial, fiscal, and telecommunications reform legislation, among others, with the long-term aim to improve competitiveness and economic growth across the Mexican economy. Since 2015, Mexico has held public auctions of oil and gas exploration and development rights and for long-term electric power generation contracts. Mexico has also issued permits for private sector import, distribution, and retail sales of refined petroleum products in an effort to attract private investment into the energy sector and boost production.

Since 2013, Mexico's economic growth has averaged 2% annually, falling short of private-sector expectations that President PENA NIETO's sweeping reforms would bolster economic prospects. Growth is predicted to remain below potential given falling oil production, weak oil prices, structural issues such as low productivity, high inequality, a large informal sector employing over half of the workforce, weak rule of law, and corruption. Mexico's economy remains vulnerable to uncertainty surrounding the future of NAFTA — because the United States is its top trading partner and the two countries share integrated supply chains — and to potential shifts in domestic policies following the inauguration of a new a president in December 2018.

GDP (PURCHASING POWER PARITY):

$2.463 trillion (2017 est.)

$2.413 trillion (2016 est.)

$2.346 trillion (2015 est.)

note: data are in 2017 dollars

country comparison to the world: 11

GDP (OFFICIAL EXCHANGE RATE):

$1.151 trillion (2017 est.)

GDP - REAL GROWTH RATE:

2% (2017 est.)

2.9% (2016 est.)

3.3% (2015 est.)

country comparison to the world: 152

GDP - PER CAPITA (PPP):

$19,900 (2017 est.)

$19,700 (2016 est.)

$19,400 (2015 est.)

note: data are in 2017 dollars

country comparison to the world: 90

GROSS NATIONAL SAVING:

21.4% of GDP (2017 est.)

21.6% of GDP (2016 est.)

20.7% of GDP (2015 est.)

country comparison to the world: 85

GDP - COMPOSITION, BY END USE:

household consumption: 67% (2017 est.)

government consumption: 11.8% (2017 est.)

investment in fixed capital: 22.3% (2017 est.)

investment in inventories: 0.8% (2017 est.)

exports of goods and services: 37.8% (2017 est.)

imports of goods and services: -39.7% (2017 est.)

GDP - COMPOSITION, BY SECTOR OF ORIGIN:

agriculture: 3.6% (2017 est.)

industry: 31.9% (2017 est.)

services: 64.5% (2017 est.)

AGRICULTURE - PRODUCTS:

corn, wheat, soybeans, rice, beans, cotton, coffee, fruit, tomatoes; beef, poultry, dairy products; wood products

INDUSTRIES:

food and beverages, tobacco, chemicals, iron and steel, petroleum, mining, textiles, clothing, motor vehicles, consumer durables, tourism

INDUSTRIAL PRODUCTION GROWTH RATE:

-0.6% (2017 est.)

country comparison to the world: 174

LABOR FORCE:

54.51 million (2017 est.)

country comparison to the world: 12

LABOR FORCE - BY OCCUPATION:

agriculture: 13.4%

industry: 24.1%

services: 61.9% (2011)

UNEMPLOYMENT RATE:

3.4% (2017 est.)

3.9% (2016 est.)

note: underemployment may be as high as 25%

country comparison to the world: 42

POPULATION BELOW POVERTY LINE:

46.2% (2014 est.)

note: from a food-based definition of poverty; asset-based poverty amounted to more than 47%

HOUSEHOLD INCOME OR CONSUMPTION BY PERCENTAGE SHARE:

lowest 10%: 2%

highest 10%: 40% (2014)

DISTRIBUTION OF FAMILY INCOME - GINI INDEX:

48.2 (2014)

48.3 (2008)

country comparison to the world: 24

BUDGET:

revenues: 261.4 billion (2017 est.)

expenditures: 273.8 billion (2017 est.)

TAXES AND OTHER REVENUES:

22.7% (of GDP) (2017 est.)

country comparison to the world: 131

BUDGET SURPLUS (+) OR DEFICIT (-):

-1.1% (of GDP) (2017 est.)

country comparison to the world: 83

PUBLIC DEBT:

54.3% of GDP (2017 est.)

56.8% of GDP (2016 est.)

country comparison to the world: 82

FISCAL YEAR:

calendar year

INFLATION RATE (CONSUMER PRICES):

6% (2017 est.)

2.8% (2016 est.)

country comparison to the world: 186

CENTRAL BANK DISCOUNT RATE:

7.25% (31 December 2017)

5.75% (31 December 2016)

country comparison to the world: 44

COMMERCIAL BANK PRIME LENDING RATE:

7.34% (31 December 2017 est.)

4.72% (31 December 2016 est.)

country comparison to the world: 113

STOCK OF NARROW MONEY:

$215.5 billion (31 December 2017 est.)

$186.6 billion (31 December 2016 est.)

country comparison to the world: 24

STOCK OF BROAD MONEY:

$215.5 billion (31 December 2017 est.)

$186.6 billion (31 December 2016 est.)

country comparison to the world: 24

STOCK OF DOMESTIC CREDIT:

$431.6 billion (31 December 2017 est.)

$393.8 billion (31 December 2016 est.)

country comparison to the world: 28

MARKET VALUE OF PUBLICLY TRADED SHARES:

$402.3 billion (31 December 2015 est.)

$480.2 billion (31 December 2014 est.)

$526 billion (31 December 2013 est.)

country comparison to the world: 25

CURRENT ACCOUNT BALANCE:

-$19.35 billion (2017 est.)

-$23.32 billion (2016 est.)

country comparison to the world: 198

EXPORTS:

$409.8 billion (2017 est.)

$374.3 billion (2016 est.)

country comparison to the world: 12

EXPORTS - PARTNERS:

US 79.9% (2017)

EXPORTS - COMMODITIES:

manufactured goods, electronics, vehicles and auto parts, oil and oil products, silver, plastics, fruits, vegetables, coffee, cotton; Mexico is the world's leading producer of silver

IMPORTS:

$420.8 billion (2017 est.)

$387.4 billion (2016 est.)

country comparison to the world: 14

IMPORTS - COMMODITIES:

metalworking machines, steel mill products, agricultural machinery, electrical equipment, automobile parts for assembly and repair, aircraft, aircraft parts, plastics, natural gas and oil products

IMPORTS - PARTNERS:

US 46.4%, China 17.7%, Japan 4.3% (2017)

RESERVES OF FOREIGN EXCHANGE AND GOLD:

$175.3 billion (31 December 2017 est.)

$178.4 billion (31 December 2016 est.)

note: Mexico also maintains access to an $88 million Flexible Credit Line with the IMF

country comparison to the world: 14
DEBT - EXTERNAL:
$445.8 billion (31 December 2017 est.)
$450.2 billion (31 December 2016 est.)
country comparison to the world: 28
STOCK OF DIRECT FOREIGN INVESTMENT - AT HOME:
$554.3 billion (31 December 2017 est.)
$473.5 billion (31 December 2016 est.)
country comparison to the world: 16
STOCK OF DIRECT FOREIGN INVESTMENT - ABROAD:
$243.8 billion (31 December 2017 est.)
$148.6 billion (31 December 2016 est.)
country comparison to the world: 25
EXCHANGE RATES:
Mexican pesos (MXN) per US dollar -
18.26 (2017 est.)
18.664 (2016 est.)
18.664 (2015 est.)
15.848 (2014 est.)
13.292 (2013 est.)

ENERGY :: MEXICO

ELECTRICITY ACCESS:
electrification - total population: 100% (2016)
ELECTRICITY - PRODUCTION:
302.7 billion kWh (2016 est.)
country comparison to the world: 13
ELECTRICITY - CONSUMPTION:
258.7 billion kWh (2016 est.)
country comparison to the world: 14
ELECTRICITY - EXPORTS:
7.308 billion kWh (2016 est.)
country comparison to the world: 27
ELECTRICITY - IMPORTS:
3.532 billion kWh (2016 est.)
country comparison to the world: 47
ELECTRICITY - INSTALLED GENERATING CAPACITY:
72.56 million kW (2016 est.)
country comparison to the world: 17
ELECTRICITY - FROM FOSSIL FUELS:
71% of total installed capacity (2016 est.)
country comparison to the world: 106
ELECTRICITY - FROM NUCLEAR FUELS:
2% of total installed capacity (2017 est.)
country comparison to the world: 27
ELECTRICITY - FROM HYDROELECTRIC PLANTS:
17% of total installed capacity (2017 est.)
country comparison to the world: 96
ELECTRICITY - FROM OTHER RENEWABLE SOURCES:
9% of total installed capacity (2017 est.)
country comparison to the world: 82
CRUDE OIL - PRODUCTION:
1.852 million bbl/day (2018 est.)
country comparison to the world: 13
CRUDE OIL - EXPORTS:
1.214 million bbl/day (2017 est.)
country comparison to the world: 11
CRUDE OIL - IMPORTS:
0 bbl/day (2017 est.)
country comparison to the world: 166
CRUDE OIL - PROVED RESERVES:
6.63 billion bbl (1 January 2018 est.)
country comparison to the world: 19
REFINED PETROLEUM PRODUCTS - PRODUCTION:
844,600 bbl/day (2017 est.)
country comparison to the world: 23
REFINED PETROLEUM PRODUCTS - CONSUMPTION:
1.984 million bbl/day (2017 est.)
country comparison to the world: 11
REFINED PETROLEUM PRODUCTS - EXPORTS:
155,800 bbl/day (2017 est.)
country comparison to the world: 35
REFINED PETROLEUM PRODUCTS - IMPORTS:
867,500 bbl/day (2017 est.)
country comparison to the world: 10
NATURAL GAS - PRODUCTION:
31.57 billion cu m (2017 est.)
country comparison to the world: 24
NATURAL GAS - CONSUMPTION:
81.61 billion cu m (2017 est.)
country comparison to the world: 9
NATURAL GAS - EXPORTS:
36.81 million cu m (2017 est.)
country comparison to the world: 51
NATURAL GAS - IMPORTS:
50.12 billion cu m (2017 est.)
country comparison to the world: 8
NATURAL GAS - PROVED RESERVES:
279.8 billion cu m (1 January 2018 est.)
country comparison to the world: 38
CARBON DIOXIDE EMISSIONS FROM CONSUMPTION OF ENERGY:
454.1 million Mt (2017 est.)
country comparison to the world: 14

COMMUNICATIONS :: MEXICO

TELEPHONES - FIXED LINES:
total subscriptions: 20,602,668
subscriptions per 100 inhabitants: 17 (2017 est.)
country comparison to the world: 13
TELEPHONES - MOBILE CELLULAR:
total subscriptions: 114,326,842
subscriptions per 100 inhabitants: 92 (2017 est.)
country comparison to the world: 14
TELEPHONE SYSTEM:
general assessment: adequate telephone service for business and government; improving quality and increasing mobile cellular availability, with mobile subscribers far outnumbering fixed-line subscribers; domestic satellite system with 120 earth stations; extensive microwave radio relay network; considerable use of fiber-optic cable and coaxial cable; two main MNOs despite efforts for competition; preparation for 5G and LTE-M services; Mexico's first local Internet Exchange Point opens in Mexico City (2018)
domestic: competition has spurred the mobile-cellular market; fixed-line teledensity exceeds 17 per 100 persons; mobile-cellular teledensity is about 92 per 100 persons (2018)
international: country code - 52; Columbus-2 fiber-optic submarine cable with access to the US, Virgin Islands, Canary Islands, Spain, and Italy; the Americas Region Caribbean Ring System (ARCOS-1) and the MAYA-1 submarine cable system together provide access to Central America, parts of South America and the Caribbean, and the US; satellite earth stations - 120 (32 Intelsat, 2 Solidaridad (giving Mexico improved access to South America, Central America, and much of the US as well as enhancing domestic communications), 1 Panamsat, numerous Inmarsat mobile earth stations); linked to Central American Microwave System of trunk connections (2016)

BROADCAST MEDIA:

telecom reform in 2013 enabled the creation of new broadcast television channels after decades of a quasi-monopoly; Mexico has 821 TV stations and 1,745 radio stations and most are privately owned; the Televisa group once had a virtual monopoly in TV broadcasting, but new broadcasting groups and foreign satellite and cable operators are now available; in 2016, Mexico became the first country in Latin America to complete the transition from analog to digital transmissions, allowing for better image and audio quality and a wider selection of programming from networks

INTERNET COUNTRY CODE:

.mx

INTERNET USERS:

total: 73,334,032

percent of population: 59.5% (July 2016 est.)

country comparison to the world: 7

BROADBAND - FIXED SUBSCRIPTIONS:

total: 17,131,820

subscriptions per 100 inhabitants: 14 (2017 est.)

country comparison to the world: 11

MILITARY AND SECURITY :: MEXICO

MILITARY EXPENDITURES:

0.54% of GDP (2018)

0.47% of GDP (2017)

0.56% of GDP (2016)

0.66% of GDP (2015)

0.66% of GDP (2014)

country comparison to the world: 146

MILITARY AND SECURITY FORCES:

Secretariat of National Defense (Secretaria de Defensa Nacional, Sedena): Army (Ejercito), Mexican Air Force (Fuerza Aerea Mexicana, FAM); Secretariat of the Navy (Secretaria de Marina, Semar): Mexican Navy (Armada de Mexico (ARM), includes Naval Air Force (FAN), Mexican Naval Infantry Corps (Cuerpo de Infanteria de Marina, Mexmar or CIM)); Ministry of Security and Citizen Protection: Federal Police, National Guard (2019)

Note: the National Guard was formed in 2019 and consists of personnel from the Federal Police and military police units of the Army and Navy

MILITARY SERVICE AGE AND OBLIGATION:

18 years of age for compulsory military service (selection for service determined by lottery; conscript service obligation is 12 months; 16 years of age with consent for voluntary enlistment; cadets enrolled in military schools from the age of 15 are considered members of the armed forces; women are eligible for voluntary military service (2012)

TRANSPORTATION :: MEXICO

NATIONAL AIR TRANSPORT SYSTEM:

number of registered air carriers: 21 (2015)

inventory of registered aircraft operated by air carriers: 357 (2015)

annual passenger traffic on registered air carriers: 45,560,063 (2015)

annual freight traffic on registered air carriers: 713,985,467 mt-km (2015)

CIVIL AIRCRAFT REGISTRATION COUNTRY CODE PREFIX:

XA (2016)

AIRPORTS:

1,714 (2013)

country comparison to the world: 3

AIRPORTS - WITH PAVED RUNWAYS:

total: 243 (2017)

over 3,047 m: 12 (2017)

2,438 to 3,047 m: 32 (2017)

1,524 to 2,437 m: 80 (2017)

914 to 1,523 m: 86 (2017)

under 914 m: 33 (2017)

AIRPORTS - WITH UNPAVED RUNWAYS:

total: 1,471 (2013)

over 3,047 m: 1 (2013)

2,438 to 3,047 m: 1 (2013)

1,524 to 2,437 m: 42 (2013)

914 to 1,523 m: 281 (2013)

under 914 m: 1,146 (2013)

HELIPORTS:

1 (2013)

PIPELINES:

15,986 km natural gas (2019), 10,365 km oil (2017), 8,946 km refined products (2016)

RAILWAYS:

total: 20,825 km (2017)

standard gauge: 20,825 km 1.435-m gauge (27 km electrified) (2017)

country comparison to the world: 14

ROADWAYS:

total: 398,148 km (2017)

paved: 174,911 km (includes 10,362 km of expressways) (2017)

unpaved: 223,237 km (2017)

country comparison to the world: 18

WATERWAYS:

2,900 km (navigable rivers and coastal canals mostly connected with ports on the country's east coast) (2012)

country comparison to the world: 33

MERCHANT MARINE:

total: 617

by type: bulk carrier 6, general cargo 11, oil tanker 35, other 565 (2018)

country comparison to the world: 34

PORTS AND TERMINALS:

major seaport(s): Altamira, Coatzacoalcos, Lazaro Cardenas, Manzanillo, Veracruz

oil terminal(s): Cayo Arcas terminal, Dos Bocas terminal

cruise port(s): Cancun, Cozumel, Ensenada

container port(s) (TEUs): Manzanillo (2,830,370), Lazaro Cardenas (1,149,079) (2017)

LNG terminal(s) (import): Altamira, Ensenada

TRANSNATIONAL ISSUES :: MEXICO

DISPUTES - INTERNATIONAL:

abundant rainfall in recent years along much of the Mexico-US border region has ameliorated periodically strained water-sharing arrangements; the US has intensified security measures to monitor and control legal and illegal personnel, transport, and commodities across its border with Mexico; Mexico must deal with thousands of impoverished Guatemalans and other Central Americans who cross the porous border looking for work in Mexico and the US; Belize and Mexico are working to solve minor border demarcation discrepancies arising from inaccuracies in the 1898 border treaty

REFUGEES AND INTERNALLY DISPLACED PERSONS:

refugees (country of origin): 5,155 (El Salvador) (2018); 64,053 (Venezuela) (economic and political crisis; includes Venezuelans who have claimed asylum or have received alternative legal stay) (2019)

IDPs: 338,000 (government's quashing of Zapatista uprising in 1994 in eastern Chiapas Region; drug cartel violence and government's military response since 2007; violence between and within indigenous groups) (2018)

stateless persons: 13 (2018)

ILLICIT DRUGS:

major drug-producing and transit nation; Mexico is estimated to be the world's third largest producer of opium with poppy cultivation in 2015 estimated to be 28,000 hectares yielding a potential production of 475 metric tons of raw opium; government conducts the largest independent illicit-crop eradication program in the world; continues as the primary transshipment country for US-bound cocaine from South America, with an estimated 95% of annual cocaine movements toward the US stopping in Mexico; major drug syndicates control the majority of drug trafficking throughout the country; producer and distributor of ecstasy; significant money-laundering center; major supplier of heroin and largest foreign supplier of marijuana and methamphetamine to the US market

AUSTRALIA - OCEANIA :: MICRONESIA FEDERATED STATES OF

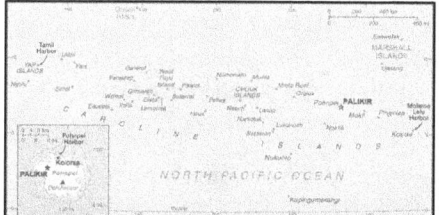

INTRODUCTION :: MICRONESIA, FEDERATED STATES OF

BACKGROUND:

The Caroline Islands are a widely scattered archipelago in the western Pacific Ocean; they became part of a UN Trust Territory under US administration following World War II. The eastern four island groups adopted a constitution in 1979 and chose to become the Federated States of Micronesia (FSM). (The westernmost island group became Palau.) Independence came in 1986 under a Compact of Free Association (COFA) with the US, which was amended in 2004. The COFA has been a force for stability and democracy in the FSM since it came into force in 1986. Present concerns include economic uncertainty after 2023 when direct US economic assistance is scheduled to end, large-scale unemployment, overfishing, overdependence on US foreign aid, and state perceptions of inequitable allocation of US aid.

As a signatory to the COFA with the US, eligible Micronesians can live, work, and study in any part of the US and its territories without a visa - this privilege reduces stresses on the island economy and the environment. Micronesians serve in the US armed forces and military recruiting from the Federated States of Micronesia, per capita, is higher than many US states.

GEOGRAPHY :: MICRONESIA, FEDERATED STATES OF

LOCATION:
Oceania, island group in the North Pacific Ocean, about three-quarters of the way from Hawaii to Indonesia

GEOGRAPHIC COORDINATES:
6 55 N, 158 15 E

MAP REFERENCES:
Oceania

AREA:
total: 702 sq km

land: 702 sq km

water: 0 sq km (fresh water only)

note: includes Pohnpei (Ponape), Chuuk (Truk) Islands, Yap Islands, and Kosrae (Kosaie)

country comparison to the world: 192

AREA - COMPARATIVE:
four times the size of Washington, DC (land area only)

LAND BOUNDARIES:
0 km

COASTLINE:
6,112 km

MARITIME CLAIMS:
territorial sea: 12 nm

exclusive economic zone: 200 nm

CLIMATE:
tropical; heavy year-round rainfall, especially in the eastern islands; located on southern edge of the typhoon belt with occasionally severe damage

TERRAIN:
islands vary geologically from high mountainous islands to low, coral atolls; volcanic outcroppings on Pohnpei, Kosrae, and Chuuk

ELEVATION:
lowest point: Pacific Ocean 0 m

highest point: Nanlaud on Pohnpei 782 m

NATURAL RESOURCES:
timber, marine products, deep-seabed minerals, phosphate

LAND USE:
agricultural land: 25.5% (2011 est.)

arable land: 2.3% (2011 est.) / **permanent crops:** 19.7% (2011 est.) / **permanent pasture:** 3.5% (2011 est.)

forest: 74.5% (2011 est.)

other: 0% (2011 est.)

IRRIGATED LAND:
0 sq km NA (2012)

POPULATION DISTRIBUTION:
the majority of the populaton lives in the coastal areas of the high islands; the mountainous interior is largely uninhabited; less than half of the population lives in urban areas

NATURAL HAZARDS:
typhoons (June to December)

ENVIRONMENT - CURRENT ISSUES:
overfishing; climate change; water pollution, toxic pollution from mining; solid waste disposal

ENVIRONMENT - INTERNATIONAL AGREEMENTS:
party to: Biodiversity, Climate Change, Climate Change-Kyoto Protocol, Desertification, Hazardous Wastes, Law of the Sea, Ozone Layer Protection

signed, but not ratified: none of the selected agreements

GEOGRAPHY - NOTE:
composed of four major island groups totaling 607 islands

PEOPLE AND SOCIETY :: MICRONESIA, FEDERATED STATES OF

POPULATION:
103,643 (July 2018 est.)

country comparison to the world: 194

NATIONALITY:
noun: Micronesian(s)

adjective: Micronesian; Chuukese, Kosraen(s), Pohnpeian(s), Yapese

ETHNIC GROUPS:
Chuukese/Mortlockese 49.3%, Pohnpeian 29.8%, Kosraean 6.3%, Yapese 5.7%, Yap outer islanders 5.1%, Polynesian 1.6%, Asian 1.4%, other 0.8% (2010 est.)

LANGUAGES:
English (official and common language), Chuukese, Kosrean, Pohnpeian, Yapese, Ulithian, Woleaian, Nukuoro, Kapingamarangi

RELIGIONS:
Roman Catholic 54.7%, Protestant 41.1% (includes Congregational 38.5%, Baptist 1.1%, Seventh Day Adventist 0.8%, Assembly of God 0.7%), Mormon 1.5%, other 1.9%, none 0.7%, unspecified 0.1% (2010 est.)

AGE STRUCTURE:
0-14 years: 29.81% (male 15,707 /female 15,186)

15-24 years: 19.38% (male 10,068 /female 10,020)

25-54 years: 39.57% (male 19,799 /female 21,208)

55-64 years: 7.09% (male 3,574 /female 3,777)

65 years and over: 4.15% (male 1,943 /female 2,361) (2018 est.)

DEPENDENCY RATIOS:
total dependency ratio: 62.4 (2015 est.)

youth dependency ratio: 55.3 (2015 est.)

elderly dependency ratio: 7.1 (2015 est.)

potential support ratio: 14.1 (2015 est.)

MEDIAN AGE:
total: 25.5 years (2018 est.)

male: 24.7 years

female: 26.2 years

country comparison to the world: 156

POPULATION GROWTH RATE:
-0.55% (2018 est.)

country comparison to the world: 223

BIRTH RATE:
19.6 births/1,000 population (2018 est.)

country comparison to the world: 80

DEATH RATE:
4.2 deaths/1,000 population (2018 est.)

country comparison to the world: 208

NET MIGRATION RATE:
-20.9 migrant(s)/1,000 population (2018 est.)

country comparison to the world: 224

POPULATION DISTRIBUTION:
the majority of the populaton lives in the coastal areas of the high islands; the mountainous interior is largely uninhabited; less than half of the population lives in urban areas

URBANIZATION:
urban population: 22.8% of total population (2019)

rate of urbanization: 1.05% annual rate of change (2015-20 est.)

MAJOR URBAN AREAS - POPULATION:
7,000 PALIKIR (capital) (2018)

SEX RATIO:
at birth: 1.05 male(s)/female

0-14 years: 1.03 male(s)/female

15-24 years: 1 male(s)/female

25-54 years: 0.93 male(s)/female

55-64 years: 0.95 male(s)/female

65 years and over: 0.82 male(s)/female

total population: 0.97 male(s)/female (2018 est.)

MATERNAL MORTALITY RATE:
88 deaths/100,000 live births (2017 est.)

country comparison to the world: 75

INFANT MORTALITY RATE:
total: 19.1 deaths/1,000 live births (2018 est.)

male: 21.2 deaths/1,000 live births

female: 16.9 deaths/1,000 live births

country comparison to the world: 81

LIFE EXPECTANCY AT BIRTH:
total population: 73.4 years (2018 est.)

male: 71.3 years

female: 75.6 years

country comparison to the world: 137

TOTAL FERTILITY RATE:
2.37 children born/woman (2018 est.)

country comparison to the world: 83

DRINKING WATER SOURCE:
improved:

urban: 94.8% of population

rural: 87.4% of population

total: 89% of population

unimproved:

urban: 5.2% of population

rural: 12.6% of population

total: 11% of population (2015 est.)

CURRENT HEALTH EXPENDITURE:
12.6% (2016)

PHYSICIANS DENSITY:
0.19 physicians/1,000 population (2009)

HOSPITAL BED DENSITY:
3.2 beds/1,000 population (2009)

SANITATION FACILITY ACCESS:
improved:

urban: 85.1% of population (2015 est.)

rural: 49% of population (2015 est.)

total: 57.1% of population (2015 est.)

unimproved:

urban: 14.9% of population (2015 est.)

rural: 51% of population (2015 est.)

total: 42.9% of population (2015 est.)

HIV/AIDS - ADULT PREVALENCE RATE:
NA

HIV/AIDS - PEOPLE LIVING WITH HIV/AIDS:
NA

HIV/AIDS - DEATHS:
NA

MAJOR INFECTIOUS DISEASES:
note: active local transmission of Zika virus by Aedes species mosquitoes has been identified in this country (as of August 2016); it poses an important risk (a large number of cases possible) among US citizens if bitten by an infective mosquito; other less common ways to get Zika are through sex, via blood transfusion, or during pregnancy, in which the pregnant woman passes Zika virus to her fetus

OBESITY - ADULT PREVALENCE RATE:

45.8% (2016)

country comparison to the world: 10

EDUCATION EXPENDITURES:

12.5% of GDP (2015)

country comparison to the world: 2

UNEMPLOYMENT, YOUTH AGES 15-24:

total: 18.9%

male: 10.4%

female: 29.9% (2014)

country comparison to the world: 71

GOVERNMENT :: MICRONESIA, FEDERATED STATES OF

COUNTRY NAME:

conventional long form: Federated States of Micronesia

conventional short form: none

local long form: Federated States of Micronesia

local short form: none

former: New Philippines; Caroline Islands; Trust Territory of the Pacific Islands, Ponape, Truk, and Yap Districts

abbreviation: FSM

etymology: the term "Micronesia" is a 19th-century construct of two Greek words, "micro" (small) and "nesoi" (islands), and refers to thousands of small islands in the western Pacific Ocean

GOVERNMENT TYPE:

federal republic in free association with the US

CAPITAL:

name: Palikir

geographic coordinates: 6 55 N, 158 09 E

time difference: UTC+11 (16 hours ahead of Washington, DC, during Standard Time)

note: Micronesia has two time zones

ADMINISTRATIVE DIVISIONS:

4 states; Chuuk (Truk), Kosrae (Kosaie), Pohnpei (Ponape), Yap

INDEPENDENCE:

3 November 1986 (from the US-administered UN trusteeship)

NATIONAL HOLIDAY:

Constitution Day, 10 May (1979)

CONSTITUTION:

history: drafted June 1975, ratified 1 October 1978, entered into force 10 May 1979

amendments: proposed by Congress, by a constitutional convention, or by public petition; passage requires approval by at least three-fourths majority vote in at least three fourths of the states; amended 1990; note – at least every 10 years as part of a general or special election, voters are asked whether to hold a constitution convention; a majority of affirmative votes is required to proceed (2018)

LEGAL SYSTEM:

mixed legal system of common and customary law

INTERNATIONAL LAW ORGANIZATION PARTICIPATION:

has not submitted an ICJ jurisdiction declaration; non-party state to the ICCt

CITIZENSHIP:

citizenship by birth: no

citizenship by descent only: at least one parent must be a citizen of FSM

dual citizenship recognized: no

residency requirement for naturalization: 5 years

SUFFRAGE:

18 years of age; universal

EXECUTIVE BRANCH:

chief of state: President David W. PANUELO (since 11 May 2019); Vice President Yosiwo P. GEORGE (since 11 May 2015); note - the president is both chief of state and head of government

head of government: President David W. PANUELO (since 11 May 2019); Vice President Yosiwo P. GEORGE (since 11 May 2015)

cabinet: Cabinet includes the vice president and the heads of the 8 executive departments

elections/appointments: president and vice president indirectly elected by Congress from among the 4 'at large' senators for a 4-year term (eligible for a second term); election last held on 11 May 2019 (next to be held in 2023)

election results: David W. PANUELO elected president by Congress; Yosiwo P. GEORGE reelected vice president

LEGISLATIVE BRANCH:

description: unicameral Congress (14 seats; 10 members directly elected in single-seat constituencies by simple majority vote to serve 2-year terms and 4 at-large members directly elected from each of the 4 states by proportional representation vote to serve 4-year terms)

elections: last held on 5 March 2019 (next to be held in March 2021)

election results: percent of vote - NA; seats - independent 14; composition - men 14, women 0

JUDICIAL BRANCH:

highest courts: Federated States of Micronesia (FSM) Supreme Court (consists of the chief justice and not more than 5 associate justices and organized into appellate and criminal divisions)

judge selection and term of office: justices appointed by the FSM president with the approval of two-thirds of Congress; justices appointed for life

subordinate courts: the highest state-level courts are: Chuuk Supreme Court; Korsae State Court; Pohnpei State Court; Yap State Court

POLITICAL PARTIES AND LEADERS:

no formal parties

INTERNATIONAL ORGANIZATION PARTICIPATION:

ACP, ADB, AOSIS, FAO, G-77, IBRD, ICAO, ICRM, IDA, IFC, IFRCS, IMF, IOC, IOM, IPU, ITSO, ITU, MIGA, OPCW, PIF, Sparteca, SPC, UN, UNCTAD, UNESCO, WHO, WMO

DIPLOMATIC REPRESENTATION IN THE US:

Ambassador Akillino Harris SUSAIA (since 24 April 2017)

chancery: 1725 N Street NW, Washington, DC 20036

telephone: [1] (202) 223-4383

FAX: [1] (202) 223-4391

consulate(s) general: Honolulu, Tamuning (Guam)

DIPLOMATIC REPRESENTATION FROM THE US:

chief of mission: Ambassador Robert Annan RILEY III (since 16 August 2016)

telephone: [691] 320-2187

embassy: 1986 U.S. Embassy Place, Kolonia, Pohnpei, FM 96941 mailing address: P. O. Box 1286, Kolonia, Pohnpei, 96941; U.S. Embassy in Micronesia, 4120 Kolonia Place, Washington, D.C. 20521-4120

FAX: [691] 320-2186

FLAG DESCRIPTION:

light blue with four white five-pointed stars centered; the stars are arranged in a diamond pattern; blue symbolizes the Pacific Ocean, the stars represent the four island groups of Chuuk, Kosrae, Pohnpei, and Yap

NATIONAL SYMBOL(S):

four, five-pointed, white stars on a light blue field; national colors: light blue, white

NATIONAL ANTHEM:

name: Patriots of Micronesia

lyrics/music: unknown

note: adopted 1991; also known as "Across All Micronesia"; the music is based on the 1820 German patriotic song "Ich hab mich ergeben", which was the West German national anthem from 1949-1950; variants of this tune are used in Johannes Brahms' "Festival Overture" and Gustav Mahler's "Third Symphony"

ECONOMY :: MICRONESIA, FEDERATED STATES OF

ECONOMY - OVERVIEW:

Economic activity consists largely of subsistence farming and fishing, and government, which employs two-thirds of the adult working population and receives funding largely - 58% in 2013 – from Compact of Free Association assistance provided by the US. The islands have few commercially valuable mineral deposits. The potential for tourism is limited by isolation, lack of adequate facilities, and limited internal air and water transportation.

Under the terms of the original Compact, the US provided $1.3 billion in grants and aid from 1986 to 2001. The US and the Federated States of Micronesia (FSM) negotiated a second (amended) Compact agreement in 2002-03 that took effect in 2004. The amended Compact runs for a 20-year period to 2023; during which the US will provide roughly $2.1 billion to the FSM. The amended Compact also develops a trust fund for the FSM that will provide a comparable income stream beyond 2024 when Compact grants end.

The country's medium-term economic outlook appears fragile because of dependence on US assistance and lackluster performance of its small and stagnant private sector.

GDP (PURCHASING POWER PARITY):

$348 million (2017 est.)

$341.1 million (2016 est.)

$331.4 million (2015 est.)

note: data are in 2017 dollars

country comparison to the world: 215

GDP (OFFICIAL EXCHANGE RATE):

$328 million (2017 est.)

GDP - REAL GROWTH RATE:

2% (2017 est.)

2.9% (2016 est.)

3.9% (2015 est.)

country comparison to the world: 153

GDP - PER CAPITA (PPP):

$3,400 (2017 est.)

$3,300 (2016 est.)

$3,200 (2015 est.)

note: data are in 2017 dollars

country comparison to the world: 189

GDP - COMPOSITION, BY END USE:

household consumption: 83.5% (2013 est.)

government consumption: 48.4% (2016 est.)

investment in fixed capital: 29.5% (2016 est.)

investment in inventories: 1.9% (2016 est.)

exports of goods and services: 27.5% (2016 est.)

imports of goods and services: -77% (2016 est.)

GDP - COMPOSITION, BY SECTOR OF ORIGIN:

agriculture: 26.3% (2013 est.)

industry: 18.9% (2013 est.)

services: 54.8% (2013 est.)

AGRICULTURE - PRODUCTS:

taro, yams, coconuts, bananas, cassava (manioc, tapioca), sakau (kava), Kosraen citrus, betel nuts, black pepper, fish, pigs, chickens

INDUSTRIES:

tourism, construction; specialized aquaculture, craft items (shell and wood)

INDUSTRIAL PRODUCTION GROWTH RATE:

NA

LABOR FORCE:

37,920 (2010 est.)

country comparison to the world: 200

LABOR FORCE - BY OCCUPATION:

agriculture: 0.9%

industry: 5.2%

services: 93.9% (2013 est.)

note: two-thirds of the labor force are government employees

UNEMPLOYMENT RATE:

16.2% (2010 est.)

country comparison to the world: 177

POPULATION BELOW POVERTY LINE:

26.7% (2000 est.)

HOUSEHOLD INCOME OR CONSUMPTION BY PERCENTAGE SHARE:

lowest 10%: NA

highest 10%: NA

DISTRIBUTION OF FAMILY INCOME - GINI INDEX:

61.1 (2013 est.)

country comparison to the world: 3

BUDGET:

revenues: 213.8 million (FY12/13 est.)

expenditures: 192.1 million (FY12/13 est.)

TAXES AND OTHER REVENUES:

65.2% (of GDP) (FY12/13 est.)

country comparison to the world: 7

BUDGET SURPLUS (+) OR DEFICIT (-):

6.6% (of GDP) (FY12/13 est.)

country comparison to the world: 4

PUBLIC DEBT:

24.5% of GDP (2017 est.)

25.3% of GDP (2016 est.)

country comparison to the world: 176

FISCAL YEAR:

1 October - 30 September

INFLATION RATE (CONSUMER PRICES):

0.5% (2017 est.)

0.5% (2016 est.)

country comparison to the world: 28

COMMERCIAL BANK PRIME LENDING RATE:

15.73% (31 December 2017 est.)

15.7% (31 December 2016 est.)

country comparison to the world: 34

STOCK OF NARROW MONEY:

$NA (31 December 2016)

$44.07 million (31 December 2015 est.)

$196 million (31 December 2013 est.)

country comparison to the world: 190

STOCK OF BROAD MONEY:

$178.3 million (31 December 2015 est.)

$225.2 million (31 December 2013 est.)

country comparison to the world: 189

STOCK OF DOMESTIC CREDIT:

$56.98 million (31 December 2017 est.)

-$103 million (31 December 2015 est.)

country comparison to the world: 189

MARKET VALUE OF PUBLICLY TRADED SHARES:

NA

CURRENT ACCOUNT BALANCE:

$12 million (2017 est.)

$11 million (2016 est.)

country comparison to the world: 63

EXPORTS:

$88.3 million (2013 est.)

country comparison to the world: 197

EXPORTS - COMMODITIES:

fish, sakau (kava), betel nuts, black pepper

IMPORTS:

$167.8 million (2015 est.)

$258.5 million (2013 est.)

country comparison to the world: 212

IMPORTS - COMMODITIES:

food, beverages, clothing, computers, household electronics, appliances, manufactured goods, automobiles, machinery and equipment, furniture, tools

RESERVES OF FOREIGN EXCHANGE AND GOLD:

$203.7 million (31 December 2017 est.)

$135.1 million (31 December 2015 est.)

country comparison to the world: 174

DEBT - EXTERNAL:

$93.6 million (2013 est.)

$93.5 million (2012 est.)

country comparison to the world: 194

STOCK OF DIRECT FOREIGN INVESTMENT - AT HOME:

$15.8 million (2013 est.)

$34.4 million (2012 est.)

country comparison to the world: 139

EXCHANGE RATES:

the US dollar is used

ENERGY :: MICRONESIA, FEDERATED STATES OF

ELECTRICITY ACCESS:

electrification - total population: 75.4% (2016)

electrification - urban areas: 91.9% (2016)

electrification - rural areas: 70.7% (2016)

ELECTRICITY - PRODUCTION:

192 million kWh (2002)

country comparison to the world: 193

ELECTRICITY - CONSUMPTION:

178.6 million kWh (2002)

country comparison to the world: 195

ELECTRICITY - EXPORTS:

0 kWh (2013 est.)

country comparison to the world: 171

ELECTRICITY - IMPORTS:

0 kWh (2013 est.)

country comparison to the world: 175

ELECTRICITY - INSTALLED GENERATING CAPACITY:

18,000 kW (2015 est.)

country comparison to the world: 206

ELECTRICITY - FROM FOSSIL FUELS:

96% of total installed capacity (2015 est.)

country comparison to the world: 41

ELECTRICITY - FROM NUCLEAR FUELS:

0% of total installed capacity (2015 est.)

country comparison to the world: 143

ELECTRICITY - FROM HYDROELECTRIC PLANTS:

1% of total installed capacity (2013 est.)

country comparison to the world: 149

ELECTRICITY - FROM OTHER RENEWABLE SOURCES:

3% of total installed capacity (2013 est.)

country comparison to the world: 127

CRUDE OIL - PRODUCTION:

0 bbl/day (2014)

country comparison to the world: 174

CRUDE OIL - EXPORTS:

0 bbl/day (2014)

country comparison to the world: 165

CRUDE OIL - IMPORTS:

0 bbl/day (2014)

country comparison to the world: 167

CRUDE OIL - PROVED RESERVES:

0 bbl (1 January 2014)

country comparison to the world: 169

REFINED PETROLEUM PRODUCTS - PRODUCTION:

0 bbl/day (2014)

country comparison to the world: 178

REFINED PETROLEUM PRODUCTS - EXPORTS:

0 bbl/day

country comparison to the world: 182

NATURAL GAS - PRODUCTION:

0 cu m (2014)

country comparison to the world: 171

NATURAL GAS - PROVED RESERVES:

0 cu m

country comparison to the world: 170

CARBON DIOXIDE EMISSIONS FROM CONSUMPTION OF ENERGY:

105 Mt (2010 est.)

country comparison to the world: 214

COMMUNICATIONS :: MICRONESIA, FEDERATED STATES OF

TELEPHONES - FIXED LINES:

total subscriptions: 6,947

subscriptions per 100 inhabitants: 7 (2017 est.)

country comparison to the world: 202

TELEPHONES - MOBILE CELLULAR:

total subscriptions: 23,114

subscriptions per 100 inhabitants: 22 (2017 est.)

country comparison to the world: 209

TELEPHONE SYSTEM:

general assessment: adequate system (2016)

domestic: islands interconnected by shortwave radiotelephone (used mostly for government purposes), satellite (Intelsat) ground stations, and some coaxial and fiber-optic cable; mobile-cellular service available on the major islands (2016)

international: country code - 691; landing points for the Chuukk-Pohnpei Cable and HANTRU-1 submarine cable system linking the Federated States of Micronesia and the US; satellite earth stations - 5 Intelsat (Pacific Ocean) (2019)

BROADCAST MEDIA:

no TV broadcast stations; each state has a multi-channel cable service with TV transmissions carrying roughly 95% imported programming and 5% local programming; about a half-dozen radio stations (2009)

INTERNET COUNTRY CODE:

.fm

INTERNET USERS:

total: 33,000

percent of population: 31.5% (July 2016 est.)

country comparison to the world: 201

BROADBAND - FIXED SUBSCRIPTIONS:

total: 3,776

subscriptions per 100 inhabitants: 4 (2017 est.)

country comparison to the world: 179

MILITARY AND SECURITY :: MICRONESIA, FEDERATED STATES OF

MILITARY AND SECURITY FORCES:

no military forces; Federated States of Micronesia National Police (2019)

MILITARY - NOTE:

defense is the responsibility of the US

TRANSPORTATION :: MICRONESIA, FEDERATED STATES OF

CIVIL AIRCRAFT REGISTRATION COUNTRY CODE PREFIX:

V6 (2016)

AIRPORTS:

6 (2013)

country comparison to the world: 173

AIRPORTS - WITH PAVED RUNWAYS:

total: 6 (2017)

1,524 to 2,437 m: 4 (2017)

914 to 1,523 m: 2 (2017)

ROADWAYS:

note - paved and unpaved circumferential roads, most interior roads are unpaved

MERCHANT MARINE:

total: 63

by type: general cargo 40, oil tanker 6, other 17 (2018)

country comparison to the world: 105

PORTS AND TERMINALS:

major seaport(s): Colonia (Tamil Harbor), Molsron Lele Harbor, Pohnepi Harbor

TRANSNATIONAL ISSUES :: MICRONESIA, FEDERATED STATES OF

DISPUTES - INTERNATIONAL:

none

ILLICIT DRUGS:

major consumer of cannabis

EUROPE :: MOLDOVA

INTRODUCTION :: MOLDOVA

BACKGROUND:

A large portion of present day Moldovan territory became a province of the Russian Empire in 1812 and then unified with Romania in 1918 in the aftermath of World War I. This territory was then incorporated into the Soviet Union at the close of World War II. Although Moldova has been independent from the Soviet Union since 1991, Russian forces have remained on Moldovan territory east of the Nistru River supporting the breakaway region of Transnistria, whose population is roughly equally composed of ethnic Ukrainians, Russians, and Moldovans.

Years of Communist Party rule in Moldova from 2001-2009 ultimately ended with election-related violent protests and a rerun of parliamentary elections in 2009. Since then, a series of pro-European ruling coalitions have governed Moldova. As a result of the country's most recent legislative election in February 2019, parliamentary seats are split among the left-leaning Socialist Party (35 seats), the ruling Democratic Party (30 seats), and the center-right opposition ACUM bloc (26 seats). After the elections, ideological differences among the three main political parties led to a prolonged government formation process. The parties have until June 2019 to form a government or snap elections will be called.

GEOGRAPHY :: MOLDOVA

LOCATION:
Eastern Europe, northeast of Romania

GEOGRAPHIC COORDINATES:
47 00 N, 29 00 E

MAP REFERENCES:
Europe

AREA:
total: 33,851 sq km

land: 32,891 sq km

water: 960 sq km

country comparison to the world: 140

AREA - COMPARATIVE:
slightly larger than Maryland

LAND BOUNDARIES:
total: 1,885 km

border countries (2): Romania 683 km, Ukraine 1202 km

COASTLINE:
0 km (landlocked)

MARITIME CLAIMS:
none (landlocked)

CLIMATE:
moderate winters, warm summers

TERRAIN:
rolling steppe, gradual slope south to Black Sea

ELEVATION:
mean elevation: 139 m

lowest point: Dniester (Nistru) 2 m

highest point: Dealul Balanesti 430 m

NATURAL RESOURCES:
lignite, phosphorites, gypsum, limestone, arable land

LAND USE:
agricultural land: 74.9% (2011 est.)

arable land: 55.1% (2011 est.) / permanent crops: 9.1% (2011 est.) / permanent pasture: 10.7% (2011 est.)

forest: 11.9% (2011 est.)

other: 13.2% (2011 est.)

IRRIGATED LAND:
2,283 sq km (2012)

POPULATION DISTRIBUTION:
pockets of agglomeration exist throughout the country, the largest being in the center of the country around the capital of Chisinau, followed by Tiraspol and Balti

NATURAL HAZARDS:
landslides

ENVIRONMENT - CURRENT ISSUES:
heavy use of agricultural chemicals, has contaminated soil and groundwater; extensive soil erosion and declining soil fertility from poor farming methods

ENVIRONMENT - INTERNATIONAL AGREEMENTS:
party to: Air Pollution, Air Pollution-Persistent Organic Pollutants,

Biodiversity, Climate Change, Climate Change-Kyoto Protocol, Desertification, Endangered Species, Hazardous Wastes, Ozone Layer Protection, Ship Pollution, Wetlands

signed, but not ratified: none of the selected agreements

GEOGRAPHY - NOTE:

landlocked; well endowed with various sedimentary rocks and minerals including sand, gravel, gypsum, and limestone

PEOPLE AND SOCIETY :: MOLDOVA

POPULATION:

3,437,720 (July 2018 est.)

country comparison to the world: 132

NATIONALITY:

noun: Moldovan(s)

adjective: Moldovan

ETHNIC GROUPS:

Moldovan 75.1%, Romanian 7%, Ukrainian 6.6%, Gagauz 4.6%, Russian 4.1%, Bulgarian 1.9%, other 0.8% (2014 est.)

LANGUAGES:

Moldovan/Romanian 80.2% (official) (56.7% identify their mother tongue as Moldovan, which is virtually the same as Romanian; 23.5% identify Romanian as their mother tongue), Russian 9.7%, Gagauz 4.2% (a Turkish language), Ukrainian 3.9%, Bulgarian 1.5%, Romani 0.3%, other 0.2% (2014 est.)

note: data represent mother tongue

RELIGIONS:

Orthodox 90.1%, other Christian 2.6%, other 0.1%, agnostic (2014 est.)

AGE STRUCTURE:

0-14 years: 18.29% (male 324,002 /female 304,737)

15-24 years: 11.84% (male 210,988 /female 196,063)

25-54 years: 43.29% (male 752,758 /female 735,471)

55-64 years: 13.5% (male 213,410 /female 250,755)

65 years and over: 13.08% (male 176,252 /female 273,284) (2018 est.)

DEPENDENCY RATIOS:

total dependency ratio: 34.5 (2015 est.)

youth dependency ratio: 21.2 (2015 est.)

elderly dependency ratio: 13.4 (2015 est.)

potential support ratio: 7.5 (2015 est.)

MEDIAN AGE:

total: 37 years (2018 est.)

male: 35.3 years

female: 38.9 years

country comparison to the world: 71

POPULATION GROWTH RATE:

-1.06% (2018 est.)

country comparison to the world: 226

BIRTH RATE:

11.2 births/1,000 population (2018 est.)

country comparison to the world: 175

DEATH RATE:

12.6 deaths/1,000 population (2018 est.)

country comparison to the world: 15

NET MIGRATION RATE:

-9.3 migrant(s)/1,000 population (2018 est.)

country comparison to the world: 215

POPULATION DISTRIBUTION:

pockets of agglomeration exist throughout the country, the largest being in the center of the country around the capital of Chisinau, followed by Tiraspol and Balti

URBANIZATION:

urban population: 42.7% of total population (2019)

rate of urbanization: -0.07% annual rate of change (2015-20 est.)

MAJOR URBAN AREAS - POPULATION:

504,000 CHISINAU (capital) (2019)

SEX RATIO:

at birth: 1.06 male(s)/female

0-14 years: 1.06 male(s)/female

15-24 years: 1.08 male(s)/female

25-54 years: 1.02 male(s)/female

55-64 years: 0.85 male(s)/female

65 years and over: 0.64 male(s)/female

total population: 0.95 male(s)/female (2018 est.)

MOTHER'S MEAN AGE AT FIRST BIRTH:

24 years (2014 est.)

MATERNAL MORTALITY RATE:

19 deaths/100,000 live births (2017 est.)

country comparison to the world: 125

INFANT MORTALITY RATE:

total: 11.7 deaths/1,000 live births (2018 est.)

male: 13.4 deaths/1,000 live births

female: 9.8 deaths/1,000 live births

country comparison to the world: 121

LIFE EXPECTANCY AT BIRTH:

total population: 71.3 years (2018 est.)

male: 67.4 years

female: 75.4 years

country comparison to the world: 153

TOTAL FERTILITY RATE:

1.57 children born/woman (2018 est.)

country comparison to the world: 187

CONTRACEPTIVE PREVALENCE RATE:

59.5% (2012)

DRINKING WATER SOURCE:

improved:

urban: 96.9% of population

rural: 81.4% of population

total: 88.4% of population

unimproved:

urban: 3.1% of population

rural: 18.6% of population

total: 11.6% of population (2015 est.)

CURRENT HEALTH EXPENDITURE:

9% (2016)

PHYSICIANS DENSITY:

3.2 physicians/1,000 population (2015)

HOSPITAL BED DENSITY:

5.8 beds/1,000 population (2013)

SANITATION FACILITY ACCESS:

improved:

urban: 87.8% of population (2015 est.)

rural: 67.1% of population (2015 est.)

total: 76.4% of population (2015 est.)

unimproved:

urban: 12.2% of population (2015 est.)

rural: 32.9% of population (2015 est.)

total: 23.6% of population (2015 est.)

HIV/AIDS - ADULT PREVALENCE RATE:

0.6% (2018 est.)

country comparison to the world: 62

HIV/AIDS - PEOPLE LIVING WITH HIV/AIDS:
17,000 (2018 est.)

country comparison to the world: 88

HIV/AIDS - DEATHS:
<1000 (2018 est.)

OBESITY - ADULT PREVALENCE RATE:
18.9% (2016)

country comparison to the world: 115

CHILDREN UNDER THE AGE OF 5 YEARS UNDERWEIGHT:
2.2% (2012)

country comparison to the world: 111

EDUCATION EXPENDITURES:
6.7% of GDP (2017)

country comparison to the world: 19

LITERACY:
definition: age 15 and over can read and write

total population: 99.4%

male: 99.7%

female: 99.1% (2015 est.)

SCHOOL LIFE EXPECTANCY (PRIMARY TO TERTIARY EDUCATION):
total: 12 years

male: 11 years

female: 12 years (2015)

UNEMPLOYMENT, YOUTH AGES 15-24:
total: 7.4%

male: 7.5%

female: 7.2% (2018 est.)

country comparison to the world: 151

GOVERNMENT :: MOLDOVA

COUNTRY NAME:
conventional long form: Republic of Moldova

conventional short form: Moldova

local long form: Republica Moldova

local short form: Moldova

former: Moldavian Soviet Socialist Republic, Moldovan Soviet Socialist Republic

etymology: named for the Moldova River in neighboring eastern Romania

GOVERNMENT TYPE:
parliamentary republic

CAPITAL:
name: Chisinau in Romanian (Kishinev in Russian)

geographic coordinates: 47 00 N, 28 51 E

time difference: UTC+2 (7 hours ahead of Washington, DC, during Standard Time)

daylight saving time: +1hr, begins last Sunday in March; ends last Sunday in October

note: pronounced KEE-shee-now (KIH-shi-nyov)

etymology: origin unclear but may derive from the archaic Romanian word "chisla" ("spring" or "water source") and "noua" ("new") because the original settlement was built at the site of a small spring

ADMINISTRATIVE DIVISIONS:
32 raions (raioane, singular - raion), 3 municipalities (municipii, singular - municipiul), 1 autonomous territorial unit (unitatea teritoriala autonoma), and 1 territorial unit (unitatea teritoriala)

raions: Anenii Noi, Basarabeasca, Briceni, Cahul, Cantemir, Calarasi, Causeni, Cimislia, Criuleni, Donduseni, Drochia, Dubasari, Edinet, Falesti, Floresti, Glodeni, Hincesti, Ialoveni, Leova, Nisporeni, Ocnita, Orhei, Rezina, Riscani, Singerei, Soldanesti, Soroca, Stefan Voda, Straseni, Taraclia, Telenesti, Ungheni;

municipalities: Balti, Bender, Chisinau;

autonomous territorial unit: Gagauzia;

territorial unit: Stinga Nistrului (Transnistria)

INDEPENDENCE:
27 August 1991 (from the Soviet Union)

NATIONAL HOLIDAY:
Independence Day, 27 August (1991)

CONSTITUTION:
history: previous 1978; latest adopted 29 July 1994, effective 27 August 1994

amendments: proposed by voter petition (at least 200,000 eligible voters), by at least one third of Parliament members, or by the government; passage requires two-thirds majority vote of Parliament within one year of initial proposal; revisions to constitutional articles on sovereignty, independence, and neutrality require majority vote by referendum; articles on fundamental rights and freedoms cannot be amended; amended several times, last in 2010; note – in early 2016, the Moldovan Constitutional Court decision returned the country to direct presidential elections, reversing a 2000 constitutional amendment that allowed Parliament to select the president (2016)

LEGAL SYSTEM:
civil law system with Germanic law influences; Constitutional Court review of legislative acts

INTERNATIONAL LAW ORGANIZATION PARTICIPATION:
has not submitted an ICJ jurisdiction declaration; accepts ICCt jurisdiction

CITIZENSHIP:
citizenship by birth: no

citizenship by descent only: at least one parent must be a citizen of Moldova

dual citizenship recognized: no

residency requirement for naturalization: 10 years

SUFFRAGE:
18 years of age; universal

EXECUTIVE BRANCH:
chief of state: President Igor DODON (since 23 December 2016); note – in 2017-19, DODON was temporarily suspended several times by the Moldovan Constitutional Court for rejecting ministerial appointments and for refusing to sign legislation

head of government: Prime Minister Ion CHICU (since 14 November 2019)

cabinet: Cabinet proposed by the prime minister-designate, nominated by the president, approved through a vote of confidence in Parliament

elections/appointments: president directly elected for a 4-year term (eligible for a second term); election last held on 13 November 2016 (next to be held in fall 2020); prime minister designated by the president upon consultation with Parliament; within 15 days from designation, the prime minister-designate must request a vote of confidence for his/her proposed work program from the Parliament

election results: Igor DODON elected president; percent of vote - Igor DODON (PSRM) 52.2%, Maia

SANDU (PAS) 47.8%; Ion CHICU designated prime minister; Parliament vote - 62 of 101

LEGISLATIVE BRANCH:

description: unicameral Parliament (101 seats; 51 members directly elected in single-seat constituencies by simple majority vote and 50 members directly elected in a single, nationwide constituency by closed party-list proportional representation vote; all members serve 4-year terms

elections: last held on 24 February 2019 (next scheduled for February 2023)

election results: percent of vote by party - PSRM 31.2%, ACUM (PPDA + PAS) 26.8%, PDM 23.6%, PS 8.3%, other 10.1%; seats by party - PSRM 35, ACUM (PPDA + PAS) 26, PDM 30, PS 7, independent 3; composition - men 78, women 23, percent of women 22.8%

JUDICIAL BRANCH:

highest courts: Supreme Court of Justice (consists of the chief judge, 3 deputy-chief judges, 45 judges, and 7 assistant judges); Constitutional Court (consists of the court president and 6 judges); note - the Constitutional Court is autonomous to the other branches of government; the Court interprets the Constitution and reviews the constitutionality of parliamentary laws and decisions, decrees of the president, and acts of the government

judge selection and term of office: Supreme Court of Justice judges appointed by the president upon the recommendation of the Superior Council of Magistracy, an 11-member body of judicial officials; all judges serve 4-year renewable terms; Constitutional Court judges appointed 2 each by Parliament, the president, and the Higher Council of Magistracy for 6-year terms; court president elected by other court judges for a 3-year term

subordinate courts: Courts of Appeal; Court of Business Audit; municipal courts

POLITICAL PARTIES AND LEADERS:

represented in Parliament:
Action and Solidarity Party or PAS [Maia SANDU]
Democratic Party of Moldova or PDM [Vladimir PLAHOTNIUC]
Dignity and Truth Platform or PPDA [Andrei NASTASE]
NOW Platform or ACUM (PPDA + PAS)
Shor Party or PS [Ilan SHOR]
Socialist Party of the Republic of Moldova or PSRM [Zinaida GRECEANII]

not represented in Parliament, participated in recent elections (2014-2019):
Anti-Mafia Movement or MPA [Sergiu MOCANU]
Centrist Union of Moldova or UCM [Mihai PETRACHE]
Christian Democratic People's Party or PPCD [Victor CIOBANU]
Communist Party of the Republic of Moldova or PCRM [Vladimir VORONIN]
Conservative Party or PC [Natalia NIRCA]
Democracy at Home Party or PDA [Vasile COSTIUC]
Democratic Action Party or PAD [Mihai GODEA]
Ecologist Green Party or PVE [Anatolie PROHNITCHI]
European People's Party of Moldova or EPPM [Iurie LEANCA]
Law and Justice Party or PLD [Nicolae ALEXEI]
Liberal Democratic Party of Moldova or PLDM [Tudor DELIU]
Liberal Party or PL [Dorin CHIRTOACA]
"Motherland" Party or PP [Sergiu BIRIUCOV]
National Liberal Party or PNL [Vitalia PAVLICENKO]
Our Home Moldova or PCNM [Grigore PETRENCO]
Our Party or PN [Renato USATII]
Party of National Unity [Anatol SALARU]
People's Party of Moldova or PPRM [Alexandru OLEINIC]
Regions Party of Moldova or PRM [Alexandr KALININ]
Socialist People's Party of Moldova or PPSM [Victor STEPANIUC]

INTERNATIONAL ORGANIZATION PARTICIPATION:

BSEC, CD, CE, CEI, CIS, EAEC (observer), EAPC, EBRD, FAO, GCTU, GUAM, IAEA, IBRD, ICAO, ICC (NGOs), ICCt, ICRM, IDA, IFAD, IFC, IFRCS, ILO, IMF, IMO, Interpol, IOC, IOM, IPU, ISO (correspondent), ITU, ITUC (NGOs), MIGA, OIF, OPCW, OSCE, PFP, SELEC, UN, UNCTAD, UNESCO, UNHCR, UNIDO, Union Latina, UNMIL, UNMISS, UNOCI, UNWTO, UPU, WCO, WHO, WIPO, WMO, WTO

DIPLOMATIC REPRESENTATION IN THE US:

Ambassador Cristina BALAN (since 22 June 2018)

chancery: 2101 S Street NW, Washington, DC 20008

telephone: [1] (202) 667-1130

FAX: [1] (202) 667-1204

DIPLOMATIC REPRESENTATION FROM THE US:

chief of mission: Ambassador Dereck J. HOGAN (since 15 October 2018)

telephone: [373] (22) 40-8300

embassy: 103 Mateevici Street, Chisinau MD-2009

mailing address: use embassy street address

FAX: [373] (22) 23-3044

FLAG DESCRIPTION:

three equal vertical bands of Prussian blue (hoist side), chrome yellow, and vermilion red; emblem in center of flag is of a Roman eagle of dark gold (brown) outlined in black with a red beak and talons carrying a yellow cross in its beak and a green olive branch in its right talons and a yellow scepter in its left talons; on its breast is a shield divided horizontally red over blue with a stylized aurochs head, star, rose, and crescent all in black-outlined yellow; based on the color scheme of the flag of Romania - with which Moldova shares a history and culture - but Moldova's blue band is lighter; the reverse of the flag displays a mirrored image of the coat of arms

note: one of only three national flags that differ on their obverse and reverse sides - the others are Paraguay and Saudi Arabia

NATIONAL SYMBOL(S):

aurochs (a type of wild cattle); national colors: blue, yellow, red

NATIONAL ANTHEM:

name: "Limba noastra" (Our Language)

lyrics/music: Alexei MATEEVICI/Alexandru CRISTEA

note: adopted 1994

ECONOMY :: MOLDOVA

ECONOMY - OVERVIEW:

Despite recent progress, Moldova remains one of the poorest countries in Europe. With a moderate climate and productive farmland, Moldova's economy relies heavily on its agriculture sector, featuring fruits, vegetables, wine, wheat, and tobacco. Moldova also depends on annual remittances of about $1.2 billion - almost 15% of GDP - from the roughly one million Moldovans working in Europe, Israel, Russia, and elsewhere.

With few natural energy resources, Moldova imports almost all of its energy supplies from Russia and Ukraine. Moldova's dependence on Russian energy is underscored by a more than $6 billion debt to Russian natural gas supplier Gazprom, largely the result of unreimbursed natural gas consumption in the breakaway region of Transnistria. Moldova and Romania inaugurated the Ungheni-Iasi natural gas interconnector project in August 2014. The 43-kilometer pipeline between Moldova and Romania, allows for both the import and export of natural gas. Several technical and regulatory delays kept gas from flowing into Moldova until March 2015. Romanian gas exports to Moldova are largely symbolic. In 2018, Moldova awarded a tender to Romanian Transgaz to construct a pipeline connecting Ungheni to Chisinau, bringing the gas to Moldovan population centers. Moldova also seeks to connect with the European power grid by 2022.

The government's stated goal of EU integration has resulted in some market-oriented progress. Moldova experienced better than expected economic growth in 2017, largely driven by increased consumption, increased revenue from agricultural exports, and improved tax collection. During fall 2014, Moldova signed an Association Agreement and a Deep and Comprehensive Free Trade Agreement with the EU (AA/DCFTA), connecting Moldovan products to the world's largest market. The EU AA/DCFTA has contributed to significant growth in Moldova's exports to the EU. In 2017, the EU purchased over 65% of Moldova's exports, a major change from 20 years previously when the Commonwealth of Independent States (CIS) received over 69% of Moldova's exports. A $1 billion asset-stripping heist of Moldovan banks in late 2014 delivered a significant shock to the economy in 2015; the subsequent bank bailout increased inflationary pressures and contributed to the depreciation of the leu and a minor recession. Moldova's growth has also been hampered by endemic corruption, which limits business growth and deters foreign investment, and Russian restrictions on imports of Moldova's agricultural products. The government's push to restore stability and implement meaningful reform led to the approval in 2016 of a $179 million three-year IMF program focused on improving the banking and fiscal environments, along with additional assistance programs from the EU, World Bank, and Romania. Moldova received two IMF tranches in 2017, totaling over $42.5 million.

Over the longer term, Moldova's economy remains vulnerable to corruption, political uncertainty, weak administrative capacity, vested bureaucratic interests, energy import dependence, Russian political and economic pressure, heavy dependence on agricultural exports, and unresolved separatism in Moldova's Transnistria region.

GDP (PURCHASING POWER PARITY):

$23.72 billion (2017 est.)

$22.69 billion (2016 est.)

$21.75 billion (2015 est.)

note: data are in 2017 dollars

country comparison to the world: 143

GDP (OFFICIAL EXCHANGE RATE):

$9.556 billion (2017 est.)

GDP - REAL GROWTH RATE:

4.5% (2017 est.)

4.3% (2016 est.)

-0.4% (2015 est.)

country comparison to the world: 65

GDP - PER CAPITA (PPP):

$6,700 (2017 est.)

$6,400 (2016 est.)

$6,100 (2015 est.)

note: data are in 2017 dollars

country comparison to the world: 162

GROSS NATIONAL SAVING:

13.5% of GDP (2017 est.)

15.9% of GDP (2016 est.)

14.5% of GDP (2015 est.)

country comparison to the world: 143

GDP - COMPOSITION, BY END USE:

household consumption: 85.8% (2017 est.)

government consumption: 19% (2017 est.)

investment in fixed capital: 21.9% (2017 est.)

investment in inventories: 1.4% (2017 est.)

exports of goods and services: 42.5% (2017 est.)

imports of goods and services: -70.7% (2017 est.)

GDP - COMPOSITION, BY SECTOR OF ORIGIN:

agriculture: 17.7% (2017 est.)

industry: 20.3% (2017 est.)

services: 62% (2017 est.)

AGRICULTURE - PRODUCTS:

vegetables, fruits, grapes, grain, sugar beets, sunflower seeds, tobacco; beef, milk; wine

INDUSTRIES:

sugar processing, vegetable oil, food processing, agricultural machinery; foundry equipment, refrigerators and freezers, washing machines; hosiery, shoes, textiles

INDUSTRIAL PRODUCTION GROWTH RATE:

3% (2017 est.)

country comparison to the world: 104

LABOR FORCE:

1.295 million (2017 est.)

country comparison to the world: 136

LABOR FORCE - BY OCCUPATION:

agriculture: 32.3%

industry: 12%

services: 55.7% (2017 est.)

UNEMPLOYMENT RATE:

4.1% (2017 est.)

4.2% (2016 est.)

country comparison to the world: 53

POPULATION BELOW POVERTY LINE:

9.6% (2015 est.)

HOUSEHOLD INCOME OR CONSUMPTION BY PERCENTAGE SHARE:

lowest 10%: 4.2%

highest 10%: 22.1% (2014 est.)

DISTRIBUTION OF FAMILY INCOME - GINI INDEX:

26.8 (2015 est.)

26.8 (2014 est.)

country comparison to the world: 146

BUDGET:

revenues: 2.886 billion (2017 est.)

expenditures: 2.947 billion (2017 est.)

note: National Public Budget

TAXES AND OTHER REVENUES:

30.2% (of GDP) (2017 est.)

country comparison to the world: 77

BUDGET SURPLUS (+) OR DEFICIT (-):

-0.6% (of GDP) (2017 est.)

country comparison to the world: 65

PUBLIC DEBT:

31.5% of GDP (2017 est.)

35.8% of GDP (2016 est.)

country comparison to the world: 163

FISCAL YEAR:

calendar year

INFLATION RATE (CONSUMER PRICES):

6.6% (2017 est.)

6.4% (2016 est.)

country comparison to the world: 191

CENTRAL BANK DISCOUNT RATE:

6.5% (31 December 2017)

9% (31 December 2016)

note: this is the basic rate on short-term operations

country comparison to the world: 60

COMMERCIAL BANK PRIME LENDING RATE:

10.36% (31 December 2017 est.)

14.28% (31 December 2016 est.)

country comparison to the world: 84

STOCK OF NARROW MONEY:

$2.026 billion (31 December 2017 est.)

$1.406 billion (31 December 2016 est.)

country comparison to the world: 134

STOCK OF BROAD MONEY:

$2.026 billion (31 December 2017 est.)

$1.406 billion (31 December 2016 est.)

country comparison to the world: 142

STOCK OF DOMESTIC CREDIT:

$2.135 billion (31 December 2017 est.)

$1.942 billion (31 December 2016 est.)

country comparison to the world: 148

MARKET VALUE OF PUBLICLY TRADED SHARES:

$18.42 million (31 December 2015 est.)

$9.723 million (31 December 2015 est.)

$50.47 million (31 December 2014 est.)

country comparison to the world: 123

CURRENT ACCOUNT BALANCE:

-$602 million (2017 est.)

-$268 million (2016 est.)

country comparison to the world: 123

EXPORTS:

$1.858 billion (2017 est.)

$2.045 billion (2016 est.)

country comparison to the world: 143

EXPORTS - PARTNERS:

Romania 24.6%, Russia 13.7%, Italy 9.1%, Germany 6.2%, Ukraine 5.3%, UK 4.6%, Poland 4.6% (2017)

EXPORTS - COMMODITIES:

foodstuffs, textiles, machinery

IMPORTS:

$4.427 billion (2017 est.)

$3.635 billion (2016 est.)

country comparison to the world: 136

IMPORTS - COMMODITIES:

mineral products and fuel, machinery and equipment, chemicals, textiles

IMPORTS - PARTNERS:

Romania 15.5%, Ukraine 11.4%, Russia 10.6%, China 10.4%, Germany 8.9%, Italy 6.9%, Turkey 6.1% (2017)

RESERVES OF FOREIGN EXCHANGE AND GOLD:

$2.803 billion (31 December 2017 est.)

$2.206 billion (31 December 2016 est.)

country comparison to the world: 111

DEBT - EXTERNAL:

$6.549 billion (31 December 2017 est.)

$6.138 billion (31 December 2016 est.)

country comparison to the world: 126

STOCK OF DIRECT FOREIGN INVESTMENT - AT HOME:

$3.701 billion (31 December 2017 est.)

$3.581 billion (31 December 2016 est.)

country comparison to the world: 112

STOCK OF DIRECT FOREIGN INVESTMENT - ABROAD:

$252.7 million (31 December 2017)

$206.1 million (31 December 2016)

country comparison to the world: 106

EXCHANGE RATES:

Moldovan lei (MDL) per US dollar -

18.49 (2017 est.)

19.924 (2016 est.)

19.924 (2015 est.)

19.83 (2014 est.)

14.036 (2013 est.)

ENERGY :: MOLDOVA

ELECTRICITY ACCESS:

electrification - total population: 100% (2016)

ELECTRICITY - PRODUCTION:

5.49 billion kWh (2016 est.)

country comparison to the world: 118

ELECTRICITY - CONSUMPTION:

4.4 billion kWh (2016 est.)

country comparison to the world: 125

ELECTRICITY - EXPORTS:

0 kWh (2016 est.)

country comparison to the world: 172

ELECTRICITY - IMPORTS:

4 million kWh (2016 est.)

country comparison to the world: 116

ELECTRICITY - INSTALLED GENERATING CAPACITY:

515,000 kW (2016 est.)

note: excludes Transnistria

country comparison to the world: 148

ELECTRICITY - FROM FOSSIL FUELS:

86% of total installed capacity (2016 est.)

country comparison to the world: 67

ELECTRICITY - FROM NUCLEAR FUELS:

0% of total installed capacity (2017 est.)

country comparison to the world: 144

ELECTRICITY - FROM HYDROELECTRIC PLANTS:

12% of total installed capacity (2017 est.)

country comparison to the world: 112

ELECTRICITY - FROM OTHER RENEWABLE SOURCES:

2% of total installed capacity (2017 est.)

country comparison to the world: 142

CRUDE OIL - PRODUCTION:

0 bbl/day (2018 est.)

country comparison to the world: 175

CRUDE OIL - EXPORTS:

0 bbl/day (2015 est.)

country comparison to the world: 166

CRUDE OIL - IMPORTS:

20 bbl/day (2015 est.)

country comparison to the world: 83

CRUDE OIL - PROVED RESERVES:

0 bbl (1 January 2018 est.)

country comparison to the world: 170

REFINED PETROLEUM PRODUCTS - PRODUCTION:

232 bbl/day (2015 est.)

country comparison to the world: 107

REFINED PETROLEUM PRODUCTS - CONSUMPTION:

18,000 bbl/day (2016 est.)

country comparison to the world: 148

REFINED PETROLEUM PRODUCTS - EXPORTS:

275 bbl/day (2015 est.)

country comparison to the world: 116

REFINED PETROLEUM PRODUCTS - IMPORTS:

18,160 bbl/day (2015 est.)

country comparison to the world: 130

NATURAL GAS - PRODUCTION:

11.33 million cu m (2017 est.)

country comparison to the world: 92

NATURAL GAS - CONSUMPTION:

2.52 billion cu m (2017 est.)

note: excludes breakaway Transnistria

country comparison to the world: 78

NATURAL GAS - EXPORTS:

0 cu m (2017 est.)

country comparison to the world: 152

NATURAL GAS - IMPORTS:

2.52 billion cu m (2017 est.)

note: excludes breakaway Transnistria

country comparison to the world: 46

NATURAL GAS - PROVED RESERVES:

NA cu m (1 January 2017 est.)

CARBON DIOXIDE EMISSIONS FROM CONSUMPTION OF ENERGY:

7.653 million Mt (2017 est.)

country comparison to the world: 121

COMMUNICATIONS :: MOLDOVA

TELEPHONES - FIXED LINES:

total subscriptions: 1,143,852

subscriptions per 100 inhabitants: 33 (2017 est.)

country comparison to the world: 73

TELEPHONES - MOBILE CELLULAR:

total subscriptions: 3,662,968

subscriptions per 100 inhabitants: 105 (2017 est.)

country comparison to the world: 132

TELEPHONE SYSTEM:

general assessment: the mobile market has extended the reach of service to outside the cities and across most of the country; endeavors to join the EU have promoted regulatory issues to be in line with EU principles and standards; market is competitive with 80 ISPs active; LTE services available and mobile broadband growth (2018)

domestic: competition among mobile telephone providers has spurred subscriptions; little interest in expanding fixed-line service 33 per 100; mobile-cellular teledensity sits at 105 per 100 persons (2018)

international: country code - 373; service through Romania and Russia via landline; satellite earth stations - at least 3 (Intelsat, Eutelsat, and Intersputnik)

BROADCAST MEDIA:

state-owned national radio-TV broadcaster operates 1 TV and 1 radio station; a total of nearly 70 terrestrial TV channels and some 50 radio stations are in operation; Russian and Romanian channels also are available (2019)

INTERNET COUNTRY CODE:

.md

INTERNET USERS:

total: 2,492,444

percent of population: 71% (July 2016 est.)

country comparison to the world: 104

BROADBAND - FIXED SUBSCRIPTIONS:

total: 584,330

subscriptions per 100 inhabitants: 17 (2017 est.)

country comparison to the world: 78

MILITARY AND SECURITY :: MOLDOVA

MILITARY EXPENDITURES:

0.35% of GDP (2018)

0.37% of GDP (2017)

0.44% of GDP (2016)

0.35% of GDP (2015)

0.35% of GDP (2014)

country comparison to the world: 152

MILITARY AND SECURITY FORCES:

National Army: Land Forces Command, Air Forces Command (includes air defense unit); Carabinieri Troops (a component of the Ministry of Internal Affairs that also has official status as a service of the Armed Forces during wartime) (2017)

MILITARY SERVICE AGE AND OBLIGATION:

18-27 years of age for compulsory or voluntary military service; male registration required at age 16; 1-year service obligation; note - Moldova intends to abolish military conscription by 2021. (2019)

TRANSPORTATION :: MOLDOVA

NATIONAL AIR TRANSPORT SYSTEM:

number of registered air carriers: 3 (2015)

inventory of registered aircraft operated by air carriers: 12 (2015)

annual passenger traffic on registered air carriers: 1,005,942 (2015)

annual freight traffic on registered air carriers: 489,630 mt-km (2015)

CIVIL AIRCRAFT REGISTRATION COUNTRY CODE PREFIX:

ER (2016)

AIRPORTS:

7 (2013)

country comparison to the world: 169

AIRPORTS - WITH PAVED RUNWAYS:

total: 5 (2017)

over 3,047 m: 1 (2017)

2,438 to 3,047 m: 2 (2017)

1,524 to 2,437 m: 2 (2017)

AIRPORTS - WITH UNPAVED RUNWAYS:

total: 2 (2013)

1,524 to 2,437 m: 1 (2013)

under 914 m: 1 (2013)

PIPELINES:

1916 km gas (2014)

RAILWAYS:

total: 1,171 km (2014)

standard gauge: 14 km 1.435-m gauge (2014)

broad gauge: 1,157 km 1.520-m gauge (2014)

country comparison to the world: 87

ROADWAYS:

total: 9,352 km (2012)

paved: 8,835 km (2012)

unpaved: 517 km (2012)

country comparison to the world: 131

WATERWAYS:

558 km (in public use on Danube, Dniester and Prut Rivers) (2011)

country comparison to the world: 82

MERCHANT MARINE:

total: 151

by type: bulk carrier 3, container ship 3, general cargo 113, oil tanker 8, other 24 (2018)

country comparison to the world: 71

TRANSNATIONAL ISSUES :: MOLDOVA

DISPUTES - INTERNATIONAL:

Moldova and Ukraine operate joint customs posts to monitor the transit of people and commodities through Moldova's break-away Transnistria region, which remains under the auspices of an Organization for Security and Cooperation in Europe-mandated peacekeeping mission comprised of Moldovan, Transnistrian, Russian, and Ukrainian troops

REFUGEES AND INTERNALLY DISPLACED PERSONS:

refugees (country of origin): 6,779 applicants for forms of legal stay other than asylum (Ukraine) (2015)

stateless persons: 4,451 (2018)

ILLICIT DRUGS:

limited cultivation of opium poppy and cannabis, mostly for CIS consumption; transshipment point for illicit drugs from Southwest Asia via Central Asia to Russia, Western Europe, and possibly the US; widespread crime and underground economic activity

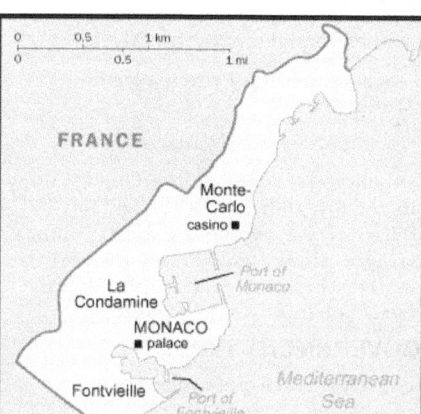

EUROPE :: MONACO

INTRODUCTION :: MONACO

BACKGROUND:

The Genoese built a fortress on the site of present day Monaco in 1215. The current ruling GRIMALDI family first seized control in 1297 but was not able to permanently secure its holding until 1419. Economic development was spurred in the late 19th century with a railroad linkup to France and the opening of a casino. Since then, the principality's mild climate, splendid scenery, and gambling facilities have made Monaco world famous as a tourist and recreation center.

GEOGRAPHY :: MONACO

LOCATION:
Western Europe, bordering the Mediterranean Sea on the southern coast of France, near the border with Italy

GEOGRAPHIC COORDINATES:
43 44 N, 7 24 E

MAP REFERENCES:
Europe

AREA:
total: 2 sq km
land: 2 sq km
water: 0 sq km
country comparison to the world: 255

AREA - COMPARATIVE:
about three times the size of the National Mall in Washington, DC

LAND BOUNDARIES:
total: 6 km
border countries (1): France 6 km

COASTLINE:
4.1 km

MARITIME CLAIMS:
territorial sea: 12 nm
exclusive economic zone: 12 nm

CLIMATE:
Mediterranean with mild, wet winters and hot, dry summers

TERRAIN:
hilly, rugged, rocky

ELEVATION:
lowest point: Mediterranean Sea 0 m
highest point: Chemin des Revoires on Mont Agel 162 m

NATURAL RESOURCES:
none

LAND USE:
agricultural land: 1% (2011 est.)
arable land: 0% (2011 est.) / permanent crops: 1% (2011 est.) / permanent pasture: 0% (2011 est.)
forest: 0% (2011 est.)
other: 99% (2011 est.)

IRRIGATED LAND:
0 sq km (2012)

POPULATION DISTRIBUTION:
the second most densely populated country in the world (after Macau); its entire population living on 2 square km

NATURAL HAZARDS:
none

ENVIRONMENT - CURRENT ISSUES:
no serious issues; actively monitors pollution levels in air and water

ENVIRONMENT - INTERNATIONAL AGREEMENTS:
party to: Air Pollution, Air Pollution-Sulfur 94, Air Pollution-Volatile Organic Compounds, Biodiversity, Climate Change, Climate Change-Kyoto Protocol, Desertification, Endangered Species, Hazardous Wastes, Law of the Sea, Marine Dumping, Ozone Layer Protection, Ship Pollution, Wetlands, Whaling
signed, but not ratified: none of the selected agreements

GEOGRAPHY - NOTE:
second-smallest independent state in the world (after the Holy See); smallest country with a coastline; almost entirely urban

PEOPLE AND SOCIETY :: MONACO

POPULATION:
30,727 (July 2018 est.)
note: immigrants make up almost 55% of the total population, according to UN data (2017)
country comparison to the world: 217

NATIONALITY:
noun: Monegasque(s) or Monacan(s)
adjective: Monegasque or Monacan

ETHNIC GROUPS:
Monegasque 32.1%, French 19.9%, Italian 15.3%, British 5%, Belgian 2.3%, Swiss 2%, German 1.9%, Russian 1.8%, American 1.1%, Dutch 1.1%, Moroccan 1%, other 16.6%

note: data represent population by country of birth

French 24.9%, Monegasque 22.5%, Italian 21.9%, British 7.5%, Swiss 3.2%, Belgian 2.9%, German 2.4%, Russian 2%, Dutch 1.5%, Portuguese 1.4%, Greek 1.1%, American 1%, other 7.7%

note: data represent population by nationality (2016 est.)

LANGUAGES:
French (official), English, Italian, Monegasque

RELIGIONS:
Roman Catholic 90% (official), other 10%

AGE STRUCTURE:
0-14 years: 10.27% (male 1,622 /female 1,533)

15-24 years: 9.39% (male 1,498 /female 1,387)

25-54 years: 32.15% (male 4,964 /female 4,916)

55-64 years: 15.04% (male 2,305 /female 2,315)

65 years and over: 33.15% (male 4,530 /female 5,657) (2018 est.)

MEDIAN AGE:
total: 53.8 years (2018 est.)

male: 52.4 years

female: 55.3 years

country comparison to the world: 1

POPULATION GROWTH RATE:
0.3% (2018 est.)

country comparison to the world: 170

BIRTH RATE:
6.5 births/1,000 population (2018 est.)

country comparison to the world: 226

DEATH RATE:
10.1 deaths/1,000 population (2018 est.)

country comparison to the world: 36

NET MIGRATION RATE:
6.5 migrant(s)/1,000 population (2018 est.)

country comparison to the world: 16

POPULATION DISTRIBUTION:
the second most densely populated country in the world (after Macau); its entire population living on 2 square km

URBANIZATION:
urban population: 100% of total population (2019)

rate of urbanization: 0.51% annual rate of change (2015-20 est.)

MAJOR URBAN AREAS - POPULATION:
39,000 MONACO (capital) (2018)

SEX RATIO:
at birth: 1.04 male(s)/female

0-14 years: 1.06 male(s)/female

15-24 years: 1.08 male(s)/female

25-54 years: 1.01 male(s)/female

55-64 years: 1 male(s)/female

65 years and over: 0.8 male(s)/female

total population: 0.94 male(s)/female (2018 est.)

INFANT MORTALITY RATE:
total: 1.8 deaths/1,000 live births (2018 est.)

male: 2.1 deaths/1,000 live births

female: 1.6 deaths/1,000 live births

country comparison to the world: 223

LIFE EXPECTANCY AT BIRTH:
total population: 89.4 years (2018 est.)

male: 85.5 years

female: 93.4 years

country comparison to the world: 1

TOTAL FERTILITY RATE:
1.54 children born/woman (2018 est.)

country comparison to the world: 191

DRINKING WATER SOURCE:
improved:

urban: 100% of population

total: 100% of population

unimproved:

urban: 0% of population

total: 0% of population (2015 est.)

CURRENT HEALTH EXPENDITURE:
1.7% (2016)

PHYSICIANS DENSITY:
6.56 physicians/1,000 population (2014)

HOSPITAL BED DENSITY:
13.8 beds/1,000 population (2012)

SANITATION FACILITY ACCESS:
improved:

urban: 100% of population (2015 est.)

total: 100% of population (2015 est.)

unimproved:

urban: 0% of population (2015 est.)

total: 0% of population (2015 est.)

HIV/AIDS - ADULT PREVALENCE RATE:
NA

HIV/AIDS - PEOPLE LIVING WITH HIV/AIDS:
NA

HIV/AIDS - DEATHS:
NA

EDUCATION EXPENDITURES:
1.4% of GDP (2016)

country comparison to the world: 172

UNEMPLOYMENT, YOUTH AGES 15-24:
total: 26.6%

male: 25.7%

female: 27.9% (2016 est.)

country comparison to the world: 42

GOVERNMENT :: MONACO

COUNTRY NAME:
conventional long form: Principality of Monaco

conventional short form: Monaco

local long form: Principaute de Monaco

local short form: Monaco

etymology: founded as a Greek colony in the 6th century B.C., the name derives from two Greek words "monos" (single, alone) and "oikos" (house) to convey the sense of a people "living apart" or in a "single habitation"

GOVERNMENT TYPE:
constitutional monarchy

CAPITAL:
name: Monaco

geographic coordinates: 43 44 N, 7 25 E

time difference: UTC+1 (6 hours ahead of Washington, DC, during Standard Time)

daylight saving time: +1hr, begins last Sunday in March; ends last Sunday in October

ADMINISTRATIVE DIVISIONS:
none; there are no first-order administrative divisions as defined by the US Government, but there are 4 quarters (quartiers, singular - quartier); Fontvieille, La Condamine,

Monaco-Ville, Monte-Carlo; note - Moneghetti, a part of La Condamine, is sometimes called the 5th quarter of Monaco

INDEPENDENCE:
1419 (beginning of permanent rule by the House of GRIMALDI)

NATIONAL HOLIDAY:
National Day (Saint Rainier's Day), 19 November (1857)

CONSTITUTION:
history: previous 1911 (suspended 1959); latest adopted 17 December 1962

amendments: proposed by joint agreement of the chief of state (the prince) and the National Council; passage requires two-thirds majority vote of National Council members; amended 2002 (2016)

LEGAL SYSTEM:
civil law system influenced by French legal tradition

INTERNATIONAL LAW ORGANIZATION PARTICIPATION:
has not submitted an ICJ jurisdiction declaration; non-party state to the ICCt

CITIZENSHIP:
citizenship by birth: no

citizenship by descent only: the father must be a citizen of Monaco; in the case of a child born out of wedlock, the mother must be a citizen and father unknown

dual citizenship recognized: no

residency requirement for naturalization: 10 years

SUFFRAGE:
18 years of age; universal

EXECUTIVE BRANCH:
chief of state: Prince ALBERT II (since 6 April 2005)

head of government: Minister of State Serge TELLE (since 1 February 2016)

cabinet: Council of Government under the authority of the monarch

elections/appointments: the monarchy is hereditary; minister of state appointed by the monarch from a list of three French national candidates presented by the French Government

LEGISLATIVE BRANCH:
description: unicameral National Council or Conseil National (24 seats; 16 members directly elected in multi-seat constituencies by simple majority vote and 8 directly elected by proportional representation vote; members serve 5-year terms)

elections: last held on 11 February 2018 (next to be held in February 2023)

election results: percent of vote by party - Priorite Monaco 57.7%, Horizon Monaco 26.1%, Union Monegasque 16.2%; seats by party - Priorite Monaco 21, Horizon Monaco 2, Union Monegasque 1; composition - men 16, women 8, percent of women 33.3%

JUDICIAL BRANCH:
highest courts: Supreme Court (consists of 5 permanent members and 2 substitutes)

judge selection and term of office: Supreme Court members appointed by the monarch upon the proposals of the National Council, State Council, Crown Council, Court of Appeal, and Trial Court

subordinate courts: Court of Appeal; Civil Court of First Instance

POLITICAL PARTIES AND LEADERS:
Horizon Monaco [Laurent NOUVION]
Priorite Monaco [Stephane VALERI]
Renaissance [SBM (public corporation)]
Union Monegasque [Jean-Francois ROBILLON]

INTERNATIONAL ORGANIZATION PARTICIPATION:
CD, CE, FAO, IAEA, ICAO, ICC (national committees), ICRM, IFRCS, IHO, IMO, IMSO, Interpol, IOC, IPU, ITSO, ITU, OAS (observer), OIF, OPCW, OSCE, Schengen Convention (de facto member), UN, UNCTAD, UNESCO, UNIDO, Union Latina, UNWTO, UPU, WHO, WIPO, WMO

DIPLOMATIC REPRESENTATION IN THE US:
Ambassador Maguy MACCARIO-DOYLE (since 3 December 2013)

chancery: 3400 International Drive NW, Suite 2K-100, Washington, DC 20008

telephone: (202) 234-1530

FAX: (202) 244-7656

consulate(s) general: New York

DIPLOMATIC REPRESENTATION FROM THE US:
the US does not have an embassy in Monaco; the US Ambassador to France is accredited to Monaco; the US Consul General in Marseille (France), under the authority of the US Ambassador to France, handles diplomatic and consular matters concerning Monaco

FLAG DESCRIPTION:
two equal horizontal bands of red (top) and white; the colors are those of the ruling House of Grimaldi and have been in use since 1339, making the flag one of the world's oldest national banners

note: similar to the flag of Indonesia which is longer and the flag of Poland which is white (top) and red

NATIONAL SYMBOL(S):
red and white lozenges (diamond shapes); national colors: red, white

NATIONAL ANTHEM:
name: "A Marcia de Muneghu" (The March of Monaco)

lyrics/music: Louis NOTARI/Charles ALBRECHT

note: music adopted 1867, lyrics adopted 1931; although French is commonly spoken, only the Monegasque lyrics are official; the French version is known as "Hymne Monegasque" (Monegasque Anthem); the words are generally only sung on official occasions

ECONOMY :: MONACO

ECONOMY - OVERVIEW:
Monaco, bordering France on the Mediterranean coast, is a popular resort, attracting tourists to its casino and pleasant climate. The principality also is a banking center and has successfully sought to diversify into services and small, high-value-added, nonpolluting industries. The state retains monopolies in a number of sectors, including tobacco, the telephone network, and the postal service. Living standards are high, roughly comparable to those in prosperous French metropolitan areas.

The state has no income tax and low business taxes and thrives as a tax haven both for individuals who have established residence and for foreign companies that have set up businesses and offices. Monaco, however, is not a tax-free shelter; it charges nearly 20% value-added tax, collects stamp duties, and companies face a 33% tax on profits unless they can show that three-quarters of profits are generated within the principality. Monaco was formally removed from the OECD's "grey list" of uncooperative tax jurisdictions in late 2009, but continues to face international pressure to abandon its banking secrecy laws and help combat tax evasion. In October 2014, Monaco officially became the 84th jurisdiction participating in the OECD's Multilateral Convention on Mutual Administrative Assistance in Tax Matters, an effort to combat offshore tax avoidance and evasion.

Monaco's reliance on tourism and banking for its economic growth has left it vulnerable to downturns in France and other European economies which are the principality's main trade partners. In 2009, Monaco's GDP fell by 11.5% as the euro-zone crisis precipitated a sharp drop in tourism and retail activity and home sales. A modest recovery ensued in 2010 and intensified in 2013, with GDP growth of more than 9%, but Monaco's economic prospects remain uncertain.

GDP (PURCHASING POWER PARITY):
$7.672 billion (2015 est.)

$7.279 billion (2014 est.)

$6.79 billion (2013 est.)

note: data are in 2015 US dollars

country comparison to the world: 165

GDP (OFFICIAL EXCHANGE RATE):
$6.006 billion (2015 est.) (2015 est.)

GDP - REAL GROWTH RATE:
5.4% (2015 est.)

7.2% (2014 est.)

9.6% (2013 est.)

country comparison to the world: 40

GDP - PER CAPITA (PPP):
$115,700 (2015 est.)

$109,200 (2014 est.)

$101,900 (2013 est.)

country comparison to the world: 3

GDP - COMPOSITION, BY SECTOR OF ORIGIN:
agriculture: 0% (2013)

industry: 14% (2013)

services: 86% (2013)

AGRICULTURE - PRODUCTS:
none

INDUSTRIES:
banking, insurance, tourism, construction, small-scale industrial and consumer products

INDUSTRIAL PRODUCTION GROWTH RATE:
6.8% (2015)

country comparison to the world: 33

LABOR FORCE:
52,000 (2014 est.)

note: includes all foreign workers

country comparison to the world: 190

LABOR FORCE - BY OCCUPATION:
agriculture: 0%

industry: 16.1%

services: 83.9% (2012 est.)

UNEMPLOYMENT RATE:
2% (2012)

country comparison to the world: 19

POPULATION BELOW POVERTY LINE:
NA

HOUSEHOLD INCOME OR CONSUMPTION BY PERCENTAGE SHARE:
lowest 10%: NA

highest 10%: NA

BUDGET:
revenues: 896.3 million (2011 est.)

expenditures: 953.6 million (2011 est.)

TAXES AND OTHER REVENUES:
14.9% (of GDP) (2011 est.)

country comparison to the world: 196

BUDGET SURPLUS (+) OR DEFICIT (-):
-1% (of GDP) (2011 est.)

country comparison to the world: 80

FISCAL YEAR:
calendar year

INFLATION RATE (CONSUMER PRICES):
1.5% (2010)

country comparison to the world: 84

MARKET VALUE OF PUBLICLY TRADED SHARES:
NA

EXPORTS:
$964.6 million (2017 est.)

$1.115 billion (2011)

note: full customs integration with France, which collects and rebates Monegasque trade duties; also participates in EU market system through customs union with France

country comparison to the world: 162

IMPORTS:
$1.371 billion (2017 est.)

$1.162 billion (2011 est.)

note: full customs integration with France, which collects and rebates Monegasque trade duties; also participates in EU market system through customs union with France

country comparison to the world: 176

DEBT - EXTERNAL:
NA

EXCHANGE RATES:
euros (EUR) per US dollar -

0.885 (2017 est.)

0.903 (2016 est.)

0.9214 (2015 est.)

0.885 (2014 est.)

0.7634 (2013 est.)

ENERGY :: MONACO

ELECTRICITY ACCESS:
electrification - total population: 100% (2016)

COMMUNICATIONS :: MONACO

TELEPHONES - FIXED LINES:
total subscriptions: 47,013

subscriptions per 100 inhabitants: 153 (2017 est.)

country comparison to the world: 159

TELEPHONES - MOBILE CELLULAR:
total subscriptions: 32,978

subscriptions per 100 inhabitants: 108 (2017 est.)

country comparison to the world: 206

TELEPHONE SYSTEM:
general assessment: modern automatic telephone system; the country's sole fixed-line operator offers a full range of services to residential and business customers; competitive mobile telephony market (2018)

domestic: fixed-line 153 per 100 and mobile-cellular teledensity exceeds 108 per 100 persons (2018)

international: country code - 377; landing points for the EIG and Italy-Monaco submarine cables connecting Monaco to Europe, Africa, the Middle East and Asia; no satellite earth stations; connected by cable into the French communications system (2019)

BROADCAST MEDIA:

TV Monte-Carlo operates a TV network; cable TV available; Radio Monte-Carlo has extensive radio networks in France and Italy with French-language broadcasts to France beginning in the 1960s and Italian-language broadcasts to Italy beginning in the 1970s; other radio stations include Riviera Radio and Radio Monaco

INTERNET COUNTRY CODE:

.mc

INTERNET USERS:

total: 29,116

percent of population: 95.2% (July 2016 est.)

country comparison to the world: 202

BROADBAND - FIXED SUBSCRIPTIONS:

total: 19,258

subscriptions per 100 inhabitants: 63 (2017 est.)

country comparison to the world: 152

MILITARY AND SECURITY :: MONACO

MILITARY AND SECURITY FORCES:

no regular military forces; Ministry of Interior: Compagnie des Carabiniers du Prince (Prince's Company of Carabiniers (Palace Guard)), Corps des Sapeurs-pompiers de Monaco (Fire and Emergency), Police Department (2019)

MILITARY - NOTE:

defense is the responsibility of France

TRANSPORTATION :: MONACO

CIVIL AIRCRAFT REGISTRATION COUNTRY CODE PREFIX:

3A (2016)

HELIPORTS:

1 (2012)

RAILWAYS:

note: Monaco has a single railway station but does not operate its own train service; the French operator SNCF operates rail services in Monaco

ROADWAYS:

PORTS AND TERMINALS:

major seaport(s): Hercules Port

TRANSNATIONAL ISSUES :: MONACO

DISPUTES - INTERNATIONAL:

none

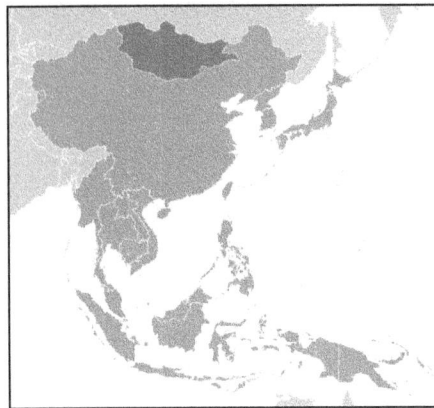

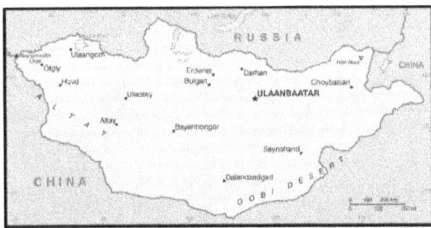

EAST ASIA / SOUTHEAST ASIA :: MONGOLIA

INTRODUCTION :: MONGOLIA

BACKGROUND:

The Mongols gained fame in the 13th century when under Chinggis KHAAN they established a huge Eurasian empire through conquest. After his death the empire was divided into several powerful Mongol states, but these broke apart in the 14th century. The Mongols eventually retired to their original steppe homelands and in the late 17th century came under Chinese rule. Mongolia declared its independence from the Manchu-led Qing Empire in 1911 and achieved limited autonomy until 1919, when it again came under Chinese control. The Mongolian Revolution of 1921 ended Chinese dominance, and a communist regime, the Mongolian People's Republic, took power in 1924.

The modern country of Mongolia, represents only part of the Mongols' historical homeland; today, more ethnic Mongolians live in the Inner Mongolia Autonomous Region in the People's Republic of China than in Mongolia. Since the country's peaceful democratic revolution in 1990, the ex-communist Mongolian People's Revolutionary Party (MPRP) - which took the name Mongolian People's Party (MPP) in 2010 - has competed for political power with the Democratic Party (DP) and several other smaller parties, including a new party formed by former President ENKHBAYAR, which confusingly adopted for itself the MPRP name. In the country's most recent parliamentary elections in June 2016, Mongolians handed the MPP overwhelming control of Parliament, largely pushing out the DP, which had overseen a sharp decline in Mongolia's economy during its control of Parliament in the preceding years. Mongolians elected a DP member, Khaltmaa BATTULGA, as president in 2017.

GEOGRAPHY :: MONGOLIA

LOCATION:
Northern Asia, between China and Russia

GEOGRAPHIC COORDINATES:
46 00 N, 105 00 E

MAP REFERENCES:
Asia

AREA:
total: 1,564,116 sq km

land: 1,553,556 sq km

water: 10,560 sq km

country comparison to the world: 20

AREA - COMPARATIVE:
slightly smaller than Alaska; more than twice the size of Texas

LAND BOUNDARIES:
total: 8,082 km

border countries (2): China 4630 km, Russia 3452 km

COASTLINE:
0 km (landlocked)

MARITIME CLAIMS:
none (landlocked)

CLIMATE:
desert; continental (large daily and seasonal temperature ranges)

TERRAIN:
vast semidesert and desert plains, grassy steppe, mountains in west and southwest; Gobi Desert in south-central

ELEVATION:
mean elevation: 1,528 m

lowest point: Hoh Nuur 560 m

highest point: Nayramadlin Orgil (Khuiten Peak) 4,374 m

NATURAL RESOURCES:
oil, coal, copper, molybdenum, tungsten, phosphates, tin, nickel, zinc, fluorspar, gold, silver, iron

LAND USE:
agricultural land: 73% (2011 est.)

arable land: 0.4% (2011 est.) / permanent crops: 0% (2011 est.) / permanent pasture: 72.6% (2011 est.)

forest: 7% (2011 est.)

other: 20% (2011 est.)

IRRIGATED LAND:
840 sq km (2012)

POPULATION DISTRIBUTION:
sparsely distributed population throughout the country; the capital of Ulaanbaatar and the northern city of Darhan support the highest population densities

NATURAL HAZARDS:
dust storms; grassland and forest fires; drought; "zud," which is harsh winter conditions

ENVIRONMENT - CURRENT ISSUES:
limited natural freshwater resources in some areas; the burning of soft coal in power plants and the lack of enforcement of environmental laws leads to air pollution in Ulaanbaatar; deforestation and overgrazing increase soil erosion from wind and rain; water pollution; desertification and mining activities have a deleterious effect on the environment

ENVIRONMENT - INTERNATIONAL AGREEMENTS:
party to: Biodiversity, Climate Change, Climate Change-Kyoto Protocol, Desertification, Endangered Species, Environmental Modification, Hazardous Wastes, Law of the Sea, Ozone Layer Protection, Ship Pollution, Wetlands, Whaling

signed, but not ratified: none of the selected agreements

GEOGRAPHY - NOTE:

landlocked; strategic location between China and Russia

PEOPLE AND SOCIETY :: MONGOLIA

POPULATION:

3,103,428 (July 2018 est.)

note: Mongolia is one of the least densely populated countries in the world (2 people per sq km); twice as many ethnic Mongols (some 6 million) live in Inner Mongolia (Nei Mongol) in neighboring China

country comparison to the world: 135

NATIONALITY:

noun: Mongolian(s)

adjective: Mongolian

ETHNIC GROUPS:

Khalkh 84.5%, Kazak 3.9%, Dorvod 2.4%, Bayad 1.7%, Buryat-Bouriates 1.3%, Zakhchin 1%, other 5.2% (2015 est.)

LANGUAGES:

Mongolian 90% (official) (Khalkha dialect is predominant), Turkic, Russian (1999)

RELIGIONS:

Buddhist 53%, Muslim 3%, Shamanist 2.9%, Christian 2.2%, other 0.4%, none 38.6% (2010 est.)

AGE STRUCTURE:

0-14 years: 27% (male 427,225 /female 410,579)

15-24 years: 15.67% (male 246,198 /female 240,040)

25-54 years: 45.49% (male 683,475 /female 728,149)

55-64 years: 7.43% (male 105,085 /female 125,502)

65 years and over: 4.42% (male 55,447 /female 81,728) (2018 est.)

DEPENDENCY RATIOS:

total dependency ratio: 48.5 (2015 est.)

youth dependency ratio: 42.7 (2015 est.)

elderly dependency ratio: 5.8 (2015 est.)

potential support ratio: 17.3 (2015 est.)

MEDIAN AGE:

total: 28.8 years (2018 est.)

male: 28 years

female: 29.6 years

country comparison to the world: 129

POPULATION GROWTH RATE:

1.11% (2018 est.)

country comparison to the world: 99

BIRTH RATE:

18.2 births/1,000 population (2018 est.)

country comparison to the world: 92

DEATH RATE:

6.3 deaths/1,000 population (2018 est.)

country comparison to the world: 152

NET MIGRATION RATE:

-0.8 migrant(s)/1,000 population (2018 est.)

country comparison to the world: 136

POPULATION DISTRIBUTION:

sparsely distributed population throughout the country; the capital of Ulaanbaatar and the northern city of Darhan support the highest population densities

URBANIZATION:

urban population: 68.5% of total population (2019)

rate of urbanization: 1.63% annual rate of change (2015-20 est.)

MAJOR URBAN AREAS - POPULATION:

1.553 million ULAANBAATAR (capital) (2019)

SEX RATIO:

at birth: 1.05 male(s)/female

0-14 years: 1.04 male(s)/female

15-24 years: 1.03 male(s)/female

25-54 years: 0.94 male(s)/female

55-64 years: 0.84 male(s)/female

65 years and over: 0.68 male(s)/female

total population: 0.96 male(s)/female (2018 est.)

MOTHER'S MEAN AGE AT FIRST BIRTH:

20.5 years (2008 est.)

note: median age at first birth among women 20-24

MATERNAL MORTALITY RATE:

45 deaths/100,000 live births (2017 est.)

country comparison to the world: 97

INFANT MORTALITY RATE:

total: 20.5 deaths/1,000 live births (2018 est.)

male: 23.5 deaths/1,000 live births

female: 17.3 deaths/1,000 live births

country comparison to the world: 80

LIFE EXPECTANCY AT BIRTH:

total population: 70.2 years (2018 est.)

male: 66 years

female: 74.7 years

country comparison to the world: 160

TOTAL FERTILITY RATE:

2.04 children born/woman (2018 est.)

country comparison to the world: 110

CONTRACEPTIVE PREVALENCE RATE:

54.6% (2013)

DRINKING WATER SOURCE:

improved:

urban: 66.4% of population

rural: 59.2% of population

total: 64.4% of population

unimproved:

urban: 33.6% of population

rural: 40.8% of population

total: 35.6% of population (2015 est.)

CURRENT HEALTH EXPENDITURE:

3.8% (2016)

PHYSICIANS DENSITY:

2.89 physicians/1,000 population (2016)

HOSPITAL BED DENSITY:

7 beds/1,000 population (2012)

SANITATION FACILITY ACCESS:

improved:

urban: 66.4% of population (2015 est.)

rural: 42.6% of population (2015 est.)

total: 59.7% of population (2015 est.)

unimproved:

urban: 33.6% of population (2015 est.)

rural: 57.4% of population (2015 est.)

total: 40.3% of population (2015 est.)

HIV/AIDS - ADULT PREVALENCE RATE:

<.1% (2018 est.)

HIV/AIDS - PEOPLE LIVING WITH HIV/AIDS:

<1000 (2018 est.)

HIV/AIDS - DEATHS:

<100 (2018 est.)

OBESITY - ADULT PREVALENCE RATE:

20.6% (2016)

country comparison to the world: 96

CHILDREN UNDER THE AGE OF 5 YEARS UNDERWEIGHT:

0.9% (2016)

country comparison to the world: 123

EDUCATION EXPENDITURES:

4.1% of GDP (2017)

country comparison to the world: 105

LITERACY:

definition: age 15 and over can read and write

total population: 98.4%

male: 98.2%

female: 98.6% (2015 est.)

SCHOOL LIFE EXPECTANCY (PRIMARY TO TERTIARY EDUCATION):

total: 15 years

male: 14 years

female: 16 years (2015)

UNEMPLOYMENT, YOUTH AGES 15-24:

total: 17.9%

male: 15%

female: 22.6% (2017 est.)

country comparison to the world: 77

GOVERNMENT :: MONGOLIA

COUNTRY NAME:

conventional long form: none

conventional short form: Mongolia

local long form: none

local short form: Mongol Uls

former: Outer Mongolia, Mongolian People's Republic

etymology: the name means "Land of the Mongols" in Latin; the Mongolian name Mongol Uls translates as "Mongol State"

GOVERNMENT TYPE:

semi-presidential republic

CAPITAL:

name: Ulaanbaatar

geographic coordinates: 47 55 N, 106 55 E

time difference: UTC+8 (13 hours ahead of Washington, DC, during Standard Time)

daylight saving time: +1hr, begins last Saturday in March; ends last Saturday in September

note: Mongolia has two time zones - Ulaanbaatar Time (8 hours in advance of UTC) and Hovd Time (7 hours in advance of UTC)

etymology: the name means "red hero" in Mongolian and honors national hero Damdin Sukhbaatar, leader of the partisan army that with Soviet Red Army help, liberated Mongolia from Chinese occupation in the early 1920s

ADMINISTRATIVE DIVISIONS:

21 provinces (aymguud, singular - aymag) and 1 municipality* (singular - hot); Arhangay, Bayanhongor, Bayan-Olgiy, Bulgan, Darhan-Uul, Dornod, Dornogovi, Dundgovi, Dzavhan (Zavkhan), Govi-Altay, Govisumber, Hentiy, Hovd, Hovsgol, Omnogovi, Orhon, Ovorhangay, Selenge, Suhbaatar, Tov, Ulaanbaatar*, Uvs

INDEPENDENCE:

29 December 1911 (independence declared from China; in actuality, autonomy attained); 11 July 1921 (from China)

NATIONAL HOLIDAY:

Naadam (games) holiday (commemorates independence from China in the 1921 Revolution), 11-15 July; Constitution Day (marks the date that the Mongolian People's Republic was created under a new constitution), 26 November (1924)

CONSTITUTION:

history: several previous; latest adopted 13 January 1992, effective 12 February 1992

amendments: proposed by the State Great Hural, by the president of the republic, by the government, or by petition submitted to the State Great Hural by the Constitutional Court; conducting referenda on proposed amendments requires at least two-thirds majority vote of the State Great Hural; passage of amendments by the State Great Hural requires at least three-quarters majority vote; passage by referendum requires majority participation of qualified voters and a majority of votes; amended 1999, 2000 (2019)

LEGAL SYSTEM:

civil law system influenced by Soviet and Romano-Germanic legal systems; constitution ambiguous on judicial review of legislative acts

INTERNATIONAL LAW ORGANIZATION PARTICIPATION:

has not submitted an ICJ jurisdiction declaration; accepts ICCt jurisdiction

CITIZENSHIP:

citizenship by birth: no

citizenship by descent only: both parents must be citizens of Mongolia; one parent if born within Mongolia

dual citizenship recognized: no

residency requirement for naturalization: 5 years

SUFFRAGE:

18 years of age; universal

EXECUTIVE BRANCH:

chief of state: President Khaltmaa BATTULGA (since 10 July 2017)

head of government: Prime Minister Ukhnaa KHURELSUKH (since 4 October 2017); Deputy Prime Minister Ulziisaikhan ENKHTUVSHIN (since 18 October 2017); note - Prime Minister Jargaltulga ERDENEBAT (since 8 July 2016) was voted out of office by the Parliament on 7 September 2017

cabinet: Cabinet nominated by the prime minister in consultation with the president, confirmed by the State Great Hural (parliament)

elections/appointments: presidential candidates nominated by political parties represented in the State Great Hural and directly elected by simple majority popular vote for a 4-year term (eligible for a second term); election last held on 26 June 2017 with a runoff held 7 July 2017 (next to be held in 2021); following legislative elections, the leader of the majority party or majority coalition is usually elected prime minister by the State Great Hural

election results: Khaltmaa BATTULGA elected president in second round; percent of vote in first round - Khaltmaa BATTULGA (DP) 38.1%, Miyegombo ENKHBOLD (MPP) 30.3%, Sainkhuu GANBAATAR (MPRP) 30.2%, invalid 1.4%; percent of vote in second round - Khaltmaa BATTULGA 55.2%, Miyegombo ENKHBOLD 44.8%

LEGISLATIVE BRANCH:

description: unicameral State Great Hural or Ulsyn Ikh Khural (76 seats; members directly elected in single-seat constituencies by simple majority vote; each constituency requires at least 50% voter participation for the poll to be valid; members serve 4-year terms)

elections: last held on 29 June 2016 (next to be held in June 2020)

election results: percent of vote by party - MPP 45.1%, DP 33.1%, MPRP 8.0%, independent 4.8%, other 9.0%; seats by party - MPP 65, DP 9, MPRP 1, independent 1; composition - men 63, women 13, percent of women 17.1%

JUDICIAL BRANCH:

highest courts: Supreme Court (consists of the Chief Justice and 24 judges organized into civil, criminal, and administrative chambers); Constitutional Court or Tsets

(consists of the chairman and 8 members)

judge selection and term of office: Supreme Court chief justice and judges appointed by the president upon recommendation by the General Council of Courts - a 14-member body of judges and judicial officials - to the State Great Hural; appointment is for life; chairman of the Constitutional Court elected from among its members; members appointed from nominations by the State Great Hural - 3 each by the president, the State Great Hural, and the Supreme Court; appointment is 6 years; chairmanship limited to a single renewable 3-year term

subordinate courts: aimag (provincial) and capital city appellate courts; soum, inter-soum, and district courts; Administrative Cases Courts

POLITICAL PARTIES AND LEADERS:

Democratic Party or DP [Sodnomzundui ERDENE]
Mongolian National Democratic Party or MNDP [Bayanjargal TSOGTGEREL]
Mongolian People's Party or MPP [Ukhnaa KHURELSUKH]
Mongolian People's Revolutionary Party or MPRP [Nambar ENKHBAYAR]

INTERNATIONAL ORGANIZATION PARTICIPATION:

ADB, ARF, CD, CICA, CP, EBRD, EITI (compliant country), FAO, G-77, IAEA, IBRD, ICAO, ICC (NGOs), ICCt, ICRM, IDA, IFAD, IFC, IFRCS, ILO, IMF, IMO, IMSO, Interpol, IOC, IOM, IPU, ISO, ITSO, ITU, ITUC, MIGA, MINURSO, MONUSCO, NAM, OPCW, OSCE, SCO (observer), UN, UNAMID, UNCTAD, UNESCO, UNIDO, UNISFA, UNMISS, UNWTO, UPU, WCO, WHO, WIPO, WMO, WTO

DIPLOMATIC REPRESENTATION IN THE US:

Ambassador Yondon OTGONBAYAR (since 28 March 2018)

chancery: 2833 M Street NW, Washington, DC 20007

telephone: [1] (202) 333-7117

FAX: [1] (202) 298-9227

consulate(s) general: New York, San Francisco

DIPLOMATIC REPRESENTATION FROM THE US:

chief of mission: Ambassador Michael S. KLECHESKI (since 22 February 2019)

telephone: [976] 7007-6001

embassy: Denver Street #3, 11th Micro-District, Big Ring Road, Ulaanbaatar, 14190 Mongolia

mailing address: P.O. Box 341, Ulaanbaatar 14192

FAX: [976] 7007-6016

FLAG DESCRIPTION:

three, equal vertical bands of red (hoist side), blue, and red; centered on the hoist-side red band in yellow is the national emblem ("soyombo" - a columnar arrangement of abstract and geometric representation for fire, sun, moon, earth, water, and the yin-yang symbol); blue represents the sky, red symbolizes progress and prosperity

NATIONAL SYMBOL(S):

soyombo emblem; national colors: red, blue, yellow

NATIONAL ANTHEM:

name: "Mongol ulsyn toriin duulal" (National Anthem of Mongolia)

lyrics/music: Tsendiin DAMDINSUREN/Bilegiin DAMDINSUREN and Luvsanjamts MURJORJ

note: music adopted 1950, lyrics adopted 2006; lyrics altered on numerous occasions

ECONOMY :: MONGOLIA

ECONOMY - OVERVIEW:

Foreign direct investment in Mongolia's extractive industries – which are based on extensive deposits of copper, gold, coal, molybdenum, fluorspar, uranium, tin, and tungsten - has transformed Mongolia's landlocked economy from its traditional dependence on herding and agriculture. Exports now account for more than 40% of GDP. Mongolia depends on China for more than 60% of its external trade - China receives some 90% of Mongolia's exports and supplies Mongolia with more than one-third of its imports. Mongolia also relies on Russia for 90% of its energy supplies, leaving it vulnerable to price increases. Remittances from Mongolians working abroad, particularly in South Korea, are significant.

Soviet assistance, at its height one-third of GDP, disappeared almost overnight in 1990 and 1991 at the time of the dismantlement of the USSR. The following decade saw Mongolia endure both deep recession, because of political inaction, and natural disasters, as well as strong economic growth, because of market reforms and extensive privatization of the formerly state-run economy. The country opened a fledgling stock exchange in 1991. Mongolia joined the WTO in 1997 and seeks to expand its participation in regional economic and trade regimes.

Growth averaged nearly 9% per year in 2004-08 largely because of high copper prices globally and new gold production. By late 2008, Mongolia was hit by the global financial crisis and Mongolia's real economy contracted 1.3% in 2009. In early 2009, the IMF reached a $236 million Stand-by Arrangement with Mongolia and it emerged from the crisis with a stronger banking sector and better fiscal management. In October 2009, Mongolia passed long-awaited legislation on an investment agreement to develop the Oyu Tolgoi (OT) mine, among the world's largest untapped copper-gold deposits. However, a dispute with foreign investors developing OT called into question the attractiveness of Mongolia as a destination for foreign investment. This caused a severe drop in FDI, and a slowing economy, leading to the dismissal of Prime Minister Norovyn ALTANKHUYAG in November 2014. The economy had grown more than 10% per year between 2011 and 2013 - largely on the strength of commodity exports and high government spending - before slowing to 7.8% in 2014, and falling to the 2% level in 2015. Growth rebounded from a brief 1.6% contraction in the third quarter of 2016 to 5.8% during the first three quarters of 2017, largely due to rising commodity prices.

The May 2015 agreement with Rio Tinto to restart the OT mine and the subsequent $4.4 billion finance package signing in December 2015 stemmed the loss of investor confidence. The current government has made restoring investor trust and reviving the economy its top priority, but has failed to invigorate the economy in the face of the large drop-off in foreign direct investment, mounting external debt, and a sizeable budget deficit. Mongolia secured a $5.5 billion financial assistance package from the IMF and a host of international creditors in May 2017, which is expected to improve Mongolia's long-term fiscal and economic stability as long as Ulaanbaatar can advance the agreement's difficult contingent reforms, such as consolidating the government's off-balance sheet liabilities and rehabilitating the Mongolian banking sector.

GDP (PURCHASING POWER PARITY):

$39.73 billion (2017 est.)

$37.81 billion (2016 est.)

$37.38 billion (2015 est.)

note: data are in 2017 dollars

country comparison to the world: 120

GDP (OFFICIAL EXCHANGE RATE):

$11.14 billion (2017 est.)

GDP - REAL GROWTH RATE:

5.1% (2017 est.)

1.2% (2016 est.)

2.4% (2015 est.)

country comparison to the world: 48

GDP - PER CAPITA (PPP):

$13,000 (2017 est.)

$12,500 (2016 est.)

$12,600 (2015 est.)

note: data are in 2017 dollars

country comparison to the world: 120

GROSS NATIONAL SAVING:

26.9% of GDP (2017 est.)

23.1% of GDP (2016 est.)

22.4% of GDP (2015 est.)

country comparison to the world: 46

GDP - COMPOSITION, BY END USE:

household consumption: 49.2% (2017 est.)

government consumption: 12.3% (2017 est.)

investment in fixed capital: 23.8% (2017 est.)

investment in inventories: 12.4% (2017 est.)

exports of goods and services: 59.5% (2017 est.)

imports of goods and services: -57.1% (2017 est.)

GDP - COMPOSITION, BY SECTOR OF ORIGIN:

agriculture: 12.1% (2017 est.)

industry: 38.2% (2017 est.)

services: 49.7% (2017 est.)

AGRICULTURE - PRODUCTS:

wheat, barley, vegetables, forage crops; sheep, goats, cattle, camels, horses

INDUSTRIES:

construction and construction materials; mining (coal, copper, molybdenum, fluorspar, tin, tungsten, gold); oil; food and beverages; processing of animal products, cashmere and natural fiber manufacturing

INDUSTRIAL PRODUCTION GROWTH RATE:

-1% (2017 est.)

country comparison to the world: 176

LABOR FORCE:

1.241 million (2017 est.)

country comparison to the world: 137

LABOR FORCE - BY OCCUPATION:

agriculture: 31.1%

industry: 18.5%

services: 50.5% (2016)

UNEMPLOYMENT RATE:

8% (2017 est.)

7.9% (2016 est.)

country comparison to the world: 116

POPULATION BELOW POVERTY LINE:

29.6% (2016 est.)

HOUSEHOLD INCOME OR CONSUMPTION BY PERCENTAGE SHARE:

lowest 10%: 13.7%

highest 10%: 5.7% (2017)

DISTRIBUTION OF FAMILY INCOME - GINI INDEX:

34 (2017)

36.5 (2008)

country comparison to the world: 104

BUDGET:

revenues: 2.967 billion (2017 est.)

expenditures: 3.681 billion (2017 est.)

TAXES AND OTHER REVENUES:

26.6% (of GDP) (2017 est.)

country comparison to the world: 106

BUDGET SURPLUS (+) OR DEFICIT (-):

-6.4% (of GDP) (2017 est.)

country comparison to the world: 187

PUBLIC DEBT:

91.4% of GDP (2017 est.)

90% of GDP (2016 est.)

country comparison to the world: 24

FISCAL YEAR:

calendar year

INFLATION RATE (CONSUMER PRICES):

4.6% (2017 est.)

0.5% (2016 est.)

country comparison to the world: 169

CENTRAL BANK DISCOUNT RATE:

11% (25 December 2017)

14% (19 December 2016)

country comparison to the world: 19

COMMERCIAL BANK PRIME LENDING RATE:

20.01% (31 December 2017 est.)

19.74% (31 December 2016 est.)

country comparison to the world: 14

STOCK OF NARROW MONEY:

$1.164 billion (31 December 2017 est.)

$862.7 million (31 December 2016 est.)

country comparison to the world: 152

STOCK OF BROAD MONEY:

$1.164 billion (31 December 2017 est.)

$862.7 million (31 December 2016 est.)

country comparison to the world: 157

STOCK OF DOMESTIC CREDIT:

$7.542 billion (31 December 2017 est.)

$7.312 billion (31 December 2016 est.)

country comparison to the world: 117

MARKET VALUE OF PUBLICLY TRADED SHARES:

$632.6 million (31 December 2015 est.)

$766.1 million (31 December 2014 est.)

$1.095 billion (31 December 2013 est.)

country comparison to the world: 109

CURRENT ACCOUNT BALANCE:

-$1.155 billion (2017 est.)

-$700 million (2016 est.)

country comparison to the world: 146

EXPORTS:

$5.834 billion (2017 est.)

$4.916 billion (2016 est.)

country comparison to the world: 104

EXPORTS - PARTNERS:

China 85%, UK 10.7% (2017)

EXPORTS - COMMODITIES:

copper, apparel, livestock, animal products, cashmere, wool, hides, fluorspar, other nonferrous metals, coal, crude oil

IMPORTS:

$4.345 billion (2017 est.)

$3.466 billion (2016 est.)

country comparison to the world: 137

IMPORTS - COMMODITIES:

machinery and equipment, fuel, cars, food products, industrial consumer goods, chemicals, building materials, cigarettes and tobacco, appliances, soap and detergent

IMPORTS - PARTNERS:

China 32.6%, Russia 28.1%, Japan 8.4%, US 4.8%, South Korea 4.6% (2017)

RESERVES OF FOREIGN EXCHANGE AND GOLD:

$3.016 billion (31 December 2017 est.)

$1.296 billion (31 December 2016 est.)

country comparison to the world: 109
DEBT - EXTERNAL:
$25.33 billion (31 December 2017 est.)
$24.63 billion (31 December 2016 est.)
country comparison to the world: 88
STOCK OF DIRECT FOREIGN INVESTMENT - AT HOME:
$18.02 billion (31 December 2017 est.)
$16.28 billion (31 December 2016 est.)
country comparison to the world: 83
STOCK OF DIRECT FOREIGN INVESTMENT - ABROAD:
$495 million (31 December 2017 est.)
$455.2 million (31 December 2016 est.)
country comparison to the world: 97
EXCHANGE RATES:
togrog/tugriks (MNT) per US dollar -
2,378.1 (2017 est.)
2,140.3 (2016 est.)
2,140.3 (2015 est.)
1,970.3 (2014 est.)
1,817.9 (2013 est.)

ENERGY :: MONGOLIA

ELECTRICITY ACCESS:
electrification - total population: 81.8% (2016)
electrification - urban areas: 95.8% (2016)
electrification - rural areas: 44.2% (2016)
ELECTRICITY - PRODUCTION:
5.339 billion kWh (2016 est.)
country comparison to the world: 120
ELECTRICITY - CONSUMPTION:
5.932 billion kWh (2016 est.)
country comparison to the world: 115
ELECTRICITY - EXPORTS:
51 million kWh (2015 est.)
country comparison to the world: 87
ELECTRICITY - IMPORTS:
1.446 billion kWh (2016 est.)
country comparison to the world: 62
ELECTRICITY - INSTALLED GENERATING CAPACITY:
1.134 million kW (2016 est.)
country comparison to the world: 125
ELECTRICITY - FROM FOSSIL FUELS:
87% of total installed capacity (2016 est.)
country comparison to the world: 63

ELECTRICITY - FROM NUCLEAR FUELS:
0% of total installed capacity (2017 est.)
country comparison to the world: 145
ELECTRICITY - FROM HYDROELECTRIC PLANTS:
2% of total installed capacity (2017 est.)
country comparison to the world: 140
ELECTRICITY - FROM OTHER RENEWABLE SOURCES:
11% of total installed capacity (2017 est.)
country comparison to the world: 79
CRUDE OIL - PRODUCTION:
20,000 bbl/day (2018 est.)
country comparison to the world: 66
CRUDE OIL - EXPORTS:
14,360 bbl/day (2015 est.)
country comparison to the world: 56
CRUDE OIL - IMPORTS:
0 bbl/day (2015 est.)
country comparison to the world: 168
CRUDE OIL - PROVED RESERVES:
NA bbl (1 January 2017)
REFINED PETROLEUM PRODUCTS - PRODUCTION:
0 bbl/day (2015 est.)
country comparison to the world: 179
REFINED PETROLEUM PRODUCTS - CONSUMPTION:
27,000 bbl/day (2016 est.)
country comparison to the world: 124
REFINED PETROLEUM PRODUCTS - EXPORTS:
0 bbl/day (2015 est.)
country comparison to the world: 183
REFINED PETROLEUM PRODUCTS - IMPORTS:
24,190 bbl/day (2015 est.)
country comparison to the world: 109
NATURAL GAS - PRODUCTION:
0 cu m (2017 est.)
country comparison to the world: 172
NATURAL GAS - CONSUMPTION:
0 cu m (2017 est.)
country comparison to the world: 176
NATURAL GAS - EXPORTS:
0 cu m (2017 est.)
country comparison to the world: 153
NATURAL GAS - IMPORTS:
0 cu m (2017 est.)
country comparison to the world: 158
NATURAL GAS - PROVED RESERVES:

0 cu m (1 January 2014 est.)
country comparison to the world: 171
CARBON DIOXIDE EMISSIONS FROM CONSUMPTION OF ENERGY:
19.86 million Mt (2017 est.)
country comparison to the world: 86

COMMUNICATIONS :: MONGOLIA

TELEPHONES - FIXED LINES:
total subscriptions: 292,594
subscriptions per 100 inhabitants: 10 (2017 est.)
country comparison to the world: 114
TELEPHONES - MOBILE CELLULAR:
total subscriptions: 3,886,167
subscriptions per 100 inhabitants: 127 (2017 est.)
country comparison to the world: 129
TELEPHONE SYSTEM:
general assessment: network is improving with international direct dialing available in many areas; a fiber-optic network has been installed that is improving broadband and communication services between major urban centers with multiple companies providing inter-city fiber-optic cable services; compared to other Asian countries, Mongolia's growth in telecommunications is moderate; mobile broadband is growing with 4 competitive MNOs (mobile network operators) along with better tarrifs; 3G mobile broadband products are very popular with 4G services by 2022; in May 2018 a South Korean company completed the sale of 40% stake back to Mongolian government (2018)
domestic: very low fixed-line teledensity 10 per 100; there are four mobile-cellular providers and subscribership is increasing with 131 per 100 persons (2018)
international: country code - 976; satellite earth stations - 7 (2016)
BROADCAST MEDIA:
following a law passed in 2005, Mongolia's state-run radio and TV provider converted to a public service provider; also available are 68 radio and 160 TV stations, including multi-channel satellite and cable TV providers; transmissions of multiple international broadcasters are available (2019)
INTERNET COUNTRY CODE:
.mn
INTERNET USERS:
total: 674,949

percent of population: 22.3% (July 2016 est.)

country comparison to the world: 142

BROADBAND - FIXED SUBSCRIPTIONS:

total: 285,093

subscriptions per 100 inhabitants: 9 (2017 est.)

country comparison to the world: 98

MILITARY AND SECURITY :: MONGOLIA

MILITARY EXPENDITURES:

0.68% of GDP (2018)

0.72% of GDP (2017)

0.92% of GDP (2016)

0.87% of GDP (2015)

0.86% of GDP (2014)

country comparison to the world: 136

MILITARY AND SECURITY FORCES:

Mongolian Armed Forces (Mongol ulsyn zevsegt huchin): Mongolian Army, Mongolian Air Force (2019)

MILITARY SERVICE AGE AND OBLIGATION:

18-27 years of age for compulsory and voluntary military service; 1-year conscript service obligation in army or air forces or police for males only; after conscription, soldiers can contract into military service for 2 or 4 years; citizens can also voluntarily join the armed forces (2017)

MILITARY - NOTE:

The Mongolian Armed Forces also includes a National Center for Emergency and Disaster Relief to coordinate the military's efforts as first-responders for earthquakes, wildfires, and forest fires; contagious diseases; and snow and dust storms as well as severe winters (known as *zud*).

Paramilitary forces: Border Guards, Internal Security Troops (2017)

TRANSPORTATION :: MONGOLIA

NATIONAL AIR TRANSPORT SYSTEM:

number of registered air carriers: 3 (2015)

inventory of registered aircraft operated by air carriers: 12 (2015)

annual passenger traffic on registered air carriers: 541,129 (2015)

annual freight traffic on registered air carriers: 7,130,148 mt-km (2015)

CIVIL AIRCRAFT REGISTRATION COUNTRY CODE PREFIX:

JU (2016)

AIRPORTS:

44 (2013)

country comparison to the world: 98

AIRPORTS - WITH PAVED RUNWAYS:

total: 15 (2017)

over 3,047 m: 2 (2017)

2,438 to 3,047 m: 10 (2017)

1,524 to 2,437 m: 3 (2017)

AIRPORTS - WITH UNPAVED RUNWAYS:

total: 29 (2013)

over 3,047 m: 2 (2013)

2,438 to 3,047 m: 2 (2013)

1,524 to 2,437 m: 24 (2013)

under 914 m: 1 (2013)

HELIPORTS:

1 (2013)

RAILWAYS:

total: 1,815 km (2017)

broad gauge: 1,815 km 1.520-m gauge (2017)

note: national operator Ulaanbaatar Railway is jointly owned by the Mongolian Government and by the Russian State Railway

country comparison to the world: 78

ROADWAYS:

total: 113,200 km (2017)

paved: 10,600 km (2017)

unpaved: 102,600 km (2017)

country comparison to the world: 44

WATERWAYS:

580 km (the only waterway in operation is Lake Hovsgol) (135 km); Selenge River (270 km) and Orhon River (175 km) are navigable but carry little traffic; lakes and rivers ice free from May to September) (2010)

country comparison to the world: 81

MERCHANT MARINE:

total: 265

by type: bulk carrier 4, container ship 3, general cargo 107, oil tanker 68, other 83 (2018)

country comparison to the world: 55

TRANSNATIONAL ISSUES :: MONGOLIA

DISPUTES - INTERNATIONAL:

none

REFUGEES AND INTERNALLY DISPLACED PERSONS:

stateless persons: 17 (2018)

EUROPE :: MONTENEGRO

INTRODUCTION :: MONTENEGRO

BACKGROUND:

The use of the name Crna Gora or Black Mountain (Montenegro) began in the 13th century in reference to a highland region in the Serbian province of Zeta. The later medieval state of Zeta maintained its existence until 1496 when Montenegro finally fell under Ottoman rule. Over subsequent centuries, Montenegro managed to maintain a level of autonomy within the Ottoman Empire. From the 16th to 19th centuries, Montenegro was a theocracy ruled by a series of bishop princes; in 1852, it transformed into a secular principality. Montenegro was recognized as an independent sovereign principality at the Congress of Berlin in 1878. After World War I, during which Montenegro fought on the side of the Allies, Montenegro was absorbed by the Kingdom of Serbs, Croats, and Slovenes, which became the Kingdom of Yugoslavia in 1929. At the conclusion of World War II, it became a constituent republic of the Socialist Federal Republic of Yugoslavia. When the latter dissolved in 1992, Montenegro joined with Serbia, creating the Federal Republic of Yugoslavia and, after 2003, shifting to a looser State Union of Serbia and Montenegro. In May 2006, Montenegro invoked its right under the Constitutional Charter of Serbia and Montenegro to hold a referendum on independence from the two-state union. The vote for severing ties with Serbia barely exceeded 55% - the threshold set by the EU - allowing Montenegro to formally restore its independence on 3 June 2006. In 2017, Montenegro joined NATO and is currently completing its EU accession process, having officially applied to join the EU in December 2008.

GEOGRAPHY :: MONTENEGRO

LOCATION:
Southeastern Europe, between the Adriatic Sea and Serbia

GEOGRAPHIC COORDINATES:
42 30 N, 19 18 E

MAP REFERENCES:
Europe

AREA:
total: 13,812 sq km

land: 13,452 sq km

water: 360 sq km

country comparison to the world: 162

AREA - COMPARATIVE:
slightly smaller than Connecticut; slightly larger than twice the size of Delaware

LAND BOUNDARIES:
total: 680 km

border countries (5): Albania 186 km, Bosnia and Herzegovina 242 km, Croatia 19 km, Kosovo 76 km, Serbia 157 km

COASTLINE:
293.5 km

MARITIME CLAIMS:
territorial sea: 12 nm

continental shelf: defined by treaty

CLIMATE:
Mediterranean climate, hot dry summers and autumns and relatively cold winters with heavy snowfalls inland

TERRAIN:
highly indented coastline with narrow coastal plain backed by rugged high limestone mountains and plateaus

ELEVATION:
mean elevation: 1,086 m

lowest point: Adriatic Sea 0 m

highest point: Bobotov Kuk 2,522 m

NATURAL RESOURCES:
bauxite, hydroelectricity

LAND USE:
agricultural land: 38.2% (2011 est.)

arable land: 12.9% (2011 est.) / permanent crops: 1.2% (2011 est.) / permanent pasture: 24.1% (2011 est.)

forest: 40.4% (2011 est.)

other: 21.4% (2011 est.)

IRRIGATED LAND:
24 sq km (2012)

POPULATION DISTRIBUTION:
highest population density is concentrated in the south, southwest; the extreme eastern border is the least populated area

NATURAL HAZARDS:
destructive earthquakes

ENVIRONMENT - CURRENT ISSUES:
pollution of coastal waters from sewage outlets, especially in tourist-related areas such as Kotor; serious air pollution in Podgorica, Pljevlja and Niksie; air pollution in Pljevlja is caused by the nearby lignite power plant and the domestic use of coal and wood for household heating

ENVIRONMENT - INTERNATIONAL AGREEMENTS:

party to: Air Pollution, Biodiversity, Climate Change, Climate Change-Kyoto Protocol, Desertification, Hazardous Wastes, Law of the Sea, Marine Dumping, Marine Life Conservation, Ozone Layer Protection, Ship Pollution

signed, but not ratified: none of the selected agreements

GEOGRAPHY - NOTE:
strategic location along the Adriatic coast

PEOPLE AND SOCIETY :: MONTENEGRO

POPULATION:
614,249 (July 2018 est.)

country comparison to the world: 169

NATIONALITY:
noun: Montenegrin(s)

adjective: Montenegrin

ETHNIC GROUPS:
Montenegrin 45%, Serbian 28.7%, Bosniak 8.7%, Albanian 4.9%, Muslim 3.3%, Romani 1%, Croat 1%, other 2.6%, unspecified 4.9% (2011 est.)

LANGUAGES:
Serbian 42.9%, Montenegrin (official) 37%, Bosnian 5.3%, Albanian 5.3%, Serbo-Croat 2%, other 3.5%, unspecified 4% (2011 est.)

RELIGIONS:
Orthodox 72.1%, Muslim 19.1%, Catholic 3.4%, atheist 1.2%, other 1.5%, unspecified 2.6% (2011 est.)

AGE STRUCTURE:
0-14 years: 18.22% (male 58,219 /female 53,718)

15-24 years: 13.05% (male 41,406 /female 38,755)

25-54 years: 40.16% (male 122,940 /female 123,746)

55-64 years: 13.47% (male 40,661 /female 42,089)

65 years and over: 15.09% (male 39,899 /female 52,816) (2018 est.)

DEPENDENCY RATIOS:
total dependency ratio: 47.8 (2015 est.)

youth dependency ratio: 27.3 (2015 est.)

elderly dependency ratio: 20.5 (2015 est.)

potential support ratio: 4.9 (2015 est.)

MEDIAN AGE:
total: 38.9 years (2018 est.)

male: 37.4 years

female: 40.4 years

country comparison to the world: 57

POPULATION GROWTH RATE:
-0.34% (2018 est.)

country comparison to the world: 218

BIRTH RATE:
11.9 births/1,000 population (2018 est.)

country comparison to the world: 168

DEATH RATE:
10.4 deaths/1,000 population (2018 est.)

country comparison to the world: 30

NET MIGRATION RATE:
-4.9 migrant(s)/1,000 population (2018 est.)

country comparison to the world: 193

POPULATION DISTRIBUTION:
highest population density is concentrated in the south, southwest; the extreme eastern border is the least populated area

URBANIZATION:
urban population: 67.2% of total population (2019)

rate of urbanization: 0.54% annual rate of change (2015-20 est.)

MAJOR URBAN AREAS - POPULATION:
177,000 PODGORICA (capital) (2018)

SEX RATIO:
at birth: 1.04 male(s)/female

0-14 years: 1.08 male(s)/female

15-24 years: 1.07 male(s)/female

25-54 years: 0.99 male(s)/female

55-64 years: 0.97 male(s)/female

65 years and over: 0.76 male(s)/female

total population: 0.97 male(s)/female (2018 est.)

MOTHER'S MEAN AGE AT FIRST BIRTH:
26.3 years (2010 est.)

MATERNAL MORTALITY RATE:
6 deaths/100,000 live births (2017 est.)

country comparison to the world: 162

CONTRACEPTIVE PREVALENCE RATE:
23.3% (2013)

DRINKING WATER SOURCE:
improved:

urban: 100% of population

rural: 99.2% of population

total: 99.7% of population

unimproved:

urban: 0% of population

rural: 0.8% of population

total: 0.3% of population (2015 est.)

CURRENT HEALTH EXPENDITURE:
7.6% (2016)

PHYSICIANS DENSITY:
2.33 physicians/1,000 population (2015)

HOSPITAL BED DENSITY:
4 beds/1,000 population (2012)

SANITATION FACILITY ACCESS:
improved:

urban: 98% of population (2015 est.)

rural: 92.2% of population (2015 est.)

total: 95.9% of population (2015 est.)

unimproved:

urban: 2% of population (2015 est.)

rural: 7.8% of population (2015 est.)

total: 4.1% of population (2015 est.)

HIV/AIDS - ADULT PREVALENCE RATE:
0.1% (2018 est.)

country comparison to the world: 127

HIV/AIDS - PEOPLE LIVING WITH HIV/AIDS:
<500 (2018 est.)

HIV/AIDS - DEATHS:
<100 (2018 est.)

MAJOR INFECTIOUS DISEASES:
degree of risk: intermediate (2016)

food or waterborne diseases: bacterial diarrhea (2016)

vectorborne diseases: Crimean-Congo hemorrhagic fever (2016)

OBESITY - ADULT PREVALENCE RATE:
23.3% (2016)

country comparison to the world: 66

CHILDREN UNDER THE AGE OF 5 YEARS UNDERWEIGHT:
1% (2013)

country comparison to the world: 122

EDUCATION EXPENDITURES:

NA

LITERACY:

definition: age 15 and over can read and write

total population: 98.7%

male: 99.5%

female: 98% (2015 est.)

SCHOOL LIFE EXPECTANCY (PRIMARY TO TERTIARY EDUCATION):

total: 15 years

male: 15 years

female: 15 years (2017)

UNEMPLOYMENT, YOUTH AGES 15-24:

total: 31.7%

male: 30.7%

female: 33.1% (2017 est.)

country comparison to the world: 28

GOVERNMENT :: MONTENEGRO

COUNTRY NAME:

conventional long form: none

conventional short form: Montenegro

local long form: none

local short form: Crna Gora

former: People's Republic of Montenegro, Socialist Republic of Montenegro, Republic of Montenegro

etymology: the country's name locally as well as in most Western European languages means "black mountain" and refers to the dark coniferous forests on Mount Lovcen and the surrounding area

GOVERNMENT TYPE:

parliamentary republic

CAPITAL:

name: Podgorica; note - Cetinje retains the status of "Old Royal Capital"

geographic coordinates: 42 26 N, 19 16 E

time difference: UTC+1 (6 hours ahead of Washington, DC, during Standard Time)

daylight saving time: +1 hr, begins last Sunday in March; ends last Sunday in October

etymology: the name translates as "beneath Gorica"; the meaning of Gorica is "hillock"; the reference is to the small hill named Gorica that the city is built around

ADMINISTRATIVE DIVISIONS:

24 municipalities (opstine, singular - opstina); Andrijevica, Bar, Berane, Bijelo Polje, Budva, Cetinje, Danilovgrad, Gusinje, Herceg-Novi, Kolasin, Kotor, Mojkovac, Niksic, Petnijica, Plav, Pljevlja, Pluzine, Podgorica, Rozaje, Savnik, Tivat, Tuzi, Ulcinj, Zabljak

INDEPENDENCE:

3 June 2006 (from the State Union of Serbia and Montenegro); notable earlier dates: 13 March 1852 (Principality of Montenegro established); 13 July 1878 (Congress of Berlin recognizes Montenegrin independence); 28 August 1910 (Kingdom of Montenegro established)

NATIONAL HOLIDAY:

National Day, 13 July (1878, the day the Berlin Congress recognized Montenegro as the 27th independent state in the world, and 1941, the day the Montenegrins staged an uprising against fascist occupiers and sided with the partisan communist movement)

CONSTITUTION:

history: several previous; latest adopted 22 October 2007

amendments: proposed by the president of Montenegro, by the government, or by at least 25 members of the Assembly; passage of draft proposals requires two-thirds majority vote of the Assembly, followed by a public hearing; passage of draft amendments requires two-thirds majority vote of the Assembly; changes to certain constitutional articles, such as sovereignty, state symbols, citizenship, and constitutional change procedures, require three-fifths majority vote in a referendum; amended 2013, 2014 (2016)

LEGAL SYSTEM:

civil law

INTERNATIONAL LAW ORGANIZATION PARTICIPATION:

has not submitted an ICJ jurisdiction declaration; accepts ICCt jurisdiction

CITIZENSHIP:

citizenship by birth: no

citizenship by descent only: at least one parent must be a citizen of Montenegro

dual citizenship recognized: no

residency requirement for naturalization: 10 years

SUFFRAGE:

18 years of age; universal

EXECUTIVE BRANCH:

chief of state: President Milo DJUKANOVIC (since 20 May 2018)

head of government: Prime Minister Dusko MARKOVIC (since 28 November 2016)

cabinet: Ministers act as cabinet

elections/appointments: president directly elected by absolute majority popular vote in 2 rounds if needed for a 5-year term (eligible for a second term); election last held on 15 April 2018 (next to be held in 2023); prime minister nominated by the president, approved by the Assembly

election results: Milo DJUKANOVIC elected president in the first round; percent of vote - Milo DJUKANOVIC (DPS) 53.9%, Mladen BOJANIC (independent) 33.4%, Draginja VUKSANOVIC (SDP) 8.2%, Marko MILACIC (PRAVA) 2.8%, other 1.7%

LEGISLATIVE BRANCH:

description: unicameral Assembly or Skupstina (81 seats; members directly elected in a single nationwide constituency by proportional representation vote; members serve 4-year terms)

elections: last held on 16 October 2016 (next to be held by October 2020)

election results: percent of vote by party/coalition - DPS 41.4%, DF 20.3%, Key Coalition, 11.1%, DCG 10.0%, SDP 5.2%, SD 3.3%, BS, 3.2%, Albanians Decisively 1.3%, HGI .5%, other 3.7%; seats by party/coalition - DPS 36, DF 18, Key Coalition 9, DCG 8, SDP 4, SD 2, BS 2, Albanians Decisively 1, HGI 1; composition - men 62, women 19, percent of women 23.5%

JUDICIAL BRANCH:

highest courts: Supreme Court or Vrhovni Sud (consists of the court president, deputy president, and 15 judges); Constitutional Court or Ustavni Sud (consists of the court president and 7 judges)

judge selection and term of office: Supreme Court president proposed by general session of the Supreme Court and elected by the Judicial Council, a 9-member body consisting of judges, lawyers designated by the Assembly, and the minister of judicial affairs;

Supreme Court president elected for a single renewable, 5-year term; other judges elected by the Judicial Council for life; Constitutional Court judges - 2 proposed by the president of Montenegro and 5 by the Assembly, and elected by the Assembly; court president elected from among the court members; court president elected for a 3-year term, other judges serve 9-year terms

subordinate courts: Administrative Courts; Appellate Court; Commercial Courts; High Courts; basic courts

POLITICAL PARTIES AND LEADERS:

Albanians Decisively [Genci NIMANBEGU] (electoral coalition included FORCA, AA, DUA)
Albanian Alternative or AA [Nik DJELOSAJ]
Bosniak Party or BS [Rafet HUSOVIC]
Croatian Civic Initiative or HGI [Marija VUCINOVIC]
Democratic Alliance or DEMOS [Miodrag LEKIC]
Democratic Front or DF [collective leadership] (coalition includes NOVA, PZP, DNP, RP)
Democratic Montenegro or DCG [Aleksa BECIC]
Democratic Party of Socialists or DPS [Milo DJUKANOVIC]
Democratic People's Party or DNP [Milan KNEZEVIC]
Democratic Union of Albanians or DUA [Mehmet ZENKA]
Key Coalition [Miodrag LEKIC] (includes DEMOS, SNP, URA]
Liberal Party or LP [Andrija POPOVIC]
Movement for Change or PZP [Nebojsa MEDOJEVIC]
New Democratic Power or FORCA [Nazif CUNGU]
New Serb Democracy or NOVA [Andrija MANDIC]
Social Democratic Party or SDP [Ranko KRIVOKAPIC]
Social Democrats or SD [Ivan BRAJOVIC]
Socialist People's Party or SNP [Vladimir JOKOVIC]
True Montenegro or PRAVA [Marko MILACIC]
United Montenegro or UCG [Goran DANILOVIC] (split from DEMOS)
United Reform Action or URA [Dritan ABAZOVIC]
Workers' Party or RP [Janko VUCINIC]

INTERNATIONAL ORGANIZATION PARTICIPATION:

CE, CEI, EAPC, EBRD, FAO, IAEA, IBRD, ICAO, ICC (NGOs), ICCt, ICRM, IDA, IFC, IFRCS, IHO, ILO, IMF, IMO, IMSO, Interpol, IOC, IOM, IPU, ISO (correspondent), ITSO, ITU, ITUC (NGOs), MIGA, OAS (observer), OIF (observer), OPCW, OSCE, PCA, PFP, SELEC, UN, UNCTAD, UNESCO, UNHCR, UNIDO, UNWTO, UPU, WCO, WHO, WIPO, WMO, WTO

DIPLOMATIC REPRESENTATION IN THE US:

Ambassador Nebojsa KALUDEROVIC (since 18 January 2017)

chancery: 1610 New Hampshire Avenue NW, Washington, DC, 20009

telephone: [1] (202) 234-6108

FAX: [1] (202) 234-6109

consulate(s) general: New York

DIPLOMATIC REPRESENTATION FROM THE US:

chief of mission: Ambassador Judy Rising REINKE (since 20 December 2018)

telephone: [382] 20-410-500

embassy: Dzona Dzeksona 2, 81000 Podgorica, Montenegro

mailing address: use embassy street address

FAX: [382] 20-241-358

FLAG DESCRIPTION:

a red field bordered by a narrow golden-yellow stripe with the Montenegrin coat of arms centered; the arms consist of a double-headed golden eagle - symbolizing the unity of church and state - surmounted by a crown; the eagle holds a golden scepter in its right claw and a blue orb in its left; the breast shield over the eagle shows a golden lion passant on a green field in front of a blue sky; the lion is a symbol of episcopal authority and harkens back to the three and a half centuries when Montenegro was ruled as a theocracy

NATIONAL SYMBOL(S):

double-headed eagle; national colors: red, gold

NATIONAL ANTHEM:

name: "Oj, svijetla majska zoro" (Oh, Bright Dawn of May)

lyrics/music: Sekula DRLJEVIC/unknown, arranged by Zarko MIKOVIC

note: adopted 2004; music based on a Montenegrin folk song

ECONOMY :: MONTENEGRO

ECONOMY - OVERVIEW:

Montenegro's economy is transitioning to a market system. Around 90% of Montenegrin state-owned companies have been privatized, including 100% of banking, telecommunications, and oil distribution. Tourism, which accounts for more than 20% of Montenegro's GDP, brings in three times as many visitors as Montenegro's total population every year. Several new luxury tourism complexes are in various stages of development along the coast, and a number are being offered in connection with nearby boating and yachting facilities. In addition to tourism, energy and agriculture are considered two distinct pillars of the economy. Only 20% of Montenegro's hydropower potential is utilized. Montenegro plans to become a net energy exporter, and the construction of an underwater cable to Italy, which will be completed by the end of 2018, will help meet its goal.

Montenegro uses the euro as its domestic currency, though it is not an official member of the euro zone. In January 2007, Montenegro joined the World Bank and IMF, and in December 2011, the WTO. Montenegro began negotiations to join the EU in 2012, having met the conditions set down by the European Council, which called on Montenegro to take steps to fight corruption and organized crime.

The government recognizes the need to remove impediments in order to remain competitive and open the economy to foreign investors. Net foreign direct investment in 2017 reached $848 million and investment per capita is one of the highest in Europe, due to a low corporate tax rate. The biggest foreign investors in Montenegro in 2017 were Norway, Russia, Italy, Azerbaijan and Hungary.

Montenegro is currently planning major overhauls of its road and rail networks, and possible expansions of its air transportation system. In 2014, the Government of Montenegro selected two Chinese companies to construct a 41 km-long section of the country's highway system, which will become part of China's Belt and Road Initiative. Cheaper borrowing costs have stimulated Montenegro's growing debt, which currently sits at 65.9% of GDP, with a forecast, absent fiscal consolidation, to increase to 80% once the repayment to China's Ex/Im Bank of a €800 million highway loan begins in 2019. Montenegro first instituted a value-added tax (VAT) in April 2003, and introduced differentiated VAT rates of 17% and 7% (for tourism) in January 2006. The Montenegrin Government increased the non-tourism Value Added Tax (VAT) rate to 21% as of January 2018, with the goal of reducing its public debt.

GDP (PURCHASING POWER PARITY):

$11.08 billion (2017 est.)

$10.63 billion (2016 est.)

$10.32 billion (2015 est.)

note: data are in 2017 dollars

country comparison to the world: 160

GDP (OFFICIAL EXCHANGE RATE):

$4.784 billion (2017 est.)

GDP - REAL GROWTH RATE:

4.3% (2017 est.)

2.9% (2016 est.)

3.4% (2015 est.)

country comparison to the world: 69

GDP - PER CAPITA (PPP):

$17,800 (2017 est.)

$17,100 (2016 est.)

$16,600 (2015 est.)

note: data are in 2017 dollars

country comparison to the world: 99

GROSS NATIONAL SAVING:

13.2% of GDP (2017 est.)

9.9% of GDP (2016 est.)

9.1% of GDP (2015 est.)

country comparison to the world: 144

GDP - COMPOSITION, BY END USE:

household consumption: 76.8% (2016 est.)

government consumption: 19.6% (2016 est.)

investment in fixed capital: 23.2% (2016 est.)

investment in inventories: 2.9% (2016 est.)

exports of goods and services: 40.5% (2016 est.)

imports of goods and services: -63% (2016 est.)

GDP - COMPOSITION, BY SECTOR OF ORIGIN:

agriculture: 7.5% (2016 est.)

industry: 15.9% (2016 est.)

services: 76.6% (2016 est.)

AGRICULTURE - PRODUCTS:

tobacco, potatoes, citrus fruits, olives and related products, grapes; sheep, wine

INDUSTRIES:

steelmaking, aluminum, agricultural processing, consumer goods, tourism

INDUSTRIAL PRODUCTION GROWTH RATE:

-4.2% (2017 est.)

country comparison to the world: 194

LABOR FORCE:

273,200 (2017 est.)

country comparison to the world: 167

LABOR FORCE - BY OCCUPATION:

agriculture: 7.9%

industry: 17.1%

services: 75% (2017 est.)

UNEMPLOYMENT RATE:

16.1% (2017 est.)

17.1% (2016 est.)

country comparison to the world: 176

POPULATION BELOW POVERTY LINE:

8.6% (2013 est.)

HOUSEHOLD INCOME OR CONSUMPTION BY PERCENTAGE SHARE:

lowest 10%: 3.5%

highest 10%: 25.7% (2014 est.)

DISTRIBUTION OF FAMILY INCOME - GINI INDEX:

31.9 (2014 est.)

32.3 (2013 est.)

country comparison to the world: 122

BUDGET:

revenues: 1.78 billion (2017 est.)

expenditures: 2.05 billion (2017 est.)

TAXES AND OTHER REVENUES:

37.2% (of GDP) (2017 est.)

country comparison to the world: 55

BUDGET SURPLUS (+) OR DEFICIT (-):

-5.6% (of GDP) (2017 est.)

country comparison to the world: 175

PUBLIC DEBT:

67.2% of GDP (2017 est.)

66.4% of GDP (2016 est.)

note: data cover general government debt, and includes debt instruments issued (or owned) by government entities other than the treasury; the data include treasury debt held by foreign entities; the data include debt issued by subnational entities, as well as intragovernmental debt; intragovernmental debt consists of treasury borrowings from surpluses in the social funds, such as for retirement, medical care, and unemployment; debt instruments for the social funds are not sold at public auctions

country comparison to the world: 55

FISCAL YEAR:

calendar year

INFLATION RATE (CONSUMER PRICES):

2.4% (2017 est.)

-0.3% (2016 est.)

country comparison to the world: 120

COMMERCIAL BANK PRIME LENDING RATE:

6.81% (31 December 2017 est.)

7.45% (31 December 2016 est.)

country comparison to the world: 123

STOCK OF NARROW MONEY:

$1.284 billion (31 December 2016 est.)

$1.072 billion (31 December 2015 est.)

country comparison to the world: 150

STOCK OF BROAD MONEY:

$2.37 billion (31 December 2016 est.)

$2.235 billion (31 December 2015 est.)

country comparison to the world: 137

STOCK OF DOMESTIC CREDIT:

$3.239 billion (31 December 2017 est.)

$2.547 billion (31 December 2016 est.)

country comparison to the world: 137

MARKET VALUE OF PUBLICLY TRADED SHARES:

$3.425 billion (31 December 2017 est.)

$3.027 billion (31 December 2016 est.)

$3.246 billion (31 December 2015 est.)

country comparison to the world: 90

CURRENT ACCOUNT BALANCE:

-$780 million (2017 est.)

-$710 million (2016 est.)

country comparison to the world: 133

EXPORTS:

$422.2 million (2017 est.)

$362 million (2016 est.)

country comparison to the world: 181

IMPORTS:

$2.618 billion (2017 est.)

$2.29 billion (2016 est.)

country comparison to the world: 155

RESERVES OF FOREIGN EXCHANGE AND GOLD:

$1.077 billion (31 December 2017 est.)

$846.5 million (31 December 2016 est.)

country comparison to the world: 131

DEBT - EXTERNAL:

$2.516 billion (31 December 2017 est.)

$2.224 billion (31 December 2016 est.)

country comparison to the world: 149

STOCK OF DIRECT FOREIGN INVESTMENT - AT HOME:

$737.7 million (31 December 2017 est.)

$763.4 million (31 December 2016 est.)

country comparison to the world: 125

STOCK OF DIRECT FOREIGN INVESTMENT - ABROAD:

$39.77 million (31 December 2017 est.)

$213.1 million (31 December 2016 est.)

country comparison to the world: 115

EXCHANGE RATES:

euros (EUR) per US dollar -

0.885 (2017 est.)

0.903 (2016 est.)

0.9214 (2015 est.)

0.885 (2014 est.)

0.7634 (2013 est.)

ENERGY :: MONTENEGRO

ELECTRICITY ACCESS:

electrification - total population: 100% (2016)

ELECTRICITY - PRODUCTION:

3.045 billion kWh (2016 est.)

country comparison to the world: 132

ELECTRICITY - CONSUMPTION:

2.808 billion kWh (2016 est.)

country comparison to the world: 138

ELECTRICITY - EXPORTS:

914 million kWh (2016 est.)

country comparison to the world: 59

ELECTRICITY - IMPORTS:

1.21 billion kWh (2016 est.)

country comparison to the world: 65

ELECTRICITY - INSTALLED GENERATING CAPACITY:

890,000 kW (2016 est.)

country comparison to the world: 133

ELECTRICITY - FROM FOSSIL FUELS:

23% of total installed capacity (2016 est.)

country comparison to the world: 192

ELECTRICITY - FROM NUCLEAR FUELS:

0% of total installed capacity (2017 est.)

country comparison to the world: 146

ELECTRICITY - FROM HYDROELECTRIC PLANTS:

69% of total installed capacity (2017 est.)

country comparison to the world: 18

ELECTRICITY - FROM OTHER RENEWABLE SOURCES:

8% of total installed capacity (2017 est.)

country comparison to the world: 88

CRUDE OIL - PRODUCTION:

0 bbl/day (2018 est.)

country comparison to the world: 176

CRUDE OIL - EXPORTS:

0 bbl/day (2015 est.)

country comparison to the world: 167

CRUDE OIL - IMPORTS:

0 bbl/day (2015 est.)

country comparison to the world: 169

CRUDE OIL - PROVED RESERVES:

0 bbl (1 January 2018 est.)

country comparison to the world: 171

REFINED PETROLEUM PRODUCTS - PRODUCTION:

0 bbl/day (2015 est.)

country comparison to the world: 180

REFINED PETROLEUM PRODUCTS - CONSUMPTION:

6,000 bbl/day (2016 est.)

country comparison to the world: 172

REFINED PETROLEUM PRODUCTS - EXPORTS:

357 bbl/day (2015 est.)

country comparison to the world: 114

REFINED PETROLEUM PRODUCTS - IMPORTS:

6,448 bbl/day (2015 est.)

country comparison to the world: 163

NATURAL GAS - PRODUCTION:

0 cu m (2017 est.)

country comparison to the world: 173

NATURAL GAS - CONSUMPTION:

0 cu m (2017 est.)

country comparison to the world: 177

NATURAL GAS - EXPORTS:

0 cu m (2017 est.)

country comparison to the world: 154

NATURAL GAS - IMPORTS:

0 cu m (2017 est.)

country comparison to the world: 159

NATURAL GAS - PROVED RESERVES:

0 cu m (2016 est.)

country comparison to the world: 172

CARBON DIOXIDE EMISSIONS FROM CONSUMPTION OF ENERGY:

2.287 million Mt (2017 est.)

country comparison to the world: 156

COMMUNICATIONS :: MONTENEGRO

TELEPHONES - FIXED LINES:

total subscriptions: 152,155

subscriptions per 100 inhabitants: 24 (2017 est.)

country comparison to the world: 128

TELEPHONES - MOBILE CELLULAR:

total subscriptions: 1,044,674

subscriptions per 100 inhabitants: 163 (2017 est.)

country comparison to the world: 158

TELEPHONE SYSTEM:

general assessment: modern telecommunications system with access to European satellites; telecom sector in-line with EU norms which means competition, access and tariff structures; DSL, cable, leased line, fiber and wireless; seasonal tourist have boosted mobile penetration; LTE technologies available (2018)

domestic: GSM mobile-cellular service, available through multiple providers with national coverage, is growing; fixed-line 24 per 100 and mobile-cellular 163 per 100 persons (2018)

international: country code - 382; 2 international switches connect the national system

BROADCAST MEDIA:

state-funded national radio-TV broadcaster operates 2 terrestrial TV networks, 1 satellite TV channel, and 2 radio networks; 4 local public TV stations and 14 private TV stations; 14 local public radio stations, 35 private radio stations, and several on-line media (2019)

INTERNET COUNTRY CODE:

.me

INTERNET USERS:

total: 450,442

percent of population: 69.9% (July 2016 est.)

country comparison to the world: 150

BROADBAND - FIXED SUBSCRIPTIONS:

total: 137,426

subscriptions per 100 inhabitants: 21 (2017 est.)

country comparison to the world: 115

MILITARY AND SECURITY :: MONTENEGRO

MILITARY EXPENDITURES:

1.67% of GDP (2019 est.)

1.7% of GDP (2018)

1.66% of GDP (2017)

1.61% of GDP (2016)

1.38% of GDP (2015)

country comparison to the world: 69

MILITARY AND SECURITY FORCES:

Armed Forces of the Republic of Montenegro: Army of Montenegro (includes Ground Troops (Kopnena Vojska), Montenegrin Navy (Mornarica Crne Gore, MCG)), Air Force (2019)

MILITARY SERVICE AGE AND OBLIGATION:

18 is the legal minimum age for voluntary military service; no conscription (2012)

TRANSPORTATION :: MONTENEGRO

NATIONAL AIR TRANSPORT SYSTEM:

number of registered air carriers: 1 (2015)

inventory of registered aircraft operated by air carriers: 6 (2015)

annual passenger traffic on registered air carriers: 526,980 (2015)

annual freight traffic on registered air carriers: 0 mt-km (2015)

CIVIL AIRCRAFT REGISTRATION COUNTRY CODE PREFIX:

4O (2016)

AIRPORTS:

5 (2013)

country comparison to the world: 181

AIRPORTS - WITH PAVED RUNWAYS:

total: 5 (2017)

2,438 to 3,047 m: 2 (2017)

1,524 to 2,437 m: 1 (2017)

914 to 1,523 m: 1 (2017)

under 914 m: 1 (2017)

HELIPORTS:

1 (2012)

RAILWAYS:

total: 250 km (2017)

standard gauge: 250 km 1.435-m gauge (224 km electrified) (2017)

country comparison to the world: 125

ROADWAYS:

total: 7,762 km (2010)

paved: 7,141 km (2010)

unpaved: 621 km (2010)

country comparison to the world: 134

MERCHANT MARINE:

total: 12

by type: bulk carrier 4, other 8 (2018)

country comparison to the world: 147

PORTS AND TERMINALS:

major seaport(s): Bar

TERRORISM :: MONTENEGRO

TERRORIST GROUPS - FOREIGN BASED:

Aum Shinrikyo (AUM):
aim(s): enhance its networks in Montenegro for recruitment and fundraising
area(s) of operation: maintains a limited presence; membership drastically depleted in March 2016 when authorities expelled 58 foreign members (2018)

TRANSNATIONAL ISSUES :: MONTENEGRO

DISPUTES - INTERNATIONAL:

Kosovo ratified the border demarcation agreement with Montenegro in March 2018, but the actual demarcation has not been completed

REFUGEES AND INTERNALLY DISPLACED PERSONS:

stateless persons: 145 (2018)

note: 13,960 estimated refugee and migrant arrivals (January 2015-December 2019)

CENTRAL AMERICA :: MONTSERRAT

INTRODUCTION :: MONTSERRAT

BACKGROUND:
English and Irish colonists from St. Kitts first settled on Montserrat in 1632; the first African slaves arrived three decades later. The British and French fought for possession of the island for most of the 18th century, but it finally was confirmed as a British possession in 1783. The island's sugar plantation economy was converted to small farm landholdings in the mid-19th century. Much of this island was devastated and two-thirds of the population fled abroad because of the eruption of the Soufriere Hills Volcano that began on 18 July 1995. Montserrat has endured volcanic activity since, with the last eruption occurring in 2013.

GEOGRAPHY :: MONTSERRAT

LOCATION:
Caribbean, island in the Caribbean Sea, southeast of Puerto Rico

GEOGRAPHIC COORDINATES:
16 45 N, 62 12 W

MAP REFERENCES:
Central America and the Caribbean

AREA:
total: 102 sq km

land: 102 sq km

water: 0 sq km

country comparison to the world: 226

AREA - COMPARATIVE:
about 0.6 times the size of Washington, DC

LAND BOUNDARIES:
0 km

COASTLINE:
40 km

MARITIME CLAIMS:
territorial sea: 12 nm

exclusive fishing zone: 200 nm

CLIMATE:
tropical; little daily or seasonal temperature variation

TERRAIN:
volcanic island, mostly mountainous, with small coastal lowland

ELEVATION:
lowest point: Caribbean Sea 0 m

highest point: Soufriere Hills volcano pre-eruption height was 915 m; current lava dome is subject to periodic build up and collapse; estimated dome height was 1,050 m in 2015

NATURAL RESOURCES:
NEGL

LAND USE:
agricultural land: 30% (2011 est.)

arable land: 20% (2011 est.) / permanent crops: 0% (2011 est.) / permanent pasture: 10% (2011 est.)

forest: 25% (2011 est.)

other: 45% (2011 est.)

IRRIGATED LAND:
0 sq km (2012)

POPULATION DISTRIBUTION:
only the northern half of the island is populated, the southern portion is uninhabitable due to volcanic activity

NATURAL HAZARDS:
volcanic eruptions; severe hurricanes (June to November)

volcanism: Soufriere Hills volcano (915 m), has erupted continuously since 1995; a massive eruption in 1997 destroyed most of the capital, Plymouth, and resulted in approximately half of the island becoming uninhabitable; the island of Montserrat is part of the volcanic island arc of the Lesser Antilles that extends from Saba in the north to Grenada in the south

ENVIRONMENT - CURRENT ISSUES:
land erosion occurs on slopes that have been cleared for cultivation

GEOGRAPHY - NOTE:
the island is entirely volcanic in origin and comprised of three major volcanic centers of differing ages

PEOPLE AND SOCIETY :: MONTSERRAT

POPULATION:
5,315 (July 2018 est.)

note: an estimated 8,000 refugees left the island following the resumption of volcanic activity in July 1995; some have returned

country comparison to the world: 228

NATIONALITY:
noun: Montserratian(s)

adjective: Montserratian

ETHNIC GROUPS:
African/black 88.4%, mixed 3.7%, hispanic/Spanish 3%, caucasian/white 2.7%, East Indian/Indian 1.5%, other 0.7% (2011 est.)

LANGUAGES:
English

RELIGIONS:

Protestant 67.1% (includes Anglican 21.8%, Methodist 17%, Pentecostal 14.1%, Seventh Day Adventist 10.5%, and Church of God 3.7%), Roman Catholic 11.6%, Rastafarian 1.4%, other 6.5%, none 2.6%, unspecified 10.8% (2001 est.)

AGE STRUCTURE:

0-14 years: 15.99% (male 436 /female 414)

15-24 years: 21.39% (male 588 /female 549)

25-54 years: 47.58% (male 1,224 /female 1,305)

55-64 years: 8.81% (male 214 /female 254)

65 years and over: 6.23% (male 191 /female 140) (2018 est.)

MEDIAN AGE:

total: 33.8 years (2018 est.)

male: 33.1 years

female: 34.4 years

country comparison to the world: 90

POPULATION GROWTH RATE:

0.43% (2018 est.)

country comparison to the world: 159

BIRTH RATE:

10.5 births/1,000 population (2018 est.)

country comparison to the world: 186

DEATH RATE:

6.2 deaths/1,000 population (2018 est.)

country comparison to the world: 158

NET MIGRATION RATE:

0 migrant(s)/1,000 population (2018 est.)

country comparison to the world: 93

POPULATION DISTRIBUTION:

only the northern half of the island is populated, the southern portion is uninhabitable due to volcanic activity

URBANIZATION:

urban population: 9.1% of total population (2019)

rate of urbanization: 0.64% annual rate of change (2015-20 est.)

SEX RATIO:

at birth: 1.04 male(s)/female

0-14 years: 1.05 male(s)/female

15-24 years: 1.07 male(s)/female

25-54 years: 0.94 male(s)/female

55-64 years: 0.84 male(s)/female

65 years and over: 1.36 male(s)/female

total population: 1 male(s)/female (2018 est.)

INFANT MORTALITY RATE:

total: 11.9 deaths/1,000 live births (2018 est.)

male: 9.4 deaths/1,000 live births

female: 14.5 deaths/1,000 live births

country comparison to the world: 116

LIFE EXPECTANCY AT BIRTH:

total population: 74.8 years (2018 est.)

male: 76.1 years

female: 73.5 years

country comparison to the world: 121

TOTAL FERTILITY RATE:

1.34 children born/woman (2018 est.)

country comparison to the world: 216

DRINKING WATER SOURCE:

improved:

urban: 99% of population

rural: 99% of population

total: 99% of population

unimproved:

urban: 1% of population

rural: 1% of population

total: 1% of population (2015 est.)

SANITATION FACILITY ACCESS:

improved:

urban: 82.9% of population (2007 est.)

rural: 82.9% of population (2007 est.)

total: 82.9% of population (2007 est.)

unimproved:

urban: 17.1% of population (2007 est.)

rural: 17.1% of population (2007 est.)

total: 17.1% of population (2007 est.)

HIV/AIDS - ADULT PREVALENCE RATE:

NA

HIV/AIDS - PEOPLE LIVING WITH HIV/AIDS:

NA

HIV/AIDS - DEATHS:

NA

EDUCATION EXPENDITURES:

5.1% of GDP (2009)

country comparison to the world: 61

GOVERNMENT :: MONTSERRAT

COUNTRY NAME:

conventional long form: none

conventional short form: Montserrat

etymology: island named by explorer Christopher COLUMBUS in 1493 after the Benedictine abbey Santa Maria de Montserrat, near Barcelona, Spain

DEPENDENCY STATUS:

overseas territory of the UK

GOVERNMENT TYPE:

parliamentary democracy; self-governing overseas territory of the UK

CAPITAL:

name: Plymouth; note - Plymouth was abandoned in 1997 because of volcanic activity; interim government buildings have been built at Brades Estate, the de facto capital, in the Carr's Bay/Little Bay vicinity at the northwest end of Montserrat

geographic coordinates: 16 42 N, 62 13 W

time difference: UTC-4 (1 hour ahead of Washington, DC, during Standard Time)

etymology and note: now entirely deserted because of volcanic activity, the city was originally named after Plymouth, England; de jure, Plymouth remains the capital city of Montserrat; it is therefore the only ghost town that serves as the capital of a political entity

ADMINISTRATIVE DIVISIONS:

3 parishes; Saint Anthony, Saint Georges, Saint Peter

INDEPENDENCE:

none (overseas territory of the UK)

NATIONAL HOLIDAY:

Birthday of Queen ELIZABETH II, usually celebrated the Monday after the second Saturday in June (1926)

CONSTITUTION:

history: previous 1960; latest effective 1 September 2010 (The Montserrat Constitution Order 2010)

amendments: amended 2011 (2018)

LEGAL SYSTEM:

English common law

CITIZENSHIP:

see United Kingdom

SUFFRAGE:

18 years of age; universal

EXECUTIVE BRANCH:

chief of state: Queen ELIZABETH II (since 6 February 1952); represented by Governor Andrew PEARCE (since 1 February 2018)

head of government: Premier Donaldson ROMERO (since 12 September 2014); note - effective with The Constitution Order 2010, effective October 2010, the office of premier replaced the office of chief minister

cabinet: Executive Council consists of the governor, the premier, 3 other ministers, the attorney general, and the finance secretary

elections/appointments: the monarchy is hereditary; governor appointed by the monarch; following legislative elections, the leader of the majority party usually becomes premier

LEGISLATIVE BRANCH:

description: unicameral Legislative Assembly (11 seats; 9 members directly elected in a single constituency by absolute majority vote in 2 rounds to serve 5-year terms and 2 ex-officio members - the attorney general and financial secretary)

elections: last held on 11 September 2014 (next scheduled for 30 September 2019)

election results: percent of vote by party - PDM 50.0%, MCAP 35.4%, other 14.6%; seats by party - PDM 7, MCAP 2; composition - men 7, women 2, percent of women 22.2%

JUDICIAL BRANCH:

highest courts: the Eastern Caribbean Supreme Court (ECSC) is the superior court of the Organization of Eastern Caribbean States; the ECSC - headquartered on St. Lucia - consists of the Court of Appeal - headed by the chief justice and 4 judges - and the High Court with 18 judges; the Court of Appeal is itinerant, traveling to member states on a schedule to hear appeals from the High Court and subordinate courts; High Court judges reside in the member states, with 1 assigned to Montserrat; Montserrat is also a member of the Caribbean Court of Justice

judge selection and term of office: chief justice of Eastern Caribbean Supreme Court appointed by the Her Majesty, Queen ELIZABETH II; other justices and judges appointed by the Judicial and Legal Services Commission, and independent body of judicial officials; Court of Appeal justices appointed for life with mandatory retirement at age 65; High Court judges appointed for life with mandatory retirement at age 62

subordinate courts: magistrate's court

POLITICAL PARTIES AND LEADERS:

Movement for Change and Prosperity or MCAP [Easton Taylor FARRELL]
People's Democratic Movement or PDM [Donaldson ROMERO]

INTERNATIONAL ORGANIZATION PARTICIPATION:

Caricom, CDB, Interpol (subbureau), OECS, UPU

DIPLOMATIC REPRESENTATION IN THE US:

none (overseas territory of the UK)

DIPLOMATIC REPRESENTATION FROM THE US:

none (overseas territory of the UK)

FLAG DESCRIPTION:

blue with the flag of the UK in the upper hoist-side quadrant and the Montserratian coat of arms centered in the outer half of the flag; the arms feature a woman in green dress, Erin, the female personification of Ireland, standing beside a yellow harp and embracing a large dark cross with her right arm; Erin and the harp are symbols of Ireland reflecting the territory's Irish ancestry; blue represents awareness, trustworthiness, determination, and righteousness

NATIONAL ANTHEM:

note: as a territory of the UK, "God Save the Queen" is official (see United Kingdom)

ECONOMY :: MONTSERRAT

ECONOMY - OVERVIEW:

Severe volcanic activity, which began in July 1995, has put a damper on this small, open economy. A catastrophic eruption in June 1997 closed the airport and seaports, causing further economic and social dislocation. Two-thirds of the 12,000 inhabitants fled the island. Some began to return in 1998 but lack of housing limited the number. The agriculture sector continued to be affected by the lack of suitable land for farming and the destruction of crops.

Prospects for the economy depend largely on developments in relation to the volcanic activity and on public sector construction activity. Half of the island remains uninhabitable. In January 2013, the EU announced the disbursement of a $55.2 million aid package to Montserrat in order to boost the country's economic recovery, with a specific focus on public finance management, public sector reform, and prudent economic management. Montserrat is tied to the EU through the UK. Although the UK is leaving the EU, Montserrat's aid will not be affected as Montserrat maintains a direct agreement with the EU regarding aid.

GDP (PURCHASING POWER PARITY):

$167.4 million (2011 est.)

$155.9 million (2010 est.)

$162.7 million (2009 est.)

country comparison to the world: 223

GDP (OFFICIAL EXCHANGE RATE):

$167.4 million (2011 est.) (2011 est.)

GDP - REAL GROWTH RATE:

7.4% (2011 est.)

-4.2% (2010 est.)

country comparison to the world: 15

GDP - PER CAPITA (PPP):

$34,000 (2011 est.)

$31,100 (2010 est.)

$32,300 (2009 est.)

country comparison to the world: 60

GDP - COMPOSITION, BY END USE:

household consumption: 90.8% (2017 est.)

government consumption: 50.4% (2017 est.)

investment in fixed capital: 17.9% (2017 est.)

investment in inventories: -0.1% (2017 est.)

exports of goods and services: 29.5% (2017 est.)

imports of goods and services: -88.6% (2017 est.)

GDP - COMPOSITION, BY SECTOR OF ORIGIN:

agriculture: 1.9% (2017 est.)

industry: 7.8% (2017 est.)

services: 90.3% (2017 est.)

AGRICULTURE - PRODUCTS:

cabbages, carrots, cucumbers, tomatoes, onions, peppers; livestock products

INDUSTRIES:

tourism, rum, textiles, electronic appliances

INDUSTRIAL PRODUCTION GROWTH RATE:

-21% (2017 est.)

country comparison to the world: 200

LABOR FORCE:

4,521 (2012)

country comparison to the world: 222

LABOR FORCE - BY OCCUPATION:

agriculture: 1.4%

industry: 12.7%

services: 85.9% (2017 est.)

UNEMPLOYMENT RATE:

5.6% (2017 est.)

6% (1998 est.)

country comparison to the world: 83

POPULATION BELOW POVERTY LINE:

NA

HOUSEHOLD INCOME OR CONSUMPTION BY PERCENTAGE SHARE:

lowest 10%: NA

highest 10%: NA

BUDGET:

revenues: 66.67 million (2017 est.)

expenditures: 47.04 million (2017 est.)

FISCAL YEAR:

1 April - 31 March

INFLATION RATE (CONSUMER PRICES):

1.2% (2017 est.)

-0.2% (2016 est.)

country comparison to the world: 66

CENTRAL BANK DISCOUNT RATE:

10.99% (31 December 2010)

6.5% (31 December 2009)

country comparison to the world: 20

COMMERCIAL BANK PRIME LENDING RATE:

6.95% (31 December 2017 est.)

7.21% (31 December 2016 est.)

country comparison to the world: 120

STOCK OF NARROW MONEY:

$28.33 million (31 December 2017 est.)

$23.04 million (31 December 2016 est.)

country comparison to the world: 192

STOCK OF BROAD MONEY:

$28.33 million (31 December 2017 est.)

$23.04 million (31 December 2016 est.)

country comparison to the world: 195

STOCK OF DOMESTIC CREDIT:

$5.185 million (31 December 2017 est.)

$1.481 million (31 December 2016 est.)

country comparison to the world: 190

CURRENT ACCOUNT BALANCE:

-$15.4 million (2017 est.)

-$12.2 million (2016 est.)

country comparison to the world: 71

EXPORTS:

$4.4 million (2017 est.)

$5.2 million (2016 est.)

country comparison to the world: 218

EXPORTS - PARTNERS:

US 29%, France 23%, Saint Kitts and Nevis 22.2% (2017)

EXPORTS - COMMODITIES:

electronic components, plastic bags, apparel; hot peppers, limes, live plants; cattle

IMPORTS:

$39.44 million (2017 est.)

$36.1 million (2016 est.)

country comparison to the world: 221

IMPORTS - COMMODITIES:

machinery and transportation equipment, foodstuffs, manufactured goods, fuels, lubricants

IMPORTS - PARTNERS:

US 72.8%, Trinidad and Tobago 6%, UK 4.1% (2017)

RESERVES OF FOREIGN EXCHANGE AND GOLD:

$47.58 million (31 December 2017 est.)

$51.47 million (31 December 2015 est.)

country comparison to the world: 187

DEBT - EXTERNAL:

$8.9 million (1997)

country comparison to the world: 200

EXCHANGE RATES:

East Caribbean dollars (XCD) per US dollar -

2.7 (2017 est.)

2.7 (2016 est.)

2.7 (2015 est.)

2.7 (2014 est.)

2.7 (2013 est.)

ENERGY :: MONTSERRAT

ELECTRICITY - PRODUCTION:

24 million kWh (2016 est.)

country comparison to the world: 211

ELECTRICITY - CONSUMPTION:

22.32 million kWh (2016 est.)

country comparison to the world: 211

ELECTRICITY - EXPORTS:

0 kWh (2016 est.)

country comparison to the world: 173

ELECTRICITY - IMPORTS:

0 kWh (2016 est.)

country comparison to the world: 176

ELECTRICITY - INSTALLED GENERATING CAPACITY:

5,000 kW (2016 est.)

country comparison to the world: 213

ELECTRICITY - FROM FOSSIL FUELS:

100% of total installed capacity (2016 est.)

country comparison to the world: 13

ELECTRICITY - FROM NUCLEAR FUELS:

0% of total installed capacity (2017 est.)

country comparison to the world: 147

ELECTRICITY - FROM HYDROELECTRIC PLANTS:

0% of total installed capacity (2017 est.)

country comparison to the world: 187

ELECTRICITY - FROM OTHER RENEWABLE SOURCES:

0% of total installed capacity (2017 est.)

country comparison to the world: 202

CRUDE OIL - PRODUCTION:

0 bbl/day (2018 est.)

country comparison to the world: 177

CRUDE OIL - EXPORTS:

0 bbl/day (2015 est.)

country comparison to the world: 168

CRUDE OIL - IMPORTS:

0 bbl/day (2015 est.)

country comparison to the world: 170

CRUDE OIL - PROVED RESERVES:

0 bbl (1 January 2018 est.)

country comparison to the world: 172

REFINED PETROLEUM PRODUCTS - PRODUCTION:

0 bbl/day (2015 est.)

country comparison to the world: 181

REFINED PETROLEUM PRODUCTS - CONSUMPTION:

400 bbl/day (2016 est.)

country comparison to the world: 212

REFINED PETROLEUM PRODUCTS - EXPORTS:

0 bbl/day (2015 est.)

country comparison to the world: 184

REFINED PETROLEUM PRODUCTS - IMPORTS:

406 bbl/day (2015 est.)

country comparison to the world: 208

NATURAL GAS - PRODUCTION:

0 cu m (2017 est.)

country comparison to the world: 174

NATURAL GAS - CONSUMPTION:

0 cu m (2017 est.)

country comparison to the world: 178

NATURAL GAS - EXPORTS:

0 cu m (2017 est.)

country comparison to the world: 155

NATURAL GAS - IMPORTS:

0 cu m (2017 est.)

country comparison to the world: 160

NATURAL GAS - PROVED RESERVES:

0 cu m (1 January 2014 est.)

country comparison to the world: 173

CARBON DIOXIDE EMISSIONS FROM CONSUMPTION OF ENERGY:

57,180 Mt (2017 est.)

country comparison to the world: 210

COMMUNICATIONS :: MONTSERRAT

TELEPHONES - FIXED LINES:

total subscriptions: 3,000

subscriptions per 100 inhabitants: 57 (July 2016 est.)

country comparison to the world: 209

TELEPHONES - MOBILE CELLULAR:

total subscriptions: 5,000

subscriptions per 100 inhabitants: 95 (July 2016 est.)

country comparison to the world: 214

TELEPHONE SYSTEM:

general assessment: modern and fully digitalized; high dependency on tourism and offshore financial services; operators expand FttP (Fiber to Home) services; LTE launches and operators invest in mobile networks (2018)

domestic: fixed-line 57 per 100 and mobile-cellular teledensity 95 per 100 persons (2018)

international: country code - 1-664; landing point for the ECFS optic submarine cable with links to 14 other islands in the eastern Caribbean extending from the British Virgin Islands to Trinidad (2019)

BROADCAST MEDIA:

Radio Montserrat, a public radio broadcaster, transmits on 1 station and has a repeater transmission to a second station; repeater transmissions from the GEM Radio Network of Trinidad and Tobago provide another 2 radio stations; cable and satellite TV available (2007)

INTERNET COUNTRY CODE:

.ms

INTERNET USERS:

total: 2,860

percent of population: 54.6% (July 2016 est.)

country comparison to the world: 219

MILITARY AND SECURITY :: MONTSERRAT

MILITARY AND SECURITY FORCES:

no regular military forces; Royal Montserrat Defence Force (ceremonial, civil defense duties), Montserrat Police Force (2019)

MILITARY - NOTE:

defense is the responsibility of the UK

TRANSPORTATION :: MONTSERRAT

NATIONAL AIR TRANSPORT SYSTEM:

number of registered air carriers: 1 (2015)

inventory of registered aircraft operated by air carriers: 3 (2015)

CIVIL AIRCRAFT REGISTRATION COUNTRY CODE PREFIX:

VP-M (2016)

AIRPORTS:

1 (2013)

country comparison to the world: 229

AIRPORTS - WITH PAVED RUNWAYS:

total: 1 (2017)

under 914 m: 1 (2017)

ROADWAYS:

note: volcanic eruptions that began in 1995 destroyed most of the 227 km road system; a new road infrastructure has been built on the north end of the island

PORTS AND TERMINALS:

major seaport(s): Little Bay, Plymouth

TRANSNATIONAL ISSUES :: MONTSERRAT

DISPUTES - INTERNATIONAL:

none

ILLICIT DRUGS:

transshipment point for South American narcotics destined for the US and Europe

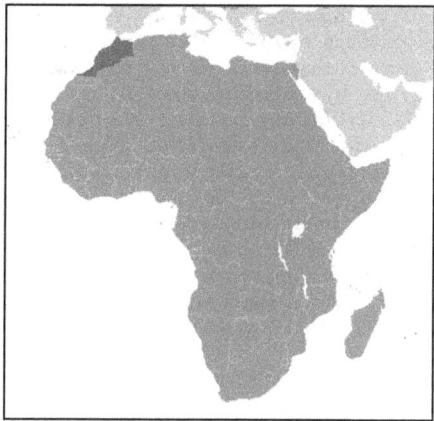

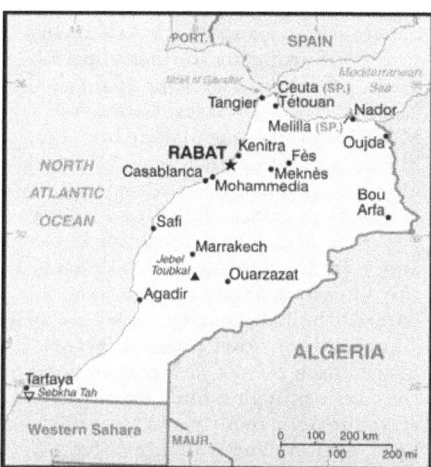

AFRICA :: MOROCCO

INTRODUCTION :: MOROCCO

BACKGROUND:

In 788, about a century after the Arab conquest of North Africa, a series of Moroccan Muslim dynasties began to rule in Morocco. In the 16th century, the Sa'adi monarchy, particularly under Ahmad al-MANSUR (1578-1603), repelled foreign invaders and inaugurated a golden age. The Alaouite Dynasty, to which the current Moroccan royal family belongs, dates from the 17th century. In 1860, Spain occupied northern Morocco and ushered in a half-century of trade rivalry among European powers that saw Morocco's sovereignty steadily erode; in 1912, the French imposed a protectorate over the country. A protracted independence struggle with France ended successfully in 1956. The internationalized city of Tangier and most Spanish possessions were turned over to the new country that same year. Sultan MOHAMMED V, the current monarch's grandfather, organized the new state as a constitutional monarchy and in 1957 assumed the title of king. Since Spain's 1976 withdrawal from what is today called Western Sahara, Morocco has extended its de facto administrative control to roughly 75% of this territory; however, the UN does not recognize Morocco as the administering power for Western Sahara. The UN since 1991 has monitored a cease-fire between Morocco and the Polisario Front - an organization advocating the territory's independence - and restarted negotiations over the status of the territory in December 2018.

King MOHAMMED VI in early 2011 responded to the spread of pro-democracy protests in the region by implementing a reform program that included a new constitution, passed by popular referendum in July 2011, under which some new powers were extended to parliament and the prime minister, but ultimate authority remains in the hands of the monarch. In November 2011, the Justice and Development Party (PJD) - a moderate Islamist party - won the largest number of seats in parliamentary elections, becoming the first Islamist party to lead the Moroccan Government. In September 2015, Morocco held its first direct elections for regional councils, one of the reforms included in the 2011 constitution. The PJD again won the largest number of seats in nationwide parliamentary elections in October 2016.

GEOGRAPHY :: MOROCCO

LOCATION:
Northern Africa, bordering the North Atlantic Ocean and the Mediterranean Sea, between Algeria and Western Sahara

GEOGRAPHIC COORDINATES:
32 00 N, 5 00 W

MAP REFERENCES:
Africa

AREA:
total: 446,550 sq km

land: 446,300 sq km

water: 250 sq km

country comparison to the world: 59

AREA - COMPARATIVE:
slightly more than three times the size of New York; slightly larger than California

LAND BOUNDARIES:
total: 2,362.5 km

border countries (4): Algeria 1900 km, Western Sahara 444 km, Spain (Ceuta) 8 km, Spain (Melilla) 10.5 km

note: an additional 75-meter border segment exists between Morocco and the Spanish exclave of Penon de Velez de la Gomera

COASTLINE:
1,835 km

MARITIME CLAIMS:
territorial sea: 12 nm

exclusive economic zone: 200 nm

contiguous zone: 24 nm

continental shelf: 200-m depth or to the depth of exploitation

CLIMATE:
Mediterranean, becoming more extreme in the interior

TERRAIN:
mountainous northern coast (Rif Mountains) and interior (Atlas Mountains) bordered by large plateaus with intermontane valleys, and fertile coastal plains

ELEVATION:
mean elevation: 909 m

lowest point: Sebkha Tah -59 m

highest point: Jebel Toubkal 4,165 m

NATURAL RESOURCES:

phosphates, iron ore, manganese, lead, zinc, fish, salt

LAND USE:

agricultural land: 67.5% (2011 est.)

arable land: 17.5% (2011 est.) / permanent crops: 2.9% (2011 est.) / permanent pasture: 47.1% (2011 est.)

forest: 11.5% (2011 est.)

other: 21% (2011 est.)

IRRIGATED LAND:

14,850 sq km (2012)

POPULATION DISTRIBUTION:

the highest population density is found along the Atlantic and Mediterranean coasts; a number of densely populated agglomerations are found scattered through the Atlas Mountains

NATURAL HAZARDS:

northern mountains geologically unstable and subject to earthquakes; periodic droughts; windstorms; flash floods; landslides

ENVIRONMENT - CURRENT ISSUES:

land degradation/desertification (soil erosion resulting from farming of marginal areas, overgrazing, destruction of vegetation); water and soil pollution due to dumping of industrial wastes into the ocean and inland water sources, and onto the land

ENVIRONMENT - INTERNATIONAL AGREEMENTS:

party to: Biodiversity, Climate Change, Climate Change-Kyoto Protocol, Desertification, Endangered Species, Hazardous Wastes, Law of the Sea, Marine Dumping, Ozone Layer Protection, Ship Pollution, Wetlands, Whaling

signed, but not ratified: Environmental Modification

GEOGRAPHY - NOTE:

strategic location along Strait of Gibraltar; the only African nation to have both Atlantic and Mediterranean coastlines

PEOPLE AND SOCIETY :: MOROCCO

POPULATION:

34,314,130 (July 2018 est.)

country comparison to the world: 40

NATIONALITY:

noun: Moroccan(s)

adjective: Moroccan

ETHNIC GROUPS:

Arab-Berber 99%, other 1%

LANGUAGES:

Arabic (official), Berber languages (Tamazight (official), Tachelhit, Tarifit), French (often the language of business, government, and diplomacy)

note: the proportion of Berber speakers is disputed

RELIGIONS:

Muslim 99% (official; virtually all Sunni, <0.1% Shia), other 1% (includes Christian, Jewish, and Baha'i); note - Jewish about 6,000 (2010 est.)

DEMOGRAPHIC PROFILE:

Morocco is undergoing a demographic transition. Its population is growing but at a declining rate, as people live longer and women have fewer children. Infant, child, and maternal mortality rates have been reduced through better health care, nutrition, hygiene, and vaccination coverage, although disparities between urban and rural and rich and poor households persist. Morocco's shrinking child cohort reflects the decline of its total fertility rate from 5 in mid-1980s to 2.2 in 2010, which is a result of increased female educational attainment, higher contraceptive use, delayed marriage, and the desire for smaller families. Young adults (persons aged 15-29) make up almost 26% of the total population and represent a potential economic asset if they can be gainfully employed. Currently, however, many youths are unemployed because Morocco's job creation rate has not kept pace with the growth of its working-age population. Most youths who have jobs work in the informal sector with little security or benefits.

During the second half of the 20th century, Morocco became one of the world's top emigration countries, creating large, widely dispersed migrant communities in Western Europe. The Moroccan Government has encouraged emigration since its independence in 1956, both to secure remittances for funding national development and as an outlet to prevent unrest in rebellious (often Berber) areas. Although Moroccan labor migrants earlier targeted Algeria and France, the flood of Moroccan "guest workers" from the mid-1960s to the early 1970s spread widely across northwestern Europe to fill unskilled jobs in the booming manufacturing, mining, construction, and agriculture industries. Host societies and most Moroccan migrants expected this migration to be temporary, but deteriorating economic conditions in Morocco related to the 1973 oil crisis and tighter European immigration policies resulted in these stays becoming permanent.

A wave of family migration followed in the 1970s and 1980s, with a growing number of second generation Moroccans opting to become naturalized citizens of their host countries. Spain and Italy emerged as new destination countries in the mid-1980s, but their introduction of visa restrictions in the early 1990s pushed Moroccans increasingly to migrate either legally by marrying Moroccans already in Europe or illegally to work in the underground economy. Women began to make up a growing share of these labor migrants. At the same time, some higher-skilled Moroccans went to the US and Quebec, Canada.

In the mid-1990s, Morocco developed into a transit country for asylum seekers from sub-Saharan Africa and illegal labor migrants from sub-Saharan Africa and South Asia trying to reach Europe via southern Spain, Spain's Canary Islands, or Spain's North African enclaves, Ceuta and Melilla. Forcible expulsions by Moroccan and Spanish security forces have not deterred these illegal migrants or calmed Europe's security concerns. Rabat remains unlikely to adopt an EU agreement to take back third-country nationals who have entered the EU illegally via Morocco. Thousands of other illegal migrants have chosen to stay in Morocco until they earn enough money for further travel or permanently as a "second-best" option. The launching of a regularization program in 2014 legalized the status of some migrants and granted them equal access to education, health care, and work, but xenophobia and racism remain obstacles.

AGE STRUCTURE:

0-14 years: 25.47% (male 4,441,554 /female 4,298,715)

15-24 years: 16.83% (male 2,873,939 /female 2,902,206)

25-54 years: 42.41% (male 7,039,912 /female 7,513,651)

55-64 years: 8.33% (male 1,404,527 /female 1,454,304)

65 years and over: 6.95% (male 1,081,035 /female 1,304,287) (2018 est.)

DEPENDENCY RATIOS:

total dependency ratio: 51.6 (2015 est.)

youth dependency ratio: 41.9 (2015 est.)

elderly dependency ratio: 9.7 (2015 est.)

potential support ratio: 10.3 (2015 est.)

MEDIAN AGE:

total: 29.7 years (2018 est.)

male: 29 years

female: 30.3 years

country comparison to the world: 121

POPULATION GROWTH RATE:

0.95% (2018 est.)

country comparison to the world: 115

BIRTH RATE:

17.5 births/1,000 population (2018 est.)

country comparison to the world: 100

DEATH RATE:

4.9 deaths/1,000 population (2018 est.)

country comparison to the world: 197

NET MIGRATION RATE:

-3.1 migrant(s)/1,000 population (2018 est.)

country comparison to the world: 179

POPULATION DISTRIBUTION:

the highest population density is found along the Atlantic and Mediterranean coasts; a number of densely populated agglomerations are found scattered through the Atlas Mountains

URBANIZATION:

urban population: 63% of total population (2019)

rate of urbanization: 2.14% annual rate of change (2015-20 est.)

MAJOR URBAN AREAS - POPULATION:

3.716 million Casablanca, 1.865 million RABAT (capital), 1.204 million Fes, 1.157 million Tangier, 989,000 Marrakech, 906,000 Agadir (2019)

SEX RATIO:

at birth: 1.05 male(s)/female

0-14 years: 1.03 male(s)/female

15-24 years: 0.99 male(s)/female

25-54 years: 0.94 male(s)/female

55-64 years: 0.97 male(s)/female

65 years and over: 0.83 male(s)/female

total population: 0.96 male(s)/female (2018 est.)

MATERNAL MORTALITY RATE:

70 deaths/100,000 live births (2017 est.)

country comparison to the world: 84

INFANT MORTALITY RATE:

total: 21.1 deaths/1,000 live births (2018 est.)

male: 25 deaths/1,000 live births

female: 16.9 deaths/1,000 live births

country comparison to the world: 78

LIFE EXPECTANCY AT BIRTH:

total population: 77.3 years (2018 est.)

male: 74.2 years

female: 80.5 years

country comparison to the world: 75

TOTAL FERTILITY RATE:

2.09 children born/woman (2018 est.)

country comparison to the world: 103

CONTRACEPTIVE PREVALENCE RATE:

70.8% (2018)

DRINKING WATER SOURCE:

improved:

urban: 98.7% of population

rural: 65.3% of population

total: 85.4% of population

unimproved:

urban: 1.3% of population

rural: 34.7% of population

total: 14.6% of population (2015 est.)

CURRENT HEALTH EXPENDITURE:

5.8% (2016)

PHYSICIANS DENSITY:

0.73 physicians/1,000 population (2017)

HOSPITAL BED DENSITY:

1.1 beds/1,000 population (2014)

SANITATION FACILITY ACCESS:

improved:

urban: 84.1% of population (2015 est.)

rural: 65.5% of population (2015 est.)

total: 76.7% of population (2015 est.)

unimproved:

urban: 15.9% of population (2015 est.)

rural: 34.5% of population (2015 est.)

total: 23.3% of population (2015 est.)

HIV/AIDS - ADULT PREVALENCE RATE:

<.1% (2018 est.)

HIV/AIDS - PEOPLE LIVING WITH HIV/AIDS:

21,000 (2018 est.)

country comparison to the world: 84

HIV/AIDS - DEATHS:

<500 (2018 est.)

OBESITY - ADULT PREVALENCE RATE:

26.1% (2016)

country comparison to the world: 45

CHILDREN UNDER THE AGE OF 5 YEARS UNDERWEIGHT:

2.9% (2011)

country comparison to the world: 102

EDUCATION EXPENDITURES:

5.3% of GDP (2009)

country comparison to the world: 54

LITERACY:

definition: age 15 and over can read and write

total population: 68.5%

male: 78.6%

female: 58.8% (2015 est.)

SCHOOL LIFE EXPECTANCY (PRIMARY TO TERTIARY EDUCATION):

total: 13 years

male: 14 years

female: 13 years (2017)

UNEMPLOYMENT, YOUTH AGES 15-24:

total: 22.2%

male: 20%

female: 22.8% (2016 est.)

country comparison to the world: 61

GOVERNMENT :: MOROCCO

COUNTRY NAME:

conventional long form: Kingdom of Morocco

conventional short form: Morocco

local long form: Al Mamlakah al Maghribiyah

local short form: Al Maghrib

former: French Protectorate in Morocco, Spanish Protectorate in Morocco

etymology: the English name "Morocco" derives from, respectively, the Spanish and Portuguese names "Marruecos" and "Marrocos," which stem from "Marrakesh" the Latin name for the former capital of ancient Morocco; the Arabic name "Al Maghrib" translates as "The West"

GOVERNMENT TYPE:
parliamentary constitutional monarchy

CAPITAL:
name: Rabat

geographic coordinates: 34 01 N, 6 49 W

time difference: UTC 0 (5 hours ahead of Washington, DC, during Standard Time)

daylight saving time: +1 hr, begins last Sunday in March; ends last Sunday in October

etymology: name derives from the Arabic title "Ribat el-Fath," meaning "stronghold of victory," applied to the newly constructed citadel in 1170

ADMINISTRATIVE DIVISIONS:
11 regions (recognized); Beni Mellal-Khenifra, Casablanca-Settat, Draa-Tafilalet, Fes-Meknes, Guelmim-Oued Noun, Laayoune-Sakia al Hamra, Oriental, Marrakech-Safi, Rabat-Sale-Kenitra, Souss-Massa, Tanger-Tetouan-Al Hoceima

note: Morocco claims the territory of Western Sahara, the political status of which is considered undetermined by the US Government; portions of the regions Guelmim-Oued Noun and Laayoune-Sakia al Hamra as claimed by Morocco lie within Western Sahara; Morocco also claims a 12th region, Dakhla-Oued ed Dahab, that falls entirely within Western Sahara

INDEPENDENCE:
2 March 1956 (from France)

NATIONAL HOLIDAY:
Throne Day (accession of King MOHAMMED VI to the throne), 30 July (1999)

CONSTITUTION:
history: several previous; latest drafted 17 June 2011, approved by referendum 1 July 2011; note - sources disagree on whether the 2011 referendum was for a new constitution or for reforms to the previous constitution

amendments: proposed by the king, by the prime minister, or by members in either chamber of Parliament; passage requires at least two-thirds majority vote by both chambers and approval in a referendum; the king can opt to submit self-initiated proposals directly to a referendum (2016)

LEGAL SYSTEM:
mixed legal system of civil law based on French civil law and Islamic (sharia) law; judicial review of legislative acts by Constitutional Court

INTERNATIONAL LAW ORGANIZATION PARTICIPATION:
has not submitted an ICJ jurisdiction declaration; non-party state to the ICCt

CITIZENSHIP:
citizenship by birth: no

citizenship by descent only: the father must be a citizen of Morocco; if the father is unknown or stateless, the mother must be a citizen

dual citizenship recognized: yes

residency requirement for naturalization: 5 years

SUFFRAGE:
18 years of age; universal

EXECUTIVE BRANCH:
chief of state: King MOHAMMED VI (since 30 July 1999)

head of government: Prime Minister Saad-Eddine al-OTHMANI (since 17 March 2017)

cabinet: Council of Ministers chosen by the prime minister in consultation with Parliament and appointed by the monarch

elections/appointments: the monarchy is hereditary; prime minister appointed by the monarch from the majority party following legislative elections

LEGISLATIVE BRANCH:
description: bicameral Parliament consists of:
Chamber of Advisors (120 seats; members indirectly elected by an electoral college of local councils, professional organizations, and labor unions; members serve 6-year terms)
Chamber of Representatives (395 seats; 305 members directly elected in multi-seat constituencies by proportional representation vote and 90 directly elected in a single nationwide constituency by proportional representation vote; members serve 5-year terms); note - in the national constituency, 60 seats are reserved for women and 30 reserved for those under age 40

elections:
Chamber of Advisors - last held on 2 October 2015 (next to be held in fall 2021)
Chamber of Representatives - last held on 7 October 2016 (next to be held in fall 2021)

election results:
Chamber of Advisors - percent of vote by party - NA; seats by party - NA; composition - men 106, women 14, percent of women 11.7%
Chamber of Representatives - percent of vote by party NA; seats by party - PJD 125, PAM 102, PI 46, RNI 37, MP 27, USFP 20, UC 19, PPS 12, MDS 3, other 4; composition - men 314, women 81, percent of women 20.5%; note - total Parliament percent of women 18.4%

JUDICIAL BRANCH:
highest courts: Supreme Court or Court of Cassation (consists of 5-judge panels organized into civil, family matters, commercial, administrative, social, and criminal sections); Constitutional Court (consists of 12 members)

judge selection and term of office: Supreme Court judges appointed by the Superior Council of Judicial Power, a 20-member body presided by the monarch, which includes the Supreme Court president, the prosecutor general, representatives of the appeals and first instance courts (among them 1 woman magistrate), the president of the National Council of the Rights of Man, and 5 "notable persons" appointed by the monarch; judges appointed for life; Constitutional Court members - 6 designated by the monarch and 6 elected by Parliament; court president appointed by the monarch from among the court members; members serve 9-year nonrenewable terms

subordinate courts: courts of appeal; High Court of Justice; administrative and commercial courts; regional and sadad courts (for religious, civil and administrative, and penal adjudication); first instance courts

POLITICAL PARTIES AND LEADERS:
Action Party or PA [Mohammed EL IDRISSI]

Amal (hope) Party [Mohamed BANI]
An-Nahj Ad-Dimocrati or An-Nahj [Mustapha BRAHMA]
Authenticity and Modernity Party or PAM [Ilyas al-OMARI]
Constitutional Union Party or UC [Mohamed SAJID]
Democratic and Social Movement or MDS [Abdessamad ARCHANE]
Democratic Forces Front or FFD [Mustapha BENALI]
Democratic Oath Party or SD
Democratic Socialist Vanguard Party or PADS [Abderrahman BENAMROU]
Democratic Society Party [Zhour CHAKKAFI]
Environment and Development Party or PED [Karim HRITAN]
Green Left Party [Mohamed FARES]
Istiqlal (Independence) Party or PI [Nizar BARAKA]
Ittihadi National Congress or CNI [Abdesalam EL AZIZ]
Labor Party or PT
Moroccan Liberal Party or PML [Mohammed ZIANE]
Moroccan Union for Democracy or UMD [Jamal MANDRI]
National Rally of Independents or RNI [Aziz AKHANNOUCH]
Neo-Democrats Party [Mohamed DARIF]
Party of Development Reform or PRD [Abderrahmane EL KOHEN]
Party of Justice and Development or PJD [Saad Eddine al-OTHMANI]
Party of Liberty and Social Justice [Miloud MOUSSAOUI]
Popular Movement or MP [Mohand LAENSER]
Progress and Socialism Party or PPS [Nabil BENABDELLAH]
Renaissance and Virtue Party [Mohamed KHALIDI]
Renaissance Party [Said EL GHENNIOUI]
Renewal and Equity Party or PRE [Chakir ACHEHABAR]
Shoura (consultation) and Istiqlal Party [Ahmed BELGHAZI]
Social Center Party or PCS [Lahcen MADIH]
Socialist Party [Abdelmajid BOUZOUBAA]
Socialist Union of Popular Forces or USFP [Driss LACHGAR]
Unified Socialist Party or GSU [Nabila MOUNIB]
Unity and Democracy Party [Ahmed FITRI]

INTERNATIONAL ORGANIZATION PARTICIPATION:

ABEDA, AfDB, AFESD, AMF, AMU, CAEU, CD, EBRD, FAO, G-11, G-77, IAEA, IBRD, ICAO, ICC (national committees), ICRM, IDA, IDB, IFAD, IFC, IFRCS, IHO, ILO, IMF, IMO, IMSO, Interpol, IOC, IOM, IPU, ISO, ITSO, ITU, ITUC (NGOs), LAS, MIGA, MONUSCO, NAM, OAS (observer), OIC, OIF, OPCW, OSCE (partner), Pacific Alliance (observer), Paris Club (associate), PCA, SICA (observer), UN, UNCTAD, UNESCO, UNHCR, UNIDO, UNOCI, UNSC (temporary), UNWTO, UPU, WCO, WHO, WIPO, WMO, WTO

DIPLOMATIC REPRESENTATION IN THE US:

Ambassador Lalla Joumala ALAOUI (since 24 April 2017)

chancery: 3508 International Drive NW, Washington, DC 20008

telephone: [1] (202) 462-7979

FAX: [1] (202) 462-7643

consulate(s) general: New York

DIPLOMATIC REPRESENTATION FROM THE US:

chief of mission: Ambassador David GREENE (since 5 August 2019)

telephone: [212] 537 637 200

embassy: Km 5.7 Avenue Mohammed VI, Souissi, Rabat 10170

mailing address: Unit 9400, Box Front Office, DPO AE 09718

FAX: [212] 537 637 201

consulate(s) general: Casablanca

FLAG DESCRIPTION:

red with a green pentacle (five-pointed, linear star) known as Sulayman's (Solomon's) seal in the center of the flag; red and green are traditional colors in Arab flags, although the use of red is more commonly associated with the Arab states of the Persian Gulf; the pentacle represents the five pillars of Islam and signifies the association between God and the nation; design dates to 1912

NATIONAL SYMBOL(S):

pentacle symbol, lion; national colors: red, green

NATIONAL ANTHEM:

name: "Hymne Cherifien" (Hymn of the Sharif)

lyrics/music: Ali Squalli HOUSSAINI/Leo MORGAN

note: music adopted 1956, lyrics adopted 1970

ECONOMY :: MOROCCO

ECONOMY - OVERVIEW:

Morocco has capitalized on its proximity to Europe and relatively low labor costs to work towards building a diverse, open, market-oriented economy. Key sectors of the economy include agriculture, tourism, aerospace, automotive, phosphates, textiles, apparel, and subcomponents. Morocco has increased investment in its port, transportation, and industrial infrastructure to position itself as a center and broker for business throughout Africa. Industrial development strategies and infrastructure improvements - most visibly illustrated by a new port and free trade zone near Tangier - are improving Morocco's competitiveness.

In the 1980s, Morocco was a heavily indebted country before pursuing austerity measures and pro-market reforms, overseen by the IMF. Since taking the throne in 1999, King MOHAMMED VI has presided over a stable economy marked by steady growth, low inflation, and gradually falling unemployment, although poor harvests and economic difficulties in Europe contributed to an economic slowdown. To boost exports, Morocco entered into a bilateral Free Trade Agreement with the US in 2006 and an Advanced Status agreement with the EU in 2008. In late 2014, Morocco eliminated subsidies for gasoline, diesel, and fuel oil, dramatically reducing outlays that weighed on the country's budget and current account. Subsidies on butane gas and certain food products remain in place. Morocco also seeks to expand its renewable energy capacity with a goal of making renewable more than 50% of installed electricity generation capacity by 2030.

Despite Morocco's economic progress, the country suffers from high unemployment, poverty, and illiteracy, particularly in rural areas. Key economic challenges for Morocco include reforming the education system and the judiciary.

GDP (PURCHASING POWER PARITY):

$298.6 billion (2017 est.)

$286.8 billion (2016 est.)

$283.6 billion (2015 est.)

note: data are in 2017 dollars

country comparison to the world: 57

GDP (OFFICIAL EXCHANGE RATE):

$109.3 billion (2017 est.)

GDP - REAL GROWTH RATE:
4.1% (2017 est.)
1.1% (2016 est.)
4.6% (2015 est.)
country comparison to the world: 74

GDP - PER CAPITA (PPP):
$8,600 (2017 est.)
$8,300 (2016 est.)
$8,300 (2015 est.)
note: data are in 2017 dollars
country comparison to the world: 147

GROSS NATIONAL SAVING:
30.1% of GDP (2017 est.)
28.9% of GDP (2016 est.)
28.8% of GDP (2015 est.)
country comparison to the world: 31

GDP - COMPOSITION, BY END USE:
household consumption: 58% (2017 est.)
government consumption: 18.9% (2017 est.)
investment in fixed capital: 28.4% (2017 est.)
investment in inventories: 4.2% (2017 est.)
exports of goods and services: 37.1% (2017 est.)
imports of goods and services: -46.6% (2017 est.)

GDP - COMPOSITION, BY SECTOR OF ORIGIN:
agriculture: 14% (2017 est.)
industry: 29.5% (2017 est.)
services: 56.5% (2017 est.)

AGRICULTURE - PRODUCTS:
barley, wheat, citrus fruits, grapes, vegetables, olives; livestock; wine

INDUSTRIES:
automotive parts, phosphate mining and processing, aerospace, food processing, leather goods, textiles, construction, energy, tourism

INDUSTRIAL PRODUCTION GROWTH RATE:
2.8% (2017 est.)
country comparison to the world: 110

LABOR FORCE:
12 million (2017 est.)
country comparison to the world: 48

LABOR FORCE - BY OCCUPATION:
agriculture: 39.1%
industry: 20.3%
services: 40.5% (2014 est.)

UNEMPLOYMENT RATE:
10.2% (2017 est.)
9.9% (2016 est.)
country comparison to the world: 143

POPULATION BELOW POVERTY LINE:
15% (2007 est.)

HOUSEHOLD INCOME OR CONSUMPTION BY PERCENTAGE SHARE:
lowest 10%: 2.7%
highest 10%: 33.2% (2007)

DISTRIBUTION OF FAMILY INCOME - GINI INDEX:
40.9 (2007 est.)
39.5 (1999 est.)
country comparison to the world: 61

BUDGET:
revenues: 22.81 billion (2017 est.)
expenditures: 26.75 billion (2017 est.)

TAXES AND OTHER REVENUES:
20.9% (of GDP) (2017 est.)
country comparison to the world: 144

BUDGET SURPLUS (+) OR DEFICIT (-):
-3.6% (of GDP) (2017 est.)
country comparison to the world: 150

PUBLIC DEBT:
65.1% of GDP (2017 est.)
64.9% of GDP (2016 est.)
country comparison to the world: 58

FISCAL YEAR:
calendar year

INFLATION RATE (CONSUMER PRICES):
0.8% (2017 est.)
1.6% (2016 est.)
country comparison to the world: 43

CENTRAL BANK DISCOUNT RATE:
6.5% (31 December 2010)
3.31% (31 December 2009)
country comparison to the world: 61

COMMERCIAL BANK PRIME LENDING RATE:
5.6% (31 December 2017 est.)
5.73% (31 December 2016 est.)
country comparison to the world: 131

STOCK OF NARROW MONEY:
$87.13 billion (31 December 2017 est.)
$74.7 billion (31 December 2016 est.)
country comparison to the world: 42

STOCK OF BROAD MONEY:
$87.13 billion (31 December 2017 est.)
$74.7 billion (31 December 2016 est.)
country comparison to the world: 42

STOCK OF DOMESTIC CREDIT:
$124.4 billion (31 December 2017 est.)
$109.3 billion (31 December 2016 est.)
country comparison to the world: 52

MARKET VALUE OF PUBLICLY TRADED SHARES:
$45.93 billion (31 December 2015 est.)
$52.75 billion (31 December 2014 est.)
$53.83 billion (31 December 2013 est.)
country comparison to the world: 53

CURRENT ACCOUNT BALANCE:
-$3.92 billion (2017 est.)
-$4.363 billion (2016 est.)
country comparison to the world: 177

EXPORTS:
$21.48 billion (2017 est.)
$22.66 billion (2016 est.)
country comparison to the world: 70

EXPORTS - PARTNERS:
Spain 23.2%, France 22.6%, Italy 4.5%, US 4.2% (2017)

EXPORTS - COMMODITIES:
clothing and textiles, automobiles, electric components, inorganic chemicals, transistors, crude minerals, fertilizers (including phosphates), petroleum products, citrus fruits, vegetables, fish

IMPORTS:
$39.64 billion (2017 est.)
$36.59 billion (2016 est.)
country comparison to the world: 60

IMPORTS - COMMODITIES:
crude petroleum, textile fabric, telecommunications equipment, wheat, gas and electricity, transistors, plastics

IMPORTS - PARTNERS:
Spain 16.7%, France 12.2%, China 9.2%, US 6.9%, Germany 6%, Italy 5.9%, Turkey 4.5% (2017)

RESERVES OF FOREIGN EXCHANGE AND GOLD:
$26.27 billion (31 December 2017 est.)
$25.37 billion (31 December 2016 est.)
country comparison to the world: 53

DEBT - EXTERNAL:
$51.48 billion (31 December 2017 est.)

$44.65 billion (31 December 2016 est.)

country comparison to the world: 65

STOCK OF DIRECT FOREIGN INVESTMENT - AT HOME:

$63.17 billion (31 December 2017 est.)

$54.78 billion (31 December 2016 est.)

country comparison to the world: 55

STOCK OF DIRECT FOREIGN INVESTMENT - ABROAD:

$5.351 billion (31 December 2017 est.)

$5.203 billion (31 December 2016 est.)

country comparison to the world: 75

EXCHANGE RATES:

Moroccan dirhams (MAD) per US dollar -

9.639 (2017 est.)

9.7787 (2016 est.)

9.7787 (2015 est.)

9.7351 (2014 est.)

8.3798 (2013 est.)

ENERGY :: MOROCCO

ELECTRICITY ACCESS:

electrification - total population: 100% (2016)

ELECTRICITY - PRODUCTION:

28.75 billion kWh (2016 est.)

country comparison to the world: 68

ELECTRICITY - CONSUMPTION:

28.25 billion kWh (2016 est.)

country comparison to the world: 64

ELECTRICITY - EXPORTS:

165 million kWh (2015 est.)

country comparison to the world: 79

ELECTRICITY - IMPORTS:

5.289 billion kWh (2016 est.)

country comparison to the world: 37

ELECTRICITY - INSTALLED GENERATING CAPACITY:

8.303 million kW (2016 est.)

country comparison to the world: 68

ELECTRICITY - FROM FOSSIL FUELS:

68% of total installed capacity (2016 est.)

country comparison to the world: 114

ELECTRICITY - FROM NUCLEAR FUELS:

0% of total installed capacity (2017 est.)

country comparison to the world: 148

ELECTRICITY - FROM HYDROELECTRIC PLANTS:

16% of total installed capacity (2017 est.)

country comparison to the world: 101

ELECTRICITY - FROM OTHER RENEWABLE SOURCES:

15% of total installed capacity (2017 est.)

country comparison to the world: 60

CRUDE OIL - PRODUCTION:

160 bbl/day (2018 est.)

country comparison to the world: 98

CRUDE OIL - EXPORTS:

0 bbl/day (2015 est.)

country comparison to the world: 169

CRUDE OIL - IMPORTS:

61,160 bbl/day (2015 est.)

country comparison to the world: 53

CRUDE OIL - PROVED RESERVES:

684,000 bbl (1 January 2018 est.)

country comparison to the world: 97

REFINED PETROLEUM PRODUCTS - PRODUCTION:

66,230 bbl/day (2017 est.)

country comparison to the world: 74

REFINED PETROLEUM PRODUCTS - CONSUMPTION:

278,000 bbl/day (2016 est.)

country comparison to the world: 44

REFINED PETROLEUM PRODUCTS - EXPORTS:

9,504 bbl/day (2015 est.)

country comparison to the world: 83

REFINED PETROLEUM PRODUCTS - IMPORTS:

229,300 bbl/day (2015 est.)

country comparison to the world: 30

NATURAL GAS - PRODUCTION:

87.78 million cu m (2017 est.)

country comparison to the world: 82

NATURAL GAS - CONSUMPTION:

1.218 billion cu m (2017 est.)

country comparison to the world: 89

NATURAL GAS - EXPORTS:

0 cu m (2017 est.)

country comparison to the world: 156

NATURAL GAS - IMPORTS:

1.133 billion cu m (2017 est.)

country comparison to the world: 61

NATURAL GAS - PROVED RESERVES:

1.444 billion cu m (1 January 2018 est.)

country comparison to the world: 97

CARBON DIOXIDE EMISSIONS FROM CONSUMPTION OF ENERGY:

55.4 million Mt (2017 est.)

country comparison to the world: 56

COMMUNICATIONS :: MOROCCO

TELEPHONES - FIXED LINES:

total subscriptions: 2,046,390

subscriptions per 100 inhabitants: 6 (2017 est.)

country comparison to the world: 57

TELEPHONES - MOBILE CELLULAR:

total subscriptions: 43,916,066

subscriptions per 100 inhabitants: 129 (2017 est.)

country comparison to the world: 32

TELEPHONE SYSTEM:

general assessment: good system composed of open-wire lines, cables, and microwave radio relay links; principal switching centers are Casablanca and Rabat; national network nearly 100% digital using fiber-optic links; improved rural service employs microwave radio relay; one of the most state-of-the-art markets in Africa; high mobile penetration rates in the region with low cost for broadband Internet access; LTE and VoD (Video on Demand) launched (2018)

domestic: fixed-line teledensity is 6 per 100 persons; mobile-cellular subscribership exceeds 129 per 100 persons (2018)

international: country code - 212; landing point for the Atlas Offshore, Estepona-Tetouan, Canalink and SEA-ME-WE-3 fiber-optic telecommunications undersea cables that provide connectivity to Asia, Africa, the Middle East, Europe and Australia; satellite earth stations - 2 Intelsat (Atlantic Ocean) and 1 Arabsat; microwave radio relay to Gibraltar, Spain, and Western Sahara (2019)

BROADCAST MEDIA:

2 TV broadcast networks with state-run Radio-Television Marocaine (RTM) operating one network and the state partially owning the other; foreign TV broadcasts are available via satellite dish; 3 radio broadcast networks with RTM operating one; the government-owned network includes 10 regional radio channels in addition to its national service (2019)

INTERNET COUNTRY CODE:

.ma

INTERNET USERS:

total: 19,611,643

percent of population: 58.3% (July 2016 est.)

country comparison to the world: 34

BROADBAND - FIXED SUBSCRIPTIONS:

total: 1,378,867

subscriptions per 100 inhabitants: 4 (2017 est.)

country comparison to the world: 64

COMMUNICATIONS - NOTE:

the University of al-Quarawiyyin Library in Fez is recognized as the oldest existing, continually operating library in the world, dating back to A.D. 859; among its holdings are approximately 4,000 ancient Islamic manuscripts (2018)

MILITARY AND SECURITY :: MOROCCO

MILITARY EXPENDITURES:

3.1% of GDP (2018)

3.19% of GDP (2017)

3.21% of GDP (2016)

3.23% of GDP (2015)

3.68% of GDP (2014)

country comparison to the world: 21

MILITARY AND SECURITY FORCES:

Royal Armed Forces: Royal Moroccan Army, Royal Moroccan Navy (includes Coast Guard, marines), Royal Moroccan Air Force, Royal Morroccan Gendarmerie, Morroccan Royal Guard (provides security for the royal family; officially part of the Royal Army); Force Auxiliaire (a paramilitary force under the Ministry of Interior that supplements the military and the police as needed) (2019)

MILITARY SERVICE AGE AND OBLIGATION:

19 years of age for compulsory military service; both sexes are obligated to military service; conscript service obligation - 12 months (2019)

TRANSPORTATION :: MOROCCO

NATIONAL AIR TRANSPORT SYSTEM:

number of registered air carriers: 4 (2015)

inventory of registered aircraft operated by air carriers: 65 (2015)

annual passenger traffic on registered air carriers: 6,786,850 (2015)

annual freight traffic on registered air carriers: 47,828,227 mt-km (2015)

CIVIL AIRCRAFT REGISTRATION COUNTRY CODE PREFIX:

CN (2016)

AIRPORTS:

55 (2013)

country comparison to the world: 85

AIRPORTS - WITH PAVED RUNWAYS:

total: 31 (2017)

over 3,047 m: 11 (2017)

2,438 to 3,047 m: 9 (2017)

1,524 to 2,437 m: 7 (2017)

914 to 1,523 m: 4 (2017)

AIRPORTS - WITH UNPAVED RUNWAYS:

total: 24 (2013)

2,438 to 3,047 m: 1 (2013)

1,524 to 2,437 m: 7 (2013)

914 to 1,523 m: 11 (2013)

under 914 m: 5 (2013)

HELIPORTS:

1 (2013)

PIPELINES:

944 km gas, 270 km oil, 175 km refined products (2013)

RAILWAYS:

total: 2,067 km (2014)

standard gauge: 2,067 km 1.435-m gauge (1,022 km electrified) (2014)

country comparison to the world: 73

ROADWAYS:

total: 57,300 km (2018)

country comparison to the world: 79

MERCHANT MARINE:

total: 87

by type: container ship 7, general cargo 6, oil tanker 3, other 71 (2018)

country comparison to the world: 93

PORTS AND TERMINALS:

major seaport(s): Casablanca, Jorf Lasfar, Mohammedia, Safi, Tangier

container port(s) (TEUs): Tangier (3,312,409) (2017)

LNG terminal(s) (import): Jorf Lasfar

TRANSNATIONAL ISSUES :: MOROCCO

DISPUTES - INTERNATIONAL:

claims and administers Western Sahara whose sovereignty remains unresolved; Morocco protests Spain's control over the coastal enclaves of Ceuta, Melilla, and Penon de Velez de la Gomera, the islands of Penon de Alhucemas and Islas Chafarinas, and surrounding waters; both countries claim Isla Perejil (Leila Island); discussions have not progressed on a comprehensive maritime delimitation, setting limits on resource exploration and refugee interdiction, since Morocco's 2002 rejection of Spain's unilateral designation of a median line from the Canary Islands; Morocco serves as one of the primary launching areas of illegal migration into Spain from North Africa; Algeria's border with Morocco remains an irritant to bilateral relations, each nation accusing the other of harboring militants and arms smuggling; the National Liberation Front's assertions of a claim to Chirac Pastures in southeastern Morocco is a dormant dispute

ILLICIT DRUGS:

the world's largest producer and exporter of cannabis; total production for 2015-2016 growing season estimated to be 700 metric tons; shipments of hashish mostly directed to Western Europe; transit point for cocaine from South America destined for Western Europe; significant consumer of cannabis

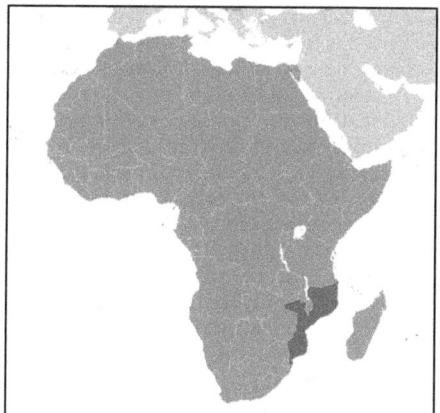

AFRICA :: MOZAMBIQUE

INTRODUCTION :: MOZAMBIQUE

BACKGROUND:

Almost five centuries as a Portuguese colony came to a close with independence in 1975. Large-scale emigration, economic dependence on South Africa, a severe drought, and a prolonged civil war hindered the country's development until the mid-1990s. The ruling Front for the Liberation of Mozambique (FRELIMO) party formally abandoned Marxism in 1989, and a new constitution the following year provided for multiparty elections and a free market economy. A UN-negotiated peace agreement between FRELIMO and rebel Mozambique National Resistance (RENAMO) forces ended the fighting in 1992. In 2004, Mozambique underwent a delicate transition as Joaquim CHISSANO stepped down after 18 years in office. His elected successor, Armando GUEBUZA, served two terms and then passed executive power to Filipe NYUSI in 2015. RENAMO's residual armed forces have intermittently engaged in a low-level insurgency since 2012, although a late December 2016 ceasefire held throughout 2018 and has facilitated efforts toward a peacebuilding initiative and a constitutional amendment to devolve some governance to the provinces. Since October 2017, the northern province of Cabo Delgado has experienced violent extremist attacks.

GEOGRAPHY :: MOZAMBIQUE

LOCATION:

Southeastern Africa, bordering the Mozambique Channel, between South Africa and Tanzania

GEOGRAPHIC COORDINATES:

18 15 S, 35 00 E

MAP REFERENCES:

Africa

AREA:

total: 799,380 sq km

land: 786,380 sq km

water: 13,000 sq km

country comparison to the world: 36

AREA - COMPARATIVE:

slightly more than five times the size of Georgia; slightly less than twice the size of California

LAND BOUNDARIES:

total: 4,783 km

border countries (6): Malawi 1498 km, South Africa 496 km, Eswatini 108 km, Tanzania 840 km, Zambia 439 km, Zimbabwe 1402 km

COASTLINE:

2,470 km

MARITIME CLAIMS:

territorial sea: 12 nm

exclusive economic zone: 200 nm

CLIMATE:

tropical to subtropical

TERRAIN:

mostly coastal lowlands, uplands in center, high plateaus in northwest, mountains in west

ELEVATION:

mean elevation: 345 m

lowest point: Indian Ocean 0 m

highest point: Monte Binga 2,436 m

NATURAL RESOURCES:

coal, titanium, natural gas, hydropower, tantalum, graphite

LAND USE:

agricultural land: 56.3% (2011 est.)

arable land: 6.4% (2011 est.) / permanent crops: 0.3% (2011 est.) / permanent pasture: 49.6% (2011 est.)

forest: 43.7% (2011 est.)

other: 0% (2011 est.)

IRRIGATED LAND:

1,180 sq km (2012)

POPULATION DISTRIBUTION:

three large populations clusters are found along the southern coast between Maputo and Inhambane, in the central area between Beira and Chimoio along the Zambezi River, and in and around the northern cities of Nampula, Cidade de Nacala, and Pemba; the northwest and southwest are the least populated areas

NATURAL HAZARDS:

severe droughts; devastating cyclones and floods in central and southern provinces

ENVIRONMENT - CURRENT ISSUES:

increased migration of the population to urban and coastal areas with adverse environmental consequences; desertification; soil erosion; deforestation; water pollution caused by artisanal mining; pollution of surface and coastal waters; wildlife preservation (elephant poaching for ivory)

ENVIRONMENT - INTERNATIONAL AGREEMENTS:

party to: Biodiversity, Climate Change, Climate Change-Kyoto Protocol, Desertification, Endangered Species, Hazardous Wastes, Law of the Sea, Ozone Layer Protection, Ship Pollution, Wetlands

signed, but not ratified: none of the selected agreements

GEOGRAPHY - NOTE:

the Zambezi River flows through the north-central and most fertile part of the country

PEOPLE AND SOCIETY :: MOZAMBIQUE

POPULATION:

27,233,789 (July 2018 est.)

note: estimates for this country explicitly take into account the effects of excess mortality due to AIDS; this can result in lower life expectancy, higher infant mortality, higher death rates, lower population growth rates, and changes in the distribution of population by age and sex than would otherwise be expected

country comparison to the world: 50

NATIONALITY:

noun: Mozambican(s)

adjective: Mozambican

ETHNIC GROUPS:

African 99.66% (Makhuwa, Tsonga, Lomwe, Sena, and others), Euro-African 0.2%, Indian 0.08%, European 0.06%

LANGUAGES:

Emakhuwa 26.1%, Portuguese (official) 16.6%, Xichangana 8.6%, Cinyanja 8.1, Cisena 7.1%, Elomwe 7.1%, Echuwabo 4.7%, Cindau 3.8%, Xitswa 3.8%, other Mozambican languages 11.8%, other 0.5%, unspecified 1.8% (2017 est.)

RELIGIONS:

Roman Catholic 27.2%, Muslim 18.9%, Zionist Christian 15.6%, Evangelical/Pentecostal 15.3%, Anglican 1.7%, other 4.8%, none 13.9%, unspecified 2.5% (2017 est.)

DEMOGRAPHIC PROFILE:

Mozambique is a poor, sparsely populated country with high fertility and mortality rates and a rapidly growing youthful population – 45% of the population is younger than 15. Mozambique's high poverty rate is sustained by natural disasters, disease, high population growth, low agricultural productivity, and the unequal distribution of wealth. The country's birth rate is among the world's highest, averaging around more than 5 children per woman (and higher in rural areas) for at least the last three decades. The sustained high level of fertility reflects gender inequality, low contraceptive use, early marriages and childbearing, and a lack of education, particularly among women. The high population growth rate is somewhat restrained by the country's high HIV/AIDS and overall mortality rates. Mozambique ranks among the worst in the world for HIV/AIDS prevalence, HIV/AIDS deaths, and life expectancy at birth.

Mozambique is predominantly a country of emigration, but internal, rural-urban migration has begun to grow. Mozambicans, primarily from the country's southern region, have been migrating to South Africa for work for more than a century. Additionally, approximately 1.7 million Mozambicans fled to Malawi, South Africa, and other neighboring countries between 1979 and 1992 to escape from civil war. Labor migrants have usually been men from rural areas whose crops have failed or who are unemployed and have headed to South Africa to work as miners; multiple generations of the same family often become miners. Since the abolition of apartheid in South Africa in 1991, other job opportunities have opened to Mozambicans, including in the informal and manufacturing sectors, but mining remains their main source of employment.

AGE STRUCTURE:

0-14 years: 44.52% (male 6,097,116 /female 6,028,416)

15-24 years: 21.6% (male 2,905,254 /female 2,977,732)

25-54 years: 27.62% (male 3,525,755 /female 3,995,264)

55-64 years: 3.37% (male 442,990 /female 475,900)

65 years and over: 2.88% (male 359,624 /female 425,738) (2018 est.)

DEPENDENCY RATIOS:

total dependency ratio: 93.5 (2015 est.)

youth dependency ratio: 87.5 (2015 est.)

elderly dependency ratio: 6.1 (2015 est.)

potential support ratio: 16.5 (2015 est.)

MEDIAN AGE:

total: 17.3 years (2018 est.)

male: 16.7 years

female: 17.8 years

country comparison to the world: 220

POPULATION GROWTH RATE:

2.46% (2018 est.)

country comparison to the world: 25

BIRTH RATE:

37.8 births/1,000 population (2018 est.)

country comparison to the world: 11

DEATH RATE:

11.4 deaths/1,000 population (2018 est.)

country comparison to the world: 22

NET MIGRATION RATE:

-1.8 migrant(s)/1,000 population (2018 est.)

country comparison to the world: 159

POPULATION DISTRIBUTION:

three large populations clusters are found along the southern coast between Maputo and Inhambane, in the central area between Beira and Chimoio along the Zambezi River, and in and around the northern cities of Nampula, Cidade de Nacala, and Pemba; the northwest and southwest are the least populated areas

URBANIZATION:

urban population: 36.5% of total population (2019)

rate of urbanization: 4.35% annual rate of change (2015-20 est.)

MAJOR URBAN AREAS - POPULATION:

1.669 million Matola, 1.104 million MAPUTO (capital), 811,000 Nampula (2019)

SEX RATIO:

at birth: 1.02 male(s)/female

0-14 years: 1.01 male(s)/female

15-24 years: 0.98 male(s)/female

25-54 years: 0.88 male(s)/female

55-64 years: 0.93 male(s)/female

65 years and over: 0.84 male(s)/female

total population: 0.96 male(s)/female (2018 est.)

MOTHER'S MEAN AGE AT FIRST BIRTH:

18.9 years (2011 est.)

median age at first birth among women 25-29

MATERNAL MORTALITY RATE:

289 deaths/100,000 live births (2017 est.)

country comparison to the world: 39

INFANT MORTALITY RATE:

total: 64 deaths/1,000 live births (2018 est.)

male: 66 deaths/1,000 live births

female: 62 deaths/1,000 live births

country comparison to the world: 11

LIFE EXPECTANCY AT BIRTH:

total population: 54.1 years (2018 est.)

male: 53.3 years

female: 54.9 years

country comparison to the world: 218

TOTAL FERTILITY RATE:

5.02 children born/woman (2018 est.)

country comparison to the world: 12

CONTRACEPTIVE PREVALENCE RATE:

27.1% (2015)

DRINKING WATER SOURCE:

improved:

urban: 80.6% of population

rural: 37% of population

total: 51.1% of population

unimproved:

urban: 19.4% of population

rural: 63% of population

total: 48.9% of population (2015 est.)

CURRENT HEALTH EXPENDITURE:

5.1% (2016)

PHYSICIANS DENSITY:

0.07 physicians/1,000 population (2017)

HOSPITAL BED DENSITY:

0.7 beds/1,000 population (2011)

SANITATION FACILITY ACCESS:

improved:

urban: 42.4% of population (2015 est.)

rural: 10.1% of population (2015 est.)

total: 20.5% of population (2015 est.)

unimproved:

urban: 57.6% of population (2015 est.)

rural: 89.9% of population (2015 est.)

total: 79.5% of population (2015 est.)

HIV/AIDS - ADULT PREVALENCE RATE:

12.6% (2018 est.)

country comparison to the world: 6

HIV/AIDS - PEOPLE LIVING WITH HIV/AIDS:

2.2 million (2018 est.)

country comparison to the world: 2

HIV/AIDS - DEATHS:

53,900 (2018 est.)

country comparison to the world: 3

MAJOR INFECTIOUS DISEASES:

degree of risk: very high (2016)

food or waterborne diseases: bacterial and protozoal diarrhea, hepatitis A, and typhoid fever (2016)

vectorborne diseases: malaria and dengue fever (2016)

water contact diseases: schistosomiasis (2016)

animal contact diseases: rabies (2016)

OBESITY - ADULT PREVALENCE RATE:

7.2% (2016)

country comparison to the world: 160

CHILDREN UNDER THE AGE OF 5 YEARS UNDERWEIGHT:

15.6% (2011)

country comparison to the world: 41

EDUCATION EXPENDITURES:

6.5% of GDP (2013)

country comparison to the world: 23

LITERACY:

definition: age 15 and over can read and write

total population: 56%

male: 70.8%

female: 43.1% (2015 est.)

SCHOOL LIFE EXPECTANCY (PRIMARY TO TERTIARY EDUCATION):

total: 10 years

male: 10 years

female: 9 years (2017)

UNEMPLOYMENT, YOUTH AGES 15-24:

total: 7.4%

male: 7.7%

female: 7.1% (2015 est.)

country comparison to the world: 152

GOVERNMENT :: MOZAMBIQUE

COUNTRY NAME:

conventional long form: Republic of Mozambique

conventional short form: Mozambique

local long form: Republica de Mocambique

local short form: Mocambique

former: Portuguese East Africa, People's Republic of Mozambique

etymology: named for the offshore island of Mozambique; the island was apparently named after Mussa al-BIK, an influential Arab slave trader who set himself up as sultan on the island in the 15th century

GOVERNMENT TYPE:
presidential republic

CAPITAL:
name: Maputo

geographic coordinates: 25 57 S, 32 35 E

time difference: UTC+2 (7 hours ahead of Washington, DC, during Standard Time)

etymology: reputedly named after the Maputo River, which drains into Maputo Bay south of the city

ADMINISTRATIVE DIVISIONS:
10 provinces (provincias, singular - provincia), 1 city (cidade)*; Cabo Delgado, Gaza, Inhambane, Manica, Maputo, Cidade de Maputo*, Nampula, Niassa, Sofala, Tete, Zambezia

INDEPENDENCE:
25 June 1975 (from Portugal)

NATIONAL HOLIDAY:
Independence Day, 25 June (1975)

CONSTITUTION:
history: previous 1975, 1990; latest adopted 16 November 2004, effective 21 December 2004

amendments: proposed by the president of the republic or supported by at least one third of the Assembly of the Republic membership; passage of amendments affecting constitutional provisions, including the independence and sovereignty of the state, the republican form of government, basic rights and freedoms, and universal suffrage, requires at least a two-thirds majority vote by the Assembly and approval in a referendum; referenda not required for passage of other amendments; amended 2007, 2018 (2018)

LEGAL SYSTEM:
mixed legal system of Portuguese civil law and customary law; note - in rural, apply where applicable predominantly Muslim villages with no formal legal system, Islamic law may be applied

INTERNATIONAL LAW ORGANIZATION PARTICIPATION:
has not submitted an ICJ jurisdiction declaration; non-party state to the ICCt

CITIZENSHIP:
citizenship by birth: no

citizenship by descent only: at least one parent must be a citizen of Mozambique

dual citizenship recognized: no

residency requirement for naturalization: 5 years

SUFFRAGE:
18 years of age; universal

EXECUTIVE BRANCH:
chief of state: President Filipe Jacinto NYUSI (since 15 January 2015, re-elected 15 Oct 2019) (2019)

head of government: President Filipe Jacinto NYUSI (since 15 January 2015); Prime Minister Carlos Agostinho DO ROSARIO (since 17 January 2015) (2019)

cabinet: Cabinet appointed by the president

elections/appointments: president elected directly by absolute majority popular vote in 2 rounds if needed for a 5-year term (eligible for 2 consecutive terms); election last held on 15 October 2019 (next to be held on 15 October 2024); prime minister appointed by the president (2019)

election results: Filipe NYUSI elected president in first round; percent of vote - Filipe NYUSI (FRELIMO) 73.0%, Ossufo MOMADE (RENAMO) 21.9%, Daviz SIMANGO (MDM) 5.1% (2019)

LEGISLATIVE BRANCH:
description: unicameral Assembly of the Republic or Assembleia da Republica (250 seats; 248 members elected in multi-seat constituencies by party-list proportional representation vote and 2 single members representing Mozambicans abroad directly elected by simple majority vote; members serve 5-year terms) (2019)

elections: last held on 15 October 2019 (next to be held on 15 October 2024) (2019)

election results: percent of vote by party - FRELIMO 58%, RENAMO 36%, MDM 7%; seats by party - FRELIMO 144, RENAMO 89, MDM 17; composition - men 151, women 99, percent of women 39.6% (2019)

JUDICIAL BRANCH:
highest courts: Supreme Court (consists of the court president, vice president, and 5 judges); Constitutional Council (consists of 7 judges); note - the Higher Council of the Judiciary Magistracy is responsible for judiciary management and discipline

judge selection and term of office: Supreme Court president appointed by the president of the republic; vice president appointed by the president in consultation with the Higher Council of the Judiciary (CSMJ) and ratified by the Assembly of the Republic; other judges elected by the Assembly; judges serve 5-year renewable terms; Constitutional Council judges appointed - 1 by the president, 5 by the Assembly, and 1 by the CSMJ; judges serve 5-year nonrenewable terms

subordinate courts: Administrative Court (capital city only); provincial courts or Tribunais Judicias de Provincia; District Courts or Tribunais Judicias de Districto; customs courts; maritime courts; courts marshal; labor courts; community courts

POLITICAL PARTIES AND LEADERS:
Democratic Movement of Mozambique (Movimento Democratico de Mocambique) or MDM [Daviz SIMANGO]
Front for the Liberation of Mozambique (Frente de Liberatacao de Mocambique) or FRELIMO [Filipe NYUSI]
Mozambican National Resistance (Resistencia Nacional Mocambicana) or RENAMO [Ossufo MOMADE]
Optimistic Party for the Development of Mozambique or Podemos [Helder Mendonca]

INTERNATIONAL ORGANIZATION PARTICIPATION:
ACP, AfDB, AU, C, CD, CPLP, EITI (compliant country), FAO, G-77, IAEA, IBRD, ICAO, ICC (NGOs), ICRM, IDA, IDB, IFAD, IFC, IFRCS, IHO, ILO, IMF, IMO, IMSO, Interpol, IOC, IOM, IPU, ISO (correspondent), ITSO, ITU, ITUC (NGOs), MIGA, NAM, OIC, OIF (observer), OPCW, SADC, UN, UNCTAD, UNESCO, UNHCR, UNIDO, Union Latina, UNISFA, UNWTO, UPU, WCO, WFTU (NGOs), WHO, WIPO, WMO, WTO

DIPLOMATIC REPRESENTATION IN THE US:
Ambassador Carlos DOS SANTOS (since 28 January 2016)

chancery: 1525 New Hampshire Avenue NW, Washington, DC 20036 telephone: [1] (202) 293-7146

FAX: [1] (202) 835-0245

DIPLOMATIC REPRESENTATION FROM THE US:

chief of mission: Ambassador Dennis W. HEARNE (since 22 February 2019)

telephone: [258] (21) 49 2797

embassy: Avenida Kenneth Kuanda 193, Caixa Postal, 783, Maputo

mailing address: P.O. Box 783, Maputo

FAX: [258] (21) 49 0114

FLAG DESCRIPTION:

three equal horizontal bands of green (top), black, and yellow with a red isosceles triangle based on the hoist side; the black band is edged in white; centered in the triangle is a yellow five-pointed star bearing a crossed rifle and hoe in black superimposed on an open white book; green represents the riches of the land, white peace, black the African continent, yellow the country's minerals, and red the struggle for independence; the rifle symbolizes defense and vigilance, the hoe refers to the country's agriculture, the open book stresses the importance of education, and the star represents Marxism and internationalism

note: one of only two national flags featuring a firearm, the other is Guatemala

NATIONAL SYMBOL(S):

national colors: green, black, yellow, white, red

NATIONAL ANTHEM:

name: "Patria Amada" (Lovely Fatherland)

lyrics/music: Salomao J. MANHICA/unknown

note: adopted 2002

ECONOMY :: MOZAMBIQUE

ECONOMY - OVERVIEW:

At independence in 1975, Mozambique was one of the world's poorest countries. Socialist policies, economic mismanagement, and a brutal civil war from 1977 to 1992 further impoverished the country. In 1987, the government embarked on a series of macroeconomic reforms designed to stabilize the economy. These steps, combined with donor assistance and with political stability since the multi-party elections in 1994, propelled the country's GDP, in purchasing power parity terms, from $4 billion in 1993 to about $37 billion in 2017. Fiscal reforms, including the introduction of a value-added tax and reform of the customs service, have improved the government's revenue collection abilities. In spite of these gains, about half the population remains below the poverty line and subsistence agriculture continues to employ the vast majority of the country's work force.

Mozambique's once substantial foreign debt was reduced through forgiveness and rescheduling under the IMF's Heavily Indebted Poor Countries (HIPC) and Enhanced HIPC initiatives. However, in 2016, information surfaced revealing that the Mozambican Government was responsible for over $2 billion in government-backed loans secured between 2012-14 by state-owned defense and security companies without parliamentary approval or national budget inclusion; this prompted the IMF and international donors to halt direct budget support to the Government of Mozambique. An international audit was performed on Mozambique's debt in 2016-17, but debt restructuring and resumption of donor support have yet to occur.

Mozambique grew at an average annual rate of 6%-8% in the decade leading up to 2015, one of Africa's strongest performances, but the sizable external debt burden, donor withdrawal, elevated inflation, and currency depreciation contributed to slower growth in 2016-17.

Two major International consortiums, led by American companies ExxonMobil and Anadarko, are seeking approval to develop massive natural gas deposits off the coast of Cabo Delgado province, in what has the potential to become the largest infrastructure project in Africa. . The government predicts sales of liquefied natural gas from these projects could generate several billion dollars in revenues annually sometime after 2022.

GDP (PURCHASING POWER PARITY):

$37.09 billion (2017 est.)

$35.76 billion (2016 est.)

$34.46 billion (2015 est.)

note: data are in 2017 dollars

country comparison to the world: 122

GDP (OFFICIAL EXCHANGE RATE):

$12.59 billion (2017 est.)

GDP - REAL GROWTH RATE:

3.7% (2017 est.)

3.8% (2016 est.)

6.6% (2015 est.)

country comparison to the world: 91

GDP - PER CAPITA (PPP):

$1,300 (2017 est.)

$1,200 (2016 est.)

$1,200 (2015 est.)

note: data are in 2017 dollars

country comparison to the world: 222

GROSS NATIONAL SAVING:

16.8% of GDP (2017 est.)

-1.2% of GDP (2016 est.)

5% of GDP (2015 est.)

country comparison to the world: 123

GDP - COMPOSITION, BY END USE:

household consumption: 69.7% (2017 est.)

government consumption: 27.2% (2017 est.)

investment in fixed capital: 21.7% (2017 est.)

investment in inventories: 13.9% (2017 est.)

exports of goods and services: 38.3% (2017 est.)

imports of goods and services: -70.6% (2017 est.)

GDP - COMPOSITION, BY SECTOR OF ORIGIN:

agriculture: 23.9% (2017 est.)

industry: 19.3% (2017 est.)

services: 56.8% (2017 est.)

AGRICULTURE - PRODUCTS:

cotton, cashew nuts, sugarcane, tea, cassava (manioc, tapioca), corn, coconuts, sisal, citrus and tropical fruits, potatoes, sunflowers; beef, poultry

INDUSTRIES:

aluminum, petroleum products, chemicals (fertilizer, soap, paints), textiles, cement, glass, asbestos, tobacco, food, beverages

INDUSTRIAL PRODUCTION GROWTH RATE:

4.9% (2017 est.)

country comparison to the world: 61

LABOR FORCE:

12.9 million (2017 est.)

country comparison to the world: 45

LABOR FORCE - BY OCCUPATION:

agriculture: 74.4%

industry: 3.9%

services: 21.7% (2015 est.)

UNEMPLOYMENT RATE:

24.5% (2017 est.)

25% (2016 est.)

country comparison to the world: 196

POPULATION BELOW POVERTY LINE:

46.1% (2015 est.)

HOUSEHOLD INCOME OR CONSUMPTION BY PERCENTAGE SHARE:

lowest 10%: 1.9%

highest 10%: 36.7% (2008)

DISTRIBUTION OF FAMILY INCOME - GINI INDEX:

45.6 (2008)

47.3 (2002)

country comparison to the world: 39

BUDGET:

revenues: 3.356 billion (2017 est.)

expenditures: 4.054 billion (2017 est.)

TAXES AND OTHER REVENUES:

26.7% (of GDP) (2017 est.)

country comparison to the world: 105

BUDGET SURPLUS (+) OR DEFICIT (-):

-5.6% (of GDP) (2017 est.)

country comparison to the world: 176

PUBLIC DEBT:

102.1% of GDP (2017 est.)

121.6% of GDP (2016 est.)

country comparison to the world: 15

FISCAL YEAR:

calendar year

INFLATION RATE (CONSUMER PRICES):

15.3% (2017 est.)

19.2% (2016 est.)

country comparison to the world: 212

CENTRAL BANK DISCOUNT RATE:

19% (4 November 2017)

23.25% (31 December 2016)

country comparison to the world: 8

COMMERCIAL BANK PRIME LENDING RATE:

27.86% (31 December 2017 est.)

21.18% (31 December 2016 est.)

country comparison to the world: 8

STOCK OF NARROW MONEY:

$3.817 billion (31 December 2017 est.)

$3.411 billion (31 December 2016 est.)

country comparison to the world: 112

STOCK OF BROAD MONEY:

$3.817 billion (31 December 2017 est.)

$3.411 billion (31 December 2016 est.)

country comparison to the world: 117

STOCK OF DOMESTIC CREDIT:

$4.337 billion (31 December 2017 est.)

$4.242 billion (31 December 2016 est.)

country comparison to the world: 131

MARKET VALUE OF PUBLICLY TRADED SHARES:

NA

CURRENT ACCOUNT BALANCE:

-$2.824 billion (2017 est.)

-$4.28 billion (2016 est.)

country comparison to the world: 174

EXPORTS:

$4.725 billion (2017 est.)

$3.328 billion (2016 est.)

country comparison to the world: 111

EXPORTS - PARTNERS:

India 28.1%, Netherlands 24.4%, South Africa 16.7% (2017)

EXPORTS - COMMODITIES:

aluminum, prawns, cashews, cotton, sugar, citrus, timber; bulk electricity

IMPORTS:

$5.223 billion (2017 est.)

$4.733 billion (2016 est.)

country comparison to the world: 124

IMPORTS - COMMODITIES:

machinery and equipment, vehicles, fuel, chemicals, metal products, foodstuffs, textiles

IMPORTS - PARTNERS:

South Africa 36.8%, China 7%, UAE 6.8%, India 6.2%, Portugal 4.4% (2017)

RESERVES OF FOREIGN EXCHANGE AND GOLD:

$3.361 billion (31 December 2017 est.)

$2.081 billion (31 December 2016 est.)

country comparison to the world: 106

DEBT - EXTERNAL:

$10.91 billion (31 December 2017 est.)

$10.48 billion (31 December 2016 est.)

country comparison to the world: 110

EXCHANGE RATES:

meticais (MZM) per US dollar -

64.4 (2017 est.)

63.067 (2016 est.)

63.067 (2015 est.)

39.983 (2014 est.)

31.367 (2013 est.)

ENERGY :: MOZAMBIQUE

ELECTRICITY ACCESS:

population without electricity: 21 million (2017)

electrification - total population: 24.2% (2016)

electrification - urban areas: 64.2% (2016)

electrification - rural areas: 5% (2016)

ELECTRICITY - PRODUCTION:

18.39 billion kWh (2016 est.)

country comparison to the world: 79

ELECTRICITY - CONSUMPTION:

11.57 billion kWh (2016 est.)

country comparison to the world: 90

ELECTRICITY - EXPORTS:

12.88 billion kWh (2015 est.)

country comparison to the world: 16

ELECTRICITY - IMPORTS:

9.928 billion kWh (2016 est.)

country comparison to the world: 25

ELECTRICITY - INSTALLED GENERATING CAPACITY:

2.626 million kW (2016 est.)

country comparison to the world: 102

ELECTRICITY - FROM FOSSIL FUELS:

16% of total installed capacity (2016 est.)

country comparison to the world: 199

ELECTRICITY - FROM NUCLEAR FUELS:

0% of total installed capacity (2017 est.)

country comparison to the world: 149

ELECTRICITY - FROM HYDROELECTRIC PLANTS:

83% of total installed capacity (2017 est.)

country comparison to the world: 12

ELECTRICITY - FROM OTHER RENEWABLE SOURCES:

1% of total installed capacity (2017 est.)

country comparison to the world: 161

CRUDE OIL - PRODUCTION:

0 bbl/day (2018 est.)

country comparison to the world: 178

CRUDE OIL - EXPORTS:

0 bbl/day (2015 est.)

country comparison to the world: 170

CRUDE OIL - IMPORTS:

0 bbl/day (2015 est.)

country comparison to the world: 171

CRUDE OIL - PROVED RESERVES:

0 bbl (1 January 2018 est.)

country comparison to the world: 173

REFINED PETROLEUM PRODUCTS - PRODUCTION:

0 bbl/day (2015 est.)

country comparison to the world: 182

REFINED PETROLEUM PRODUCTS - CONSUMPTION:

26,000 bbl/day (2016 est.)

country comparison to the world: 128

REFINED PETROLEUM PRODUCTS - EXPORTS:

0 bbl/day (2015 est.)

country comparison to the world: 185

REFINED PETROLEUM PRODUCTS - IMPORTS:

25,130 bbl/day (2015 est.)

country comparison to the world: 107

NATURAL GAS - PRODUCTION:

6.003 billion cu m (2017 est.)

country comparison to the world: 47

NATURAL GAS - CONSUMPTION:

1.841 billion cu m (2017 est.)

country comparison to the world: 84

NATURAL GAS - EXPORTS:

4.162 billion cu m (2017 est.)

country comparison to the world: 32

NATURAL GAS - IMPORTS:

0 cu m (2017 est.)

country comparison to the world: 161

NATURAL GAS - PROVED RESERVES:

2.832 trillion cu m (1 January 2018 est.)

country comparison to the world: 13

CARBON DIOXIDE EMISSIONS FROM CONSUMPTION OF ENERGY:

11.12 million Mt (2017 est.)

country comparison to the world: 102

COMMUNICATIONS :: MOZAMBIQUE

TELEPHONES - FIXED LINES:

total subscriptions: 80,545

subscriptions per 100 inhabitants: less than 1 (2017 est.)

country comparison to the world: 144

TELEPHONES - MOBILE CELLULAR:

total subscriptions: 11,875,506

subscriptions per 100 inhabitants: 45 (2017 est.)

country comparison to the world: 77

TELEPHONE SYSTEM:

general assessment: the mobile segment has shown strong growth given competition; poor fixed-line infrastructure means most Internet access is through mobile accounts; DSL, cable broadband, WiMAX (broadband over long distances), 3G and some fibre broadband available; LTE services launched (2018)

domestic: extremely low fixed-line teledensity contrasts with rapid growth in the mobile-cellular network; operators provide coverage that includes all the main cities and key roads; fixed-line less than 1 per 100 and 45 per 100 mobile-cellular teledensity (2018)

international: country code - 258; landing points for the EASSy and SEACOM/ Tata TGN-Eurasia fiber-optic submarine cable systems linking numerous east African countries, the Middle East and Asia ; satellite earth stations - 5 Intelsat (2 Atlantic Ocean and 3 Indian Ocean) (2019)

BROADCAST MEDIA:

1 state-run TV station supplemented by private TV station; Portuguese state TV's African service, RTP Africa, and Brazilian-owned TV Miramar are available; state-run radio provides nearly 100% territorial coverage and broadcasts in multiple languages; a number of privately owned and community-operated stations; transmissions of multiple international broadcasters are available (2019)

INTERNET COUNTRY CODE:

.mz

INTERNET USERS:

total: 4,543,284

percent of population: 17.5% (July 2016 est.)

country comparison to the world: 81

BROADBAND - FIXED SUBSCRIPTIONS:

total: 41,653

subscriptions per 100 inhabitants: less than 1 (2017 est.)

country comparison to the world: 133

MILITARY AND SECURITY :: MOZAMBIQUE

MILITARY EXPENDITURES:

0.99% of GDP (2018)

1.02% of GDP (2017)

1.03% of GDP (2016)

0.81% of GDP (2015)

1.02% of GDP (2014)

country comparison to the world: 118

MILITARY AND SECURITY FORCES:

Armed Defense Forces of Mozambique (Forcas Armadas de Defesa de Mocambique, FADM): Mozambique Army, Mozambique Navy (Marinha de Guerra de Mocambique, MGM), Mozambique Air Force (Forca Aerea de Mocambique, FAM) (2019)

MILITARY SERVICE AGE AND OBLIGATION:

registration for military service is mandatory for all males and females at 18 years of age; 18-35 years of age for selective compulsory military service; 18 years of age for voluntary service; 2-year service obligation; women may serve as officers or enlisted (2019)

TRANSPORTATION :: MOZAMBIQUE

NATIONAL AIR TRANSPORT SYSTEM:

number of registered air carriers: 3 (2015)

inventory of registered aircraft operated by air carriers: 16 (2015)

annual passenger traffic on registered air carriers: 686,892 (2015)

annual freight traffic on registered air carriers: 5,138,916 mt-km (2015)

CIVIL AIRCRAFT REGISTRATION COUNTRY CODE PREFIX:

C9 (2016)

AIRPORTS:

98 (2013)

country comparison to the world: 57

AIRPORTS - WITH PAVED RUNWAYS:

total: 21 (2017)

over 3,047 m: 1 (2017)

2,438 to 3,047 m: 2 (2017)

1,524 to 2,437 m: 9 (2017)

914 to 1,523 m: 5 (2017)

under 914 m: 4 (2017)

AIRPORTS - WITH UNPAVED RUNWAYS:

total: 77 (2013)

2,438 to 3,047 m: 1 (2013)

1,524 to 2,437 m: 9 (2013)

914 to 1,523 m: 29 (2013)

under 914 m: 38 (2013)

PIPELINES:

972 km gas, 278 km refined products (2013)

RAILWAYS:

total: 4,787 km (2014)

narrow gauge: 4,787 km 1.067-m gauge (2014)

country comparison to the world: 41

ROADWAYS:

total: 31,083 km (2015)

paved: 7,365 km (2015)

unpaved: 23,718 km (2015)

country comparison to the world: 96

WATERWAYS:

460 km (Zambezi River navigable to Tete and along Cahora Bassa Lake) (2010)

country comparison to the world: 85

MERCHANT MARINE:

total: 27

by type: general cargo 10, other 17 (2018)

country comparison to the world: 132

PORTS AND TERMINALS:

major seaport(s): Beira, Maputo, Nacala

TRANSNATIONAL ISSUES :: MOZAMBIQUE

DISPUTES - INTERNATIONAL:

South Africa has placed military units to assist police operations along the border of Lesotho, Zimbabwe, and Mozambique to control smuggling, poaching, and illegal migration

REFUGEES AND INTERNALLY DISPLACED PERSONS:

refugees (country of origin): 9,802 (Democratic Republic of Congo) (refugees and asylum seekers), 7,841 (Burundi) (refugees and asylum seekers) (2019)

IDPs: 14,000 (violence between the government and an opposition group, violence associated with extremists groups in 2018) (2018)

ILLICIT DRUGS:

southern African transit point for South Asian hashish and heroin, and South American cocaine probably destined for the European and South African markets; producer of cannabis (for local consumption) and methaqualone (for export to South Africa); corruption and poor regulatory capability make the banking system vulnerable to money laundering, but the lack of a well-developed financial infrastructure limits the country's utility as a money-laundering center

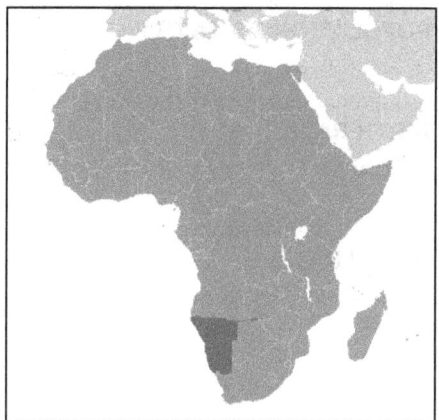

AFRICA :: NAMIBIA

INTRODUCTION :: NAMIBIA

BACKGROUND:

Namibia gained independence in 1990. Prior to independence, apartheid South Africa occupied the former German colony known as South-West Africa during World War I and administered it as a mandate until after World War II, when it annexed the territory. In 1966, the Marxist South-West Africa People's Organization (SWAPO) guerrilla group launched a war of independence for the area that became Namibia, but it was not until 1988 that South Africa agreed to end its administration in accordance with a UN peace plan for the entire region. Namibia has been governed by SWAPO since the country won independence, though the party has dropped much of its Marxist ideology. President Hage GEINGOB was elected in 2014 in a landslide victory, replacing Hifikepunye POHAMBA who stepped down after serving two terms. SWAPO retained its parliamentary super majority in the 2014 elections and established a system of gender parity in parliamentary positions.

GEOGRAPHY :: NAMIBIA

LOCATION:
Southern Africa, bordering the South Atlantic Ocean, between Angola and South Africa

GEOGRAPHIC COORDINATES:
22 00 S, 17 00 E

MAP REFERENCES:
Africa

AREA:
total: 824,292 sq km

land: 823,290 sq km

water: 1,002 sq km

country comparison to the world: 35

AREA - COMPARATIVE:
almost seven times the size of Pennsylvania; slightly more than half the size of Alaska

LAND BOUNDARIES:
total: 4,220 km

border countries (4): Angola 1427 km, Botswana 1544 km, South Africa 1005 km, Zambia 244 km

COASTLINE:
1,572 km

MARITIME CLAIMS:
territorial sea: 12 nm

exclusive economic zone: 200 nm

contiguous zone: 24 nm

CLIMATE:
desert; hot, dry; rainfall sparse and erratic

TERRAIN:
mostly high plateau; Namib Desert along coast; Kalahari Desert in east

ELEVATION:
mean elevation: 1,141 m

lowest point: Atlantic Ocean 0 m

highest point: Konigstein on Brandberg 2,573 m

NATURAL RESOURCES:
diamonds, copper, uranium, gold, silver, lead, tin, lithium, cadmium, tungsten, zinc, salt, hydropower, fish, note, suspected deposits of oil, coal, and iron ore

LAND USE:
agricultural land: 47.2% (2011 est.)

arable land: 1% (2011 est.) / permanent crops: 0% (2011 est.) / permanent pasture: 46.2% (2011 est.)

forest: 8.8% (2011 est.)

other: 44% (2011 est.)

IRRIGATED LAND:
80 sq km (2012)

POPULATION DISTRIBUTION:
population density is very low, with the largest clustering found in the extreme north-central area along the border with Angola

NATURAL HAZARDS:
prolonged periods of drought

ENVIRONMENT - CURRENT ISSUES:
depletion and degradation of water and aquatic resources; desertification; land degradation; loss of biodiversity and biotic resources; wildlife poaching

ENVIRONMENT - INTERNATIONAL AGREEMENTS:
party to: Antarctic-Marine Living Resources, Biodiversity, Climate Change, Climate Change-Kyoto Protocol, Desertification, Endangered Species, Hazardous Wastes, Law of the Sea, Ozone Layer Protection, Wetlands

signed, but not ratified: none of the selected agreements

GEOGRAPHY - NOTE:
the Namib Desert, after which the country is named, is considered to be the oldest desert in the world; Namibia is the first country in the world to incorporate the protection of the environment into its constitution; some 14% of the land is protected, including virtually the entire Namib

Desert coastal strip; Namib-Naukluft National Park (49,768 sq km), is the largest game park in Africa and one of the largest in the world

PEOPLE AND SOCIETY :: NAMIBIA

POPULATION:
2,533,224 (July 2018 est.)

note: estimates for this country explicitly take into account the effects of excess mortality due to AIDS; this can result in lower life expectancy, higher infant mortality, higher death rates, lower population growth rates, and changes in the distribution of population by age and sex than would otherwise be expected

country comparison to the world: 142

NATIONALITY:
noun: Namibian(s)

adjective: Namibian

ETHNIC GROUPS:
Ovambo 50%, Kavangos 9%, Herero 7%, Damara 7%, European and African ancestry 6.5%, European 6%, Nama 5%, Caprivian 4%, San 3%, Baster 2%, Tswana .5%

LANGUAGES:
Oshiwambo languages 49.7%, Nama/Damara 11%, Kavango languages 10.4%, Afrikaans 9.4% (common language of most of the population), Herero languages 9.2%, Zambezi languages 4.9%, English (official) 2.3%, other African languages 1.5%, other European languages .7%, other 1% (2016 est.)

note: Namibia has 13 recognized national languages, including 10 indigenous African languages and 3 Indo-European languages

RELIGIONS:
Christian 80% to 90% (at least 50% Lutheran), indigenous beliefs 10% to 20%

DEMOGRAPHIC PROFILE:
Planning officials view Namibia's reduced population growth rate as sustainable based on the country's economic growth over the past decade. Prior to independence in 1990, Namibia's relatively small population grew at about 3% annually, but declining fertility and the impact of HIV/AIDS slowed this growth to 1.4% by 2011, rebounding to close to 2% by 2016. Namibia's fertility rate has fallen over the last two decades – from about 4.5 children per woman in 1996 to 3.4 in 2016 – due to increased contraceptive use, higher educational attainment among women, and greater female participation in the labor force. The average age at first birth has stayed fairly constant, but the age at first marriage continues to increase, indicating a rising incidence of premarital childbearing.

The majority of Namibians are rural dwellers (about 55%) and live in the better-watered north and northeast parts of the country. Migration, historically male-dominated, generally flows from northern communal areas – non-agricultural lands where blacks were sequestered under the apartheid system – to agricultural, mining, and manufacturing centers in the center and south. After independence from South Africa, restrictions on internal movement eased, and rural-urban migration increased, bolstering urban growth.

Some Namibians – usually persons who are better-educated, more affluent, and from urban areas – continue to legally migrate to South Africa temporarily to visit family and friends and, much less frequently, to pursue tertiary education or better economic opportunities. Namibians concentrated along the country's other borders make unauthorized visits to Angola, Zambia, Zimbabwe, or Botswana, to visit family and to trade agricultural goods. Few Namibians express interest in permanently settling in other countries; they prefer the safety of their homeland, have a strong national identity, and enjoy a well-supplied retail sector. Although Namibia is receptive to foreign investment and cross-border trade, intolerance toward non-citizens is widespread.

AGE STRUCTURE:
0-14 years: 36.54% (male 467,392 /female 458,190)

15-24 years: 20.34% (male 257,190 /female 257,984)

25-54 years: 34.74% (male 421,849 /female 458,118)

55-64 years: 4.46% (male 50,459 /female 62,478)

65 years and over: 3.93% (male 42,381 /female 57,183) (2018 est.)

DEPENDENCY RATIOS:
total dependency ratio: 68.1 (2015 est.)

youth dependency ratio: 62.2 (2015 est.)

elderly dependency ratio: 5.8 (2015 est.)

potential support ratio: 17.1 (2015 est.)

MEDIAN AGE:
total: 21.4 years (2018 est.)

male: 20.7 years

female: 22.2 years

country comparison to the world: 182

POPULATION GROWTH RATE:
1.91% (2018 est.)

country comparison to the world: 52

BIRTH RATE:
26.8 births/1,000 population (2018 est.)

country comparison to the world: 45

DEATH RATE:
7.7 deaths/1,000 population (2018 est.)

country comparison to the world: 101

NET MIGRATION RATE:
0 migrant(s)/1,000 population (2018 est.)

country comparison to the world: 94

POPULATION DISTRIBUTION:
population density is very low, with the largest clustering found in the extreme north-central area along the border with Angola

URBANIZATION:
urban population: 51% of total population (2019)

rate of urbanization: 4.2% annual rate of change (2015-20 est.)

MAJOR URBAN AREAS - POPULATION:
417,000 WINDHOEK (capital) (2019)

SEX RATIO:
at birth: 1.03 male(s)/female

0-14 years: 1.02 male(s)/female

15-24 years: 1 male(s)/female

25-54 years: 0.92 male(s)/female

55-64 years: 0.81 male(s)/female

65 years and over: 0.74 male(s)/female

total population: 0.96 male(s)/female (2018 est.)

MOTHER'S MEAN AGE AT FIRST BIRTH:
21.5 years (2013 est.)

note: median age at first birth among women 25-29

MATERNAL MORTALITY RATE:

195 deaths/100,000 live births (2017 est.)

country comparison to the world: 48

INFANT MORTALITY RATE:

total: 33.8 deaths/1,000 live births (2018 est.)

male: 36 deaths/1,000 live births

female: 31.6 deaths/1,000 live births

country comparison to the world: 54

LIFE EXPECTANCY AT BIRTH:

total population: 64.4 years (2018 est.)

male: 62.7 years

female: 66.2 years

country comparison to the world: 189

TOTAL FERTILITY RATE:

3.21 children born/woman (2018 est.)

country comparison to the world: 47

CONTRACEPTIVE PREVALENCE RATE:

56.1% (2013)

DRINKING WATER SOURCE:

improved:

urban: 98.2% of population

rural: 84.6% of population

total: 91% of population

unimproved:

urban: 1.8% of population

rural: 15.4% of population

total: 9% of population (2015 est.)

CURRENT HEALTH EXPENDITURE:

9.1% (2016)

HOSPITAL BED DENSITY:

2.7 beds/1,000 population (2009)

SANITATION FACILITY ACCESS:

improved:

urban: 54.5% of population (2015 est.)

rural: 16.8% of population (2015 est.)

total: 34.4% of population (2015 est.)

unimproved:

urban: 45.5% of population (2015 est.)

rural: 83.2% of population (2015 est.)

total: 65.6% of population (2015 est.)

HIV/AIDS - ADULT PREVALENCE RATE:

11.8% (2018 est.)

country comparison to the world: 7

HIV/AIDS - PEOPLE LIVING WITH HIV/AIDS:

200,000 (2018 est.)

country comparison to the world: 29

HIV/AIDS - DEATHS:

2,700 (2018 est.)

country comparison to the world: 39

MAJOR INFECTIOUS DISEASES:

degree of risk: high (2016)

food or waterborne diseases: bacterial diarrhea, hepatitis A, and typhoid fever (2016)

vectorborne diseases: malaria (2016)

water contact diseases: schistosomiasis (2016)

OBESITY - ADULT PREVALENCE RATE:

17.2% (2016)

country comparison to the world: 119

CHILDREN UNDER THE AGE OF 5 YEARS UNDERWEIGHT:

13.2% (2013)

country comparison to the world: 50

EDUCATION EXPENDITURES:

3.1% of GDP (2014)

country comparison to the world: 139

LITERACY:

definition: age 15 and over can read and write

total population: 81.9%

male: 79.2%

female: 84.5% (2015 est.)

UNEMPLOYMENT, YOUTH AGES 15-24:

total: 44.9%

male: 37.7%

female: 52.5% (2016 est.)

country comparison to the world: 11

GOVERNMENT :: NAMIBIA

COUNTRY NAME:

conventional long form: Republic of Namibia

conventional short form: Namibia

local long form: Republic of Namibia

local short form: Namibia

former: German South-West Africa (Deutsch-Suedwestafrika), South-West Africa

etymology: named for the coastal Namib Desert; the name "namib" means "vast place" in the Nama/Damara language

GOVERNMENT TYPE:

presidential republic

CAPITAL:

name: Windhoek

geographic coordinates: 22 34 S, 17 05 E

time difference: UTC+1 (6 hours ahead of Washington, DC, during Standard Time)

daylight saving time: +1hr, begins first Sunday in September; ends first Sunday in April

etymology: may derive from the Afrikaans word "wind-hoek" meaning "windy corner"

ADMINISTRATIVE DIVISIONS:

14 regions; Erongo, Hardap, //Karas, Kavango East, Kavango West, Khomas, Kunene, Ohangwena, Omaheke, Omusati, Oshana, Oshikoto, Otjozondjupa, Zambezi; note - the Karas Region was renamed //Karas in September 2013 to include the alveolar lateral click of the Khoekhoegowab language

INDEPENDENCE:

21 March 1990 (from South African mandate)

NATIONAL HOLIDAY:

Independence Day, 21 March (1990)

CONSTITUTION:

history: adopted 9 February 1990, entered into force 21 March 1990

amendments: initiated by the Cabinet; passage requires two-thirds majority vote of the National Assembly membership and of the National Council of Parliament and assent of the president of the republic; if the National Council fails to pass an amendment, the president can call for a referendum; passage by referendum requires two-thirds majority of votes cast; amendments that detract from or repeal constitutional articles on fundamental rights and freedoms cannot be amended, and the requisite majorities needed by Parliament to amend the constitution cannot be changed; amended 1998, 2010, 2014 (2017)

LEGAL SYSTEM:

mixed legal system of uncodified civil law based on Roman-Dutch law and customary law

INTERNATIONAL LAW ORGANIZATION PARTICIPATION: has not submitted an ICJ jurisdiction declaration; accepts ICCt jurisdiction

CITIZENSHIP:

citizenship by birth: no

citizenship by descent only: at least one parent must be a citizen of Namibia

dual citizenship recognized: no

residency requirement for naturalization: 5 years

SUFFRAGE:

18 years of age; universal

EXECUTIVE BRANCH:

chief of state: President Hage GEINGOB (since 21 March 2015); Vice President Nangola MBUMBA (since 8 February 2018); note - the president is both chief of state and head of government

head of government: President Hage GEINGOB (since 21 March 2015); Vice President Nangola MBUMBA (since 8 February 2018); Prime Minister Saara KUUGONGELWA-AMADHILA (since 21 March 2015)

cabinet: Cabinet appointed by the president from among members of the National Assembly

elections/appointments: president elected by absolute majority popular vote in 2 rounds if needed for a 5-year term (eligible for a second term); election last held on 27 November 2019 (next to be held on 27 November 2024)

election results: Hage GEINGOB elected president in the first round; percent of vote - Hage GEINGOB (SWAPO) 56.8%, Panduleni ITULA (Independent) 29.4%, McHenry VENAANI (PDM) 5.6%, Bernadus SWARTBOOI (LPM) 2.9%, Apius AUCHAB (UDF) 1.8%, Esther MUINJANGUE (NUDO) 1.5%, other 2%

LEGISLATIVE BRANCH:

description: bicameral Parliament consists of:
National Council (42 seats); members indirectly elected 3 each by the 14 regional councils to serve 5-year terms); note - the Council primarily reviews legislation passed and referred by the National Assembly
National Assembly (104 seats; 96 members directly elected in multi-seat constituencies by closed list, proportional representation vote to serve 5-year terms and 8 nonvoting members appointed by the president)

elections: National Council - elections for regional councils to determine members of the National Council held on 27 November 2015 (next to be held on 27 November 2020)
National Assembly - last held on 27 November 2014 (next to be held on 27 November 2024)

election results: National Council - percent of vote by party - NA; seats by party - SWAPO 40, NUDO 1, DPM 1; composition - men 32, women 10, percent of women 23.8%
National Assembly - percent of vote by party - SWAPO 65.5%, PDM 16.6%, LPM 4.7%, NUDO 1.9%, APP 1.8%, UDF 1.8%, RP 1.8%, NEFF 1.7%, RDP 1.1%, CDV .7%, SWANU .6%, other 1.8%; seats by party - SWAPO 63, PDM 16, LPM 4, NUDO 2, APP 2, UDF 2, RP 2, NEFF 1, RDP 1, CDV 1, SWANU 1

JUDICIAL BRANCH:

highest courts: Supreme Court (consists of the chief justice and at least 3 judges in quorum sessions)

judge selection and term of office: judges appointed by the president of Namibia upon the recommendation of the Judicial Service Commission; judges serve until age 65, but terms can be extended by the president until age 70

subordinate courts: High Court; Electoral Court, Labor Court; regional and district magistrates' courts; community courts

POLITICAL PARTIES AND LEADERS:

All People's Party or APP [Ignatius SHIXWAMENI]
Christian Democratic Voice or CDV [Gothard KANDUME]
Landless People's Movement or LPM [Bernadus SWARTBOOI]
National Unity Democratic Organization or NUDO [Estes MUINJANGUE]
Namibian Economic Freedom Fighters or NEFF [Epafras MUKWIILONGO]
Popular Democratic Movement or PDM (formerly DTA) [McHenry VENAANI]
Rally for Democracy and Progress or RDP [Steve BEZUIDERHOUDT (Acting)]
Republican Party or RP [Henk MUDGE]
South West Africa National Union or SWANU [Tangeni IIYAMBO]
South West Africa People's Organization or SWAPO [Hage GEINGOB]
United Democratic Front or UDF [Apius AUCHAB]
United People's Movement or UPM [Jan J. VAN WYK]
Workers' Revolutionary Party or WRP (formerly CPN) [MPs Salmon FLEERMUYS and Benson KAAPALA]

INTERNATIONAL ORGANIZATION PARTICIPATION:

ACP, AfDB, AU, C, CD, CPLP (associate observer), FAO, G-77, IAEA, IBRD, ICAO, ICCt, ICRM, IDA, IFAD, IFC, IFRCS, ILO, IMF, IMO, Interpol, IOC, IOM, IPU, ISO, ITSO, ITU, ITUC (NGOs), MIGA, NAM, OPCW, SACU, SADC, UN, UNAMID, UNCTAD, UNESCO, UNHCR, UNIDO, UNISFA, UNMIL, UNMISS, UNOCI, UNWTO, UPU, WCO, WHO, WIPO, WMO, WTO

DIPLOMATIC REPRESENTATION IN THE US:

Ambassador Monica NASHANDI (since 7 November 2018)

chancery: 1605 New Hampshire Avenue NW, Washington, DC 20009

telephone: [1] (202) 986-0540

FAX: [1] (202) 986-0443

DIPLOMATIC REPRESENTATION FROM THE US:

chief of mission: Ambassador Lisa A. JOHNSON (since 3 February 2018)

telephone: [264] (061) 295-8500

embassy: 14 Lossen Street, Windhoek

mailing address: Private Bag 12029 Ausspannplatz, Windhoek

FAX: [264] (061) 295-8603

FLAG DESCRIPTION:

a wide red stripe edged by narrow white stripes divides the flag diagonally from lower hoist corner to upper fly corner; the upper hoist-side triangle is blue and charged with a golden-yellow, 12-rayed sunburst; the lower fly-side triangle is green; red signifies the heroism of the people and their determination to build a future of equal opportunity for all; white stands for peace, unity, tranquility, and harmony; blue represents the Namibian sky and the Atlantic Ocean, the country's precious water resources and rain; the golden-yellow sun denotes power and existence; green symbolizes vegetation and agricultural resources

NATIONAL SYMBOL(S):

oryx (antelope); national colors: blue, red, green, white, yellow

NATIONAL ANTHEM:

name: Namibia, Land of the Brave

lyrics/music: Axali DOESEB

note: adopted 1991

ECONOMY :: NAMIBIA

ECONOMY - OVERVIEW:

Namibia's economy is heavily dependent on the extraction and processing of minerals for export. Mining accounts for about 12.5% of GDP, but provides more than 50% of foreign exchange earnings. Rich alluvial diamond deposits make Namibia a primary source for gem-quality diamonds. Marine diamond mining is increasingly important as the terrestrial diamond supply has dwindled. The rising cost of mining diamonds, especially from the sea, combined with increased diamond production in Russia and China, has reduced profit margins. Namibian authorities have emphasized the need to add value to raw materials, do more in-country manufacturing, and exploit the services market, especially in the logistics and transportation sectors.

Namibia is one of the world's largest producers of uranium. The Chinese-owned Husab uranium mine began producing uranium ore in 2017, and is expected to reach full production in August 2018 and produce 15 million pounds of uranium a year. Namibia also produces large quantities of zinc and is a smaller producer of gold and copper. Namibia's economy remains vulnerable to world commodity price fluctuations and drought.

Namibia normally imports about 50% of its cereal requirements; in drought years, food shortages are problematic in rural areas. A high per capita GDP, relative to the region, obscures one of the world's most unequal income distributions; the current government has prioritized exploring wealth redistribution schemes while trying to maintain a pro-business environment. GDP growth in 2017 slowed to about 1%, however, due to contractions in both the construction and mining sectors, as well as an ongoing drought. Growth is expected to recover modestly in 2018.

A five-year Millennium Challenge Corporation compact ended in September 2014. As an upper middle income country, Namibia is ineligible for a second compact. The Namibian economy is closely linked to South Africa with the Namibian dollar pegged one-to-one to the South African rand. Namibia receives 30%-40% of its revenues from the Southern African Customs Union (SACU); volatility in the size of Namibia's annual SACU allotment and global mineral prices complicates budget planning.

GDP (PURCHASING POWER PARITY):

$26.6 billion (2017 est.)

$26.81 billion (2016 est.)

$26.62 billion (2015 est.)

note: data are in 2017 dollars

country comparison to the world: 139

GDP (OFFICIAL EXCHANGE RATE):

$13.24 billion (2017 est.)

GDP - REAL GROWTH RATE:

-0.8% (2017 est.)

0.7% (2016 est.)

6.1% (2015 est.)

country comparison to the world: 200

GDP - PER CAPITA (PPP):

$11,200 (2017 est.)

$11,500 (2016 est.)

$11,700 (2015 est.)

note: data are in 2017 dollars

country comparison to the world: 135

GROSS NATIONAL SAVING:

16.7% of GDP (2017 est.)

9.6% of GDP (2016 est.)

19.1% of GDP (2015 est.)

country comparison to the world: 125

GDP - COMPOSITION, BY END USE:

household consumption: 68.7% (2017 est.)

government consumption: 24.5% (2017 est.)

investment in fixed capital: 16% (2017 est.)

investment in inventories: 1.6% (2017 est.)

exports of goods and services: 36.7% (2017 est.)

imports of goods and services: -47.5% (2017 est.)

GDP - COMPOSITION, BY SECTOR OF ORIGIN:

agriculture: 6.7% (2016 est.)

industry: 26.3% (2016 est.)

services: 67% (2017 est.)

AGRICULTURE - PRODUCTS:

millet, sorghum, peanuts, grapes; livestock; fish

INDUSTRIES:

meatpacking, fish processing, dairy products, pasta, beverages; mining (diamonds, lead, zinc, tin, silver, tungsten, uranium, copper)

INDUSTRIAL PRODUCTION GROWTH RATE:

-0.4% (2017 est.)

country comparison to the world: 171

LABOR FORCE:

956,800 (2017 est.)

country comparison to the world: 146

LABOR FORCE - BY OCCUPATION:

agriculture: 31%

industry: 14%

services: 54% (2013 est.)

note: about half of Namibia's people are unemployed while about two-thirds live in rural areas; roughly two-thirds of rural dwellers rely on subsistence agriculture

UNEMPLOYMENT RATE:

34% (2016 est.)

28.1% (2014 est.)

country comparison to the world: 210

POPULATION BELOW POVERTY LINE:

28.7% (2010 est.)

HOUSEHOLD INCOME OR CONSUMPTION BY PERCENTAGE SHARE:

lowest 10%: 2.4%

highest 10%: 42% (2010)

DISTRIBUTION OF FAMILY INCOME - GINI INDEX:

59.7 (2010)

70.7 (2003)

country comparison to the world: 6

BUDGET:

revenues: 4.268 billion (2017 est.)

expenditures: 5 billion (2017 est.)

TAXES AND OTHER REVENUES:

32.2% (of GDP) (2017 est.)

country comparison to the world: 68

BUDGET SURPLUS (+) OR DEFICIT (-):

-5.5% (of GDP) (2017 est.)

country comparison to the world: 173

PUBLIC DEBT:
41.3% of GDP (2017 est.)
39.5% of GDP (2016 est.)
country comparison to the world: 121

FISCAL YEAR:
1 April - 31 March

INFLATION RATE (CONSUMER PRICES):
6.1% (2017 est.)
6.7% (2016 est.)
country comparison to the world: 187

CENTRAL BANK DISCOUNT RATE:
7% (12 April 2017)
6.5% (31 December 2015)
country comparison to the world: 51

COMMERCIAL BANK PRIME LENDING RATE:
10.04% (31 December 2017 est.)
9.84% (31 December 2016 est.)
country comparison to the world: 85

STOCK OF NARROW MONEY:
$3.425 billion (31 December 2017 est.)
$2.911 billion (31 December 2016 est.)
country comparison to the world: 116

STOCK OF BROAD MONEY:
$3.425 billion (31 December 2017 est.)
$2.911 billion (31 December 2016 est.)
country comparison to the world: 122

STOCK OF DOMESTIC CREDIT:
$8.582 billion (31 December 2017 est.)
$7.038 billion (31 December 2016 est.)
country comparison to the world: 114

MARKET VALUE OF PUBLICLY TRADED SHARES:
$1.305 billion (31 December 2012 est.)
$1.152 billion (31 December 2011 est.)
$1.176 billion (31 December 2010 est.)
country comparison to the world: 103

CURRENT ACCOUNT BALANCE:
-$438 million (2017 est.)
-$1.555 billion (2016 est.)
country comparison to the world: 115

EXPORTS:
$3.995 billion (2017 est.)
$4.003 billion (2016 est.)
country comparison to the world: 118

EXPORTS - PARTNERS:
South Africa 27.1%, Botswana 14.9%, Switzerland 12%, Zambia 5.7%, China 4.6%, Italy 4.4% (2017)

EXPORTS - COMMODITIES:
diamonds, copper, gold, zinc, lead, uranium; cattle, white fish and mollusks

IMPORTS:
$5.384 billion (2017 est.)
$5.625 billion (2016 est.)
country comparison to the world: 123

IMPORTS - COMMODITIES:
foodstuffs; petroleum products and fuel, machinery and equipment, chemicals

IMPORTS - PARTNERS:
South Africa 61.4% (2017)

RESERVES OF FOREIGN EXCHANGE AND GOLD:
$2.432 billion (31 December 2017 est.)
$1.834 billion (31 December 2016 est.)
country comparison to the world: 115

DEBT - EXTERNAL:
$7.969 billion (31 December 2017 est.)
$6.904 billion (31 December 2016 est.)
country comparison to the world: 123

STOCK OF DIRECT FOREIGN INVESTMENT - AT HOME:
NA

STOCK OF DIRECT FOREIGN INVESTMENT - ABROAD:
NA

EXCHANGE RATES:
Namibian dollars (NAD) per US dollar -
13.67 (2017 est.)
14.7096 (2016 est.)
14.7096 (2015 est.)
12.7589 (2014 est.)
10.8526 (2013 est.)

ENERGY :: NAMIBIA

ELECTRICITY ACCESS:
population without electricity: 1 million (2017)
electrification - total population: 51.8% (2016)
electrification - urban areas: 77.1% (2016)
electrification - rural areas: 28.7% (2016)

ELECTRICITY - PRODUCTION:
1.403 billion kWh (2016 est.)
country comparison to the world: 145

ELECTRICITY - CONSUMPTION:
3.891 billion kWh (2016 est.)
country comparison to the world: 128

ELECTRICITY - EXPORTS:
88 million kWh (2015 est.)
country comparison to the world: 83

ELECTRICITY - IMPORTS:
3.073 billion kWh (2016 est.)
country comparison to the world: 50

ELECTRICITY - INSTALLED GENERATING CAPACITY:
535,500 kW (2016 est.)
country comparison to the world: 146

ELECTRICITY - FROM FOSSIL FUELS:
28% of total installed capacity (2016 est.)
country comparison to the world: 187

ELECTRICITY - FROM NUCLEAR FUELS:
0% of total installed capacity (2017 est.)
country comparison to the world: 150

ELECTRICITY - FROM HYDROELECTRIC PLANTS:
64% of total installed capacity (2017 est.)
country comparison to the world: 26

ELECTRICITY - FROM OTHER RENEWABLE SOURCES:
8% of total installed capacity (2017 est.)
country comparison to the world: 89

CRUDE OIL - PRODUCTION:
0 bbl/day (2018 est.)
country comparison to the world: 179

CRUDE OIL - EXPORTS:
0 bbl/day (2015 est.)
country comparison to the world: 171

CRUDE OIL - IMPORTS:
0 bbl/day (2015 est.)
country comparison to the world: 172

CRUDE OIL - PROVED RESERVES:
0 bbl (1 January 2018 est.)
country comparison to the world: 174

REFINED PETROLEUM PRODUCTS - PRODUCTION:
0 bbl/day (2015 est.)
country comparison to the world: 183

REFINED PETROLEUM PRODUCTS - CONSUMPTION:
27,000 bbl/day (2016 est.)
country comparison to the world: 125

REFINED PETROLEUM PRODUCTS - EXPORTS:
80 bbl/day (2015 est.)
country comparison to the world: 120

REFINED PETROLEUM PRODUCTS - IMPORTS:

26,270 bbl/day (2015 est.)

country comparison to the world: 105

NATURAL GAS - PRODUCTION:

0 cu m (2017 est.)

country comparison to the world: 175

NATURAL GAS - CONSUMPTION:

0 cu m (2017 est.)

country comparison to the world: 179

NATURAL GAS - EXPORTS:

0 cu m (2017 est.)

country comparison to the world: 157

NATURAL GAS - IMPORTS:

0 cu m (2017 est.)

country comparison to the world: 162

NATURAL GAS - PROVED RESERVES:

62.29 billion cu m (1 January 2018 est.)

country comparison to the world: 60

CARBON DIOXIDE EMISSIONS FROM CONSUMPTION OF ENERGY:

3.958 million Mt (2017 est.)

country comparison to the world: 139

COMMUNICATIONS :: NAMIBIA

TELEPHONES - FIXED LINES:

total subscriptions: 193,125

subscriptions per 100 inhabitants: 8 (2017 est.)

country comparison to the world: 125

TELEPHONES - MOBILE CELLULAR:

total subscriptions: 2,647,853

subscriptions per 100 inhabitants: 107 (2017 est.)

country comparison to the world: 143

TELEPHONE SYSTEM:

general assessment: good system; core fiber-optic network links most centers with digital connections; 3G and LTE services; Internet and broadband sector fairly competitive; infrastructure investment through 2021 (2018)

domestic: fixed-line still a government monopoly with plans to open to competion soon; multiple mobile-cellular providers; fixed-line subscribership of 8 per 100 and mobile-cellular 107 per 100 persons (2018)

international: country code - 264; landing points for the ACE and WACS fiber-optic submarine cable linking southern and western African countries to Europe; satellite earth stations - 4 Intelsat (2019)

BROADCAST MEDIA:

1 private and 1 state-run TV station; satellite and cable TV service available; state-run radio service broadcasts in multiple languages; about a dozen private radio stations; transmissions of multiple international broadcasters available

INTERNET COUNTRY CODE:

.na

INTERNET USERS:

total: 756,118

percent of population: 31% (July 2016 est.)

country comparison to the world: 139

BROADBAND - FIXED SUBSCRIPTIONS:

total: 63,894

subscriptions per 100 inhabitants: 3 (2017 est.)

country comparison to the world: 127

MILITARY AND SECURITY :: NAMIBIA

MILITARY EXPENDITURES:

3.35% of GDP (2018)

3.56% of GDP (2017)

3.89% of GDP (2016)

4.48% of GDP (2015)

4.2% of GDP (2014)

country comparison to the world: 18

MILITARY AND SECURITY FORCES:

Namibian Defense Force (NDF): Army, Navy, Air Force (2019)

MILITARY SERVICE AGE AND OBLIGATION:

18-25 years of age for voluntary military service; no conscription (2019)

TRANSPORTATION :: NAMIBIA

NATIONAL AIR TRANSPORT SYSTEM:

number of registered air carriers: 2 (2015)

inventory of registered aircraft operated by air carriers: 12 (2015)

annual passenger traffic on registered air carriers: 553,322 (2015)

annual freight traffic on registered air carriers: 30,302,405 mt-km (2015)

CIVIL AIRCRAFT REGISTRATION COUNTRY CODE PREFIX:

V5 (2016)

AIRPORTS:

112 (2013)

country comparison to the world: 52

AIRPORTS - WITH PAVED RUNWAYS:

total: 19 (2017)

over 3,047 m: 4 (2017)

2,438 to 3,047 m: 2 (2017)

1,524 to 2,437 m: 12 (2017)

914 to 1,523 m: 1 (2017)

AIRPORTS - WITH UNPAVED RUNWAYS:

total: 93 (2013)

1,524 to 2,437 m: 25 (2013)

914 to 1,523 m: 52 (2013)

under 914 m: 16 (2013)

RAILWAYS:

total: 2,628 km (2014)

narrow gauge: 2,628 km 1.067-m gauge (2014)

country comparison to the world: 65

ROADWAYS:

total: 48,875 km (2018)

paved: 7,893 km (2018)

unpaved: 40,982 km (2018)

country comparison to the world: 82

MERCHANT MARINE:

total: 10

by type: general cargo 1, other 9 (2018)

country comparison to the world: 150

PORTS AND TERMINALS:

major seaport(s): Luderitz, Walvis Bay

TRANSNATIONAL ISSUES :: NAMIBIA

DISPUTES - INTERNATIONAL:

concerns from international experts and local populations over the Okavango Delta ecology in Botswana and human displacement scuttled Namibian plans to construct a hydroelectric dam on Popa Falls along the Angola-Namibia border; the governments of South Africa and Namibia have not signed or ratified the text of the 1994 Surveyor's General agreement placing the boundary in the middle of the Orange River; Namibia has supported, and in 2004 Zimbabwe dropped objections to, plans between Botswana and Zambia to build a bridge over the Zambezi River, thereby de facto recognizing a short, but not clearly delimited, Botswana-Zambia boundary in the river

TRAFFICKING IN PERSONS:

current situation: Namibia is a country of origin and destination for children and, to a lesser extent, women subjected to forced labor and sex trafficking; victims, lured by promises of legitimate jobs, are forced to work in urban centers and on commercial farms; traffickers exploit Namibian children, as well as children from Angola, Zambia, and Zimbabwe, for forced labor in agriculture, cattle herding, domestic service, fishing, and street vending; children are also forced into prostitution, often catering to tourists from southern Africa and Europe; San and Zemba children are particularly vulnerable; foreign adults and Namibian adults and children are reportedly subjected to forced labor in Chinese-owned retail, construction, and fishing operations

tier rating: Tier 2 Watch List – Namibia does not fully comply with the minimum standards for the elimination of trafficking; however, it is making significant efforts to do so; Namibia was granted a waiver from an otherwise required downgrade to Tier 3 because its government has a written plan that, if implemented would constitute making significant efforts to bring itself into compliance with the minimum standards for the elimination of trafficking; in 2015, the Child Care and Protection Bill passed, criminalizing child trafficking; the government's first sex trafficking prosecution remained pending; no new prosecutions were initiated and no trafficking offenders have ever been convicted; accusations of forced labor at Chinese construction and mining companies continue to go uninvestigated; authorities failed to fully implement victim identification and referral processes, which led to the deportation of possible victims (2015)

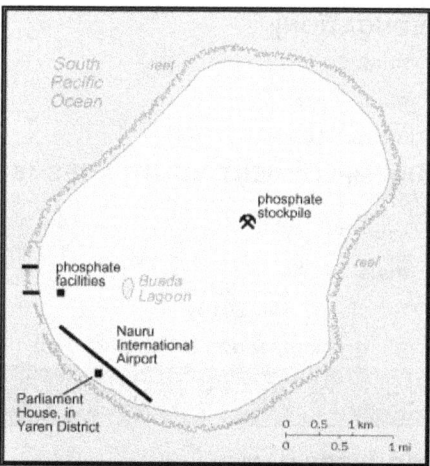

AUSTRALIA - OCEANIA :: NAURU

INTRODUCTION :: NAURU

BACKGROUND:

The exact origins of the Nauruans are unclear since their language does not resemble any other in the Pacific region. Germany annexed the island in 1888. A German-British consortium began mining the island's phosphate deposits early in the 20th century. Australian forces occupied Nauru in World War I; it subsequently became a League of Nations mandate. After the Second World War - and a brutal occupation by Japan - Nauru became a UN trust territory. It achieved independence in 1968 and joined the UN in 1999 as the world's smallest independent republic.

GEOGRAPHY :: NAURU

LOCATION:
Oceania, island in the South Pacific Ocean, south of the Marshall Islands

GEOGRAPHIC COORDINATES:
0 32 S, 166 55 E

MAP REFERENCES:
Oceania

AREA:
total: 21 sq km
land: 21 sq km
water: 0 sq km
country comparison to the world: 240

AREA - COMPARATIVE:
about 0.1 times the size of Washington, DC

LAND BOUNDARIES:
0 km

COASTLINE:
30 km

MARITIME CLAIMS:
territorial sea: 12 nm
exclusive economic zone: 200 nm
contiguous zone: 24 nm

CLIMATE:
tropical with a monsoonal pattern; rainy season (November to February)

TERRAIN:
sandy beach rises to fertile ring around raised coral reefs with phosphate plateau in center

ELEVATION:
lowest point: Pacific Ocean 0 m
highest point: Command Ridge 70 m

NATURAL RESOURCES:
phosphates, fish

LAND USE:
agricultural land: 20% (2011 est.)
arable land: 0% (2011 est.) / permanent crops: 20% (2011 est.) / permanent pasture: 0% (2011 est.)
forest: 0% (2011 est.)
other: 80% (2011 est.)

IRRIGATED LAND:
0 sq km (2012)

POPULATION DISTRIBUTION:
extensive phosphate mining made approximately 90% of the island unsuitable for farming; most people live in the fertile coastal areas, especially along the southwest coast

NATURAL HAZARDS:
periodic droughts

ENVIRONMENT - CURRENT ISSUES:
limited natural freshwater resources, roof storage tanks that collect rainwater and desalination plants provide water; a century of intensive phosphate mining beginning in 1906 left the central 90% of Nauru a wasteland; cadmium residue, phosphate dust, and other contaminants have caused air and water pollution with negative impacts on health; climate change has brought on rising sea levels and inland water shortages

ENVIRONMENT - INTERNATIONAL AGREEMENTS:
party to: Biodiversity, Climate Change, Climate Change-Kyoto Protocol, Desertification, Hazardous Wastes, Law of the Sea, Marine Dumping, Ozone Layer Protection, Whaling
signed, but not ratified: none of the selected agreements

GEOGRAPHY - NOTE:
world's smallest island country; situated just 53 km south of the Equator; Nauru is one of the three great phosphate rock islands in the Pacific Ocean - the others are Banaba (Ocean Island) in Kiribati and Makatea in French Polynesia

PEOPLE AND SOCIETY :: NAURU

POPULATION:
9,692 (July 2018 est.)
country comparison to the world: 223

NATIONALITY:
noun: Nauruan(s)
adjective: Nauruan

ETHNIC GROUPS:
Nauruan 88.9%, part Nauruan 6.6%, I-Kiribati 2%, other 2.5% (2007 est.)

LANGUAGES:

Nauruan 93% (official, a distinct Pacific Island language), English 2% (widely understood, spoken, and used for most government and commercial purposes), other 5% (includes I-Kiribati 2% and Chinese 2%) (2011 est.)

note: percentages represent main language spoken at home; Nauruan is spoken by 95% of the population, English by 66%, and other languages by 12%

RELIGIONS:
Protestant 60.4% (includes Nauru Congregational 35.7%, Assembly of God 13%, Nauru Independent Church 9.5%, Baptist 1.5%, and Seventh Day Adventist 0.7%), Roman Catholic 33%, other 3.7%, none 1.8%, unspecified 1.1% (2011 est.)

AGE STRUCTURE:
0-14 years: 31.18% (male 1,323 /female 1,699)

15-24 years: 16.37% (male 764 /female 823)

25-54 years: 43.08% (male 2,112 /female 2,063)

55-64 years: 6.51% (male 249 /female 382)

65 years and over: 2.86% (male 101 /female 176) (2018 est.)

MEDIAN AGE:
total: 26.7 years (2018 est.)

male: 27.4 years

female: 25.8 years

country comparison to the world: 149

POPULATION GROWTH RATE:
0.51% (2018 est.)

country comparison to the world: 153

BIRTH RATE:
23.2 births/1,000 population (2018 est.)

country comparison to the world: 62

DEATH RATE:
5.9 deaths/1,000 population (2018 est.)

country comparison to the world: 168

NET MIGRATION RATE:
-12.3 migrant(s)/1,000 population (2018 est.)

country comparison to the world: 218

POPULATION DISTRIBUTION:
extensive phosphate mining made approximately 90% of the island unsuitable for farming; most people live in the fertile coastal areas, especially along the southwest coast

URBANIZATION:
urban population: 100% of total population (2019)

rate of urbanization: -0.06% annual rate of change (2015-20 est.)

SEX RATIO:
at birth: 0.84 male(s)/female

0-14 years: 0.78 male(s)/female

15-24 years: 0.93 male(s)/female

25-54 years: 1.02 male(s)/female

55-64 years: 0.65 male(s)/female

65 years and over: 0.57 male(s)/female

total population: 0.88 male(s)/female (2018 est.)

INFANT MORTALITY RATE:
total: 7.7 deaths/1,000 live births (2018 est.)

male: 9.8 deaths/1,000 live births

female: 5.9 deaths/1,000 live births

country comparison to the world: 156

LIFE EXPECTANCY AT BIRTH:
total population: 67.8 years (2018 est.)

male: 63.6 years

female: 71.2 years

country comparison to the world: 170

TOTAL FERTILITY RATE:
2.76 children born/woman (2018 est.)

country comparison to the world: 62

DRINKING WATER SOURCE:
improved:

urban: 96.5% of population

total: 96.5% of population

unimproved:

urban: 3.5% of population

total: 3.5% of population (2015 est.)

CURRENT HEALTH EXPENDITURE:
11.1% (2016)

PHYSICIANS DENSITY:
1.24 physicians/1,000 population (2015)

HOSPITAL BED DENSITY:
5 beds/1,000 population (2010)

SANITATION FACILITY ACCESS:
improved:

urban: 65.6% of population (2015 est.)

total: 65.6% of population (2015 est.)

unimproved:

urban: 34.4% of population (2015 est.)

total: 34.4% of population (2015 est.)

HIV/AIDS - ADULT PREVALENCE RATE:
NA

HIV/AIDS - PEOPLE LIVING WITH HIV/AIDS:
NA

HIV/AIDS - DEATHS:
NA

OBESITY - ADULT PREVALENCE RATE:
61% (2016)

country comparison to the world: 1

EDUCATION EXPENDITURES:
NA

SCHOOL LIFE EXPECTANCY (PRIMARY TO TERTIARY EDUCATION):
total: 9 years

male: 9 years

female: 10 years (2008)

UNEMPLOYMENT, YOUTH AGES 15-24:
total: 26.6%

male: 20.9%

female: 37.5% (2013)

country comparison to the world: 43

GOVERNMENT :: NAURU

COUNTRY NAME:
conventional long form: Republic of Nauru

conventional short form: Nauru

local long form: Republic of Nauru

local short form: Nauru

former: Pleasant Island

etymology: the island name may derive from the Nauruan word "anaoero" meaning "I go to the beach"

GOVERNMENT TYPE:
parliamentary republic

CAPITAL:
name: no official capital; government offices in the Yaren District

time difference: UTC+12 (17 hours ahead of Washington, DC, during Standard Time)

ADMINISTRATIVE DIVISIONS:
14 districts; Aiwo, Anabar, Anetan, Anibare, Baitsi, Boe, Buada,

Denigomodu, Ewa, Ijuw, Meneng, Nibok, Uaboe, Yaren

INDEPENDENCE:
31 January 1968 (from the Australia-, NZ-, and UK-administered UN trusteeship)

NATIONAL HOLIDAY:
Independence Day, 31 January (1968)

CONSTITUTION:
history: effective 29 January 1968

amendments: proposed by Parliament; passage requires two-thirds majority vote of Parliament; amendments to constitutional articles, such as the republican form of government, protection of fundamental rights and freedoms, the structure and authorities of the executive and legislative branches, also requires two-thirds majority of votes in a referendum; amended 1968, 2009, 2014 (2018)

LEGAL SYSTEM:
mixed legal system of common law based on the English model and customary law

INTERNATIONAL LAW ORGANIZATION PARTICIPATION:
has not submitted an ICJ jurisdiction declaration; accepts ICCt jurisdiction

SUFFRAGE:
20 years of age; universal and compulsory

EXECUTIVE BRANCH:
chief of state: President Lionel AINGIMEA (since 27 August 2019); note - the president is both chief of state and head of government

head of government: President Lionel AINGIMEA (since 27 August 2019)

cabinet: Cabinet appointed by the president from among members of Parliament

elections/appointments: president indirectly elected by Parliament (eligible for a second term); election last held on 27 August 2019 (next to be held in 2022)

election results: Lionel AINGIMEA elected president; Parliament vote - Lionel AINGIMEA (independent) 12, David ADEANG (Nauru First) 6

LEGISLATIVE BRANCH:
description: unicameral parliament (19 seats; members directly elected in multi-seat constituencies by majority vote using the "Dowdall" counting system by which voters rank candidates on their ballots; members serve 3-year terms)

elections: last held on 24 August 2019 (next to be held in 2022)

election results: percent of vote - NA; seats - independent 19; composition - men 17, women 2, percent of women 10.5%

JUDICIAL BRANCH:
highest courts: Supreme Court (consists of the chief justice and several justices); note - in late 2017, the Nauruan Government revoked the 1976 High Court Appeals Act, which had allowed appeals beyond the Nauruan Supreme Court, and in early 2018, the government formed its own appeals court

judge selection and term of office: judges appointed by the president to serve until age 65

subordinate courts: District Court, Family Court

POLITICAL PARTIES AND LEADERS:
Democratic Party [Kennan ADEANG]
Nauru First (Naoero Amo) Party
Nauru Party (informal)

note: loose multiparty system

INTERNATIONAL ORGANIZATION PARTICIPATION:
ACP, ADB, AOSIS, C, FAO, G-77, ICAO, ICCt, IFAD, Interpol, IOC, IOM, ITU, OPCW, PIF, Sparteca, SPC, UN, UNCTAD, UNESCO, UPU, WHO

DIPLOMATIC REPRESENTATION IN THE US:
Ambassador Marlene Inemwin MOSES (since 13 March 2006)

chancery: 800 2nd Avenue, Suite 400 D, New York, NY 10017

telephone: [1] (212) 937-0074

FAX: [1] (212) 937-0079

DIPLOMATIC REPRESENTATION FROM THE US:
the US does not have an embassy in Nauru; the US Ambassador to Fiji is accredited to Nauru

FLAG DESCRIPTION:
blue with a narrow, horizontal, gold stripe across the center and a large white 12-pointed star below the stripe on the hoist side; blue stands for the Pacific Ocean, the star indicates the country's location in relation to the Equator (the gold stripe) and the 12 points symbolize the 12 original tribes of Nauru; the star's white color represents phosphate, the basis of the island's wealth

NATIONAL SYMBOL(S):
frigatebird, calophyllum flower; national colors: blue, yellow, white

NATIONAL ANTHEM:
name: "Nauru Bwiema" (Song of Nauru)

lyrics/music: Margaret HENDRIE/Laurence Henry HICKS

note: adopted 1968

ECONOMY :: NAURU

ECONOMY - OVERVIEW:
Revenues of this tiny island - a coral atoll with a land area of 21 square kilometers - traditionally have come from exports of phosphates. Few other resources exist, with most necessities being imported, mainly from Australia, its former occupier and later major source of support. Primary reserves of phosphates were exhausted and mining ceased in 2006, but mining of a deeper layer of "secondary phosphate" in the interior of the island began the following year. The secondary phosphate deposits may last another 30 years. Earnings from Nauru's export of phosphate remains an important source of income. Few comprehensive statistics on the Nauru economy exist; estimates of Nauru's GDP vary widely.

The rehabilitation of mined land and the replacement of income from phosphates are serious long-term problems. In anticipation of the exhaustion of Nauru's phosphate deposits, substantial amounts of phosphate income were invested in trust funds to help cushion the transition and provide for Nauru's economic future.

Although revenue sources for government are limited, the opening of the Australian Regional Processing Center for asylum seekers since 2012 has sparked growth in the economy. Revenue derived from fishing licenses under the "vessel day scheme" has also boosted government income. Housing, hospitals, and other capital plant are deteriorating. The cost to Australia of keeping the Nauruan government and economy afloat continues to climb.

GDP (PURCHASING POWER PARITY):
$160 million (2017 est.)

$153.9 million (2016 est.)

$139.4 million (2015 est.)

note: data are in 2015 dollars

country comparison to the world: 224

GDP (OFFICIAL EXCHANGE RATE):

$114 million (2017 est.)

GDP - REAL GROWTH RATE:

4% (2017 est.)

10.4% (2016 est.)

2.8% (2015 est.)

country comparison to the world: 80

GDP - PER CAPITA (PPP):

$12,300 (2017 est.)

$11,800 (2016 est.)

$11,600 (2015 est.)

note: data are in 2015 US dollars

country comparison to the world: 129

GDP - COMPOSITION, BY END USE:

household consumption: 98% (2016 est.)

government consumption: 37.6% (2016 est.)

investment in fixed capital: 42.2% (2016 est.)

exports of goods and services: 11.2% (2016 est.)

imports of goods and services: -89.1% (2016 est.)

GDP - COMPOSITION, BY SECTOR OF ORIGIN:

agriculture: 6.1% (2009 est.)

industry: 33% (2009 est.)

services: 60.8% (2009 est.)

AGRICULTURE - PRODUCTS:

coconuts

INDUSTRIES:

phosphate mining, offshore banking, coconut products

INDUSTRIAL PRODUCTION GROWTH RATE:

NA

LABOR FORCE:

NA

LABOR FORCE - BY OCCUPATION:

note: most of the labor force is employed in phosphate mining, public administration, education, and transportation

UNEMPLOYMENT RATE:

23% (2011 est.)

90% (2004 est.)

country comparison to the world: 193

POPULATION BELOW POVERTY LINE:

NA

HOUSEHOLD INCOME OR CONSUMPTION BY PERCENTAGE SHARE:

lowest 10%: NA

highest 10%: NA

BUDGET:

revenues: 103 million (2017 est.)

expenditures: 113.4 million (2017 est.)

TAXES AND OTHER REVENUES:

90.3% (of GDP) (2017 est.)

country comparison to the world: 2

BUDGET SURPLUS (+) OR DEFICIT (-):

-9.2% (of GDP) (2017 est.)

country comparison to the world: 206

PUBLIC DEBT:

62% of GDP (2017 est.)

65% of GDP (2016 est.)

country comparison to the world: 71

FISCAL YEAR:

1 July - 30 June

INFLATION RATE (CONSUMER PRICES):

5.1% (2017 est.)

8.2% (2016 est.)

country comparison to the world: 172

CURRENT ACCOUNT BALANCE:

$5 million (2017 est.)

$2 million (2016 est.)

country comparison to the world: 64

EXPORTS:

$125 million (2013 est.)

$110.3 million (2012 est.)

country comparison to the world: 194

EXPORTS - PARTNERS:

Nigeria 38.6%, Japan 16.6%, Australia 15.9%, South Korea 13.7%, NZ 5.7% (2017)

EXPORTS - COMMODITIES:

phosphates

IMPORTS:

$64.9 million (2016 est.)

$143.1 million (2013 est.)

country comparison to the world: 219

IMPORTS - COMMODITIES:

food, fuel, manufactures, building materials, machinery

IMPORTS - PARTNERS:

Australia 67.5%, Fiji 9.2%, India 8.1%, Singapore 5.4% (2017)

DEBT - EXTERNAL:

$33.3 million (2004 est.)

country comparison to the world: 199

EXCHANGE RATES:

Australian dollars (AUD) per US dollar -

1.311 (2017 est.)

1.3452 (2016 est.)

1.3452 (2015 est.)

1.3291 (2014 est.)

1.1094 (2013 est.)

ENERGY :: NAURU

ELECTRICITY - PRODUCTION:

24 million kWh (2016 est.)

country comparison to the world: 212

ELECTRICITY - CONSUMPTION:

22.32 million kWh (2016 est.)

country comparison to the world: 212

ELECTRICITY - EXPORTS:

0 kWh (2016 est.)

country comparison to the world: 174

ELECTRICITY - IMPORTS:

0 kWh (2016 est.)

country comparison to the world: 177

ELECTRICITY - INSTALLED GENERATING CAPACITY:

7,000 kW (2016 est.)

country comparison to the world: 211

ELECTRICITY - FROM FOSSIL FUELS:

86% of total installed capacity (2016 est.)

country comparison to the world: 68

ELECTRICITY - FROM NUCLEAR FUELS:

0% of total installed capacity (2017 est.)

country comparison to the world: 151

ELECTRICITY - FROM HYDROELECTRIC PLANTS:

0% of total installed capacity (2017 est.)

country comparison to the world: 188

ELECTRICITY - FROM OTHER RENEWABLE SOURCES:

14% of total installed capacity (2017 est.)

country comparison to the world: 63

CRUDE OIL - PRODUCTION:

0 bbl/day (2018 est.)

country comparison to the world: 180

CRUDE OIL - EXPORTS:

0 bbl/day (2015 est.)

country comparison to the world: 172

CRUDE OIL - IMPORTS:

0 bbl/day (2015 est.)

country comparison to the world: 173

CRUDE OIL - PROVED RESERVES:

0 bbl (1 January 2018 est.)

country comparison to the world: 175

REFINED PETROLEUM PRODUCTS - PRODUCTION:

0 bbl/day (2015 est.)

country comparison to the world: 184

REFINED PETROLEUM PRODUCTS - CONSUMPTION:

470 bbl/day (2016 est.)

country comparison to the world: 210

REFINED PETROLEUM PRODUCTS - EXPORTS:

0 bbl/day (2015 est.)

country comparison to the world: 186

REFINED PETROLEUM PRODUCTS - IMPORTS:

449 bbl/day (2015 est.)

country comparison to the world: 206

NATURAL GAS - PRODUCTION:

0 cu m (2017 est.)

country comparison to the world: 176

NATURAL GAS - CONSUMPTION:

0 cu m (2017 est.)

country comparison to the world: 180

NATURAL GAS - EXPORTS:

0 cu m (2017 est.)

country comparison to the world: 158

NATURAL GAS - IMPORTS:

0 cu m (2017 est.)

country comparison to the world: 163

NATURAL GAS - PROVED RESERVES:

0 cu m (1 January 2014 est.)

country comparison to the world: 174

CARBON DIOXIDE EMISSIONS FROM CONSUMPTION OF ENERGY:

76,540 Mt (2017 est.)

country comparison to the world: 208

COMMUNICATIONS :: NAURU

TELEPHONES - FIXED LINES:

total subscriptions: 1,900

subscriptions per 100 inhabitants: 14 (July 2016 est.)

country comparison to the world: 215

TELEPHONES - MOBILE CELLULAR:

total subscriptions: 9,900

subscriptions per 100 inhabitants: 87 (July 2016 est.)

country comparison to the world: 212

TELEPHONE SYSTEM:

general assessment: adequate local and international radiotelephone communication provided via Australian facilities; geography is a challenge for the islands; there is a need to service the tourism sector and thus the South Pacific Islands economy; mobile technology is booming (2018)

domestic: fixed-line 14 per 100 and mobile-cellular 87 per 100 (2018)

international: country code - 674; satellite earth station - 1 Intelsat (Pacific Ocean)

BROADCAST MEDIA:

1 government-owned TV station broadcasting programs from New Zealand sent via satellite or on videotape; 1 government-owned radio station, broadcasting on AM and FM, utilizes Australian and British programs (2019)

INTERNET COUNTRY CODE:

.nr

INTERNET USERS:

total: 5,100

percent of population: 53.5% (July 2016 est.)

country comparison to the world: 213

MILITARY AND SECURITY :: NAURU

MILITARY AND SECURITY FORCES:

no regular military forces (2019)

MILITARY - NOTE:

Nauru maintains no defense forces; under an informal agreement, defense is the responsibility of Australia

TRANSPORTATION :: NAURU

NATIONAL AIR TRANSPORT SYSTEM:

number of registered air carriers: 1 (2015)

inventory of registered aircraft operated by air carriers: 5 (2015)

annual passenger traffic on registered air carriers: 38,858 (2015)

annual freight traffic on registered air carriers: 7,793,474 mt-km (2015)

CIVIL AIRCRAFT REGISTRATION COUNTRY CODE PREFIX:

C2 (2016)

AIRPORTS:

1 (2013)

country comparison to the world: 230

AIRPORTS - WITH PAVED RUNWAYS:

total: 1 (2017)

1,524 to 2,437 m: 1 (2017)

ROADWAYS:

total: 30 km (2002)

paved: 24 km (2002)

unpaved: 6 km (2002)

country comparison to the world: 211

PORTS AND TERMINALS:

major seaport(s): Nauru

TRANSNATIONAL ISSUES :: NAURU

DISPUTES - INTERNATIONAL:

none

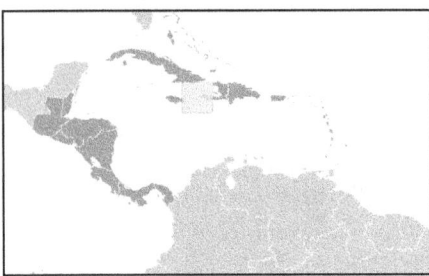

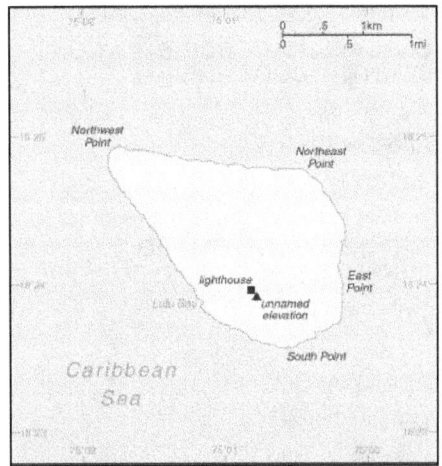

CENTRAL AMERICA :: NAVASSA ISLAND

INTRODUCTION :: NAVASSA ISLAND

BACKGROUND:
This uninhabited island was claimed by the US in 1857 for its guano. Mining took place between 1865 and 1898. The lighthouse, built in 1917, was shut down in 1996 and administration of Navassa Island transferred from the US Coast Guard to the Department of the Interior, Office of Insular Affairs. A 1998 scientific expedition to the island described it as a "unique preserve of Caribbean biodiversity." The following year it became a National Wildlife Refuge and annual scientific expeditions have continued.

GEOGRAPHY :: NAVASSA ISLAND

LOCATION:
Caribbean, island in the Caribbean Sea, 30 nm west of Tiburon Peninsula of Haiti

GEOGRAPHIC COORDINATES:
18 25 N, 75 02 W

MAP REFERENCES:
Central America and the Caribbean

AREA:
total: 5.4 sq km

land: 5.4 sq km

water: 0 sq km

country comparison to the world: 249

AREA - COMPARATIVE:
about nine times the size of the National Mall in Washington, DC

LAND BOUNDARIES:
0 km

COASTLINE:
8 km

MARITIME CLAIMS:
territorial sea: 12 nm

exclusive economic zone: 200 nm

CLIMATE:
marine, tropical

TERRAIN:
raised flat to undulating coral and limestone plateau; ringed by vertical white cliffs (9 to 15 m high)

ELEVATION:
lowest point: Caribbean Sea 0 m

highest point: 200 m NNW of lighthouse 85 m

NATURAL RESOURCES:
guano (mining discontinued in 1898)

LAND USE:
agricultural land: 0% (2011 est.)

arable land: 0% (2011 est.) / permanent crops: 0% (2011 est.) / permanent pasture: 0% (2011 est.)

forest: 0% (2011 est.)

other: 100% (2011 est.)

NATURAL HAZARDS:
hurricanes

ENVIRONMENT - CURRENT ISSUES:
some coral bleaching

GEOGRAPHY - NOTE:
strategic location 160 km south of the US Naval Base at Guantanamo Bay, Cuba; mostly exposed rock with numerous solution holes (limestone sinkholes) but with enough grassland to support goat herds; dense stands of fig trees, scattered cactus

PEOPLE AND SOCIETY :: NAVASSA ISLAND

POPULATION:
uninhabited; transient Haitian fishermen and others camp on the island

EDUCATION EXPENDITURES:
NA

GOVERNMENT :: NAVASSA ISLAND

COUNTRY NAME:
conventional long form: none

conventional short form: Navassa Island

etymology: the flat island was named "Navaza" by some of Christopher COLUMBUS' sailors in 1504; the name derives from the Spanish term "nava" meaning "flat land, plain, or field"

DEPENDENCY STATUS:
unorganized, unincorporated territory of the US; administered by the Fish and Wildlife Service, US Department of the Interior from the Caribbean Islands National Wildlife Refuge in Boqueron, Puerto Rico; in September 1996, the Coast Guard ceased operations and maintenance of the Navassa Island Light, a 46-meter-tall lighthouse on the southern side of the island; Haiti has claimed the island since the 19th century

LEGAL SYSTEM:
the laws of the US apply where applicable

DIPLOMATIC REPRESENTATION FROM THE US:

none (territory of the US)

FLAG DESCRIPTION:

the flag of the US is used

ECONOMY :: NAVASSA ISLAND

ECONOMY - OVERVIEW:

Subsistence fishing and commercial trawling occur within refuge waters.

MILITARY AND SECURITY :: NAVASSA ISLAND

MILITARY - NOTE:

defense is the responsibility of the US

TRANSPORTATION :: NAVASSA ISLAND

ROADWAYS:

PORTS AND TERMINALS:

none; offshore anchorage only

TRANSNATIONAL ISSUES :: NAVASSA ISLAND

DISPUTES - INTERNATIONAL:

claimed by Haiti, source of subsistence fishing

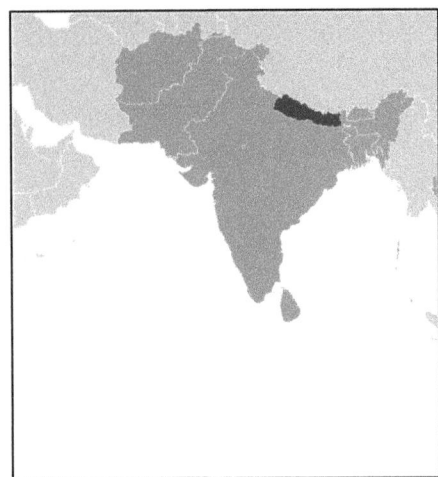

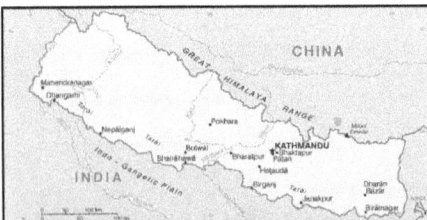

SOUTH ASIA :: NEPAL

INTRODUCTION :: NEPAL

BACKGROUND:

During the late 18th-early 19th centuries, the principality of Gorkha united many of the other principalities and states of the sub-Himalayan region into a Nepali Kingdom. Nepal retained its independence following the Anglo-Nepalese War of 1814-16 and the subsequent peace treaty laid the foundations for two centuries of amicable relations between Britain and Nepal. (The Brigade of Gurkhas continues to serve in the British Army to the present day.) In 1951, the Nepali monarch ended the century-old system of rule by hereditary premiers and instituted a cabinet system that brought political parties into the government. That arrangement lasted until 1960, when political parties were again banned, but was reinstated in 1990 with the establishment of a multiparty democracy within the framework of a constitutional monarchy.

An insurgency led by Maoists broke out in 1996. During the ensuing 10-year civil war between Maoist and government forces, the monarchy dissolved the cabinet and parliament and re-assumed absolute power in 2002, after the crown prince massacred the royal family in 2001. A peace accord in 2006 led to the promulgation of an interim constitution in 2007. Following a nationwide Constituent Assembly (CA) election in 2008, the newly formed CA declared Nepal a federal democratic republic, abolished the monarchy, and elected the country's first president. After the CA failed to draft a constitution by a 2012 deadline set by the Supreme Court, then-Prime Minister Baburam BHATTARAI dissolved the CA. Months of negotiations ensued until 2013 when the major political parties agreed to create an interim government headed by then-Chief Justice Khil Raj REGMI with a mandate to hold elections for a new CA. Elections were held in 2013, in which the Nepali Congress won the largest share of seats in the CA and in 2014 formed a coalition government with the second-place Communist Party of Nepal-Unified Marxist-Leninist (UML) and with Nepali Congress (NC) President Sushil KOIRALA serving as prime minister. Nepal's new constitution came into effect in 2015, at which point the CA became the Parliament. Khagda Prasad Sharma OLI served as the first post-constitution prime minister from 2015 to 2016. OLI resigned ahead of a no-confidence motion against him, and Parliament elected Communist Party of Nepal-Maoist (CPN-M) leader Pushpa Kamal DAHAL (aka "Prachanda") prime minister. The constitution provided for a transitional period during which three sets of elections – local, provincial, and national – needed to take place. The first local elections in 20 years occurred in three phases between May and September 2017, and state and federal elections proceeded in two phases in November and December 2017. The parties headed by OLI and DAHAL ran in coalition and swept the parliamentary elections, and OLI, who led the larger of the two parties, was sworn in as prime minister in February 2018. In May 2018, OLI and DAHAL merged their parties - the UML and CPN-M - to establish the Nepal Communist Party (NCP), which is now the ruling party in Parliament.

GEOGRAPHY :: NEPAL

LOCATION:

Southern Asia, between China and India

GEOGRAPHIC COORDINATES:

28 00 N, 84 00 E

MAP REFERENCES:

Asia

AREA:

total: 147,181 sq km

land: 143,351 sq km

water: 3,830 sq km

country comparison to the world: 96

AREA - COMPARATIVE:

slightly larger than New York state

LAND BOUNDARIES:

total: 3,159 km

border countries (2): China 1389 km, India 1770 km

COASTLINE:

0 km (landlocked)

MARITIME CLAIMS:

none (landlocked)

CLIMATE:

varies from cool summers and severe winters in north to subtropical summers and mild winters in south

TERRAIN:

Tarai or flat river plain of the Ganges in south; central hill region with rugged Himalayas in north

ELEVATION:

mean elevation: 2,565 m

lowest point: Kanchan Kalan 70 m

highest point: Mount Everest (highest peak in Asia and highest point on earth above sea level) 8,848 m

NATURAL RESOURCES:

quartz, water, timber, hydropower, scenic beauty, small deposits of lignite, copper, cobalt, iron ore

LAND USE:

agricultural land: 28.8% (2011 est.)

arable land: 15.1% (2011 est.) / permanent crops: 1.2% (2011 est.) / permanent pasture: 12.5% (2011 est.)

forest: 25.4% (2011 est.)

other: 45.8% (2011 est.)

IRRIGATED LAND:

13,320 sq km (2012)

POPULATION DISTRIBUTION:

most of the population is divided nearly equally between a concentration in the southern-most plains of the Tarai region and the central hilly region; overall density is quite low

NATURAL HAZARDS:

severe thunderstorms; flooding; landslides; drought and famine depending on the timing, intensity, and duration of the summer monsoons

ENVIRONMENT - CURRENT ISSUES:

deforestation (overuse of wood for fuel and lack of alternatives); forest degradation; soil erosion; contaminated water (with human and animal wastes, agricultural runoff, and industrial effluents); unmanaged solid-waste; wildlife conservation; vehicular emissions

ENVIRONMENT - INTERNATIONAL AGREEMENTS:

party to: Biodiversity, Climate Change, Climate Change-Kyoto Protocol, Desertification, Endangered Species, Hazardous Wastes, Law of the Sea, Ozone Layer Protection, Tropical Timber 83, Tropical Timber 94, Wetlands

signed, but not ratified: Marine Life Conservation

GEOGRAPHY - NOTE:

landlocked; strategic location between China and India; contains eight of world's 10 highest peaks, including Mount Everest and Kanchenjunga - the world's tallest and third tallest mountains - on the borders with China and India respectively

PEOPLE AND SOCIETY :: NEPAL

POPULATION:

29,717,587 (July 2018 est.)

country comparison to the world: 47

NATIONALITY:

noun: Nepali (singular and plural)

adjective: Nepali

ETHNIC GROUPS:

Chhettri 16.6%, Brahman-Hill 12.2%, Magar 7.1%, Tharu 6.6%, Tamang 5.8%, Newar 5%, Kami 4.8%, Muslim 4.4%, Yadav 4%, Rai 2.3%, Gurung 2%, Damai/Dholii 1.8%, Thakuri 1.6%, Limbu 1.5%, Sarki 1.4%, Teli 1.4%, Chamar/Harijan/Ram 1.3%, Koiri/Kushwaha 1.2%, other 19% (2011 est.)

note: 125 caste/ethnic groups were reported in the 2011 national census

LANGUAGES:

Nepali (official) 44.6%, Maithali 11.7%, Bhojpuri 6%, Tharu 5.8%, Tamang 5.1%, Newar 3.2%, Bajjika 3%, Magar 3%, Doteli 3%, Urdu 2.6%, Avadhi 1.9%, Limbu 1.3%, Gurung 1.2%, Baitadeli 1%, other 6.4%, unspecified 0.2% (2011 est.)

note: 123 languages reported as mother tongue in 2011 national census; many in government and business also speak English

RELIGIONS:

Hindu 81.3%, Buddhist 9%, Muslim 4.4%, Kirant 3.1%, Christian 1.4%, other 0.5%, unspecified 0.2% (2011 est.)

AGE STRUCTURE:

0-14 years: 29.54% (male 4,578,768 /female 4,198,913)

15-24 years: 21.52% (male 3,250,614 /female 3,145,807)

25-54 years: 37.18% (male 4,987,071 /female 6,061,616)

55-64 years: 6.42% (male 917,342 /female 991,937)

65 years and over: 5.34% (male 785,893 /female 799,626) (2018 est.)

DEPENDENCY RATIOS:

total dependency ratio: 61.4 (2015 est.)

youth dependency ratio: 52.5 (2015 est.)

elderly dependency ratio: 8.8 (2015 est.)

potential support ratio: 11.3 (2015 est.)

MEDIAN AGE:

total: 24.5 years (2018 est.)

male: 23.2 years

female: 25.8 years

country comparison to the world: 162

POPULATION GROWTH RATE:

1.09% (2018 est.)

country comparison to the world: 102

BIRTH RATE:

19.1 births/1,000 population (2018 est.)

country comparison to the world: 82

DEATH RATE:

5.6 deaths/1,000 population (2018 est.)

country comparison to the world: 176

NET MIGRATION RATE:

-2.5 migrant(s)/1,000 population (2018 est.)

country comparison to the world: 169

POPULATION DISTRIBUTION:

most of the population is divided nearly equally between a concentration in the southern-most plains of the Tarai region and the central hilly region; overall density is quite low

URBANIZATION:

urban population: 20.2% of total population (2019)

rate of urbanization: 3.15% annual rate of change (2015-20 est.)

MAJOR URBAN AREAS - POPULATION:

1.376 million KATHMANDU (capital) (2019)

SEX RATIO:

at birth: 1.06 male(s)/female

0-14 years: 1.09 male(s)/female

15-24 years: 1.03 male(s)/female

25-54 years: 0.82 male(s)/female

55-64 years: 0.92 male(s)/female

65 years and over: 0.98 male(s)/female

total population: 0.96 male(s)/female (2018 est.)

MOTHER'S MEAN AGE AT FIRST BIRTH:

20.8 years (2016 est.)

note: median age at first birth among women 25-29

MATERNAL MORTALITY RATE:

186 deaths/100,000 live births (2017 est.)

country comparison to the world: 49

INFANT MORTALITY RATE:

total: 26.9 deaths/1,000 live births (2018 est.)

male: 28.2 deaths/1,000 live births

female: 25.6 deaths/1,000 live births

country comparison to the world: 67

LIFE EXPECTANCY AT BIRTH:

total population: 71.3 years (2018 est.)

male: 70.6 years

female: 72 years

country comparison to the world: 154

TOTAL FERTILITY RATE:

2.07 children born/woman (2018 est.)

country comparison to the world: 105

CONTRACEPTIVE PREVALENCE RATE:

52.6% (2016/17)

DRINKING WATER SOURCE:

improved:

urban: 90.9% of population

rural: 91.8% of population

total: 91.6% of population

unimproved:

urban: 9.1% of population

rural: 8.2% of population

total: 8.4% of population (2015 est.)

CURRENT HEALTH EXPENDITURE:

6.3% (2016)

PHYSICIANS DENSITY:

0.65 physicians/1,000 population (2017)

HOSPITAL BED DENSITY:

3 beds/1,000 population (2012)

SANITATION FACILITY ACCESS:

improved:

urban: 56% of population (2015 est.)

rural: 43.5% of population (2015 est.)

total: 45.8% of population (2015 est.)

unimproved:

urban: 44% of population (2015 est.)

rural: 56.5% of population (2015 est.)

total: 54.2% of population (2015 est.)

HIV/AIDS - ADULT PREVALENCE RATE:

0.1% (2018 est.)

country comparison to the world: 128

HIV/AIDS - PEOPLE LIVING WITH HIV/AIDS:

30,000 (2018 est.)

country comparison to the world: 73

HIV/AIDS - DEATHS:

900 (2018 est.)

country comparison to the world: 62

MAJOR INFECTIOUS DISEASES:

degree of risk: high (2016)

food or waterborne diseases: bacterial diarrhea, hepatitis A and E, and typhoid fever (2016)

vectorborne diseases: Japanese encephalitis, malaria, and dengue fever (2016)

OBESITY - ADULT PREVALENCE RATE:

4.1% (2016)

country comparison to the world: 187

CHILDREN UNDER THE AGE OF 5 YEARS UNDERWEIGHT:

27.2% (2016)

country comparison to the world: 15

EDUCATION EXPENDITURES:

5.1% of GDP (2017)

country comparison to the world: 62

LITERACY:

definition: age 15 and over can read and write

total population: 63.9%

male: 76.4%

female: 53.1% (2015 est.)

SCHOOL LIFE EXPECTANCY (PRIMARY TO TERTIARY EDUCATION):

total: 12 years

male: 12 years

female: 13 years (2017)

UNEMPLOYMENT, YOUTH AGES 15-24:

GOVERNMENT :: NEPAL

COUNTRY NAME:

conventional long form: Federal Democratic Republic of Nepal

conventional short form: Nepal

local long form: Sanghiya Loktantrik Ganatantra Nepal

local short form: Nepal

etymology: the Newar people of the Kathmandu Valley and surrounding areas apparently gave their name to the country; the terms "Nepal," "Newar," "Nepar," and "Newal" are phonetically different forms of the same word

GOVERNMENT TYPE:

federal parliamentary republic

CAPITAL:

name: Kathmandu

geographic coordinates: 27 43 N, 85 19 E

time difference: UTC+5.75 (10.75 hours ahead of Washington, DC, during Standard Time)

etymology: name derives from the Kasthamandap temple that stood in Durbar Square; in Sanskrit, "kastha" means "wood" and "mandapa" means "pavilion"; the three-story structure was made entirely of wood, without iron nails or supports, and dated to the late 16th century; it collapsed during a 2015 earthquake

ADMINISTRATIVE DIVISIONS:

7 provinces; Gandaki Pradesh, Karnali Pradesh, Province No. One, Province No. Two, Province No. Three, Province No. Five, Sudurpashchim Pradesh

INDEPENDENCE:

1768 (unified by Prithvi Narayan SHAH)

NATIONAL HOLIDAY:

Constitution Day, 20 September (2015); note - marks the promulgation of Nepal's constitution in 2015 and replaces the previous 28 May Republic Day as the official national day in Nepal; the Gregorian day fluctuates based on Nepal's Hindu calendar

CONSTITUTION:

history: several previous; latest approved by the Second Constituent Assembly 16 September 2015, signed by the president and effective 20 September 2015

amendments: proposed as a bill by either house of the Federal Parliament; bills affecting a state border or powers delegated to a state must be submitted to the affected state assembly; passage of such bills requires a majority vote of that state assembly membership; bills not requiring state assembly consent require at least two-thirds majority vote by the membership of both houses of the Federal Parliament; parts of the constitution on the sovereignty, territorial integrity, independence, and sovereignty vested in the people cannot be amended; last amended 2016 (2019)

LEGAL SYSTEM:

English common law and Hindu legal concepts; note - new criminal and civil codes came into effect on 17 August 2018

INTERNATIONAL LAW ORGANIZATION PARTICIPATION:

has not submitted an ICJ jurisdiction declaration; non-party state to the ICCt

CITIZENSHIP:

citizenship by birth: yes

citizenship by descent only: yes

dual citizenship recognized: no

residency requirement for naturalization: 15 years

SUFFRAGE:

18 years of age; universal

EXECUTIVE BRANCH:

head of government: Prime Minister Khadga Prasad (KP) Sharma OLI (since 15 February 2018); deputy prime ministers Ishwar POKHREL, Upendra YADAV (since 1 June 2018)

cabinet: Council of Ministers appointed by the prime minister; cabinet dominated by the Nepal Communist Party

elections/appointments: president indirectly elected by an electoral college of the Federal Parliament and of the state assemblies for a 5-year term (eligible for a second term); election last held 13 March 2018 (next to be held in 2023); prime minister indirectly elected by the Federal Parliament

election results: Bidhya Devi BHANDARI reelected president; electoral vote - Bidhya Devi BHANDARI (CPN-UML) 39,275, Kumari Laxmi RAI (NC) 11,730

head of state: President Bidhya Devi BANDHARI (since 29 October 2015); Vice President Nanda Bahadar PUN (since 31 October 2015)

LEGISLATIVE BRANCH:

description: bicameral Federal Parliament consists of:
National Assembly (59 seats; 56 members, including at least 3 women, 1 Dalit, 1 member with disabilities, or 1 minority indirectly elected by an electoral college of state and municipal government leaders, and 3 members, including 1 woman, nominated by the president of Nepal on the recommendation of the government; members serve 6-year terms with renewal of one-third of the membership every 2 years)
House of Representatives (275 seats; 165 members directly elected in single-seat constituencies by simple majority vote and 110 members directly elected in a single nationwide constituency by party-list proportional representation vote; members serve 5-year terms)

elections:
first election for the National Assembly held on 7 February 2018 (next to be held in 2024)
first election for House of Representatives held on 26 November and 7 December 2017 (next to be held in 2022)

election results:
National Assembly - percent of vote by party - NA; seats by party - NCP 42, NC 13, FSFN 2, RJPN 2; composition - men 37, women 22, percent of women 37.3%
House of Representatives - percent of vote by party - NA; seats by party - NCP 174, NC 63, RJPN 17, FSFN 16, other 4, independent 1; composition - men 185, women 90, percent of women 32.7%; note - total Federal Parliament percent of women 33.5%

JUDICIAL BRANCH:

highest courts: Supreme Court (consists of the chief justice and up to 20 judges)

judge selection and term of office: Supreme Court chief justice appointed by the president upon the recommendation of the Constitutional Council, a 5-member, high-level advisory body headed by the prime minister; other judges appointed by the president upon the recommendation of the Judicial Council, a 5-member advisory body headed by the chief justice; the chief justice serves a 6-year term; judges serve until age 65

subordinate courts: High Court; district courts

POLITICAL PARTIES AND LEADERS:

the Election Commission of Nepal granted ballot access under the proportional system to 88 political parties for the November-December 2017 House of Representatives election to the Federal Parliament; of these, the following 8 parties won seats:
Federal Socialist Forum, Nepal or FSFN [Upendra YADAV]
Naya Shakti Party, Nepal [Baburam BHATTARAI]
Nepal Communist Party or NCP [Khadga Prasad OLI, Pushpa Kamal DAHAL]
Nepali Congress or NC [Sher Bahadur DEUBA]
Nepal Mazdoor Kisan Party [Narayan Man BIJUKCHHE]
Rastriya Janamorcha [Chitra Bahadur K.C.]
Rastriya Janata Party or RJPN [Mahanta THAKUR]
Rastriya Prajatantra party or RPP [Kamal THAPA]

INTERNATIONAL ORGANIZATION PARTICIPATION:

ADB, BIMSTEC, CD, CP, FAO, G-77, IAEA, IBRD, ICAO, ICC (NGOs), ICRM, IDA, IFAD, IFC, IFRCS, ILO, IMF, IMO, Interpol, IOC, IOM, IPU, ISO, ITSO, ITU, ITUC (NGOs), MIGA, MINURSO, MINUSMA, MINUSTAH, MONUSCO, NAM, OPCW, SAARC, SACEP, UN, UNAMID, UNCTAD, UNDOF, UNESCO, UNIDO, UNIFIL, UNMIL, UNMISS, UNOCI, UNTSO, UNWTO, UPU, WCO, WFTU (NGOs), WHO, WIPO, WMO, WTO

DIPLOMATIC REPRESENTATION IN THE US:

Ambassador Arjun Kumar KARKI (since 18 May 2015)

chancery: 2730 34th Place NW, Washington, DC 20007

telephone: [1] (202) 667-4550

FAX: [1] (202) 667-5534

consulate(s) general: Chicago (IL), New York

DIPLOMATIC REPRESENTATION FROM THE US:

chief of mission: Ambassador Randy BERRY (since 25 October 2018)

telephone: [977] (1) 423-4000

embassy: Maharajgunj, Kathmandu, Nepal

mailing address: US Embassy, Maharajgunj Chakrapath, Kathmandu, Nepal 44600

FAX: [977] (1) 400-7272

FLAG DESCRIPTION:

crimson red with a blue border around the unique shape of two overlapping right triangles; the smaller, upper triangle bears a white stylized moon and the larger, lower triangle displays a white 12-pointed sun; the color red represents the rhododendron (Nepal's national flower) and is a sign of victory and bravery, the blue border signifies peace and harmony; the two right triangles are a combination of two single pennons (pennants) that originally symbolized the Himalaya Mountains while their charges represented the families of the king (upper) and the prime minister, but today they are understood to denote Hinduism and Buddhism, the country's two main religions; the moon represents the serenity of the Nepalese people and the shade and cool weather in the Himalayas, while the sun depicts the heat and higher temperatures of the lower parts of Nepal; the moon and the sun are also said to express the hope that the nation will endure as long as these heavenly bodies

note: Nepal is the only country in the world whose flag is not rectangular or square

NATIONAL SYMBOL(S):

rhododendron blossom; national color: red

NATIONAL ANTHEM:

name: "Sayaun Thunga Phool Ka" (Hundreds of Flowers)

lyrics/music: Pradeep Kumar RAI/Ambar GURUNG

note: adopted 2007; after the abolition of the monarchy in 2006, a new anthem was required because of the previous anthem's praise for the king

ECONOMY :: NEPAL

ECONOMY - OVERVIEW:

Nepal is among the least developed countries in the world, with about one-quarter of its population living below the poverty line. Nepal is heavily dependent on remittances, which amount to as much as 30% of GDP. Agriculture is the mainstay of the economy, providing a livelihood for almost two-thirds of the population but accounting for less than a third of GDP. Industrial activity mainly involves the processing of agricultural products, including pulses, jute, sugarcane, tobacco, and grain.

Nepal has considerable scope for exploiting its potential in hydropower, with an estimated 42,000 MW of commercially feasible capacity. Nepal has signed trade and investment agreements with India, China, and other countries, but political uncertainty and a difficult business climate have hampered foreign investment. The United States and Nepal signed a $500 million Millennium Challenge Corporation Compact in September 2017 which will expand Nepal's electricity infrastructure and help maintain transportation infrastructure.

Massive earthquakes struck Nepal in early 2015, which damaged or destroyed infrastructure and homes and set back economic development. Although political gridlock and lack of capacity have hindered post-earthquake recovery, government-led reconstruction efforts have progressively picked up speed, although many hard hit areas still have seen little assistance. Additional challenges to Nepal's growth include its landlocked geographic location, inconsistent electricity supply, and underdeveloped transportation infrastructure.

GDP (PURCHASING POWER PARITY):

$79.19 billion (2017 est.)

$73.39 billion (2016 est.)

$72.96 billion (2015 est.)

note: data are in 2017 dollars

country comparison to the world: 95

GDP (OFFICIAL EXCHANGE RATE):

$24.88 billion (2017 est.)

GDP - REAL GROWTH RATE:

7.9% (2017 est.)

0.6% (2016 est.)

3.3% (2015 est.)

country comparison to the world: 9

GDP - PER CAPITA (PPP):

$2,700 (2017 est.)

$2,500 (2016 est.)

$2,500 (2015 est.)

note: data are in 2017 dollars

country comparison to the world: 195

GROSS NATIONAL SAVING:

45.4% of GDP (2017 est.)

40.2% of GDP (2016 est.)

44% of GDP (2015 est.)

country comparison to the world: 7

GDP - COMPOSITION, BY END USE:

household consumption: 78% (2017 est.)

government consumption: 11.7% (2017 est.)

investment in fixed capital: 33.8% (2017 est.)

investment in inventories: 8.7% (2017 est.)

exports of goods and services: 9.8% (2017 est.)

imports of goods and services: -42% (2017 est.)

GDP - COMPOSITION, BY SECTOR OF ORIGIN:

agriculture: 27% (2017 est.)

industry: 13.5% (2017 est.)

services: 59.5% (2017 est.)

AGRICULTURE - PRODUCTS:

pulses, rice, corn, wheat, sugarcane, jute, root crops; milk, water buffalo meat

INDUSTRIES:

tourism, carpets, textiles; small rice, jute, sugar, and oilseed mills; cigarettes, cement and brick production

INDUSTRIAL PRODUCTION GROWTH RATE:

12.4% (2017 est.)

country comparison to the world: 7

LABOR FORCE:

16.81 million (2017 est.)

note: severe lack of skilled labor

country comparison to the world: 37

LABOR FORCE - BY OCCUPATION:

agriculture: 69%

industry: 12%

services: 19% (2015 est.)

UNEMPLOYMENT RATE:

3% (2017 est.)

3.2% (2016 est.)

country comparison to the world: 36

POPULATION BELOW POVERTY LINE:

25.2% (2011 est.)

HOUSEHOLD INCOME OR CONSUMPTION BY PERCENTAGE SHARE:

lowest 10%: 3.2%

highest 10%: 29.5% (2011)

DISTRIBUTION OF FAMILY INCOME - GINI INDEX:

32.8 (2010)

47.2 (2008 est.)

country comparison to the world: 115

BUDGET:

revenues: 5.925 billion (2017 est.)

expenditures: 5.945 billion (2017 est.)

TAXES AND OTHER REVENUES:
23.8% (of GDP) (2017 est.)

country comparison to the world: 122

BUDGET SURPLUS (+) OR DEFICIT (-):
-0.1% (of GDP) (2017 est.)

country comparison to the world: 48

PUBLIC DEBT:
26.4% of GDP (2017 est.)

27.9% of GDP (2016 est.)

country comparison to the world: 171

FISCAL YEAR:
16 July - 15 July

INFLATION RATE (CONSUMER PRICES):
4.5% (2017 est.)

9.9% (2016 est.)

country comparison to the world: 168

CENTRAL BANK DISCOUNT RATE:
7% (30 July 2017)

7% (30 July 2016)

country comparison to the world: 52

COMMERCIAL BANK PRIME LENDING RATE:
11.3% (31 December 2017 est.)

8.9% (31 December 2016 est.)

country comparison to the world: 73

STOCK OF NARROW MONEY:
$5.505 billion (31 December 2017 est.)

$4.857 billion (31 December 2016 est.)

country comparison to the world: 98

STOCK OF BROAD MONEY:
$5.505 billion (31 December 2017 est.)

$4.857 billion (31 December 2016 est.)

country comparison to the world: 101

STOCK OF DOMESTIC CREDIT:
$21.99 billion (31 December 2017 est.)

$17.94 billion (31 December 2016 est.)

country comparison to the world: 89

MARKET VALUE OF PUBLICLY TRADED SHARES:
$17.57 billion (31 October 2017 est.)

$19.4 billion (31 October 2016 est.)

$11.37 billion (31 October 2015 est.)

country comparison to the world: 67

CURRENT ACCOUNT BALANCE:
-$93 million (2017 est.)

$1.339 billion (2016 est.)

country comparison to the world: 84

EXPORTS:
$818.7 million (2017 est.)

$761.6 million (2016 est.)

country comparison to the world: 169

EXPORTS - PARTNERS:
India 53.1%, US 11.8%, Turkey 7.2% (2017)

EXPORTS - COMMODITIES:
clothing, pulses, carpets, textiles, juice, jute goods

IMPORTS:
$10 billion (2017 est.)

$8.764 billion (2016 est.)

country comparison to the world: 101

IMPORTS - COMMODITIES:
petroleum products, machinery and equipment, gold, electrical goods, medicine

IMPORTS - PARTNERS:
India 70.2%, China 7.5% (2017)

RESERVES OF FOREIGN EXCHANGE AND GOLD:
$9.091 billion (31 December 2017 est.)

$8.506 billion (31 December 2016 est.)

country comparison to the world: 76

DEBT - EXTERNAL:
$5.849 billion (31 December 2017 est.)

$4.321 billion (31 December 2016 est.)

country comparison to the world: 129

STOCK OF DIRECT FOREIGN INVESTMENT - AT HOME:
$103 million (31 July 2013 est.)

country comparison to the world: 138

STOCK OF DIRECT FOREIGN INVESTMENT - ABROAD:
NA

EXCHANGE RATES:
Nepalese rupees (NPR) per US dollar -

104 (2017 est.)

107.38 (2016 est.)

107.38 (2015 est.)

102.41 (2014 est.)

99.53 (2013 est.)

ENERGY :: NEPAL

ELECTRICITY ACCESS:
population without electricity: 3 million (2017)

electrification - total population: 90.7% (2016)

electrification - urban areas: 94.5% (2016)

electrification - rural areas: 85.2% (2016)

ELECTRICITY - PRODUCTION:
4.244 billion kWh (2016 est.)

country comparison to the world: 125

ELECTRICITY - CONSUMPTION:
4.983 billion kWh (2016 est.)

country comparison to the world: 124

ELECTRICITY - EXPORTS:
2.69 million kWh (FY 2017 est.)

country comparison to the world: 94

ELECTRICITY - IMPORTS:
2.175 billion kWh (2016 est.)

country comparison to the world: 57

ELECTRICITY - INSTALLED GENERATING CAPACITY:
943,100 kW (2016 est.)

country comparison to the world: 130

ELECTRICITY - FROM FOSSIL FUELS:
5% of total installed capacity (2016 est.)

country comparison to the world: 203

ELECTRICITY - FROM NUCLEAR FUELS:
0% of total installed capacity (2017 est.)

country comparison to the world: 152

ELECTRICITY - FROM HYDROELECTRIC PLANTS:
92% of total installed capacity (2017 est.)

country comparison to the world: 10

ELECTRICITY - FROM OTHER RENEWABLE SOURCES:
3% of total installed capacity (2017 est.)

country comparison to the world: 128

CRUDE OIL - PRODUCTION:
0 bbl/day (2018 est.)

country comparison to the world: 181

CRUDE OIL - EXPORTS:
0 bbl/day (2015 est.)

country comparison to the world: 173

CRUDE OIL - IMPORTS:
0 bbl/day (2015 est.)

country comparison to the world: 174

CRUDE OIL - PROVED RESERVES:
0 bbl (1 January 2018 est.)

country comparison to the world: 176

REFINED PETROLEUM PRODUCTS - PRODUCTION:
0 bbl/day (2015 est.)

country comparison to the world: 185

REFINED PETROLEUM PRODUCTS - CONSUMPTION:

27,000 bbl/day (2016 est.)

country comparison to the world: 126

REFINED PETROLEUM PRODUCTS - EXPORTS:

0 bbl/day (2015 est.)

country comparison to the world: 187

REFINED PETROLEUM PRODUCTS - IMPORTS:

26,120 bbl/day (2015 est.)

country comparison to the world: 106

NATURAL GAS - PRODUCTION:

0 cu m (2017 est.)

country comparison to the world: 177

NATURAL GAS - CONSUMPTION:

0 cu m (2017 est.)

country comparison to the world: 181

NATURAL GAS - EXPORTS:

0 cu m (2017 est.)

country comparison to the world: 159

NATURAL GAS - IMPORTS:

0 cu m (2017 est.)

country comparison to the world: 164

NATURAL GAS - PROVED RESERVES:

0 cu m (1 January 2014 est.)

country comparison to the world: 175

CARBON DIOXIDE EMISSIONS FROM CONSUMPTION OF ENERGY:

8.396 million Mt (2017 est.)

country comparison to the world: 115

COMMUNICATIONS :: NEPAL

TELEPHONES - FIXED LINES:

total subscriptions: 861,299

subscriptions per 100 inhabitants: 3 (2017 est.)

country comparison to the world: 77

TELEPHONES - MOBILE CELLULAR:

total subscriptions: 32,120,305

subscriptions per 100 inhabitants: 109 (July 2016 est.)

country comparison to the world: 41

TELEPHONE SYSTEM:

general assessment: mountainous topography hinders development of telecom infrastructure; fair radiotelephone communication service; 20% of the market share is fixed (wired) broadband, 2% is fixed (wireless) broadband, and 78% is mobile broadband (2019); fixed broadband is low due to limited number of fixed lines and preeminence of the mobile platform; accelerated mobile broadband penetration the last five years; 90% of the population will have access to broadband by 2020 (2018)

domestic: mobile service has been extended to all 75 districts covering 90% of Nepal's land area; 3G coverage is available in 20 major cities (2019); disparity between high coverage in cities and coverage available in underdeveloped rural regions; fixed-line 3 per 100 persons and mobile-cellular 109 per 100 persons (2018)

international: country code - 977; Nepal, China and Tibet connected across borders with underground and all-dielectric self-supporting (ADSS) fiber-optic cables; radiotelephone communications; microwave and fiber landlines to India; satellite earth station - 1 Intelsat (Indian Ocean) (2019)

BROADCAST MEDIA:

state operates 3 TV stations, as well as national and regional radio stations; 117 television channels are licensed, among those 71 are cable television channels, three are distributed through Direct-To-Home (DTH) system, and four are digital terrestrial; 736 FM radio stations are licensed and at least 314 of those radio stations are community radio stations (2019)

INTERNET COUNTRY CODE:

.np

INTERNET USERS:

total: 5,716,419

percent of population: 19.7% (July 2016 est.)

country comparison to the world: 69

BROADBAND - FIXED SUBSCRIPTIONS:

total: 224,184

subscriptions per 100 inhabitants: 1 (2017 est.)

country comparison to the world: 105

MILITARY AND SECURITY :: NEPAL

MILITARY EXPENDITURES:

1.44% of GDP (2018)

1.55% of GDP (2017)

1.7% of GDP (2016)

1.56% of GDP (2015)

1.63% of GDP (2014)

country comparison to the world: 78

MILITARY AND SECURITY FORCES:

Nepal Army (includes Air Wing); Nepal Armed Police Force (under the Ministry of Interior; paramilitary force responsible for border and internal security, including counter-insurgency, and assisting the Army in the event of an external invasion) (2019)

MILITARY SERVICE AGE AND OBLIGATION:

18 years of age for voluntary military service (including women); no conscription (2019)

TRANSPORTATION :: NEPAL

NATIONAL AIR TRANSPORT SYSTEM:

number of registered air carriers: 4 (2015)

inventory of registered aircraft operated by air carriers: 15 (2015)

annual passenger traffic on registered air carriers: 510,341 (2015)

annual freight traffic on registered air carriers: 4,536,371 mt-km (2015)

CIVIL AIRCRAFT REGISTRATION COUNTRY CODE PREFIX:

9N (2016)

AIRPORTS:

47 (2013)

country comparison to the world: 93

AIRPORTS - WITH PAVED RUNWAYS:

total: 11 (2017)

over 3,047 m: 1 (2017)

1,524 to 2,437 m: 3 (2017)

914 to 1,523 m: 6 (2017)

under 914 m: 1 (2017)

AIRPORTS - WITH UNPAVED RUNWAYS:

total: 36 (2013)

1,524 to 2,437 m: 1 (2013)

914 to 1,523 m: 6 (2013)

under 914 m: 29 (2013)

RAILWAYS:

total: 59 km (2018)

narrow gauge: 59 km 0.762-m gauge (2018)

country comparison to the world: 131

ROADWAYS:

total: 27,990 km (2016)

paved: 11,890 km (2016)

unpaved: 16,100 km (2016)

country comparison to the world: 98

TERRORISM :: NEPAL

TERRORIST GROUPS - FOREIGN BASED:

Indian Mujahedeen (IM): aim(s): enhance networks in Nepal to carry out attacks against Indians in Nepal and India
area(s) of operation: maintains active hubs of small, loosely connected networks (2018)

TRANSNATIONAL ISSUES :: NEPAL

DISPUTES - INTERNATIONAL:

joint border commission continues to work on contested sections of boundary with India, including the 400 sq km dispute over the source of the Kalapani River; India has instituted a stricter border regime to restrict transit of illegal cross-border activities

REFUGEES AND INTERNALLY DISPLACED PERSONS:

refugees (country of origin): 13,509 (Tibet/China), 6,626 (Bhutan) (2018)

stateless persons: undetermined (2016); note - the UNHCR is working with the Nepali Government to address the large number of individuals lacking citizenship certificates in Nepal; smaller numbers of Bhutanese Hindu refugees of Nepali origin (the Lhotshampa) who were stripped of Bhutanese nationality and forced to flee their country in the late 1980s and early 1990s - and undocumented Tibetan refugees who arrived in Nepal prior to the 1990s - are considered stateless

ILLICIT DRUGS:

illicit producer of cannabis and hashish for the domestic and international drug markets; transit point for opiates from Southeast Asia to the West

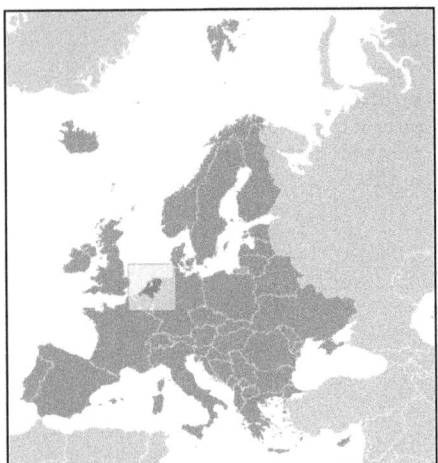

EUROPE :: NETHERLANDS

INTRODUCTION :: NETHERLANDS

BACKGROUND:
The Dutch United Provinces declared their independence from Spain in 1579; during the 17th century, they became a leading seafaring and commercial power, with settlements and colonies around the world. After a 20-year French occupation, a Kingdom of the Netherlands was formed in 1815. In 1830, Belgium seceded and formed a separate kingdom. The Netherlands remained neutral in World War I, but suffered German invasion and occupation in World War II. A modern, industrialized nation, the Netherlands is also a large exporter of agricultural products. The country was a founding member of NATO and the EEC (now the EU) and participated in the introduction of the euro in 1999. In October 2010, the former Netherlands Antilles was dissolved and the three smallest islands - Bonaire, Sint Eustatius, and Saba - became special municipalities in the Netherlands administrative structure. The larger islands of Sint Maarten and Curacao joined the Netherlands and Aruba as constituent countries forming the Kingdom of the Netherlands.

In February 2018, the Sint Eustatius island council (governing body) was dissolved and replaced by a government commissioner to restore the integrity of public administration. According to the Dutch Government, the intervention will be as "short as possible and as long as needed."

GEOGRAPHY :: NETHERLANDS

LOCATION:
Western Europe, bordering the North Sea, between Belgium and Germany

GEOGRAPHIC COORDINATES:
52 30 N, 5 45 E

MAP REFERENCES:
Europe

AREA:
total: 41,543 sq km

land: 33,893 sq km

water: 7,650 sq km

country comparison to the world: 135

AREA - COMPARATIVE:
slightly less than twice the size of New Jersey

LAND BOUNDARIES:
total: 1,053 km

border countries (2): Belgium 478 km, Germany 575 km

COASTLINE:
451 km

MARITIME CLAIMS:
territorial sea: 12 nm

contiguous zone: 24 nm

exclusive fishing zone: 200 nm

CLIMATE:
temperate; marine; cool summers and mild winters

TERRAIN:
mostly coastal lowland and reclaimed land (polders); some hills in southeast

ELEVATION:
mean elevation: 30 m

lowest point: Zuidplaspolder -7 m

highest point: Mount Scenery (on the island of Saba in the Caribbean, now considered an integral part of the Netherlands following the dissolution of the Netherlands Antilles) 862 m

note: the highest point on continental Netherlands is Vaalserberg at 322 m

NATURAL RESOURCES:
natural gas, petroleum, peat, limestone, salt, sand and gravel, arable land

LAND USE:
agricultural land: 55.1% (2011 est.)

arable land: 29.8% (2011 est.) / permanent crops: 1.1% (2011 est.) / permanent pasture: 24.2% (2011 est.)

forest: 10.8% (2011 est.)

other: 34.1% (2011 est.)

IRRIGATED LAND:
4,860 sq km (2012)

POPULATION DISTRIBUTION:
an area known as the Randstad, anchored by the cities of Amsterdam, Rotterdam, the Hague, and Utrecht, is the most densely populated region; the north tends to be less dense, though sizeable communities can be found throughout the entire country

NATURAL HAZARDS:
flooding

volcanism: Mount Scenery (887 m), located on the island of Saba in the Caribbean, last erupted in 1640;; Round Hill (601 m), a dormant volcano also known as The Quill, is located on the island of St. Eustatius in the Caribbean;; these islands are at the northern end of the volcanic island arc of the Lesser Antilles that extends south to Grenada

ENVIRONMENT - CURRENT ISSUES:

water and air pollution are significant environmental problems; pollution of the country's rivers from industrial and agricultural chemicals, including heavy metals, organic compounds, nitrates, and phosphates; air pollution from vehicles and refining activities

ENVIRONMENT - INTERNATIONAL AGREEMENTS:

party to: Air Pollution, Air Pollution-Nitrogen Oxides, Air Pollution-Persistent Organic Pollutants, Air Pollution-Sulfur 85, Air Pollution-Sulfur 94, Air Pollution-Volatile Organic Compounds, Antarctic-Environmental Protocol, Antarctic-Marine Living Resources, Antarctic Treaty, Biodiversity, Climate Change, Climate Change-Kyoto Protocol, Desertification, Endangered Species, Environmental Modification, Hazardous Wastes, Law of the Sea, Marine Dumping, Marine Life Conservation, Ozone Layer Protection, Ship Pollution, Tropical Timber 83, Tropical Timber 94, Wetlands, Whaling

signed, but not ratified: none of the selected agreements

GEOGRAPHY - NOTE:

located at mouths of three major European rivers (Rhine, Maas or Meuse, and Schelde); about a quarter of the country lies below sea level and only about half of the land exceeds one meter above sea level

PEOPLE AND SOCIETY :: NETHERLANDS

POPULATION:

17,151,228 (July 2018 est.)

country comparison to the world: 66

NATIONALITY:

noun: Dutchman(men), Dutchwoman(women)

adjective: Dutch

ETHNIC GROUPS:

Dutch 76.9%, EU 6.4%, Turkish 2.4%, Moroccan 2.3%, Indonesian 2.1%, German 2.1%, Surinamese 2%, Polish 1%, other 4.8% (2018 est.)

LANGUAGES:

Dutch (official)

note: Frisian is an official language in Fryslan province; Frisian, Low Saxon, Limburgish, Romani, and Yiddish have protected status under the European Charter for Regional or Minority Languages; Dutch is the official language of the three special municipalities of the Caribbean Netherlands; English is a recognized regional language on Sint Eustatius and Saba; Papiamento is a recognized regional language on Bonaire

RELIGIONS:

Roman Catholic 23.6%, Protestant 14.9% (includes Dutch Reformed 6.4%, Protestant Church of The Netherlands 5.6%, Calvinist 2.9%), Muslim 5.1%, other 5.6% (includes Hindu, Buddhist, Jewish), none 50.7% (2017 est.)

AGE STRUCTURE:

0-14 years: 16.28% (male 1,428,837 /female 1,362,686)

15-24 years: 12.03% (male 1,052,357 /female 1,011,710)

25-54 years: 39.18% (male 3,371,698 /female 3,348,595)

55-64 years: 13.41% (male 1,143,824 /female 1,155,751)

65 years and over: 19.1% (male 1,487,278 /female 1,788,492) (2018 est.)

DEPENDENCY RATIOS:

total dependency ratio: 53.1 (2015 est.)

youth dependency ratio: 25.6 (2015 est.)

elderly dependency ratio: 27.4 (2015 est.)

potential support ratio: 3.6 (2015 est.)

MEDIAN AGE:

total: 42.7 years (2018 est.)

male: 41.6 years

female: 43.8 years

country comparison to the world: 26

POPULATION GROWTH RATE:

0.38% (2018 est.)

country comparison to the world: 164

BIRTH RATE:

10.9 births/1,000 population (2018 est.)

country comparison to the world: 181

DEATH RATE:

9 deaths/1,000 population (2018 est.)

country comparison to the world: 62

NET MIGRATION RATE:

1.9 migrant(s)/1,000 population (2018 est.)

country comparison to the world: 51

POPULATION DISTRIBUTION:

an area known as the Randstad, anchored by the cities of Amsterdam, Rotterdam, the Hague, and Utrecht, is the most densely populated region; the north tends to be less dense, though sizeable communities can be found throughout the entire country

URBANIZATION:

urban population: 91.9% of total population (2019)

rate of urbanization: 0.74% annual rate of change (2015-20 est.)

MAJOR URBAN AREAS - POPULATION:

1.14 million AMSTERDAM (capital), 1.009 million Rotterdam (2019)

SEX RATIO:

at birth: 1.05 male(s)/female

0-14 years: 1.05 male(s)/female

15-24 years: 1.04 male(s)/female

25-54 years: 1.01 male(s)/female

55-64 years: 0.99 male(s)/female

65 years and over: 0.83 male(s)/female

total population: 0.98 male(s)/female (2018 est.)

MOTHER'S MEAN AGE AT FIRST BIRTH:

29.6 years (2015 est.)

MATERNAL MORTALITY RATE:

5 deaths/100,000 live births (2017 est.)

country comparison to the world: 169

INFANT MORTALITY RATE:

total: 3.5 deaths/1,000 live births (2018 est.)

male: 3.8 deaths/1,000 live births

female: 3.3 deaths/1,000 live births

country comparison to the world: 199

LIFE EXPECTANCY AT BIRTH:

total population: 81.5 years (2018 est.)

male: 79.3 years

female: 83.8 years

country comparison to the world: 27

TOTAL FERTILITY RATE:

1.78 children born/woman (2018 est.)

country comparison to the world: 153

CONTRACEPTIVE PREVALENCE RATE:

73% (2013)

note: percent of women aged 18-45

DRINKING WATER SOURCE:

improved:

urban: 100% of population

rural: 100% of population

total: 100% of population

unimproved:

urban: 0% of population

rural: 0% of population

total: 0% of population (2015 est.)

CURRENT HEALTH EXPENDITURE:
10.4% (2016)

PHYSICIANS DENSITY:
3.51 physicians/1,000 population (2016)

HOSPITAL BED DENSITY:
4.7 beds/1,000 population (2009)

SANITATION FACILITY ACCESS:
improved:

urban: 97.5% of population (2015 est.)

rural: 99.9% of population (2015 est.)

total: 97.7% of population (2015 est.)

unimproved:

urban: 2.5% of population (2015 est.)

rural: 0.1% of population (2015 est.)

total: 2.3% of population (2015 est.)

HIV/AIDS - ADULT PREVALENCE RATE:
0.2% (2017 est.)

country comparison to the world: 108

HIV/AIDS - PEOPLE LIVING WITH HIV/AIDS:
23,000 (2017 est.)

country comparison to the world: 81

HIV/AIDS - DEATHS:
100 (2018 est.)

country comparison to the world: 65

OBESITY - ADULT PREVALENCE RATE:
20.4% (2016)

country comparison to the world: 99

EDUCATION EXPENDITURES:
5.4% of GDP (2015)

country comparison to the world: 46

SCHOOL LIFE EXPECTANCY (PRIMARY TO TERTIARY EDUCATION):
total: 18 years

male: 18 years

female: 18 years (2016)

UNEMPLOYMENT, YOUTH AGES 15-24:
total: 8.9%

male: 9%

female: 8.8% (2017 est.)

country comparison to the world: 135

GOVERNMENT :: NETHERLANDS

COUNTRY NAME:
conventional long form: Kingdom of the Netherlands

conventional short form: Netherlands

local long form: Koninkrijk der Nederlanden

local short form: Nederland

abbreviation: NL

etymology: the country name literally means "the lowlands" and refers to the geographic features of the land being both flat and down river from higher areas (i.e., at the estuaries of the Scheldt, Meuse, and Rhine Rivers; only about half of the Netherlands is more than 1 meter above sea level)

GOVERNMENT TYPE:
parliamentary constitutional monarchy; part of the Kingdom of the Netherlands

CAPITAL:
name: Amsterdam; note - The Hague is the seat of government

geographic coordinates: 52 21 N, 4 55 E

time difference: UTC+1 (6 hours ahead of Washington, DC, during Standard Time)

daylight saving time: +1hr, begins last Sunday in March; ends last Sunday in October

note: time descriptions apply to the continental Netherlands only, for the constituent countries in the Caribbean, the time difference is UTC-4

etymology: the original Dutch name, Amstellerdam, meaning "a dam on the Amstel River," dates to the 13th century; over time the name simplified to Amsterdam

ADMINISTRATIVE DIVISIONS:
12 provinces (provincies, singular - provincie); Drenthe, Flevoland, Fryslan (Friesland), Gelderland, Groningen, Limburg, Noord-Brabant (North Brabant), Noord-Holland (North Holland), Overijssel, Utrecht, Zeeland (Zealand), Zuid-Holland (South Holland)

note: the Netherlands is one of four constituent countries of the Kingdom of the Netherlands; the other three, Aruba, Curacao, and Sint Maarten, are all islands in the Caribbean; while all four parts are considered equal partners, in practice, most of the Kingdom's affairs are administered by the Netherlands, which makes up about 98% of the Kingdom's total land area and population

note: three other Caribbean islands, Bonaire, Sint Eustatius, and Saba, are considered to be special municipalities of the Netherlands proper

DEPENDENT AREAS:
Aruba, Curacao, Sint Maarten

INDEPENDENCE:
23 January 1579 (the northern provinces of the Low Countries conclude the Union of Utrecht breaking with Spain; on 26 July 1581, they formally declared their independence with an Act of Abjuration; however, it was not until 30 January 1648 and the Peace of Westphalia that Spain recognized this independence)

NATIONAL HOLIDAY:
King's Day (birthday of King WILLEM-ALEXANDER), 27 April (1967); note - King's or Queen's Day are observed on the ruling monarch's birthday; currently celebrated on 26 April if 27 April is a Sunday

CONSTITUTION:
history: previous 1597, 1798; latest adopted 24 August 1815 (substantially revised in 1848)

amendments: proposed as an Act of Parliament by or on behalf of the king or by the Second Chamber of the States General; the Second Chamber is dissolved after its first reading of the Act; passage requires a second reading by both the First Chamber and the newly elected Second Chamber, followed by at least two-thirds majority vote of both chambers, and ratification by the king; amended many times, last in 2010 (2016)

LEGAL SYSTEM:
civil law system based on the French system; constitution does not permit judicial review of acts of the States General

INTERNATIONAL LAW ORGANIZATION PARTICIPATION:
accepts compulsory ICJ jurisdiction with reservations; accepts ICCt jurisdiction

CITIZENSHIP:

citizenship by birth: no

citizenship by descent only: at least one parent must be a citizen of the Netherlands

dual citizenship recognized: no

residency requirement for naturalization: 5 years

SUFFRAGE:

18 years of age; universal

EXECUTIVE BRANCH:

chief of state: King WILLEM-ALEXANDER (since 30 April 2013); Heir Apparent Princess Catharina-Amalia (daughter of King WILLEM-ALEXANDER, born 7 December 2003)

head of government: Prime Minister Mark RUTTE (since 14 October 2010); Deputy Prime Ministers (since 26 October 2017) Hugo DE JONGE, Karin Kajsa OLLONGREN, and Carola SCHOUTEN (since 26 October 2017); note - Mark RUTTE heads his third cabinet put in place since 26 October 2017

cabinet: Council of Ministers appointed by the monarch

elections/appointments: the monarchy is hereditary; following Second Chamber elections, the leader of the majority party or majority coalition is usually appointed prime minister by the monarch; deputy prime ministers are appointed by the monarch

LEGISLATIVE BRANCH:

description: bicameral States General or Staten Generaal consists of: First Chamber or Eerste Kamer (75 seats; members indirectly elected by the country's 12 provincial council members by proportional representation vote; members serve 4-year terms) Second Chamber or Tweede Kamer (150 seats; members directly elected in multi-seat constituencies by proportional representation vote to serve up to 4-year terms)

elections:
First Chamber - last held on 27 May 2019 (next to be held on NA May 2023)
Second Chamber - last held on 15 March 2017 (next to be held 15 March 2021)

election results:
First Chamber - percent of vote by party - NA; seats by party - FvD 12, VVD 12, CDA 9, GL 8, D66 7, MvdA 6, PVV 5, SP 4, CU 4, other 8; composition - men 49, women 26, percent of women 34.7%
Second Chamber - percent of vote by party - VVD 21.3%, PVV 13.1%, CDA 12.4%, D66 12.2%, GL 9.1%, SP 9.1%, PvdA 5.7%, CU 3.4%, PvdD 3.2%, 50 Plus 3.1%, other 7.4%; seats by party - VVD 33, PVV 20, CDA 19, D66 19, GL 14, SP 14, PvdA 9, CU 5, PvdD 5, 50 Plus 4, other 8; composition - men 96, women 54, percent of women 36%; note - total States General percent of women 35.6%

JUDICIAL BRANCH:

highest courts: Supreme Court or Hoge Raad (consists of 41 judges: the president, 6 vice presidents, 31 justices or raadsheren, and 3 justices in exceptional service, referred to as buitengewone dienst); the court is divided into criminal, civil, tax, and ombuds chambers

judge selection and term of office: justices appointed by the monarch from a list provided by the Second Chamber of the States General; justices appointed for life or until mandatory retirement at age 70

subordinate courts: courts of appeal; district courts, each with up to 5 subdistrict courts; Netherlands Commercial Court

POLITICAL PARTIES AND LEADERS:

Christian Democratic Appeal or CDA [Sybrand VAN HAERSMA BUMA]
Christian Union or CU [Gert-Jan SEGERS]
Democrats 66 or D66 [Rob JETTEN]
Denk [Tunahan KUZU]
50 Plus [Henk KROL]
Forum for Democracy or FvD [Thierry BAUDET]
Green Left or GL [Jesse KLAVER]
Labor Party or PvdA [Lodewijk ASSCHER]
Party for Freedom or PVV [Geert WILDERS]
Party for the Animals or PvdD [Marianne THIEME]
People's Party for Freedom and Democracy or VVD [Mark RUTTE]
Reformed Political Party or SGP [Kees VAN DER STAAIJ]
Socialist Party or SP [Emile ROEMER]
plus a few minor parties

INTERNATIONAL ORGANIZATION PARTICIPATION:

ADB (nonregional member), AfDB (nonregional member), Arctic Council (observer), Australia Group, Benelux, BIS, CBSS (observer), CD, CE, CERN, EAPC, EBRD, ECB, EIB, EITI (implementing country), EMU, ESA, EU, FAO, FATF, G-10, IADB, IAEA, IBRD, ICAO, ICC (national committees), ICCt, ICRM, IDA, IEA, IFAD, IFC, IFRCS, IGAD (partners), IHO, ILO, IMF, IMO, IMSO, Interpol, IOC, IOM, IPU, ISO, ITSO, ITU, ITUC (NGOs), MIGA, MINUSMA, NATO, NEA, NSG, OAS (observer), OECD, OPCW, OSCE, Pacific Alliance (observer), Paris Club, PCA, Schengen Convention, SELEC (observer), UN, UNCTAD, UNDOF, UNESCO, UNHCR, UNIDO, UNMISS, UNRWA, UN Security Council (temporary), UNTSO, UNWTO, UPU, WCO, WHO, WIPO, WMO, WTO, ZC

DIPLOMATIC REPRESENTATION IN THE US:

Ambassador Hendrik Jan Jurriaan SCHUWER (since 17 September 2015)

chancery: 4200 Linnean Avenue NW, Washington, DC 20008

telephone: [1] (202) 244-5300, [1] 877-388-2443

FAX: [1] (202) 362-3430

consulate(s) general: Chicago, Miami, New York, San Francisco

DIPLOMATIC REPRESENTATION FROM THE US:

chief of mission: Ambassador Peter HOEKSTRA (since 10 January 2018)

telephone: [31] (70) 310-2209

embassy: John Adams Park 1, 2244 BZ Wassenaar

mailing address: PSC 71, Box 1000, APO AE 09715

FAX: [31] (70) 310-2207

consulate(s) general: Amsterdam

FLAG DESCRIPTION:

three equal horizontal bands of red (bright vermilion; top), white, and blue (cobalt); similar to the flag of Luxembourg, which uses a lighter blue and is longer; the colors were derived from those of WILLIAM I, Prince of Orange, who led the Dutch Revolt against Spanish sovereignty in the latter half of the 16th century; originally the upper band was orange, but because its dye tended to turn red over time, the red shade was eventually made the permanent color; the banner is perhaps the oldest tricolor in continuous use

NATIONAL SYMBOL(S):

lion, tulip; national color: orange

NATIONAL ANTHEM:

name: "Het Wilhelmus" (The William)

lyrics/music: Philips VAN MARNIX van Sint Aldegonde (presumed)/unknown

note: adopted 1932, in use since the 17th century, making it the oldest national anthem in the world; also known as "Wilhelmus van Nassouwe" (William of Nassau), it is in the form of an acrostic, where the first letter of each stanza spells the name of the leader of the Dutch Revolt

ECONOMY :: NETHERLANDS

ECONOMY - OVERVIEW:

The Netherlands, the sixth-largest economy in the European Union, plays an important role as a European transportation hub, with a consistently high trade surplus, stable industrial relations, and low unemployment. Industry focuses on food processing, chemicals, petroleum refining, and electrical machinery. A highly mechanized agricultural sector employs only 2% of the labor force but provides large surpluses for food-processing and underpins the country's status as the world's second largest agricultural exporter.

The Netherlands is part of the euro zone, and as such, its monetary policy is controlled by the European Central Bank. The Dutch financial sector is highly concentrated, with four commercial banks possessing over 80% of banking assets, and is four times the size of Dutch GDP.

In 2008, during the financial crisis, the government budget deficit hit 5.3% of GDP. Following a protracted recession from 2009 to 2013, during which unemployment doubled to 7.4% and household consumption contracted for four consecutive years, economic growth began inching forward in 2014. Since 2010, Prime Minister Mark RUTTE's government has implemented significant austerity measures to improve public finances and has instituted broad structural reforms in key policy areas, including the labor market, the housing sector, the energy market, and the pension system. In 2017, the government budget returned to a surplus of 0.7% of GDP, with economic growth of 3.2%, and GDP per capita finally surpassed pre-crisis levels. The fiscal policy announced by the new government in the 2018-2021 coalition plans for increases in government consumption and public investment, fueling domestic demand and household consumption and investment. The new government's policy also plans to increase demand for workers in the public and private sector, forecasting a further decline in the unemployment rate, which hit 4.8% in 2017.

GDP (PURCHASING POWER PARITY):

$924.4 billion (2017 est.)

$898.6 billion (2016 est.)

$879.4 billion (2015 est.)

note: data are in 2017 dollars

country comparison to the world: 27

GDP (OFFICIAL EXCHANGE RATE):

$832.2 billion (2017 est.)

GDP - REAL GROWTH RATE:

2.9% (2017 est.)

2.2% (2016 est.)

2% (2015 est.)

country comparison to the world: 118

GDP - PER CAPITA (PPP):

$53,900 (2017 est.)

$52,800 (2016 est.)

$51,900 (2015 est.)

note: data are in 2017 dollars

country comparison to the world: 23

GROSS NATIONAL SAVING:

31.2% of GDP (2017 est.)

28.5% of GDP (2016 est.)

28.8% of GDP (2015 est.)

country comparison to the world: 28

GDP - COMPOSITION, BY END USE:

household consumption: 44.3% (2017 est.)

government consumption: 24.2% (2017 est.)

investment in fixed capital: 20.5% (2017 est.)

investment in inventories: 0.2% (2017 est.)

exports of goods and services: 83% (2017 est.)

imports of goods and services: -72.3% (2017 est.)

GDP - COMPOSITION, BY SECTOR OF ORIGIN:

agriculture: 1.6% (2017 est.)

industry: 17.9% (2017 est.)

services: 70.2% (2017 est.)

AGRICULTURE - PRODUCTS:

vegetables, ornamentals, dairy, poultry and livestock products; propagation materials

INDUSTRIES:

agroindustries, metal and engineering products, electrical machinery and equipment, chemicals, petroleum, construction, microelectronics, fishing

INDUSTRIAL PRODUCTION GROWTH RATE:

3.3% (2017 est.)

country comparison to the world: 96

LABOR FORCE:

7.969 million (2017 est.)

country comparison to the world: 63

LABOR FORCE - BY OCCUPATION:

agriculture: 1.2%

industry: 17.2%

services: 81.6% (2015 est.)

UNEMPLOYMENT RATE:

4.9% (2017 est.)

6% (2016 est.)

country comparison to the world: 69

POPULATION BELOW POVERTY LINE:

8.8% (2015 est.)

HOUSEHOLD INCOME OR CONSUMPTION BY PERCENTAGE SHARE:

lowest 10%: 2.3%

highest 10%: 24.9% (2014 est.)

DISTRIBUTION OF FAMILY INCOME - GINI INDEX:

30.3 (2015 est.)

25.1 (2013 est.)

country comparison to the world: 134

BUDGET:

revenues: 361.4 billion (2017 est.)

expenditures: 352.4 billion (2017 est.)

TAXES AND OTHER REVENUES:

43.4% (of GDP) (2017 est.)

country comparison to the world: 27

BUDGET SURPLUS (+) OR DEFICIT (-):

1.1% (of GDP) (2017 est.)

country comparison to the world: 32

PUBLIC DEBT:

56.5% of GDP (2017 est.)

61.3% of GDP (2016 est.)

note: data cover general government debt and include debt instruments issued (or owned) by government entities other than the treasury; the data include treasury debt held by foreign entities; the data include debt issued by subnational entities, as well as intragovernmental debt; intragovernmental debt consists of treasury borrowings from surpluses in the social funds, such as for retirement, medical care, and unemployment; debt instruments for the social funds are not sold at public auctions

country comparison to the world: 78

FISCAL YEAR:

calendar year

INFLATION RATE (CONSUMER PRICES):

1.3% (2017 est.)

0.1% (2016 est.)

country comparison to the world: 70

CENTRAL BANK DISCOUNT RATE:

0% (31 December 2016)

0.05% (31 December 2015)

note: this is the European Central Bank's rate on the marginal lending facility, which offers overnight credit to banks in the euro area

country comparison to the world: 158

COMMERCIAL BANK PRIME LENDING RATE:

1.33% (31 December 2017 est.)

1.47% (31 December 2016 est.)

country comparison to the world: 192

STOCK OF NARROW MONEY:

$419 billion (31 December 2017 est.)

$364.9 billion (31 December 2016 est.)

note: see entry for the European Union for money supply for the entire euro area; the European Central Bank (ECB) controls monetary policy for the 18 members of the Economic and Monetary Union (EMU); individual members of the EMU do not control the quantity of money circulating within their own borders

country comparison to the world: 13

STOCK OF BROAD MONEY:

$419 billion (31 December 2017 est.)

$364.9 billion (31 December 2016 est.)

country comparison to the world: 13

STOCK OF DOMESTIC CREDIT:

$1.687 trillion (31 December 2017 est.)

$1.547 trillion (31 December 2016 est.)

country comparison to the world: 14

MARKET VALUE OF PUBLICLY TRADED SHARES:

$652.7 billion (31 December 2015 est.)

$735.1 billion (31 December 2014 est.)

$675 billion (31 December 2013 est.)

country comparison to the world: 17

CURRENT ACCOUNT BALANCE:

$87.46 billion (2017 est.)

$62.92 billion (2016 est.)

country comparison to the world: 4

EXPORTS:

$555.6 billion (2017 est.)

$495.4 billion (2016 est.)

country comparison to the world: 6

EXPORTS - PARTNERS:

Germany 24.2%, Belgium 10.7%, UK 8.8%, France 8.8%, Italy 4.2% (2017)

EXPORTS - COMMODITIES:

machinery and transport equipment, chemicals, mineral fuels; food and livestock, manufactured goods

IMPORTS:

$453.8 billion (2017 est.)

$402.9 billion (2016 est.)

country comparison to the world: 10

IMPORTS - COMMODITIES:

machinery and transport equipment, chemicals, fuels, foodstuffs, clothing

IMPORTS - PARTNERS:

China 16.4%, Germany 15.3%, Belgium 8.5%, US 6.9%, UK 5.1%, Russia 4.3% (2017)

RESERVES OF FOREIGN EXCHANGE AND GOLD:

$38.44 billion (31 December 2017 est.)

$38.21 billion (31 December 2015 est.)

country comparison to the world: 46

DEBT - EXTERNAL:

$4.063 trillion (31 December 2016 est.)

$4.054 trillion (31 December 2015 est.)

country comparison to the world: 5

STOCK OF DIRECT FOREIGN INVESTMENT - AT HOME:

$5.499 trillion (31 December 2017 est.)

$4.759 trillion (31 December 2016 est.)

country comparison to the world: 1

STOCK OF DIRECT FOREIGN INVESTMENT - ABROAD:

$6.579 trillion (31 December 2017 est.)

$5.623 trillion (31 December 2016 est.)

country comparison to the world: 1

EXCHANGE RATES:

euros (EUR) per US dollar -

0.885 (2017 est.)

0.903 (2016 est.)

0.9214 (2015 est.)

0.885 (2014 est.)

0.7634 (2013 est.)

ENERGY :: NETHERLANDS

ELECTRICITY ACCESS:

electrification - total population: 100% (2016)

ELECTRICITY - PRODUCTION:

109.3 billion kWh (2016 est.)

country comparison to the world: 33

ELECTRICITY - CONSUMPTION:

108.8 billion kWh (2016 est.)

country comparison to the world: 32

ELECTRICITY - EXPORTS:

19.34 billion kWh (2016 est.)

country comparison to the world: 8

ELECTRICITY - IMPORTS:

24.26 billion kWh (2016 est.)

country comparison to the world: 7

ELECTRICITY - INSTALLED GENERATING CAPACITY:

34.17 million kW (2016 est.)

country comparison to the world: 29

ELECTRICITY - FROM FOSSIL FUELS:

75% of total installed capacity (2016 est.)

country comparison to the world: 95

ELECTRICITY - FROM NUCLEAR FUELS:

1% of total installed capacity (2017 est.)

country comparison to the world: 31

ELECTRICITY - FROM HYDROELECTRIC PLANTS:

0% of total installed capacity (2017 est.)

country comparison to the world: 189

ELECTRICITY - FROM OTHER RENEWABLE SOURCES:

23% of total installed capacity (2017 est.)

country comparison to the world: 32

CRUDE OIL - PRODUCTION:

18,000 bbl/day (2018 est.)

country comparison to the world: 67

CRUDE OIL - EXPORTS:

7,984 bbl/day (2017 est.)

country comparison to the world: 62

CRUDE OIL - IMPORTS:

1.094 million bbl/day (2017 est.)

country comparison to the world: 10

CRUDE OIL - PROVED RESERVES:

81.13 million bbl (1 January 2018 est.)

country comparison to the world: 72

REFINED PETROLEUM PRODUCTS - PRODUCTION:

1.282 million bbl/day (2017 est.)

country comparison to the world: 17

REFINED PETROLEUM PRODUCTS - CONSUMPTION:

954,500 bbl/day (2017 est.)

country comparison to the world: 23

REFINED PETROLEUM PRODUCTS - EXPORTS:

2.406 million bbl/day (2017 est.)

country comparison to the world: 3

REFINED PETROLEUM PRODUCTS - IMPORTS:

2.148 million bbl/day (2017 est.)

country comparison to the world: 3

NATURAL GAS - PRODUCTION:

45.33 billion cu m (2017 est.)

note: the Netherlands has curbed gas production due to seismic activity in the province of Groningen, largest source of gas reserves

country comparison to the world: 17

NATURAL GAS - CONSUMPTION:

43.38 billion cu m (2017 est.)

country comparison to the world: 21

NATURAL GAS - EXPORTS:

51.25 billion cu m (2017 est.)

country comparison to the world: 8

NATURAL GAS - IMPORTS:

51 billion cu m (2017 est.)

country comparison to the world: 7

NATURAL GAS - PROVED RESERVES:

801.4 billion cu m (1 January 2018 est.)

country comparison to the world: 26

CARBON DIOXIDE EMISSIONS FROM CONSUMPTION OF ENERGY:

250.2 million Mt (2017 est.)

country comparison to the world: 26

COMMUNICATIONS :: NETHERLANDS

TELEPHONES - FIXED LINES:

total subscriptions: 6.551 million

subscriptions per 100 inhabitants: 38 (2017 est.)

country comparison to the world: 26

TELEPHONES - MOBILE CELLULAR:

total subscriptions: 20.532 million

subscriptions per 100 inhabitants: 120 (2017 est.)

country comparison to the world: 55

TELEPHONE SYSTEM:

general assessment: highly developed and well maintained; while fixed-line voice market is in decline the VoIP (voice over Internet protocal) and mobile platforms advance; one of the highest fixed broadband penetration rates in the world; government investments; preparations for 5G trials, plans for 3G network shutdown in 2022; LTE-A services; MNOs and banks launch m-payments system (2018)

domestic: extensive fixed-line, fiber-optic network; large cellular telephone system with five major operators utilizing the third generation of the Global System for Mobile Communications technology; one in five households now use Voice over the Internet Protocol services; fixed-line 38 per 100 and mobile-cellular 120 per 100 persons (2018)

international: country code - 31; landing points for Farland North, TAT-14, Circe North, Concerto, Ulysses 2, AC-1, UK-Netherlands 14, and COBRAcable submarine cables which provide links to the US and Europe; satellite earth stations - 5 (3 Intelsat - 1 Indian Ocean and 2 Atlantic Ocean, 1 Eutelsat, and 1 Inmarsat) (2019)

BROADCAST MEDIA:

more than 90% of households are connected to cable or satellite TV systems that provide a wide range of domestic and foreign channels; public service broadcast system includes multiple broadcasters, 3 with a national reach and the remainder operating in regional and local markets; 2 major nationwide commercial television companies, each with 3 or more stations, and many commercial TV stations in regional and local markets; nearly 600 radio stations with a mix of public and private stations providing national or regional coverage

INTERNET COUNTRY CODE:

.nl

INTERNET USERS:

total: 15,385,203

percent of population: 90.4% (July 2016 est.)

country comparison to the world: 39

BROADBAND - FIXED SUBSCRIPTIONS:

total: 7,210,800

subscriptions per 100 inhabitants: 42 (2017 est.)

country comparison to the world: 22

MILITARY AND SECURITY :: NETHERLANDS

MILITARY EXPENDITURES:

1.24% of GDP (2018)

1.16% of GDP (2017)

1.16% of GDP (2016)

1.13% of GDP (2015)

1.16% of GDP (2014)

country comparison to the world: 102

MILITARY AND SECURITY FORCES:

Royal Netherlands Army, Royal Netherlands Navy (includes Naval Air Service and Marine Corps), Royal Netherlands Air Force (Koninklijke Luchtmacht, KLu), Royal Marechaussee (Military Police) (2019)

MILITARY SERVICE AGE AND OBLIGATION:

17 years of age for an all-volunteer force (2016)

TRANSPORTATION :: NETHERLANDS

NATIONAL AIR TRANSPORT SYSTEM:

number of registered air carriers: 8 (2015)

inventory of registered aircraft operated by air carriers: 244 (2015)

annual passenger traffic on registered air carriers: 34,870,204 (2015)

annual freight traffic on registered air carriers: 5,292,794,685 mt-km (2015)

CIVIL AIRCRAFT REGISTRATION COUNTRY CODE PREFIX:

PH (2016)

AIRPORTS:

29 (2013)

country comparison to the world: 118

AIRPORTS - WITH PAVED RUNWAYS:

total: 23 (2017)

over 3,047 m: 3 (2017)

2,438 to 3,047 m: 11 (2017)

1,524 to 2,437 m: 1 (2017)

914 to 1,523 m: 6 (2017)

under 914 m: 2 (2017)

AIRPORTS - WITH UNPAVED RUNWAYS:

total: 6 (2013)

914 to 1,523 m: 4 (2013)

under 914 m: 2 (2013)

HELIPORTS:

1 (2013)

PIPELINES:

14000 km gas, 2500 km oil and refined products, 3000 km chemicals (2016)

RAILWAYS:

total: 3,058 km (2016)

standard gauge: 3,058 km 1.435-m gauge (2,314 km electrified) (2016)

country comparison to the world: 61

ROADWAYS:

total: 139,124 km (includes 3,654 km of expressways) (2016)

country comparison to the world: 37

WATERWAYS:

6,237 km (navigable by ships up to 50 tons) (2012)

country comparison to the world: 21

MERCHANT MARINE:

total: 1,233

by type: bulk carrier 13, container ship 41, general cargo 586, oil tanker 21, other 572 (2018)

country comparison to the world: 23

PORTS AND TERMINALS:

major seaport(s): IJmuiden, Vlissingen

container port(s) (TEUs): Rotterdam (13,734,000) (2017)

LNG terminal(s) (import): Rotterdam

river port(s): Amsterdam (Nordsee Kanaal); Moerdijk (Hollands Diep River); Rotterdam (Rhine River); Terneuzen (Western Scheldt River)

TRANSNATIONAL ISSUES :: NETHERLANDS

DISPUTES - INTERNATIONAL:

none

REFUGEES AND INTERNALLY DISPLACED PERSONS:

refugees (country of origin): 32,092 (Syria), 15,478 (Somalia), 14,931 (Eritrea), 9,259 (Iraq), 6,267 (Afghanistan) (2017)

stateless persons: 1,951 (2018)

ILLICIT DRUGS:

major European producer of synthetic drugs, including ecstasy, and cannabis cultivator; important gateway for cocaine, heroin, and hashish entering Europe; major source of US-bound ecstasy and a significant consumer of ecstasy; a large financial sector vulnerable to money laundering

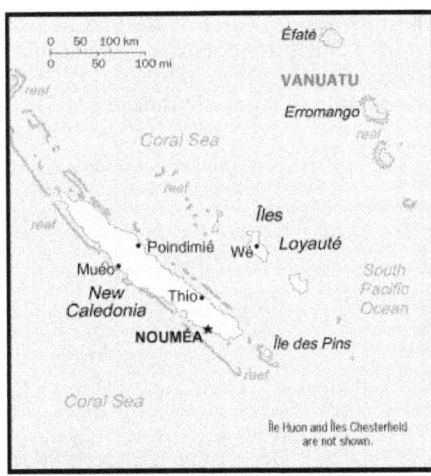

AUSTRALIA - OCEANIA :: NEW CALEDONIA

INTRODUCTION :: NEW CALEDONIA

BACKGROUND:
Settled by both Britain and France during the first half of the 19th century, the island became a French possession in 1853. It served as a penal colony for four decades after 1864. Agitation for independence during the 1980s and early 1990s ended in the 1998 Noumea Accord, which over two decades transferred an increasing amount of governing responsibility from France to New Caledonia. In a referendum held in November 2018, residents rejected independence and decided to retain their territorial status, although two additional referendums may occur in 2020 and 2022, per the Noumea Accord.

GEOGRAPHY :: NEW CALEDONIA

LOCATION:
Oceania, islands in the South Pacific Ocean, east of Australia

GEOGRAPHIC COORDINATES:
21 30 S, 165 30 E

MAP REFERENCES:
Oceania

AREA:
total: 18,575 sq km
land: 18,275 sq km
water: 300 sq km
country comparison to the world: 156

AREA - COMPARATIVE:
slightly smaller than New Jersey

LAND BOUNDARIES:
0 km

COASTLINE:
2,254 km

MARITIME CLAIMS:
territorial sea: 12 nm
exclusive economic zone: 200 nm

CLIMATE:
tropical; modified by southeast trade winds; hot, humid

TERRAIN:
coastal plains with interior mountains

ELEVATION:
lowest point: Pacific Ocean 0 m
highest point: Mont Panie 1,628 m

NATURAL RESOURCES:
nickel, chrome, iron, cobalt, manganese, silver, gold, lead, copper

LAND USE:
agricultural land: 10.4% (2011 est.)
arable land: 0.4% (2011 est.) / permanent crops: 0.2% (2011 est.) / permanent pasture: 9.8% (2011 est.)
forest: 45.9% (2011 est.)
other: 43.7% (2011 est.)

IRRIGATED LAND:
100 sq km (2012)

POPULATION DISTRIBUTION:
most of the populace lives in the southern part of the main island, in and around the capital of Noumea

NATURAL HAZARDS:
cyclones, most frequent from November to March

volcanism: Matthew and Hunter Islands are historically active

ENVIRONMENT - CURRENT ISSUES:
preservation of coral reefs; prevention of invasive species; limiting erosion caused by nickel mining and forest fires

GEOGRAPHY - NOTE:
consists of the main island of New Caledonia (one of the largest in the Pacific Ocean), the archipelago of Iles Loyaute, and numerous small, sparsely populated islands and atolls

PEOPLE AND SOCIETY :: NEW CALEDONIA

POPULATION:
282,754 (July 2018 est.)
country comparison to the world: 183

NATIONALITY:
noun: New Caledonian(s)
adjective: New Caledonian

ETHNIC GROUPS:
Kanak 39.1%, European 27.1%, Wallisian, Futunian 8.2%, Tahitian 2.1%, Indonesian 1.4%, Ni-Vanuatu 1%, Vietnamese 0.9%, other 17.7%, unspecified 2.5% (2014 est.)

LANGUAGES:
French (official), 33 Melanesian-Polynesian dialects

RELIGIONS:
Roman Catholic 60%, Protestant 30%, other 10%

AGE STRUCTURE:
0-14 years: 22.19% (male 32,057 /female 30,675)
15-24 years: 16.16% (male 23,355 /female 22,349)

25-54 years: 43.66% (male 62,227 /female 61,215)

55-64 years: 8.57% (male 11,713 /female 12,530)

65 years and over: 9.42% (male 11,790 /female 14,843) (2018 est.)

DEPENDENCY RATIOS:

total dependency ratio: 48.3 (2015 est.)

youth dependency ratio: 33.9 (2015 est.)

elderly dependency ratio: 14.4 (2015 est.)

potential support ratio: 6.9 (2015 est.)

MEDIAN AGE:

total: 32.3 years (2018 est.)

male: 31.5 years

female: 33 years

country comparison to the world: 103

POPULATION GROWTH RATE:

1.3% (2018 est.)

country comparison to the world: 85

BIRTH RATE:

14.8 births/1,000 population (2018 est.)

country comparison to the world: 128

DEATH RATE:

5.7 deaths/1,000 population (2018 est.)

country comparison to the world: 175

NET MIGRATION RATE:

3.9 migrant(s)/1,000 population (2018 est.)

note: there has been steady emigration from Wallis and Futuna to New Caledonia

country comparison to the world: 34

POPULATION DISTRIBUTION:

most of the populace lives in the southern part of the main island, in and around the capital of Noumea

URBANIZATION:

urban population: 71.1% of total population (2019)

rate of urbanization: 1.89% annual rate of change (2015-20 est.)

MAJOR URBAN AREAS - POPULATION:

198,000 NOUMEA (capital) (2018)

SEX RATIO:

at birth: 1.05 male(s)/female

0-14 years: 1.05 male(s)/female

15-24 years: 1.05 male(s)/female

25-54 years: 1.02 male(s)/female

55-64 years: 0.93 male(s)/female

65 years and over: 0.79 male(s)/female

total population: 1 male(s)/female (2018 est.)

INFANT MORTALITY RATE:

total: 5.2 deaths/1,000 live births (2018 est.)

male: 6.1 deaths/1,000 live births

female: 4.2 deaths/1,000 live births

country comparison to the world: 174

LIFE EXPECTANCY AT BIRTH:

total population: 78 years (2018 est.)

male: 74.1 years

female: 82.2 years

country comparison to the world: 65

TOTAL FERTILITY RATE:

1.92 children born/woman (2018 est.)

country comparison to the world: 130

DRINKING WATER SOURCE:

improved:

urban: 98.5% of population

rural: 98.5% of population

total: 98.5% of population

unimproved:

urban: 1.5% of population

rural: 1.5% of population

total: 1.5% of population (2015 est.)

PHYSICIANS DENSITY:

2.22 physicians/1,000 population (2009)

SANITATION FACILITY ACCESS:

improved:

urban: 100% of population (2015 est.)

rural: 100% of population (2015 est.)

total: 100% of population (2015 est.)

unimproved:

urban: 0% of population (2015 est.)

rural: 0% of population (2015 est.)

total: 0% of population (2015 est.)

HIV/AIDS - ADULT PREVALENCE RATE:

NA

HIV/AIDS - PEOPLE LIVING WITH HIV/AIDS:

NA

HIV/AIDS - DEATHS:

NA

MAJOR INFECTIOUS DISEASES:

note: active local transmission of Zika virus by Aedes species mosquitoes has been identified in this country (as of August 2016); it poses an important risk (a large number of cases possible) among US citizens if bitten by an infective mosquito; other less common ways to get Zika are through sex, via blood transfusion, or during pregnancy, in which the pregnant woman passes Zika virus to her fetus

EDUCATION EXPENDITURES:

NA

LITERACY:

definition: age 15 and over can read and write

total population: 96.9%

male: 97.3%

female: 96.5% (2015 est.)

UNEMPLOYMENT, YOUTH AGES 15-24:

total: 38.4%

male: 37.1%

female: 40% (2014 est.)

country comparison to the world: 16

GOVERNMENT :: NEW CALEDONIA

COUNTRY NAME:

conventional long form: Territory of New Caledonia and Dependencies

conventional short form: New Caledonia

local long form: Territoire des Nouvelle-Caledonie et Dependances

local short form: Nouvelle-Caledonie

etymology: British explorer Captain James COOK discovered and named New Caledonia in 1774; he used the appellation because the northeast of the island reminded him of Scotland (Caledonia is the Latin designation for Scotland)

DEPENDENCY STATUS:

special collectivity (or a sui generis collectivity) of France since 1998; note - an independence referendum took place on 4 November 2018 with a majority voting to reject independence in favor of maintaining the status quo; two additional referenda, still unscheduled, may occur in 2020 and 2022

GOVERNMENT TYPE:

parliamentary democracy (Territorial Congress); an overseas collectivity of France

CAPITAL:

name: Noumea

geographic coordinates: 22 16 S, 166 27 E

time difference: UTC+11 (16 hours ahead of Washington, DC, during Standard Time)

ADMINISTRATIVE DIVISIONS:

3 provinces; Province Iles (Islands Province), Province Nord (North Province), and Province Sud (South Province)

INDEPENDENCE:

none (overseas collectivity of France); note - in an independence referendum on 4 November 2018, the majority voted to reject independence in favor of maintaining the status quo

NATIONAL HOLIDAY:

Fete de la Federation, 14 July (1790); note - the local holiday is New Caledonia Day, 24 September (1853)

CONSTITUTION:

history: 4 October 1958 (French Constitution with changes as reflected in the Noumea Accord of 5 May 1998)

amendments: French constitution amendment procedures apply

LEGAL SYSTEM:

civil law system based on French civil law

CITIZENSHIP:

see France

SUFFRAGE:

18 years of age; universal

EXECUTIVE BRANCH:

chief of state: President Emmanuel MACRON (since 14 May 2017); represented by High Commissioner Laurent PREVOST (since 5 August 2019)

head of government: President of the Government Thierry SANTA (since 9 July 2019); Temporary Vice President Gilbert TUIENON (since 9 July 2019); note - Temporary Vice President Gilbert TUIENON was elected so that the new government could take over; Philippe GERMAIN's government remained caretaker government until the new government was settled

cabinet: Cabinet elected from and by the Territorial Congress

elections/appointments: French president directly elected by absolute majority popular vote in 2 rounds if needed for a 5-year term (eligible for a second term); high commissioner appointed by the French president on the advice of the French Ministry of Interior; president of New Caledonia elected by Territorial Congress for a 5-year term (no term limits); election last held on 13 June 2017 (next to be held in 2022)

election results: Thierry SANTA elected president by Territorial Congress with 6 votes out of 11

LEGISLATIVE BRANCH:

description: unicameral Territorial Congress or Congrès du Territoire (54 seats; members indirectly selected proportionally by the partisan makeup of the 3 Provincial Assemblies or Assemblés Provinciales; members of the 3 Provincial Assemblies directly elected by proportional representation vote; members serve 5-year terms); note - the Customary Senate is the assembly of the various traditional councils of the Kanaks, the indigenous population, which rules on laws affecting the indigenous population New Caledonia indirectly elects 2 members to the French Senate by an electoral colleges for a 6-year term with one seat renewed every 3 years and directly elects 2 members to the French National Assembly by absolute majority vote in 2 rounds if needed for a 5-year term

elections:
Territorial Congress - last held on 12 May 2019 (next to be held in May 2024)
French Senate - election last held on 24 September 2017 (next to be held not later than 2019)

French National Assembly - election last held on 11 and 18 June 2017 (next to be held by June 2022)

election results:

Territorial Congress - percent of vote by party - N/A; seats by party -Future With Confidence 18, UNI 9, UC 9, CE 7, FLNKS 6, Oceanic Awakening 3, PT 1, LKS 1 (Anti-Independence 28, Pro-Independence 26); composition - men 30, women 24, percent of women 44.4%

French Senate - percent of vote by party - NA; seats by party - UMP 2

French National Assembly - percent of vote by party - NA; seats by party - CE 2

JUDICIAL BRANCH:

highest courts: Court of Appeal in Noumea or Cour d'Appel; organized into civil, commercial, social, and pre-trial investigation chambers; court bench normally includes the court president and 2 counselors); Administrative Court (number of judges NA); note - final appeals beyond the Court of Appeal are referred to the Court of Cassation or Cour de Cassation (in Paris); final appeals beyond the Administrative Court are referred to the Administrative Court of Appeal (in Paris)

judge selection and term of office: judge appointment and tenure based on France's judicial system

subordinate courts: Courts of First Instance include: civil, juvenile, commercial, labor, police, criminal, assizes, and also a pre-trial investigation chamber; Joint Commerce Tribunal; administrative courts

POLITICAL PARTIES AND LEADERS:

Build Our Rainbow Nation
Caledonia Together or CE [Philippe GERMAIN]
Caledonian Union or UC [Daniel GOA]
Future Together (l'Avenir Ensemble) [Harold MARTIN]
Kanak Socialist Front for National Liberation or FLNKS (alliance includes PALIKA, UNI, UC, and UPM) [Victor TUTUGORO]
Labor Party (Parti Travailliste) or PT [Louis Kotra UREGEI]
National Union for Independence (Union Nationale pour l'Independance) or UNI
Party of Kanak Liberation (Parti de Liberation Kanak) or PALIKA [Paul NEAOUTYINE]
Socialist Kanak Liberation or LKS [Nidoish NAISSELINE]
The Republicans (formerly The Rally or UMP) [interim leader Thierry SANTA]
Union for Caledonia in France

INTERNATIONAL ORGANIZATION PARTICIPATION:

ITUC (NGOs), PIF (associate member), SPC, UPU, WFTU (NGOs), WMO

DIPLOMATIC REPRESENTATION IN THE US:

none (overseas territory of France)

DIPLOMATIC REPRESENTATION FROM THE US:

none (overseas territory of France)

FLAG DESCRIPTION:

New Caledonia has two official flags; alongside the flag of France, the Kanak (indigenous Melanesian) flag has equal status; the latter consists of three equal horizontal bands of blue (top), red, and green; a large yellow disk - diameter two-thirds the height of the flag - shifted slightly to the hoist side is edged in black and displays a black fleche faitiere symbol, a native rooftop adornment

NATIONAL SYMBOL(S):

fleche faitiere (native rooftop adornment), kagu bird; national colors: gray, red

NATIONAL ANTHEM:

name: "Soyons unis, devenons freres" (Let Us Be United, Let Us Become Brothers)

lyrics/music: Chorale Melodia (a local choir)

note: adopted 2008; contains a mixture of lyrics in both French and Nengone (an indigenous language); as a self-governing territory of France, in addition to the local anthem, "La Marseillaise" is official (see France)

ECONOMY :: NEW CALEDONIA

ECONOMY - OVERVIEW:

New Caledonia has 11% of the world's nickel reserves, representing the second largest reserves on the planet. Only a small amount of the land is suitable for cultivation, and food accounts for about 20% of imports. In addition to nickel, substantial financial support from France - equal to more than 15% of GDP - and tourism are keys to the health of the economy.

With the gradual increase in the production of two new nickel plants in 2015, average production of metallurgical goods stood at a record level of 94 thousand tons. However, the sector is exposed to the high volatility of nickel prices, which have been in decline since 2016. In 2017, one of the three major mining firms on the island, Vale, put its operations up for sale, triggering concerns of layoffs ahead of the 2018 independence referendum.

GDP (PURCHASING POWER PARITY):

$11.11 billion (2017 est.)

$10.89 billion (2016 est.)

$10.77 billion (2015 est.)

note: data are in 2015 dollars

country comparison to the world: 159

GDP (OFFICIAL EXCHANGE RATE):

$9.77 billion (2017 est.)

GDP - REAL GROWTH RATE:

2% (2017 est.)

1.1% (2016 est.)

3.2% (2015 est.)

country comparison to the world: 154

GDP - PER CAPITA (PPP):

$31,100 (2015 est.)

$32,100 (2014 est.)

$29,800 (2012 est.)

country comparison to the world: 66

GDP - COMPOSITION, BY END USE:

household consumption: 64.3% (2017 est.)

government consumption: 24% (2017 est.)

investment in fixed capital: 38.4% (2017 est.)

investment in inventories: 0% (2017 est.)

exports of goods and services: 18.7% (2017 est.)

imports of goods and services: -45.5% (2017 est.)

GDP - COMPOSITION, BY SECTOR OF ORIGIN:

agriculture: 1.4% (2017 est.)

industry: 26.4% (2017 est.)

services: 72.1% (2017 est.)

AGRICULTURE - PRODUCTS:

vegetables; beef, venison, other livestock products; fish

INDUSTRIES:

nickel mining and smelting

INDUSTRIAL PRODUCTION GROWTH RATE:

3.5% (2017 est.)

country comparison to the world: 87

LABOR FORCE:

119,500 (2016 est.)

country comparison to the world: 181

LABOR FORCE - BY OCCUPATION:

agriculture: 2.7%

industry: 22.4%

services: 74.9% (2010)

UNEMPLOYMENT RATE:

14.7% (2014)

14% (2009)

country comparison to the world: 171

POPULATION BELOW POVERTY LINE:

17% (2008)

HOUSEHOLD INCOME OR CONSUMPTION BY PERCENTAGE SHARE:

lowest 10%: NA

highest 10%: NA

BUDGET:

revenues: 1.995 billion (2015 est.)

expenditures: 1.993 billion (2015 est.)

TAXES AND OTHER REVENUES:

20.4% (of GDP) (2015 est.)

country comparison to the world: 147

BUDGET SURPLUS (+) OR DEFICIT (-):

0% (of GDP) (2015 est.)

country comparison to the world: 45

PUBLIC DEBT:

6.5% of GDP (2015 est.)

6.5% of GDP (2014 est.)

country comparison to the world: 203

FISCAL YEAR:

calendar year

INFLATION RATE (CONSUMER PRICES):

1.4% (2017 est.)

0.6% (2016 est.)

country comparison to the world: 79

STOCK OF DOMESTIC CREDIT:

$9.522 billion (2015 est.)

country comparison to the world: 107

MARKET VALUE OF PUBLICLY TRADED SHARES:

NA

CURRENT ACCOUNT BALANCE:

-$1.469 billion (2014 est.)

-$1.861 billion (2013 est.)

country comparison to the world: 156

EXPORTS:

$2.207 billion (2014 est.)

country comparison to the world: 138

EXPORTS - PARTNERS:

China 25.4%, Japan 16.6%, South Korea 14.8%, France 8.2%, Belgium 5%, US 4.6% (2017)

EXPORTS - COMMODITIES:
ferronickels, nickel ore, fish

IMPORTS:
$2.715 billion (2015 est.)

$4.4 billion (2014 est.)

country comparison to the world: 154

IMPORTS - COMMODITIES:
machinery and equipment, fuels, chemicals, foodstuffs

IMPORTS - PARTNERS:
France 24.2%, Singapore 13.1%, China 9.2%, Australia 7.1%, South Korea 5.2%, Malaysia 4.7%, NZ 4.4%, US 4.4% (2017)

DEBT - EXTERNAL:
$112 million (31 December 2013 est.)

$79 million (31 December 1998 est.)

country comparison to the world: 192

STOCK OF DIRECT FOREIGN INVESTMENT - AT HOME:
$16.43 billion (2015 est.)

$14.55 billion (2014 est.)

country comparison to the world: 87

STOCK OF DIRECT FOREIGN INVESTMENT - ABROAD:
$658.2 million (2015 est.)

$593.8 million (2014 est.)

country comparison to the world: 94

EXCHANGE RATES:
Comptoirs Francais du Pacifique francs (XPF) per US dollar -

110.2 (2017 est.)

107.84 (2016 est.)

107.84 (2015 est.)

89.85 (2013 est.)

90.56 (2012 est.)

ENERGY :: NEW CALEDONIA

ELECTRICITY ACCESS:
electrification - total population: 100% (2016)

ELECTRICITY - PRODUCTION:
2.945 billion kWh (2016 est.)

country comparison to the world: 133

ELECTRICITY - CONSUMPTION:
2.739 billion kWh (2016 est.)

country comparison to the world: 139

ELECTRICITY - EXPORTS:
0 kWh (2016 est.)

country comparison to the world: 175

ELECTRICITY - IMPORTS:
0 kWh (2016 est.)

country comparison to the world: 178

ELECTRICITY - INSTALLED GENERATING CAPACITY:
996,200 kW (2016 est.)

country comparison to the world: 128

ELECTRICITY - FROM FOSSIL FUELS:
87% of total installed capacity (2016 est.)

country comparison to the world: 64

ELECTRICITY - FROM NUCLEAR FUELS:
0% of total installed capacity (2017 est.)

country comparison to the world: 153

ELECTRICITY - FROM HYDROELECTRIC PLANTS:
8% of total installed capacity (2017 est.)

country comparison to the world: 123

ELECTRICITY - FROM OTHER RENEWABLE SOURCES:
6% of total installed capacity (2017 est.)

country comparison to the world: 101

CRUDE OIL - PRODUCTION:
0 bbl/day (2018 est.)

country comparison to the world: 182

CRUDE OIL - EXPORTS:
0 bbl/day (2015 est.)

country comparison to the world: 174

CRUDE OIL - IMPORTS:
0 bbl/day (2015 est.)

country comparison to the world: 175

CRUDE OIL - PROVED RESERVES:
0 bbl (1 January 2018 est.)

country comparison to the world: 177

REFINED PETROLEUM PRODUCTS - PRODUCTION:
0 bbl/day (2015 est.)

country comparison to the world: 186

REFINED PETROLEUM PRODUCTS - CONSUMPTION:
20,000 bbl/day (2016 est.)

country comparison to the world: 142

REFINED PETROLEUM PRODUCTS - EXPORTS:
0 bbl/day (2015 est.)

country comparison to the world: 188

REFINED PETROLEUM PRODUCTS - IMPORTS:
19,100 bbl/day (2015 est.)

country comparison to the world: 124

NATURAL GAS - PRODUCTION:
0 cu m (2017 est.)

country comparison to the world: 178

NATURAL GAS - CONSUMPTION:
0 cu m (2017 est.)

country comparison to the world: 182

NATURAL GAS - EXPORTS:
0 cu m (2017 est.)

country comparison to the world: 160

NATURAL GAS - IMPORTS:
0 cu m (2017 est.)

country comparison to the world: 165

NATURAL GAS - PROVED RESERVES:
0 cu m (1 January 2014 est.)

country comparison to the world: 176

CARBON DIOXIDE EMISSIONS FROM CONSUMPTION OF ENERGY:
6.165 million Mt (2017 est.)

country comparison to the world: 128

COMMUNICATIONS :: NEW CALEDONIA

TELEPHONES - FIXED LINES:
total subscriptions: 92,000

subscriptions per 100 inhabitants: 34 (July 2016 est.)

country comparison to the world: 142

TELEPHONES - MOBILE CELLULAR:
total subscriptions: 246,000

subscriptions per 100 inhabitants: 91 (July 2016 est.)

country comparison to the world: 179

TELEPHONE SYSTEM:
general assessment: well advanced telecoms sector; 4G network services (2018)

domestic: fixed-line 34 per 100 and mobile-cellular telephone subscribership 91 per 100 persons (2018)

international: country code - 687; landing points for the Gondwana-1 and Picot-1 providing connectivity via submarine cables around New Caledonia and to Australia; satellite earth station - 1 Intelsat (Pacific Ocean) (2019)

BROADCAST MEDIA:
the publicly owned French Overseas Network (RFO), which operates in France's overseas departments and territories, broadcasts over the RFO Nouvelle-Calédonie TV and radio

stations; a small number of privately owned radio stations also broadcast

INTERNET COUNTRY CODE:

.nc

INTERNET USERS:

total: 201,000

percent of population: 74% (July 2016 est.)

country comparison to the world: 169

MILITARY AND SECURITY :: NEW CALEDONIA

MILITARY AND SECURITY FORCES:

no regular military forces; France bases land, air, and naval forces on New Caledonia (Forces Armées de la Nouvelle-Calédonie, FANC) (2019)

MILITARY - NOTE:

defense is the responsibility of France

TRANSPORTATION :: NEW CALEDONIA

NATIONAL AIR TRANSPORT SYSTEM:

number of registered air carriers: 2 (registered in France) (2015)

inventory of registered aircraft operated by air carriers: 10 (registered in France) (2015)

AIRPORTS:

25 (2013)

country comparison to the world: 129

AIRPORTS - WITH PAVED RUNWAYS:

total: 12 (2017)

over 3,047 m: 1 (2017)

914 to 1,523 m: 10 (2017)

under 914 m: 1 (2017)

AIRPORTS - WITH UNPAVED RUNWAYS:

total: 13 (2013)

914 to 1,523 m: 5 (2013)

under 914 m: 8 (2013)

HELIPORTS:

8 (2013)

ROADWAYS:

total: 5,622 km (2006)

country comparison to the world: 142

MERCHANT MARINE:

total: 10

by type: general cargo 2, other 8 (2018)

country comparison to the world: 151

PORTS AND TERMINALS:

major seaport(s): Noumea

TRANSNATIONAL ISSUES :: NEW CALEDONIA

DISPUTES - INTERNATIONAL:

Matthew and Hunter Islands east of New Caledonia claimed by France and Vanuatu

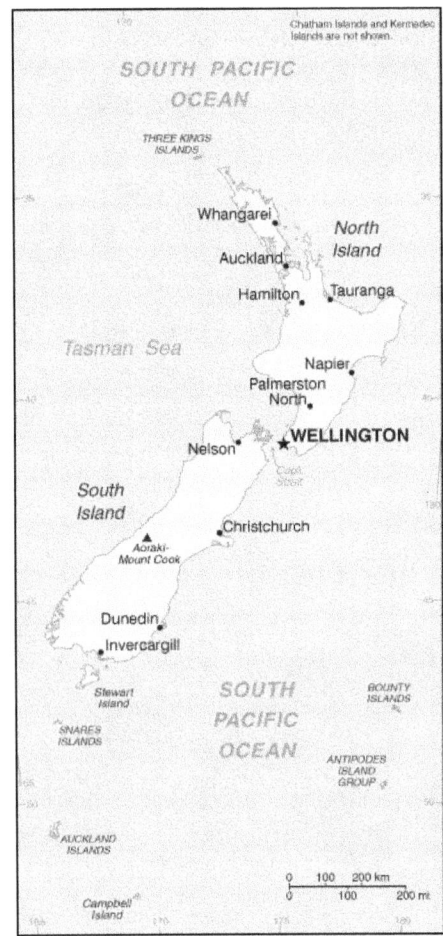

AUSTRALIA - OCEANIA :: NEW ZEALAND

INTRODUCTION :: NEW ZEALAND

BACKGROUND:

The Polynesian Maori reached New Zealand sometime between A.D. 1250 and 1300. In 1840, their chieftains entered into a compact with Great Britain, the Treaty of Waitangi, in which they ceded sovereignty to Queen Victoria while retaining territorial rights. That same year, the British began the first organized colonial settlement. A series of land wars between 1843 and 1872 ended with the defeat of the native peoples. The British colony of New Zealand became an independent dominion in 1907 and supported the UK militarily in both world wars. New Zealand's full participation in a number of defense alliances lapsed by the 1980s. In recent years, the government has sought to address longstanding Maori grievances.

GEOGRAPHY :: NEW ZEALAND

LOCATION:
Oceania, islands in the South Pacific Ocean, southeast of Australia

GEOGRAPHIC COORDINATES:
41 00 S, 174 00 E

MAP REFERENCES:
Oceania

AREA:
total: 268,838 sq km

land: 264,537 sq km

water: 4,301 sq km

note: includes Antipodes Islands, Auckland Islands, Bounty Islands, Campbell Island, Chatham Islands, and Kermadec Islands

country comparison to the world: 77

AREA - COMPARATIVE:
almost twice the size of North Carolina; about the size of Colorado

LAND BOUNDARIES:
0 km

COASTLINE:
15,134 km

MARITIME CLAIMS:
territorial sea: 12 nm

exclusive economic zone: 200 nm

contiguous zone: 24 nm

continental shelf: 200 nm or to the edge of the continental margin

CLIMATE:
temperate with sharp regional contrasts

TERRAIN:
predominately mountainous with large coastal plains

ELEVATION:
mean elevation: 388 m

lowest point: Pacific Ocean 0 m

highest point: Aoraki/Mount Cook 3,724 m; note - the mountain's height was 3,764 m until 14 December 1991 when it lost about 10 m in an avalanche of rock and ice; erosion of the ice cap since then has brought the height down another 30 m

NATURAL RESOURCES:
natural gas, iron ore, sand, coal, timber, hydropower, gold, limestone

LAND USE:
agricultural land: 43.2% (2011 est.)

arable land: 1.8% (2011 est.) / permanent crops: 0.3% (2011 est.) / permanent pasture: 41.1% (2011 est.)

forest: 31.4% (2011 est.)

other: 25.4% (2011 est.)

IRRIGATED LAND:
7,210 sq km (2012)

POPULATION DISTRIBUTION:
over three-quarters of New Zealanders, including the indigenous Maori, live on the North Island, primarily in urban areas

NATURAL HAZARDS:
earthquakes are common, though usually not severe; volcanic activity

volcanism: significant volcanism on North Island; Ruapehu (2,797 m), which last erupted in 2007, has a history of large eruptions in the past century; Taranaki has the potential to produce dangerous avalanches and lahars; other historically active volcanoes include Okataina, Raoul Island, Tongariro, and White Island; see note 2 under "Geography - note"

ENVIRONMENT - CURRENT ISSUES:

water quality and availability; rapid urbanisation; deforestation; soil erosion and degradation; native flora and fauna hard-hit by invasive species; negative effects of climate change

ENVIRONMENT - INTERNATIONAL AGREEMENTS:

party to: Antarctic-Environmental Protocol, Antarctic-Marine Living Resources, Antarctic Treaty, Biodiversity, Climate Change, Climate Change-Kyoto Protocol, Desertification, Endangered Species, Environmental Modification, Hazardous Wastes, Law of the Sea, Marine Dumping, Ozone Layer Protection, Ship Pollution, Tropical Timber 83, Tropical Timber 94, Wetlands, Whaling

signed, but not ratified: Antarctic Seals, Marine Life Conservation

GEOGRAPHY - NOTE:

note 1: consists of two main islands and a number of smaller islands; South Island, the larger main island, is the 12th largest island in the world and is divided along its length by the Southern Alps; North Island is the 14th largest island in the world and is not as mountainous, but it is marked by volcanism

note 2: New Zealand lies along the Ring of Fire, a belt of active volcanoes and earthquake epicenters bordering the Pacific Ocean; up to 90% of the world's earthquakes and some 75% of the world's volcanoes occur within the Ring of Fire

note 3: almost 90% of the population lives in cities and over three-quarters on North Island; Wellington is the southernmost national capital in the world

PEOPLE AND SOCIETY :: NEW ZEALAND

POPULATION:

4,545,627 (July 2018 est.)

country comparison to the world: 126

NATIONALITY:

noun: New Zealander(s)

adjective: New Zealand

ETHNIC GROUPS:

European 64.1%, Maori 16.5%, Chinese 4.9%, Indian 4.7%, Samoan 3.9%, Tongan 1.8%, Cook Islands Maori 1.7%, English 1.5%, Filipino 1.5%, New Zealander 1%, other 13.7% (2018 est.)

note: based on the 2018 census of the usually resident population; percentages add up to more than 100% because respondents were able to identify more than one ethnic group

LANGUAGES:

English (de facto official) 95.4%, Maori (de jure official) 4%, Samoan 2.2%, Northern Chinese 2%, Hindi 1.5%, French 1.2%, Yue 1.1%, New Zealand Sign Language (de jure official) .5%, other or not stated 17.2% (2018 est.)

note: shares sum to 124.1% due to multiple responses on the 2018 census

RELIGIONS:

Christian 37.3% (Catholic 10.1%, Anglican 6.8%, Presbyterian and Congregational 5.2%, Pentecostal 1.8%, Methodist 1.6%, Mormon 1.2%, other 10.7%), Hindu 2.7%, Maori 1.3%, Muslim, 1.3%, Buddhist 1.1%, other religion 1.6% (includes Judaism, Spiritualism and New Age religions, Baha'i, Asian religions other than Buddhism), no religion 48.6%, objected to answering 6.7% (2018 est.)

note: based on the 2018 census of the usually resident population; percentages add up to more than 100% because respondents were able to identify more than one religion

AGE STRUCTURE:

0-14 years: 19.62% (male 457,071 /female 434,789)

15-24 years: 13.16% (male 307,574 /female 290,771)

25-54 years: 39.58% (male 902,909 /female 896,398)

55-64 years: 12.06% (male 266,855 /female 281,507)

65 years and over: 15.57% (male 327,052 /female 380,701) (2018 est.)

DEPENDENCY RATIOS:

total dependency ratio: 52.9 (2015 est.)

youth dependency ratio: 30.5 (2015 est.)

elderly dependency ratio: 22.4 (2015 est.)

potential support ratio: 4.5 (2015 est.)

MEDIAN AGE:

total: 38.1 years (2018 est.)

male: 37.2 years

female: 39 years

country comparison to the world: 62

POPULATION GROWTH RATE:

0.77% (2018 est.)

country comparison to the world: 133

BIRTH RATE:

13.1 births/1,000 population (2018 est.)

country comparison to the world: 145

DEATH RATE:

7.6 deaths/1,000 population (2018 est.)

country comparison to the world: 106

NET MIGRATION RATE:

2.2 migrant(s)/1,000 population (2018 est.)

country comparison to the world: 47

POPULATION DISTRIBUTION:

over three-quarters of New Zealanders, including the indigenous Maori, live on the North Island, primarily in urban areas

URBANIZATION:

urban population: 86.6% of total population (2019)

rate of urbanization: 1.01% annual rate of change (2015-20 est.)

MAJOR URBAN AREAS - POPULATION:

1.582 million Auckland, 413,000 WELLINGTON (capital) (2019)

SEX RATIO:

at birth: 1.05 male(s)/female

0-14 years: 1.05 male(s)/female

15-24 years: 1.06 male(s)/female

25-54 years: 1.01 male(s)/female

55-64 years: 0.95 male(s)/female

65 years and over: 0.86 male(s)/female

total population: 0.99 male(s)/female (2018 est.)

MOTHER'S MEAN AGE AT FIRST BIRTH:

27.8 years (2009 est.)

note: median age at first birth

MATERNAL MORTALITY RATE:

9 deaths/100,000 live births (2017 est.)

country comparison to the world: 148

INFANT MORTALITY RATE:

total: 4.4 deaths/1,000 live births (2018 est.)

male: 4.9 deaths/1,000 live births

female: 3.8 deaths/1,000 live births

country comparison to the world: 183

LIFE EXPECTANCY AT BIRTH:

total population: 81.4 years (2018 est.)

male: 79.2 years

female: 83.6 years

country comparison to the world: 30

TOTAL FERTILITY RATE:

2.01 children born/woman (2018 est.)

country comparison to the world: 116

DRINKING WATER SOURCE:

improved:

urban: 100% of population

rural: 100% of population

total: 100% of population

unimproved:

urban: 0% of population

rural: 0% of population

total: 0% of population (2015 est.)

CURRENT HEALTH EXPENDITURE:

9.2% (2016)

PHYSICIANS DENSITY:

3.03 physicians/1,000 population (2016)

HOSPITAL BED DENSITY:

2.8 beds/1,000 population (2013)

HIV/AIDS - ADULT PREVALENCE RATE:

0.1% (2018 est.)

country comparison to the world: 129

HIV/AIDS - PEOPLE LIVING WITH HIV/AIDS:

3,600 (2018 est.)

country comparison to the world: 125

HIV/AIDS - DEATHS:

<100 (2018 est.)

OBESITY - ADULT PREVALENCE RATE:

30.8% (2016)

country comparison to the world: 22

EDUCATION EXPENDITURES:

6.3% of GDP (2016)

country comparison to the world: 29

SCHOOL LIFE EXPECTANCY (PRIMARY TO TERTIARY EDUCATION):

total: 19 years

male: 18 years

female: 20 years (2016)

UNEMPLOYMENT, YOUTH AGES 15-24:

total: 12.7%

male: 12.4%

female: 13% (2017 est.)

country comparison to the world: 110

GOVERNMENT :: NEW ZEALAND

COUNTRY NAME:

conventional long form: none

conventional short form: New Zealand

abbreviation: NZ

etymology: Dutch explorer Abel TASMAN was the first European to reach New Zealand in 1642; he named it Staten Landt, but Dutch cartographers renamed it Nova Zeelandia in 1645 after the Dutch province of Zeeland; British explorer Captain James COOK subsequently anglicized the name to New Zealand when he mapped the islands in 1769

GOVERNMENT TYPE:

parliamentary democracy under a constitutional monarchy; a Commonwealth realm

CAPITAL:

name: Wellington

geographic coordinates: 41 18 S, 174 47 E

time difference: UTC+12 (17 hours ahead of Washington, DC, during Standard Time)

daylight saving time: +1hr, begins last Sunday in September; ends first Sunday in April

note: New Zealand has two time zones: New Zealand standard time (UTC+12) and Chatham Islands time (45 minutes in advance of New Zealand standard time; UTC+12:45)

etymology: named in 1840 after Arthur Wellesley, the first Duke of Wellington and victorious general at the Battle of Waterloo

ADMINISTRATIVE DIVISIONS:

16 regions and 1 territory*; Auckland, Bay of Plenty, Canterbury, Chatham Islands*, Gisborne, Hawke's Bay, Manawatu-Wanganui, Marlborough, Nelson, Northland, Otago, Southland, Taranaki, Tasman, Waikato, Wellington, West Coast

DEPENDENT AREAS:

Cook Islands, Niue, Tokelau

INDEPENDENCE:

26 September 1907 (from the UK)

NATIONAL HOLIDAY:

Waitangi Day (Treaty of Waitangi established British sovereignty over New Zealand), 6 February (1840); Anzac Day (commemorated as the anniversary of the landing of troops of the Australian and New Zealand Army Corps during World War I at Gallipoli, Turkey), 25 April (1915)

CONSTITUTION:

history: New Zealand has no single constitution document; the Constitution Act 1986, effective 1 January 1987, includes only part of the uncodified constitution; others include a collection of statutes or "acts of Parliament," the Treaty of Waitangi, Orders in Council, letters patent, court decisions, and unwritten conventions

amendments: proposed as bill by Parliament or by referendum called either by the government or by citizens; passage of a bill as an act normally requires two separate readings with committee reviews in between to make changes and corrections, a third reading approved by the House of Representatives membership or by the majority of votes in a referendum, and assent of the governor-general; passage of amendments to reserved constitutional provisions affecting the term of Parliament, electoral districts, and voting restrictions requires approval by 75% of the House membership or the majority of votes in a referendum; amended many times, last in 2014 (2018)

LEGAL SYSTEM:

common law system, based on English model, with special legislation and land courts for the Maori

INTERNATIONAL LAW ORGANIZATION PARTICIPATION:

accepts compulsory ICJ jurisdiction with reservations; accepts ICCt jurisdiction

CITIZENSHIP:

citizenship by birth: no

citizenship by descent only: at least one parent must be a citizen of New Zealand

dual citizenship recognized: yes

residency requirement for naturalization: 3 years

SUFFRAGE:

18 years of age; universal

EXECUTIVE BRANCH:

chief of state: Queen ELIZABETH II (since 6 February 1952); represented by Governor-General Dame Patricia Lee REDDY (since 28 September 2016)

head of government: Prime Minister Jacinda ARDERN (since 26 October 2017); Deputy Prime Minister Winston PETERS (since 26 October 2017)

cabinet: Executive Council appointed by the governor-general on the recommendation of the prime minister

elections/appointments: the monarchy is hereditary; governor-general appointed by the monarch on the advice of the prime minister; following legislative elections, the leader of the majority party or majority coalition usually appointed prime minister by the governor-general; deputy prime minister appointed by the governor-general; note - Prime Minister ARDERN heads up a minority coalition government consisting of the Labor and New Zealand First parties with confidence and supply support from the Green Party

LEGISLATIVE BRANCH:

description: unicameral House of Representatives - commonly called Parliament (usually 120 seats; 71 members directly elected in single-seat constituencies, including 7 Maori constituencies, by simple majority vote and 49 directly elected by proportional representation vote; members serve 3-year terms)

elections: last held on 23 September 2017 (next to be held by November 2020)

election results: percent of vote by party - National Party 44.5%, Labor Party 36.9%, NZ First 7.2%, Green Party 6.3%, ACT Party 0.5%; seats by party - National Party 56, Labor Party 46, NZ First 9, Green Party 8, ACT Party 1; composition - men 74, women 46, percent of women 38.3%

JUDICIAL BRANCH:

highest courts: Supreme Court (consists of 5 justices, including the chief justice); note - the Supreme Court in 2004 replaced the Judicial Committee of the Privy Council (in London) as the final appeals court

judge selection and term of office: justices appointed by the governor-general upon the recommendation of the attorney- general; justices appointed until compulsory retirement at age 70

subordinate courts: Court of Appeal; High Court; tribunals and authorities; district courts; specialized courts for issues related to employment, environment, family, Maori lands, youth, military; tribunals

POLITICAL PARTIES AND LEADERS:

ACT New Zealand [David SEYMOUR]
Green Party [James SHAW]
Mana Movement [Hone HARAWIRA] (formerly Mana Party)
Maori Party [Che WILSON and Kaapua SMITH]
New Zealand First Party or NZ First [Winston PETERS]
New Zealand Labor Party [Jacinda ARDERN]
New Zealand National Party [Simon BRIDGES]
United Future New Zealand [Damian LIGHT]

INTERNATIONAL ORGANIZATION PARTICIPATION:

ADB, ANZUS, APEC, ARF, ASEAN (dialogue partner), Australia Group, BIS, C, CD, CP, EAS, EBRD, FAO, FATF, IAEA, IBRD, ICAO, ICC (national committees), ICCt, ICRM, IDA, IEA, IFAD, IFC, IFRCS, IHO, ILO, IMF, IMO, IMSO, Interpol, IOC, IOM, IPU, ISO, ITSO, ITU, ITUC (NGOs), MIGA, NSG, OECD, OPCW, Pacific Alliance (observer), Paris Club (associate), PCA, PIF, SICA (observer), Sparteca, SPC, UN, UNCTAD, UNESCO, UNHCR, UNIDO, UNMISS, UNTSO, UPU, WCO, WFTU (NGOs), WHO, WIPO, WMO, WTO

DIPLOMATIC REPRESENTATION IN THE US:

Ambassador Timothy John GROSER (since 28 January 2016)

chancery: 37 Observatory Circle NW, Washington, DC 20008

telephone: [1] (202) 328-4800

FAX: [1] (202) 667-5227

consulate(s) general: Honolulu (HI), Los Angeles, New York

DIPLOMATIC REPRESENTATION FROM THE US:

chief of mission: Ambassador Scott P. BROWN (since 27 June 2017) note - also accredited to Samoa

telephone: [64] (4) 462-6000

embassy: 29 Fitzherbert Terrace, Thorndon, Wellington

mailing address: P. O. Box 1190, Wellington; PSC 467, Box 1, APO AP 96531-1034

FAX: [64] (4) 499-0490

consulate(s) general: Auckland

FLAG DESCRIPTION:

blue with the flag of the UK in the upper hoist-side quadrant with four red five-pointed stars edged in white centered in the outer half of the flag; the stars represent the Southern Cross constellation

NATIONAL SYMBOL(S):

Southern Cross constellation (four, five-pointed stars), kiwi (bird), silver fern; national colors: black, white, red (ochre)

NATIONAL ANTHEM:

name: God Defend New Zealand

lyrics/music: Thomas BRACKEN [English], Thomas Henry SMITH [Maori]/John Joseph WOODS

note: adopted 1940 as national song, adopted 1977 as co-national anthem; New Zealand has two national anthems with equal status; as a commonwealth realm, in addition to "God Defend New Zealand," "God Save the Queen" serves as a national anthem (see United Kingdom); "God Save the Queen" normally played only when a member of the royal family or the governor-general is present; in all other cases, "God Defend New Zealand" is played

ECONOMY :: NEW ZEALAND

ECONOMY - OVERVIEW:

Over the past 40 years, the government has transformed New Zealand from an agrarian economy, dependent on concessionary British market access, to a more industrialized, free market economy that can compete globally. This dynamic growth has boosted real incomes, but left behind some at the bottom of the ladder and broadened and deepened the technological capabilities of the industrial sector.

Per capita income rose for 10 consecutive years until 2007 in purchasing power parity terms, but fell in 2008-09. Debt-driven consumer spending drove robust growth in the first half of the decade, fueling a large balance of payments deficit that posed a challenge for policymakers. Inflationary pressures caused the central bank to raise its key rate steadily from January 2004 until it was among the highest in the OECD in 2007 and 2008. The higher rate attracted international capital inflows, which strengthened the currency and housing market while aggravating the current account deficit. Rising house prices, especially in Auckland, have become a political issue in recent years, as well as a policy challenge in 2016 and 2017, as the ability to afford housing has declined for many.

Expanding New Zealand's network of free trade agreements remains a top foreign policy priority. New Zealand was an early promoter of the Trans-Pacific Partnership (TPP) and was the second country to ratify the agreement in May 2017. Following the United States' withdrawal from the TPP in January 2017, on 10 November 2017 the remaining 11 countries agreed on the core elements of a modified agreement, which they renamed the Comprehensive and Progressive Agreement for Trans-Pacific Partnership (CPTPP). In November 2016, New Zealand opened negotiations to upgrade its FTA with China; China is one of New Zealand's most important trading partners.

GDP (PURCHASING POWER PARITY):

$189 billion (2017 est.)

$183.4 billion (2016 est.)

$176.1 billion (2015 est.)

note: data are in 2017 dollars

country comparison to the world: 68

GDP (OFFICIAL EXCHANGE RATE):

$201.4 billion (2017 est.)

GDP - REAL GROWTH RATE:

3% (2017 est.)

4.1% (2016 est.)

4.2% (2015 est.)

country comparison to the world: 114

GDP - PER CAPITA (PPP):

$39,000 (2017 est.)

$38,600 (2016 est.)

$37,900 (2015 est.)

note: data are in 2017 dollars

country comparison to the world: 48

GROSS NATIONAL SAVING:

21% of GDP (2017 est.)

21.5% of GDP (2016 est.)

20.2% of GDP (2015 est.)

country comparison to the world: 89

GDP - COMPOSITION, BY END USE:

household consumption: 57.2% (2017 est.)

government consumption: 18.2% (2017 est.)

investment in fixed capital: 23.4% (2017 est.)

investment in inventories: 0.3% (2017 est.)

exports of goods and services: 27% (2017 est.)

imports of goods and services: -26.1% (2017 est.)

GDP - COMPOSITION, BY SECTOR OF ORIGIN:

agriculture: 5.7% (2017 est.)

industry: 21.5% (2017 est.)

services: 72.8% (2017 est.)

AGRICULTURE - PRODUCTS:

dairy products, sheep, beef, poultry, fruit, vegetables, wine, seafood, wheat and barley

INDUSTRIES:

agriculture, forestry, fishing, logs and wood articles, manufacturing, mining, construction, financial services, real estate services, tourism

INDUSTRIAL PRODUCTION GROWTH RATE:

1.8% (2017 est.)

country comparison to the world: 137

LABOR FORCE:

2.655 million (2017 est.)

country comparison to the world: 113

LABOR FORCE - BY OCCUPATION:

agriculture: 6.6%

industry: 20.7%

services: 72.7% (2017 est.)

UNEMPLOYMENT RATE:

4.7% (2017 est.)

5.1% (2016 est.)

country comparison to the world: 68

POPULATION BELOW POVERTY LINE:

NA

HOUSEHOLD INCOME OR CONSUMPTION BY PERCENTAGE SHARE:

lowest 10%: NA

highest 10%: NA

DISTRIBUTION OF FAMILY INCOME - GINI INDEX:

36.2 (1997)

country comparison to the world: 89

BUDGET:

revenues: 74.11 billion (2017 est.)

expenditures: 70.97 billion (2017 est.)

TAXES AND OTHER REVENUES:

36.8% (of GDP) (2017 est.)

country comparison to the world: 56

BUDGET SURPLUS (+) OR DEFICIT (-):

1.6% (of GDP) (2017 est.)

country comparison to the world: 21

PUBLIC DEBT:

31.7% of GDP (2017 est.)

33.5% of GDP (2016 est.)

country comparison to the world: 162

FISCAL YEAR:

1 April - 31 March

note: this is the fiscal year for tax purposes

INFLATION RATE (CONSUMER PRICES):

1.9% (2017 est.)

0.6% (2016 est.)

country comparison to the world: 98

CENTRAL BANK DISCOUNT RATE:

1.75% (31 December 2017)

1.75% (31 December 2016)

country comparison to the world: 124

COMMERCIAL BANK PRIME LENDING RATE:

5.1% (31 December 2017 est.)

5.02% (31 December 2016 est.)

country comparison to the world: 149

STOCK OF NARROW MONEY:

$46.52 billion (31 December 2017 est.)

$42.01 billion (31 December 2016 est.)

country comparison to the world: 55

STOCK OF BROAD MONEY:

$46.52 billion (31 December 2017 est.)

$42.01 billion (31 December 2016 est.)

country comparison to the world: 55

STOCK OF DOMESTIC CREDIT:

$304.2 billion (31 December 2017 est.)

$284.7 billion (31 December 2016 est.)

country comparison to the world: 36

MARKET VALUE OF PUBLICLY TRADED SHARES:

$80.05 billion (31 December 2015 est.)

$74.35 billion (31 December 2015 est.)

$74.42 billion (31 December 2014 est.)

country comparison to the world: 46

CURRENT ACCOUNT BALANCE:

-$5.471 billion (2017 est.)

-$4.171 billion (2016 est.)

country comparison to the world: 186

EXPORTS:

$37.35 billion (2017 est.)

$33.61 billion (2016 est.)

country comparison to the world: 57

EXPORTS - PARTNERS:

China 22.4%, Australia 16.4%, US 9.9%, Japan 6.1% (2017)

EXPORTS - COMMODITIES:

dairy products, meat and edible offal, logs and wood articles, fruit, crude oil, wine

IMPORTS:

$39.74 billion (2017 est.)

$35.53 billion (2016 est.)

country comparison to the world: 59

IMPORTS - COMMODITIES:

petroleum and products, mechanical machinery, vehicles and parts, electrical machinery, textiles

IMPORTS - PARTNERS:

China 19%, Australia 12.1%, US 10.5%, Japan 7.3%, Germany 5.3%, Thailand 4.6% (2017)

RESERVES OF FOREIGN EXCHANGE AND GOLD:

$20.68 billion (31 December 2017 est.)

$17.81 billion (31 December 2016 est.)

country comparison to the world: 58

DEBT - EXTERNAL:

$91.62 billion (31 December 2017 est.)

$84.03 billion (31 December 2016 est.)

country comparison to the world: 51

STOCK OF DIRECT FOREIGN INVESTMENT - AT HOME:

$84.19 billion (31 December 2017 est.)

$70.4 billion (31 December 2016 est.)

country comparison to the world: 48

STOCK OF DIRECT FOREIGN INVESTMENT - ABROAD:

$16.74 billion (31 December 2016 est.)

$18.03 billion (31 December 2015 est.)

country comparison to the world: 58

EXCHANGE RATES:

New Zealand dollars (NZD) per US dollar -

1.416 (2017 est.)

1.4341 (2016 est.)

1.4341 (2015 est.)

1.4279 (2014 est.)

1.2039 (2013 est.)

ENERGY :: NEW ZEALAND

ELECTRICITY ACCESS:

electrification - total population: 100% (2016)

ELECTRICITY - PRODUCTION:

42.53 billion kWh (2016 est.)

country comparison to the world: 56

ELECTRICITY - CONSUMPTION:

39.5 billion kWh (2016 est.)

country comparison to the world: 55

ELECTRICITY - EXPORTS:

0 kWh (2016 est.)

country comparison to the world: 176

ELECTRICITY - IMPORTS:

0 kWh (2016 est.)

country comparison to the world: 179

ELECTRICITY - INSTALLED GENERATING CAPACITY:

9.301 million kW (2016 est.)

country comparison to the world: 63

ELECTRICITY - FROM FOSSIL FUELS:

23% of total installed capacity (2016 est.)

country comparison to the world: 193

ELECTRICITY - FROM NUCLEAR FUELS:

0% of total installed capacity (2017 est.)

country comparison to the world: 154

ELECTRICITY - FROM HYDROELECTRIC PLANTS:

58% of total installed capacity (2017 est.)

country comparison to the world: 29

ELECTRICITY - FROM OTHER RENEWABLE SOURCES:

20% of total installed capacity (2017 est.)

country comparison to the world: 40

CRUDE OIL - PRODUCTION:

24,000 bbl/day (2018 est.)

country comparison to the world: 64

CRUDE OIL - EXPORTS:

26,440 bbl/day (2017 est.)

country comparison to the world: 48

CRUDE OIL - IMPORTS:

108,900 bbl/day (2017 est.)

country comparison to the world: 43

CRUDE OIL - PROVED RESERVES:

51.8 million bbl (1 January 2018 est.)

country comparison to the world: 76

REFINED PETROLEUM PRODUCTS - PRODUCTION:

115,100 bbl/day (2017 est.)

country comparison to the world: 65

REFINED PETROLEUM PRODUCTS - CONSUMPTION:

169,100 bbl/day (2017 est.)

country comparison to the world: 61

REFINED PETROLEUM PRODUCTS - EXPORTS:

1,782 bbl/day (2017 est.)

country comparison to the world: 106

REFINED PETROLEUM PRODUCTS - IMPORTS:

56,000 bbl/day (2017 est.)

country comparison to the world: 76

NATURAL GAS - PRODUCTION:

5.097 billion cu m (2017 est.)

country comparison to the world: 51

NATURAL GAS - CONSUMPTION:

5.182 billion cu m (2017 est.)

country comparison to the world: 57

NATURAL GAS - EXPORTS:

0 cu m (2017 est.)

country comparison to the world: 161

NATURAL GAS - IMPORTS:

0 cu m (2017 est.)

country comparison to the world: 166

NATURAL GAS - PROVED RESERVES:

33.7 billion cu m (1 January 2018 est.)

country comparison to the world: 67

CARBON DIOXIDE EMISSIONS FROM CONSUMPTION OF ENERGY:

37.75 million Mt (2017 est.)

country comparison to the world: 68

COMMUNICATIONS :: NEW ZEALAND

TELEPHONES - FIXED LINES:

total subscriptions: 1.368 million

subscriptions per 100 inhabitants: 30 (2017 est.)

country comparison to the world: 66

TELEPHONES - MOBILE CELLULAR:

total subscriptions: 6.4 million

subscriptions per 100 inhabitants: 142 (2017 est.)

country comparison to the world: 110

TELEPHONE SYSTEM:

general assessment: excellent domestic and international systems; mobile and P2P services soar; LTE rates some of the fastest in the world; investment and development of infrastructure enable network capabilities to propel the digital economy, digital media sector along with e-government, e-commerce across the country (2018)

domestic: fixed-line 30 per 100 and mobile-cellular telephone subscribership 142 per 100 persons (2018)

international: country code - 64; landing points for the Southern Cross NEXT, Aqualink, Nelson-Levin, SCCN and Hawaiki submarine cable system providing links to Australia, Fiji, American Samoa, Kiribati, Samo, Tokelau, US and around New Zealand; satellite earth stations - 8 (1 Inmarsat - Pacific Ocean, 7 other) (2019)

BROADCAST MEDIA:

state-owned Television New Zealand operates multiple TV networks and state-owned Radio New Zealand operates 3 radio networks and an external shortwave radio service to the South Pacific region; a small number of national commercial TV and radio stations and many regional commercial television and radio stations are available; cable and satellite TV systems are available, as are a range of streaming services (2019)

INTERNET COUNTRY CODE:

.nz

INTERNET USERS:

total: 3,958,642

percent of population: 88.5% (July 2016 est.)

country comparison to the world: 88

BROADBAND - FIXED SUBSCRIPTIONS:

total: 1.582 million

subscriptions per 100 inhabitants: 35 (2017 est.)

country comparison to the world: 59

MILITARY AND SECURITY :: NEW ZEALAND

MILITARY EXPENDITURES:

1.16% of GDP (2018)

1.21% of GDP (2017)

1.18% of GDP (2016)

1.15% of GDP (2015)

1.18% of GDP (2014)

country comparison to the world: 109

MILITARY AND SECURITY FORCES:

New Zealand Defence Force (NZDF): New Zealand Army, Royal New Zealand Navy, Royal New Zealand Air Force (2019)

MILITARY SERVICE AGE AND OBLIGATION:

17 years of age for voluntary military service; soldiers cannot be deployed until the age of 18; no conscription (2019)

TRANSPORTATION :: NEW ZEALAND

NATIONAL AIR TRANSPORT SYSTEM:

number of registered air carriers: 6 (2015)

inventory of registered aircraft operated by air carriers: 123 (2015)

annual passenger traffic on registered air carriers: 15,304,409 (2015)

annual freight traffic on registered air carriers: 999,384,961 mt-km (2015)

CIVIL AIRCRAFT REGISTRATION COUNTRY CODE PREFIX:

ZK (2016)

AIRPORTS:

123 (2013)

country comparison to the world: 48

AIRPORTS - WITH PAVED RUNWAYS:

total: 39 (2017)

over 3,047 m: 2 (2017)

2,438 to 3,047 m: 1 (2017)

1,524 to 2,437 m: 12 (2017)

914 to 1,523 m: 23 (2017)

under 914 m: 1 (2017)

AIRPORTS - WITH UNPAVED RUNWAYS:

total: 84 (2013)

1,524 to 2,437 m: 3 (2013)

914 to 1,523 m: 33 (2013)

under 914 m: 48 (2013)

PIPELINES:

331 km condensate, 2500 km gas, 172 km liquid petroleum gas, 288 km oil, 198 km refined products (2018)

RAILWAYS:

total: 4,128 km (2018)

narrow gauge: 4,128 km 1.067-m gauge (506 km electrified) (2018)

country comparison to the world: 46

ROADWAYS:

total: 94,000 km (2017)

paved: 61,600 km (includes 199 km of expressways) (2017)

unpaved: 32,400 km (2017)

country comparison to the world: 53

MERCHANT MARINE:

total: 111

by type: general cargo 15, oil tanker 6, other 90 (2018)

country comparison to the world: 81

PORTS AND TERMINALS:

major seaport(s): Auckland, Lyttelton, Manukau Harbor, Marsden Point, Tauranga, Wellington

TRANSNATIONAL ISSUES :: NEW ZEALAND

DISPUTES - INTERNATIONAL:

asserts a territorial claim in Antarctica (Ross Dependency)

ILLICIT DRUGS:

significant consumer of amphetamines

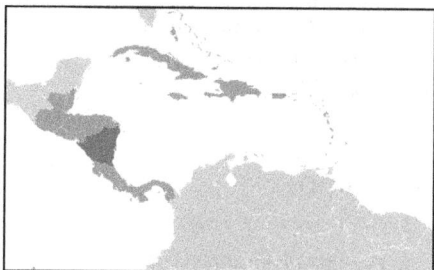

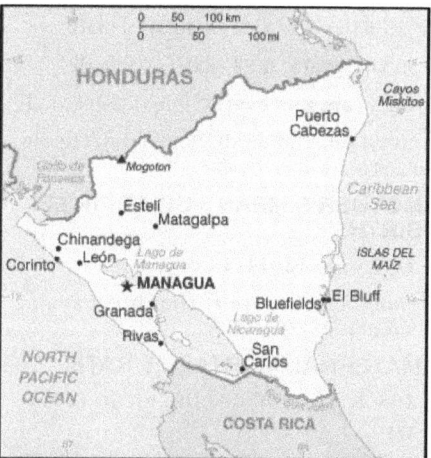

CENTRAL AMERICA :: NICARAGUA

INTRODUCTION :: NICARAGUA

BACKGROUND:

The Pacific coast of Nicaragua was settled as a Spanish colony from Panama in the early 16th century. Independence from Spain was declared in 1821 and the country became an independent republic in 1838. Britain occupied the Caribbean Coast in the first half of the 19th century, but gradually ceded control of the region in subsequent decades. Violent opposition to governmental manipulation and corruption spread to all classes by 1978 and resulted in a short-lived civil war that brought the Marxist Sandinista guerrillas led by Daniel ORTEGA Saavedra to power in 1979. Nicaraguan aid to leftist rebels in El Salvador prompted the US to sponsor anti-Sandinista contra guerrillas through much of the 1980s. After losing free and fair elections in 1990, 1996, and 2001, former Sandinista President Daniel ORTEGA was elected president in 2006, 2011, and most recently in 2016. Municipal, regional, and national-level elections since 2008 have been marred by widespread irregularities. Democratic institutions have weakened under the ORTEGA administration as the president has garnered full control over all branches of government, especially after cracking down on a nationwide antigovernment protest movement in 2018.

GEOGRAPHY :: NICARAGUA

LOCATION:
Central America, bordering both the Caribbean Sea and the North Pacific Ocean, between Costa Rica and Honduras

GEOGRAPHIC COORDINATES:
13 00 N, 85 00 W

MAP REFERENCES:
Central America and the Caribbean

AREA:
total: 130,370 sq km

land: 119,990 sq km

water: 10,380 sq km

country comparison to the world: 99

AREA - COMPARATIVE:
slightly larger than Pennsylvania; slightly smaller than New York state

LAND BOUNDARIES:
total: 1,253 km

border countries (2): Costa Rica 313 km, Honduras 940 km

COASTLINE:
910 km

MARITIME CLAIMS:
territorial sea: 12 nm

contiguous zone: 24 nm

continental shelf: natural prolongation

CLIMATE:
tropical in lowlands, cooler in highlands

TERRAIN:
extensive Atlantic coastal plains rising to central interior mountains; narrow Pacific coastal plain interrupted by volcanoes

ELEVATION:
mean elevation: 298 m

lowest point: Pacific Ocean 0 m

highest point: Mogoton 2,085 m

NATURAL RESOURCES:
gold, silver, copper, tungsten, lead, zinc, timber, fish

LAND USE:
agricultural land: 42.2% (2011 est.)

arable land: 12.5% (2011 est.) / permanent crops: 2.5% (2011 est.) / permanent pasture: 27.2% (2011 est.)

forest: 25.3% (2011 est.)

other: 32.5% (2011 est.)

IRRIGATED LAND:
1,990 sq km (2012)

POPULATION DISTRIBUTION:
the overwhelming majority of the population resides in the western half of the country, with much of the urban growth centered in the capital city of Managua; coastal areas also show large population clusters

NATURAL HAZARDS:
destructive earthquakes; volcanoes; landslides; extremely susceptible to hurricanes

volcanism: significant volcanic activity; Cerro Negro (728 m), which last erupted in 1999, is one of Nicaragua's most active volcanoes; its lava flows and ash have been known to cause significant damage to farmland and buildings; other historically active volcanoes include Concepcion, Cosiguina, Las Pilas, Masaya, Momotombo, San Cristobal, and Telica

ENVIRONMENT - CURRENT ISSUES:
deforestation; soil erosion; water pollution; drought

ENVIRONMENT - INTERNATIONAL AGREEMENTS:
party to: Biodiversity, Climate Change, Climate Change-Kyoto

Protocol, Desertification, Endangered Species, Environmental Modification, Hazardous Wastes, Law of the Sea, Ozone Layer Protection, Ship Pollution, Wetlands, Whaling

signed, but not ratified: none of the selected agreements

GEOGRAPHY - NOTE:

largest country in Central America; contains the largest freshwater body in Central America, Lago de Nicaragua

PEOPLE AND SOCIETY :: NICARAGUA

POPULATION:

6,085,213 (July 2018 est.)

country comparison to the world: 111

NATIONALITY:

noun: Nicaraguan(s)

adjective: Nicaraguan

ETHNIC GROUPS:

mestizo (mixed Amerindian and white) 69%, white 17%, black 9%, Amerindian 5%

LANGUAGES:

Spanish (official) 95.3%, Miskito 2.2%, Mestizo of the Caribbean coast 2%, other 0.5% (2005 est.)

note: English and indigenous languages found on the Caribbean coast

RELIGIONS:

Roman Catholic 50%, Evangelical 33.2%, other 2.9%, unspecified 13.2%, none 0.7% (2017 est.)

DEMOGRAPHIC PROFILE:

Despite being one of the poorest countries in Latin America, Nicaragua has improved its access to potable water and sanitation and has ameliorated its life expectancy, infant and child mortality, and immunization rates. However, income distribution is very uneven, and the poor, agriculturalists, and indigenous people continue to have less access to healthcare services. Nicaragua's total fertility rate has fallen from around 6 children per woman in 1980 to below replacement level today, but the high birth rate among adolescents perpetuates a cycle of poverty and low educational attainment.

Nicaraguans emigrate primarily to Costa Rica and to a lesser extent the United States. Nicaraguan men have been migrating seasonally to Costa Rica to harvest bananas and coffee since the early 20th century. Political turmoil, civil war, and natural disasters from the 1970s through the 1990s dramatically increased the flow of refugees and permanent migrants seeking jobs, higher wages, and better social and healthcare benefits. Since 2000, Nicaraguan emigration to Costa Rica has slowed and stabilized. Today roughly 300,000 Nicaraguans are permanent residents of Costa Rica - about 75% of the foreign population - and thousands more migrate seasonally for work, many illegally.

AGE STRUCTURE:

0-14 years: 26.65% (male 827,585 /female 794,086)

15-24 years: 20.67% (male 632,847 /female 624,811)

25-54 years: 41.04% (male 1,186,467 /female 1,310,957)

55-64 years: 6.19% (male 173,674 /female 202,765)

65 years and over: 5.46% (male 147,324 /female 184,697) (2018 est.)

DEPENDENCY RATIOS:

total dependency ratio: 54.1 (2015 est.)

youth dependency ratio: 46.3 (2015 est.)

elderly dependency ratio: 7.8 (2015 est.)

potential support ratio: 12.8 (2015 est.)

MEDIAN AGE:

total: 26.2 years (2018 est.)

male: 25.3 years

female: 27.1 years

country comparison to the world: 150

POPULATION GROWTH RATE:

0.97% (2018 est.)

country comparison to the world: 113

BIRTH RATE:

17.5 births/1,000 population (2018 est.)

country comparison to the world: 101

DEATH RATE:

5.2 deaths/1,000 population (2018 est.)

country comparison to the world: 191

NET MIGRATION RATE:

-2.6 migrant(s)/1,000 population (2018 est.)

country comparison to the world: 172

POPULATION DISTRIBUTION:

the overwhelming majority of the population resides in the western half of the country, with much of the urban growth centered in the capital city of Managua; coastal areas also show large population clusters

URBANIZATION:

urban population: 58.8% of total population (2019)

rate of urbanization: 1.45% annual rate of change (2015-20 est.)

MAJOR URBAN AREAS - POPULATION:

1.055 million MANAGUA (capital) (2019)

SEX RATIO:

at birth: 1.05 male(s)/female

0-14 years: 1.04 male(s)/female

15-24 years: 1.01 male(s)/female

25-54 years: 0.91 male(s)/female

55-64 years: 0.86 male(s)/female

65 years and over: 0.8 male(s)/female

total population: 0.95 male(s)/female (2018 est.)

MOTHER'S MEAN AGE AT FIRST BIRTH:

19.2 years (2011/12 est.)

note: median age at first birth among women 25-29

MATERNAL MORTALITY RATE:

198 deaths/100,000 live births (2017 est.)

country comparison to the world: 47

INFANT MORTALITY RATE:

total: 17.7 deaths/1,000 live births (2018 est.)

male: 20.4 deaths/1,000 live births

female: 15 deaths/1,000 live births

country comparison to the world: 89

LIFE EXPECTANCY AT BIRTH:

total population: 73.7 years (2018 est.)

male: 71.5 years

female: 76.1 years

country comparison to the world: 134

TOTAL FERTILITY RATE:

1.87 children born/woman (2018 est.)

country comparison to the world: 140

CONTRACEPTIVE PREVALENCE RATE:

80.4% (2011/12)

DRINKING WATER SOURCE:

improved:

urban: 99.3% of population

rural: 69.4% of population

total: 87% of population

unimproved:

urban: 0.7% of population

rural: 30.6% of population

total: 13% of population (2015 est.)

CURRENT HEALTH EXPENDITURE:

8.7% (2016)

PHYSICIANS DENSITY:

1.01 physicians/1,000 population (2018)

HOSPITAL BED DENSITY:

0.9 beds/1,000 population (2014)

SANITATION FACILITY ACCESS:

improved:

urban: 76.5% of population (2015 est.)

rural: 55.7% of population (2015 est.)

total: 67.9% of population (2015 est.)

unimproved:

urban: 23.5% of population (2015 est.)

rural: 44.3% of population (2015 est.)

total: 32.1% of population (2015 est.)

HIV/AIDS - ADULT PREVALENCE RATE:

0.2% (2018 est.)

country comparison to the world: 109

HIV/AIDS - PEOPLE LIVING WITH HIV/AIDS:

9,400 (2018 est.)

country comparison to the world: 102

HIV/AIDS - DEATHS:

200 (2018 est.)

country comparison to the world: 64

MAJOR INFECTIOUS DISEASES:

degree of risk: high (2016)

food or waterborne diseases: bacterial diarrhea, hepatitis A, and typhoid fever (2016)

vectorborne diseases: dengue fever and malaria (2016)

note: active local transmission of Zika virus by Aedes species mosquitoes has been identified in this country (as of August 2016); it poses an important risk (a large number of cases possible) among US citizens if bitten by an infective mosquito; other less common ways to get Zika are through sex, via blood transfusion, or during pregnancy, in which the pregnant woman passes Zika virus to her fetus

OBESITY - ADULT PREVALENCE RATE:

23.7% (2016)

country comparison to the world: 63

CHILDREN UNDER THE AGE OF 5 YEARS UNDERWEIGHT:

4.6% (2012)

country comparison to the world: 86

EDUCATION EXPENDITURES:

4.3% of GDP (2017)

country comparison to the world: 98

LITERACY:

definition: age 15 and over can read and write

total population: 82.8%

male: 82.4%

female: 83.2% (2015 est.)

UNEMPLOYMENT, YOUTH AGES 15-24:

total: 8.5%

male: 6.4%

female: 12.9% (2014 est.)

country comparison to the world: 141

GOVERNMENT :: NICARAGUA

COUNTRY NAME:

conventional long form: Republic of Nicaragua

conventional short form: Nicaragua

local long form: Republica de Nicaragua

local short form: Nicaragua

etymology: Nicarao was the name of the largest indigenous settlement at the time of Spanish arrival; conquistador Gil GONZALEZ Davila, who explored the area (1622-23), combined the name of the community with the Spanish word "agua" (water), referring to the two large lakes in the west of the country (Lake Managua and Lake Nicaragua)

GOVERNMENT TYPE:

presidential republic

CAPITAL:

name: Managua

geographic coordinates: 12 08 N, 86 15 W

time difference: UTC-6 (1 hour behind Washington, DC, during Standard Time)

etymology: may derive from the indigenous Nahuatl term "mana-ahuac," which translates as "adjacent to the water" or a site "surrounded by water"; the city is situated on the southwestern shore of Lake Managua

ADMINISTRATIVE DIVISIONS:

15 departments (departamentos, singular - departamento) and 2 autonomous regions* (regiones autonomistas, singular - region autonoma); Boaco, Carazo, Chinandega, Chontales, Costa Caribe Norte*, Costa Caribe Sur*, Esteli, Granada, Jinotega, Leon, Madriz, Managua, Masaya, Matagalpa, Nueva Segovia, Rio San Juan, Rivas

INDEPENDENCE:

15 September 1821 (from Spain)

NATIONAL HOLIDAY:

Independence Day, 15 September (1821)

CONSTITUTION:

history: several previous; latest adopted 19 November 1986, effective 9 January 1987

amendments: proposed by the president of the republic or assent of at least half of the National Assembly membership; passage requires approval by 60% of the membership of the next elected Assembly and promulgation by the president of the republic; amended several times, last in 2014 (2018)

LEGAL SYSTEM:

civil law system; Supreme Court may review administrative acts

INTERNATIONAL LAW ORGANIZATION PARTICIPATION:

accepts compulsory ICJ jurisdiction with reservations; non-party state to the ICCt

CITIZENSHIP:

citizenship by birth: yes

citizenship by descent only: yes

dual citizenship recognized: no, except in cases where bilateral agreements exist

residency requirement for naturalization: 4 years

SUFFRAGE:

16 years of age; universal

EXECUTIVE BRANCH:

chief of state: President Jose Daniel ORTEGA Saavedra (since 10 January 2007); Vice President Rosario MURILLO Zambrana (since 10 January 2017); note - the president is both chief of state and head of government

head of government: President Jose Daniel ORTEGA Saavedra (since 10 January 2007); Vice President Rosario MURILLO Zambrana (since 10 January 2017)

cabinet: Council of Ministers appointed by the president

elections/appointments: president and vice president directly elected on the same ballot by simple majority popular vote for a 5-year term (no term limits as of 2014); election last held on 6 November 2016 (next to be held by November 2021)

election results: Jose Daniel ORTEGA Saavedra reelected president; percent of vote - Jose Daniel ORTEGA Saavedra (FSLN) 72.4%, Maximino RODRIGUEZ (PLC) 15%, Jose del Carmen ALVARADO (PLI) 4.5%, Saturnino CERRATO Hodgson (ALN) 4.3%, other 3.7%

LEGISLATIVE BRANCH:

description: unicameral National Assembly or Asamblea Nacional (92 seats; 70 members in multi-seat constituencies and 20 members in a single nationwide constituency directly elected by proportional representation vote; 2 seats reserved for the previous president and the runner-up candidate in the previous presidential election; members serve 5-year terms)

elections: last held on 6 November 2016 (next to be held by November 2021)

election results: percent of vote by party - NA; seats by party - FSLN 71, PLC 14, ALN 2, PLI 2, APRE 1, PC 1, YATAMA 1; composition - men 50, women 42, percent of women 45.7%

JUDICIAL BRANCH:

highest courts: Supreme Court or Corte Suprema de Justicia (consists of 16 judges organized into administrative, civil, criminal, and constitutional chambers)

judge selection and term of office: Supreme Court judges elected by the National Assembly to serve 5-year staggered terms

subordinate courts: Appeals Court; first instance civil, criminal, and labor courts; military courts are independent of the Supreme Court

POLITICAL PARTIES AND LEADERS:

Alliance for the Republic or APRE [Carlos CANALES]
Conservative Party or PC [Alfredo CESAR]
Independent Liberal Party or PLI [Jose del Carmen ALVARADO]
Liberal Constitutionalist Party or PLC [Maria Haydee OSUNA]
Nicaraguan Liberal Alliance or ALN [Alejandro MEJIA Ferreti]
Sandinista National Liberation Front or FSLN [Jose Daniel ORTEGA Saavedra]
Sandinista Renovation Movement or MRS [Suyen BARAHONA]
Sons of Mother Earth or YATAMA [Brooklyn RIVERA]

INTERNATIONAL ORGANIZATION PARTICIPATION:

BCIE, CACM, CD, CELAC, FAO, G-77, IADB, IAEA, IBRD, ICAO, ICRM, IDA, IFAD, IFC, IFRCS, ILO, IMF, IMO, Interpol, IOC, IOM, IPU, ISO (correspondent), ITSO, ITU, ITUC (NGOs), LAES, LAIA (observer), MIGA, NAM, OAS, OPANAL, OPCW, PCA, Petrocaribe, SICA, UN, UNCTAD, UNESCO, UNHCR, UNIDO, Union Latina, UNWTO, UPU, WCO, WHO, WIPO, WMO, WTO

DIPLOMATIC REPRESENTATION IN THE US:

Ambassador Francisco Obadiah CAMPBELL Hooker (since 28 June 2010)

chancery: 1627 New Hampshire Avenue NW, Washington, DC 20009

telephone: [1] (202) 939-6570, 6573

FAX: [1] (202) 939-6545

consulate(s) general: Houston, Los Angeles, Miami, New York, San Francisco

DIPLOMATIC REPRESENTATION FROM THE US:

chief of mission: Ambassador Kevin K. SULLIVAN (since 18 December 2018)

telephone: [505] 2252-7100, 2252-7888; 2252-7100 or 8767-7100 (after hours)

embassy: Kilometer 5.5 Carretera Sur, Managua

mailing address: American Embassy Managua, APO AA 34021

FAX: [505] 2252-7250

FLAG DESCRIPTION:

three equal horizontal bands of blue (top), white, and blue with the national coat of arms centered in the white band; the coat of arms features a triangle encircled by the words REPUBLICA DE NICARAGUA on the top and AMERICA CENTRAL on the bottom; the banner is based on the former blue-white-blue flag of the Federal Republic of Central America; the blue bands symbolize the Pacific Ocean and the Caribbean Sea, while the white band represents the land between the two bodies of water

note: similar to the flag of El Salvador, which features a round emblem encircled by the words REPUBLICA DE EL SALVADOR EN LA AMERICA CENTRAL centered in the white band; also similar to the flag of Honduras, which has five blue stars arranged in an X pattern centered in the white band

NATIONAL SYMBOL(S):

turquoise-browed motmot (bird); national colors: blue, white

NATIONAL ANTHEM:

name: "Salve a ti, Nicaragua" (Hail to Thee, Nicaragua)

lyrics/music: Salomon Ibarra MAYORGA/traditional, arranged by Luis Abraham DELGADILLO

note: although only officially adopted in 1971, the music was approved in 1918 and the lyrics in 1939; the tune, originally from Spain, was used as an anthem for Nicaragua from the 1830s until 1876

ECONOMY :: NICARAGUA

ECONOMY - OVERVIEW:

Nicaragua, the poorest country in Central America and the second poorest in the Western Hemisphere, has widespread underemployment and poverty. GDP growth of 4.5% in 2017 was insufficient to make a significant difference. Textiles and agriculture combined account for nearly 50% of Nicaragua's exports. Beef, coffee, and gold are Nicaragua's top three export commodities.

The Dominican Republic-Central America-United States Free Trade Agreement has been in effect since April 2006 and has expanded export opportunities for many Nicaraguan agricultural and manufactured goods.

In 2013, the government granted a 50-year concession with the option for an additional 50 years to a newly formed Chinese-run company to finance and build an inter-oceanic canal and related projects, at an estimated cost of $50 billion. The canal construction has not started.

GDP (PURCHASING POWER PARITY):
$36.4 billion (2017 est.)

$34.71 billion (2016 est.)

$33.17 billion (2015 est.)

note: data are in 2017 dollars

country comparison to the world: 124

GDP (OFFICIAL EXCHANGE RATE):
$13.81 billion (2017 est.)

GDP - REAL GROWTH RATE:
4.9% (2017 est.)

4.7% (2016 est.)

4.8% (2015 est.)

country comparison to the world: 54

GDP - PER CAPITA (PPP):
$5,900 (2017 est.)

$5,600 (2016 est.)

$5,500 (2015 est.)

note: data are in 2017 dollars

country comparison to the world: 165

GROSS NATIONAL SAVING:
24% of GDP (2017 est.)

23.2% of GDP (2016 est.)

23.6% of GDP (2015 est.)

country comparison to the world: 69

GDP - COMPOSITION, BY END USE:
household consumption: 69.9% (2017 est.)

government consumption: 15.3% (2017 est.)

investment in fixed capital: 28.1% (2017 est.)

investment in inventories: 1.7% (2017 est.)

exports of goods and services: 41.2% (2017 est.)

imports of goods and services: -55.4% (2017 est.)

GDP - COMPOSITION, BY SECTOR OF ORIGIN:
agriculture: 15.5% (2017 est.)

industry: 24.4% (2017 est.)

services: 60% (2017 est.)

AGRICULTURE - PRODUCTS:
coffee, bananas, sugarcane, rice, corn, tobacco, cotton, sesame, soya, beans, beef, veal, pork, poultry, dairy products, shrimp, lobsters, peanuts

INDUSTRIES:
food processing, chemicals, machinery and metal products, knit and woven apparel, petroleum refining and distribution, beverages, footwear, wood, electric wire harness manufacturing, mining

INDUSTRIAL PRODUCTION GROWTH RATE:
3.5% (2017 est.)

country comparison to the world: 88

LABOR FORCE:
3.046 million (2017 est.)

country comparison to the world: 103

LABOR FORCE - BY OCCUPATION:
agriculture: 31%

industry: 18%

services: 50% (2011 est.)

UNEMPLOYMENT RATE:
6.4% (2017 est.)

6.2% (2016 est.)

note: underemployment was 46.5% in 2008

country comparison to the world: 95

POPULATION BELOW POVERTY LINE:
29.6% (2015 est.)

HOUSEHOLD INCOME OR CONSUMPTION BY PERCENTAGE SHARE:
lowest 10%: 1.8%

highest 10%: 47.1% (2014)

DISTRIBUTION OF FAMILY INCOME - GINI INDEX:
47.1 (2014)

45.8 (2009)

country comparison to the world: 27

BUDGET:
revenues: 3.871 billion (2017 est.)

expenditures: 4.15 billion (2017 est.)

TAXES AND OTHER REVENUES:
28% (of GDP) (2017 est.)

country comparison to the world: 97

BUDGET SURPLUS (+) OR DEFICIT (-):
-2% (of GDP) (2017 est.)

country comparison to the world: 106

PUBLIC DEBT:
33.3% of GDP (2017 est.)

31.2% of GDP (2016 est.)

note: official data; data cover general government debt and include debt instruments issued (or owned) by Government entities other than the treasury; the data include treasury debt held by foreign entities, as well as intragovernmental debt; intragovernmental debt consists of treasury borrowings from surpluses in the social funds, such as retirement, medical care, and unemployment, debt instruments for the social funds are not sold at public auctions; Nicaragua rebased its GDP figures in 2012, which reduced the figures for debt as a percentage of GDP

country comparison to the world: 157

FISCAL YEAR:
calendar year

INFLATION RATE (CONSUMER PRICES):
3.9% (2017 est.)

3.5% (2016 est.)

country comparison to the world: 153

CENTRAL BANK DISCOUNT RATE:
3% (31 December 2010)

country comparison to the world: 112

COMMERCIAL BANK PRIME LENDING RATE:
10.8% (31 December 2017 est.)

11.44% (31 December 2016 est.)

country comparison to the world: 76

STOCK OF NARROW MONEY:
$1.162 billion (31 December 2017 est.)

$1.043 billion (31 December 2016 est.)

country comparison to the world: 153

STOCK OF BROAD MONEY:
$1.162 billion (31 December 2017 est.)

$1.043 billion (31 December 2016 est.)

country comparison to the world: 158

STOCK OF DOMESTIC CREDIT:
$6.461 billion (31 December 2017 est.)

$6.159 billion (31 December 2016 est.)

country comparison to the world: 122

MARKET VALUE OF PUBLICLY TRADED SHARES:
$1.568 billion (31 December 2016)

$1.209 billion (31 December 2015)

$995 million (31 December 2014)

country comparison to the world: 102

CURRENT ACCOUNT BALANCE:
-$694 million (2017 est.)

-$989 million (2016 est.)

country comparison to the world: 127

EXPORTS:
$3.819 billion (2017 est.)

$3.772 billion (2016 est.)

country comparison to the world: 120

EXPORTS - PARTNERS:

US 44.2%, El Salvador 6.4%, Venezuela 5.5%, Costa Rica 5.5% (2017)

EXPORTS - COMMODITIES:

coffee, beef, gold, sugar, peanuts, shrimp and lobster, tobacco, cigars, automobile wiring harnesses, textiles, apparel

IMPORTS:

$6.613 billion (2017 est.)

$6.384 billion (2016 est.)

country comparison to the world: 117

IMPORTS - COMMODITIES:

consumer goods, machinery and equipment, raw materials, petroleum products

IMPORTS - PARTNERS:

US 20.8%, China 14.3%, Mexico 11.1%, Costa Rica 7.9%, Guatemala 7%, El Salvador 5.6% (2017)

RESERVES OF FOREIGN EXCHANGE AND GOLD:

$2.758 billion (31 December 2017 est.)

$2.448 billion (31 December 2016 est.)

country comparison to the world: 113

DEBT - EXTERNAL:

$11.31 billion (31 December 2017 est.)

$10.87 billion (31 December 2016 est.)

country comparison to the world: 109

EXCHANGE RATES:

cordobas (NIO) per US dollar -

30.11 (2017 est.)

28.678 (2016 est.)

28.678 (2015 est.)

27.257 (2014 est.)

26.01 (2013 est.)

ENERGY :: NICARAGUA

ELECTRICITY ACCESS:

electrification - total population: 81.8% (2016)

electrification - urban areas: 99.2% (2016)

electrification - rural areas: 56.6% (2016)

ELECTRICITY - PRODUCTION:

4.454 billion kWh (2016 est.)

country comparison to the world: 124

ELECTRICITY - CONSUMPTION:

3.59 billion kWh (2016 est.)

country comparison to the world: 132

ELECTRICITY - EXPORTS:

17.87 million kWh (2016 est.)

country comparison to the world: 91

ELECTRICITY - IMPORTS:

205 million kWh (2016 est.)

country comparison to the world: 93

ELECTRICITY - INSTALLED GENERATING CAPACITY:

1.551 million kW (2016 est.)

country comparison to the world: 123

ELECTRICITY - FROM FOSSIL FUELS:

56% of total installed capacity (2016 est.)

country comparison to the world: 139

ELECTRICITY - FROM NUCLEAR FUELS:

0% of total installed capacity (2017 est.)

country comparison to the world: 155

ELECTRICITY - FROM HYDROELECTRIC PLANTS:

9% of total installed capacity (2017 est.)

country comparison to the world: 120

ELECTRICITY - FROM OTHER RENEWABLE SOURCES:

35% of total installed capacity (2017 est.)

country comparison to the world: 9

CRUDE OIL - PRODUCTION:

0 bbl/day (2018 est.)

country comparison to the world: 183

CRUDE OIL - EXPORTS:

0 bbl/day (2015 est.)

country comparison to the world: 175

CRUDE OIL - IMPORTS:

16,180 bbl/day (2015 est.)

country comparison to the world: 69

CRUDE OIL - PROVED RESERVES:

0 bbl (1 January 2018 est.)

country comparison to the world: 178

REFINED PETROLEUM PRODUCTS - PRODUCTION:

14,720 bbl/day (2015 est.)

country comparison to the world: 95

REFINED PETROLEUM PRODUCTS - CONSUMPTION:

37,000 bbl/day (2016 est.)

country comparison to the world: 115

REFINED PETROLEUM PRODUCTS - EXPORTS:

460 bbl/day (2015 est.)

country comparison to the world: 111

REFINED PETROLEUM PRODUCTS - IMPORTS:

20,120 bbl/day (2015 est.)

country comparison to the world: 121

NATURAL GAS - PRODUCTION:

0 cu m (2017 est.)

country comparison to the world: 179

NATURAL GAS - CONSUMPTION:

0 cu m (2017 est.)

country comparison to the world: 183

NATURAL GAS - EXPORTS:

0 cu m (2017 est.)

country comparison to the world: 162

NATURAL GAS - IMPORTS:

0 cu m (2017 est.)

country comparison to the world: 167

NATURAL GAS - PROVED RESERVES:

0 cu m (1 January 2015 est.)

country comparison to the world: 177

CARBON DIOXIDE EMISSIONS FROM CONSUMPTION OF ENERGY:

5.405 million Mt (2017 est.)

country comparison to the world: 132

COMMUNICATIONS :: NICARAGUA

TELEPHONES - FIXED LINES:

total subscriptions: 375,856

subscriptions per 100 inhabitants: 6 (2017 est.)

country comparison to the world: 105

TELEPHONES - MOBILE CELLULAR:

total subscriptions: 8,179,876

subscriptions per 100 inhabitants: 136 (2017 est.)

country comparison to the world: 99

TELEPHONE SYSTEM:

general assessment: system being upgraded by foreign investment; nearly all installed telecommunications capacity now uses digital technology, owing to investments since privatization of the formerly state-owned telecommunications company; lowest fixed-line teledensity and mobile penetration in Central America; a Russian state corporation is operating in the area; LTE service in 60 towns and cities (2018)

domestic: since privatization, access to fixed-line and mobile-cellular services has improved; fixed-line teledensity roughly 6 per 100 persons; mobile-cellular telephone subscribership has increased to 136 per 100 persons (2018) international: country code - 505; landing point for the ARCOS fiber-optic submarine cable which provides connectivity to South and Central America, parts of the Caribbean, and the US; satellite earth stations - 1 Intersputnik (Atlantic Ocean region) and 1 Intelsat (Atlantic Ocean) (2019)

BROADCAST MEDIA:

multiple terrestrial TV stations, supplemented by cable TV in most urban areas; nearly all are government-owned or affiliated; more than 300 radio stations, both government-affiliated and privately owned (2019)

INTERNET COUNTRY CODE:

.ni

INTERNET USERS:

total: 1,466,152

percent of population: 24.6% (July 2016 est.)

country comparison to the world: 122

BROADBAND - FIXED SUBSCRIPTIONS:

total: 210,124

subscriptions per 100 inhabitants: 3 (2017 est.)

country comparison to the world: 108

MILITARY AND SECURITY :: NICARAGUA

MILITARY EXPENDITURES:

0.61% of GDP (2018)

0.62% of GDP (2017)

0.64% of GDP (2016)

0.78% of GDP (2015)

0.69% of GDP (2014)

country comparison to the world: 140

MILITARY AND SECURITY FORCES:

National Army of Nicaragua (Ejercito Nacional de Nicaragua, ENN; includes Navy, Air Force) (2019)

MILITARY SERVICE AGE AND OBLIGATION:

18-30 years of age for voluntary military service; no conscription; tour of duty 18-36 months; requires Nicaraguan nationality and 6th-grade education (2012)

TRANSPORTATION :: NICARAGUA

NATIONAL AIR TRANSPORT SYSTEM:

number of registered air carriers: 1 (2015)

inventory of registered aircraft operated by air carriers: 2 (2015)

annual passenger traffic on registered air carriers: 61,031 (2015)

annual freight traffic on registered air carriers: 0 mt-km (2015)

CIVIL AIRCRAFT REGISTRATION COUNTRY CODE PREFIX:

YN (2016)

AIRPORTS:

147 (2013)

country comparison to the world: 40

AIRPORTS - WITH PAVED RUNWAYS:

total: 12 (2017)

2,438 to 3,047 m: 3 (2017)

1,524 to 2,437 m: 2 (2017)

914 to 1,523 m: 3 (2017)

under 914 m: 4 (2017)

AIRPORTS - WITH UNPAVED RUNWAYS:

total: 135 (2013)

1,524 to 2,437 m: 1 (2013)

914 to 1,523 m: 15 (2013)

under 914 m: 119 (2013)

PIPELINES:

54 km oil (2013)

ROADWAYS:

total: 23,897 km (2014)

paved: 3,346 km (2014)

unpaved: 20,551 km (2014)

country comparison to the world: 105

WATERWAYS:

2,220 km (navigable waterways as well as the use of the large Lake Managua and Lake Nicaragua; rivers serve only the sparsely populated eastern part of the country) (2011)

country comparison to the world: 39

MERCHANT MARINE:

total: 5

by type: general cargo 1, oil tanker 1, other 3 (2018)

country comparison to the world: 163

PORTS AND TERMINALS:

major seaport(s): Bluefields, Corinto

TRANSNATIONAL ISSUES :: NICARAGUA

DISPUTES - INTERNATIONAL:

the 1992 ICJ ruling for El Salvador and Honduras advised a tripartite resolution to establish a maritime boundary in the Gulf of Fonseca, which considers Honduran access to the Pacific; Nicaragua and Costa Rica regularly file border dispute cases over the delimitations of the San Juan River and the northern tip of Calero Island to the ICJ; there is an ongoing case in the ICJ to determine Pacific and Atlantic ocean maritime borders as well as land borders; in 2009, the ICJ ruled that Costa Rican vessels carrying out police activities could not use the river, but official Costa Rican vessels providing essential services to riverside inhabitants and Costa Rican tourists could travel freely on the river; in 2011, the ICJ provisionally ruled that both countries must remove personnel from the disputed area; in 2013, the ICJ rejected Nicaragua's 2012 suit to halt Costa Rica's construction of a highway paralleling the river on the grounds of irreparable environmental damage; in 2013, the ICJ, regarding the disputed territory, ordered that Nicaragua should refrain from dredging or canal construction and refill and repair damage caused by trenches connecting the river to the Caribbean and upheld its 2010 ruling that Nicaragua must remove all personnel; in early 2014, Costa Rica brought Nicaragua to the ICJ over offshore oil concessions in the disputed region; Nicaragua filed a case against Colombia in 2013 over the delimitation of the Continental shelf beyond the 200 nautical miles from the Nicaraguan coast, as well as over the alleged violation by Colombia of Nicaraguan maritime space in the Caribbean Sea

ILLICIT DRUGS:

transshipment point for cocaine destined for the US and transshipment point for arms-for-drugs dealing

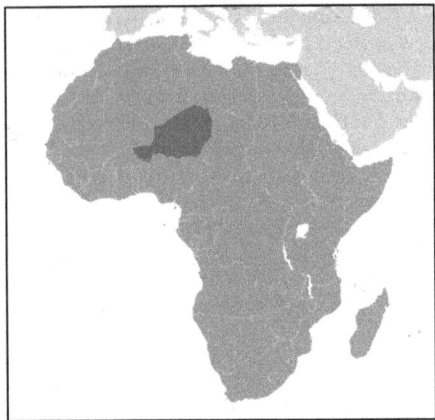

AFRICA :: NIGER

INTRODUCTION :: NIGER

BACKGROUND:
Niger became independent from France in 1960 and experienced single-party and military rule until 1991, when Gen. Ali SAIBOU was forced by public pressure to allow multiparty elections, which resulted in a democratic government in 1993. Political infighting brought the government to a standstill and in 1996 led to a coup by Col. Ibrahim BARE. In 1999, BARE was killed in a counter coup by military officers who restored democratic rule and held elections that brought Mamadou TANDJA to power in December of that year. TANDJA was reelected in 2004 and in 2009 spearheaded a constitutional amendment allowing him to extend his term as president. In February 2010, military officers led a coup that deposed TANDJA and suspended the constitution. ISSOUFOU Mahamadou was elected in April 2011 following the coup and reelected to a second term in early 2016. Niger is one of the poorest countries in the world with minimal government services and insufficient funds to develop its resource base, and is ranked last in the world on the United Nations Development Programme's Human Development Index. The largely agrarian and subsistence-based economy is frequently disrupted by extended droughts common to the Sahel region of Africa. The Nigerien Government continues its attempts to diversify the economy through increased oil production and mining projects. A Tuareg rebellion emerged in 2007 and ended in 2009. Niger is facing increased security concerns on its borders from various external threats including insecurity in Libya, spillover from the conflict in Mali, and violent extremism in northeastern Nigeria.

GEOGRAPHY :: NIGER

LOCATION:
Western Africa, southeast of Algeria

GEOGRAPHIC COORDINATES:
16 00 N, 8 00 E

MAP REFERENCES:
Africa

AREA:
total: 1.267 million sq km

land: 1,266,700 sq km

water: 300 sq km

country comparison to the world: 23

AREA - COMPARATIVE:
slightly less than twice the size of Texas

LAND BOUNDARIES:
total: 5,834 km

border countries (7): Algeria 951 km, Benin 277 km, Burkina Faso 622 km, Chad 1196 km, Libya 342 km, Mali 838 km, Nigeria 1608 km

COASTLINE:
0 km (landlocked)

MARITIME CLAIMS:
none (landlocked)

CLIMATE:
desert; mostly hot, dry, dusty; tropical in extreme south

TERRAIN:
predominately desert plains and sand dunes; flat to rolling plains in south; hills in north

ELEVATION:
mean elevation: 474 m

lowest point: Niger River 200 m

highest point: Idoukal-n-Taghes 2,022 m

NATURAL RESOURCES:
uranium, coal, iron ore, tin, phosphates, gold, molybdenum, gypsum, salt, petroleum

LAND USE:
agricultural land: 35.1% (2011 est.)

arable land: 12.3% (2011 est.) / permanent crops: 0.1% (2011 est.) / permanent pasture: 22.7% (2011 est.)

forest: 1% (2011 est.)

other: 63.9% (2011 est.)

IRRIGATED LAND:
1,000 sq km (2012)

POPULATION DISTRIBUTION:
majority of the populace is located in the southernmost extreme of the country along the border with Nigeria and Benin

NATURAL HAZARDS:
recurring droughts

ENVIRONMENT - CURRENT ISSUES:
overgrazing; soil erosion; deforestation; desertification; contaminated water; inadequate potable water; wildlife populations (such as elephant, hippopotamus, giraffe, and lion) threatened because of poaching and habitat destruction

ENVIRONMENT - INTERNATIONAL AGREEMENTS:
party to: Biodiversity, Climate Change, Climate Change-Kyoto Protocol, Desertification, Endangered

Species, Environmental Modification, Hazardous Wastes, Ozone Layer Protection, Wetlands

signed, but not ratified: Law of the Sea

GEOGRAPHY - NOTE:

landlocked; one of the hottest countries in the world; northern four-fifths is desert, southern one-fifth is savanna, suitable for livestock and limited agriculture

PEOPLE AND SOCIETY :: NIGER

POPULATION:

19,866,231 (July 2018 est.)

country comparison to the world: 59

NATIONALITY:

noun: Nigerien(s)

adjective: Nigerien

ETHNIC GROUPS:

Hausa 53.1%, Zarma/Songhai 21.2%, Tuareg 11%, Fulani (Peuhl) 6.5%, Kanuri 5.9%, Gurma 0.8%, Arab 0.4%, Tubu 0.4%, other/unavailable 0.9% (2006 est.)

LANGUAGES:

French (official), Hausa, Djerma

RELIGIONS:

Muslim 99.3%, Christian 0.3%, animist 0.2%, none 0.1% (2012 est.)

DEMOGRAPHIC PROFILE:

Niger has the highest total fertility rate (TFR) of any country in the world, averaging close to 7 children per woman in 2016. A slight decline in fertility over the last few decades has stalled. This leveling off of the high fertility rate is in large part a product of the continued desire for large families. In Niger, the TFR is lower than the desired fertility rate, which makes it unlikely that contraceptive use will increase. The high TFR sustains rapid population growth and a large youth population – almost 70% of the populace is under the age of 25. Gender inequality, including a lack of educational opportunities for women and early marriage and childbirth, also contributes to high population growth.

Because of large family sizes, children are inheriting smaller and smaller parcels of land. The dependence of most Nigeriens on subsistence farming on increasingly small landholdings, coupled with declining rainfall and the resultant shrinkage of arable land, are all preventing food production from keeping up with population growth.

For more than half a century, Niger's lack of economic development has led to steady net outmigration. In the 1960s, Nigeriens mainly migrated to coastal West African countries to work on a seasonal basis. Some headed to Libya and Algeria in the 1970s to work in the booming oil industry until its decline in the 1980s. Since the 1990s, the principal destinations for Nigerien labor migrants have been West African countries, especially Burkina Faso and Cote d'Ivoire, while emigration to Europe and North America has remained modest. During the same period, Niger's desert trade route town Agadez became a hub for West African and other sub-Saharan migrants crossing the Sahara to North Africa and sometimes onward to Europe.

More than 60,000 Malian refugees have fled to Niger since violence between Malian government troops and armed rebels began in early 2012. Ongoing attacks by the Boko Haram Islamist insurgency, dating to 2013 in northern Nigeria and February 2015 in southeastern Niger, have pushed tens of thousands of Nigerian refugees and Nigerien returnees across the border to Niger and to displace thousands of locals in Niger's already impoverished Diffa region.

AGE STRUCTURE:

0-14 years: 48.68% (male 4,878,031 /female 4,793,021)

15-24 years: 19.36% (male 1,899,879 /female 1,945,806)

25-54 years: 26.02% (male 2,581,597 /female 2,587,913)

55-64 years: 3.3% (male 340,032 /female 315,142)

65 years and over: 2.64% (male 268,072 /female 256,738) (2018 est.)

DEPENDENCY RATIOS:

total dependency ratio: 111.6 (2015 est.)

youth dependency ratio: 106.2 (2015 est.)

elderly dependency ratio: 5.4 (2015 est.)

potential support ratio: 18.6 (2015 est.)

MEDIAN AGE:

total: 15.5 years (2018 est.)

male: 15.4 years

female: 15.7 years

country comparison to the world: 228

POPULATION GROWTH RATE:

3.16% (2018 est.)

country comparison to the world: 7

BIRTH RATE:

43.6 births/1,000 population (2018 est.)

country comparison to the world: 2

DEATH RATE:

11.5 deaths/1,000 population (2018 est.)

country comparison to the world: 20

NET MIGRATION RATE:

-0.5 migrant(s)/1,000 population (2018 est.)

country comparison to the world: 125

POPULATION DISTRIBUTION:

majority of the populace is located in the southernmost extreme of the country along the border with Nigeria and Benin

URBANIZATION:

urban population: 16.5% of total population (2019)

rate of urbanization: 4.27% annual rate of change (2015-20 est.)

MAJOR URBAN AREAS - POPULATION:

1.252 million NIAMEY (capital) (2019)

SEX RATIO:

at birth: 1.03 male(s)/female

0-14 years: 1.02 male(s)/female

15-24 years: 0.98 male(s)/female

25-54 years: 1 male(s)/female

55-64 years: 1.08 male(s)/female

65 years and over: 1.04 male(s)/female

total population: 1.01 male(s)/female (2018 est.)

MOTHER'S MEAN AGE AT FIRST BIRTH:

18.1 years (2012 est.)

note: median age at first birth among women 25-29

MATERNAL MORTALITY RATE:

509 deaths/100,000 live births (2017 est.)

country comparison to the world: 20

INFANT MORTALITY RATE:

total: 79.4 deaths/1,000 live births (2018 est.)

male: 83.7 deaths/1,000 live births

female: 75 deaths/1,000 live births

country comparison to the world: 5

LIFE EXPECTANCY AT BIRTH:

total population: 56.3 years (2018 est.)

male: 55 years

female: 57.7 years

country comparison to the world: 216

TOTAL FERTILITY RATE:

6.35 children born/woman (2018 est.)

country comparison to the world: 1

CONTRACEPTIVE PREVALENCE RATE:

11% (2018)

DRINKING WATER SOURCE:

improved:

urban: 100% of population

rural: 48.6% of population

total: 58.2% of population

unimproved:

urban: 0% of population

rural: 51.4% of population

total: 41.8% of population (2015 est.)

CURRENT HEALTH EXPENDITURE:

6.2% (2016)

PHYSICIANS DENSITY:

0.05 physicians/1,000 population (2014)

SANITATION FACILITY ACCESS:

improved:

urban: 37.9% of population (2015 est.)

rural: 4.6% of population (2015 est.)

total: 10.9% of population (2015 est.)

unimproved:

urban: 62.1% of population (2015 est.)

rural: 95.4% of population (2015 est.)

total: 89.1% of population (2015 est.)

HIV/AIDS - ADULT PREVALENCE RATE:

0.3% (2018 est.)

country comparison to the world: 93

HIV/AIDS - PEOPLE LIVING WITH HIV/AIDS:

36,000 (2018 est.)

country comparison to the world: 70

HIV/AIDS - DEATHS:

1,200 (2018 est.)

country comparison to the world: 58

MAJOR INFECTIOUS DISEASES:

degree of risk: very high (2016)

food or waterborne diseases: bacterial and protozoal diarrhea, hepatitis A, and typhoid fever (2016)

vectorborne diseases: malaria and dengue fever (2016)

water contact diseases: schistosomiasis (2016)

animal contact diseases: rabies (2016)

respiratory diseases: meningococcal meningitis (2016)

OBESITY - ADULT PREVALENCE RATE:

5.5% (2016)

country comparison to the world: 177

CHILDREN UNDER THE AGE OF 5 YEARS UNDERWEIGHT:

31.4% (2016)

country comparison to the world: 9

EDUCATION EXPENDITURES:

3.5% of GDP (2017)

country comparison to the world: 127

LITERACY:

definition: age 15 and over can read and write

total population: 19.1%

male: 27.3%

female: 11% (2015 est.)

SCHOOL LIFE EXPECTANCY (PRIMARY TO TERTIARY EDUCATION):

total: 6 years

male: 7 years

female: 6 years (2017)

UNEMPLOYMENT, YOUTH AGES 15-24:

total: 0.7%

male: 0.9%

female: 0.4% (2014 est.)

country comparison to the world: 180

GOVERNMENT :: NIGER

COUNTRY NAME:

conventional long form: Republic of Niger

conventional short form: Niger

local long form: Republique du Niger

local short form: Niger

etymology: named for the Niger River that passes through the southwest of the country; from a native term "Ni Gir" meaning "River Gir"

note: pronounced nee-zher

GOVERNMENT TYPE:

semi-presidential republic

CAPITAL:

name: Niamey

geographic coordinates: 13 31 N, 2 07 E

time difference: UTC+1 (6 hours ahead of Washington, DC, during Standard Time)

ADMINISTRATIVE DIVISIONS:

7 regions (regions, singular - region) and 1 capital district* (communaute urbaine); Agadez, Diffa, Dosso, Maradi, Niamey*, Tahoua, Tillaberi, Zinder

INDEPENDENCE:

3 August 1960 (from France)

NATIONAL HOLIDAY:

Republic Day, 18 December (1958); note - commemorates the founding of the Republic of Niger which predated independence from France in 1960

CONSTITUTION:

history: several previous; passed by referendum 31 October 2010, entered into force 25 November 2010

amendments: proposed by the president of the republic or by the National Assembly; consideration of amendments requires at least three-fourths majority vote by the Assembly; passage requires at least four-fifths majority vote; if disapproved, the proposed amendment is dropped or submitted to a referendum; constitutional articles on the form of government, the multiparty system, the separation of state and religion, disqualification of Assembly members, amendment procedures, and amnesty of participants in the 2010 coup cannot be amended; amended 2011 (2017)

LEGAL SYSTEM:

mixed legal system of civil law, based on French civil law, Islamic law, and customary law

INTERNATIONAL LAW ORGANIZATION PARTICIPATION:

has not submitted an ICJ jurisdiction declaration; accepts ICCt jurisdiction

CITIZENSHIP:

citizenship by birth: no

citizenship by descent only: at least one parent must be a citizen of Niger

dual citizenship recognized: yes

residency requirement for naturalization: unknown

SUFFRAGE:

18 years of age; universal

EXECUTIVE BRANCH:

chief of state: President ISSOUFOU Mahamadou (since 7 April 2011)

head of government: Prime Minister Brigi RAFINI (since 7 April 2011)

cabinet: Cabinet appointed by the president

elections/appointments: president directly elected by absolute majority popular vote in 2 rounds if needed for a 5-year term (eligible for a second term); election last held on 21 February 2016 with a runoff on 20 March 2016 (next to be held in 2021); prime minister appointed by the president, authorized by the National Assembly

election results: ISSOUFOU Mahamadou reelected president in second round; percent of vote in first round - ISSOUFOU Mahamadou (PNDS-Tarrayya) 48.6%, Hama AMADOU (MODEN/FA Lumana Africa) 17.8%, Seini OUMAROU (MNSD-Nassara) 11.3%, other 22.3%; percent of vote in second round - ISSOUFOU Mahamadou 92%, Hama AMADOU 8%

LEGISLATIVE BRANCH:

description: unicameral National Assembly or Assemblee Nationale (171 seats; 158 members directly elected from 8 multi-member constituencies in 7 regions and Niamey by party-list proportional representation, 8 reserved for minorities elected in special single-seat constituencies by simple majority vote, 5 seats reserved for Nigeriens living abroad - 1 seat per continent - elected in single-seat constituencies by simple majority vote; members serve 5-year terms); note - the number of National Assembly seats increased from 113 to 171 in the February 2016 legislative election

elections: last held on 21 February 2016 (next to be held in 2021)

election results: percent of vote by party - PNDS-Tarrayya 44.1%, MODEN/FA Lumana 14.7%, MNSD-Nassara 11.8%, MPR-Jamhuriya 7.1%, MNRD Hankuri-PSDN Alheri 3.5%, MPN-Kishin Kassa 2.9%, ANDP-Zaman Lahiya 2.4%, RSD-Gaskiya 2.4%, CDS-Rahama 1.8%, CPR-Inganci 1.8%, RDP-Jama'a 1.8%, AMEN AMIN 1.8%, other 3.9%; seats by party - PNDS-Tarrayya 75, MODEN/FA Lumana 25, MNSD-Nassara 20, MPR-Jamhuriya 12, MNRD Hankuri-PSDN Alheri 6, MPN-Kishin Kassa 5, ANDP-Zaman Lahiya 4, RSD-Gaskiya 4, CDS-Rahama 3, CPR-Inganci 3, RDP-Jama'a 3, RDP-Jama'a 3, AMEN AMIN 3, other 8; composition - men 146, women 24 percent of women 14.6%

JUDICIAL BRANCH:

highest courts: Constitutional Court (consists of 7 judges); High Court of Justice (consists of 7 members)

judge selection and term of office: Constitutional Court judges nominated/elected - 1 by the president of the Republic, 1 by the president of the National Assembly, 2 by peer judges, 2 by peer lawyers, 1 law professor by peers, and 1 from within Nigerien society; all appointed by the president; judges serve 6-year nonrenewable terms with one-third of membership renewed every 2 years; High Judicial Court members selected from among the legislature and judiciary; members serve 5-year terms

subordinate courts: Court of Cassation; Council of State; Court of Finances; various specialized tribunals and customary courts

POLITICAL PARTIES AND LEADERS:

Alliance of Movements for the Emergence of Niger or AMEN AMIN [Omar Hamidou TCHIANA]
Congress for the Republic or CPR-Inganci [Kassoum MOCTAR]
Democratic Alliance for Niger or ADN-Fusaha [Habi Mahamadou SALISSOU]
Democratic and Social Convention-Rahama or CDS-Rahama [Abdou LABO]
National Movement for the Development of Society-Nassara or MNSD-Nassara [Seini OUMAROU]
Nigerien Alliance for Democracy and Progress-Zaman Lahiya or ANDP-Zaman Lahiya [Moussa Moumouni DJERMAKOYE]
Nigerien Democratic Movement for an African Federation or MODEN/FA Lumana [Hama AMADOU]
Nigerien Movement for Democratic Renewal or MNRD-Hankuri [Mahamane OUSMANE]
Nigerien Party for Democracy and Socialism or PNDS-Tarrayya [Mahamadou ISSOUFOU]
Nigerien Patriotic Movement or MPN-Kishin Kassa [Ibrahim YACOUBA]
Party for Socialism and Democracy in Niger or PSDN-Alheri
Patriotic Movement for the Republic or MPR-Jamhuriya [Albade ABOUBA]
Rally for Democracy and Progress-Jama'a or RDP-Jama'a [Hamid ALGABID]
Social and Democratic Rally or RSD-Gaskiyya [Amadou CHEIFFOU]
Social Democratic Party or PSD-Bassira [Mohamed BEN OMAR]
Union for Democracy and the Republic-Tabbat or UDR-Tabbat [Amadou Boubacar CISSE]

note: the SPLM and SPLM-DC are banned political parties

INTERNATIONAL ORGANIZATION PARTICIPATION:

ACP, AfDB, AU, CD, ECOWAS, EITI (compliant country), Entente, FAO, FZ, G-77, IAEA, IBRD, ICAO, ICCt, ICRM, IDA, IDB, IFAD, IFC, IFRCS, ILO, IMF, Interpol, IOC, IOM, IPU, ISO (correspondent), ITSO, ITU, ITUC (NGOs), MIGA, MINUSMA, MONUSCO, NAM, OIC, OIF, OPCW, UN, UNCTAD, UNESCO, UNIDO, UNMIL, UNOCI, UNWTO, UPU, WADB (regional), WAEMU, WCO, WFTU (NGOs), WHO, WIPO, WMO, WTO

DIPLOMATIC REPRESENTATION IN THE US:

Ambassador Hassana ALIDOU (since 23 February 2015)

chancery: 2204 R Street NW, Washington, DC 20008

telephone: [1] (202) 483-4224 through 4227

FAX: [1] (202) 483-3169

DIPLOMATIC REPRESENTATION FROM THE US:

chief of mission: Ambassador Eric P. WHITAKER (since 26 January 2018)

telephone: [227] 20-72-26-61

embassy: BP 11201, Rue Des Ambassades, Niamey

mailing address: 2420 Niamey Place, Washington DC 20521-2420

FAX: [227] 20-73-55-60

FLAG DESCRIPTION:

three equal horizontal bands of orange (top), white, and green with a small orange disk centered in the white band; the orange band denotes the drier northern regions of the Sahara; white stands for purity and innocence; green symbolizes hope and the fertile and productive southern and western areas, as well as the Niger River; the orange disc represents the sun and the sacrifices made by the people note: similar to the flag of India, which has a blue spoked wheel centered in the white band

NATIONAL SYMBOL(S):

zebu; national colors: orange, white, green

NATIONAL ANTHEM:

name: "La Nigerienne" (The Nigerien)

lyrics/music: Maurice Albert THIRIET/Robert JACQUET and Nicolas Abel Francois FRIONNET

note: adopted 1961

ECONOMY :: NIGER

ECONOMY - OVERVIEW:

Niger is a landlocked, sub-Saharan nation, whose economy centers on subsistence crops, livestock, and some of the world's largest uranium deposits. Agriculture contributes approximately 40% of GDP and provides livelihood for over 80% of the population. The UN ranked Niger as the second least developed country in the world in 2016 due to multiple factors such as food insecurity, lack of industry, high population growth, a weak educational sector, and few prospects for work outside of subsistence farming and herding.

Since 2011 public debt has increased due to efforts to scale-up public investment, particularly that related to infrastructure, as well as due to increased security spending. The government relies on foreign donor resources for a large portion of its fiscal budget. The economy in recent years has been hurt by terrorist activity near its uranium mines and by instability in Mali and in the Diffa region of the country; concerns about security have resulted in increased support from regional and international partners on defense. Low uranium prices, demographics, and security expenditures may continue to put pressure on the government's finances.

The Government of Niger plans to exploit oil, gold, coal, and other mineral resources to sustain future growth. Although Niger has sizable reserves of oil, the prolonged drop in oil prices has reduced profitability. Food insecurity and drought remain perennial problems for Niger, and the government plans to invest more in irrigation. Niger's three-year $131 million IMF Extended Credit Facility (ECF) agreement for the years 2012-15 was extended until the end of 2016. In February 2017, the IMF approved a new 3-year $134 million ECF. In June 2017, The World Bank's International Development Association (IDA) granted Niger $1 billion over three years for IDA18, a program to boost the country's development and alleviate poverty. A $437 million Millennium Challenge Account compact for Niger, commencing in FY18, will focus on large-scale irrigation infrastructure development and community-based, climate-resilient agriculture, while promoting sustainable increases in agricultural productivity and sales.

Formal private sector investment needed for economic diversification and growth remains a challenge, given the country's limited domestic markets, access to credit, and competitiveness. Although President ISSOUFOU is courting foreign investors, including those from the US, as of April 2017, there were no US firms operating in Niger. In November 2017, the National Assembly passed the 2018 Finance Law that was geared towards raising government revenues and moving away from international support.

GDP (PURCHASING POWER PARITY):

$21.86 billion (2017 est.)

$20.84 billion (2016 est.)

$19.87 billion (2015 est.)

note: data are in 2017 dollars

country comparison to the world: 146

GDP (OFFICIAL EXCHANGE RATE):

$8.224 billion (2017 est.)

GDP - REAL GROWTH RATE:

4.9% (2017 est.)

4.9% (2016 est.)

4.3% (2015 est.)

country comparison to the world: 55

GDP - PER CAPITA (PPP):

$1,200 (2017 est.)

$1,100 (2016 est.)

$1,100 (2015 est.)

note: data are in 2017 dollars

country comparison to the world: 224

GROSS NATIONAL SAVING:

22.4% of GDP (2017 est.)

20.6% of GDP (2016 est.)

21.2% of GDP (2015 est.)

country comparison to the world: 80

GDP - COMPOSITION, BY END USE:

household consumption: 70.2% (2017 est.)

government consumption: 9.4% (2017 est.)

investment in fixed capital: 38.6% (2017 est.)

investment in inventories: 0% (2017 est.)

exports of goods and services: 16.4% (2017 est.)

imports of goods and services: -34.6% (2017 est.)

GDP - COMPOSITION, BY SECTOR OF ORIGIN:

agriculture: 41.6% (2017 est.)

industry: 19.5% (2017 est.)

services: 38.7% (2017 est.)

AGRICULTURE - PRODUCTS:

cowpeas, cotton, peanuts, millet, sorghum, cassava (manioc, tapioca), rice; cattle, sheep, goats, camels, donkeys, horses, poultry

INDUSTRIES:

uranium mining, petroleum, cement, brick, soap, textiles, food processing, chemicals, slaughterhouses

INDUSTRIAL PRODUCTION GROWTH RATE:

6% (2017 est.)

country comparison to the world: 41

LABOR FORCE:

6.5 million (2017 est.)

country comparison to the world: 70

LABOR FORCE - BY OCCUPATION:

agriculture: 79.2%

industry: 3.3%

services: 17.5% (2012 est.)

UNEMPLOYMENT RATE:

0.3% (2017 est.)

0.3% (2016 est.)

country comparison to the world: 3

POPULATION BELOW POVERTY LINE:

45.4% (2014 est.)

HOUSEHOLD INCOME OR CONSUMPTION BY PERCENTAGE SHARE:

lowest 10%: 3.2%

highest 10%: 26.8% (2014)

DISTRIBUTION OF FAMILY INCOME - GINI INDEX:

34 (2014)

50.5 (1995)

country comparison to the world: 105

BUDGET:

revenues: 1.757 billion (2017 est.)

expenditures: 2.171 billion (2017 est.)

TAXES AND OTHER REVENUES:

21.4% (of GDP) (2017 est.)

country comparison to the world: 140

BUDGET SURPLUS (+) OR DEFICIT (-):

-5% (of GDP) (2017 est.)

country comparison to the world: 169

PUBLIC DEBT:

45.3% of GDP (2017 est.)

45.2% of GDP (2016 est.)

country comparison to the world: 115

FISCAL YEAR:

calendar year

INFLATION RATE (CONSUMER PRICES):

2.4% (2017 est.)

0.2% (2016 est.)

country comparison to the world: 121

CENTRAL BANK DISCOUNT RATE:

4.25% (31 December 2015)

4.25% (31 December 2014)

country comparison to the world: 95

COMMERCIAL BANK PRIME LENDING RATE:

5.4% (31 December 2017 est.)

5.3% (31 December 2016 est.)

country comparison to the world: 137

STOCK OF NARROW MONEY:

$1.804 billion (31 December 2017 est.)

$1.511 billion (31 December 2016 est.)

country comparison to the world: 136

STOCK OF BROAD MONEY:

$1.804 billion (31 December 2017 est.)

$1.511 billion (31 December 2016 est.)

country comparison to the world: 145

STOCK OF DOMESTIC CREDIT:

$1.506 billion (31 December 2017 est.)

$1.196 billion (31 December 2016 est.)

country comparison to the world: 162

MARKET VALUE OF PUBLICLY TRADED SHARES:

NA

CURRENT ACCOUNT BALANCE:

-$1.16 billion (2017 est.)

-$1.181 billion (2016 est.)

country comparison to the world: 147

EXPORTS:

$4.143 billion (2017 est.)

$1.101 billion (2016 est.)

country comparison to the world: 116

EXPORTS - PARTNERS:

France 30.2%, Thailand 18.3%, Malaysia 9.9%, Nigeria 8.3%, Mali 5%, Switzerland 4.9% (2017)

EXPORTS - COMMODITIES:

uranium ore, livestock, cowpeas, onions

IMPORTS:

$1.829 billion (2017 est.)

$1.715 billion (2016 est.)

country comparison to the world: 171

IMPORTS - COMMODITIES:

foodstuffs, machinery, vehicles and parts, petroleum, cereals

IMPORTS - PARTNERS:

France 28.8%, China 14.4%, Malaysia 5.7%, Nigeria 5.4%, Thailand 5.3%, US 5.1%, India 4.9% (2017)

RESERVES OF FOREIGN EXCHANGE AND GOLD:

$1.314 billion (31 December 2017 est.)

$1.186 billion (31 December 2016 est.)

country comparison to the world: 126

DEBT - EXTERNAL:

$3.728 billion (31 December 2017 est.)

$2.926 billion (31 December 2016 est.)

country comparison to the world: 140

EXCHANGE RATES:

Communaute Financiere Africaine francs (XOF) per US dollar -

605.3 (2017 est.)

593.01 (2016 est.)

593.01 (2015 est.)

591.45 (2014 est.)

494.42 (2013 est.)

ENERGY :: NIGER

ELECTRICITY ACCESS:

population without electricity: 19 million (2017)

electrification - total population: 16.2% (2016)

electrification - urban areas: 65.4% (2016)

electrification - rural areas: 4.7% (2016)

ELECTRICITY - PRODUCTION:

494.7 million kWh (2016 est.)

country comparison to the world: 167

ELECTRICITY - CONSUMPTION:

1.065 billion kWh (2016 est.)

country comparison to the world: 153

ELECTRICITY - EXPORTS:

0 kWh (2016 est.)

country comparison to the world: 177

ELECTRICITY - IMPORTS:

779 million kWh (2016 est.)

country comparison to the world: 74

ELECTRICITY - INSTALLED GENERATING CAPACITY:

184,000 kW (2016 est.)

country comparison to the world: 168

ELECTRICITY - FROM FOSSIL FUELS:

95% of total installed capacity (2016 est.)

country comparison to the world: 45

ELECTRICITY - FROM NUCLEAR FUELS:

0% of total installed capacity (2017 est.)

country comparison to the world: 156

ELECTRICITY - FROM HYDROELECTRIC PLANTS:

0% of total installed capacity (2017 est.)

country comparison to the world: 190

ELECTRICITY - FROM OTHER RENEWABLE SOURCES:

5% of total installed capacity (2017 est.)

country comparison to the world: 108

CRUDE OIL - PRODUCTION:

9,000 bbl/day (2018 est.)

country comparison to the world: 79

CRUDE OIL - EXPORTS:

0 bbl/day (2015 est.)

country comparison to the world: 176

CRUDE OIL - IMPORTS:

0 bbl/day (2015 est.)

country comparison to the world: 176

CRUDE OIL - PROVED RESERVES:

150 million bbl (1 January 2018 est.)

country comparison to the world: 61

REFINED PETROLEUM PRODUCTS - PRODUCTION:

15,280 bbl/day (2015 est.)

country comparison to the world: 94

REFINED PETROLEUM PRODUCTS - CONSUMPTION:

14,000 bbl/day (2016 est.)

country comparison to the world: 156

REFINED PETROLEUM PRODUCTS - EXPORTS:

5,422 bbl/day (2015 est.)

country comparison to the world: 90

REFINED PETROLEUM PRODUCTS - IMPORTS:

3,799 bbl/day (2015 est.)

country comparison to the world: 180

NATURAL GAS - PRODUCTION:

0 cu m (2017 est.)

country comparison to the world: 180

NATURAL GAS - CONSUMPTION:

0 cu m (2017 est.)

country comparison to the world: 184

NATURAL GAS - EXPORTS:

0 cu m (2017 est.)

country comparison to the world: 163

NATURAL GAS - IMPORTS:

0 cu m (2017 est.)

country comparison to the world: 168

NATURAL GAS - PROVED RESERVES:

0 cu m (1 January 2016 est.)

country comparison to the world: 178

CARBON DIOXIDE EMISSIONS FROM CONSUMPTION OF ENERGY:

2.534 million Mt (2017 est.)

country comparison to the world: 154

COMMUNICATIONS :: NIGER

TELEPHONES - FIXED LINES:

total subscriptions: 114,352

subscriptions per 100 inhabitants: 1 (2017 est.)

country comparison to the world: 139

TELEPHONES - MOBILE CELLULAR:

total subscriptions: 8,778,884

subscriptions per 100 inhabitants: 46 (2017 est.)

country comparison to the world: 90

TELEPHONE SYSTEM:

general assessment: small system of wire, radio telephone communications, and microwave radio relay links concentrated in southwestern Niger; mobile services stronger than fixed telecoms; broadband penetration inconsequential; LTE license secured for the future; government tax of telecom sector (2018)

domestic: fixed-line 1 per 100 persons and mobile-cellular teledensity remains 46 per 100 persons despite a rapidly increasing cellular subscribership base; domestic satellite system with 3 earth stations and 1 planned (2018)

international: country code - 227; satellite earth stations - 2 Intelsat (1 Atlantic Ocean and 1 Indian Ocean)

BROADCAST MEDIA:

state-run TV station; 3 private TV stations provide a mix of local and foreign programming; state-run radio has only radio station with national coverage; about 30 private radio stations operate locally; as many as 100 community radio stations broadcast; transmissions of multiple international broadcasters are available

INTERNET COUNTRY CODE:

.ne

INTERNET USERS:

total: 805,702

percent of population: 4.3% (July 2016 est.)

country comparison to the world: 138

BROADBAND - FIXED SUBSCRIPTIONS:

total: 8,650

subscriptions per 100 inhabitants: less than 1 (2017 est.)

country comparison to the world: 171

MILITARY AND SECURITY :: NIGER

MILITARY EXPENDITURES:

2.45% of GDP (2018)

2.47% of GDP (2017)

2.22% of GDP (2016)

1.78% of GDP (2014)

1.38% of GDP (2013)

country comparison to the world: 34

MILITARY AND SECURITY FORCES:

Nigerien Armed Forces (Forces Armees Nigeriennes, FAN): Army, Nigerien Air Force (Force Aerienne du Niger), Niger Gendarmerie (GN); Ministry of Interior: Niger National Guard (GNN) (2019)

MILITARY SERVICE AGE AND OBLIGATION:

18 is the legal minimum age for compulsory or voluntary military service; enlistees must be Nigerien citizens and unmarried; 2-year service term; women may serve in health care (2017)

TRANSPORTATION :: NIGER

NATIONAL AIR TRANSPORT SYSTEM:

number of registered air carriers: 2 (2015)

inventory of registered aircraft operated by air carriers: 2 (2015)

annual passenger traffic on registered air carriers: 15,242 (2015)

annual freight traffic on registered air carriers: 0 mt-km (2015)

CIVIL AIRCRAFT REGISTRATION COUNTRY CODE PREFIX:

5U (2016)

AIRPORTS:

30 (2013)

country comparison to the world: 116

AIRPORTS - WITH PAVED RUNWAYS:

total: 10 (2017)

2,438 to 3,047 m: 3 (2017)

1,524 to 2,437 m: 6 (2017)

914 to 1,523 m: 1 (2017)

AIRPORTS - WITH UNPAVED RUNWAYS:

total: 20 (2013)

1,524 to 2,437 m: 3 (2013)

914 to 1,523 m: 15 (2013)

under 914 m: 2 (2013)

HELIPORTS:

1 (2013)

PIPELINES:

464 km oil

ROADWAYS:

total: 18,949 km (2010)

paved: 3,912 km (2010)

unpaved: 15,037 km (2010)

country comparison to the world: 116

WATERWAYS:

300 km (the Niger, the only major river, is navigable to Gaya between September and March) (2012)

country comparison to the world: 93

MERCHANT MARINE:

total: 1

by type: other 1 (2018)

country comparison to the world: 174

TERRORISM :: NIGER

TERRORIST GROUPS - HOME BASED:

Islamic State of Iraq and ash-sham networks in the Greater Sahara (ISGS): aim(s): replace regional governments with an Islamic state
area(s) of operation: mostly concentrated along the Mali-Niger border region; targets primarily security forces (2018)

Islamic State of Iraq and ash-Sham (ISIS)-West Africa: aim(s): implement ISIS's strict interpretation of Sharia; replace the Nigerian Government with an Islamic state
area(s) of operation: based primarily in the southeast along the border with Nigeria, with its largest presence in northeast Nigeria and the Lake Chad region; targets primarily regional military installations, especially in the southeastern Diffa region (2018)

TERRORIST GROUPS - FOREIGN BASED:

al-Mulathamun Battalion: aim(s): replace several African governments, including Niger's government, with an Islamic state
area(s) of operation: conducts attacks against Nigerien military and security personnel; targets Westerners for kidnappings for ransom (2018)

al-Qa'ida-affiliated Jama'at Nusrat al-Islam wal-Muslimin (JNIM): aim(s): establish an Islamic state centered in Mali
area(s) of operation: primarily based in northern and central Mali; targets Western and local interests in West Africa and Sahel; has claimed responsibility for attacks in Mali, Niger, and Burkina Faso
note: pledged allegiance to al-Qa'ida and AQIM; holds Western hostages; wages attacks against security and peacekeeping forces in Mali (2018)

Boko Haram: aim(s): establish an Islamic caliphate across Africa
area(s) of operation: conducts kidnappings, bombings, and assaults; responsible for displacing thousands of people and contributing to food insecurity
note: violently opposes any political or social activity associated with Western society, including voting, attending secular schools, and wearing Western dress (2018)

TRANSNATIONAL ISSUES :: NIGER

DISPUTES - INTERNATIONAL:

Libya claims about 25,000 sq km in a currently dormant dispute in the Tommo region; location of Benin-Niger-Nigeria tripoint is unresolved; only Nigeria and Cameroon have heeded the Lake Chad Commission's admonition to ratify the delimitation treaty that also includes the Chad-Niger and Niger-Nigeria boundaries; the dispute with Burkina Faso was referred to the ICJ in 2010

REFUGEES AND INTERNALLY DISPLACED PERSONS:

refugees (country of origin): 161,359 (Nigeria), 56,499 (Mali) (2019)

IDPs: 187,359 (includes the regions of Diffa, Tillaberi, and Tahoua; unknown how many of the 11,000 people displaced by clashes between government forces and the Tuareg militant group, Niger Movement for Justice, in 2007 are still displaced; inter-communal violence; Boko Haram attacks in southern Niger, 2015) (2019)

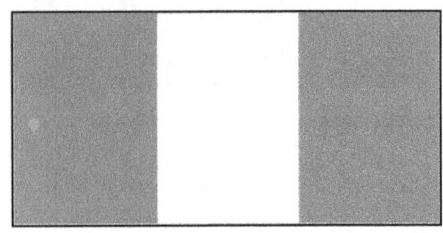

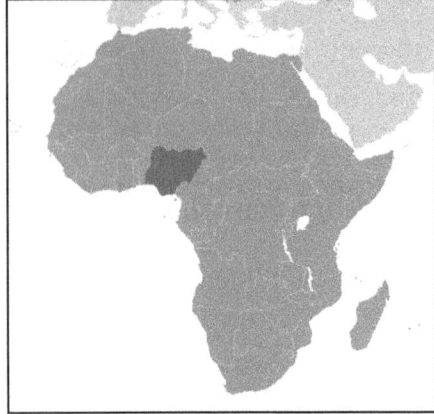

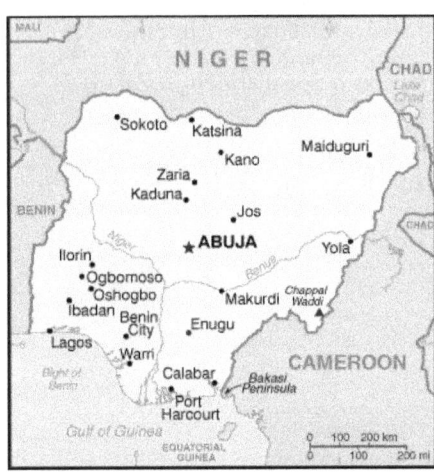

AFRICA :: NIGERIA

INTRODUCTION :: NIGERIA

BACKGROUND:
British influence and control over what would become Nigeria and Africa's most populous country grew through the 19th century. A series of constitutions after World War II granted Nigeria greater autonomy. After independence in 1960, politics were marked by coups and mostly military rule, until the death of a military head of state in 1998 allowed for a political transition. In 1999, a new constitution was adopted and a peaceful transition to civilian government was completed. The government continues to face the daunting task of institutionalizing democracy and reforming a petroleum-based economy, whose revenues have been squandered through corruption and mismanagement. In addition, Nigeria continues to experience longstanding ethnic and religious tensions. Although both the 2003 and 2007 presidential elections were marred by significant irregularities and violence, Nigeria is currently experiencing its longest period of civilian rule since independence. The general elections of 2007 marked the first civilian-to-civilian transfer of power in the country's history and the elections of 2011 were generally regarded as credible. The 2015 election was heralded for the fact that the then-umbrella opposition party, the All Progressives Congress, defeated the long-ruling People's Democratic Party that had governed since 1999 and assumed the presidency after a peaceful transfer of power. Successful presidential and legislative elections were held in early 2019.

GEOGRAPHY :: NIGERIA

LOCATION:
Western Africa, bordering the Gulf of Guinea, between Benin and Cameroon

GEOGRAPHIC COORDINATES:
10 00 N, 8 00 E

MAP REFERENCES:
Africa

AREA:
total: 923,768 sq km

land: 910,768 sq km

water: 13,000 sq km

country comparison to the world: 33

AREA - COMPARATIVE:
about six times the size of Georgia; slightly more than twice the size of California

LAND BOUNDARIES:
total: 4,477 km

border countries (4): Benin 809 km, Cameroon 1975 km, Chad 85 km, Niger 1608 km

COASTLINE:
853 km

MARITIME CLAIMS:
territorial sea: 12 nm

exclusive economic zone: 200 nm

continental shelf: 200-m depth or to the depth of exploitation

CLIMATE:
varies; equatorial in south, tropical in center, arid in north

TERRAIN:
southern lowlands merge into central hills and plateaus; mountains in southeast, plains in north

ELEVATION:
mean elevation: 380 m

lowest point: Atlantic Ocean 0 m

highest point: Chappal Waddi 2,419 m

NATURAL RESOURCES:
natural gas, petroleum, tin, iron ore, coal, limestone, niobium, lead, zinc, arable land

LAND USE:
agricultural land: 78% (2011 est.)

arable land: 37.3% (2011 est.) / permanent crops: 7.4% (2011 est.) / permanent pasture: 33.3% (2011 est.)

forest: 9.5% (2011 est.)

other: 12.5% (2011 est.)

IRRIGATED LAND:
2,930 sq km (2012)

POPULATION DISTRIBUTION:
largest population of any African nation; significant population clusters are scattered throughout the country, with the highest density areas being in the south and southwest

NATURAL HAZARDS:
periodic droughts; flooding

ENVIRONMENT - CURRENT ISSUES:
serious overpopulation and rapid urbanization have led to numerous environmental problems; urban air and water pollution; rapid deforestation; soil degradation; loss of arable land; oil pollution - water, air, and soil have suffered serious damage from oil spills

ENVIRONMENT - INTERNATIONAL AGREEMENTS:
party to: Biodiversity, Climate Change, Climate Change-Kyoto Protocol, Desertification, Endangered Species, Hazardous Wastes, Law of the Sea, Marine Dumping, Marine Life

Conservation, Ozone Layer Protection, Ship Pollution, Wetlands

signed, but not ratified: none of the selected agreements

GEOGRAPHY - NOTE:

the Niger River enters the country in the northwest and flows southward through tropical rain forests and swamps to its delta in the Gulf of Guinea

PEOPLE AND SOCIETY :: NIGERIA

POPULATION:

203,452,505 (July 2018 est.)

note: estimates for this country explicitly take into account the effects of excess mortality due to AIDS; this can result in lower life expectancy, higher infant mortality, higher death rates, lower population growth rates, and changes in the distribution of population by age and sex than would otherwise be expected

country comparison to the world: 7

NATIONALITY:

noun: Nigerian(s)

adjective: Nigerian

ETHNIC GROUPS:

Hausa 30%, Yoruba 15.5%, Igbo (Ibo) 15.2%, Fulani 6%, Tiv 2.4%, Kanuri/Beriberi 2.4%, Ibibio 1.8%, Ijaw/Izon 1.8%, other 24.7% (2018 est.)

note: Nigeria, Africa's most populous country, is composed of more than 250 ethnic groups

LANGUAGES:

English (official), Hausa, Yoruba, Igbo (Ibo), Fulani, over 500 additional indigenous languages

RELIGIONS:

Muslim 53.5%, Roman Catholic 10.6%, other Christian 35.3%, other .6% (2018 est.)

DEMOGRAPHIC PROFILE:

Nigeria's population is projected to grow from more than 186 million people in 2016 to 392 million in 2050, becoming the world's fourth most populous country. Nigeria's sustained high population growth rate will continue for the foreseeable future because of population momentum and its high birth rate. Abuja has not successfully implemented family planning programs to reduce and space births because of a lack of political will, government financing, and the availability and affordability of services and products, as well as a cultural preference for large families. Increased educational attainment, especially among women, and improvements in health care are needed to encourage and to better enable parents to opt for smaller families.

Nigeria needs to harness the potential of its burgeoning youth population in order to boost economic development, reduce widespread poverty, and channel large numbers of unemployed youth into productive activities and away from ongoing religious and ethnic violence. While most movement of Nigerians is internal, significant emigration regionally and to the West provides an outlet for Nigerians looking for economic opportunities, seeking asylum, and increasingly pursuing higher education. Immigration largely of West Africans continues to be insufficient to offset emigration and the loss of highly skilled workers. Nigeria also is a major source, transit, and destination country for forced labor and sex trafficking.

AGE STRUCTURE:

0-14 years: 42.45% (male 44,087,799 /female 42,278,742)

15-24 years: 19.81% (male 20,452,045 /female 19,861,371)

25-54 years: 30.44% (male 31,031,253 /female 30,893,168)

55-64 years: 4.04% (male 4,017,658 /female 4,197,739)

65 years and over: 3.26% (male 3,138,206 /female 3,494,524) (2018 est.)

DEPENDENCY RATIOS:

total dependency ratio: 88.2 (2015 est.)

youth dependency ratio: 83 (2015 est.)

elderly dependency ratio: 5.1 (2015 est.)

potential support ratio: 19.4 (2015 est.)

MEDIAN AGE:

total: 18.3 years (2018 est.)

male: 18.1 years

female: 18.6 years

country comparison to the world: 210

POPULATION GROWTH RATE:

2.54% (2018 est.)

country comparison to the world: 21

BIRTH RATE:

35.2 births/1,000 population (2018 est.)

country comparison to the world: 20

DEATH RATE:

9.6 deaths/1,000 population (2018 est.)

country comparison to the world: 46

NET MIGRATION RATE:

-0.2 migrant(s)/1,000 population (2018 est.)

country comparison to the world: 110

POPULATION DISTRIBUTION:

largest population of any African nation; significant population clusters are scattered throughout the country, with the highest density areas being in the south and southwest

URBANIZATION:

urban population: 51.2% of total population (2019)

rate of urbanization: 4.23% annual rate of change (2015-20 est.)

MAJOR URBAN AREAS - POPULATION:

13.904 million Lagos, 3.906 million Kano, 3.464 million Ibadan, 3.095 million ABUJA (capital), 2.873 million Port Harcourt, 1.676 million Benin City (2019)

SEX RATIO:

at birth: 1.06 male(s)/female

0-14 years: 1.04 male(s)/female

15-24 years: 1.03 male(s)/female

25-54 years: 1 male(s)/female

55-64 years: 0.96 male(s)/female

65 years and over: 0.9 male(s)/female

total population: 1.02 male(s)/female (2018 est.)

MOTHER'S MEAN AGE AT FIRST BIRTH:

20.3 years (2013 est.)

note: median age at first birth among women 25-29

MATERNAL MORTALITY RATE:

917 deaths/100,000 live births (2017 est.)

country comparison to the world: 4

INFANT MORTALITY RATE:

total: 63.3 deaths/1,000 live births (2018 est.)

male: 69.1 deaths/1,000 live births

female: 57.3 deaths/1,000 live births

country comparison to the world: 13

LIFE EXPECTANCY AT BIRTH:

total population: 59.3 years (2018 est.)

male: 57.5 years

female: 61.1 years

country comparison to the world: 211

TOTAL FERTILITY RATE:

4.85 children born/woman (2018 est.)

country comparison to the world: 16

CONTRACEPTIVE PREVALENCE RATE:

27.6% (2018)

DRINKING WATER SOURCE:

improved:

urban: 80.8% of population

rural: 57.3% of population

total: 68.5% of population

unimproved:

urban: 19.2% of population

rural: 42.7% of population

total: 31.5% of population (2015 est.)

CURRENT HEALTH EXPENDITURE:

3.6% (2016)

PHYSICIANS DENSITY:

0.38 physicians/1,000 population (2013)

SANITATION FACILITY ACCESS:

improved:

urban: 32.8% of population (2015 est.)

rural: 25.4% of population (2015 est.)

total: 29% of population (2015 est.)

unimproved:

urban: 67.2% of population (2015 est.)

rural: 74.6% of population (2015 est.)

total: 71% of population (2015 est.)

HIV/AIDS - ADULT PREVALENCE RATE:

1.5% (2018 est.)

country comparison to the world: 31

HIV/AIDS - PEOPLE LIVING WITH HIV/AIDS:

1.9 million (2018 est.)

country comparison to the world: 4

HIV/AIDS - DEATHS:

53,200 (2017 est.)

country comparison to the world: 4

MAJOR INFECTIOUS DISEASES:

degree of risk: very high (2016)

food or waterborne diseases: bacterial and protozoal diarrhea, hepatitis A and E, and typhoid fever (2016)

vectorborne diseases: malaria, dengue fever, and yellow fever (2016)

water contact diseases: leptospirosis and schistosomiasis (2016)

animal contact diseases: rabies (2016)

respiratory diseases: meningococcal meningitis (2016)

aerosolized dust or soil contact diseases: Lassa fever (2016)

note - on 7 October 2019, the Centers for Disease Control and Prevention issued a Travel Health Notice for a Yellow Fever outbreak in Nigeria; a large, ongoing outbreak of yellow fever in Nigeria began in September 2017; the outbreak is now spread throughout the country with the Nigerian Ministry of Health reporting cases of the disease in all 36 states and the Federal Capital Territory; the CDC recommends travelers going to Nigeria should receive vaccination against yellow fever at least 10 days before travel and should take steps to prevent mosquito bites while there; those never vaccinated against yellow fever should avoid travel to Nigeria during the outbreak

OBESITY - ADULT PREVALENCE RATE:

8.9% (2016)

country comparison to the world: 145

CHILDREN UNDER THE AGE OF 5 YEARS UNDERWEIGHT:

31.5% (2016)

country comparison to the world: 8

EDUCATION EXPENDITURES:

NA

LITERACY:

definition: age 15 and over can read and write

total population: 59.6%

male: 69.2%

female: 49.7% (2015 est.)

SCHOOL LIFE EXPECTANCY (PRIMARY TO TERTIARY EDUCATION):

total: 9 years

male: 9 years

female: 8 years (2011)

UNEMPLOYMENT, YOUTH AGES 15-24:

total: 12.4%

male: NA

female: NA (2016 est.)

country comparison to the world: 112

GOVERNMENT :: NIGERIA

COUNTRY NAME:

conventional long form: Federal Republic of Nigeria

conventional short form: Nigeria

etymology: named for the Niger River that flows through the west of the country to the Atlantic Ocean; from a native term "Ni Gir" meaning "River Gir"

GOVERNMENT TYPE:

federal presidential republic

CAPITAL:

name: Abuja

geographic coordinates: 9 05 N, 7 32 E

time difference: UTC+1 (6 hours ahead of Washington, DC, during Standard Time)

etymology: Abuja is a planned capital city, it replaced Lagos in 1991; situated in the center of the country, Abuja takes its name from a nearby town, now renamed Suleja

ADMINISTRATIVE DIVISIONS:

36 states and 1 territory*; Abia, Adamawa, Akwa Ibom, Anambra, Bauchi, Bayelsa, Benue, Borno, Cross River, Delta, Ebonyi, Edo, Ekiti, Enugu, Federal Capital Territory*, Gombe, Imo, Jigawa, Kaduna, Kano, Katsina, Kebbi, Kogi, Kwara, Lagos, Nasarawa, Niger, Ogun, Ondo, Osun, Oyo, Plateau, Rivers, Sokoto, Taraba, Yobe, Zamfara

INDEPENDENCE:

1 October 1960 (from the UK)

NATIONAL HOLIDAY:

Independence Day (National Day), 1 October (1960)

CONSTITUTION:

history: several previous; latest adopted 5 May 1999, effective 29 May 1999

amendments: proposed by the National Assembly; passage requires at least two-thirds majority vote of both houses and approval by the Houses of Assembly of at least two thirds of the states; amendments to constitutional articles on the creation of a new state, fundamental constitutional rights, or constitution-amending procedures requires at least four-fifths majority vote by both houses of the National Assembly and approval by the Houses of Assembly in at least two thirds of the states; passage of amendments limited to the creation of a new state require at least two-thirds majority vote by the proposing National Assembly house and approval by the Houses of Assembly in two thirds of the states; amended several times, last in 2018 (2018)

LEGAL SYSTEM:

mixed legal system of English common law, Islamic law (in 12 northern states), and traditional law

INTERNATIONAL LAW ORGANIZATION PARTICIPATION:

accepts compulsory ICJ jurisdiction with reservations; accepts ICCt jurisdiction

CITIZENSHIP:

citizenship by birth: no

citizenship by descent only: at least one parent must be a citizen of Nigeria

dual citizenship recognized: yes

residency requirement for naturalization: 15 years

SUFFRAGE:

18 years of age; universal

EXECUTIVE BRANCH:

chief of state: President Maj. Gen. (ret.) Muhammadu BUHARI (since 29 May 2015); Vice President Oluyemi "Yemi" OSINBAJO (since 29 May 2015); note - the president is both chief of state, head of government, and commander-in-chief of the armed forces

head of government: President Maj.Gen. (ret.) Muhammadu BUHARI (since 29 May 2015); Vice President Oluyemi "Yemi" OSINBAJO (since 29 May 2015)

cabinet: Federal Executive Council appointed by the president but constrained constitutionally to include at least one member from each of the 36 states

elections/appointments: president directly elected by qualified majority popular vote and at least 25% of the votes cast in 24 of Nigeria's 36 states; president elected for a 4-year term (eligible for a second term); election last held on 23 February 2019 (next to be held in February 2023); note: the election was scheduled for 16 February 2019, but postponed on 16 February 2019

election results: Muhammadu BUHARI elected president; percent of vote - Muhammadu BUHARI (APC) 53%, Atiku ABUBAKER (PDP) 39%, other 8%

LEGISLATIVE BRANCH:

description: bicameral National Assembly consists of:
Senate (109 seats - 3 each for the 36 states and 1 for Abuja-Federal Capital Territory; members directly elected in single-seat constituencies by simple majority vote to serve 4-year terms) House of Representatives (360 seats; members directly elected in single-seat constituencies by simple majority vote to serve 4-year terms)

elections: Senate - last held on 23 February 2019 (next to be held on 23 February 2023); note: election was scheduled for 16 February 2019 but was postponed on 15 February 2019 House of Representatives - last held on 23 February 2019 (next to be held on 23 February 2023); note: election was scheduled for 16 February 2019 but was postponed on 15 February 2019

election results: Senate - percent of vote by party - NA; seats by party - APC 65, PDP 39, YPP 1, TBD 3; composition - men 103, women 6, percent of women 5.5%
House of Representatives - percent of vote by party - NA; seats by party - APC 217, PDP 115, other 20, TBD 8; composition - men 346, women 14, percent of women 3.9%; note - total National Assembly percent of women 4.3%

JUDICIAL BRANCH:

highest courts: Supreme Court (consists of the chief justice and 15 justices)

judge selection and term of office: judges appointed by the president upon the recommendation of the National Judicial Council, a 23-member independent body of federal and state judicial officials; judge appointments confirmed by the Senate; judges serve until age 70

subordinate courts: Court of Appeal; Federal High Court; High Court of the Federal Capital Territory; Sharia Court of Appeal of the Federal Capital Territory; Customary Court of Appeal of the Federal Capital Territory; state court system similar in structure to federal system

POLITICAL PARTIES AND LEADERS:

Accord Party or ACC [Mohammad Lawal MALADO]
All Progressives Congress or APC [Adams OSHIOMHOLE]
All Progressives Grand Alliance or APGA [Victor Ike OYE]
Democratic Peoples Party or DPP [Biodun OGUNBIYI]
Labor Party or LP [Alhai Abdulkadir ABDULSALAM]
Peoples Democratic Party or PDP [Uche SECONDUS]
Young Progressive Party or YPP [Kingsley MOGHALU]

INTERNATIONAL ORGANIZATION PARTICIPATION:

ACP, AfDB, AU, C, CD, D-8, ECOWAS, EITI (compliant country), FAO, G-15, G-24, G-77, IAEA, IBRD, ICAO, ICC (national committees), ICCt, ICRM, IDA, IDB, IFAD, IFC, IFRCS, IHO, ILO, IMF, IMO, IMSO, Interpol, IOC, IOM, IPU, ISO, ITSO, ITU, ITUC (NGOs), MIGA, MINURSO, MINUSMA, MONUSCO, NAM, OAS (observer), OIC, OPCW, OPEC, PCA, UN, UNAMID, UNCTAD, UNESCO, UNHCR, UNIDO, UNIFIL, UNISFA, UNITAR, UNMIL, UNMISS, UNOCI, UNWTO, UPU, WCO, WFTU (NGOs), WHO, WIPO, WMO, WTO

DIPLOMATIC REPRESENTATION IN THE US:

Ambassador Sylvanus Adiewere NSOFOR (since 29 November 2017)

chancery: 3519 International Court NW, Washington, DC 20008

telephone: [1] (202) 516-4277

FAX: [1] (202) 362-6541

consulate(s) general: Atlanta, New York

DIPLOMATIC REPRESENTATION FROM THE US:

chief of mission: Ambassador W. Stuart SYMINGTON (since 1 December 2016)

telephone: [234] (9) 461-4000

embassy: Plot 1075 Diplomatic Drive, Central District Area, Abuja

mailing address: P. O. Box 5760, Garki, Abuja

FAX: [234] (9) 461-4036

consulate(s): Lagos

FLAG DESCRIPTION:

three equal vertical bands of green (hoist side), white, and green; the color green represents the forests and abundant natural wealth of the country, white stands for peace and unity

NATIONAL SYMBOL(S):

eagle; national colors: green, white

NATIONAL ANTHEM:

name: Arise Oh Compatriots, Nigeria's Call Obey

lyrics/music: John A. ILECHUKWU, Eme Etim AKPAN, B.A. OGUNNAIKE, Sotu OMOIGUI and P.O. ADERIBIGBE/Benedict Elide ODIASE

note: adopted 1978; lyrics are a mixture of the five top entries in a national contest

ECONOMY :: NIGERIA

ECONOMY - OVERVIEW:

Nigeria is Sub Saharan Africa's largest economy and relies heavily on oil as its main source of foreign exchange earnings and government revenues. Following the 2008-09 global financial crises, the banking sector was effectively recapitalized and regulation enhanced. Since then, Nigeria's economic growth has been driven by growth in agriculture, telecommunications, and services. Economic diversification and strong growth have not translated into a significant decline in poverty levels; over 62% of Nigeria's over 180 million people still live in extreme poverty.

Despite its strong fundamentals, oil-rich Nigeria has been hobbled by inadequate power supply, lack of infrastructure, delays in the passage of legislative reforms, an inefficient property registration system, restrictive trade policies, an inconsistent regulatory environment, a slow and ineffective judicial system, unreliable dispute resolution mechanisms, insecurity, and pervasive corruption. Regulatory constraints and security risks have limited new investment in oil and natural gas, and Nigeria's oil production had been contracting every year since 2012 until a slight rebound in 2017.

President BUHARI, elected in March 2015, has established a cabinet of economic ministers that includes several technocrats, and he has announced plans to increase transparency, diversify the economy away from oil, and improve fiscal management, but has taken a primarily protectionist approach that favors domestic producers at the expense of consumers. President BUHARI ran on an anti-corruption platform, and has made some headway in alleviating corruption, such as implementation of a Treasury Single Account that allows the government to better manage its resources and a more transparent government payroll and personnel system that eliminated duplicate and "ghost workers." The government also is working to develop stronger public-private partnerships for roads, agriculture, and power.

Nigeria entered recession in 2016 as a result of lower oil prices and production, exacerbated by militant attacks on oil and gas infrastructure in the Niger Delta region, coupled with detrimental economic policies, including foreign exchange restrictions. GDP growth turned positive in 2017 as oil prices recovered and output stabilized.

GDP (PURCHASING POWER PARITY):

$1.121 trillion (2017 est.)

$1.112 trillion (2016 est.)

$1.13 trillion (2015 est.)

note: data are in 2017 dollars

country comparison to the world: 24

GDP (OFFICIAL EXCHANGE RATE):

$376.4 billion (2017 est.)

GDP - REAL GROWTH RATE:

0.8% (2017 est.)

-1.6% (2016 est.)

2.7% (2015 est.)

country comparison to the world: 187

GDP - PER CAPITA (PPP):

$5,900 (2017 est.)

$6,100 (2016 est.)

$6,300 (2015 est.)

note: data are in 2017 dollars

country comparison to the world: 166

GROSS NATIONAL SAVING:

18.2% of GDP (2017 est.)

16% of GDP (2016 est.)

12.3% of GDP (2015 est.)

country comparison to the world: 110

GDP - COMPOSITION, BY END USE:

household consumption: 80% (2017 est.)

government consumption: 5.8% (2017 est.)

investment in fixed capital: 14.8% (2017 est.)

investment in inventories: 0.7% (2017 est.)

exports of goods and services: 11.9% (2017 est.)

imports of goods and services: -13.2% (2017 est.)

GDP - COMPOSITION, BY SECTOR OF ORIGIN:

agriculture: 21.1% (2016 est.)

industry: 22.5% (2016 est.)

services: 56.4% (2017 est.)

AGRICULTURE - PRODUCTS:

cocoa, peanuts, cotton, palm oil, corn, rice, sorghum, millet, cassava (manioc, tapioca), yams, rubber; cattle, sheep, goats, pigs; timber; fish

INDUSTRIES:

crude oil, coal, tin, columbite; rubber products, wood; hides and skins, textiles, cement and other construction materials, food products, footwear, chemicals, fertilizer, printing, ceramics, steel

INDUSTRIAL PRODUCTION GROWTH RATE:

2.2% (2017 est.)

country comparison to the world: 126

LABOR FORCE:

60.08 million (2017 est.)

country comparison to the world: 10

LABOR FORCE - BY OCCUPATION:

agriculture: 70%

industry: 10%

services: 20% (1999 est.)

UNEMPLOYMENT RATE:

16.5% (2017 est.)

13.9% (2016 est.)

country comparison to the world: 178

POPULATION BELOW POVERTY LINE:

70% (2010 est.)

HOUSEHOLD INCOME OR CONSUMPTION BY PERCENTAGE SHARE:

lowest 10%: 1.8%

highest 10%: 38.2% (2010 est.)

DISTRIBUTION OF FAMILY INCOME - GINI INDEX:

48.8 (2013)

50.6 (1997)

country comparison to the world: 21

BUDGET:

revenues: 12.92 billion (2017 est.)

expenditures: 19.54 billion (2017 est.)

TAXES AND OTHER REVENUES:

3.4% (of GDP) (2017 est.)

country comparison to the world: 220

BUDGET SURPLUS (+) OR DEFICIT (-):

-1.8% (of GDP) (2017 est.)

country comparison to the world: 99

PUBLIC DEBT:

21.8% of GDP (2017 est.)

19.6% of GDP (2016 est.)

country comparison to the world: 185

FISCAL YEAR:

calendar year

INFLATION RATE (CONSUMER PRICES):

16.5% (2017 est.)

15.7% (2016 est.)

country comparison to the world: 213

CENTRAL BANK DISCOUNT RATE:

4.25% (31 December 2010)

6% (31 December 2009)

country comparison to the world: 96

COMMERCIAL BANK PRIME LENDING RATE:

17.58% (31 December 2017 est.)

16.87% (31 December 2016 est.)

country comparison to the world: 25

STOCK OF NARROW MONEY:

$36.13 billion (31 December 2017 est.)

$37.02 billion (31 December 2016 est.)

country comparison to the world: 58

STOCK OF BROAD MONEY:

$36.13 billion (31 December 2017 est.)

$37.02 billion (31 December 2016 est.)

country comparison to the world: 58

STOCK OF DOMESTIC CREDIT:

$84.66 billion (31 December 2017 est.)

$88.2 billion (31 December 2016 est.)

country comparison to the world: 58

MARKET VALUE OF PUBLICLY TRADED SHARES:

$53.07 billion (31 December 2016 est.)

$63.47 billion (31 December 2014 est.)

$80.61 billion (31 December 2013 est.)

country comparison to the world: 51

CURRENT ACCOUNT BALANCE:

$10.38 billion (2017 est.)

$2.714 billion (2016 est.)

country comparison to the world: 21

EXPORTS:

$1.146 billion (2017 est.)

$34.7 billion (2016 est.)

country comparison to the world: 155

EXPORTS - PARTNERS:

India 30.6%, US 12.1%, Spain 6.6%, China 5.6%, France 5.5%, Netherlands 4.4%, Indonesia 4.4% (2017)

EXPORTS - COMMODITIES:

petroleum and petroleum products 95%, cocoa, rubber (2012 est.)

IMPORTS:

$32.67 billion (2017 est.)

$35.24 billion (2016 est.)

country comparison to the world: 63

IMPORTS - COMMODITIES:

machinery, chemicals, transport equipment, manufactured goods, food and live animals

IMPORTS - PARTNERS:

China 21.1%, Belgium 8.7%, US 8.4%, South Korea 7.5%, UK 4.4% (2017)

RESERVES OF FOREIGN EXCHANGE AND GOLD:

$38.77 billion (31 December 2017 est.)

$25.84 billion (31 December 2016 est.)

country comparison to the world: 45

DEBT - EXTERNAL:

$40.96 billion (31 December 2017 est.)

$31.41 billion (31 December 2016 est.)

country comparison to the world: 73

STOCK OF DIRECT FOREIGN INVESTMENT - AT HOME:

$116.9 billion (31 December 2017 est.)

$113.4 billion (31 December 2016 est.)

country comparison to the world: 44

STOCK OF DIRECT FOREIGN INVESTMENT - ABROAD:

$16.93 billion (31 December 2017 est.)

$15.65 billion (31 December 2016 est.)

country comparison to the world: 57

EXCHANGE RATES:

nairas (NGN) per US dollar -

323.5 (2017 est.)

253 (2016 est.)

253 (2015 est.)

192.73 (2014 est.)

158.55 (2013 est.)

ENERGY :: NIGERIA

ELECTRICITY ACCESS:

population without electricity: 77 million (2017)

electrification - total population: 59.3% (2016)

electrification - urban areas: 86% (2016)

electrification - rural areas: 41.1% (2016)

ELECTRICITY - PRODUCTION:

29.35 billion kWh (2016 est.)

country comparison to the world: 67

ELECTRICITY - CONSUMPTION:

24.72 billion kWh (2016 est.)

country comparison to the world: 69

ELECTRICITY - EXPORTS:

0 kWh (2016 est.)

country comparison to the world: 178

ELECTRICITY - IMPORTS:

0 kWh (2016 est.)

country comparison to the world: 180

ELECTRICITY - INSTALLED GENERATING CAPACITY:

10.52 million kW (2016 est.)

country comparison to the world: 58

ELECTRICITY - FROM FOSSIL FUELS:

80% of total installed capacity (2016 est.)

country comparison to the world: 83

ELECTRICITY - FROM NUCLEAR FUELS:

0% of total installed capacity (2017 est.)

country comparison to the world: 157

ELECTRICITY - FROM HYDROELECTRIC PLANTS:

19% of total installed capacity (2017 est.)

country comparison to the world: 91

ELECTRICITY - FROM OTHER RENEWABLE SOURCES:

0% of total installed capacity (2017 est.)

country comparison to the world: 203

CRUDE OIL - PRODUCTION:

1.989 million bbl/day (2018 est.)

country comparison to the world: 11

CRUDE OIL - EXPORTS:

2.096 million bbl/day (2015 est.)

country comparison to the world: 6

CRUDE OIL - IMPORTS:

0 bbl/day (2015 est.)

country comparison to the world: 177

CRUDE OIL - PROVED RESERVES:

37.45 billion bbl (1 January 2018 est.)

country comparison to the world: 10

REFINED PETROLEUM PRODUCTS - PRODUCTION:

35,010 bbl/day (2017 est.)

country comparison to the world: 83

REFINED PETROLEUM PRODUCTS - CONSUMPTION:

325,000 bbl/day (2016 est.)

country comparison to the world: 41

REFINED PETROLEUM PRODUCTS - EXPORTS:

2,332 bbl/day (2015 est.)

country comparison to the world: 102

REFINED PETROLEUM PRODUCTS - IMPORTS:

223,400 bbl/day (2015 est.)

country comparison to the world: 31

NATURAL GAS - PRODUCTION:

44.48 billion cu m (2017 est.)

country comparison to the world: 18

NATURAL GAS - CONSUMPTION:

17.24 billion cu m (2017 est.)

country comparison to the world: 41

NATURAL GAS - EXPORTS:

27.21 billion cu m (2017 est.)

country comparison to the world: 13

NATURAL GAS - IMPORTS:

0 cu m (2017 est.)

country comparison to the world: 169

NATURAL GAS - PROVED RESERVES:

5.475 trillion cu m (1 January 2018 est.)

country comparison to the world: 8

CARBON DIOXIDE EMISSIONS FROM CONSUMPTION OF ENERGY:

104 million Mt (2017 est.)

country comparison to the world: 42

COMMUNICATIONS :: NIGERIA

TELEPHONES - FIXED LINES:

total subscriptions: 139,344

subscriptions per 100 inhabitants: less than 1 (2017 est.)

country comparison to the world: 134

TELEPHONES - MOBILE CELLULAR:

total subscriptions: 144,920,170

subscriptions per 100 inhabitants: 76 (2017 est.)

country comparison to the world: 9

TELEPHONE SYSTEM:

general assessment: one of the larger telecom markets in Africa; foreign investment; market competition; LTE technologies available but GSM technology dominate; unified licensing regime; government committed to expanding broadband penetration; in Q1 2018, the Nigerian Communications Commission approved seven licenses to telecom companies to deploy fiber optic cable in the six geopolitical zones and Lagos (2018)

domestic: fixed-line subscribership remains less than 1 per 100 persons; mobile-cellular services growing rapidly, in part responding to the shortcomings of the fixed-line network; multiple cellular providers operate nationally with subscribership base over 76 per 100 persons (2018)

international: country code - 234; landing point for the SAT-3/WASC, NCSCS, MainOne, Glo-1 & 2, ACE, and Equiano fiber-optic submarine cable that provides connectivity to Europe and South and West Africa; satellite earth stations - 3 Intelsat (2 Atlantic Ocean and 1 Indian Ocean) (2019)

BROADCAST MEDIA:

nearly 70 federal government-controlled national and regional TV stations; all 36 states operate TV stations; several private TV stations operational; cable and satellite TV subscription services are available; network of federal government-controlled national, regional, and state radio stations; roughly 40 state government-owned radio stations typically carry their own programs except for news broadcasts; about 20 private radio stations; transmissions of international broadcasters are available; digital broadcasting migration process completed in three states in 2018 (2019)

INTERNET COUNTRY CODE:

.ng

INTERNET USERS:

total: 47,759,904

percent of population: 25.7% (July 2016 est.)

country comparison to the world: 14

BROADBAND - FIXED SUBSCRIPTIONS:

total: 74,004

subscriptions per 100 inhabitants: less than 1 (2017 est.)

country comparison to the world: 124

MILITARY AND SECURITY :: NIGERIA

MILITARY EXPENDITURES:

0.51% of GDP (2018)

0.43% of GDP (2017)

0.43% of GDP (2016)

0.42% of GDP (2015)

0.42% of GDP (2014)

country comparison to the world: 147

MILITARY AND SECURITY FORCES:

Nigerian Armed Forces: Army, Navy (includes Coast Guard), Air Force; Ministry of Interior: Nigeria Security and Civil Defence Corps (NSCDC, a paramilitary agency commissioned to assist the military in the management of threats to internal security, including attacks and natural disasters) (2019)

MILITARY SERVICE AGE AND OBLIGATION:

18 years of age for voluntary military service; no conscription (2012)

MARITIME THREATS:

the International Maritime Bureau reports the territorial and offshore waters in the Niger Delta and Gulf of Guinea as very high risk for piracy and armed robbery of ships; in 2018, 48 commercial vessels were boarded or attacked compared with 33 attacks in 2017; in 2018, 29 ships were boarded eight of which were underway, 12 were fired upon, and 78 crew members were abducted; Nigerian pirates have extended the range of their attacks to as far away as Cote d'Ivoire and as far as 170 nm offshore; the Maritime Administration of the US Department of Transportation has issued a Maritime Advisory (2019-010-Gulf of Guinea-Piracy/Armed Robbery/Kidnapping for Ransom) effective 19 July 2019, which states in part "Piracy, armed robbery, and kidnapping for ransom (KFR) continue to serve as significant threats to U.S. flagged vessels transiting or operating in the Gulf of Guinea (GoG). ...According to the Office of Naval Intelligence's "Weekly Piracy Reports" 72 reported incidents of piracy and armed robbery at sea occurred in the GoG region this year as of July 9, 2019. Attacks, kidnappings for ransom (KFR), and boardings to steal valuables from the ships and crews are the most common types of incidents with approximately 75 percent of all incidents taking place off Nigeria. During the first six months of 2019, there were 15 kidnapping and 3 hijackings in the GoG."

TRANSPORTATION :: NIGERIA

NATIONAL AIR TRANSPORT SYSTEM:

number of registered air carriers: 16 (2015)

inventory of registered aircraft operated by air carriers: 73 (2015)

annual passenger traffic on registered air carriers: 3,223,459 (2015)

annual freight traffic on registered air carriers: 22,400,657 mt-km (2015)

CIVIL AIRCRAFT REGISTRATION COUNTRY CODE PREFIX:

5N (2016)

AIRPORTS:

54 (2013)

country comparison to the world: 88

AIRPORTS - WITH PAVED RUNWAYS:

total: 40 (2017)

over 3,047 m: 10 (2017)

2,438 to 3,047 m: 12 (2017)

1,524 to 2,437 m: 9 (2017)

914 to 1,523 m: 6 (2017)

under 914 m: 3 (2017)

AIRPORTS - WITH UNPAVED RUNWAYS:

total: 14 (2013)

1,524 to 2,437 m: 2 (2013)

914 to 1,523 m: 9 (2013)

under 914 m: 3 (2013)

HELIPORTS:

5 (2013)

PIPELINES:

124 km condensate, 4045 km gas, 164 km liquid petroleum gas, 4441 km oil, 3940 km refined products (2013)

RAILWAYS:

total: 3,798 km (2014)

standard gauge: 293 km 1.435-m gauge (2014)

narrow gauge: 3,505 km 1.067-m gauge (2014)

note: as of the end of 2018, there were only six operational locomotives in Nigeria primarily used for passenger service; the majority of the rail lines are in a severe state of disrepair and need to be replaced

country comparison to the world: 54

ROADWAYS:

total: 195,000 km (2017)

paved: 60,000 km (2017)

unpaved: 135,000 km (2017)

country comparison to the world: 29

WATERWAYS:

8,600 km (Niger and Benue Rivers and smaller rivers and creeks) (2011)

country comparison to the world: 15

MERCHANT MARINE:

total: 576

by type: general cargo 14, oil tanker 90, other 472 (2018)

country comparison to the world: 36

PORTS AND TERMINALS:

major seaport(s): Bonny Inshore Terminal, Calabar, Lagos

LNG terminal(s) (export): Bonny Island

TERRORISM :: NIGERIA

TERRORIST GROUPS - HOME BASED:

Boko Haram: aim(s): replace the Nigerian Government with an Islamic state under strict sharia and, ultimately, establish an Islamic caliphate across Africa; avenge military offenses against the group and destroy any political or social activity associated with Western society; conducts attacks against primarily civilian and regional military targets
area(s) of operation: headquartered in the northeast
note: since 2009, fighters have killed tens of thousands of Nigerians during hundreds of attacks and disrupted trade and farming in the northeast, causing a risk of famine and displacing millions of people; violently opposes any political or social activity associated with Western society, including voting, attending secular schools, and wearing Western dress (2018)

Islamic State of Iraq and ash-Sham (ISIS)-West Africa: aim(s): implement ISIS's strict interpretation of Sharia; replace the Nigerian Government with an Islamic state
area(s) of operation: based primarily in the north along the border with Niger, with its largest presence in the northeast and the Lake Chad region; targets primarily regional military installations and civilians (2018)

TRANSNATIONAL ISSUES :: NIGERIA

DISPUTES - INTERNATIONAL:

Joint Border Commission with Cameroon reviewed 2002 ICJ ruling on the entire boundary and bilaterally resolved differences, including June 2006 Greentree Agreement that immediately cedes sovereignty of the Bakassi Peninsula to Cameroon with a phaseout of Nigerian control within two years while resolving patriation issues; the ICJ ruled on an equidistance settlement of Cameroon-Equatorial Guinea-Nigeria maritime boundary in the Gulf of Guinea, but imprecisely defined coordinates in the ICJ decision and a sovereignty dispute between Equatorial Guinea and Cameroon over an island at the mouth of the Ntem River all contribute to the delay in implementation; only Nigeria and Cameroon have heeded the Lake Chad Commission's admonition to ratify the delimitation treaty which also includes the Chad-Niger and Niger-Nigeria boundaries; location of Benin-Niger-Nigeria tripoint is unresolved

REFUGEES AND INTERNALLY DISPLACED PERSONS:

refugees (country of origin): 44,524 (Cameroon) (2019)

IDPs: 2,018,513 (northeast Nigeria; Boko Haram attacks and counterinsurgency efforts in northern Nigeria; communal violence between Christians and Muslims in the middle belt region, political violence; flooding; forced evictions; cattle rustling; competition for resources) (2019)

ILLICIT DRUGS:

a transit point for heroin and cocaine intended for European, East Asian, and North American markets; consumer of amphetamines; safe haven for Nigerian narcotraffickers operating worldwide; major money-laundering center; massive corruption and criminal activity; Nigeria has improved some anti-money-laundering controls, resulting in its removal from the Financial Action Task Force's (FATF's) Noncooperative Countries and Territories List in June 2006; Nigeria's anti-money-laundering regime continues to be monitored by FATF

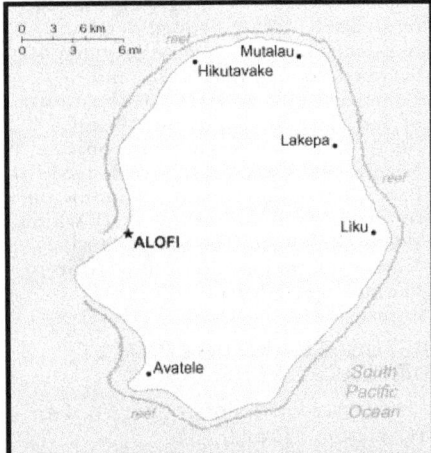

AUSTRALIA - OCEANIA :: NIUE

INTRODUCTION :: NIUE

BACKGROUND:

Niue's remoteness, as well as cultural and linguistic differences between its Polynesian inhabitants and those of the adjacent Cook Islands, has caused it to be separately administered by New Zealand. The population of the island has trended downwards over recent decades (from a peak of 5,200 in 1966 to 1,618 in 2017) with substantial emigration to New Zealand 2,400 km to the southwest.

GEOGRAPHY :: NIUE

LOCATION:

Oceania, island in the South Pacific Ocean, east of Tonga

GEOGRAPHIC COORDINATES:

19 02 S, 169 52 W

MAP REFERENCES:

Oceania

AREA:

total: 260 sq km

land: 260 sq km

water: 0 sq km

country comparison to the world: 213

AREA - COMPARATIVE:

1.5 times the size of Washington, DC

LAND BOUNDARIES:

0 km

COASTLINE:

64 km

MARITIME CLAIMS:

territorial sea: 12 nm

exclusive economic zone: 200 nm

CLIMATE:

tropical; modified by southeast trade winds

TERRAIN:

steep limestone cliffs along coast, central plateau

ELEVATION:

lowest point: Pacific Ocean 0 m

highest point: unnamed elevation 1.4 km east of Hikutavake 80 m

NATURAL RESOURCES:

arable land, fish

LAND USE:

agricultural land: 19.1% (2011 est.)

arable land: 3.8% (2011 est.) / permanent crops: 11.5% (2011 est.) / permanent pasture: 3.8% (2011 est.)

forest: 71.2% (2011 est.)

other: 9.7% (2011 est.)

IRRIGATED LAND:

0 sq km (2012)

POPULATION DISTRIBUTION:

population distributed around the peripheral coastal areas of the island

NATURAL HAZARDS:

tropical cyclones

ENVIRONMENT - CURRENT ISSUES:

increasing attention to conservationist practices to counter loss of soil fertility from traditional slash and burn agriculture

ENVIRONMENT - INTERNATIONAL AGREEMENTS:

party to: Biodiversity, Climate Change, Climate Change-Kyoto Protocol, Desertification, Law of the Sea, Ozone Layer Protection

GEOGRAPHY - NOTE:

one of world's largest coral islands; the only major break in the surrounding coral reef occurs in the central western part of the coast

PEOPLE AND SOCIETY :: NIUE

POPULATION:

1,618 (July 2017 est.)

note: because of the island's limited economic and educational opportunities, Niueans have emigrated for decades - primarily to New Zealand, but also to Australia and other Pacific island states; Niue's population peaked in 1966 at 5,194, but by 2005 had fallen to 1,508; since then it has rebounded slightly; as of 2013, 23,883 people of Niuean ancestry lived in New Zealand - with more than 20% Niue-born; this means that there are about 15 times as many persons of Niuean living in New Zealand as in Niue, possibly the most eccentric population distribution in the world

country comparison to the world: 233

NATIONALITY:

noun: Niuean(s)

adjective: Niuean

ETHNIC GROUPS:

Niuean 66.5%, part-Niuean 13.4%, non-Niuean 20.1% (includes 12% European and Asian and 8% other Pacific Islanders) (2011 est.)

LANGUAGES:

Niuean (official) 46% (a Polynesian language closely related to Tongan and Samoan), Niuean and English 32%, English (official) 11%, Niuean and others 5%, other 6% (2011 est.)

RELIGIONS:

Ekalesia Niue (Congregational Christian Church of Niue - a Protestant church founded by missionaries from the London Missionary Society) 67%, other Protestant 3% (includes Seventh Day Adventist 1%, Presbyterian 1%, and Methodist 1%), Mormon 10%, Roman

Catholic 10%, Jehovah's Witnesses 2%, other 6%, none 2% (2011 est.)

POPULATION GROWTH RATE:

-0.03% (2014 est.)

country comparison to the world: 199

POPULATION DISTRIBUTION:

population distributed around the peripheral coastal areas of the island

URBANIZATION:

urban population: 45.5% of total population (2019)

rate of urbanization: 1.69% annual rate of change (2015-20 est.)

MAJOR URBAN AREAS - POPULATION:

1,000 ALOFI (capital) (2018)

SEX RATIO:

NA

INFANT MORTALITY RATE:

total: NA (2018)

male: NA

female: NA

LIFE EXPECTANCY AT BIRTH:

total population: NA (2017 est.)

male: NA

female: NA

TOTAL FERTILITY RATE:

NA

DRINKING WATER SOURCE:

improved:

urban: 98.4% of population

rural: 98.6% of population

total: 98.5% of population

unimproved:

urban: 1.6% of population

rural: 1.4% of population

total: 1.5% of population (2015 est.)

CURRENT HEALTH EXPENDITURE:

6.3% (2015)

PHYSICIANS DENSITY:

SANITATION FACILITY ACCESS:

improved:

urban: 100% of population (2015 est.)

rural: 100% of population (2015 est.)

total: 100% of population (2015 est.)

unimproved:

urban: 0% of population (2015 est.)

rural: 0% of population (2015 est.)

total: 0% of population (2015 est.)

HIV/AIDS - ADULT PREVALENCE RATE:

NA

HIV/AIDS - PEOPLE LIVING WITH HIV/AIDS:

NA

HIV/AIDS - DEATHS:

NA

OBESITY - ADULT PREVALENCE RATE:

50% (2016)

country comparison to the world: 6

EDUCATION EXPENDITURES:

NA

GOVERNMENT :: NIUE

COUNTRY NAME:

conventional long form: none

conventional short form: Niue

former: Savage Island

etymology: the origin of the name is obscure; in Niuean, the word supposedly translates as "behold the coconut"

note: pronunciation falls between nyu-way and new-way, but not like new-wee

DEPENDENCY STATUS:

self-governing in free association with New Zealand since 1974; Niue is fully responsible for internal affairs; New Zealand retains responsibility for external affairs and defense; however, these responsibilities confer no rights of control and are only exercised at the request of the Government of Niue

GOVERNMENT TYPE:

parliamentary democracy

CAPITAL:

name: Alofi

geographic coordinates: 19 01 S, 169 55 W

time difference: UTC-11 (6 hours behind Washington, DC, during Standard Time)

ADMINISTRATIVE DIVISIONS:

none; note - there are no first-order administrative divisions as defined by the US Government, but there are 14 villages at the second order

INDEPENDENCE:

19 October 1974 (Niue became a self-governing state in free association with New Zealand)

NATIONAL HOLIDAY:

Waitangi Day (Treaty of Waitangi established British sovereignty over New Zealand), 6 February (1840)

CONSTITUTION:

history: several previous (New Zealand colonial statutes); latest 19 October 1974 (Niue Constitution Act 1974)

amendments: proposed by the Assembly; passage requires at least two-thirds majority vote of the Assembly membership in each of three readings and approval by the majority of votes in a referendum; passage of amendments to a number of sections, including Niue's self-governing status, British nationality and New Zealand citizenship, external affairs and defense, economic and administrative assistance by New Zealand, and amendment procedures, requires at least two-thirds majority vote by the Assembly and at least two thirds of votes in a referendum; amended 1992, 2007 (2017)

LEGAL SYSTEM:

English common law

SUFFRAGE:

18 years of age; universal

EXECUTIVE BRANCH:

chief of state: Queen ELIZABETH II (since 6 February 1952); represented by Governor-General of New Zealand Dame Patricia Lee REDDY (since 28 September 2016); the UK and New Zealand are represented by New Zealand High Commissioner Kirk YATES (since May 2018)

head of government: Premier Sir Toke TALAGI (since 18 June 2008)

cabinet: Cabinet chosen by the premier

elections/appointments: the monarchy is hereditary; premier indirectly elected by the Legislative Assembly for a 3-year term; election last held on 12 May 2017 (next to be held in 2020)

election results: Toke TALAGI reelected premier; Legislative Assembly vote - Toke TALAGI (independent) 15, O'Love JACOBSEN (independent) 5

LEGISLATIVE BRANCH:

description: unicameral Assembly or Fono Ekepule (20 seats; 14 members directly elected in single-seat constituencies by simple majority vote and 6 directly elected from the National Register or "common roll" by majority vote; members serve 3-year terms)

elections: last held on 6 May 2017 (next to be held in 2020)

election results: percent of vote by party - NA; seats by party - independent 20; composition - men 15, women 5, percent of women 25%

JUDICIAL BRANCH:

highest courts: Court of Appeal (consists of the chief justice and up to 3 judges); note - the Judicial Committee of the Privy Council (in London) is the final appeal court beyond the Niue Court of Appeal

judge selection and term of office: Niue chief justice appointed by the governor general on the advice of the Cabinet and tendered by the premier; other judges appointed by the governor general on the advice of the Cabinet and tendered by the chief justice and the minister of justice; judges serve until age 68

subordinate courts: High Court

note: Niue is a participant in the Pacific Judicial Development Program, which is designed to build governance and the rule of law in 15 Pacific island countries

POLITICAL PARTIES AND LEADERS:

Alliance of Independents or AI
Niue People's Action Party or NPP [Young VIVIAN]

INTERNATIONAL ORGANIZATION PARTICIPATION:

ACP, AOSIS, FAO, IFAD, OPCW, PIF, Sparteca, SPC, UNESCO, UPU, WHO, WIPO, WMO

DIPLOMATIC REPRESENTATION IN THE US:

none (self-governing territory in free association with New Zealand)

DIPLOMATIC REPRESENTATION FROM THE US:

none (self-governing territory in free association with New Zealand)

FLAG DESCRIPTION:

yellow with the flag of the UK in the upper hoist-side quadrant; the flag of the UK bears five yellow five-pointed stars - a large star on a blue disk in the center and a smaller star on each arm of the bold red cross; the larger star stands for Niue, the smaller stars recall the Southern Cross constellation on the New Zealand flag and symbolize links with that country; yellow represents the bright sunshine of Niue and the warmth and friendship between Niue and New Zealand

NATIONAL SYMBOL(S):

yellow, five-pointed star; national color: yellow

NATIONAL ANTHEM:

name: "Ko e Iki he Lagi" (The Lord in Heaven)

lyrics/music: unknown/unknown, prepared by Sioeli FUSIKATA

note: adopted 1974

ECONOMY :: NIUE

ECONOMY - OVERVIEW:

The economy suffers from the typical Pacific island problems of geographic isolation, few resources, and a small population. The agricultural sector consists mainly of subsistence gardening, although some cash crops are grown for export. Industry consists primarily of small factories for processing passion fruit, lime oil, honey, and coconut cream. The sale of postage stamps to foreign collectors is an important source of revenue.

Government expenditures regularly exceed revenues, and the shortfall is made up by critically needed grants from New Zealand that are used to pay wages to public employees. Economic aid allocation from New Zealand in FY13/14 was US$10.1 million. Niue has cut government expenditures by reducing the public service by almost half.

The island in recent years has suffered a serious loss of population because of emigration to New Zealand. Efforts to increase GDP include the promotion of tourism and financial services, although the International Banking Repeal Act of 2002 resulted in the termination of all offshore banking licenses.

GDP (PURCHASING POWER PARITY):

$10.01 million (2003 est.)

country comparison to the world: 228

GDP (OFFICIAL EXCHANGE RATE):

$10.01 million (2003) (2003)

GDP - REAL GROWTH RATE:

6.2% (2003 est.)

country comparison to the world: 32

GDP - PER CAPITA (PPP):

$5,800 (2003 est.)

country comparison to the world: 168

GDP - COMPOSITION, BY SECTOR OF ORIGIN:

agriculture: 23.5% (2003)

industry: 26.9% (2003)

services: 49.5% (2003)

AGRICULTURE - PRODUCTS:

coconuts, passion fruit, honey, limes, taro, yams, cassava (manioc, tapioca), sweet potatoes; pigs, poultry, beef cattle

INDUSTRIES:

handicrafts, food processing

INDUSTRIAL PRODUCTION GROWTH RATE:

NA

LABOR FORCE:

663 (2001)

country comparison to the world: 230

LABOR FORCE - BY OCCUPATION:

note: most work on family plantations; paid work exists only in government service, small industry, and the Niue Development Board

UNEMPLOYMENT RATE:

12% (2001)

country comparison to the world: 159

POPULATION BELOW POVERTY LINE:

NA

HOUSEHOLD INCOME OR CONSUMPTION BY PERCENTAGE SHARE:

lowest 10%: NA

highest 10%: NA

BUDGET:

revenues: 15.07 million (FY04/05)

expenditures: 16.33 million (FY04/05)

BUDGET SURPLUS (+) OR DEFICIT (-):

-12.6% (of GDP) (FY04/05)

country comparison to the world: 215

FISCAL YEAR:

1 April - 31 March

INFLATION RATE (CONSUMER PRICES):

4% (2005)

country comparison to the world: 155

EXPORTS:

$201,400 (2004 est.)

country comparison to the world: 221

EXPORTS - COMMODITIES:

canned coconut cream, copra, honey, vanilla, passion fruit products, pawpaws, root crops, limes, footballs, stamps, handicrafts

IMPORTS:

$9.038 million (2004 est.)

country comparison to the world: 223

IMPORTS - COMMODITIES:

food, live animals, manufactured goods, machinery, fuels, lubricants, chemicals, drugs

DEBT - EXTERNAL:

$418,000 (2002 est.)

country comparison to the world: 202

EXCHANGE RATES:

New Zealand dollars (NZD) per US dollar -

1.416 (2017 est.)

1.4279 (2016 est.)
1.4279 (2015)
1.4279 (2014 est.)
1.2039 (2013 est.)

ENERGY :: NIUE

ELECTRICITY - PRODUCTION:
3 million kWh (2016 est.)

country comparison to the world: 216

ELECTRICITY - CONSUMPTION:
2.79 million kWh (2016 est.)

country comparison to the world: 215

ELECTRICITY - EXPORTS:
0 kWh (2016 est.)

country comparison to the world: 179

ELECTRICITY - IMPORTS:
0 kWh (2016 est.)

country comparison to the world: 181

ELECTRICITY - INSTALLED GENERATING CAPACITY:
2,300 kW (2016 est.)

country comparison to the world: 214

ELECTRICITY - FROM FOSSIL FUELS:
87% of total installed capacity (2016 est.)

country comparison to the world: 65

ELECTRICITY - FROM NUCLEAR FUELS:
0% of total installed capacity (2017 est.)

country comparison to the world: 158

ELECTRICITY - FROM HYDROELECTRIC PLANTS:
0% of total installed capacity (2017 est.)

country comparison to the world: 191

ELECTRICITY - FROM OTHER RENEWABLE SOURCES:
13% of total installed capacity (2017 est.)

country comparison to the world: 68

CRUDE OIL - PRODUCTION:
0 bbl/day (2018 est.)

country comparison to the world: 184

CRUDE OIL - EXPORTS:
0 bbl/day (2015 est.)

country comparison to the world: 177

CRUDE OIL - IMPORTS:
0 bbl/day (2015 est.)

country comparison to the world: 178

CRUDE OIL - PROVED RESERVES:
0 bbl (1 January 2018 est.)

country comparison to the world: 179

REFINED PETROLEUM PRODUCTS - PRODUCTION:
0 bbl/day (2017 est.)

country comparison to the world: 187

REFINED PETROLEUM PRODUCTS - CONSUMPTION:
50 bbl/day (2016 est.)

country comparison to the world: 215

REFINED PETROLEUM PRODUCTS - EXPORTS:
0 bbl/day (2015 est.)

country comparison to the world: 189

REFINED PETROLEUM PRODUCTS - IMPORTS:
54 bbl/day (2015 est.)

country comparison to the world: 211

NATURAL GAS - PRODUCTION:
0 cu m (2017 est.)

country comparison to the world: 181

NATURAL GAS - CONSUMPTION:
0 cu m (2017 est.)

country comparison to the world: 185

NATURAL GAS - EXPORTS:
0 cu m (2017 est.)

country comparison to the world: 164

NATURAL GAS - IMPORTS:
0 cu m (2017 est.)

country comparison to the world: 170

NATURAL GAS - PROVED RESERVES:
0 cu m (1 January 2014 est.)

country comparison to the world: 179

CARBON DIOXIDE EMISSIONS FROM CONSUMPTION OF ENERGY:
7,252 Mt (2017 est.)

country comparison to the world: 213

COMMUNICATIONS :: NIUE

TELEPHONE SYSTEM:

general assessment: sole provider services for over 1000 landlines and fixed wireless lines; cellular telephone service operates on AMPS and GSM platforms; difficult geography presents challenges for rural areas (2018)

domestic: single-line (fixed line) telephone system connects all villages (and virtually all households) on island (2018)

international: country code - 683; landing point for the Manatua submarine cable linking Niue to several South Pacific Ocean Islands (2019)

BROADCAST MEDIA:
1 government-owned TV station with many of the programs supplied by Television New Zealand; 1 government-owned radio station broadcasting in AM and FM (2019)

INTERNET COUNTRY CODE:
.nu

INTERNET USERS:
total: 1,090

percent of population: 91.6% (July 2016 est.)

country comparison to the world: 222

MILITARY AND SECURITY :: NIUE

MILITARY AND SECURITY FORCES:
no regular indigenous military forces; Police Force (2019)

MILITARY - NOTE:
defense is the responsibility of New Zealand

TRANSPORTATION :: NIUE

AIRPORTS:
1 (2013)

country comparison to the world: 231

AIRPORTS - WITH PAVED RUNWAYS:
total: 1 (2017)

1,524 to 2,437 m: 1 (2017)

AIRPORTS - WITH UNPAVED RUNWAYS:
total: 1 (2013)

1,524 to 2,437 m: 1 (2013)

ROADWAYS:
total: 234 km (2017)

paved: 210 km (2017)

unpaved: 24 km

country comparison to the world: 200

PORTS AND TERMINALS:
major seaport(s): Alofi

TRANSNATIONAL ISSUES :: NIUE

DISPUTES - INTERNATIONAL:
none

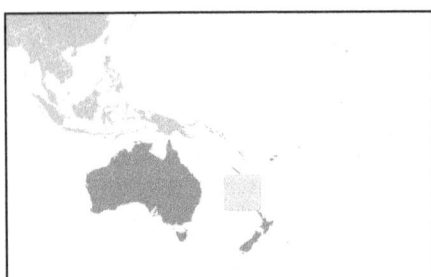
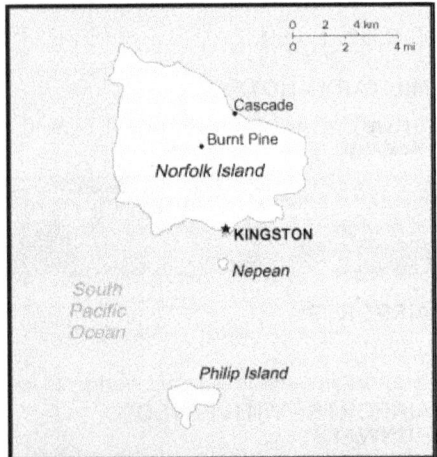

AUSTRALIA - OCEANIA :: NORFOLK ISLAND

INTRODUCTION :: NORFOLK ISLAND

BACKGROUND:
Two British attempts at establishing the island as a penal colony (1788-1814 and 1825-55) were ultimately abandoned. In 1856, the island was resettled by Pitcairn Islanders, descendants of the Bounty mutineers and their Tahitian companions.

GEOGRAPHY :: NORFOLK ISLAND

LOCATION:
Oceania, island in the South Pacific Ocean, east of Australia

GEOGRAPHIC COORDINATES:
29 02 S, 167 57 E

MAP REFERENCES:
Oceania

AREA:
total: 36 sq km
land: 36 sq km
water: 0 sq km
country comparison to the world: 235

AREA - COMPARATIVE:
about 0.2 times the size of Washington, DC

LAND BOUNDARIES:
0 km

COASTLINE:
32 km

MARITIME CLAIMS:
territorial sea: 12 nm
exclusive fishing zone: 200 nm

CLIMATE:
subtropical; mild, little seasonal temperature variation

TERRAIN:
volcanic island with mostly rolling plains

ELEVATION:
lowest point: Pacific Ocean 0 m
highest point: Mount Bates 319 m

NATURAL RESOURCES:
fish

LAND USE:
agricultural land: 25% (2011 est.)
arable land: 0% (2011 est.) / permanent crops: 0% (2011 est.) / permanent pasture: 25% (2011 est.)
forest: 11.5% (2011 est.)
other: 63.5% (2011 est.)

IRRIGATED LAND:
0 sq km (2012)

POPULATION DISTRIBUTION:
population concentrated around the capital of Kingston

NATURAL HAZARDS:
tropical cyclones (especially May to July)

ENVIRONMENT - CURRENT ISSUES:
inadequate solid waste management; most freshwater obtained through rainwater catchment; preservation of unique ecosystem

GEOGRAPHY - NOTE:
most of the 32 km coastline consists of almost inaccessible cliffs, but the land slopes down to the sea in one small southern area on Sydney Bay, where the capital of Kingston is situated

PEOPLE AND SOCIETY :: NORFOLK ISLAND

POPULATION:
1,748 (2016 est.)
country comparison to the world: 232

NATIONALITY:
noun: Norfolk Islander(s)
adjective: Norfolk Islander(s)

ETHNIC GROUPS:
Australian 22.8%, English 22.4%, Pitcairn 20%, Scottish 6%, Irish 5.2%

(2011 est.)

note: respondents were able to identify up to two ancestries; percentages represent a proportion of all responses from people in Norfolk Island, including those who did not identify an ancestry; only top responses are shown

LANGUAGES:
English (official) 44.9%, Norfolk (also known as Norfuk or Norf'k, which is a mixture of 18th century English and ancient Tahitian) 40.3%, Fijian 1.8%, other 6.8%, unspecified 6.2% (2016 est.)

note: data represent language spoken at home

RELIGIONS:
Protestant 46.8% (Anglican 33.6%, Uniting Church in Australia 12.8%, Seventh Day Adventist 3.2%), Roman Catholic 12.6%, other Christian 2.9%, other 1.4%, none 26.7%, unspecified 9.5% (2016 est.)

POPULATION GROWTH RATE:
0.01% (2014 est.)
country comparison to the world: 191

POPULATION DISTRIBUTION:

population concentrated around the capital of Kingston

SEX RATIO:

NA

INFANT MORTALITY RATE:

total: NA (2018)

male: NA

female: NA

LIFE EXPECTANCY AT BIRTH:

total population: NA (2017 est.)

male: NA

female: NA

TOTAL FERTILITY RATE:

NA

HIV/AIDS - ADULT PREVALENCE RATE:

NA

HIV/AIDS - PEOPLE LIVING WITH HIV/AIDS:

NA

HIV/AIDS - DEATHS:

NA

EDUCATION EXPENDITURES:

NA

GOVERNMENT :: NORFOLK ISLAND

COUNTRY NAME:

conventional long form: Territory of Norfolk Island

conventional short form: Norfolk Island

etymology: named by British explorer Captain James COOK after Mary HOWARD, Duchess of Norfolk, in 1774

DEPENDENCY STATUS:

self-governing territory of Australia; administered from Canberra by the Department of Regional Australia, Local Government, Arts, and Sport

GOVERNMENT TYPE:

non-self-governing overseas territory of Australia; note - the Norfolk Island Regional Council, which began operations 1 July 2016, is responsible for planning and managing a variety of public services, including those funded by the Government of Australia

CAPITAL:

name: Kingston

geographic coordinates: 29 03 S, 167 58 E

time difference: UTC+11 (16 hours ahead of Washington, DC, during Standard Time)

etymology: the name is a blending of the words "king's" and "town"; the British king at the time of the town's settlement in the late 18th century was George III

ADMINISTRATIVE DIVISIONS:

none (territory of Australia)

INDEPENDENCE:

none (territory of Australia)

NATIONAL HOLIDAY:

Bounty Day (commemorates the arrival of Pitcairn Islanders), 8 June (1856)

CONSTITUTION:

history: previous 1913, 1957; latest effective 7 August 1979

amendments: amended many times, last in 2015 (2017)

LEGAL SYSTEM:

English common law and the laws of Australia

CITIZENSHIP:

see Australia

SUFFRAGE:

18 years of age; universal

EXECUTIVE BRANCH:

chief of state: Queen ELIZABETH II (since 6 February 1952); represented by Governor General of the Commonwealth of Australia General Sir Peter COSGROVE (since 28 March 2014)

head of government: Administrator Eric HUTCHINSON (since 1 April 2017)

cabinet: Executive Council consists of 4 Legislative Assembly members

elections/appointments: the monarchy is hereditary; governor general appointed by the monarch; administrator appointed by the governor general of Australia for a 2-year term and represents the monarch and Australia

LEGISLATIVE BRANCH:

description: unicameral Norfolk Island Regional Council (5 seats; councillors directly elected by simple majority vote to serve 4-year terms); mayor elected annually by the councillors

elections: elections last held 28 May 2016 (next to be held in 2020)

election results: seats by party - independent 5; composition - men 4, women 1, percent of women 20%

note: following an administrative restructuring of local government, the Legislative Assembly was dissolved on 18 June 2015 and replaced by an interim Norfolk Island Advisory Council effective 1 July 2015; the Advisory Council consisted of 5 members appointed by the Norfolk Island administrator based on nominations from the community; following elections on 28 May 2016, the new Norfolk Island Regional Council commenced operations on 1 July 2016

JUDICIAL BRANCH:

highest courts: Supreme Court of Norfolk Island (consists of the chief justice and several justices); note - appeals beyond the Supreme Court of Norfolk Island are heard by the Federal Court and the High Court of Australia

judge selection and term of office: justices appointed by the governor general of Australia from among justices of the Federal Court of Australia; justices serve until mandatory retirement at age 70

subordinate courts: Petty Court of Sessions; specialized courts, including a Coroner's Court and the Employment Tribunal

POLITICAL PARTIES AND LEADERS:

Norfolk Island Labor Party [Mike KELLY]

Norfolk Liberals [John BROWN]

INTERNATIONAL ORGANIZATION PARTICIPATION:

UPU

DIPLOMATIC REPRESENTATION IN THE US:

none (territory of Australia)

DIPLOMATIC REPRESENTATION FROM THE US:

none (territory of Australia)

FLAG DESCRIPTION:

three vertical bands of green (hoist side), white, and green with a large green Norfolk Island pine tree centered in the slightly wider white band; green stands for the rich vegetation on the island, and the pine tree - endemic to the island - is a symbol of Norfolk Island note: somewhat reminiscent of the flag of Canada with its use of only two colors and depiction of a prominent local floral symbol in the central white band; also resembles the green and white triband of Nigeria

NATIONAL SYMBOL(S):
Norfolk Island pine

NATIONAL ANTHEM:
name: Come Ye Blessed

lyrics/music: New Testament/John Prindle SCOTT

note: the local anthem, whose lyrics consist of the words from Matthew 25:34-36, 40, is also known as "The Pitcairn Anthem;" the island does not recognize "Advance Australia Fair" (which other Australian territories use); instead "God Save the Queen" is official (see United Kingdom)

ECONOMY :: NORFOLK ISLAND

ECONOMY - OVERVIEW:
Norfolk Island is suffering from a severe economic downturn. Tourism, the primary economic activity, is the main driver of economic growth. The agricultural sector has become self-sufficient in the production of beef, poultry, and eggs.

GDP (PURCHASING POWER PARITY):
NA

AGRICULTURE - PRODUCTS:
Norfolk Island pine seed, Kentia palm seed, cereals, vegetables, fruit; cattle, poultry

INDUSTRIES:
tourism, light industry, ready mixed concrete

LABOR FORCE:
978 (2006)

country comparison to the world: 229

LABOR FORCE - BY OCCUPATION:
agriculture: 6%

industry: 14%

services: 80% (2006 est.)

BUDGET:
revenues: 4.6 million (FY99/00)

expenditures: 4.8 million (FY99/00)

FISCAL YEAR:
1 July - 30 June

EXPORTS:
NA

EXPORTS - COMMODITIES:
postage stamps, seeds of the Norfolk Island pine and Kentia palm, small quantities of avocados

IMPORTS:
$NA

IMPORTS - COMMODITIES:
NA

DEBT - EXTERNAL:
NA

EXCHANGE RATES:
Australian dollars (AUD) per US dollar -

1.311 (2017 est.)

1.3291 (2016 est.)

1.3291 (2015)

1.3291 (2014 est.)

1.1094 (2013 est.)

COMMUNICATIONS :: NORFOLK ISLAND

TELEPHONE SYSTEM:
general assessment: adequate

domestic: free local calls

international: country code - 672; submarine cable links with Australia and New Zealand; satellite earth station - 1

BROADCAST MEDIA:
1 local radio station; broadcasts of several Australian radio and TV stations available via satellite (2009)

INTERNET COUNTRY CODE:
.nf

INTERNET USERS:
total: 765

percent of population: 34.6% (July 2016 est.)

country comparison to the world: 225

MILITARY AND SECURITY :: NORFOLK ISLAND

MILITARY - NOTE:
defense is the responsibility of Australia

TRANSPORTATION :: NORFOLK ISLAND

AIRPORTS:
1 (2013)

country comparison to the world: 232

AIRPORTS - WITH PAVED RUNWAYS:
total: 1 (2017)

1,524 to 2,437 m: 1 (2017)

ROADWAYS:
total: 80 km (2008)

paved: 53 km (2008)

unpaved: 27 km (2008)

country comparison to the world: 209

PORTS AND TERMINALS:
major seaport(s): Kingston

TRANSNATIONAL ISSUES :: NORFOLK ISLAND

DISPUTES - INTERNATIONAL:
none

EUROPE :: NORTH MACEDONIA

INTRODUCTION :: NORTH MACEDONIA

BACKGROUND:

North Macedonia gained its independence peacefully from Yugoslavia in 1991 under the name of "Macedonia." Greek objection to the new country's name, insisting it implied territorial pretensions to the northern Greek province of Macedonia, and democratic backsliding for several years stalled the country's movement toward Euro-Atlantic integration. Immediately after Macedonia declared independence, Greece sought to block Macedonian efforts to gain UN membership if the name "Macedonia" was used. The country was eventually admitted to the UN in 1993 as "The former Yugoslav Republic of Macedonia," and at the same time it agreed to UN-sponsored negotiations on the name dispute. In 1995, Greece lifted a 20-month trade embargo and the two countries agreed to normalize relations, but the issue of the name remained unresolved and negotiations for a solution continued. Over time, the US and over 130 other nations recognized Macedonia by its constitutional name, Republic of Macedonia. Ethnic Albanian grievances over perceived political and economic inequities escalated into a conflict in 2001 that eventually led to the internationally brokered Ohrid Framework Agreement, which ended the fighting and established guidelines for constitutional amendments and the creation of new laws that enhanced the rights of minorities. In January 2018, the government adopted a new law on languages, which elevated the Albanian language to an official language at the national level, with the Macedonian language remaining the sole official language in international relations. Relations between ethnic Macedonians and ethnic Albanians remain complicated, however.

North Macedonia's pro-Western government has used its time in office since 2017 to sign a historic deal with Greece in June 2018 to end the name dispute and revive Skopje's NATO and EU membership prospects. This followed a nearly three-year political crisis that engulfed the country but ended in June 2017 following a six-month-long government formation period after a closely contested election in December 2016. The crisis began after the 2014 legislative and presidential election, and escalated in 2015 when the opposition party began releasing wiretapped material that revealed alleged widespread government corruption and abuse. Although an EU candidate since 2005, North Macedonia has yet to open EU accession negotiations. The country still faces challenges, including fully implementing reforms to overcome years of democratic backsliding and stimulating economic growth and development. In June 2018, Macedonia and Greece signed the Prespa Accord whereby the Republic of Macedonia agreed to change its name to the Republic of North Macedonia. Following ratification by both countries, the agreement went in to force on 12 February 2019. North Macedonia signed an accession protocol to become a NATO member state in February 2019.

GEOGRAPHY :: NORTH MACEDONIA

LOCATION:
Southeastern Europe, north of Greece

GEOGRAPHIC COORDINATES:
41 50 N, 22 00 E

MAP REFERENCES:
Europe

AREA:
total: 25,713 sq km
land: 25,433 sq km
water: 280 sq km
country comparison to the world: 150

AREA - COMPARATIVE:
slightly larger than Vermont; almost four times the size of Delaware

LAND BOUNDARIES:
total: 838 km
border countries (5): Albania 181 km, Bulgaria 162 km, Greece 234 km, Kosovo 160 km, Serbia 101 km

COASTLINE:
0 km (landlocked)

MARITIME CLAIMS:
none (landlocked)

CLIMATE:
warm, dry summers and autumns; relatively cold winters with heavy snowfall

TERRAIN:
mountainous with deep basins and valleys; three large lakes, each divided by a frontier line; country bisected by the Vardar River

ELEVATION:
mean elevation: 741 m
lowest point: Vardar River 50 m
highest point: Golem Korab (Maja e Korabit) 2,764 m

NATURAL RESOURCES:

low-grade iron ore, copper, lead, zinc, chromite, manganese, nickel, tungsten, gold, silver, asbestos, gypsum, timber, arable land

LAND USE:
agricultural land: 44.3% (2011 est.)

arable land: 16.4% (2011 est.) / permanent crops: 1.4% (2011 est.) / permanent pasture: 26.5% (2011 est.)

forest: 39.8% (2011 est.)

other: 15.9% (2011 est.)

IRRIGATED LAND:
1,280 sq km (2012)

POPULATION DISTRIBUTION:
a fairly even distribution throughout most of the country, with urban areas attracting larger and denser populations

NATURAL HAZARDS:
high seismic risks

ENVIRONMENT - CURRENT ISSUES:
air pollution from metallurgical plants; Skopje has severe air pollution problems every winter as a result of industrial emissions, smoke from wood-buring stoves, and exhaust fumes from old cars

ENVIRONMENT - INTERNATIONAL AGREEMENTS:
party to: Air Pollution, Biodiversity, Climate Change, Climate Change-Kyoto Protocol, Desertification, Endangered Species, Hazardous Wastes, Law of the Sea, Ozone Layer Protection, Wetlands

signed, but not ratified: none of the selected agreements

GEOGRAPHY - NOTE:
landlocked; major transportation corridor from Western and Central Europe to Aegean Sea and Southern Europe to Western Europe

PEOPLE AND SOCIETY :: NORTH MACEDONIA

POPULATION:
2,118,945 (July 2018 est.)

country comparison to the world: 146

NATIONALITY:
noun: Macedonian(s)

adjective: Macedonian

ETHNIC GROUPS:
Macedonian 64.2%, Albanian 25.2%, Turkish 3.9%, Romani 2.7%, Serb 1.8%, other 2.2% (2002 est.)

note: North Macedonia has not conducted a census since 2002; Romani populations are usually underestimated in official statistics and may represent 6.5–13% of North Macedonia's population

LANGUAGES:
Macedonian (official) 66.5%, Albanian 25.1%, Turkish 3.5%, Romani 1.9%, Serbian 1.2%, other (includes Aromanian (Vlach) and Bosnian) 1.8% (2002 est.)

note: minority languages are co-official with Macedonian in municipalities where they are spoken by at least 20% of the population; Albanian is co-official in Tetovo, Brvenica, Vrapciste, and other municipalities; Turkish is co-official in Centar Zupa and Plasnica; Romani is co-official in Suto Orizari; Aromanian is co-official in Krusevo; Serbian is co-official in Cucer Sandevo

RELIGIONS:
Macedonian Orthodox 64.8%, Muslim 33.3%, other Christian 0.4%, other and unspecified 1.5% (2002 est.)

AGE STRUCTURE:
0-14 years: 16.24% (male 177,719 /female 166,374)

15-24 years: 13.41% (male 147,292 /female 136,851)

25-54 years: 44.55% (male 478,851 /female 465,058)

55-64 years: 12.43% (male 129,731 /female 133,645)

65 years and over: 13.38% (male 123,101 /female 160,323) (2018 est.)

DEPENDENCY RATIOS:
total dependency ratio: 41.6 (2015 est.)

youth dependency ratio: 23.8 (2015 est.)

elderly dependency ratio: 17.7 (2015 est.)

potential support ratio: 5.6 (2015 est.)

MEDIAN AGE:
total: 38.2 years (2018 est.)

male: 37.2 years

female: 39.3 years

country comparison to the world: 60

POPULATION GROWTH RATE:
0.19% (2018 est.)

country comparison to the world: 181

BIRTH RATE:
10.8 births/1,000 population (2018 est.)

country comparison to the world: 182

DEATH RATE:
9.6 deaths/1,000 population (2018 est.)

country comparison to the world: 44

NET MIGRATION RATE:
0.7 migrant(s)/1,000 population (2018 est.)

country comparison to the world: 68

POPULATION DISTRIBUTION:
a fairly even distribution throughout most of the country, with urban areas attracting larger and denser populations

URBANIZATION:
urban population: 58.2% of total population (2019)

rate of urbanization: 0.45% annual rate of change (2015-20 est.)

MAJOR URBAN AREAS - POPULATION:
590,000 SKOPJE (capital) (2019)

SEX RATIO:
at birth: 1.07 male(s)/female

0-14 years: 1.07 male(s)/female

15-24 years: 1.08 male(s)/female

25-54 years: 1.03 male(s)/female

55-64 years: 0.97 male(s)/female

65 years and over: 0.77 male(s)/female

total population: 0.99 male(s)/female (2018 est.)

MOTHER'S MEAN AGE AT FIRST BIRTH:
26.8 years (2014 est.)

MATERNAL MORTALITY RATE:
7 deaths/100,000 live births (2017 est.)

country comparison to the world: 155

INFANT MORTALITY RATE:
total: 7.8 deaths/1,000 live births (2018 est.)

male: 8.7 deaths/1,000 live births

female: 6.8 deaths/1,000 live births

country comparison to the world: 154

LIFE EXPECTANCY AT BIRTH:
total population: 75.9 years (2018 est.)

male: 73.8 years

female: 78.2 years

country comparison to the world: 96

TOTAL FERTILITY RATE:
1.49 children born/woman (2018 est.)

country comparison to the world: 198

CONTRACEPTIVE PREVALENCE RATE:
40.2% (2011)

DRINKING WATER SOURCE:
improved:

urban: 99.8% of population

rural: 98.9% of population

total: 99.4% of population

unimproved:

urban: 0.2% of population

rural: 1.1% of population

total: 0.6% of population (2015 est.)

CURRENT HEALTH EXPENDITURE:

6.3% (2016)

PHYSICIANS DENSITY:

2.87 physicians/1,000 population (2015)

HOSPITAL BED DENSITY:

4.4 beds/1,000 population (2013)

SANITATION FACILITY ACCESS:

improved:

urban: 97.2% of population (2015 est.)

rural: 82.6% of population (2015 est.)

total: 90.9% of population (2015 est.)

unimproved:

urban: 2.8% of population (2015 est.)

rural: 17.4% of population (2015 est.)

total: 9.1% of population (2015 est.)

HIV/AIDS - ADULT PREVALENCE RATE:

<.1% (2018 est.)

HIV/AIDS - PEOPLE LIVING WITH HIV/AIDS:

<500 (2018 est.)

HIV/AIDS - DEATHS:

300 (2018 est.)

country comparison to the world: 63

OBESITY - ADULT PREVALENCE RATE:

22.4% (2016)

country comparison to the world: 77

CHILDREN UNDER THE AGE OF 5 YEARS UNDERWEIGHT:

1.3% (2011)

country comparison to the world: 119

EDUCATION EXPENDITURES:

NA

LITERACY:

definition: age 15 and over can read and write

total population: 97.8%

male: 98.8%

female: 96.8% (2015 est.)

SCHOOL LIFE EXPECTANCY (PRIMARY TO TERTIARY EDUCATION):

total: 13 years

male: 13 years

female: 13 years (2015)

UNEMPLOYMENT, YOUTH AGES 15-24:

total: 46.7%

male: 45.7%

female: 48.6% (2017 est.)

country comparison to the world: 8

GOVERNMENT :: NORTH MACEDONIA

COUNTRY NAME:

conventional long form: Republic of North Macedonia

conventional short form: North Macedonia

local long form: Republika Severna Makedonija

local short form: Severna Makedonija

former: Democratic Federal Macedonia, People's Republic of Macedonia, Socialist Republic of Macedonia, Republic of Macedonia

etymology: the country name derives from the ancient kingdom of Macedon (7th to 2nd centuries B.C.)

GOVERNMENT TYPE:

parliamentary republic

CAPITAL:

name: Skopje

geographic coordinates: 42 00 N, 21 26 E

time difference: UTC+1 (6 hours ahead of Washington, DC, during Standard Time)

daylight saving time: +1hr, begins last Sunday in March; ends last Sunday in October

etymology: Skopje derives from its ancient name Scupi, the Latin designation of a classical era Greco-Roman frontier fortress town; the name may go back even further to a pre-Greek, Illyrian name

ADMINISTRATIVE DIVISIONS:

70 municipalities (opstini, singular - opstina) and 1 city* (grad); Aracinovo, Berovo, Bitola, Bogdanci, Bogovinje, Bosilovo, Brvenica, Caska, Centar Zupa, Cesinovo-Oblesevo, Cucer Sandevo, Debar, Debarca, Delcevo, Demir Hisar, Demir Kapija, Dojran, Dolneni, Gevgelija, Gostivar, Gradsko, Ilinden, Jegunovce, Karbinci, Kavadarci, Kicevo, Kocani, Konce, Kratovo, Kriva Palanka, Krivogastani, Krusevo, Kumanovo, Lipkovo, Lozovo, Makedonska Kamenica, Makedonski Brod, Mavrovo i Rostusa, Mogila, Negotino, Novaci, Novo Selo, Ohrid, Pehcevo, Petrovec, Plasnica, Prilep, Probistip, Radovis, Rankovce, Resen, Rosoman, Skopje*, Sopiste, Staro Nagoricane, Stip, Struga, Strumica, Studenicani, Sveti Nikole, Tearce, Tetovo, Valandovo, Vasilevo, Veles, Vevcani, Vinica, Vrapciste, Zelenikovo, Zelino, Zrnovci

INDEPENDENCE:

8 September 1991 (referendum by registered voters endorsed independence from Yugoslavia)

NATIONAL HOLIDAY:

Independence Day, 8 September (1991), also known as National Day

CONSTITUTION:

history: several previous; latest adopted 17 November 1991, effective 20 November 1991

amendments: proposed by the president of the republic, by the government, by at least 30 members of the Assembly, or by petition of at least 150,000 citizens; final approval requires a two-thirds majority vote by the Assembly; amended several times, last in 2019 (2019)

LEGAL SYSTEM:

civil law system; judicial review of legislative acts

INTERNATIONAL LAW ORGANIZATION PARTICIPATION:

has not submitted an ICJ jurisdiction declaration; accepts ICCt jurisdiction

CITIZENSHIP:

citizenship by birth: no

citizenship by descent only: at least one parent must be a citizen of North Macedonia

dual citizenship recognized: no

residency requirement for naturalization: 8 years

SUFFRAGE:

18 years of age; universal

EXECUTIVE BRANCH:

chief of state: President Stevo PENDAROVSKI (since 12 May 2019)

head of government: Prime Minister Zoran ZAEV (since 31 May 2017)

cabinet: Council of Ministers elected by the Assembly by simple majority vote; note - after the December 2016 election, VMRO-DPMNE won a plurality of the seats but failed to gather a majority in the Assembly to establish a government; SDSM, DUI, and the Alliance for Albanians formed an alliance; however, the president refused to give the SDSM leader the mandate to form a new government; VMRO-DPMNE blocked the election of a Speaker of the Assembly until late April 2017, when a majority of Assembly members elected Talat XHAFERI as speaker; in response, demonstrators disrupted the Assembly building, attacking journalists and Assembly members; President Gjorge IVANOV eventually gave the mandate to SDSM's Zoran ZAEV to form a new coalition government, and the Assembly confirmed the Cabinet on 31 May 2017

elections/appointments: president directly elected using a modified 2-round system; a candidate can only be elected in the first round with an absolute majority from all registered voters; in the second round, voter turnout must be at least 40% for the result to be deemed valid; president elected for a 5-year term (eligible for a second term); election last held on 21 April and 5 May 2019 (next to be held in 2024); following legislative elections, the leader of the majority party or majority coalition is usually elected prime minister by the Assembly

election results: Stevo PENDAROVSKI elected president in second round; percent of vote in first round - Stevo PENDAROVSKI (SDSM) 44.8%, Gordana SILJANOVSKA-DAVKOVA (VMRO-DPMNE) 44.2%, Blenim REKA (independent) 11.1%; percent of vote in second round - Stevo PENDAROVSKI 53.6%, Gordana SILJANOVSKA-DAVKOVA 46.4%

LEGISLATIVE BRANCH:

description: unicameral Assembly - Sobraine in Macedonian, Kuvend in Albanian (between 120 and 140 seats, currently 120; members directly elected in multi-seat constituencies by closed-list proportional representation vote; possibility of 3 directly elected in diaspora constituencies by simple majority vote provided there is sufficient voter turnout; members serve 4-year terms)

elections: last held on 11 December 2016, with a second round held in one polling station on 25 December 2016 (next to be held in 2020)

election results: percent of vote by party/coalition - VMRO-DPMNE 38.1%, SDSM coalition 36.7%, BDI 7.3%, Besa Movement 4.9%, AfA 3.1%, PDSh 2.7%, other 7.2%; seats by party - VMRO-DPMNE 51, SDSM coalition 49, BDI 10, Besa Movement 5, AfA 3, PDSh 2; note - the 3 seats for diaspora went unfilled because none of the candidates won the 6,500 minimum vote threshold

note: seats by party/coalition as of May 2019 - ruling coalition 68 (SDSM coalition 49, BDI 10, Besa Movement 3, PDSh 2, other 5), opposition coalition 52 (VMRO-DPMNE coalition 48, Besa Movement 2, AfA 2); composition - men 75, women 45, percent of women 37.5%

JUDICIAL BRANCH:

highest courts: Supreme Court (consists of 22 judges); Constitutional Court (consists of 9 judges)

judge selection and term of office: Supreme Court judges nominated by the Judicial Council, a 7-member body of legal professionals, and appointed by the Assembly; judge tenure NA; Constitutional Court judges appointed by the Assembly for nonrenewable, 9-year terms

subordinate courts: Courts of Appeal; Basic Courts

POLITICAL PARTIES AND LEADERS:

Alliance for Albanians or AfA [Ziadin SELA]
Besa Movement [Bilal KASAMI]
Democratic Party of Albanians or PDSh [Menduh THACI]
Democratic Union for Integration or BDI [Ali AHMETI]
Internal Macedonian Revolutionary Organization - Democratic Party for Macedonian National Unity or VMRO-DPMNE [Hristijan MICKOSKI]
Liberal Democratic Party or LDP [Goran MILEVSKI]
Social Democratic Union of Macedonia or SDSM [Zoran ZAEV]
Socialist Party of Macedonia or SPM [Ljubislav IVANOV-DZINGO]

note: during the 2016 parliamentary elections SDSM and VMRO-DPMNE each led coalitions

INTERNATIONAL ORGANIZATION PARTICIPATION:

BIS, CD, CE, CEI, EAPC, EBRD, EU (candidate country), FAO, IAEA, IBRD, ICAO, ICC (NGOs), ICCt, ICRM, IDA, IFAD, IFC, IFRCS, ILO, IMF, IMO, Interpol, IOC, IOM, IPU, ISO, ITU, ITUC (NGOs), MIGA, OAS (observer), OIF, OPCW, OSCE, PCA, PFP, SELEC, UN, UNCTAD, UNESCO, UNHCR, UNIDO, UNIFIL, UNWTO, UPU, WCO, WHO, WIPO, WMO, WTO

DIPLOMATIC REPRESENTATION IN THE US:

Ambassador Vasko NAUMOVSKI (since 18 November 2014)

chancery: 2129 Wyoming Avenue NW, Washington, DC 20008

telephone: [1] (202) 667-0501

FAX: [1] (202) 667-2131

consulate(s) general: Chicago, Detroit, New York

DIPLOMATIC REPRESENTATION FROM THE US:

chief of mission: Ambassador Kate Marie BYRNES (since 12 July 2019)

telephone: [389] (2) 310-2000

embassy: Str. Samoilova, Nr. 21, 1000 Skopje

mailing address: American Embassy Skopje, US Department of State, 7120 Skopje Place, Washington, DC 20521-7120 (pouch)

FAX: [389] (2) 310-2499

FLAG DESCRIPTION:

a yellow sun (the Sun of Liberty) with eight broadening rays extending to the edges of the red field; the red and yellow colors have long been associated with Macedonia

NATIONAL SYMBOL(S):

eight-rayed sun; national colors: red, yellow

NATIONAL ANTHEM:

name: "Denes nad Makedonija" (Today Over Macedonia)

lyrics/music: Vlado MALESKI/Todor SKALOVSKI

note: written in 1943 and adopted in 1991, the song previously served as the anthem of the Socialist Republic of Macedonia while part of Yugoslavia

ECONOMY :: NORTH MACEDONIA

ECONOMY - OVERVIEW:

Since its independence in 1991, Macedonia has made progress in liberalizing its economy and improving its business environment. Its low tax rates and free economic zones have helped to attract foreign investment, which is still low relative to the rest of Europe. Corruption and weak rule of law remain significant problems. Some businesses complain of opaque regulations and unequal enforcement of the law.

Macedonia's economy is closely linked to Europe as a customer for exports and source of investment, and has suffered as a result of prolonged weakness in the euro zone. Unemployment has remained consistently high at about 23%, but may be overstated based on the existence of an extensive gray market, estimated to be between 20% and 45% of GDP, which is not captured by official statistics.

Macedonia is working to build a country-wide natural gas pipeline and distribution network. Currently,

Macedonia receives its small natural gas supplies from Russia via Bulgaria. In 2016, Macedonia signed a memorandum of understanding with Greece to build an interconnector that could connect to the Trans Adriatic Pipeline that will traverse the region once complete, or to an LNG import terminal in Greece.

Macedonia maintained macroeconomic stability through the global financial crisis by conducting prudent monetary policy, which keeps the domestic currency pegged to the euro, and inflation at a low level. However, in the last two years, the internal political crisis has hampered economic performance, with GDP growth slowing in 2016 and 2017, and both domestic private and public investments declining. Fiscal policies were lax, with unproductive public expenditures, including subsidies and pension increases, and rising guarantees for the debt of state owned enterprises, and fiscal targets were consistently missed. In 2017, public debt stabilized at about 47% of GDP, still relatively low compared to its Western Balkan neighbors and the rest of Europe.

GDP (PURCHASING POWER PARITY):

$31.03 billion (2017 est.)

$31.02 billion (2016 est.)

$30.15 billion (2015 est.)

note: data are in 2017 dollars; Macedonia has a large informal sector that may not be reflected in these data

country comparison to the world: 131

GDP (OFFICIAL EXCHANGE RATE):

$11.37 billion (2017 est.)

GDP - REAL GROWTH RATE:

0% (2017 est.)

2.9% (2016 est.)

3.9% (2015 est.)

country comparison to the world: 197

GDP - PER CAPITA (PPP):

$14,900 (2017 est.)

$15,000 (2016 est.)

$14,600 (2015 est.)

note: data are in 2017 dollars

country comparison to the world: 113

GROSS NATIONAL SAVING:

30.3% of GDP (2017 est.)

29.9% of GDP (2016 est.)

28.5% of GDP (2015 est.)

country comparison to the world: 29

GDP - COMPOSITION, BY END USE:

household consumption: 65.6% (2017 est.)

government consumption: 15.6% (2017 est.)

investment in fixed capital: 13.6% (2017 est.)

investment in inventories: 20.2% (2017 est.)

exports of goods and services: 54% (2017 est.)

imports of goods and services: -69% (2017 est.)

GDP - COMPOSITION, BY SECTOR OF ORIGIN:

agriculture: 10.9% (2017 est.)

industry: 26.6% (2017 est.)

services: 62.5% (2017 est.)

AGRICULTURE - PRODUCTS:

grapes, tobacco, vegetables, fruits; milk, eggs

INDUSTRIES:

food processing, beverages, textiles, chemicals, iron, steel, cement, energy, pharmaceuticals, automotive parts

INDUSTRIAL PRODUCTION GROWTH RATE:

-7.8% (2017 est.)

country comparison to the world: 198

LABOR FORCE:

950,800 (2017 est.)

country comparison to the world: 147

LABOR FORCE - BY OCCUPATION:

agriculture: 16.2%

industry: 29.2%

services: 54.5% (2017 est.)

UNEMPLOYMENT RATE:

22.4% (2017 est.)

23.8% (2016 est.)

country comparison to the world: 191

POPULATION BELOW POVERTY LINE:

21.5% (2015 est.)

HOUSEHOLD INCOME OR CONSUMPTION BY PERCENTAGE SHARE:

lowest 10%: 1.7%

highest 10%: 25% (2015 est.)

DISTRIBUTION OF FAMILY INCOME - GINI INDEX:

33.7 (2015)

35.2 (2014)

country comparison to the world: 111

BUDGET:

revenues: 3.295 billion (2017 est.)

expenditures: 3.605 billion (2017 est.)

TAXES AND OTHER REVENUES:

29% (of GDP) (2017 est.)

country comparison to the world: 88

BUDGET SURPLUS (+) OR DEFICIT (-):

-2.7% (of GDP) (2017 est.)

country comparison to the world: 122

PUBLIC DEBT:

39.3% of GDP (2017 est.)

39.5% of GDP (2016 est.)

note: official data from Ministry of Finance; data cover central government debt; this data excludes debt instruments issued (or owned) by government entities other than the treasury; includes treasury debt held by foreign entitites; excludes debt issued by sub-national entities; there are no debt instruments sold for social funds

country comparison to the world: 134

FISCAL YEAR:

calendar year

INFLATION RATE (CONSUMER PRICES):

1.4% (2017 est.)

-0.2% (2016 est.)

country comparison to the world: 78

CENTRAL BANK DISCOUNT RATE:

3.25% (31 March 2017)

3.75% (31 December 2016)

note: series discontinued in January 2010; the discount rate has been replaced by a referent rate for calculating the penalty rate

country comparison to the world: 106

COMMERCIAL BANK PRIME LENDING RATE:

6.21% (31 December 2017 est.)

6.61% (31 December 2016 est.)

country comparison to the world: 125

STOCK OF NARROW MONEY:

$2.403 billion (31 December 2017 est.)

$1.909 billion (31 December 2016 est.)

country comparison to the world: 129

STOCK OF BROAD MONEY:

$2.403 billion (31 December 2017 est.)

$1.909 billion (31 December 2016 est.)

country comparison to the world: 136

STOCK OF DOMESTIC CREDIT:

$6.243 billion (31 December 2017 est.)

$5.01 billion (31 December 2016 est.)

country comparison to the world: 123

MARKET VALUE OF PUBLICLY TRADED SHARES:

$2.078 billion (31 December 2016)

$1.853 billion (31 December 2015)

$2.269 billion (31 December 2014)

country comparison to the world: 98

CURRENT ACCOUNT BALANCE:

-$151 million (2017 est.)

-$293 million (2016 est.)

country comparison to the world: 92

EXPORTS:

$4.601 billion (2017 est.)

$3.75 billion (2016 est.)

country comparison to the world: 113

EXPORTS - PARTNERS:

Germany 46.7%, Bulgaria 6.1%, Serbia 4.4%, Belgium 4.1% (2017)

EXPORTS - COMMODITIES:

foodstuffs, beverages, tobacco; textiles, miscellaneous manufactures, iron, steel; automotive parts

IMPORTS:

$6.63 billion (2017 est.)

$5.805 billion (2016 est.)

country comparison to the world: 116

IMPORTS - COMMODITIES:

machinery and equipment, automobiles, chemicals, fuels, food products

IMPORTS - PARTNERS:

Germany 11.9%, UK 10%, Greece 8%, Serbia 7.1%, China 5.9%, Italy 5.5%, Turkey 4.5%, Bulgaria 4.3% (2017)

RESERVES OF FOREIGN EXCHANGE AND GOLD:

$2.802 billion (31 December 2017 est.)

$2.755 billion (31 December 2016 est.)

country comparison to the world: 112

DEBT - EXTERNAL:

$8.79 billion (31 December 2017 est.)

$7.685 billion (31 December 2016 est.)

country comparison to the world: 117

STOCK OF DIRECT FOREIGN INVESTMENT - AT HOME:

$6.937 billion (31 December 2017 est.)

$6.8 billion (31 December 2016 est.)

country comparison to the world: 99

STOCK OF DIRECT FOREIGN INVESTMENT - ABROAD:

$1.169 billion (31 December 2017 est.)

$849.1 million (31 December 2016 est.)

country comparison to the world: 88

EXCHANGE RATES:

Macedonian denars (MKD) per US dollar -

55.8 (2017 est.)

55.733 (2016 est.)

55.733 (2015 est.)

55.537 (2014 est.)

46.437 (2013 est.)

ENERGY :: NORTH MACEDONIA

ELECTRICITY ACCESS:

electrification - total population: 100% (2016)

ELECTRICITY - PRODUCTION:

5.396 billion kWh (2016 est.)

country comparison to the world: 119

ELECTRICITY - CONSUMPTION:

6.42 billion kWh (2016 est.)

country comparison to the world: 112

ELECTRICITY - EXPORTS:

58.5 million kWh (2016 est.)

country comparison to the world: 84

ELECTRICITY - IMPORTS:

2.191 billion kWh (2016 est.)

country comparison to the world: 55

ELECTRICITY - INSTALLED GENERATING CAPACITY:

1.828 million kW (2016 est.)

country comparison to the world: 115

ELECTRICITY - FROM FOSSIL FUELS:

60% of total installed capacity (2016 est.)

country comparison to the world: 132

ELECTRICITY - FROM NUCLEAR FUELS:

0% of total installed capacity (2017 est.)

country comparison to the world: 133

ELECTRICITY - FROM HYDROELECTRIC PLANTS:

37% of total installed capacity (2017 est.)

country comparison to the world: 57

ELECTRICITY - FROM OTHER RENEWABLE SOURCES:

3% of total installed capacity (2017 est.)

country comparison to the world: 126

CRUDE OIL - PRODUCTION:

0 bbl/day (2018 est.)

country comparison to the world: 166

CRUDE OIL - EXPORTS:

142 bbl/day (2015 est.)

country comparison to the world: 80

CRUDE OIL - IMPORTS:

0 bbl/day (2015 est.)

country comparison to the world: 157

CRUDE OIL - PROVED RESERVES:

0 bbl (1 January 2018 est.)

country comparison to the world: 161

REFINED PETROLEUM PRODUCTS - PRODUCTION:

0 bbl/day (2015 est.)

country comparison to the world: 169

REFINED PETROLEUM PRODUCTS - CONSUMPTION:

21,000 bbl/day (2016 est.)

country comparison to the world: 138

REFINED PETROLEUM PRODUCTS - EXPORTS:

3,065 bbl/day (2015 est.)

country comparison to the world: 99

REFINED PETROLEUM PRODUCTS - IMPORTS:

23,560 bbl/day (2015 est.)

country comparison to the world: 111

NATURAL GAS - PRODUCTION:

0 cu m (2017 est.)

country comparison to the world: 162

NATURAL GAS - CONSUMPTION:

198.2 million cu m (2017 est.)

country comparison to the world: 105

NATURAL GAS - EXPORTS:

0 cu m (2017 est.)

country comparison to the world: 143

NATURAL GAS - IMPORTS:

198.2 million cu m (2017 est.)

country comparison to the world: 72

NATURAL GAS - PROVED RESERVES:

0 cu m (31 December 2016 est.)

country comparison to the world: 163

CARBON DIOXIDE EMISSIONS FROM CONSUMPTION OF ENERGY:

7.459 million Mt (2017 est.)

country comparison to the world: 123

COMMUNICATIONS :: NORTH MACEDONIA

TELEPHONES - FIXED LINES:

total subscriptions: 361,269

subscriptions per 100 inhabitants: 17 (2017 est.)

country comparison to the world: 108

TELEPHONES - MOBILE CELLULAR:

total subscriptions: 2,121,805

subscriptions per 100 inhabitants: 101 (2017 est.)

country comparison to the world: 148

TELEPHONE SYSTEM:

general assessment: being part of the EU pre-accession process has led to a stronger teledensity with closer regulatory framework and independent regulators; administrative ties with the European Union have led to progress; broadband services are widely available; more customers moving to fiber networks; 2 mobile network operators; end of roaming tariffs (2018)

domestic: fixed-line 17 per 100 and mobile-cellular 101 per 100 subscriptions (2018)

international: country code - 389

BROADCAST MEDIA:

public service TV broadcaster Macedonian Radio and Television operates 3 national terrestrial TV channels and 2 satellite TV channels; additionally, there are 10 regional TV stations that broadcast nationally using terrestrial transmitters, 54 TV channels with concession for cable TV, 9 regional TV stations with concessions for cable TV; 4 satellite TV channels broadcasting on a national level, 21 local commercial TV channels, and a large number of cable operators that offer domestic and international programming; the public radio broadcaster operates over 3 stations; there are 4 privately owned radio stations that broadcast nationally; 17 regional radio stations, and 49 local commercial radio stations (2019)

INTERNET COUNTRY CODE:

.mk

INTERNET USERS:

total: 1.475 million

percent of population: 70.4% (July 2016 est.)

country comparison to the world: 121

BROADBAND - FIXED SUBSCRIPTIONS:

total: 386,718

subscriptions per 100 inhabitants: 18 (2017 est.)

country comparison to the world: 88

MILITARY AND SECURITY :: NORTH MACEDONIA

MILITARY EXPENDITURES:

1.19% of GDP (2018)

0.99% of GDP (2017)

0.96% of GDP (2016)

1% of GDP (2015)

1.09% of GDP (2014)

country comparison to the world: 107

MILITARY AND SECURITY FORCES:

Army of the Republic of North Macedonia (ARSM; includes General Staff and subordinate Joint Operational Command, Logistic Support Command, Training and Doctrine Command, Special Ops Regiment, Electronic Surveillance Center, and Air Surveillance Center) (2019)

Note: The Joint Operations Command includes air, ground, support, and reserve forces.

MILITARY SERVICE AGE AND OBLIGATION:

18 years of age for voluntary military service; conscription abolished in 2008 (2013)

TRANSPORTATION :: NORTH MACEDONIA

CIVIL AIRCRAFT REGISTRATION COUNTRY CODE PREFIX:

Z3 (2016)

AIRPORTS:

10 (2013)

country comparison to the world: 156

AIRPORTS - WITH PAVED RUNWAYS:

total: 8 (2017)

2,438 to 3,047 m: 2 (2017)

under 914 m: 6 (2017)

AIRPORTS - WITH UNPAVED RUNWAYS:

total: 2 (2013)

914 to 1,523 m: 1 (2013)

under 914 m: 1 (2013)

PIPELINES:

262 km gas, 120 km oil (2017)

RAILWAYS:

total: 925 km (2017)

standard gauge: 925 km 1.435-m gauge (313 km electrified) (2017)

country comparison to the world: 93

ROADWAYS:

total: 14,182 km (includes 290 km of expressways) (2017)

paved: 9,633 km (2017)

unpaved: 4,549 km (2017)

country comparison to the world: 125

TRANSNATIONAL ISSUES :: NORTH MACEDONIA

DISPUTES - INTERNATIONAL:

Kosovo and North Macedonia completed demarcation of their boundary in September 2008

REFUGEES AND INTERNALLY DISPLACED PERSONS:

stateless persons: 571 (2018)

note: 483,236 estimated refugee and migrant arrivals (January 2015-December 2019); North Macedonia is predominantly a transit country and hosts fewer than 50 refugees and asylum seekers as of October 2017; 3,132 migrant arrivals in 2018

ILLICIT DRUGS:

major transshipment point for Southwest Asian heroin and hashish; minor transit point for South American cocaine destined for Europe; although not a financial center and most criminal activity is thought to be domestic, money laundering is a problem due to a mostly cash-based economy and weak enforcement

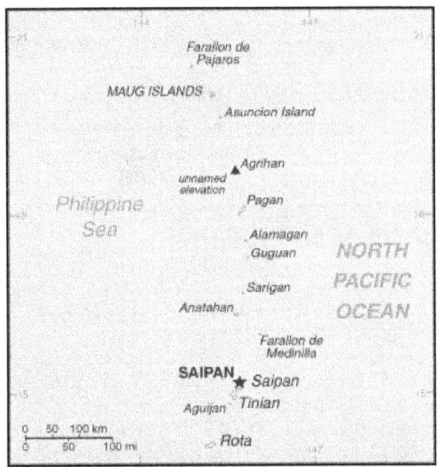

AUSTRALIA - OCEANIA :: NORTHERN MARIANA ISLANDS

INTRODUCTION :: NORTHERN MARIANA ISLANDS

BACKGROUND:

Under US administration as part of the UN Trust Territory of the Pacific, the people of the Northern Mariana Islands decided in the 1970s not to seek independence but instead to forge closer links with the US. Negotiations for territorial status began in 1972. A covenant to establish a commonwealth in political union with the US was approved in 1975, and came into force on 24 March 1976. A new government and constitution went into effect in 1978.

GEOGRAPHY :: NORTHERN MARIANA ISLANDS

LOCATION:
Oceania, islands in the North Pacific Ocean, about three-quarters of the way from Hawaii to the Philippines

GEOGRAPHIC COORDINATES:
15 12 N, 145 45 E

MAP REFERENCES:
Oceania

AREA:
total: 464 sq km
land: 464 sq km
water: 0 sq km
note: consists of 14 islands including Saipan, Rota, and Tinian
country comparison to the world: 197

AREA - COMPARATIVE:
2.5 times the size of Washington, DC

LAND BOUNDARIES:
0 km

COASTLINE:
1,482 km

MARITIME CLAIMS:
territorial sea: 12 nm
exclusive economic zone: 200 nm

CLIMATE:
tropical marine; moderated by northeast trade winds, little seasonal temperature variation; dry season December to June, rainy season July to October

TERRAIN:
the southern islands in this north-south trending archipelago are limestone, with fringing coral reefs; the northern islands are volcanic, with active volcanoes on several islands

ELEVATION:
lowest point: Pacific Ocean 0 m
highest point: unnamed elevation on Agrihan 965 m

NATURAL RESOURCES:
arable land, fish

LAND USE:
agricultural land: 6.6% (2011 est.)
arable land: 2.2% (2011 est.) / permanent crops: 2.2% (2011 est.) / permanent pasture: 2.2% (2011 est.)
forest: 65.5% (2011 est.)
other: 27.9% (2011 est.)

IRRIGATED LAND:
1 sq km (2012)

POPULATION DISTRIBUTION:
approximately 90% of the population lives on the island of Saipan

NATURAL HAZARDS:
active volcanoes on Pagan and Agrihan; typhoons (especially August to November)

ENVIRONMENT - CURRENT ISSUES:
contamination of groundwater on Saipan may contribute to disease; clean-up of landfill; protection of endangered species conflicts with development

GEOGRAPHY - NOTE:
strategic location in the North Pacific Ocean

PEOPLE AND SOCIETY :: NORTHERN MARIANA ISLANDS

POPULATION:
51,994 (July 2018 est.)
country comparison to the world: 209

NATIONALITY:
noun: NA (US citizens)
adjective: NA

ETHNIC GROUPS:
Asian 50% (includes Filipino 35.3%, Chinese 6.8%, Korean 4.2%, and other Asian 3.7%), Native Hawaiian or other Pacific Islander 34.9% (includes Chamorro 23.9%, Carolinian 4.6%, and other Native Hawaiian or Pacific Islander 6.4%), other 2.5%, two or more ethnicities or races 12.7% (2010 est.)

LANGUAGES:
Philippine languages 32.8%, Chamorro (official) 24.1%, English (official)

17%, other Pacific island languages 10.1%, Chinese 6.8%, other Asian languages 7.3%, other 1.9% (2010 est.)

RELIGIONS:

Christian (Roman Catholic majority, although traditional beliefs and taboos may still be found)

AGE STRUCTURE:

0-14 years: 26.17% (male 7,355 /female 6,252)

15-24 years: 15.71% (male 4,365 /female 3,804)

25-54 years: 39.14% (male 10,545 /female 9,805)

55-64 years: 13% (male 3,701 /female 3,057)

65 years and over: 5.98% (male 1,672 /female 1,438) (2018 est.)

MEDIAN AGE:

total: 33.4 years (2018 est.)

male: 32.4 years

female: 34.3 years

country comparison to the world: 94

POPULATION GROWTH RATE:

-0.52% (2018 est.)

country comparison to the world: 222

BIRTH RATE:

14.9 births/1,000 population (2018 est.)

country comparison to the world: 126

DEATH RATE:

4.9 deaths/1,000 population (2018 est.)

country comparison to the world: 198

NET MIGRATION RATE:

-15.2 migrant(s)/1,000 population (2018 est.)

country comparison to the world: 221

POPULATION DISTRIBUTION:

approximately 90% of the population lives on the island of Saipan

URBANIZATION:

urban population: 91.7% of total population (2019)

rate of urbanization: 0.29% annual rate of change (2015-20 est.)

MAJOR URBAN AREAS - POPULATION:

51,000 SAIPAN (capital) (2018)

SEX RATIO:

at birth: 1.17 male(s)/female

0-14 years: 1.18 male(s)/female

15-24 years: 1.15 male(s)/female

25-54 years: 1.08 male(s)/female

55-64 years: 1.21 male(s)/female

65 years and over: 1.16 male(s)/female

total population: 1.13 male(s)/female (2018 est.)

INFANT MORTALITY RATE:

total: 12.3 deaths/1,000 live births (2018 est.)

male: 14.6 deaths/1,000 live births

female: 9.6 deaths/1,000 live births

country comparison to the world: 111

LIFE EXPECTANCY AT BIRTH:

total population: 75.6 years (2018 est.)

male: 73.6 years

female: 78.1 years

country comparison to the world: 105

TOTAL FERTILITY RATE:

2.76 children born/woman (2018 est.)

country comparison to the world: 63

DRINKING WATER SOURCE:

improved:

urban: 97.5% of population

rural: 97.5% of population

total: 97.5% of population

unimproved:

urban: 2.5% of population

rural: 2.5% of population

total: 2.5% of population (2015 est.)

PHYSICIANS DENSITY:

SANITATION FACILITY ACCESS:

improved:

urban: 79.7% of population (2015 est.)

rural: 79.7% of population (2015 est.)

total: 79.7% of population (2015 est.)

unimproved:

urban: 20.3% of population (2015 est.)

rural: 20.3% of population (2015 est.)

total: 20.3% of population (2015 est.)

HIV/AIDS - ADULT PREVALENCE RATE:

NA

HIV/AIDS - PEOPLE LIVING WITH HIV/AIDS:

NA

HIV/AIDS - DEATHS:

NA

EDUCATION EXPENDITURES:

NA

GOVERNMENT :: NORTHERN MARIANA ISLANDS

COUNTRY NAME:

conventional long form: Commonwealth of the Northern Mariana Islands

conventional short form: Northern Mariana Islands

former: Trust Territory of the Pacific Islands, Mariana Islands District

abbreviation: CNMI

etymology: formally claimed and named by Spain in 1667 in honor of the Spanish Queen, MARIANA of Austria

DEPENDENCY STATUS:

commonwealth in political union with and under the sovereignty of the US; federal funds to the Commonwealth administered by the US Department of the Interior, Office of Insular Affairs

GOVERNMENT TYPE:

republican form of government with separate executive, legislative, and judicial branches; a commonwealth in political union with and under the sovereignty of the US

CAPITAL:

name: Saipan

geographic coordinates: 15 12 N, 145 45 E

time difference: UTC+10 (15 hours ahead of Washington, DC, during Standard Time)

ADMINISTRATIVE DIVISIONS:

none (commonwealth in political union with the US); there are no first-order administrative divisions as defined by the US Government, but there are 4 municipalities at the second order: Northern Islands, Rota, Saipan, Tinian

INDEPENDENCE:

none (commonwealth in political union with the US)

NATIONAL HOLIDAY:

Commonwealth Day, 8 January (1978)

CONSTITUTION:

history: partially effective 9 January 1978 (Constitution of the Commonwealth of the Northern

Mariana Islands); fully effective 4 November 1986 (Covenant Agreement)

amendments: proposed by constitutional convention, by public petition, or by the Legislature; ratification of proposed amendments requires approval by voters at the next general election or special election; amendments proposed by constitutional convention or by petition become effective if approved by a majority of voters and at least two-thirds majority of voters in each of two senatorial districts; amendments proposed by the Legislature are effective if approved by majority vote; amended several times, last in 2012 (2017)

LEGAL SYSTEM:

the laws of the US apply, except for customs and some aspects of taxation

CITIZENSHIP:

see United States

SUFFRAGE:

18 years of age; universal; note - indigenous inhabitants are US citizens but do not vote in US presidential elections

EXECUTIVE BRANCH:

chief of state: President Donald J. TRUMP (since 20 January 2017); Vice President Michael R. PENCE (since 20 January 2017)

head of government: Governor Ralph TORRES (since 29 December 2015); Lieutenant Governor Victor HOCOG (since 29 December 2015)

cabinet: Cabinet appointed by the governor with the advice and consent of the Senate

elections/appointments: president and vice president indirectly elected on the same ballot by an Electoral College of 'electors' chosen from each state; president and vice president serve a 4-year term (eligible for a second term); under the US Constitution, residents of the Northern Mariana Islands do not vote in elections for US president and vice president; however, they may vote in Democratic and Republican party presidential primary elections; governor directly elected by absolute majority vote in 2 rounds if needed; election last held on 13 November 2018 (next to be held in 2022)

election results: Ralph TORRES elected governor; percent of vote - Ralph TORRES (Republican) 62.2%, Juan BABAUTA (Independent) 37.8%; Arnold PALACIOS elected Lieutenant Governor

LEGISLATIVE BRANCH:

description: bicameral Northern Marianas Commonwealth Legislature consists of:
Senate (9 seats; members directly elected in single-seat constituencies by simple majority vote to serve 4-year terms)
House of Representatives (20 seats; members directly elected in single-seat constituencies by simple majority vote to serve 2-year terms)

the Northern Mariana Islands directly elects 1 delegate to the US House of Representatives by simple majority vote to serve a 2-year term

elections:
CNMI Senate - last held on 8 November 2016 (next to be held in November 2020)
CNMI House of Representatives - last held on 13 November 2018 (next to be held in November 2020)
Commonwealth of Northern Mariana Islands delegate to the US House of Representatives - last held on 13 November 2018 (next to be held in November 2020)

election results:
CNMI Senate - percent of vote by party - NA; seats by party - Republican Party 6, independent 3; composition - men 8, women 1, percent of women 11.1%
CNMI House of Representatives - percent of vote by party - NA; seats by party - Republican Party 13, independent 7; composition - men 17, women 3, percent of women 15%; note - total CNMI Legislature percent of women 13.8%

delegate to US House of Representatives - seat won by Democratic Party; composition - 1 man

note: the Northern Mariana Islands delegate to the US House of Representatives can vote when serving on a committee and when the House meets as the "Committee of the Whole House" but not when legislation is submitted for a "full floor" House vote

JUDICIAL BRANCH:

highest courts: Supreme Court of the Commonwealth of the Northern Mariana Islands (CNMI) (consists of the chief justice and 2 associate justices); US Federal District Court (consists of 1 judge); note - US Federal District Court jurisdiction limited to US federal laws; appeals beyond the CNMI Supreme Court are referred to the US Supreme Court

judge selection and term of office: CNMI Supreme Court judges appointed by the governor and confirmed by the CNMI Senate; judges appointed for 8-year terms and another term if directly elected in a popular election; US Federal District Court judges appointed by the US president and confirmed by the US Senate; judges appointed for renewable 10-year terms

subordinate courts: Superior Court

POLITICAL PARTIES AND LEADERS:

Democratic Party [Daniel QUITUGUA]
Republican Party [James ADA]

INTERNATIONAL ORGANIZATION PARTICIPATION:

PIF (observer), SPC, UPU

FLAG DESCRIPTION:

blue with a white, five-pointed star superimposed on a gray latte stone (the traditional foundation stone used in building) in the center, surrounded by a wreath; blue symbolizes the Pacific Ocean, the star represents the Commonwealth; the latte stone and the floral head wreath display elements of the native Chamorro culture

NATIONAL SYMBOL(S):

latte stone; national colors: blue, white

NATIONAL ANTHEM:

name: "Gi Talo Gi Halom Tasi" (In the Middle of the Sea)

lyrics/music: Jose S. PANGELINAN [Chamoru], David PETER [Carolinian]/Wilhelm GANZHORN

note: adopted 1996; the Carolinian version of the song is known as "Satil Matawal Pacifico;" as a commonwealth of the US, in addition to the local anthem, "The Star-Spangled Banner" is official (see United States)

ECONOMY :: NORTHERN MARIANA ISLANDS

ECONOMY - OVERVIEW:

The economy of the Commonwealth of the Northern Mariana Islands(CNMI) has been on the rebound in the last few years, mainly on the strength of its tourism industry. In 2016, the CNMI's real GDP increased 28.6%

over the previous year, following two years of relatively rapid growth in 2014 and 2015. Chinese and Korean tourists have supplanted Japanese tourists in the last few years. The Commonwealth is making a concerted effort to broaden its tourism by extending casino gambling from the small Islands of Tinian and Rota to the main Island of Saipan, its political and commercial center. Investment is concentrated on hotels and casinos in Saipan, the CNMI's largest island and home to about 90% of its population.

Federal grants have also contributed to economic growth and stability. In 2016, federal grants amounted to $101.4 billion which made up 26% of the CNMI government's total revenues. A small agriculture sector consists of cattle ranches and small farms producing coconuts, breadfruit, tomatoes, and melons.

Legislation is pending in the US Congress to extend the transition period to allow foreign workers to work in the CNMI on temporary visas.

GDP (PURCHASING POWER PARITY):
$1.242 billion (2016 est.)

$933 million (2015 est.)

$845 million (2014 est.)

  note: GDP estimate includes US subsidy; data are in 2013 dollars

  country comparison to the world: 203

GDP (OFFICIAL EXCHANGE RATE):
$1.242 billion (2016 est.) (2016 est.)

GDP - REAL GROWTH RATE:
28.6% (2016 est.)

3.8% (2015 est.)

3.5% (2014 est.)

  country comparison to the world: 2

GDP - PER CAPITA (PPP):
$24,500 (2016 est.)

$18,400 (2015 est.)

$16,600 (2014 est.)

  country comparison to the world: 84

GDP - COMPOSITION, BY END USE:
  household consumption: 43.1% (2016 est.)

  government consumption: 28.9% (2016 est.)

  investment in fixed capital: 26.3% (2016 est.)

  investment in inventories: NA (2016 est.)

  exports of goods and services: 73.6% (2016 est.)

  imports of goods and services: -71.9% (2016 est.)

GDP - COMPOSITION, BY SECTOR OF ORIGIN:
  agriculture: 1.7% (2016)

  industry: 58.1% (2016 est.)

  services: 40.2% (2016)

AGRICULTURE - PRODUCTS:
vegetables and melons, fruits and nuts; ornamental plants; livestock, poultry, eggs; fish and aquaculture products

INDUSTRIES:
tourism, banking, construction, fishing, handicrafts, other services

INDUSTRIAL PRODUCTION GROWTH RATE:
NA

LABOR FORCE:
27,970 (2010 est.)

  note: includes foreign workers

  country comparison to the world: 205

LABOR FORCE - BY OCCUPATION:
  agriculture: 1.9%

  industry: 10%

  services: 88.1% (2010 est.)

UNEMPLOYMENT RATE:
11.2% (2010 est.)

8% (2005 est.)

  country comparison to the world: 152

POPULATION BELOW POVERTY LINE:
NA

HOUSEHOLD INCOME OR CONSUMPTION BY PERCENTAGE SHARE:
  lowest 10%: NA

  highest 10%: NA

BUDGET:
  revenues: 389.6 million (2016 est.)

  expenditures: 344 million (2015 est.)

TAXES AND OTHER REVENUES:
31.4% (of GDP) (2016 est.)

  country comparison to the world: 72

BUDGET SURPLUS (+) OR DEFICIT (-):
3.7% (of GDP) (2016 est.)

  country comparison to the world: 11

PUBLIC DEBT:
7.1% of GDP (2017 est.)

  country comparison to the world: 201

FISCAL YEAR:
1 October - 30 September

INFLATION RATE (CONSUMER PRICES):
0.3% (2016 est.)

0.1% (2015 est.)

  country comparison to the world: 21

EXPORTS:
$914 million (2016 est.)

$520 million (2015 est.)

  country comparison to the world: 163

EXPORTS - COMMODITIES:
garments

IMPORTS:
$893 million (2016 est.)

$638 million (2015 est.)

  country comparison to the world: 187

IMPORTS - COMMODITIES:
food, construction equipment and materials, petroleum products

DEBT - EXTERNAL:
NA

EXCHANGE RATES:
the US dollar is used

ENERGY :: NORTHERN MARIANA ISLANDS

ELECTRICITY ACCESS:
  electrification - total population: 100% (2016)

ELECTRICITY - PRODUCTION:
60,600 kWh (2009)

  country comparison to the world: 217

ELECTRICITY - CONSUMPTION:
48,300 kWh (2009)

  country comparison to the world: 217

ELECTRICITY - EXPORTS:
0 kWh (2009 est.)

  country comparison to the world: 180

ELECTRICITY - IMPORTS:
0 kWh (January 2009 est.)

  country comparison to the world: 182

COMMUNICATIONS :: NORTHERN MARIANA ISLANDS

TELEPHONE SYSTEM:
  general assessment: digital fiber-optic cables and satellites connect the

islands to worldwide networks; future launch of 5G (2018)

domestic: wide variety of services available including dial-up and broadband Internet, mobile cellular, international private lines, payphones, phone cards, voicemail, and automatic call distribution systems (2018)

international: country code - 1-670; landing points for the Atisa and Mariana-Guam submarine cables linking Mariana islands to Guam; satellite earth stations - 2 Intelsat (Pacific Ocean) (2019)

BROADCAST MEDIA:

1 TV broadcast station on Saipan; multi-channel cable TV services are available on Saipan; 9 licensed radio broadcast stations (2009)

INTERNET COUNTRY CODE:

.mp

INTERNET USERS:

total: 16,000

percent of population: 30.6% (July 2016 est.)

country comparison to the world: 207

MILITARY AND SECURITY :: NORTHERN MARIANA ISLANDS

MILITARY - NOTE:

defense is the responsibility of the US

TRANSPORTATION :: NORTHERN MARIANA ISLANDS

AIRPORTS:

5 (2013)

country comparison to the world: 182

AIRPORTS - WITH PAVED RUNWAYS:

total: 3 (2017)

2,438 to 3,047 m: 2 (2017)

1,524 to 2,437 m: 1 (2017)

AIRPORTS - WITH UNPAVED RUNWAYS:

total: 2 (2013)

2,438 to 3,047 m: 1 (2013)

under 914 m: 1 (2013)

HELIPORTS:

1 (2013)

ROADWAYS:

total: 536 km (2008)

country comparison to the world: 188

MERCHANT MARINE:

total: 1

by type: other 1 (2018)

country comparison to the world: 175

PORTS AND TERMINALS:

major seaport(s): Saipan, Tinian, Rota

TRANSNATIONAL ISSUES :: NORTHERN MARIANA ISLANDS

DISPUTES - INTERNATIONAL:

none

EUROPE :: NORWAY

INTRODUCTION :: NORWAY

BACKGROUND:

Two centuries of Viking raids into Europe tapered off following the adoption of Christianity by King Olav TRYGGVASON in 994; conversion of the Norwegian kingdom occurred over the next several decades. In 1397, Norway was absorbed into a union with Denmark that lasted more than four centuries. In 1814, Norwegians resisted the cession of their country to Sweden and adopted a new constitution. Sweden then invaded Norway but agreed to let Norway keep its constitution in return for accepting the union under a Swedish king. Rising nationalism throughout the 19th century led to a 1905 referendum granting Norway independence. Although Norway remained neutral in World War I, it suffered heavy losses to its shipping. Norway proclaimed its neutrality at the outset of World War II, but was nonetheless occupied for five years by Nazi Germany (1940-45). In 1949, Norway abandoned neutrality and became a member of NATO. Discovery of oil and gas in adjacent waters in the late 1960s boosted Norway's economic fortunes. In referenda held in 1972 and 1994, Norway rejected joining the EU. Key domestic issues include immigration and integration of ethnic minorities, maintaining the country's extensive social safety net with an aging population, and preserving economic competitiveness.

GEOGRAPHY :: NORWAY

LOCATION:

Northern Europe, bordering the North Sea and the North Atlantic Ocean, west of Sweden

GEOGRAPHIC COORDINATES:

62 00 N, 10 00 E

MAP REFERENCES:

Europe

AREA:

total: 323,802 sq km

land: 304,282 sq km

water: 19,520 sq km

country comparison to the world: 69

AREA - COMPARATIVE:

slightly larger than twice the size of Georgia; slightly larger than New Mexico

LAND BOUNDARIES:

total: 2,566 km

border countries (3): Finland 709 km, Sweden 1666 km, Russia 191 km

COASTLINE:

25,148 km (includes mainland 2,650 km, as well as long fjords, numerous small islands, and minor indentations 22,498 km; length of island coastlines 58,133 km)

MARITIME CLAIMS:

territorial sea: 12 nm

exclusive economic zone: 200 nm

contiguous zone: 10 nm

continental shelf: 200 nm

CLIMATE:

temperate along coast, modified by North Atlantic Current; colder interior with increased precipitation and colder summers; rainy year-round on west coast

TERRAIN:
glaciated; mostly high plateaus and rugged mountains broken by fertile valleys; small,scattered plains; coastline deeply indented by fjords; arctic tundra in north

ELEVATION:
mean elevation: 460 m

lowest point: Norwegian Sea 0 m

highest point: Galdhopiggen 2,469 m

NATURAL RESOURCES:
petroleum, natural gas, iron ore, copper, lead, zinc, titanium, pyrites, nickel, fish, timber, hydropower

LAND USE:
agricultural land: 2.7% (2011 est.)

arable land: 2.2% (2011 est.) / permanent crops: 0% (2011 est.) / permanent pasture: 0.5% (2011 est.)

forest: 27.8% (2011 est.)

other: 69.5% (2011 est.)

IRRIGATED LAND:
900 sq km (2012)

POPULATION DISTRIBUTION:
most Norweigans live in the south where the climate is milder and there is better connectivity to mainland Europe; population clusters are found all along the North Sea coast in the southwest, and Skaggerak in the southeast; the interior areas of the north remain sparsely populated

NATURAL HAZARDS:
rockslides, avalanches

volcanism: Beerenberg (2,227 m) on Jan Mayen Island in the Norwegian Sea is the country's only active volcano

ENVIRONMENT - CURRENT ISSUES:
water pollution; acid rain damaging forests and adversely affecting lakes, threatening fish stocks; air pollution from vehicle emissions

ENVIRONMENT - INTERNATIONAL AGREEMENTS:
party to: Air Pollution, Air Pollution-Nitrogen Oxides, Air Pollution-Persistent Organic Pollutants, Air Pollution-Sulfur 85, Air Pollution-Sulfur 94, Air Pollution-Volatile Organic Compounds, Antarctic-Environmental Protocol, Antarctic-Marine Living Resources, Antarctic Seals, Antarctic Treaty, Biodiversity, Climate Change, Climate Change-Kyoto Protocol, Desertification, Endangered Species, Environmental Modification, Hazardous Wastes, Law of the Sea, Marine Dumping, Ozone Layer Protection, Ship Pollution, Tropical Timber 83, Tropical Timber 94, Wetlands, Whaling

signed, but not ratified: none of the selected agreements

GEOGRAPHY - NOTE:
about two-thirds mountains; some 50,000 islands off its much-indented coastline; strategic location adjacent to sea lanes and air routes in North Atlantic; one of the most rugged and longest coastlines in the world

PEOPLE AND SOCIETY :: NORWAY

POPULATION:
5,372,191 (July 2018 est.)

country comparison to the world: 120

NATIONALITY:
noun: Norwegian(s)

adjective: Norwegian

ETHNIC GROUPS:
Norwegian 83.2% (includes about 60,000 Sami), other European 8.3%, other 8.5% (2017 est.)

LANGUAGES:
Bokmal Norwegian (official), Nynorsk Norwegian (official), small Sami- and Finnish-speaking minorities

note: Sami has three dialects: Lule, North Sami, and South Sami; Sami is an official language in nine municipalities in Norway's three northernmost counties: Finnmark, Nordland, and Troms

RELIGIONS:
Church of Norway (Evangelical Lutheran - official) 70.6%, Muslim 3.2%, Roman Catholic 3%, other Christian 3.7%, other 2.5%, unspecified 17% (2016 est.)

AGE STRUCTURE:
0-14 years: 17.99% (male 495,403 /female 471,014)

15-24 years: 12.37% (male 340,672 /female 324,088)

25-54 years: 40.98% (male 1,136,373 /female 1,065,138)

55-64 years: 11.72% (male 318,898 /female 310,668)

65 years and over: 16.94% (male 420,178 /female 489,759) (2018 est.)

DEPENDENCY RATIOS:
total dependency ratio: 52.1 (2015 est.)

youth dependency ratio: 27.3 (2015 est.)

elderly dependency ratio: 24.8 (2015 est.)

potential support ratio: 4 (2015 est.)

note: data include Svalbard and Jan Mayen Islands

MEDIAN AGE:
total: 39.3 years (2018 est.)

male: 38.6 years

female: 40 years

country comparison to the world: 55

POPULATION GROWTH RATE:
0.94% (2018 est.)

country comparison to the world: 117

BIRTH RATE:
12.2 births/1,000 population (2018 est.)

country comparison to the world: 160

DEATH RATE:
8 deaths/1,000 population (2018 est.)

country comparison to the world: 90

NET MIGRATION RATE:
5.3 migrant(s)/1,000 population (2018 est.)

country comparison to the world: 24

POPULATION DISTRIBUTION:
most Norweigans live in the south where the climate is milder and there is better connectivity to mainland Europe; population clusters are found all along the North Sea coast in the southwest, and Skaggerak in the southeast; the interior areas of the north remain sparsely populated

URBANIZATION:
urban population: 82.6% of total population (2019)

rate of urbanization: 1.4% annual rate of change (2015-20 est.)

note: data include Svalbard and Jan Mayen Islands

MAJOR URBAN AREAS - POPULATION:
1.027 million OSLO (capital) (2019)

SEX RATIO:
at birth: 1.05 male(s)/female

0-14 years: 1.05 male(s)/female

15-24 years: 1.05 male(s)/female

25-54 years: 1.07 male(s)/female

55-64 years: 1.03 male(s)/female

65 years and over: 0.86 male(s)/female

total population: 1.02 male(s)/female (2018 est.)

MOTHER'S MEAN AGE AT FIRST BIRTH:

28.9 years (2015 est.)

note: data is calculated based on actual age at first births

MATERNAL MORTALITY RATE:

2 deaths/100,000 live births (2017 est.)

country comparison to the world: 183

INFANT MORTALITY RATE:

total: 2.5 deaths/1,000 live births (2018 est.)

male: 2.8 deaths/1,000 live births

female: 2.2 deaths/1,000 live births

country comparison to the world: 219

LIFE EXPECTANCY AT BIRTH:

total population: 82 years (2018 est.)

male: 79.9 years

female: 84.1 years

country comparison to the world: 22

TOTAL FERTILITY RATE:

1.85 children born/woman (2018 est.)

country comparison to the world: 143

DRINKING WATER SOURCE:

improved:

urban: 100% of population

rural: 100% of population

total: 100% of population

unimproved:

urban: 0% of population

rural: 0% of population

total: 0% of population (2015 est.)

CURRENT HEALTH EXPENDITURE:

10.5% (2016)

PHYSICIANS DENSITY:

4.63 physicians/1,000 population (2017)

HOSPITAL BED DENSITY:

3.8 beds/1,000 population (2015)

SANITATION FACILITY ACCESS:

improved:

urban: 98% of population (2015 est.)

rural: 98.3% of population (2015 est.)

total: 98.1% of population (2015 est.)

unimproved:

urban: 2% of population (2015 est.)

rural: 1.7% of population (2015 est.)

total: 1.9% of population (2015 est.)

HIV/AIDS - ADULT PREVALENCE RATE:

0.1% (2018 est.)

country comparison to the world: 130

HIV/AIDS - PEOPLE LIVING WITH HIV/AIDS:

5,800 (2018 est.)

country comparison to the world: 117

HIV/AIDS - DEATHS:

<100 (2018 est.)

OBESITY - ADULT PREVALENCE RATE:

23.1% (2016)

country comparison to the world: 68

EDUCATION EXPENDITURES:

7.6% of GDP (2015)

country comparison to the world: 8

SCHOOL LIFE EXPECTANCY (PRIMARY TO TERTIARY EDUCATION):

total: 18 years

male: 17 years

female: 19 years (2016)

UNEMPLOYMENT, YOUTH AGES 15-24:

total: 10.4%

male: 11.7%

female: 9% (2017 est.)

country comparison to the world: 127

GOVERNMENT :: NORWAY

COUNTRY NAME:

conventional long form: Kingdom of Norway

conventional short form: Norway

local long form: Kongeriket Norge

local short form: Norge

etymology: derives from the Old Norse words "nordr" and "vegr" meaning "northern way" and refers to the long coastline of western Norway

GOVERNMENT TYPE:

parliamentary constitutional monarchy

CAPITAL:

name: Oslo

geographic coordinates: 59 55 N, 10 45 E

time difference: UTC+1 (6 hours ahead of Washington, DC, during Standard Time)

daylight saving time: +1hr, begins last Sunday in March; ends last Sunday in October

etymology: the medieval name was spelt "Aslo"; the "as" component refered either to the Ekeberg ridge southeast of the town ("as" in modern Norwegian), or to the Aesir (Norse gods); "lo" refered to "meadow," so the most likely interpretations would have been either "the meadow beneath the ridge" or "the meadow of the gods"; both explanations are considered equally plausible

ADMINISTRATIVE DIVISIONS:

18 counties (fylker, singular - fylke); Akershus, Aust-Agder, Buskerud, Finnmark, Hedmark, Hordaland, More og Romsdal, Nordland, Oppland, Oslo, Ostfold, Rogaland, Sogn og Fjordane, Telemark, Troms, Trondelag, Vest-Agder, Vestfold

DEPENDENT AREAS:

Bouvet Island, Jan Mayen, Svalbard

INDEPENDENCE:

7 June 1905 (declared the union with Sweden dissolved); 26 October 1905 (Sweden agreed to the repeal of the union); notable earlier dates: ca. 872 (traditional unification of petty Norwegian kingdoms by HARALD Fairhair); 1397 (Kalmar Union of Denmark, Norway, and Sweden); 1524 (Denmark-Norway); 17 May 1814 (Norwegian constitution adopted); 4 November 1814 (Sweden-Norway union confirmed)

NATIONAL HOLIDAY:

Constitution Day, 17 May (1814)

CONSTITUTION:

history: drafted spring 1814, adopted 16 May 1814, signed by Constituent Assembly 17 May 1814

amendments: proposals submitted by members of Parliament or by the government within the first three years of Parliament's four-year term; passage requires two-thirds majority vote of a two-thirds quorum in the next elected Parliament; amended over 400 times, last in 2018 (2018)

LEGAL SYSTEM:

mixed legal system of civil, common, and customary law; Supreme Court can advise on legislative acts

INTERNATIONAL LAW ORGANIZATION PARTICIPATION:

accepts compulsory ICJ jurisdiction with reservations; accepts ICCt jurisdiction

CITIZENSHIP:

citizenship by birth: no

citizenship by descent only: at least one parent must be a citizen of Norway

dual citizenship recognized: no

residency requirement for naturalization: 7 years

SUFFRAGE:

18 years of age; universal

EXECUTIVE BRANCH:

chief of state: King HARALD V (since 17 January 1991); Heir Apparent Crown Prince HAAKON MAGNUS (son of the monarch, born 20 July 1973)

head of government: Prime Minister Erna SOLBERG (since 16 October 2013)

cabinet: Council of State appointed by the monarch, approved by Parliament

elections/appointments: the monarchy is hereditary; following parliamentary elections, the leader of the majority party or majority coalition usually appointed prime minister by the monarch with the approval of the parliament

LEGISLATIVE BRANCH:

description: unicameral Parliament or Storting (169 seats; members directly elected in multi-seat constituencies by proportional representation vote; members serve 4-year terms)

elections: last held on 11 September 2017 (next to be held in September 2021)

election results: percent of vote by party - Ap 27.4%, H 25%, FrP 15.2%, SP 10.3%, SV 6%, V 4.4%, KrF 4.2%, MDG 3.2%, R 2.4%, other/invalid 1.9%; seats by party - Ap 49, H 45, FrP 27, SP 19, SV 11, V 8, KrF 8, MDG 1, R 1; composition - men 99, women 70, percent of women 41.4%

JUDICIAL BRANCH:

highest courts: Supreme Court or Hoyesterett (consists of the chief justice and 18 associate justices)

judge selection and term of office: justices appointed by the monarch (King in Council) upon the recommendation of the Judicial Appointments Board; justices can serve until mandatory retirement at age 70

subordinate courts: Courts of Appeal or Lagmennsrett; regional and district courts; Conciliation Boards; ordinary and special courts; note - in addition to professionally trained judges, elected lay judges sit on the bench with professional judges in the Courts of Appeal and district courts

POLITICAL PARTIES AND LEADERS:

Center Party or Sp [Trygve Slagsvold VEDUM]
Christian Democratic Party or KrF [Kjell Ingolf ROPSTADT]
Conservative Party or H [Erna SOLBERG]
Green Party or MDG [Rasmus HANSSON and Une Aina BASTHOLM]
Labor Party or Ap [Jonas Gahr STORE]
Liberal Party or V [Trine SKEI GRANDE]
Progress Party or FrP [Siv JENSEN]
Red Party or R [Bionar MOXNES]
Socialist Left Party or SV [Audun LYSBAKKEN]

INTERNATIONAL ORGANIZATION PARTICIPATION:

ADB (nonregional member), AfDB (nonregional member), Arctic Council, Australia Group, BIS, CBSS, CD, CE, CERN, EAPC, EBRD, EFTA, EITI (implementing country), ESA, FAO, FATF, IADB, IAEA, IBRD, ICAO, ICC (national committees), ICCt, ICRM, IDA, IEA, IFAD, IFC, IFRCS, IGAD (partners), IHO, ILO, IMF, IMO, IMSO, Interpol, IOC, IOM, IPU, ISO, ITSO, ITU, ITUC (NGOs), MIGA, MINUSMA, NATO, NC, NEA, NIB, NSG, OAS (observer), OECD, OPCW, OSCE, Paris Club, PCA, Schengen Convention, UN, UNCTAD, UNESCO, UNHCR, UNIDO, UNITAR, UNMISS, UNRWA, UNTSO, UNWTO, UPU, WCO, WHO, WIPO, WMO, WTO, ZC

DIPLOMATIC REPRESENTATION IN THE US:

Ambassador Kare Reidar AAS (since 17 September 2013)

chancery: 2720 34th Street NW, Washington, DC 20008

telephone: [1] (202) 333-6000

FAX: [1] (202) 469-3990

consulate(s) general: Houston, New York, San Francisco

DIPLOMATIC REPRESENTATION FROM THE US:

chief of mission: Ambassador Kenneth BRAITHWAITE (since 8 February 2018)

telephone: [47] 21-30-85-40

embassy: Morgedalsvegen 36, 0378 Oslo

mailing address: PO Box 4075 AMB 0244 Oslo

FAX: [47] 22-44-33-63, 22-56-27-51

FLAG DESCRIPTION:

red with a blue cross outlined in white that extends to the edges of the flag; the vertical part of the cross is shifted to the hoist side in the style of the Dannebrog (Danish flag); the colors recall Norway's past political unions with Denmark (red and white) and Sweden (blue)

NATIONAL SYMBOL(S):

lion; national colors: red, white, blue

NATIONAL ANTHEM:

name: "Ja, vi elsker dette landet" (Yes, We Love This Country)

lyrics/music: lyrics/music: Bjornstjerne BJORNSON/Rikard NORDRAAK

note: adopted 1864; in addition to the national anthem, "Kongesangen" (Song of the King), which uses the tune of "God Save the Queen," serves as the royal anthem

ECONOMY :: NORWAY

ECONOMY - OVERVIEW:

Norway has a stable economy with a vibrant private sector, a large state sector, and an extensive social safety net. Norway opted out of the EU during a referendum in November 1994. However, as a member of the European Economic Area, Norway partially participates in the EU's single market and contributes sizably to the EU budget.

The country is richly endowed with natural resources such as oil and gas, fish, forests, and minerals. Norway is a leading producer and the world's second largest exporter of seafood, after China. The government manages the country's petroleum resources through extensive regulation. The petroleum sector provides about 9% of jobs, 12% of GDP, 13% of the state's revenue, and 37% of exports, according to official national estimates. Norway is one of the world's leading petroleum exporters, although oil production is close to 50% below its peak in 2000. Gas production, conversely, has more than doubled since 2000. Although oil production is historically low, it rose in 2016 for the third consecutive year due to the higher production of existing oil fields and to new fields coming on stream. Norway's domestic electricity production relies almost entirely on hydropower.

In anticipation of eventual declines in oil and gas production, Norway saves state revenue from petroleum sector activities in the world's largest sovereign wealth fund, valued at over $1 trillion at the end of 2017. To help balance the federal budget each year, the government follows a "fiscal rule," which states that spending of revenues from petroleum and fund investments shall correspond to the expected real rate of return on the fund, an amount it estimates is sustainable over time. In February 2017, the government revised the expected rate of return for the fund downward from 4% to 3%.

After solid GDP growth in the 2004-07 period, the economy slowed in 2008, and contracted in 2009, before returning to modest, positive growth from 2010 to 2017. The Norwegian economy has been adjusting to lower energy prices, as demonstrated by growth in labor force participation and employment in 2017. GDP growth was about 1.5% in 2017, driven largely by domestic demand, which has been boosted by the rebound in the labor market and supportive fiscal policies. Economic growth is expected to remain constant or improve slightly in the next few years.

GDP (PURCHASING POWER PARITY):

$381.2 billion (2017 est.)

$374 billion (2016 est.)

$370 billion (2015 est.)

note: data are in 2017 dollars

country comparison to the world: 48

GDP (OFFICIAL EXCHANGE RATE):

$398.8 billion (2017 est.)

GDP - REAL GROWTH RATE:

1.9% (2017 est.)

1.1% (2016 est.)

2% (2015 est.)

country comparison to the world: 156

GDP - PER CAPITA (PPP):

$72,100 (2017 est.)

$71,200 (2016 est.)

$71,100 (2015 est.)

note: data are in 2017 dollars

country comparison to the world: 11

GROSS NATIONAL SAVING:

34.3% of GDP (2017 est.)

33.1% of GDP (2016 est.)

35.5% of GDP (2015 est.)

country comparison to the world: 18

GDP - COMPOSITION, BY END USE:

household consumption: 44.8% (2017 est.)

government consumption: 24% (2017 est.)

investment in fixed capital: 24.1% (2017 est.)

investment in inventories: 4.8% (2017 est.)

exports of goods and services: 35.5% (2017 est.)

imports of goods and services: -33.2% (2017 est.)

GDP - COMPOSITION, BY SECTOR OF ORIGIN:

agriculture: 2.3% (2017 est.)

industry: 33.7% (2017 est.)

services: 64% (2017 est.)

AGRICULTURE - PRODUCTS:

barley, wheat, potatoes; pork, beef, veal, milk; fish

INDUSTRIES:

petroleum and gas, shipping, fishing, aquaculture, food processing, shipbuilding, pulp and paper products, metals, chemicals, timber, mining, textiles

INDUSTRIAL PRODUCTION GROWTH RATE:

1.5% (2017 est.)

country comparison to the world: 143

LABOR FORCE:

2.797 million (2017 est.)

country comparison to the world: 108

LABOR FORCE - BY OCCUPATION:

agriculture: 2.1%

industry: 19.3%

services: 78.6% (2016 est.)

UNEMPLOYMENT RATE:

4.2% (2017 est.)

4.7% (2016 est.)

country comparison to the world: 56

POPULATION BELOW POVERTY LINE:

NA

HOUSEHOLD INCOME OR CONSUMPTION BY PERCENTAGE SHARE:

lowest 10%: 3.8%

highest 10%: 21.2% (2014)

DISTRIBUTION OF FAMILY INCOME - GINI INDEX:

26.8 (2010)

25.8 (1995)

country comparison to the world: 147

BUDGET:

revenues: 217.1 billion (2017 est.)

expenditures: 199.5 billion (2017 est.)

TAXES AND OTHER REVENUES:

54.4% (of GDP) (2017 est.)

country comparison to the world: 9

BUDGET SURPLUS (+) OR DEFICIT (-):

4.4% (of GDP) (2017 est.)

country comparison to the world: 8

PUBLIC DEBT:

36.5% of GDP (2017 est.)

36.4% of GDP (2016 est.)

note: data cover general government debt and include debt instruments issued (or owned) by government entities other than the treasury; the data exclude treasury debt held by foreign entities; the data exclude debt issued by subnational entities, as well as intragovernmental debt; intragovernmental debt consists of treasury borrowings from surpluses in the social funds, such as for retirement, medical care, and unemployment; debt instruments for the social funds are not sold at public auctions

country comparison to the world: 146

FISCAL YEAR:

calendar year

INFLATION RATE (CONSUMER PRICES):

1.9% (2017 est.)

3.6% (2016 est.)

country comparison to the world: 99

CENTRAL BANK DISCOUNT RATE:

6.25% (31 December 2010)

1.75% (31 December 2009)

country comparison to the world: 67

COMMERCIAL BANK PRIME LENDING RATE:

2.89% (31 December 2017 est.)

2.96% (31 December 2016 est.)

country comparison to the world: 175

STOCK OF NARROW MONEY:

$237.7 billion (31 December 2017 est.)

$214 billion (31 December 2016 est.)

country comparison to the world: 23

STOCK OF BROAD MONEY:

$237.7 billion (31 December 2017 est.)

$214 billion (31 December 2016 est.)

country comparison to the world: 23

STOCK OF DOMESTIC CREDIT:

$640.4 billion (31 December 2017 est.)

$571.4 billion (31 December 2016 est.)

country comparison to the world: 22

MARKET VALUE OF PUBLICLY TRADED SHARES:

$193.9 billion (31 December 2015 est.)

$219.4 billion (31 December 2014 est.)

$265.4 billion (31 December 2013 est.)

country comparison to the world: 34

CURRENT ACCOUNT BALANCE:

$22.01 billion (2017 est.)

$14.09 billion (2016 est.)

country comparison to the world: 16

EXPORTS:

$102.8 billion (2017 est.)

$88.88 billion (2016 est.)

country comparison to the world: 36

EXPORTS - PARTNERS:

UK 21.1%, Germany 15.5%, Netherlands 9.9%, Sweden 6.6%, France 6.4%, Belgium 4.8%, Denmark 4.7%, US 4.6% (2017)

EXPORTS - COMMODITIES:

petroleum and petroleum products, machinery and equipment, metals, chemicals, ships, fish

IMPORTS:

$95.06 billion (2017 est.)

$74.94 billion (2016 est.)

country comparison to the world: 36

IMPORTS - COMMODITIES:

machinery and equipment, chemicals, metals, foodstuffs

IMPORTS - PARTNERS:

Sweden 11.4%, Germany 11%, China 9.8%, US 6.8%, South Korea 6.7%, Denmark 5.4%, UK 4.7% (2017)

RESERVES OF FOREIGN EXCHANGE AND GOLD:

$65.92 billion (31 December 2017 est.)

$57.46 billion (31 December 2015 est.)

country comparison to the world: 34

DEBT - EXTERNAL:

$642.3 billion (31 March 2016 est.)

$640.1 billion (31 March 2015 est.)

note: Norway is a net external creditor

country comparison to the world: 17

STOCK OF DIRECT FOREIGN INVESTMENT - AT HOME:

$236.5 billion (31 December 2017 est.)

$219.1 billion (31 December 2016 est.)

country comparison to the world: 27

STOCK OF DIRECT FOREIGN INVESTMENT - ABROAD:

$196.3 billion (31 December 2017 est.)

$191.7 billion (31 December 2016 est.)

country comparison to the world: 28

EXCHANGE RATES:

Norwegian kroner (NOK) per US dollar -

8.308 (2017 est.)

8.3978 (2016 est.)

8.3978 (2015 est.)

8.0646 (2014 est.)

6.3021 (2013 est.)

ENERGY :: NORWAY

ELECTRICITY ACCESS:

electrification - total population: 100% (2016)

ELECTRICITY - PRODUCTION:

147.7 billion kWh (2016 est.)

country comparison to the world: 29

ELECTRICITY - CONSUMPTION:

122.2 billion kWh (2016 est.)

country comparison to the world: 29

ELECTRICITY - EXPORTS:

15.53 billion kWh (2016 est.)

country comparison to the world: 12

ELECTRICITY - IMPORTS:

5.741 billion kWh (2016 est.)

country comparison to the world: 34

ELECTRICITY - INSTALLED GENERATING CAPACITY:

33.86 million kW (2016 est.)

country comparison to the world: 30

ELECTRICITY - FROM FOSSIL FUELS:

3% of total installed capacity (2016 est.)

country comparison to the world: 208

ELECTRICITY - FROM NUCLEAR FUELS:

0% of total installed capacity (2017 est.)

country comparison to the world: 159

ELECTRICITY - FROM HYDROELECTRIC PLANTS:

93% of total installed capacity (2017 est.)

country comparison to the world: 8

ELECTRICITY - FROM OTHER RENEWABLE SOURCES:

4% of total installed capacity (2017 est.)

country comparison to the world: 115

CRUDE OIL - PRODUCTION:

1.517 million bbl/day (2018 est.)

country comparison to the world: 15

CRUDE OIL - EXPORTS:

1.383 million bbl/day (2017 est.)

country comparison to the world: 10

CRUDE OIL - IMPORTS:

36,550 bbl/day (2017 est.)

country comparison to the world: 58

CRUDE OIL - PROVED RESERVES:

6.376 billion bbl (1 January 2018)

country comparison to the world: 20

REFINED PETROLEUM PRODUCTS - PRODUCTION:

371,600 bbl/day (2017 est.)

country comparison to the world: 38

REFINED PETROLEUM PRODUCTS - CONSUMPTION:

205,300 bbl/day (2017 est.)

country comparison to the world: 57

REFINED PETROLEUM PRODUCTS - EXPORTS:

432,800 bbl/day (2017 est.)

country comparison to the world: 20

REFINED PETROLEUM PRODUCTS - IMPORTS:

135,300 bbl/day (2017 est.)

country comparison to the world: 43

NATURAL GAS - PRODUCTION:

123.9 billion cu m (2017 est.)

country comparison to the world: 7

NATURAL GAS - CONSUMPTION:

4.049 billion cu m (2017 est.)

country comparison to the world: 65

NATURAL GAS - EXPORTS:

120.2 billion cu m (2017 est.)

country comparison to the world: 3

NATURAL GAS - IMPORTS:

5.663 million cu m (2017 est.)

country comparison to the world: 77
NATURAL GAS - PROVED RESERVES:

1.782 trillion cu m (1 January 2018 est.)

country comparison to the world: 20
CARBON DIOXIDE EMISSIONS FROM CONSUMPTION OF ENERGY:

39.8 million Mt (2017 est.)

country comparison to the world: 65

COMMUNICATIONS :: NORWAY

TELEPHONES - FIXED LINES:

total subscriptions: 745,182

subscriptions per 100 inhabitants: 14 (2017 est.)

country comparison to the world: 84

TELEPHONES - MOBILE CELLULAR:

total subscriptions: 5,721,255

subscriptions per 100 inhabitants: 108 (2017 est.)

country comparison to the world: 117

TELEPHONE SYSTEM:

general assessment: modern in all respects; one of the most advanced telecommunications networks in Europe; forward leaning in LTE-A developments; looking to close 3G and 2G networks by 2025 and preparing for 5G; broadband penetration rate is among the best in Europe (2018)

domestic: Norway has a domestic satellite system; the prevalence of rural areas encourages the wide use of mobile-cellular systems; fixed-line 14 per 100 and mobile-cellular 108 per 100 (2018)

international: country code - 47; landing points for the Svalbard Undersea Cable System, Polar Circle Cable, Bodo-Rost Cable, NOR5KE Viking, Celtic Norse, Tempnet Offshore FOC Network, England Cable, Denmark-Norway6, Havfrue/AEC-2, Skagerrak 4, and the Skagenfiber West & East submarine cables providing links to other Nordic countries, Europe and the US; satellite earth stations - NA Eutelsat, NA Intelsat (Atlantic Ocean), and 1 Inmarsat (Atlantic and Indian Ocean regions); note - Norway shares the Inmarsat earth station with the other Nordic countries (Denmark, Finland, Iceland, and Sweden) (2019)

BROADCAST MEDIA:

state-owned public radio-TV broadcaster operates 3 nationwide TV stations, 3 nationwide radio stations, and 16 regional radio stations; roughly a dozen privately owned TV stations broadcast nationally and roughly another 25 local TV stations broadcasting; nearly 75% of households have access to multi-channel cable or satellite TV; 2 privately owned radio stations broadcast nationwide and another 240 stations operate locally; Norway is the first country in the world to phase out FM radio in favor of Digital Audio Broadcasting (DAB), a process scheduled for completion in late 2017 (2019)

INTERNET COUNTRY CODE:

.no

INTERNET USERS:

total: 5,122,904

percent of population: 97.3% (July 2016 est.)

country comparison to the world: 75

BROADBAND - FIXED SUBSCRIPTIONS:

total: 2,134,105

subscriptions per 100 inhabitants: 40 (2017 est.)

country comparison to the world: 51

MILITARY AND SECURITY :: NORWAY

MILITARY EXPENDITURES:

1.61% of GDP (2018)

1.62% of GDP (2017)

1.62% of GDP (2016)

1.5% of GDP (2015)

1.47% of GDP (2014)

country comparison to the world: 71

MILITARY AND SECURITY FORCES:

Norwegian Armed Forces: Norwegian Army (Haeren), Royal Norwegian Navy (Kongelige Norske Sjoeforsvaret; includes Coastal Rangers and Coast Guard (Kystvakt)), Royal Norwegian Air Force (Kongelige Norske Luftforsvaret), Home Guard (Heimevernet, HV) (2019)

MILITARY SERVICE AGE AND OBLIGATION:

19-35 years of age for male and female selective compulsory military service; 17 years of age for male volunteers (16 in wartime); 18 years of age for women; 19-month service obligation; conscripts first serve 12 months from 19-28, and then up to 4-5 refresher training periods until age 35, 44, 55, or 60 depending on rank and function. (2019)

TRANSPORTATION :: NORWAY

NATIONAL AIR TRANSPORT SYSTEM:

number of registered air carriers: 3 (2015)

inventory of registered aircraft operated by air carriers: 106 (2015)

annual passenger traffic on registered air carriers: 12,277,220 (2015)

annual freight traffic on registered air carriers: 0 mt-km (2015)

CIVIL AIRCRAFT REGISTRATION COUNTRY CODE PREFIX:

LN (2016)

AIRPORTS:

95 (2013)

country comparison to the world: 61

AIRPORTS - WITH PAVED RUNWAYS:

total: 67 (2017)

2,438 to 3,047 m: 14 (2017)

1,524 to 2,437 m: 10 (2017)

914 to 1,523 m: 22 (2017)

under 914 m: 21 (2017)

AIRPORTS - WITH UNPAVED RUNWAYS:

total: 28 (2013)

914 to 1,523 m: 6 (2013)

under 914 m: 22 (2013)

HELIPORTS:

1 (2013)

PIPELINES:

8520 km gas, 1304 km oil/condensate (2017)

RAILWAYS:

total: 4,200 km (2019)

standard gauge: 4,200 km 1.435-m gauge (2,480 km electrified) (2019)

country comparison to the world: 45

ROADWAYS:

total: 94,902 km (includes 455 km of expressways) (2018)

country comparison to the world: 52

WATERWAYS:

1,577 km (2010)

country comparison to the world: 51

MERCHANT MARINE:

total: 1,581

by type: bulk carrier 102, general cargo 249, oil tanker 81, other 1149 (2018)

country comparison to the world: 17

PORTS AND TERMINALS:

major seaport(s): Bergen, Haugesund, Maaloy, Mongstad, Narvik, Sture

LNG terminal(s) (export): Kamoy, Kollsnes, Melkoya Island

LNG terminal(s) (import): Fredrikstad, Mosjoen

TRANSNATIONAL ISSUES :: NORWAY

DISPUTES - INTERNATIONAL:

Norway asserts a territorial claim in Antarctica (Queen Maud Land and its continental shelf); Denmark (Greenland) and Norway have made submissions to the Commission on the Limits of the Continental Shelf (CLCS) and Russia is collecting additional data to augment its 2001 CLCS submission; Norway and Russia signed a comprehensive maritime boundary agreement in 2010

REFUGEES AND INTERNALLY DISPLACED PERSONS:

refugees (country of origin): 15,246 (Eritrea), 13,914 (Syria), 7,183 (Somalia), 6,065 (Afghanistan) (2018)

stateless persons: 2,809 (2018)

MIDDLE EAST :: OMAN

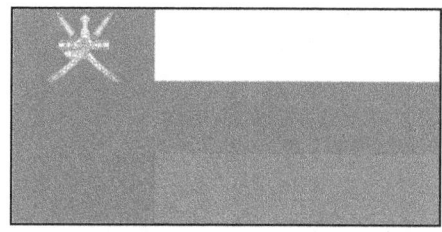

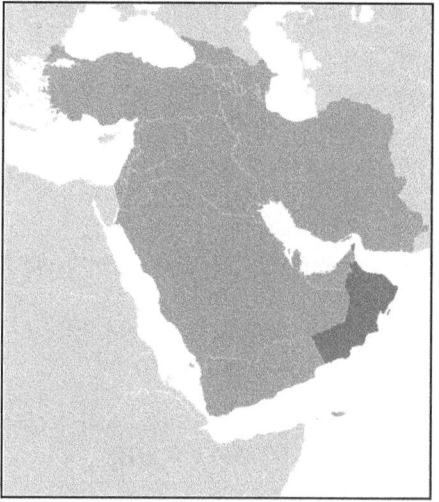

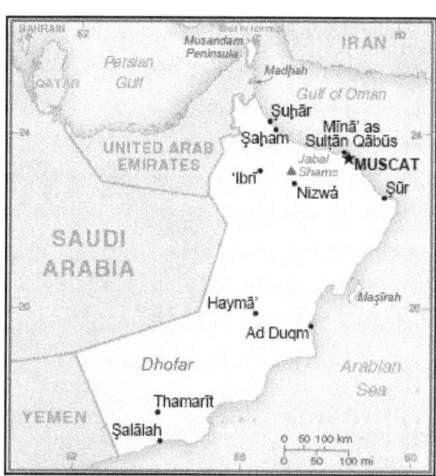

INTRODUCTION :: OMAN

BACKGROUND:
The inhabitants of the area of Oman have long prospered from Indian Ocean trade. In the late 18th century, the nascent sultanate in Muscat signed the first in a series of friendship treaties with Britain. Over time, Oman's dependence on British political and military advisors increased, although the sultanate never became a British colony. In 1970, QABOOS bin Said Al-Said overthrew his father, and has since ruled as sultan. Sultan QABOOS has no children and has not designated a successor publicly; the Basic Law of 1996 outlines Oman's succession procedure. Sultan QABOOS' extensive modernization program opened the country to the outside world, and the sultan has prioritized strategic ties with the UK and US. Oman's moderate, independent foreign policy has sought to maintain good relations with its neighbors and to avoid external entanglements.

Inspired by the popular uprisings that swept the Middle East and North Africa beginning in January 2011, some Omanis staged demonstrations, calling for more jobs and economic benefits and an end to corruption. In response to those protester demands, QABOOS in 2011 pledged to implement economic and political reforms, such as granting Oman's bicameral legislative body more power and authorizing direct elections for its lower house, which took place in November 2011. Additionally, the Sultan increased unemployment benefits, and, in August 2012, issued a royal directive mandating the speedy implementation of a national job creation plan for thousands of public and private sector Omani jobs. As part of the government's efforts to decentralize authority and allow greater citizen participation in local governance, Oman successfully conducted its first municipal council elections in December 2012. Announced by the sultan in 2011, the municipal councils have the power to advise the Royal Court on the needs of local districts across Oman's 11 governorates.

GEOGRAPHY :: OMAN

LOCATION:
Middle East, bordering the Arabian Sea, Gulf of Oman, and Persian Gulf, between Yemen and the UAE

GEOGRAPHIC COORDINATES:
21 00 N, 57 00 E

MAP REFERENCES:
Middle East

AREA:
total: 309,500 sq km

land: 309,500 sq km

water: 0 sq km

country comparison to the world: 72

AREA - COMPARATIVE:
twice the size of Georgia; slightly smaller than Kansas

LAND BOUNDARIES:
total: 1,561 km

border countries (3): Saudi Arabia 658 km, UAE 609 km, Yemen 294 km

COASTLINE:
2,092 km

MARITIME CLAIMS:
territorial sea: 12 nm

exclusive economic zone: 200 nm

contiguous zone: 24 nm

CLIMATE:
dry desert; hot, humid along coast; hot, dry interior; strong southwest summer monsoon (May to September) in far south

TERRAIN:
central desert plain, rugged mountains in north and south

ELEVATION:
mean elevation: 310 m

lowest point: Arabian Sea 0 m

highest point: Jabal Shams 3,004 m

NATURAL RESOURCES:
petroleum, copper, asbestos, some marble, limestone, chromium, gypsum, natural gas

LAND USE:
agricultural land: 4.7% (2011 est.)

arable land: 0.1% (2011 est.) / permanent crops: 0.1% (2011 est.) / permanent pasture: 4.5% (2011 est.)

forest: 0% (2011 est.)

other: 95.3% (2011 est.)

IRRIGATED LAND:
590 sq km (2012)

POPULATION DISTRIBUTION:
the vast majority of the population is located in and around the Al Hagar Mountains in the north of the country; another smaller cluster is found around the city of Salalah in the

far south; most of the country remains sparsely poplulated

NATURAL HAZARDS:

summer winds often raise large sandstorms and dust storms in interior; periodic droughts

ENVIRONMENT - CURRENT ISSUES:

limited natural freshwater resources; high levels of soil and water salinity in the coastal plains; beach pollution from oil spills; industrial effluents seeping into the water tables and aquifers; desertificaiton due to high winds driving desert sand into arable lands

ENVIRONMENT - INTERNATIONAL AGREEMENTS:

party to: Biodiversity, Climate Change, Climate Change-Kyoto Protocol, Desertification, Hazardous Wastes, Law of the Sea, Marine Dumping, Ozone Layer Protection, Ship Pollution, Whaling

signed, but not ratified: none of the selected agreements

GEOGRAPHY - NOTE:

consists of Oman proper and two northern exclaves, Musandam and Al Madhah; the former is a peninsula that occupies a strategic location adjacent to the Strait of Hormuz, a vital transit point for world crude oil

PEOPLE AND SOCIETY :: OMAN

POPULATION:

4,613,241 (July 2017 est. est.)

note: immigrants make up approximately 45% of the total population (2017)

country comparison to the world: 125

NATIONALITY:

noun: Omani(s)

adjective: Omani

ETHNIC GROUPS:

Arab, Baluchi, South Asian (Indian, Pakistani, Sri Lankan, Bangladeshi), African

LANGUAGES:

Arabic (official), English, Baluchi, Swahili, Urdu, Indian dialects

RELIGIONS:

Muslim 85.9%, Christian 6.5%, Hindu 5.5%, Buddhist 0.8%, Jewish <0.1%, other 1%, unaffiliated 0.2% (2010 est.)

note: Omani citizens represent approximately 56.4% of the population and are overwhelming Muslim (Ibadhi and Sunni sects each constitute about 45% and Shia about 5%); Christians, Hindus, and Buddhists account for roughly 5% of Omani citizens

AGE STRUCTURE:

0-14 years: 30.1% (male 539,202 /female 512,416)

15-24 years: 18.26% (male 334,784 /female 303,172)

25-54 years: 44.15% (male 886,080 /female 656,734)

55-64 years: 3.94% (male 73,233 /female 64,450)

65 years and over: 3.55% (male 60,354 /female 63,691) (2018 est.)

DEPENDENCY RATIOS:

total dependency ratio: 32.4 (2015 est.)

youth dependency ratio: 29.4 (2015 est.)

elderly dependency ratio: 3.1 (2015 est.)

potential support ratio: 32.6 (2015 est.)

MEDIAN AGE:

total: 25.8 years (2018 est.)

male: 26.8 years

female: 24.5 years

country comparison to the world: 154

POPULATION GROWTH RATE:

2% (2018 est.)

country comparison to the world: 47

BIRTH RATE:

23.7 births/1,000 population (2018 est.)

country comparison to the world: 54

DEATH RATE:

3.3 deaths/1,000 population (2018 est.)

country comparison to the world: 219

NET MIGRATION RATE:

-0.4 migrant(s)/1,000 population (2018 est.)

country comparison to the world: 123

POPULATION DISTRIBUTION:

the vast majority of the population is located in and around the Al Hagar Mountains in the north of the country; another smaller cluster is found around the city of Salalah in the far south; most of the country remains sparsely poplulated

URBANIZATION:

urban population: 85.4% of total population (2019)

rate of urbanization: 5.25% annual rate of change (2015-20 est.)

MAJOR URBAN AREAS - POPULATION:

1.502 million MUSCAT (capital) (2019)

SEX RATIO:

at birth: 1.05 male(s)/female

0-14 years: 1.05 male(s)/female

15-24 years: 1.1 male(s)/female

25-54 years: 1.35 male(s)/female

55-64 years: 1.14 male(s)/female

65 years and over: 0.95 male(s)/female

total population: 1.18 male(s)/female (2018 est.)

MATERNAL MORTALITY RATE:

19 deaths/100,000 live births (2017 est.)

country comparison to the world: 126

INFANT MORTALITY RATE:

total: 12.4 deaths/1,000 live births (2018 est.)

male: 12.7 deaths/1,000 live births

female: 12.1 deaths/1,000 live births

country comparison to the world: 109

LIFE EXPECTANCY AT BIRTH:

total population: 75.9 years (2018 est.)

male: 73.9 years

female: 78 years

country comparison to the world: 97

TOTAL FERTILITY RATE:

2.8 children born/woman (2018 est.)

country comparison to the world: 61

CONTRACEPTIVE PREVALENCE RATE:

29.7% (2014)

DRINKING WATER SOURCE:

improved:

urban: 95.5% of population

rural: 86.1% of population

total: 93.4% of population

unimproved:

urban: 4.5% of population

rural: 13.9% of population

total: 6.6% of population (2015 est.)

CURRENT HEALTH EXPENDITURE:

4.3% (2016)

PHYSICIANS DENSITY:

1.97 physicians/1,000 population (2017)

HOSPITAL BED DENSITY:

1.6 beds/1,000 population (2014)

SANITATION FACILITY ACCESS:

improved:

  urban: 97.3% of population (2015 est.)

  rural: 94.7% of population (2015 est.)

  total: 96.7% of population (2015 est.)

unimproved:

  urban: 2.7% of population (2015 est.)

  rural: 5.3% of population (2015 est.)

  total: 3.3% of population (2015 est.)

HIV/AIDS - ADULT PREVALENCE RATE:

0.2% (2018)

country comparison to the world: 110

HIV/AIDS - PEOPLE LIVING WITH HIV/AIDS:

3,200 (2018)

country comparison to the world: 129

HIV/AIDS - DEATHS:

100 (2018)

country comparison to the world: 66

OBESITY - ADULT PREVALENCE RATE:

27% (2016)

country comparison to the world: 39

CHILDREN UNDER THE AGE OF 5 YEARS UNDERWEIGHT:

9.7% (2014)

country comparison to the world: 63

EDUCATION EXPENDITURES:

6.7% of GDP (2017)

country comparison to the world: 20

LITERACY:

  definition: age 15 and over can read and write

  total population: 96.1%

  male: 97.4%

  female: 93.2% (2017 est.)

SCHOOL LIFE EXPECTANCY (PRIMARY TO TERTIARY EDUCATION):

  total: 15 years

  male: 14 years

  female: 15 years (2016)

UNEMPLOYMENT, YOUTH AGES 15-24:

  total: 13.7%

  male: 10.3%

  female: 33.9% (2016)

  country comparison to the world: 101

GOVERNMENT :: OMAN

COUNTRY NAME:

  conventional long form: Sultanate of Oman

  conventional short form: Oman

  local long form: Saltanat Uman

  local short form: Uman

  former: Sultanate of Muscat and Oman

  etymology: the origin of the name is uncertain, but it apparently dates back at least 2,000 years since an "Omana" is mentioned by Pliny the Elder (1st century A.D.) and an "Omanon" by Ptolemy (2nd century A.D.)

GOVERNMENT TYPE:

absolute monarchy

CAPITAL:

  name: Muscat

  geographic coordinates: 23 37 N, 58 35 E

  time difference: UTC+4 (9 hours ahead of Washington, DC, during Standard Time)

  etymology: the name, whose meaning is uncertain, traces back almost two millennia; two 2nd century A.D. scholars, the geographer Ptolemy and the historian Arrian, both mention an Arabian Sea coastal town of Moscha, which most likely referred to Muscat

ADMINISTRATIVE DIVISIONS:

11 governorates (muhafazat, singular - muhafaza); Ad Dakhiliyah, Al Buraymi, Al Wusta, Az Zahirah, Janub al Batinah (Al Batinah South), Janub ash Sharqiyah (Ash Sharqiyah South), Masqat (Muscat), Musandam, Shamal al Batinah (Al Batinah North), Shamal ash Sharqiyah (Ash Sharqiyah North), Zufar (Dhofar)

INDEPENDENCE:

1650 (expulsion of the Portuguese)

NATIONAL HOLIDAY:

National Day, 18 November; note - coincides with the birthday of Sultan QABOOS, 18 November (1940)

CONSTITUTION:

  history: promulgated by royal decree 6 November 1996 (the Basic Law of the Sultanate of Oman serves as the constitution) amended by royal decree in 2011

  amendments: promulgated by the sultan or proposed by the Council of Oman and drafted by a technical committee as stipulated by royal decree and then promulgated through royal decree; amended by royal decree in 2011 (2016)

LEGAL SYSTEM:

mixed legal system of Anglo-Saxon law and Islamic law

INTERNATIONAL LAW ORGANIZATION PARTICIPATION:

has not submitted an ICJ jurisdiction declaration; non-party state to the ICCt

CITIZENSHIP:

  citizenship by birth: no

  citizenship by descent only: the father must be a citizen of Oman

  dual citizenship recognized: no

  residency requirement for naturalization: unknown

SUFFRAGE:

21 years of age; universal; note - members of the military and security forces by law cannot vote

EXECUTIVE BRANCH:

  chief of state: Sultan and Prime Minister QABOOS bin Said Al-Said (sultan since 23 July 1970 and prime minister since 23 July 1972); note - the monarch is both chief of state and head of government

  head of government: Sultan and Prime Minister QABOOS bin Said Al-Said (sultan since 23 July 1970 and prime minister since 23 July 1972)

  cabinet: Cabinet appointed by the monarch

  elections/appointments: members of the Ruling Family Council determine a successor from the sultan's extended family; if the Council cannot form a consensus within 3 days of the sultan's death or incapacitation, the Defense Council will relay a predetermined heir as chosen by the sultan

LEGISLATIVE BRANCH:

  description: bicameral Council of Oman or Majlis Oman consists of: Council of State or Majlis al-Dawla (85 seats including the chairman; members appointed by the sultan from among former government officials and prominent educators, businessmen, and citizens) Consultative Council or Majlis al-

Shura (84 seats; members directly elected in single- and 2-seat constituencies by simple majority popular vote to serve renewable 4-year terms); note - since political reforms in 2011, legislation from the Consultative Council is submitted to the Council of State for review by the Royal Court

elections: Council of State - last appointments on 7 November 2015 (next - NA)
Consultative Assembly - last held on 27 October 2019 (next to be held in October 2023)

election results:
Council of State - composition - men 72, women 13, percent of women 15.3%
Consultative Council percent of vote by party - NA; seats by party - NA (organized political parties in Oman are legally banned); composition men 83, women 2, percent of women 2.4%; note - total Council of Oman percent of women 8.8%

JUDICIAL BRANCH:

highest courts: Supreme Court (consists of 5 judges)

judge selection and term of office: judges nominated by the 9-member Supreme Judicial Council (chaired by the monarch) and appointed by the monarch; judges appointed for life

subordinate courts: Courts of Appeal; Administrative Court; Courts of First Instance; sharia courts; magistrates' courts; military courts

POLITICAL PARTIES AND LEADERS:

none; note - organized political parties are legally banned in Oman, and loyalties tend to form around tribal affiliations

INTERNATIONAL ORGANIZATION PARTICIPATION:

ABEDA, AFESD, AMF, CAEU, FAO, G-77, GCC, IAEA, IBRD, ICAO, ICC (NGOs), IDA, IDB, IFAD, IFC, IHO, ILO, IMF, IMO, IMSO, Interpol, IOC, IPU, ISO, ITSO, ITU, LAS, MIGA, NAM, OIC, OPCW, UN, UNCTAD, UNESCO, UNIDO, UNWTO, UPU, WCO, WFTU (NGOs), WHO, WIPO, WMO, WTO

DIPLOMATIC REPRESENTATION IN THE US:

Ambassador Hunaina bint Sultan bin Ahmad al-MUGHAIRI (since 2 December 2005)

chancery: 2535 Belmont Road, NW, Washington, DC 20008

telephone: [1] (202) 387-1980

FAX: [1] (202) 745-4933

DIPLOMATIC REPRESENTATION FROM THE US:

chief of mission: Ambassador Marc J. SIEVERS (since 15 December 2016)

telephone: [968] 24-643-400

embassy: P.C. 115, Madinat Al Sultan Qaboos, Muscat

mailing address: P.O. Box 202, P.C. 115, Madinat Al Sultan Qaboos, Muscat

FAX: [968] 24-643-740

FLAG DESCRIPTION:

three horizontal bands of white (top), red, and green of equal width with a broad, vertical, red band on the hoist side; the national emblem (a khanjar dagger in its sheath superimposed on two crossed swords in scabbards) in white is centered near the top of the vertical band; white represents peace and prosperity, red recalls battles against foreign invaders, and green symbolizes the Jebel al Akhdar (Green Mountains) and fertility

NATIONAL SYMBOL(S):

khanjar dagger superimposed on two crossed swords; national colors: red, white, green

NATIONAL ANTHEM:

name: "Nashid as-Salaam as-Sultani" (The Sultan's Anthem)

lyrics/music: Rashid bin Uzayyiz al KHUSAIDI/James Frederick MILLS, arranged by Bernard EBBINGHAUS

note: adopted 1932; new lyrics written after QABOOS bin Said al Said gained power in 1970; first performed by the band of a British ship as a salute to the Sultan during a 1932 visit to Muscat; the bandmaster of the HMS Hawkins was asked to write a salutation to the Sultan on the occasion of his ship visit

ECONOMY :: OMAN

ECONOMY - OVERVIEW:

Oman is heavily dependent on oil and gas resources, which can generate between and 68% and 85% of government revenue, depending on fluctuations in commodity prices. In 2016, low global oil prices drove Oman's budget deficit to $13.8 billion, or approximately 20% of GDP, but the budget deficit is estimated to have reduced to 12% of GDP in 2017 as Oman reduced government subsidies. As of January 2018, Oman has sufficient foreign assets to support its currency's fixed exchange rates. It is issuing debt to cover its deficit.

Oman is using enhanced oil recovery techniques to boost production, but it has simultaneously pursued a development plan that focuses on diversification, industrialization, and privatization, with the objective of reducing the oil sector's contribution to GDP. The key components of the government's diversification strategy are tourism, shipping and logistics, mining, manufacturing, and aquaculture.

Muscat also has notably focused on creating more Omani jobs to employ the rising number of nationals entering the workforce. However, high social welfare benefits - that had increased in the wake of the 2011 Arab Spring - have made it impossible for the government to balance its budget in light of current oil prices. In response, Omani officials imposed austerity measures on its gasoline and diesel subsidies in 2016. These spending cuts have had only a moderate effect on the government's budget, which is projected to again face a deficit of $7.8 billion in 2018.

GDP (PURCHASING POWER PARITY):

$190.1 billion (2017 est.)

$191.9 billion (2016 est.)

$182.8 billion (2015 est.)

note: data are in 2017 dollars

country comparison to the world: 67

GDP (OFFICIAL EXCHANGE RATE):

$70.78 billion (2017 est.)

GDP - REAL GROWTH RATE:

-0.9% (2017 est.)

5% (2016 est.)

4.7% (2015 est.)

country comparison to the world: 201

GDP - PER CAPITA (PPP):

$46,000 (2017 est.)

$47,900 (2016 est.)

$48,400 (2015 est.)

note: data are in 2017 dollars

country comparison to the world: 37

GROSS NATIONAL SAVING:

16.1% of GDP (2017 est.)

10.5% of GDP (2016 est.)

14.3% of GDP (2015 est.)

country comparison to the world: 127

GDP - COMPOSITION, BY END USE:

household consumption: 36.8% (2017 est.)

government consumption: 26.2% (2017 est.)

investment in fixed capital: 27.8% (2017 est.)

investment in inventories: 3% (2017 est.)

exports of goods and services: 51.5% (2017 est.)

imports of goods and services: -46.6% (2017 est.)

GDP - COMPOSITION, BY SECTOR OF ORIGIN:

agriculture: 1.8% (2017 est.)

industry: 46.4% (2017 est.)

services: 51.8% (2017 est.)

AGRICULTURE - PRODUCTS:

dates, limes, bananas, alfalfa, vegetables; camels, cattle; fish

INDUSTRIES:

crude oil production and refining, natural and liquefied natural gas production; construction, cement, copper, steel, chemicals, optic fiber

INDUSTRIAL PRODUCTION GROWTH RATE:

-3% (2017 est.)

country comparison to the world: 188

LABOR FORCE:

2.255 million (2016 est.)

note: about 60% of the labor force is non-national

country comparison to the world: 119

LABOR FORCE - BY OCCUPATION:

agriculture: 4.7% NA

industry: 49.6% NA

services: 45% NA (2016 est.)

UNEMPLOYMENT RATE:

NA

POPULATION BELOW POVERTY LINE:

NA

HOUSEHOLD INCOME OR CONSUMPTION BY PERCENTAGE SHARE:

lowest 10%: NA

highest 10%: NA

BUDGET:

revenues: 22.14 billion (2017 est.)

expenditures: 31.92 billion (2017 est.)

TAXES AND OTHER REVENUES:

31.3% (of GDP) (2017 est.)

country comparison to the world: 73

BUDGET SURPLUS (+) OR DEFICIT (-):

-13.8% (of GDP) (2017 est.)

country comparison to the world: 216

PUBLIC DEBT:

46.9% of GDP (2017 est.)

32.5% of GDP (2016 est.)

note: excludes indebtedness of state-owned enterprises

country comparison to the world: 113

FISCAL YEAR:

calendar year

INFLATION RATE (CONSUMER PRICES):

1.6% (2017 est.)

1.1% (2016 est.)

country comparison to the world: 90

CENTRAL BANK DISCOUNT RATE:

2% (31 December 2010)

0.05% (31 December 2009)

country comparison to the world: 119

COMMERCIAL BANK PRIME LENDING RATE:

5.2% (31 December 2017 est.)

5.08% (31 December 2016 est.)

country comparison to the world: 148

STOCK OF NARROW MONEY:

$12.85 billion (31 December 2017 est.)

$12.95 billion (31 December 2016 est.)

country comparison to the world: 79

STOCK OF BROAD MONEY:

$12.85 billion (31 December 2017 est.)

$12.95 billion (31 December 2016 est.)

country comparison to the world: 80

STOCK OF DOMESTIC CREDIT:

$48.47 billion (31 December 2017 est.)

$46.47 billion (31 December 2016 est.)

country comparison to the world: 67

MARKET VALUE OF PUBLICLY TRADED SHARES:

$41.12 billion (31 December 2015 est.)

$37.83 billion (31 December 2014 est.)

$36.77 billion (31 December 2013 est.)

country comparison to the world: 57

CURRENT ACCOUNT BALANCE:

-$10.76 billion (2017 est.)

-$12.32 billion (2016 est.)

country comparison to the world: 192

EXPORTS:

$103.3 billion (2017 est.)

$27.54 billion (2016 est.)

country comparison to the world: 35

EXPORTS - PARTNERS:

China 43.7%, UAE 11%, South Korea 7.9%, Saudi Arabia 4.2% (2017)

EXPORTS - COMMODITIES:

petroleum, reexports, fish, metals, textiles

IMPORTS:

$24.12 billion (2017 est.)

$21.29 billion (2016 est.)

country comparison to the world: 71

IMPORTS - COMMODITIES:

machinery and transport equipment, manufactured goods, food, livestock, lubricants

IMPORTS - PARTNERS:

UAE 35.5%, US 27.8%, Brazil 4% (2017)

RESERVES OF FOREIGN EXCHANGE AND GOLD:

$16.09 billion (31 December 2017 est.)

$20.26 billion (31 December 2016 est.)

country comparison to the world: 64

DEBT - EXTERNAL:

$46.27 billion (31 December 2017 est.)

$27.05 billion (31 December 2016 est.)

country comparison to the world: 70

STOCK OF DIRECT FOREIGN INVESTMENT - AT HOME:

NA

STOCK OF DIRECT FOREIGN INVESTMENT - ABROAD:

NA

EXCHANGE RATES:

Omani rials (OMR) per US dollar -

0.3845 (2017 est.)

0.3845 (2016 est.)

0.3845 (2015 est.)

0.3845 (2014 est.)

0.3845 (2013 est.)

ENERGY :: OMAN

ELECTRICITY ACCESS:

electrification - total population: 99% (2016)

electrification - urban areas: 100% (2016)

electrification - rural areas: 93% (2016)

ELECTRICITY - PRODUCTION:
32.16 billion kWh (2016 est.)

country comparison to the world: 62

ELECTRICITY - CONSUMPTION:
28.92 billion kWh (2016 est.)

country comparison to the world: 63

ELECTRICITY - EXPORTS:
0 kWh (2016 est.)

country comparison to the world: 181

ELECTRICITY - IMPORTS:
0 kWh (2016 est.)

country comparison to the world: 183

ELECTRICITY - INSTALLED GENERATING CAPACITY:
8.167 million kW (2016 est.)

country comparison to the world: 70

ELECTRICITY - FROM FOSSIL FUELS:
100% of total installed capacity (2016 est.)

country comparison to the world: 14

ELECTRICITY - FROM NUCLEAR FUELS:
0% of total installed capacity (2017 est.)

country comparison to the world: 160

ELECTRICITY - FROM HYDROELECTRIC PLANTS:
0% of total installed capacity (2017 est.)

country comparison to the world: 192

ELECTRICITY - FROM OTHER RENEWABLE SOURCES:
0% of total installed capacity (2017 est.)

country comparison to the world: 204

CRUDE OIL - PRODUCTION:
979,000 bbl/day (2018 est.)

country comparison to the world: 21

CRUDE OIL - EXPORTS:
844,100 bbl/day (2015 est.)

country comparison to the world: 14

CRUDE OIL - IMPORTS:
0 bbl/day (2015 est.)

country comparison to the world: 179

CRUDE OIL - PROVED RESERVES:
5.373 billion bbl (1 January 2018 est.)

country comparison to the world: 21

REFINED PETROLEUM PRODUCTS - PRODUCTION:
229,600 bbl/day (2015 est.)

country comparison to the world: 48

REFINED PETROLEUM PRODUCTS - CONSUMPTION:
188,000 bbl/day (2016 est.)

country comparison to the world: 59

REFINED PETROLEUM PRODUCTS - EXPORTS:
33,700 bbl/day (2015 est.)

country comparison to the world: 60

REFINED PETROLEUM PRODUCTS - IMPORTS:
6,041 bbl/day (2015 est.)

country comparison to the world: 165

NATURAL GAS - PRODUCTION:
31.23 billion cu m (2017 est.)

country comparison to the world: 26

NATURAL GAS - CONSUMPTION:
21.94 billion cu m (2017 est.)

country comparison to the world: 35

NATURAL GAS - EXPORTS:
11.16 billion cu m (2017 est.)

country comparison to the world: 20

NATURAL GAS - IMPORTS:
1.982 billion cu m (2017 est.)

country comparison to the world: 53

NATURAL GAS - PROVED RESERVES:
651.3 billion cu m (1 January 2018 est.)

country comparison to the world: 28

CARBON DIOXIDE EMISSIONS FROM CONSUMPTION OF ENERGY:
68.94 million Mt (2017 est.)

country comparison to the world: 52

COMMUNICATIONS :: OMAN

TELEPHONES - FIXED LINES:
total subscriptions: 497,716

subscriptions per 100 inhabitants: 11 (2017 est.)

country comparison to the world: 95

TELEPHONES - MOBILE CELLULAR:
total subscriptions: 6,943,910

subscriptions per 100 inhabitants: 151 (2017 est.)

country comparison to the world: 107

TELEPHONE SYSTEM:
general assessment: modern system consisting of open-wire, microwave, and radiotelephone communication stations; coaxial cable; domestic satellite system with 8 earth stations; both 3G and 4G LTE networks; exploring 5G options; competition among mobile network operators (MNO) (2018)

domestic: fixed-line 11 per 100 and mobile-cellular 151 per 100, subscribership both increasing with fixed-line phone service gradually being introduced to remote villages using wireless local loop systems (2018)

international: country code - 968; landing points for GSA, AAE-1, SeaMeWe-5, Tata TGN-Gulf, FALCON, GBICS/MENA, MENA/Guld Bridge International, TW1, BBG, EIG, OMRAN/EPEG, and POI submarine cables providing connectivity to Asia, Africa, the Middle East, Southeast Asia and Europe; satellite earth stations - 2 Intelsat (Indian Ocean) (2019)

BROADCAST MEDIA:
1 state-run TV broadcaster; TV stations transmitting from Saudi Arabia, the UAE, Iran, and Yemen available via satellite TV; state-run radio operates multiple stations; first private radio station began operating in 2007 and several additional stations now operating (2019)

INTERNET COUNTRY CODE:
.om

INTERNET USERS:
total: 2,342,483

percent of population: 69.8% (July 2016 est.)

country comparison to the world: 106

BROADBAND - FIXED SUBSCRIPTIONS:
total: 348,926

subscriptions per 100 inhabitants: 8 (2017 est.)

country comparison to the world: 91

MILITARY AND SECURITY :: OMAN

MILITARY EXPENDITURES:
8.17% of GDP (2018)

9.56% of GDP (2017)

11.97% of GDP (2016)

10.79% of GDP (2015)

10.14% of GDP (2014)

country comparison to the world: 2

MILITARY AND SECURITY FORCES:
Sultan's Armed Forces (SAF): Royal Army of Oman (RAO), Royal Navy of

Oman (RNO), Royal Air Force of Oman (RAFO), Royal Guard of Oman (RGO) (2019)

The Royal Oman Police Coast Guard is separate from the SAF.

MILITARY SERVICE AGE AND OBLIGATION:

18-30 years of age for voluntary military service; no conscription (2012)

MARITIME THREATS:

the Maritime Administration of the US Department of Transportation has issued a Maritime Advisory (2019-012-Persian Gulf, Strait of Hormuz, Gulf of Oman, Arabian Sea, Red Sea-Threats to US and International Shipping from Iran) effective 7 August 2019, which states in part that "heightened military activities and increased political tensions in this region continue to present risk to commercial shipping...there is a continued possibility that Iran and/or its regional proxies could take actions against US and partner interests in the region;" at present, Iran has seized two foreign-flagged tankers in the Persian Gulf; the US and UK navies have established Operation Sentinel to provide escorts for commercial shipping transiting the Persian Gulf, Strait of Hormuz, and Gulf of Oman

TRANSPORTATION :: OMAN

NATIONAL AIR TRANSPORT SYSTEM:

number of registered air carriers: 1 (2015)

inventory of registered aircraft operated by air carriers: 45 (2015)

annual passenger traffic on registered air carriers: 6,365,784 (2015)

annual freight traffic on registered air carriers: 412,234,008 mt-km (2015)

CIVIL AIRCRAFT REGISTRATION COUNTRY CODE PREFIX:

A4O (2016)

AIRPORTS:

132 (2013)

country comparison to the world: 44

AIRPORTS - WITH PAVED RUNWAYS:

total: 13 (2017)

over 3,047 m: 7 (2017)

2,438 to 3,047 m: 5 (2017)

914 to 1,523 m: 1 (2017)

AIRPORTS - WITH UNPAVED RUNWAYS:

total: 119 (2013)

over 3,047 m: 2 (2013)

2,438 to 3,047 m: 7 (2013)

1,524 to 2,437 m: 51 (2013)

914 to 1,523 m: 33 (2013)

under 914 m: 26 (2013)

HELIPORTS:

3 (2013)

PIPELINES:

106 km condensate, 4224 km gas, 3558 km oil, 33 km oil/gas/water, 264 km refined products (2013)

RAILWAYS:

ROADWAYS:

total: 60,230 km (2012)

paved: 29,685 km (includes 1,943 km of expressways) (2012)

unpaved: 30,545 km (2012)

country comparison to the world: 74

MERCHANT MARINE:

total: 51

by type: general cargo 9, other 42 (2018)

country comparison to the world: 114

PORTS AND TERMINALS:

major seaport(s): Mina' Qabus, Salalah, Suhar

container port(s) (TEUs): Salalah (3,946,421) (2017)

LNG terminal(s) (export): Qalhat

TRANSNATIONAL ISSUES :: OMAN

DISPUTES - INTERNATIONAL:

boundary agreement reportedly signed and ratified with UAE in 2003 for entire border, including Oman's Musandam Peninsula and Al Madhah exclave, but details of the alignment have not been made public

REFUGEES AND INTERNALLY DISPLACED PERSONS:

refugees (country of origin): 5,000 (Yemen) (2017)

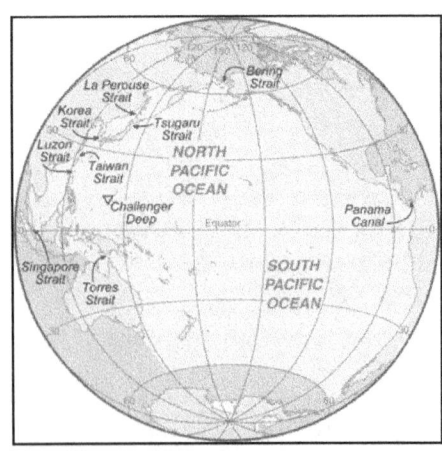

OCEANS :: PACIFIC OCEAN

INTRODUCTION :: PACIFIC OCEAN

BACKGROUND:
The Pacific Ocean is the largest of the world's five oceans (followed by the Atlantic Ocean, Indian Ocean, Southern Ocean, and Arctic Ocean). Strategically important access waterways include the La Perouse, Tsugaru, Tsushima, Taiwan, Singapore, and Torres Straits. The decision by the International Hydrographic Organization in the spring of 2000 to delimit a fifth ocean, the Southern Ocean, removed the portion of the Pacific Ocean south of 60 degrees south.

GEOGRAPHY :: PACIFIC OCEAN

LOCATION:
body of water between the Southern Ocean, Asia, Australia, and the Western Hemisphere

GEOGRAPHIC COORDINATES:
0 00 N, 160 00 W

MAP REFERENCES:
Political Map of the World

AREA:
total: 155.557 million sq km

note: includes Bali Sea, Bering Sea, Bering Strait, Coral Sea, East China Sea, Gulf of Alaska, Gulf of Tonkin, Philippine Sea, Sea of Japan, Sea of Okhotsk, South China Sea, Tasman Sea, and other tributary water bodies

AREA - COMPARATIVE:
about 15 times the size of the US; covers about 28% of the global surface; almost equal to the total land area of the world

COASTLINE:
135,663 km

CLIMATE:
planetary air pressure systems and resultant wind patterns exhibit remarkable uniformity in the south and east; trade winds and westerly winds are well-developed patterns, modified by seasonal fluctuations; tropical cyclones (hurricanes) may form south of Mexico from June to October and affect Mexico and Central America; continental influences cause climatic uniformity to be much less pronounced in the eastern and western regions at the same latitude in the North Pacific Ocean; the western Pacific is monsoonal - a rainy season occurs during the summer months, when moisture-laden winds blow from the ocean over the land, and a dry season during the winter months, when dry winds blow from the Asian landmass back to the ocean; tropical cyclones (typhoons) may strike southeast and east Asia from May to December

TERRAIN:
surface dominated by two large gyres (broad, circular systems of currents), one in the northern Pacific and another in the southern Pacific; in the northern Pacific, sea ice forms in the Bering Sea and Sea of Okhotsk in winter; in the southern Pacific, sea ice from Antarctica reaches its northernmost extent in October; the ocean floor in the eastern Pacific is dominated by the East Pacific Rise, while the western Pacific is dissected by deep trenches, including the Mariana Trench, which is the world's deepest at 10,924 m

major surface currents: clockwise North Pacific Gyre formed by the warm northward flowing Kuroshio Current in the west, the eastward flowing North Pacific Current in the north, the southward flowing cold California Current in the east, and the westward flowing North Equatorial Current in the south; the counterclockwise South Pacific Gyre composed of the southward flowing warm East Australian Current in the west, the eastward flowing South Pacific Current in the south, the northward flowing cold Peru (Humbolt) Current in the east, and the westward flowing South Equatorial Current in the north

ELEVATION:
mean depth: -2,970 m

lowest point: Challenger Deep in the Mariana Trench -10,924 m

highest point: sea level

NATURAL RESOURCES:
oil and gas fields, polymetallic nodules, sand and gravel aggregates, placer deposits, fish

NATURAL HAZARDS:
surrounded by a zone of violent volcanic and earthquake activity sometimes referred to as the "Pacific Ring of Fire"; subject to tropical cyclones (typhoons) in southeast and east Asia from May to December (most frequent from July to October); tropical cyclones (hurricanes) may form south of Mexico and strike Central America and Mexico from June to October (most common in August and September); cyclical El Nino/La Nina phenomenon occurs in the equatorial Pacific, influencing weather in the Western Hemisphere and the western Pacific; ships subject to superstructure icing in extreme north from October to May; persistent fog in the northern Pacific can be a maritime hazard from June to December

ENVIRONMENT - CURRENT ISSUES:
pollution (such as sewage, runoff from land and toxic waste); habitat destruction; over-fishing; climate change leading to sea level rise, ocean acidification, and warming; endangered marine species include the dugong, sea lion, sea otter, seals, turtles, and whales; oil pollution in Philippine Sea and South China Sea

GEOGRAPHY - NOTE:
the major chokepoints are the Bering Strait, Panama Canal, Luzon Strait, and the Singapore Strait; the Equator divides the Pacific Ocean into the North Pacific Ocean and the South Pacific Ocean; dotted with low coral islands and rugged volcanic islands in the southwestern Pacific Ocean; much of the Pacific Ocean's rim lies along the Ring of Fire, a belt of active

volcanoes and earthquake epicenters that accounts for up to 90% of the world's earthquakes and some 75% of the world's volcanoes

GOVERNMENT :: PACIFIC OCEAN

COUNTRY NAME:
etymology: named by Portuguese explorer Ferdinand MAGELLAN during the Spanish circumnavigation of the world in 1521; encountering favorable winds upon reaching the ocean, he called it "Mar Pacifico," which means "peaceful sea" in both Portuguese and Spanish

ECONOMY :: PACIFIC OCEAN

ECONOMY - OVERVIEW:
The Pacific Ocean is a major contributor to the world economy and particularly to those nations its waters directly touch. It provides low-cost sea transportation between East and West, extensive fishing grounds, offshore oil and gas fields, minerals, and sand and gravel for the construction industry. In 1996, over 60% of the world's fish catch came from the Pacific Ocean. Exploitation of offshore oil and gas reserves is playing an ever-increasing role in the energy supplies of the US, Australia, NZ, China, and Peru. The high cost of recovering offshore oil and gas, combined with the wide swings in world prices for oil since 1985, has led to fluctuations in new drillings.

MARINE FISHERIES:
the Pacific Ocean fisheries are the most important in the world accounting for 59%, or 46,706,536 mt, of the global marine capture in 2016; of the six regions delineated by the Food and Agriculture Organization in the Pacific Ocean, the following are the most important:

Northwest Pacific region (Region 61) is the world's most important fishery producing 28% of the global catch or 22,411,224 mt in 2016; it encompasses the waters north of 20º north latitude and west of 175º west longitude with the major producers including China (14,776,769 mt), Japan (2,896,073 mt), South Korea (944,558 mt), and Taiwan (378,990 mt); the principal catches include Alaska Pollock, Japanese anchovy, chub mackerel, and scads

Western Central Pacific region (Region 71) is the world's second most important fishing region producing 16%, or 12,742,955 mt, of the global catch in 2016; tuna is the most important species in this region; the region includes the waters between 20º North and 25º South latitude and west of 175º West longitude with the major producers including Indonesia (4,704,382 mt), Vietnam (2,678,406 mt), Philippines (1,865,213 mt), Thailand (950,219 mt), and Malaysia (792,163 mt); the principal catches include Skipjack and Yellowfin tuna, sardinellas, and cephalopods

Southeast Pacific region (Region 87) is the third major Pacific fishery and fifth largest in the world producing 8%, or 6,329,328 mt, of the global catch in 2016; this region includes the nutrient rich upwelling waters off the west coast of South America between 5º North and 60º South latitude and east of 120º West longitude with the major producers including Peru (3,774,887 mt), Chile (1,495,359 mt), and Ecuador (612,755 mt); the principal catches include Peruvian anchovy (50% of the catch), Jumbo flying squid, and Chilean jack mackerel

Pacific Northeast region (Region 67) is the fourth largest Pacific Ocean fishery and eighth largest in the world producing 4% of the global catch or 3,092,529 mt in 2016; this region encompasses the waters north of 40º North latitude and east of 175º West longitude including the Gulf of Alaska and Bering Sea with the major producers including the US (2,900,835 mt), Canada (180,664 mt), and Russia (11,030 mt); the principal catches include Alaska pollock, Pacific cod, and North Pacific hake

MILITARY AND SECURITY :: PACIFIC OCEAN

MARITIME THREATS:
the International Maritime Bureau reports the territorial waters of littoral states and offshore waters in the South China Sea as high risk for piracy and armed robbery against ships; an emerging threat area lies in the Celebes and Sulu Seas between the Philippines and Malaysia where three crew were kidnapped or taken hostage in 2018; numerous commercial vessels have been attacked and hijacked both at anchor and while underway; hijacked vessels are often disguised and cargoes stolen; crew and passengers are often held for ransom, murdered, or cast adrift; the Maritime Administration (MARAD) of the US Department of Transportation has issued a Maritime Advisory (2019-011-Sulu and Celebes Seas-Piracy/Armed Robbery/Terrorism) which states in part "In 2018, there were at least 12 reported boardings, attempted boardings, attacks, hijackings, and kidnappings in the Sulu and Celebes Seas. Recent kidnapping incidents in this area were reportedly linked to the Abu Sayyaf Group (ASG), a violent Islamic separatist group operating in the southern Philippines..." and advises ships to adhere to counter-piracy practices to minimize risk

TRANSPORTATION :: PACIFIC OCEAN

ROADWAYS:
PORTS AND TERMINALS:
major seaport(s): Bangkok (Thailand), Hong Kong (China), Kao-hsiung (Taiwan), Los Angeles (US), Manila (Philippines), Pusan (South Korea), San Francisco (US), Seattle (US), Shanghai (China), Singapore, Sydney (Australia), Vladivostok (Russia), Wellington (NZ), Yokohama (Japan)

TRANSNATIONAL ISSUES :: PACIFIC OCEAN

DISPUTES - INTERNATIONAL:
some maritime disputes (see littoral states)

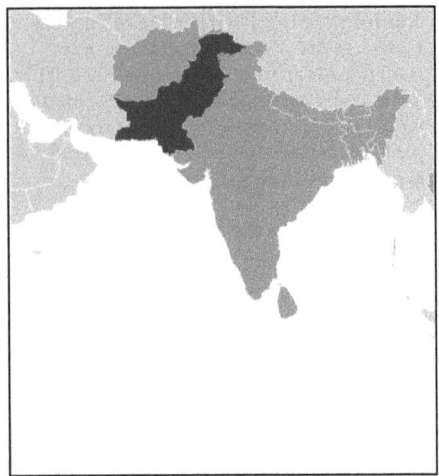

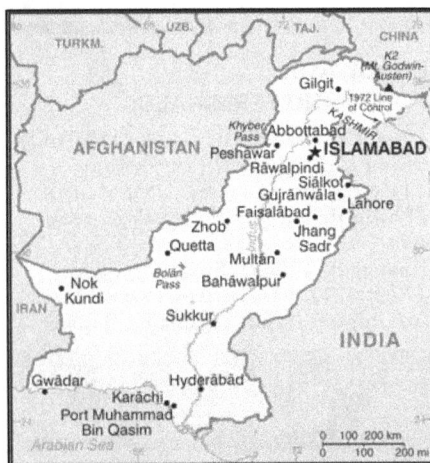

SOUTH ASIA :: PAKISTAN

INTRODUCTION :: PAKISTAN

BACKGROUND:

The Indus Valley civilization, one of the oldest in the world and dating back at least 5,000 years, spread over much of what is presently Pakistan. During the second millennium B.C., remnants of this culture fused with the migrating Indo-Aryan peoples. The area underwent successive invasions in subsequent centuries from the Persians, Greeks, Scythians, Arabs (who brought Islam), Afghans, and Turks. The Mughal Empire flourished in the 16th and 17th centuries; the British came to dominate the region in the 18th century. The separation in 1947 of British India into the Muslim state of Pakistan (with West and East sections) and largely Hindu India was never satisfactorily resolved, and India and Pakistan fought two wars and a limited conflict - in 1947-48, 1965, and 1999 respectively - over the disputed Kashmir territory. A third war between these countries in 1971 - in which India assisted an indigenous movement reacting to the marginalization of Bengalis in Pakistani politics - resulted in East Pakistan becoming the separate nation of Bangladesh.

In response to Indian nuclear weapons testing, Pakistan conducted its own tests in mid-1998. India-Pakistan relations improved in the mid-2000s but have been rocky since the November 2008 Mumbai attacks and have been further strained by attacks in India by militants believed to be based in Pakistan. Imran KHAN took office as prime minister in 2018 after the Pakistan Tehreek-e-Insaaf (PTI) party won a plurality of seats in the July 2018 general elections. Pakistan has been engaged in a decades-long armed conflict with militant groups that target government institutions and civilians, including the Tehreek-e-Taliban Pakistan (TTP) and other militant networks.

GEOGRAPHY :: PAKISTAN

LOCATION:
Southern Asia, bordering the Arabian Sea, between India on the east and Iran and Afghanistan on the west and China in the north

GEOGRAPHIC COORDINATES:
30 00 N, 70 00 E

MAP REFERENCES:
Asia

AREA:
total: 796,095 sq km

land: 770,875 sq km

water: 25,220 sq km

country comparison to the world: 37

AREA - COMPARATIVE:
slightly more than five times the size of Georgia; slightly less than twice the size of California

LAND BOUNDARIES:
total: 7,257 km

border countries (4): Afghanistan 2670 km, China 438 km, India 3190 km, Iran 959 km

COASTLINE:
1,046 km

MARITIME CLAIMS:
territorial sea: 12 nm

exclusive economic zone: 200 nm

contiguous zone: 24 nm

continental shelf: 200 nm or to the edge of the continental margin

CLIMATE:
mostly hot, dry desert; temperate in northwest; arctic in north

TERRAIN:
divided into three major geographic areas: the northern highlands, the Indus River plain in the center and east, and the Balochistan Plateau in the south and west

ELEVATION:
mean elevation: 900 m

lowest point: Arabian Sea 0 m

highest point: K2 (Mt. Godwin-Austen) 8,611 m

NATURAL RESOURCES:
arable land, extensive natural gas reserves, limited petroleum, poor quality coal, iron ore, copper, salt, limestone

LAND USE:
agricultural land: 35.2% (2011 est.)

arable land: 27.6% (2011 est.) / permanent crops: 1.1% (2011 est.) / permanent pasture: 6.5% (2011 est.)

forest: 2.1% (2011 est.)

other: 62.7% (2011 est.)

IRRIGATED LAND:
202,000 sq km (2012)

POPULATION DISTRIBUTION:
the Indus River and its tributaries attract most of the settlement, with Punjab province the most densely populated

NATURAL HAZARDS:
frequent earthquakes, occasionally severe especially in north and west;

flooding along the Indus after heavy rains (July and August)

ENVIRONMENT - CURRENT ISSUES:
water pollution from raw sewage, industrial wastes, and agricultural runoff; limited natural freshwater resources; most of the population does not have access to potable water; deforestation; soil erosion; desertification; air pollution and noise pollution in urban areas

ENVIRONMENT - INTERNATIONAL AGREEMENTS:
party to: Biodiversity, Climate Change, Climate Change-Kyoto Protocol, Desertification, Endangered Species, Environmental Modification, Hazardous Wastes, Law of the Sea, Marine Dumping, Ozone Layer Protection, Ship Pollution, Wetlands

signed, but not ratified: Marine Life Conservation

GEOGRAPHY - NOTE:
controls Khyber Pass and Bolan Pass, traditional invasion routes between Central Asia and the Indian Subcontinent

PEOPLE AND SOCIETY :: PAKISTAN

POPULATION:
207,862,518 (July 2017 est.) (July 2018 est.)

note: provisional results of Pakistan's 2017 national census estimate the country's total population to be 207,774,000

country comparison to the world: 6

NATIONALITY:
noun: Pakistani(s)

adjective: Pakistani

ETHNIC GROUPS:
Punjabi 44.7%, Pashtun (Pathan) 15.4%, Sindhi 14.1%, Saraiki 8.4%, Muhajirs 7.6%, Balochi 3.6%, other 6.3%

LANGUAGES:
Punjabi 48%, Sindhi 12%, Saraiki (a Punjabi variant) 10%, Pashto (alternate name, Pashtu) 8%, Urdu (official) 8%, Balochi 3%, Hindko 2%, Brahui 1%, English (official; lingua franca of Pakistani elite and most government ministries), Burushaski, and other 8%

RELIGIONS:
Muslim (official) 96.4% (Sunni 85-90%, Shia 10-15%), other (includes Christian and Hindu) 3.6% (2010 est.)

AGE STRUCTURE:
0-14 years: 30.76% (male 32,828,078 /female 31,118,626)

15-24 years: 20.94% (male 22,446,320 /female 21,076,265)

25-54 years: 38.04% (male 41,021,803 /female 38,039,766)

55-64 years: 5.7% (male 5,979,712 /female 5,871,574)

65 years and over: 4.56% (male 4,399,926 /female 5,080,448) (2018 est.)

DEPENDENCY RATIOS:
total dependency ratio: 65.3 (2015 est.)

youth dependency ratio: 57.9 (2015 est.)

elderly dependency ratio: 7.4 (2015 est.)

potential support ratio: 13.5 (2015 est.)

MEDIAN AGE:
total: 24.1 years (2018 est.)

male: 24.1 years

female: 24.2 years

country comparison to the world: 166

POPULATION GROWTH RATE:
1.41% (2018 est.)

country comparison to the world: 79

BIRTH RATE:
21.6 births/1,000 population (2018 est.)

country comparison to the world: 73

DEATH RATE:
6.3 deaths/1,000 population (2018 est.)

country comparison to the world: 153

NET MIGRATION RATE:
-1.2 migrant(s)/1,000 population (2018 est.)

country comparison to the world: 146

POPULATION DISTRIBUTION:
the Indus River and its tributaries attract most of the settlement, with Punjab province the most densely populated

URBANIZATION:
urban population: 36.9% of total population (2019)

rate of urbanization: 2.53% annual rate of change (2015-20 est.)

MAJOR URBAN AREAS - POPULATION:
15.741 million Karachi, 12.188 million Lahore, 3.385 million Faisalabad, 2.196 million Rawalpindi, 2.169 million Gujranwala, 1.095 million ISLAMABAD (capital) (2019)

SEX RATIO:
at birth: 1.05 male(s)/female

0-14 years: 1.05 male(s)/female

15-24 years: 1.07 male(s)/female

25-54 years: 1.08 male(s)/female

55-64 years: 1.02 male(s)/female

65 years and over: 0.87 male(s)/female

total population: 1.05 male(s)/female (2018 est.)

MOTHER'S MEAN AGE AT FIRST BIRTH:
23.6 years (2017/18 est.)

note: median age at first birth among women 25-29

MATERNAL MORTALITY RATE:
140 deaths/100,000 live births (2017 est.)

country comparison to the world: 61

INFANT MORTALITY RATE:
total: 50.4 deaths/1,000 live births (2018 est.)

male: 53.5 deaths/1,000 live births

female: 47.1 deaths/1,000 live births

country comparison to the world: 28

LIFE EXPECTANCY AT BIRTH:
total population: 68.4 years (2018 est.)

male: 66.4 years

female: 70.5 years

country comparison to the world: 167

TOTAL FERTILITY RATE:
2.55 children born/woman (2018 est.)

country comparison to the world: 76

CONTRACEPTIVE PREVALENCE RATE:
34.2% (2017/18)

DRINKING WATER SOURCE:
improved:

urban: 93.9% of population

rural: 89.9% of population

total: 91.4% of population

unimproved:

urban: 6.1% of population

rural: 10.1% of population

total: 8.6% of population (2015 est.)

CURRENT HEALTH EXPENDITURE:
2.8% (2016)

PHYSICIANS DENSITY:
0.98 physicians/1,000 population (2015)

HOSPITAL BED DENSITY:
0.6 beds/1,000 population (2014)

SANITATION FACILITY ACCESS:

improved:

urban: 83.1% of population (2015 est.)

rural: 51.1% of population (2015 est.)

total: 63.5% of population (2015 est.)

unimproved:

urban: 16.9% of population (2015 est.)

rural: 48.9% of population (2015 est.)

total: 36.5% of population (2015 est.)

HIV/AIDS - ADULT PREVALENCE RATE:

0.1% (2018 est.)

country comparison to the world: 131

HIV/AIDS - PEOPLE LIVING WITH HIV/AIDS:

160,000 (2018 est.)

country comparison to the world: 34

HIV/AIDS - DEATHS:

6,400 (2018 est.)

country comparison to the world: 23

MAJOR INFECTIOUS DISEASES:

degree of risk: high (2016)

food or waterborne diseases: bacterial diarrhea, hepatitis A and E, and typhoid fever (2016)

vectorborne diseases: dengue fever and malaria (2016)

animal contact diseases: rabies (2016)

OBESITY - ADULT PREVALENCE RATE:

8.6% (2016)

country comparison to the world: 150

CHILDREN UNDER THE AGE OF 5 YEARS UNDERWEIGHT:

23.1% (2018)

country comparison to the world: 24

EDUCATION EXPENDITURES:

2.8% of GDP (2017)

country comparison to the world: 151

LITERACY:

definition: age 15 and over can read and write

total population: 57.9%

male: 69.5%

female: 45.8% (2015 est.)

SCHOOL LIFE EXPECTANCY (PRIMARY TO TERTIARY EDUCATION):

total: 8 years

male: 9 years

female: 8 years (2017)

UNEMPLOYMENT, YOUTH AGES 15-24:

total: 7.8%

male: 8.2%

female: 6.8% (2018 est.)

country comparison to the world: 148

GOVERNMENT :: PAKISTAN

COUNTRY NAME:

conventional long form: Islamic Republic of Pakistan

conventional short form: Pakistan

local long form: Jamhuryat Islami Pakistan

local short form: Pakistan

former: West Pakistan

etymology: the word "pak" means "pure" in Persian or Pashto, while the Persian suffix "-stan" means "place of" or "country," so the word Pakistan literally means "Land of the Pure"

GOVERNMENT TYPE:

federal parliamentary republic

CAPITAL:

name: Islamabad

geographic coordinates: 33 41 N, 73 03 E

time difference: UTC+5 (10 hours ahead of Washington, DC, during Standard Time)

etymology: derived from two words: "Islam," an Urdu word referring to the religion of Islam, and "-abad," a Persian suffix indicating an "inhabited place" or "city," to render the meaning "City of Islam"

ADMINISTRATIVE DIVISIONS:

4 provinces, 2 Pakistan-administered areas*, and 1 capital territory**; Azad Kashmir*, Balochistan, Gilgit-Baltistan*, Islamabad Capital Territory**, Khyber Pakhtunkhwa, Punjab, Sindh

INDEPENDENCE:

14 August 1947 (from British India)

NATIONAL HOLIDAY:

Pakistan Day (also referred to as Pakistan Resolution Day or Republic Day), 23 March (1940); note - commemorates both the adoption of the Lahore Resolution by the All-India Muslim League during its 22-24 March 1940 session, which called for the creation of independent Muslim states, and the adoption of the first constitution of Pakistan on 23 March 1956 during the transition to the Islamic Republic of Pakistan

CONSTITUTION:

history: several previous; latest endorsed 12 April 1973, passed 19 April 1973, entered into force 14 August 1973 (suspended and restored several times)

amendments: proposed by the Senate or by the National Assembly; passage requires at least two-thirds majority vote of both houses; amended many times, last in 2018 (2018)

LEGAL SYSTEM:

common law system with Islamic law influence

INTERNATIONAL LAW ORGANIZATION PARTICIPATION:

accepts compulsory ICJ jurisdiction with reservations; non-party state to the ICCt

CITIZENSHIP:

citizenship by birth: yes

citizenship by descent only: at least one parent must be a citizen of Pakistan

dual citizenship recognized: yes, but limited to select countries

residency requirement for naturalization: 4 out of the previous 7 years and including the 12 months preceding application

SUFFRAGE:

18 years of age; universal; note - there are joint electorates and reserved parliamentary seats for women and non-Muslims

EXECUTIVE BRANCH:

chief of state: President Arif ALVI (since 9 September 2018)

head of government: Prime Minister Imran KHAN (since 18 August 2018)

cabinet: Cabinet appointed by the president upon the advice of the prime minister

elections/appointments: president indirectly elected by the Electoral College consisting of members of the Senate, National Assembly, and provincial assemblies for a 5-year term (limited to 2 consecutive terms); election last held on 4 September 2018 (next to be held in 2023); prime minister elected by the National Assembly on 17 August 2018

election results: Arif ALVI elected president; Electoral College vote - Arif ALVI (PTI) 352, Fazl-ur-REHMAN (MMA) 184, Aitzaz AHSAN (PPP) 124; Imran KHAN elected prime minister; National Assembly vote - Imran KHAN (PTI) 176, Shehbaz SHARIF (PML-N) 96

LEGISLATIVE BRANCH:

description: bicameral Parliament or Majlis-e-Shueera consists of:

Senate (104 seats; members indirectly elected by the 4 provincial assemblies and the territories' representatives by proportional representation vote; members serve 6-year terms with one-half of the membership renewed every 3 years)
National Assembly (342 seats; 272 members directly elected in single-seat constituencies by simple majority vote and 70 members - 60 women and 10 non-Muslims - directly elected by proportional representation vote; all members serve 5-year terms)and the Consultative Council or Majlis al-Shura (85 seats; members directly elected in single- and 2-seat constituencies by simple majority popular vote to serve renewable 4-year terms)

elections:
Senate - last held on 3 March 2018 (next to be held in March 2021)
National Assembly - last held on 25 July 2018 (next to be held on 25 July 2023)

election results:
Senate - percent of vote by party - NA; seats by party - PML-N 15, PPP 12, PTI 6, PkMAP 2, NP 2, JUI-F 2, JI 1, MQM-P 1, PML-F 1, independent 10
National Assembly - percent of votes by party - PTI 31.9%, PML-N 24.4%, PPP 13.1%, MMA 4.8%, MQM 1.4%, PML-Q 1%, BAP 0.6%, BNP 0.4%, other 11.1%,independent 11.4%; seats by party - PTI 157, PML-N 84, PPP 54, MMA 16, MQM 7, BAP 5, PML-Q 5, BNP 4, other 5, independent 4; 1 seat vacant

note: since political reforms in 2011, legislation from the Consultative Council is submitted to the Council of State for review by the Royal Court) and the National Assembly (342 seats; 272 members directly elected in single-seat constituencies by simple majority vote and 70 members - 60 women and 10 non-Muslims - directly elected by proportional representation vote; all members serve 5-year terms)

JUDICIAL BRANCH:

highest courts: Supreme Court of Pakistan (consists of the chief justice and 16 judges)

judge selection and term of office: justices nominated by an 8-member parliamentary committee upon the recommendation of the Judicial Commission, a 9-member body of judges and other judicial professionals, and appointed by the president; justices can serve until age 65

subordinate courts: High Courts; Federal Shariat Court; provincial and district civil and criminal courts; specialized courts for issues, such as taxation, banking, and customs

POLITICAL PARTIES AND LEADERS:

Awami National Party or ANP [Asfandyar Wali KHAN]
Awami Muslim League or AML [Sheikh Rashid AHMED]
Balochistan National Party-Awami or BNP-A [Mir Israr Ullah ZEHRI]
Balochistan National Party-Mengal or BNP-M [Sardar Akhtar Jan MENGAL]
Grand Democratic Alliance or GDA (alliance of several parties)
Jamhoori Wattan Party or JWP [Shahzain BUGTI]
Jamaat-i Islami or JI [Sirajul HAQ]
Jamiat-i Ulema-i Islam Fazl-ur Rehman or JUI-F [Fazlur REHMAN]
Muttahida Quami Movement-London or MQM-L [Altaf HUSSAIN] (MQM split into two factions in 2016)
Muttahida Quami Movement-Pakistan or MQM-P [Dr. Khalid Maqbool SIDDIQUI] (MQM split into two factions in 2016)
Muttahida Majlis-e-Amal or MMA [Fazl-ur- REHMAN] (alliance of several parties)
National Party or NP [Mir Hasil Khan BIZENJO]
Pakhtunkhwa Milli Awami Party or PMAP or PkMAP [Mahmood Khan ACHAKZAI]
Pakistan Muslim League-Functional or PML-F [Pir PAGARO or Syed Shah Mardan SHAH-II]
Pakistan Muslim League-Nawaz or PML-N [Shehbaz SHARIF]
Pakistan Muslim League – Quaid-e-Azam Group or PML-Q [Chaudhry Shujaat HUSSAIN]
Pakistan Peoples Party or PPP [Bilawal BHUTTO ZARDARI, Asif Ali ZARDARI]
Pakistan Tehrik-e Insaaf or PTI (Pakistan Movement for Justice) [Imran KHAN]Pak Sarzameen Party or PSP [Mustafa KAMAL]
Quami Watan Party or QWP [Aftab Ahmed Khan SHERPAO]

note: political alliances in Pakistan shift frequently

INTERNATIONAL ORGANIZATION PARTICIPATION:

ADB, ARF, ASEAN (dialogue partner), C, CICA, CP, D-8, ECO, FAO, G-11, G-24, G-77, IAEA, IBRD, ICAO, ICC (national committees), ICRM, IDA, IDB, IFAD, IFC, IFRCS, IHO, ILO, IMF, IMO, IMSO, Interpol, IOC, IOM, IPU, ISO, ITSO, ITU, ITUC (NGOs), MIGA, MINURSO, MONUSCO, NAM, OAS (observer), OIC, OPCW, PCA, SAARC, SACEP, SCO (observer), UN, UNAMID, UNCTAD, UNESCO, UNHCR, UNIDO, UNMIL, UNOCI, UNWTO, UPU, WCO, WFTU (NGOs), WHO, WIPO, WMO, WTO

DIPLOMATIC REPRESENTATION IN THE US:

Ambassador Asad Majeed KHAN (since 11 January 2019)

chancery: 3517 International Court NW, Washington, DC 20008

telephone: [1] (202) 243-6500

FAX: [1] (202) 686-1534

consulate(s) general: Chicago, Houston, Los Angeles, New York

consulate(s): Louisville (KY), San Francisco

DIPLOMATIC REPRESENTATION FROM THE US:

chief of mission: Ambassador (vacant); Charge d'Affaires Ambassador Paul W. JONES (since 24 September 2018)

telephone: [92] 51-201-4000

embassy: Diplomatic Enclave, Ramna 5, Islamabad

mailing address: 8100 Islamabad Place, Washington, DC 20521-8100

FAX: [92] 51-227-6427

consulate(s) general: Karachi, Lahore, Peshawar

FLAG DESCRIPTION:

green with a vertical white band (symbolizing the role of religious minorities) on the hoist side; a large white crescent and star are centered in the green field; the crescent, star, and color green are traditional symbols of Islam

NATIONAL SYMBOL(S):

five-pointed star between the horns of a waxing crescent moon, jasmine; national colors: green, white

NATIONAL ANTHEM:

name: "Qaumi Tarana" (National Anthem)

lyrics/music: Abu-Al-Asar Hafeez JULLANDHURI/Ahmed Ghulamali CHAGLA

note: adopted 1954; also known as "Pak sarzamin shad bad" (Blessed Be the Sacred Land)

ECONOMY :: PAKISTAN

ECONOMY - OVERVIEW:

Decades of internal political disputes and low levels of foreign investment have led to underdevelopment in Pakistan. Pakistan has a large English-speaking population, with English-language skills less prevalent outside urban centers. Despite some progress in recent years in both security and energy, a challenging security environment, electricity shortages, and a burdensome investment climate have traditionally deterred investors.

Agriculture accounts for one-fifth of output and two-fifths of employment. Textiles and apparel account for more than half of Pakistan's export earnings; Pakistan's failure to diversify its exports has left the country vulnerable to shifts in world demand. Pakistan's GDP growth has gradually increased since 2012, and was 5.3% in 2017. Official unemployment was 6% in 2017, but this fails to capture the true picture, because much of the economy is informal and underemployment remains high. Human development continues to lag behind most of the region.

In 2013, Pakistan embarked on a $6.3 billion IMF Extended Fund Facility, which focused on reducing energy shortages, stabilizing public finances, increasing revenue collection, and improving its balance of payments position. The program concluded in September 2016. Although Pakistan missed several structural reform criteria, it restored macroeconomic stability, improved its credit rating, and boosted growth. The Pakistani rupee has remained relatively stable against the US dollar since 2015, though it declined about 10% between November 2017 and March 2018. Balance of payments concerns have reemerged, however, as a result of a significant increase in imports and weak export and remittance growth.

Pakistan must continue to address several longstanding issues, including expanding investment in education, healthcare, and sanitation; adapting to the effects of climate change and natural disasters; improving the country's business environment; and widening the country's tax base. Given demographic challenges, Pakistan's leadership will be pressed to implement economic reforms, promote further development of the energy sector, and attract foreign investment to support sufficient economic growth necessary to employ its growing and rapidly urbanizing population, much of which is under the age of 25.

In an effort to boost development, Pakistan and China are implementing the "China-Pakistan Economic Corridor" (CPEC) with $60 billion in investments targeted towards energy and other infrastructure projects. Pakistan believes CPEC investments will enable growth rates of over 6% of GDP by laying the groundwork for increased exports. CPEC-related obligations, however, have raised IMF concern about Pakistan's capital outflows and external financing needs over the medium term.

GDP (PURCHASING POWER PARITY):

$1.061 trillion (2017 est.)

$1.007 trillion (2016 est.)

$962.8 billion (2015 est.)

note: data are in 2017 dollars data are for fiscal years

country comparison to the world: 25

GDP (OFFICIAL EXCHANGE RATE):

$305 billion (2017 est.)

GDP - REAL GROWTH RATE:

5.4% (2017 est.)

4.6% (2016 est.)

4.1% (2015 est.)

note: data are for fiscal years

country comparison to the world: 41

GDP - PER CAPITA (PPP):

$5,400 (2017 est.)

$5,200 (2016 est.)

$5,100 (2015 est.)

note: data are in 2017 dollars data are for fiscal years

country comparison to the world: 171

GROSS NATIONAL SAVING:

12% of GDP (2017 est.)

13.9% of GDP (2016 est.)

14.7% of GDP (2015 est.)

note: data are for fiscal years

country comparison to the world: 151

GDP - COMPOSITION, BY END USE:

household consumption: 82% (2017 est.)

government consumption: 11.3% (2017 est.)

investment in fixed capital: 14.5% (2017 est.)

investment in inventories: 1.6% (2017 est.)

exports of goods and services: 8.2% (2017 est.)

imports of goods and services: -17.6% (2017 est.)

GDP - COMPOSITION, BY SECTOR OF ORIGIN:

agriculture: 24.4% (2016 est.)

industry: 19.1% (2016 est.)

services: 56.5% (2017 est.)

AGRICULTURE - PRODUCTS:

cotton, wheat, rice, sugarcane, fruits, vegetables; milk, beef, mutton, eggs

INDUSTRIES:

textiles and apparel, food processing, pharmaceuticals, surgical instruments, construction materials, paper products, fertilizer, shrimp

INDUSTRIAL PRODUCTION GROWTH RATE:

5.4% (2017 est.)

country comparison to the world: 53

LABOR FORCE:

63.89 million (2017 est.)

note: extensive export of labor, mostly to the Middle East, and use of child labor

country comparison to the world: 9

LABOR FORCE - BY OCCUPATION:

agriculture: 42.3%

industry: 22.6%

services: 35.1% (FY2015 est.)

UNEMPLOYMENT RATE:

6% (2017 est.)

6% (2016 est.)

note: Pakistan has substantial underemployment

country comparison to the world: 90

POPULATION BELOW POVERTY LINE:

29.5% (FY2013 est.)

HOUSEHOLD INCOME OR CONSUMPTION BY PERCENTAGE SHARE:

lowest 10%: 4%

highest 10%: 26.1% (FY2013)

DISTRIBUTION OF FAMILY INCOME - GINI INDEX:

30.7 (FY2013)

30.9 (FY2011)

country comparison to the world: 130

BUDGET:

revenues: 46.81 billion (2017 est.)

expenditures: 64.49 billion (2017 est.)

note: data are for fiscal years

TAXES AND OTHER REVENUES:

15.4% (of GDP) (2017 est.)

country comparison to the world: 190

BUDGET SURPLUS (+) OR DEFICIT (-):

-5.8% (of GDP) (2017 est.)

country comparison to the world: 178

PUBLIC DEBT:

67% of GDP (2017 est.)

67.6% of GDP (2016 est.)

country comparison to the world: 56

FISCAL YEAR:

1 July - 30 June

INFLATION RATE (CONSUMER PRICES):

4.1% (2017 est.)

2.9% (2016 est.)

CENTRAL BANK DISCOUNT RATE:

5.75% (15 November 2016)

6% (15 November 2015)

country comparison to the world: 71

COMMERCIAL BANK PRIME LENDING RATE:

6.98% (31 December 2017 est.)

6.94% (31 December 2016 est.)

country comparison to the world: 119

STOCK OF NARROW MONEY:

$109.9 billion (31 December 2017 est.)

$103.5 billion (31 December 2016 est.)

country comparison to the world: 36

STOCK OF BROAD MONEY:

$109.9 billion (31 December 2017 est.)

$103.5 billion (31 December 2016 est.)

country comparison to the world: 36

STOCK OF DOMESTIC CREDIT:

$155.9 billion (31 December 2017 est.)

$145.2 billion (31 December 2016 est.)

country comparison to the world: 48

MARKET VALUE OF PUBLICLY TRADED SHARES:

$43.68 billion (31 December 2012 est.)

$32.76 billion (31 December 2011 est.)

$38.17 billion (31 December 2010 est.)

country comparison to the world: 54

CURRENT ACCOUNT BALANCE:

-$12.44 billion (2017 est.)

-$4.867 billion (2016 est.)

country comparison to the world: 194

EXPORTS:

$32.88 billion (2017 est.)

$21.97 billion (2016 est.)

country comparison to the world: 61

EXPORTS - PARTNERS:

US 17.7%, UK 7.7%, China 6%, Germany 5.8%, Afghanistan 5.2%, UAE 4.5%, Spain 4.1% (2017)

EXPORTS - COMMODITIES:

textiles (garments, bed linen, cotton cloth, yarn), rice, leather goods, sporting goods, chemicals, manufactures, surgical instruments, carpets and rugs

IMPORTS:

$53.11 billion (2017 est.)

$42.69 billion (2016 est.)

country comparison to the world: 51

IMPORTS - COMMODITIES:

petroleum, petroleum products, machinery, plastics, transportation equipment, edible oils, paper and paperboard, iron and steel, tea

IMPORTS - PARTNERS:

China 27.4%, UAE 13.7%, US 4.9%, Indonesia 4.3%, Saudi Arabia 4.2% (2017)

RESERVES OF FOREIGN EXCHANGE AND GOLD:

$18.46 billion (31 December 2017 est.)

$22.05 billion (31 December 2016 est.)

country comparison to the world: 62

DEBT - EXTERNAL:

$82.19 billion (31 December 2017 est.)

$70.45 billion (31 December 2016 est.)

country comparison to the world: 55

STOCK OF DIRECT FOREIGN INVESTMENT - AT HOME:

$43.21 billion (31 December 2017 est.)

$39.06 billion (31 December 2016 est.)

country comparison to the world: 62

STOCK OF DIRECT FOREIGN INVESTMENT - ABROAD:

$1.983 billion (31 December 2017 est.)

$2.094 billion (31 December 2016 est.)

country comparison to the world: 83

EXCHANGE RATES:

Pakistani rupees (PKR) per US dollar -

105.1 (2017 est.)

104.769 (2016 est.)

104.769 (2015 est.)

102.769 (2014 est.)

101.1 (2013 est.)

ENERGY :: PAKISTAN

ELECTRICITY ACCESS:

population without electricity: 52 million (2017)

electrification - total population: 74% (2017)

electrification - urban areas: 90% (2017)

electrification - rural areas: 64% (2017)

ELECTRICITY - PRODUCTION:

109.7 billion kWh (2016 est.)

country comparison to the world: 32

ELECTRICITY - CONSUMPTION:

92.33 billion kWh (2016 est.)

country comparison to the world: 34

ELECTRICITY - EXPORTS:

0 kWh (2016 est.)

country comparison to the world: 182

ELECTRICITY - IMPORTS:

490 million kWh (2016 est.)

country comparison to the world: 80

ELECTRICITY - INSTALLED GENERATING CAPACITY:

26.9 million kW (2016 est.)

country comparison to the world: 35

ELECTRICITY - FROM FOSSIL FUELS:

62% of total installed capacity (2016 est.)

country comparison to the world: 125

ELECTRICITY - FROM NUCLEAR FUELS:

5% of total installed capacity (2017 est.)

country comparison to the world: 22

ELECTRICITY - FROM HYDROELECTRIC PLANTS:

27% of total installed capacity (2017 est.)

country comparison to the world: 74

ELECTRICITY - FROM OTHER RENEWABLE SOURCES:

7% of total installed capacity (2017 est.)

country comparison to the world: 94

CRUDE OIL - PRODUCTION:

90,000 bbl/day (2018 est.)

country comparison to the world: 45

CRUDE OIL - EXPORTS:

13,150 bbl/day (2015 est.)

country comparison to the world: 58

CRUDE OIL - IMPORTS:

168,200 bbl/day (2015 est.)

country comparison to the world: 34

CRUDE OIL - PROVED RESERVES:

332.2 million bbl (1 January 2018 est.)

country comparison to the world: 52

REFINED PETROLEUM PRODUCTS - PRODUCTION:

291,200 bbl/day (2015 est.)

country comparison to the world: 43

REFINED PETROLEUM PRODUCTS - CONSUMPTION:

557,000 bbl/day (2016 est.)

country comparison to the world: 33

REFINED PETROLEUM PRODUCTS - EXPORTS:

25,510 bbl/day (2015 est.)

country comparison to the world: 68

REFINED PETROLEUM PRODUCTS - IMPORTS:

264,500 bbl/day (2015 est.)

country comparison to the world: 27

NATURAL GAS - PRODUCTION:

39.05 billion cu m (2017 est.)

country comparison to the world: 21

NATURAL GAS - CONSUMPTION:

45.05 billion cu m (2017 est.)

country comparison to the world: 20

NATURAL GAS - EXPORTS:

0 cu m (2017 est.)

country comparison to the world: 165

NATURAL GAS - IMPORTS:

6.003 billion cu m (2017 est.)

country comparison to the world: 32

NATURAL GAS - PROVED RESERVES:

588.8 billion cu m (1 January 2018 est.)

country comparison to the world: 30

CARBON DIOXIDE EMISSIONS FROM CONSUMPTION OF ENERGY:

179.5 million Mt (2017 est.)

country comparison to the world: 33

COMMUNICATIONS :: PAKISTAN

TELEPHONES - FIXED LINES:

total subscriptions: 2,940,243

subscriptions per 100 inhabitants: 1 (2017 est.)

country comparison to the world: 47

TELEPHONES - MOBILE CELLULAR:

total subscriptions: 144,525,637

subscriptions per 100 inhabitants: 71 (2017 est.)

country comparison to the world: 10

TELEPHONE SYSTEM:

general assessment: the telecommunications infrastructure is improving, with investments in mobile-cellular networks increasing, but fixed-line subscriptions declining; system consists of microwave radio relay, coaxial cable, fiber-optic cable, cellular, and satellite networks; 4G mobile services broadly available; 5G not before 2030; mobile platform and mobile broadband doing well (2018)

domestic: mobile-cellular subscribership has skyrocketed; more than 90% of Pakistanis live within areas that have cell phone coverage; fiber-optic networks are being constructed throughout the country to increase broadband access, though broadband penetration in Pakistan is still relatively low; fixed-line 1 per 100 and mobile-cellular 71 per 100 persons (2018)

international: country code - 92; landing points for the SEA-ME-WE-3, -4, -5, AAE-1, IMEWE, Orient Express, PEACE Cable, and TW1 submarine cable systems that provide links to Europe, Africa, the Middle East, Asia, Southeast Asia, and Australia; satellite earth stations - 3 Intelsat (1 Atlantic Ocean and 2 Indian Ocean); 3 operational international gateway exchanges (1 at Karachi and 2 at Islamabad); microwave radio relay to neighboring countries (2019)

BROADCAST MEDIA:

media is government regulated; 1 dominant state-owned TV broadcaster, Pakistan Television Corporation (PTV), operates a network consisting of 8 channels; private TV broadcasters are permitted; to date 69 foreign satellite channels are operational; the state-owned radio network operates more than 30 stations; nearly 200 commercially licensed, privately owned radio stations provide programming mostly limited to music and talk shows (2019)

INTERNET COUNTRY CODE:

.pk

INTERNET USERS:

total: 31,338,715

percent of population: 15.5% (July 2016 est.)

country comparison to the world: 23

BROADBAND - FIXED SUBSCRIPTIONS:

total: 1,829,673

subscriptions per 100 inhabitants: 1 (2017 est.)

country comparison to the world: 53

MILITARY AND SECURITY :: PAKISTAN

MILITARY EXPENDITURES:

4.03% of GDP (2018)

3.77% of GDP (2017)

3.59% of GDP (2016)

3.55% of GDP (2015)

3.48% of GDP (2014)

country comparison to the world: 10

MILITARY AND SECURITY FORCES:

Pakistan Army (includes National Guard), Pakistan Navy (includes marines, Maritime Security Agency), Pakistan Air Force (Pakistan Fizaia); Ministry of Interior paramilitary forces: Frontier Corps, Pakistan Rangers (2019)

MILITARY SERVICE AGE AND OBLIGATION:

16-23 years of age for voluntary military service; soldiers cannot be deployed for combat until age 18; women serve in all three armed forces; reserve obligation to age 45 for enlisted men, age 50 for officers (2019)

TRANSPORTATION :: PAKISTAN

NATIONAL AIR TRANSPORT SYSTEM:

number of registered air carriers: 4 (2015)

inventory of registered aircraft operated by air carriers: 67 (2015)

annual passenger traffic on registered air carriers: 8,467,827 (2015)

annual freight traffic on registered air carriers: 183,177,313 mt-km (2015)

CIVIL AIRCRAFT REGISTRATION COUNTRY CODE PREFIX:

AP (2016)

AIRPORTS:

151 (2013)

country comparison to the world: 37

AIRPORTS - WITH PAVED RUNWAYS:

total: 108 (2017)

over 3,047 m: 15 (2017)

2,438 to 3,047 m: 20 (2017)

1,524 to 2,437 m: 43 (2017)

914 to 1,523 m: 20 (2017)

under 914 m: 10 (2017)

AIRPORTS - WITH UNPAVED RUNWAYS:

total: 43 (2013)

2,438 to 3,047 m: 1 (2013)

1,524 to 2,437 m: 9 (2013)

914 to 1,523 m: 9 (2013)

under 914 m: 24 (2013)

HELIPORTS:

23 (2013)

PIPELINES:

12,984 km gas, 3,470 km oil, 1,170 km refined products (2019)

RAILWAYS:

total: 11,881 km (2019)

narrow gauge: 389 km 1.000-m gauge (2019)

broad gauge: 11,492 km 1.676-m gauge (293 km electrified) (2019)

country comparison to the world: 22

ROADWAYS:

total: 263,775 km (2019)

paved: 185,063 km (includes 708 km of expressways) (2019)

unpaved: 78,712 km (2019)

country comparison to the world: 22

MERCHANT MARINE:

total: 53

by type: bulk carrier 5, oil tanker 7, other 41 (2018)

country comparison to the world: 113

PORTS AND TERMINALS:

major seaport(s): Karachi, Port Muhammad Bin Qasim

container port(s) (TEUs): Karachi (2,224,000) (2017)

LNG terminal(s) (import): Port Qasim

TERRORISM :: PAKISTAN

TERRORIST GROUPS - HOME BASED:

al-Qa'ida (AQ): aim(s): eject Western influence from the Islamic world, unite the worldwide Muslim community, overthrow governments perceived as un-Islamic and, ultimately, establish a pan-Islamic caliphate under a strict Salafi Muslim interpretation of sharia
area(s) of operation: presence in Pakistan's Federally Administered Tribal Areas (FATA) near the Pakistan-Afghanistan border (2018)

al-Qa'ida in the Indian Subcontinent (AQIS): aim(s): establish an Islamic caliphate in the Indian subcontinent
area(s) of operation: operational throughout the country, targeting military and security personnel; responsible for numerous attacks in Karachi; stages attacks in Afghanistan, India, and Bangladesh, where the group is the most active (2018)

Haqqani Network (HQN): aim(s): enhance its operational networks and capabilities for staging cross-border attacks in Afghanistan; replace the Afghan Government with an Islamic state operating according to a strict Salafi Muslim interpretation of sharia
area(s) of operation: headquartered in the Federally Administered Tribal Areas (FATA) region located across from Afghanistan's southeastern border; fighters have staged numerous cross-border operations from Kurram and North Waziristan Agency in the FATA into Afghanistan, targeting Afghan, US, and NATO forces and other Afghan Government personnel and Westerners for attack or kidnappings for ransom (2018)

Harakat ul-Jihad-i-Islami (HUJI): aim(s): overthrow the Pakistan Government and implement sharia throughout the country
area(s) of operation: headquartered in Pakistan, where the group operates several camps; remains heavily active in the southern area of Azad Kashmir (2018)

Harakat ul-Mujahidin (HUM): aim(s): annex Kashmir to Pakistan and establish an Islamic state in Kashmir
area(s) of operation: headquartered in Islamabad, with an operational presence in Muzaffarabad in Azad Kashmir, where operatives stage attacks against India; maintains training and paramilitary camps in the country's Federally Administered Tribal Areas (FATA) region (2018)

Jaish-e-Mohammed (JEM): aim(s): unite Kashmir with Pakistan, install sharia in Pakistan, and drive foreign forces from Afghanistan
area(s) of operation: headquartered in Punjab Province; stages attacks against Indian forces, primarily in Jammu and Kashmir State (2018)

Jaysh al Adl: aim(s): seeks greater autonomy for Balochis in Pakistan and Iran
area(s) of operation: headquartered in Balochistan Province, where operatives stage attacks inside Iran against Shia Muslims, primarily targets Iranian soldiers and security personnel
note: formerly known as Jundallah (2018)

Lashkar i Jhangvi (LJ): aim(s): exterminate Shia Muslims, rid the region of Western influence and, ultimately, establish an Islamic state in Pakistan under sharia
area(s) of operation: has a growing presence in Karachi, the capital of Sindh Province; loosely coordinated cells are spread across the country, primarily in Punjab and Balochistan provinces, Karachi, and in the Federally Administered Tribal Areas (FATA) region; majority of attacks are against local and foreign Shia Muslims and government personnel and facilities (2018)

Lashkar-e Tayyiba (LT): aim(s): return the Indian state of Jammu and Kashmir to Pakistan and foment Islamic insurgency in India; enhance its recruitment networks and paramilitary training in South Asia; and, ultimately, implement Islamic rule throughout South Asia
area(s) of operation: headquartered in Lahore, Punjab Province, with an operational presence throughout the country; active in both the Pakistan-administered and India-administered Kashmir regions
note: does not conduct attacks within Pakistan; often operates under the guise of its charitable affiliates, including Jamaat-ud-Dawa (2018)

TERRORIST GROUPS - FOREIGN BASED:

Indian Mujahedeen (IM): aim(s): stated goal is to carry out terrorist attacks against Indians for perceived atrocities against Indian Muslims following the 2002 Gujarat riots
area(s) of operation: Punjab and Sindh Provinces and Pakistan-controlled Kashmir (2018)

Islamic State of Iraq and ash-Sham-Khorasan (ISIS-K): aim(s): establish an Islamic caliphate in the Afghanistan-Pakistan region; oppose Pakistan Government and Westerners; oppose Shia Muslim population
area(s) of operation: maintains an operational and recruitment presence throughout the country, primarily along the Pakistan-Afghanistan border to stage attacks inside Afghanistan and Pakistan
note: recruits from among the local population and other militant groups such as Tehrik-e Taliban Pakistan, the Afghan Taliban, and the Islamic Movement of Uzbekistan (2018)

Tehrik-e-Taliban Pakistan (TTP): aim(s): remove Pakistani forces from the Federally Administered Tribal Areas (FATA) region; overthrow the Pakistan Government to implement TTP's strict interpretation of sharia
area(s) of operation: maintains a large presence in Karachi, the capital of Sindh Province; trains and deploys fighters in the tribal belt in the Pashtun areas along the Pakistan-Afghanistan border, especially in Kunar and Paktika provinces where TTP has established sanctuaries; operationally active in the North Waziristan, South Waziristan, and Balochistan regions; targets Pakistan Government officials and military, security, and police personnel, as well as Westerners, pro-government tribal elders, Shia Muslims, and education figures and advocates (2018)

TRANSNATIONAL ISSUES :: PAKISTAN

DISPUTES - INTERNATIONAL:

various talks and confidence-building measures cautiously have begun to defuse tensions over Kashmir, particularly since the October 2005 earthquake in the region; Kashmir nevertheless remains the site of the world's largest and most militarized territorial dispute with portions under the de facto administration of China (Aksai Chin), India (Jammu and Kashmir), and Pakistan (Azad Kashmir and Northern Areas); UN Military Observer Group in India and Pakistan has maintained a small group of peacekeepers since 1949; India does not recognize Pakistan's ceding historic Kashmir lands to China in 1964; India and Pakistan have maintained their 2004 cease-fire in Kashmir and initiated discussions on defusing the armed standoff in the Siachen glacier region; Pakistan protests India's fencing the highly militarized Line of Control and construction of the Baglihar Dam on the Chenab River in Jammu and Kashmir, which is part of the larger dispute on water sharing of the Indus River and its tributaries; to defuse tensions and prepare for discussions on a maritime boundary, India and Pakistan seek technical resolution of the disputed boundary in Sir Creek estuary at the mouth of the Rann of Kutch in the Arabian Sea; Pakistani maps continue to show the Junagadh claim in India's Gujarat State; since 2002, with UN assistance, Pakistan has repatriated 3.8 million Afghan refugees, leaving about 2.6 million; Pakistan has sent troops across and built fences along some remote tribal areas of its treaty-defined Durand Line border with Afghanistan, which serve as bases for foreign terrorists and other illegal activities; Afghan, Coalition, and Pakistan military meet periodically to clarify the alignment of the boundary on the ground and on maps

REFUGEES AND INTERNALLY DISPLACED PERSONS:

refugees (country of origin): 2.58-2.68 million (1.4 million registered, 1.18-1.28 million undocumented) (Afghanistan) (2017)

IDPs: 119,000 (primarily those who remain displaced by counter-terrorism and counter-insurgency operations and violent conflict between armed non-state groups in the Federally Administered Tribal Areas and Khyber-Paktunkwa Province; more than 1 million displaced in northern Waziristan in 2014; individuals also have been displaced by repeated monsoon floods) (2018)

TRAFFICKING IN PERSONS:

current situation: Pakistan is a source, transit, and destination country for men, women, and children subjected to forced labor and sex trafficking; the largest human trafficking problem is bonded labor in agriculture, brickmaking and, to a lesser extent, fishing, mining and carpet-making; children are bought, sold, rented, and placed in forced begging rings, domestic service, small shops, brick-making factories, or prostitution; militant groups also force children to spy, fight, or die as suicide bombers, kidnapping the children or getting them from poor parents through sale or coercion; women and girls are forced into prostitution or marriages; Pakistani adults migrate to the Gulf States and African and European states for low-skilled jobs and sometimes become victims of forced labor, debt bondage, or prostitution; foreign adults and children, particularly from Afghanistan, Bangladesh, and Sri Lanka, may be subject to forced labor, and foreign women may be sex trafficked in Pakistan, with refugees and ethnic minorities being most vulnerable

tier rating: Tier 2 Watch List – Pakistan does not fully comply with the minimum standards for the elimination of trafficking; however, it is making significant efforts to do so; the government lacks political will and capacity to fully address human trafficking, as evidenced by ineffective law enforcement efforts, official complicity, penalization of victims, and the continued conflation of migrant smuggling and human trafficking by many officials; not all forms of trafficking are prohibited; an anti-trafficking bill drafted in 2013 to address gaps in existing legislation remains pending, and a national action plan drafted in 2014 is not finalized; feudal landlords and brick kiln owners use their political influence to protect their involvement in bonded labor, while some police personnel have taken bribes to ignore prostitution that may have included sex trafficking; authorities began to use standard procedures for the identification and referral of trafficking victims, but it is not clear how widely these methods were practiced; in other instances, police were reluctant to assist NGOs with rescues and even punished victims for crimes committed as a direct result of being trafficked (2015)

ILLICIT DRUGS:

significant transit area for Afghan drugs, including heroin, opium, morphine, and hashish, bound for Iran, Western markets, the Gulf States, Africa, and Asia; financial crimes related to drug trafficking, terrorism, corruption, and smuggling remain problems; opium poppy cultivation estimated to be 930 hectares in 2015; federal and provincial authorities continue to conduct anti-poppy campaigns that utilizes forced eradication, fines, and arrests

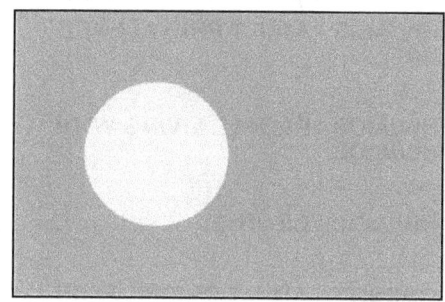

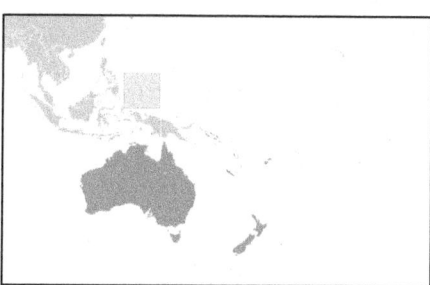

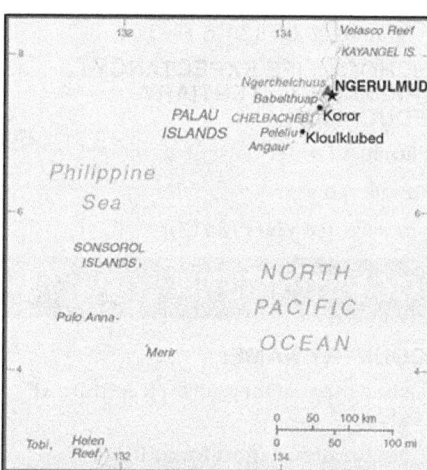

AUSTRALIA - OCEANIA :: PALAU

INTRODUCTION :: PALAU

BACKGROUND:
After three decades as part of the UN Trust Territory of the Pacific under US administration, this westernmost cluster of the Caroline Islands opted for independence in 1978 rather than join the Federated States of Micronesia. A Compact of Free Association with the US was approved in 1986 but not ratified until 1993. It entered into force the following year when the islands gained independence.

GEOGRAPHY :: PALAU

LOCATION:
Oceania, group of islands in the North Pacific Ocean, southeast of the Philippines

GEOGRAPHIC COORDINATES:
7 30 N, 134 30 E

MAP REFERENCES:
Oceania

AREA:
total: 459 sq km
land: 459 sq km
water: 0 sq km
country comparison to the world: 198

AREA - COMPARATIVE:
slightly more than 2.5 times the size of Washington, DC

LAND BOUNDARIES:
0 km

COASTLINE:
1,519 km

MARITIME CLAIMS:
territorial sea: 12 nm
exclusive economic zone: 200 nm
contiguous zone: 24 nm
continental shelf: 200 nm

CLIMATE:
tropical; hot and humid; wet season May to November

TERRAIN:
varying topography from the high, mountainous main island of Babelthuap to low, coral islands usually fringed by large barrier reefs

ELEVATION:
lowest point: Pacific Ocean 0 m
highest point: Mount Ngerchelchuus 242 m

NATURAL RESOURCES:
forests, minerals (especially gold), marine products, deep-seabed minerals

LAND USE:
agricultural land: 10.8% (2011 est.)
arable land: 2.2% (2011 est.) / permanent crops: 4.3% (2011 est.) / permanent pasture: 4.3% (2011 est.)
forest: 87.6% (2011 est.)
other: 1.6% (2011 est.)

IRRIGATED LAND:
0 sq km (2012)

POPULATION DISTRIBUTION:
most of the population is located on the southern end of the main island of Babelthuap

NATURAL HAZARDS:
typhoons (June to December)

ENVIRONMENT - CURRENT ISSUES:
inadequate facilities for disposal of solid waste; threats to the marine ecosystem from sand and coral dredging, illegal and destructive fishing practices, and overfishing; climate change contributes to rising sea level and coral bleaching; drought

ENVIRONMENT - INTERNATIONAL AGREEMENTS:
party to: Biodiversity, Climate Change, Climate Change-Kyoto Protocol, Desertification, Hazardous Wastes, Law of the Sea, Ozone Layer Protection, Wetlands, Whaling
signed, but not ratified: none of the selected agreements

GEOGRAPHY - NOTE:
westernmost archipelago in the Caroline chain, consists of six island groups totaling more than 300 islands; includes World War II battleground of Beliliou (Peleliu) and world-famous Rock Islands

PEOPLE AND SOCIETY :: PALAU

POPULATION:
21,516 (July 2018 est.)
country comparison to the world: 219

NATIONALITY:
noun: Palauan(s)
adjective: Palauan

ETHNIC GROUPS:
Palauan (Micronesian with Malayan and Melanesian admixtures) 73%, Carolinian 2%, Asian 21.7%, caucasian 1.2%, other 2.1% (2015 est.)

LANGUAGES:
Palauan (official on most islands) 65.2%, other Micronesian 1.9%, English (official) 19.1%, Filipino 9.9%, Chinese 1.2%, other 2.8% (2015 est.)

note: Sonsoralese is official in Sonsoral; Tobian is official in Tobi; Angaur and Japanese are official in Angaur

RELIGIONS:

Roman Catholic 45.3%, Protestant 34.9% (includes Evangelical 26.4%, Seventh Day Adventist 6.9%, Assembly of God .9%, Baptist .7%), Modekngei 5.7% (indigenous to Palau), Muslim 3%, Mormon 1.5%, other 9.7% (2015 est.)

AGE STRUCTURE:

0-14 years: 19.37% (male 2,149 /female 2,019)

15-24 years: 16.4% (male 1,768 /female 1,760)

25-54 years: 45.74% (male 6,016 /female 3,826)

55-64 years: 9.99% (male 765 /female 1,384)

65 years and over: 8.5% (male 464 /female 1,365) (2018 est.)

MEDIAN AGE:

total: 33.6 years (2018 est.)

male: 32.8 years

female: 35.3 years

country comparison to the world: 92

POPULATION GROWTH RATE:

0.4% (2018 est.)

country comparison to the world: 162

BIRTH RATE:

11.3 births/1,000 population (2018 est.)

country comparison to the world: 173

DEATH RATE:

8.2 deaths/1,000 population (2018 est.)

country comparison to the world: 85

NET MIGRATION RATE:

0.8 migrant(s)/1,000 population (2018 est.)

country comparison to the world: 66

POPULATION DISTRIBUTION:

most of the population is located on the southern end of the main island of Babelthuap

URBANIZATION:

urban population: 80.5% of total population (2019)

rate of urbanization: 1.77% annual rate of change (2015-20 est.)

MAJOR URBAN AREAS - POPULATION:

277 NGERULMUD (capital) (2018)

SEX RATIO:

at birth: 1.06 male(s)/female

0-14 years: 1.06 male(s)/female

15-24 years: 1 male(s)/female

25-54 years: 1.57 male(s)/female

55-64 years: 0.55 male(s)/female

65 years and over: 0.34 male(s)/female

total population: 1.08 male(s)/female (2018 est.)

INFANT MORTALITY RATE:

total: 10.3 deaths/1,000 live births (2018 est.)

male: 11.8 deaths/1,000 live births

female: 8.8 deaths/1,000 live births

country comparison to the world: 133

LIFE EXPECTANCY AT BIRTH:

total population: 73.6 years (2018 est.)

male: 70.4 years

female: 77 years

country comparison to the world: 136

TOTAL FERTILITY RATE:

1.7 children born/woman (2018 est.)

country comparison to the world: 171

DRINKING WATER SOURCE:

improved:

urban: 97% of population

rural: 86% of population

total: 95.3% of population

unimproved:

urban: 3% of population

rural: 14% of population

total: 4.7% of population (2011 est.)

CURRENT HEALTH EXPENDITURE:

11.7% (2016)

PHYSICIANS DENSITY:

1.19 physicians/1,000 population (2014)

HOSPITAL BED DENSITY:

4.8 beds/1,000 population (2010)

SANITATION FACILITY ACCESS:

improved:

urban: 100% of population (2015 est.)

rural: 100% of population (2015 est.)

total: 100% of population (2015 est.)

unimproved:

urban: 0% of population (2015 est.)

rural: 0% of population (2015 est.)

total: 0% of population (2015 est.)

HIV/AIDS - ADULT PREVALENCE RATE:

NA

HIV/AIDS - PEOPLE LIVING WITH HIV/AIDS:

NA

HIV/AIDS - DEATHS:

NA

OBESITY - ADULT PREVALENCE RATE:

55.3% (2016)

country comparison to the world: 3

EDUCATION EXPENDITURES:

NA

LITERACY:

definition: age 15 and over can read and write

total population: 96.6%

male: 96.8%

female: 96.3% (2015 est.)

SCHOOL LIFE EXPECTANCY (PRIMARY TO TERTIARY EDUCATION):

total: 17 years

male: 16 years

female: 18 years (2013)

GOVERNMENT :: PALAU

COUNTRY NAME:

conventional long form: Republic of Palau

conventional short form: Palau

local long form: Beluu er a Belau

local short form: Belau

former: Trust Territory of the Pacific Islands, Palau District

etymology: from the Palauan name for the islands, Belau, which likely derives from the Palauan word "beluu" meaning "village"

GOVERNMENT TYPE:

presidential republic in free association with the US

CAPITAL:

name: Ngerulmud

geographic coordinates: 7 30 N, 134 37 E

time difference: UTC+9 (14 hours ahead of Washington, DC, during Standard Time) etymology: the Palauan meaning is "place of fermented 'mud'" ('mud' being the native name for the keyhole angelfish); the site of the new capitol (established in 2006) had been a large hill overlooking the ocean, Ngerulmud, on which women would communally gather to offer fermented angelfish to the gods

ADMINISTRATIVE DIVISIONS:

16 states; Aimeliik, Airai, Angaur, Hatohobei, Kayangel, Koror, Melekeok, Ngaraard, Ngarchelong, Ngardmau, Ngatpang, Ngchesar, Ngeremlengui, Ngiwal, Peleliu, Sonsorol

INDEPENDENCE:

1 October 1994 (from the US-administered UN trusteeship)

NATIONAL HOLIDAY:

Constitution Day, 9 July (1981), day of a national referendum to pass the new constitution; Independence Day, 1 October (1994)

CONSTITUTION:

history: ratified 9 July 1980, effective 1 January 1981

amendments: proposed by a constitutional convention (held at least once every 15 years with voter approval), by public petition of at least 25% of eligible voters, or by a resolution adopted by at least three fourths of National Congress members; passage requires approval by a majority of votes in at least three fourths of the states in the next regular general election; amended 1992, 2004, 2008 (2017)

LEGAL SYSTEM:

mixed legal system of civil, common, and customary law

INTERNATIONAL LAW ORGANIZATION PARTICIPATION:

has not submitted an ICJ jurisdiction declaration; non-party state to the ICCt

CITIZENSHIP:

citizenship by birth: no

citizenship by descent only: at least one parent must be a citizen of Palau

dual citizenship recognized: no

residency requirement for naturalization: note - no procedure for naturalization

SUFFRAGE:

18 years of age; universal

EXECUTIVE BRANCH:

chief of state: President Tommy REMENGESAU (since 17 January 2013); Vice President Raynold OILUCH (since 19 January 2017); note - the president is both chief of state and head of government

head of government: President Tommy REMENGESAU (since 17 January 2013); Vice President Raynold OILUCH (since 19 January 2017)

cabinet: Cabinet appointed by the president with the advice and consent of the Senate; also includes the vice president; the Council of Chiefs consists of chiefs from each of the states who advise the president on issues concerning traditional laws, customs, and their relationship to the constitution and laws of Palau

elections/appointments: president and vice president directly elected on separate ballots by absolute majority popular vote in 2 rounds if needed for a 4-year term (eligible for a second term); election last held on 1 November 2016 (next to be held in November 2020)

election results: Tommy REMENGESAU reelected president; percent of vote - Tommy REMENGESAU (independent) 51.3%, Surangel WHIPPS, Jr.(independent) 48.7%; Raynold OILUCH elected vice president

LEGISLATIVE BRANCH:

description: bicameral National Congress or Olbiil Era Kelulau consists of:
Senate (13 seats; members directly elected in single-seat constituencies by majority vote to serve 4-year terms) House of Delegates (16 seats; members directly elected in single-seat constituencies by simple majority vote to serve 4-year terms)

elections:
Senate - last held on 1 November 2016 (next to be held in November 2020) House of Delegates - last held on 1 November 2016 (next to be held in November 2020)

election results:
Senate - percent of vote - NA; seats - independent 13; composition - men 11, women 2, percent of women 15.4% House of Delegates - percent of vote - NA; seats - independent 16; composition - men 14, women 2, percent of women 12.5%; note - total National Congress percent of women 13.8%

JUDICIAL BRANCH:

highest courts: Supreme Court (consists of the chief justice and 3 associate justices organized into appellate trial divisions; the Supreme Court organization also includes the Common Pleas and Land Courts)

judge selection and term of office: justices nominated by a 7-member independent body consisting of judges, presidential appointees, and lawyers and appointed by the president; judges can serve until mandatory retirement at age 65

subordinate courts: National Court and other 'inferior' courts

POLITICAL PARTIES AND LEADERS:

none

INTERNATIONAL ORGANIZATION PARTICIPATION:

ACP, ADB, AOSIS, FAO, IAEA, IBRD, ICAO, ICRM, IDA, IFC, IFRCS, ILO, IMF, IMO, IMSO, IOC, IPU, MIGA, OPCW, PIF, Sparteca, SPC, UN, UNAMID, UNCTAD, UNESCO, WHO

DIPLOMATIC REPRESENTATION IN THE US:

Ambassador Hersey KYOTA (since 12 November 1997)

chancery: 1701 Pennsylvania Avenue NW, Suite 300, Washington, DC 20036

telephone: [1] (202) 452-6814

FAX: [1] (202) 452-6281

consulate(s): Tamuning (Guam)

DIPLOMATIC REPRESENTATION FROM THE US:

chief of mission: Ambassador Amy HYATT (since 9 March 2015)

telephone: [680] 587-2920

embassy: Omsangel/Beklelachieb, Airai, Palau 96940

mailing address: P. O. Box 6028, Koror, Republic of Palau 96940

FAX: [680] 587-2911

FLAG DESCRIPTION:

light blue with a large yellow disk shifted slightly to the hoist side; the blue color represents the ocean, the disk represents the moon; Palauans consider the full moon to be the optimum time for human activity; it is also considered a symbol of peace, love, and tranquility

NATIONAL SYMBOL(S):

bai (native meeting house); national colors: blue, yellow

NATIONAL ANTHEM:

name: "Belau rekid" (Our Palau)

lyrics/music: multiple/Ymesei O. EZEKIEL

note: adopted 1980

ECONOMY :: PALAU

ECONOMY - OVERVIEW:

The economy is dominated by tourism, fishing, and subsistence agriculture. Government is a major employer of the work force relying on financial assistance from the US under the Compact of Free Association (Compact) with the US that took effect after the end of the UN trusteeship on 1 October 1994. The US provided Palau with roughly $700 million in aid for the first 15 years following commencement of the Compact in 1994 in return for unrestricted access to its land and waterways for strategic purposes. The population enjoys a per capita income roughly double that of the Philippines and much of Micronesia.

Business and leisure tourist arrivals reached a record 167,966 in 2015, a 14.4% increase over the previous year, but fell to 138,408 in 2016. Long-run prospects for tourism have been bolstered by the expansion of air travel in the Pacific, the rising prosperity of industrial East Asia, and the willingness of foreigners to finance infrastructure development. Proximity to Guam, the region's major destination for tourists from East Asia, and a regionally competitive tourist infrastructure enhance Palau's advantage as a destination.

GDP (PURCHASING POWER PARITY):

$264 million (2017 est.)

$274.2 million (2016 est.)

$274.1 million (2015 est.)

note: data are in 2017 dollars

country comparison to the world: 217

GDP (OFFICIAL EXCHANGE RATE):

$292 million (2017 est.)

GDP - REAL GROWTH RATE:

-3.7% (2017 est.)

0% (2016 est.)

10.1% (2015 est.)

country comparison to the world: 215

GDP - PER CAPITA (PPP):

$14,700 (2017 est.)

$15,200 (2016 est.)

$15,200 (2015 est.)

note: data are in 2017 dollars

country comparison to the world: 115

GROSS NATIONAL SAVING:

48.7% of GDP (2016 est.)

50.1% of GDP (2015 est.)

country comparison to the world: 2

GDP - COMPOSITION, BY END USE:

household consumption: 60.5% (2016 est.)

government consumption: 27.2% (2016 est.)

investment in fixed capital: 22.7% (2016 est.)

investment in inventories: 1.9% (2016 est.)

exports of goods and services: 55.2% (2016 est.)

imports of goods and services: -67.6% (2016 est.)

GDP - COMPOSITION, BY SECTOR OF ORIGIN:

agriculture: 3% (2016 est.)

industry: 19% (2016 est.)

services: 78% (2016 est.)

AGRICULTURE - PRODUCTS:

coconuts, cassava (manioc, tapioca), sweet potatoes; fish, pigs, chickens, eggs, bananas, papaya, breadfruit, calamansi, soursop, Polynesian chestnuts, Polynesian almonds, mangoes, taro, guava, beans, cucumbers, squash/pumpkins (various), eggplant, green onions, kangkong (watercress), cabbages (various), radishes, betel nuts, melons, peppers, noni, okra

INDUSTRIES:

tourism, fishing, subsistence agriculture

INDUSTRIAL PRODUCTION GROWTH RATE:

NA

LABOR FORCE:

11,610 (2016)

country comparison to the world: 216

LABOR FORCE - BY OCCUPATION:

agriculture: 1.2%

industry: 12.4%

services: 86.4% (2016)

UNEMPLOYMENT RATE:

1.7% (2015 est.)

4.1% (2012)

country comparison to the world: 15

POPULATION BELOW POVERTY LINE:

24.9% NA (2006)

HOUSEHOLD INCOME OR CONSUMPTION BY PERCENTAGE SHARE:

lowest 10%: NA

highest 10%: NA

BUDGET:

revenues: 193 million (2012 est.)

expenditures: 167.3 million (2012 est.)

TAXES AND OTHER REVENUES:

66.1% (of GDP) (2016 est.)

country comparison to the world: 6

BUDGET SURPLUS (+) OR DEFICIT (-):

8.8% (of GDP) (2016 est.)

country comparison to the world: 3

PUBLIC DEBT:

24.1% of GDP (2016 est.)

21.6% of GDP (2015)

country comparison to the world: 179

FISCAL YEAR:

1 October - 30 September

INFLATION RATE (CONSUMER PRICES):

0.9% (2017 est.)

-1% (2016 est.)

country comparison to the world: 46

MARKET VALUE OF PUBLICLY TRADED SHARES:

NA

CURRENT ACCOUNT BALANCE:

-$53 million (2017 est.)

-$36 million (2016 est.)

country comparison to the world: 79

EXPORTS:

$23.17 billion (2017 est.)

$14.8 million (2015 est.)

country comparison to the world: 69

EXPORTS - PARTNERS:

Japan 51.3%, US 15.8%, India 13.8%, Guam 8% (2017)

EXPORTS - COMMODITIES:

shellfish, tuna, other fish (many species)

IMPORTS:

$4.715 billion (2018 est.)

$4.079 billion (2017 est.)

country comparison to the world: 134

IMPORTS - COMMODITIES:
machinery and equipment, fuels, metals; foodstuffs

IMPORTS - PARTNERS:
US 33.4%, Guam 15.8%, Japan 15.7%, China 13.5%, South Korea 5.3% (2017)

RESERVES OF FOREIGN EXCHANGE AND GOLD:
$0 (31 December 2017 est.)

$580.9 million (31 December 2015 est.)

country comparison to the world: 193

DEBT - EXTERNAL:
$18.38 billion (31 December 2014 est.)

$16.47 billion (31 December 2013 est.)

country comparison to the world: 94

STOCK OF DIRECT FOREIGN INVESTMENT - AT HOME:
(31 December 2009 est.)

EXCHANGE RATES:
the US dollar is used

ENERGY :: PALAU

ELECTRICITY ACCESS:
electrification - total population: 99.3% (2016)

electrification - urban areas: 99.6% (2016)

electrification - rural areas: 97.2% (2016)

COMMUNICATIONS :: PALAU

TELEPHONES - FIXED LINES:
total subscriptions: 7,204

subscriptions per 100 inhabitants: 34 (July 2016 est.)

country comparison to the world: 201

TELEPHONES - MOBILE CELLULAR:
total subscriptions: 24,000

subscriptions per 100 inhabitants: 112 (July 2016 est.)

country comparison to the world: 208

TELEPHONE SYSTEM:
general assessment: well-developed mobile sector recently boosted by satellite network capacity upgrades; 3G services available with satellite; lack of telecom regulations; (2018)

domestic: fixed-line 34 per 100 and mobile-cellular services 112 per 100 persons (2018)

international: country code - 680; landing point for the SEA-US submarine cable linking Palau, Philippines, Micronesia, Indonesia, Hawaii (US), Guam (US) and California (US); satellite earth station - 1 Intelsat (Pacific Ocean) (2019)

BROADCAST MEDIA:
no broadcast TV stations; a cable TV network covers the major islands and provides access to 4 local cable stations, rebroadcasts (on a delayed basis) of a number of US stations, as well as access to a number of real-time satellite TV channels; about a half dozen radio stations (1 government-owned) (2019)

INTERNET COUNTRY CODE:
.pw

INTERNET USERS:
total: 7,650

percent of population: 36% (July 2016 est.)

country comparison to the world: 211

MILITARY AND SECURITY :: PALAU

MILITARY AND SECURITY FORCES:
no regular military forces; the Ministry of Justice includes divisions/bureaus for public security, police functions, and maritime law enforcement. (2019)

MILITARY - NOTE:
Under a 1994 Compact of Free Association between Palau and the US, the US until 2044 is responsible for the defense of Palaus and the US military is granted access to the islands, but it has not stationed any military forces there. (2019)

TRANSPORTATION :: PALAU

NATIONAL AIR TRANSPORT SYSTEM:
number of registered air carriers: 1 (2015)

inventory of registered aircraft operated by air carriers: 1 (2015)

AIRPORTS:
3 (2013)

country comparison to the world: 196

AIRPORTS - WITH PAVED RUNWAYS:
total: 1 (2017)

1,524 to 2,437 m: 1 (2017)

AIRPORTS - WITH UNPAVED RUNWAYS:
total: 2 (2013)

1,524 to 2,437 m: 2 (2013)

ROADWAYS:
total: 125 km (2018)

paved: 89 km (2018)

unpaved: 36 km (2018)

country comparison to the world: 205

PORTS AND TERMINALS:
major seaport(s): Koror

TRANSNATIONAL ISSUES :: PALAU

DISPUTES - INTERNATIONAL:
maritime delineation negotiations continue with Philippines, Indonesia

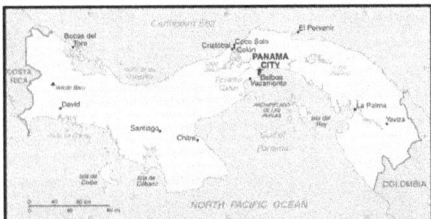

CENTRAL AMERICA :: PANAMA

INTRODUCTION :: PANAMA

BACKGROUND:

Explored and settled by the Spanish in the 16th century, Panama broke with Spain in 1821 and joined a union of Colombia, Ecuador, and Venezuela - named the Republic of Gran Colombia. When the latter dissolved in 1830, Panama remained part of Colombia. With US backing, Panama seceded from Colombia in 1903 and promptly signed a treaty with the US allowing for the construction of a canal and US sovereignty over a strip of land on either side of the structure (the Panama Canal Zone). The Panama Canal was built by the US Army Corps of Engineers between 1904 and 1914. In 1977, an agreement was signed for the complete transfer of the Canal from the US to Panama by the end of the century. Certain portions of the Zone and increasing responsibility over the Canal were turned over in the subsequent decades. With US help, dictator Manuel NORIEGA was deposed in 1989. The entire Panama Canal, the area supporting the Canal, and remaining US military bases were transferred to Panama by the end of 1999. An ambitious expansion project to more than double the Canal's capacity - by allowing for more Canal transits and larger ships - was carried out between 2007 and 2016.

GEOGRAPHY :: PANAMA

LOCATION:
Central America, bordering both the Caribbean Sea and the North Pacific Ocean, between Colombia and Costa Rica

GEOGRAPHIC COORDINATES:
9 00 N, 80 00 W

MAP REFERENCES:
Central America and the Caribbean

AREA:
total: 75,420 sq km

land: 74,340 sq km

water: 1,080 sq km

country comparison to the world: 119

AREA - COMPARATIVE:
slightly smaller than South Carolina

LAND BOUNDARIES:
total: 687 km

border countries (2): Colombia 339 km, Costa Rica 348 km

COASTLINE:
2,490 km

MARITIME CLAIMS:
territorial sea: 12 nm

exclusive economic zone: 200 nm or edge of continental margin

contiguous zone: 24 nm

CLIMATE:
tropical maritime; hot, humid, cloudy; prolonged rainy season (May to January), short dry season (January to May)

TERRAIN:
interior mostly steep, rugged mountains with dissected, upland plains; coastal plains with rolling hills

ELEVATION:
mean elevation: 360 m

lowest point: Pacific Ocean 0 m

highest point: Volcan Baru 3,475 m

NATURAL RESOURCES:
copper, mahogany forests, shrimp, hydropower

LAND USE:
agricultural land: 30.5% (2011 est.)

arable land: 7.3% (2011 est.) / permanent crops: 2.5% (2011 est.) / permanent pasture: 20.7% (2011 est.)

forest: 43.6% (2011 est.)

other: 25.9% (2011 est.)

IRRIGATED LAND:
321 sq km (2012)

POPULATION DISTRIBUTION:
population is concentrated towards the center of the country, particularly around the Canal, but a sizeable segment of the populace also lives in the far west around David; the eastern third of the country is sparsely inhabited

NATURAL HAZARDS:
occasional severe storms and forest fires in the Darien area

ENVIRONMENT - CURRENT ISSUES:
water pollution from agricultural runoff threatens fishery resources; deforestation of tropical rain forest; land degradation and soil erosion threatens siltation of Panama Canal; air pollution in urban areas; mining threatens natural resources

ENVIRONMENT - INTERNATIONAL AGREEMENTS:
party to: Biodiversity, Climate Change, Climate Change-Kyoto Protocol, Desertification, Endangered Species, Environmental Modification, Hazardous Wastes, Law of the Sea, Marine Dumping, Ozone Layer Protection, Ship Pollution, Tropical Timber 83, Tropical Timber 94, Wetlands, Whaling

signed, but not ratified: Marine Life Conservation

GEOGRAPHY - NOTE:
strategic location on eastern end of isthmus forming land bridge connecting North and South America; controls Panama Canal that links North Atlantic Ocean via Caribbean Sea with North Pacific Ocean

PEOPLE AND SOCIETY :: PANAMA

POPULATION:
3,800,644 (July 2018 est.)

country comparison to the world: 131

NATIONALITY:
noun: Panamanian(s)

adjective: Panamanian

ETHNIC GROUPS:
mestizo (mixed Amerindian and white) 65%, Native American 12.3% (Ngabe 7.6%, Kuna 2.4%, Embera 0.9%, Bugle 0.8%, other 0.4%, unspecified 0.2%), black or African descent 9.2%, mulatto 6.8%, white 6.7% (2010 est.)

LANGUAGES:
Spanish (official), indigenous languages (including Ngabere (or Guaymi), Buglere, Kuna, Embera, Wounaan, Naso (or Teribe), and Bri Bri), Panamanian English Creole (similar to Jamaican English Creole; a mixture of English and Spanish with elements of Ngabere; also known as Guari Guari and Colon Creole), English, Chinese (Yue and Hakka), Arabic, French Creole, other (Yiddish, Hebrew, Korean, Japanese)

note: many Panamanians are bilingual

RELIGIONS:
Roman Catholic 85%, Protestant 15%

DEMOGRAPHIC PROFILE:
Panama is a country of demographic and economic contrasts. It is in the midst of a demographic transition, characterized by steadily declining rates of fertility, mortality, and population growth, but disparities persist based on wealth, geography, and ethnicity. Panama has one of the fastest growing economies in Latin America and dedicates substantial funding to social programs, yet poverty and inequality remain prevalent. The indigenous population accounts for a growing share of Panama's poor and extreme poor, while the non-indigenous rural poor have been more successful at rising out of poverty through rural-to-urban labor migration. The government's large expenditures on untargeted, indirect subsidies for water, electricity, and fuel have been ineffective, but its conditional cash transfer program has shown some promise in helping to decrease extreme poverty among the indigenous population.

Panama has expanded access to education and clean water, but the availability of sanitation and, to a lesser extent, electricity remains poor. The increase in secondary schooling - led by female enrollment - is spreading to rural and indigenous areas, which probably will help to alleviate poverty if educational quality and the availability of skilled jobs improve. Inadequate access to sanitation contributes to a high incidence of diarrhea in Panama's children, which is one of the main causes of Panama's elevated chronic malnutrition rate, especially among indigenous communities.

AGE STRUCTURE:
0-14 years: 26.13% (male 506,953 /female 486,129)

15-24 years: 16.84% (male 326,207 /female 313,894)

25-54 years: 40.35% (male 776,395 /female 757,008)

55-64 years: 8.11% (male 152,894 /female 155,353)

65 years and over: 8.57% (male 149,415 /female 176,396) (2018 est.)

DEPENDENCY RATIOS:
total dependency ratio: 54.8 (2015 est.)

youth dependency ratio: 43.1 (2015 est.)

elderly dependency ratio: 11.7 (2015 est.)

potential support ratio: 8.5 (2015 est.)

MEDIAN AGE:
total: 29.5 years (2018 est.)

male: 29 years

female: 29.9 years

country comparison to the world: 123

POPULATION GROWTH RATE:
1.24% (2018 est.)

country comparison to the world: 89

BIRTH RATE:
17.6 births/1,000 population (2018 est.)

country comparison to the world: 97

DEATH RATE:
5 deaths/1,000 population (2018 est.)

country comparison to the world: 195

NET MIGRATION RATE:
-0.2 migrant(s)/1,000 population (2018 est.)

country comparison to the world: 111

POPULATION DISTRIBUTION:
population is concentrated towards the center of the country, particularly around the Canal, but a sizeable segment of the populace also lives in the far west around David; the eastern third of the country is sparsely inhabited

URBANIZATION:
urban population: 68.1% of total population (2019)

rate of urbanization: 2.06% annual rate of change (2015-20 est.)

MAJOR URBAN AREAS - POPULATION:
1.822 million PANAMA CITY (capital) (2019)

SEX RATIO:
at birth: 1.04 male(s)/female

0-14 years: 1.04 male(s)/female

15-24 years: 1.04 male(s)/female

25-54 years: 1.03 male(s)/female

55-64 years: 0.98 male(s)/female

65 years and over: 0.85 male(s)/female

total population: 1.01 male(s)/female (2018 est.)

MATERNAL MORTALITY RATE:
52 deaths/100,000 live births (2017 est.)

country comparison to the world: 93

INFANT MORTALITY RATE:
total: 9.6 deaths/1,000 live births (2018 est.)

male: 10.3 deaths/1,000 live births

female: 8.9 deaths/1,000 live births

country comparison to the world: 137

LIFE EXPECTANCY AT BIRTH:
total population: 78.9 years (2018 est.)

male: 76.1 years

female: 81.9 years

country comparison to the world: 58

TOTAL FERTILITY RATE:
2.28 children born/woman (2018 est.)

country comparison to the world: 89

CONTRACEPTIVE PREVALENCE RATE:
62.8% (2013)

DRINKING WATER SOURCE:
improved:

urban: 97.7% of population

rural: 86.6% of population

total: 94.7% of population

unimproved:

urban: 2.3% of population

rural: 11.4% of population

total: 5.3% of population (2015 est.)

CURRENT HEALTH EXPENDITURE:

7.3% (2016)

PHYSICIANS DENSITY:

1.57 physicians/1,000 population (2016)

HOSPITAL BED DENSITY:

2.3 beds/1,000 population (2013)

SANITATION FACILITY ACCESS:

improved:

urban: 83.5% of population (2015 est.)

rural: 58% of population (2015 est.)

total: 75% of population (2015 est.)

unimproved:

urban: 16.5% of population (2015 est.)

rural: 42% of population (2015 est.)

total: 25% of population (2015 est.)

HIV/AIDS - ADULT PREVALENCE RATE:

0.9% (2018 est.)

country comparison to the world: 52

HIV/AIDS - PEOPLE LIVING WITH HIV/AIDS:

26,000 (2018 est.)

country comparison to the world: 78

HIV/AIDS - DEATHS:

<500 (2018 est.)

MAJOR INFECTIOUS DISEASES:

degree of risk: intermediate (2016)

food or waterborne diseases: bacterial diarrhea (2016)

vectorborne diseases: dengue fever (2016)

note: active local transmission of Zika virus by Aedes species mosquitoes has been identified in this country (as of August 2016); it poses an important risk (a large number of cases possible) among US citizens if bitten by an infective mosquito; other less common ways to get Zika are through sex, via blood transfusion, or during pregnancy, in which the pregnant woman passes Zika virus to her fetus

OBESITY - ADULT PREVALENCE RATE:

22.7% (2016)

country comparison to the world: 73

CHILDREN UNDER THE AGE OF 5 YEARS UNDERWEIGHT:

EDUCATION EXPENDITURES:

3.2% of GDP (2011)

country comparison to the world: 133

LITERACY:

definition: age 15 and over can read and write

total population: 95%

male: 95.7%

female: 94.4% (2015 est.)

SCHOOL LIFE EXPECTANCY (PRIMARY TO TERTIARY EDUCATION):

total: 13 years

male: 12 years

female: 13 years (2015)

UNEMPLOYMENT, YOUTH AGES 15-24:

total: 10.8%

male: 8.3%

female: 14.9% (2017 est.)

country comparison to the world: 121

GOVERNMENT :: PANAMA

COUNTRY NAME:

conventional long form: Republic of Panama

conventional short form: Panama

local long form: Republica de Panama

local short form: Panama

etymology: named after the capital city which was itself named after a former indigenous fishing village

GOVERNMENT TYPE:

presidential republic

CAPITAL:

name: Panama City

geographic coordinates: 8 58 N, 79 32 W

time difference: UTC-5 (same time as Washington, DC, during Standard Time)

etymology: according to tradition, the name derives from a former fishing area near the present capital - an indigenous village and its adjacent beach - that were called "Panama" meaning "an abundance of fish"

ADMINISTRATIVE DIVISIONS:

10 provinces (provincias, singular - provincia) and 3 indigenous regions* (comarcas); Bocas del Toro, Chiriqui, Cocle, Colon, Darien, Embera-Wounaan*, Herrera, Guna Yala*, Los Santos, Ngobe-Bugle*, Panama, Panama Oeste, Veraguas

INDEPENDENCE:

3 November 1903 (from Colombia; became independent from Spain on 28 November 1821)

NATIONAL HOLIDAY:

Independence Day (Separation Day), 3 November (1903)

CONSTITUTION:

history: several previous; latest effective 11 October 1972

amendments: proposed by the National Assembly, by the Cabinet, or by the Supreme Court of Justice; passage requires approval by one of two procedures: 1) absolute majority vote of the Assembly membership in each of three readings and by absolute majority vote of the next elected Assembly in a single reading without textual modifications; 2) absolute majority vote of the Assembly membership in each of three readings, followed by absolute majority vote of the next elected Assembly in each of three readings with textual modifications, and approval in a referendum; amended several times, last in 2004 (2018)

LEGAL SYSTEM:

civil law system; judicial review of legislative acts in the Supreme Court of Justice

INTERNATIONAL LAW ORGANIZATION PARTICIPATION:

accepts compulsory ICJ jurisdiction with reservations; accepts ICCt jurisdiction

CITIZENSHIP:

citizenship by birth: yes

citizenship by descent only: yes

dual citizenship recognized: no

residency requirement for naturalization: 5 years

SUFFRAGE:

18 years of age; universal

EXECUTIVE BRANCH:

chief of state: President Laurentino "Nito" CORTIZO Cohen (since 1 July 2019); Vice President Jose Gabriel CARRIZO Jaen (since 1 July 2019); note - the president is both chief of state and head of government

head of government: President Laurentino "Nito" CORTIZO Cohen (since 1 July 2019); Vice President Jose Gabriel CARRIZO Jaen (since 1 July 2019)

cabinet: Cabinet appointed by the president

elections/appointments: president and vice president directly elected on the same ballot by simple majority popular vote for a 5-year term; president eligible for a single non-consecutive term); election last held on 5 May 2019 (next to be held in 2024)

election results: Laurentino "Nito" CORTIZO Cohen elected president; percent of vote - Laurentino CORTIZO Cohen (PRD) 33.3%, Romulo ROUX (CD) 31%, Ricardo LOMBANA (independent) 18.8%, Jose BLANDON (Panamenista Party) 10.8%, Ana Matilde GOMEZ Ruiloba (independent) 4.8%, other 1.3%

LEGISLATIVE BRANCH:

description: unicameral National Assembly or Asamblea Nacional (71 seats; 45 members directly elected in multi-seat constituencies - populous towns and cities - by proportional representation vote and 26 directly elected in single-seat constituencies - outlying rural districts - by plurality vote; members serve 5-year terms)

elections: last held on 4 May 2014 (next to be held in May 2019)

election results: percent of vote by party - CD 33.7%, PRD 31.5%, Panamenista Party 20%, MOLIRENA 7.2%, PP 3.3%, other 1%, independent 3%; seats by party - PRD 30, CD 25, Panamenista 12, MOLIRENA 2, PP 1, independent 1; composition - men 58, women 13, percent of women 18.3%

note: an alliance between the Panamenista Party and Democratic Revolutionary Party (PRD) fractured after the 2014 election, but a loose coalition composed of Panamenista and moderate PRD and CD legislators generally work together to support the president's agenda

JUDICIAL BRANCH:

highest courts: Supreme Court of Justice or Corte Suprema de Justicia (consists of 9 magistrates and 9 alternates and divided into civil, criminal, administrative, and general business chambers)

judge selection and term of office: magistrates appointed by the president for staggered 10-year terms

subordinate courts: appellate courts or Tribunal Superior; Labor Supreme Courts; Court of Audit; circuit courts or Tribunal Circuital (2 each in 9 of the 10 provinces); municipal courts; electoral, family, maritime, and adolescent courts

POLITICAL PARTIES AND LEADERS:

Democratic Change or CD [Romulo ROUX]
Democratic Revolutionary Party or PRD [Benicio ROBINSON]
Nationalist Republican Liberal Movement or MOLIRENA [Francisco "Pancho" ALEMAN]
Panamenista Party [Jose Luis "Popi" VARELA Rodriguez] (formerly the Arnulfista Party)
Popular Party or PP [Juan Carlos ARANGO Reese] (formerly Christian Democratic Party or PDC)

INTERNATIONAL ORGANIZATION PARTICIPATION:

BCIE, CAN (observer), CD, CELAC, FAO, G-77, IADB, IAEA, IBRD, ICAO, ICC (national committees), ICCt, ICRM, IDA, IFAD, IFC, IFRCS, ILO, IMF, IMO, IMSO, Interpol, IOC, IOM, IPU, ISO, ITSO, ITU, ITUC (NGOs), LAES, LAIA, MIGA, NAM, OAS, OPANAL, OPCW, Pacific Alliance (observer), PCA, SICA, UN, UNASUR (observer), UNCTAD, UNESCO, UNIDO, Union Latina, UNWTO, UPU, WCO, WFTU (NGOs), WHO, WIPO, WMO, WTO

DIPLOMATIC REPRESENTATION IN THE US:

Ambassador Emanuel Arturo GONZALEZ-REVILLA Lince (since 18 September 2014)

chancery: 2862 McGill Terrace NW, Washington, DC 20007

telephone: [1] (202) 483-1407

FAX: [1] (202) 483-8413

consulate(s) general: Houston, Miami, Los Angeles, New Orleans, New York, Philadelphia, Tampa, Washington DC

DIPLOMATIC REPRESENTATION FROM THE US:

chief of mission: Ambassador (vacant), Charge d'Affairs Roxanne CABRAL (since 9 March 2018)

telephone: [507] 317-5000

embassy: Edificio 783, Avenida Demetrio Basilio Lakas Avenue, Clayton, Panama

mailing address: American Embassy Panama, Unit 0945, APO AA 34002; American Embassy Panama, 9100 Panama City PL, Washington, DC 20521-9100

FAX: [507] 317-5445 (2018)

FLAG DESCRIPTION:

divided into four, equal rectangles; the top quadrants are white (hoist side) with a blue five-pointed star in the center and plain red; the bottom quadrants are plain blue (hoist side) and white with a red five-pointed star in the center; the blue and red colors are those of the main political parties (Conservatives and Liberals respectively) and the white denotes peace between them; the blue star stands for the civic virtues of purity and honesty, the red star signifies authority and law

NATIONAL SYMBOL(S):

harpy eagle; national colors: blue, white, red

NATIONAL ANTHEM:

name: "Himno Istmeno" (Isthmus Hymn)

lyrics/music: Jeronimo DE LA OSSA/Santos A. JORGE

note: adopted 1925

ECONOMY :: PANAMA

ECONOMY - OVERVIEW:

Panama's dollar-based economy rests primarily on a well-developed services sector that accounts for more than three-quarters of GDP. Services include operating the Panama Canal, logistics, banking, the Colon Free Trade Zone, insurance, container ports, flagship registry, and tourism and Panama is a center for offshore banking. Panama's transportation and logistics services sectors, along with infrastructure development projects, have boosted economic growth; however, public debt surpassed $37 billion in 2016 because of excessive government spending and public works projects. The US-Panama Trade Promotion Agreement was approved by Congress and signed into law in October 2011, and entered into force in October 2012.

Future growth will be bolstered by the Panama Canal expansion project that began in 2007 and was completed in 2016 at a cost of $5.3 billion - about 10-15% of current GDP. The expansion project more than doubled the Canal's capacity, enabling it to accommodate high-capacity vessels such as tankers and neopanamax vessels that are too large to traverse the existing canal. The US and China are the top users of the Canal.

Strong economic performance has not translated into broadly shared prosperity, as Panama has the second worst income distribution in Latin America. About one-fourth of the population lives in poverty; however, from 2006 to 2012 poverty was reduced by 10 percentage points.

GDP (PURCHASING POWER PARITY):

$104.1 billion (2017 est.)

$98.82 billion (2016 est.)

$94.12 billion (2015 est.)

note: data are in 2017 dollars

country comparison to the world: 83

GDP (OFFICIAL EXCHANGE RATE):

$61.84 billion (2017 est.)

GDP - REAL GROWTH RATE:

5.4% (2017 est.)

5% (2016 est.)

5.8% (2015 est.)

country comparison to the world: 42

GDP - PER CAPITA (PPP):

$25,400 (2017 est.)

$24,500 (2016 est.)

$23,700 (2015 est.)

note: data are in 2017 dollars

country comparison to the world: 80

GROSS NATIONAL SAVING:

38.9% of GDP (2017 est.)

39.2% of GDP (2016 est.)

36.8% of GDP (2015 est.)

country comparison to the world: 10

GDP - COMPOSITION, BY END USE:

household consumption: 45.6% (2017 est.)

government consumption: 10.7% (2017 est.)

investment in fixed capital: 42.9% (2017 est.)

investment in inventories: 3% (2017 est.)

exports of goods and services: 41.9% (2017 est.)

imports of goods and services: -44.2% (2017 est.)

GDP - COMPOSITION, BY SECTOR OF ORIGIN:

agriculture: 2.4% (2017 est.)

industry: 15.7% (2017 est.)

services: 82% (2017 est.)

AGRICULTURE - PRODUCTS:

bananas, rice, corn, coffee, sugarcane, vegetables; livestock; shrimp

INDUSTRIES:

construction, brewing, cement and other construction materials, sugar milling

INDUSTRIAL PRODUCTION GROWTH RATE:

6.3% (2017 est.)

country comparison to the world: 38

LABOR FORCE:

1.633 million (2017 est.)

note: shortage of skilled labor, but an oversupply of unskilled labor

country comparison to the world: 129

LABOR FORCE - BY OCCUPATION:

agriculture: 17%

industry: 18.6%

services: 64.4% (2009 est.)

UNEMPLOYMENT RATE:

6% (2017 est.)

5.5% (2016 est.)

country comparison to the world: 91

POPULATION BELOW POVERTY LINE:

23% (2015 est.)

HOUSEHOLD INCOME OR CONSUMPTION BY PERCENTAGE SHARE:

lowest 10%: 1.1%

highest 10%: 38.9% (2014 est.)

DISTRIBUTION OF FAMILY INCOME - GINI INDEX:

50.7 (2014 est.)

56.1 (2003)

country comparison to the world: 14

BUDGET:

revenues: 12.43 billion (2017 est.)

expenditures: 13.44 billion (2017 est.)

TAXES AND OTHER REVENUES:

20.1% (of GDP) (2017 est.)

country comparison to the world: 152

BUDGET SURPLUS (+) OR DEFICIT (-):

-1.6% (of GDP) (2017 est.)

country comparison to the world: 94

PUBLIC DEBT:

37.8% of GDP (2017 est.)

37.4% of GDP (2016 est.)

country comparison to the world: 138

FISCAL YEAR:

calendar year

INFLATION RATE (CONSUMER PRICES):

0.9% (2017 est.)

0.7% (2016 est.)

country comparison to the world: 47

COMMERCIAL BANK PRIME LENDING RATE:

7.52% (31 December 2017 est.)

7.53% (31 December 2016 est.)

country comparison to the world: 112

STOCK OF NARROW MONEY:

$8.347 billion (31 December 2017 est.)

$8.249 billion (31 December 2016 est.)

country comparison to the world: 87

STOCK OF BROAD MONEY:

$8.347 billion (31 December 2017 est.)

$8.249 billion (31 December 2016 est.)

country comparison to the world: 89

STOCK OF DOMESTIC CREDIT:

$51.05 billion (31 December 2017 est.)

$46.41 billion (31 December 2016 est.)

country comparison to the world: 66

MARKET VALUE OF PUBLICLY TRADED SHARES:

$12.54 billion (31 December 2012 est.)

$10.68 billion (31 December 2011 est.)

$8.348 billion (31 December 2010 est.)

country comparison to the world: 71

CURRENT ACCOUNT BALANCE:

-$3.036 billion (2017 est.)

-$3.16 billion (2016 est.)

country comparison to the world: 176

EXPORTS:

$15.5 billion (2017 est.)

$14.7 billion (2016 est.)

note: includes the Colon Free Zone

country comparison to the world: 75

EXPORTS - PARTNERS:

US 18.9%, Netherlands 16.6%, China 6.5%, Costa Rica 5.4%, India 5.1%, Vietnam 5% (2017)

EXPORTS - COMMODITIES:

fruit and nuts, fish, iron and steel waste, wood

IMPORTS:

$21.91 billion (2017 est.)

$20.51 billion (2016 est.)

note: includes the Colon Free Zone

country comparison to the world: 73

IMPORTS - COMMODITIES:
fuels, machinery, vehicles, iron and steel rods, pharmaceuticals

IMPORTS - PARTNERS:
US 24.4%, China 9.8%, Mexico 4.9% (2017)

RESERVES OF FOREIGN EXCHANGE AND GOLD:
$2.703 billion (31 December 2017 est.)
$3.878 billion (31 December 2016 est.)
country comparison to the world: 114

DEBT - EXTERNAL:
$91.53 billion (31 December 2017 est.)
$83.81 billion (31 December 2016 est.)
country comparison to the world: 52

STOCK OF DIRECT FOREIGN INVESTMENT - AT HOME:
$56.7 billion (31 December 2017 est.)
$50.62 billion (31 December 2016 est.)
country comparison to the world: 57

STOCK OF DIRECT FOREIGN INVESTMENT - ABROAD:
$11.38 billion (31 December 2017 est.)
$10.71 billion (31 December 2016 est.)
country comparison to the world: 62

EXCHANGE RATES:
balboas (PAB) per US dollar -
1 (2017 est.)
1 (2016 est.)
1 (2015 est.)
1 (2014 est.)
1 (2013 est.)

ENERGY :: PANAMA

ELECTRICITY ACCESS:
electrification - total population: 93.4% (2016)
electrification - urban areas: 99.4% (2016)
electrification - rural areas: 81.3% (2016)

ELECTRICITY - PRODUCTION:
10.6 billion kWh (2016 est.)
country comparison to the world: 101

ELECTRICITY - CONSUMPTION:
8.708 billion kWh (2016 est.)
country comparison to the world: 103

ELECTRICITY - EXPORTS:
139 million kWh (2015 est.)
country comparison to the world: 80

ELECTRICITY - IMPORTS:
30 million kWh (2016 est.)
country comparison to the world: 110

ELECTRICITY - INSTALLED GENERATING CAPACITY:
3.4 million kW (2016 est.)
country comparison to the world: 97

ELECTRICITY - FROM FOSSIL FUELS:
36% of total installed capacity (2016 est.)
country comparison to the world: 175

ELECTRICITY - FROM NUCLEAR FUELS:
0% of total installed capacity (2017 est.)
country comparison to the world: 161

ELECTRICITY - FROM HYDROELECTRIC PLANTS:
51% of total installed capacity (2017 est.)
country comparison to the world: 36

ELECTRICITY - FROM OTHER RENEWABLE SOURCES:
13% of total installed capacity (2017 est.)
country comparison to the world: 69

CRUDE OIL - PRODUCTION:
0 bbl/day (2018 est.)
country comparison to the world: 185

CRUDE OIL - EXPORTS:
0 bbl/day (2015 est.)
country comparison to the world: 178

CRUDE OIL - IMPORTS:
0 bbl/day (2015 est.)
country comparison to the world: 180

CRUDE OIL - PROVED RESERVES:
0 bbl (1 January 2018)
country comparison to the world: 180

REFINED PETROLEUM PRODUCTS - PRODUCTION:
0 bbl/day (2015 est.)
country comparison to the world: 188

REFINED PETROLEUM PRODUCTS - CONSUMPTION:
146,000 bbl/day (2016 est.)
country comparison to the world: 67

REFINED PETROLEUM PRODUCTS - EXPORTS:
66 bbl/day (2015 est.)
country comparison to the world: 121

REFINED PETROLEUM PRODUCTS - IMPORTS:
129,200 bbl/day (2015 est.)
country comparison to the world: 45

NATURAL GAS - PRODUCTION:
0 cu m (2017 est.)
country comparison to the world: 182

NATURAL GAS - CONSUMPTION:
0 cu m (2017 est.)
country comparison to the world: 186

NATURAL GAS - EXPORTS:
0 cu m (2017 est.)
country comparison to the world: 166

NATURAL GAS - IMPORTS:
0 cu m (2017 est.)
country comparison to the world: 171

NATURAL GAS - PROVED RESERVES:
0 cu m (1 January 2014 est.)
country comparison to the world: 180

CARBON DIOXIDE EMISSIONS FROM CONSUMPTION OF ENERGY:
26.08 million Mt (2017 est.)
country comparison to the world: 79

COMMUNICATIONS :: PANAMA

TELEPHONES - FIXED LINES:
total subscriptions: 603,638
subscriptions per 100 inhabitants: 16 (2017 est.)
country comparison to the world: 91

TELEPHONES - MOBILE CELLULAR:
total subscriptions: 5,977,641
subscriptions per 100 inhabitants: 159 (2017 est.)
country comparison to the world: 114

TELEPHONE SYSTEM:
general assessment: domestic and international facilities well-developed; investment from international operators; competion among operators helps reduce price of services; launches LTE services; (2018)

domestic: fixed-line 16 per 100 and mobile-cellular telephone 159 per 100 and subscribership has increased rapidly (2018)

international: country code - 507; landing points for the PAN-AM, ARCOS, SAC, AURORA, PCCS, PAC, and the MAYA-1, submarine cable systems that together provide links to the US and parts of the Caribbean, Central America, and South America; satellite earth stations - 2 Intelsat (Atlantic Ocean); connected to the Central American Microwave System (2019)

BROADCAST MEDIA:

multiple privately owned TV networks and a government-owned educational TV station; multi-channel cable and satellite TV subscription services are available; more than 100 commercial radio stations (2019)

INTERNET COUNTRY CODE:

.pa

INTERNET USERS:

total: 2,000,833

percent of population: 54% (July 2016 est.)

country comparison to the world: 112

BROADBAND - FIXED SUBSCRIPTIONS:

total: 446,076

subscriptions per 100 inhabitants: 12 (2017 est.)

country comparison to the world: 83

MILITARY AND SECURITY :: PANAMA

MILITARY AND SECURITY FORCES:

no regular military forces; Panamanian Public Security Forces (subordinate to the Ministry of Public Security), comprising the National Police (PNP), National Air-Naval Service (SENAN), National Border Service (SENAFRONT) (2019)

MILITARY - NOTE:

on 10 February 1990, the government of then President Guillermo ENDARA abolished Panama's military and reformed the security apparatus by creating the Panamanian Public Forces; in October 1994, Panama's National Assembly approved a constitutional amendment prohibiting the creation of a standing military force but allowing the temporary establishment of special police units to counter acts of "external aggression"

TRANSPORTATION :: PANAMA

NATIONAL AIR TRANSPORT SYSTEM:

number of registered air carriers: 4 (2015)

inventory of registered aircraft operated by air carriers: 103 (2015)

annual passenger traffic on registered air carriers: 12,018,103 (2015)

annual freight traffic on registered air carriers: 121,567,075 mt-km (2015)

CIVIL AIRCRAFT REGISTRATION COUNTRY CODE PREFIX:

HP (2016)

AIRPORTS:

117 (2013)

country comparison to the world: 50

AIRPORTS - WITH PAVED RUNWAYS:

total: 57 (2017)

over 3,047 m: 1 (2017)

2,438 to 3,047 m: 3 (2017)

1,524 to 2,437 m: 3 (2017)

914 to 1,523 m: 20 (2017)

under 914 m: 30 (2017)

AIRPORTS - WITH UNPAVED RUNWAYS:

total: 60 (2013)

1,524 to 2,437 m: 1 (2013)

914 to 1,523 m: 8 (2013)

under 914 m: 51 (2013)

HELIPORTS:

3 (2013)

PIPELINES:

128 km oil (2013)

RAILWAYS:

total: 77 km (2014)

standard gauge: 77 km 1.435-m gauge (2014)

country comparison to the world: 128

ROADWAYS:

WATERWAYS:

800 km (includes the 82-km Panama Canal that is being widened) (2011)

country comparison to the world: 71

MERCHANT MARINE:

total: 7,914

by type: bulk carrier 2585, container ship 590, general cargo 1327, oil tanker 808, other 2604 (2018)

country comparison to the world: 2

PORTS AND TERMINALS:

major seaport(s): Balboa, Colon, Cristobal

container port(s) (TEUs): Balboa (2,905,049), Colon (3,891,209) (2017)

TRANSNATIONAL ISSUES :: PANAMA

DISPUTES - INTERNATIONAL:

organized illegal narcotics operations in Colombia operate within the remote border region with Panama

REFUGEES AND INTERNALLY DISPLACED PERSONS:

refugees (country of origin): 15,614 (Colombia) (2016), 85,571 (Venezuela) (economic and political crisis; includes Venezuelans who have claimed asylum or have received alternative legal stay) (2019)

ILLICIT DRUGS:

major cocaine transshipment point and primary money-laundering center for narcotics revenue; money-laundering activity is especially heavy in the Colon Free Zone; offshore financial center; negligible signs of coca cultivation; monitoring of financial transactions is improving; official corruption remains a major problem

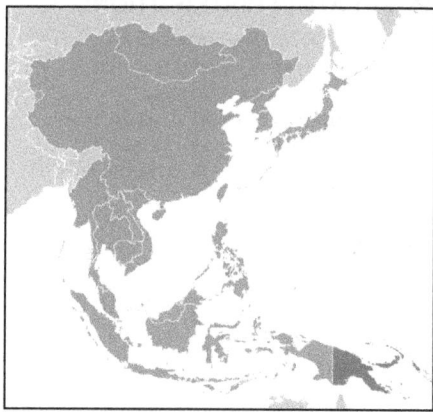
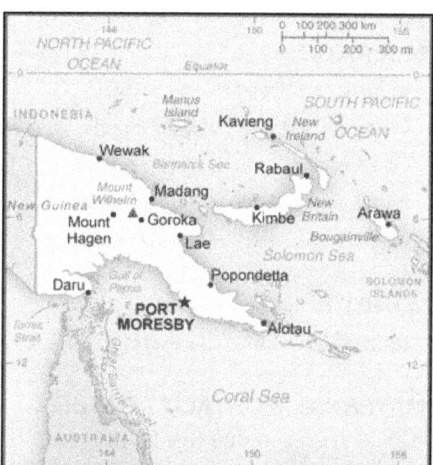

EAST ASIA / SOUTHEAST ASIA :: PAPUA NEW GUINEA

INTRODUCTION :: PAPUA NEW GUINEA

BACKGROUND:
The eastern half of the island of New Guinea - second largest in the world - was divided between Germany (north) and the UK (south) in 1885. The latter area was transferred to Australia in 1902, which occupied the northern portion during World War I and continued to administer the combined areas until independence in 1975. A nine-year secessionist revolt on the island of Bougainville ended in 1997 after claiming some 20,000 lives. Since 2001, Bougainville has experienced autonomy; a referendum asking the population if they would like independence or greater self rule is tentatively scheduled for October 2019.

GEOGRAPHY :: PAPUA NEW GUINEA

LOCATION:
Oceania, group of islands including the eastern half of the island of New Guinea between the Coral Sea and the South Pacific Ocean, east of Indonesia

GEOGRAPHIC COORDINATES:
6 00 S, 147 00 E

MAP REFERENCES:
Oceania

AREA:
total: 462,840 sq km

land: 452,860 sq km

water: 9,980 sq km

country comparison to the world: 56

AREA - COMPARATIVE:
slightly larger than California

LAND BOUNDARIES:
total: 824 km

border countries (1): Indonesia 824 km

COASTLINE:
5,152 km

MARITIME CLAIMS:
territorial sea: 12 nm

continental shelf: 200-m depth or to the depth of exploitation

exclusive fishing zone: 200 nm measured from claimed archipelagic baselines

CLIMATE:
tropical; northwest monsoon (December to March), southeast monsoon (May to October); slight seasonal temperature variation

TERRAIN:
mostly mountains with coastal lowlands and rolling foothills

ELEVATION:
mean elevation: 667 m

lowest point: Pacific Ocean 0 m

highest point: Mount Wilhelm 4,509 m

NATURAL RESOURCES:
gold, copper, silver, natural gas, timber, oil, fisheries

LAND USE:
agricultural land: 2.6% (2011 est.)

arable land: 0.7% (2011 est.) / permanent crops: 1.5% (2011 est.) / permanent pasture: 0.4% (2011 est.)

forest: 63.1% (2011 est.)

other: 34.3% (2011 est.)

IRRIGATED LAND:
0 sq km (2012)

POPULATION DISTRIBUTION:
population concentrated in the highlands and eastern coastal areas on the island of New Guinea; predominantly a rural distribution with only about one-fifth of the population residing in urban areas

NATURAL HAZARDS:
active volcanism; the country is subject to frequent and sometimes severe earthquakes; mud slides; tsunamis

volcanism: severe volcanic activity; Ulawun (2,334 m), one of Papua New Guinea's potentially most dangerous volcanoes, has been deemed a Decade Volcano by the International Association of Volcanology and Chemistry of the Earth's Interior, worthy of study due to its explosive history and close proximity to human populations; Rabaul (688 m) destroyed the city of Rabaul in 1937 and 1994; Lamington erupted in 1951 killing 3,000 people; Manam's 2004 eruption forced the island's abandonment; other historically active volcanoes include Bam, Bagana, Garbuna, Karkar, Langila, Lolobau, Long Island, Pago, St. Andrew Strait, Victory, and

Waiowa; see note 2 under "Geography - note"

ENVIRONMENT - CURRENT ISSUES:

rain forest loss as a result of growing commercial demand for tropical timber; unsustainable logging practices result in soil erosion, water quality degredation, and loss of habitat and biodiversity; large-scale mining projects cause adverse impacts on forests and water quality (discharge of heavy metals, cyanide, and acids into rivers); severe drought; inappropriate farming practices accelerate land degradion (soil erosion, siltation, loss of soil fertility); destructive fishing practices and coastal pollution due to run-off from land-based activities and oil spills

ENVIRONMENT - INTERNATIONAL AGREEMENTS:

party to: Antarctic Treaty, Biodiversity, Climate Change, Climate Change-Kyoto Protocol, Desertification, Endangered Species, Environmental Modification, Hazardous Wastes, Law of the Sea, Marine Dumping, Ozone Layer Protection, Ship Pollution, Tropical Timber 83, Tropical Timber 94, Wetlands

signed, but not ratified: none of the selected agreements

GEOGRAPHY - NOTE:

note 1: shares island of New Guinea with Indonesia; generally east-west trending highlands break up New Guinea into diverse ecoregions; one of world's largest swamps along southwest coast

note 2: Papua New Guinea is one of the countries along the Ring of Fire, a belt of active volcanoes and earthquake epicenters bordering the Pacific Ocean; up to 90% of the world's earthquakes and some 75% of the world's volcanoes occur within the Ring of Fire

PEOPLE AND SOCIETY :: PAPUA NEW GUINEA

POPULATION:

7,027,332 (July 2018 est.)

country comparison to the world: 105

NATIONALITY:

noun: Papua New Guinean(s)

adjective: Papua New Guinean

ETHNIC GROUPS:

Melanesian, Papuan, Negrito, Micronesian, Polynesian

LANGUAGES:

Tok Pisin (official), English (official), Hiri Motu (official), some 839 indigenous languages spoken (about 12% of the world's total); many languages have fewer than 1,000 speakers

note: Tok Pisin, a creole language, is widely used and understood; English is spoken by 1%-2%; Hiri Motu is spoken by less than 2%

RELIGIONS:

Protestant 64.3% (Evangelical Lutheran 18.4%, Seventh Day Adventist 12.9%, Pentecostal 10.4%, United Church 10.3%, Evangelical Alliance 5.9%, Anglican 3.2%, Baptist 2.8%, Salvation Army .4%), Roman Catholic 26%, other Christian 5.3%, non-Christian 1.4%, unspecified 3.1% (2011 est.)

note: data represent only the citizen population; roughly .3% of the population are non-citizens, consisting of Christian 52% (predominantly Roman Catholic), other 10.7%, none 37.3%

AGE STRUCTURE:

0-14 years: 32.94% (male 1,178,509/female 1,136,069)

15-24 years: 19.94% (male 710,166/female 690,848)

25-54 years: 37.13% (male 1,338,558/female 1,271,008)

55-64 years: 5.59% (male 201,271/female 191,833)

65 years and over: 4.4% (male 153,922/female 155,148) (2018 est.)

DEPENDENCY RATIOS:

total dependency ratio: 67.4 (2015 est.)

youth dependency ratio: 61.3 (2015 est.)

elderly dependency ratio: 6.1 (2015 est.)

potential support ratio: 16.4 (2015 est.)

MEDIAN AGE:

total: 23.4 years (2018 est.)

male: 23.5 years

female: 23.4 years

country comparison to the world: 171

POPULATION GROWTH RATE:

1.67% (2018 est.)

country comparison to the world: 61

BIRTH RATE:

23.3 births/1,000 population (2018 est.)

country comparison to the world: 60

DEATH RATE:

6.6 deaths/1,000 population (2018 est.)

country comparison to the world: 141

NET MIGRATION RATE:

0 migrant(s)/1,000 population (2018 est.)

country comparison to the world: 95

POPULATION DISTRIBUTION:

population concentrated in the highlands and eastern coastal areas on the island of New Guinea; predominantly a rural distribution with only about one-fifth of the population residing in urban areas

URBANIZATION:

urban population: 13.2% of total population (2019)

rate of urbanization: 2.51% annual rate of change (2015-20 est.)

MAJOR URBAN AREAS - POPULATION:

375,000 PORT MORESBY (capital) (2019)

SEX RATIO:

at birth: 1.05 male(s)/female

0-14 years: 1.04 male(s)/female

15-24 years: 1.03 male(s)/female

25-54 years: 1.05 male(s)/female

55-64 years: 1.05 male(s)/female

65 years and over: 0.99 male(s)/female

total population: 1.04 male(s)/female (2018 est.)

MATERNAL MORTALITY RATE:

145 deaths/100,000 live births (2017 est.)

country comparison to the world: 58

INFANT MORTALITY RATE:

total: 35.3 deaths/1,000 live births (2018 est.)

male: 38.6 deaths/1,000 live births

female: 31.7 deaths/1,000 live births

country comparison to the world: 49

LIFE EXPECTANCY AT BIRTH:

total population: 67.5 years (2018 est.)

male: 65.3 years

female: 69.8 years

country comparison to the world: 171

TOTAL FERTILITY RATE:

2.97 children born/woman (2018 est.)

country comparison to the world: 54

DRINKING WATER SOURCE:

improved:

urban: 88% of population

rural: 32.8% of population

total: 40% of population

unimproved:

urban: 12% of population

rural: 67.2% of population

total: 60% of population (2015 est.)

CURRENT HEALTH EXPENDITURE:

2% (2016)

PHYSICIANS DENSITY:

0.05 physicians/1,000 population (2010)

SANITATION FACILITY ACCESS:

improved:

urban: 56.4% of population (2015 est.)

rural: 13.3% of population (2015 est.)

total: 18.9% of population (2015 est.)

unimproved:

urban: 43.6% of population (2015 est.)

rural: 86.7% of population (2015 est.)

total: 81.1% of population (2015 est.)

HIV/AIDS - ADULT PREVALENCE RATE:

0.8% (2018 est.)

country comparison to the world: 55

HIV/AIDS - PEOPLE LIVING WITH HIV/AIDS:

45,000 (2018 est.)

country comparison to the world: 62

HIV/AIDS - DEATHS:

1,100 (2017 est.)

country comparison to the world: 60

MAJOR INFECTIOUS DISEASES:

degree of risk: very high (2016)

food or waterborne diseases: bacterial diarrhea, hepatitis A, and typhoid fever (2016)

vectorborne diseases: dengue fever and malaria (2016)

note: active local transmission of Zika virus by Aedes species mosquitoes has been identified in this country (as of August 2016); it poses an important risk (a large number of cases possible) among US citizens if bitten by an infective mosquito; other less common ways to get Zika are through sex, via blood transfusion, or during pregnancy, in which the pregnant woman passes Zika virus to her fetus

OBESITY - ADULT PREVALENCE RATE:

21.3% (2016)

country comparison to the world: 91

CHILDREN UNDER THE AGE OF 5 YEARS UNDERWEIGHT:

27.8% (2010)

country comparison to the world: 14

EDUCATION EXPENDITURES:

NA

LITERACY:

definition: age 15 and over can read and write

total population: 64.2%

male: 65.6%

female: 62.8% (2015 est.)

UNEMPLOYMENT, YOUTH AGES 15-24:

total: 3.6%

male: 4.3%

female: 3% (2010 est.)

country comparison to the world: 172

PEOPLE - NOTE:

the indigenous population of Papua New Guinea (PNG) is one of the most heterogeneous in the world; PNG has several thousand separate communities, most with only a few hundred people; divided by language, customs, and tradition, some of these communities have engaged in low-scale tribal conflict with their neighbors for millennia; the advent of modern weapons and modern migrants into urban areas has greatly magnified the impact of this lawlessness

GOVERNMENT :: PAPUA NEW GUINEA

COUNTRY NAME:

conventional long form: Independent State of Papua New Guinea

conventional short form: Papua New Guinea

local short form: Papuaniugini

former: Territory of Papua and New Guinea

abbreviation: PNG

etymology: the word "papua" derives from the Malay "papuah" describing the frizzy hair of the Melanesians; Spanish explorer Ynigo ORTIZ de RETEZ applied the term "Nueva Guinea" to the island of New Guinea in 1545 after noting the resemblance of the locals to the peoples of the Guinea coast of Africa

GOVERNMENT TYPE:

parliamentary democracy under a constitutional monarchy; a Commonwealth realm

CAPITAL:

name: Port Moresby

geographic coordinates: 9 27 S, 147 11 E

time difference: UTC+10 (15 hours ahead of Washington, DC, during Standard Time)

note: Papua New Guinea has two time zones, including Bougainville (UTC+11)

etymology: named in 1873 by Captain John Moresby (1830-1922) in honor of his father, British Admiral Sir Fairfax Moresby (1786-1877)

ADMINISTRATIVE DIVISIONS:

20 provinces, 1 autonomous region*, and 1 district**; Bougainville*, Central, Chimbu, Eastern Highlands, East New Britain, East Sepik, Enga, Gulf, Hela, Jiwaka, Madang, Manus, Milne Bay, Morobe, National Capital**, New Ireland, Northern, Southern Highlands, Western, Western Highlands, West New Britain, West Sepik

INDEPENDENCE:

16 September 1975 (from the Australia-administered UN trusteeship)

NATIONAL HOLIDAY:

Independence Day, 16 September (1975)

CONSTITUTION:

history: adopted 15 August 1975, effective at independence 16 September 1975

amendments: proposed by the National Parliament; passage has prescribed majority vote requirements depending on the constitutional sections being amended – absolute majority, two-thirds majority, or three-fourths majority; amended many times, last in 2014 (2018)

LEGAL SYSTEM:

mixed legal system of English common law and customary law

INTERNATIONAL LAW ORGANIZATION PARTICIPATION: has not submitted an ICJ jurisdiction declaration; non-party state to the ICCt

CITIZENSHIP:

citizenship by birth: no

citizenship by descent only: at least one parent must be a citizen of Papua New Guinea

dual citizenship recognized: no

residency requirement for naturalization: 8 years

SUFFRAGE:

18 years of age; universal

EXECUTIVE BRANCH:

chief of state: Queen ELIZABETH II (since 6 February 1952); represented by Governor General Grand Chief Sir Bob DADAE (since 28 February 2017)

head of government: Prime Minister James MARAPE (since 30 May 2019); Deputy Prime Minister Charles ABEL (since 4 August 2017)

cabinet: National Executive Council appointed by the governor general on the recommendation of the prime minister

elections/appointments: the monarchy is hereditary; governor general nominated by the National Parliament and appointed by the chief of state; following legislative elections, the leader of the majority party or majority coalition usually appointed prime minister by the governor general pending the outcome of a National Parliament vote

election results: Peter Paire O'NEILL (PNC) reelected prime minister; National Parliament vote - 60 to 46

LEGISLATIVE BRANCH:

description: unicameral National Parliament (111 seats; members directly elected in single-seat constituencies - 89 local, 20 provinicial, the autonomous province of Bouganville, and the National Capital District - by majority preferential vote; members serve 5-year terms); note - the constitution allows up to 126 seats

elections: last held from 24 June 2017 to 8 July 2017 (next to be held in June 2022)

election results: percent of vote by party - PNC 37%; NA 13%; Pangu 14%; URP 11%; PPP 4%; SDP 4%; Independents 3%; and smaller parties 14%; seats by party - NA; composition - men 108, women 3, percent of women 3%

JUDICIAL BRANCH:

highest courts: Supreme Court (consists of the chief justice, deputy chief justice, 35 justices, and 5 acting justices); National Courts (consists of 13 courts located in the provincial capitals, with a total of 19 resident judges)

judge selection and term of office: Supreme Court chief justice appointed by the governor general upon advice of the National Executive Council (cabinet) after consultation with the National Justice Administration minister; deputy chief justice and other justices appointed by the Judicial and Legal Services Commission, a 5-member body that includes the Supreme Court chief and deputy chief justices, the chief ombudsman, and a member of the National Parliament; full-time citizen judges appointed for 10-year renewable terms; non-citizen judges initially appointed for 3-year renewable terms and after first renewal can serve until age 70; appointment and tenure of National Court resident judges NA

subordinate courts: district, village, and juvenile courts, military courts, taxation courts, coronial courts, mining warden courts, land courts, traffic courts, committal courts, grade five courts

POLITICAL PARTIES AND LEADERS:

National Alliance Party or NAP [Patrick PRUAITCH]
Papua and Niugini Union Party or PANGU [Sam BASIL]
Papua New Guinea Party or PNGP [Belden NAMAH]
People's National Congress Party or PNC [Peter Paire O'NEILL]
People's Party or PP [Peter IPATAS]
People's Progress Party or PPP [Sir Julius CHAN]
Social Democratic Party or SDP [Powes PARKOP]
Triumph Heritage Empowerment Party or THE [Don POLYE]
United Resources Party or URP [William DUMA]

note: as of 8 July 2017, 45 political parties were registered

INTERNATIONAL ORGANIZATION PARTICIPATION:

ACP, ADB, AOSIS, APEC, ARF, ASEAN (observer), C, CD, CP, EITI (candidate country), FAO, G-77, IAEA, IBRD, ICAO, ICRM, IDA, IFAD, IFC, IFRCS, IHO, ILO, IMF, IMO, Interpol, IOC, IOM, IPU, ISO (correspondent), ITSO, ITU, MIGA, NAM, OPCW, PIF, Sparteca, SPC, UN, UNCTAD, UNESCO, UNIDO, UNMISS, UNWTO, UPU, WCO, WFTU (NGOs), WHO, WIPO, WMO, WTO

DIPLOMATIC REPRESENTATION IN THE US:

Ambassador (vacant); Charge D'Affaires Elias Rahuromo WOHENGU (since 30 September 2017)

chancery: 1779 Massachusetts Avenue NW, Suite 805, Washington, DC 20036

telephone: [1] (202) 745-3680

FAX: [1] (202) 745-3679

DIPLOMATIC REPRESENTATION FROM THE US:

chief of mission: Ambassador Catherine EBERT-GRAY (since 23 February 2016); note - also accredited to the Solomon Islands and Vanuatu

telephone: [675] 321-1455

embassy: P.O. Box 1492, Port Moresby

mailing address: 4240 Port Moresby Place, US Department of State, Washington DC 20521-4240

FAX: [675] 321-3423

FLAG DESCRIPTION:

divided diagonally from upper hoist-side corner; the upper triangle is red with a soaring yellow bird of paradise centered; the lower triangle is black with five, white, five-pointed stars of the Southern Cross constellation centered; red, black, and yellow are traditional colors of Papua New Guinea; the bird of paradise - endemic to the island of New Guinea - is an emblem of regional tribal culture and represents the emergence of Papua New Guinea as a nation; the Southern Cross, visible in the night sky, symbolizes Papua New Guinea's connection with Australia and several other countries in the South Pacific

NATIONAL SYMBOL(S):

bird of paradise; national colors: red, black

NATIONAL ANTHEM:

name: O Arise All You Sons

lyrics/music: Thomas SHACKLADY

note: adopted 1975

ECONOMY :: PAPUA NEW GUINEA

ECONOMY - OVERVIEW:

Papua New Guinea (PNG) is richly endowed with natural resources, but exploitation has been hampered by rugged terrain, land tenure issues, and the high cost of developing infrastructure. The economy has a small formal sector, focused mainly on the export of those natural resources, and an informal sector, employing the majority of the population. Agriculture provides a subsistence livelihood for 85% of the people. The global financial crisis had little impact because of continued foreign demand for PNG's commodities.

Mineral deposits, including copper, gold, and oil, account for nearly two-thirds of export earnings. Natural gas reserves amount to an estimated 155 billion cubic meters. Following construction of a $19 billion liquefied natural gas (LNG) project, PNG LNG, a consortium led by ExxonMobil, began exporting liquefied natural gas to Asian markets in May 2014. The project was delivered on time and only slightly above budget. The success of the project has encouraged other companies to look at similar LNG projects. French supermajor Total is hopes to begin construction on the Papua LNG project by 2020. Due to lower global commodity prices, resource revenues of all types have fallen dramatically. PNG's government has recently been forced to adjust spending levels downward.

Numerous challenges still face the government of Peter O'NEILL, including providing physical security for foreign investors, regaining investor confidence, restoring integrity to state institutions, promoting economic efficiency by privatizing moribund state institutions, and maintaining good relations with Australia, its former colonial ruler. Other socio-cultural challenges could upend the economy including chronic law and order and land tenure issues. In August, 2017, PNG launched its first-ever national trade policy, PNG Trade Policy 2017-2032. The policy goal is to maximize trade and investment by increasing exports, to reduce imports, and to increase foreign direct investment (FDI).

GDP (PURCHASING POWER PARITY):

$30.19 billion (2017 est.)

$29.44 billion (2016 est.)

$28.98 billion (2015 est.)

note: data are in 2017 dollars

country comparison to the world: 132

GDP (OFFICIAL EXCHANGE RATE):

$19.82 billion (2017 est.)

GDP - REAL GROWTH RATE:

2.5% (2017 est.)

1.6% (2016 est.)

5.3% (2015 est.)

country comparison to the world: 131

GDP - PER CAPITA (PPP):

$3,700 (2017 est.)

$3,600 (2016 est.)

$3,700 (2015 est.)

note: data are in 2017 dollars

country comparison to the world: 184

GROSS NATIONAL SAVING:

36.8% of GDP (2017 est.)

38% of GDP (2016 est.)

33.7% of GDP (2015 est.)

country comparison to the world: 14

GDP - COMPOSITION, BY END USE:

household consumption: 43.7% (2017 est.)

government consumption: 19.7% (2017 est.)

investment in fixed capital: 10% (2017 est.)

investment in inventories: 0.4% (2017 est.)

exports of goods and services: 49.3% (2017 est.)

imports of goods and services: -22.3% (2017 est.)

GDP - COMPOSITION, BY SECTOR OF ORIGIN:

agriculture: 22.1% (2017 est.)

industry: 42.9% (2017 est.)

services: 35% (2017 est.)

AGRICULTURE - PRODUCTS:

coffee, cocoa, copra, palm kernels, tea, sugar, rubber, sweet potatoes, fruit, vegetables, vanilla; poultry, pork; shellfish

INDUSTRIES:

copra crushing, palm oil processing, plywood production, wood chip production; mining (gold, silver, copper); crude oil and petroleum products; construction, tourism, livestock (pork, poultry, cattle), dairy products, spice products (turmeric, vanilla, ginger, cardamom, chili, pepper, citronella, and nutmeg), fisheries products

INDUSTRIAL PRODUCTION GROWTH RATE:

3.3% (2017 est.)

country comparison to the world: 97

LABOR FORCE:

3.681 million (2017 est.)

country comparison to the world: 97

LABOR FORCE - BY OCCUPATION:

agriculture: 85%

industry: NA

services: NA

UNEMPLOYMENT RATE:

2.5% (2017 est.)

2.5% (2016 est.)

country comparison to the world: 26

POPULATION BELOW POVERTY LINE:

37% (2002 est.)

HOUSEHOLD INCOME OR CONSUMPTION BY PERCENTAGE SHARE:

lowest 10%: 1.7%

highest 10%: 40.5% (1996)

DISTRIBUTION OF FAMILY INCOME - GINI INDEX:

50.9 (1996)

country comparison to the world: 13

BUDGET:

revenues: 3.638 billion (2017 est.)

expenditures: 4.591 billion (2017 est.)

TAXES AND OTHER REVENUES:

18.4% (of GDP) (2017 est.)

country comparison to the world: 160

BUDGET SURPLUS (+) OR DEFICIT (-):

-4.8% (of GDP) (2017 est.)

country comparison to the world: 168

PUBLIC DEBT:

36.9% of GDP (2017 est.)

36.9% of GDP (2016 est.)

country comparison to the world: 144

FISCAL YEAR:

calendar year

INFLATION RATE (CONSUMER PRICES):

5.4% (2017 est.)

6.7% (2016 est.)

country comparison to the world: 177

CENTRAL BANK DISCOUNT RATE:

14% (31 December 2010)

6.92% (31 December 2009)

country comparison to the world: 15

COMMERCIAL BANK PRIME LENDING RATE:

8.4% (31 December 2017 est.)

8.38% (31 December 2016 est.)

country comparison to the world: 99

STOCK OF NARROW MONEY:

$5.409 billion (31 December 2017 est.)

$5.05 billion (31 December 2016 est.)

country comparison to the world: 99

STOCK OF BROAD MONEY:

$5.409 billion (31 December 2017 est.)

$5.05 billion (31 December 2016 est.)

country comparison to the world: 102

STOCK OF DOMESTIC CREDIT:

$7.091 billion (31 December 2017 est.)

$7.223 billion (31 December 2016 est.)

country comparison to the world: 119

MARKET VALUE OF PUBLICLY TRADED SHARES:

$10.71 billion (31 December 2012 est.)

$8.999 billion (31 December 2011 est.)

$9.742 billion (31 December 2010 est.)

country comparison to the world: 74

CURRENT ACCOUNT BALANCE:

$4.859 billion (2017 est.)

$4.569 billion (2016 est.)

country comparison to the world: 29

EXPORTS:

$8.522 billion (2017 est.)

$9.224 billion (2016 est.)

country comparison to the world: 96

EXPORTS - PARTNERS:

Australia 18.9%, Singapore 17.5%, Japan 13.8%, China 12.7%, Philippines 4.7%, Netherlands 4.2%, India 4.2% (2017)

EXPORTS - COMMODITIES:

liquefied natural gas, oil, gold, copper ore, nickel, cobalt logs, palm oil, coffee, cocoa, copra, spice (turmeric, vanilla, ginger, and cardamom), crayfish, prawns, tuna, sea cucumber

IMPORTS:

$1.876 billion (2017 est.)

$2.077 billion (2016 est.)

country comparison to the world: 170

IMPORTS - COMMODITIES:

machinery and transport equipment, manufactured goods, food, fuels, chemicals

IMPORTS - PARTNERS:

Australia 30.1%, China 17.3%, Singapore 10.2%, Malaysia 8.2%, Indonesia 4% (2017)

RESERVES OF FOREIGN EXCHANGE AND GOLD:

$1.735 billion (31 December 2017 est.)

$1.656 billion (31 December 2016 est.)

country comparison to the world: 123

DEBT - EXTERNAL:

$17.94 billion (31 December 2017 est.)

$18.28 billion (31 December 2016 est.)

country comparison to the world: 95

STOCK OF DIRECT FOREIGN INVESTMENT - AT HOME:

NA

STOCK OF DIRECT FOREIGN INVESTMENT - ABROAD:

NA

EXCHANGE RATES:

kina (PGK) per US dollar -

3.179 (2017 est.)

3.133 (2016 est.)

3.133 (2015 est.)

2.7684 (2014 est.)

2.4614 (2013 est.)

ENERGY :: PAPUA NEW GUINEA

ELECTRICITY ACCESS:

electrification - total population: 22.9% (2016)

electrification - urban areas: 72.7% (2016)

electrification - rural areas: 15.5% (2016)

ELECTRICITY - PRODUCTION:

3.481 billion kWh (2016 est.)

country comparison to the world: 129

ELECTRICITY - CONSUMPTION:

3.237 billion kWh (2016 est.)

country comparison to the world: 134

ELECTRICITY - EXPORTS:

0 kWh (2017 est.)

country comparison to the world: 183

ELECTRICITY - IMPORTS:

0 kWh (2016 est.)

country comparison to the world: 184

ELECTRICITY - INSTALLED GENERATING CAPACITY:

900,900 kW (2016 est.)

country comparison to the world: 131

ELECTRICITY - FROM FOSSIL FUELS:

63% of total installed capacity (2016 est.)

country comparison to the world: 123

ELECTRICITY - FROM NUCLEAR FUELS:

0% of total installed capacity (2017 est.)

country comparison to the world: 162

ELECTRICITY - FROM HYDROELECTRIC PLANTS:

30% of total installed capacity (2017 est.)

country comparison to the world: 69

ELECTRICITY - FROM OTHER RENEWABLE SOURCES:

7% of total installed capacity (2017 est.)

country comparison to the world: 95

CRUDE OIL - PRODUCTION:

45,000 bbl/day (2018 est.)

country comparison to the world: 55

CRUDE OIL - EXPORTS:

55,600 bbl/day (2015 est.)

country comparison to the world: 41

CRUDE OIL - IMPORTS:

22,220 bbl/day (2015 est.)

country comparison to the world: 62

CRUDE OIL - PROVED RESERVES:

183.8 million bbl (1 January 2018 est.)

country comparison to the world: 57

REFINED PETROLEUM PRODUCTS - PRODUCTION:

22,170 bbl/day (2015 est.)

country comparison to the world: 88

REFINED PETROLEUM PRODUCTS - CONSUMPTION:

37,000 bbl/day (2016 est.)

country comparison to the world: 116

REFINED PETROLEUM PRODUCTS - EXPORTS:

0 bbl/day (2015 est.)

country comparison to the world: 190

REFINED PETROLEUM PRODUCTS - IMPORTS:

17,110 bbl/day (2015 est.)

country comparison to the world: 134

NATURAL GAS - PRODUCTION:

11.18 billion cu m (2017 est.)

country comparison to the world: 39

NATURAL GAS - CONSUMPTION:

99.11 million cu m (2017 est.)

country comparison to the world: 109

NATURAL GAS - EXPORTS:

11.1 billion cu m (2017 est.)

country comparison to the world: 21

NATURAL GAS - IMPORTS:

0 cu m (2017 est.)

country comparison to the world: 172

NATURAL GAS - PROVED RESERVES:

210.5 billion cu m (1 January 2018 est.)

country comparison to the world: 41

CARBON DIOXIDE EMISSIONS FROM CONSUMPTION OF ENERGY:

6.082 million Mt (2017 est.)

country comparison to the world: 129

COMMUNICATIONS :: PAPUA NEW GUINEA

TELEPHONES - FIXED LINES:

total subscriptions: 154,000

subscriptions per 100 inhabitants: 2 (July 2016 est.)

country comparison to the world: 127

TELEPHONES - MOBILE CELLULAR:

total subscriptions: 3.782 million

subscriptions per 100 inhabitants: 55 (July 2016 est.)

country comparison to the world: 130

TELEPHONE SYSTEM:

general assessment: services are minimal; facilities provide radiotelephone and telegraph, coastal radio, aeronautical radio, and international radio communication services; a great deal of the population is under served in telecommunications; terrain, living conditions and economice stability is not high; 3G and 4G LTE in urban areas (2018)

domestic: access to telephone services is not widely available; fixed-line 2 per 100 and mobile-cellular 55 per 100 person, teledensity has increased (2018)

international: country code - 675; landing points for the Kumul Domestic Submarine Cable System, PNG-LNG, APNG-2, CSCS and the PPC-1 submarine cables to Australia, Guam, PNG and Solomon Islands; satellite earth station - 1 Intelsat (Pacific Ocean); international radio communication service (2019)

BROADCAST MEDIA:

4 TV stations: 1 commercial station operating since 1987, 1 state-run station launched in 2008, 1 digital free-to-view network launched in 2014, and 1 satellite network Click TV (PNGTV) launched in 2015; the state-run National Broadcasting Corporation operates 3 radio networks with multiple repeaters and about 20 provincial stations; several commercial radio stations with multiple transmission points as well as several community stations; transmissions of several international broadcasters are accessible (2018)

INTERNET COUNTRY CODE:

.pg

INTERNET USERS:

total: 652,071

percent of population: 9.6% (July 2016 est.)

country comparison to the world: 144

BROADBAND - FIXED SUBSCRIPTIONS:

total: 17,000

subscriptions per 100 inhabitants: less than 1 (2017 est.)

country comparison to the world: 155

MILITARY AND SECURITY :: PAPUA NEW GUINEA

MILITARY EXPENDITURES:

0.27% of GDP (2018)

0.34% of GDP (2017)

0.39% of GDP (2016)

0.47% of GDP (2015)

0.49% of GDP (2014)

country comparison to the world: 155

MILITARY AND SECURITY FORCES:

Papua New Guinea Defense Force (PNGDF, includes land, maritime, and air elements) (2019)

MILITARY SERVICE AGE AND OBLIGATION:

16 years of age for voluntary military service (with parental consent); no conscription; graduation from grade 12 required (2013)

TRANSPORTATION :: PAPUA NEW GUINEA

NATIONAL AIR TRANSPORT SYSTEM:

number of registered air carriers: 6 (2015)

inventory of registered aircraft operated by air carriers: 47 (2015)

annual passenger traffic on registered air carriers: 2,062,584 (2015)

annual freight traffic on registered air carriers: 34,827,034 mt-km (2015)

CIVIL AIRCRAFT REGISTRATION COUNTRY CODE PREFIX:

P2 (2016)

AIRPORTS:

561 (2013)

country comparison to the world: 12

AIRPORTS - WITH PAVED RUNWAYS:

total: 21 (2017)

over 3,047 m: 1 (2017)

2,438 to 3,047 m: 2 (2017)

1,524 to 2,437 m: 12 (2017)

914 to 1,523 m: 5 (2017)

under 914 m: 1 (2017)

AIRPORTS - WITH UNPAVED RUNWAYS:

total: 540 (2013)

1,524 to 2,437 m: 11 (2013)

914 to 1,523 m: 53 (2013)

under 914 m: 476 (2013)

HELIPORTS:

2 (2013)

PIPELINES:

264 km oil (2013)

ROADWAYS:

total: 9,349 km (2011)

paved: 3,000 km (2011)

unpaved: 6,349 km (2011)

country comparison to the world: 132

WATERWAYS:

11,000 km (2011)

country comparison to the world: 12

MERCHANT MARINE:

total: 173

by type: container ship 7, general cargo 79, oil tanker 3, other 84 (2018)

country comparison to the world: 65

PORTS AND TERMINALS:

major seaport(s): Kimbe, Lae, Madang, Rabaul, Wewak

LNG terminal(s) (export): Port Moresby

TRANSNATIONAL ISSUES :: PAPUA NEW GUINEA

DISPUTES - INTERNATIONAL:

relies on assistance from Australia to keep out illegal cross-border activities from primarily Indonesia, including goods smuggling, illegal narcotics trafficking, and squatters and secessionists

REFUGEES AND INTERNALLY DISPLACED PERSONS:

refugees (country of origin): 9,368 (Indonesia) (2018)

IDPs: 12,000 (natural disasters, tribal conflict, inter-communal violence, development projects) (2017)

TRAFFICKING IN PERSONS:

current situation: Papua New Guinea is a source and destination country for men, women, and children subjected to sex trafficking and forced labor; foreign and Papua New Guinean women and children are subjected to sex trafficking, domestic servitude, forced begging, and street vending; parents may sell girls into forced marriages to settle debts or as peace offerings or trade them to another tribe to forge a political alliance, leaving them vulnerable to forced domestic service, or, in urban areas, they may prostitute their children for income or to pay school fees; Chinese, Malaysian, and local men are forced to labor in logging and mining camps through debt bondage schemes; migrant women from Indonesia, Malaysia, Thailand, China, and the Philippines are subjected to sex trafficking and domestic servitude at logging and mining camps, fisheries, and entertainment sites

tier rating: Tier 2 Watch List - Papua New Guinea does not fully comply with the minimum standards for the elimination of trafficking; however, it is making significant efforts to do so; the Criminal Code Amendment of 2013, which prohibits all forms of trafficking was brought into force in 2014; the government also formed an anti-trafficking committee, which drafted a national action plan; despite corruption problems, trafficking-related crimes were prosecuted in village courts rather than criminal courts, resulting in restitution to the victim but no prison time for offenders; the government did not investigate, prosecute, or convict any officials or law enforcement personnel complicit in trafficking offenses; the government made no efforts to proactively identify trafficking victims, has no formal victim identification and referral mechanism, and does not provide care facilities to victims or funding to shelters run by NGOs or international organizations (2015)

ILLICIT DRUGS:

major consumer of cannabis

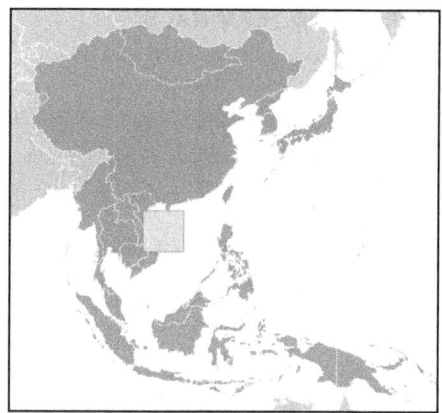

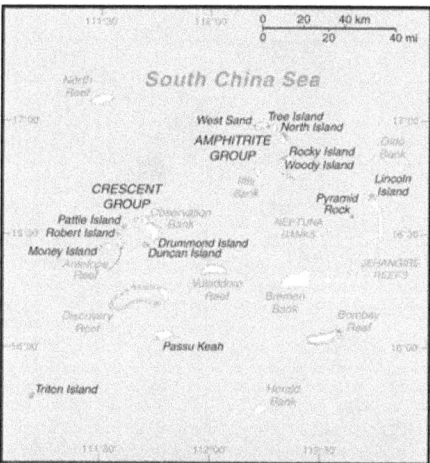

EAST ASIA / SOUTHEAST ASIA :: PARACEL ISLANDS

INTRODUCTION :: PARACEL ISLANDS

BACKGROUND:
The Paracel Islands are surrounded by productive fishing grounds and by potential oil and gas reserves. In 1932, French Indochina annexed the islands and set up a weather station on Pattle Island; maintenance was continued by its successor, Vietnam. China has occupied all the Paracel Islands since 1974, when its troops seized a South Vietnamese garrison occupying the western islands. China built a military installation on Woody Island with an airfield and artificial harbor. The islands also are claimed by Taiwan and Vietnam.

GEOGRAPHY :: PARACEL ISLANDS

LOCATION:
Southeastern Asia, group of small islands and reefs in the South China Sea, about one-third of the way from central Vietnam to the northern Philippines

GEOGRAPHIC COORDINATES:
16 30 N, 112 00 E

MAP REFERENCES:
Southeast Asia

AREA:
total: 7.75 sq km ca.
land: 7.75 sq km ca.
water: 0 sq km
country comparison to the world: 244

AREA - COMPARATIVE:
land area is about 13 times the size of the National Mall in Washington, DC

LAND BOUNDARIES:
0 km

COASTLINE:
518 km

MARITIME CLAIMS:
NA

CLIMATE:
tropical

TERRAIN:
mostly low and flat

ELEVATION:
lowest point: South China Sea 0 m
highest point: unnamed location on Rocky Island 14 m

NATURAL RESOURCES:
none

LAND USE:
agricultural land: 0% (2011 est.)
arable land: 0% (2011 est.) / permanent crops: 0% (2011 est.) / permanent pasture: 0% (2011 est.)
forest: 0% (2011 est.)
other: 100% (2011 est.)

IRRIGATED LAND:
0 sq km (2012)

POPULATION DISTRIBUTION:
a population of over 1,000 Chinese resides on Woody Island, the largest of the Paracels; there are scattered Chinese garrisons on some other islands

NATURAL HAZARDS:
typhoons

ENVIRONMENT - CURRENT ISSUES:
China's use of dredged sand and coral to build artificial islands harms reef systems; ongoing human activities, including military operations, infrastructure construction, and tourism endangers local ecosystem including birds, fish, marine mammals, and marine reptiles

GEOGRAPHY - NOTE:
composed of 130 small coral islands and reefs divided into the northeast Amphitrite Group and the western Crescent Group

PEOPLE AND SOCIETY :: PARACEL ISLANDS

POPULATION:
1,440 (2014 est.)
note: Chinese activity has increased in recent years, particularly on Woody Island, where the population exceeds 1,000; there are scattered Chinese garrisons on some other islands
country comparison to the world: 234

POPULATION DISTRIBUTION:
a population of over 1,000 Chinese resides on Woody Island, the largest of the Paracels; there are scattered Chinese garrisons on some other islands

GOVERNMENT :: PARACEL ISLANDS

COUNTRY NAME:
conventional long form: none
conventional short form: Paracel Islands
etymology: Portuguese navigators began to refer to the "Ilhas do Pracel" in the 16th century as a designation of low lying islets, sandbanks, and reefs scattered over a wide area; over time the name changed to "parcel" and then "paracel"

ECONOMY :: PARACEL ISLANDS

ECONOMY - OVERVIEW:
The islands have the potential for oil and gas development. Waters around the islands support commercial fishing, but the islands themselves are not populated on a permanent basis.

MILITARY AND SECURITY :: PARACEL ISLANDS

MILITARY - NOTE:
occupied by China

TRANSPORTATION :: PARACEL ISLANDS

AIRPORTS:
1 (2013)
country comparison to the world: 233

AIRPORTS - WITH PAVED RUNWAYS:
total: 1 (2017)
1,524 to 2,437 m: 1 (2017)

ROADWAYS:
PORTS AND TERMINALS:
small Chinese port facilities on Woody Island and Duncan Island

TRANSNATIONAL ISSUES :: PARACEL ISLANDS

DISPUTES - INTERNATIONAL:
occupied by China, also claimed by Taiwan and Vietnam

SOUTH AMERICA :: PARAGUAY

INTRODUCTION :: PARAGUAY

BACKGROUND:
Paraguay achieved its independence from Spain in 1811. In the disastrous War of the Triple Alliance (1865-70) - between Paraguay and Argentina, Brazil, and Uruguay - Paraguay lost two-thirds of its adult males and much of its territory. The country stagnated economically for the next half century. Following the Chaco War of 1932-35 with Bolivia, Paraguay gained a large part of the Chaco lowland region. The 35-year military dictatorship of Alfredo STROESSNER ended in 1989, and Paraguay has held relatively free and regular presidential elections since the country's return to democracy.

GEOGRAPHY :: PARAGUAY

LOCATION:
Central South America, northeast of Argentina, southwest of Brazil

GEOGRAPHIC COORDINATES:
23 00 S, 58 00 W

MAP REFERENCES:
South America

AREA:
total: 406,752 sq km

land: 397,302 sq km

water: 9,450 sq km

country comparison to the world: 61

AREA - COMPARATIVE:
about three times the size of New York state; slightly smaller than California

LAND BOUNDARIES:
total: 4,655 km

border countries (3): Argentina 2531 km, Bolivia 753 km, Brazil 1371 km

COASTLINE:
0 km (landlocked)

MARITIME CLAIMS:
none (landlocked)

CLIMATE:
subtropical to temperate; substantial rainfall in the eastern portions, becoming semiarid in the far west

TERRAIN:
grassy plains and wooded hills east of Rio Paraguay; Gran Chaco region west of Rio Paraguay mostly low, marshy plain near the river, and dry forest and thorny scrub elsewhere

ELEVATION:
mean elevation: 178 m

lowest point: junction of Rio Paraguay and Rio Parana 46 m

highest point: Cerro Pero 842 m

NATURAL RESOURCES:
hydropower, timber, iron ore, manganese, limestone

LAND USE:
agricultural land: 53.8% (2011 est.)

arable land: 10.8% (2011 est.) / permanent crops: 0.2% (2011 est.) / permanent pasture: 42.8% (2011 est.)

forest: 43.8% (2011 est.)

other: 2.4% (2011 est.)

IRRIGATED LAND:
1,362 sq km (2012)

POPULATION DISTRIBUTION:
most of the population resides in the eastern half of the country; to the west lies the Gran Chaco (a semi-arid lowland plain), which accounts for 60% of the land territory, but only 2% of the overall population

NATURAL HAZARDS:
local flooding in southeast (early September to June); poorly drained plains may become boggy (early October to June)

ENVIRONMENT - CURRENT ISSUES:
deforestation; water pollution; rivers suffer from toxic dumping; tanneries release mercury and chromium into rivers and streams; loss of wetlands; inadequate means for waste disposal pose health risks for many urban residents

ENVIRONMENT - INTERNATIONAL AGREEMENTS:
party to: Biodiversity, Climate Change, Climate Change-Kyoto Protocol, Desertification, Endangered Species, Hazardous Wastes, Law of the Sea, Ozone Layer Protection, Wetlands

signed, but not ratified: none of the selected agreements

GEOGRAPHY - NOTE:
landlocked; lies between Argentina, Bolivia, and Brazil; population concentrated in eastern and southern part of country

PEOPLE AND SOCIETY :: PARAGUAY

POPULATION:

7,025,763 (July 2018 est.)

country comparison to the world: 106

NATIONALITY:

noun: Paraguayan(s)

adjective: Paraguayan

ETHNIC GROUPS:

mestizo (mixed Spanish and Amerindian) 95%, other 5%

LANGUAGES:

Spanish (official) and Guarani (official) 46.3%, only Guarani 34%, only Spanish 15.2%, other (includes Portuguese, German, other indigenous languages) 4.1%, no response .4% (2012 est.)

note: data represent predominant household language

RELIGIONS:

Roman Catholic 89.6%, Protestant 6.2%, other Christian 1.1%, other or unspecified 1.9%, none 1.1% (2002 census)

DEMOGRAPHIC PROFILE:

Paraguay falls below the Latin American average in several socioeconomic categories, including immunization rates, potable water, sanitation, and secondary school enrollment, and has greater rates of income inequality and child and maternal mortality. Paraguay's poverty rate has declined in recent years but remains high, especially in rural areas, with more than a third of the population below the poverty line. However, the well-being of the poor in many regions has improved in terms of housing quality and access to clean water, telephone service, and electricity. The fertility rate continues to drop, declining sharply from an average 4.3 births per woman in the late 1990s to about 2 in 2013, as a result of the greater educational attainment of women, increased use of contraception, and a desire for smaller families among young women.

Paraguay is a country of emigration; it has not attracted large numbers of immigrants because of political instability, civil wars, years of dictatorship, and the greater appeal of neighboring countries. Paraguay first tried to encourage immigration in 1870 in order to rebound from the heavy death toll it suffered during the War of the Triple Alliance, but it received few European and Middle Eastern immigrants. In the 20th century, limited numbers of immigrants arrived from Lebanon, Japan, South Korea, and China, as well as Mennonites from Canada, Russia, and Mexico. Large flows of Brazilian immigrants have been arriving since the 1960s, mainly to work in agriculture. Paraguayans continue to emigrate to Argentina, Brazil, Uruguay, the United States, Italy, Spain, and France.

AGE STRUCTURE:

0-14 years: 24.13% (male 862,803 /female 832,325)

15-24 years: 18.8% (male 664,086 /female 656,947)

25-54 years: 41.59% (male 1,461,657 /female 1,460,565)

55-64 years: 8.13% (male 290,719 /female 280,328)

65 years and over: 7.35% (male 242,783 /female 273,550) (2018 est.)

DEPENDENCY RATIOS:

total dependency ratio: 56.6 (2015 est.)

youth dependency ratio: 47.2 (2015 est.)

elderly dependency ratio: 9.4 (2015 est.)

potential support ratio: 10.6 (2015 est.)

MEDIAN AGE:

total: 28.7 years (2018 est.)

male: 28.5 years

female: 28.9 years

country comparison to the world: 131

POPULATION GROWTH RATE:

1.17% (2018 est.)

country comparison to the world: 93

BIRTH RATE:

16.6 births/1,000 population (2018 est.)

country comparison to the world: 107

DEATH RATE:

4.8 deaths/1,000 population (2018 est.)

country comparison to the world: 201

NET MIGRATION RATE:

-0.1 migrant(s)/1,000 population (2018 est.)

country comparison to the world: 106

POPULATION DISTRIBUTION:

most of the population resides in the eastern half of the country; to the west lies the Gran Chaco (a semi-arid lowland plain), which accounts for 60% of the land territory, but only 2% of the overall population

URBANIZATION:

urban population: 61.9% of total population (2019)

rate of urbanization: 1.71% annual rate of change (2015-20 est.)

MAJOR URBAN AREAS - POPULATION:

3.279 million ASUNCION (capital) (2019)

SEX RATIO:

at birth: 1.05 male(s)/female

0-14 years: 1.04 male(s)/female

15-24 years: 1.01 male(s)/female

25-54 years: 1 male(s)/female

55-64 years: 1.04 male(s)/female

65 years and over: 0.89 male(s)/female

total population: 1.01 male(s)/female (2018 est.)

MOTHER'S MEAN AGE AT FIRST BIRTH:

22.9 years (2008 est.)

note: median age at first birth among women 25-29

MATERNAL MORTALITY RATE:

84 deaths/100,000 live births (2017 est.)

country comparison to the world: 77

INFANT MORTALITY RATE:

total: 18.1 deaths/1,000 live births (2018 est.)

male: 21.4 deaths/1,000 live births

female: 14.7 deaths/1,000 live births

country comparison to the world: 86

LIFE EXPECTANCY AT BIRTH:

total population: 77.6 years (2018 est.)

male: 74.9 years

female: 80.4 years

country comparison to the world: 68

TOTAL FERTILITY RATE:

1.9 children born/woman (2018 est.)

country comparison to the world: 132

CONTRACEPTIVE PREVALENCE RATE:

68.4% (2016)

DRINKING WATER SOURCE:

improved:

urban: 100% of population

rural: 94.9% of population

total: 98% of population

unimproved:

urban: 0% of population

rural: 5.1% of population

total: 2% of population (2015 est.)

CURRENT HEALTH EXPENDITURE:
8% (2016)

PHYSICIANS DENSITY:
1.37 physicians/1,000 population (2018)

HOSPITAL BED DENSITY:
1.3 beds/1,000 population (2011)

SANITATION FACILITY ACCESS:
improved:

urban: 95.5% of population (2015 est.)

rural: 78.4% of population (2015 est.)

total: 88.6% of population (2015 est.)

unimproved:

urban: 4.5% of population (2015 est.)

rural: 21.6% of population (2015 est.)

total: 11.4% of population (2015 est.)

HIV/AIDS - ADULT PREVALENCE RATE:
0.5% (2018 est.)

country comparison to the world: 71

HIV/AIDS - PEOPLE LIVING WITH HIV/AIDS:
21,000 (2018 est.)

country comparison to the world: 85

HIV/AIDS - DEATHS:
<1000 (2018 est.)

MAJOR INFECTIOUS DISEASES:
degree of risk: intermediate (2016)

food or waterborne diseases: bacterial diarrhea, hepatitis A, and typhoid fever (2016)

vectorborne diseases: dengue fever (2016)

note: active local transmission of Zika virus by Aedes species mosquitoes has been identified in this country (as of August 2016); it poses an important risk (a large number of cases possible) among US citizens if bitten by an infective mosquito; other less common ways to get Zika are through sex, via blood transfusion, or during pregnancy, in which the pregnant woman passes Zika virus to her fetus

OBESITY - ADULT PREVALENCE RATE:
20.3% (2016)

country comparison to the world: 100

CHILDREN UNDER THE AGE OF 5 YEARS UNDERWEIGHT:
1.3% (2016)

country comparison to the world: 120

EDUCATION EXPENDITURES:
4.5% of GDP (2016)

country comparison to the world: 89

LITERACY:
definition: age 15 and over can read and write

total population: 94.7%

male: 95.5%

female: 93.8% (2016 est.)

SCHOOL LIFE EXPECTANCY (PRIMARY TO TERTIARY EDUCATION):
total: 12 years

male: 12 years

female: 13 years (2010)

UNEMPLOYMENT, YOUTH AGES 15-24:
total: 14.5%

male: 11.8%

female: 18.7% (2018 est.)

country comparison to the world: 98

GOVERNMENT :: PARAGUAY

COUNTRY NAME:
conventional long form: Republic of Paraguay

conventional short form: Paraguay

local long form: Republica del Paraguay

local short form: Paraguay

etymology: the precise meaning of the name Paraguay is unclear, but it seems to derive from the river of the same name; one explanation has the name meaning "water of the Payagua" (an indigenous tribe that lived along the river)

GOVERNMENT TYPE:
presidential republic

CAPITAL:
name: Asuncion

geographic coordinates: 25 16 S, 57 40 W

time difference: UTC-4 (1 hour ahead of Washington, DC, during Standard Time)

daylight saving time: +1hr, begins first Sunday in October; ends last Sunday in March

etymology: the name means "assumption" and derives from the original name given to the city at its founding in 1537, Nuestra Senora Santa Maria de la Asuncion (Our Lady Saint Mary of the Assumption)

ADMINISTRATIVE DIVISIONS:
17 departments (departamentos, singular - departamento) and 1 capital city*; Alto Paraguay, Alto Parana, Amambay, Asuncion*, Boqueron, Caaguazu, Caazapa, Canindeyu, Central, Concepcion, Cordillera, Guaira, Itapua, Misiones, Neembucu, Paraguari, Presidente Hayes, San Pedro

INDEPENDENCE:
14-15 May 1811 (from Spain); note - the uprising against Spanish authorities took place during the night of 14-15 May 1811 and both days are celebrated in Paraguay

NATIONAL HOLIDAY:
Independence Day, 14-15 May (1811) (observed 15 May); 14 May is celebrated as Flag Day

CONSTITUTION:
history: several previous; latest approved and promulgated 20 June 1992

amendments: proposed at the initiative of at least one quarter of either chamber of the National Congress, by the president of the republic, or by petition of at least 30,000 voters; passage requires absolute majority vote by both chambers and approval in a referendum; amended 2011, 2014; note - in April 2017, a proposed amendment to extend presidential term limits was defeated by the lower house of the National Congress (2018)

LEGAL SYSTEM:
civil law system with influences from Argentine, Spanish, Roman, and French civil law models; judicial review of legislative acts in Supreme Court of Justice

INTERNATIONAL LAW ORGANIZATION PARTICIPATION:
accepts compulsory ICJ jurisdiction; accepts ICCt jurisdiction

CITIZENSHIP:
citizenship by birth: yes

citizenship by descent only: at least one parent must be a native-born citizen of Paraguay

dual citizenship recognized: yes

residency requirement for naturalization: 3 years

SUFFRAGE:

18 years of age; universal and compulsory until the age of 75

EXECUTIVE BRANCH:

chief of state: President Mario Abdo BENITEZ (since 15 August 2018); Vice President Hugo Adalberto VELAZQUEZ Moreno (since 15 August 2018); note - the president is both chief of state and head of government

head of government: President Mario Abdo BENITEZ (since 15 August 2018); Vice President Hugo Adalberto VELAZQUEZ Moreno (since 15 August 2018)

cabinet: Council of Ministers appointed by the president

elections/appointments: president and vice president directly elected on the same ballot by simple majority popular vote for a single 5-year term; election last held on 22 April 2018 (next to be held in April 2023)

election results: Mario Abdo BENITEZ elected president; percent of vote - Mario Abdo BENITEZ (ANR) 46.4%, Efrain ALEGRE (PLRA) 42.7%, Juan Bautista YBANEZ 3.3%, other 7.6%

LEGISLATIVE BRANCH:

description: bicameral National Congress or Congreso Nacional consists of: Chamber of Senators or Camara de Senadores (45 seats; members directly elected in a single nationwide constituency by proportional representation vote to serve 5-year terms) Chamber of Deputies or Camara de Diputados (80 seats; members directly elected in 18 multi-seat constituencies - corresponding to the country's 17 departments and capital city - by proportional representation vote to serve 5-year terms)

elections:
Chamber of Senators - last held on 22 April 2018 (next to be held in April 2023)
Chamber of Deputies - last held on 22 April 2018 (next to be held in April 2023)

election results:
Chamber of Senators - percent of vote by party/coalition - ANR 32.52%, PLRA 24.18%, FG 11.83%, PPQ 6.77%, MH 4.47%, PDP 3.66%, MCN 2.48%, UNACE 2.12%, other 11.97%; seats by party/coalition - ANR 17, PLRA 13, FG 6, PPQ 3, MH 2, PDP 2, MCN 1, UNACE 1; composition - men 36, women 9, percent of women 20%
Chamber of Deputies - percent of vote by party/coalition - ANR 39.1%, PLRA 17.74%, Ganar Alliance 12.08%, PPQ 4.46%, MH 3.19%, other 23.43%; seats by party/coalition - ANR 42, PLRA 17, Ganar Alliance 13, PPQ 3, MH 2, other 3; composition - men 66, women 14, percent of women 17.5%; note - total National Congress percent of women 18.4%

JUDICIAL BRANCH:

highest courts: Supreme Court of Justice or Corte Suprema de Justicia (consists of 9 justices divided 3 each into the Constitutional Court, Civil and Commercial Chamber, and Criminal Division)

judge selection and term of office: justices proposed by the Council of Magistrates or Consejo de la Magistratura, a 6-member independent body, and appointed by the Chamber of Senators with presidential concurrence; judges can serve until mandatory retirement at age 75

subordinate courts: appellate courts; first instance courts; minor courts, including justices of the peace

POLITICAL PARTIES AND LEADERS:

Asociacion Nacional Republicana - Colorado Party or ANR [Pedro ALLIANA]
Avanza Pais coalition or AP [Adolfo FERREIRO]
Broad Front coalition (Frente Guasu) or FG [Esperanza MARTINEZ]
Ganar Alliance (alliance between PLRA and Guasu Front)
Movimiento Cruzada Nacional or MCN
Movimiento Hagamos or MH [Antonio "Tony" APURIL]
Movimiento Union Nacional de Ciudadanos Eticos or UNACE [Jorge OVIEDO MATTO]
Partido del Movimiento al Socialismo or P-MAS [Camilo Ernesto SOARES Machado]
Partido Democratica Progresista or PDP [Rafael FILIZZOLA]
Partido Encuentro Nacional or PEN [Hermann RATZLAFFIN Klippemstein]
Partido Liberal Radical Autentico or PLRA [Efrain ALEGRE]
Partido Pais Solidario or PPS [Carlos Alberto FILIZZOLA Pallares]
Partido Popular Tekojoja or PPT [Sixto PEREIRA Galeano]
Patria Querida (Beloved Fatherland Party) or PPQ [Miguel CARRIZOSA]

INTERNATIONAL ORGANIZATION PARTICIPATION:

CAN (associate), CD, CELAC, FAO, G-11, G-77, IADB, IAEA, IBRD, ICAO, ICC (national committees), ICCt, ICRM, IDA, IFAD, IFC, IFRCS, ILO, IMF, IMO, Interpol, IOC, IOM, IPU, ISO (correspondent), ITSO, ITU, ITUC (NGOs), LAES, LAIA, Mercosur, MIGA, MINURSO, MINUSTAH, MONUSCO, NAM (observer), OAS, OPANAL, OPCW, Pacific Alliance (observer), PCA, UN, UNASUR, UNCTAD, UNESCO, UNFICYP, UNIDO, Union Latina, UNISFA, UNMIL, UNMISS, UNOCI, UNWTO, UPU, WCO, WHO, WIPO, WMO, WTO

DIPLOMATIC REPRESENTATION IN THE US:

Ambassador Manuel Maria CACERES (since 11 January 2019)

chancery: 2400 Massachusetts Avenue NW, Washington, DC 20008

telephone: [1] (202) 483-6960 through 6962

FAX: [1] (202) 234-4508

consulate(s) general: Los Angeles, Miami, New York

DIPLOMATIC REPRESENTATION FROM THE US:

chief of mission: Ambassador Lee MCCLENNY (since 20 February 2018)

telephone: [595] (21) 213-715

embassy: 1776 Avenida Mariscal Lopez, Casilla Postal 402, Asuncion

mailing address: Unit 4711, DPO AA 34036-0001

FAX: [595] (21) 213-728

FLAG DESCRIPTION:

three equal, horizontal bands of red (top), white, and blue with an emblem centered in the white band; unusual flag in that the emblem is different on each side; the obverse (hoist side at the left) bears the national coat of arms (a yellow five-pointed star within a green wreath capped by the words REPUBLICA DEL PARAGUAY, all within two circles); the reverse (hoist side at the right) bears a circular seal of the treasury (a yellow lion below a red Cap of Liberty and the words PAZ Y JUSTICIA (Peace and Justice)); red symbolizes bravery and patriotism, white represents integrity and peace, and blue denotes liberty and generosity

note: the three color bands resemble those on the flag of the Netherlands; one of only three national flags that differ on their obverse and reverse sides - the others are Moldova and Saudi Arabia

NATIONAL SYMBOL(S):
lion; national colors: red, white, blue

NATIONAL ANTHEM:
name: "Paraguayos, Republica o muerte!" (Paraguayans, The Republic or Death!)

lyrics/music: Francisco Esteban ACUNA de Figueroa/disputed

note: adopted 1934, in use since 1846; officially adopted following its re-arrangement in 1934

ECONOMY :: PARAGUAY

ECONOMY - OVERVIEW:
Landlocked Paraguay has a market economy distinguished by a large informal sector, featuring re-export of imported consumer goods to neighboring countries, as well as the activities of thousands of microenterprises and urban street vendors. A large percentage of the population, especially in rural areas, derives its living from agricultural activity, often on a subsistence basis. Because of the importance of the informal sector, accurate economic measures are difficult to obtain.

On a per capita basis, real income has grown steadily over the past five years as strong world demand for commodities, combined with high prices and favorable weather, supported Paraguay's commodity-based export expansion. Paraguay is the fifth largest soy producer in the world. Drought hit in 2008, reducing agricultural exports and slowing the economy even before the onset of the global recession. The economy fell 3.8% in 2009, as lower world demand and commodity prices caused exports to contract. Severe drought and outbreaks of hoof-and-mouth disease in 2012 led to a brief drop in beef and other agricultural exports. Since 2014, however, Paraguay's economy has grown at a 4% average annual rate due to strong production and high global prices, at a time when other countries in the region have contracted.

The Paraguayan Government recognizes the need to diversify its economy and has taken steps in recent years to do so. In addition to looking for new commodity markets in the Middle East and Europe, Paraguayan officials have promoted the country's low labor costs, cheap energy from its massive Itaipu Hydroelectric Dam, and single-digit tax rate on foreign firms. As a result, the number of factories operating in the country – mostly transplants from Brazil - has tripled since 2014.

Corruption, limited progress on structural reform, and deficient infrastructure are the main obstacles to long-term growth. Judicial corruption is endemic and is seen as the greatest barrier to attracting more foreign investment. Paraguay has been adverse to public debt throughout its history, but has recently sought to finance infrastructure improvements to attract foreign investment.

GDP (PURCHASING POWER PARITY):
$88.91 billion (2017 est.)

$84.87 billion (2016 est.)

$81.36 billion (2015 est.)

note: data are in 2017 dollars

country comparison to the world: 91

GDP (OFFICIAL EXCHANGE RATE):
$38.94 billion (2017 est.)

GDP - REAL GROWTH RATE:
4.8% (2017 est.)

4.3% (2016 est.)

3.1% (2015 est.)

country comparison to the world: 58

GDP - PER CAPITA (PPP):
$12,800 (2017 est.)

$12,400 (2016 est.)

$12,000 (2015 est.)

note: data are in 2017 dollars

country comparison to the world: 123

GROSS NATIONAL SAVING:
18.6% of GDP (2017 est.)

20.9% of GDP (2016 est.)

20% of GDP (2015 est.)

country comparison to the world: 108

GDP - COMPOSITION, BY END USE:
household consumption: 66.7% (2017 est.)

government consumption: 11.3% (2017 est.)

investment in fixed capital: 17.3% (2017 est.)

investment in inventories: 0.3% (2017 est.)

exports of goods and services: 46.6% (2017 est.)

imports of goods and services: -42.2% (2017 est.)

GDP - COMPOSITION, BY SECTOR OF ORIGIN:
agriculture: 17.9% (2017 est.)

industry: 27.7% (2017 est.)

services: 54.5% (2017 est.)

AGRICULTURE - PRODUCTS:
cotton, sugarcane, soybeans, corn, wheat, tobacco, cassava (manioc, tapioca), fruits, vegetables; beef, pork, eggs, milk; timber

INDUSTRIES:
sugar processing, cement, textiles, beverages, wood products, steel, base metals, electric power

INDUSTRIAL PRODUCTION GROWTH RATE:
2% (2017 est.)

country comparison to the world: 132

LABOR FORCE:
3.428 million (2017 est.)

country comparison to the world: 101

LABOR FORCE - BY OCCUPATION:
agriculture: 26.5%

industry: 18.5%

services: 55% (2008)

UNEMPLOYMENT RATE:
5.7% (2017 est.)

6% (2016 est.)

country comparison to the world: 85

POPULATION BELOW POVERTY LINE:
22.2% (2015 est.)

HOUSEHOLD INCOME OR CONSUMPTION BY PERCENTAGE SHARE:
lowest 10%: 1.5%

highest 10%: 37.6% (2013 est.)

DISTRIBUTION OF FAMILY INCOME - GINI INDEX:
51.7 (2014)

53.2 (2009)

country comparison to the world: 11

BUDGET:

revenues: 5.524 billion (2017 est.)

expenditures: 5.968 billion (2017 est.)

TAXES AND OTHER REVENUES:

14.2% (of GDP) (2017 est.)

country comparison to the world: 202

BUDGET SURPLUS (+) OR DEFICIT (-):

-1.1% (of GDP) (2017 est.)

country comparison to the world: 84

PUBLIC DEBT:

19.5% of GDP (2017 est.)

18.9% of GDP (2016 est.)

country comparison to the world: 191

FISCAL YEAR:

calendar year

INFLATION RATE (CONSUMER PRICES):

3.6% (2017 est.)

4.1% (2016 est.)

country comparison to the world: 144

CENTRAL BANK DISCOUNT RATE:

5.5% (31 December 2012)

6% (31 December 2011)

country comparison to the world: 76

COMMERCIAL BANK PRIME LENDING RATE:

17% (31 December 2017 est.)

18.08% (31 December 2016 est.)

country comparison to the world: 28

STOCK OF NARROW MONEY:

$5.117 billion (31 December 2017 est.)

$4.307 billion (31 December 2016 est.)

country comparison to the world: 103

STOCK OF BROAD MONEY:

$5.117 billion (31 December 2017 est.)

$4.307 billion (31 December 2016 est.)

country comparison to the world: 106

STOCK OF DOMESTIC CREDIT:

$12.91 billion (31 December 2017 est.)

$12.18 billion (31 December 2016 est.)

country comparison to the world: 104

MARKET VALUE OF PUBLICLY TRADED SHARES:

$962.3 million (31 December 2012 est.)

$958.1 million (31 December 2011 est.)

$42 million (31 December 2010 est.)

country comparison to the world: 106

CURRENT ACCOUNT BALANCE:

-$298 million (2017 est.)

$416 million (2016 est.)

country comparison to the world: 104

EXPORTS:

$11.73 billion (2017 est.)

$10.86 billion (2016 est.)

country comparison to the world: 84

EXPORTS - PARTNERS:

Brazil 31.9%, Argentina 15.9%, Chile 6.9%, Russia 5.9% (2017)

EXPORTS - COMMODITIES:

soybeans, livestock feed, cotton, meat, edible oils, wood, leather, gold

IMPORTS:

$11.35 billion (2017 est.)

$9.617 billion (2016 est.)

country comparison to the world: 96

IMPORTS - COMMODITIES:

road vehicles, consumer goods, tobacco, petroleum products, electrical machinery, tractors, chemicals, vehicle parts

IMPORTS - PARTNERS:

China 31.3%, Brazil 23.4%, Argentina 12.9%, US 7.4% (2017)

RESERVES OF FOREIGN EXCHANGE AND GOLD:

$7.877 billion (31 December 2017 est.)

$6.881 billion (31 December 2016 est.)

country comparison to the world: 79

DEBT - EXTERNAL:

$17.7 billion (31 December 2017 est.)

$16.48 billion (31 December 2016 est.)

country comparison to the world: 96

STOCK OF DIRECT FOREIGN INVESTMENT - AT HOME:

$6.235 billion (31 December 2017 est.)

$5.276 billion (31 December 2016 est.)

country comparison to the world: 103

STOCK OF DIRECT FOREIGN INVESTMENT - ABROAD:

$705.1 million (31 December 2017 est.)

$591.3 million (31 December 2016 est.)

country comparison to the world: 92

EXCHANGE RATES:

guarani (PYG) per US dollar -

5,628.1 (2017 est.)

5,680.7 (2016 est.)

5,680.7 (2015 est.)

5,160.4 (2014 est.)

4,462.2 (2013 est.)

ENERGY :: PARAGUAY

ELECTRICITY ACCESS:

electrification - total population: 98.4% (2016)

electrification - urban areas: 99.9% (2016)

electrification - rural areas: 96.1% (2016)

ELECTRICITY - PRODUCTION:

63.13 billion kWh (2016 est.)

country comparison to the world: 45

ELECTRICITY - CONSUMPTION:

10.9 billion kWh (2016 est.)

country comparison to the world: 92

ELECTRICITY - EXPORTS:

41.13 billion kWh (2015 est.)

country comparison to the world: 4

ELECTRICITY - IMPORTS:

0 kWh (2016 est.)

country comparison to the world: 185

ELECTRICITY - INSTALLED GENERATING CAPACITY:

8.87 million kW (2016 est.)

country comparison to the world: 65

ELECTRICITY - FROM FOSSIL FUELS:

0% of total installed capacity (2016 est.)

country comparison to the world: 214

ELECTRICITY - FROM NUCLEAR FUELS:

0% of total installed capacity (2017 est.)

country comparison to the world: 163

ELECTRICITY - FROM HYDROELECTRIC PLANTS:

99% of total installed capacity (2017 est.)

country comparison to the world: 3

ELECTRICITY - FROM OTHER RENEWABLE SOURCES:

1% of total installed capacity (2017 est.)

country comparison to the world: 162

CRUDE OIL - PRODUCTION:

0 bbl/day (2018 est.)

country comparison to the world: 186

CRUDE OIL - EXPORTS:

0 bbl/day (2015 est.)

country comparison to the world: 179

CRUDE OIL - IMPORTS:

0 bbl/day (2015 est.)

country comparison to the world: 181

CRUDE OIL - PROVED RESERVES:

0 bbl (1 January 2018 est.)

country comparison to the world: 181

REFINED PETROLEUM PRODUCTS - PRODUCTION:

0 bbl/day (2015 est.)

country comparison to the world: 189

REFINED PETROLEUM PRODUCTS - CONSUMPTION:

43,000 bbl/day (2016 est.)

country comparison to the world: 112

REFINED PETROLEUM PRODUCTS - EXPORTS:

0 bbl/day (2015 est.)

country comparison to the world: 191

REFINED PETROLEUM PRODUCTS - IMPORTS:

40,760 bbl/day (2015 est.)

country comparison to the world: 89

NATURAL GAS - PRODUCTION:

0 cu m (2017 est.)

country comparison to the world: 183

NATURAL GAS - CONSUMPTION:

0 cu m (2017 est.)

country comparison to the world: 187

NATURAL GAS - EXPORTS:

0 cu m (2017 est.)

country comparison to the world: 167

NATURAL GAS - IMPORTS:

0 cu m (2017 est.)

country comparison to the world: 173

NATURAL GAS - PROVED RESERVES:

0 cu m (1 January 2014 est.)

country comparison to the world: 181

CARBON DIOXIDE EMISSIONS FROM CONSUMPTION OF ENERGY:

7.74 million Mt (2017 est.)

country comparison to the world: 117

COMMUNICATIONS :: PARAGUAY

TELEPHONES - FIXED LINES:

total subscriptions: 290,109

subscriptions per 100 inhabitants: 4 (2017 est.)

country comparison to the world: 116

TELEPHONES - MOBILE CELLULAR:

total subscriptions: 7,468,275

subscriptions per 100 inhabitants: 108 (2017 est.)

country comparison to the world: 102

TELEPHONE SYSTEM:

general assessment: the fixed-line market is a state monopoly and fixed-line telephone service is meager; principal switching center is in Asuncion; DSL, cable modem, FttP (fiber to the home) and WiMAX technologies available; competition in mobile market among 4 operators; 18 mobile phones for every fixed-line service phone (2018)

domestic: deficiencies in provision of fixed-line service have resulted in a rapid expansion of mobile-cellular services fostered by competition among multiple providers; Internet market also open to competition; fixed-line 4 per 100 and mobile-cellular 108 per 100 (2018)

international: country code - 595; Paraguay's landlocked position means they must depend on neighbors for interconnection with submarine cable networks, making it cost more for broadband services; satellite earth station - 1 Intelsat (Atlantic Ocean) (2019)

BROADCAST MEDIA:

6 privately owned TV stations; about 75 commercial and community radio stations; 1 state-owned radio network (2019)

INTERNET COUNTRY CODE:

.py

INTERNET USERS:

total: 3,524,045

percent of population: 51.3% (July 2016 est.)

country comparison to the world: 92

BROADBAND - FIXED SUBSCRIPTIONS:

total: 278,169

subscriptions per 100 inhabitants: 4 (2017 est.)

country comparison to the world: 99

MILITARY AND SECURITY :: PARAGUAY

MILITARY EXPENDITURES:

0.93% of GDP (2018)

0.89% of GDP (2017)

0.95% of GDP (2016)

1.07% of GDP (2015)

0.99% of GDP (2014)

country comparison to the world: 125

MILITARY AND SECURITY FORCES:

Armed Forces Command (Commando de las Fuerzas Militares): Army, National Navy (Armada Nacional, includes marines), Paraguayan Air Force (Fuerza Aerea Paraguay, FAP) (2019)

MILITARY SERVICE AGE AND OBLIGATION:

18 years of age for compulsory and voluntary military service; conscript service obligation is 12 months for Army, 24 months for Navy; volunteers for the Air Force must be younger than 22 years of age with a secondary school diploma (2016)

TRANSPORTATION :: PARAGUAY

NATIONAL AIR TRANSPORT SYSTEM:

number of registered air carriers: 1 (2015)

inventory of registered aircraft operated by air carriers: 5 (2015)

annual passenger traffic on registered air carriers: 452,004 (2015)

annual freight traffic on registered air carriers: 1,641,624 mt-km (2015)

CIVIL AIRCRAFT REGISTRATION COUNTRY CODE PREFIX:

ZP (2016)

AIRPORTS:

799 (2013)

country comparison to the world: 9

AIRPORTS - WITH PAVED RUNWAYS:

total: 15 (2017)

over 3,047 m: 3 (2017)

1,524 to 2,437 m: 7 (2017)

914 to 1,523 m: 5 (2017)

AIRPORTS - WITH UNPAVED RUNWAYS:

total: 784 (2013)

1,524 to 2,437 m: 23 (2013)

914 to 1,523 m: 290 (2013)

under 914 m: 471 (2013)

RAILWAYS:

total: 30 km (2014)

standard gauge: 30 km 1.435-m gauge (2014)

country comparison to the world: 133

ROADWAYS:

total: 74,676 km (2017)

paved: 6,167 km (2017)

unpaved: 68,509 km (2017)

country comparison to the world: 65

WATERWAYS:

3,100 km (primarily on the Paraguay and Paraná River systems) (2012)

country comparison to the world: 32

MERCHANT MARINE:

total: 80

by type: container ship 3, general cargo 23, oil tanker 6, other 48 (2018)

note: as of 2017, Paraguay registered 2,012 fluvial vessels of which 1,741 were commercial barges

country comparison to the world: 99

PORTS AND TERMINALS:

river port(s): Asuncion, Villeta, San Antonio, Encarnacion (Parana)

TRANSNATIONAL ISSUES :: PARAGUAY

DISPUTES - INTERNATIONAL:

unruly region at convergence of Argentina-Brazil-Paraguay borders is locus of money laundering, smuggling, arms and illegal narcotics trafficking, and fundraising for violent extremist organizations

ILLICIT DRUGS:

major illicit producer of cannabis, most or all of which is consumed in Brazil, Argentina, and Chile; transshipment country for Andean cocaine headed for Brazil, other Southern Cone markets, and Europe; weak border controls, extensive corruption and money-laundering activity, especially in the Tri-Border Area; weak anti-money-laundering laws and enforcement

INTRODUCTION :: PERU

BACKGROUND:

Ancient Peru was the seat of several prominent Andean civilizations, most notably that of the Incas whose empire was captured by Spanish conquistadors in 1533. Peru declared its independence in 1821, and remaining Spanish forces were defeated in 1824. After a dozen years of military rule, Peru returned to democratic leadership in 1980, but experienced economic problems and the growth of a violent insurgency. President Alberto FUJIMORI's election in 1990 ushered in a decade that saw a dramatic turnaround in the economy and significant progress in curtailing guerrilla activity. Nevertheless, the president's increasing reliance on authoritarian measures and an economic slump in the late 1990s generated mounting dissatisfaction with his regime, which led to his resignation in 2000. A caretaker government oversaw a new election in the spring of 2001, which installed Alejandro TOLEDO Manrique as the new head of government - Peru's first democratically elected president of indigenous ethnicity. The presidential election of 2006 saw the return of Alan GARCIA Perez who, after a disappointing presidential term from 1985 to 1990, oversaw a robust economic rebound. Former army officer Ollanta HUMALA Tasso was elected president in June 2011, and carried on the sound, market-oriented economic policies of the three preceding administrations. Poverty and unemployment levels have fallen dramatically in the last decade, and today Peru boasts one of the best performing economies in Latin America. Pedro Pablo KUCZYNSKI Godard won a very narrow presidential runoff election in June 2016. Facing impeachment after evidence surfaced of his involvement in a vote-buying scandal, President KUCZYNSKI offered his resignation on 21 March 2018. Two days later, First Vice President Martin Alberto VIZCARRA Cornejo was sworn in as president.

GEOGRAPHY :: PERU

LOCATION:

Western South America, bordering the South Pacific Ocean, between Chile and Ecuador

GEOGRAPHIC COORDINATES:

10 00 S, 76 00 W

MAP REFERENCES:

South America

AREA:

total: 1,285,216 sq km

land: 1,279,996 sq km

water: 5,220 sq km

country comparison to the world: 21

AREA - COMPARATIVE:

almost twice the size of Texas; slightly smaller than Alaska

LAND BOUNDARIES:

total: 7,062 km

border countries (5): Bolivia 1212 km, Brazil 2659 km, Chile 168 km, Colombia 1494 km, Ecuador 1529 km

COASTLINE:

2,414 km

MARITIME CLAIMS:

territorial sea: 200 nm

continental shelf: 200 nm

CLIMATE:

varies from tropical in east to dry desert in west; temperate to frigid in Andes

TERRAIN:

western coastal plain (costa), high and rugged Andes in center (sierra), eastern lowland jungle of Amazon Basin (selva)

ELEVATION:

mean elevation: 1,555 m

lowest point: Pacific Ocean 0 m

highest point: Nevado Huascaran 6,746 m

NATURAL RESOURCES:

copper, silver, gold, petroleum, timber, fish, iron ore, coal, phosphate, potash, hydropower, natural gas

LAND USE:

agricultural land: 18.8% (2011 est.)

arable land: 3.1% (2011 est.) / permanent crops: 1.1% (2011 est.) / permanent pasture: 14.6% (2011 est.)

forest: 53% (2011 est.)

other: 28.2% (2011 est.)

IRRIGATED LAND:

25,800 sq km (2012)

POPULATION DISTRIBUTION:

approximately one-third of the population resides along the desert coastal belt in the west, with a strong focus on the capital city of Lima; the Andean highlands, or sierra, which is strongly identified with the country's Amerindian population, contains roughly half of the overall population; the eastern slopes of the Andes, and adjoining rainforest, are sparsely populated

NATURAL HAZARDS:

earthquakes, tsunamis, flooding, landslides, mild volcanic activity

volcanism: volcanic activity in the Andes Mountains; Ubinas (5,672 m), which last erupted in 2009, is the country's most active volcano; other historically active volcanoes include El Misti, Huaynaputina, Sabancaya, and Yucamane; see note 2 under "Geography - note"

ENVIRONMENT - CURRENT ISSUES:

deforestation (some the result of illegal logging); overgrazing of the slopes of the costa and sierra leading to soil erosion; desertification; air pollution in Lima; pollution of rivers and coastal waters from municipal and mining wastes; overfishing

ENVIRONMENT - INTERNATIONAL AGREEMENTS:

party to: Antarctic-Environmental Protocol, Antarctic-Marine Living Resources, Antarctic Treaty, Biodiversity, Climate Change, Climate Change-Kyoto Protocol, Desertification, Endangered Species, Hazardous Wastes, Marine Dumping, Ozone Layer Protection, Ship Pollution, Tropical Timber 83, Tropical Timber 94, Wetlands, Whaling

signed, but not ratified: none of the selected agreements

GEOGRAPHY - NOTE:

note 1: shares control of Lago Titicaca, world's highest navigable lake, with Bolivia; a remote slope of Nevado Mismi, a 5,316 m peak, is the ultimate source of the Amazon River

note 2: Peru is one of the countries along the Ring of Fire, a belt of active volcanoes and earthquake epicenters bordering the Pacific Ocean; up to 90% of the world's earthquakes and some 75% of the world's volcanoes occur within the Ring of Fire

note 3: on 19 February 1600, Mount Huaynaputina in the southern Peruvian Andes erupted in the largest volcanic explosion in South America in historical times; intermittent eruptions lasted until 5 March 1600 and pumped an estimated 16 to 32 million metric tons of particulates into the atmosphere reducing the amount of sunlight reaching the earth's surface and affecting weather worldwide; over the next two and a half years, millions died around the globe in famines from bitterly cold winters, cool summers, and the loss of crops and animals

note 4: the southern regions of Peru and the extreme northwestern part of Bolivia are considered to be the place of origin for the common potato

PEOPLE AND SOCIETY :: PERU

POPULATION:

31,331,228 (July 2018 est.)

country comparison to the world: 44

NATIONALITY:

noun: Peruvian(s)

adjective: Peruvian

ETHNIC GROUPS:

mestizo (mixed Amerindian and white) 60.2%, Amerindian 25.8%, white 5.9%, African descent 3.6%, other (includes Chinese and Japanese descent) 1.2%, unspecified 3.3% (2017 est.)

LANGUAGES:

Spanish (official) 82.9%, Quechua (official) 13.6%, Aymara (official) 1.6%, Ashaninka 0.3%, other native languages (includes a large number of minor Amazonian languages) 0.8%, other (includes foreign languages and sign language) 0.2%, none .1%, unspecified .7% (2017 est.)

RELIGIONS:

Roman Catholic 60%, Christian 14.6% (includes evangelical 11.1%, other 3.5%), other .3%, none 4%, unspecified 21.1% (2017 est.)

DEMOGRAPHIC PROFILE:

Peru's urban and coastal communities have benefited much more from recent economic growth than rural, Afro-Peruvian, indigenous, and poor populations of the Amazon and mountain regions. The poverty rate has dropped substantially during the last decade but remains stubbornly high at about 30% (more than 55% in rural areas). After remaining almost static for about a decade, Peru's malnutrition rate began falling in 2005, when the government introduced a coordinated strategy focusing on hygiene, sanitation, and clean water. School enrollment has improved, but achievement scores reflect ongoing problems with educational quality. Many poor children temporarily or permanently drop out of school to help support their families. About a quarter to a third of Peruvian children aged 6 to 14 work, often putting in long hours at hazardous mining or construction sites.

Peru was a country of immigration in the 19th and early 20th centuries, but has become a country of emigration in the last few decades. Beginning in the 19th century, Peru brought in Asian contract laborers mainly to work on coastal plantations. Populations of Chinese and Japanese descent - among the largest in Latin America - are economically and culturally influential in Peru today. Peruvian emigration began rising in the 1980s due to an economic crisis and a violent internal conflict, but outflows have stabilized in the last few years as economic conditions have improved. Nonetheless, more than 2 million Peruvians have emigrated in the last decade, principally to the US, Spain, and Argentina.

AGE STRUCTURE:

0-14 years: 26.01% (male 4,147,404 /female 4,001,069)

15-24 years: 17.96% (male 2,820,562 /female 2,806,280)

25-54 years: 40.47% (male 6,081,748 /female 6,597,405)

55-64 years: 7.95% (male 1,201,272 /female 1,289,734)

65 years and over: 7.61% (male 1,125,850 /female 1,259,904) (2018 est.)

DEPENDENCY RATIOS:

total dependency ratio: 53.2 (2015 est.)

youth dependency ratio: 42.7 (2015 est.)

elderly dependency ratio: 10.5 (2015 est.)

potential support ratio: 9.6 (2015 est.)

MEDIAN AGE:

total: 28.4 years (2018 est.)

male: 27.6 years

female: 29.1 years

country comparison to the world: 137

POPULATION GROWTH RATE:

0.94% (2018 est.)

country comparison to the world: 118

BIRTH RATE:

17.6 births/1,000 population (2018 est.)

country comparison to the world: 98

DEATH RATE:

6.1 deaths/1,000 population (2018 est.)

country comparison to the world: 159

NET MIGRATION RATE:

-2.1 migrant(s)/1,000 population (2018 est.)

country comparison to the world: 164

POPULATION DISTRIBUTION:

approximately one-third of the population resides along the desert coastal belt in the west, with a strong focus on the capital city of Lima; the Andean highlands, or sierra, which is strongly identified with the country's Amerindian population, contains roughly half of the overall population; the eastern slopes of the Andes, and adjoining rainforest, are sparsely populated

URBANIZATION:

urban population: 78.1% of total population (2019)

rate of urbanization: 1.44% annual rate of change (2015-20 est.)

MAJOR URBAN AREAS - POPULATION:

10.555 million LIMA (capital), 911,000 Arequipa, 851,000 Trujillo (2019)

SEX RATIO:

at birth: 1.05 male(s)/female

0-14 years: 1.04 male(s)/female

15-24 years: 1.01 male(s)/female

25-54 years: 0.92 male(s)/female

55-64 years: 0.93 male(s)/female

65 years and over: 0.89 male(s)/female

total population: 0.96 male(s)/female (2018 est.)

MOTHER'S MEAN AGE AT FIRST BIRTH:

22.2 years (2013 est.)

note: median age at first birth among women 25-29

MATERNAL MORTALITY RATE:

88 deaths/100,000 live births (2017 est.)

country comparison to the world: 76

INFANT MORTALITY RATE:

total: 17.8 deaths/1,000 live births (2018 est.)

male: 19.9 deaths/1,000 live births

female: 15.6 deaths/1,000 live births

country comparison to the world: 88

LIFE EXPECTANCY AT BIRTH:

total population: 74.2 years (2018 est.)

male: 72.1 years

female: 76.4 years

country comparison to the world: 128

TOTAL FERTILITY RATE:

2.1 children born/woman (2018 est.)

country comparison to the world: 101

CONTRACEPTIVE PREVALENCE RATE:

75.4% (2017)

DRINKING WATER SOURCE:

improved:

urban: 91.4% of population

rural: 69.2% of population

total: 86.7% of population

unimproved:

urban: 8.6% of population

rural: 30.8% of population

total: 13.3% of population (2015 est.)

CURRENT HEALTH EXPENDITURE:

5.1% (2016)

PHYSICIANS DENSITY:

1.27 physicians/1,000 population (2016)

HOSPITAL BED DENSITY:

1.6 beds/1,000 population (2014)

SANITATION FACILITY ACCESS:

improved:

urban: 82.5% of population (2015 est.)

rural: 53.2% of population (2015 est.)

total: 76.2% of population (2015 est.)

unimproved:

urban: 17.5% of population (2015 est.)

rural: 46.8% of population (2015 est.)

total: 23.8% of population (2015 est.)

HIV/AIDS - ADULT PREVALENCE RATE:

0.3% (2018 est.)

country comparison to the world: 94

HIV/AIDS - PEOPLE LIVING WITH HIV/AIDS:

79,000 (2018 est.)

country comparison to the world: 49

HIV/AIDS - DEATHS:

1,000 (2018 est.)

country comparison to the world: 61

MAJOR INFECTIOUS DISEASES:

degree of risk: very high (2016)

food or waterborne diseases: bacterial diarrhea, hepatitis A, and typhoid fever (2016)

vectorborne diseases: dengue fever, malaria, and Bartonellosis (Oroya fever) (2016)

note: active local transmission of Zika virus by Aedes species mosquitoes has been identified in this country (as of August 2016); it poses an important risk (a large number of cases possible) among US citizens if bitten by an infective mosquito; other less common ways to get Zika are through sex, via blood transfusion, or during pregnancy, in which the pregnant woman passes Zika virus to her fetus

OBESITY - ADULT PREVALENCE RATE:

19.7% (2016)

country comparison to the world: 110

CHILDREN UNDER THE AGE OF 5 YEARS UNDERWEIGHT:

3.2% (2017)

country comparison to the world: 96

EDUCATION EXPENDITURES:

3.9% of GDP (2017)

country comparison to the world: 114

LITERACY:

definition: age 15 and over can read and write

total population: 94.2%

male: 97.2%

female: 91.2% (2016 est.)

SCHOOL LIFE EXPECTANCY (PRIMARY TO TERTIARY EDUCATION):

total: 15 years

male: 14 years

female: 15 years (2016)

UNEMPLOYMENT, YOUTH AGES 15-24:

total: 14.7%

male: 14.3%

female: 15% (2018 est.)

country comparison to the world: 96

GOVERNMENT :: PERU

COUNTRY NAME:

conventional long form: Republic of Peru

conventional short form: Peru

local long form: Republica del Peru

local short form: Peru

etymology: exact meaning is obscure, but the name may derive from a native word "biru" meaning "river"

GOVERNMENT TYPE:

presidential republic

CAPITAL:

name: Lima

geographic coordinates: 12 03 S, 77 03 W

time difference: UTC-5 (same time as Washington, DC, during Standard Time)

etymology: the word "Lima" derives from the Spanish pronunciation of "Limaq," the native name for the valley in which the city was founded in 1535; "limaq" means "talker" in coastal Quechua and referred to an oracle that was situated in the valley but which was eventually destroyed by the Spanish and replaced with a church

ADMINISTRATIVE DIVISIONS:

25 regions (regiones, singular - region) and 1 province* (provincia); Amazonas, Ancash, Apurimac, Arequipa, Ayacucho, Cajamarca, Callao, Cusco, Huancavelica, Huanuco, Ica, Junin, La Libertad, Lambayeque, Lima, Lima*, Loreto, Madre de Dios, Moquegua, Pasco, Piura, Puno, San Martin, Tacna, Tumbes, Ucayali

note: Callao, the largest port in Peru, is also referred to as a constitutional province, the only province of the Callao region

INDEPENDENCE:

28 July 1821 (from Spain)

NATIONAL HOLIDAY:

Independence Day, 28-29 July (1821)

CONSTITUTION:

history: several previous; latest promulgated 29 December 1993, enacted 31 December 1993

amendments: proposed by Congress, by the president of the republic with the approval of the "Cabinet," or by petition of at least 0.3% of voters; passage requires absolute majority approval by the Congress membership, followed by approval in a referendum; a referendum is not required if Congress approves the amendment by greater than two-thirds majority vote in each of two successive sessions; amended many times, last in 2018 (2018)

LEGAL SYSTEM:

civil law system

INTERNATIONAL LAW ORGANIZATION PARTICIPATION:

accepts compulsory ICJ jurisdiction with reservations; accepts ICCt jurisdiction

CITIZENSHIP:

citizenship by birth: yes

citizenship by descent only: yes

dual citizenship recognized: yes

residency requirement for naturalization: 2 years

SUFFRAGE:

18 years of age; universal and compulsory until the age of 70

EXECUTIVE BRANCH:

chief of state: President Martin Alberto VIZCARRA Cornejo (since 23 March 2018); First Vice President (vacant); Second Vice President (vacant); note - the 21 March 2018 resignation of President Pedro Pablo KUCZYNSKI Godard (since 28 July 2016) was accepted by parliament on 23 March 2018; the president is both chief of state and head of government

head of government: President Martin Alberto VIZCARRA Cornejo (since 23 March 2018); First Vice President (vacant); Second Vice President (vacant)

cabinet: Council of Ministers appointed by the president

elections/appointments: president directly elected by absolute majority popular vote in 2 rounds if needed for a 5-year term (eligible for nonconsecutive terms); election last held on 10 April 2016 with a runoff on 5 June 2016 (next to be held in April 2021)

election results: Pedro Pablo KUCZYNSKI Godard elected president in second round; percent of vote in first round - Keiko FUJIMORI Higuchi (Fuerza Popular) 39.9%, Pedro Pablo KUCZYNSKI Godard (Peruanos Por el Kambio) 21.1%, Veronika MENDOZA (Broad Front) 18.7%, Alfredo BARNECHEA (Popular Action) 7%, Alan GARCIA (APRA) 5.8%, other 7.5%; percent of vote in second round - Pedro Pablo KUCZYNSKI Godard 50.1%, Keiko FUJIMORI Higuchi 49.9%

note: Prime Minister Vicente Antonio ZEBALLOS Salinas (since 30 September 2019) does not exercise executive power; this power rests with the president

LEGISLATIVE BRANCH:

description: unicameral Congress of the Republic of Peru or Congreso de la Republica del Peru (130 seats; members directly elected in multi-seat constituencies by closed party-list proportional representation vote to serve 5-year terms); note - a referendum held in December 2018 approved a single consecutive term for Congress members

elections: last held on 10 April 2016 with run-off election on 6 June 2016 (next to be held in April 2021)

election results: percent of vote by party/coalition - Fuerza Popular 36.3%, PPK 16.5%, Frente Amplio 13.9%, APP 9.2%; APRA 8.3%; AP 7.2%, other 8.6%; seats by party/coalition - Fuerza Popular 73, Frente Amplio 20, PPK 18, APP 9; APRA 5; AP 5; composition - men 94, women 36, percent of women 27.7%

JUDICIAL BRANCH:

highest courts: Supreme Court (consists of 16 judges and divided into civil, criminal, and constitutional-social sectors)

judge selection and term of office: justices proposed by the National Council of the Judiciary or National Judicial Council (a 7-member independent body), nominated by the president, and confirmed by the Congress (all appointments reviewed by the Council every 7 years); justices can serve until mandatory retirement at age 70

subordinate courts: Court of Constitutional Guarantees; Superior Courts or Cortes Superiores; specialized civil, criminal, and mixed courts; 2 types of peace courts in which professional judges and selected members of the local communities preside

POLITICAL PARTIES AND LEADERS:

Alliance for Progress (Alianza para el Progreso) or APP [Cesar ACUNA Peralta]American Popular Revolutionary Alliance or APRA Broad Front (Frente Amplio; also

known as El Frente Amplio por Justicia, Vida y Libertad) (coalition includes Nuevo Peru [Veronika Mendoza], Tierra y Libertad [Marco ARANA Zegarra], and Fuerza Social [Susana VILLARAN de la Puente]
Fuerza Popular (formerly Fuerza 2011) [Keiko FUJIMORI Higuchi]
National Solidarity (Solidaridad Nacional) or SN [Luis CASTANEDA Lossio]
Peru Posible or PP (coalition includes Accion Popular and Somos Peru) [Alejandro TOLEDO Manrique]
Peruvian Aprista Party (Partido Aprista Peruano) or PAP [Javier VELASQUEZ Quesquen] (also referred to by its original name Alianza Popular Revolucionaria Americana or APRA)
Peruvian Nationalist Party [Ollanta HUMALA]
Peruvians for Change (Peruanos Por el Kambio) or PPK [Pedro Pablo KUCZYNSKI]
Popular Action (Accion Popular) or AP [Mesias GUEVARA Amasifuen]
Popular Christian Party (Partido Popular Cristiano) or PPC [Lourdes FLORES Nano]

INTERNATIONAL ORGANIZATION PARTICIPATION:

APEC, BIS, CAN, CD, CELAC, EITI (compliant country), FAO, G-24, G-77, IADB, IAEA, IBRD, ICAO, ICC (NGOs), ICCt, ICRM, IDA, IFAD, IFC, IFRCS, IHO, ILO, IMF, IMO, IMSO, Interpol, IOC, IOM, IPU, ISO, ITSO, ITU, ITUC (NGOs), LAES, LAIA, Mercosur (associate), MIGA, MINUSTAH, MONUSCO, NAM, OAS, OPANAL, OPCW, Pacific Alliance, PCA, SICA (observer), UN, UNAMID, UNASUR, UNCTAD, UNESCO, UNHCR, UNIDO, Union Latina, UNISFA, UNMISS, UNOCI, UN Security Council (temporary), UNWTO, UPU, WCO, WFTU (NGOs), WHO, WIPO, WMO, WTO

DIPLOMATIC REPRESENTATION IN THE US:

Ambassador Carlos Jose PAREJA Rios (since 16 September 2016)

chancery: 1700 Massachusetts Avenue NW, Washington, DC 20036

telephone: [1] (202) 833-9860 through 9869

FAX: [1] (202) 659-8124

consulate(s) general: Atlanta, Boston, Chicago, Dallas, Denver, Hartford (CT), Houston, Los Angeles, Miami, New York, Paterson (NJ), San Francisco, Washington DC

DIPLOMATIC REPRESENTATION FROM THE US:

chief of mission: Ambassador Krishna R. URS (since 18 October 2017)

telephone: [51] (1) 618-2000

embassy: Avenida La Encalada, Cuadra 17 s/n, Surco, Lima 33

mailing address: P. O. Box 1995, Lima 1; American Embassy (Lima), APO AA 34031-5000

FAX: [51] (1) 618-2397

FLAG DESCRIPTION:

three equal, vertical bands of red (hoist side), white, and red with the coat of arms centered in the white band; the coat of arms features a shield bearing a vicuna (representing fauna), a cinchona tree (the source of quinine, signifying flora), and a yellow cornucopia spilling out coins (denoting mineral wealth); red recalls blood shed for independence, white symbolizes peace

NATIONAL SYMBOL(S):

vicuna (a camelid related to the llama); national colors: red, white

NATIONAL ANTHEM:

name: "Himno Nacional del Peru" (National Anthem of Peru)

lyrics/music: Jose DE LA TORRE Ugarte/Jose Bernardo ALZEDO

note: adopted 1822; the song won a national anthem contest

ECONOMY :: PERU

ECONOMY - OVERVIEW:

Peru's economy reflects its varied topography - an arid lowland coastal region, the central high sierra of the Andes, and the dense forest of the Amazon. A wide range of important mineral resources are found in the mountainous and coastal areas, and Peru's coastal waters provide excellent fishing grounds. Peru is the world's second largest producer of silver and copper.

The Peruvian economy grew by an average of 5.6% per year from 2009-13 with a stable exchange rate and low inflation. This growth was due partly to high international prices for Peru's metals and minerals exports, which account for 55% of the country's total exports. Growth slipped from 2014 to 2017, due to weaker world prices for these resources. Despite Peru's strong macroeconomic performance, dependence on minerals and metals exports and imported foodstuffs makes the economy vulnerable to fluctuations in world prices.

Peru's rapid expansion coupled with cash transfers and other programs have helped to reduce the national poverty rate by over 35 percentage points since 2004, but inequality persists and continued to pose a challenge for the Ollanta HUMALA administration, which championed a policy of social inclusion and a more equitable distribution of income. Poor infrastructure hinders the spread of growth to Peru's non-coastal areas. The HUMALA administration passed several economic stimulus packages in 2014 to bolster growth, including reforms to environmental regulations in order to spur investment in Peru's lucrative mining sector, a move that was opposed by some environmental groups. However, in 2015, mining investment fell as global commodity prices remained low and social conflicts plagued the sector.

Peru's free trade policy continued under the HUMALA administration; since 2006, Peru has signed trade deals with the US, Canada, Singapore, China, Korea, Mexico, Japan, the EU, the European Free Trade Association, Chile, Thailand, Costa Rica, Panama, Venezuela, Honduras, concluded negotiations with Guatemala and the Trans-Pacific Partnership, and begun trade talks with El Salvador, India, and Turkey. Peru also has signed a trade pact with Chile, Colombia, and Mexico, called the Pacific Alliance, that seeks integration of services, capital, investment and movement of people. Since the US-Peru Trade Promotion Agreement entered into force in February 2009, total trade between Peru and the US has doubled. President Pedro Pablo KUCZYNSKI succeeded HUMALA in July 2016 and is focusing on economic reforms and free market policies aimed at boosting investment in Peru. Mining output increased significantly in 2016-17, which helped Peru attain one of the highest GDP growth rates in Latin America, and Peru should maintain strong growth in 2018. However, economic performance was depressed by delays in infrastructure mega-projects and the start of a corruption scandal associated with a Brazilian firm. Massive flooding in early 2017 also was a drag on growth, offset somewhat by additional public spending aimed at recovery efforts.

GDP (PURCHASING POWER PARITY):

$430.3 billion (2017 est.)

$420 billion (2016 est.)

$403.7 billion (2015 est.)

note: data are in 2017 dollars

country comparison to the world: 46

GDP (OFFICIAL EXCHANGE RATE):

$214.2 billion (2017 est.)

GDP - REAL GROWTH RATE:

2.5% (2017 est.)

4% (2016 est.)

3.3% (2015 est.)

country comparison to the world: 132

GDP - PER CAPITA (PPP):

$13,500 (2017 est.)

$13,300 (2016 est.)

$13,000 (2015 est.)

note: data are in 2017 dollars

country comparison to the world: 119

GROSS NATIONAL SAVING:

19.8% of GDP (2017 est.)

19.5% of GDP (2016 est.)

19% of GDP (2015 est.)

country comparison to the world: 100

GDP - COMPOSITION, BY END USE:

household consumption: 64.9% (2017 est.)

government consumption: 11.7% (2017 est.)

investment in fixed capital: 21.7% (2017 est.)

investment in inventories: -0.2% (2017 est.)

exports of goods and services: 24% (2017 est.)

imports of goods and services: -22% (2017 est.)

GDP - COMPOSITION, BY SECTOR OF ORIGIN:

agriculture: 7.6% (2017 est.)

industry: 32.7% (2017 est.)

services: 59.9% (2017 est.)

AGRICULTURE - PRODUCTS:

artichokes, asparagus, avocados, blueberries, coffee, cocoa, cotton, sugarcane, rice, potatoes, corn, plantains, grapes, oranges, pineapples, guavas, bananas, apples, lemons, pears, coca, tomatoes, mangoes, barley, medicinal plants, quinoa, palm oil, marigolds, onions, wheat, dry beans; poultry, beef, pork, dairy products; guinea pigs; fish

INDUSTRIES:

mining and refining of minerals; steel, metal fabrication; petroleum extraction and refining, natural gas and natural gas liquefaction; fishing and fish processing, cement, glass, textiles, clothing, food processing, beer, soft drinks, rubber, machinery, electrical machinery, chemicals, furniture

INDUSTRIAL PRODUCTION GROWTH RATE:

2.7% (2017 est.)

country comparison to the world: 113

LABOR FORCE:

17.03 million (2017 est.)

note: individuals older than 14 years of age

country comparison to the world: 36

LABOR FORCE - BY OCCUPATION:

agriculture: 25.8%

industry: 17.4%

services: 56.8% (2011)

UNEMPLOYMENT RATE:

6.9% (2017 est.)

6.7% (2016 est.)

note: data are for metropolitan Lima; widespread underemployment

country comparison to the world: 104

POPULATION BELOW POVERTY LINE:

22.7% (2014 est.)

HOUSEHOLD INCOME OR CONSUMPTION BY PERCENTAGE SHARE:

lowest 10%: 1.4%

highest 10%: 36.1% (2010 est.)

DISTRIBUTION OF FAMILY INCOME - GINI INDEX:

45.3 (2012)

51 (2005)

country comparison to the world: 40

BUDGET:

revenues: 58.06 billion (2017 est.)

expenditures: 64.81 billion (2017 est.)

TAXES AND OTHER REVENUES:

27.1% (of GDP) (2017 est.)

country comparison to the world: 103

BUDGET SURPLUS (+) OR DEFICIT (-):

-3.1% (of GDP) (2017 est.)

country comparison to the world: 135

PUBLIC DEBT:

25.4% of GDP (2017 est.)

24.5% of GDP (2016 est.)

note: data cover general government debt, and includes debt instruments issued by government entities other than the treasury; the data exclude treasury debt held by foreign entities; the data include debt issued by subnational entities

country comparison to the world: 174

FISCAL YEAR:

calendar year

INFLATION RATE (CONSUMER PRICES):

2.8% (2017 est.)

3.6% (2016 est.)

note: data are for metropolitan Lima, annual average

country comparison to the world: 128

CENTRAL BANK DISCOUNT RATE:

4.25% (31 December 2016 est.)

5.05% (31 December 2012)

country comparison to the world: 97

COMMERCIAL BANK PRIME LENDING RATE:

16.6% (31 December 2017 est.)

16.47% (31 December 2016 est.)

note: domestic currency lending rate, 90 day maturity

country comparison to the world: 29

STOCK OF NARROW MONEY:

$33.41 billion (31 December 2017 est.)

$31.08 billion (31 December 2016 est.)

country comparison to the world: 61

STOCK OF BROAD MONEY:

$33.41 billion (31 December 2017 est.)

$31.08 billion (31 December 2016 est.)

country comparison to the world: 61

STOCK OF DOMESTIC CREDIT:

$56.7 billion (31 December 2017 est.)

$52.8 billion (31 December 2016 est.)

country comparison to the world: 62

MARKET VALUE OF PUBLICLY TRADED SHARES:

$56.56 billion (31 December 2015 est.)

$78.84 billion (31 December 2014 est.)

$80.98 billion (31 December 2013 est.)

country comparison to the world: 49

CURRENT ACCOUNT BALANCE:

-$2.414 billion (2017 est.)

-$5.239 billion (2016 est.)

country comparison to the world: 172
EXPORTS:
$44.92 billion (2017 est.)

$37.02 billion (2016 est.)

country comparison to the world: 54
EXPORTS - PARTNERS:
China 26.5%, US 15.2%, Switzerland 5.2%, South Korea 4.4%, Spain 4.1%, India 4.1% (2017)
EXPORTS - COMMODITIES:
copper, gold, lead, zinc, tin, iron ore, molybdenum, silver; crude petroleum and petroleum products, natural gas; coffee, asparagus and other vegetables, fruit, apparel and textiles, fishmeal, fish, chemicals, fabricated metal products and machinery, alloys
IMPORTS:
$38.65 billion (2017 est.)

$35.13 billion (2016 est.)

country comparison to the world: 62
IMPORTS - COMMODITIES:
petroleum and petroleum products, chemicals, plastics, machinery, vehicles, TV sets, power shovels, front-end loaders, telephones and telecommunication equipment, iron and steel, wheat, corn, soybean products, paper, cotton, vaccines and medicines
IMPORTS - PARTNERS:
China 22.3%, US 20.1%, Brazil 6%, Mexico 4.4% (2017)
RESERVES OF FOREIGN EXCHANGE AND GOLD:
$63.83 billion (31 December 2017 est.)

$61.81 billion (31 December 2016 est.)

country comparison to the world: 35
DEBT - EXTERNAL:
$66.25 billion (31 December 2017 est.)

$66.76 billion (31 December 2016 est.)

country comparison to the world: 60
STOCK OF DIRECT FOREIGN INVESTMENT - AT HOME:
$98.24 billion (31 December 2017 est.)

$91.48 billion (31 December 2016 est.)

country comparison to the world: 46
STOCK OF DIRECT FOREIGN INVESTMENT - ABROAD:
$5.447 billion (31 December 2017 est.)

$4.255 billion (31 December 2016 est.)

country comparison to the world: 74
EXCHANGE RATES:
nuevo sol (PEN) per US dollar -

3.265 (2017 est.)

3.3751 (2016 est.)

3.3751 (2015 est.)

3.185 (2014 est.)

2.8383 (2013 est.)

ENERGY :: PERU

ELECTRICITY ACCESS:
population without electricity: 2 million (2017)

electrification - total population: 95% (2017)

electrification - urban areas: 97% (2017)

electrification - rural areas: 89% (2017)
ELECTRICITY - PRODUCTION:
50.13 billion kWh (2016 est.)

country comparison to the world: 54
ELECTRICITY - CONSUMPTION:
44.61 billion kWh (2016 est.)

country comparison to the world: 53
ELECTRICITY - EXPORTS:
55 million kWh (2015 est.)

country comparison to the world: 86
ELECTRICITY - IMPORTS:
22 million kWh (2016 est.)

country comparison to the world: 112
ELECTRICITY - INSTALLED GENERATING CAPACITY:
14.73 million kW (2016 est.)

country comparison to the world: 51
ELECTRICITY - FROM FOSSIL FUELS:
61% of total installed capacity (2016 est.)

country comparison to the world: 128
ELECTRICITY - FROM NUCLEAR FUELS:
0% of total installed capacity (2017 est.)

country comparison to the world: 164
ELECTRICITY - FROM HYDROELECTRIC PLANTS:
35% of total installed capacity (2017 est.)

country comparison to the world: 60
ELECTRICITY - FROM OTHER RENEWABLE SOURCES:
4% of total installed capacity (2017 est.)

country comparison to the world: 116
CRUDE OIL - PRODUCTION:
49,000 bbl/day (2018 est.)

country comparison to the world: 54
CRUDE OIL - EXPORTS:
7,995 bbl/day (2015 est.)

country comparison to the world: 61
CRUDE OIL - IMPORTS:
86,060 bbl/day (2015 est.)

country comparison to the world: 46
CRUDE OIL - PROVED RESERVES:
434.9 million bbl (1 January 2018 est.)

country comparison to the world: 47
REFINED PETROLEUM PRODUCTS - PRODUCTION:
166,600 bbl/day (2015 est.)

country comparison to the world: 57
REFINED PETROLEUM PRODUCTS - CONSUMPTION:
250,000 bbl/day (2016 est.)

country comparison to the world: 50
REFINED PETROLEUM PRODUCTS - EXPORTS:
62,640 bbl/day (2015 est.)

country comparison to the world: 49
REFINED PETROLEUM PRODUCTS - IMPORTS:
65,400 bbl/day (2015 est.)

country comparison to the world: 71
NATURAL GAS - PRODUCTION:
12.99 billion cu m (2017 est.)

country comparison to the world: 37
NATURAL GAS - CONSUMPTION:
7.483 billion cu m (2017 est.)

country comparison to the world: 53
NATURAL GAS - EXPORTS:
5.505 billion cu m (2017 est.)

country comparison to the world: 28
NATURAL GAS - IMPORTS:
0 cu m (2017 est.)

country comparison to the world: 174
NATURAL GAS - PROVED RESERVES:
455.9 billion cu m (1 January 2018 est.)

country comparison to the world: 32
CARBON DIOXIDE EMISSIONS FROM CONSUMPTION OF ENERGY:
55.94 million Mt (2017 est.)

country comparison to the world: 55

COMMUNICATIONS :: PERU

TELEPHONES - FIXED LINES:
total subscriptions: 3,082,036

subscriptions per 100 inhabitants: 10 (2017 est.)

country comparison to the world: 46

TELEPHONES - MOBILE CELLULAR:

total subscriptions: 38,915,386

subscriptions per 100 inhabitants: 125 (2017 est.)

country comparison to the world: 37

TELEPHONE SYSTEM:

general assessment: adequate for most requirements; nationwide microwave radio relay system and a domestic satellite system with 12 earth stations; 3G network and new LTE services begun; 2019 the year to try 5G; Peru is seen as a potential market for growth in broadband with government work with fiber-optic backbone to remote areas (2018)

domestic: fixed-line teledensity is only about 10 per 100 persons; mobile-cellular teledensity, spurred by competition among multiple providers, now 125 telephones per 100 persons (2018)

international: country code - 51; landing points for the SAM-1, IGW, American Movil-Telxius, SAC and PAN-AM submarine cable systems provide links to parts of Central and South America, the Caribbean, and US; satellite earth stations - 2 Intelsat (Atlantic Ocean) (2019)

BROADCAST MEDIA:

10 major TV networks of which only one, Television Nacional de Peru, is state owned; multi-channel cable TV services are available; in excess of 2,000 radio stations including a substantial number of indigenous language stations (2019)

INTERNET COUNTRY CODE:

.pe

INTERNET USERS:

total: 13,975,422

percent of population: 45.5% (July 2016 est.)

country comparison to the world: 42

BROADBAND - FIXED SUBSCRIPTIONS:

total: 2,310,217

subscriptions per 100 inhabitants: 7 (2017 est.)

country comparison to the world: 50

MILITARY AND SECURITY :: PERU

MILITARY EXPENDITURES:

1.19% of GDP (2018)

1.24% of GDP (2017)

1.3% of GDP (2016)

1.72% of GDP (2015)

1.59% of GDP (2014)

country comparison to the world: 108

MILITARY AND SECURITY FORCES:

Peruvian Army (Ejercito del Peru), Peruvian Navy (Marina de Guerra del Peru, MGP, includes naval air, naval infantry, and Coast Guard), Air Force of Peru (Fuerza Aerea del Peru, FAP) (2019)

MILITARY SERVICE AGE AND OBLIGATION:

18-50 years of age for male and 18-45 years of age for female voluntary military service; no conscription (2012)

MARITIME THREATS:

the International Maritime Bureau reports the territorial waters of Peru are a risk for armed robbery against ships; in 2018, four attacks against commercial vessels were reported, a slight increase from the two reported in 2017; most of these occured in the main port of Callao

TRANSPORTATION :: PERU

NATIONAL AIR TRANSPORT SYSTEM:

number of registered air carriers: 7 (2015)

inventory of registered aircraft operated by air carriers: 35 (2015)

annual passenger traffic on registered air carriers: 13,907,948 (2015)

annual freight traffic on registered air carriers: 223,643,434 mt-km (2015)

CIVIL AIRCRAFT REGISTRATION COUNTRY CODE PREFIX:

OB (2016)

AIRPORTS:

191 (2013)

country comparison to the world: 30

AIRPORTS - WITH PAVED RUNWAYS:

total: 59 (2017)

over 3,047 m: 5 (2017)

2,438 to 3,047 m: 21 (2017)

1,524 to 2,437 m: 16 (2017)

914 to 1,523 m: 12 (2017)

under 914 m: 5 (2017)

AIRPORTS - WITH UNPAVED RUNWAYS:

total: 132 (2013)

2,438 to 3,047 m: 1 (2013)

1,524 to 2,437 m: 19 (2013)

914 to 1,523 m: 30 (2013)

under 914 m: 82 (2013)

HELIPORTS:

5 (2013)

PIPELINES:

786 km extra heavy crude, 1526 km gas, 679 km liquid petroleum gas, 1033 km oil, 15 km refined products (2013)

RAILWAYS:

total: 1,854 km (2014)

standard gauge: 1,730.4 km 1.435-m gauge (34 km electrified) (2014)

narrow gauge: 124 km 0.914-m gauge (2014)

country comparison to the world: 76

ROADWAYS:

total: 140,672 km (18,699 km paved) (2012)

note: includes 24,593 km of national roads (14,748 km paved), 24,235 km of departmental roads (2,340 km paved), and 91,844 km of local roads (1,611 km paved)

country comparison to the world: 36

WATERWAYS:

8,808 km (8,600 km of navigable tributaries on the Amazon River system and 208 km on Lago Titicaca) (2011)

country comparison to the world: 14

MERCHANT MARINE:

total: 95

by type: container ship 2, oil tanker 13, other 80 (2018)

country comparison to the world: 90

PORTS AND TERMINALS:

major seaport(s): Callao, Matarani, Paita

oil terminal(s): Conchan oil terminal, La Pampilla oil terminal

container port(s) (TEUs): Callao (2,250,200) (2017)

river port(s): Iquitos, Pucallpa, Yurimaguas (Amazon)

TERRORISM :: PERU

TERRORIST GROUPS - HOME BASED:

Shining Path (Sendero Luminoso, SL):
aim(s): generate revenue by providing security for narcotics trafficking and growing coca to produce cocaine; historically, SL's goal has been to replace Peruvian institutions with a peasant revolutionary regime
area(s) of operation: headquartered in the Valley of the Apurimac, Ene, and Mantaro River (VRAEM) region (2018)

TRANSNATIONAL ISSUES :: PERU

DISPUTES - INTERNATIONAL:

Chile and Ecuador rejected Peru's November 2005 unilateral legislation to shift the axis of their joint treaty-defined maritime boundaries along the parallels of latitude to equidistance lines which favor Peru; organized illegal narcotics operations in Colombia have penetrated Peru's shared border; Peru rejects Bolivia's claim to restore maritime access through a sovereign corridor through Chile along the Peruvian border

REFUGEES AND INTERNALLY DISPLACED PERSONS:

refugees (country of origin): 946,020 (Venezuela) (economic and political crisis; includes Venezuelans who have claimed asylum or have received alternative legal stay) (2019)

IDPs: 59,000 (civil war from 1980-2000; most IDPs are indigenous peasants in Andean and Amazonian regions; as of 2011, no new information on the situation of these IDPs) (2017)

ILLICIT DRUGS:

until 1996 the world's largest coca leaf producer, Peru is now the world's second largest producer of coca leaf, though it lags far behind Colombia; cultivation of coca in Peru was estimated at 44,000 hectares in 2016, a decrease of 16 per cent over 2015; second largest producer of cocaine, estimated at 410 metric tons of potential pure cocaine in 2016; finished cocaine is shipped out from Pacific ports to the international drug market; increasing amounts of base and finished cocaine, however, are being moved to Brazil, Chile, Argentina, and Bolivia for use in the Southern Cone or transshipment to Europe and Africa; increasing domestic drug consumption

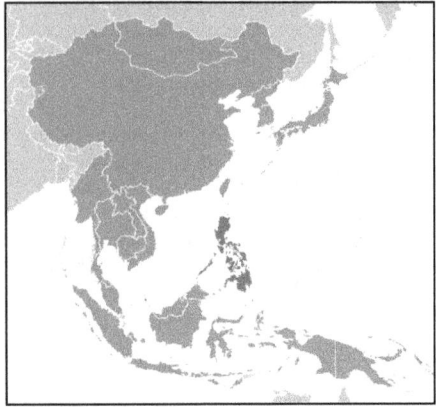

EAST ASIA / SOUTHEAST ASIA :: PHILIPPINES

INTRODUCTION :: PHILIPPINES

BACKGROUND:

The Philippine Islands became a Spanish colony during the 16th century; they were ceded to the US in 1898 following the Spanish-American War. In 1935 the Philippines became a self-governing commonwealth. Manuel QUEZON was elected president and was tasked with preparing the country for independence after a 10-year transition. In 1942 the islands fell under Japanese occupation during World War II, and US forces and Filipinos fought together during 1944-45 to regain control. On 4 July 1946 the Republic of the Philippines attained its independence. A 21-year rule by Ferdinand MARCOS ended in 1986, when a "people power" movement in Manila ("EDSA 1") forced him into exile and installed Corazon AQUINO as president. Her presidency was hampered by several coup attempts that prevented a return to full political stability and economic development. Fidel RAMOS was elected president in 1992. His administration was marked by increased stability and by progress on economic reforms. In 1992, the US closed its last military bases on the islands. Joseph ESTRADA was elected president in 1998. He was succeeded by his vice-president, Gloria MACAPAGAL-ARROYO, in January 2001 after ESTRADA's stormy impeachment trial on corruption charges broke down and another "people power" movement ("EDSA 2") demanded his resignation. MACAPAGAL-ARROYO was elected to a six-year term as president in May 2004. Her presidency was marred by several corruption allegations but the Philippine economy was one of the few to avoid contraction following the 2008 global financial crisis, expanding each year of her administration. Benigno AQUINO III was elected to a six-year term as president in May 2010 and was succeeded by Rodrigo DUTERTE in May 2016.

The Philippine Government faces threats from several groups, some of which are on the US Government's Foreign Terrorist Organization list. Manila has waged a decades-long struggle against ethnic Moro insurgencies in the southern Philippines, which led to a peace accord with the Moro National Liberation Front and a separate agreement with a break away faction, the Moro Islamic Liberation Front. The decades-long Maoist-inspired New People's Army insurgency also operates through much of the country. In 2017, Philippine armed forces battled an ISIS-Philippines siege in Marawi City, driving DUTERTE to declare martial law in the region. The Philippines faces increased tension with China over disputed territorial and maritime claims in the South China Sea.

GEOGRAPHY :: PHILIPPINES

LOCATION:

Southeastern Asia, archipelago between the Philippine Sea and the South China Sea, east of Vietnam

GEOGRAPHIC COORDINATES:

13 00 N, 122 00 E

MAP REFERENCES:

Southeast Asia

AREA:

total: 300,000 sq km

land: 298,170 sq km

water: 1,830 sq km

country comparison to the world: 74

AREA - COMPARATIVE:

slightly less than twice the size of Georgia; slightly larger than Arizona

LAND BOUNDARIES:

0 km

COASTLINE:

36,289 km

MARITIME CLAIMS:

territorial sea: irregular polygon extending up to 100 nm from coastline as defined by 1898 treaty; since late 1970s has also claimed polygonal-shaped area in South China Sea as wide as 285 nm

exclusive economic zone: 200 nm

continental shelf: to the depth of exploitation

CLIMATE:
tropical marine; northeast monsoon (November to April); southwest monsoon (May to October)

TERRAIN:
mostly mountains with narrow to extensive coastal lowlands

ELEVATION:
mean elevation: 442 m

lowest point: Philippine Sea 0 m

highest point: Mount Apo 2,954 m

NATURAL RESOURCES:
timber, petroleum, nickel, cobalt, silver, gold, salt, copper

LAND USE:
agricultural land: 41% (2011 est.)

arable land: 18.2% (2011 est.) / **permanent crops:** 17.8% (2011 est.) / **permanent pasture:** 5% (2011 est.)

forest: 25.9% (2011 est.)

other: 33.1% (2011 est.)

IRRIGATED LAND:
16,270 sq km (2012)

POPULATION DISTRIBUTION:
population concentrated where good farmlands lie; highest concentrations are northwest and south-central Luzon, the southeastern extension of Luzon, and the islands of the Visayan Sea, particularly Cebu and Negros; Manila is home to one-eighth of the entire national population

NATURAL HAZARDS:
astride typhoon belt, usually affected by 15 and struck by five to six cyclonic storms each year; landslides; active volcanoes; destructive earthquakes; tsunamis

volcanism: significant volcanic activity; Taal (311 m), which has shown recent unrest and may erupt in the near future, has been deemed a Decade Volcano by the International Association of Volcanology and Chemistry of the Earth's Interior, worthy of study due to its explosive history and close proximity to human populations; Mayon (2,462 m), the country's most active volcano, erupted in 2009 forcing over 33,000 to be evacuated; other historically active volcanoes include Biliran, Babuyan Claro, Bulusan, Camiguin, Camiguin de Babuyanes, Didicas, Iraya, Jolo, Kanlaon, Makaturing, Musuan, Parker, Pinatubo, and Ragang; see note 2 under "Geography - note"

ENVIRONMENT - CURRENT ISSUES:
uncontrolled deforestation especially in watershed areas; illegal mining and logging; soil erosion; air and water pollution in major urban centers; coral reef degradation; increasing pollution of coastal mangrove swamps that are important fish breeding grounds; coastal erosion; dynamite fishing; wildlife extinction

ENVIRONMENT - INTERNATIONAL AGREEMENTS:
party to: Biodiversity, Climate Change, Climate Change-Kyoto Protocol, Desertification, Endangered Species, Hazardous Wastes, Law of the Sea, Marine Dumping, Ozone Layer Protection, Ship Pollution, Tropical Timber 83, Tropical Timber 94, Wetlands, Whaling

signed, but not ratified: Air Pollution-Persistent Organic Pollutants

GEOGRAPHY - NOTE:
note 1: for decades, the Philippine archipelago was reported as having 7,107 islands; in 2016, the national mapping authority reported that hundreds of new islands had been discovered and increased the number of islands to 7,641 - though not all of the new islands have been verified; the country is favorably located in relation to many of Southeast Asia's main water bodies: the South China Sea, Philippine Sea, Sulu Sea, Celebes Sea, and Luzon Strait

note 2: Philippines is one of the countries along the Ring of Fire, a belt of active volcanoes and earthquake epicenters bordering the Pacific Ocean; up to 90% of the world's earthquakes and some 75% of the world's volcanoes occur within the Ring of Fire

note 3: the Philippines sits astride the Pacific typhoon belt and an average of 9 typhoons make landfall on the islands each year - with about 5 of these being destructive; the country is the most exposed in the world to tropical storms

PEOPLE AND SOCIETY :: PHILIPPINES

POPULATION:
105,893,381 (July 2018 est.)

country comparison to the world: 13

NATIONALITY:
noun: Filipino(s)

adjective: Philippine

ETHNIC GROUPS:
Tagalog 24.4%, Bisaya/Binisaya 11.4%, Cebuano 9.9%, Ilocano 8.8%, Hiligaynon/Ilonggo 8.4%, Bikol/Bicol 6.8%, Waray 4%, other local ethnicity 26.1%, other foreign ethnicity .1% (2010 est.)

LANGUAGES:
unspecified Filipino (official; based on Tagalog) and English (official); eight major dialects - Tagalog, Cebuano, Ilocano, Hiligaynon or Ilonggo, Bicol, Waray, Pampango, and Pangasinan

RELIGIONS:
Roman Catholic 80.6%, Protestant 8.2% (includes Philippine Council of Evangelical Churches 2.7%, National Council of Churches in the Philippines 1.2%, other Protestant 4.3%), other Christian 3.4%, Muslim 5.6%, tribal religions .2%, other 1.9%, none .1% (2010 est.)

AGE STRUCTURE:
0-14 years: 33.07% (male 17,870,983 /female 17,151,096)

15-24 years: 19.17% (male 10,360,704 /female 9,934,798)

25-54 years: 37.11% (male 19,987,460 /female 19,312,673)

55-64 years: 6.04% (male 2,932,572 /female 3,462,832)

65 years and over: 4.61% (male 2,001,964 /female 2,878,299) (2018 est.)

DEPENDENCY RATIOS:
total dependency ratio: 58.2 (2015 est.)

youth dependency ratio: 51 (2015 est.)

elderly dependency ratio: 7.2 (2015 est.)

potential support ratio: 13.8 (2015 est.)

MEDIAN AGE:
total: 23.7 years (2018 est.)

male: 23.3 years

female: 24.2 years

country comparison to the world: 169

POPULATION GROWTH RATE:
1.55% (2018 est.)

country comparison to the world: 70

BIRTH RATE:

23.4 births/1,000 population (2018 est.)

country comparison to the world: 58

DEATH RATE:

6.1 deaths/1,000 population (2018 est.)

country comparison to the world: 160

NET MIGRATION RATE:

-1.9 migrant(s)/1,000 population (2018 est.)

country comparison to the world: 162

POPULATION DISTRIBUTION:

population concentrated where good farmlands lie; highest concentrations are northwest and south-central Luzon, the southeastern extension of Luzon, and the islands of the Visayan Sea, particularly Cebu and Negros; Manila is home to one-eighth of the entire national population

URBANIZATION:

urban population: 47.1% of total population (2019)

rate of urbanization: 1.99% annual rate of change (2015-20 est.)

MAJOR URBAN AREAS - POPULATION:

13.699 million MANILA (capital), 1.785 million Davao, 967,000 Cebu City, 905,000 Zamboanga, 859,000 Antipolo (2019)

SEX RATIO:

at birth: 1.05 male(s)/female

0-14 years: 1.04 male(s)/female

15-24 years: 1.04 male(s)/female

25-54 years: 1.03 male(s)/female

55-64 years: 0.85 male(s)/female

65 years and over: 0.7 male(s)/female

total population: 1.01 male(s)/female (2018 est.)

MOTHER'S MEAN AGE AT FIRST BIRTH:

22.8 years (2017 est.)

note: median age at first birth among women 25-29

MATERNAL MORTALITY RATE:

121 deaths/100,000 live births (2017 est.)

country comparison to the world: 64

INFANT MORTALITY RATE:

total: 20.9 deaths/1,000 live births (2018 est.)

male: 23.8 deaths/1,000 live births

female: 17.9 deaths/1,000 live births

country comparison to the world: 79

LIFE EXPECTANCY AT BIRTH:

total population: 69.6 years (2018 est.)

male: 66.1 years

female: 73.3 years

country comparison to the world: 162

TOTAL FERTILITY RATE:

2.99 children born/woman (2018 est.)

country comparison to the world: 52

CONTRACEPTIVE PREVALENCE RATE:

54.1% (2017)

DRINKING WATER SOURCE:

improved:

urban: 93.7% of population

rural: 90.3% of population

total: 91.8% of population

unimproved:

urban: 6.3% of population

rural: 9.7% of population

total: 8.2% of population (2015 est.)

CURRENT HEALTH EXPENDITURE:

4.4% (2016)

PHYSICIANS DENSITY:

1.28 physicians/1,000 population (2010)

HOSPITAL BED DENSITY:

1 beds/1,000 population (2011)

SANITATION FACILITY ACCESS:

improved:

urban: 77.9% of population (2015 est.)

rural: 70.8% of population (2015 est.)

total: 73.9% of population (2015 est.)

unimproved:

urban: 22.1% of population (2015 est.)

rural: 29.2% of population (2015 est.)

total: 26.1% of population (2015 est.)

HIV/AIDS - ADULT PREVALENCE RATE:

0.1% (2018 est.)

country comparison to the world: 132

HIV/AIDS - PEOPLE LIVING WITH HIV/AIDS:

77,000 (2018 est.)

country comparison to the world: 50

HIV/AIDS - DEATHS:

1,200 (2018 est.)

country comparison to the world: 59

MAJOR INFECTIOUS DISEASES:

degree of risk: high (2016)

food or waterborne diseases: bacterial diarrhea, hepatitis A, and typhoid fever (2016)

vectorborne diseases: dengue fever and malaria (2016)

water contact diseases: leptospirosis (2016)

note - on 8 October 2019, the Centers for Disease Control and Prevention issued a Travel Health Notice regarding a polio outbreak in the Philippines; CDC recommends that all travelers to the Philippines be vaccinated fully against polio; before traveling to the Philippines, adults who completed their routine polio vaccine series as children should receive a single, lifetime adult booster dose of polio vaccine

OBESITY - ADULT PREVALENCE RATE:

6.4% (2016)

country comparison to the world: 168

CHILDREN UNDER THE AGE OF 5 YEARS UNDERWEIGHT:

21.5% (2015)

country comparison to the world: 26

EDUCATION EXPENDITURES:

2.7% of GDP (2009)

country comparison to the world: 155

LITERACY:

definition: age 15 and over can read and write

total population: 96.3%

male: 95.8%

female: 96.8% (2015 est.)

SCHOOL LIFE EXPECTANCY (PRIMARY TO TERTIARY EDUCATION):

total: 13 years

male: 12 years

female: 13 years (2013)

UNEMPLOYMENT, YOUTH AGES 15-24:

total: 7.5%

male: 6.6%

female: 8.9% (2017 est.)

country comparison to the world: 150

GOVERNMENT :: PHILIPPINES

COUNTRY NAME:

conventional long form: Republic of the Philippines

conventional short form: Philippines

local long form: Republika ng Pilipinas

local short form: Pilipinas

etymology: named in honor of King PHILLIP II of Spain by Spanish explorer Ruy LOPEZ de VILLALOBOS, who visited some of the islands in 1543

GOVERNMENT TYPE:

presidential republic

CAPITAL:

name: Manila

geographic coordinates: 14 36 N, 120 58 E

time difference: UTC+8 (13 hours ahead of Washington, DC, during Standard Time)

etymology: derives from the Tagalog "may-nila" meaning "where there is indigo" and refers to the presence of indigo-yielding plants growing in the area surrounding the original settlement

ADMINISTRATIVE DIVISIONS:

80 provinces and 39 chartered cities

provinces: Abra, Agusan del Norte, Agusan del Sur, Aklan, Albay, Antique, Apayao, Aurora, Basilan, Bataan, Batanes, Batangas, Biliran, Benguet, Bohol, Bukidnon, Bulacan, Cagayan, Camarines Norte, Camarines Sur, Camiguin, Capiz, Catanduanes, Cavite, Cebu, Compostela, Cotabato, Davao del Norte, Davao del Sur, Davao Oriental, Dinagat Islands, Eastern Samar, Guimaras, Ifugao, Ilocos Norte, Ilocos Sur, Iloilo, Isabela, Kalinga, Laguna, Lanao del Norte, Lanao del Sur, La Union, Leyte, Maguindanao, Marinduque, Masbate, Mindoro Occidental, Mindoro Oriental, Misamis Occidental, Misamis Oriental, Mountain, Negros Occidental, Negros Oriental, Northern Samar, Nueva Ecija, Nueva Vizcaya, Palawan, Pampanga, Pangasinan, Quezon, Quirino, Rizal, Romblon, Samar, Sarangani, Siquijor, Sorsogon, South Cotabato, Southern Leyte, Sultan Kudarat, Sulu, Surigao del Norte, Surigao del Sur, Tarlac, Tawi-Tawi, Zambales, Zamboanga del Norte, Zamboanga del Sur, Zamboanga Sibugay;

chartered cities: Angeles, Antipolo, Bacolod, Baguio, Butuan, Cagayan de Oro, Caloocan, Cebu, Cotabato, Dagupan, Davao, General Santos, Iligan, Iloilo, Lapu-Lapu, Las Pinas, Lucena, Makati, Malabon, Mandaluyong, Mandaue, Manila, Marikina, Muntinlupa, Naga, Navotas, Olongapo, Ormoc, Paranaque, Pasay, Pasig, Puerto Princesa, Quezon, San Juan, Santiago, Tacloban, Taguig, Valenzuela, Zamboanga

(2012)

INDEPENDENCE:

4 July 1946 (from the US)

NATIONAL HOLIDAY:

Independence Day, 12 June (1898); note - 12 June 1898 was date of declaration of independence from Spain; 4 July 1946 was date of independence from the US

CONSTITUTION:

history: several previous; latest ratified 2 February 1987, effective 11 February 1987

amendments: proposed by Congress if supported by three fourths of the membership, by a constitutional convention called by Congress, or by public petition; passage by either of the three proposal methods requires a majority vote in a national referendum; note - the constitution has not been amended since its enactment in 1987 (2017)

LEGAL SYSTEM:

mixed legal system of civil, common, Islamic (sharia), and customary law

INTERNATIONAL LAW ORGANIZATION PARTICIPATION:

accepts compulsory ICJ jurisdiction with reservations; withdrew from the ICCt in March 2019

CITIZENSHIP:

citizenship by birth: no

citizenship by descent only: at least one parent must be a citizen of the Philippines

dual citizenship recognized: no

residency requirement for naturalization: 10 years

SUFFRAGE:

18 years of age; universal

EXECUTIVE BRANCH:

chief of state: President Rodrigo DUTERTE (since 30 June 2016); Vice President Leni ROBREDO (since 30 June 2016); note - the president is both chief of state and head of government

head of government: President Rodrigo DUTERTE (since 30 June 2016); Vice President Leni ROBREDO (since 30 June 2016)

cabinet: Cabinet appointed by the president with the consent of the Commission of Appointments, an independent body of 25 Congressional members including the Senate president (ex officio chairman), appointed by the president

elections/appointments: president and vice president directly elected on separate ballots by simple majority popular vote for a single 6-year term; election last held on 9 May 2016 (next to be held in May 2022)

election results: Rodrigo DUTERTE elected president; percent of vote - Rodrigo DUTERTE (PDP-Laban) 39%, Manuel "Mar" ROXAS (LP) 23.5%, Grace POE (independent) 21.4%, Jejomar BINAY (UNA) 12.7%, Miriam Defensor SANTIAGO (PRP) 3.4%; Leni ROBREDO elected vice president; percent of vote Leni ROBREDO (LP) 35.1%, Bongbong MARCOS (independent) 34.5%, Alan CAYETANO 14.4%, Francis ESCUDERO (independent) 12%, Antonio TRILLANES (independent) 2.1%, Gregorio HONASAN (UNA) 1.9%

LEGISLATIVE BRANCH:

description: bicameral Congress or Kongreso consists of:
Senate or Senado (24 seats; members directly elected in multi-seat constituencies by majority vote; members serve 6-year terms with one-half of the membership renewed every 3 years)
House of Representatives or Kapulungan Ng Mga Kinatawan (297 seats; 238 members directly elected in single-seat constituencies by simple majority vote and 59 representing minorities directly elected by party-list proportional representation vote; members serve 3-year terms)

elections:
Senate - elections last held on 9 May 2016 (next to be held on 13 May 2019)
House of Representatives - elections last held on 9 May 2016 (next to be held on 13 May 2019)

election results:
Senate - percent of vote by party - LP 31.3%, NPC 10.1%, UNA 7.6%, Akbayan 5.0%, other 30.9%, independent 15.1%; seats by party - LP 6, NPC 3, UNA 4, Akbayan 1, other 10; composition - men 18, women 6, percent of women 25%

House of Representatives - percent of vote by party - LP 41.7%, NPC 17.0%, UNA 6.6%, NUP 9.7%, NP 9.4%, independent 6.0%, others 10.1%; seats by party - LP 115, NPC 42, NUP 23, NP 24, UNA 11, other 19, independent 4, party-list 59; composition - men 210, women 87, percent of women 29.8%; note - total Congress percent of women 29.4%

JUDICIAL BRANCH:

highest courts: Supreme Court (consists of a chief justice and 14 associate justices)

judge selection and term of office: justices are appointed by the president on the recommendation of the Judicial and Bar Council, a constitutionally created, 6-member body that recommends Supreme Court nominees; justices serve until age 70

subordinate courts: Court of Appeals; Sandiganbayan (special court for corruption cases of government officials); Court of Tax Appeals; regional, metropolitan, and municipal trial courts; sharia courts

POLITICAL PARTIES AND LEADERS:

Akbayon [Machris CABREROS]
Laban ng Demokratikong Pilipino (Struggle of Filipino Democrats) or LDP [Edgardo ANGARA]
Lakas ng EDSA-Christian Muslim Democrats or Lakas-CMD [Ferdinand Martin ROMUALDEZ]
Liberal Party or LP [Francis PANGILINAN]
Nacionalista Party or NP [Manuel "Manny" VILLAR]
Nationalist People's Coalition or NPC [Eduardo COJUNGCO, Jr.]
National Unity Party or NUP [Albert GARCIA]
PDP-Laban [Aquilino PIMENTEL III]
People's Reform Party or PRP [Narcisco SANTIAGO]
Puwersa ng Masang Pilipino (Force of the Philippine Masses) or PMP [Joseph ESTRADA]
United Nationalist Alliance or UNA

INTERNATIONAL ORGANIZATION PARTICIPATION:

ADB, APEC, ARF, ASEAN, BIS, CD, CICA (observer), CP, EAS, FAO, G-24, G-77, IAEA, IBRD, ICAO, ICC (national committees), ICCt, ICRM, IDA, IFAD, IFC, IFRCS, IHO, ILO, IMF, IMO, IMSO, Interpol, IOC, IOM, IPU, ISO, ITSO, ITU, ITUC (NGOs), MIGA, MINUSTAH, NAM, OAS (observer), OPCW, PCA, PIF (partner), UN, UNCTAD, UNESCO, UNHCR, UNIDO, Union Latina, UNMIL, UNMOGIP, UNOCI, UNWTO, UPU, WCO, WFTU (NGOs), WHO, WIPO, WMO, WTO

DIPLOMATIC REPRESENTATION IN THE US:

Ambassador Jose Manuel del Gallego ROMUALDEZ (since 29 November 2017)

chancery: 1600 Massachusetts Avenue NW, Washington, DC 20036

telephone: [1] (202) 467-9300

FAX: [1] (202) 328-7614

consulate(s) general: Chicago, Honolulu, Los Angeles, New York, Saipan (Northern Mariana Islands), San Francisco, Tamuning (Guam)

DIPLOMATIC REPRESENTATION FROM THE US:

chief of mission: Ambassador Sung KIM (since 6 December 2016)

telephone: [63] (2) 301-2000

embassy: 1201 Roxas Boulevard, Manila 1000

mailing address: PSC 500, FPO AP 96515-1000

FAX: [63] (2) 301-2017

FLAG DESCRIPTION:

two equal horizontal bands of blue (top) and red; a white equilateral triangle is based on the hoist side; the center of the triangle displays a yellow sun with eight primary rays; each corner of the triangle contains a small, yellow, five-pointed star; blue stands for peace and justice, red symbolizes courage, the white equal-sided triangle represents equality; the rays recall the first eight provinces that sought independence from Spain, while the stars represent the three major geographical divisions of the country: Luzon, Visayas, and Mindanao; the design of the flag dates to 1897

note: in wartime the flag is flown upside down with the red band at the top

NATIONAL SYMBOL(S):

three stars and sun, Philippine eagle; national colors: red, white, blue, yellow

NATIONAL ANTHEM:

name: "Lupang Hinirang" (Chosen Land)

lyrics/music: Jose PALMA (revised by Felipe PADILLA de Leon)/Julian FELIPE

note: music adopted 1898, original Spanish lyrics adopted 1899, Filipino (Tagalog) lyrics adopted 1956; although the original lyrics were written in Spanish, later English and Filipino versions were created; today, only the Filipino version is used

ECONOMY :: PHILIPPINES

ECONOMY - OVERVIEW:

The economy has been relatively resilient to global economic shocks due to less exposure to troubled international securities, lower dependence on exports, relatively resilient domestic consumption, large remittances from about 10 million overseas Filipino workers and migrants, and a rapidly expanding services industry. During 2017, the current account balance fell into the negative range, the first time since the 2008 global financial crisis, in part due to an ambitious new infrastructure spending program announced this year. However, international reserves remain at comfortable levels and the banking system is stable.

Efforts to improve tax administration and expenditures management have helped ease the Philippines' debt burden and tight fiscal situation. The Philippines received investment-grade credit ratings on its sovereign debt under the former AQUINO administration and has had little difficulty financing its budget deficits. However, weak absorptive capacity and implementation bottlenecks have prevented the government from maximizing its expenditure plans. Although it has improved, the low tax-to-GDP ratio remains a constraint to supporting increasingly higher spending levels and sustaining high and inclusive growth over the longer term.

Economic growth has accelerated, averaging over 6% per year from 2011 to 2017, compared with 4.5% under the MACAPAGAL-ARROYO government; and competitiveness rankings have improved. Although 2017 saw a new record year for net foreign direct investment inflows, FDI to the Philippines has continued to lag regional peers, in part because the Philippine constitution and other laws limit foreign investment and restrict foreign ownership in important activities/sectors - such as land ownership and public utilities.

Although the economy grew at a rapid pace under the AQUINO government, challenges to achieving more inclusive growth remain. Wealth is concentrated in the hands of the rich. The unemployment rate declined from 7.3% to 5.7% between 2010 and 2017; while there has been some improvement, underemployment remains high at around 17% to 18% of the employed population. At least 40% of the employed work in the informal sector. Poverty afflicts more than a fifth of the total population but is as high as 75% in some areas of the southern Philippines. More than 60% of the poor reside in rural areas, where the incidence of poverty (about 30%) is more severe - a challenge to raising rural farm and non-farm incomes. Continued efforts are needed to improve governance, the judicial system, the regulatory environment, the infrastructure, and the overall ease of doing business.

2016 saw the election of President Rodrigo DUTERTE, who has pledged to make inclusive growth and poverty reduction his top priority. DUTERTE believes that illegal drug use, crime and corruption are key barriers to economic development. The administration wants to reduce the poverty rate to 17% and graduate the economy to upper-middle income status by the end of President DUTERTE's term in 2022. Key themes under the government's Ten-Point Socioeconomic Agenda include continuity of macroeconomic policy, tax reform, higher investments in infrastructure and human capital development, and improving competitiveness and the overall ease of doing business. The administration sees infrastructure shortcomings as a key barrier to sustained economic growth and has pledged to spend $165 billion on infrastructure by 2022. Although the final outcome has yet to be seen, the current administration is shepherding legislation for a comprehensive tax reform program to raise revenues for its ambitious infrastructure spending plan and to promote a more equitable and efficient tax system. However, the need to finance rehabilitation and reconstruction efforts in the southern region of Mindanao following the 2017 Marawi City siege may compete with other spending on infrastructure.

GDP (PURCHASING POWER PARITY):

$877.2 billion (2017 est.)

$822.2 billion (2016 est.)

$769.3 billion (2015 est.)

note: data are in 2017 dollars

country comparison to the world: 29

GDP (OFFICIAL EXCHANGE RATE):

$313.6 billion (2017 est.)

GDP - REAL GROWTH RATE:

6.7% (2017 est.)

6.9% (2016 est.)

6.1% (2015 est.)

country comparison to the world: 29

GDP - PER CAPITA (PPP):

$8,400 (2017 est.)

$8,000 (2016 est.)

$7,600 (2015 est.)

note: data are in 2017 dollars

country comparison to the world: 148

GROSS NATIONAL SAVING:

24.3% of GDP (2017 est.)

24% of GDP (2016 est.)

23.7% of GDP (2015 est.)

country comparison to the world: 67

GDP - COMPOSITION, BY END USE:

household consumption: 73.5% (2017 est.)

government consumption: 11.3% (2017 est.)

investment in fixed capital: 25.1% (2017 est.)

investment in inventories: 0.1% (2017 est.)

exports of goods and services: 31% (2017 est.)

imports of goods and services: -40.9% (2017 est.)

GDP - COMPOSITION, BY SECTOR OF ORIGIN:

agriculture: 9.6% (2017 est.)

industry: 30.6% (2017 est.)

services: 59.8% (2017 est.)

AGRICULTURE - PRODUCTS:

rice, fish, livestock, poultry, bananas, coconut/copra, corn, sugarcane, mangoes, pineapple, cassava

INDUSTRIES:

semiconductors and electronics assembly, business process outsourcing, food and beverage manufacturing, construction, electric/gas/water supply, chemical products, radio/television/communications equipment and apparatus, petroleum and fuel, textile and garments, non-metallic minerals, basic metal industries, transport equipment

INDUSTRIAL PRODUCTION GROWTH RATE:

7.2% (2017 est.)

country comparison to the world: 30

LABOR FORCE:

42.78 million (2017 est.)

country comparison to the world: 15

LABOR FORCE - BY OCCUPATION:

agriculture: 25.4%

industry: 18.3%

services: 56.3% (2017 est.)

UNEMPLOYMENT RATE:

5.7% (2017 est.)

5.5% (2016 est.)

country comparison to the world: 86

POPULATION BELOW POVERTY LINE:

21.6% (2017 est.)

HOUSEHOLD INCOME OR CONSUMPTION BY PERCENTAGE SHARE:

lowest 10%: 3.2%

highest 10%: 29.5% (2015 est.)

DISTRIBUTION OF FAMILY INCOME - GINI INDEX:

44.4 (2015 est.)

46 (2012 est.)

country comparison to the world: 45

BUDGET:

revenues: 49.07 billion (2017 est.)

expenditures: 56.02 billion (2017 est.)

TAXES AND OTHER REVENUES:

15.6% (of GDP) (2017 est.)

country comparison to the world: 188

BUDGET SURPLUS (+) OR DEFICIT (-):

-2.2% (of GDP) (2017 est.)

country comparison to the world: 109

PUBLIC DEBT:

39.9% of GDP (2017 est.)

39% of GDP (2016 est.)

country comparison to the world: 128

FISCAL YEAR:

calendar year

INFLATION RATE (CONSUMER PRICES):

2.9% (2017 est.)

1.3% (2016 est.)

country comparison to the world: 131

CENTRAL BANK DISCOUNT RATE:

3.56% (31 December 2017)

3.56% (31 December 2016)

country comparison to the world: 101

COMMERCIAL BANK PRIME LENDING RATE:

5.63% (31 December 2017 est.)

5.64% (31 December 2016 est.)

country comparison to the world: 130

STOCK OF NARROW MONEY:

$71.13 billion (31 December 2017 est.)

$61.62 billion (31 December 2016 est.)

country comparison to the world: 47

STOCK OF BROAD MONEY:

$71.13 billion (31 December 2017 est.)

$61.62 billion (31 December 2016 est.)

country comparison to the world: 47

STOCK OF DOMESTIC CREDIT:

$209.8 billion (31 December 2017 est.)

$184.6 billion (31 December 2016 est.)

country comparison to the world: 45

MARKET VALUE OF PUBLICLY TRADED SHARES:

$352.2 billion (31 December 2017 est.)

$290.4 billion (31 December 2017 est.)

$286.1 billion (31 December 2015 est.)

country comparison to the world: 29

CURRENT ACCOUNT BALANCE:

-$2.518 billion (2017 est.)

-$1.199 billion (2016 est.)

country comparison to the world: 173

EXPORTS:

$48.2 billion (2017 est.)

$57.41 billion (2016 est.)

country comparison to the world: 52

EXPORTS - PARTNERS:

Japan 16.4%, US 14.6%, Hong Kong 13.7%, China 11%, Singapore 6.1%, Thailand 4.3%, Germany 4.1%, South Korea 4% (2017)

EXPORTS - COMMODITIES:

semiconductors and electronic products, machinery and transport equipment, wood manufactures, chemicals, processed food and beverages, garments, coconut oil, copper concentrates, seafood, bananas/fruits

IMPORTS:

$89.39 billion (2017 est.)

$78.28 billion (2016 est.)

country comparison to the world: 39

IMPORTS - COMMODITIES:

electronic products, mineral fuels, machinery and transport equipment, iron and steel, textile fabrics, grains, chemicals, plastic

IMPORTS - PARTNERS:

China 18.1%, Japan 11.4%, South Korea 8.8%, US 7.4%, Thailand 7.1%, Indonesia 6.7%, Singapore 5.9% (2017)

RESERVES OF FOREIGN EXCHANGE AND GOLD:

$81.57 billion (31 December 2017 est.)

$80.69 billion (31 December 2016 est.)

country comparison to the world: 29

DEBT - EXTERNAL:

$76.18 billion (31 December 2017 est.)

$74.76 billion (31 December 2016 est.)

country comparison to the world: 57

STOCK OF DIRECT FOREIGN INVESTMENT - AT HOME:

$78.79 billion (31 December 2017 est.)

$64.51 billion (31 December 2016 est.)

country comparison to the world: 50

STOCK OF DIRECT FOREIGN INVESTMENT - ABROAD:

$47.82 billion (31 December 2017 est.)

$43.89 billion (31 December 2016 est.)

country comparison to the world: 44

EXCHANGE RATES:

Philippine pesos (PHP) per US dollar -

50.4 (2017 est.)

47.493 (2016 est.)

47.493 (2015 est.)

45.503 (2014 est.)

44.395 (2013 est.)

ENERGY :: PHILIPPINES

ELECTRICITY ACCESS:

population without electricity: 12 million (2017)

electrification - total population: 88% (2017)

electrification - urban areas: 98% (2017)

electrification - rural areas: 80% (2017)

ELECTRICITY - PRODUCTION:

86.59 billion kWh (2016 est.)

country comparison to the world: 36

ELECTRICITY - CONSUMPTION:

78.3 billion kWh (2016 est.)

country comparison to the world: 37

ELECTRICITY - EXPORTS:

0 kWh (2017 est.)

country comparison to the world: 184

ELECTRICITY - IMPORTS:

0 kWh (2016 est.)

country comparison to the world: 186

ELECTRICITY - INSTALLED GENERATING CAPACITY:

22.13 million kW (2016 est.)

country comparison to the world: 39

ELECTRICITY - FROM FOSSIL FUELS:

67% of total installed capacity (2016 est.)

country comparison to the world: 116

ELECTRICITY - FROM NUCLEAR FUELS:

0% of total installed capacity (2017 est.)

country comparison to the world: 165

ELECTRICITY - FROM HYDROELECTRIC PLANTS:

17% of total installed capacity (2017 est.)

country comparison to the world: 97

ELECTRICITY - FROM OTHER RENEWABLE SOURCES:

16% of total installed capacity (2017 est.)

country comparison to the world: 54

CRUDE OIL - PRODUCTION:

13,000 bbl/day (2018 est.)

country comparison to the world: 76

CRUDE OIL - EXPORTS:

16,450 bbl/day (2015 est.)

country comparison to the world: 52

CRUDE OIL - IMPORTS:

211,400 bbl/day (2015 est.)

country comparison to the world: 30

CRUDE OIL - PROVED RESERVES:

138.5 million bbl (1 January 2018 est.)

country comparison to the world: 64

REFINED PETROLEUM PRODUCTS - PRODUCTION:

215,500 bbl/day (2015 est.)

country comparison to the world: 50

REFINED PETROLEUM PRODUCTS - CONSUMPTION:

424,000 bbl/day (2016 est.)

country comparison to the world: 36

REFINED PETROLEUM PRODUCTS - EXPORTS:

26,710 bbl/day (2015 est.)

REFINED PETROLEUM PRODUCTS - IMPORTS:

211,400 bbl/day (2015 est.)

country comparison to the world: 33

NATURAL GAS - PRODUCTION:

3.058 billion cu m (2017 est.)

country comparison to the world: 58

NATURAL GAS - CONSUMPTION:

3.143 billion cu m (2017 est.)

country comparison to the world: 72

NATURAL GAS - EXPORTS:

0 cu m (2017 est.)

country comparison to the world: 168

NATURAL GAS - IMPORTS:

0 cu m (2017 est.)

country comparison to the world: 175

NATURAL GAS - PROVED RESERVES:

98.54 billion cu m (1 January 2018 est.)

country comparison to the world: 51

CARBON DIOXIDE EMISSIONS FROM CONSUMPTION OF ENERGY:

117.2 million Mt (2017 est.)

country comparison to the world: 38

COMMUNICATIONS :: PHILIPPINES

TELEPHONES - FIXED LINES:

total subscriptions: 4,163,282

subscriptions per 100 inhabitants: 4 (2017 est.)

country comparison to the world: 34

TELEPHONES - MOBILE CELLULAR:

total subscriptions: 115,824,982

subscriptions per 100 inhabitants: 111 (2017 est.)

country comparison to the world: 13

TELEPHONE SYSTEM:

general assessment: good international radiotelephone and submarine cable services; domestic and interisland service adequate; National Broadband Plan to improve connectivity in rural areas underway; 4G available now in some areas with 5G pilots planned to commence in 2019-2020 (2018)

domestic: telecommunications infrastructure includes the following platforms: fixed line, mobile cellular, cable TV, over-the-air TV, radio and Very Small Aperture Terminal (VSAT), fiber-optic cable, and satellite for redundant international connectivity; fixed-line 4 per 100 and mobile-cellular 111 per 100 (2018)

international: country code - 63; landing points for the NDTN, TGN-IA, AAG, PLCN, EAC-02C, DFON, SJC, APCN-2, SeaMeWe, Boracay-Palawan Submarine Cable System, Palawa-Illoilo Cable System, NDTN, SEA-US, SSSFOIP, ASE and JUPITAR submarine cables that together provide connectivity to the US, Southeast Asia, Asia, Europe, Africa, the Middle East, and Australia (2019)

BROADCAST MEDIA:

multiple national private TV and radio networks; multi-channel satellite and cable TV systems available; more than 400 TV stations; about 1,500 cable TV providers with more than 2 million subscribers, and some 1,400 radio stations; the Philippines adopted Japan's Integrated Service Digital Broadcast – Terrestrial standard for digital terrestrial television in November 2013 and is scheduled to complete the switch from analog to digital broadcasting by the end of 2023 (2019)

INTERNET COUNTRY CODE:

.ph

INTERNET USERS:

total: 56,956,436

percent of population: 55.5% (July 2016 est.)

country comparison to the world: 12

BROADBAND - FIXED SUBSCRIPTIONS:

total: 3,399,291

subscriptions per 100 inhabitants: 3 (2017 est.)

country comparison to the world: 35

MILITARY AND SECURITY :: PHILIPPINES

MILITARY EXPENDITURES:

1.13% of GDP (2018)

1.2% of GDP (2017)

1.43% of GDP (2016)

1.14% of GDP (2015)

1.09% of GDP (2014)

country comparison to the world: 110

MILITARY AND SECURITY FORCES:

Armed Forces of the Philippines (AFP): Army, Navy (includes Marine Corps), Air Force (2019)

the Philippine Coast Guard is an armed and uniformed service under the Department of Transportation; it would be attached to the AFP in wartime; the Philippine National Police Force (PNP) falls under the Ministry of Interior and Local Government

MILITARY SERVICE AGE AND OBLIGATION:

18-23 years of age (officers 21-29) for voluntary military service; no conscription (2019)

MARITIME THREATS:

the International Maritime Bureau reports the territorial and offshore waters in the South China Sea as high risk for piracy and armed robbery against ships; during 2018, 10 attacks were reported in and around the Philippines including six ships that were boarded, one fired upon, and three crewman kidnapped for ransom; an emerging threat area lies in the Celebes and Sulu Seas between the Philippines and Malaysia where it is believed the pirates involved are associated with the Abu Sayyaf Group (ASG) terrorist organization; numerous commercial vessels have been attacked and hijacked both at anchor and while underway; hijacked vessels are often disguised and cargo diverted to ports in East Asia; crews have been murdered or cast adrift; the Maritime Administration (MARAD) of the US Department of Transportation has issued a Maritime Advisory (2019-011-Sulu and Celebes Seas-Piracy/Armed Robbery/Terrorism) which states in part "In 2018, there were at least 12 reported boardings, attempted boardings, attacks, hijackings, and kidnappings in the Sulu and Celebes Seas. Recent kidnapping incidents in this area were reportedly linked to the Abu Sayyaf Group (ASG), a violent Islamic separatist group operating in the southern Philippines..." and advises ships to adhere to counter-piracy practices to minimize risk

TRANSPORTATION :: PHILIPPINES

NATIONAL AIR TRANSPORT SYSTEM:

number of registered air carriers: 11 (2015)

inventory of registered aircraft operated by air carriers: 158 (2015) annual passenger traffic on registered air carriers: 32,230,986 (2015)

annual freight traffic on registered air carriers: 484,190,968 mt-km (2015)

CIVIL AIRCRAFT REGISTRATION COUNTRY CODE PREFIX:

RP (2016)

AIRPORTS:

247 (2013)

country comparison to the world: 24

AIRPORTS - WITH PAVED RUNWAYS:

total: 89 (2017)

over 3,047 m: 4 (2017)

2,438 to 3,047 m: 8 (2017)

1,524 to 2,437 m: 33 (2017)

914 to 1,523 m: 34 (2017)

under 914 m: 10 (2017)

AIRPORTS - WITH UNPAVED RUNWAYS:

total: 158 (2013)

1,524 to 2,437 m: 3 (2013)

914 to 1,523 m: 56 (2013)

under 914 m: 99 (2013)

HELIPORTS:

2 (2013)

PIPELINES:

530 km gas, 138 km oil (non-operational), 185 km refined products (2017)

RAILWAYS:

total: 77 km (2017)

standard gauge: 49 km 1.435-m gauge (2017)

narrow gauge: 28 km 1.067-m gauge (2017)

country comparison to the world: 129

ROADWAYS:

total: 216,387 km (2014)

paved: 61,093 km (2014)

unpaved: 155,294 km (2014)

country comparison to the world: 25

WATERWAYS:

3,219 km (limited to vessels with draft less than 1.5 m) (2011)

country comparison to the world: 30

MERCHANT MARINE:

total: 1,615

by type: bulk carrier 58, container ship 43, general cargo 654, oil tanker 191, other 669 (2018)

country comparison to the world: 16

PORTS AND TERMINALS:

major seaport(s): Batangas, Cagayan de Oro, Cebu, Davao, Liman, Manila

container port(s) (TEUs): Manila (4,782,240) (2017)

TERRORISM :: PHILIPPINES

TERRORIST GROUPS - HOME BASED:

Abu Sayyaf Group (ASG): aim(s): establish an Islamic State in the Philippines' Mindanao Island and the Sulu Archipelago, and ultimately, an Islamic caliphate across Southeast Asia
area(s) of operation: southern Philippines in Mindanao and the Sulu Archipelago region (2018)

Communist Party of the Philippines/New People's Army (CPP/NPA): aim(s): destabilize the Philippines' economy to inspire the populace to revolt against the government and, ultimately, overthrow the Philippine Government
area(s) of operation: operates throughout most of the country, primarily in rural regions, with its strongest presence in the Sierra Madre Mountains, rural Luzon, Visayas, and parts of northern and eastern Mindanao; maintains cells in Manila, Davao City, and other metropolitan areas (2018)

Islamic State of Iraq and ash-Sham (ISIS) network in Philippines: aim(s): replace the Philippine Government with an Islamic state and implement ISIS's strict interpretation of sharia
area(s) of operation: Mindanao and the Sulu Archipelago region (2018)

TERRORIST GROUPS - FOREIGN BASED:

Jemaah Islamiyah (JI): aim(s): enhance its networks in the Philippines and, ultimately, overthrow the Philippine Government and establish a pan-Islamic state across Southeast Asia
area(s) of operation: maintains an operational and recruitment presence, especially in the south (2018)

TRANSNATIONAL ISSUES :: PHILIPPINES

DISPUTES - INTERNATIONAL:

Philippines claims sovereignty over Scarborough Reef (also claimed by China together with Taiwan) and over certain of the Spratly Islands, known locally as the Kalayaan (Freedom) Islands, also claimed by China, Malaysia, Taiwan, and Vietnam; the 2002 "Declaration on the Conduct of Parties in the South China Sea," has eased tensions in the Spratly Islands but falls short of a legally binding "code of conduct" desired by several of the disputants; in March 2005, the national oil companies of China, the Philippines, and Vietnam signed a joint accord to conduct marine seismic activities in the Spratly Islands; Philippines retains a dormant claim to Malaysia's Sabah State in northern Borneo based on the Sultanate of Sulu's granting the Philippines Government power of attorney to pursue a sovereignty claim on his behalf; maritime delimitation negotiations continue with Palau

REFUGEES AND INTERNALLY DISPLACED PERSONS:

IDPs: 301,000 (government troops fighting the Moro Islamic Liberation Front, the Abu Sayyaf Group, and the New People's Army; clan feuds; natural disasters) (2018)

stateless persons: 1,068 (2018); note - stateless persons are descendants of Indonesian migrants

ILLICIT DRUGS:

domestic methamphetamine production has been a growing problem in recent years despite government crackdowns; major consumer of amphetamines; longstanding marijuana producer mainly in rural areas where Manila's control is limited

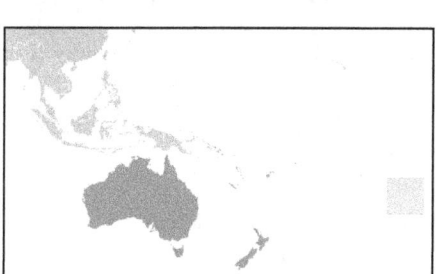

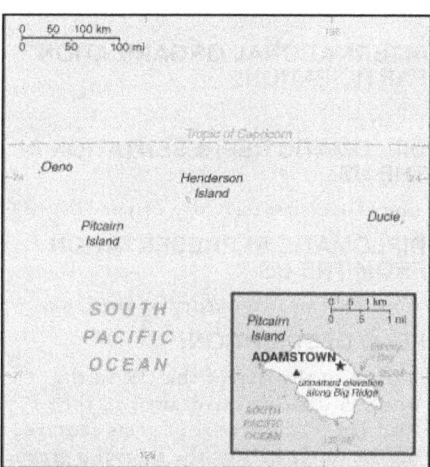

AUSTRALIA - OCEANIA :: PITCAIRN ISLANDS

INTRODUCTION :: PITCAIRN ISLANDS

BACKGROUND:

Pitcairn Island was discovered in 1767 by the British and settled in 1790 by the Bounty mutineers and their Tahitian companions. Pitcairn was the first Pacific island to become a British colony (in 1838) and today remains the last vestige of that empire in the South Pacific. Outmigration, primarily to New Zealand, has thinned the population from a peak of 233 in 1937 to less than 50 today.

GEOGRAPHY :: PITCAIRN ISLANDS

LOCATION:

Oceania, islands in the South Pacific Ocean, about midway between Peru and New Zealand

GEOGRAPHIC COORDINATES:

25 04 S, 130 06 W

MAP REFERENCES:

Oceania

AREA:

total: 47 sq km

land: 47 sq km

water: 0 sq km

country comparison to the world: 234

AREA - COMPARATIVE:

about three-tenths the size of Washington, DC

LAND BOUNDARIES:

0 km

COASTLINE:

51 km

MARITIME CLAIMS:

territorial sea: 12 nm

exclusive economic zone: 200 nm

CLIMATE:

tropical; hot and humid; modified by southeast trade winds; rainy season (November to March)

TERRAIN:

rugged volcanic formation; rocky coastline with cliffs

ELEVATION:

lowest point: Pacific Ocean 0 m

highest point: Palwala Valley Point on Big Ridge 347 m

NATURAL RESOURCES:

miro trees (used for handicrafts), fish, note, manganese, iron, copper, gold, silver, and zinc have been discovered offshore

LAND USE:

agricultural land: 0% (2011 est.)

arable land: 0% (2011 est.) / permanent crops: 0% (2011 est.) / permanent pasture: 0% (2011 est.)

forest: 74.5% (2011 est.)

other: 25.5% (2011 est.)

IRRIGATED LAND:

0 sq km (2012)

POPULATION DISTRIBUTION:

less than 50 inhabitants on Pitcairn Island, most reside near the village of Adamstown

NATURAL HAZARDS:

occasional tropical cyclones (especially November to March), but generally only heavy tropical storms; landslides

ENVIRONMENT - CURRENT ISSUES:

deforestation (only a small portion of the original forest remains because of burning and clearing for settlement)

GEOGRAPHY - NOTE:

Britain's most isolated dependency; only the larger island of Pitcairn is inhabited but it has no port or natural harbor; supplies must be transported by rowed longboat from larger ships stationed offshore

PEOPLE AND SOCIETY :: PITCAIRN ISLANDS

POPULATION:

54 (July 2016 est.)

country comparison to the world: 238

NATIONALITY:

noun: Pitcairn Islander(s)

adjective: Pitcairn Islander

ETHNIC GROUPS:

other descendants of the Bounty mutineers and their Tahitian wives

LANGUAGES:

English (official), Pitkern (mixture of an 18th century English dialect and a Tahitian dialect)

RELIGIONS:

Seventh-Day Adventist 100%

POPULATION GROWTH RATE:

0% (2014 est.)

country comparison to the world: 194

POPULATION DISTRIBUTION:

less than 50 inhabitants on Pitcairn Island, most reside near the village of Adamstown

URBANIZATION:

urban population: 0% of total population (2012)

rate of urbanization: NA

SEX RATIO:

NA

INFANT MORTALITY RATE:

total: NA (2018)

male: NA

female: NA

LIFE EXPECTANCY AT BIRTH:

total population: NA (2017 est.)

male: NA

female: NA

TOTAL FERTILITY RATE:

NA

HIV/AIDS - ADULT PREVALENCE RATE:

NA

HIV/AIDS - PEOPLE LIVING WITH HIV/AIDS:

NA

HIV/AIDS - DEATHS:

NA

GOVERNMENT :: PITCAIRN ISLANDS

COUNTRY NAME:

conventional long form: Pitcairn, Henderson, Ducie, and Oeno Islands

conventional short form: Pitcairn Islands

etymology: named after Midshipman Robert PITCAIRN who first sighted the island in 1767

DEPENDENCY STATUS:

overseas territory of the UK

GOVERNMENT TYPE:

parliamentary democracy

CAPITAL:

name: Adamstown

geographic coordinates: 25 04 S, 130 05 W

time difference: UTC-9 (4 hours behind Washington, DC, during Standard Time)

etymology: named after John Adams (1767-1829), the last survivor of the Bounty mutineers who settled on Pitcairn Island in January 1790

ADMINISTRATIVE DIVISIONS:

none (overseas territory of the UK)

INDEPENDENCE:

none (overseas territory of the UK)

NATIONAL HOLIDAY:

Birthday of Queen ELIZABETH II, second Saturday in June (1926); Discovery Day (Pitcairn Day), 2 July (1767)

CONSTITUTION:

history: several previous; latest drafted 10 February 2010, presented 17 February 2010, effective 4 March 2010

LEGAL SYSTEM:

local island by-laws

CITIZENSHIP:

see United Kingdom

SUFFRAGE:

18 years of age; universal with three years residency

EXECUTIVE BRANCH:

chief of state: Queen ELIZABETH II (since 6 February 1952); represented by UK High Commissioner to New Zealand and Governor (nonresident) of the Pitcairn Islands Laura CLARK (since 25 January 2018)

head of government: Mayor and Chairman of the Island Council Shawn CHRISTIAN (since 9 November 2016)

cabinet: none

elections/appointments: the monarchy is hereditary; governor and commissioner appointed by the monarch; island mayor directly elected by majority popular vote for a 3-year term; election last held on 9 November 2016 (next to be held not later than December 2019)

election results: Shawn CHRISTIAN reelected mayor and chairman of the Island Council; Island Council vote - NA

LEGISLATIVE BRANCH:

description: unicameral Island Council (10 seats; 4 members directly elected by proportional representation vote, 1 nominated by the elected Council members, 2 appointed by the governor, and 3 ex-officio members - the governor, deputy governor, and commissioner; elected members serve 1-year terms)

elections: last held in November 2017 (next to be held not later than December 2019)

election results: percent of vote - NA; seats - 5 independent; composition - men 5, women 5, percent of women 50%

JUDICIAL BRANCH:

highest courts: Pitcairn Court of Appeal (consists of the court president, 2 judges, and the Supreme Court chief justice, an ex-officio member); Pitcairn Supreme Court (consists of the chief justice and 2 judges); note - appeals beyond the Pitcairn Court of Appeal are referred to the Judicial Committee of the Privy Council (in London)

judge selection and term of office: all judges of both courts appointed by the governor of the Pitcairn Islands on the instructions of the Queen of England through the Secretary of State; all judges can serve until retirement, normally at age 75

subordinate courts: Magistrate's Court

POLITICAL PARTIES AND LEADERS:

none

INTERNATIONAL ORGANIZATION PARTICIPATION:

SPC, UPU

DIPLOMATIC REPRESENTATION IN THE US:

none (overseas territory of the UK)

DIPLOMATIC REPRESENTATION FROM THE US:

none (overseas territory of the UK)

FLAG DESCRIPTION:

blue with the flag of the UK in the upper hoist-side quadrant and the Pitcairn Islander coat of arms centered on the outer half of the flag; the green, yellow, and blue of the shield represents the island rising from the ocean; the green field features a yellow anchor surmounted by a bible (both the anchor and the bible were items found on the HMS Bounty); sitting on the crest is a Pitcairn Island wheelbarrow from which springs a flowering twig of miro (a local plant)

NATIONAL ANTHEM:

name: We From Pitcairn Island

lyrics/music: unknown/Frederick M. LEHMAN

note: serves as a local anthem; as a territory of the UK, "God Save the Queen" is official (see United Kingdom)

ECONOMY :: PITCAIRN ISLANDS

ECONOMY - OVERVIEW:

The inhabitants of this tiny isolated economy exist on fishing, subsistence farming, handicrafts, and postage stamps. The fertile soil of the valleys produces a wide variety of fruits and vegetables, including citrus, sugarcane, watermelons, bananas, yams, and beans. Bartering is an important part of the economy. The major sources of revenue are the sale of postage stamps to collectors and the sale of handicrafts to passing ships.

GDP (PURCHASING POWER PARITY):

NA

AGRICULTURE - PRODUCTS:

honey; wide variety of fruits and vegetables; goats, chickens; fish

INDUSTRIES:

postage stamps, handicrafts, beekeeping, honey

LABOR FORCE:

15 (2004)

country comparison to the world: 232

LABOR FORCE - BY OCCUPATION:

note: no business community in the usual sense; some public works; subsistence farming and fishing

BUDGET:

revenues: 746,000 (FY04/05)

expenditures: 1.028 million (FY04/05)

FISCAL YEAR:

1 April - 31 March

EXPORTS:

NA

EXPORTS - COMMODITIES:

honey, fruits, vegetables, curios, postage stamps

IMPORTS:

NA

IMPORTS - COMMODITIES:

fuel oil, machinery, building materials, flour, sugar, other foodstuffs

STOCK OF DIRECT FOREIGN INVESTMENT - AT HOME:

(31 December 2009 est.)

EXCHANGE RATES:

New Zealand dollars (NZD) per US dollar -

1.416 (2017 est.)

1.4279 (2016 est.)

1.4279 (2015)

1.4279 (2014 est.)

1.2039 (2013 est.)

COMMUNICATIONS :: PITCAIRN ISLANDS

TELEPHONE SYSTEM:

general assessment: satellite-based phone services; rural connectivity a challenge (2018)

domestic: local phone service with international connections via Internet (2018)

international: country code - 872; satellite earth station - 1 (Inmarsat)

BROADCAST MEDIA:

satellite TV from Fiji-based Sky Pacific offering a wide range of international channels

INTERNET COUNTRY CODE:

.pn

INTERNET USERS:

total: 54

percent of population: 100% (July 2016 est.)

country comparison to the world: 226

BROADBAND - FIXED SUBSCRIPTIONS:

COMMUNICATIONS - NOTE:

satellite-based local phone service and broadband Internet connections available in all homes

MILITARY AND SECURITY :: PITCAIRN ISLANDS

MILITARY - NOTE:

defense is the responsibility of the UK

TRANSPORTATION :: PITCAIRN ISLANDS

ROADWAYS:

total: 0 km

country comparison to the world: 215

PORTS AND TERMINALS:

major seaport(s): Adamstown (on Bounty Bay)

TRANSNATIONAL ISSUES :: PITCAIRN ISLANDS

DISPUTES - INTERNATIONAL:

none

EUROPE :: POLAND

INTRODUCTION :: POLAND

BACKGROUND:

Poland's history as a state began near the middle of the 10th century. By the mid-16th century, the Polish-Lithuanian Commonwealth ruled a vast tract of land in Central and Eastern Europe. During the 18th century, internal disorders weakened the nation, and in a series of agreements between 1772 and 1795, Russia, Prussia, and Austria partitioned Poland among themselves. Poland regained its independence in 1918 only to be overrun by Germany and the Soviet Union in World War II. It became a Soviet satellite state following the war. Labor turmoil in 1980 led to the formation of the independent trade union "Solidarity" that over time became a political force with over 10 million members. Free elections in 1989 and 1990 won Solidarity control of the parliament and the presidency, bringing the communist era to a close. A "shock therapy" program during the early 1990s enabled the country to transform its economy into one of the most robust in Central Europe. Poland joined NATO in 1999 and the EU in 2004. With its transformation to a democratic, market-oriented country largely completed and with large investments in defense, energy, and other infrastructure, Poland is an increasingly active member of Euro-Atlantic organizations.

GEOGRAPHY :: POLAND

LOCATION:
Central Europe, east of Germany

GEOGRAPHIC COORDINATES:
52 00 N, 20 00 E

MAP REFERENCES:
Europe

AREA:
total: 312,685 sq km

land: 304,255 sq km

water: 8,430 sq km

country comparison to the world: 71

AREA - COMPARATIVE:
about twice the size of Georgia; slightly smaller than New Mexico

LAND BOUNDARIES:
total: 3,071 km

border countries (7): Belarus 418 km, Czech Republic 796 km, Germany 467 km, Lithuania 104 km, Russia (Kaliningrad Oblast) 210 km, Slovakia 541 km, Ukraine 535 km

COASTLINE:
440 km

MARITIME CLAIMS:
territorial sea: 12 nm

exclusive economic zone: defined by international treaties

CLIMATE:
temperate with cold, cloudy, moderately severe winters with frequent precipitation; mild summers with frequent showers and thundershowers

TERRAIN:
mostly flat plain; mountains along southern border

ELEVATION:
mean elevation: 173 m

lowest point: near Raczki Elblaskie -2 m

highest point: Rysy 2,499 m

NATURAL RESOURCES:
coal, sulfur, copper, natural gas, silver, lead, salt, amber, arable land

LAND USE:
agricultural land: 48.2% (2011 est.)

arable land: 36.2% (2011 est.) / permanent crops: 1.3% (2011 est.) / permanent pasture: 10.7% (2011 est.)

forest: 30.6% (2011 est.)

other: 21.2% (2011 est.)

IRRIGATED LAND:
970 sq km (2012)

POPULATION DISTRIBUTION:
population concentrated in the southern area around Krakow and the central area around Warsaw and Lodz, with an extension to the northern coastal city of Gdansk

NATURAL HAZARDS:
flooding

ENVIRONMENT - CURRENT ISSUES:
decreased emphasis on heavy industry and increased environmental concern by post-communist governments has improved environment; air pollution remains serious because of emissions from burning low-quality coals in homes and from coal-fired power plants; the resulting acid rain causes forest damage; water pollution from industrial and municipal sources is a problem, as is disposal of hazardous wastes

ENVIRONMENT - INTERNATIONAL AGREEMENTS:
party to: Air Pollution, Antarctic-Environmental Protocol, Antarctic-Marine Living Resources, Antarctic

Seals, Antarctic Treaty, Biodiversity, Climate Change, Climate Change-Kyoto Protocol, Desertification, Endangered Species, Environmental Modification, Hazardous Wastes, Law of the Sea, Marine Dumping, Ozone Layer Protection, Ship Pollution, Wetlands

signed, but not ratified: Air Pollution-Nitrogen Oxides, Air Pollution-Persistent Organic Pollutants, Air Pollution-Sulfur 94

GEOGRAPHY - NOTE:
historically, an area of conflict because of flat terrain and the lack of natural barriers on the North European Plain

PEOPLE AND SOCIETY :: POLAND

POPULATION:
38,420,687 (July 2018 est.)

country comparison to the world: 37

NATIONALITY:
noun: Pole(s)

adjective: Polish

ETHNIC GROUPS:
Polish 96.9%, Silesian 1.1%, German 0.2%, Ukrainian 0.1%, other and unspecified 1.7% (2011 est.)

note: represents ethnicity declared first

LANGUAGES:
Polish (official) 98.2%, Silesian 1.4%, other 1.1%, unspecified 1.3% (2011 est.)

note: data represents the language spoken at home; shares sum to more than 100% because some respondents gave more than one answer on the census; Poland ratified the European Charter for Regional or Minority Languages in 2009 recognizing Kashub as a regional language, Czech, Hebrew, Yiddish, Belarusian, Lithuanian, German, Armenian, Russian, Slovak, and Ukrainian as national minority languages, and Karaim, Lemko, Romani (Polska Roma and Bergitka Roma), and Tatar as ethnic minority languages

RELIGIONS:
Catholic 85.9% (includes Roman Catholic 85.6% and Greek Catholic, Armenian Catholic, and Byzantine-Slavic Catholic .3%), Orthodox 1.3% (almost all are Polish Autocephalous Orthodox), Protestant 0.4% (mainly Augsburg Evangelical and Pentacostal), other 0.4% (includes Jehovah's Witness, Buddhist, Hare Krishna, Gaudiya Vaishnavism, Muslim, Jewish, Mormon), unspecified 12.1% (2017 est.)

AGE STRUCTURE:
0-14 years: 14.8% (male 2,924,077 /female 2,762,634)

15-24 years: 10.34% (male 2,040,043 /female 1,932,009)

25-54 years: 43.44% (male 8,431,045 /female 8,260,124)

55-64 years: 13.95% (male 2,538,566 /female 2,819,544)

65 years and over: 17.47% (male 2,663,364 /female 4,049,281) (2018 est.)

DEPENDENCY RATIOS:
total dependency ratio: 43.9 (2015 est.)

youth dependency ratio: 21.4 (2015 est.)

elderly dependency ratio: 22.5 (2015 est.)

potential support ratio: 4.5 (2015 est.)

MEDIAN AGE:
total: 41.1 years (2018 est.)

male: 39.4 years

female: 42.8 years

country comparison to the world: 44

POPULATION GROWTH RATE:
-0.16% (2018 est.)

country comparison to the world: 206

BIRTH RATE:
9.3 births/1,000 population (2018 est.)

country comparison to the world: 202

DEATH RATE:
10.5 deaths/1,000 population (2018 est.)

country comparison to the world: 29

NET MIGRATION RATE:
-0.4 migrant(s)/1,000 population (2018 est.)

country comparison to the world: 124

POPULATION DISTRIBUTION:
population concentrated in the southern area around Krakow and the central area around Warsaw and Lodz, with an extension to the northern coastal city of Gdansk

URBANIZATION:
urban population: 60% of total population (2019)

rate of urbanization: -0.25% annual rate of change (2015-20 est.)

MAJOR URBAN AREAS - POPULATION:
1.776 million WARSAW (capital), 768,000 Krakow (2019)

SEX RATIO:
at birth: 1.06 male(s)/female

0-14 years: 1.06 male(s)/female

15-24 years: 1.06 male(s)/female

25-54 years: 1.02 male(s)/female

55-64 years: 0.9 male(s)/female

65 years and over: 0.66 male(s)/female

total population: 0.94 male(s)/female (2018 est.)

MOTHER'S MEAN AGE AT FIRST BIRTH:
27.4 years (2014 est.)

MATERNAL MORTALITY RATE:
2 deaths/100,000 live births (2017 est.)

country comparison to the world: 184

INFANT MORTALITY RATE:
total: 4.4 deaths/1,000 live births (2018 est.)

male: 4.7 deaths/1,000 live births

female: 3.9 deaths/1,000 live births

country comparison to the world: 184

LIFE EXPECTANCY AT BIRTH:
total population: 77.9 years (2018 est.)

male: 74.1 years

female: 82 years

country comparison to the world: 67

TOTAL FERTILITY RATE:
1.36 children born/woman (2018 est.)

country comparison to the world: 214

CONTRACEPTIVE PREVALENCE RATE:
62.3% (2014)

DRINKING WATER SOURCE:
improved:

urban: 99.3% of population

rural: 96.9% of population

total: 98.3% of population

unimproved:

urban: 0.7% of population

rural: 3.1% of population

total: 1.7% of population (2015 est.)

CURRENT HEALTH EXPENDITURE:

6.5% (2016)

PHYSICIANS DENSITY:

2.4 physicians/1,000 population (2016)

HOSPITAL BED DENSITY:

6.5 beds/1,000 population (2013)

SANITATION FACILITY ACCESS:

improved:

urban: 97.5% of population (2015 est.)

rural: 96.7% of population (2015 est.)

total: 97.2% of population (2015 est.)

unimproved:

urban: 2.5% of population (2015 est.)

rural: 3.3% of population (2015 est.)

total: 2.8% of population (2015 est.)

HIV/AIDS - ADULT PREVALENCE RATE:

NA

HIV/AIDS - PEOPLE LIVING WITH HIV/AIDS:

NA

HIV/AIDS - DEATHS:

NA

MAJOR INFECTIOUS DISEASES:

degree of risk: intermediate (2016)

vectorborne diseases: tickborne encephalitis (2016)

OBESITY - ADULT PREVALENCE RATE:

23.1% (2016)

country comparison to the world: 69

EDUCATION EXPENDITURES:

4.8% of GDP (2015)

country comparison to the world: 76

LITERACY:

definition: age 15 and over can read and write

total population: 99.8%

male: 99.9%

female: 99.7% (2015 est.)

SCHOOL LIFE EXPECTANCY (PRIMARY TO TERTIARY EDUCATION):

total: 16 years

male: 16 years

female: 17 years (2016)

UNEMPLOYMENT, YOUTH AGES 15-24:

total: 14.8%

male: 14.6%

female: 15.1% (2017 est.)

country comparison to the world: 94

GOVERNMENT :: POLAND

COUNTRY NAME:

conventional long form: Republic of Poland

conventional short form: Poland

local long form: Rzeczpospolita Polska

local short form: Polska

former: Polish People's Republic

etymology: name derives from the Polanians, a west Slavic tribe that united several surrounding Slavic groups (9th-10th centuries A.D.) and who passed on their name to the country; the name of the tribe likely comes from the Slavic "pole" (field or plain), indicating the flat nature of their country

GOVERNMENT TYPE:

parliamentary republic

CAPITAL:

name: Warsaw

geographic coordinates: 52 15 N, 21 00 E

time difference: UTC+1 (6 hours ahead of Washington, DC, during Standard Time)

daylight saving time: +1hr, begins last Sunday in March; ends last Sunday in October

etymology: the origin of the name is unknown; the Polish designation "Warszawa" was the name of a fishing village and several legends/traditions link the city's founding to a man named Wars or Warsz

ADMINISTRATIVE DIVISIONS:

16 voivodships [provinces] (wojewodztwa, singular - wojewodztwo); Dolnoslaskie (Lower Silesia), Kujawsko-Pomorskie (Kuyavia-Pomerania), Lodzkie (Lodz), Lubelskie (Lublin), Lubuskie (Lubusz), Malopolskie (Lesser Poland), Mazowieckie (Masovia), Opolskie (Opole), Podkarpackie (Subcarpathia), Podlaskie, Pomorskie (Pomerania), Slaskie (Silesia), Swietokrzyskie (Holy Cross), Warminsko-Mazurskie (Warmia-Masuria), Wielkopolskie (Greater Poland), Zachodniopomorskie (West Pomerania)

INDEPENDENCE:

11 November 1918 (republic proclaimed); notable earlier dates: 966 (adoption of Christianity, traditional founding date), 1 July 1569 (Polish-Lithuanian Commonwealth created)

NATIONAL HOLIDAY:

Constitution Day, 3 May (1791)

CONSTITUTION:

history: several previous; latest adopted 2 April 1997, approved by referendum 25 May 1997, effective 17 October 1997

amendments: proposed by at least one fifth of Sejm deputies, by the Senate, or by the president of the republic; passage requires at least two-thirds majority vote in the Sejm and absolute majority vote in the Senate; amendments to articles relating to sovereignty, personal freedoms, and constitutional amendment procedures also require passage by majority vote in a referendum; amended 2006, 2009 (2019)

LEGAL SYSTEM:

civil law system; judicial review of legislative, administrative, and other governmental acts; constitutional law rulings of the Constitutional Tribunal are final

INTERNATIONAL LAW ORGANIZATION PARTICIPATION:

accepts compulsory ICJ jurisdiction with reservations; accepts ICCt jurisdiction

CITIZENSHIP:

citizenship by birth: no

citizenship by descent only: both parents must be citizens of Poland

dual citizenship recognized: no

residency requirement for naturalization: 5 years

SUFFRAGE:

18 years of age; universal

EXECUTIVE BRANCH:

chief of state: President Andrzej DUDA (since 6 August 2015)

head of government: Prime Minister Mateusz MORAWIECKI (since 11 December 2017); Deputy Prime Ministers Piotr GLINSKI and Jaroslaw GOWIN (since 16 November 2015), Jacek SASIN (since 4 June 2019)

cabinet: Council of Ministers proposed by the prime minister, appointed by the president, and approved by the Sejm

elections/appointments: president directly elected by absolute majority popular vote in 2 rounds if needed for a 5-year term (eligible for a second term); election last held on 10 May 2015 with a second round on 24 May 2015 (next to be held in May 2020); prime minister, deputy prime ministers, and Council of Ministers appointed by the president and confirmed by the Sejm

election results: Andrzej DUDA elected president in runoff; percent of vote - Andrzej DUDA (independent) 51.5%, Bronislaw KOMOROWSKI (independent) 48.5%

LEGISLATIVE BRANCH:

description: bicameral legislature consists of:
Senate or Senat (100 seats; members directly elected in single-seat constituencies by simple majority vote to serve 4-year terms)
Sejm (460 seats; members elected in multi-seat constituencies by party-list proportional representation vote with 5% threshold of total votes needed for parties and 8% for coalitions to gain seats; minorities exempt from threshold; members serve 4-year terms)

elections:
Senate - last held on 13 October 2019 (next to be held in October 2023)
Sejm - last held on 13 October 2019 (next to be held in October 2023)

election results:
Senate - percent of vote by party - NA; seats by party - PiS 48, KO 43, PSL 3, SLD 2, independent 4; composition - men 87, women 13, percent of women 13%
Sejm - percent of vote by party - PiS 43.6%, KO 27.4%, SLD 12.6%, PSL 8.5% Confederation 6.8%, other 1.1%; seats by party - PiS 235, KO 134, SLD 49, PSL 30, KWiN 11, MN 1; men 334, women 126, percent of women 27.4%; note - total legislature percent of women 24.8%

note: the designation National Assembly or Zgromadzenie Narodowe is only used on those rare occasions when the 2 houses meet jointly

JUDICIAL BRANCH:

highest courts: Supreme Court or Sad Najwyzszy (consists of the first president of the Supreme Court and 120 justices organized in criminal, civil, labor and social insurance, and extraordinary appeals and public affairs and disciplinary chambers); Constitutional Tribunal (consists of 15 judges, including the court president and vice president)

judge selection and term of office: president of the Supreme Court nominated by the General Assembly of the Supreme Court and selected by the president of Poland; other judges nominated by the 25-member National Judicial Council and appointed by the president of Poland; judges serve until retirement, usually at age 65, but tenure can be extended; Constitutional Tribunal judges chosen by the Sejm for 9-year terms

subordinate courts: administrative courts; military courts; local, regional and appellate courts subdivided into military, civil, criminal, labor, and family courts

POLITICAL PARTIES AND LEADERS:

Civic Coalition or KO [Grzegorz SCHETYNA]
Confederation Liberty and Independence or KWiN [Janusz KORWIN-MIKKE, Robert WINNICKI, Grzegorz BRAUN]
Democratic Left Alliance or SLD [Wlodzimierz CZARZASTY]
German Minority or MN [Ryszard GALLA]
Kukiz 15 or K15 [Pawel KUKIZ]
Law and Justice or PiS [Jaroslaw KACZYNSKI]
TERAZ! (NOW!) [Ryszard PETRU]
Nowoczesna (Modern) or N [Katarzyna LUBNAUER]
Polish People's Party or PSL [Wladyslaw KOSINIAK-KAMYSZ]
Razem (Together) [collective leadership]
Wiosna (Spring) [Robert BIEDRON]

INTERNATIONAL ORGANIZATION PARTICIPATION:

Arctic Council (observer), Australia Group, BIS, BSEC (observer), CBSS, CD, CE, CEI, CERN, EAPC, EBRD, ECB, EIB, ESA, EU, FAO, IAEA, IBRD, ICAO, ICC (national committees), ICCt, ICRM, IDA, IEA, IFC, IFRCS, IHO, ILO, IMF, IMO, IMSO, Interpol, IOC, IOM, IPU, ISO, ITSO, ITU, ITUC (NGOs), MIGA, MONUSCO, NATO, NEA, NSG, OAS (observer), OECD, OIF (observer), OPCW, OSCE, PCA, Schengen Convention, UN, UNCTAD, UNESCO, UNHCR, UNIDO, UNMIL, UNMISS, UNOCI, UN Security Council (temporary), UNWTO, UPU, WCO, WFTU (NGOs), WHO, WIPO, WMO, WTO, ZC

DIPLOMATIC REPRESENTATION IN THE US:

Ambassador Piotr Antoni WILCZEK (since 18 January 2017)

chancery: 2640 16th Street NW, Washington, DC 20009

telephone: [1] (202) 499-1700

FAX: [1] (202) 328-6271

consulate(s) general: Chicago, Los Angeles, New York

DIPLOMATIC REPRESENTATION FROM THE US:

chief of mission: Ambassador Georgette MOSBACHER (since 6 September 2018)

telephone: [48] (22) 504-2000

embassy: Aleje Ujazdowskie 29/31 00-540 Warsaw

mailing address: American Embassy Warsaw, US Department of State, Washington, DC 20521-5010 (pouch)

FAX: [48] (22) 504-2226

consulate(s) general: Krakow

FLAG DESCRIPTION:

two equal horizontal bands of white (top) and red; colors derive from the Polish emblem - a white eagle on a red field

note: similar to the flags of Indonesia and Monaco which are red (top) and white

NATIONAL SYMBOL(S):

white crowned eagle; national colors: white, red

NATIONAL ANTHEM:

name: "Mazurek Dabrowskiego" (Dabrowski's Mazurka)

lyrics/music: Jozef WYBICKI/traditional

note: adopted 1927; the anthem, commonly known as "Jeszcze Polska nie zginela" (Poland Has Not Yet Perished), was written in 1797; the lyrics resonate strongly with Poles because they reflect the numerous occasions in which the nation's lands have been occupied

ECONOMY :: POLAND

ECONOMY - OVERVIEW:

Poland has the sixth-largest economy in the EU and has long had a reputation as a business-friendly country with largely sound macroeconomic policies. Since 1990,

Poland has pursued a policy of economic liberalization. During the 2008-09 economic slowdown Poland was the only EU country to avoid a recession, in part because of the government's loose fiscal policy combined with a commitment to rein in spending in the medium-term Poland is the largest recipient of EU development funds and their cyclical allocation can significantly impact the rate of economic growth.

The Polish economy performed well during the 2014-17 period, with the real GDP growth rate generally exceeding 3%, in part because of increases in government social spending that have helped to accelerate consumer-driven growth. However, since 2015, Poland has implemented new business restrictions and taxes on foreign-dominated economic sectors, including banking and insurance, energy, and healthcare, that have dampened investor sentiment and has increased the government's ownership of some firms. The government reduced the retirement age in 2016 and has had mixed success in introducing new taxes and boosting tax compliance to offset the increased costs of social spending programs and relieve upward pressure on the budget deficit. Some credit ratings agencies estimate that Poland during the next few years is at risk of exceeding the EU's 3%-of-GDP limit on budget deficits, possibly impacting its access to future EU funds. Poland's economy is projected to perform well in the next few years in part because of an anticipated cyclical increase in the use of its EU development funds and continued, robust household spending.

Poland faces several systemic challenges, which include addressing some of the remaining deficiencies in its road and rail infrastructure, business environment, rigid labor code, commercial court system, government red tape, and burdensome tax system, especially for entrepreneurs. Additional long-term challenges include diversifying Poland's energy mix, strengthening investments in innovation, research, and development, as well as stemming the outflow of educated young Poles to other EU member states, especially in light of a coming demographic contraction due to emigration, persistently low fertility rates, and the aging of the Solidarity-era baby boom generation.

GDP (PURCHASING POWER PARITY):

$1.126 trillion (2017 est.)

$1.076 trillion (2016 est.)

$1.045 trillion (2015 est.)

note: data are in 2017 dollars

country comparison to the world: 23

GDP (OFFICIAL EXCHANGE RATE):

$524.8 billion (2017 est.)

GDP - REAL GROWTH RATE:

4.7% (2017 est.)

3% (2016 est.)

3.8% (2015 est.)

country comparison to the world: 60

GDP - PER CAPITA (PPP):

$29,600 (2017 est.)

$28,300 (2016 est.)

$27,500 (2015 est.)

note: data are in 2017 dollars

country comparison to the world: 69

GROSS NATIONAL SAVING:

20% of GDP (2017 est.)

19.2% of GDP (2016 est.)

19.9% of GDP (2015 est.)

country comparison to the world: 97

GDP - COMPOSITION, BY END USE:

household consumption: 58.6% (2017 est.)

government consumption: 17.7% (2017 est.)

investment in fixed capital: 17.7% (2017 est.)

investment in inventories: 2% (2017 est.)

exports of goods and services: 54% (2017 est.)

imports of goods and services: -49.9% (2017 est.)

GDP - COMPOSITION, BY SECTOR OF ORIGIN:

agriculture: 2.4% (2017 est.)

industry: 40.2% (2017 est.)

services: 57.4% (2017 est.)

AGRICULTURE - PRODUCTS:

potatoes, fruits, vegetables, wheat; poultry, eggs, pork, dairy

INDUSTRIES:

machine building, iron and steel, coal mining, chemicals, shipbuilding, food processing, glass, beverages, textiles

INDUSTRIAL PRODUCTION GROWTH RATE:

7.5% (2017 est.)

country comparison to the world: 28

LABOR FORCE:

17.6 million (2017 est.)

country comparison to the world: 35

LABOR FORCE - BY OCCUPATION:

agriculture: 11.5%

industry: 30.4%

services: 57.6% (2015)

UNEMPLOYMENT RATE:

4.9% (2017 est.)

6.2% (2016 est.)

country comparison to the world: 70

POPULATION BELOW POVERTY LINE:

17.6% (2015 est.)

HOUSEHOLD INCOME OR CONSUMPTION BY PERCENTAGE SHARE:

lowest 10%: 3%

highest 10%: 23.9% (2015 est.)

DISTRIBUTION OF FAMILY INCOME - GINI INDEX:

30.8 (2015)

33.7 (2008)

country comparison to the world: 128

BUDGET:

revenues: 207.5 billion (2017 est.)

expenditures: 216.2 billion (2017 est.)

TAXES AND OTHER REVENUES:

39.5% (of GDP) (2017 est.)

country comparison to the world: 45

BUDGET SURPLUS (+) OR DEFICIT (-):

-1.7% (of GDP) (2017 est.)

country comparison to the world: 96

PUBLIC DEBT:

50.6% of GDP (2017 est.)

54.2% of GDP (2016 est.)

note: data cover general government debt and include debt instruments issued (or owned) by government entities other than the treasury; the data include treasury debt held by foreign entities, the data include subnational entities, as well as intragovernmental debt; intragovernmental debt consists of treasury borrowings from surpluses in the social funds, such as for retirement, medical care, and unemployment; debt instruments for the social funds are not sold at public auctions

country comparison to the world: 100
FISCAL YEAR:
calendar year
INFLATION RATE (CONSUMER PRICES):
2% (2017 est.)
-0.6% (2016 est.)
country comparison to the world: 106
CENTRAL BANK DISCOUNT RATE:
1.5% (31 December 2017)
1.5% (31 December 2016)
country comparison to the world: 127
COMMERCIAL BANK PRIME LENDING RATE:
4.8% (31 December 2017 est.)
4.74% (31 December 2016 est.)
country comparison to the world: 153
STOCK OF NARROW MONEY:
$260.4 billion (31 December 2017 est.)
$195.1 billion (31 December 2016 est.)
country comparison to the world: 20
STOCK OF BROAD MONEY:
$260.4 billion (31 December 2017 est.)
$195.1 billion (31 December 2016 est.)
country comparison to the world: 20
STOCK OF DOMESTIC CREDIT:
$419.7 billion (31 December 2017 est.)
$336.6 billion (31 December 2016 est.)
country comparison to the world: 30
MARKET VALUE OF PUBLICLY TRADED SHARES:
$397 billion (31 December 2017 est.)
$265.4 billion (31 December 2016 est.)
$277.4 billion (31 December 2015 est.)
country comparison to the world: 26
CURRENT ACCOUNT BALANCE:
$1.584 billion (2017 est.)
-$1.369 billion (2016 est.)
country comparison to the world: 46
EXPORTS:
$224.6 billion (2017 est.)
$195.7 billion (2016 est.)
country comparison to the world: 23
EXPORTS - PARTNERS:
Germany 27.4%, Czech Republic 6.4%, UK 6.4%, France 5.6%, Italy 4.9%, Netherlands 4.4% (2017)
EXPORTS - COMMODITIES:
machinery and transport equipment 37.8%, intermediate manufactured goods 23.7%, miscellaneous manufactured goods 17.1%, food and live animals 7.6% (2012 est.)

IMPORTS:
$223.8 billion (2017 est.)
$193.2 billion (2016 est.)
country comparison to the world: 23
IMPORTS - COMMODITIES:
machinery and transport equipment 38%, intermediate manufactured goods 21%, chemicals 15%, minerals, fuels, lubricants, and related materials 9% (2011 est.)
IMPORTS - PARTNERS:
Germany 27.9%, China 8%, Russia 6.4%, Netherlands 6%, Italy 5.3%, France 4.2%, Czech Republic 4% (2017)
RESERVES OF FOREIGN EXCHANGE AND GOLD:
$113.3 billion (31 December 2017 est.)
$114.4 billion (31 December 2016 est.)
country comparison to the world: 22
DEBT - EXTERNAL:
$241 billion (31 December 2017 est.)
$347.8 billion (31 December 2016 est.)
country comparison to the world: 31
STOCK OF DIRECT FOREIGN INVESTMENT - AT HOME:
$282.6 billion (31 December 2017 est.)
$224.5 billion (31 December 2016 est.)
country comparison to the world: 23
STOCK OF DIRECT FOREIGN INVESTMENT - ABROAD:
$72.87 billion (31 December 2017 est.)
$64.52 billion (31 December 2016 est.)
country comparison to the world: 38
EXCHANGE RATES:
zlotych (PLN) per US dollar -
3.748 (2017 est.)
3.9459 (2016 est.)
3.9459 (2015 est.)
3.7721 (2014 est.)
3.1538 (2013 est.)

ENERGY :: POLAND

ELECTRICITY ACCESS:
electrification - total population: 100% (2016)
ELECTRICITY - PRODUCTION:
156.9 billion kWh (2016 est.)
country comparison to the world: 25
ELECTRICITY - CONSUMPTION:
149.4 billion kWh (2016 est.)
country comparison to the world: 24

ELECTRICITY - EXPORTS:
12.02 billion kWh (2016)
country comparison to the world: 17
ELECTRICITY - IMPORTS:
14.02 billion kWh (2016 est.)
country comparison to the world: 17
ELECTRICITY - INSTALLED GENERATING CAPACITY:
38.11 million kW (2016 est.)
country comparison to the world: 28
ELECTRICITY - FROM FOSSIL FUELS:
79% of total installed capacity (2016 est.)
country comparison to the world: 87
ELECTRICITY - FROM NUCLEAR FUELS:
0% of total installed capacity (2017 est.)
country comparison to the world: 166
ELECTRICITY - FROM HYDROELECTRIC PLANTS:
2% of total installed capacity (2017 est.)
country comparison to the world: 141
ELECTRICITY - FROM OTHER RENEWABLE SOURCES:
19% of total installed capacity (2017 est.)
country comparison to the world: 44
CRUDE OIL - PRODUCTION:
21,000 bbl/day (2018 est.)
country comparison to the world: 65
CRUDE OIL - EXPORTS:
4,451 bbl/day (2017 est.)
country comparison to the world: 66
CRUDE OIL - IMPORTS:
493,100 bbl/day (2017 est.)
country comparison to the world: 19
CRUDE OIL - PROVED RESERVES:
126 million bbl (1 January 2018)
country comparison to the world: 66
REFINED PETROLEUM PRODUCTS - PRODUCTION:
554,200 bbl/day (2017 est.)
country comparison to the world: 30
REFINED PETROLEUM PRODUCTS - CONSUMPTION:
649,600 bbl/day (2017 est.)
country comparison to the world: 30
REFINED PETROLEUM PRODUCTS - EXPORTS:
104,800 bbl/day (2017 est.)
country comparison to the world: 43

REFINED PETROLEUM PRODUCTS - IMPORTS:

222,300 bbl/day (2017 est.)

country comparison to the world: 32

NATURAL GAS - PRODUCTION:

5.748 billion cu m (2017 est.)

country comparison to the world: 49

NATURAL GAS - CONSUMPTION:

20.1 billion cu m (2017 est.)

country comparison to the world: 38

NATURAL GAS - EXPORTS:

1.246 billion cu m (2017 est.)

country comparison to the world: 39

NATURAL GAS - IMPORTS:

15.72 billion cu m (2017 est.)

country comparison to the world: 20

NATURAL GAS - PROVED RESERVES:

79.79 billion cu m (1 January 2018 est.)

country comparison to the world: 56

CARBON DIOXIDE EMISSIONS FROM CONSUMPTION OF ENERGY:

359 million Mt (2017 est.)

country comparison to the world: 18

COMMUNICATIONS :: POLAND

TELEPHONES - FIXED LINES:

total subscriptions: 8,143,145

subscriptions per 100 inhabitants: 24 (July 2016 est.)

country comparison to the world: 21

TELEPHONES - MOBILE CELLULAR:

total subscriptions: 49,828,596

subscriptions per 100 inhabitants: 130 (2017 est.)

country comparison to the world: 30

TELEPHONE SYSTEM:

general assessment: modernization of the telecommunications network has accelerated with market-based competition; fixed-line service, dominated by the former state-owned company, is dwarfed by the growth in mobile-cellular services; regulatory is framed by EU principles of competition; mobile penetration is above European average; 5G trials begin; LTE-B and VoWi-Fi technologies; launch of 1Gb/s cable services (2018)

domestic: several nation-wide networks provide mobile-cellular service; coverage is generally good; fixed-line 24 per 100 service lags in rural areas, mobile-cellular 130 per 100 persons (2018)

international: country code - 48; landing points for the Baltica and the Denmark-Poland2 submarine cables connecting Poland, Denmark and Sweden; international direct dialing with automated exchanges; satellite earth station - 1 with access to Intelsat, Eutelsat, Inmarsat, and Intersputnik (2019)

BROADCAST MEDIA:

state-run public TV operates 2 national channels supplemented by 16 regional channels and several niche channels; privately owned entities operate several national TV networks and a number of special interest channels; many privately owned channels broadcasting locally; roughly half of all households are linked to either satellite or cable TV systems providing access to foreign television networks; state-run public radio operates 5 national networks and 17 regional radio stations; 2 privately owned national radio networks, several commercial stations broadcasting to multiple cities, and many privately owned local radio stations (2019)

INTERNET COUNTRY CODE:

.pl

INTERNET USERS:

total: 28,237,820

percent of population: 73.3% (July 2016 est.)

country comparison to the world: 27

BROADBAND - FIXED SUBSCRIPTIONS:

total: 7,053,333

subscriptions per 100 inhabitants: 18 (2017 est.)

country comparison to the world: 23

MILITARY AND SECURITY :: POLAND

MILITARY EXPENDITURES:

1.99% of GDP (2018 est.)

1.9% of GDP (2017)

1.94% of GDP (2016)

2.14% of GDP (2015)

1.9% of GDP (2014)

country comparison to the world: 49

MILITARY AND SECURITY FORCES:

Polish Armed Forces: Land Forces (Wojska Ladowe), Navy (Marynarka Wojenna), Air Force (Sily Powietrzne), Special Forces (Wojska Specjalne), Territorial Defense Force (Wojska Obrony Terytorialnej) (2019)

note: Territorial Defense Force only began recruitment in winter 2016

MILITARY SERVICE AGE AND OBLIGATION:

18-28 years of age for male and female voluntary military service; conscription phased out in 2009-12; professional soldiers serve on a permanent basis (for an unspecified period of time) or on a contract basis (for a specified period of time); initial contract period is 24 months; women serve in the military on the same terms as men (2019)

MILITARY - NOTE:

Coast guard duties fall under the Border Guard, which is controlled by the Ministry of the Interior (2019)

TRANSPORTATION :: POLAND

NATIONAL AIR TRANSPORT SYSTEM:

number of registered air carriers: 6 (2015)

inventory of registered aircraft operated by air carriers: 92 (2015)

annual passenger traffic on registered air carriers: 4,841,128 (2015)

annual freight traffic on registered air carriers: 120,016,466 mt-km (2015)

CIVIL AIRCRAFT REGISTRATION COUNTRY CODE PREFIX:

SP (2016)

AIRPORTS:

126 (2013)

country comparison to the world: 47

AIRPORTS - WITH PAVED RUNWAYS:

total: 87 (2017)

over 3,047 m: 5 (2017)

2,438 to 3,047 m: 30 (2017)

1,524 to 2,437 m: 36 (2017)

914 to 1,523 m: 10 (2017)

under 914 m: 6 (2017)

AIRPORTS - WITH UNPAVED RUNWAYS:

total: 39 (2013)

1,524 to 2,437 m: 1 (2013)

914 to 1,523 m: 17 (2013)

under 914 m: 21 (2013)

HELIPORTS:

6 (2013)

PIPELINES:

14198 km gas, 1374 km oil, 2483 km refined products (2016)

RAILWAYS:

total: 19,231 km (2016)

standard gauge: 18,836 km 1.435-m gauge (11,874 km electrified) (2016)

broad gauge: 395 km 1.524-m gauge (2016)

country comparison to the world: 16

ROADWAYS:

total: 420,000 km (2016)

paved: 291,000 km (includes 1,492 km of expressways, 1,559 of motorways) (2016)

unpaved: 129,000 km (2016)

country comparison to the world: 17

WATERWAYS:

3,997 km (navigable rivers and canals) (2009)

country comparison to the world: 27

MERCHANT MARINE:

total: 148

by type: bulk carrier 1, container ship 1, general cargo 13, oil tanker 7, other 126 (2018)

country comparison to the world: 72

PORTS AND TERMINALS:

major seaport(s): Gdansk, Gdynia, Swinoujscie

container port(s) (TEUs): Gdansk (1,593,761) (2017)

LNG terminal(s) (import): Swinoujscie

river port(s): Szczecin (River Oder)

TRANSNATIONAL ISSUES :: POLAND

DISPUTES - INTERNATIONAL:

as a member state that forms part of the EU's external border, Poland has implemented the strict Schengen border rules to restrict illegal immigration and trade along its eastern borders with Belarus and Ukraine

REFUGEES AND INTERNALLY DISPLACED PERSONS:

refugees (country of origin): 9,893 (Russia) (2018)

stateless persons: 10,825 (2018)

ILLICIT DRUGS:

despite diligent counternarcotics measures and international information sharing on cross-border crimes, a major illicit producer of synthetic drugs for the international market; minor transshipment point for Southwest Asian heroin and Latin American cocaine to Western Europe

www.ingramcontent.com/pod-product-compliance
Lightning Source LLC
Chambersburg PA
CBHW081151020426

42333CB00020B/2475